W9-BJQ-882

The Adventures in Literature Program

═══════

ADVENTURES FOR READERS: BOOK ONE
Teacher's Manual
Test Booklet
Reading/Writing Workshop, Grade 7

ADVENTURES FOR READERS: BOOK TWO
Teacher's Manual
Test Booklet
Reading/Writing Workshop, Grade 8

ADVENTURES IN READING
Teacher's Manual
Test Booklet
Reading/Writing Workshop, Grade 9

ADVENTURES IN APPRECIATION
Teacher's Manual
Test Booklet
Reading/Writing Workshop, Grade 10

ADVENTURES IN AMERICAN LITERATURE
Teacher's Manual
Test Booklet
Lessons in Critical Reading and Writing:
Henry James's *Washington Square* and *Daisy Miller*

ADVENTURES IN ENGLISH LITERATURE
Teacher's Manual
Test Booklet
Lessons in Critical Reading and Writing.
Shakespeare's *Hamlet*

ADVENTURES IN MODERN LITERATURE
Teacher's Manual
Test Booklet

ADVENTURES IN WORLD LITERATURE
Teacher's Manual
Test Booklet
Lessons in Critical Reading and Writing:
Three Masters of Russian Fiction

LAURENCE PERRINE
Southern Methodist University, Dallas, Texas
The Short Story, Poetry

ROBERT JAMESON
The Haverford School, Haverford, Pennsylvania
Nonfiction, Composition and Language Program, "Practice in Reading and Writing"

RITA SILVERI
Chicago City College, Wright Branch. Formerly of Steinmetz High School,
Chicago, Illinois
GENERAL TEACHING CONSULTANT
The King Arthur Legend, The Bridge of San Luis Rey, *and* Silas Marner
Teacher's Manual

G. B. HARRISON
University of Michigan, Ann Arbor, Michigan
Shakespeare

A. R. GURNEY, JR.
Massachusetts Institute of Technology, Cambridge, Massachusetts
Drama

V. S. PRITCHETT
London
The Novel

WALTER LOBAN
University of California, Berkeley, California
CONSULTANT

THOMAS M. FOLDS
Dean of Education
Metropolitan Museum of Art, New York, New York
Fine Arts Program

ADVENTURES
in Appreciation

CLASSIC EDITION

Harcourt Brace Jovanovich

NEW YORK CHICAGO SAN FRANCISCO ATLANTA DALLAS *and* LONDON

LAURENCE PERRINE is Professor of English at Southern Methodist University in Dallas, Texas. Mr. Perrine received a master's degree from Oberlin College and a Ph.D. from Yale University. He is the author of *Sound and Sense: An Introduction to Poetry* and *Story and Structure;* and coauthor of *Poetry: A Closer Look* and *100 American Poems of the Twentieth Century.*

ROBERT JAMESON is Chairman of the English Department at The Haverford School, Haverford, Pennsylvania. Mr. Jameson received an A.B. from Harvard College and has been a Visiting Associate Professor of English at Trinity College, Hartford, Connecticut. He is the Director of Reading for the College Board Advanced Placement Program, has written widely on educational subjects, and is the editor of *Essays Old and New.*

RITA SILVERI, formerly of Steinmetz High School, teaches at Chicago City College, Wright Branch, in Chicago, Illinois. She served as Chairman of the Department of English at Harrison High School in Chicago, and has contributed widely to educational journals.

G. B. HARRISON is Emeritus Professor of English at the University of Michigan. Editor of *Shakespeare: The Complete Works,* his other books include *The Elizabethan and Jacobean Journals, Introducing Shakespeare,* and *Shakespeare's Tragedies.*

A. R. GURNEY, JR. is an Associate Professor of English at the Massachusetts Institute of Technology. He is a graduate of the Yale School of Drama and has produced and published several plays.

V. S. PRITCHETT is an English novelist, short story writer, and literary critic. He has worked also as a newspaper correspondent and has lectured on the novel at Princeton University. Among his works are *The Living Novel, Books in General, London Perceived,* and *New York Proclaimed.*

WALTER LOBAN is Supervisor of the Teaching of English and Associate Professor of Education at the University of California in Berkeley. He has taught English at various Midwestern public schools and universities, teaches on the television program "Focus on America," and is a coauthor of *Teaching Language Through Literature.* He has been an editor of six editions of *Adventures in Appreciation.*

THOMAS M. FOLDS is Dean of Education at the Metropolitan Museum of Art in New York. A graduate of Yale College and the Yale School of Fine Arts, Mr. Folds has been an instructor of English and Art Director at the Phillips Exeter Academy, New Hampshire, and a Professor of Art and Chairman of the Department of Art at Northwestern University.

Front cover photo by Susan McCartney.
Coin used as colophon courtesy of The American Numismatic Society.

Copyright © 1973, 1968 by Harcourt Brace Jovanovich, Inc.

PRINTED IN THE UNITED STATES OF AMERICA

ISBN 0–15–335139–X

CONTENTS

THE SHORT STORY

THE ESSAY

BIOGRAPHY

POETRY

DRAMA

THE KING ARTHUR LEGEND

THE NOVEL

The Fine Arts Program

Adventures in Appreciation

THE SHORT STORY

THERE ARE two reasons for reading imaginative literature and two tests for judging it: pleasure and insight. The first and most important test of a story, poem, or play is, "Does it bring enjoyment?" If it doesn't, we want no more of it. But we must ask, "Enjoyment to whom?" The best story in the world will bring no enjoyment to a person who doesn't know how to read it. Many excellent stories bring no enjoyment to us because we are unskilled as readers, or because we haven't experienced enough, or are insufficiently developed in imagination, sympathy, or compassion—because we aren't human enough. Thus, not only do *we* judge literature, but good literature judges *us*. We say to a story or poem, "Are you enjoyable? If not, go away." But a great story or poem says to us, "Can you enjoy me? If not, go away, perfect yourself, then come back and try again."

The second test for the worth of imaginative literature is, "Does it yield insight? Do we know more, after reading it, about the world we live in, about our fellow human beings, about ourselves?" The paradox of imaginative literature is that, though it deals with imaginary events and imaginary people, it can communicate real truth—not just factual truth, but truth delivered living and whole to our senses, our emotions, and our imaginations as well as to our minds. Literature which brings such understanding is significant literature. For the good reader it is also the most enjoyable literature, because the enjoyment it brings increases his understanding. Reading good literature is thus both a source of enjoyment and a means of enlarging our experience, extending our sympathies, and deepening our understanding. As such, it is both a means and an end of education, for though we read imaginative literature for enjoyment, we also read it to make ourselves more fully human.

The short stories which follow have proved their capacity for providing pleasure by already having pleased many readers. Most of them also, though in varying degrees, offer insight into the quality and nature of human experience.

PLOT

In order to read stories well—to get from them all that they are capable of giving—we need some awareness of the elements of which they are composed and of the means an author uses to reach his reader. Among the most important of these are *plot, character, theme, irony,* and *symbol.*

Plot is the sequence of incidents or actions in a story. Whatever the characters do, or whatever happens to them, constitutes *plot.*

In some stories the plot does little more than create excitement. The principal interest in these stories is in what happens, and the reader is hurried breathlessly from one crisis to another. Such stories rely heavily on suspense, danger, mystery, action, physical conflict, and surprise. In other stories—generally the more significant ones—plot also serves to exhibit character and to reveal some truth about life. In such stories the plot may still be exciting, but it doesn't exist just for its own sake.

The most important element in plot is usually *conflict.* Conflict may be *external* or *internal;* it may be physical, intellectual, emotional, or moral. A story may pit man against his environment, against other men, or against his own unreasonable impulses or desires. In the richest stories there is usually more than one kind of conflict. The conflict of the main character with other men or with nature may be complicated by conflicts within himself. A story ordinarily ends when its main conflict is *resolved;* that is, when one side or the other triumphs, and the main character either succeeds or fails. In some stories, however, the conflict is left unresolved, just as conflicts in real life often have no definite conclusions.

A plot may be either realistic or fantastic. It may start from an ordinary, everyday situation or from a highly unusual, or even supernatural one. Each kind of initial situation is capable of providing pleasure, revealing character, or giving insight into some kind of truth. All the succeeding events, however, should proceed logically from that initial situation; and all the characters' actions should be consistent with their individual natures. A good plot is governed by an inner logic. It may begin with a far-fetched coincidence, but it will not ordinarily end with one. It may take place in a world of one-eyed giants, but the giants must act in a consistent and believable fashion. The reader has a right to demand that a story be true to its own original conditions. Though the beginning of a story may be improbable, the end should be probable in light of the beginning.

Finally, in a good plot nothing is included which is not necessary to the author's intention. Each incident or episode should be more than interesting in itself: it should be part of an overall design. If an incident can be omitted without harm to the story, the plot is to some degree defective. Just as a wall is more than a heap of bricks, so a good plot is more than a collection of incidents. A good plot has a design, or pattern. Its whole is greater than the sum of its parts.

Contents of the Dead Man's Pockets

JACK FINNEY

At the little living-room desk Tom Benecke rolled two sheets of flimsy [1] and a heavier top sheet, carbon paper sandwiched between them, into his portable. *Interoffice Memo*, the top sheet was headed, and he typed tomorrow's date just below this; then he glanced at a creased yellow sheet, covered with his own handwriting, beside the typewriter. "Hot in here," he muttered to himself. Then, from the short hallway at his back, he heard the muffled clang of wire coat hangers in the bedroom closet, and at this reminder of what his wife was doing he thought: Hot, no—guilty conscience.

He got up, shoving his hands into the back pockets of his gray wash slacks, stepped to the living-room window beside the desk, and stood breathing on the glass, watching the expanding circlet of mist, staring down through the autumn night at Lexington Avenue,[2] eleven stories below. He was a tall, lean, dark-haired young man

in a pullover sweater, who looked as though he had played not football, probably, but basketball in college. Now he placed the heels of his hands against the top edge of the lower window frame and shoved upward. But as usual the window didn't budge, and he had to lower his hands and then shoot them hard upward to jolt the window open a few inches. He dusted his hands, muttering.

But still he didn't begin his work. He crossed the room to the hallway entrance and, leaning against the doorjamb, hands shoved into his back pockets again, he called, "Clare?" When his wife answered, he said, "Sure you don't mind going alone?"

"No." Her voice was muffled, and he knew her head and shoulders were in the bedroom closet. Then the tap of her high heels sounded on the wood floor and she appeared at the end of the little hallway, wearing a slip, both hands raised to one ear, clipping on an earring. She smiled at him—a slender, very pretty girl with light brown, almost blonde, hair—her prettiness emphasized by the pleasant nature that showed in her face. "It's just that I hate you to miss this movie; you wanted to see it too."

"Yeah, I know." He ran his fingers through his hair. "Got to get this done though."

She nodded, accepting this. Then, glancing at the desk across the living room, she said, "You work too much, though, Tom—and too hard."

He smiled. "You won't mind though, will you, when the money comes rolling in and I'm known as the Boy Wizard of Wholesale Groceries?"

"I guess not." She smiled and turned back toward the bedroom.

At his desk again, Tom lighted a cigarette; then a few moments later as Clare appeared, dressed and ready to leave, he

[1] **flimsy:** a thin paper used in typing carbon copies.

[2] **Lexington Avenue:** one of the main streets of New York City.

set it on the rim of the ash tray. "Just after seven," she said. "I can make the beginning of the first feature."

He walked to the front-door closet to help her on with her coat. He kissed her then and, for an instant, holding her close, smelling the perfume she had used, he was tempted to go with her; it was not actually true that he had to work tonight, though he very much wanted to. This was his own project, unannounced as yet in his office, and it could be postponed. But then they won't see it till Monday, he thought once again, and if I give it to the boss tomorrow he might read it over the weekend. . . . "Have a good time," he said aloud. He gave his wife a little swat and opened the door for her, feeling the air from the building hallway, smelling faintly of floor wax, stream past his face.

He watched her walk down the hall, flicked a hand in response as she waved, and then he started to close the door, but it resisted for a moment. As the door opening narrowed, the current of warm air from the hallway, channeled through this smaller opening now, suddenly rushed past him with accelerated force. Behind him he heard the slap of the window curtains against the wall and the sound of paper fluttering from his desk, and he had to push to close the door.

Turning, he saw a sheet of white paper drifting to the floor in a series of arcs, and another sheet, yellow, moving toward the window, caught in the dying current flowing through the narrow opening. As he watched, the paper struck the bottom edge of the window and hung there for an instant, plastered against the glass and wood. Then as the moving air stilled completely, the curtains swinging back from the wall to hang free again, he saw the yellow sheet drop to the window ledge and slide over out of sight.

He ran across the room, grasped the bottom edge of the window, and tugged, staring through the glass. He saw the yellow sheet, dimly now in the darkness outside, lying on the ornamental ledge a yard below the window. Even as he watched, it was moving, scraping slowly along the ledge, pushed by the breeze that pressed steadily against the building wall. He heaved on the window with all his strength and it shot open with a bang, the window weight rattling in the casing. But the paper was past his reach and, leaning out into the night, he watched it scud steadily along the ledge to the south, half-plastered against the building wall. Above the muffled sound of the street traffic far below, he could hear the dry scrape of its movement, like a leaf on the pavement.

The living room of the next apartment to the south projected a yard or more farther out toward the street than this one; because of this the Beneckes paid seven and a half dollars less rent than their neighbors. And now the yellow sheet, sliding along the stone ledge, nearly invisible in the night, was stopped by the projecting blank wall of the next apartment. It lay motionless, then, in the corner formed by the two walls—a good five yards away, pressed firmly against the ornate corner ornament of the ledge, by the breeze that moved past Tom Benecke's face.

He knelt at the window and stared at the yellow paper for a full minute or more, waiting for it to move, to slide off the ledge and fall, hoping he could follow its course to the street, and then hurry down in the elevator and retrieve it. But it didn't move, and then he saw that the paper was caught firmly between a projection of the convoluted corner ornament and the ledge. He thought about the poker from the fireplace, then the broom, then the mop—discarding each thought as it occurred to him. There was nothing in the

apartment long enough to reach that paper.

It was hard for him to understand that he actually had to abandon it—it was ridiculous—and he began to curse. Of all the papers on his desk, why did it have to be this one in particular! On four long Saturday afternoons he had stood in supermarkets counting the people who passed certain displays, and the results were scribbled on that yellow sheet. From stacks of trade publications, gone over page by page in snatched half-hours at work and during evenings at home, he had copied facts, quotations, and figures onto that sheet. And he had carried it with him to the Public Library on Fifth Avenue, where he'd spent a dozen lunch hours and early evenings adding more. All were needed to support and lend authority to his idea for a new grocery-store display method; without them his idea was a mere opinion. And there they all lay in his own improvised shorthand—countless hours of work—out there on the ledge.

For many seconds he believed he was going to abandon the yellow sheet, that there was nothing else to do. The work

could be duplicated. But it would take two months, and the time to present this idea was *now,* for use in the spring displays. He struck his fist on the window ledge. Then he shrugged. Even though his plan were adopted, he told himself, it wouldn't bring him a raise in pay—not immediately, anyway, or as a direct result. It won't bring me a promotion either, he argued—not of itself.

But just the same, and he couldn't escape the thought, this and other independent projects, some already done and others planned for the future, would gradually mark him out from the score of other young men in his company. They were the way to change from a name on the payroll to a name in the minds of the company officials. They were the beginning of the long, long climb to where he was determined to be, at the very top. And he knew he was going out there in the darkness, after the yellow sheet fifteen feet beyond his reach.

By a kind of instinct, he instantly began making his intention acceptable to himself by laughing at it. The mental picture of himself sidling along the ledge outside was absurd—it was actually comical—and he smiled. He imagined himself describing it; it would make a good story at the office and, it occurred to him, would add a special interest and importance to his memorandum, which would do it no harm at all.

To simply go out and get his paper was an easy task—he could be back here with it in less than two minutes—and he knew he wasn't deceiving himself. The ledge, he saw, measuring it with his eye, was about as wide as the length of his shoe, and perfectly flat. And every fifth row of brick in the face of the building, he remembered—leaning out, he verified this —was indented half an inch, enough for the tips of his fingers, enough to maintain

balance easily. It occurred to him that if this ledge and wall were only a yard above ground—as he knelt at the window staring out, this thought was the final confirmation of his intention—he could move along the ledge indefinitely.

On a sudden impulse, he got to his feet, walked to the front closet, and took out an old tweed jacket; it would be cold outside. He put it on and buttoned it as he crossed the room rapidly toward the open window. In the back of his mind he knew he'd better hurry and get this over with before he thought too much, and at the window he didn't allow himself to hesitate.

He swung a leg over the sill, then felt for and found the ledge a yard below the window with his foot. Gripping the bottom of the window frame very tightly and carefully, he slowly ducked his head under it, feeling on his face the sudden change from the warm air of the room to the chill outside. With infinite care he brought out his other leg, his mind concentrating on what he was doing. Then he slowly stood erect. Most of the putty, dried out and brittle, had dropped off the bottom edging of the window frame, he found, and the flat wooden edging provided a good gripping surface, a half-inch or more deep, for the tips of his fingers.

Now, balanced easily and firmly, he stood on the ledge outside in the slight, chill breeze, eleven stories above the street, staring into his own lighted apartment, odd and different-seeming now.

First his right hand, then his left, he carefully shifted his finger-tip grip from the puttyless window edging to an indented row of bricks directly to his right. It was hard to take the first shuffling sideways step then—to make himself move—and the fear stirred in his stomach, but he did it, again by not allowing himself time to think. And now—with his chest, stomach, and the left side of his face pressed against the rough cold brick—his lighted apartment was suddenly gone, and it was much darker out here than he had thought.

Without pause he continued—right foot, left foot, right foot, left—his shoe soles shuffling and scraping along the rough stone, never lifting from it, fingers sliding along the exposed edging of brick. He moved on the balls of his feet, heels lifted slightly; the ledge was not quite as wide as he'd expected. But leaning slightly inward toward the face of the building and pressed against it, he could feel his balance firm and secure, and moving along the ledge was quite as easy as he had thought it would be. He could hear the buttons of his jacket scraping steadily along the rough bricks and feel them catch momentarily, tugging a little, at each mortared crack. He simply did not permit himself to look down, though the compulsion to do so never left him; nor did he allow himself actually to think. Mechanically—right foot, left foot, over and again—he shuffled along crabwise, watching the projecting wall ahead loom steadily closer. . . .

Then he reached it and, at the corner—he'd decided how he was going to pick up the paper—he lifted his right foot and placed it carefully on the ledge that ran along the projecting wall at a right angle to the ledge on which his other foot rested. And now, facing the building, he stood in the corner formed by the two walls, one foot on the ledging of each, a hand on the shoulder-high indentation of each wall. His forehead was pressed directly into the corner against the cold bricks, and now he carefully lowered first one hand, then the other, perhaps a foot farther down, to the next indentation in the rows of bricks.

Very slowly, sliding his forehead down the trough of the brick corner and bending his knees, he lowered his body toward

the paper lying between his outstretched feet. Again he lowered his fingerholds another foot and bent his knees still more, thigh muscles taut, his forehead sliding and bumping down the brick V. Half-squatting now, he dropped his left hand to the next indentation and then slowly reached with his right hand toward the paper between his feet.

He couldn't quite touch it, and his knees now were pressed against the wall; he could bend them no farther. But by ducking his head another inch lower, the top of his head now pressed against the bricks, he lowered his right shoulder and his fingers had the paper by a corner, pulling it loose. At the same instant he saw, between his legs and far below, Lexington Avenue stretched out for miles ahead.

He saw, in that instant, the Loew's theater sign, blocks ahead past Fiftieth Street; the miles of traffic signals, all green now; the lights of cars and street lamps; countless neon signs; and the moving black dots of people. And a violent instantaneous explosion of absolute terror roared through him. For a motionless instant he saw himself externally—bent practically double, balanced on this narrow ledge, nearly half his body projecting out above the street far below—and he began to tremble violently, panic flaring through his mind and muscles, and he felt the blood rush from the surface of his skin.

In the fractional moment before horror paralyzed him, as he stared between his legs at that terrible length of street far beneath him, a fragment of his mind raised his body in a spasmodic jerk to an upright position again, but so violently that his head scraped hard against the wall, bouncing off it, and his body swayed outward to the knife edge of balance, and he very nearly plunged backward and fell. Then he was leaning far into the corner again, squeezing and pushing into it, not only his

face but his chest and stomach, his back arching; and his finger tips clung with all the pressure of his pulling arms to the shoulder-high half-inch indentation in the bricks.

He was more than trembling now; his whole body was racked with a violent shuddering beyond control, his eyes squeezed so tightly shut it was painful, though he was past awareness of that. His teeth were exposed in a frozen grimace, the strength draining like water from his knees and calves. It was extremely likely, he knew, that he would faint, slump down along the wall, his face scraping, and then drop backward, a limp weight, out into nothing. And to save his life he concentrated on holding on to consciousness, drawing deliberate deep breaths of cold air into his lungs, fighting to keep his senses aware.

Then he knew that he would not faint, but he could not stop shaking nor open his eyes. He stood where he was, breathing deeply, trying to hold back the terror of the glimpse he had had of what lay below him; and he knew he had made a mistake in not making himself stare down at the street, getting used to it and accepting it, when he had first stepped out onto the ledge.

It was impossible to walk back. He simply could not do it. He couldn't bring himself to make the slightest movement. The strength was gone from his legs; his shivering hands—numb, cold, and desperately rigid—had lost all deftness; his easy ability to move and balance was gone. Within a step or two, if he tried to move, he knew that he would stumble and fall.

Seconds passed, with the chill faint wind pressing the side of his face, and he could hear the toned-down volume of the street traffic far beneath him. Again and again it slowed and then stopped, almost

to silence; then presently, even this high, he would hear the click of the traffic signals and the subdued roar of the cars starting up again. During a lull in the street sounds, he called out. Then he was shouting "*Help!*" so loudly it rasped his throat. But he felt the steady pressure of the wind, moving between his face and the blank wall, snatch up his cries as he uttered them, and he knew they must sound directionless and distant. And he remembered how habitually, here in New York, he himself heard and ignored shouts in the night. If anyone heard him, there was no sign of it, and presently Tom Benecke knew he had to try moving; there was nothing else he could do.

Eyes squeezed shut, he watched scenes in his mind like scraps of motion-picture film—he could not stop them. He saw himself stumbling suddenly sideways as he crept along the ledge and saw his upper body arc outward, arms flailing. He was a dangling shoestring caught between the ledge and the sole of his other shoe, saw a foot start to move, to be stopped with a jerk, and felt his balance leaving him. He saw himself falling with a terrible speed as his body revolved in the air, knees clutched tight to his chest, eyes squeezed shut, moaning softly.

Out of utter necessity, knowing that any of these thoughts might be reality in the very next seconds, he was slowly able to shut his mind against every thought but what he now began to do. With fear-soaked slowness, he slid his left foot an inch or two toward his own impossibly distant window. Then he slid the fingers of his shivering left hand a corresponding distance. For a moment he could not bring himself to lift his right foot from one ledge to the other; then he did it, and became aware of the harsh exhalation of air from his throat and realized that he was panting. As his right hand, then, began to slide along the brick edging, he was astonished to feel the yellow paper pressed to the bricks underneath his stiff fingers, and he uttered a terrible, abrupt bark that might have been a laugh or a moan. He opened his mouth and took the paper in his teeth, pulling it out from under his fingers.

By a kind of trick—by concentrating his entire mind on first his left foot, then his left hand, then the other foot, then the other hand—he was able to move, almost imperceptibly, trembling steadily, very nearly without thought. But he could feel the terrible strength of the pent-up horror on just the other side of the flimsy barrier he had erected in his mind; and he knew that if it broke through he would lose this thin artificial control of his body.

During one slow step he tried keeping his eyes closed; it made him feel safer, shutting him off a little from the fearful reality of where he was. Then a sudden rush of giddiness swept over him and he had to open his eyes wide, staring sideways at the cold rough brick and angled lines of mortar, his cheek tight against the building. He kept his eyes open then, knowing that if he once let them flick outward, to stare for an instant at the lighted windows across the street, he would be past help.

He didn't know how many dozens of tiny sidling steps he had taken, his chest, belly, and face pressed to the wall; but he knew the slender hold he was keeping on his mind and body was going to break. He had a sudden mental picture of his apartment on just the other side of this wall—warm, cheerful, incredibly spacious. And he saw himself striding through it, lying down on the floor on his back, arms spread wide, reveling in its unbelievable security. The impossible remoteness of this utter safety, the contrast between it and where he now stood, was more than he could bear. And the barrier broke then,

and the fear of the awful height he stood on coursed through his nerves and muscles.

A fraction of his mind knew he was going to fall, and he began taking rapid blind steps with no feeling of what he was doing, sidling with a clumsy desperate swiftness, fingers scrabbling along the brick, almost hopelessly resigned to the sudden backward pull and swift motion outward and down. Then his moving left hand slid onto not brick but sheer emptiness, an impossible gap in the face of the wall, and he stumbled.

His right foot smashed into his left anklebone; he staggered sideways, began falling, and the claw of his hand cracked against glass and wood, slid down it, and his finger tips were pressed hard on the puttyless edging of his window. His right hand smacked gropingly beside it as he fell to his knees; and, under the full weight and direct downward pull of his sagging body, the open window dropped shudderingly in its frame till it closed and his wrists struck the sill and were jarred off.

For a single moment he knelt, knee bones against stone on the very edge of the ledge, body swaying and touching nowhere else, fighting for balance. Then he lost it, his shoulders plunging backward, and he flung his arms forward, his hands smashing against the window casing on either side; and—his body moving backward—his fingers clutched the narrow wood stripping of the upper pane.

For an instant he hung suspended between balance and falling, his finger tips pressed onto the quarter-inch wood strips. Then, with utmost delicacy, with a focused concentration of all his senses, he increased even further the strain on his finger tips hooked to these slim edgings of wood. Elbows slowly bending, he began to draw the full weight of his upper body forward, knowing that the instant his fingers slipped off these quarter-inch strips he'd plunge backward and be falling. Elbows imperceptibly bending, body shaking with the strain, the sweat starting from his forehead in great sudden drops, he pulled, his entire being and thought concentrated in his finger tips. Then suddenly, the strain slackened and ended, his chest touching the window sill, and he was kneeling on the ledge, his forehead pressed to the glass of the closed window.

Dropping his palms to the sill, he stared into his living room—at the red-brown davenport across the room, and a magazine he had left there; at the pictures on the walls and the gray rug; the entrance to the hallway; and at his papers, typewriter, and desk, not two feet from his nose. A movement from his desk caught his eye and he saw that it was a thin curl of blue smoke; his cigarette, the ash long, was still burning in the ash tray where he'd left it—this was past all belief—only a few minutes before.

His head moved, and in faint reflection from the glass before him he saw the yellow paper clenched in his front teeth. Lifting a hand from the sill he took it from his mouth; the moistened corner parted from the paper, and he spat it out.

For a moment, in the light from the living room, he stared wonderingly at the yellow sheet in his hand and then crushed it into the side pocket of his jacket.

He couldn't open the window. It had been pulled not completely closed, but its lower edge was below the level of the outside sill; there was no room to get his fingers underneath it. Between the upper sash and the lower was a gap not wide enough—reaching up, he tried—to get his fingers into; he couldn't push it open. The upper window panel, he knew from long experience, was impossible to move, frozen tight with dried paint.

Very carefully observing his balance, the finger tips of his left hand again hooked to the narrow stripping of the window casing, he drew back his right hand, palm facing the glass, and then struck the glass with the heel of his hand.

His arm rebounded from the pane, his body tottering. He knew he didn't dare strike a harder blow.

But in the security and relief of his new position, he simply smiled; with only a sheet of glass between him and the room just before him, it was not possible that there wasn't a way past it. Eyes narrowing, he thought for a few moments about what to do. Then his eyes widened, for nothing occurred to him. But still he felt calm: the trembling, he realized, had stopped. At the back of his mind there still lay the thought that once he was again in his home, he could give release to his feelings. He actually *would* lie on the floor, rolling, clenching tufts of the rug in his hands. He would literally run across the room, free to move as he liked, jumping on the floor, testing and reveling in its absolute security, letting the relief flood through him, draining the fear from

his mind and body. His yearning for this was astonishingly intense, and somehow he understood that he had better keep this feeling at bay.

He took a half dollar from his pocket and struck it against the pane, but without any hope that the glass would break and with very little disappointment when it did not. After a few moments of thought he drew his leg onto the ledge and picked loose the knot of his shoelace. He slipped off the shoe and, holding it across the instep. drew back his arm as far as he dared and struck the leather heel against the glass. The pane rattled, but he knew he'd been a long way from breaking it. His foot was cold and he slipped the shoe back on. He shouted again, experimentally, and then once more, but there was no answer.

The realization suddenly struck him that he might have to wait here till Clare came home, and for a moment the thought was funny. He could see Clare opening the front door, withdrawing her key from the lock, closing the door behind her, and then glancing up to see him crouched on the other side of the window. He could see her rush across the room, face astounded and frightened, and hear himself shouting instructions: "Never mind how I got here! Just open the wind—" She couldn't open it, he remembered, she'd never been able to; she'd always had to call him. She'd have to get the building superintendent or a neighbor, and he pictured himself smiling, and answering their questions as he climbed in. "I just wanted to get a breath of fresh air, so——"

He couldn't possibly wait here till Clare came home. It was the second feature she'd wanted to see, and she'd left in time to see the first. She'd be another three hours or—He glanced at his watch; Clare had been gone eight minutes. It wasn't possible, but only

eight minutes ago he had kissed his wife good-by. She wasn't even at the theater yet!

It would be four hours before she could possibly be home, and he tried to picture himself kneeling out here, finger tips hooked to these narrow strippings, while first one movie, preceded by a slow listing of credits, began, developed, reached its climax, and then finally ended. There'd be a newsreel next, maybe, and then an animated cartoon, and then interminable scenes from coming pictures. And then, once more, the beginning of a full-length picture—while all the time he hung out here in the night.

He might possibly get to his feet, but he was afraid to try. Already his legs were cramped, his thigh muscles tired; his knees hurt, his feet felt numb, and his hands were stiff. He couldn't possibly stay out here for four hours, or anywhere near it. Long before that his legs and arms would give out; he would be forced to try changing his position often—stiffly, clumsily, his coordination and strength gone —and he would fall. Quite realistically, he knew that he would fall; no one could stay out here on this ledge for four hours.

A dozen windows in the apartment building across the street were lighted. Looking over his shoulder, he could see the top of a man's head behind the newspaper he was reading; in another window he saw the blue-gray flicker of a television screen. No more than twenty-odd yards from his back were scores of people, and if just one of them would walk idly to his window and glance out. . . . For some moments he stared over his shoulder at the lighted rectangles, waiting. But no one appeared. The man reading his paper turned a page and then continued his reading. A figure passed another of the windows and was immediately gone.

In the inside pocket of his jacket he found a little sheaf of papers, and he pulled one out and looked at it in the light from the living room. It was an old letter, an advertisement of some sort; his name and address, in purple ink, were on a label pasted to the envelope. Gripping one end of the envelope in his teeth, he twisted it into a tight curl. From his shirt pocket he brought out a book of matches. He didn't dare let go the casing with both hands but, with the twist of paper in his teeth, he opened the matchbook with his free hand; then he bent one of the matches in two without tearing it from the folder, its red-tipped end now touching the striking surface. With his thumb, he rubbed the red tip across the striking area.

He did it again, then again, and still again, pressing harder each time, and the match suddenly flared, burning his thumb. But he kept it alight, cupping the matchbook in his hand and shielding it with his body. He held the flame to the paper in his mouth till it caught. Then he snuffed out the match flame with his thumb and forefinger, careless of the burn, and replaced the book in his pocket. Taking the paper twist in his hand, he held it flame down, watching the flame crawl up the paper, till it flared bright. Then he held it behind him over the street, moving it from side to side, watching it over his shoulder, the flame flickering and guttering in the wind.

There were three letters in his pocket and he lighted each of them, holding each till the flame touched his hand and then dropping it to the street below. At one point, watching over his shoulder while the last of the letters burned, he saw the man across the street put down his paper and stand—even seeming to glance toward Tom's window. But when he moved, it was only to walk across the room and disappear from sight.

There were a dozen coins in Tom

Benecke's pocket and he dropped them, three or four at a time. But if they struck anyone, or if anyone noticed their falling, no one connected them with their source.

His arms had begun to tremble from the steady strain of clinging to this narrow perch, and he did not know what to do now and was terribly frightened. Clinging to the window stripping with one hand, he again searched his pockets. But now —he had left his wallet on his dresser when he'd changed clothes—there was nothing left but the yellow sheet. It occurred to him irrelevantly that his death on the sidewalk below would be an eternal mystery; the window closed—why, how, and from where could he have fallen? No one would be able to identify his body for a time, either—the thought was somehow unbearable and increased his fear. All they'd find in his pockets would be the yellow sheet. *Contents of the dead man's pockets,* he thought, *one sheet of paper bearing penciled notations—incomprehensible.*

He understood fully that he might actually be going to die; his arms, maintaining his balance on the ledge, were trembling steadily now. And it occurred to him then with all the force of a revelation that, if he fell, all he was ever going to have out of life he would then, abruptly, have had. Nothing, then, could ever be changed; and nothing more—no least experience or pleasure—could ever be added to his life. He wished, then, that he had not allowed his wife to go off by herself tonight—and on similar nights. He thought of all the evenings he had spent away from her, working; and he regretted them. He thought wonderingly of his fierce ambition and of the direction his life had taken; he thought of the hours he'd spent by himself, filling the yellow sheet that had brought him out here.

Contents of the dead man's pockets, he thought with sudden fierce anger, *a wasted life.*

He was simply not going to cling here till he slipped and fell; he told himself that now. There was one last thing he could try; he had been aware of it for some moments, refusing to think about it, but now he faced it. Kneeling here on the ledge, the finger tips of one hand pressed to the narrow strip of wood, he could, he knew, draw his other hand back a yard perhaps, fist clenched tight, doing it very slowly till he sensed the outer limit of balance, then, as hard as he was able from the distance, he could drive his fist forward against the glass. If it broke, his fist smashing through, he was safe; he might cut himself badly, and probably would, but with his arm inside the room, he would be secure. But if the glass did not break, the rebound, flinging his arm back, would topple him off the ledge. He was certain of that.

He tested his plan. The fingers of his left hand clawlike on the little stripping, he drew back his other fist until his body began teetering backward. But he had no leverage now—he could feel that there would be no force to his swing—and he moved his fist slowly forward till he rocked forward on his knees again and could sense that this swing would carry its greatest force. Glancing down, however, measuring the distance from his fist to the glass, he saw it was less than two feet.

It occurred to him that he could raise his arm over his head, to bring it down against the glass. But, experimenting in slow motion, he knew it would be an awkward girl-like blow without the force of a driving punch, and not nearly enough to break the glass.

Facing the window, he had to drive a blow from the shoulder, he knew now, at

a distance of less than two feet; and he did not know whether it would break through the heavy glass. It might; he could picture it happening, he could feel it in the nerves of his arm. And it might not; he could feel that too—feel his fist striking this glass and being instantaneously flung back by the unbreaking pane, feel the fingers of his other hand breaking loose, nails scraping along the casing as he fell.

He waited, arm drawn back, fist balled, but in no hurry to strike; this pause, he knew, might be an extension of his life. And to live even a few seconds longer, he felt, even out here on this ledge in the night, was infinitely better than to die a moment earlier than he had to. His arm grew tired, and he brought it down.

Then he knew that it was time to make the attempt. He could not kneel here hesitating indefinitely till he lost all courage to act, waiting till he slipped off the ledge. Again he drew back his arm, knowing this time that he would not bring it down till he struck. His elbow protruding over Lexington Avenue far below, the fingers of his other hand pressed down bloodlessly tight against the narrow stripping, he waited, feeling the sick tenseness and terrible excitement building. It grew and swelled toward the moment of action, his nerves tautening. He thought of Clare—just a wordless, yearning thought—and then drew his arm back just a bit more, fist so tight his fingers pained him, and knowing he was going to do it. Then with full power, with every last scrap of strength he could bring to bear, he shot his arm forward toward the glass, and he said, *"Clare!"*

He heard the sound, felt the blow, felt himself falling forward, and his hand closed on the living-room curtains, the shards and fragments of glass showering onto the floor. And then, kneeling there on the ledge, an arm thrust into the room up to the shoulder, he began picking away the protruding slivers and great wedges of glass from the window frame, tossing them in onto the rug. And, as he grasped the edges of the empty window frame and climbed into his home, he was grinning in triumph.

He did not lie down on the floor or run through the apartment, as he had promised himself; even in the first few moments it seemed to him natural and normal that he should be where he was. He simply turned to his desk, pulled the crumpled yellow sheet from his pocket, and laid it down where it had been, smoothing it out; then he absently laid a pencil across it to weight it down. He shook his head wonderingly, and turned to walk toward the closet.

There he got out his topcoat and hat and, without waiting to put them on, opened the front door and stepped out, to go find his wife. He turned to pull the door closed and the warm air from the hall rushed through the narrow opening again. As he saw the yellow paper, the pencil flying, scooped off the desk and, unimpeded by the glassless window, sail out into the night and out of his life, Tom Benecke burst into laughter and then closed the door behind him.

FOR STUDY AND DISCUSSION

1. Why was the yellow paper so important to Tom? How did he underestimate the difficulty of getting it off the ledge?

2. How is suspense created in this story? Describe the crises, or critical moments, that occur while Tom is on the ledge. What makes each new crisis seem more critical than the one before?

3. In what part of the story was the author especially successful in making you actually *feel* Tom's experience? How did he do this? Where in the story did Tom's reactions seem especially true to life?

4. What are Tom's virtues as man and husband? What are his shortcomings? How does he change as a result of his experience on the ledge? Why does he change? Why does he laugh when the yellow paper flies out the window the second time?

5. There are two aspects to the setting in this story: the Beneckes' apartment—familiar, warm, and safe; and the ledge—strange, frightening, and dangerous. How does each part of the setting affect Tom's actions, and the plot?

6. What are the conflicts in the story? Is there conflict between Tom and his wife? between Tom and nature? between Tom and himself? Which do you think is most important in the story? Why?

7. What comments on work and on ambition are made in this story? What seems to be the author's attitude toward ambition? Do you agree or disagree? Why?

LANGUAGE AND VOCABULARY

The events of "Contents of the Dead Man's Pockets" take little more than ten minutes, although to both Tom Benecke and the reader they seem to take far longer. Since this story is told in strictly chronological order, the author had to make especially careful use of connectives (connecting words). Note the importance of these connectives in the first three paragraphs: "then ... Then ... Now ... as usual ... then ... still ... When ..."

Look again at the connectives (words or phrases) that Finney uses in describing Tom's experience on the ledge. Make a list of the connecting words used in any part of that experience: reaching the yellow paper; picking it up; breaking the window; getting back into the room. How do these "little words" help you follow the story? Rewrite one of the paragraphs, omitting the connectives. What happens to the clear line of the story?

FOR COMPOSITION

The power of "Contents of the Dead Man's Pockets" comes from its account of Tom Benecke's harrowing experience on the ledge. Notice the details Finney used in achieving his effects. Then imagine yourself in a similar tight spot: for instance, you have broken through thin ice just out of reach of shore, or have wandered into quicksand, or have fallen off a boat and come up under a raft or float. Describe in detail how you would get out of this scrape. Try to make your reader *feel* your experience as vividly as Finney made you feel Tom Benecke's.

ABOUT THE AUTHOR

Jack Finney (1911–) was born in Milwaukee and graduated from Knox College in Galesburg, Illinois. While getting his start as a writer, he worked in an advertising agency in New York. Finney has written novels, short stories, and novelettes. Two of his novels, *Five Against the House* (1954) and *The Body Snatchers* (1955), have been made into movies. Finney now lives in California.

To Build a Fire

JACK LONDON

Day had broken cold and gray, exceedingly cold and gray, when the man turned aside from the main Yukon[1] trail and climbed the high earth bank, where a dim and little-traveled trail led eastward through the fat spruce timberland. It was a steep bank, and he paused for breath at the top, excusing the act to himself by looking at his watch. It was nine o'clock. There was no sun nor hint of sun, though there was not a cloud in the sky. It was a clear day, and yet there seemed an intangible pall over the face of things, a subtle gloom that made the day dark, and that was due to the absence of sun. This fact did not worry the man. He was used to the lack of sun. It had been days since he had seen the sun, and he knew that a few more days must pass before that cheerful orb, due south, would just peep above the skyline and dip immediately from view.

The man flung a look back along the way he had come. The Yukon lay a mile wide and hidden under three feet of ice. On top of this ice were as many feet of snow. It was all pure white, rolling in gentle undulations where the ice jams of the freeze-up had formed. North and south, as far as his eye could see, it was unbroken white, save for a dark hairline that curved and twisted from around the spruce-covered island to the south, and that curved and twisted away into the north, where it disappeared behind another spruce-covered island. This dark hairline was the trail—the main trail—that led south five hundred miles to the Chilcoot Pass, Dyea, and salt water; and that led north seventy miles to Dawson, and still on to the north a thousand miles to Nulato,[2] and finally to St. Michael on Bering Sea, a thousand miles and half a thousand more.

But all this—the mysterious, far-reaching hairline trail, the absence of sun from the sky, the tremendous cold, and the strangeness and weirdness of it all—made no impression on the man. It was not because he was long used to it. He was a newcomer in the land, a *chechaquo*[3] and this was his first winter. The trouble with him was that he was without imagination. He was quick and alert in the things of life, but only in the things, and not in the significances. Fifty degrees below zero meant eighty-odd degrees of frost. Such fact impressed him as being cold and uncomfortable, and that was all. It did not lead him to meditate upon his frailty as a creature of temperature, and upon man's frailty in general, able only to live within certain narrow limits of heat and cold; and from there on it did not lead him to the conjectural field of immortality and man's place in the universe. Fifty degrees below zero stood for a bite of frost that hurt and that must be guarded against by the use of mittens, earflaps, warm moccasins, and thick socks. Fifty degrees below zero was to him just precisely fifty degrees below zero. That there should be anything more

[1] **Yukon** (yoo′kon): a territory in northwestern Canada, bordering on Alaska. The Yukon is also the name of the large river running through the territory.

"To Build a Fire" by Jack London. Reprinted by permission of I. Milo Shepard.

[2] **Dawson, Nulato:** towns on the Yukon.
[3] *chechaquo:* tenderfoot.

to it than that was a thought that never entered his head.

As he turned to go on, he spat speculatively. There was a sharp, explosive crackle that startled him. He spat again. And again, in the air, before it could fall to the snow, the spittle crackled. He knew that at fifty below spittle crackled on the snow, but this spittle had crackled in the air. Undoubtedly it was colder than fifty below—how much colder he did not know. But the temperature did not matter. He was bound for the old claim on the left fork of Henderson Creek, where the boys were already. They had come over across the divide from the Indian Creek country, while he had come the roundabout way to take a look at the possibilities of getting out logs in the spring from the islands in the Yukon. He would be in to camp by six o'clock; a bit after dark, it was true, but the boys would be there, a fire would be going, and a hot supper would be ready. As for lunch, he pressed his hand against the protruding bundle under his jacket. It was also under his shirt, wrapped up in a handkerchief and lying against the naked skin. It was the only way to keep the biscuits from freezing. He smiled agreebly to himself as he thought of those biscuits, each cut open and sopped in bacon grease, and each enclosing a generous slice of fried bacon.

He plunged in among the big spruce trees. The trail was faint. A foot of snow had fallen since the last sled had passed over, and he was glad he was without a sled, traveling light. In fact, he carried nothing but the lunch wrapped in the handkerchief. He was surprised, however, at the cold. It certainly was cold, he concluded, as he rubbed his numb nose and cheekbones with his mittened hand. He was a warm-whiskered man, but the hair on his face did not protect the high cheekbones and the eager nose that thrust itself aggressively into the frosty air.

At the man's heels trotted a dog, a big native husky, the proper wolf dog, gray-coated and without any visible or temperamental difference from its brother, the wild wolf. The animal was depressed by the tremendous cold. It knew that it was no time for traveling. Its instinct told it a truer tale than was told to the man by the man's judgment. In reality, it was not merely colder than fifty below zero; it was colder than sixty below, than seventy below. It was seventy-five below zero. Since the freezing point is thirty-two above zero, it meant that one hundred and seven degrees of frost obtained. The dog did not know anything about thermometers. Possibly in its brain there was no sharp consciousness of a condition of very cold such as was in the man's brain. But the brute had its instinct. It experienced a vague but menacing apprehension that subdued it and made it slink

along at the man's heels, and that made it question eagerly every unwonted [1] movement of the man as if expecting him to go into camp or to seek shelter somewhere and build a fire. The dog had learned fire, and it wanted fire, or else to burrow under the snow and cuddle its warmth away from the air.

The frozen moisture of its breathing had settled on its fur in a fine powder of frost, and especially were its jowls, muzzle, and eyelashes whitened by its crystaled breath. The man's red beard and mustache were likewise frosted, but more solidly, the deposit taking the form of ice and increasing with every warm, moist breath he exhaled. Also, the man was chewing tobacco, and the muzzle of ice held his lips so rigidly that he was unable to clear his chin when he expelled the juice. The result was that a crystal beard of the color and solidity of amber was increasing its length on his chin. If he fell down it would shatter itself, like glass, into brittle fragments. But he did not mind the appendage. It was the penalty all tobacco chewers paid in that country, and he had been out before in two cold snaps. They had not been so cold as this, he knew, but by the spirit [2] thermometer at Sixty Mile he knew they had been registered at fifty below and at fifty-five.

He held on through the level stretch of woods for several miles, crossed a wide flat of niggerheads, [3] and dropped down a bank to the frozen bed of a small stream. This was Henderson Creek, and he knew he was ten miles from the forks. He looked at his watch. It was ten o'clock. He was making four miles an hour, and he calculated that he would arrive at the forks at half-past twelve.

[1] **unwonted:** unusual.
[2] **spirit:** alcohol.
[3] **niggerheads:** dark-colored clumps of sedge grass or tundra, common in frozen Arctic wastes.

He decided to celebrate that event by eating his lunch there.

The dog dropped in again at his heels, with a tail drooping discouragement, as the man swung along the creek bed. The furrow of the old sled trail was plainly visible, but a dozen inches of snow covered the marks of the last runners. In a month no man had come up or down that silent creek. The man held steadily on. He was not much given to thinking, and just then particularly he had nothing to think about save that he would eat lunch at the forks and that at six o'clock he would be in camp with the boys. There was nobody to talk to; and, had there been, speech would have been impossible because of the ice muzzle on his mouth. So he continued monotonously to chew tobacco and to increase the length of his amber beard.

Once in a while the thought reiterated itself that it was very cold and that he had never experienced such cold. As he walked along he rubbed his cheekbones and nose with the back of his mittened hand. He did this automatically, now and again changing hands. But rub as he would, the instant he stopped his cheekbones went numb, and the following instant the end of his nose went numb. He was sure to frost his cheeks; he knew that, and experienced a pang of regret that he had not devised a nose strap of that sort Bud wore in cold snaps. Such a strap passed across the cheeks, as well, and saved them. But it didn't matter much, after all. What were frosted cheeks? A bit painful, that was all; they were never serious.

Empty as the man's mind was of thoughts, he was keenly observant, and he noticed the changes in the creek, and curves and bends and timber jams, and always he sharply noted where he placed his feet. Once, coming around a bend, he shied abruptly, like a startled horse,

curved away from the place where he had been walking, and retreated several paces back along the trail. The creek, he knew, was frozen clear to the bottom—no creek could contain water in that arctic winter —but he knew also that there were springs that bubbled out from the hillsides and ran along under the snow and on top of the ice of the creek. He knew that the coldest snaps never froze these springs, and he knew likewise their danger. They were traps. They hid pools of water under the snow that might be three inches deep, or three feet. Sometimes a skin of ice half an inch thick covered them, and in turn was covered by the snow. Sometimes there were alternate layers of water and ice skin, so that when one broke through he kept on breaking through for a while, sometimes wetting himself almost to the waist.

That was why he had shied in such panic. He had felt the give under his feet and heard the crackle of a snow-hidden ice skin. And to get his feet wet in such a temperature meant trouble and danger. At the very least it meant delay, for he would be forced to stop and build a fire, and under its protection to bare his feet while he dried his socks and moccasins. He stood and studied the creek bed and its banks, and decided that the flow of water came from the right. He reflected awhile, rubbing his nose and cheeks, then skirted to the left, stepping gingerly and testing the footing for each step. Once clear of the danger, he took a fresh chew of tobacco and swung along at his four-mile gait.

In the course of the next two hours he came upon several similar traps. Usually the snow above the hidden pools had a sunken, candied appearance that advertised the danger. Once again, however, he had a close call; and once, suspecting danger, he compelled the dog to go on in front. The dog did not want to go. It hung back until the man shoved it forward, and then it went quickly across the white, unbroken surface. Suddenly it broke through, floundered to one side, and got away to firmer footing. It had wet its forefeet and legs, and almost immediately the water that clung to it turned to ice. It made quick efforts to lick the ice off its legs, then dropped down in the snow and began to bite out the ice that had formed between the toes. This was a matter of instinct. To permit the ice to remain would mean sore feet. It did not know this. It merely obeyed the mysterious prompting that arose from the deep

crypts of its being. But the man knew, having achieved a judgment on the subject, and he removed the mitten from his right hand and helped tear out the ice particles. He did not expose his fingers more than a minute, and was astonished at the swift numbness that smote [1] them. It certainly was cold. He pulled on the mitten hastily and beat the hand savagely across his chest.

At twelve o'clock the day was at its brightest. Yet the sun was too far south on its winter journey to clear the horizon.

[1] **smote:** struck suddenly and with great force.

The bulge of the earth intervened between it and Henderson Creek, where the man walked under a clear sky at noon and cast no shadow. At half-past twelve, to the minute, he arrived at the forks of the creek. He was pleased at the speed he had made. If he kept it up, he would certainly be with the boys by six. He unbuttoned his jacket and shirt and drew forth his lunch. The action consumed no more than a quarter of a minute, yet in that brief moment the numbness laid hold of the exposed fingers. He did not put the mitten on, but, instead, struck the fingers a dozen sharp smashes against his leg. Then he sat down on a snow-covered log to eat. The sting that followed upon the striking of his fingers against his leg ceased so quickly that he was startled. He had had no chance to take a bite of biscuit. He struck the fingers repeatedly and returned them to the mitten, baring the other hand for the purpose of eating. He tried to take a mouthful, but the ice muzzle prevented. He had forgotten to build a fire and thaw out. He chuckled at his foolishness, and as he chuckled he noted the numbness creeping into the exposed fingers. Also, he noted that the stinging which had first come to his toes when he sat down was already passing away. He wondered whether his toes were warm or numb. He moved them inside the moccasins and decided that they were numb.

He pulled the mitten on hurriedly and stood up. He was a bit frightened. He stamped up and down until the stinging returned into the feet. It certainly was cold, was his thought. That man from Sulphur Creek had spoken the truth when telling how cold it sometimes got in the country. And he had laughed at him at the time! That showed one must not be too sure of things. There was no mistake about it, it *was* cold. He strode up and down, stamping his feet and threshing his arms, until reassured by the returning warmth. Then he got out matches and proceeded to make a fire. From the undergrowth, where high water of the previous spring had lodged a supply of seasoned twigs, he got his firewood, Working carefully from a small beginning, he soon had a roaring fire, over which he thawed the ice from his face and in the protection of which he ate his biscuits. For the moment the cold of space was outwitted. The dog took satisfaction in the fire, stretching out close enough for warmth and far enough away to escape being singed.

When the man had finished, he filled his pipe and took his comfortable time over a smoke. Then he pulled on his mittens, settled the earflaps of his cap firmly about his ears, and took the creek trail up the left fork. The dog was disappointed and yearned back toward the fire. This man did not know cold. Possibly all the generations of his ancestry had been ignorant of cold, of real cold, of cold one hundred and seven degrees below freezing point. But the dog knew; all its ancestry knew, and it had inherited the knowledge. And it knew that it was not good to walk abroad in such fearful cold. It was the time to lie snug in a hole in the snow and wait for a curtain of cloud to be drawn across the face of outer space whence this cold came. On the other hand, there was no keen intimacy between the dog and man. The one was the toil slave of the other, and the only caress it had ever received were the caresses of the whiplash and of harsh and menacing throat sounds that threatened the whiplash. So the dog made no effort to communicate its apprehension to the man. It was not concerned in the welfare of the man; it was for its own sake that it yearned back toward the fire. But the man whistled, and spoke to it with the sound of whiplashes, and the dog swung in at the man's heels and followed after.

The man took a chew of tobacco and proceeded to start a new amber beard. Also, his moist breath quickly powdered with white his mustache, eyebrows, and lashes. There did not seem to be so many springs on the left fork of the Henderson, and for half an hour the man saw no signs of any. And then it happened. At a place where there were no signs, where the soft, unbroken snow seemed to advertise solidity beneath, the man broke through. It was not deep. He wet himself halfway to the knees before he floundered out to the firm crust.

He was angry, and cursed his luck aloud. He had hoped to get into camp with the boys at six o'clock, and this would delay him an hour, for he would have to build a fire and dry out his footgear. This was imperative at that low temperature —he knew that much; and he turned aside to the bank, which he climbed. On top, tangled in the underbrush about the trunks of several small spruce trees, was a high-water deposit of dry firewood—sticks and twigs, principally, but also larger portions of seasoned branches and fine, dry, last year's grasses. He threw down several large pieces on top of the snow. This served for a foundation and prevented the young flame from drowning itself in the snow it otherwise would melt. The flame he got by touching a match to a small shred of birch bark that he took from his pocket. This burned even more readily than paper. Placing it on the foundation, he fed the young flame with wisps of dry grass and with the tiniest dry twigs.

He worked slowly and carefully, keenly aware of his danger. Gradually, as the flame grew stronger, he increased the size of the twigs with which he fed it. He squatted in the snow, pulling the twigs out from their entanglement in the brush and feeding directly to the flame. He knew there must be no failure. When it is sev-enty-five below zero, a man must not fail in his first attempt to build a fire—that is, if his feet are wet. If his feet are dry, and he fails, he can run along the trail for half a mile and restore his circulation. But the circulation of wet and freezing feet cannot be restored by running when it is seventy-five below. No matter how fast he runs, the wet feet will freeze the harder.

All this the man knew. The oldtimer on Sulphur Creek had told him about it the previous fall, and now he was appreciating the advice. Already all sensation had gone out of his feet. To build the fire he had been forced to remove his mittens, and the fingers had quickly gone numb. His pace of four miles an hour had kept his heart pumping blood to the surface of his body and to all the extremities. But the instant he stopped, the action of the pump eased down. The cold of space smote the unprotected tip of the planet, and he, being on that unprotected tip, received the full force of the blow. The blood of his body recoiled before it. The blood was alive, like the dog, and like the dog it wanted to hide away and cover itself up from the fearful cold. So long as he walked four miles an hour, he pumped that blood, willy-nilly, to the surface; but now it ebbed away and sank down into the recesses of his body. The extremities were the first to feel its absence. His wet

feet froze the faster, and his exposed fingers numbed the faster, though they had not yet begun to freeze. Nose and cheeks were already freezing, while the skin of all his body chilled as it lost its blood.

But he was safe. Toes and nose and cheeks would be only touched by the frost, for the fire was beginning to burn with strength. He was feeding it with twigs the size of his finger. In another minute he would be able to feed it with branches the size of his wrist, and then he could remove his wet footgear, and, while it dried, he could keep his naked feet warm by the fire, rubbing them at first, of course, with snow. The fire was a success. He was safe. He remembered the advice of the oldtimer on Sulphur Creek, and smiled. The oldtimer had been very serious in laying down the law that no man must travel alone in the Klondike after fifty below. Well, here he was; he had had the accident; he was alone; and he had saved himself. Those oldtimers were rather womanish, some of them, he thought. All a man had to do was keep his head, and he was all right. Any man who was a man could travel alone. But it was surprising, the rapidity with which his cheeks and nose were freezing. And he had not thought his fingers could go lifeless in so short a time. Lifeless they were, for he could scarcely make them move together to grip a twig, and they seemed remote from his body and from him. When he touched a twig, he had to look and see whether or not he had hold of it. The wires were pretty well down between him and his finger ends.

All of which counted for little. There was the fire, snapping and crackling and promising life with every dancing flame. He started to untie his moccasins. They were coated with ice; the thick German socks were like sheaths of iron halfway to the knees; and the moccasin strings

were like rods of steel all twisted and knotted as by some conflagration. For a moment he tugged with his numb fingers, then, realizing the folly of trying to work with that lifeless flesh, he drew his sheath knife.

But before he could cut the strings, it happened. It was his own fault or, rather, his mistake. He should not have built the fire under the spruce tree. He should have built it in the open. But it had been easier to pull the twigs from the brush and drop them directly on the fire. Now the tree under which he had done this carried a weight of snow on its boughs. No wind had blown for weeks, and each bough was fully freighted. Each time he had pulled a twig he had communicated a slight agitation to the tree—an imperceptible agitation, so far as he was concerned, but an agitation sufficient to bring about the disaster. High up in the tree one bough capsized its load of snow. This fell on the boughs beneath, capsizing them. This process continued, spreading out and involving the whole tree. It grew like an avalanche, and it descended without warning upon the man and the fire, and the fire was blotted out! Where it had burned there was now spread a mantle of fresh and disordered snow.

The man was shocked. It was as though he had just heard his own sentence of death. For a moment he sat and stared at the spot where the fire had been. Then he grew very calm. Perhaps the oldtimer on Sulphur Creek was right. If he had only

had a trail mate he would have been in no danger now. The trail mate could have built the fire. Well, it was up to him to build the fire over again, and this second time there must be no failure. Even if he succeeded, he would most likely lose some toes. His feet must be badly frozen by now, and there would be some time before the second fire was ready.

Such were his thoughts, but he did not sit and think them. He was busy all the time they were passing through his mind. He made a new foundation for a fire, this time in the open, where no treacherous tree could blot it out. Next, he gathered dry grasses and tiny twigs from the high-water flotsam. He could not bring his fingers together to pull them out, but he was able to gather them by the handful. In this way he got many rotten twigs and bits of green moss that were undesirable, but it was the best he could do. He worked methodically, even collecting an armful of the larger branches to be used later when the fire gathered strength. And all the while the dog sat and watched him, a certain yearning wistfulness in its eyes, for it looked upon him as the fire provider, and the fire was slow in coming.

When all was ready, the man reached in his pocket for a second piece of birch bark. He knew the bark was there, and though he could not feel it with his fingers, he could hear its crisp rustling as he fumbled for it. Try as he would, he could not clutch hold of it. And all the time, in his consciousness, was the knowledge that each instant his feet were freezing. This thought tended to put him in a panic, but he fought against it and kept calm. He pulled up his mittens with his teeth, and threshed his arms back and forth, beating his hands with all his might against his sides. He did this sitting down, and he stood up to do it; and all the while the dog sat in the snow, its wolf brush of a tail curled around warmly over its forefeet, its sharp wolf ears pricked forward intently as it watched the man. And the man, as he beat and threshed with his arms and hands, felt a great surge of envy as he regarded the creature that was warm and secure in its natural covering.

After a time he was aware of the first faraway signals of sensation in his beaten fingers. The faint tingling grew stronger till it evolved into a stinging ache that was excruciating, but which the man hailed with satisfaction. He stripped the mitten from his right hand and fetched forth the birch bark. The exposed fingers were quickly going numb again. Next he brought out his bunch of sulphur matches. But the tremendous cold had already driven the life out of his fingers. In his effort to separate one match from the others, the whole bunch fell in the snow. He tried to pick it out of the snow, but failed. The dead fingers could neither touch nor clutch. He was very careful. He drove the thought of his freezing feet, and nose, and cheeks out of his mind, devoting his whole soul to the matches. He watched, using the sense of vision in place of that of touch, and when he saw his fingers on each side of the bunch, he closed them—that is, he willed to close them, for the wires were down, and the fingers did not obey. He pulled the mitten on the right hand, and beat it fiercely against his knee. Then, with both mittened hands, he scooped the bunch of matches, along with much snow, into his lap. Yet he was no better off.

After some manipulation he managed to get the bunch between the heels of his mittened hands. In this fashion he carried it to his mouth. The ice crackled and snapped when by a violent effort he opened his mouth. He drew the lower jaw in, curled the upper lip out of the way, and scraped the bunch with his upper

teeth in order to separate a match. He succeeded in getting one, which he dropped on his lap. He was no better off. He could not pick it up. Then he devised a way. He picked it up in his teeth and scratched it on his leg. Twenty times he scratched it before he succeeded in lighting it. As it flamed he held it with his teeth to the birch bark. But the burning brimstone went up his nostrils and into his lungs, causing him to cough spasmodically. The match fell into the snow and went out.

The oldtimer on Sulphur Creek was right, he thought in the moment of controlled despair that ensued: after fifty below, a man should travel with a partner. He beat his hands, but failed in exciting any sensation. Suddenly he bared both hands, removing the mittens with his teeth. He caught the whole bunch between the heels of his hands. His arm muscles not being frozen enabled him to press the hand heels tightly against the matches. Then he scratched the bunch along his leg. It flared into flame, seventy sulphur matches at once! There was no wind to blow them out. He kept his head to one side to escape the strangling fumes, and held the blazing bunch to the birch bark. As he so held it, he became aware of sensation in his hand. His flesh was burning. He could smell it. Deep down below the surface he could feel it. The sensation developed into pain that grew acute. And still he endured it, holding the flame of the matches clumsily to the bark that

would not light readily because his own burning hands were in the way, absorbing most of the flame.

At last, when he could endure no more, he jerked his hands apart. The blazing matches fell sizzling into the snow, but the birch bark was alight. He began laying dry grasses and the tiniest twigs on the flame. He could not pick and choose, for he had to lift the fuel between the heels of his hands. Small pieces of rotten wood and green moss clung to the twigs, and he bit them off as well as he could with his teeth. He cherished the flame carefully and awkwardly. It meant life, and it must not perish. The withdrawal of blood from the surface of his body now made him begin to shiver, and he grew more awkward. A large piece of green moss fell squarely on the little fire. He tried to poke it out with his fingers, but his shivering frame made him poke too far, and he disrupted the nucleus of the little fire, the burning grasses and tiny twigs separating and scattering. He tried to poke them together again, but in spite of the tenseness of the effort, his shivering got away from him, and the twigs were hopelessly scattered. Each twig gushed a puff of smoke and went out. The fire provider had failed. As he looked apathetically about him, his eyes chanced on the dog, sitting across the ruins of the fire from him, in the snow, making restless, hunching movements, slightly lifting one forefoot and then the

other, shifting its weight back and forth on them with wistful eagerness and eyeing the fire provider expectantly.

The sight of the dog put a wild idea into his head. He remembered the tale of the man, caught in a blizzard, who killed a steer, and crawled inside the carcass, and so was saved. He would kill the dog and bury his hands in the warm body until the numbness went out of them. Then he could build another fire. He spoke to the dog, calling it to him; but in his voice was a strange note of fear that frightened the animal, who had never known the man to speak in such a way before. Something was the matter, and its suspicious nature sensed danger—it knew not what danger, but somewhere, somehow, in its brain arose an apprehension of the man. It flattened its ears down at the sound of the man's voice, and its restless, hunching movements and the liftings and shiftings of its forefeet became more pronounced; but it would not come to the man. He got

on his hands and knees and crawled toward the dog. This unusual posture again excited suspicion, and the animal sidled mincingly away.

The man sat up in the snow for a moment and struggled for calmness. Then he pulled on his mittens, by means of his

teeth, and got upon his feet. He glanced down at first in order to assure himself that he was really standing up, for the absence of sensation in his feet left him unrelated to the earth. His erect position in itself started to drive the webs of suspicion from the dog's mind; and when he spoke peremptorily, with the sound of whiplashes in his voice, the dog rendered its customary allegiance and came to him. As it came within reaching distance, the man lost his control. His arms flashed out to the dog, and he experienced genuine surprise when he discovered that his hands could not clutch, that there was neither bend nor feeling in the fingers. He had forgotten for the moment that they were frozen and that they were freezing more and more. All this happened quickly, and before the animal could get away, he encircled its body with his arms. He sat down in the snow, and in this fashion held the dog, while it snarled and whined and struggled.

But it was all he could do, hold its body encircled in his arms and sit there. He realized that he could not kill the dog. There was no way to do it. With his helpless hands he could neither draw nor hold his sheath knife nor throttle the animal. He released it, and it plunged wildly away, with tail between its legs, and still snarling. It halted forty feet away and surveyed him curiously, with ears sharply pricked forward. The man looked down at his hands in order to locate them, and found them hanging on the ends of his arms. It struck him as curious that one should have to use his eyes in order to find out where his hands were. He began threshing his arms back and forth, beating the mittened hands against his sides. He did this for five minutes, violently, and his heart pumped enough blood up to the surface to put a stop to his shivering. But no sensation was

aroused in the hands. He had an impression that they hung like weights on the ends of his arms, but when he tried to run the impression down, he could not find it.

A certain fear of death, dull and oppressive, came to him. This fear quickly became poignant as he realized that it was no longer a mere matter of freezing his fingers and toes, or of losing his hands and feet, but that it was a matter of life and death, with the chances against him. This threw him into a panic, and he turned and ran up the creek bed along the old, dim trail. The dog joined in behind and kept up with him. He ran blindly, without intention, in fear such as he had never known in his life. Slowly, as he ploughed and floundered through the snow, he began to see things again—the banks of the creek, the old timber jams, the leafless aspens, and the sky. The running made him feel better. He did not shiver. Maybe, if he ran on, his feet would thaw out; and, anyway, if he ran far enough, he would reach camp and the boys. Without doubt he would lose some fingers and toes and some of his face; but the boys would take care of him, and save the rest of him when he got there. And at the same time there was another thought in his mind that said he would never get to the camp and the boys; that it was too many miles away, that he would soon be stiff and dead. This thought he kept in the background and refused to consider. Sometimes it pushed itself forward and demanded to be heard, but he thrust it back and strove to think of other things.

It struck him as curious that he could run at all on feet so frozen that he could not feel them when they struck the earth and took the weight of his body. He seemed to himself to skim along above the surface, and to have no connection with the earth. Somewhere he had once seen a winged Mercury,[1] and he wondered if Mercury felt as he felt when skimming over the earth.

His theory of running until he reached camp and the boys had one flaw in it: he lacked the endurance. Several times he stumbled, and finally he tottered, crumpled up, and fell. When he tried to rise, he failed. He must sit and rest, he decided, and next time he would merely walk and keep on going. As he sat and regained his breath, he noted that he was feeling quite warm and comfortable. He was not shivering, and it even seemed that a warm glow had come to his chest and trunk. And yet, when he touched his nose or cheeks, there was no sensation. Running would not thaw them out. Nor would it thaw out his hands and feet. Then the thought came to him that the frozen portions of his body must be extending. He tried to keep this thought down, to forget it, to think of something else; he was aware of the panicky feeling that it caused, and he was afraid of the panic. But the thought asserted itself, and persisted, until it produced a vision of his body totally frozen. This was too much, and he made another wild run along the trail. Once he slowed down to a walk, but the thought of the freezing extending itself made him run again.

And all the time the dog ran with him, at his heels. When he fell down a second time, it curled its tail over its forefeet and sat in front of him, facing him, curiously eager and intent. The warmth and security of the animal angered him, and he cursed it till it flattened down its ears appeasingly. This time the shivering came more quickly upon the man. He was losing in his battle with the frost. It was creeping into his body from all sides. The thought of it

[1] **Mercury:** in Roman mythology, the messenger of the gods, who wore winged sandals and ran with incredible speed.

drove him on, but he ran no more than a hundred feet, when he staggered and pitched headlong. It was his last panic. When he had recovered his breath and control, he sat up and entertained in his mind the conception of meeting death with dignity. However, the conception did not come to him in such terms. His idea of it was that he had been making a fool of himself, running around like a chicken with its head cut off—such was the simile that occurred to him. Well, he was bound to freeze anyway, and he might as well take it decently. With this new-found peace of mind came the first glimmerings of drowsiness. A good idea, he thought, to sleep off to death. It was like taking an anesthetic. Freezing was not so bad as people thought. There were lots worse ways to die.

He pictured the boys finding his body the next day. Suddenly he found himself with them, coming along the trail and looking for himself. And, still with them, he came around a turn in the trail and found himself lying in the snow. He did not belong with himself any more, for even then he was out of himself, standing with the boys and looking at himself in the snow. It certainly was cold, was his thought. When he got back to the States he could tell the folks what real cold was. He drifted on from this to a vision of the old-timer on Sulphur Creek. He could see him quite clearly, warm and comfortable.

"You were right, old hoss; you were right," the man mumbled to the old-timer of Sulphur Creek.

Then the man drowsed off into what seemed to him the most comfortable and satisfying sleep he had ever known. The dog sat facing him and waiting. The brief day drew to a close in a long, slow twilight. There were no signs of a fire to be made, and besides, never in the dog's experience had it known a man to sit like that in the snow and make no fire. As the twilight drew on, its eager yearning for the fire mastered it. With a great lifting and shifting of forefeet, it whined softly, then flattened its ears down in anticipation of being chidden by the man. But the man remained silent. Later, the dog whined loudly. And still later it crept close to the man and caught the scent of death. This made the animal bristle and back away. A little longer it delayed, howling under the stars that leaped and danced and shone brightly in the cold sky. Then it turned and trotted up the trail in the direction of the camp it knew, where were the other food providers and fire providers.

FOR STUDY AND DISCUSSION

1. Where in the story does the man first become aware of the danger of the cold? How does this awareness affect his later actions? If he had realized the danger earlier and more fully, what might he have done differently?

2. What are the chief conflicts in the story? Is there conflict between man and dog? between man and nature? between man and himself?

3. What is the relationship between the man and his dog? What essential difference between them enables the dog to escape the man's fate?

4. The author tells us that the man was "without imagination" and "not much given to thinking." What does he tell us indirectly about the man's weaknesses of character? What are his strengths of character? What mistakes does he make that lead to his destruction? Are they mistakes of judgment only, or are they due largely to his character?

5. What does the story suggest about the kind of man who is most likely to survive challenges and trials? Which does London feel is more important—physical strength or an awareness of the possible consequences of one's actions? Do you agree? Why or why not?

6. What does the story suggest about man's place in nature? What purpose do you think

the author might have had in not giving his character a name?

7. The plot of this story is a simple one: a man making a trek in the Arctic freezes to death because he is unable to build a fire. Which moments in the story are the most exciting? Do they also suggest a wider meaning?

SUSPENSE AND PLOT

Compare the creation of suspense in "Contents of the Dead Man's Pockets" and "To Build a Fire." In which story were you more uncertain of the outcome? Which story do you think would have held your attention better if you had known its outcome from the start?

Would "To Build a Fire" be a better story if it had a happy ending? Would "Contents of the Dead Man's Pockets" be better if it had an unhappy one? Why or why not? Would changing the ending of either story change its meaning?

Which story—"Contents of the Dead Man's Pockets" or "To Build a Fire"—is more powerful and meaningful? What makes it so?

LANGUAGE AND VOCABULARY

You may have been taught that repeating words is a sin in writing—and it is, when the effect is one of monotony. Yet the repetition of words can be one of a writer's most effective devices. In "To Build a Fire," Jack London uses simple words over and over again for a single dominant effect. To make the reader feel the cold and see the bleak landscape, he pounds these words into the reader's mind. What is the dominant impression of each of the following passages? What repeated word or words is responsible for each impression?

"Day had broken cold and gray, exceedingly cold and gray. . ."

"There was no sun nor hint of sun . . . a subtle gloom that made the day dark, and that was due to the absence of sun. . . . He was used to the lack of sun. It had been days since he had seen the sun . . ."

"It certainly was cold . . . It certainly was cold . . . It certainly was cold . . ."

What is the effect of London's mentioning so often, in the same words, the oldtimer on Sulphur Creek? Would he have done better to call the old prospector something slightly different each time?

FOR COMPOSITION

1. "But before he could cut the strings, it happened. It was his own fault or, rather, his mistake. He should not have built the fire under the spruce tree." All of us have undertaken some action which seemed well on the way to success, only to have the whole thing ruined by a careless mistake or lack of planning. In a short narrative based on your own experience, tell how something seemed to be a complete success and then suddenly came to nothing. The incident need not be a matter of life or death, as it was to the man in London's story.

2. The dominant mood of this story is one of grim hopelessness. In a short essay about the story, explain with specific examples some of the ways in which London builds up this mood. Do not limit your discussion to repetition.

ABOUT THE AUTHOR

Jack London (1876–1916) lived a life as colorful and adventurous as the novels and short stories that made him famous. Born in poverty in San Francisco, he had to make his own way in life, but became in his lifetime well known throughout the world. By the time he published his first book at the age of twenty-four, he had been a hobo, a longshoreman, an oyster pirate, a seaman before the mast, and a prospector for gold in Alaska. He had also served, for vagrancy, a month at hard labor in New York State, and had been jailed in California for speaking at a socialist meeting. His experiences in the Klondike gold rush of 1896 gave him the background for "To Build a Fire" and other stories. In general, his fiction features physical conflict, "the survival of the fittest," and sympathy for the underprivileged. His best-known novels are *The Call of the Wild* and *Martin Eden*.

CHARACTER

Plot in a short story consists largely of what the characters do. What the characters do, in a good short story, is determined by what they are. In other words, in good fiction, plot is determined by character.

One of the great pleasures of reading fiction is getting acquainted with new people. We can meet in fiction a wider range and variety of people than we could ever know in life, and often the characters in fiction are more interesting than the people we meet in life. They are more interesting because we can know them better. Fiction, for two reasons, allows us to see more deeply into the inner nature of a character than we usually can in life. First, it places its characters in crucial situations, which test them and expose their nature more clearly than would ordinary situations. Second, the author can, when he wishes, take us inside a character and let us experience at first-hand inner thoughts and feelings which in life we could only guess at from outward actions. Of course, fictional characters are imaginary people and have only imaginary existence. Yet if their author has drawn them accurately, we can, by understanding them, gain a better appreciation of real people. Indeed, we may come to understand ourselves better by reading about characters who are like us in certain ways.

If fiction is to give us these benefits, however, it must be written by an author who is deeply interested in human nature. Not all fiction is. Some writers are satisfied to engage our momentary interest in following the adventures of a brave, resourceful hero or in sharing the good fortune of a beautiful heroine. Such a writer is likely to present us with oversimplified characters who have none of the complexity of real people. To be believable, a character cannot be either all good or all bad; we know that real people are not like that. Also, a character must be consistent in his actions: he must not act one way on one occasion and an entirely different way on another. In addition, his actions should be clearly motivated: that is, we should be able to understand the reasons for his acting as he does. If a character changes during the course of the story, we should be able to understand why he changes. Sudden changes of heart for no apparent reason are more commonly found in third-rate than in first-rate fiction.

An author may present his characters ("characterize" them) either *directly*, by simply telling us what a character is like, or *indirectly*, by showing us what the character does or says or thinks or feels. If a character is to be fully convincing, the author must do a good deal of showing as well as telling. He must *dramatize* his characters—show them speaking and acting. What we are *told* about a character will have little force unless we are *shown* the character behaving as he has been described. Modern writers often rely entirely on indirect presentation. Although this method puts a greater burden on the reader, who must decide for himself what a character is like, it can greatly increase the speed and vividness of a story.

The Revolt of "Mother"

MARY E. WILKINS FREEMAN

A revolution has occurred in American life since 1891, when this story was first published. Today women can vote; they engage in business and in the professions; and they claim equality with men in all areas of life. But in New England in the last century, woman's place was in the home. The husband was lord and master of the household, and a social order such as we have today would have been regarded by most people as a violation of the laws of nature.

FATHER!"

"What is it?"

"What are them men diggin' over there in the field for?"

There was a sudden dropping and enlarging of the lower part of the old man's face, as if some heavy weight had settled therein; he shut his mouth tight and went on harnessing the great bay mare. He hustled the collar on to her neck with a jerk.

"Father!"

The old man slapped the saddle upon the mare's back.

"Look here, Father, I want to know what them men are diggin' over in the field for, an' I'm goin' to know."

"I wish you'd go into the house,

"The Revolt of 'Mother'" from *A New England Nun and Other Stories* by Mary E. Wilkins Freeman. Reprinted by permission of Harper & Row, Publishers.

Mother, an' 'tend to your own affairs," the old man said then. He ran his words together, and his speech was almost as inarticulate as a growl.

But the woman understood; it was her native tongue. "I ain't goin' into the house till you tell me what them men are doin' over there in the field," said she.

Then she stood waiting. She was a small woman, short and straight-waisted like a child in her brown cotton gown. Her forehead was mild and benevolent between the smooth curves of gray hair; there were meek downward lines about her nose and mouth; but her eyes, fixed upon the old man, looked as if the meekness had been the result of her own will, never of the will of another.

They were in the barn, standing before the wide open doors. The spring air, full of the smell of growing grass and unseen blossoms, came in their faces. The deep yard in front was littered with farm wagons and piles of wood; on the edges, close to the fence and the house, the grass was a vivid green, and there were some dandelions.

The old man glanced doggedly at his wife as he tightened the last buckles on the harness. She looked as immovable to him as one of the rocks in his pasture land, bound to the earth with generations of blackberry vines. He slapped the reins over the horse, and started forth from the barn.

"*Father!*" said she.

The old man pulled up. "What is it?"

"I want to know what them men are diggin' over there in that field for."

"They're diggin' a cellar, I s'pose, if you've got to know."

"A cellar for what?"

"A barn."

"A barn? You ain't goin' to build a barn over there where we was goin' to have a house, Father?"

The old man said not another word. He hurried the horse into the farm wagon and clattered out of the yard, jouncing as sturdily on his seat as a boy.

The woman stood a moment looking after him, then she went out of the barn across a corner of the yard to the house. The house, standing at right angles with the great barn and a long reach of sheds and outbuildings, was infinitesimal compared with them. It was scarcely as commodious for people as the little boxes under the barn eaves were for doves.

A pretty girl's face, pink and delicate as a flower, was looking out of one of the house windows. She was watching three men who were digging over in the field which bounded the yard near the road line. She turned quietly when the woman entered.

"What are they digging for, Mother?" said she. "Did he tell you?"

"They're diggin' for—a cellar for a new barn."

"Oh, Mother, he ain't going to build another barn?"

"That's what he says."

A boy stood before the kitchen glass combing his hair. He combed slowly and painstakingly, arranging his brown hair in a smooth hillock over his forehead. He did not seem to pay any attention to the conversation.

"Sammy, did you know Father was going to build a new barn?" asked the girl.

The boy combed assiduously.

"Sammy!"

He turned and showed a face like his father's under his smooth crest of hair. "Yes, I s'pose I did," he said reluctantly.

"How long have you known it?" asked his mother.

"'Bout three months, I guess."

"Why didn't you tell of it?"

"Didn't think 'twould do no good."

"I don't see what Father wants another barn for," said the girl, in her sweet, slow voice. She turned again to the window and stared out at the digging men in the field. Her tender, sweet face was full of gentle distress. Her forehead was as bald and innocent as a baby's, with the light hair strained back from it in a row of curl papers. She was quite large, but her soft curves did not look as if they covered muscles.

Her mother looked sternly at the boy. "Is he goin' to buy more cows?" said she.

The boy did not reply; he was tying his shoes.

"Sammy, I want you to tell me if he's goin' to buy more cows."

"I s'pose he is."

"How many?"

"Four, I guess."

His mother said nothing more. She went into the pantry, and there was a clatter of dishes. The boy got his cap from a nail behind the door, took an old arithmetic from the shelf, and started for school. He was lightly built, but clumsy. He went out of the yard with a curious spring in the hips, that made his loose homemade jacket tilt up in the rear.

The girl went to the sink and began to wash the dishes that were piled up there. Her mother came promptly out of the pantry and shoved her aside. "You wipe 'em," said she; "I'll wash. There's a good many this mornin'."

The mother plunged her hands vigorously into the water; the girl wiped the plates slowly and dreamily. "Mother," said she, "don't you think it's too bad Father's going to build that new barn, much as we need a decent house to live in?"

Her mother scrubbed a dish fiercely. "You ain't found out yet we're women-folks, Nanny Penn," said she. "You ain't seen enough of menfolks yet to. One of these days you'll find it out, an' then you'll know that we know only what menfolks think we do, so far as any use of it goes, an' how we'd ought to reckon menfolks in with Providence [1] an' not complain of what they do any more than we do of the weather."

"I don't care; I don't believe George is anything like that, anyhow," said Nanny.

[1] **Providence:** the ruling power in the world; God.

Her delicate face flushed pink, her lips pouted softly, as if she were going to cry.

"You wait an' see. I guess George Eastman ain't no better than other men. You hadn't ought to judge Father, though. He can't help it, 'cause he don't look at things jest the way we do. An' we've been pretty comfortable here, after all. The roof don't leak—ain't never but once—that's one thing. Father's kept it shingled right up."

"I do wish we had a parlor."

"I guess it won't hurt George Eastman any to come to see you in a nice clean kitchen. I guess a good many girls don't have as good a place as this. Nobody's ever heard me complain."

"I ain't complained either, Mother."

"Well, I don't think you'd better, a good father an' a good home as you've got. S'pose your father made you go out an' work for your livin'? Lots of girls have to that ain't no stronger an' better able to than you be."

Sarah Penn washed the frying pan with a conclusive air. She scrubbed the outside of it as faithfully as the inside. She was a masterly keeper of her box of a house. Her one living room never seemed to have in it any of the dust which the friction of life with inanimate matter produces. She swept, and there seemed to be no dirt to go before the broom; she cleaned, and one could see no difference. She was like an artist so perfect that he has apparently no art. Today she got out a mixing bowl and a board and rolled some pies, and there was no more flour upon her than upon her daughter who was doing finer work. Nanny was to be married in the fall, and she was sewing on some white cambric and embroidery. She sewed industriously while her mother cooked; her soft milk-white hands and wrists showed whiter than her delicate work.

"We must have the stove moved out

in the shed before long," said Mrs. Penn. "Talk about not havin' things, it's been a real blessin' to be able to put a stove up in that shed in hot weather. Father did one good thing when he fixed that stovepipe out there."

Sarah Penn's face as she rolled her pies had that expression of meek vigor which might have characterized one of the New Testament saints. She was making mince pies. Her husband, Adoniram Penn, liked them better than any other kind. She baked twice a week. Adoniram often liked a piece of pie between meals. She hurried this morning. It had been later than usual when she began, and she wanted to have a pie baked for dinner. However deep a resentment she might be forced to hold against her husband, she would never fail in sedulous attention to his wants.

Nobility of character manifests itself at loopholes when it is not provided with large doors. Sarah Penn's showed itself today in flaky dishes of pastry. So she made the pies faithfully, while across the table she could see, when she glanced up from her work, the sight that rankled in her patient and steadfast soul—the digging of the cellar of the new barn in the place where Adoniram forty years ago had promised her their new house should stand.

The pies were done for dinner. Adoniram and Sammy were home a few minutes after twelve o'clock. The dinner was eaten with serious haste. There was never much conversation at the table in the Penn family. Adoniram asked a blessing, and they ate promptly, then rose up and went about their work.

Sammy went back to school, taking soft sly lopes out of the yard like a rabbit. He wanted a game of marbles before school and feared his father would give him some chores to do. Adoniram has-

tened to the door and called after him, but he was out of sight.

"I don't see what you let him go for, Mother," said he. "I wanted him to help me unload that wood."

Adoniram went to work out in the yard unloading wood from the wagon. Sarah put away the dinner dishes, while Nanny took down her curl papers and changed her dress. She was going down to the store to buy some more embroidery and thread.

When Nanny was gone, Mrs. Penn went to the door. "Father!" she called.

"Well, what is it!"

"I want to see you jest a minute, Father."

"I can't leave this wood nohow. I've got to git it unloaded an' go for a load of gravel afore two o'clock. Sammy had ought to helped me. You hadn't ought to let him go to school so early."

"I want to see you jest a minute."

"I tell ye I can't, nohow, Mother."

"Father, you come here." Sarah Penn stood in the door like a queen; she held her head as if it bore a crown; there was that patience which makes authority royal in her voice. Adoniram went.

Mrs. Penn led the way into the kitchen and pointed to a chair. "Sit down, Father," said she; "I've got somethin' I want to say to you."

He sat down heavily; his face was quite stolid, but he looked at her with restive eyes. "Well, what is it, Mother?"

"I want to know what you're buildin' that new barn for, Father?"

"I ain't got nothin' to say about it."

"It can't be you think you need another barn?"

"I tell ye I ain't got nothin' to say about it, Mother; an' I ain't goin' to say nothin'."

"Be you goin' to buy more cows?"

Adoniram did not reply; he shut his mouth tight.

"I know you be, as well as I want to. Now, Father, look here"—Sarah Penn had not sat down; she stood before her husband in the humble fashion of a Scripture woman [1]—"I'm goin' to talk real plain to you; I never have sence I married you, but I'm goin' to now. I ain't never complained, an' I ain't goin' to complain now, but I'm goin' to talk plain. You see this room here, Father; you look at it well. You see there ain't no carpet on the floor, an' you see the paper is all dirty an' droppin' off the walls. We ain't had no new paper on it for ten year, an' then I put it on myself, an' it didn't cost but ninepence a roll. You see this room, Father; it's all the one I've had to work in an' eat in an' sit in sence we was married. There ain't another woman in the whole town whose husband ain't got half the means you have but what's got better. It's all the room Nanny's got to have her company in; an' there ain't one of her mates but what's got better, an' their fathers not so able as hers is.

It's all the room she'll have to be married in. What would you have thought, Father, if we had had our weddin' in a room no better than this? I was married in my mother's parlor, with a carpet on the floor, an' stuffed furniture, an' a mahogany card table. An' this is all the room my daughter will have to be married in. Look here, Father!"

Sarah Penn went across the room as though it were a tragic stage. She flung open a door and disclosed a tiny bedroom, only large enough for a bed and bureau, with a path between. "There, Father," said she—"there's all the room I've had to sleep in forty year. All my children were born there—the two that died, an' the two that's livin'. I was sick with a fever there."

She stepped to another door and opened it. It led into the small, ill-lighted pantry. "Here," said she, "is all the buttery I've got—every place I've got for my dishes, to set away my victuals [2] in, an' to keep my milk pans in. Father, I've been takin' care of the milk of six cows in this place, an'

[1] **Scripture woman:** a woman of Biblical times, when women were considered merely the servants or helpers of their husbands.

[2] **victuals** (vit'lz): food.

now you're going to build a new barn, an' keep more cows, an' give me more to do in it."

She threw open another door. A narrow crooked flight of stairs wound upward from it. "There, Father," said she, "I want you to look at the stairs that go up to them two unfinished chambers that are all the places our son an' daughter have had to sleep in all their lives. There ain't a prettier girl in town nor a more lady-like one than Nanny, an' that's the place she has to sleep in. It ain't so good as your horse's stall; it ain't so warm an' tight."

Sarah Penn went back and stood before her husband. "Now, Father," said she, "I want to know if you think you're doin' right an' accordin' to what you profess. Here, when we was married, forty year ago, you promised me faithful that we should have a new house built in that lot over in the field before the year was out. You said you had money enough, an' you wouldn't ask me to live in no such place as this. It is forty year now, an' you've been makin' more money, an' I've been savin' of it for you ever sence, an' you ain't built no house yet. You've built sheds an' cow houses an' one new barn an' now you're goin' to build another. Father, I want to know if you think it's

right. You're lodgin' your dumb beasts better than you are your own flesh an' blood. I want to know if you think it's right."

"I ain't got nothin' to say."

"You can't say nothin' without ownin' it ain't right, Father. An' there's another thing—I ain't complained; I've got along forty year, an' I s'pose I should forty more, if it wa'n't for that—if we don't have another house, Nanny she can't live with us after she's married. She'll have to go somewheres else to live away from us, an' it don't seem as if I could have it so, noways, Father. She wa'n't ever strong. She's got considerable color, but there wa'n't never any backbone to her. I've always took the heft of everything off her, an' she ain't fit to keep house an' do everything herself. She'll be all worn out inside of a year. Think of her doin' all the washin' an' ironin' an' bakin' with them soft white hands an' arms, an' sweepin'! I can't have it so, noways, Father."

Mrs. Penn's face was burning; her mild eyes gleamed. She had pleaded her little cause like a Webster;[1] she had ranged from severity to pathos; but her opponent employed that obstinate silence which makes eloquence futile with mocking echoes. Adoniram arose clumsily.

"Father, ain't you got nothin' to say?" said Mrs. Penn.

"I've got to go off after that load of gravel. I can't stan' here talkin' all day."

"Father, won't you think it over an' have a house built there instead of a barn?"

"I ain't got nothin' to say."

Adoniram shuffled out. Mrs. Penn went into her bedroom. When she came out, her eyes were red. She had a roll of un-bleached cotton cloth. She spread it out on the kitchen table and began cutting out some shirts for her husband. The men

[1] **Webster:** Daniel Webster (1782–1852), famous American orator and public speaker.

over in the field had a team to help them this afternoon; she could hear their halloos. She had a scanty pattern for the shirts; she had to plan and piece the sleeves.

Nanny came home with her embroidery and sat down with her needlework. She had taken down her curl papers and there was a soft roll of fair hair like an aureole [1] over her forehead; her face was as delicately fine and clear as porcelain. Suddenly she looked up, and the tender red flamed all over her face and neck. "Mother," said she.

"What say?"

"I've been thinking—I don't see how we're goin' to have any—wedding in this room. I'd be ashamed to have his folks come if we didn't have anybody else."

"Mebbe we can have some new paper before then; I can put it on. I guess you won't have no call to be ashamed of your belongin's."

"We might have the wedding in the new barn," said Nanny, with gentle pettishness. "Why, Mother, what makes you look so?"

Mrs. Penn had started, and was staring at her with a curious expression. She turned again to her work and spread out a pattern carefully on the cloth. "Nothin'," said she.

Presently Adoniram clattered out of the yard in his two-wheeled dump cart, standing as proudly upright as a Roman charioteer. Mrs. Penn opened the door and stood there a minute looking out; the halloos of the men sounded louder.

It seemed to her all through the spring months that she heard nothing but the halloos and the noises of saws and hammers. The new barn grew fast. It was a

[1] **aureole** (ôr'ē·ōl): halo, radiant crown.

fine edifice for this little village. Men came on pleasant Sundays, in their meeting suits and clean shirt bosoms, and stood around it admiringly. Mrs. Penn did not speak of it, and Adoniram did not mention it to her, although sometimes, upon a return from inspecting it, he bore himself with injured dignity.

"It's a strange thing how your mother feels about the new barn," he said, confidentially, to Sammy one day.

Sammy only grunted after an odd fashion for a boy; he had learned it from his father.

The barn was all completed ready for use by the third week in July. Adoniram had planned to move his stock in on Wednesday; on Tuesday he received a letter which changed his plans. He came in with it early in the morning. "Sammy's been to the post office," said he, "an' I've got a letter from Hiram." Hiram was Mrs. Penn's brother, who lived in Vermont.

"Well," said Mrs. Penn, "what does he say about the folks?"

"I guess they're all right. He says he thinks if I come up country right off there's a chance to buy jest the kind of a horse I want." He stared reflectively out of the window at the new barn.

Mrs. Penn was making pies. She went on clapping the rolling pin into the crust, although she was very pale, and her heart beat loudly.

"I dun' know but what I'd better go," said Adoniram. "I hate to go off jest now, right in the midst of hayin', but the ten-acre lot's cut, an' I guess Rufus an' the others can git along without me three or four days. I can't get a horse round here to suit me, nohow, an' I've got to have another for all that wood haulin' in the fall. I told Hiram to watch out, an' if he got wind of a good horse to let me know. I guess I'd better go."

"I'll get out your clean shirt an' collar," said Mrs. Penn calmly.

She laid out Adoniram's Sunday suit and his clean clothes on the bed in the little bedroom. She got his shaving water and razor ready. At last she buttoned on his collar and fastened his black cravat.

Adoniram never wore his collar and cravat except on extra occasions. He held his head high, with a rasped dignity. When he was all ready, with his coat and hat brushed, and a lunch of pie and cheese in a paper bag, he hesitated on the threshold of the door. He looked at his wife, and his manner was defiantly apologetic. "If them cows come today, Sammy can drive 'em into the new barn," said he; "an' when they bring the hay up, they can pitch it in there."

"Well," replied Mrs. Penn.

Adoniram set his shaven face ahead and started. When he had cleared the doorstep, he turned and looked back with a kind of nervous solemnity. "I shall be back by Saturday if nothin' happens," said he.

"Do be careful, Father," replied his wife.

She stood in the door with Nanny at her elbow and watched him out of sight. Her eyes had a strange, doubtful expression in them; her peaceful forehead was contracted. She went in and about her baking again. Nanny sat sewing. Her wedding day was drawing nearer, and she was getting pale and thin with her steady sewing. Her mother kept glancing at her.

"Have you got that pain in your side this mornin'?" she asked.

"A little."

Mrs. Penn's face, as she worked, changed, her perplexed forehead smoothed, her eyes were steady, her lips firmly set. She formed a maxim for herself, although incoherently with her unlettered thoughts. "Unsolicited opportunities are the guideposts of the Lord to the new roads of life," she repeated in effect, and she made up her mind to her course of action.

"S'posin' I *had* wrote to Hiram," she muttered once, when she was in the pantry—"s'posin' I had wrote an' asked him if he knew of any horse? But I didn't an' Father's goin' wa'n't none of my doin'. It looks like a providence."[1] Her voice rang out quite loud at the last.

"What you talkin' about, Mother?" called Nanny.

"Nothin'."

Mrs. Penn hurried her baking; at eleven o'clock it was all done. The load of hay from the west field came slowly down the cart track and drew up at the new barn. Mrs. Penn ran out. "Stop!" she screamed —"stop!"

The men stopped and looked; Sammy upreared from the top of the load and stared at his mother.

"Stop!" she cried out again. "Don't you put the hay in that barn; put it in the old one."

"Why, he said to put it in here," re-

[1] **a providence:** a colloquial expression referring to an event brought about by fate or by God's will.

turned one of the haymakers, wonderingly. He was a young man, a neighbor's son, whom Adoniram hired by the year to help on the farm.

"Don't you put the hay in the new barn; there's room enough in the old one, ain't there?" said Mrs. Penn.

"Room enough," returned the hired man, in his thick, rustic tones. "Didn't need the new barn, nohow, far as room's concerned. Well, I s'pose he changed his mind." He took hold of the horses' bridles.

Mrs. Penn went back to the house. Soon the kitchen windows were darkened, and a fragrance like warm honey came into the room.

Nanny laid down her work. "I thought father wanted them to put the hay into the new barn?" she said wonderingly.

"It's all right," replied her mother.

Sammy slid down from the load of hay and came in to see if dinner was ready.

"I ain't goin' to get a regular dinner today, as long as Father's gone," said his mother. "I've let the fire go out. You can have some bread an' milk an' pie. I thought we could get along." She set out some bowls of milk, some bread, and a pie on the kitchen table. "You better eat your dinner now," said she. "You might jest as well get through with it. I want you to help me afterward."

Nanny and Sammy stared at each other. There was something strange in their mother's manner. Mrs. Penn did not eat anything herself. She went into the pantry, and they heard her moving dishes while they ate. Presently she came out with a pile of plates. She got the clothes basket out of the shed and packed them in it. Nanny and Sammy watched. She brought out cups and saucers and put them in with the plates.

"What you goin' to do, Mother?" inquired Nanny, in a timid voice. A sense of something unusual made her tremble, as if it were a ghost. Sammy rolled his eyes over his pie.

"You'll see what I'm goin' to do," replied Mrs. Penn. "If you're through, Nanny, I want you to go upstairs an' pack up your things; an' I want you, Sammy, to help me take down the bed in the bedroom."

"Oh, Mother, what for?" gasped Nanny.

"You'll see."

During the next few hours a feat was performed by the simple, pious New England mother which was equal in its way to Wolfe's storming of the Heights of Abraham.[1] It took no more genius and audacity of bravery for Wolfe to cheer his wondering soldiers up those steep precipices, under the sleeping eyes of the enemy, than for Sarah Penn, at the head of her children, to move all their little household goods into the new barn while her husband was away.

Nanny and Sammy followed their mother's instructions without a murmur; indeed, they were overawed. There is a certain uncanny and superhuman quality about all such purely original undertakings as their mother's was to them. Nanny went back and forth with her light loads, and Sammy tugged with sober energy.

At five o'clock in the afternoon the little house in which the Penns had lived for forty years had emptied itself into the new barn.

Every builder builds somewhat for unknown purposes and is in a measure a prophet. The architect of Adoniram Penn's barn, while he designed it for the comfort of four-footed animals, had planned better than he knew for the comfort of humans. Sarah Penn saw at a glance its possibili-

[1] **the Heights of Abraham:** a plain atop steep cliffs outside the city of Quebec; site of a battle in 1759 in which the English General Wolfe defeated the French forces under General Montcalm.

ties. Those great box stalls, with quilts hung before them, would make better bedrooms than the one she had occupied for forty years, and there was a tight carriage room. The harness room, with its chimney and shelves, would make a kitchen of her dreams. The great middle space would make a parlor, by and by, fit for a palace. Upstairs there was as much room as down. With partitions and windows, what a house would there be! Sarah looked at the row of stanchions before the allotted space for the cows and reflected that she would have her front entry there.

At six o'clock the stove was up in the harness room, the kettle was boiling, and the table was set for tea. It looked almost as homelike as the abandoned house across the yard had ever done. The young hired man milked, and Sarah directed him calmly to bring the milk to the new barn. He came gaping, dropping little blots of foam from the brimming pails on the grass. Before the next morning he had spread the story of Adoniram Penn's wife moving into the new barn all over the little village. Men assembled in the store and

talked it over, women with shawls over their heads scuttled into each other's houses before their work was done. Any deviation from the ordinary course of life in this quiet town was enough to stop all progress in it. Everybody paused to look at the staid, independent figure on the side track. There was a difference of opinion with regard to her. Some held her to be insane; some, of a lawless and rebellious spirit.

Friday the minister went to see her. It was in the forenoon, and she was at the barn door shelling peas for dinner. She looked up and returned his salutation with dignity, then she went on with her work. She did not invite him in. The saintly expression of her face remained fixed, but there was an angry flush over it.

The minister stood awkwardly before her and talked. She handled the peas as if they were bullets. At last she looked up, and her eyes showed the spirit that her meek front had covered for a lifetime.

"There ain't no use talkin', Mr. Hersey," said she. "I've thought it all over, an' I believe I'm doin' what's right. I've made it the subject of prayer, an' it's betwixt me an' the Lord an' Adoniram. There ain't no call for nobody else to worry about it."

"Well, of course, if you have brought it to the Lord in prayer and feel satisfied that you are doing right, Mrs. Penn," said the minister, helplessly. His thin gray-bearded face was pathetic. He was a sickly man; his youthful confidence had cooled; he had to scourge himself up to some of his pastoral duties as relentlessly as a Catholic ascetic, and then he was prostrated by the smart.

"I think it's right jest as much as I think it was right for our forefathers to come over from the old country 'cause they didn't have what belonged to 'em," said Mrs. Penn. She arose. The barn threshold might have been Plymouth

Rock from her bearing. "I don't doubt you mean well, Mr. Hersey," said she, "but there are things people hadn't ought to interfere with. I've been a member of the church for over forty years. I've got my own mind an' my own feet, an' I'm goin' to think my own thoughts an' go my own ways, an' nobody but the Lord is goin' to dictate to me unless I've a mind to have him. Won't you come in an' set down? How is Mis' Hersey?"

"She is well, I thank you," replied the minister. He added some more perplexed apologetic remarks; then he retreated.

He could expound the intricacies of every character study in the Scriptures, he was competent to grasp the Pilgrim Fathers and all historical innovators, but Sarah Penn was beyond him. He could deal with primal cases, but parallel ones worsted him. But, after all, although it was aside from his province, he wondered more how Adoniram Penn would deal with his wife than how the Lord would. Everybody shared the wonder. When Adoniram's four new cows arrived, Sarah ordered three to be put in the old barn, the other in the house shed where the cooking stove had stood. That added to the excitement. It was whispered that all four cows were domiciled in the house.

Toward sunset on Saturday, when Adoniram was expected home, there was a knot of men in the road near the new barn. The hired man had milked, but he still hung around the premises. Sarah Penn had supper all ready. There were brown bread and baked beans and a custard pie; it was the supper that Adoniram loved on a Saturday night. She had on a clean calico, and she bore herself imperturbably. Nanny and Sammy kept close at her heels. Their eyes were large, and Nanny was full of nervous tremors. Still there was to them more pleasant excitement than anything else. An inborn con-

fidence in their mother over their father asserted itself.

Sammy looked out of the harness-room window. "There he is," he announced, in an awed whisper. He and Nanny peeped around the casing. Mrs. Penn kept on about her work. The children watched Adoniram leave the new horse standing in the drive while he went to the house door. It was fastened. Then he went around to the shed. That door was seldom locked, even when the family was away. The thought how her father would be confronted by the cow flashed upon Nanny. There was a hysterical sob in her throat. Adoniram emerged from the shed and stood looking about in a dazed fashion. His lips moved. He was saying something, but they could not hear what it was. The hired man was peeping around a corner of the old barn, but nobody saw him.

Adoniram took the new horse by the bridle and led him across the yard to the new barn. Nanny and Sammy slunk close to their mother. The barn doors rolled back, and there stood Adoniram, with the long mild face of the great Canadian farm horse looking over his shoulder.

Nanny kept behind her mother, but Sammy stepped suddenly forward and stood in front of her.

Adoniram stared at the group. "What on airth you all down here for?" said he. "What's the matter over to the house?"

"We've come here to live, Father," said Sammy. His shrill voice quavered out bravely.

"What"—Adoniram sniffed—"what is it smells like cookin'?" said he. He stepped forward and looked in the open door of the harness room. Then he turned to his wife. His old bristling face was pale and frightened. "What on airth does this mean, Mother?" he gasped.

"You come in here, Father," said

Sarah. She led the way into the harness room and shut the door. "Now, Father," said she, "you needn't be scared. I ain't crazy. There ain't nothin' to be upset over. But we've come here to live, an' we're goin' to live here. We've got jest as good a right here as new horses an' cows. The house wa'n't fit for us to live in any longer, an' I made up my mind I wa'n't goin' to stay there. I've done my duty by you forty year, an' I'm goin' to do it now; but I'm goin' to live here. You've got to put in some windows and partitions; an' you'll have to buy some furniture."

"Why, Mother!" the old man gasped.

"You'd better take your coat off an' get washed—there's the washbasin—and then we'll have supper."

"Why, Mother!"

Sammy went past the window, leading the new horse to the old barn. The old man saw him and shook his head speechlessly. He tried to take off his coat, but his arms seemed to lack the power. His wife helped him. She poured some water into the tin basin and put in a piece of soap. She got the comb and brush and smoothed his thin gray hair after he had washed. Then she put the beans, hot bread, and tea on the table. Sammy came in, and the family drew up. Adoniram sat looking dazedly at his plate, and they waited.

"Ain't you goin' to ask a blessin', Father?" said Sarah. And the old man bent his head and mumbled.

All through the meal he stopped eating at intervals and stared furtively at his wife, but he ate well. The home food tasted good to him, and his old frame was too sturdily healthy to be affected by his mind. But after supper he went out and sat down on the step of the smaller door at the right of the barn, through which he had meant his Jerseys to pass in stately file, but which Sarah designed for her front house door, and he leaned his head on his hands.

After the supper dishes were cleared away and the milk pans washed, Sarah went out to him. The twilight was deepening. There was a clear green glow in the sky. Before them stretched the smooth level of field; in the distance was a cluster of haystacks like the huts of a village; the air was very cool and calm and sweet. The landscape might have been an ideal one of peace.

Sarah bent over and touched her husband on one of his thin, sinewy shoulders. "Father!"

The old man's shoulder heaved; he was weeping.

"Why, don't do so, Father," said Sarah.

"I'll—put up the—partitions, an'—everything you—want, Mother."

Sarah put her apron up to her face; she was overcome by her own triumph.

Adoniram was like a fortress whose walls had no active resistance and went down the instant the right besieging tools were used. "Why, Mother," he said, hoarsely, "I hadn't no idee you was so set on't as all this comes to."

FOR STUDY AND DISCUSSION

1. The three stories you have read so far have featured strong central conflicts of different kinds: man against himself ("Contents of the Dead Man's Pockets"), man against nature ("To Build a Fire"), and man against man—or, in this case, woman ("The Revolt of 'Mother'"). Which story puts the greatest emphasis on characterization? Why is individual characterization more important to this story than to the other two?

2. What kind of person is "Mother"? In what ways are she and her husband very much alike? In what ways are they different? Mrs. Penn has tact as well as a strong will. Show where her revolt would have failed without both of these qualities.

3. How does Mrs. Penn regard the prevailing opinion about "menfolks" and "womenfolks"? To what extent does she accept it?

4. What is Mrs. Penn's attitude toward "Father"? Does she love him? hate him? resent him? respect him? Explain.

5. When does the idea of moving into the barn first occur to Mrs. Penn? When does she finally decide to go through with it? Why does she feel she is doing the right thing?

6. How does the community regard Mrs. Penn's revolt? Do they share the author's sympathy for her? Why do they feel as they do?

7. What kind of man is Father? What does he value most in life? Would you call him a selfish man? Why does he refuse to answer his wife's questions about the digging? Why does he give in so easily at the end?

8. Describe the personalities of Nanny and Sammy. Which of them is more like their mother? Which is more like their father? Which one changes during the story? How?

9. Is the characterization in this story mainly direct or indirect? Can you find any examples of direct characterization? At what points in the story are we taken into the thoughts or feelings of one of the characters in a way that would be impossible in life?

10. Are the actions of the characters consistent? Mrs. Penn has apparently never before defied her husband in forty years of marriage. Does she have sufficient reason to revolt? What qualities in her help to make her revolt, after all those years, believable?

11. "The Revolt of 'Mother'" is actually about a rather minor incident in domestic life. How does the author make this incident take on heroic proportions? What would you say is her attitude toward the everyday lives of ordinary men and women?

LANGUAGE AND VOCABULARY

Much of "The Revolt of 'Mother'" is dialogue, and nearly all of the dialogue is *dialect* —the carefully reproduced speech of a particular region—in this case, rural New England. The author's use of down-to-earth speech patterns helps you to *hear* the words as well as see them on the page. Hearing the way the characters speak reveals much about them.

For example, what difference between mother and daughter is suggested by the following? (Listen to the sound of the words.)
> "I don't care; I don't believe George is anything like that, anyhow."
> "You wait an' see. I guess George Eastman ain't no better than other men. You hadn't ought to judge Father, though."

What do you learn about Father from his favorite expression, "I ain't got nothin' to say about it"? What do his last words—"Why, Mother, I hadn't no idee you was so set on't as all this comes to"—suggest about his way of thinking?

In the long lecture that Mother gives Father, what does her way of speaking reveal about her character? Explain, pointing out specific words and phrases.

2. Very often in this story, the author uses words that help to give a picture of one of the characters. How does each of the following expressions help to characterize the character involved?
> "Sarah Penn washed the frying pan with a *conclusive* air."
> "Sarah Penn's face . . . had that expression of *meek vigor* which might have characterized one of the New Testament saints."
> "He looked at his wife, and his manner was *defiantly apologetic*."
> "She *flung* open a door . . ."
> "There is a certain *uncanny and superhuman* quality about all such purely original undertakings . . ."
> "Adoniram was like a *fortress* whose walls had no active resistance . . ."

ABOUT THE AUTHOR

Mary E. Wilkins Freeman (1852–1930) was born in Randolph, Massachusetts, to an old New England family. In delicate health during much of her life, she was too frail to have much formal schooling. Except for ten years in West Brattleboro, Vermont, she lived the first fifty years of her life in Randolph, and for several years she was a secretary to Oliver Wendell Holmes. Though she wrote a dozen novels, she is best known for her short stories, particularly those in *A Humble Romance* and *A New England Nun*. Her characteristic subject is rural and village New England life.

The Leader of the People

JOHN STEINBECK

On Saturday afternoon Billy Buck, the ranch hand, raked together the last of the old year's haystack and pitched small forkfuls over the wire fence to a few mildly interested cattle. High in the air small clouds like puffs of cannon smoke were driven eastward by the March wind. The wind could be heard whishing in the brush on the ridge crests, but no breath of it penetrated down into the ranch cup.

The little boy, Jody, emerged from the house eating a thick piece of buttered bread. He saw Billy working on the last of the haystack. Jody tramped down scuffing his shoes in a way he had been told was destructive to good shoe leather. A flock of white pigeons flew out of the black cypress tree as Jody passed, and circled the tree and landed again. A half-grown tortoise-shell cat leaped from the bunkhouse porch, galloped on stiff legs across the road, whirled and galloped back again. Jody picked up a stone to help the game along, but he was too late, for the cat was under the porch before the stone could be discharged. He threw the stone into the cypress tree and started the white pigeons on another whirling flight.

Arriving at the used-up haystack, the boy leaned against the barbed wire fence. "Will that be all of it, do you think?" he asked.

The middle-aged ranch hand stopped his careful raking and stuck his fork into the ground. He took off his black hat and smoothed down his hair. "Nothing left of it that isn't soggy from ground moisture," he said. He replaced his hat and rubbed his dry leathery hands together.

"Ought to be plenty mice," Jody suggested.

"Lousy with them," said Billy. "Just crawling with mice."

"Well, maybe, when you get all through, I could call the dogs and hunt the mice."

"Sure, I guess you could," said Billy Buck. He lifted a forkful of the damp ground-hay and threw it into the air. Instantly three mice leaped out and burrowed frantically under the hay again.

Jody sighed with satisfaction. Those plump, sleek, arrogant mice were doomed. For eight months they had lived and multiplied in the haystack. They had been immune from cats, from traps, from poison, and from Jody. They had grown smug in their security, overbearing, and fat. Now the time of disaster had come; they would not survive another day.

Billy looked up at the top of the hills that surrounded the ranch. "Maybe you better ask your father before you do it," he suggested.

"Well, where is he? I'll ask him now."

"He rode up to the ridge ranch after dinner. He'll be back pretty soon."

Jody slumped against the fence post. "I don't think he'd care."

As Billy went back to his work he said ominously, "You'd better ask him anyway. You know how he is."

Jody did know. His father, Carl Tiflin, insisted upon giving permission for anything that was done on the ranch, whether it was important or not. Jody sagged far-

ther against the post until he was sitting on the ground. He looked up at the little puffs of wind-driven cloud. "Is it like to rain, Billy?"

"It might. The wind's good for it, but not strong enough."

"Well, I hope it don't rain until after I kill those mice."

Jody turned back and looked at the side-hill where the road from the outside world came down. The hill was washed with lean March sunshine. Silver thistles, blue lupins, and a few poppies bloomed among the sage bushes. Halfway up the hill Jody could see Doubletree Mutt, the black dog, digging in a squirrel hole. He paddled for a while and then paused to kick bursts of dirt out between his hind legs, and he dug with an earnestness which belied the knowledge he must have had that no dog had ever caught a squirrel by digging in a hole.

Suddenly, while Jody watched, the black dog stiffened and backed out of the hole and looked up the hill toward the cleft in the ridge where the road came through. Jody looked up too. For a moment Carl Tiflin on horseback stood out against the pale sky and then he moved down the road toward the house. He carried something white in his hand.

The boy started to his feet, "He's got a letter," Jody cried. He trotted away toward the ranch house, for the letter would probably be read aloud and he wanted to be there. He reached the house before his father did, and ran in. He heard Carl dismount from his creaking saddle and slap the horse on the side to send it to the barn where Billy would unsaddle it and turn it out.

Jody ran into the kitchen. "We got a letter!" he cried.

His mother looked up from a pan of beans. "Who has?"

"Father has. I saw it in his hand."

Carl strode into the kitchen then, and Jody's mother asked, "Who's the letter from Carl?"

He frowned quickly. "How did you know there was a letter?"

She nodded her head in the boy's direction. "Big-Britches Jody told me."

Jody was embarrassed.

His father looked down at him contemptuously. "He *is* getting to be a Big-Britches," Carl said. "He's minding everybody's business but his own. Got his big nose into everything."

Mrs. Tiflin relented a little. "Well, he hasn't enough to keep him busy. Who's the letter from?"

Carl still frowned on Jody. "I'll keep him busy if he isn't careful." He held out a sealed letter. "I guess it's from your father."

Mrs. Tiflin took a hairpin from her head and slit open the flap. Her lips pursed judiciously. Jody saw her eyes snap back and forth over the lines. "He says," she translated, "he says he's going to drive out Saturday to stay for a little while. Why, this is Saturday. The letter must have been delayed." She looked at the postmark. "This was mailed day before yesterday. It should have been here yesterday." She looked up questioningly at her husband, and then her face darkened angrily. "Now what have you got that look on you for? He doesn't come often."

Carl turned his eyes away from her anger. He could be stern with her most of the time, but when occasionally her temper arose, he could not combat it.

"What's the matter with you?" she demanded again.

In his explanation there was a tone of apology Jody himself might have used. "It's just that he talks," Carl said lamely. "Just talks."

"Well, what of it? You talk yourself."

"Sure I do. But your father only talks about one thing."

"Indians!" Jody broke in excitedly. "Indians and crossing the plains!"

Carl turned fiercely on him. "You get out, Mr. Big-Britches! Go on, now! Get out!"

Jody went miserably out the back door and closed the screen with elaborate quietness. Under the kitchen window his shamed, downcast eyes fell upon a curiously shaped stone, a stone of such fascination that he squatted down and picked it up and turned it over in his hands.

The voices came clearly to him through the open kitchen window. "Jody's right," he heard his father say. "Just Indians and crossing the plains. I've heard that story about how the horses got driven off about a thousand times. He just goes on and on, and he never changes a word in the things he tells."

When Mrs. Tiflin answered her tone was so changed that Jody, outside the window, looked up from his study of the stone. Her voice had become soft and explanatory. Jody knew how her face would have changed to match the tone. She said quietly, "Look at it this way, Carl. That was the big thing in my father's life. He led a wagon train clear across the plains to the coast, and when it was finished, his life was done. It was a big thing to do, but it didn't last long enough. Look!" she continued, "it's as though he was born to do that, and after he finished it, there wasn't anything more for him to do but think about it and talk about it. If there'd been any farther west to go, he'd have gone. He's told me so himself. But at last there was the ocean. He lives right by the ocean where he had to stop."

She had caught Carl, caught him and entangled him in her soft tone.

"I've seen him," he agreed quietly. "He goes down and stares off west over the ocean." His voice sharpened a little. "And then he goes up to the Horseshoe Club in Pacific Grove, and he tells people how the Indians drove off the horses."

She tried to catch him again. "Well, it's everything to him. You might be patient with him and pretend to listen."

Carl turned impatiently away. "Well, if it gets too bad, I can always go down to the bunkhouse and sit with Billy," he said irritably. He walked through the house and slammed the front door after him.

Jody ran to his chores. He dumped the grain to the chickens without chasing any of them He gathered the eggs from the nests. He trotted into the house with the wood and interlaced it so carefully in the

woodbox that two armloads seemed to fill it to overflowing.

His mother had finished the beans by now. She stirred up the fire and brushed off the stove top with a turkey wing. Jody peered cautiously at her to see whether any rancor toward him remained. "Is he coming today?" Jody asked.

"That's what his letter said."

"Maybe I better walk up the road to meet him."

Mrs. Tiflin clanged the stove lid shut. "That would be nice," she said. "He'd probably like to be met."

"I guess I'll just do it then."

Outside, Jody whistled shrilly to the dogs. "Come on up the hill," he commanded. The two dogs waved their tails and ran ahead. Along the roadside the sage had tender new tips. Jody tore off some pieces and rubbed them on his hands until the air was filled with the sharp wild smell. With a rush the dogs leaped from the road and yapped into the brush after a rabbit. That was the last Jody saw of them, for when they failed to catch the rabbit, they went back home.

Jody plodded on up the hill toward the ridge top. When he reached the little cleft where the road came through, the afternoon wind struck him and blew up his hair and ruffled his shirt. He looked down on the little hills and ridges below and then out at the huge green Salinas Valley. He could see the white town of Salinas far out in the flat and the flash of its windows under the waning sun. Directly below him, in an oak tree, a crow congress had convened. The tree was black with crows all cawing at once.

Then Jody's eyes followed the wagon road down from the ridge where he stood, and lost it behind a hill, and picked it up again on the other side. On that distant stretch he saw a cart slowly pulled by a bay horse. It disappeared behind the hill.

Jody sat down on the ground and watched the place where the cart would reappear again. The wind sang on the hilltops and the puffball clouds hurried eastward.

Then the cart came into sight and stopped. A man dressed in black dismounted from the seat and walked to the horse's head. Although it was so far away, Jody knew he had unhooked the checkrein, for the horse's head dropped forward. The horse moved on, and the man walked slowly up the hill beside it. Jody gave a glad cry and ran down the road toward them. The squirrels bumped along off the road, and a road runner flirted its tail and raced over the edge of the hill and sailed out like a glider.

Jody tried to leap into the middle of his shadow at every step. A stone rolled under his foot and he went down. Around a little bend he raced, and there, a short distance ahead, were his grandfather and the cart. The boy dropped from his unseemly running and approached at a dignified walk.

The horse plodded stumble-footed up the hill and the old man walked beside it. In the lowering sun their giant shadows flickered darkly behind them. The grandfather was dressed in a black broadcloth suit and he wore kid congress gaiters [1] and a black tie on a short, hard collar. He carried his black slouch hat in his hand. His white beard was cropped close and his white eyebrows overhung his eyes like mustaches. The blue eyes were sternly merry. About the whole face and figure there was a granite dignity, so that every motion seemed an impossible thing. Once at rest, it seemed the old man would be stone, would never move again. His steps were slow and certain. Once made, no step could ever be retraced; once headed in a direction, the path would

[1] **kid congress gaiters:** high boots made of kidskin.

never bend nor the pace increase nor slow.

When Jody appeared around the bend, Grandfather waved his hat slowly in welcome, and he called, "Why, Jody! Come down to meet me, have you?"

Jody sidled near and turned and matched his step to the old man's step and stiffened his body and dragged his heels a little. "Yes, sir," he said. "We got your letter only today."

"Should have been here yesterday," said Grandfather. "It certainly should. How are all the folks?"

"They're fine, sir." He hesitated and then suggested shyly. "Would you like to come on a mouse hunt tomorrow, sir?"

"Mouse hunt, Jody?" Grandfather chuckled. "Have the people of this generation come down to hunting mice? They aren't very strong, the new people, but I hardly thought mice would be game for them."

"No, sir. It's just play. The haystack's gone. I'm going to drive out the mice to the dogs. And you can watch, or even beat the hay a little."

The stern, merry eyes turned down on him. "I see. You don't eat them, then. You haven't come to that yet."

Jody explained, "The dogs eat them, sir. It wouldn't be much like hunting Indians, I guess."

"No, not much—but then later, when the troops were hunting Indians and shooting children and burning teepees, it wasn't much different from your mouse hunt."

They topped the rise and started down into the ranch cup, and they lost the sun from their shoulders. "You've grown," Grandfather said. "Nearly an inch, I should say."

"More," Jody boasted. "Where they mark me on the door, I'm up more than an inch since Thanksgiving even."

Grandfather's rich throaty voice said, "Maybe you're getting too much water and turning to pith and stalk. Wait until you head out, and then we'll see."

Jody looked quickly into the old man's face to see whether his feelings should be hurt, but there was no will to injure, no punishing nor putting-in-your-place light in the keen blue eyes. "We might kill a pig," Jody suggested.

"Oh, no! I couldn't let you do that. You're just humoring me. It isn't the time and you know it."

"You know Riley, the big boar, sir?"

"Yes, I remember Riley well."

"Well, Riley ate a hole into that same haystack, and it fell down on him and smothered him."

"Pigs do that when they can," said Grandfather.

"Riley was a nice pig, for a boar, sir. I rode him sometimes, and he didn't mind."

A door slammed at the house below them, and they saw Jody's mother standing on the porch waving her apron in welcome. And they saw Carl Tiflin walking up from the barn to be at the house for the arrival.

The sun had disappeared from the hills by now. The blue smoke from the house chimney hung in flat layers in the purpling ranch cup. The puffball clouds, dropped by the falling wind, hung listlessly in the sky.

Billy Buck came out of the bunkhouse and flung a wash basin of soapy water on the ground. He had been shaving in midweek, for Billy held Grandfather in reverence, and Grandfather said that Billy was one of the few men of the new generation who had not gone soft. Although Billy was in middle age, Grandfather considered him a boy. Now Billy was hurrying toward the house too.

When Jody and Grandfather arrived,

the three were waiting for them in front of the yard gate.

Carl said, "Hello, sir. We've been looking for you."

Mrs. Tiflin kissed Grandfather on the side of his beard and stood still while his big hand patted her shoulder. Billy shook hands solemnly, grinning under his straw mustache. "I'll put up your horse," said Billy, and he led the rig away.

Grandfather watched him go, and then, turning back to the group, he said as he had said a hundred times before, "There's a good boy. I knew his father, old Mule-tail Buck. I never knew why they called him Mule-tail except he packed mules."

Mrs. Tiflin turned and led the way into the house. "How long are you going to stay, Father? Your letter didn't say."

"Well, I don't know. I thought I'd stay about two weeks. But I never stay as long as I think I'm going to."

In a short while they were sitting at the white oilcloth table eating their supper. The lamp with the tin reflector hung over the table. Outside the dining-room windows the big moths battered softly against the glass.

Grandfather cut his steak into tiny pieces and chewed slowly. "I'm hungry," he said. "Driving out here got my appetite up. It's like when we were crossing. We all got so hungry every night we could hardly wait to let the meat get done. I could eat about five pounds of buffalo meat every night."

"It's moving around does it," said Billy. "My father was a government packer. I helped him when I was a kid. Just the two of us could about clean up a deer's ham."

"I knew your father, Billy," said Grandfather. "A fine man he was. They called him Mule-tail Buck. I don't know why except he packed mules."

"That was it," Billy agreed. "He packed mules."

Grandfather put down his knife and fork and looked around the table. "I remember one time we ran out of meat—" His voice dropped to a curious low sing-song, dropped into a tonal groove the story had worn for itself. "There was no buffalo, no antelope, not even rabbits. The hunters couldn't even shoot a coyote. That was the time for the leader to be on the watch. I was the leader, and I kept my eyes open. Know why? Well, just the minute the people began to get hungry they'd start slaughtering the team oxen. Do you believe that? I've heard of parties that just ate up their draft cattle. Started from the middle and worked toward the ends. Finally they'd eat the lead pair, and then the wheelers. The leader of a party had to keep them from doing that."

In some manner a big moth got into the room and circled the hanging kerosene lamp. Billy got up and tried to clap it between his hands. Carl struck with a cupped palm and caught the moth and broke it. He walked to the window and dropped it out.

"As I was saying," Grandfather began again, but Carl interrupted him. "You'd better eat some more meat. All the rest of us are ready for our pudding."

Jody saw a flash of anger in his mother's eyes. Grandfather picked up his knife and fork. "I'm pretty hungry, all right," he said. "I'll tell you about that later."

When supper was over, when the family and Billy Buck sat in front of the fireplace in the other room, Jody anxiously watched Grandfather. He saw the signs he knew. The bearded head leaned forward; the eyes lost their sternness and looked wonderingly into the fire; the big lean fingers laced themselves on the black knees. "I wonder," he began, "I just wonder whether I ever told you how those thieving Piutes drove off thirty-five of our horses."

"I think you did," Carl interrupted. "Wasn't it just before you went up into the Tahoe country?"

Grandfather turned quickly toward his son-in-law. "That's right. I guess I must have told you that story."

"Lots of times," Carl said cruelly, and he avoided his wife's eyes. But he felt the angry eyes on him, and he said, "Course I'd like to hear it again."

Grandfather looked back at the fire. His fingers unlaced and laced again. Jody knew how he felt, how his insides were collapsed and empty. Hadn't Jody been called a Big-Britches that very afternoon? He arose to heroism and opened himself to the term Big-Britches again. "Tell about Indians," he said softly.

Grandfather's eyes grew stern again. "Boys always want to hear about Indians. It was a job for men, but boys want to hear about it. Well, let's see. Did I ever tell you how I wanted each wagon to carry a long iron plate?"

Everyone but Jody remained silent. Jody said, "No. You didn't."

"Well, when the Indians attacked, we always put the wagons in a circle and fought from between the wheels. I thought that if every wagon carried a long plate with rifle holes, the men could stand the plates on the outside of the wheels when the wagons were in the circle and they would be protected. It would save lives and that would make up for the extra weight of the iron. But of course the party wouldn't do it. No party had done it before and they couldn't see why they should go to the expense. They lived to regret it, too."

Jody looked at his mother and knew from her expression that she was not listening at all. Carl picked at a callus

on his thumb and Billy Buck watched a spider crawling up the wall.

Grandfather's tone dropped into its narrative groove again. Jody knew in advance exactly what words would fall. The story droned on, speeded up for the attack, grew sad over the wounds, struck a dirge at the burials on the great plains. Jody sat quietly watching Grandfather. The stern blue eyes were detached. He looked as though he were not very interested in the story himself.

When it was finished, when the pause had been politely respected as the frontier of the story, Billy Buck stood up and stretched and hitched his trousers. "I guess I'll turn in," he said. Then he faced Grandfather. "I've got an old powder horn and a cap and ball pistol down to the bunkhouse. Did I ever show them to you?"

Grandfather nodded slowly. "Yes, I think you did, Billy. Reminds me of a pistol I had when I was leading the people across." Billy stood politely until the little story was done, and then he said, "Good night," and went out of the house.

Carl Tiflin tried to turn the conversation then. "How's the country between here and Monterey? I've heard it's pretty dry."

"It is dry," said Grandfather. "There's not a drop of water in the Laguna Seca. But it's a long pull from '87. The whole country was powder then, and in '61 I believe all the coyotes starved to death. We had fifteen inches of rain this year."

"Yes, but it all came too early. We could do with some now." Carl's eyes fell on Jody. "Hadn't you better be getting to bed?"

Jody stood up obediently. "Can I kill the mice in the old haystack, sir?"

"Mice? Oh! Sure, kill them all off. Billy said there isn't any good hay left."

Jody exchanged a secret and satis-fying look with Grandfather. "I'll kill every one tomorrow," he promised.

Jody lay in his bed and thought of the impossible world of Indians and buffaloes, a world that had ceased to be forever. He wished he could have been living in the heroic time, but he knew he was not of heroic timber. No one living now, save possibly Billy Buck, was worthy to do the things that had been done. A race of giants had lived then, fearless men, men of a staunchness unknown in this day. Jody thought of the wide plains and of the wagons moving across like centipedes. He thought of Grandfather on a huge white horse, marshaling the people. Across his mind marched the great phantoms, and they marched off the earth and they were gone.

He came back to the ranch for a moment, then. He heard the dull rushing sound that space and silence make. He heard one of the dogs, out in the doghouse, scratching a flea and bumping his elbow against the floor with every stroke. Then the wind arose again and the black cypress groaned and Jody went to sleep.

He was up half an hour before the triangle sounded for breakfast. His mother was rattling the stove to make the flames roar when Jody went through the kitchen. "You're up early," she said. "Where are you going?"

"Out to get a good stick. We're going to kill the mice today."

"Who is 'we'?"

"Why, Grandfather and I."

"So you've got him in it. You always like to have someone in with you in case there's blame to share."

"I'll be right back," said Jody. "I just want to have a good stick ready for after breakfast."

He closed the screen door after him and went out into the cool blue morning. The birds were noisy in the dawn and the ranch

cats came down from the hill like blunt snakes. They had been hunting gophers in the dark, and although the four cats were full of gopher meat, they sat in a semicircle at the back door and mewed piteously for milk. Doubletree Mutt and Smasher moved sniffing along the edge of the brush, performing the duty with rigid ceremony, but when Jody whistled, their heads jerked up and their tails waved. They plunged down to him, wriggling their skins and yawning. Jody patted their heads seriously and moved on to the weathered scrap pile. He selected an old broom handle and a short piece of inch-square scrap wood. From his pocket he took a shoelace and tied the ends of the sticks loosely together to make a flail. He whistled his new weapon through the air and struck the ground experimentally, while the dogs leaped aside and whined with apprehension.

Jody turned and started down past the house toward the old haystack ground to look over the field of slaughter, but Billy Buck, sitting patiently on the back steps, called to him, "You better come back. It's only a couple of minutes till breakfast."

Jody changed his course and moved toward the house. He leaned his flail against the steps. "That's to drive the mice out," he said. "I'll bet they're fat, I'll bet they don't know what's going to happen to them today."

"No, nor you either," Billy remarked philosophically, "nor me, nor anyone."

Jody was staggered by this thought. He knew it was true. His imagination twitched away from the mouse hunt. Then his mother came out on the back porch and struck the triangle, and all thoughts fell in a heap.

Grandfather hadn't appeared at the table when they sat down. Billy nodded at his empty chair. "He's all right? He isn't sick?"

"He takes a long time to dress," said Mrs. Tiflin. "He combs his whiskers and rubs up his shoes and brushes his clothes."

Carl scattered sugar on his mush. "A man that's led a wagon train across the plains has got to be pretty careful how he dresses."

Mrs. Tiflin turned on him. "Don't do that, Carl! Please don't!" There was more of threat than of request in her tone. And the threat irritated Carl.

"Well, how many times do I have to listen to the story of the iron plates, and the thirty-five horses? That time's done. Why can't he forget it, now it's done?" He grew angrier while he talked and his voice rose. "Why does he have to tell them over and over? He came across the plains. All right! Now it's finished. Nobody wants to hear about it over and over."

The door into the kitchen closed softly. The four at the table sat frozen. Carl laid his mush spoon on the table and touched his chin with his fingers.

Then the kitchen door opened and Grandfather walked in. His mouth smiled tightly and his eyes squinted. "Good morning," he said, and he sat down and looked at his mush dish.

Carl could not leave it there. "Did— did you hear what I said?"

Grandfather jerked a little nod.

"I don't know what got into me, sir. I didn't mean it. I was just being funny."

Jody glanced in shame at his mother, and he saw that she was looking at Carl, and that she wasn't breathing. It was an awful thing that he was doing. He was tearing himself to pieces to talk like that. It was a terrible thing to him to retract a word, but to retract it in shame was infinitely worse.

Grandfather looked sidewise. "I'm trying to get right side up," he said gently. "I'm not being mad. I don't mind

what you said, but it might be true, and I would mind that."

"It isn't true," said Carl. "I'm not feeling well this morning. I'm sorry I said it."

"Don't be sorry, Carl. An old man doesn't see things sometimes. Maybe you're right. The crossing is finished. Maybe it should be forgotten, now it's done."

Carl got up from the table. "I've had enough to eat. I'm going to work. Take your time, Billy!" He walked quickly out of the dining room. Billy gulped the rest of his food and followed soon after. But Jody could not leave his chair.

"Won't you tell any more stories?" Jody asked.

"Why, sure I'll tell them, but only when—I'm sure people want to hear them."

"I like to hear them, sir."

"Oh! Of course you do, but you're a little boy. It was a job for men, but only little boys like to hear about it."

Jody got up from his place. "I'll wait outside for you, sir. I've got a good stick for those mice."

He waited by the gate until the old man came out on the porch. "Let's go down and kill the mice now," Jody called.

"I think I'll just sit in the sun, Jody. You go kill the mice."

"You can use my stick if you like."

"No, I'll just sit here a while."

Jody turned disconsolately away and walked down toward the old haystack. He tried to whip up his enthusiasm with thoughts of the fat juicy mice. He beat the ground with his flail. The dogs coaxed and whined about him, but he could not go. Back at the house he could see Grandfather sitting on the porch, looking small and thin and black.

Jody gave up and went to sit on the steps at the old man's feet.

"Back already? Did you kill the mice?"

"No, sir. I'll kill them some other day."

The morning flies buzzed close to the ground and the ants dashed about in front of the steps. The heavy smell of sage slipped down the hill. The porch boards grew warm in the sunshine.

Jody hardly knew when Grandfather started to talk. "I shouldn't stay here, feeling the way I do." He examined his strong old hands. "I feel as though the crossing wasn't worth doing." His eyes moved up the sidehill and stopped on a motionless hawk perched on a dead limb. "I tell those old stories, but they're not what I want to tell. I only know how I want people to feel when I tell them.

"It wasn't Indians that were important, nor adventures, nor even getting out here. It was a whole bunch of people made into one big crawling beast. And I was the head. It was westering and westering. Every man wanted something for himself, but the big beast that was all of them wanted only westering. I was the leader, but if I hadn't been there, someone else would have been the head. The thing had to have a head.

"Under the little bushes the shadows

were black at white noonday. When we saw the mountains at last, we cried—all of us. But it wasn't getting here that mattered, it was movement and westering.

"We carried life out here and set it down the way those ants carry eggs. And I was the leader. The westering was as big as God, and the slow steps that made the movement piled up and piled up until the continent was crossed.

"Then we came down to the sea, and it was done." He stopped and wiped his eyes until the rims were red. "That's what I should be telling instead of stories."

When Jody spoke, Grandfather started and looked down at him. "Maybe I could lead the people some day," Jody said.

The old man smiled. "There's no place to go. There's the ocean to stop you. There's a line of old men along the shore hating the ocean because it stopped them."

"In boats I might, sir."

"No place to go, Jody. Every place is taken. But that's not the worst—no, not the worst. Westering has died out of the people. Westering isn't a hunger any more. It's all done. Your father is right. It is finished." He laced his fingers on his knee and looked at them.

Jody felt very sad. "If you'd like a glass of lemonade I could make it for you."

Grandfather was about to refuse, and then he saw Jody's face. "That would be nice," he said. "Yes, it would be nice to drink lemonade."

Jody ran into the kitchen where his mother was wiping the last of the breakfast dishes. "Can I have a lemon to make a lemonade for Grandfather?"

His mother mimicked—"And another lemon to make a lemonade for you."

"No, ma'am. I don't want one."

"Jody! You're sick!" Then she stopped suddenly. "Take a lemon out of the cooler," she said softly. "Here, I'll reach the squeezer down to you."

1. Do you think the author wants us to respect Grandfather, as Billy Buck does, or to see him as tedious and useless, as Carl Tiflin does? What makes you think so? Do Billy Buck and Mrs. Tiflin find Grandfather's stories any less tedious than Carl does? Why do they pretend to be interested? Where in the story does Grandfather show his largeness of spirit? Where does he show that he still has a strongly disciplined will?

2. Is Grandfather's desire to tell over and over the stories of the westward movement in which he was a "leader of the people" chiefly an egotistic—that is, a self-centered or selfish —one? Is his telling these stories a way of making himself seem important? What does Grandfather feel was the most important thing about his adventure?

3. Who is a more admirable person—Carl Tiflin or Grandfather? How does the author indicate the difference between them? Is his characterization of Carl entirely unsympathetic? Where in the story does Carl behave admirably? Why does his life, on the whole, seem "smaller" than Grandfather's?

4. Why is Mrs. Tiflin more sympathetic to Grandfather than Carl is? Which of them has greater insight into the feelings of other people? How is this shown in their treatment of each other?

5. What kind of person is Billy Buck? What is his attitude toward Jody? toward Grandfather? Do you think the author wants us to respect Billy? What in the story makes you think so?

6. Which actions of Jody's show you what he is like? In what ways is he a typical boy? What boyish action causes his parents to call him a "Big-Britches"? Do you think this word is a good description of Jody? Why or why not?

7. At the beginning of the story Jody is planning a mouse hunt and looking forward to Grandfather's tales about hunting Indians. How does Jody's attitude toward hunting Indians differ from Grandfather's? How is Jody's idea of crossing the plains and being a leader of the people different from Grandfather's?

8. How does Jody mature during the course of the story? What does he learn about life and people? How does his behavior at the very end of the story differ from his behavior at the beginning? Why does he give up the mouse hunt? Why does he want to make lemonade for Grandfather? What has caused this change in him?

9. Besides contrasting some very different people, this story contrasts two different times in American history. What is the difference between these times? What connection does Steinbeck make between the nature of the times and the nature of the people produced by them?

10. What does this story say about the most satisfying kinds of human relationships?

CHARACTER AND CHARACTERIZATION

Which of these stories—"The Revolt of 'Mother'" or "The Leader of the People"— is more direct in its characterization? Which author tells you directly more about his characters? Which one lets you form your own conclusions on the basis of what the characters themselves say and do and what the other characters say about them? Support your answer by citing paragraphs from the stories.

Which character, from both these stories, do you feel you know best as a person? Look back at the story to see how the author introduced that character and built up his (or her) personality in the story. Which clues told you the most about his personality? Which details of speech or behavior did the most to make him seem alive and real?

LANGUAGE AND VOCABULARY

In addition to the use of dialect (see page 41), another important aspect of the sound of a story is the different tones of voice that suggest characters' feelings. Here again the reader has to hear the words as well as see them. Different tones of voice, of course, provide much of our understanding about the characters in a play, but tone of voice can be as vital in a story as it is in a play. In a story, however, which is usually read and not spoken, the writer has to provide hints from time to time about the tone of voice that he intends to imply. A writer often does this with a carefully chosen word or phrase to introduce lines of dialogue. Study the following "signals" that Steinbeck uses in "The Leader of the People." What does each of the following quotations tell you about the tone of voice the speaker will use?

"He frowned quickly."
"His father looked down at him contemptuously."
"Mrs. Tiflin relented a little."
"then her face darkened angrily."
"Carl turned fiercely on him."

Find some other "signal" phrases or sentences in the story. How does each one help you to hear the speaker's tone?

FOR COMPOSITION

Grandfather tells Jody, "There's no place to go. . . . Westering isn't a hunger any more. It's all done." Do you think he is right? Is it true that in our day all the frontiers have been crossed? In a short composition, tell why you agree or disagree. If you disagree, describe some kinds of "westering" that are yet to be done.

ABOUT THE AUTHOR

John Steinbeck (1902–1968) was born and grew up in the fertile valley of Salinas, Monterey County, California—the setting of "The Leader of the People." After high school, where he starred in track and basketball, he attended Stanford University for four years, specializing in marine biology. Before becoming established as a writer, he worked as a hod carrier, ranch hand, painter's apprentice, fruit picker, caretaker, surveyor, and chemist. His best-known novel, *The Grapes of Wrath,* is about the migration of the "Okies" from the dust bowl of Oklahoma to the valleys of California during the Depression of the 1930's. "The Leader of the People" is one of four stories about the boy Jody which have been grouped together under the title *The Red Pony.* For many years, Steinbeck lived on Long Island near New York City. He was awarded the Nobel prize for literature in 1962.

THEME

The theme of a story is its controlling idea or central insight: the single large generalization that the story suggests about life. Not all stories have theme. If a story is written purely to entertain, it will often not have theme. But every story that has a single point of view and an important purpose— every story in which the author has faithfully attempted to reveal life—has theme, or central meaning.

The theme of a story is not necessarily an idea which the author consciously decided to write about before beginning to write. A writer does not, as a rule, write a story in order to illustrate a truth. Rather, he tries to write truthfully about life as he sees it, and his particular way of looking at things gives his story a central focus and purpose. We must not, then, usually expect to find theme stated outright in a story. Sometimes it may be, but more often we must state it for ourselves, taking into account all the elements of the story, especially character and plot.

The theme of a story is not usually a "moral." A moral is a useful bit of advice about life, such as "A stitch in time saves nine," or "There's no use crying over spilt milk," or "Crime never pays." Of course, *if* a story has a moral, then the moral is the theme. But stories are not sermons, and most short-story writers are not interested in "preaching" to their readers. They are interested, rather, in illuminating human experience by faithfully recording a particular series of incidents that suggests a larger meaning. In attempting to determine the theme of a story, we should ask not what it *teaches,* but what it *reveals*.

There is no single "right" way to state the theme of a story. We should simply be sure that our statement of theme truly expresses the story's underlying idea. The theme of Jack London's "To Build a Fire" might be stated in several ways: "At seventy-five degrees below zero a man's life may depend on his ability to build a fire"; or "Subfreezing weather in the Arctic is treacherous and can be fatal to those who underestimate its dangers"; or "Man is a frail creature, able to live safely only within narrow limits of heat and cold." Though each of these statements emphasizes a slightly different aspect of the story, each gets at its central meaning. Notice, by the way, that theme in itself is abstract and unexciting. Only when embodied in a story does it take on life. The theme merely states dryly to our conscious mind what the story makes us deeply feel.

One good way of getting at theme is to ask what a story is *about* and then translate the answer into a general statement. Jack Finney's story "Contents of the Dead Man's Pockets" is about a man who decides, after a close scrape with death on an eleventh-story apartment ledge, to spend more time with his wife instead of doing extra work to get ahead. Translating this into a generalization, we come out with something like this: "A narrow escape from death can cause a man to realize that ambition for future success in

business is less important than love and companionship here and now." Or, reducing this statement even further: "Ambition and business success are less important than love, companionship, and enjoyment of life."

We do not have to state a story's theme in order to appreciate it as a story any more than the author had to state the theme in order to write the story. Nevertheless, our ability to state theme is one of the best tests of whether we really understand a story. In stating theme, always state it in the form of a complete sentence, with a subject and verb, to be sure that it is a complete thought. Also, be sure to make your statement a generalization, not a comment on specific characters or a specific situation. On the other hand, be careful not to make too large a generalization. Remember that the themes of most stories are more accurately expressed in terms such as *may, sometimes,* or *some men* than in terms such as *must, never,* or *all men.*

The Ship That Found Herself

RUDYARD KIPLING

We now, held in captivity,
　Spring to our labor nor grieve!
See now, how it is blesseder,
　Brothers, to give than receive!
Keep trust, wherefore ye were made,
　Paying the duty ye owe;
For a clean thrust and the sheer of the blade
　Shall carry us where we should go.
Song of the Engines

IT WAS her first voyage, and though she was but a cargo steamer of twelve hundred tons, she was the very best of her kind, the outcome of forty years of experiments and improvements in framework and machinery; and her designers and owner thought as much of her as

"The Ship That Found Herself" from *Day's Work* by Rudyard Kipling. Reprinted by permission of Doubleday & Company, Inc.

though she had been the *Lucania*.[1] Anyone can make a floating hotel that will pay expenses, if he puts enough money into the saloon and charges for private baths, suites of rooms, and such like; but in these days of competition and low freights every square inch of a cargo boat must be built for cheapness, great hold-capacity, and a certain steady speed. This boat was, perhaps, two hundred and forty feet long and thirty-two feet wide, with arrangements that enabled her to carry cattle on her main and sheep on her upper deck if she wanted to; but her great glory was the amount of cargo that she could store away in her holds. Her owners—they were a very well-known Scotch firm—came round with her from the north, where she had been launched and christened and fitted, to Liverpool, where she was to take cargo for New York; and the owner's daughter, Miss Frazier, went to and fro on the clean decks, admiring the new paint and the brass work and the patent winches, and particularly the strong, straight bow, over which she had cracked a bottle of cham-

[1] **the** *Lucania:* one of the first twin-screw steamers, whose top speed of twenty-two knots (twenty-five miles an hour) made it the most famous ship of its day.

pagne when she named the steamer the *Dimbula*. It was a beautiful September afternoon, and the boat in all her newness —she was painted lead color with a red funnel—looked very fine indeed. Her house flag was flying, and her whistle from time to time acknowledged the salutes of friendly boats, who saw that she was new to the High and Narrow Seas and wished to make her welcome.

"And now," said Miss Frazier delightedly to the captain, "she's a real ship, isn't she? It seems only the other day Father gave the order for her, and now —and now—isn't she a beauty!" The girl was proud of the firm and talked as though she were the controlling partner.

"Oh, she's no so bad," the skipper replied cautiously. "But I'm sayin' that it takes more than christenin' to mak' a ship. In the nature o' things, Miss Frazier,

if ye follow me, she's just irons and rivets and plates put into the form of a ship. She has to find herself yet."

"I thought Father said she was exceptionally well found."

"So she is," said the skipper, with a laugh. "But it's this way wi' ships, Miss Frazier. She's all here, but the parrts of her have not learned to work together yet. They've had no chance."

"The engines are working beautifully. I can hear them."

"Yes, indeed. But there's more than engines to a ship. Every inch of her, ye'll understand, has to be livened up and made to work wi' its neighbor—sweetenin' her, we call it, technically."

"And how will you do it?" the girl asked.

"We can no more than drive and steer her, and so forth; but if we have rough

weather this trip—it's likely—she'll learn the rest by heart! For a ship, ye'll obsairve, Miss Frazier, is in no sense a reegid body closed at both ends. She's a highly complex structure o' various an' conflictin' strains, wi' tissues that must give an' tak' accordin' to her personal modulus of elasteecity."[1] Mr. Buchanan, the chief engineer, was coming toward them. "I'm sayin' to Miss Frazier, here, that our little *Dimbula* has to be sweetened yet, and nothin' but a gale will do it. How's all wi' your engines, Buck?"

"Well enough—true by plumb[2] an' rule, o' course; but there's no spontaneeity yet." He turned to the girl. "Take my word, Miss Frazier, and maybe ye'll comprehend later; even after a pretty girl's christened a ship it does not follow that there's such a thing as a ship under the men that work her."

"I was sayin' the very same, Mr. Buchanan," the skipper interrupted.

"That's more metaphysical than I can follow," said Miss Frazier, laughing.

"Why so? Ye're good Scotch, an'—I knew your mother's father, he was fra' Dumfries—ye've a vested right in metapheesics,[3] Miss Frazier, just as ye have in the *Dimbula,*" the engineer said.

"Eh, well, we must go down to the deep watters, an' earn Miss Frazier her deevidends. Will you not come to my cabin for tea?" said the skipper. "We'll be in dock the night, and when you're goin' back to Glasgie[4] ye can think of us loadin' her down an' drivin' her forth—all for your sake."

[1] **modulus of elasteecity:** that is, modulus of elasticity, the amount of flexibility within a plate or beam.

[2] **plumb:** a plumb line, used to test vertical straightness.

[3] **vested . . . metapheesics:** that is, vested . . . metaphysics. Scotland is known for its philosophers and metaphysicians, who speculate on the nature and meaning of life.

[4] **Glasgie:** Glasgow.

In the next few days they stowed some two thousand tons' dead weight into the *Dimbula* and took her out from Liverpool. As soon as she met the lift of the open water, she naturally began to talk. If you lay your ear to the side of the cabin the next time you are in a steamer, you will hear hundreds of little voices in every direction, thrilling and buzzing, and whispering and popping, and gurgling and sobbing and squeaking exactly like a telephone in a thunderstorm. Wooden ships shriek and growl and grunt, but iron vessels throb and quiver through all their hundreds of ribs and thousands of rivets. The *Dimbula* was very strongly built, and every piece of her had a letter or number, or both, to describe it; and every piece had been hammered, or forged, or rolled, or punched by man, and had lived in the roar and rattle of the shipyard for months. Therefore, every piece had its own separate voice in exact proportion to the amount of trouble spent upon it. Cast iron, as a rule, says very little; but mild steel plates and wrought iron, and rib and beams that have been much bent and welded and riveted, talk continuously. Their conversation, of course, is not half as wise as our human talk, because they are all, though they do not know it, bound down one to the other in a black darkness, where they cannot tell what is happening near them, nor what will overtake them next.

As soon as she had cleared the Irish coast a sullen, gray-headed old wave of the Atlantic climbed leisurely over her straight bow and sat down on her steam capstan[5] used for hauling up the anchor. Now the capstan and the engine that drove it had been newly painted red and green; besides which, nobody likes being ducked.

[5] **capstan:** a cylinder used for moving or raising heavy weights.

"Don't you do that again," the capstan sputtered through the teeth of his cogs. "Hi! Where's the fellow gone?"

The wave had slouched overside with a plop and a chuckle; but "Plenty more where he came from," said a brother wave, and went through and over the capstan, who was bolted firmly to an iron plate on the iron deck beams below.

"Can't you keep still up there?" said the deck beams. "What's the matter with you? One minute you weigh twice as much as you ought to, and the next you don't!"

"It isn't my fault," said the capstan. "There's a green brute outside that comes and hits me on the head."

"Tell that to the shipwrights. You've been in position for months and you've never wriggled like this before. If you aren't careful you'll strain us."

"Talking of strain," said a low, rasping, unpleasant voice, "are any of you fellows —you deck beams, we mean—aware that those exceedingly ugly knees of yours happen to be riveted into our structure —ours?"

"Who might you be?" the deck beams inquired.

"Oh, nobody in particular," was the answer. "We're only the port and starboard upper-deck stringers; and if you persist in heaving and hiking like this, we shall be reluctantly compelled to take steps."

Now the stringers of the ship are long iron girders, so to speak, that run lengthways from stern to bow. They keep the iron frames (what are called ribs in a wooden ship) in place, and also help to hold the ends of the deck beams, which go from side to side of the ship. Stringers always consider themselves most important, because they are so long.

"You will take steps—will you?" This was a long echoing rumble. It came from the frames—scores and scores of them, each one about eighteen inches distant from the next, and each riveted to the stringers in four places. "We think you will have a certain amount of trouble in that"; and thousands and thousands of little rivets that held everything together whispered: "You will. You will! Stop quivering and be quiet. Hold on, brethren! Hold on! Hot Punches! What's that?"

Rivets have no teeth, so they cannot chatter with fright; but they did their best as a fluttering jar swept along the ship from stern to bow, and she shook like a rat in a terrier's mouth.

An unusually severe pitch, for the sea was rising, had lifted the big throbbing screw nearly to the surface, and it was spinning round in a kind of soda water— half sea and half air—going much faster than was proper, because there was no deep water for it to work in. As it sank again, the engines—and they were triple expansion, three cylinders in a row— snorted through all their three pistons. "Was that a joke, you fellow outside? It's an uncommonly poor one. How are we to do our work if you fly off the handle that way?"

"I didn't fly off the handle," said the screw, twirling huskily at the end of the screw shaft. "If I had, you'd have been scrap iron by this time. The sea dropped away from under me, and I had nothing to catch on to. That's all."

"That's all, d'you call it?" said the thrust block, whose business it is to take the push of the screw; for if a screw had nothing to hold it back it would crawl right into the engine room. (It is the holding back of the screwing action that gives the drive to a ship.) "I know I do my work deep down and out of sight, but I warn you I expect justice. All I ask for is bare justice. Why can't you push steadily and evenly, instead of whizzing like a whirli-

gig and making me hot under all my collars." The thrust block had six collars, each faced with brass, and he did not wish to get them heated.

All the bearings that supported the fifty feet of screw shaft as it ran to the stern whispered: "Justice—give us justice."

"I can only give you what I can get," the screw answered. "Look out! It's coming again!"

He rose with a roar as the *Dimbula* plunged, and "whack—flack—whack—whack" went the engines, furiously, for they had little to check them.

"I'm the noblest outcome of human ingenuity—Mr. Buchanan says so," squealed the high-pressure cylinder. "This is simply ridiculous!" The piston went up savagely, and choked, for half the steam behind it was mixed with dirty water. "Help! Oiler! Fitter! Stoker! Help! I'm choking," it gasped. "Never in the history of maritime invention has such a calamity overtaken one so young and strong. And if I go, who's to drive the ship?"

"Hush! oh, hush!" whispered the Steam, who, of course, had been to sea many times before. He used to spend his leisure ashore in a cloud, or a gutter, or a flowerpot, or a thunderstorm, or anywhere else where water was needed. "That's only a little priming, a little carrying-over, as they call it. It'll happen all night, on and off. I don't say it's nice, but it's the best we can do under the circumstances."

"What difference can circumstances make? I'm here to do my work—on clean, dry steam. Blow circumstances!" the cylinder roared.

"The circumstances will attend to the blowing. I've worked on the North Atlantic run a good many times—it's going to be rough before morning."

"It isn't distressingly calm now," said the extra-strong frames—they were called web frames—in the engine room. "There's an upward thrust that we don't understand, and there's a twist that is very bad for our brackets and diamond plates, and there's a sort of west-north-westerly pull that follows the twist, which seriously annoys us. We mention this because we happened to cost a good deal of money, and we feel sure that the owner would not approve of our being treated in this frivolous way."

"I'm afraid the matter is out of the owner's hands for the present," said the Steam, slipping into the condenser. "You're left to your own devices till the weather betters."

"I wouldn't mind the weather," said a flat bass voice below; "it's this confounded cargo that's breaking my heart. I'm the garboard strake, and I'm twice as thick as most of the others, and I ought to know something."

The garboard strake is the lowest plate in the bottom of a ship, and the *Dimbula's* garboard strake was nearly three quarters of an inch mild steel.

"The sea pushes me up in a way I should never have expected," the strake grunted, "and the cargo pushes me down, and, between the two, I don't know what I'm supposed to do."

"When in doubt, hold on," rumbled the Steam, making head in the boilers.

"Yes; but there's only dark, and cold, and hurry, down here; and how do I know whether the other plates are doing their duty? Those bulwark plates up above, I've heard, ain't more than five sixteenths of an inch thick—scandalous, I call it."

"I agree with you," said a huge web frame by the main cargo hatch. He was deeper and thicker than all the others, and curved halfway across the ship in the shape of half an arch, to support the deck

where deck beams would have been in the way of cargo coming up and down. "I work entirely unsupported, and I observe that I am the sole strength of this vessel, so far as my vision extends. The responsibility, I assure you, is enormous. I believe the money value of the cargo is over one hundred and fifty thousand pounds.[1] Think of that!"

"And every pound of it is dependent on my personal exertions." Here spoke a sea valve that communicated directly with the water outside, and was seated not very far from the garboard strake. "I rejoice to think that I am a Prince-Hyde Valve, with best Para rubber facings. Five patents cover me—I mention this without pride—five separate and several patents, each one finer than the other. At present I am screwed fast. Should I open, you would immediately be swamped. This is incontrovertible!"

Patent things always use the longest words they can. It is a trick that they pick up from their inventors.

"That's news," said a big centrifugal bilge pump. "I had an idea that you were employed to clean decks and things with. At least, I've used you for that more than once. I forget the precise number, in thousands, of gallons which I am guaranteed to throw per hour; but I assure you, my complaining friends, that there is not the least danger. I alone am capable of clearing any water that may find its way here. By my Biggest Deliveries, we pitched then!"

The sea was getting up in a workmanlike style. It was a dead westerly gale, blown from under a ragged opening of green sky, narrowed on all sides by fat, gray clouds; and the wind bit like pincers as it fretted the spray into lacework on the flanks of the waves.

"I tell you what it is," the foremast telephoned down its wire stays. "I'm up here, and I can take a dispassionate view of things. There's an organized conspiracy against us. I'm sure of it, because every single one of these waves is heading directly for our bows. The whole sea is concerned in it—and so's the wind. It's awful!"

"What's awful?" said a wave, drowning the capstan for the hundredth time.

"This organized conspiracy on your part," the capstan gurgled, taking his cue from the mast.

"Organized bubbles and spindrift! There has been a depression[2] in the Gulf of Mexico. Excuse me!" He leaped overside; but his friends took up the tale one after another.

"Which has advanced—" That wave hove green water over the funnel.

"As far as Cape Hatteras—" He drenched the bridge.

"And is now going out to sea—to sea—to sea!" The third wave went free in three surges, making a clean sweep of a boat, which turned bottom up and sank in the darkening troughs alongside, while the broken falls whipped the davits.

"That's all there is to it," seethed the white water roaring through the scuppers.[3] "There's no animus[4] in our proceedings. We're only meteorological corollaries."

"Is it going to get any worse?" said the bow anchor chained down to the deck, where he could only breathe once in five minutes.

"Not knowing, can't say. Wind may blow a bit by midnight. Thanks awfully. Good-by."

[1] **pounds:** A pound at the time was about five dollars in American money.

[2] **depression:** a region of low air pressure surrounded by higher pressures.

[3] **scuppers:** openings which allow water falling on deck to flow overboard.

[4] **animus:** hostile or unfriendly feelings.

The wave that spoke so politely had traveled some distance aft and found itself all mixed up on the deck amidships, which was a well deck sunk between high bulwarks. One of the bulwark plates, which was hung on hinges to open outward, had swung out, and passed the bulk of the water back to the sea again with a clean smack.

"Evidently that's what I'm made for," said the plate closing again with a sputter of pride. "Oh no, you don't, my friend!"

The top of a wave was trying to get in from the outside, but as the plate did not open in that direction, the defeated water spurted back.

"Not bad for five sixteenths of an inch," said the bulwark plate. "My work, I see, is laid down for the night"; and it began opening and shutting with the motion of the ship as it was designed to do.

"We are not what you might call idle," groaned all the frames together, as the *Dimbula* climbed a big wave, lay on her side at the top, and shot into the next hollow, twisting in the descent. A huge swell pushed up exactly under her middle, and her bow and stern hung free with nothing to support them. Then one joking wave caught her up at the bow, and another at the stern, while the rest of the water slunk away from under her just to see how she would like it; so she was held up at her two ends only, and the weight of the cargo and the machinery fell on the groaning iron keels and bilge stringers.

"Ease off! Ease off, there!" roared the garboard strake. "I want one eighth of an inch fair play. D'you hear me, you rivets!"

"Ease off! Ease off!" cried the bilge stringers. "Don't hold us so tight to the frames!"

"Ease off!" grunted the deck beams, as the *Dimbula* rolled fearfully. "You've cramped our knees into the stringers, and we can't move. Ease off, you flat-headed little nuisances."

Then two converging seas hit the bows, one on each side, and fell away in torrents of streaming thunder.

"Ease off!" shouted the forward collision bulkhead. "I want to crumple up, but I'm stiffened in every direction. Ease off, you dirty little forge filings. Let me breathe!"

All the hundreds of plates that are riveted to the frames and make the outside skin of every steamer echoed the call, for each plate wanted to shift and creep a little, and each plate, according to its position, complained against the rivets.

"We can't help it! We can't help it!" they murmured in reply. "We're put here to hold you, and we're going to do it; you never pull us twice in the same direction. If you'd say what you were going to do next, we'd try to meet your views."

"As far as I could feel," said the upper-deck planking, and that was four inches thick, "every single iron near me was pushing or pulling in opposite directions. Now, what's the sense of that? My friends, let us all pull together."

"Pull any way you please," roared the funnel, "so long as you don't try your experiments on me. I need seven wire ropes, all pulling in different directions, to hold me steady. Isn't that so?"

"We believe you, my boy!" whistled the funnel stays through their clinched teeth, as they twanged in the wind from the top of the funnel to the deck.

"Nonsense! We must all pull together," the decks repeated. "Pull lengthways."

"Very good," said the stringers; "then stop pushing sideways when you get wet. Be content to run gracefully fore and aft, and curve in at the ends as we do."

"No—no curves at the end! A very slight workmanlike curve from side to

side, with a good grip at each knee, and little pieces welded on," said the deck beams.

"Fiddle!" cried the iron pillars of the deep, dark hold. "Who ever heard of curves? Stand up straight; be a perfectly round column, and carry tons of good solid weight—like that! There!" A big sea smashed on the deck above, and the pillars stiffened themselves to the load.

"Straight up and down is not bad," said the frames, who ran that way in the sides of the ship, "but you must also expand yourselves sideways. Expansion is the law of life, children. Open out! open out!"

"Come back!" said the deck beams savagely, as the upward heave of the sea made the frames try to open. "Come back to your bearings, you slack-jawed irons!"

"Rigidity! Rigidity! Rigidity!" thumped the engines. "Absolute, unvarying rigidity —rigidity!"

"You see!" whined the rivets in chorus. "No two of you will ever pull alike, and —and you blame it all on us. We only know how to go through a plate and bite down on both sides so that it can't, and mustn't, and shan't move."

"I've got one fraction of an inch play, at any rate," said the garboard strake, triumphantly. So he had, and all the bottom of the ship felt the easier for it.

"Then we're no good," sobbed the bottom rivets. "We were ordered—we were ordered—never to give; and we've given, and sea will come in, and we'll all go to the bottom together! First we're blamed for everything unpleasant, and now we haven't the consolation of having done our work."

"Don't say I told you," whispered the Steam consolingly; "but, between you and me and the last cloud I came from, it was bound to happen sooner or later. You had to give a fraction, and you've given with-out knowing it. Now, hold on, as before."

"What's the use?" a few hundred rivets chattered. "We've given—we've given; and the sooner we confess that we can't keep the ship together, and go off our little heads, the easier it will be. No rivet forged can stand this strain."

"No one rivet was ever meant to. Share it among you," the Steam answered.

"The others can have my share. I'm going to pull out," said a rivet in one of the forward plates.

"If you go, others will follow," hissed the Steam. "There's nothing so contagious in a boat as rivets going. Why, I knew a little chap like you—he was an eighth of an inch fatter, though—on a steamer—to be sure, she was only nine hundred tons, now I come to think of it—in exactly the same place as you are. He pulled out in a bit of a bobble of a sea, not half as bad as this, and he started all his friends on the same butt strap, and the plates opened like a furnace door, and I had to climb into the nearest fog bank, while the boat went down."

"Now that's peculiarly disgraceful," said the rivet. "Fatter than me, was he, and in a steamer half our tonnage? Reedy little peg! I blush for the family, sir." He settled himself more firmly than ever in his place, and the Steam chuckled.

"You see," he went on, quite gravely, "a rivet, and especially a rivet in your position, is really the one indispensable part of the ship."

The Steam did not say that he had whispered the very same thing to every single piece of iron aboard. There is no sense in telling too much truth.

And all that while the little *Dimbula* pitched and chopped, and swung and slewed, and lay down as though she were going to die, and got up as though she had been stung, and threw her nose round and round in circles half a dozen times as she

dipped; for the gale was at its worst. It was inky black, in spite of the tearing white froth on the waves, and, to top everything, the rain began to fall in sheets, so that you could not see your hand before your face. This did not make much difference to the iron work below, but it troubled the foremast a good deal.

"Now it's all finished," he said dismally. "The conspiracy is too strong for us. There is nothing left but to——"

"Hurraar! Brrrraaah! Brrrrrrp!" roared the Steam through the foghorn, till the decks quivered. "Don't be frightened, below. It's only me, just throwing out a few words, in case any one happens to be rolling round tonight."

"You don't mean to say there's any one except us on the sea in such weather?" said the funnel in a husky snuffle.

"Scores of 'em," said the Steam, clearing its throat; "Rrrrrraaa! Brraaaaa! Prrrp! It's a trifle windy up here and, Great Boilers! how it rains!"

"We're drowning," said the scuppers. They had been doing nothing else all night, but this steady thrash of rain above them seemed to be the end of the world.

"That's all right. We'll be easier in an hour or two. First the wind and then the rain: Soon you may make sail again! Grrraaaaaah! Drrraaaa! Drrrp! I have a notion that the sea is going down already. If it does you'll learn something about rolling. We've only pitched till now. By the way, aren't you chaps in the hold a little easier than you were?"

There was just as much groaning and straining as ever, but it was not so loud or squeaky in tone; and when the ship quivered she did not jar stiffly, like a poker hit on the floor, but gave with a supple little waggle, like a perfectly balanced golf club.

"We have made a most amazing discovery," said the stringers, one after another. "A discovery that entirely changes the situation. We have found, for the first time in the history of ship-building, that the inward pull of the deck beams and the outward thrust of the frames lock us, as it were, more closely in our places, and enables us to endure a strain which is entirely without parallel in the records of marine architecture."

The Steam turned a laugh quickly into a roar up the foghorn. "What massive intellects you great stringers have," he said softly, when he had finished.

"We also," began the deck beams, "are discoverers and geniuses. We are of opinion that the support of the hold pillars materially helps us. We find that we lock up on them when we are subjected to a heavy and singular weight of sea above."

Here the *Dimbula* shot down a hollow, lying almost on her side—righting at the bottom with a wrench and a spasm.

"In these cases—are you aware of this, Steam?—the plating at the bows, and particularly at the stern—we would also mention the floors beneath us—help us to resist any tendency to spring." The frames spoke in the solemn, awed voice which people use when they have just come across something entirely new for the very first time.

"I'm only a poor puffy little flutterer," said the Steam, "but I have to stand a good deal of pressure in my business. It's all tremendously interesting. Tell us some more. You fellows are so strong."

"Watch us and you'll see," said the bow plates, proudly. "Ready, behind there! Here's the Father and Mother of Waves coming! Sit tight, rivets all!" A great sluicing comber thundered by, but through the scuffle and confusion the Steam could hear the low, quick cries of the ironwork as the various strains took them—cries like these: "Easy, now—easy! Now push

for all your strength! Hold out! Give a fraction! Hold up! Pull in! Shove crossways! Mind the strain at the ends! Grip, now! Bite tight! Let the water get away from under—and there she goes!"

The wave raced off into the darkness, shouting, "Not bad, that, if it's your first run!" and the drenched and ducked ship throbbed to the beat of the engines inside her. All three cylinders were white with the salt spray that had come down through the engine-room hatch; there was white fur on the canvas-bound steam pipes, and even the bright work deep below was speckled and soiled; but the cylinders had learned to make the most of steam that was half water, and were pounding along cheerfully.

"How's the noblest outcome of human ingenuity hitting it?" said the Steam, as he whirled through the engine room.

"Nothing for nothing in this world of woe," the cylinders answered, as though they had been working for centuries, "and precious little for seventy-five pounds' head. We've made two knots this last hour and a quarter! Rather humiliating for eight hundred horsepower, isn't it?"

"Well, it's better than drifting astern, at any rate. You seem rather less—how shall I put it?—stiff in the back than you were."

"If you'd been hammered as we've been this night, you wouldn't be stiff—iff—iff, either. Theoreti—retti—retti—cally, of course, rigidity is the thing. Purrr—purr—practically, there has to be a little give and take. We found that out by working on our sides for five minutes at a stretch—chch—chh. How's the weather?"

"Sea's going down fast," said the Steam.

"Good business," said the high-pressure cylinder. "Whack her up, boys. They've given us five pounds more steam"; and he began humming the first

bars of "Said the young Obadiah to the old Obadiah," [1] which, as you may have noticed, is a pet tune among engines not built for high speed. Racing liners with twin screws sing "The Turkish Patrol" and the overture to "The Bronze Horse," and "Madame Angot," till something goes wrong, and then they render Gounod's "Funeral March of a Marionette," with variations.

"You'll learn a song of your own some fine day," said the Steam, as he flew up the foghorn for one last bellow.

Next day the sky cleared and the sea dropped a little, and the *Dimbula* began to roll from side to side till every inch of iron in her was sick and giddy. But luckily they did not all feel ill at the same time: otherwise she would have opened out like a wet paper box.

The Steam whistled warnings as he went about his business: it is in this short, quick roll and tumble that follows a heavy sea that most of the accidents happen, for then everything thinks that the worst is over and goes off guard. So he orated and chattered till the beams and frames and floors and stringers and things had learned how to lock down and lock up on one another and endure this new kind of strain.

They found ample time to practice, for they were sixteen days at sea, and it was foul weather till within a hundred miles of New York. The *Dimbula* picked up her pilot and came in covered with salt and red rust. Her funnel was dirty gray from top to bottom; two boats had been carried away; three copper ventilators looked like hats after a fight with the police; the bridge had a dimple in the middle of it; the house that covered the steam

[1] Said the young Obadiah to the old Obadiah,
"I am dry, Obadiah, I am dry."
Said the old Obadiah to the young Obadiah,
"So am I, Obadiah, so am I."

steering gear was split as with hatchets; there was a bill for small repairs in the engine room almost as long as the screw shaft; the forward cargo hatch fell into bucket staves when they raised the iron crossbars; and the steam capstan had been badly wrenched on its bed. Altogether, as the skipper said, it was "a pretty general average."

"But she's soupled,"[1] he said to Mr. Buchanan. "For all her dead weight she rode like a yacht. Ye mind that last blow off the Banks? I am proud of her, Buck."

"It's vara good," said the chief engineer, looking along the disheveled decks. "Now, a man judgin' superfeecially would say we were a wreck, but we know otherwise —by experience."

Naturally everything in the *Dimbula* fairly stiffened with pride, and the fore-mast and the forward collision-bulkhead, who are pushing creatures, begged the Steam to warn the Port of New York of their arrival. "Tell those big boats all about us," they said. "They seem to take

[1] **soupled:** suppled, "broken in."

us quite as a matter of course."

It was a glorious, clear, dead calm morning, and in single file, with less than half a mile between each, their bands playing and their tugboats shouting and waving handkerchiefs, were the *Majestic,* the *Paris,* the *Touraine,* the *Servia,* the *Kaiser Wilhelm II,* and the *Werkendam,* all statelily going out to sea. As the *Dimbula* shifted her helm to give the great boats clear way, the Steam (who knows far too much to mind making an exhibition of himself now and then) shouted:

"Oyez! Oyez! Oyez! Princes, Dukes, and Barons of the High Seas! Know ye by these presents, we are the *Dimbula* fifteen days nine hours from Liverpool, having crossed the Atlantic with three thousand ton of cargo for the first time in our career! We have not foundered. We are here. 'Eer! 'Eer! We are not disabled. But we have had a time wholly unparalleled in the annals of shipbuilding! Our decks were swept! We pitched; we rolled! We thought we were going to die! Hi! Hi! But we didn't. We wish to give notice that we have come to New York

all the way across the Atlantic, through the worst weather in the world; and we are the *Dimbula!* We are—arr—ha—ha—ha-r-r-r!"

The beautiful line of boats swept by as steadily as the procession of the Seasons. The *Dimbula* heard the *Majestic* say, "Hmph!" and the *Paris* grunted, "How!" and the *Touraine* said, "Oui!" with a little coquettish flicker of steam; and the *Servia* said, "Haw!" and the *Kaiser* and the *Werkendam* said, "Hoch!" Dutch-fashion—and that was absolutely all.

"I did my best," said the Steam, gravely, "but I don't think they were much impressed with us, somehow. Do you?"

"It's simply disgusting," said the bow plates. "They might have seen what we've been through. There isn't a ship on the sea that has suffered as we have—is there, now?"

"Well, I wouldn't go so far as that," said the Steam, "because I've worked on some of those boats and sent them through weather quite as bad as the fortnight that we've had, in six days; and some of them are a little over ten thousand tons, I believe. Now I've seen the *Majes-*

tic, for instance, ducked from her bows to her funnel; and I've helped the *Arizona,* I think she was, to back off an iceberg she met with one dark night; and I had to run out of the *Paris's* engine room, one day, because there was thirty foot of water in it. Of course, I don't deny—" The Steam shut off suddenly, as a tugboat, loaded with a political club and a brass band, that had been to see a New York Senator off to Europe, crossed their bows, going to Hoboken. There was a long silence that reached, without a break, from the cutwater to the propeller blades of the *Dimbula.*

Then a new, big voice said slowly and thickly, as though the owner had just waked up: "It's my conviction that I have made a fool of myself."

The Steam knew what had happened at once; for when a ship finds herself all the talking of the separate pieces ceases and melts into one voice, which is the soul of the ship.

"Who are you?" he said, with a laugh.

"I am the *Dimbula,* of course. I've never been anything else except that—and a fool!"

The tugboat, which was doing its very

best to be run down, got away just in time, its band playing clashily and brassily a popular but impolite air:

In the days of old Rameses—are you on?
In the days of old Rameses—are you on?
In the days of old Rameses,
That story had paresis,[1]
Are you on—are you on—are you on?

"Well, I'm glad you've found yourself," said the Steam. "To tell the truth I was a little tired of talking to all those ribs and stringers. Here's Quarantine. After that we'll go to our wharf and clean up a little, and—next month we'll do it all over again."

[1] **paresis** (pə·rē′sis): paralysis.

FOR STUDY AND DISCUSSION

1. The principal characters of this story are *things*. How does Kipling make them into characters? Which parts of the ship do you think he is most successful in bringing alive?

2. What does each part of the ship, at the beginning of the voyage, think of its own role in the functioning of the ship? Of what does each part complain?

3. How does the Steam, the only old-timer aboard, keep things running and holding together? At what points especially does the Steam show its wisdom?

4. At what point in the story does the ship begin to find itself? What does each of the parts discover about its functioning?

5. What does the *Dimbula* mean by declaring that she has made a fool of herself? Is this discovery perhaps the beginning of wisdom?

6. In most stories the controlling idea, or theme, is not stated explicitly. In this story it is. What is the story's theme? State it in a single sentence.

7. What did the author have to know about a ship before he could write this story? Which details are especially effective in making you see or hear the storm and the working of the ship's parts? Which show most clearly that Kipling had experienced a storm at sea?

LANGUAGE AND VOCABULARY

Kipling's story is full of technical terms. Many of these are defined in context, but quite a few are not. Here are some of the words you may need to look up. What is the meaning of each?

funnel	condenser	falls
screw	bulwark	davits
rivets	valve	bulkhead
bearings	stays	bilge
piston	bridge	hatch

Why is a builder of ships called a *shipwright*? (Look up the derivation of the word.) Why do you think a writer of plays is called a *playwright*?

How would a *centrifugal* bilge pump work?

FOR COMPOSITION

Write a character sketch of Steam or one of the other parts of the ship. Describe in detail what kind of "character" he is, illustrating your description by referring to what he says and does.

ABOUT THE AUTHOR

Rudyard Kipling (1865–1936) lived for considerable periods of time on four different continents and made use of each—as well as the oceans in between—as background for his fiction. Born in Bombay, India, he learned Hindustani along with English. At the age of six he was sent to England, where he attended school until he was seventeen. On rejoining his parents in India, he became subeditor of the *Lahore Civil and Military Gazette,* in which he published his first short stories. After his return to England in 1889, he married an American girl, and from 1892 to 1896 lived in Brattleboro, Vermont. Most of the rest of his life he lived in England, but for some ten years spent his winters in South Africa. Kipling is famous for his short stories —such as "The Man Who Would Be King," "The Brushwood Boy," "Wee Willie Winkie"; his novels—such as *Captains Courageous, Kim;* his children's books—*Just-So Stories, The Jungle Books;* and his poetry. He won the Nobel prize for literature in 1907.

Land

SINCLAIR LEWIS

HE WAS NAMED Sidney, for the sake of elegance, just as his parents had for elegance in their Brooklyn parlor a golden-oak combination bookcase, desk, and shield-shaped mirror. But Sidney Dow was descended from generations of Georges and Johns, of Lorens and Lukes and Nathans.

He was little esteemed in the slick bustle of his city school. He seemed a loutish boy, tall and heavy and slow-spoken, and he was a worry to his father. For William Dow was an ambitious parent. Born on a Vermont farm, William felt joyously that he had done well in the great city of Brooklyn. He had, in 1885, when Sidney was born, a real bathroom with a fine tin tub, gas lights, and a handsome phaeton [1] with red wheels, instead of the washtub in the kitchen for Saturday-night baths, the kerosene lamps, and the heavy old buggy which his father still used in Vermont. Instead of being up at five-thirty, he could loll abed till a quarter of seven, and he almost never, he chuckled in gratification at his progress, was in his office before a quarter to eight.

But the luxury of a red-wheeled carriage and late lying did not indicate that Wil-

[1] **phaeton** (fā′ə·tən): a light four-wheeled carriage.

"Land" from *Selected Short Stories of Sinclair Lewis*. Copyright 1931 by Sinclair Lewis, copyright renewed 1959 by Michael Lewis. Reprinted by permission of Howard W. Gould, Administrator, Estate of Michael Lewis.

liam's Yankee shrewdness had been cozened by urban vice, or that he was any less solid and respectable than old George, his own father. He was a deacon in the Universalist church, he still said grace before meals, and he went to the theater only when Ben-Hur was appearing.

For his son, Sidney, William Dow had even larger ambitions. William himself had never gone to high school, and his business was only a cautious real-estate and insurance agency, his home a squatting two-story brick house in a red, monotonous row. But Sidney—he should go to college, he should be a doctor or a preacher or a lawyer, he should travel in Europe, he should live in a three-story graystone house in the Forties in Manhattan, he should have a dress suit and wear it to respectable but expensive hops! [2]

William had once worn dress clothes at an Odd Fellows' ball, but they had been rented.

To enable Sidney to attain all these graces, William toiled and sacrificed and prayed. American fathers have always been as extraordinary as Scotch fathers in their heroic ambitions for their sons— and sometimes as unscrupulous and as unwise. It bruised William and often it made him naggingly unkind to see that Sidney, the big slug, did not "appreciate how his parents were trying to do for him and give him every opportunity." When they had a celebrated Columbia Heights physician as guest for dinner, Sidney merely gawked at him and did not at all try to make an impression.

"Suffering cats! You might have been one of your uncles still puttering around with dirty pitchforks back on the farm! What are you going to do with yourself, anyway?" raged William.

[2] **hops:** dances.

"I guess maybe I'd like to be a truck driver," mumbled Sidney.

Yet, even so, William should not have whipped him. It only made him sulkier.

To Sidney Dow, at sixteen, his eagerest memories were of occasional weeks he had spent with his grandfather and uncles on the Vermont farm, and the last of these was seven years back now. He remembered Vermont as an enchanted place, with curious and amusing animals— cows, horses, turkeys. He wanted to return, but his father seemed to hate the place. Of Brooklyn, Sidney liked nothing save livery stables [1] and occasional agreeable gang fights, with stones inside iced snowballs. He hated school, where he had to cramp his big knees under trifling desks, where irritable lady teachers tried to make him see the importance of A's going more rapidly than B to the town of X, a town in which he was even less interested than in Brooklyn—school where hour on hour he looked over the top of his geography and stolidly hated the whiskers of Longfellow, Lowell, and Whittier. He hated the stiff, clean collar and the itchy, clean winter underwear connected with Sunday school. He hated hot evenings smelling of tarry pavements, and cold evenings when the pavements were slippery.

But he didn't know that he hated any of these things. He knew only that his father must be right in saying that he was a bad, disobedient, ungrateful young whelp, and in his heart he was as humble as in his speech he was sullen.

Then, at sixteen, he came to life suddenly, on an early June morning, on his grandfather's farm. His father had sent him up to Vermont for the summer, had indeed exiled him, saying grimly, "I

[1] **livery stables:** stables with horses and carriages for hire.

guess after you live in that tumble-down big old shack and work in the fields and have to get up early, instead of lying abed till your majesty is good and ready to have the girl wait on you—I guess that next fall you'll appreciate your nice home and school and church here, young man!" So sure of himself was his father that Sidney was convinced he was going to encounter hardship on the farm, and all the way up, in the smarting air of the smoker on the slow train, he wanted to howl. The train arrived at ten in the evening, and he was met by his uncle Rob, a man rugged as a pine trunk and about as articulate.

"Well! Come for the summer!" said Uncle Rob; and after they had driven three miles: "Got new calf—yeh, new calf"; and after a mile more; "Your pa all right?" And that was all the conversation of Uncle Rob.

Seven years it was since Sidney had been in any country wilder than Far Rockaway, and the silent hills of night intimidated him. It was a roaring silence, a silence full of stifled threats. The hills that cut the stars so high up on either side the road seemed walls that would topple and crush him, as a man would crush a mosquito between his two palms. And once he cried out when, in the milky light from the lantern swung beneath the wagon, he saw a porcupine lurch into the road before them. It was dark, chill, unfriendly and, to the boy, reared to the

lights and cheery voices of the city, even though he hated them, it was appallingly lonely.

His grandfather's house was dark when they arrived. Uncle Rob drove into the barn, jerked his thumb at a ladder up to the haymow and muttered. "Y'sleep up there. Not allowed t' smoke. Take this lantern when we've unharnessed. Sure to put it out. No smoking in the barn. Too tired to help?"

Too tired? Sidney would have been glad to work till daylight if Uncle Rob would but stay with him. He was in a panic at the thought of being left in the ghostly barn where, behind the pawing of horses and the nibble of awakened cows, there were the sounds of anonymous wild animals—scratchings, squeaks, patterings overhead. He made the task as slow as possible, though actually he was handy with horses, for the livery stables of Brooklyn had been his favorite refuge and he had often been permitted to help the hostlers, quite free.

"Gee, Uncle Rob, I guess I'm kind of all thumbs about unharnessing and like that. Seven years since I been here on the farm."

"That so? G'night. Careful of that lantern now. And no smoking!"

The barn was blank as a blind face. The lantern was flickering, and in that witching light the stalls and the heap of sleighs, plows, old harness, at the black wall of the barn were immense and terrifying. The barn was larger than his whole house in Brooklyn, and ten times as large it seemed in the dimness. He could not see clear to the back wall, and he imagined abominable monsters lurking there. He dashed at the ladder up to the haymow, the lantern handle in his teeth and his imitation-leather satchel in one hand.

And the haymow, rising to the darkness

of its hand-hewn rafters, seemed vaster and more intimidating than the space below. In one corner a space had been cleared of hay for a cot, with a blanket and a pea-green comforter, and for a chair and a hinged box. Sidney dashed at the cot and crawled into it, waiting only to take off his shoes and jacket. Till the lantern flame died down to a red rim of charred wick, he kept it alight. Then utter darkness leaped upon him.

A rooster crowed, and he startled. Past him things scampered and chittered. The darkness seemed to swing in swift eddies under the rafters, the smell of dry hay choked him—and he awoke to light slipping in silver darts through cracks in the roof, and to jubilant barn swallows diving and twittering.

"Gee, I must have fell asleep!" he thought. He went down the ladder, and now, first, he saw the barn.

Like many people slow of thought and doubtful of speech, Sidney Dow had moments of revelation as complete as those of a prophet, when he beheld a scene or a person or a problem in its entirety, with none of the confusing thoughts of glibber and more clever people with their minds forever running off on many tracks. He saw the barn— really saw it, instead of merely glancing at it, like a normal city boy. He saw that the beams, hand-hewn, gray with sixty years, were beautiful; that the sides of the stalls, polished with rubbing by the shoulders of cattle dead these fifty years, were beautiful; that the harrow,[1] with its trim spikes kept sharp and rustless, was beautiful; that most beautiful of all were the animals—cows and horses, chickens that walked with bobbing heads through the straw, and a calf tethered to the wall. The calf capered with alarm as he ap-

[1] **harrow:** a machine for plowing.

proached it; then stood considering him with great eyes, letting him stroke its head and at last licking his hand. He slouched to the door of the barn and looked down the valley. More radiant in that early morning light than even the mountain tops covered with maples and hemlock were the upland clearings with white houses and red barns.

"Gosh, it looks nice! It's—it's sort of— it looks nice! I didn't hardly get it when I was here before. But gee"—with all the scorn of sixteen—"I was just a kid then!"

With Uncle Rob he drove the cows to pasture; with Uncle Ben he plowed; with his grandfather, sourly philanthropic behind his beard, he split wood. He found an even greater menagerie than in the barn—turkeys, geese, ducks, pigs and, in the woods and mowings, an exciting remnant of woodchucks, chipmunks, rabbits, and infrequent deer. With all of them—uncles and grandfather, beasts, wild or tame—he felt at home. They did not expect him to chatter and show off, as had his gang in Brooklyn; they accepted him. That, perhaps, more than any an-

cestral stoutness, more than the beauty of the land, made a farmer of him. He was a natural hermit, and here he could be a hermit without seeming queer.

And a good farmer he was—slow but tireless, patient, unannoyed by the endless work, happy to go to bed early and be up at dawn. For a few days his back felt as though he were burning at the stake, but after that he could lift all day in the hayfield or swing the scythe or drive the frisky young team. He was a good farmer, and he slept at night. The noises which on his first night had fretted his city-tortured nerves were soporific now, and when he heard the sound of a distant train, the barking of a dog on the next farm, he inarticulately told himself that they were lovely.

"You're pretty fair at working," said Uncle Rob, and that was praise almost hysterical.

Indeed, in one aspect of labor, Sidney was better than any of them, even the pine-carved Uncle Rob. He could endure wet dawns, wild winds, all-day drenching. It seems to be true that farmers are more upset by bad weather than most outdoor

workers—sailors, postmen, carpenters, brakemen, teamsters. Perhaps it is because they are less subject to higher authority; except for chores and getting in the hay, they can more nearly do things in their own time, and they build up a habit of taking shelter on nasty days. Whether or no, it was true that just the city crises that had vexed Sidney, from icy pavements to sudden fire alarms, had given him the ability to stand discomforts and the unexpected, like a little Cockney [1] surprisingly stolid in the trenches.

He learned the silent humor of the authentic Yankee. Evenings he sat with neighbors on the bench before the general store. To a passing stranger they seemed to be saying nothing, but when the stranger had passed, Uncle Rob would drawl, "Well, if I had fly nets on my hosses, guess I'd look stuck-up too!" and the others would chuckle with contempt at the alien.

This, thought Sidney, was good talk—not like the smart gabble of the city. It was all beautiful, and he knew it, though in his vocabulary there was no such word as "beautiful," and when he saw the most flamboyant sunset he said only, "Guess going to be clear tomorrow."

And so he went back to Brooklyn, not as to his home but as to prison, and as a prison corridor he saw the narrow street with little houses like little cells.

Five minutes after he had entered the house, his father laughed. "Well, did you get enough of farming? I guess you'll appreciate your school now! I won't rub it in, but I swear, how Rob and Ben can stand it——"

"I kind of liked it, Dad. I think I'll be a farmer. I—kind of liked it."

His father had black side whiskers, and between them he had thin cheeks that seemed, after Uncle Rob and Uncle Ben, pallid as the underside of a toadstool. They flushed now, and William shouted:

"You're an idiot! What have I done to have a son who is an idiot? The way I've striven and worked and economized to give you a chance to get ahead, to do something worthwhile, and then you want to slip right back and be ordinary, like your uncles! So you think you'd like it! You're a fool! Sure you like it in summer, but if you knew it like I do—rousted out to do the chores five o'clock of a January morning, twenty below zero, and maybe have to dig through two feet of snow to get to the barn! Have to tramp down to the store, snowstorm so thick you can't see five feet in front of you!"

"I don't guess I'd mind it much."

"Oh, you don't! Don't be a fool! And no nice company like here—go to bed with the chickens, a winter night, and no nice lodge meeting or church supper or lectures like there is here!"

"Don't care so much for those things. Everybody talking all the while. I like it quiet, like in the country."

"Well, you will care so much for those things, or I'll care you, my fine young man! I'm not going to let you slump back into being a rube like Ben, and don't you forget it! I'll make you work at your books! I'll make you learn to appreciate good society and dressing proper and getting ahead in the world and amounting to something! Yes, sir, amounting to something! Do you think for one moment that after the struggle I've gone through to give you a chance—the way I studied in a country school and earned my way through business college and went to work at five dollars a week in a real-estate office and studied and economized and worked late, so I could give you this nice house and advantages and opportunity——No, sir! You're going to be a law-

[1] **Cockney:** a native of the London slums.

yer or a doctor or somebody that amounts to something, and not a rube!"

It would have been too much to expect of Sidney's imagination that he should have seen anything fine and pathetic in William's fierce ambition. That did not move him, but rather fear. He could have broken his father in two, but the passion in this blenched filing case of a man was such that it hypnotized him.

For days, miserably returned to high school, he longed for the farm. But his mother took him aside and begged: "You mustn't oppose your father so, dearie. He knows what's best for you, and it would just break his heart if he thought you were going to be a common person and not have something to show for all his efforts."

So Sidney came to feel that it was some wickedness in him that made him prefer trees and winds and meadows and the kind cattle to trolley cars and offices and people who made little, flat, worried jokes all day long.

He barely got through high school. His summer vacations he spent in warehouses, hoisting boxes. He failed to enter medical school, botched his examinations shockingly—feeling wicked at betraying his father's ambitions—and his father pushed him into a second-rate dental school with sketchy requirements, a school now blessedly out of existence.

"Maybe you'd be better as a dentist anyway. Requires a lot of manipulation, and I will say you're good with your hands," his father said, in relief that now Sidney was on the highway to fortune and respectability.

But Sidney's hands, deft with hammer and nails, with reins or hoe or spade, were too big, too awkward for the delicate operations of dentistry. And in school he hated the long-winded books with their queer names and shocking colored plates of man's inwards. The workings of a liver

did not interest him. He had never seen a liver, save that of a slain chicken. He would turn from these mysteries to a catalog of harvesting machinery or vegetable seed. So with difficulty he graduated from this doubtful school, and he was uneasy at the pit of his stomach, even when his father, much rejoicing now, bought for him a complete dental outfit, and rented an office, on the new frontier of the Bronx, in the back part of a three-story red-brick apartment house.

His father and mother invited their friends over from Brooklyn to admire the office, and served them coffee and cake. Not many of them came, which was well, for the office was not large. It was really a single room, divided by a curtain to make a reception hall. The operating room had pink-calcimined walls and, for adornment, Sidney's diploma and a calendar from a dental supply house which showed, with no apparent appropriateness, a view of Pike's Peak.

When they had all gone, mouthing congratulations, Sidney looked wistfully out on the old pasture land which, fifteen years later, was to be filled solidly with tall, cheap apartment houses and huge avenues with delicatessen shops and movie palaces. Already these pastures were doomed and abandoned. Cows no longer grazed there. Gaunt billboards lined the roads and behind their barricades were unkempt waste lands of ashes and sodden newspapers. But they were open grass, and they brought back the valleys and uplands of Vermont. His great arms were hungry for the strain of plowing, and he sighed and turned back to his shining new kit of tools.

The drill he picked up was absurd against his wide red palm. All at once he was certain that he knew no dentistry, and that he never would; that he would botch every case; that dreadful things would happen—suits for malpractice—— [1]

Actually, as a few and poorly paying neighborhood patients began to come in, the dreadful things didn't happen. Sidney was slow, but he was careful; if he did no ingenious dental jeweling, he did nothing worse. He learned early what certain dentists and doctors never learn—that nature has not yet been entirely supplanted by the professions. It was not his patients who suffered; it was he.

All day long to have to remain indoors, to stand in one place, bent over gaping mouths, to fiddle with tiny instruments, to produce unctuous sounds of sympathy for cranks who complained of trivial aches, to try to give brisk and confident advice which was really selling talk—all this tortured him.

Then, within one single year, his mother died, his grandfather died on the Vermont farm, Uncle Rob and Uncle Ben moved West, and Sidney met the most wonderful girl in the world. The name of this particular most wonderful girl in the world, who unquestionably had more softness and enchantment and funny little ways of saying things than Helen of Troy, was Mabelle Ellen Pflugmann, and she was cultured; she loved the theater, but rarely attended it; loved also the piano, but hadn't time, she explained, to keep up her practice, because, her father's laundry being in a state of debility, for several years she had temporarily been cashier at the Kwiturwurry Lunch.

They furnished a four-room apartment and went to Vermont for their honeymoon. His grandfather's farm—Sidney wasn't quite sure just who had bought it—was rented out to what the neighborhood considered foreigners—that is, Vermonters from way over beyond the Ridge, fifteen miles away. They took in Sidney and Mabelle. She enjoyed it. She told how sick she had become of the smell and dish clatter of the ole lunch and horrid customers who were always trying to make love to her. She squealed equally over mountains and ducklings, sunsets and wild strawberries, and as for certain inconveniences—washing with a pitcher and bowl, sleeping in a low room smelling of the chicken run, and having supper in the kitchen with the menfolks in shirt sleeves—she said it was just too darling for words—it was, in fact, sweet. But after ten days of the fortnight [2] on which they had planned, she thought perhaps they had better get back to New York and make sure all the furniture had arrived.

They were happy in marriage. Mabelle saw him, and made him see himself, as a man strong and gallant but shy and blundering. He needed mothering, she said, and he got it and was convinced that he

[1] **malpractice:** improper treatment of a patient through ignorance or neglect.

[2] **fortnight:** two weeks.

liked it. He was less gruff with his patients, and he had many more of them, for Mabelle caused him to be known socially. Till marriage he had lived in a furnished room, and all evening he had prowled alone, or read dentistry journals and seed catalogs. Now Mabelle arranged jolly little parties—beer and Welsh rabbit [1] and a game of five hundred.[2] If at the Kwiturwurry Lunch she had met many light fellows, West Farms Lotharios,[3] she had also met estimable but bohemian families of the neighborhood—big traveling men whose territory took them as far west as Denver, assistant buyers from the downtown department stores, and the office manager of a large insurance agency.

Mabelle, a chatelaine [4] now, wanted to shine among them, and wanted Sidney to shine. And he, feeling a little cramped in a new double-breasted blue serge coat, solemnly served the beer, and sometimes a guest perceived that here was an honest and solid dentist upon whom to depend. And once they gave a theater party—six seats at a vaudeville house.

Yet Sidney was never, when he awoke mornings, excited about the adventure of standing with bent, aching shoulders over patients all this glorious coming day.

They had two children in three years and began to worry a little about the rent bill and the grocery bill, and Sidney was considerably less independent with grumbling patients than he had been. His broad shoulders had a small stoop, and he said quite humbly, "Well, I'll try my best to fix 'em to your satisfaction, Mrs. Smallberg," and sometimes his thick fingers tapped nervously on his chin as he talked. And he envied now, where once he had

[1] **Welsh rabbit:** Welsh rarebit (pronounced like "rabbit") is a cheese dish.
[2] **five hundred:** a card game much like bridge.
[3] **Lotharios:** gay young men.
[4] **chatelaine** (shat'ə·lān): the mistress of a fashionable household.

despised them, certain dental-school classmates who knew little of dentistry, but who were slick dressers and given to verbal chuckings under the chin, who had made money and opened three-room offices with chintz chairs in the waiting room. Sidney still had his old office, with no assistant, and the jerry-built tenement looked a little shabby now beside the six-story apartment houses of yellow brick trimmed with marble which had sprung up all about it.

Then their children, Rob and Willabette, were eight and six years old, and Mabelle began to nag Sidney over the children's lack of clothes as pretty as those of their lovely little friends at school.

And his dental engine—only a treadle affair at that—was worn out. And his elbows were always shiny. And in early autumn his father died.

His father died, muttering, "You've been a good boy, Sid, and done what I told you to. You can understand and appreciate now why I kept you from being just a farmer and gave you a chance to be a professional man. I don't think Mabelle comes from an awful good family, but she's a spunky little thing, and real bright,

and she'll keep you up to snuff. Maybe some day your boy will be a great, rich banker or surgeon. Keep him away from his Vermont relations—no ambition, those folks. My chest feels so tight! Bless you, Sid!"

He was his father's sole heir. When the will was read in the shabby lawyer's office in Brooklyn, he was astonished to find that his father had still owned— that he himself now owned—the ancestral Vermont home. His slow-burning imagination lighted. He was touched by the belief that his father, for all his pretended hatred of the place, had cherished it and had wanted his son to own it. Not till afterward did he learn from Uncle Rob that William, when his own father had died, had, as eldest son, been given the choice of the farm or half the money in the estate, and had taken the farm to keep Sidney away from it. He had been afraid that if his brothers had it they would welcome Sidney as a partner before he became habituated as a dentist. But in his last days, apparently, William felt that Sidney was safely civilized now and caught. With the farm Sidney inherited some three thousand dollars—not more, for the Brooklyn home was mortgaged.

Instantly and ecstatically, while the lawyer droned senseless advice, Sidney decided to go home. The tenant on his farm—his!—had only two months more on his lease. He'd take it over. The three thousand dollars would buy eight cows— well, say ten—with a cream separator, a tractor, a light truck, and serve to put the old buildings into condition adequate for a few years. He'd do the repairing himself! He arched his hands with longing for the feel of a hammer or a crowbar.

In the hall outside the lawyer's office, Mabelle crowed: "Isn't it—oh, Sid, you do know how sorry I am your father's passed on, but won't it be just lovely! The farm must be worth four thousand dollars. We'll be just as sensible as can be—not blow it all in, like lots of people would. We'll invest the seven thousand, and that ought to give us three hundred and fifty dollars a year—think of it, an extra dollar every day! You can get a dress suit now, and at last I'll have some decent dresses for the evening, and we'll get a new suit for Rob right away—how soon can you get the money? did he say?—and I saw some lovely little dresses for Willabette and the cutest slippers, and now we can get a decent bridge table instead of that rickety old thing, and——"

As she babbled, which she did, at length, on the stairs down from the office, Sidney realized wretchedly that it was going to take an eloquence far beyond him to convert her to farming and the joys of the land. He was afraid of her, as he had been of his father.

"There's a drugstore over across. Let's go over and have an ice-cream soda," he said mildly. "Gosh, it's hot for September! Up on the farm now it would be cool, and the leaves are just beginning to turn. They're awful pretty—all red and yellow."

"Oh, you and your old farm!" But in her joy she was amiable.

They sat at the bright-colored little table in the drugstore, with cheery colored drinks between them. But the scene should have been an ancient castle at midnight, terrible with wind and lightning, for suddenly they were not bright nor cheery, but black with tragedy.

There was no manner of use in trying to cajole her. She could never understand how he hated the confinement of his dental office; she would say, "Why, you get the chance of meeting all sorts of nice, interesting people, while I have to stay home," and not perceive that he did not want to meet nice, interesting people. He wanted silence and the smell of earth!

And he was under her spell as he had been under his father's. Only violently could he break it. He spoke softly enough, looking at the giddy marble of the soda counter, but he spoke sternly:

"Look here, May. This is our chance. You bet your sweet life we're going to be sensible and not blow in our stake! And we're not going to blow it in on a lot of clothes and a lot of fool bridge parties for a lot of fool folks that don't care one red hoot about us except what they get out of us! For that matter, if we were going to stay on in New York——"

"Which we most certainly are, young man!"

"Will you listen to me? I inherited this dough, not you! Gee, I don't want to be mean, May, but you got to listen to reason, and as I'm saying, if we were going to stay in the city, the first thing I'd spend money for would be a new dental engine— an electric one.

"Need it like the mischief—lose patients when they see me pumping that old one and think I ain't up-to-date—which I ain't, but that's no skin off their nose!"

Even the volatile Mabelle was silent at the unprecedented length and vigor of his oration.

"But we're not going to stay. No, sir! We're going back to the old farm, and the kids will be brought up in the fresh air instead of a lot of alleys. Go back and farm it——"

She exploded then, and as she spoke she looked at him with eyes hot with hatred, the first hatred he had ever known in her:

"Are you crazy? Go back to that hole? Have my kids messing around a lot of manure and dirty animals and out working in the hayfield like a lot of cattle? And attend a little one-room school with a boob for a teacher? And play with a lot of nitwit brats? Not on your life they

won't! I've got some ambition for 'em, even if you haven't!"

"Why, May, I thought you liked Vermont and the farm! You were crazy about it on our honeymoon, and you said——"

"I did not! I hated it even then. I just said I liked it to make you happy. That stifling little bedroom, and kerosene lamps, and bugs, and no bathroom, and those fools of farmers in their shirt sleeves— Oh, it was fierce! If you go, you go without the kids and me! I guess I can still earn a living! And I guess there's still plenty of other men would like to marry me when I divorce you! And I mean it!"

She did, and Sidney knew she did. He collapsed as helplessly as he had with his father.

"Well, of course, if you can't stand it—" he muttered.

"Well, I'm glad you're beginning to come to your senses! Honest, I think you were just crazy with the heat! But listen, here's what I'll do: I won't kick about your getting the electric dental doodingus if it don't cost too much. Now how do you go about selling the farm?"

There began for this silent man a secret life of plotting and of lies. Somehow—he could not see how—he must persuade her to go to the farm. Perhaps she would die— But he was shocked at this thought, for he loved her and believed her to be the best woman living, as conceivably she may have been. But he did not obey her and sell the farm. He lied. He told her that a Vermont real-estate dealer had written that just this autumn there was no market for farms, but next year would be excellent. And the next year he repeated the lie and rented the farm to Uncle Rob, who had done well enough on Iowa cornland but was homesick for the hills and sugar groves and placid maples of Vermont. Himself, Sidney did not go to the farm. It was not permitted.

Mabelle was furious that he had not sold, that they had only the three thousand —which was never invested—for clothes and bridge prizes and payments on the car and, after a good deal of irritated talk, his electric dental engine.

If he had always been sullenly restless in his little office, now he was raging. He felt robbed. The little back room, the view—not even of waste land now, but of the center of a cheap block and the back of new tenements—the anguish of patients, which crucified his heavy, unspoken sympathy for them, and that horrible, unending series of wide-stretched mouths and bad molars and tongues—it was intolerable. He thought of meadows scattered with daisies and devil's paintbrush, of dark, healing thundershowers pouring up the long valley. He must go home to the land!

From the landlord who owned his office he got, in the spring a year and a half after his father's death, the right to garden a tiny patch amid the litter and cement areaways in the center of the block. Mabelle laughed at him, but he stayed late every evening to cultivate each inch of his pocket paradise—a large man, with huge feet, setting them carefully down in a plot ten feet square.

The earth understood him, as it does such men, and before the Long Island market gardeners had anything to display, Sidney had a row of beautiful radish plants. A dozen radishes, wrapped in a tabloid newspaper, he took home one night, and he said vaingloriously to Mabelle, "You'll never get any radishes like these in the market! Right out of our own garden!"

She ate one absently. He braced himself to hear a jeering "You and your old garden!" What he did hear was, in its uncaring, still worse: "Yes, they're all right, I guess."

He'd show her! He'd make her see him as a great farmer! And with that ambition he lost every scruple. He plotted. And this was the way of that plotting:

Early in July he said, and casually, "Well, now we got the darn car all paid for, we ought to use it. Maybe we might take the kids this summer and make a little tour for a couple weeks or so."

"Where?"

She sounded suspicious, and in his newborn guile he droned, "Oh, wherever you'd like. I hear it's nice up around Niagara Falls and the Great Lakes. Maybe come back by way of Pennsylvania, and see Valley Forge and all them famous historical sites."

"Well, yes, perhaps. The Golheims made a tour last summer and—they make me sick!—they never stop talking about it."

They went. And Mabelle enjoyed it. She was by no means always a nagger and an improver; she was so only when her interests or what she deemed the interests of her children were threatened. She made jokes about the towns through which they passed—any community of less than fifty thousand was to her New Yorkism a "hick hole"—and she even sang jazz and admired his driving, which was bad.

They had headed north, up the Hudson. At Glens Falls he took the highway to the right, instead of left toward the Great Lakes, and she, the city girl, the urban rustic, to whom the only directions that meant anything were East Side and West Side as applied to New York, did not notice, and she was still unsuspicious when he grumbled. "Looks to me like I'd taken the wrong road." Stopping at a filling station, he demanded, "How far is it to Lake George? We ought to be there now."

"Well, stranger, way you're headed, it'll be about twenty-five thousand miles. You're going plumb in the wrong direction."

"I'll be darned! Where are we? Didn't notice the name of the last town we went through."

"You're about a mile from Fair Haven."

"Vermont?"

"Yep."

"Well, I'll be darned! Just think of that! Can't even be trusted to stay in one state and not skid across the border line!"

Mabelle was looking suspicious, and he said with desperate gaiety, "Say, do you know what, May? We're only forty miles from our farm! Let's go have a look at it." Mabelle made a sound of protest, but he turned to the children, in the back seat amid a mess of suitcases and tools and a jack and spare inner tubes, and gloated, "Wouldn't you kids like to see the farm where I worked as a kid—where your grandfather and great-grandfather were born? And see your Granduncle Rob? And see all the little chicks, and so on?"

"Oh, yes!" they shrilled together.

With that enthusiasm from her beloved young, with the smart and uniformed young filling-station attendant listening, Mabelle's talent for being righteous and indignant was gagged. Appearances! She said lightly to the filling-station man,

"The doctor just doesn't seem to be able to keep the road at all, does he? Well, Doctor, shall we get started?"

Even when they had gone on and were alone and ready for a little sound domestic quarreling, she merely croaked, "Just the same, it seems mighty queer to me!" And after another mile of brooding, while Sidney drove silently and prayed: "Awfully queer!"

But he scarcely heard her. He was speculating, without in the least putting it into words, "I wonder if in the early summer evenings the fireflies still dart above the meadows? I wonder if the full moon, before it rises behind the hemlocks and sugar maples along the Ridge, still casts up a prophetic glory? I wonder if sleepy dogs still bark across the valley? I wonder if the night breeze slips through the mowing? I, who have for fortress and self-respect only a stuffy office room—I wonder if there are still valleys and stars and the quiet night? Or was that all only the dream of youth?"

They slept at Rutland, Sidney all impatient of the citified hotel bedroom. It was at ten in the morning—he drove in twenty minutes the distance which thirty years ago had taken Uncle Rob an hour and a half—that he drove up to the white house where, since 1800, the Dows had been born.

He could see Uncle Rob with the hayrake in the south mowing, sedately driving the old team and ignoring the visitors.

"I guess he prob'ly thinks we're bootleggers," chuckled Sidney. "Come on, you kids! Here's where your old daddy worked all one summer! Let's go! . . . Thirsty? Say, I'll give you a drink of real spring water—not none of this chlorinated city stuff! And we'll see the menagerie."

Before he had finished, Rob and Willabette had slipped over the rear doors of

the car and were looking down into the valley with little sounds of excitement. Sidney whisked out almost as quickly as they, while Mabelle climbed down with the dignity suitable to a dweller in the Bronx. He ignored her. He clucked his children round the house to the spring-fed well and pumped a bucket of water.

"Oh, it's so cold, Daddy. It's swell!" said Rob.

"You bet your life it's cold and swell. Say! Don't use words like 'swell'! They're common. But hell with that! Come on, you brats! I'll show you something!"

There were kittens, and two old, grave, courteous cats. There was a calf—heaven knows by how many generations it was descended from the calf that on a June morning, when Sidney was sixteen, had licked his fingers. There were ducklings, and young turkeys with feathers grotesquely scattered over their skins like palm trees in a desert, and unexpected more kittens, and an old, brown-and-white, tail-wagging dog, and a pen of excited little pigs.

The children squealed over all of them until Mabelle caught up, puffing a little.

"Well," she said, "the kits are kind of cute, ain't they?" Then, darkly: "Now that you've got me here, Sid, with your plans and all!"

Uncle Rob crept up, snarling, "What you folks want? . . . By gracious, if it ain't Sid! This your wife and children? Well, sir!"

It was, Sidney felt, the climax of his plot, and he cried to his son, "Rob! This is your granduncle, that you were named for. How'd you like to stay here on the farm instead of in New York?"

"Hot dog! I'd love it! Them kittens and the li'l' ducks! Oh, they're the berries! You bet I'd like to stay!"

"Oh, I'd love it!" gurgled his sister.

"You would not!" snapped Mabelle. "With no bathroom?"

"We could put one in," growled Sidney.

"On what? On all the money you'd make growing orchids and bananas here, I guess! You kids—how'd you like to walk two miles to school, through the snow, in winter?"

"Oh, that would be slick! Maybe we could kill a deer," said young Rob.

"Yes, and maybe a field mouse could kill you, you dumbbell! Sure! Lovely! All evening with not a doggone thing to do after supper!"

"Why, we'd go to the movies! Do you go to the movies often, Granduncle Rob?"

"Well, afraid in winter you wouldn't get to go to the movies at all. Pretty far into town," hesitated Uncle Rob.

"Not—go—to—the—movies?" screamed the city children, incredulous. It was the most terrible thing they had ever heard of.

Rob, Jr., mourned, "Oh, gee, that wouldn't be so good! Say, how do the hicks learn anything if they don't go to the movies? But still, we could go in the summer, Ma, and in the winter it would be elegant, with sliding and hunting and everything. I'd love it!"

Mabelle cooked supper, banging the pans a good deal and emitting opinions of a house that had no porcelain sink, no water taps, no refrigerator, no gas or

electricity. She was silent through supper, silent as Sidney, silent as Uncle Rob. But Sidney was exultant. With the children for allies, he would win. And the children themselves, they were hysterical. Until Mabelle screamed for annoyance; they leaped up from the table, to come back with the most unspeakable and un-Bronxian objects—a cat affectionately carried by his hind leg, but squealing with misunderstanding of the affection, a dead mole, an unwiped oil can, a muck-covered spade.

"But, Mother," they protested, "in the city you never find anything, except maybe a dead lemon."

She shooed them off to bed at eight; herself, sniffily, she disappeared at nine, muttering to Sidney, "I hope you and your boy friend, Uncle Rob, chew the rag all night and get it out of your systems!"

He was startled, for indeed the next step of his plot did concern Uncle Rob and secret parleys.

For half an hour he walked the road, almost frightened by the intensity of stillness. He could fancy catamounts [1] in the birch clumps. But between spasms of skittish city nerves he stretched out his arms, arched back his hands, breathed consciously. This was not just air, necessary meat for the lungs; it was a spirit that filled him.

He knew that he must not tarry after nine-thirty for his intrigue with Uncle Rob. Uncle Rob was seventy-five, and in seventy-five times three hundred and sixty-five evenings he had doubtless stayed up later than nine-thirty o'clock several times—dancing with the little French Canuck [2] girls at Potsdam Forge as a young man, sitting up with a sick cow since then, or stuck in the mud on his way back from Sunday-evening meeting. But

[1] **catamounts:** mountain lions, cougars.
[2] **Canuck:** Canadian.

those few times were epochal. Uncle Rob did not hold with roistering and staying up till all hours just for the vanities of the flesh.

Sidney crept up the stairs to Uncle Rob's room.

Mabelle and Sidney had the best bedroom, on the ground floor; young Rob and Bette had Grampa's room, on the second; Uncle Rob lived in the attic.

City folks might have wondered why Uncle Rob, tenant and controller of the place, should have hidden in the attic, with three good bedrooms below him. It was simple. Uncle Rob had always lived there since he was a boy.

Up the narrow stairs, steep as a rock face, Sidney crept, and knocked.

"Who's there!" A sharp voice, a bit uneasy. How many years was it since Uncle Rob had heard anyone knock at his bedroom door?

"It's me, Rob—Sid."

"Oh, well—well, guess you can come in. Wait'll I unlock the door."

Sidney entered his uncle's room for the first time in his life. The hill people, anywhere in the world, do not intrude or encourage intrusion.

Perhaps to fastidious and alien persons Uncle Rob's room would have seemed unlovely. It was lighted by a kerosene lamp, smoking a little, with the wick burned down on one side. There was, for furniture, only a camp cot, with a kitchen chair, a washstand and a bureau. But to make up for this paucity, the room was rather littered. On the washstand, beside a pitcher dry from long disuse, there were a mail-order catalogue, a few packets of seed, a lone overshoe, a ball of twine, a bottle of applejack, and a Spanish War veteran's medal. The walls and ceiling were of plaster so old that they showed in black lines the edges of every lath.

And Sidney liked it—liked the sim-

plicity, liked the freedom from neatness and order and display, liked and envied the old-bach [1] quality of it all.

Uncle Rob, lying on the bed, had prepared for slumber by removing his shoes and outer clothing. He blinked at Sidney's amazing intrusion, but he said amiably enough, "Well, boy?"

"Uncle Rob, can't tell you how glad I am to be back at the old place!"

"H'm."

"Look, I— Golly, I feel skittish as a young colt! Hardly know the old doc, my patients wouldn't! Rob, you got to help me. Mabelle don't want to stay here and farm it—maybe me and you partners, eh? But the kids and I are crazy to. How I hate that ole city! So do the kids."

"Yeh?"

"Sure they do. Didn't you hear how they said they wouldn't mind tramping to school and not having any movies?"

"Sid, maybe you'll understand kids when you get to be a granddad. Kids will always agree with anything that sounds exciting. Rob thinks it would be dandy to hoof it two miles through the snow to school. He won't! Not once he's done it!" Uncle Rob thrust his hands behind his skinny, bark-brown old neck on the

maculate [2] pillow. He was making perhaps the longest oration of his life. The light flickered, and a spider moved indignantly in its web in a corner. "No," said Uncle Rob, "he won't like it. I never did. And the schoolmaster used to lick me. I hated it, crawling through that snow and then get licked because you're late. And jiminy—haven't thought of it for thirty years, I guess, maybe forty, but I remember how some big fellow would dare you to put your tongue to your lunch pail, and it was maybe thirty below, and your tongue stuck to it and it took the hide right off! No, I never liked any of it, especially chores."

"Rob, listen! I'm serious! The kids will maybe kind of find it hard at first, but they'll get to like it, and they'll grow up real folks and not city saps. It'll be all right with them. I'll see to that. It's Mabelle. Listen, Rob, I've got a swell idea about her, and I want you to help me. You get hold of the ladies of the township—the Grange members and the Methodist ladies and like that. You tell 'em Mabelle is a swell city girl, and it would be dandy for the neighborhood if they could get her to stay here. She's grand, but she does kind of fall for flattery, and in the Bronx she ain't so important, and if these ladies came and told her they thought she was the cat's pajamas, maybe she'd fall for it, and then I guess maybe she might stay, if the ladies came——"

"They wouldn't!"

Uncle Rob had been rubbing his long and prickly chin and curling his toes in his gray socks.

"What do you mean?"

"Well, first place, the ladies round here would be onto your Mabelle. They ain't so backwoods as they was in your time. Take Mrs. Craig. Last three winters, her

[1] **old-bach:** old bachelor-ish.

[2] **maculate:** stained.

and her husband, Frank, have packed up the flivver and gone to Florida. But that ain't it. Fact is, Sid, I kind of sympathize with Mabelle."

"What do you mean?"

"Well, I never was strong for farming. Hard life, Sid. Always thought I'd like to keep store or something in the city. You forget how hard the work is here. You with your easy job, just filling a few teeth! No, I can't help you, Sid."

"I see. All right. Sorry for disturbing you."

As he crept downstairs in bewilderment, Sidney prayed—he who so rarely prayed—"O Lord, doesn't anybody but me love the land any more? What is going to happen to us? Why, all our life comes from the land!"

He knew that in the morning he would beg Mabelle to stay for a fortnight—and that she would not stay. It was his last night here. So all night long, slow and silent, he walked the country roads, looking at hemlock branches against the sky, solemnly shaking his head and wondering why he could never rid himself of this sinfulness of longing for the land; why he could never be grown-up and ambitious and worthy, like his father and Mabelle and Uncle Rob.

FOR STUDY AND DISCUSSION

1. What kind of values has William Dow—that is, what kind of things does he consider important? Do you think the author would agree with William's feeling that "he had done well in the great city of Brooklyn"? William wants his son to "amount to something." What does "amounting to something" mean to him?

2. In addition to William's love of "respectability" and his "heroic ambitions" for his son, what other characteristics does he show? What is he like as a father? Why does Lewis call him "a blenched filing case of a man"?

3. Why are William's ambitions for Sidney "unwise"? What effect do they have on Sidney? How do they affect his idea of himself? his chances for happiness?

4. In what ways is Sidney different from his father in character and personality? Does either Sidney or his father ever realize how different they are?

5. What are Mabelle's tastes and values? What is her idea of a good time? Is she more like Sidney or his father? What makes you think so? What evidence of Mabelle's real nature does Lewis give when she is first introduced? How is Sidney's relationship with Mabelle like his relationship with his father?

6. How is Uncle Rob different from Sidney's father? Is he as different at heart as he at first seems? How does he turn out to be like his brother William?

7. What are the principal conflicts in the story? How is each of them resolved? Besides the conflicts between characters and within Sidney himself, there might be said to be a thematic conflict between city and country. Does the author take sides in this conflict? Does he suggest that life in the country is definitely better than life in the city, or just that it is better for some people?

8. Might the central conflict of the story be stated in terms of people's values—what they most want? for instance, as: "A 'respectable' life and a lot of money, or . . ." or what?

9. If you were asked to state, very briefly, what this story is about, you might say: "It is about a city man who all his life had a longing for the land but was never able to fulfill it." How would you change this statement to make it into a general statement of theme? Try beginning with a more general subject, such as "Some men . . ."

10. Could the theme of "Land" be stated in other ways? Could you make an even broader generalization out of your statement by replacing "the land" with "a certain kind of life"? Could you make it narrower by adding something about families? about fathers and wives? about "respectability"? Do you feel that one of these statements fits the story better than the rest, or are they all about equally good?

THEME AND MEANING

As you know, a story's theme is simply a general statement or summing up of its author's attitude or main idea and can never fully express the story's meaning. Of the two stories used to illustrate theme—"The Ship That Found Herself" and "Land"—which do you feel has a more complex meaning? One way of getting at the answer to this question is to ask yourself which story is easier to sum up as a theme. A story with a complex meaning is less likely to be quickly and easily summed up into a single statement than a story that was written primarily to prove a particular point. Comparing the two "theme" stories with this in mind, which would you say has a more complex meaning? Apply the same test to the two stories used to illustrate plot and the two used to illustrate character. Is the story with the more complex theme necessarily the superior story? Why or why not?

LANGUAGE AND VOCABULARY

1. Colloquial English is the English we use in speaking, and slang is a special kind of colloquial speech. Slang words are usually strong and colorful: sometimes they turn into "good English" by being used more and more frequently by more and more people; sometimes they go out of style and are quickly forgotten. Slang and other informal words figure prominently in the dialogue of "Land." A number of these words are printed below. Which are familiar to you? Which do you have to look up in the dictionary to be sure of their exact meaning?

shack	hick	care a hoot
gee	crank	dumbbell
stuck-up	spunky	cute
rube	blow (money)	bootlegger

What does the dictionary have to say about the following words, which may sound as slangy as those above?

whelp	gabble	nitwit	citified
slouch	botch	brat	shoo

2. While there is a good deal of informal language in this story, Lewis also uses language that is poetic and full of metaphors. In describing the barn at the Vermont farm, for instance, he writes as follows:

"The barn was blank *as a blind face.*"
"in that *witching light . . .*"
"Then utter darkness *leaped upon him.*"
"The darkness seemed to *swing in swift eddies . . .*"
"light *slipping in silver darts . . .*"
"*jubilant* barn swallows . . ."

What is the literal, dictionary meaning of the italicized words? What do they mean as used here? What picture is suggested by each expression

FOR COMPOSITION

Both Steinbeck's "The Leader of the People" and Lewis's "Land" have something to say about a man's feeling for nature. Write a short essay comparing these two stories, showing how Grandfather's attitude toward "westering" and Sidney's attitude toward the farm are alike and how they differ.

ABOUT THE AUTHOR

Sinclair Lewis (1885–1951), the son of a country doctor, was born and grew up in Sauk Center, Minnesota. From there he went to Yale University, where he edited the literary magazine and began to write. Before becoming established as a novelist, he held a variety of jobs with newspapers, magazines, and publishing houses in New York, Iowa, California, and Washington. An undistinguished writer until 1920, he then decided to write a novel just to please himself. Paradoxically, it pleased almost everybody. *Main Street* was both a commercial and a critical success, and was the first in a series of novels in which Lewis satirized various aspects of American life. *Babbitt, Arrowsmith, Elmer Gantry,* and *Dodsworth* are the best known of these. The last name of George F. Babbitt, the prosperous real-estate dealer and hero of *Babbitt,* has become so well known that the dictionary lists it as a synonym for a member of the middle class whose chief interests in life are making money and climbing the social ladder. In 1930 Lewis became the first American to win the Nobel prize for literature.

IRONY

Often the hinge on which a story turns—and therefore an important clue to its meaning—is the author's use of irony. Irony does not occur in all stories, but it is extremely important when it does.

All irony involves a difference, or discrepancy, between what appears to be and what really is—that is, between appearance and reality. The simplest kind of irony is *verbal irony*. In verbal irony a speaker or writer says the opposite of what he means; he speaks "tongue in cheek," as we say. In "The Ship That Found Herself," Steam uses verbal irony when it announces grandly to all the ships in New York harbor: "We have had a time wholly unparalleled in the annals of shipbuilding!" Steam, of course, knows perfectly well that the *Dimbula's* experience has been paralleled thousands of times, but it good-naturedly expresses the feeling of all the first-timers aboard that their experience has been unique.

Another, usually more important, kind of irony is *dramatic irony*. In dramatic irony the discrepancy is not between what someone says and what he means, but between what a character says (or thinks) and what the reader knows is true. In dramatic irony the speaker is not aware of the full import of what he is saying; his words suggest, to the alert reader, more than he knows and more than he intends. In the same story, Kipling uses dramatic irony when the piston on the *Dimbula* cries out during the storm, "Help! I'm choking. Never in the history of maritime invention has such a calamity overtaken one so young and strong." Unlike Steam, the piston is utterly serious, but to the reader, who knows better, its outcry indicates the piston's childishness, inexperience, and feelings of self-importance.

Verbal irony and dramatic irony are sometimes difficult to tell apart, but the classification is unimportant as long as the intent is understood. When Sinclair Lewis tells us in "Land" that "Sidney met the most wonderful girl in the world," he is stating Sidney's opinion, not his own; and at the same time he is poking fun at the similar feelings of nearly all young men in love. Lewis underlines the irony by giving the girl the somewhat ridiculous name of Mabelle Ellen Pflugmann. When he goes on to say of her, "She was cultured; she loved the theater, but rarely attended it; loved also the piano, but hadn't time, she explained, to keep up her practice . . ." his words really whisper in our ears, "Mabelle *said* she loved the theater and the piano, but of course you and I know that anyone who really loves something finds time for it no matter how busy he may be." Thus through irony Lewis exposes the shallowness and pretense of Mabelle's "culture" and makes clear to us the extent to which Sidney has been taken in.

A third kind of irony often used in fiction is *irony of situation*. In irony of situation the discrepancy is not between words and meanings, but between events and our expectations; this kind of irony is thus part of the plot

structure of the story. Irony of situation occurs when a situation turns out to be quite different from what we had supposed or would have expected. In "Land," irony of situation occurs when Sidney's father sends him off to the farm to make him appreciate the comforts of his city home, only to have Sidney love the outdoor life and return less satisfied than ever with the city. Another example of irony of situation is when Sidney approaches Uncle Rob for support in his campaign to move to the farm, only to find that Uncle Rob himself has no liking for the farm and would rather live in the city. In both cases the unexpected outcome drives home certain truths about human nature.

All three kinds of irony are means by which an author can convey meaning forcefully and in few words. Irony enables a writer to express his attitudes indirectly, in passing, at the same time that he is relating his story.

The Verger

SOMERSET MAUGHAM

THERE HAD BEEN a christening that afternoon at St. Peter's, Neville Square, and Albert Edward Foreman still wore his verger's [1] gown. He kept his new one, its folds as full and stiff as though it were made not of alpaca but of perennial bronze, for funerals and weddings (St. Peter's, Neville Square, was a church much favored by the fashionable for these ceremonies) and now he wore only his second best. He wore it with complacence, for it was the dignified symbol of his office, and without it (when he took it off to go home) he had the disconcerting sensation of being somewhat insufficiently clad. He took pains with it; he pressed it and ironed it himself. During the sixteen

years he had been verger of this church he had had a succession of such gowns, but he had never been able to throw them away when they were worn out and the complete series, neatly wrapped up in brown paper, lay in the bottom drawer of the wardrobe in his bedroom.

The verger busied himself quietly, replacing the painted wooden cover on the marble font, taking away a chair that had been brought for an infirm old lady, and waited for the vicar to have finished in the vestry so that he could tidy up in there and go home. Presently he saw him walk across the chancel, genuflect in front of the high altar, and come down the aisle; but he still wore his cassock.

"What's he 'anging about for?" the verger said to himself. "Don't 'e know I want my tea?"

The vicar had been but recently appointed, a red-faced energetic man in the early forties, and Albert Edward still regretted his predecessor, a clergyman of the old school who preached leisurely sermons in a silvery voice and dined out a great deal with his more aristocratic parishioners.[2] He liked things in church

[1] **verger's:** A verger is a caretaker of the interior of a church.

[2] **parishioners:** members of the minister's parish or church.

to be just so, but he never fussed; he was not like this new man who wanted to have his finger in every pie. But Albert Edward was tolerant. St. Peter's was in a very good neighborhood and the parishioners were a very nice class of people. The new vicar had come from the East End and he couldn't be expected to fall in all at once with the discreet ways of his fashionable congregation.

"All this 'ustle," said Albert Edward. "But give 'im time, he'll learn."

When the vicar had walked down the aisle so far that he could address the verger without raising his voice more than was becoming in a place of worship he stopped.

"Foreman, will you come into the vestry for a minute. I have something to say to you."

"Very good, sir."

The vicar waited for him to come up and they walked up the church together.

"A very nice christening, I thought, sir. Funny 'ow the baby stopped cryin' the moment you took him."

"I've noticed they very often do," said the vicar, with a little smile. "After all I've had a good deal of practice with them."

It was a source of subdued pride to him that he could nearly always quiet a whimpering infant by the manner in which he held it and he was not unconscious of the amused admiration with which mothers and nurses watched him settle the baby in the crook of his surpliced arm. The verger knew that it pleased him to be complimented on his talent.

The vicar preceded Albert Edward into the vestry. Albert Edward was a trifle surprised to find the two churchwardens there. He had not seen them come in. They gave him pleasant nods.

"Good afternoon, my lord. Good afternoon, sir," he said to one after the other.

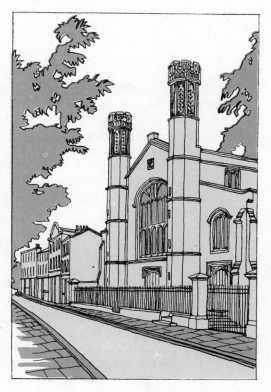

They were elderly men, both of them, and they had been churchwardens almost as long as Albert Edward had been verger. They were sitting now at a handsome refectory table [1] that the old vicar had brought many years before from Italy and the vicar sat down in the vacant chair between them. Albert Edward faced them, the table between him and them, and wondered with slight uneasiness what was the matter. He remembered still the occasion on which the organist had got into trouble and the bother they had all had to hush things up. In a church like St. Peter's, Neville Square, they couldn't afford a scandal. On the vicar's red face was a look of resolute benignity, but the others bore an expression that was slightly troubled.

[1] **refectory table:** a long, heavy table.

"He's been naggin' them, he 'as," said the verger to himself. "He's jockeyed them into doin' something, but they don't 'alf like it. That's what it is, you mark my words."

But his thoughts did not appear on Albert Edward's clean-cut and distinguished features. He stood in a respectful but not obsequious attitude. He had been in service [1] before he was appointed to his ecclesiastical office, but only in very good houses, and his deportment was irreproachable. Starting as a page boy in the household of a merchant prince he had risen by due degrees from the position of fourth to first footman, for a year he had been single-handed butler to a widowed peeress and, till the vacancy occurred at St. Peter's, butler with two men under him in the house of a retired ambassador. He was tall, spare, grave and dignified. He looked, if not like a duke, at least like an actor of the old school who specialized in dukes' parts. He had tact, firmness, and self-assurance. His character was unimpeachable.

The vicar began briskly.

"Foreman, we've got something rather unpleasant to say to you. You've been here a great many years and I think his lordship and the general agree with me that you've fulfilled the duties of your office to the satisfaction of everybody concerned."

The two churchwardens nodded.

"But a most extraordinary circumstance came to my knowledge the other day and I felt it my duty to impart it to the churchwardens. I discovered to my astonishment that you could neither read nor write."

The verger's face betrayed no sign of embarrassment.

"The last vicar knew that, sir," he replied. "He said it didn't make no difference. He always said there was a great deal too much education in the world for 'is taste."

"It's the most amazing thing I ever heard," cried the general. "Do you mean to say that you've been verger of this church for sixteen years and never learned to read or write?"

"I went into service when I was twelve, sir. The cook in the first place tried to teach me at once, but I didn't seem to 'ave the knack for it, and then what with one thing and another I never seemed to 'ave the time. I've never really found the want of it. I think a lot of these young fellows waste a rare lot of time readin' when they might be doin' something useful."

"But don't you want to know the news?" said the other churchwarden. "Don't you ever want to write a letter?"

"No, me lord, I seem to manage very well without. And of late years now they've all these pictures in the papers I get to know what's goin' on pretty well. Me wife's quite a scholar and if I want to write a letter she writes it for me. It's not as if I was a bettin' man."

The two churchwardens gave the vicar a troubled glance and then looked down at the table.

"Well, Foreman, I've talked the matter over with these gentlemen and they quite agree with me that the situation is impossible. At a church like St. Peter's, Neville Square, we cannot have a verger who can neither read nor write."

Albert Edward's thin, sallow face reddened and he moved uneasily on his feet, but he made no reply.

"Understand me, Foreman, I have no complaint to make against you. You do your work quite satisfactorily; I have the highest opinion both of your character and of your capacity; but we haven't the right to take the risk of some accident that

[1] **in service:** a servant.

might happen owing to your lamentable ignorance. It's a matter of prudence as well as of principle."

"But couldn't you learn, Foreman?" asked the general.

"No, sir, I'm afraid I couldn't, not now. You see I'm not as young as I was and if I couldn't seem able to get the letters in me 'ead when I was a nipper I don't think there's much chance of it now."

"We don't want to be harsh with you, Foreman," said the vicar. "But the churchwardens and I have quite made up our minds. We'll give you three months and if at the end of that time you cannot read and write I'm afraid you'll have to go."

Albert Edward had never liked the new vicar. He'd said from the beginning that they'd made a mistake when they gave him St. Peter's. He wasn't the type of man they wanted with a classy congregation like that. And now he straightened himself a little. He knew his value and he wasn't going to allow himself to be put upon.

"I'm very sorry, sir, I'm afraid it's no good. I'm too old a dog to learn new tricks. I've lived a good many years without knowin' 'ow to read and write and without wishin' to praise myself, self-praise is no recommendation, I don't mind sayin' I've done my duty in that state of life in which it 'as pleased a merciful providence to place me, and if I *could* learn now I don't know as I'd want to."

"In that case, Foreman, I'm afraid you must go."

"Yes, sir, I quite understand. I shall be 'appy to 'and in my resignation as soon as you've found somebody to take my place."

But when Albert Edward with his usual politeness had closed the church door behind the vicar and the two churchwardens he could not sustain the air of unruffled dignity with which he had borne the blow inflicted upon him and his lips quivered. He walked slowly back to the vestry and hung up on its proper peg his verger's gown. He sighed as he thought of all the grand funerals and smart weddings it had seen. He tidied everything up, put on his coat, and hat in hand walked down the aisle. He locked the church door behind him. He strolled across the square, but deep in his sad thoughts he did not take the street that led him home, where a nice strong cup of tea awaited him; he took the wrong turning. He walked slowly along. His heart was heavy. He did not know what he should do with himself. He did not fancy the notion of going back to domestic service; after being his own master for so many years, for the vicar and the churchwardens could say what they liked, it was he that had run St. Peter's, Neville Square, he could scarcely demean himself by accepting a situation.[1] He had saved a tidy sum, but not enough to live on without doing something, and life seemed to cost more every year. He had never thought to be troubled with such questions. The vergers of St. Peter's, like the popes of Rome, were there for life. He had often thought of the pleasant reference the vicar would make in his sermon at evensong[2] the first Sunday after his death to the long and faithful service and the exemplary character of their late verger Albert Edward Foreman. He sighed deeply. Albert Edward was a nonsmoker and a total abstainer, but with a certain latitude; that is to say he liked a glass of beer with his dinner and when he was tired he enjoyed a cigarette. It occurred to him now that one would comfort him and since he did not carry them he looked about him for a shop where he could buy a packet of Gold

[1] **situation:** a position as servant.
[2] **evensong:** the evening church service.

Flakes. He did not at once see one and walked on a little. It was a long street, with all sorts of shops in it, but there was not a single one where you could buy cigarettes.

"That's strange," said Albert Edward.

To make sure he walked right up the street again. No, there was no doubt about it. He stopped and looked reflectively up and down.

"I can't be the only man as walks along this street and wants a fag,"[1] he said. "I shouldn't wonder but what a fellow might do very well with a little shop here. Tobacco and sweets, you know."

He gave a sudden start.

"That's an idea," he said. "Strange 'ow things come to you when you least expect it."

He turned, walked home, and had his tea.

"You're very silent this afternoon, Albert," his wife remarked.

"I'm thinkin'," he said.

He considered the matter from every point of view and next day he went along the street and by good luck found a little shop to let that looked as though it would exactly suit him. Twenty-four hours later he had taken it and when a month after that he left St. Peter's, Neville Square, forever, Albert Edward Foreman set up in business as a tobacconist and news-agent. His wife said it was a dreadful comedown after being verger of St. Peter's, but he answered that you had to move with the times, the church wasn't what it was, and 'enceforward he was going to render unto Caesar what was Caesar's. Albert Edward did very well. He did so well that in a year or so it struck him that he might take a second shop and put a manager in. He looked for another long street that hadn't got a tobacconist in it

and when he found it, and a shop to let, took it and stocked it. This was a success too. Then it occurred to him that if he could run two he could run half a dozen, so he began walking about London, and whenever he found a long street that had no tobacconist and a shop to let he took it. In the course of ten years he had acquired no less than ten shops and he was making money hand over fist. He went round to all of them himself every Monday, collected the week's takings, and took them to the bank.

One morning when he was there paying in a bundle of notes and a heavy bag of silver the cashier told him that the manager would like to see him. He was shown into an office and the manager shook hands with him.

"Mr. Foreman, I wanted to have a talk to you about the money you've got on deposit with us. D'you know exactly how much it is?"

"Not within a pound[2] or two, but I've got a pretty rough idea."

"Apart from what you paid in this morning it's a little over thirty thousand pounds. That's a very large sum to have on deposit and I should have thought you'd do better to invest it."

"I wouldn't want to take no risk, sir. I know it's safe in the bank."

"You needn't have the least anxiety. We'll make you out a list of absolutely gilt-edged securities.[3] They'll bring you in a better rate of interest than we can possibly afford to give you."

A troubled look settled on Mr. Foreman's distinguished face.

"I've never 'ad anything to do with stocks and shares and I'd 'ave to leave it all in your 'ands," he said.

[1] **fag:** cigarette.

[2] **pound:** now worth just under three dollars.

[3] **gilt-edged securities:** the highest quality of stocks and bonds, those which appear safest from a sudden drop in value.

The manager smiled.

"We'll do everything. All you'll have to do next time you come in is just sign the transfers."

"I could do that all right," said Albert uncertainly. "But 'ow should I know what I was signin'?"

"I suppose you can read," said the manager a trifle sharply.

Mr. Foreman gave him a disarming smile.

"Well, sir, that's just it. I can't. I know it sounds funny like, but there it is, I can't read or write, only me name, an' I only learned to do that when I went into business."

The manager was so surprised that he jumped up from his chair.

"That's the most extraordinary thing I ever heard."

"You see, it's like this, sir, I never 'ad the opportunity until it was too late and then some'ow I wouldn't. I got obstinate like."

The manager stared at him as though he were a prehistoric monster.

"And do you mean to say that you've built up this important business and amassed a fortune of thirty thousand pounds without being able to read or write? Good God, man, what would you be now if you had been able to?"

"I can tell you that, sir," said Mr. Foreman, a little smile on his still aristocratic features. "I'd be verger of St. Peter's, Neville Square."

FOR STUDY AND DISCUSSION

1. Describe the character of Albert Edward Foreman. What are his virtues? What are his prejudices? At the beginning of the story, what is his attitude toward his position in life? How has he "risen" from his former occupation? What does his attitude toward St. Peter's Church, his own position, and the old and new vicars tell us about what he values most in life?

2. What is the chief difference between the old vicar and the new one? Which one do you think Maugham regards more highly? Albert describes the new vicar as a man "who wanted to have his finger in every pie." How might someone more friendly to the new vicar describe this characteristic?

3. Compare the characters of the verger and the new vicar. In what ways is the verger superior to his master? What might this have to do with the vicar's desire to replace the verger with someone who can read and write?

4. Why does Albert's wife regard it as a dreadful comedown for him to become an independent shopkeeper after being verger of St. Peter's? In what sense is it a comedown? In what sense is it not? He answers her that "'enceforward he was going to render unto Caesar what was Caesar's." What is the source of this saying? How does it fit Albert's situa-

tion? Would you call his final position a come-down? Why or why not?

5. To what degree is Albert's rise from un-employed verger to successful businessman due to good luck? To what degree is it due to shrewd good sense and orderly habits?

6. The plot of this story pivots on an irony of situation. What is it? Why is it ironic?

7. Because the irony of situation is so cen-tral to the story, it is necessarily connected with its theme. State the theme of "The Ver-ger." How many different ways can it be stated?

8. Besides being pivotal to the plot and theme, the central irony of this story enables the author to make indirect comments on character. What comment does the ending of the story make on the values of the vicar and the churchwardens?

9. In addition to the central irony, there are a number of minor ironies that make small but important contributions to the story. What is ironic about each of the following?

Maugham's comment on the new vicar: "It was a source of subdued pride to him that he could nearly always quiet a whimper-ing infant by the manner in which he held it . . ."

The bank manager's remark to Albert: "I suppose you can read."

Albert's explanation: "Me wife's quite a scholar and if I want to write a letter she writes it for me."

LANGUAGE AND VOCABULARY

As you know, in verbal irony a speaker says the opposite of what he means. In Somerset Maugham's "The Verger" we see a use of language much like verbal irony: characters whose manner of speaking is quite different from what we might expect.

Albert Edward Foreman, the verger, is a dignified man, quiet and well-mannered, but he speaks in the lower-class Cockney dialect and uses bad grammar. The vicar, on the other hand, is a busybody who wants "to have his finger in every pie," but he speaks in a cultured manner and uses formal words. What does the speech of each of these men tell you about his real nature? What does it suggest about why

they dislike each other? How does Albert Edward's way of speaking help to make his success as a shopkeeper believable?

To understand more fully the effect Maugham achieves with the speech of his characters, rewrite one or two of Albert Ed-ward's speeches in standard English. Read aloud the rewritten dialogue as part of the story. How do the changes affect your reac-tion to Albert Edward and your sympathies with the characters in the story?

FOR COMPOSITION

The last scene in Maugham's story—in which Albert Edward talks with the manager of the bank—could serve as a model for a scene in which a completely unexpected fact about someone is brought to light, with dra-matic results. Write the dialogue for such a scene, perhaps taking place in a classroom or at home, with fictional characters who might or might not be based on real people. If you can, try to make your revelation an ironic one.

ABOUT THE AUTHOR

Somerset Maugham (1874–1965), born in Paris of British parents, was left an orphan at the age of ten and went to England to live with his uncle, a clergyman. He studied for one year at the University of Heidelberg in Germany before returning to England to study medicine. Although he qualified as a physician and surgeon in 1897, his main in-terest was writing, and he never practiced medicine except for a year as an intern in the London slums. After ten years of relative obscurity and poverty, he won success as a dramatist and very quickly earned a fortune that enabled him to travel widely. He went around the world several times and spent extensive periods in the South Seas, the scene of many of his stories. During World War I he served as a secret agent in the British In-telligence and carried out missions in France, Italy, and Russia. His greatest work is the largely autobiographical novel *Of Human Bondage*. His best-known play is *The Circle*, a drawing-room comedy. His most famous short story is "Rain."

The Duke's Children

FRANK O'CONNOR

I COULD NEVER see precisely what was supposed to be exaggerated in the plots of novelists like Dickens. To this day I can still read about some mysterious street urchin, brought up to poverty and vice by a rag picker, who turns out to be the missing heir to an earldom, and see nothing peculiar about it. To me, it all seems the most natural thing in the world.

Having always been Mother's pet, I was comparatively grown-up when the truth about my own birth broke on me first. In fact, I was already at work as a messenger boy on the railway. Naturally, I had played with the idea as I had played with scores of other ideas, but suddenly, almost in a day, every other possibility disappeared, and I knew I had nothing whatever in common with the two commonplace creatures with whom my fate had become so strangely linked.

It wasn't only their poverty that repelled me, though that was bad enough, or the tiny terrace house we lived in, with its twelve-foot square of garden in front, its crumbling stumps of gateposts and low wall that had lost its railing. It was their utter commonness, their squabbles about money, their low friends and fatuous conversations. You could see that no breath

of fineness had ever touched them. They seemed like people who had been crippled from birth and never known what it was to walk or run or dance. Though I might be—for the moment, at least—only a messenger, I had those long spells when by some sort of instinct I knew who I really was, could stand aside and watch myself come up the road after my day's work with relaxed and measured steps, turning my head slowly to greet some neighbor and raising my cap with a grace and charm that came of centuries of breeding. Not only could I see myself like that; there were even times when I could hear an interior voice that preceded and dictated each movement as though it were a fragment of a storybook: "He raised his cap gracefully while his face broke into a thoughtful smile."

And then, as I turned the corner, I would see Father at the gate in his house clothes, a ragged trousers and vest, an old cap that came down over his eyes, and boots cut into something that resembled sandals and that he insisted on calling his "slippers." Father was a creature of habit. No sooner was he out of his working clothes than he was peppering [1] for his evening paper, and if the newsboy were five minutes late, Father muttered: "I don't know what's coming over that boy at all!" and drifted down to the main road to listen for him. When the newsboy did at last appear, Father would grab the paper from his hand and almost run home, putting on his spectacles awkwardly as he ran and triumphantly surveying the promised treat of the headlines.

And suddenly everything would go black on me, and I would take the chair by the open back door while Father, sitting at the other end, uttered little exclamations of joy or rage and Mother asked anxiously how I had got on during the day.

[1] **peppering:** impatient.

Most of the time I could reply only in monosyllables. How could I tell her that nothing had happened at work that was not as common as the things that happened at home: nothing but those moments of blinding illumination when I was alone in the station yard on a spring morning with sunlight striking the cliffs above the tunnel, and, picking my way between the rails and the trucks, I realized that it was not for long, that I was a duke or earl, lost, stolen, or strayed from my proper home, and that I had only to be discovered for everything to fall into its place? Illumination came only when I had escaped; most often when I crossed the yard on my way from work and dawdled in the passenger station before the book-

stall, or watched a passenger train go out on its way to Queenstown or Dublin [1] and realized that one day some train like that would take me back to my true home and patrimony.

These gloomy silences used to make Father mad. He was a talkative man, and every little incident of his day turned into narrative and drama for him. He seemed forever to be meeting old comrades of his army days whom he had not met for fifteen years, and astounding changes had always taken place in them in the meantime. When one of his old friends called, or even when some woman from across the square dropped in for a cup of tea, he would leave everything, even his newspaper, to talk. His corner by the window permitting him no room for drama, he would stamp about the tiny kitchen, pausing at the back door to glance up at the sky or by the other door into the little hallway to see who was passing outside in the Square. It irritated him when I got up in the middle of all this, took my cap, and went quietly out. It irritated him even more if I read while he and the others talked, and, when some question was addressed to me, put down my book and gazed at him blankly. He was so coarse in grain that he regarded it as insolence. He had no experience of dukes, and had never heard that interior voice which dictated my movements and words. "Slowly the lad lowered the book in which he had been immersed and gazed wonderingly at the man who called himself his father."

One evening I was coming home from work when a girl spoke to me. She was a girl called Nancy Harding whose elder brother I knew slightly. I had never spoken to her—indeed, there were not many girls

[1] **Queenstown . . . Dublin:** Queenstown, now called Cobh, is a seaport on the southern coast of Ireland; Dublin, a port on the eastern coast, is the capital of Ireland.

I did speak to. I was too conscious of the fact that, though my jacket was good enough, my trousers were an old blue pair of Father's, cut down and with a big patch in the seat. But Nancy, emerging from a house near the quarry, hailed me as if we were old friends and walked with me up the road. She was slim and dark-haired with an eager and inconsequent manner, and her chatter bewildered and charmed me. My own conversation was of a rather portentous sort.

"I was down with Madge Regan, getting the answers for my homework," she explained. "I don't know what's wrong with me, but I can't do those blooming old sums. Where were you?"

"Oh, I was at work," I answered.

"At work?" she exclaimed in astonishment. "Till this hour?"

"I have to work from eight to seven," I said modestly.

"But aren't they terrible hours?" she said.

"Ah, I'm only filling in time," I explained lightly. "I don't expect to be there long."

This was prophetic, because I was sacked a couple of months later, but at the same time I just wanted to make it clear if there was any exploitation being done it was I and not the railway company that was doing it. We walked slowly, and she stood under the gas lamp at the end of the Square with me. Darkness or day, it was funny how people made a rendezvous [1] of gas lamps. They were our playrooms when we were kids and our clubs as we became older. And then, for the first time, I heard the words running through my head as though they were dictating to someone else behind myself. "Pleased with his quiet conversation and well-bred voice, she wondered if he could really be

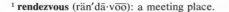

[1] **rendezvous** (rän′dā·vōō): a meeting place.

the son of the Delaneys at all." Up to this, the voice had paid no attention to other people; now that it had begun to expand its activities it took on a new reality, and I longed to repeat the experience.

I had several opportunities, because we met like that a couple of times when I was coming home from work. I was not observant, and it wasn't until years after that it struck me that she might have been waiting for me at the same house at the same time. And one evening, when we were standing under our gas lamp, I talked a little too enthusiastically about some storybook, and Nancy asked for the loan of it. I was pleased with her attention but alarmed at the thought of her seeing where I lived.

"I'll bring it with me tomorrow," I said.

"Ah, come on and get it for me now," she said coaxingly, and I glanced over my shoulder and saw Father at the gate, his head cocked, listening for the newsboy. I felt suddenly sick. I knew such a nice girl couldn't possibly want to meet Father, but I didn't see how I was to get the book without introducing them. We went up the little uneven avenue together.

"This is Nancy Harding, Dad," I said in an offhand tone. "I just want to get a book for her."

"Oh, come in, girl, come in," he said, smiling amiably. "Sit down, can't you, while you're waiting?" Father's sociability almost caused him to forget the newsboy. "Min," he called to Mother, "you keep an eye on the paper," and he set a chair in the middle of the kitchen floor. As I searched in the front room for the book, which in my desperation I could not find, I heard Mother go for the paper and Father talking away like mad to Nancy, and when I went into the kitchen, there he was in his favorite chair, the paper lying unopened on the table beside him while he told an endless, pointless story about old times in the neighborhood. Father had been born in the neighborhood, which he seemed to think a matter for pride, but if there was one of Father's favorite subjects I could not stand, it was the still wilder and more sordid life people had lived there when he was growing up. This story was about a wake [1]—all his juiciest stories were about wakes—and a tired woman getting jealous of the corpse in the bed. He was so pleased with Nancy's attention that he was dramatizing even more than usual, and I stood silent in the kitchen door for several minutes with a ducal air of scorn before he even noticed me. As I saw Nancy to the road I felt humiliated to the depths of my being. I noticed that the hallway was streaming with damp, that our gate was only a pair of brick stumps from which the cement had fallen away, and that the Square, which had never been adopted by the Council, was full of washing. There were two washerwomen on the terrace, each with a line of her own.

But that wasn't the worst. One evening when I came home, Mother said joyously:

"Oh, your dad ran into that nice little Harding girl on his way home."

"Oh, did he?" I asked indifferently, though feeling I had been kicked hard in the stomach.

"Oh, my goodness!" Father exclaimed, letting down his paper for a moment and crowing. "The way that one talks! Spatter! spatter! spatter! And, by the way," he added, looking at me over his glasses, "her Aunt Lil used to be a great friend of your mother's at one time. Her mother was a Clancy. I knew there was something familiar about her face."

"I'd never have recognized it," Mother said gravely. "Such a quiet little woman as Miss Clancy used to be."

"Oh, begor,[2] there's nothing quiet about that niece," chortled Father, but he did not sound disapproving. Father liked young people with something to say for themselves—not like me.

I was mortified. It was bad enough not seeing Nancy myself, but to have her meet Father like that, in his working clothes coming from the manure factory down the Glen, and hear him—as I had no doubt she did hear him—talk in his ig-

[1] **wake:** a watch or vigil at the side of someone who has just died.

[2] **begor** (bē'gôr): a mild Irish oath.

norant way about me was too much. I could not help contrasting Father with Mr. Harding, whom I occasionally met coming from work and whom I looked at with a respect that bordered on reverence. He was a small man with a face like a clenched fist, always very neatly dressed, and he usually carried his newspaper rolled up like a baton and sometimes hit his thigh with it as he strode briskly home.

One evening when I glanced shyly at him, he nodded in his brusque way. Everything about him was brusque, keen, and soldierly, and when I saw that he recognized me I swung into step beside him. He was like a military procession with a brass band, the way he always set the pace for anyone who accompanied him.

"Where are you working now?" he asked sharply with a side glance at me.

"Oh, on the railway still," I said. "Just for a few months, anyway."

"And what are you doing there?"

"Oh, just helping in the office," I replied lightly. I knew this was not exactly true, but I hated to tell anybody that I was only a messenger boy. "Of course, I study in my spare time," I added hastily. It was remarkable how the speeding up of my pace seemed to speed up my romancing as well. There was something breathless about the man that left me breathless, too. "I thought of taking the Indian Civil Service exam[1] or something of the sort. There's no future in railways."

"Isn't there?" he asked with some surprise.

"Not really," I answered indifferently. "Another few years and it will all be trucks. I really do it only as a stopgap. I wouldn't like to take any permanent job unless I could travel. Outside Ireland, I

mean. You see, languages are my major interest."

"Are they?" he asked in the same tone. "How many do you know?"

"Oh, only French and German at the moment—I mean, enough to get round with," I said. The pace was telling on me. I felt I wasn't making the right impression. Maybe to be a proper linguist you needed to know a dozen languages. I mended my hand as best I could. "I'm going to do Italian and Spanish this winter if I get time. You can't get anywhere in the modern world without Spanish. After English it's the most spoken of them all."

"Go on!" he said.

I wasn't altogether pleased with the results of this conversation. The moment I had left him, I slowed down to a gentle stroll, and this made me realize that the quick march had committed me farther than I liked to go. All I really knew of foreign languages was a few odd words

[1] **Indian Civil Service exam:** an examination that, while Britain ruled India, was required of British subjects for appointment to government service in India.

THE DUKE'S CHILDREN **97**

and phrases, like echoes of some dream of my lost fatherland, which I learned and repeated to myself with a strange, dreamy pleasure. It was not prudent to pretend that I knew the languages thoroughly. After all, Mr. Harding had three daughters, all well educated. People were always being asked to his house, and I had even been encouraging myself with the prospect of being asked as well. But now, if I were invited, it would be mainly because of my supposed knowledge of foreign languages, and when Nancy or one of her sisters burst into fluent French or German my few poetic phrases would not be much help. I needed something more practical, something to do with railways, for preference. I had an old French phrase book, which I had borrowed from somebody, and I determined to learn as much as I could of this by heart.

I worked hard, spurred on by an unexpected meeting with Nancy's eldest sister, Rita, who suddenly stopped and spoke to me on the road, though to my astonishment and relief she spoke in English.

Then, one evening when I was on my usual walk, which in those days nearly always brought me somewhere near Nancy's house, I ran into her going in, and we stood at the street corner near her home. I was pleased with this because Rita came out soon afterward and said in a conspiratorial tone: "Why don't ye grab the sofa before Kitty gets it?" which made Nancy blush, and then her father passed and nodded to us. I waved back to him, but Nancy had turned her back as he appeared so that she did not see him. I drew her attention to him striding down the road, but somehow this only put her in mind of my father.

"I saw him again the other day," she said with a smile that hurt me.

"Did you?" I asked with a sniff.

"What was he talking about? His soldiering days?"

"No," she said with interest. "Does he talk about them?"

"Does he ever talk about anything else?" I replied wearily. "I have that last war off by heart. It seems to have been the only thing that ever happened to him."

"He knows a terrible lot, though, doesn't he?" she asked.

"He's concealed it pretty well," I replied. "The man is an out-and-out failure, and he's managed to turn Mother into one as well. I suppose she had whatever brains there were between them—which wasn't much, I'm afraid."

"Go on!" said Nancy with a bewildered air. "Then why did she marry him?"

"'Echo answers why,'" I said with a laugh at being able to get in a phrase that had delighted me in some storybook. "Oh, I supposed it was the usual thing."

Nancy blushed again and made to leave.

"Well, it's well to be you," she said, "knowing what's wrong with him. God alone knows what's wrong with mine."

I was sorry she had to go in such a hurry, but pleased with the impression of culture and sophistication I had managed to convey, and I looked forward to showing off a bit more when I went to one of their Sunday evening parties. With that, and some really practical French, I could probably get anywhere.

At the same time it struck me that they were very slow about asking me, and my evening walks past their house took on a sort of stubborn defiance. At least, I wouldn't let them ignore me. It wasn't until weeks later that the bitter truth dawned on me—that I was not being invited because nobody wanted me there. Nancy had seen my home and talked to my parents; her sisters and father had seen me; and all of them had seen my cut-down trousers with the patch on the seat.

It mattered nothing to them even if I spoke French and German like an angel, even if I were liable to be sent off to India in the next few months. They did not think I was their class.

Those were the bitterest weeks of my life. With a sort of despair I took my evening walk in the early winter days past their house, but never saw anybody, and as I turned up the muddy lane behind it and heard the wind moaning in the branches, and looked down across the sloping field to their house, nestling in the hollow with the light shining brilliantly in the kitchen, where the girls did their homework, it seemed to be full of all the beauty I would never know. Sometimes, when I was leaning over the lane wall and watching it, it even seemed possible that I was what they thought, not the son of a duke but the son of a laborer in the manure factory; but at other times, as I was walking home by myself, tired and dispirited, the truth blazed up angrily in me again, and I knew that when it became known, the Hardings would be the first to regret their blindness. At such times I was al-ways making brilliant loveless matches and then revealing coldly to Nancy that I had never cared for anyone but her.

It was at the lowest depth of my misery that I was introduced to a girl called May Dwyer, and somehow, from the first moment, I found that there was no need for me to indulge in invention. Invention and May would never have gone together. She had a directness of approach I had never met with before in a girl. The very first evening I saw her home she asked me if I could afford the tram [1] fare. That shocked me, but afterwards I was grateful. Then she asked me in to see her parents, which scared me stiff, but I promised to come in another night when it wasn't so late, and at once she told me which evenings she was free. It was not forward-ness or lightness in her; it was all part of a directness that made her immediately both a companion and a sweetheart. I owe her a lot, for without her I might still be airing my French and German to any woman who attracted me.

[1] **tram:** streetcar.

Even when I did go in with her for a cup of tea, I felt at home after the first few minutes. Her father was a long, sad

Civil Servant,[1] and her mother a bright, direct little woman not unlike May herself, and whatever he said, the pair of them argued with and jeered him unmercifully. This only made him hang his head lower, but suddenly, after I had been talking for awhile, he began to argue with me about the state of the country, which seemed to cause him a lot of concern. In those days I was very optimistic on the subject, and I put my hands deep in my trousers pockets and answered him back politely but firmly. Then he caught me out on a matter of fact, and suddenly he gave a great crow of delight and went out to bring in two bottles of Guinness.[2] By this time I was so much in my element that I accepted the Guinness: I always have loved a good argument.

May said when I was leaving, "Do you ever stop once you start?"

"It's not so often I meet an intelligent talker," I said loftily.

"When you've heard as much of my old fellow as I have, maybe you won't think he's so intelligent," she said, but she did not sound indignant, and I had an impression that she was really quite pleased at having brought home a young fellow who could entertain her father. It gave her the feeling that she was really all the time an intellectual, but had met

[1] **Civil Servant:** government employee.
[2] **Guinness:** a heavy malt drink, called stout.

the wrong sort of boy. In the years I was courting her we quarreled often, but between her father and me it was a case of love at first sight. After I was fired from the railway, it was he who got me another job and insisted on my looking after it. The poor devil had always been pining for a man in the house.

Then one evening I ran into Nancy Harding, whom I had not seen for months. It was an embarrassing moment because I realized at once that my fantasy had all come true. If I had not actually made a brilliant match, I had as good as done so, and yet she was my first and purest love.

"I hear you and May Dwyer are very great these days," she said, and something in her tone struck me as peculiar. Afterward I realized that it was the tone I was supposed to adopt when I broke the news to her.

"I've seen quite a lot of her," I admitted.

"You weren't long getting hooked," she went on with a smile that somehow did not come off.

"I don't know about being 'hooked,' as you call it," I said, getting on my dignity at once. "She asked me to her house and I went, that's all."

"Oh, we know all about it," said Nancy, and this time there was no mistaking the malice in her tone. "You don't have to tell me anything."

"Well, there isn't so much to tell," I replied with a bland smile.

"And I suppose she talks French and German like a native?" asked Nancy.

This reference to the falsehoods I had told did hurt me. I had known they were indiscreet, but it hadn't occurred to me that they would become a joke in the Harding family.

"I don't honestly know what you're talking about, Nancy," I said weakly. "May asked me to her house and I went,

just as I'd have gone to yours if you'd asked me. That's all there is to it."

"Oh, is that all?" she asked in her commonest tone, and suddenly, to my astonishment, I saw tears in her eyes. "And if you had a house like mine you wouldn't mind asking people there either, would you? And sisters like mine! And a father like mine! It's all very well for you to grouse [1] about your old fellow, but if you had one like mine you'd have something to talk about. Blooming old pig, wouldn't open his mouth to you. 'Tis easy for you to talk, Larry Delaney!"

And then she shot away from me to conceal her tears, and I was left standing there on the pavement, stunned. Too stunned really to have done anything about it. It had all happened too suddenly, and been too great an intrusion on my fantasy for me to grasp it at all. I was so astonished and upset that, though I was to have met May that night, I didn't go. Instead I went for a lonely walk by myself, over the hills to the river, to think what I should do about it. In the end, of course, I did nothing at all; I had no experience to indicate to me what I could do; and it was not until years later that I ever realized that the reason I had cared so much for Nancy was that she, like myself, was one of the duke's children, one of those outcasts of a lost fatherland who go through life living above and beyond themselves like some image of man's original aspiration.

[1] **grouse:** grumble or complain.

FOR STUDY AND DISCUSSION

1. When did Larry Delaney realize what he calls "the truth" about his birth? What do you think the change from "Mother's pet" to messenger boy had to do with this realization?

2. Where did Larry get his romantic notions about elegant breeding? What kind of person does he imagine himself to be? What did the plots of "novelists like Dickens" contribute to his view of the world and his own condition?

3. What is Larry's attitude toward his father? Do you think he has reason to be ashamed of his family? Why or why not? What does Larry think of Nancy's father? What does Nancy think of her father, and how does she react to Larry's father? What is ironic about their attitudes?

4. Why did Nancy turn her back on her father while talking to Larry on the street corner? For what reason is Larry never invited to the Hardings' house? What does he *think* is the reason? What is ironic about this misunderstanding?

5. What does May Dwyer do for Larry that Nancy Harding could not do? Why is she able to do this? What does Larry's relation with May's father show about his changing character?

6. This story uses all three kinds of irony. Central to the plot is a double irony of situation involving Larry Delaney and Nancy Harding. What is ironic about the results of their similar attitudes and expectations?

7. Because his mature attitudes are different from his youthful ones, the older Larry uses a noticeable amount of verbal irony in telling his story. For instance, in the second paragraph, he says, "I was comparatively grown-up when the truth about my own birth broke on me first." Which word in this sentence is ironic? Where else in this same paragraph does the author use verbal irony?

8. Also because of the difference between his mature and youthful attitudes, many of young Larry's thoughts and remarks in the story are examples of dramatic irony. Perhaps the best examples are the thoughts that Larry modeled on his reading, such as: "He raised his cap gracefully while his face broke into a thoughtful smile." How does young Larry's impression of himself, as suggested by these passages, differ from the impression they give of him?

9. In the passages modeled on Larry's reading, Frank O'Connor makes fun, not only of Larry, but of a certain kind of fiction. How does this fiction differ from his own, judging from what you have seen of it in this story?

10. Have you ever gone through a phase in which you imagined you were special by birth or by nature? Do you think O'Connor has hit on a universal human experience? What connection might the lasting popularity of stories like "Cinderella" have with this experience?

IRONY AND ILLUSION

As we have seen, both dramatic irony and irony of situation involve someone's false impression of the way things really are. The false impression or illusion may be held either by the reader or by a character in the story. In "The Verger" the irony backfires on all the characters in the story who misjudged Albert Edward's abilities, and we, who have been led to suspect the truth, enjoy a well-deserved last laugh at their foolishness. In "The Duke's Children" the irony is more complex and involves a whole network of illusions. Which characters in the story have the most unreal illusion about themselves and their impression on other people? How are these illusions finally shattered by an ironic turn of events?

LANGUAGE AND VOCABULARY

1. The language of most good stories is notable for its concreteness—its use of clear, specific words. Highly specific language, however, is not always appropriate to a story. To suggest the fantasy world of Larry Delaney, a world which is rather vague even to Larry, Frank O'Connor uses a great many abstract words—words that are hard to pin down to a single, specific meaning. Consider the following quotations from "The Duke's Children" and these questions about them: What do the words actually say? What specific pictures do they call to mind? What do they suggest, by their vagueness, about the person using them?

"I was comparatively grown-up when the truth about my own birth broke on me first."

"It was their utter commonness, their squabbles about money, their low friends and fatuous conversations."

"her chatter bewildered and charmed me. My own conversation was of a rather portentous sort."

"if there was one of Father's favorite subjects I could not stand, it was the still wilder and more sordid life people had lived there when he was growing up."

" 'And if you had a house like mine you wouldn't mind asking people there either, would you?' "

2. In addition to using abstract language to describe Larry's world, O'Connor uses concrete images to keep the story itself convincingly real. Find examples of concrete pictures in the story, such as the first sentence of paragraph 3. What function do these concrete details serve as compared with Larry's vague imaginings?

FOR COMPOSITION

1. "Pride goeth before destruction, and a haughty spirit before a fall." In a well-organized composition, explain briefly how this well-known Biblical statement fits the character of Larry Delaney, his problems, and their solution.

2. Devoting a single paragraph to each man, characterize Larry's and Nancy's fathers as you think they really were.

ABOUT THE AUTHOR

Frank O'Connor (1903–1966), born Michael O'Donovan in the Irish city of Cork, is known to the world by his pen name. He did his earliest writing, as a boy, in Gaelic, the ancient language of the Irish, and at the age of twelve he put together a "collected edition" of his work—poems, biographies, and essays on Irish history. He attended school in Cork, but, coming from a poor family, was unable to go to a university. He worked as a librarian in County Cork and later in Dublin, where, for a time, he was a director of the famous Abbey Theatre. In the early 1920's he took part in the Irish struggle for political freedom, and his first book of short stories, *The Guests of the Nation,* was based on that experience. Though he has done many kinds of writing, O'Connor is best known for his short stories— rich, humorous, realistic accounts of Irish life. During the latter part of his life he spent much of his time in the United States.

SYMBOL

A symbol, in literature, is something which means more than itself. It is an object, a person, a situation, or an action which suggests or represents a wider meaning. A simple example is name-symbolism. Usually a name simply identifies a person; but if, in addition, it tells us something *about* the person (such as the name *Patience* applied to a patient woman), then the name has a symbolic meaning.

An object, person, or action, like a name, may suggest a further meaning. When the *Dimbula,* in Kipling's story, speaks for the first time with one voice, this action symbolizes that the ship has found itself—that its parts have learned to work together as a single unit. In Jack Finney's story the sheet of yellow paper covered with facts and figures comes to represent, to us as well as to Tom Benecke, an absurd and meaningless way of life. It does so when Tom imagines his dead body lying on the sidewalk eleven stories below:

> "All they'd find in his pockets would be the yellow sheet. *Contents of the dead man's pockets,* he thought, *one sheet of paper bearing penciled notations—incomprehensible."*

Finney underlines the symbolism for us a few sentences later:

> *"Contents of the dead man's pockets,* he thought with sudden fierce anger, *a wasted life."*

Ordinarily authors do not explain their symbols as directly as Finney explains the yellow sheet of paper. Many writers would have stopped with the first of the two passages quoted and have expected the reader to supply for himself the meaning indicated by the second. Often, moreover, a symbol may have more than one meaning, may suggest a whole range of meanings. This capability for multiple meaning makes symbolism an extraordinarily rich fictional device. It also places a large responsibility on the reader. We must be careful not to let our fancies run away with us and so see symbols everywhere. Symbols do not occur in all stories, and they cannot mean just anything. Their status as symbols and the meanings given them must be clearly supported by the story in which they occur.

In general, symbols are used in one of two ways in fiction. First of all, they may be used unobtrusively to enrich or broaden the meaning of a story. Used in this way, they may have their effect on us without our actually ever recognizing them as symbols or thinking about what they represent. Even if we miss the symbolism entirely, this kind of story will still make sense. On the other hand, symbols may be used to bear the full weight of a story's meaning. A story of this kind will not be understood unless we have, at least to some extent, recognized the author's symbols and explored their meanings.

A White Heron

SARAH ORNE JEWETT

I

THE WOODS were already filled with shadows one June evening, just before eight o'clock, though a bright sunset still glimmered faintly among the trunks of the trees. A little girl was driving home her cow, a plodding, dilatory, provoking creature in her behavior, but a valued companion for all that. They were going away from the western light, and striking deep into the dark woods, but their feet were familiar with the path, and it was no matter whether their eyes could see it or not.

There was hardly a night the summer through when the old cow could be found waiting at the pasture bars; on the contrary, it was her greatest pleasure to hide herself away among the high huckleberry bushes, and though she wore a loud bell she had made the discovery that if one stood perfectly still it would not ring. So Sylvia had to hunt for her until she found her, and call Co'! Co'! with never an answering Moo, until her childish patience was quite spent. If the creature had not given good milk and plenty of it, the case would have seemed very different to her owners. Besides, Sylvia had all the time there was, and very little use to make of it. Sometimes in pleasant weather it was a consolation to look upon the cow's pranks as an intelligent attempt to play hide and seek, and as the child had no playmates she lent herself to this amusement with a good deal of zest. Though this chase had been so long that the wary animal herself had given an unusual signal of her whereabouts, Sylvia had only laughed when she came upon Mistress Moolly at the swamp side, and urged her affectionately homeward with a twig of birch leaves. The old cow was not inclined to wander farther, she even turned in the right direction for once as they left the pasture, and stepped along the road at a good pace. She was quite ready to be milked now and seldom stopped to browse. Sylvia wondered what her grandmother would say because they were so late. It was a great while since she had left home at half past five o'clock, but everybody knew the difficulty of making this errand a short one. Mrs. Tilley had chased the horned torment too many summer evenings herself to blame anyone else for lingering, and was only thankful as she waited that she had Sylvia, nowadays, to give such valuable assistance. The good woman suspected that Sylvia loitered occasionally on her own account; there never was such a child for straying about out of doors since the world was made! Everybody said that it was a good change for a little maid who had tried to grow for eight years in a crowded manufacturing town, but, as for Sylvia herself, it seemed as if she never had been alive at all before she came to live at the farm. She thought often with wistful compassion of a wretched dry geranium that belonged to a town neighbor.

"'Afraid of folks,'" old Mrs. Tilley said to herself, with a smile, after she had made the unlikely choice of Sylvia from her daughter's houseful of children, and was returning to the farm. "'Afraid of folks,' they said! I guess she won't be troubled no great with 'em up to the old place!" When they reached the door of the lonely

house and stopped to unlock it, and the cat came to purr loudly and rub against them, a deserted pussy, indeed, but fat with young robins, Sylvia whispered that this was a beautiful place to live in and she never should wish to go home.

The companions followed the shady woodroad, the cow taking slow steps and the child very fast ones. The cow stopped long at the brook to drink, as if the pasture were not half a swamp, and Sylvia stood still and waited, letting her bare feet cool themselves in the shoal water, while the great twilight moths struck softly against her. She waded on through the brook as the cow moved away, and listened to the thrushes with a heart that beat fast with pleasure. There was a stirring in the great boughs overhead. They were full of little birds and beasts that seemed to be wide-awake and going about their world, or else saying good night to each other in sleepy twitters. Sylvia herself felt sleepy as she walked along. However, it was not much farther to the house, and the air was soft and sweet. She was not often in the woods so late as this, and it made her feel as if she were a part of the gray shadows and the moving leaves. She was just thinking how long it seemed since she first came to the farm a year ago and wondering if everything went on in the noisy town just the same as when she was there; the thought of the great red-faced boy who used to chase and frighten her made her hurry along the path to escape from the shadow of the trees.

Suddenly this little woods-girl is horror-stricken to hear a clear whistle not very far away. Not a bird's whistle, which would have a sort of friendliness, but a boy's whistle, determined and somewhat aggressive. Sylvia left the cow to whatever sad fate might await her and stepped discreetly aside into the bushes, but she was just too late. The enemy had discovered her and called out in a very cheerful and persuasive tone, "Halloa, little girl, how far is it to the road?" and trembling Sylvia answered almost inaudibly, "A good ways."

She did not dare to look boldly at the tall young man, who carried a gun over his shoulder, but she came out of her bush and again followed the cow, while he walked alongside.

"I have been hunting for some birds," the stranger said kindly, "and I have lost my way and need a friend very much. Don't be afraid," he added gallantly. "Speak up and tell me what your name is and whether you think I can spend the night at your house and go out gunning early in the morning."

Sylvia was more alarmed than before. Would not her grandmother consider her much to blame? But who could have foreseen such an accident as this? It did not appear to be her fault, and she hung her head as if the stem of it were broken, but managed to answer, "Sylvy," with much effort when her companion again asked her name.

Mrs. Tilley was standing in the doorway when the trio came into view. The cow gave a loud moo by way of explanation.

"Yes, you'd better speak up for yourself, you old trial! Where'd she tuck herself away this time, Sylvy?" Sylvia kept an awed silence; she knew by instinct that her grandmother did not comprehend the gravity of the situation. She must be mistaking the stranger for one of the farmer lads of the region.

The young man stood his gun beside the door and dropped a heavy game bag beside it; then he bade Mrs. Tilley good evening and repeated his wayfarer's story and asked if he could have a night's lodging.

"Put me anywhere you like," he said. "I must be off early in the morning, before day; but I am very hungry, indeed. You can give me some milk at any rate, that's plain."

"Dear sakes, yes," responded the host-

ess, whose long slumbering hospitality seemed to be easily awakened. "You might fare better if you went out on the main road a mile or so, but you're welcome to what we've got. I'll milk right off, and you make yourself at home. You can sleep on husks or feathers," she proffered graciously. "I raised them all myself. There's good pasturing for geese just below here toward the ma'sh. Now step round and set a plate for the gentleman, Sylvy!" And Sylvia promptly stepped. She was glad to have something to do, and she was hungry herself.

It was a surprise to find so clean and comfortable a little dwelling in this New England wilderness. The young man had known the horrors of its most primitive housekeeping and the dreary squalor of that level of society which does not rebel at the companionship of hens. This was the best thrift of an old-fashioned farmstead, though on such a small scale that it seemed like a hermitage. He listened eagerly to the old woman's quaint talk, he watched Sylvia's pale face and shining gray eyes with ever growing enthusiasm, and insisted that this was the best supper he had eaten for a month; then, afterward,

the new-made friends sat down in the doorway together while the moon came up.

Soon it would be berry time, and Sylvia was a great help at picking. The cow was a good milker, though a plaguy[1] thing to keep track of, the hostess gossiped frankly, adding presently that she had buried four children, so that Sylvia's mother and a son (who might be dead) in California were all the children she had left. "Dan, my boy, was a great hand to go gunning," she explained sadly. "I never wanted for pa'tridges or gray squer'ls while he was to home. He's been a great wand'rer, I expect, and he's no hand to write letters. There, I don't blame him, I'd ha' seen the world myself if it had been so I could.

"Sylvia takes after him," the grandmother continued affectionately, after a minute's pause. "There ain't a foot o' ground she don't know her way over, and the wild creatur's counts her one o' themselves. Squer'ls she'll tame to come an' feed right out o' her hands, and all sorts o' birds. Last winter she got the jaybirds to bangeing[2] here, and I believe she'd 'a' scanted herself of her own meals to have plenty to throw out amongst 'em if I hadn't kep' watch. Anything but crows, I tell her, I'm willin' to help support—though Dan he went an' tamed one o' them that did seem to have reason same as folks. It was round here a good spell after he went away. Dan an' his father they didn't hitch[3]—but he never held up his head ag'in after Dan had dared him an' gone off."

The guest did not notice this hint of family sorrows in his eager interest in something else.

"So Sylvy knows all about birds, does

[1] **plaguy** (plā'gē): annoying, troublesome.
[2] **bangeing** (ban'jing): loitering, gathering around.
[3] **hitch:** get along.

she?" he exclaimed, as he looked round at the little girl who sat, very demure but increasingly sleepy, in the moonlight. "I am making a collection of birds myself. I have been at it ever since I was a boy." (Mrs. Tilley smiled.) "There are two or three very rare ones I have been hunting for these five years. I mean to get them on my own ground if they can be found."

"Do you cage 'em up?" asked Mrs. Tilley doubtfully, in response to this enthusiastic announcement.

"Oh, no, they're stuffed and preserved, dozens and dozens of them," said the ornithologist, "and I have shot or snared every one myself. I caught a glimpse of a white heron three miles from here on Saturday, and I have followed it in this direction. They have never been found in this district at all. The little white heron, it is," and he turned again to look at Sylvia with the hope of discovering that the rare bird was one of her acquaintances.

But Sylvia was watching a hoptoad in the narrow footpath.

"You would know the heron if you saw it," the stranger continued eagerly. "A queer tall white bird with soft feathers and long thin legs. And it would have a nest perhaps in the top of a high tree, made of sticks, something like a hawk's nest."

Sylvia's heart gave a wild beat; she knew that strange white bird, and had once stolen softly near where it stood in some bright green swamp grass, away over at the other side of the woods. There was an open place where the sunshine always seemed strangely yellow and hot, where tall, nodding rushes grew, and her grandmother had warned her that she might sink in the soft black mud underneath and never be heard of more. Not far beyond were the salt marshes and beyond those was the sea, the sea which Sylvia wondered and dreamed about, but never had looked upon, though its great

voice could often be heard above the noise of the woods on stormy nights.

"I can't think of anything I should like so much as to find that heron's nest," the handsome stranger was saying. "I would give ten dollars to anybody who could show it to me," he added desperately, "and I mean to spend my whole vacation hunting for it if need be. Perhaps it was only migrating, or had been chased out of its own region by some bird of prey."

Mrs. Tilley gave amazed attention to all this, but Sylvia still watched the toad, not divining, as she might have done at some calmer time, that the creature wished to get to its hole under the doorstep, and was much hindered by the unusual spectators at that hour of the evening. No amount of thought, that night, could decide how many wished-for treasures the ten dollars, so lightly spoken of, would buy.

The next day the young sportsman hovered about the woods, and Sylvia kept him company, having lost her first fear of the friendly lad, who proved to be most kind and sympathetic. He told her many things about the birds and what they knew and where they lived and what they did with themselves. And he gave her a jack-knife, which she thought as great a treasure as if she were a desert islander. All day long he did not once make her troubled or afraid except when he brought down some unsuspecting singing creature from its bough. Sylvia would have liked him vastly better without his gun; she could not understand why he killed the very birds he seemed to like so much. But as the day waned, Sylvia still watched the young man with loving admiration. She had never seen anybody so charming and delightful; the woman's heart, asleep in the child, was vaguely thrilled by a dream of love. Some premonition of that great power stirred and swayed these young

foresters who traversed the solemn woodlands with soft-footed silent care. They stopped to listen to a bird's song; they pressed forward again eagerly, parting the branches—speaking to each other rarely and in whispers; the young man going first and Sylvia following, fascinated, a few steps behind, with her gray eyes dark with excitement.

She grieved because the longed-for white heron was elusive, but she did not lead the guest, she only followed, and there was no such thing as speaking first. The sound of her own unquestioned voice would have terrified her—it was hard enough to answer yes or no when there was need of that. At last evening began to fall, and they drove the cow home together, and Sylvia smiled with pleasure when they came to the place where she heard the whistle and was afraid only the night before.

II

Half a mile from home, at the farther edge of the woods, where the land was highest, a great pine tree stood, the last of its generation. Whether it was left for a boundary mark, or for what reason, no one could say; the woodchoppers who had felled its mates were dead and gone long ago, and a whole forest of sturdy trees, pines, and oaks and maples had grown again. But the stately head of this old pine towered above them all and made a landmark for sea and shore miles and miles away. Sylvia knew it well. She had always believed that whoever climbed to the top of it could see the ocean; and the little girl had often laid her hand on the great rough trunk and looked up wistfully at those dark boughs that the wind always stirred, no matter how hot and still the air might be below. Now she thought of the tree with a new excitement, for why, if one climbed it at break of day, could

not one see all the world, and easily discover whence the white heron flew, and mark the place, and find the hidden nest?

What a spirit of adventure, what wild ambition! What fancied triumph and delight and glory for the later morning when she could make known the secret! It was almost too real and too great for the childish heart to bear.

All night the door of the little house stood open, and the whippoorwills came and sang upon the very step. The young sportsman and his old hostess were sound asleep, but Sylvia's great design kept her broad awake and watching. She forgot to think of sleep. The short summer night seemed as long as the winter darkness, and at last when the whippoorwills ceased, and she was afraid the morning would after all come too soon, she stole out of the house and followed the pasture path through the woods, hastening toward the open ground beyond, listening with a sense of comfort and companionship to the drowsy twitter of a half-awakened bird, whose perch she had jarred in passing. Alas, if the great wave of human interest which flooded for the first time this dull little life should sweep away the satisfactions of an existence heart to heart with nature and the dumb life of the forest!

There was the huge tree asleep yet in the paling moonlight, and small and hopeful Sylvia began with utmost bravery to mount to the top of it, with tingling, eager blood coursing the channels of her whole frame, with her bare feet and fingers, that pinched and held like bird's claws to the monstrous ladder reaching up, up, almost to the sky itself. First she must mount the white oak tree that grew alongside, where she was almost lost among the dark branches and green leaves heavy and wet with dew; a bird fluttered off its nest, and a red squirrel ran to and fro and scolded pettishly at the harmless housebreaker. Sylvia felt her way easily. She had often climbed there and knew that higher still one of the oak's upper branches chafed against the pine trunk, just where its lower boughs were set close together. There, when she made the dangerous pass from one tree to the other, the great enterprise would really begin.

She crept out along the swaying oak limb at last and took the daring step across into the old pine tree. The way was harder than she thought; she must reach far and hold fast, the sharp dry twigs caught and held her and scratched her like angry talons, the pitch made her thin little fingers clumsy and stiff as she went round and round the tree's great stem, higher

and higher upward. The sparrows and robins in the woods below were beginning to wake and twitter to the dawn, yet it seemed much lighter there aloft in the pine tree, and the child knew that she must hurry if her project were to be of any use.

The tree seemed to lengthen itself out as she went up and to reach farther and farther upward. It was like a great mainmast to the voyaging earth; it must truly have been amazed that morning through all its ponderous frame as it felt this determined spark of human spirit creeping and climbing from higher branch to branch. Who knows how steadily the least twigs held themselves to advantage this light, weak creature on her way! The old pine must have loved his new dependent. More than all the hawks, and bats, and moths, and even the sweet-voiced thrushes, was the brave, beating heart of the solitary gray-eyed child. And the tree stood still and held away the winds that June morning while the dawn grew bright in the east.

Sylvia's face was like a pale star, if one had seen it from the ground, when the last thorny bough was past, and she stood trembling and tired but wholly triumphant, high in the treetop. Yes, there was the sea with the dawning sun making a golden dazzle over it, and toward that glorious east flew two hawks with slow-moving pinions. How low they looked in the air from that height when before one had only seen them far up and dark against the blue sky. Their gray feathers were as soft as moths; they seemed only a little way from the tree, and Sylvia felt as if she too could go flying away among the clouds. Westward, the woodlands and farms reached miles and miles into the distance; here and there were church steeples and white villages; truly it was a vast and awesome world.

The birds sang louder and louder. At last the sun came up bewilderingly bright. Sylvia could see the white sails of ships out at sea, and the clouds that were purple and rose-colored and yellow at first began to fade away. Where was the white heron's nest in the sea of green branches, and was this wonderful sight and pageant of the world the only reward for having climbed to such a giddy height? Now look down again, Sylvia, where the green marsh is set among the shining birches and dark hemlocks; there where you saw the white heron once you will see him again; look, look! a white spot of him like a single floating feather comes up from the dead hemlock and grows larger, and rises, and comes close at last, and goes by the landmark pine with steady sweep of wing and outstretched slender neck and crested head. And wait! do not move a foot or a finger, little girl, do not send an arrow of light and consciousness from your two eager eyes, for the heron has perched on a pine bough not far beyond yours, and cries back to his mate on the nest, and plumes his feathers for the new day!

The child gives a long sigh a minute later when a company of shouting cat-

birds comes also to the tree, and vexed by their fluttering and lawlessness the solemn heron goes away. She knows his secret now, the wild, light, slender bird that floats and wavers and goes back like an arrow presently to his home in the green world beneath. Then Sylvia, well satisfied, makes her perilous way down again, not daring to look far below the branch she stands on, ready to cry sometimes because her fingers ache and her lamed feet slip. Wondering over and over again what the stranger would say to her, and what he would think when she told him how to find his way straight to the heron's nests.

"Sylvy, Sylvy!" called the busy old grandmother again and again, but nobody answered, and the small husk bed was empty, and Sylvia had disappeared.

The guest waked from a dream, and remembering his day's pleasure hurried to dress himself that it might sooner begin. He was sure from the way the shy little girl looked once or twice yesterday that she had at least seen the white heron, and now she must really be persuaded to tell. Here she comes now, paler than ever, and her worn old frock is torn and tattered and smeared with pine pitch. The grandmother and the sportsman stand in the door together and question her, and the splendid moment has come to speak of the dead hemlock tree by the green marsh.

But Sylvia does not speak after all, though the old grandmother fretfully rebukes her, and the young man's kind appealing eyes are looking straight in her own. He can make them rich with money; he has promised it, and they are poor now. He is so well worth making happy, and he waits to hear the story she can tell.

No, she must keep silence! What is it that suddenly forbids her and makes her dumb? Has she been nine years growing, and now, when the great world for the first time puts out a hand to her, must she thrust it aside for a bird's sake? The murmur of the pine's green branches is in her ears, she remembers how the white heron came flying through the golden air and how they watched the sea and the morning together, and Sylvia cannot speak; she cannot tell the heron's secret and give its life away.

Dear loyalty, that suffered a sharp pang as the guest went away disappointed later in the day, that could have served and followed him and loved him as a dog loves! Many a night Sylvia heard the echo of his whistle haunting the pasture path as she came home with the loitering cow. She forgot even her sorrow at the sharp report of his gun and the piteous sight of thrushes and sparrows dropping silent to the ground, their songs hushed and their pretty feathers stained and wet with blood. Were the birds better friends than their hunter might have been—who can tell? Whatever treasures were lost to her, woodlands and summertime, remember! Bring your gifts and graces and tell your secrets to this lonely country child!

FOR STUDY AND DISCUSSION

1. What kind of girl is Sylvia at the beginning of the story? List her characteristics. How old is she? What has been her past experience of life? What does the author tell us about her in describing the way she treats the cow?

2. How does Sylvia react to the young stranger? Why? On closer acquaintance, how does she come to feel toward him? Where does she most clearly show her feelings? How is your attitude toward him affected by the fact that he is an ornithologist rather than an ordinary hunter?

3. What is the central conflict of the story? Is it between two characters or between two opposing desires within one character? What is at stake on each side of the conflict? Where in the story is this shown?

4. Many plants, birds, and animals are mentioned in the story. Most of them are simply details that help to describe the setting or indicate something about Sylvia or her life. A few of them, however, suggest a wider meaning. What do you think is symbolized by the "wretched dry geranium" that belonged to Sylvia's town neighbor? How does it differ from the flowers and animals in the woods? What might be symbolized by the tall pine tree that Sylvia must climb to find out the whereabouts of the white heron?

5. The central symbol in the story, of course, is the white heron. Why does Sylvia, after she has discovered its nesting place, not reveal this secret to her new friend? What beyond itself has the white heron come to stand for in her mind?

6. In making her decision, is Sylvia merely choosing between doing a favor for a charming young man and betraying a beautiful white bird, or is she choosing between two ways of life—two opposing sets of values? How will her future life be influenced by her decision? How has the author made Sylvia's decision symbolic?

7. How do you think the author wants us to feel about Sylvia's choice? In the author's opinion, is it the right choice? What makes you think so?

8. Could Sylvia just as well have been named Jane, or Mary Ann, or Shirley? Look up the meaning of *sylvan*. What does the name *Sylvia* symbolize in the story?

LANGUAGE AND VOCABULARY

To help us experience Sylvia's difficulties and her feelings as she climbs the tall pine, the author makes a particularly careful use of descriptive language. How do the following phrases add to your impression of Sylvia's ordeal?

"with tingling, eager blood coursing the channels of her whole frame . . ."

"with her bare feet and fingers, that pinched and held like bird's claws . . ."

"the monstrous ladder reaching up, up, almost to the sky itself."

"the sharp dry twigs caught and held her and scratched her like angry talons . . ."

"The tree . . . was like a great mainmast to the voyaging earth . . ."

FOR COMPOSITION

1. Like Sylvia in this story, many of us have had an experience in which an animal or a plant—some living thing—has had an important meaning in our lives. If you have had such an experience, write a brief account of how this living thing affected you. Plan your writing carefully, and include only the really significant details of the story.

2. Compare the theme and conflict of this story with those of Sinclair Lewis's "Land." How are the two stories similar? How are they different?

ABOUT THE AUTHOR

Sarah Orne Jewett (1849–1909), the daughter of a distinguished doctor and professor, was born, grew up, lived, and died in South Berwick, Maine. Delicate in health, she received little formal education, but read widely in her father's library and gained an intimate knowledge of the Maine countryside and Maine people by accompanying her father on his visits to patients on farms and in fishing villages. She published her first story at the age of nineteen, and one year later began appearing regularly in the *Atlantic Monthly*. Her first book of stories, *Deephaven*, published in 1877, brought her to the attention of the literary world and gained her the acquaintance of famous writers in both America and England. Though she made several trips to Europe and visited Boston frequently, she spent most of her life in the house where she was born. Her books, of which the best-known is *The Country of the Pointed Firs,* record sympathetically and truthfully a rural and village New England way of life that was disappearing even as she wrote about it.

EUROPEAN PAINTING

Fifteenth-Century Painting

We of the twentieth century have become well accustomed to the idea of "progress." We are constantly reminded to be up to date, to keep abreast of the latest news and ideas. In fact, we take it for granted that life tomorrow may be quite different from what it is today. Suppose, however, we were living in a time in which the world had just begun to change, after centuries of firmly established traditions. If, for example, we had lived in fifteenth-century Italy, we would have been able to sense the end of an old world and the beginning of a new one.

While the two leading powers of medieval feudalism, France and England, were in the middle of a long, exhausting war, some interesting changes were taking place in other parts of the world. A number of Italian city-states had become centers of an expanding international commerce. There was a new feeling of opportunity and adventure. The people of these city-states realized that the Middle Ages, as they called the preceding centuries of feudalism, were over. Italians were now looking to the future, but also to the distant past. They hoped for a "renaissance," or rebirth, of the days of the great Roman Empire.

Ancient Roman culture soon became the accepted standard for art and fashion in Italy. PLATE 1 shows one painter's conception of how a fifteenth-century Italian city might have looked if it were built in the style of classical Roman architecture. Here is a typically Italian concern for clear visual order. The buildings and the patterns of inlaid marble in the city square have been arranged to balance symmetrically in the picture. But notice that the artist has also created a realistic effect of depth by making all the receding lines converge toward a single "vanishing point" at our eye level. Italian Renaissance artists were the first to develop such a system of "linear perspective," which approximates on a flat surface the way our eyes interpret depth in the real world.

By financing the work of painters, sculptors, and architects, wealthy Italian merchants became important patrons of Renaissance art. In PLATE 2 we see Benozzo Gozzoli's equestrian portrait of one of the greatest patrons

of them all, Lorenzo de' Medici. Lorenzo the Magnificent, as he was called, was the third-generation head of a powerful family which ruled the city-state of Florence for sixty years of the fifteenth century. Gozzoli has characterized Lorenzo as a handsomer man than he really was, for his intention was to glorify him as a person of wealth and refinement and to display some of the pageantry of Florentine life. This scene is only a small detail from a painting which covers all four walls of the Medici family chapel.

Florence was the main center of Italian art during the 1400's. Some painters who worked there, however, originally came from other parts of Italy—for example, Piero della Francesca, who was raised in the nearby region of Umbria. You can see how different Piero's type of painting was from Gozzoli's in his portrait of the Duke of Urbino (PLATE 3). Here the artist portrayed his sitter as he actually appeared, broken nose and all. Piero has given depth to his landscape by contrasting the bright red color of the Duke's hat and coat with the pale tones of the valleys in the distance.

Another important artist of this period was Antonio Pollaiuolo, who was particularly interested in the anatomy and movement of the human body. In his painting of Apollo and Daphne (PLATE 4), for instance, the god is shown desperately trying to embrace the lovely nymph, who eludes him by turning into a tree. Yet despite the complicated action, these two figures seem to be perfectly poised and balanced. Pollaiuolo has transformed the awkward motions of a physical struggle into a graceful rhythm of line and form, which is extended even into the curving patterns of the landscape.

Vittore Carpaccio was one of several famous Renaissance artists from Venice who painted colorful scenes of contemporary life in that wealthy trading city. PLATE 5 shows an episode from the legendary story of St. Ursula that Carpaccio placed in a fifteenth-century setting. He has given us a visual report of the costumes of the day, types of Venetian buildings, and even the typical crowd across the canal which has gathered to witness a public event.

Although the early Renaissance was fundamentally Italian, another important development was taking place at the same time in a small section of northern Europe called Flanders. Flemish painters had discovered that they could blend colors more smoothly by mixing their pigments with oil. Jan van Eyck, the most famous of all fifteenth-century Flemish masters, used this technique to achieve an extraordinary kind of realism. His painting, *Giovanni Arnolfini and His Bride* (PLATE 6), for example, is remarkable for its clarity of detail. But notice also its incredibly soft gradations of tones, its beautiful effects of light and shadow. It almost seems as if we were standing in this room before the bridal couple in the same spot from which Van Eyck painted their portrait. If you ever have an opportunity to see the original painting in London, you will be able to make out the reflection of Van Eyck's own figure in the circular mirror shown on the back wall.

PLATE 1. LUCIANO DA LAURANA (1420/25–1479): *Piazza of an Italian City*. About 1475. Tempera panel, $32\frac{11}{16}$ x $86\frac{9}{16}$ inches. (The Walters Art Gallery, Baltimore)

PLATE 2. BENOZZO GOZZOLI (Florentine, about 1421–1497): *Lorenzo de' Medici*, detail from the *Procession of the Magi*. 1459. Fresco. Entire wall is 12 feet 5⅝ inches by 16 feet 9 inches. (Riccardi Palace, Florence)

PLATE 3. PIERO DELLA FRANCESCA (Umbrian, about 1416–1492): *Duke of Urbino*. About 1470. Tempera on wood panel, 18½ x 13 inches. (Uffizi, Florence)

PLATE 4. ANTONIO POLLAIUOLO (Florentine, about 1432–about 1498): *Apollo and Daphne.*
Oil on wood panel, $11\frac{5}{8}$ x $7\frac{7}{8}$ inches. (Reproduced by courtesy of the Trustees, The National
Gallery, London)

118

PLATE 5. VITTORE CARPACCIO (Venetian, active 1490–about 1526): *The Betrothed Pair Taking Leave of Their Parents*, from *The Story of Saint Ursula*. About 1490–1495. Oil on canvas, 9 feet 1 inch by 20 feet. (Academy, Venice)

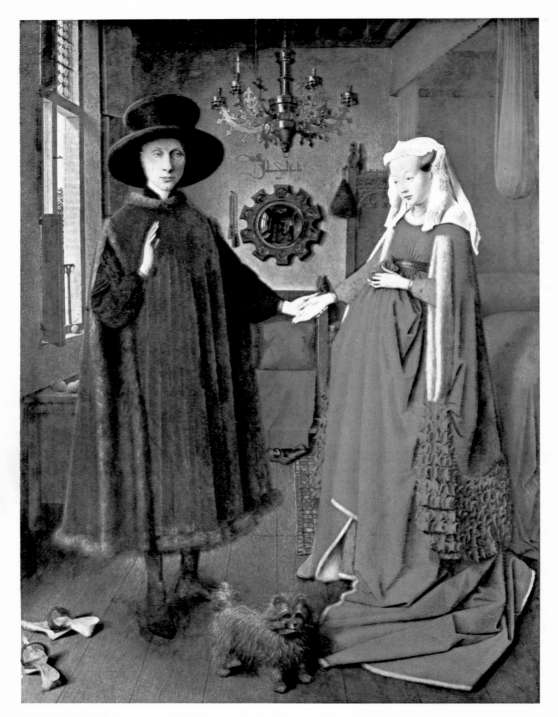

PLATE 6. JAN VAN EYCK (Flemish, about 1390–1441): *Giovanni Arnolfini and His Bride*.
1434. Oil on oak panel, $32\frac{3}{8}$ x $24\frac{1}{8}$ inches. (Reproduced by courtesy of the Trustees, The National
Gallery, London)

120

The Masque of the Red Death

EDGAR ALLAN POE

Although the meaning and final effect of "A White Heron" is enriched by the author's use of symbols, we do not have to identify and pin down those symbols to a definite meaning in order to understand the story. In the story that follows, however, the author's symbols are much more important to the story's meaning and must be consciously recognized and understood. Unless you can recognize and understand its major symbols, the story will have little significance.

THE "RED DEATH" had long devastated the country. No pestilence had ever been so fatal or so hideous. Blood was its Avatar [1] and its seal—the redness and the horror of blood. There were sharp pains, and sudden dizziness, and then profuse bleeding at the pores, with dissolution. The scarlet stains upon the body and especially upon the face of the victim were the pest ban which shut him out from the aid and from the sympathy of his fellow-men. And the whole seizure, progress, and termination of the disease were the incidents of half an hour.

But the Prince Prospero was happy and dauntless and sagacious. When his dominions were half-depopulated, he summoned to his presence a thousand hale and light-hearted friends from among the knights and dames of his court and with these retired to the deep seclusion of one of his castellated abbeys. This was an extensive and magnificent structure, the creation of the prince's own eccentric yet august taste. A strong and lofty wall girdled it in. This wall had gates of iron. The courtiers, having entered, brought furnaces and massy hammers and welded the bolts. They resolved to leave means neither of ingress nor egress to the sudden impulses of despair or of frenzy from within. The abbey was amply provisioned. With such precautions the courtiers might bid defiance to contagion. The external world could take care of itself. In the meantime it was folly to grieve or to think. The prince had provided all the appliances of pleasure. There were buffoons, there were improvisatori,[2] there were ballet dancers, there were musicians, there was Beauty, there was wine. All these and security were within. Without was the "Red Death."

It was toward the close of the fifth or sixth month of his seclusion, and while the pestilence raged most furiously abroad, that the Prince Prospero entertained his thousand friends at a masked ball of the most unusual magnificence.

It was a voluptuous scene, that masquerade. But first let me tell of the rooms in which it was held. There were seven—an imperial suite. In many palaces, however, such suites form a long and straight vista, while the folding doors slide back nearly to the walls on either hand, so that the view of the whole extent is scarcely impeded. Here the case was very different, as might have been expected from the duke's love of the bizarre. The apartments were so irregularly disposed that the vision embraced but little more than one

[1] **Avatar:** a visible sign or embodiment of an invisible force.

[2] **improvisatori** (ĕm′prô·vē·zä·tō′rē): improvisers of verse.

at a time. There was a sharp turn at every twenty or thirty yards and at each turn a novel effect. To the right and left, in the middle of each wall, a tall and narrow Gothic window looked out upon a closed corridor which pursued the windings of the suite. These windows were of stained glass whose color varied in accordance with the prevailing hue of the decorations of the chamber into which it opened. That at the eastern extremity was hung, for example, in blue—and vividly blue were its windows. The second chamber was purple in its ornaments and tapestries, and here the panes were purple. The third was green throughout, and so were the casements. The fourth was furnished and lighted with orange—the fifth with white—the sixth with violet. The seventh apartment was closely shrouded in black velvet tapestries that hung all over the ceiling and down the walls, falling in heavy folds upon a carpet of the same material and hue. But in this chamber only, the color of the windows failed to correspond with the decorations. The panes here were scarlet—a deep blood color. Now in no

one of the seven apartments was there any lamp or candelabrum amid the profusion of golden ornaments that lay scattered to and fro or depended from the roof. There was no light of any kind emanating from lamp or candle within the suite of chambers. But in the corridors that followed the suite, there stood, opposite to each window, a heavy tripod, bearing a brazier of fire, that projected its rays through the tinted glass and so glaringly illumined the room. And thus were produced a multitude of gaudy and fantastic appearances. But in the western or black chamber the effect of the firelight that streamed upon the dark hangings through the blood-tinted panes was ghastly in the extreme and produced so wild a look upon the countenances of those who entered, that there were few of the company bold enough to set foot within its precincts at all.

It was in this apartment, also, that there stood against the western wall a gigantic clock of ebony. Its pendulum swung to and fro with a dull, heavy, monotonous clang; and when the minute hand made the circuit of the face and the hour was to be stricken, there came from the brazen lungs of the clock a sound which was clear and loud and deep and exceedingly musical, but of so peculiar a note and emphasis that, at each lapse of an hour, the musicians of the orchestra were constrained to pause, momentarily, in their performance, to hearken to the sound; and thus the waltzers perforce ceased their evolutions; and there was a brief disconcert of the whole gay company; and, while the chimes of the clock yet rang, it was observed that the giddiest grew pale and the more aged and sedate passed their hands over their brows as if in confused revery or meditation. But when the echoes had fully ceased, a light laughter at once pervaded the assembly; the musicians looked at each other and smiled as if at their own ner-

vousness and folly and made whispering vows, each to the other, that the next chiming of the clock should produce in them no similar emotion; and then, after the lapse of sixty minutes (which embrace three thousand and six hundred seconds of the Time that flies), there came yet another chiming of the clock, and then were the same disconcert and tremulousness and meditation as before.

But, in spite of these things, it was a gay and magnificent revel. The tastes of the duke were peculiar. He had a fine eye for colors and effects. He disregarded the *decora* [1] of mere fashion. His plans were bold and fiery, and his conceptions glowed with barbaric luster. There are some who would have thought him mad. His followers felt that he was not. It was necessary to hear and see and touch him to be *sure* that he was not.

He had directed, in great part, the movable embellishments of the seven chambers, upon occasion of this great fete; and it was his own guiding taste which had given character to the masqueraders. Be sure they were grotesque. There were much glare and glitter and piquancy and phantasm—much of what has been since seen in *Hernani.* [2] There were arabesque figures with unsuited limbs and appointments. There were delirious fancies such as the madman fashions. There were much of the beautiful, much of the wanton, much of the bizarre, something of the terrible, and not a little of that which might have excited disgust. To and fro in the seven chambers there stalked, in fact, a multitude of dreams. And these—the dreams—writhed in and about, taking hue from the rooms and causing the wild music of the orchestra to seem as the echo of their steps. And, anon, there strikes the ebony clock which

[1] *decora:* ornaments.
[2] *Hernani:* a romantic play by Victor Hugo.

stands in the hall of the velvet. And then, for a moment, all is still, and all is silent save the voice of the clock. The dreams are stiff-frozen as they stand. But the echoes of the chime die away—they have endured but an instant—and a light, half-subdued laughter floats after them as they depart. And now again the music swells, and the dreams live and writhe to and fro more merrily than ever, taking hue from the many-tinted windows through which stream the rays from the tripods. But to the chamber which lies most westwardly of the seven there are now none of the maskers who venture; for the night is waning away; and there flows a ruddier light through the blood-colored panes; and the blackness of the sable drapery appals; and to him whose foot falls upon the sable carpet, there comes from the near clock of ebony a muffled peal more solemnly emphatic than any which reaches *their* ears who indulge in the more remote gaieties of the other apartments.

But these other apartments were densely crowded, and in them beat feverishly the heart of life. And the revel went whirlingly on, until at length there commenced the sounding of midnight upon the clock. And then the music ceased, as I have told; and the evolutions of the waltzers were quieted; and there was an uneasy cessation of all things as before. But now there were twelve strokes to be sounded by the bell of the clock; and thus it happened, perhaps, that more of thought crept, with more of time, into the meditations of the thoughtful among those who reveled. And thus too, it happened, perhaps, that before the last echoes of the last chime had utterly sunk into silence, there were many individuals in the crowd who had found leisure to become aware of the presence of a masked figure which had arrested the attention of no single individual before. And the rumor of this

company, indeed, seemed now deeply to feel that in the costume and bearing of the stranger neither wit nor propriety existed. The figure was tall and gaunt and shrouded from head to foot in the habiliments of the grave. The mask which concealed the visage was made so nearly to resemble the countenance of a stiffened corpse that the closest scrutiny must have had difficulty in detecting the cheat. And yet all this might have been endured, if not approved, by the mad revelers around. But the mummer had gone so far as to assume the type of the Red Death. His vesture was dabbled in *blood*—and his broad brow, with all the features of the face, was besprinkled with the scarlet horror.

When the eyes of Prince Prospero fell upon this spectral image (which with a slow and solemn movement, as if more fully to sustain its role, stalked to and fro among the waltzers) he was seen to be convulsed, in the first moment with a strong shudder either of terror or distaste; but, in the next, his brow reddened with rage.

"Who dares"—he demanded hoarsely of the courtiers who stood near him—"who dares insult us with this blasphemous mockery? Seize him and unmask him—that we may know whom we have to hang, at sunrise, from the battlements!"

It was in the eastern or blue chamber in which stood the Prince Prospero as he uttered these words. They rang throughout the seven rooms loudly and clearly, for the prince was a bold and robust man, and the music had become hushed at the waving of his hand.

It was in the blue room where stood the prince, with a group of pale courtiers by his side. At first, as he spoke, there was a slight rushing movement of this group in the direction of the intruder, who, at the moment was also near at hand, and

new presence having spread itself whisperingly around, there arose at length from the whole company a buzz, or murmur, expressive of disapprobation and surprise—then, finally, of terror, of horror, and of disgust.

In an assembly of phantasms such as I have painted, it may well be supposed that no ordinary appearance could have excited such sensation. In truth the masquerade license of the night was nearly unlimited; but the figure in question had out-Heroded Herod [1] and gone beyond the bounds of even the prince's indefinite decorum. There are chords in the hearts of the most reckless which cannot be touched without emotion. Even with the utterly lost, to whom life and death are equally jests, there are matters of which no jest can be made. The whole

[1] **out-Heroded Herod:** overplayed his part. The phrase comes from Shakespeare's *Hamlet,* in which Hamlet warns a group of actors not to over-act their parts.

now, with deliberate and stately step, made closer approach to the speaker. But from a certain nameless awe with which the mad assumptions of the mummer had inspired the whole party, there were found none who put forth hand to seize him; so that, unimpeded, he passed within a yard of the prince's person; and, while the vast assembly, as if with one impulse, shrank from the centers of the rooms to the walls, he made his way uninterruptedly, but with the same solemn and measured step which had distinguished him from the first, through the blue chamber to the purple—through the purple to the green—through the green to the orange—through this again to the white —and even thence to the violet ere a decided movement had been made to arrest him. It was then, however, that the Prince Prospero, maddening with rage and the shame of his own momentary cowardice, rushed hurriedly through the six chambers, while none followed him on account of a deadly terror that had seized upon all. He bore aloft a drawn dagger and had approached, in rapid impetuosity, to within three or four feet of the retreating figure, when the latter, having attained the extremity of the velvet apartment, turned suddenly and confronted his pursuer. There was a sharp cry—and the dagger dropped gleaming upon the sable carpet, upon which, instantly afterward, fell prostrate in death the Prince Prospero. Then, summoning the wild courage of despair, a throng of the revelers at once threw themselves into the black apartment and, seizing the mummer, whose tall figure stood erect and motionless within the shadow of the ebony clock, gasped in unutterable horror at finding the grave cerements and corpselike mask, which they handled with so violent a rudeness, untenanted by any tangible form.

And now was acknowledged the presence of the Red Death. He had come like a thief in the night. And one by one dropped the revelers in the blood-bedewed halls of their revel and died each in the despairing posture of his fall. And the life of the ebony clock went out with that of the last of the gay. And the flames of the tripods expired. And Darkness and Decay and the Red Death held illimitable dominion over all.

FOR STUDY AND DISCUSSION

1. What is the significance of Prince Prospero's name? (What is the meaning of *prosperous?*) How is the meaning of the Prince's name suggested by his actions in the story?

2. What kind of life do Prince Prospero and his courtiers attempt to lead in their retreat? Why is their activity so intense and feverish? What is the connection between their feverish activity and their welding the bolts on the iron gates?

3. What is suggested by the seven rooms of the imperial suite? What is the significance of their proceeding from east to west? of their

progressing from blue to black? of the fact that they are so arranged that the vision can embrace little more than one at a time?

4. What in particular is symbolized by the seventh room? What is the significance of its color? What is suggested by the fact that the stained-glass window in this room is red? Why do the maskers shun this room?

5. What is symbolized by the ebony clock? Why do the dancers pause and grow pale when the clock strikes? Why is it fitting that the strange masked figure appears when the clock strikes twelve rather than some other hour?

6. Why do you think Prince Prospero falls dead without having been struck or even touched by the masked figure? What is the cause of his death? What is the meaning of the fact that the grave cerements and corpse-like mask are found to be "untenanted by any tangible form"?

7. What symbolic meaning is suggested by each of the details in the final paragraph of the story? In what sense has the Red Death been a "thief"? How do the revelers "blood-bedew" the halls? What is symbolized by the stopping of the ebony clock? by the expiring of the flames in the tripods? What is symbolized in the final sentence: "And Darkness and Decay and the Red Death held illimitable dominion over all"? How is this sentence a symbolic summing-up of the forces opposed to Prince Prospero?

8. What is the chief conflict in this story? What is its theme? Why is Prince Prospero regarded by some people, though not by his followers, as mad? Is he, in any sense, "mad"? What makes you think so?

SYMBOL AND SYMBOLIC MEANING

As you know, a symbol is something that suggests a wider meaning. Like "loaded words"—such as *truth, brutality,* and *freedom* —symbols call forth from our minds and memories whole clusters of ideas and feelings. The stronger these associations, the more powerful the symbol. Of the symbols in "The Masque of the Red Death" and "The White Heron," which calls up the strongest associations? What do you associate with the figure of the

Red Death? of the white heron? How would different colors, such as the *black* death or the *blue* heron, affect these symbolic overtones?

LANGUAGE AND VOCABULARY

Poe's stories are rich in words which may be unfamiliar but which should be a part of our working vocabulary. Try to recall how the words below were used in the context of Poe's story; look up any that are puzzling or unfamiliar; and finally, use each word in a sentence of your own that makes clear its meaning.

pestilence	casement	propriety
dauntless	hale	gaunt
sagacious	brazen	robust
eccentric	shroud	mummer
contagion	precinct	writhe
buffoon	grotesque	dominion
Gothic	decorum	

ABOUT THE AUTHOR

Edgar Allan Poe (1809–1849) is famous for his literary criticism, his haunting poetry, and his tales of mystery and horror. The son of traveling actors, he was left an orphan at the age of two. Though an excellent athlete and a brilliant student of languages, Poe attended the University of Virginia for only one term, served two years in the army, and deliberately got himself expelled from West Point. After the death of his guardian, he went to live with an aunt, Maria Clemm, whose daughter he married before she was fourteen. His mature life was spent mostly in Baltimore, Richmond, and New York as a writer and editor on a number of newspapers and magazines. Despite suffering from poverty, alcoholism, and nervous breakdowns, he was always a hard worker. His tales "The Fall of the House of Usher" and "Ligeia" are masterpieces of the short story; "The Murders in the Rue Morgue" is the first detective story in literary history; "The Black Cat," "The Telltale Heart," and "The Pit and the Pendulum" are famous tales of horror. Among his most popular poems are "The Raven," "The Bells," "Annabel Lee," "Israfel," "The Haunted Palace," and "The City in the Sea."

STORIES FOR FURTHER EXPLORATION

The purpose of some stories is simply to thrill or entertain. If they fulfill this purpose, they are successful in what they have attempted. Such stories make the time pass pleasantly for us. They will not, however, enlarge our understanding of life and human nature.

A really good story is a journey into understanding. It not only keeps us alert and interested, it also widens our outlook, deepens our insight, and enlarges our understanding of ourselves and life. After reading a story, therefore, we should pause and ask ourselves three questions: What is this story's central purpose? How well does it fulfill that purpose? What does that achievement mean to us?

In answering these questions, we must consider all the elements of the short story that we have so far studied—plot, character, theme, irony, symbol. How do these elements work together in the following stories to enable the author to achieve his central purpose?

The Quiet Man

MAURICE WALSH

Shawn Kelvin, a blithe young lad of twenty, went to the States to seek his fortune. And fifteen years thereafter he returned to his native Kerry,[1] his blitheness sobered and his youth dried to the core, and whether he had made his fortune or whether he had not, no one could be knowing for certain. For he was a quiet man, not given to talking about himself and the things he had done. A quiet man, under middle size, with strong shoulders

[1] **Kerry:** a county in southwestern Ireland.

and deep-set blue eyes below brows darker than his dark hair—that was Shawn Kelvin. One shoulder had a trick of hunching slightly higher than the other, and some folks said that came from a habit he had of shielding his eyes in the glare of an open-hearth furnace in a place called Pittsburgh, while others said it used to be a way he had of guarding his chin that time he was a sort of sparring-partner punching bag at a boxing camp.

Shawn Kelvin came home and found that he was the last of the Kelvins and that the farm of his forefathers had added its few acres to the ranch of Big Liam O'Grady, of Moyvalla. Shawn took no action to recover his land, though O'Grady had got it meanly. He had had enough of fighting, and all he wanted now was peace. He quietly went amongst the old and kindly friends and quietly looked about him for the place and peace he wanted; and when the time came, quietly

produced the money for a neat, handy, small farm on the first warm shoulder of Knockanore Hill below the rolling curves of heather. It was not a big place but it was in good heart, and it got all the sun that was going; and, best of all, it suited Shawn to the tiptop notch of contentment; for it held the peace that tuned to his quietness, and it commanded the widest view in all Ireland—vale and mountain and the lifting green plain of the Atlantic Sea.

There, in a four-roomed, lime-washed, thatched cottage, Shawn made his life, and, though his friends hinted his needs and obligations, no thought came to him of bringing a wife into the place. Yet Fate had the thought and the dream in her loom for him. One middling imitation of a man he had to do chores for him, an ex-navy pensioner handy enough about house and byre, but with no relish for the sustained work of the field—and, indeed, as long as he kept house and byre shipshape, he found Shawn an easy master.

Shawn himself was no drudge toiler. He knew all about drudgery and the way it wears out a man's soul. He plowed a little and sowed a little, and at the end of a furrow he would lean on the handles of the cultivator, wipe his brow, if it needed wiping, and lose himself for whole minutes in the great green curve of the sea out there beyond the high black portals of Shannon mouth.[1] And sometimes of an evening he would see, under the glory of the sky, the faint smoke smudge of an American liner. Then he would smile to himself— a pitying smile—thinking of the poor devils, with dreams of fortune luring them, going out to sweat in Ironville or to stand in a breadline.[2] All these things

were behind Shawn forever.

Market days he would go down and across to Listowel town, seven miles, to do his bartering; and in the long evenings, slowly slipping into the endless summer gloaming, his friends used to climb the winding lane to see him. Only the real friends came that long road, and they were welcome—fighting men who had been out in the "Sixteen";[3] Matt Tobin the thresher, the schoolmaster, the young curate—men like that. A stone jar of malt whisky would appear on the table, and there would be a haze of smoke and a maze of warm, friendly disagreements.

"Shawn, old son," one of them might hint, "aren't you sometimes terrible lonely?"

"Never!" might retort Shawn derisively. "Why?"

"Nothing but the daylight and the wind and the sun setting with the wrath o' God."

"Just that! Well?"

"But after stirring times beyond in the States——"

"Ay! Tell me, fine man, have you ever seen a furnace in full blast?"

"A great sight."

"Great surely! But if I could jump you into a steel foundry this minute, you would be sure that God had judged you faithfully into the very hob of hell."

And then they would laugh and have another small one from the stone jar.

And on Sundays Shawn used to go to church, three miles down to the gray chapel above the black cliffs of Doon Bay. There Fate laid her lure for him.

Sitting quietly on his wooden bench or kneeling on the dusty footboard, he would fix his steadfast, deep-set eyes on the vestmented celebrant[4] and say his

[1] **Shannon mouth:** where the Shannon River empties into the Atlantic Ocean.

[2] **breadline:** People waiting in line for government bread during the worst years of the Depression in America were said to be in a breadline.

[3] **the "Sixteen";** the unsuccessful Irish rebellion against English rule in 1916.

[4] **vestmented celebrant:** the robed priest.

prayers slowly or go into that stranger trance, beyond dreams and visions, where the soul is almost at one with the unknowable.

But after a time, Shawn's eyes no longer fixed themselves on the celebrant. They went no farther than two seats ahead. A girl sat there, Sunday after Sunday she sat in front of him, and Sunday after Sunday his first casual admiration grew warmer.

She had a white nape to her neck and short red hair above it, and Shawn liked the color and wave of that flame. And he liked the set of her shoulders and the way the white neck had of leaning a little forward and she at her prayers —or her dreams. And the service over, Shawn used to stay in his seat so that he might get one quick but sure look at her face as she passed out. And he liked her face, too—the wide-set gray eyes, cheekbones firmly curved, clean-molded lips, austere yet sensitive. And he smiled pityingly at himself that one of her name should make his pulses stir—for she was an O'Grady.

One person, only, in the crowded chapel noted Shawn's look and the thought behind the look. Not the girl. Her brother, Big Liam O'Grady of Moyvalla, the very man who as good as stole the Kelvin acres. And that man smiled to himself, too—the ugly, contemptuous smile that was his by nature—and, after another habit he had, he tucked away his bit of knowledge in his mind corner against a day when it might come in useful for his own purposes.

The girl's name was Ellen—Ellen O'Grady. But in truth she was no longer a girl. She was past her first youth into that second one that had no definite ending. She might be thirty—she was no less—but there was not a lad in the countryside would say she was past her

prime. The poise of her and the firm set of her bones below clean skin saved her from the fading of mere prettiness. Though she had been sought in marriage more than once, she had accepted no one, or rather, had not been allowed to encourage anyone. Her brother saw to that.

Big Liam O'Grady was a great rawboned, sandy-haired man, with the strength of an ox and a heart no bigger than a sour apple. An overbearing man given to berserk rages. Though he was a churchgoer by habit, the true god of that man was Money—red gold, shining silver, dull copper—the trinity [1] that he worshiped in degree. He and his sister Ellen lived on the big ranch farm of Moyvalla, and Ellen was his housekeeper and maid of all work. She was a careful housekeeper, a good cook, a notable baker, and she demanded no wage. All that suited Big Liam splendidly, and so she remained single—a wasted woman.

Big Liam himself was not a marrying man. There were not many spinsters with a dowry [2] big enough to tempt him, and the few there had acquired expensive tastes—a convent education, the deplorable art of hitting jazz out of a piano, the damnable vice of cigarette smoking, the purse-emptying craze for motor cars— such things.

But in due time, the dowry and the place—with a woman tied to them— came under his nose, and Big Liam was no longer tardy. His neighbor, James Carey, died in March and left his fine farm and all on it to his widow, a youngish woman without children, a woman with a hard name for saving pennies. Big

[1] **trinity:** group of three. The author is comparing Big Liam's trinity to the Christian Trinity of the Father, the Son, and the Holy Spirit.

[2] **dowry:** the money or property a woman brings to her husband at the time of marriage.

Liam looked once at Kathy Carey and looked many times at her broad acres. Both pleased him. He took the steps required by tradition. In the very first week of the following Shrovetide,[1] he sent an accredited emissary to open formal negotiations, and that emissary came back within the hour.

"My soul," said he, "but she is the quick one! I hadn't ten words out of me when she was down my throat. 'I am in no hurry,' says she, 'to come wife to a house with another woman at the fire corner. When Ellen is in a place of her own, I will listen to what Liam O'Grady has to say.'"

"She will, I say!" Big Liam stopped him. "She will so."

There, now, was the right time to recall Shawn Kelvin and the look in his eyes. Big Liam's mind corner promptly delivered up its memory. He smiled knowingly and contemptuously. Shawn Kelvin daring to cast sheep's eyes at an O'Grady! The undersized chicken heart, who took the loss of the Kelvin acres lying down! The little Yankee runt hidden away on the shelf of Knockanore! But what of it? The required dowry would be conveniently small, and the girl would never go hungry, anyway. There was Big Liam O'Grady, far descended from many chieftains.

The very next market day at Listowel he sought out Shawn Kelvin and placed a huge, sandy-haired hand on the shoulder that hunched to meet it.

"Shawn Kelvin, a word with you! Come and have a drink."

Shawn hesitated. "Very well," he said then. He did not care for O'Grady, but he would hurt no man's feelings.

They went across to Sullivan's bar and had a drink, and Shawn paid for it. And Big Liam came directly to his subject—almost patronizingly, as if he were conferring a favor.

"I want to see Ellen settled in a place of her own," said he.

Shawn's heart lifted into his throat and stayed there. But that steadfast face with the steadfast eyes gave no sign and, moreover, he could not say a word with his heart where it was.

"Your place is small," went on the big man, "but it is handy, and no load of debt on it, as I hear. Not much of a dowry ever came to Knockanore, and not much of a dowry can I be giving with Ellen. Say two hundred pounds at the end of harvest, if prices improve. What do you say Shawn Kelvin?"

Shawn swallowed his heart, and his voice came slow and cool: "What does Ellen say?"

"I haven't asked her," said Big Liam. "But what would she say, blast it?"

"Whatever she says, she will say it herself, not you, Big Liam."

But what could Ellen say? She looked within her own heart and found it empty; she looked at the granite crag of her brother's face and contemplated herself a slowly withering spinster at his fire corner; she looked up at the swell of Knockanore Hill and saw the white cottage among the green small fields below the warm brown of the heather. Oh, but the sun would shine up there in the lengthening spring day and pleasant breezes blow in sultry summer; and finally she looked at Shawn Kelvin, that firmly built, small man with the clean face and the lustrous eyes below steadfast brow. She said a prayer to her God and sank head and shoulders in a resignation more pitiful than tears, more proud than the pride of chieftains. Romance? Welladay!

Shawn was far from satisfied with that

[1] **Shrovetide** (shrōv'tīd'): the days, usually three, immediately before Ash Wednesday, which serve as a time for confession preparatory to Lent.

resigned acceptance, but then was not the time to press for a warmer one. He knew the brother's wizened soul, guessed at the girl's clean one, and saw that she was doomed beyond hope to a fireside sordidly bought for her. Let it be his own fireside then. There were many worse ones—and God was good.

Ellen O'Grady married Shawn Kelvin. One small statement; and it holds the risk of tragedy, the chance of happiness, the probability of mere endurance—choices wide as the world.

But Big Liam O'Grady, for all his resolute promptness, did not win Kathy Carey to wife. She, foolishly enough, took to husband her own cattleman, a gay night rambler, who gave her the devil's own time and a share of happiness in the bygoing. For the first time, Big Liam discovered how mordant the wit of his neighbors could be, and to contempt for Shawn Kelvin he now added an unreasoning dislike.

Shawn Kelvin had got his precious, redhaired woman under his own roof now. He had no illusions about her feelings for him. On himself, and on himself only, lay the task of molding her into a wife and lover. Darkly, deeply, subtly, away out of sight, with gentleness, with restraint, with a consideration beyond kenning,[1] that molding must be done, and she that was being molded must never know. He hardly knew, himself.

First he turned his attention to material things. He hired a small servant maid to help her with the housework. Then he acquired a rubber-tired tub cart and half-bred gelding[2] with a reaching knee action. And on market days, husband and wife used to bowl down to Listowel, do their selling and their buying, and bowl smoothly home again, their groceries in the well of the cart and a bundle of second-hand American magazines on the seat at Ellen's side. And in the nights, before the year turned, with the wind from the plains of the Atlantic keening[3] above the chimney, they would sit at either side of the flaming peat fire, and he would read aloud strange and almost unbelievable things out of the high-colored magazines. Stories, sometimes, wholly unbelievable.

Ellen would sit and listen and smile and go on with her knitting or her sewing; and after a time it was sewing she was at mostly—small things. And when the reading was done, they would sit and talk quietly in their own quiet way. For they were both quiet. Woman though she was, she got Shawn to do most of the talking. It could be that she, too, was probing and seeking, unwrapping the man's soul to feel the texture thereof, surveying the marvel of his life as he spread it diffidently before her. He had a patient, slow, vivid way of picturing for her the things he had seen and felt. He made her see the glare of molten metal, lambent[4] yet searing, made her feel the sucking heat, made her hear the clang; she could see the roped square under the dazzle of the hooded arcs with the curling smoke layer above it, understand the explosive restraint of the game, thrill when he showed her how to stiffen wrist for the final devastating right hook. And often enough the stories were humorous, and Ellen would chuckle, or stare, or throw back her red, lovely curls in laughter. It was grand to make her laugh.

Shawn's friends, in some hesitation at first, came in ones and twos up the slope to see them. But Ellen welcomed them with her smile that was shy and, at the same time, frank, and her table was loaded for them with scones and crumpets and

[1] **kenning:** insight; understanding.
[2] **gelding** (gel'ding): a horse.
[3] **keening:** a wordless cry or wail for the dead.
[4] **lambent:** flickering brightly.

cream cakes and heather honey; and at the right time it was she herself that brought forth the decanter of whisky—no longer the half-empty stone jar—and the polished glasses. Shawn was proud as

sin of her. She would sit then and listen to their discussions and be forever surprised at the knowledgeable man her husband was—the way he would discuss war and politics and making of songs, the turn of speech that summed up a man or a situation. And sometimes she would put in a word or two and he listened too, and they would look to see if her smile commended them, and be a little chastened by the wisdom of that smile—the age-old smile of the matriarch from whom they were all descended. In no time at all, Matt Tobin the thresher, who used to think, "Poor old Shawn! Lucky she was

to get him," would whisper to the schoolmaster: "Herrin's alive! That fellow's luck would astonish nations."

Women, in the outside world, begin by loving their husbands; and then, if Fate is kind, they grow to admire them; and, if Fate is not unkind, may descend no lower than liking and enduring. And there is the end of lawful romance. Look now at Ellen O'Grady. She came up to the shelf of Knockanore and in her heart was only a nucleus of fear in a great emptiness, and that nucleus might grow into horror and disgust. But, glory of God, she, for reason piled on reason, presently found herself admiring Shawn Kelvin; and with or without reason, a quiet liking came to her for this quiet man who was so gentle and considerate; and then, one great heart-stirring dark o'night, she found herself fallen head and heels in love with her own husband. There is the sort of love that endures, but the road to it is a mighty chancy one.

A woman, loving her husband, may or may not be proud of him, but she will fight like a tiger if anyone, barring herself, belittles him. And there was one man that belittled Shawn Kelvin. Her brother, Big Liam O'Grady. At fair or market or chapel that dour giant deigned not to hide his contempt and dislike. Ellen knew why. He had lost a wife and farm; he had lost in herself a frugally cheap housekeeper; he had been made the butt of a sly humor; and for these mishaps, in some twisted way, he blamed Shawn. But —and there came in the contempt—the little Yankee runt, who dared say nothing about the lost Kelvin acres, would not now have the gall or guts to demand the dowry that was due. Lucky the hound to stean[1] an O'Grady to hungry Knockanore! Let him be satisfied with that luck!

[1] **stean:** bring.

One evening before a market day, Ellen spoke to her husband: "Has Big Liam paid you my dowry yet, Shawn?"

"Sure there's no hurry, girl," said Shawn.

"Have you ever asked him?"

"I have not. I am not looking for your dowry, Ellen."

"And Big Liam could never understand that." Her voice firmed. "You will ask him tomorrow."

"Very well so, *agrah,*" [1] agreed Shawn easily.

And the next day, in that quiet diffident way of his, he asked Big Liam. But Big Liam was brusque and blunt. He had no loose money and Kelvin would have to wait till he had. "Ask me again, Shawneen," he finished, his face in a mocking smile, and turning on his heel, he plowed his great shoulders through the crowded market.

His voice had been carelessly loud and people had heard. They laughed and talked amongst themselves. "Begogs! The devil's own boy. Big Liam! What a pup to sell! Stealing the land and keeping a grip on the fortune! Ay, and a dangerous fellow, mind you, the same Big Liam! He would smash little Shawn at the wind of a word. And devil the bit his Yankee sparring tricks would help him!"

A friend of Shawn's, Matt Tobin the thresher, heard that and lifted his voice: "I would like to be there the day Shawn Kelvin loses his temper."

"A bad day for poor Shawn!"

"It might then," said Matt Tobin, "but I would come from the other end of Kerry to see the badness that would be in it for someone."

Shawn had moved away with his wife, not heeding or not hearing.

"You see, Ellen?" he said in some dis-

comfort. "The times are hard on the big ranchers, and we don't need the money, anyway."

"Do you think Big Liam does?" Her voice had a cut in it. "He could buy you and all Knockanore and be only on the fringe of his hoard. You will ask him again."

"But, girl dear, I never wanted a dowry with you."

She liked him to say that, but far better would she like to win for him the respect and admiration that was his due. She must do that now at all costs. Shawn, drawing back now, would be the butt of his fellow men.

"You foolish lad! Big Liam would never understand your feelings, with money at stake." She smiled and a pang went through Shawn's breast. For the smile was the smile of an O'Grady, and he could not be sure whether the contempt in it was for himself or for her brother.

Shawn asked Big Liam again, unhappy in his asking, but also dimly comprehending his woman's object. And Shawn asked again a third time. The issue was become a famous one now. Men talked about it, and women too. Bets were made on it. At fair or market, if Shawn was seen approaching Big Liam, men edged closer and women edged away. Some day the big fellow would grow tired of being asked, and in one of his terrible rages half kill the little lad as he had half killed other men. A great shame! Here and there, a man advised Shawn to give up asking and put the matter in a lawyer's hands. "I couldn't do that," was Shawn's only answer. Strangely enough, none of these prudent advisers were amongst Shawn's close friends. His friends frowned and said little, but they were always about, and always amongst them was Matt Tobin.

The day at last came when Big Liam grew tired of being asked. That was the

[1] *agrah* (a·gro'): my dear.

big October cattle fair at Listowel, and he had sold twenty head of fat Polled Angus beeves at a good price. He was a hard dealer and it was late in the day before he settled at his own figure, so that the banks were closed and he was not able to make a lodgment.[1] He had, then, a great roll of bills in an inner vest pocket when he saw Shawn and Ellen coming across to where he was bargaining with Matt Tobin for a week's threshing. Besides, the day being dank, he had had a drink or two more than was good for him and the whisky had loosened his tongue and whatever he had of discretion. By the powers!—it was time and past time to deal once and for all with this little gadfly of a fellow, to show him up before the whole market. He strode to meet Shawn, and people got out of his savage way and edged in behind to lose nothing of this dangerous game.

He caught Shawn by the hunched shoulder—a rending grip—and bent down to grin in his face.

"What is it, little fellow? Don't be ashamed to ask!"

Matt Tobin was probably the only one there to notice the ease with which Shawn wrenched his shoulder free, and Matt Tobin's eyes brightened. But Shawn did nothing further and said no word. His deep-set eyes gazed steadily at the big man.

The big man showed his teeth mockingly. "Go on, you whelp! What do you want?"

"You know, O'Grady."

"I do. Listen, Shawneen!" Again he brought his handclap on the little man's shoulder. "Listen, Shawneen! If I had a dowry to give my sister, 'tis not a little shrimp like you would get her!"

His great hand gripped and he flung

Shawn backward as if he were only the image of a man filled with chaff.

Shawn went backward, but he did not fall. He gathered himself like a spring, feet under him, arms half-raised, head forward into hunched shoulder. But as quickly as the spring coiled, as quickly it slackened, and he turned away to his wife. She was there facing him, tense and keen, her face pale and set, and a gleam of the race in her eyes.

"Woman, woman!" he said in his deep voice. "Why would you and I shame ourselves like this?"

"Shawn!" she cried. "Will you let him shame you now?"

"But your own brother, Ellen—before them all?"

"And he cheating you——"

"Glory of God!" His voice was distressed. "What is his dirty money to me? Are you an O'Grady, after all?"

That stung her and she stung him back in one final effort. She placed a hand below her breast and looked *close* into his face. Her voice was low and bitter, and only he heard: "I am an O'Grady. It is a great pity that the father of this my son is a Kelvin and a coward."

The bosses [2] of Shawn Kelvin's cheekbones were like hard marble, but his voice was as soft as a dove's.

"Is that the way of it? Let us be going home then, in the name of God!"

He took her arm, but she shook his hand off; nevertheless, she walked at his side, head up, through the people that made way for them. Her brother mocked them with his great, laughing bellow.

"That fixes the pair of them!" he cried, brushed a man who laughed with him out of his way, and strode off through the fair.

There was talk then—plenty of it. "Murder, but Shawn had a narrow squeak

[1] **lodgment:** deposit.

[2] **bosses:** round protruding knobs.

that time! Did you see the way he flung him? I wager he'll give Big Liam a wide road after this. And he by way of being a boxer! That's a pound you owe me, Matt Tobin."

"I'll pay it," said Matt Tobin, and that is all he said. He stood, wide-legged, looking at the ground, his hand ruefully rubbing the back of his head and dismay and gloom on his face. His friend had failed him in the face of the people.

Shawn and Ellen went home in their tub cart and had not a single word or glance for each other on the road. And all that evening, at table or fireside, a heart-sickening silence held them in its grip. And all that night they lay side by side, still and mute. There was only one subject that possessed them and on that they dared speak no longer. They slept little. Ellen, her heart desolate, lay on her side, staring into the dark, grieving for what she had said and unable to unsay it. Shawn, on his back, contemplated things with a cold clarity. He realized that he was at the fork of life and that a finger pointed unmistakably. He must risk the very shattering of all happiness, he must do a thing so final and decisive that, once done, it could never again be questioned. Before morning he came to his decision, and it was bitter as gall. He cursed himself. "Oh, you fool! You might have known that you should never have taken an O'Grady without breaking the O'Gradys."

He got up early in the morning at his usual hour and went out, as usual, to his morning chores—rebedding and foddering the cattle, rubbing down the half-bred, helping the servant maid with the milk in the creaming pans—and, as usual, he came in to his breakfast, and ate it unhungrily and silently, which was not usual. But, thereafter he again went out to the stable, harnessed his gelding and

hitched him to the tub cart. Then he returned to the kitchen and spoke for the first time.

"Ellen, will you come with me down to see your brother?"

She hesitated, her hands thrown wide in a helpless, hopeless gesture. "Little use you going to see my brother, Shawn. 'Tis I should go and—and not come back."

"Don't blame me now or later, Ellen. It has been put on me and the thing I am going to do is the only thing to be done. Will you come?"

"Very well," she agreed tonelessly. "I will be ready in a minute."

And they went the four miles down into the vale to the big farmhouse of Moyvalla. They drove into the great square of cobbled yard and found it empty.

On one side of the square was the long, low lime-washed dwelling house; on the other, fifty yards away, the two-storied line of steadings [1] with a wide arch in the middle; and through the arch came the purr and zoom of a threshing machine. Shawn tied the half-bred to the wheel of a farm cart and, with Ellen, approached the house.

A slattern servant girl leaned over the kitchen half-door and pointed through the arch. The master was out beyond in the haggard [2]—the rickyard—and would she run across for him?

"Never mind, achara," [3] said Shawn, "I'll get him. . . . Ellen, will you go in and wait?"

"No," said Ellen, "I'll come with you." She knew her brother.

As they went through the arch, the purr and zoom grew louder and, turning

[1] **steadings:** farm buildings.

[2] **haggard** (hag'ərd) hay yard. Ricks are stacks of hay.

[3] **achara** (a·kar'a): a greeting corresponding to "Dear Sir" or "Dear Madam."

the corner, they walked into the midst of activity. A long double row of cone-pointed cornstacks stretched across the yard and, between them, Matt Tobin's portable threshing machine was busy. The smooth-flying, eight-foot driving wheel made a sleepy purr and the black driving belt ran with a sag and heave to the red-painted thresher. Up there on the platform, bare-armed men were feeding the flying drum with loosened sheaves, their hands moving in a rhythmic sway. As the toothed drum bit at the corn sheaves it made an angry snarl that changed and slowed into a satisfied zoom. The wide conveying belt was carrying the golden straw up a steep incline to where other men were building a long rick; still more men were attending to the corn shoots, shoulders bending under the weight of the sacks as they ambled across to the granary. Matt Tobin himself bent at the face of his engine, feeding the fire box with sods of hard black peat. There were not less than two score men about the place, for, as was the custom, all Big

Liam's friends and neighbors were giving him a hand with the threshing—"the day in harvest."

Big Liam came round the flank of the engine and swore. He was in his shirt sleeves, and his great forearms were covered with sandy hair.

"Look who's here!"

He was in the worst of tempers this morning. The stale dregs of yesterday's whisky were still with him, and he was in the humor that, as they say, would make a dog bite its father. He took two slow strides and halted, feet apart and head truculently forward.

"What is it this time?" he shouted. That was the un-Irish welcome he gave his sister and her husband.

Shawn and Ellen came forward steadily, and, as they came, Matt Tobin slowly throttled down his engine. Big Liam heard the change of pitch and looked angrily over his shoulder.

"What do you mean, Tobin? Get on with the work!"

"Big Liam, this is my engine, and if

you don't like it, you can leave it!" And at that he drove the throttle shut and the purr of the flywheel slowly sank.

"We will see in a minute," threatened Big Liam, and turned to the two now near at hand.

"What is it?" he growled.

"A private word with you. I won't keep you long." Shawn was calm and cold.

"You will not—on a busy morning," sneered the big man. "There is no need for private words between me and Shawn Kelvin."

"There is need," urged Shawn. "It will be best for us all if you hear what I have to say in your own house."

"Or here on my own land. Out with it! I don't care who hears!"

Shawn looked round him. Up on the thresher, up on the straw rick, men leaned idle on fork handles and looked down at him; from here and there about the stack-yard, men moved in to see, as it might be, what had caused the stoppage, but only really interested in the two brothers-in-law. He was in the midst of Clan O'Grady, for they were mostly O'Grady men—big, strong, blond men, rough, confident, proud of their breed. Matt Tobin was the only man he could call a friend. Many of the others were not unfriendly, but all had contempt in their eyes, or, what was worse, pity. Very well! Since he had to prove himself, it was fitting that he do it here amongst the O'Grady men.

Shawn brought his eyes back to Big Liam—deep, steadfast eyes that did not waver. "O'Grady," said he—and he no longer hid his contempt—"you set a great store by money."

"No harm in that. You do it yourself, Shawneen."

"Take it so! I will play that game with you, as long as you like. You would bargain your sister and cheat; I will sell my soul. Listen, you big brute! You owe me two hundred pounds. Will you pay it?" There was an iron quality in his voice that was somehow awesome. The big man, about to start forward overbearingly, restrained himself to a brutal playfulness.

"I will pay it when I am ready."

"Today."

"No; nor tomorrow."

"Right. If you break your bargain, I break mine."

"What's that?" shouted Big Liam.

"If you keep your two hundred pounds, you keep your sister."

"What is it?" shouted Big Liam again, his voice breaking in astonishment. "What is that you say?"

"You heard me. Here is your sister Ellen! Keep her!"

He was completely astounded out of his truculence. "You can't do that!"

"It is done," said Shawn.

Ellen O'Grady had been quiet as a statue at Shawn's side, but now, slow like doom, she faced him. She leaned forward and looked into his eyes and saw the pain behind the strength.

"To the mother of your son, Shawn Kelvin?" she whispered that gently to him.

His voice came cold as a stone out of a stone face: "In the face of God. Let Him judge me."

"I know—I know!" That was all she said, and walked quietly across to where Matt Tobin stood at the face of his engine.

Matt Tobin placed a hand on her arm.

"Give him time, *acolleen*," [1] he whispered urgently. "Give him his own time. He's slow but he's deadly as a tiger when he moves."

Big Liam was no fool. He knew exactly how far he could go. There was no use, at this juncture, in crushing the runt under a great fist. There was some force in the

[1] *acolleen* (ă·kol'lēn): a term of affection. In Ireland girls are often called colleens.

little fellow that defied dragooning.[1] Whatever people might think of Kelvin, public opinion would be dead against himself. Worse, his inward vision saw eyes leering in derision, mouths open in laughter. The scandal on his name would not be bounded by the four seas of Erin.[2] He must change his stance while he had time. These thoughts passed through his mind while he thudded the ground three times with ironshod heel. Now he threw up his head and bellowed his laugh.

"You fool! I was only making fun of you. What are your dirty few pounds to the likes of me? Stay where you are."

He turned, strode furiously away, and disappeared through the arch.

Shawn Kelvin was left alone in that wide ring of men. The hands had come down off the ricks and thresher to see closer. Now they moved back and aside, looked at one another, lifted eyebrows, looked at Shawn Kelvin, frowned, and shook their heads. They knew Big Liam. They knew that, yielding up the money, his savagery would break out into something little short of killing. They waited, most of them, to prevent that savagery going too far.

Shawn Kelvin did not look at anyone. He stood still as a rock, his hands deep in his pockets, one shoulder hunched forward, his eyes on the ground, and his face strangely calm. He seemed the least perturbed man there. Matt Tobin held Ellen's arm in a steadying grip and whispered in her ear: "God is good, I tell you."

Big Liam was back in two minutes. He strode straight to Shawn and halted within a pace of him.

"Look, Shawneen!" In his raised hand was a crumpled bundle of greasy bank notes. "Here is your money. Take it, and

[1] **dragooning**: compelling someone to submit by force.
[2] **Erin**: Ireland.

then see what will happen to you. Take it!" He thrust it into Shawn's hand. "Count it. Make sure you have it all—and then I will kick you out of this haggard—and look"—he thrust forward a hairy fist—"if ever I see your face again, I will drive that through it. Count it, you spawn!"

Shawn did not count it. Instead he crumpled it into a ball in his strong fingers. Then he turned on his heel and walked, with surprising slowness, to the face of the engine. He gestured with one hand to Matt Tobin, but it was Ellen, quick as a flash, who obeyed the gesture. Though the hot bar scorched her hand, she jerked open the door of the fire box and the leaping peat flames whispered out at her. And forthwith, Shawn Kelvin, with one easy sweep, threw the crumpled ball of notes into the heart of the flame. The whisper lifted one tone and one scrap of burned paper floated out of the funnel top. That was all the fuss the fire made of its work.

But there was fuss enough outside.

Big Liam O'Grady gave one mighty shout. No, it was more an anguished scream than a shout:

"My money! My good money!"

He gave two furious bounds forward,

his great arms raised to crush and kill. But his hands never touched the small man.

"You dumb ox!" said Shawn Kelvin between his teeth. That strong, hunched shoulder moved a little, but no one there could follow the terrific drive of that hooked right arm. The smack of bone on bone was sharp as whip crack, and Big Liam stopped dead, went back on his heel, swayed a moment, and staggered back three paces.

"Now and forever! Man of the Kelvins!" roared Matt Tobin.

But Big Liam was a man of iron. That blow should have laid him out on his back—blows like it had tied men to the ground for the full count. But Big Liam only shook his head, grunted like a boar, and drove in at the little man. And the little man, instead of circling away, drove in at him, compact of power.

The men of the O'Gradys saw then an exhibition that they had not knowledge enough to appreciate fully. Thousands had paid as much as ten dollars each to see the great Tiger Kelvin in action, his footwork, his timing, his hitting; and never was his action more devastating than now. He was a thunderbolt on two feet and the big man a glutton.

Big Liam never touched Shawn with clenched fist. He did not know how. Shawn, actually forty pounds lighter, drove him by sheer hitting across the yard.

Men for the first time saw a two-hundred-pound man knocked clean off his feet by a body blow. They saw for the first time the deadly restraint and explosion of skill.

Shawn set out to demolish his enemy in the briefest space of time, and it took him five minutes to do it. Five, six, eight times he knocked the big man down, and the big man came again, staggering, slavering, raving, vainly trying to rend and smash. But at last he stood swaying and clawing helplessly, and Shawn finished him with his terrible double hit—left below the breastbone and right under the jaw.

Big Liam lifted on his toes and fell flat on his back. He did not even kick as he lay.

Shawn did not waste a glance at the fallen giant. He swung full circle on the O'Grady men and his voice of iron challenged them:

"I am Shawn Kelvin, of Knockanore Hill. Is there an O'Grady amongst you thinks himself a better man? Come then."

His face was deep-carved stone, his great chest lifted, the air whistled through his nostrils; his deep-set flashing eyes dared them.

No man came.

He swung around then and walked straight to his wife. He halted before her.

His face was still of stone, but his voice quivered and had in it all the dramatic force of the Celt: [1]

"Mother of my son, will you come home with me?"

She lifted to the appeal, voice and eye:

"Is it so you ask me, Shawn Kelvin?"

His face of stone quivered at last, "As my wife only—Ellen Kelvin!"

"Very well, heart's treasure." She caught his arm in both of hers. "Let us be going home."

"In the name of God," he finished for her.

And she went with him, proud as the morning, out of that place. But a woman, she would have the last word.

"Mother of God!" she cried. "The trouble I had to make a man of him!"

"God Almighty did that for him before you were born," said Matt Tobin softly.

[1] **Celt** (selt): that is, the Celtic-speaking peoples, of whom the modern Irish, Scots, Welsh, and Bretons are the best known.

1. It is obvious early in the story that Shawn Kelvin and Liam O'Grady have different values. What does Shawn seem to value most in life? On what does Big Liam set the highest value?

2. What was ironic about Big Liam's getting Ellen married? How did this reversal add to Big Liam's dislike of Shawn?

3. How did Ellen change during the first months of her marriage? Do you think she would have forced Shawn into conflict with Big Liam if she had not fallen in love with her husband? Explain. Why did she force the issue of the dowry?

4. Why did Shawn avoid confronting Big Liam about his father's land and Ellen's dowry? What moved him to change his mind? In his place, would you have made the same decision?

5. By taking his sister back, Big Liam would have regained a good housekeeper and have rid himself of any debt to Shawn. Why wasn't Big Liam glad to take Ellen back, since his own marriage plans had failed?

6. Ellen's quickness in opening the firebox door paved the way for the happy ending. What does this action reveal about Ellen's feeling for Shawn? What does it reveal about her attitude toward money?

7. Why was the burning of his money an unbearable insult to Big Liam?

8. Will Shawn be respected by the community from now on? Which do you think ranks higher with his group—his courage in insisting on his rights or his prowess as a fighter? What in the story makes you think so?

LANGUAGE AND VOCABULARY

In this story Maurice Walsh has to make us feel and understand some powerful and complicated feelings that we may or may not have experienced ourselves. In doing this, he wastes no words and makes use of a great many figures of speech. As a result, he can say a great deal about a character in a few simple words. Point out the figures of speech in each of the following. What does each tell you about the character or characters involved?

"he returned to his native Kerry, his blitheness sobered and his youth dried to the core . . ."

"Big Liam O'Grady was a great rawboned, sandy-haired man, with the strength of an ox and a heart no bigger than a sour apple."

"Shawn Kelvin daring to cast sheep's eyes at an O'Grady! The undersized chicken heart . . . !"

"Go on, you whelp, what do you want?" (Big Liam)

The lesson here is clear: in even the shortest of stories, simple words used with care can express a great deal. No one needs to be "fancy" to write well.

FOR COMPOSITION

"Fate had the thought and the dream in her loom for him." Do you agree that Fate weaves the pattern of human destiny? In a paragraph or two, discuss the question of whether Fate, or powers beyond human control, make people what they are, or whether they "make their own breaks" and create their own destiny. Support your argument with an illustration drawn from your own experience or reading.

ABOUT THE AUTHOR

Maurice Walsh (1879–1964) described himself as "the son and the grandson and the great-great-grandson of farmers and rebels." He was born in Kerry, the county in southwestern Ireland which provides the setting for "The Quiet Man." As an employee of the Customs Excise Service, he traveled in Ireland, Scotland, Wales, and England and married a red-haired Scottish woman. His earliest efforts at writing, he said, included stories about "Australian bush-ranging, and Klondike gold-digging, and the Boer War, and other subjects with which I was closely acquainted at a distance." In 1934 he resigned as an excise officer to devote full time to writing. His stories and novels are full of romance and high adventure. "The Quiet Man" was made into one of the most successful movies of 1952.

The Storyteller

SAKI

It was a hot afternoon, and the railway carriage was correspondingly sultry, and the next stop was at Templecombe, nearly an hour ahead. The occupants of the carriage were a small girl, and a smaller girl, and a small boy. An aunt belonging to the children occupied one corner seat, and the further corner seat on the opposite side was occupied by a bachelor who was a stranger to their party, but the small girls and the small boy emphatically occupied the compartment. Both the aunt and the children were conversational in a limited, persistent way, reminding one of the attentions of a housefly that refused to be discouraged. Most of the aunt's remarks seemed to begin with "Don't," and nearly all of the children's remarks began with "Why?" The bachelor said nothing out loud.

"Don't, Cyril, don't," exclaimed the aunt, as the small boy began smacking the cushions of the seat, producing a cloud of dust at each blow.

"Come and look out of the window," she added.

The child moved reluctantly to the window. "Why are those sheep being driven out of that field?" he asked.

"I expect they are being driven to another field where there is more grass," said the aunt weakly.

"But there is lots of grass in that field," protested the boy; "there's nothing else but grass there. Aunt, there's lots of grass in that field."

"Perhaps the grass in the other field is better," suggested the aunt fatuously.

"Why is it better?" came the swift, inevitable question.

"Oh, look at those cows!" exclaimed the aunt. Nearly every field along the line had contained cows or bullocks, but she spoke as though she were drawing attention to a rarity.

"Why is the grass in the other field better?" persisted Cyril.

The frown on the bachelor's face was deepening to a scowl. He was a hard, unsympathetic man, the aunt decided in her mind. She was utterly unable to come to any satisfactory decision about the grass in the other field.

The smaller girl created a diversion by beginning to recite "On the Road to Mandalay." She only knew the first line, but she put her limited knowledge to the fullest possible use. She repeated the line over and over again in a dreamy but resolute and very audible voice; it seemed to the bachelor as though someone had had a bet with her that she could not repeat the line aloud two thousand times without stopping. Whoever it was who had made the wager was likely to lose his bet.

"Come over here and listen to a story," said the aunt, when the bachelor had looked twice at her and once at the communication cord.[1]

The children moved listlessly toward the aunt's end of the carriage. Evidently her reputation as a storyteller did not rank high in their estimation.

In a low, confidential voice, interrupted at frequent intervals by loud, petulant

"The Storyteller" from *The Complete Short Stories of Saki* (H. H. Munro). Reprinted by permission of The Viking Press, Inc. and The Bodley Head.

[1] **communication cord:** a pull on this cord summons the conductor.

questions from her listeners, she began an unenterprising and deplorably uninteresting story about a little girl who was good and made friends with everyone on account of her goodness and was finally saved from a mad bull by a number of rescuers who admired her moral character.

"Wouldn't they have saved her if she hadn't been good?" demanded the bigger of the small girls. It was exactly the question that the bachelor had wanted to ask.

"Well, yes," admitted the aunt lamely, "but I don't think they would have run quite so fast to her help if they had not liked her so much."

"It's the stupidest story I've ever heard," said the bigger of the small girls, with immense conviction.

"I didn't listen after the first bit, it was so stupid," said Cyril.

The smaller girl made no actual comment on the story, but she had long ago recommenced a murmured repetition of her favorite line.

"You don't seem to be a success as a storyteller," said the bachelor suddenly from his corner.

The aunt bristled in instant defense at this unexpected attack.

"It's a very difficult thing to tell stories that children can both understand and appreciate," she said stiffly.

"I don't agree with you," said the bachelor.

"Perhaps *you* would like to tell them a story," was the aunt's retort.

"Tell us a story," demanded the bigger of the small girls.

"Once upon a time," began the bachelor, "there was a little girl called Bertha, who was extraordinarily good."

The children's momentarily aroused interest began at once to flicker; all stories seemed dreadfully alike, no matter who told them.

"She did all that she was told, she was always truthful, she kept her clothes clean, ate milk puddings as though they were jam tarts, learned her lessons perfectly, and was polite in her manners."

"Was she pretty?" asked the bigger of the small girls.

"Not as pretty as any of you," said the bachelor, "but she was horribly good."

There was a wave of reaction in favor of the story; the word horrible in connection with goodness was a novelty that commended itself. It seemed to introduce a ring of truth that was absent from the aunt's tales of infant life.

"She was so good," continued the bachelor, "that she won several medals for goodness, which she always wore, pinned on to her dress. There was a medal for obedience, another medal for punctuality, and a third for good behavior. They were large metal medals and they clicked against one another as she walked. No other child in the town where she lived had as many as three medals, so everybody knew that she must be an extragood child."

"Horribly good," quoted Cyril.

"Everybody talked about her goodness, and the Prince of the country got to hear about it, and he said that as she was so very good she might be allowed once a week to walk in his park, which was just outside the town. It was a beautiful park, and no children were ever allowed in it, so it was a great honor for Bertha to be allowed to go there."

"Were there any sheep in the park?" demanded Cyril.

"No," said the bachelor, "there were no sheep."

"Why weren't there any sheep?" came the inevitable question arising out of that answer.

The aunt permitted herself a smile, which might almost have been described as a grin.

"There were no sheep in the park," said the bachelor, "because the Prince's mother had once had a dream that her son would either be killed by a sheep or else by a clock falling on him. For that reason the Prince never kept a sheep in his park or a clock in his palace."

The aunt suppressed a gasp of admiration.

"Was the Prince killed by a sheep or by a clock?" asked Cyril.

"He is still alive, so we can't tell whether the dream will come true" said the bachelor unconcernedly; "anyway, there were no sheep in the park, but there were lots of little pigs running all over the place."

"What color were they?"

"Black with white faces, white with black spots, black all over, gray with white patches, and some were white all over."

The storyteller paused to let a full idea of the park's treasures sink into the children's imaginations; then he resumed:

"Bertha was rather sorry to find that there were no flowers in the park. She had promised her aunts, with tears in her eyes, that she would not pick any of the kind Prince's flowers, and she had meant to keep her promise, so of course it made her feel silly to find that there were no flowers to pick."

"Why weren't there any flowers?"

"Because the pigs had eaten them all," said the bachelor promptly. "The gardeners had told the Prince that you couldn't have pigs and flowers, so he decided to have pigs and no flowers."

There was a murmur of approval at the excellence of the Prince's decision; so many people would have decided the other way.

"There were lots of other delightful things in the park. There were ponds with gold and blue and green fish in them, and trees with beautiful parrots that said clever things at a moment's notice, and humming birds that hummed all the popular tunes of the day. Bertha walked up and down and enjoyed herself immensely and thought to herself: 'If I were not so extraordinarily good I should not have been allowed to come into this beautiful park and enjoy all that there is to be seen in it,' and her three medals clinked against one

another as she walked and helped to remind her how very good she really was. Just then an enormous wolf came prowling into the park to see if it could catch a fat little pig for its supper."

"What color was it?" asked the children, amid an immediate quickening of interest.

"Mud-color all over, with a black tongue and pale gray eyes that gleamed with unspeakable ferocity. The first thing that it saw in the park was Bertha; her pinafore was so spotlessly white and clean that it could be seen from a great distance. Bertha saw the wolf and saw that it was stealing toward her, and she began to wish that she had never been allowed to come into the park. She ran as hard as she could, and the wolf came after her with huge leaps and bounds. She managed to reach a shrubbery of myrtle bushes and she hid herself in one of the thickest of the bushes. The wolf came sniffing among the branches, its black tongue lolling out of its mouth and its pale gray eyes glaring with rage. Bertha was terribly frightened and thought to herself: 'If I had not been so extraordinarily good I should have been safe in the town at this moment.' However, the scent of the myrtle was so strong that the wolf could not sniff out where Bertha was hiding, and the bushes were so thick that he might have hunted about in them for a long time without catching sight of her, so he thought he might as well go off and catch a little pig instead. Bertha was trembling very much at having the wolf prowling and sniffing so near her, and as she trembled the medal for obedience clinked against the medals for good conduct and punctuality. The wolf was just moving away when he heard the sound of the medals clinking and stopped to listen; they clinked again in a bush quite near

him. He dashed into the bush, his pale gray eyes gleaming with ferocity and triumph and dragged Bertha out and devoured her to the last morsel. All that was left of her were her shoes, bits of clothing, and the three medals for goodness."

"Were any of the little pigs killed?"

"No, they all escaped."

"The story began badly," said the smaller of the small girls, "but it had a beautiful ending."

"It is the most beautiful story that I ever heard," said the bigger of the small girls, with immense decision.

"It is the *only* beautiful story I have ever heard," said Cyril.

A dissentient [1] opinion came from the aunt.

"A most improper story to tell to young children! You have undermined the effect of years of careful teaching."

"At any rate," said the bachelor, collecting his belongings preparatory to leaving the carriage, "I kept them quiet for ten minutes, which was more than you were able to do."

"Unhappy woman!" he observed to himself as he walked down the platform of Templecombe station; "for the next six months or so those children will assail her in public with demands for an improper story!"

[1] **dissentient** (di·sen′shənt): dissenting.

FOR STUDY AND DISCUSSION

1. How are the aunt's and the bachelor's stories alike? How are they different?

2. What is the theme of the aunt's story? of the bachelor's? Which rings truer? Why? Which could be called a "moral"?

3. The bachelor's description of his heroine as "horribly good" seems to the children to introduce "a ring of truth" absent from their aunt's stories. Why? What, to them, is "horrible" about the kind of goodness he describes?

4. What does "being good" mean to the aunt? Is she good by her own standards? Would you want the children to grow up to be like her?

5. Were you glad or sorry when the little girl in the bachelor's story got eaten by the wolf? Why? What was ironic about the way she met her end?

6. Why is the bachelor more successful at answering the children's questions than the aunt? What does he use in telling his story that the aunt does not? Why is the bachelor's story more successful with the children than their aunt's?

7. The aunt accuses the bachelor of having "undermined the effect of years of careful teaching." Do you agree or disagree? What effect would you expect the bachelor's story to have on the children?

8. Do the above questions perhaps take this story too seriously? Do you think Saki wrote it primarily to make a point about children's education or to entertain his readers? What would be the effect of making the storyteller the children's father instead of a bachelor?

LANGUAGE AND VOCABULARY

When the storyteller says that Bertha was "horribly good," he gets the immediate attention of his listeners. But this is only one striking example of Saki's skillful use of adverbs in this story. What does he accomplish with each of the following words? (Look up any whose meaning you are not sure of.) How would the sentences in which they occur change if these words had been omitted?

emphatically (page 141)
reluctantly (page 141)
weakly (page 141)
fatuously (page 141)
utterly (page 141)
listlessly (page 141)
deplorably (page 142)
lamely (page 142)
stiffly (page 142)
extraordinarily (page 142)
dreadfully (page 142)

horribly (page 142)
unconcernedly (page 143)
promptly (page 143)
immensely (page 143)
spotlessly (page 144)

Much writing contains unnecessary adverbs. For instance, *"Go to bed," mother demanded firmly.* Why is *firmly* superfluous in this sentence? As Saki demonstrates, putting the right adverb in the right place makes for effective writing. How many different shades of meaning can you create by adding different adverbs to the verb in this sentence: "No," he said _____"? Make up some additional sentences whose meaning could be similarly changed by the use of various adverbs.

FOR COMPOSITION

In a single sentence, state your impression of either the aunt or the bachelor in "The Storyteller." Use this sentence as the topic sentence of a descriptive paragraph, developing your topic sentence with facts or examples from the story.

ABOUT THE AUTHOR

H. H. Munro (1870–1916) was born in Burma, the son of a Scottish inspector general of Burma police. His mother died before he was two, and he was sent to England and brought up there, with rigid strictness, by two aunts. In his early twenties, after a year's service with the Burma police, Munro went to London to write, and worked on various newspapers while he wrote a history of Russia, two novels, and several books of short stories. He traveled widely, at various times visiting Germany, France, Austria, Switzerland, Russia, and the Balkans. At the beginning of World War I he enlisted as a private, was sent to France as a corporal, and was killed in action. He is best known as a writer of very brief short stories, which combine, in various proportions, satire, humor, and sometimes horror. His pen name, Saki, means "winebearer," and was taken from "The Rubáiyát of Omar Khayyám."

A Slander

ANTON CHEKHOV

Sᴇʀɢᴇɪ Kᴀᴘɪᴛᴏɴɪᴄʜ Aʜɪɴᴇᴇᴠ, the writing master, was marrying his daughter to the teacher of history and geography. The wedding festivities were going off most successfully. In the drawing room there was singing, playing, and dancing. Waiters hired from the club were flitting distractedly about the rooms, dressed in black swallowtails [1] and dirty white ties. There was a continual hubub and din of conversation. Sitting side by side on the sofa, the teacher of mathematics, the French teacher, and the junior assessor of taxes were talking hurriedly and interrupting one another as they described to the guests cases of persons being buried alive, and gave their opinions on spiritualism. [2] None of them believed in spiritualism, but all admitted that there were many things in this world which would always be beyond the mind of man. In the next room the literature master was explaining to the visitors the cases in which a sentry has the right to fire on passers-by. The subjects, as you perceive, were alarming, but very agreeable. Persons whose social position precluded them from entering were looking in at the windows from the yard.

[1] **swallowtails:** formal dress coats with tails.
[2] **spiritualism:** the philosophical belief that all that exists is spirit.

"A Slander" by Anton Chekhov from *Horse Stealers and Other Stories* translated by Constance Garnett, copyright 1921 by Macmillan Publishing Co., Inc.; renewed 1949 by David Garnett. Reprinted by permission of the publishers, David Garnett and Chatto & Windus Ltd.

Just at midnight the master of the house went into the kitchen to see whether everything was ready for supper. The kitchen from floor to ceiling was filled with fumes composed of goose, duck, and many other odors. On two tables the accessories, the drinks and light refreshments, were set out in artistic disorder. The cook, Marfa, a red-faced woman whose figure was like a barrel with a belt around it, was bustling about the tables.

"Show me the sturgeon, [3] Marfa," said Ahineev, rubbing his hands and licking his lips. "What a perfume! I could eat up the whole kitchen. Come, show me the sturgeon."

Marfa went up to one of the benches and cautiously lifted a piece of greasy newspaper. Under the paper on an immense dish there reposed a huge sturgeon, masked in jelly and decorated with capers, olives, and carrots. Ahineev gazed at the sturgeon and gasped. His face beamed, he turned his eyes up. He bent down and with his lips emitted the sound of an ungreased wheel. After standing a moment he snapped his fingers with delight and once more smacked his lips.

"Ah-ah! the sound of a passionate kiss. . . . Who is it you're kissing out there, little Marfa?" came a voice from the next room, and in the doorway there appeared the cropped head of the assistant usher, [4] Vankin. "Who is it? A-a-h! . . . Delighted to meet you! Sergei Kapitonich! You're a fine grandfather, I must say!"

"I'm not kissing," said Ahineev in confusion. "Who told you so, you fool? I was only . . . I smacked my lips . . . in reference to . . . as an indication of . . . pleasure . . . at the sight of the fish."

"Tell that to the marines!" The intrusive face vanished, wearing a broad grin. Ahineev flushed.

[3] **sturgeon** (stûr′jən): a large fish.
[4] **usher:** an assistant teacher.

"Hang it!" he thought, "the beast will go now and talk scandal. He'll disgrace me to all the town, the brute."

Ahineev went timidly into the drawing room and looked stealthily round for Vankin. Vankin was standing by the piano, and, bending down with a jaunty air, was whispering something to the inspector's sister-in-law, who was laughing.

"Talking about me!" thought Ahineev. "About me, blast him! And she believes it . . . believes it! She laughs! Mercy on us! No, I can't let it pass . . . I can't. I must do something to prevent his being believed. . . . I'll speak to them all, and he'll be shown up for a fool and a gossip."

Ahineev scratched his head, and still overcome with embarrassment, went up to the French teacher.

"I've just been in the kitchen to see after the supper," he said to the Frenchman. "I know you are fond of fish, and I've a sturgeon, my dear fellow, beyond everything! A yard and a half long! Ha, ha, ha! And, by the way . . . I was just forgetting. . . . In the kitchen just now, with that sturgeon . . . quite a little story! I went into the kitchen just now and wanted to look at the supper dishes. I looked at the sturgeon and I smacked my lips with relish . . . at the piquancy of it. And at the very moment that fool Vankin came in and said: . . . 'Ha, ha, ha! . . . So you're kissing here!' Kissing Marfa, the cook! What a thing to imagine, silly fool! The woman is a perfect fright, like all the beasts put together, and he talks about kissing! Queer fish!"

"Who's a queer fish?" asked the mathematics teacher, coming up.

"Why he, over there—Vankin! I went into the kitchen . . ."

And he told the story of Vankin. ". . . He amused me, queer fish! I'd rather kiss a dog than Marfa, if you ask me," added Ahineev. He looked round and saw behind him the junior assessor of taxes.

"We were talking of Vankin," he said. "Queer fish, he is! He went into the kitchen, saw me beside Marfa, and began inventing all sorts of silly stories. 'Why are you kissing?' he says. He must have had a drop too much. 'And I'd rather kiss a turkeycock than Marfa,' I said, 'And I've a wife of my own, you fool,' said I. He did amuse me!"

"Who amused you?" asked the priest who taught Scripture in the school, going up to Ahineev.

"Vankin. I was standing in the kitchen, you know, looking at the sturgeon. . . ."

And so on. Within half an hour or so all the guests knew the incident of the sturgeon and Vankin.

"Let him tell away now!" thought Ahineev, rubbing his hands. "Let him! He'll begin telling his story and they'll say to him at once, 'Enough of your improbable nonsense, you fool, we know all about it!'"

And Ahineev was so relieved that in his joy he drank four glasses too many. After escorting the young people to their room, he went to bed and slept like an innocent babe, and next day he thought no more of the incident with the sturgeon. But, alas! man proposes, but God disposes. An evil tongue did its evil work, and Ahineev's strategy was of no avail. Just a week later—to be precise, on Wednesday after the third lesson—when Ahineev was standing in the middle of the teacher's room, holding forth on the vicious propensities of a boy called Visekin, the headmaster went up to him and drew him aside:

"Look here, Sergei Kapitonich," said the headmaster, "you must excuse me. . . . It's not my business; but all the same I must make you realize. . . . It's my duty. You see, there are rumors that you are romancing with that . . . cook. . . . It's nothing to do with me, but . . . flirt with her, kiss her . . . as you please, but don't let it be so public, please. I entreat you! Don't forget that you're a schoolmaster."

Ahineev turned cold and faint. He went home like a man stung by a whole swarm of bees, like a man scalded with boiling water. As he walked home, it seemed to him that the whole town was looking at him as though he were smeared with pitch. At home fresh trouble awaited him.

"Why aren't you gobbling up your food as usual?" his wife asked him at

dinner. "What are you so pensive about? Brooding over your amours?[1] Pining for your Marfa? I know all about it, Mohammedan![2] Kind friends have opened my eyes! O-o-o! . . . you savage!"

And she slapped him in the face. He got up from the table, not feeling the earth under his feet, and without his hat or coat, made his way to Vankin. He found him at home.

"You scoundrel!" he addressed him. "Why have you covered me with mud before all the town? Why did you set this slander going about me?"

"What slander? What are you talking about?"

"Who was it gossiped of my kissing Marfa? Wasn't it you? Tell me that. Wasn't it you, you brigand?"

Vankin blinked and twitched in every fiber of his battered countenance, raised his eyes to the icon[3] and articulated,

[1] amours (ə·mo͞orz′): romances.

[2] **Mohammedan:** Under the laws of the Mohammedan religion, a man can have more than one wife.

[3] **icon** (ī′kon): a sacred picture or image.

"God blast me! Strike me blind and lay me out, if I said a single word about you! May I be left without house and home, may I be stricken with worse than cholera!" [1]

Vankin's sincerity did not admit of doubt. It was evidently not he who was the author of the slander.

"But who, then, who?" Ahineev wondered, going over all his acquaintances in his mind and beating himself on the breast. "Who, then?"

[1] **cholera** (kol′ər·ə): a dreaded disease, usually fatal.

FOR STUDY AND DISCUSSION

1. What is the answer to Ahineev's final question, "Who, then?"

2. What had just happened when Vankin came into the kitchen? Why do you think he said what he did to Ahineev?

3. Ahineev vows to show Vankin up "for a fool and a gossip." Whom does he really show up as "a fool and a gossip"? What is ironic about this outcome?

4. Since Ahineev is never described directly, we must infer his character from what he says and does. What do we learn about him from his quick assumption that Vankin is whispering about him? from his feeling, after he has been reprimanded, that the whole town was looking at him?

5. What do we learn about Ahineev from the way he speaks of Marfa?

6. List, in order, all the errors of judgment, foolish actions, and moments of bewilderment that point up Ahineev's foolishness. Does he learn anything from any of them?

7. Why do the wedding guests not believe Ahineev's denials? Under the circumstances, would you? Why or why not?

8. What ironic reversal of intention is central to this story? In addition to this irony of situation, Ahineev's final question is a perfect example of dramatic irony. Why?

9. "A Slander" is about a man who, falsely accused, seeks to prove his innocence, but succeeds only in convincing everyone that he is guilty. State the theme of the story in a sentence that begins, "A man who tries too hard to . . ."

LANGUAGE AND VOCABULARY

"A Slander" contains a number of disparaging or belittling epithets. What does each of the following epithets mean? Where they occur, how do they add to the humor of the story? What do they tell about the person who uses them?

Little Marfa	Mohammedan
You fool	You savage
The beast	You scoundrel
Silly fool	You brigand
Queer fish	

FOR COMPOSITION

Life is full of ironic situations and happenings. Try to recall and describe a personal experience that was especially ironic. (Such a story is usually most effective if the teller of the story finds himself to be the victim of the irony.)

ABOUT THE AUTHOR

Anton Chekhov (1860–1904), the grandson of a serf and the son of a shopkeeper, was born and grew up in southwestern Russia. While a medical student at the University of Moscow, he supported himself, his mother, a sister, and two younger brothers by writing humorous stories for the comic weeklies. After receiving his degree at the age of twenty-four he practiced medicine only briefly, devoting himself entirely, after the publication of his first book, to a literary career. One of the most important modern dramatists and a master of the modern short story, he is known for plays such as *The Cherry Orchard, The Three Sisters,* and *The Seagull* and for stories too numerous to name. Though Chekhov was a distinguished humorist, his most characteristic work is marked by a strain of melancholy, and he is famous for his studies of frustration and disappointment.

The Piece of Yarn

GUY DE MAUPASSANT

On all the roads around Goderville, farmers and their wives were streaming into town, for this was market day. The men strode calmly along, their bodies hunching forward with each movement of their long, crooked legs, misshapen from hard labors—from leaning on the plow, which simultaneously elevated the left shoulder and threw the back out of line; from swinging the scythe, in which the need for a solid stance bowed the legs at the knees; from all the slow and laborious tasks of work in the field. Their blue smocks, starched until they glistened like varnish, embroidered at neck·and wrist with a small design in white thread, puffed out around their bony chests like balloons about to take flight with a head, two arms, and two feet attached.

The men tugged after them, at the end of a rope, a cow or a calf. And their wives, behind the animal, tried to hasten it on by flicking its rump with a small branch still bearing leaves. In the crook of their arms they carried large covered baskets from which heads of chickens and ducks protruded here and there. They walked with shorter and more lively steps than their husbands; their figures lean, erect, and wrapped in a tight-fitting shawl pinned together over their flat chests; their hair swathed in a piece of white linen and topped off by a tight brimless cap.

Now and then a farm wagon would overtake them, drawn at a brisk trot by a small sturdy horse, grotesquely jouncing two men seated side by side, and a woman in the back clinging to the frame to cushion the rough jolts.

What a milling around, what a jostling mob of people and animals there was on Goderville square! Above the surface of the assemblage protruded the horns of cattle, the high-crowned, long-furred hats of wealthy farmers, and the headdresses of their ladies. The bawling, shrill, piercing voices raised a continuous din, above which echoed an occasional hearty laugh from the robust lungs of a merry-making farmhand or the long lowing of a cow tied to a house wall.

Everything smelled of the stable, milk and manure, hay and sweat, and gave off that pungent, sour odor of man and beast so characteristic of those who work in the fields.

Maître [1] Hauchecorne, of Bréauté, had just reached Goderville and was making his way toward the square when he glimpsed a piece of yarn on the ground. Maître Hauchecorne, thrifty like the true Norman he was, thought it worthwhile to pick up anything that could be useful; and he stooped down painfully, for he suffered from rheumatism. He plucked up the thin piece of yarn and was just starting to wind it up carefully when he caught sight of Maître Malandain, the harness maker, eyeing him from his doorstep. They had once disagreed over the price of a harness, and since both had a tendency to hold grudges, they had remained on bad terms with each other. Maître Hauchecorne felt a bit humiliated

Translated by Newbury LeB. Morse from the original French of Maupassant's story, "La Ficelle."

[1] **Maître:** In the Normandy of Maupassant's time, a person who owned a bit of property was addressed as "Maître" out of courtesy.

at having been seen by his enemy scrabbling in the dirt for a bit of yarn. He quickly thrust his find under his smock, then into his trousers pocket; afterwards he pretended to search the ground for something he had lost, and at last he went off toward the marketplace with his head bent forward and his body doubled over by his aches and pains.

He lost himself at once in the shrill and slow-moving crowd, keyed up by long-drawn-out bargaining. The farmers would run their hands over the cows, go away, come back, undecided, always in fear of being taken in, never daring to commit themselves, slyly watching the seller's eye, endlessly hoping to discover the deception in the man and the defect in the beast.

The women, after placing their baskets at their feet, had drawn out their poultry, which sprawled on the ground, their feet tied together, with fear-glazed eyes and scarlet combs.

Standing rigidly, their faces giving away nothing, the women would listen to offers and hold to their prices; or else,

on impulse deciding to accept an offer, would shout after a customer who was slowly moving off: "All right, Maît' Anthime. It's yours."

Then, little by little, the square emptied, and as the bells rang the noonday angelus, those who lived too far away scattered to the inns.

At Jourdain's, the large hall was filled with diners just as the great courtyard was filled with vehicles of all descriptions: two-wheeled carts, buggies, farm wagons, carriages, nameless carryalls, yellow with mud, battered, patched together, with shafts raised heavenward like two arms or with front down and rear pointing upward.

Next to the seated diners the immense fireplace, flaming brightly, cast a lively warmth on the backs of the right-hand row. Three spits were turning, loaded with chickens, pigeons, and legs of mutton, and a delectable aroma of roasting meat and of juices trickling over the heat-browned skin wafted from the hearth, making hearts gay and mouths drool.

All the carriage aristocracy was eating

here at the table of Maît' Jourdain, innkeeper and horsedealer, a sly man who had a knack for making money.

The dishes were passed and emptied, along with jugs of yellow cider. Each man told of his dealings, what he had bought and sold. They asked one another about how they thought the crops would do. The weather was fine for hay, but a bit damp for grain.

All of a sudden the rolling beat of a drum echoed in the courtyard before the inn. At once all the diners, except a few indifferent ones, leaped to their feet, and

with mouths still full and napkins in hand, rushed to the door and windows.

When the drum roll ended, the town crier announced in a jerky voice, breaking his sentences in the wrong places:

"It is made known to the inhabitants of Goderville, and in general to all—the persons attending the market fair, that there was lost this morning, on the Beuzeville road, between—nine and ten o'clock, a black leather pocketbook containing five hundred francs [1] and some business documents. It is requested that the finder return it—to the town hall, at once, or to Maître Fortuné Houlbrèque, of Manneville. There will be a reward of twenty francs."

The man then went off. Once more in the distance the beat of the drum rolled out hollowly, followed by the receding voice of the crier.

Now everyone began to discuss the announcement, weighing the chance Maître Houlbrèque had of getting his pocketbook back.

And the meal came to an end.

They were finishing coffee when the police sergeant appeared in the doorway.

He asked: "Is Maître Hauchecorne, of Bréauté, here?"

Maître Hauchecorne, sitting at the far end of the table, spoke up: "That's me!"

And the sergeant continued: "Maître Hauchecorne, please be good enough to come with me to the town hall. The mayor wants to talk with you."

The farmer, surprised and uneasy, gulped down his after-dinner glass of brandy, got up, and, more stooped over than earlier in the morning, because his first steps after each meal were especially painful, started on his way, saying over and over:

"That's me! That's me!"

[1] **five hundred francs:** about one hundred dollars in those days, a considerable sum.

And he followed the sergeant out.

The mayor was waiting for him, presiding in an armchair. He was the local notary, a large man, grave in manner and given to pompous phrases.

"Maître Hauchecorne," he said, "you were seen this morning on the Beuzeville road picking up the pocketbook lost by Maître Houlbrèque, of Manneville."

The old farmer, struck speechless, in a panic over being suspected and not understanding why, stared at the mayor:

"Me? Me? Me pick up that pocketbook?"

"Yes, you are indeed the one."

"I swear! I don't know anything at all about it."

"You were seen."

"Seen? Me? Who says he saw me?"

"Monsieur Malandain, the harness-maker."

Then the old man remembered, understood, and, flushing with anger, said: "Hah! He saw me, that old good-for-nothing! He saw me pick up this bit of yarn. Look, Mr. Mayor." And, fumbling in the depths of his pocket, he pulled out the little piece of yarn.

But the mayor, incredulous, shook his head: "You would have me believe, Maître Hauchecorne, that Monsieur Malandain, who is a trustworthy man, mistook that piece of yarn for a pocketbook?"

The farmer, enraged, raised his hand, spit to one side to reinforce his word, and said again: "But it's God's honest truth, the sacred truth, Mister Mayor. There! On my soul and salvation, I swear."

The mayor resumed his accusation: "After having picked up the article, you kept on searching in the mud for some time to see if some coin might have slipped out."

The old man was choking with indignation and fear.

"How can anyone say such things! . . . How can anyone say such lies to ruin a man's good name! How can anyone . . ."

No matter how much he protested, no one believed him.

He was confronted by Monsieur Malandain, who repeated his statement under oath. They hurled insults at each other for a full hour. Maître Hauchecorne was searched at his own request. They found nothing on him.

Finally the mayor, completely baffled, sent him away with the warning that he was going to inform the public prosecutor and ask what should be done.

The news had spread. On leaving the town hall, the old man was surrounded and questioned with serious or good-humored curiosity, but without any hint of blame. He began to tell the story of the piece of yarn. They didn't believe him. They laughed.

He went here and there, stopped by everyone, buttonholing his acquaintances, beginning over and over again his story and his protestations, turning his pockets inside out to prove that he had nothing in them.

People said to him: "You sly old rascal, you!"

He got more and more annoyed, upset, feverish in his distress because no one believed him, not knowing what to do, and always telling his story.

Night came. It was time to go home. He set off with his three neighbors, showed them the place where he had picked up the piece of yarn, and all the way talked about his experience.

That evening he made the rounds of the village of Bréauté, telling his tale to everyone. He met no one who believed him.

He was sick about it all night.

The next day, about one in the afternoon, Marius Paumelle, a farm hand

working for Maître Breton, a landowner of Ymauville, returned the pocketbook and its contents to Maître Houlbrèque, of Manneville.

This man claimed he had actually found the article on the highway, but being unable to read, he had taken it home and given it to his employer.

The news spread through the neighborhood. Maître Hauchecorne was informed. He began immediately to make the rounds, telling his story all over again, including the ending. He was exultant.

"What made me mad," he said, "wasn't so much the accusation, you know; it was all that lying. Nothing burns you up as much as being hauled into court on the word of a liar."

All day he kept talking about his experience, retelling it on the street to passersby, in the tavern to people having a drink, outside the church on the following Sunday. He would stop complete strangers to tell them. He felt calm about it now, but something still bothered him that he could not quite figure out. People listening to him seemed to be amused. They didn't appear to be convinced. He sensed that they were making remarks behind his back.

On Tuesday of the following week he returned to the marketplace in Goderville, driven by his need to state his case.

Malandain, standing in his doorway, began to laugh when he saw him going by. Why?

He accosted a farmer from Criquetot, who didn't let him finish but punched him in the pit of the stomach and shouted in his face: "Knock it off, you old rascal!" Then he turned on his heel and walked away.

Maître Hauchecorne was struck speechless and grew more and more upset. Why would anyone call him an "old rascal"?

When he had taken his usual place at Jourdain's table, he launched into another explanation of the incident.

A horse dealer of Montivilliers shouted at him: "Oh, come off it! I'm wise to that old trick. We know all about your yarn!"

Hauchecorne stammered: "But they found the pocketbook!"

"Sure old man! Somebody found it, and somebody took it back. Seeing is believing. A real pretty tangle to unsnarl!"

The farmer was stunned. At last he understood. People were accusing him of having gotten an accomplice to return the pocketbook.

He tried to deny it. The whole table burst into laughter.

Unable to finish his dinner, he left, the butt of jokes and mockery.

He went home, feeling humiliated and indignant, strangled with anger and mental confusion, especially crushed because, as a shrewd Norman, he knew himself capable of doing what he was accused of, and even boasting about it as a good trick. In his confusion, he could not see how he could prove his innocence, since he was well known for driving a sharp bargain. He was heartsick over the injustice of being suspected.

He set about telling his experience all over again, each day embroidering his recital, with each retelling adding new reasons, more vigorous protestations, more solemn vows that he dreamed up and repeated during his hours alone, his whole mind occupied with the yarn. He

was believed less and less as his defense became more and more intricate and his explanations more and more involved.

"Ha! With such an explanation, he must be lying!" they said behind his back. He sensed this, ate his heart out, and exhausted his strength in useless efforts. He visibly began to weaken.

Jokers now encouraged him, for their amusement, to tell "The Yarn" as one encourages a soldier back from the wars to tell about his battles. His mind, hurt to the depths, began to weaken.

Toward the end of December he took to his bed.

He died during the early days of January, and, in his dying delirium, kept protesting his innocence, repeating:

"Just a bit of yarn . . . a little bit of yarn . . . see, Mr. Mayor, there it is!"

FOR STUDY AND DISCUSSION

1. Near the beginning of the story Maupassant tells us, "The farmers would run their hands over the cows, go away, come back, undecided, always in fear of being taken in, never daring to commit themselves, slyly watching the seller's eye, endlessly hoping to discover the deception in the man and the defect in the beast." Besides helping to set the scene, how do these details prepare us for what happens in the story?

2. What circumstances of Hauchecorne's picking up the yarn make him especially open to suspicion? Why does the mayor not believe his explanation?

3. How do you explain Malandain's accusation? Do you think he was deliberately lying about what he had seen? What makes you think so? Can you be sure?

4. What is the mood of the peasants who surround Hauchecorne as he leaves the mayor's office? How seriously do they regard his crime? If one of them had found the purse, what do you think he would have done with it? If Hauchecorne himself had found the purse, what do you think he would have done?

5. Why will no one believe in Hauchecorne's innocence even after the pocketbook has been returned? In answering this question, consider Hauchecorne's character, the way he goes about explaining, and the peasants' attitude toward each other.

6. Do you find Hauchecorne's death sad? Is it believable? To what extent is it the result of accident? To what extent is it brought about by character?

7. The plot of this story hinges on several ironies of situation. What is the chief one? What are some others?

8. Both "A Slander" and "The Piece of Yarn" are about a character who is falsely accused of misbehavior and who loudly protests his innocence. Why is one story comic and the other pathetic? In answering, consider not only the ending of each story but also the seriousness of the accusation, the character and behavior of the accused, and the relationship between the accused and his accuser. How do the opening paragraphs of each story prepare us for the kind of story to come?

FOR COMPOSITION

Write an essay explaining your reasons for preferring either "A Slander" or "The Piece of Yarn."

ABOUT THE AUTHOR

Guy de Maupassant (1850–1893) was born and grew up in Normandy, France, the setting for many of his stories. At the age of twenty he enlisted in the French army and saw action in the Franco-German War. On returning to civilian life, he worked as a clerk in Paris, meanwhile serving his literary apprenticeship under the great French novelist, Gustave Flaubert. Maupassant lived only ten years after striking out on his own as a writer, but during those ten years he wrote six novels and some three hundred short stories. Along with Chekhov, he is generally regarded as a master of the modern short story. Among his best-known stories are "The Necklace," "Mademoiselle Fifi," "The Duel," and "The Piece of Yarn."

By the Waters of Babylon

STEPHEN VINCENT BENÉT

The proud city of Babylon, situated between the Tigris and Euphrates rivers, was in ancient times famous for its luxury and splendor. In the early part of the sixth century B.C., its people conquered the kingdom of Judah and laid waste to the city of Jerusalem, often referred to as Zion. The Jews were exiled to Babylon, where they longed for the day when they could return to their homeland and restore their way of life, which seemed lost forever. They returned to Jerusalem in 538 B.C.

THE NORTH and the west and the south are good hunting ground, but it is forbidden to go east. It is forbidden to go to any of the Dead Places except to search for metal, and then he who touches the metal must be a priest or the son of a priest. Afterward, both the man and the metal must be purified. These are the rules and the laws; they are well made. It is forbidden to cross the great river and look upon the place that was the Place of the Gods—this is most strictly forbidden. We do not even say its name though we know its name. It is there that spirits live, and demons—it is there that there are the ashes of the Great Burning. These things

"By the Waters of Babylon" from *The Selected Works of Stephen Vincent Benét*, Holt, Rinehart and Winston, Inc., copyright 1937 by Stephen Vincent Benét. Reprinted by permission of Brandt & Brandt.

are forbidden—they have been forbidden since the beginning of time.

My father is a priest; I am the son of a priest. I have been in the Dead Places near us, with my father—at first, I was afraid. When my father went into the house to search for the metal, I stood by the door and my heart felt small and weak. It was a dead man's house, a spirit house. It did not have the smell of man, though there were old bones in a corner. But it is not fitting that a priest's son should show fear. I looked at the bones in the shadow and kept my voice still.

Then my father came out with the metal —a good, strong piece. He looked at me with both eyes but I had not run away. He gave me the metal to hold—I took it and did not die. So he knew that I was truly his son and would be a priest in my time. That was when I was very young— nevertheless, my brothers would not have done it, though they are good hunters. After that, they gave me the good piece of meat and the warm corner by the fire. My father watched over me—he was glad that I should be a priest. But when I boasted or wept without a reason, he punished me more strictly than my brothers. That was right.

After a time, I myself was allowed to go into the dead houses and search for metal. So I learned the ways of those houses—and if I saw bones, I was no longer afraid. The bones are light and old —sometimes they will fall into dust if you touch them. But that is a great sin.

I was taught the chants and the spells —I was taught how to stop the running of blood from a wound and many secrets. A priest must know many secrets—that was what my father said. If the hunters think we do all things by chants and spells, they may believe so—it does not hurt them. I was taught how to read in the old books and how to make the old writings

—that was hard and took a long time. My knowledge made me happy—it was like a fire in my heart. Most of all, I liked to hear of the Old Days and the stories of the gods. I asked myself many questions that I could not answer, but it was good to ask them. At night, I would lie awake and listen to the wind—it seemed to me that it was the voice of the gods as they flew through the air.

We are not ignorant like the Forest People—our women spin wool on the wheel, our priests wear a white robe. We do not eat grubs from the tree, we have not forgotten the old writings, although they are hard to understand. Nevertheless, my knowledge and my lack of knowledge burned in me—I wished to know more. When I was a man at last, I came to my father and said, "It is time for me to go on my journey. Give me your leave."

He looked at me for a long time, stroking his beard, then he said at last, "Yes. It is time." That night, in the house of the priesthood, I asked for and received purification. My body hurt but my spirit was a cool stone. It was my father himself who questioned me about my dreams.

He bade me look into the smoke of the fire and see—I saw and told what I saw. It was what I have always seen—a river, and, beyond it, a great Dead Place and in it the gods walking. I have always thought about that. His eyes were stern when I told him—he was no longer my father but a priest. He said, "This is a strong dream."

"It is mine," I said, while the smoke waved and my head felt light. They were singing the Star song in the outer chamber and it was like the buzzing of bees in my head.

He asked me how the gods were dressed and I told him how they were dressed. We know how they were dressed from the book, but I saw them

as if they were before me. When I had finished, he threw the sticks three times and studied them as they fell.

"This is a very strong dream," he said. "It may eat you up."

"I am not afraid," I said and looked at him with both eyes. My voice sounded thin in my ears but that was because of the smoke.

He touched me on the breast and the forehead. He gave me the bow and the three arrows.

"Take them," he said. "It is forbidden to travel east. It is forbidden to cross the river. It is forbidden to go to the Place of the Gods. All these things are forbidden."

"All these things are forbidden," I

said, but it was my voice that spoke and not my spirit. He looked at me again.

"My son," he said. "Once I had young dreams. If your dreams do not eat you up, you may be a great priest. If they eat you, you are still my son. Now go on your journey."

I went fasting, as is the law. My body hurt but not my heart. When the dawn came, I was out of sight of the village. I prayed and purified myself, waiting for a sign. The sign was an eagle. It flew east.

Sometimes signs are sent by bad spirits. I waited again on the flat rock, fasting, taking no food. I was very still—I could feel the sky above me and the earth beneath. I waited till the sun was beginning to sink. Then three deer passed in the valley, going east—they did not wind [1] me or see me. There was a white fawn with them—a very great sign.

I followed them, at a distance, waiting for what would happen. My heart was troubled about going east, yet I knew that I must go. My head hummed with my fasting—I did not even see the panther spring upon the white fawn. But, before I knew it, the bow was in my hand. I shouted and the panther lifted his head from the fawn. It is not easy to kill a panther with one arrow but the arrow went through his eye and into his brain. He died as he tried to spring—he rolled over, tearing at the ground. Then I knew I was meant to go east—I knew that was my journey. When the night came, I made my fire and roasted meat.

It is eight suns' journey to the east, and a man passes by many Dead Places. The Forest People are afraid of them but I am not. Once I made my fire on the edge of a Dead Place at night and, next morning, in the dead house, I found a good knife, little rusted. That was small to what came

afterward but it made my heart feel big. Always when I looked for game, it was in front of my arrow, and twice I passed hunting parties of the Forest People without their knowing. So I knew my magic was strong and my journey clean, in spite of the law.

Toward the setting of the eighth sun, I came to the banks of the great river. It was half-a-day's journey after I had left the god-road—we do not use the god-roads now for they are falling apart into great blocks of stone, and the forest is safer going. A long way off I had seen the water through trees but the trees were thick. At last, I came out upon an open place at the top of a cliff. There was the great river below, like a giant in the sun. It is very long, very wide. It could eat all the streams we know and still be thirsty. Its name is Ou-dis-sun, the Sacred, the Long. No man of my tribe had seen it, not even my father, the priest. It was magic and I prayed.

Then I raised my eyes and looked south. It was there, the Place of the Gods.

How can I tell what it was like—you do not know. It was there, in the red light,

[1] **wind:** smell; get the scent of.

and they were too big to be houses. It was there with the red light upon it, mighty and ruined. I knew that in another moment the gods would see me. I covered my eyes with my hands and crept back into the forest.

Surely, that was enough to do, and live. Surely it was enough to spend the night upon the cliff. The Forest People themselves do not come near. Yet, all through the night, I knew that I should have to cross the river and walk in the Place of the Gods, although the gods ate me up. My magic did not help me at all and yet there was a fire in my bowels, a fire in my mind. When the sun rose, I thought, "My journey has been clean. Now I will go home from my journey." But, even as I thought so, I knew I could not. If I went to the Place of the Gods, I would surely die, but, if I did not go, I could never be at peace with my spirit again. It is better to lose one's life than one's spirit, if one is a priest and the son of a priest.

Nevertheless, as I made the raft, the tears ran out of my eyes. The Forest People could have killed me without fight, if they had come upon me then, but they did not come. When the raft was made, I said the sayings for the dead and painted myself for death. My heart was cold as a frog and my knees like water, but the burning in my mind would not let me have peace. As I pushed the raft from the shore, I began my death song—I had the right. It was a fine song.

"I am John, son of John," I sang. "My people are the Hill People. They are the men.
I go into the Dead Places but I am not slain.
I take the metal from the Dead Places but I am not blasted.
I travel upon the god-roads and am not afraid. E-yah! I have killed the panther, I have killed the fawn!
E-yah! I have come to the great river. No man has come there before.
It is forbidden to go east, but I have gone, forbidden to go on the great river, but I am there.
Open your hearts, you spirits, and hear my song.
Now I go to the Place of the Gods, I shall not return.
My body is painted for death and my limbs weak, but my heart is big as I go to the Place of the Gods!"

All the same, when I came to the Place of the Gods, I was afraid, afraid. The current of the great river is very strong—it gripped my raft with its hands. That was magic, for the river itself is wide and calm. I could feel evil spirits about me, in the bright morning; I could feel their breath

on my neck as I was swept down the stream. Never have I been so much alone —I tried to think of my knowledge, but it was a squirrel's heap of winter nuts. There was no strength in my knowledge any more and I felt small and naked as a new-hatched bird—alone upon the great river, the servant of the gods.

Yet, after awhile, my eyes were opened and I saw. I saw both banks of the river— I saw that once there had been god-roads across it, though now they were broken and fallen like broken vines. Very great they were, and wonderful and broken— broken in the time of the Great Burning when the fire fell out of the sky. And always the current took me nearer to the Place of the Gods, and the huge ruins rose before my eyes.

I do not know the customs of rivers— we are the People of the Hills. I tried to guide my raft with the pole but it spun around. I thought the river meant to take me past the Place of the Gods and out into the Bitter Water of the legends. I grew angry then—my heart felt strong. I said aloud, "I am a priest and the son of a priest!" The gods heard me—they showed me how to paddle with the pole on one side of the raft. The current changed itself—I drew near to the Place of the Gods.

When I was very near, my raft struck and turned over. I can swim in our lakes —I swam to the shore. There was a great spike of rusted metal sticking out into the river—I hauled myself up upon it and sat there, panting. I had saved my bow and two arrows and the knife I found in the Dead Place but that was all. My raft went whirling downstream toward the Bitter Water. I looked after it, and thought if it had trod me under, at least I would be safely dead. Nevertheless, when I had dried my bowstring and restrung it, I walked forward to the Place of the Gods.

It felt like ground underfoot; it did not burn me. It is not true what some of the tales say, that the ground there burns forever, for I have been there. Here and there were the marks and stains of the Great Burning, on the ruins, that is true. But they were old marks and old stains. It is not true either, what some of our priests say, that it is an island covered with fogs and enchantments. It is not. It is a great Dead Place—greater than any Dead Place we know. Everywhere in it there are god-roads, though most are cracked and broken. Everywhere there are the ruins of the high towers of the gods.

How shall I tell what I saw? I went carefully, my strung bow in my hand, my skin ready for danger. There should have been the wailings of spirits and the shrieks of demons, but there were not. It was very silent and sunny where I had landed—the wind and the rain and the birds that drop seeds had done their work—the grass grew in the cracks of the broken stone. It is a fair island—no wonder the gods built there. If I had come there, a god, I also would have built.

How shall I tell what I saw? The towers are not all broken—here and there one still stands, like a great tree in a forest, and the birds nest high. But the towers themselves look blind, for the gods are gone. I saw a fish hawk, catching fish in the river. I saw a little dance of white butterflies over a great heap of broken stones and columns. I went there and looked about me—there was a carved stone with cut letters, broken in half. I can read letters but I could not understand these. They said UBTREAS. There was also the shattered image of a man or a god. It had been made of white stone and he wore his hair tied back like a woman's. His name was ASHING, as I read on the cracked half of a stone. I thought it wise to pray to

ASHING, though I do not know that god.

How shall I tell what I saw? There was no smell of man left, on stone or metal. Nor were there many trees in that wilderness of stone. There are many pigeons, nesting and dropping in the towers—the gods must have loved them, or, perhaps, they used them for sacrifices. There are wild cats that roam the god-roads, green-eyed, unafraid of man. At night they wail like demons but they are not demons. The wild dogs are more dangerous, for they hunt in a pack, but them I did not meet till later. Everywhere there are the carved stones, carved with magical numbers or words.

I went north—I did not try to hide myself. When a god or a demon saw me, then I would die, but meanwhile I was no longer afraid. My hunger for knowledge burned in me—there was so much that I could not understand. After awhile, I knew that my belly was hungry. I could have hunted for my meat, but I did not hunt. It is known that the gods did not hunt as we do—they got their food from enchanted boxes and jars. Sometimes these are still found in the Dead Places—once, when I was a child and foolish, I opened such a jar and tasted it and found

the food sweet. But my father found out and punished me for it strictly, for, often, that food is death. Now, though, I had long gone past what was forbidden, and I entered the likeliest towers, looking for the food of the gods.

I found it at last in the ruins of a great temple in the mid-city. A mighty temple it must have been, for the roof was painted like the sky at night with its stars—that much I could see, though the colors were faint and dim. It went down into great caves and tunnels—perhaps they kept their slaves there. But when I started to climb down, I heard the squeaking of rats, so I did not go—rats are unclean, and there must have been many tribes of them, from the squeaking. But near there, I found food, in the heart of a ruin, behind a door that still opened. I ate only the fruits from the jars—they had a very sweet taste. There was drink, too, in bottles of glass—the drink of the gods was strong and made my head swim. After I had eaten and drunk, I slept on the top of a stone, my bow at my side.

When I woke, the sun was low. Looking down from where I lay, I saw a dog sitting on his haunches. His tongue was hanging out of his mouth; he looked as if

he were laughing. He was a big dog, with a gray-brown coat, as big as a wolf. I sprang up and shouted at him but he did not move—he just sat there as if he were laughing. I did not like that. When I reached for a stone to throw, he moved swiftly out of the way of the stone. He was not afraid of me; he looked at me as if I were meat. No doubt I could have killed him with an arrow, but I did not know if there were others. Moreover, night was falling.

I looked about me—not far away there was a great, broken god-road, leading north. The towers were high enough, but not so high, and while many of the dead houses were wrecked, there were some that stood. I went toward this god-road, keeping to heights of the ruins, while the dog followed. When I had reached the god-road, I saw that there were others behind him. If I had slept later, they would have come upon me asleep and torn out my throat. As it was, they were sure enough of me; they did not hurry. When I went into the dead house, they kept watch at the entrance—doubtless they thought they would have a fine hunt. But a dog cannot open a door and I knew, from the

books, that the gods did not like to live on the ground but on high.

I had just found a door I could open when the dogs decided to rush. Ha! They were surprised when I shut the door in their faces—it was a good door, of strong metal. I could hear their foolish baying beyond it but I did not stop to answer them. I was in darkness—I found stairs and climbed. There were many stairs, turning around till my head was dizzy. At the top was another door—I found the knob and opened it. I was in a long small chamber—on one side of it was a bronze door that could not be opened, for it had no handle. Perhaps there was a magic word to open it but I did not have the word. I turned to the door in the opposite side of the wall. The lock of it was broken and I opened it and went in.

Within, there was a place of great riches. The god who lived there must have been a powerful god. The first room was a small anteroom—I waited there for some time, telling the spirits of the place that I came in peace and not as a robber. When it seemed to me that they had had time to hear me, I went on. Ah, what riches! Few, even, of the windows had been broken—it was all as it had been. The great windows that looked over the city had not been broken at all though they were dusty and streaked with many years. There were coverings on the floors, the colors not greatly faded, and the chairs were soft and deep. There were pictures upon the walls, very strange, very wonderful—I remember one of a bunch of flowers in a jar—if you came close to it, you could see nothing but bits of color, but if you stood away from it, the flowers might have been picked yesterday. It made my heart feel strange to look at this picture—and to look at the figure of a bird, in some hard clay, on a table and see it so like our birds. Everywhere there were books and writ-

ings, many in tongues that I could not read. The god who lived there must have been a wise god and full of knowledge. I felt I had right there, as I sought knowledge also.

Nevertheless, it was strange. There was a washing place but no water—perhaps the gods washed in air. There was a cooking place but no wood, and though there was a machine to cook food, there was no place to put fire in it. Nor were there candles or lamps—there were things that looked like lamps but they had neither oil nor wick. All these things were magic, but I touched them and lived—the magic had gone out of them. Let me tell one thing to show. In the washing place, a thing said "Hot" but it was not hot to the touch—another thing said "Cold" but it was not cold. This must have been a strong magic but the magic was gone. I do not understand—they had ways—I wish that I knew.

It was close and dry and dusty in their house of the gods. I have said the magic was gone but that is not true—it had gone from the magic things but it had not gone from the place. I felt the spirits about me, weighing upon me. Nor had I ever slept in a Dead Place before—and yet, tonight, I must sleep there. When I thought of it, my tongue felt dry in my throat, in spite of my wish for knowledge. Almost I would have gone down again and faced the dogs, but I did not.

I had not gone through all the rooms when the darkness fell. When it fell, I went back to the big room looking over the city and made fire. There was a place to make fire and a box with wood in it, though I do not think they cooked there. I wrapped myself in a floor covering and slept in front of the fire—I was very tired.

Now I tell what is very strong magic. I woke in the midst of the night. When I woke, the fire had gone out and I was cold.

It seemed to me that all around me there were whisperings and voices. I closed my eyes to shut them out. Some will say that I slept again, but I do not think that I slept. I could feel the spirits drawing my spirit out of my body as a fish is drawn on a line.

Why should I lie about it? I am a priest and the son of a priest. If there are spirits, as they say, in the small Dead Places near us, what spirits must there not be in that great Place of the Gods? And would not they wish to speak? After such long years? I know that I felt myself drawn as a fish is drawn on a line. I had stepped out of my body—I could see my body asleep in front of the cold fire, but it was not I. I was drawn to look out upon the city of the gods.

It should have been dark, for it was

night, but it was not dark. Everywhere there were lights—lines of light—circles and blurs of light—ten thousand torches would not have been the same. The sky itself was alight—you could barely see the stars for the glow in the sky. I thought to myself "This is strong magic" and trembled. There was a roaring in my ears like the rushing of rivers. Then my eyes grew used to the light and my ears to the sound. I knew that I was seeing the city as it had been when the gods were alive.

That was a sight indeed—yes, that was a sight: I could not have seen it in the body—my body would have died. Everywhere went the gods, on foot and in chariots—there were gods beyond number and counting and their chariots blocked the streets. They had turned night to day for their pleasure—they did not sleep with the sun. The noise of their coming and going was the noise of many waters. It was magic what they could do—it was magic what they did.

I looked out of another window—the great vines of their bridges were mended and the god-roads went east and west. Restless, restless, were the gods and always in motion! They burrowed tunnels under rivers—they flew in the air. With unbelievable tools they did giant works— no part of the earth was safe from them, for, if they wished for a thing, they summoned it from the other side of the world. And always, as they labored and rested, as they feasted and made love, there was a drum in their ears—the pulse of the giant city, beating and beating like a man's heart.

Were they happy? What is happiness to the gods? They were great, they were mighty, they were wonderful and terrible. As I looked upon them and their magic, I felt like a child—but a little more, it seemed to me, and they would pull down the moon from the sky. I saw them with wisdom beyond wisdom and knowledge beyond knowledge. And yet not all they did was well done—even I could see that—and yet their wisdom could not but grow until all was peace.

Then I saw their fate come upon them and that was terrible past speech. It came upon them as they walked the streets of their city. I have been in the fights with the Forest People—I have seen men die. But this was not like that. When gods war with gods, they use weapons we do not know. It was fire falling out of the sky and a mist that poisoned. It was the time of the Great Burning and the Destruction. They ran about like ants in the streets of their city—poor gods, poor gods! Then the towers began to fall. A few escaped—yes, a few. The legends tell it. But, even after the city had become a Dead Place, for many years the poison was still in the ground. I saw it happen, I saw the last of them die. It was darkness over the broken city and I wept.

All this, I saw. I saw it as I have told it, though not in the body. When I woke in the morning, I was hungry, but I did not think first of my hunger for my heart was perplexed and confused. I knew the reason for the Dead Places but I did not see why it had happened. It seemed to me it should not have happened, with all the magic they had. I went through the house looking for an answer. There was so much in the house I could not understand—and yet I am a priest and the son of a priest. It was like being on one side of the great river, at night, with no light to show the way.

Then I saw the dead god. He was sitting in his chair, by the window, in a room I had not entered before and, for the first moment, I thought that he was alive. Then I saw the skin on the back of his hand— it was like dry leather. The room was shut, hot, and dry—no doubt that had kept him

as he was. At first I was afraid to approach him—then the fear left me. He was sitting looking out over the city—he was dressed in the clothes of the gods. His age was neither young nor old—I could not tell his age. But there was wisdom in his face and great sadness. You could see that he would not have run away. He had sat at his window, watching his city die—then he himself had died. But it is better to lose one's life than one's spirit—and you could see from the face that his spirit had not been lost. I knew, that, if I touched him, he would fall into dust—and yet, there was something unconquered in the face.

That is all of my story, for then I knew he was a man—I knew then that they had been men, neither gods nor demons. It is a great knowledge, hard to tell and believe. They were men—they went a dark road, but they were men. I had no fear after that—I had no fear going home, though twice I fought off the dogs and once I was hunted for two days by the Forest People. When I saw my father again, I prayed and was purified. He touched my lips and my breast, he said, "You went away a boy. You come back a man and a priest." I said, "Father, they were men! I have been in the Place of the Gods and seen it! Now slay me, if it is the law—but still I know they were men."

He looked at me out of both eyes. He said, "The law is not always the same shape—you have done what you have done. I could not have done it in my time, but you come after me. Tell!"

I told and he listened. After that, I wished to tell all the people but he showed me otherwise. He said, "Truth is a hard deer to hunt. If you eat too much truth at once, you may die of the truth. It was not idly that our fathers forbade the Dead Places." He was right—it is better the truth should come little by little. I have

learned that, being a priest. Perhaps, in the old days, they ate knowledge too fast.

Nevertheless, we make a beginning. It is not for the metal alone we go to the Dead Places now—there are the books and the writings. They are hard to learn. And the magic tools are broken—but we can look at them and wonder. At least, we make a beginning. And, when I am chief priest we shall go beyond the great river. We shall go to the Place of the Gods —the place new-york—not one man but a company. We shall look for the images of the gods and find the god ASHING and the others—the gods Lincoln and Biltmore and Moses. But they were men who built the city, not gods or demons. They were men. I remember the dead man's face. They were men who were here before us. We must build again.

FOR STUDY AND DISCUSSION

1. The Place of the Gods is identified in the last paragraph, though you may have guessed it earlier. Knowing its identity, can you further identify the Ou-dis-sun? the Bitter Water? ASHING? the great underground caves and tunnels? the kind of building in which John spent the night? the gods Lincoln and Biltmore and Moses?

2. How does John show himself worthy of being a priest? What things does he do in the course of the story that other members of his tribe would not?

3. John breaks a number of tribal taboos during the course of the story. What discoveries does he make as a result of each? At the end of the story, what plans is he making to free his people of their superstitions?

4. What do you think was the "strong magic" that John experienced during the night, which drew him out of his body "as a fish is drawn on a line"?

5. As he watches the gods during this "strong magic," John asks the questions "Were they happy?" and "What is happiness to the gods?" How would you answer the first

question? the second? Earlier in the story he said, "They had turned night to day for their pleasure . . ." Does this imply a difference between pleasure and happiness? What is the difference?

6. What is meant by "fire falling out of the sky"? by "a mist that poisoned"? by "the Great Burning"? How was the Place of the Gods destroyed?

7. What does John realize when he finds the dead god? How has the vision he has seen prepared him for this realization?

8. The word *knowledge* occurs many times in this story. John, at the beginning, says of himself both "my knowledge and my lack of knowledge burned in me—I wished to know more" and "My knowledge made me happy—it was like a fire in my heart." When he is alone on the river, he says, "I tried to think of my knowledge, but it was a squirrel's heap of winter nuts." What does John learn in the course of the story about the relationship between knowledge and wisdom? How have the gods failed to understand this relationship? Do you think John will be a wise chief priest? What evidence is there even at the beginning of the story that John, apart from his knowledge, has the seeds of wisdom?

9. State a theme for this story containing the words *knowledge* and *wisdom*.

10. The title of this story is taken from Psalm 137 in the Bible: "By the waters of Babylon, there we sat down and wept, when we remembered Zion." What do you think from the context, the poet means by Zion? Look up the meanings of Zion in a dictionary. How many of them do you think the author of this story had in mind? How does the phrase used in the title apply to the city in the story?

11. Though this story pretends to be about the past, it is actually about the future. Judged as prophecy, is it optimistic or pessimistic?

LANGUAGE AND VOCABULARY

John is a "primitive" man, living at the end of another stone age and expressing himself in very simple language. Because of our wider knowledge and point of view, many of the words he uses mean one thing to him and something else to us. Thus the story is full of

dramatic irony. What do the following words mean to John? What do they mean to us?

the Dead Places	washing place
the Great Burning	cooking place
the Old Days	magic
the gods	the law
god-roads	

How does the irony of these expressions reinforce the theme of the story?

FOR COMPOSITION

1. "If you eat too much truth at once, you may die of the truth . . . Perhaps, in the old days, they ate knowledge too fast." How might either of these statements by the priest at the end of the story be applied to a situation in contemporary life? Do the newspapers or magazines ever hint that man eats knowledge too fast? Think about this question, and write an essay about some example of dying of the truth or eating knowledge too fast. Base your essay on either your own experience or current events.

2. "A little knowledge is a dangerous thing," wrote an English poet. Why might this be so? Explain, in a short composition, whether the poet's meaning is similar to the priest's or quite different.

ABOUT THE AUTHOR

Stephen Vincent Benét (1893–1943) was born in Bethlehem, Pennsylvania, the son, grandson, and great-grandson of army officers. The Benéts were a writing family, and both Stephen's brother, William Rose Benét, and his sister, Laura, were also quite well known. Stephen was brought up on various army posts, attending schools in California and Georgia, and later attending Yale University and the Sorbonne, in Paris. His best-known work is his long narrative poem on the War Between the States, *John Brown's Body,* which won the Pulitzer prize for poetry in 1929. His best-known short story, "The Devil and Daniel Webster," has become a modern classic. Another popular work, *A Book of Americans,* is a collection of ballads about popular American heroes.

Narration

Narration is the telling or relating of a sequence of events and actions as they occur in time. Often many events will be recorded in a paragraph, but usually there is one *main event*—the single most important thing that happens. As you read narrative paragraphs, learn to look for the main event.

A paragraph of *pure* narration would simply record one event after another, without describing the appearance of anything or explaining why or how these events took place. Such paragraphs, however, are rarely found. In narration, an author nearly always includes details which describe and explain the events, as in the following paragraph from "To Build a Fire":

At last, when he could endure no more, he jerked his hands apart. The blazing matches fell sizzling into the snow, but the birch bark was alight. He began laying dry grasses and the tiniest twigs on the flame. He could not pick and choose, for he had to lift the fuel between the heels of his hands. Small pieces of rotten wood and green moss clung to the twigs, and he bit them off as well as he could with his teeth. He cherished the flame carefully and awkwardly. It meant life, and it must not perish. The withdrawal of blood from the surface of his body now made him begin to shiver, and he grew more awkward. A large piece of green moss fell squarely on the little fire. He tried to poke it out with his fingers, but his shivering frame made him poke too far, and he disrupted the nucleus of the little fire, the burning grasses and tiny twigs separating and scattering. He tried to poke them together again, but in spite of the tenseness of the effort, his shivering got away from him, and the twigs were hopelessly scattered. Each twig gushed a puff of smoke and went out. The fire provider had failed. As he looked apathetically about him, his eyes chanced on the dog, sitting across the ruins of the fire from him, in the snow, making restless, hunching movements, slightly lifting one forefoot and then the other, shifting its weight back and forth on them with wistful eagerness and eyeing the fire provider expectantly. (pages 23–24)

1. What happens in this paragraph? List the events that occur. Which would you select as the *main* event? (Although in the normal procedure of reading you would not have a chance to do this, a good way to discover the main event is to try to rewrite the paragraph in just ten words.)

2. List the descriptive details in the paragraph. What explanations are included in this paragraph? Where?

PRACTICING YOUR READING

Find four other paragraphs of narration in the short stories you have read, and for each write down answers to the two questions directly above.

READING DIALOGUE

Dialogue written by a skillful writer can tell us a great deal about the person who is speaking. As in life, what a person says often is not as important as his tone of voice for understanding what he really means. A good writer has ways of making us aware of a speaker's tone. He may tell us with *direct clues* that a speaker *shouted angrily* or his voice was *hard*. Often, though, a writer will depend on the speaker's words themselves to suggest his tone. In the following paragraph from "The Leader of the People" there are several direct clues to changes in the speaker's tone. In reading, also be alert for changes in tone where no such clues are given.

When Mrs. Tiflin answered her tone was so changed that Jody, outside the window, looked up from his study of the stone. Her voice had become soft and explanatory. Jody knew how her face would have changed to match the tone. She said quietly, "Look at it this way, Carl. That was the big thing in my father's life. He led a wagon train clear across the plains to the coast, and when it was finished, his life was done. It was a big thing to do, but it didn't last long enough. Look!" she continued. "it's as though he was born to do that, and after he finished it, there wasn't anything more for him to do but think about it and talk about it. If there'd been any farther west to go, he'd have gone. He's told me so himself. But at last there was the ocean. He lives right by the ocean where he had to stop." (page 44)

1. What do you learn about Jody's mother from this paragraph?

2. Which words in the paragraph give direct clues to Mrs. Tiflin's tone? Read the paragraph aloud. Does the dialogue itself help to suggest the tone of voice in which it should be spoken?

In reading dialogue, you should always try to hear the speaker's tone of voice. You will miss much of an author's meaning if you do not sense the speaker's tone and mood. Read the following speeches aloud, trying to catch each shift and nuance in the speaker's tone:

"*Father!*" said she.

The old man pulled up. "What is it?"

"I want to know what them men are diggin' over there in that field for."

"They're diggin' a cellar, I s'pose, if you've got to know."

"A cellar for what?"

"A barn."

"A barn? You ain't goin' to build a barn over there where we was goin' to have a house, Father?" (page 29)

In the hall outside the lawyer's office, Mabelle crowed: "Isn't it—oh, Sid, you do know how sorry I am your father's passed on, but won't it be just lovely! The farm must be worth four thousand dollars. We'll be just as sensible as can be—not blow it all in, like lots of people would. We'll invest the seven thousand, and that ought to give us three hundred and fifty dollars a year—think of it, an extra dollar every day! You can get a dress suit now, and at last I'll have some decent dresses for the evening, and we'll get a new suit for Rob right away—how soon can you get the money? did he say?—and I saw some lovely little dresses for Willabette and the cutest slippers, and now we can get a decent bridge table instead of that rickety old thing, and ——" (page 76)

WRITING DIALOGUE

In writing dialogue, you should try to get a clear picture in your mind of the speaker's personality and attitudes, imagine what he (or she) would say in the particular situation he is in, and write the speech in the words you think the speaker himself would use. If the tone of a speech is not clear from the words themselves, add a clue, such as *angrily*.

1. Write a dialogue between a boy who calls for a date and a girl who turns him down. Make up your own characters and situation. What is the boy like? How does the girl feel about him? Imagine your characters completely, then write their dialogue.

2. Write a dialogue between a busy businessman and a high school student who wants a summer job. Imagine your characters' personalities, then let their conversation determine whether or not the student gets a job.

ART AND LITERATURE

Let your imagination work on the scene and people shown in one of the paintings on pages 115–20, and write a story, including dialogue, based on the situation shown.

THE ESSAY

I DOUBT IF anyone could define the essay," one writer of essays remarked, "but I see no reason why anybody should be afraid to write one if he has anything worth essaying." The variety in the essays that follow supports this statement. Yet some definition, however incomplete, is in order here.

What is an essay? Basically, it is a short piece of prose, seldom longer than five or six thousand words. (Yet some essays fill whole books, and others, such as Alexander Pope's *Essay on Man,* are written in verse.) An essay should be on a topic of interest to the writer. It is "true" in the sense that it is not fiction; it is about something the writer has really seen, or felt, or thought about. It is usually an *attempt*—that is, not an exhaustive treatment of the topic. Unless it is strictly technical, its style depends upon the personality of the writer and upon the topic under discussion. Its purpose may be to stimulate the reader's thought, to amuse, to instruct, to explain, to describe, or to convince.

In studying the following essays, which were written over a span of almost four hundred years, you will be asked to pay attention to some of the ways the authors have given structure and style to their writing. You will learn how to apply some of these devices to your own writing. Take the matter of organization, for example. You will see how your ideas can be arranged by chronology, as in Charles Dickens's description of the London streets or in John Steinbeck's narrative of his amusing war with the ospreys. You will see how the effective organization of some essays depends upon a spatial or geographical arrangement, as does Paul Horgan's sharp-focus description of the Rio Grande.

You will also see how the author's personality and his attitude toward his subject are reflected in the style of his essay. Montaigne, as a humanist, is informal and highly personal. Horgan is serious and objective in his approach. Sometimes the language is plain; sometimes it is richly colored and imaginative. You will see how some writers, such as Addison and Montaigne, use anecdotes or fictional characters to help them make their points in an interesting way.

In a famous comedy by the seventeenth-century playwright, Molière, a character is surprised and pleased to find out that he has been speaking prose all his life. Perhaps you have not been aware that you have been reading essays for years. An essay is not a strange form that exists only in textbooks. In a sense, it is any attempt at written communication. Whenever you read a letter, a sports column, a movie review, an editorial, you are reading an essay. For the most part, the essays you read every day are *familiar:* they are informal and reflect the personalities of their writers. A good essay is like good conversation. One of the rewards of reading essays is meeting people—the essayists—through the ideas that interest them.

On Liars

MICHEL DE MONTAIGNE

(1533–1592)

"So, reader," wrote Montaigne in 1580 in the preface to his first volume of *Essays,* "I am myself the substance of my book, and there is no reason why you should waste your leisure on so frivolous and unrewarding a subject." Until the age of thirty-eight, Michel Eyquem de Montaigne had been an active man of the world—busy at the court of King Henry II of France, and in the parliament of his native city, Bordeaux. Then, as he tells us, "weary of court employment and public honors," he retired to his estate near Bordeaux. There, in a small book-lined room high up in a tower, he spent most of his remaining years writing his essays and reading.

Montaigne was the real inventor of the essay and even of the word "essay" itself. To him, this word—from the French *essai,* a trial or attempt—meant a short and very personal treatment of any topic. He did not attempt to treat the topic completely, and he wrote about anything from friendship to cannibals—whatever interested him.

What interested him most was himself. No writer before Montaigne's time had ever published such intimate details about his own mind, feelings, and habits. In his conversational style, he tells us, for example, that he was small; that he slept too much; that he was bad at sports; and that he "could never speak to dogs, birds, or horses." His motto was *que sais je?*—what do I know? The modern French writer, André Gide, said of Montaigne: "What did he bring the world then that was so new? Self-knowledge—and all other knowledge seemed to him uncertain; but the human being he discovers, and uncovers, is so genuine, so true, that in him every reader of the *Essays* recognizes himself."

THERE IS no man so unsuited for the task of speaking about memory as I am, for I find scarcely a trace of it in myself, and I do not believe there is another man in the world so hideously lacking in it. All my other faculties are poor and ordinary, but in this I think I am most rare and singular and deserve to gain name and fame thereby.

Besides the natural inconvenience that I suffer on this account—for assuredly, considering how necessary it is, Plato [1] was right in calling memory a great and powerful goddess—in my country, when

"On Liars" from *Montaigne's Essays,* translated by J. M. Cohen. Reprinted by permission of Penguin Books Ltd.

[1] **Plato:** the great Greek philosopher (427?–347). (See page 277.)

they want to say that a man has no sense, they say that he has no memory; and when I complain of the shortcomings of my own, people correct me and refuse to believe me, as if I were accusing myself of being a fool. They can see no difference between memory and intellect.

This makes me look much worse off. But they wrong me, for experience shows that, on the contrary, excellent memories are often coupled with feeble judgments. They also wrong me in this, that the same words which indicate my infirmity, signify ingratitude as well—and I am nothing if I am not a good friend. They blame my affections [1] instead of my memory and turn an involuntary defect into a wilful one. "He has forgotten this request or that promise," they say. "He doesn't remember his friends. He did not remember to do this, to say that, or to keep quiet about the other, for my sake." Certainly I am prone enough to forgetfulness, but as for neglecting, out of indifference, a service which a friend has asked of me, that I do not do. Let them be content with my misfortune and not turn it into a kind of ill will, a kind quite foreign to my character.

But I find some consolation, first because I have derived from this evil my principal argument against a worse evil, which might have taken root in me: the evil of ambition. For lack of memory is an intolerable defect in anyone who takes on the burden of the world's affairs.

Then, as several similar examples of nature's workings show, she has generously strengthened other faculties in me in proportion as this one has grown weaker. I might easily have let my intelligence and judgment follow languidly in other men's footsteps, as all the world does, without exerting their own power, if other people's ideas and opinions had ever

[1] **affections:** feelings.

Michel de Montaigne

been present with me by favor of my memory.

Again, my speech is consequently briefer, for the storehouse of the memory is generally better stocked with material than that of the invention. If my memory had been good, I should have deafened all my friends with my chatter, since any subject that calls out such powers as I have of argument and development warms and extends my eloquence. This would have been lamentable, as I have learned in the case of some of my intimate friends. In proportion as their memory gives them a complete and first-hand view of their subject, so they push their narrative back into the past and burden it with useless details. If the story is a good one, they smother its virtues; if it is not, you curse their fortunate powers of memory or their unfortunate lack of judgment. Once one is well on the road, it is difficult to close a discourse and break it off. There is no better way of proving a horse's strength than by pulling him up short and sharp. Even among men who keep to the point, I find some who would like to break off but cannot. While they are searching for a

place at which to stop, they go maundering and trailing on like a man who is losing strength. Particularly dangerous are old men who retain the memory of past events but do not remember how often they have repeated them. I have known some very amusing tales to become most tiresome when told by some gentlemen whose whole audience has been sated with them a hundred times.

I find some consolation, also, in the reflection that I have, in the words of a certain ancient author,[1] a short memory for the injuries I have received. Like Darius,[2] I should need a prompter. Wishing not to forget the insult he had suffered from the Athenians, the Persian king made one of his pages come and repeat three times in his ear, each time he sat down to table: "Sire, remember the Athenians"; and it consoles me too that the places I revisit and the books I reread always smile upon me with the freshness of novelty.

Not without reason is it said that no one who is not conscious of having a sound memory should set up to be a liar. I know quite well that grammarians make a distinction between telling an untruth and lying. They say that to tell an untruth is to say something that is false, but that we suppose to be true, and that the meaning of the Latin *mentiri,* from which our French word for lying [3] derives, is to go against one's conscience, and that consequently it applies only to those who say the opposite of what they know; and it is of them I am speaking.

Now liars either invent the whole thing, or they disguise and alter an actual fact. If they disguise and alter, it is hard for them not to get mixed up when they refer to the same story again and again because,

the real facts having been the first to lodge in the memory and impress themselves upon it by way of consciousness and knowledge, they will hardly fail to spring into the mind and dislodge the false version, which cannot have as firm or assured a foothold. The circumstances, as they were first learned, will always rush back into the thoughts, driving out the memory of the false or modified details that have been added.

If liars make a complete invention, they apparently have much less reason to be afraid of tripping up, inasmuch as there is no contrary impression to clash with their fiction. But even this, being an empty thing that offers no hold, readily escapes from the memory unless it is a very reliable one. I have often had amusing proof of this, at the expense of those who profess to suit their speech only to the advantage of the business in hand and to please the great men to whom they are speaking. The circumstances to which it is their wish to subordinate their faith and their conscience being subject to various changes, their language has also to change from time to time; and so they call the same thing gray one moment and yellow the next, say one thing to one man, and another to another. Then, if these listeners happen to bring all this contrary information together as a common booty,[4] what becomes of all their fine art? Besides, they trip up so often when they are off their guard. For what memory could be strong enough to retain all the different shapes they have invented for the same subject? I have seen many in my time who have desired a reputation for this subtle kind of discretion, not seeing that the reputation and the end in view are incompatible.

Lying is indeed an accursed vice. We are men, and we have relations with one another only by speech. If we recognized

[1] **a ... author:** Cicero, speaking of Caesar.

[2] **Darius:** Montaigne refers to Darius I ("the Great"), king of Persia from 521–486 B.C. He was defeated by the Athenians in two attacks on Greece, notably at the Battle of Marathon in 490 B.C.

[3] **lying:** The French verb meaning *to lie* is *mentir.*

[4] **common booty:** Booty is plunder or gain; it is used here in the sense of "common property."

the horror and gravity of an untruth, we should more justifiably punish it with fire than any other crime. I commonly find people taking the most ill-advised pains to correct their children for their harmless faults and worrying them about heedless acts which leave no trace and have no consequences.Lying—and in a lesser degree obstinacy—are, in my opinion, the only faults whose birth and progress we should consistently oppose. They grow with a child's growth, and once the tongue has got the knack of lying, it is difficult to imagine how impossible it is to correct it. Whence it happens that we find some otherwise excellent men subject to this fault and enslaved by it. I have a decent lad as my tailor, whom I have never heard to utter a single truth, even when it would have been to his advantage.

If, like the truth, falsehood had only one face, we should know better where we are, for we should then take the opposite of what a liar said to be the truth. But the opposite of a truth has a hundred thousand shapes and a limitless field.

The Pythagoreans [1] regard good as certain and finite, and evil as boundless and uncertain. There are a thousand ways of missing the bull's-eye, only one of hitting it. I am by no means sure that I could induce myself to tell a brazen and deliberate lie even to protect myself from the most obvious and extreme danger. An ancient father [2] says that we are better off in the company of a dog we know than in that of a man whose language we do not understand. Therefore those of different nations do not regard one another as men, and how much less friendly is false speech than silence!

King Francis the First [3] boasted of having by this means drawn circles round Francesco Taverna, ambassador of Francesco Sforza, [4] Duke of Milan—a man of great reputation in the art of speech-making. Taverna had been sent to make his master's excuses to His Majesty in a matter of great importance, which was this: the King wished to have constant channels of information in Italy, from which he had recently been expelled, and especially in the Duchy of Milan. He had decided, therefore, to keep a gentleman of his own at the Duke's court, an ambassador in effect, but in appearance a private individual ostensibly there on his own personal business. For the Duke very much depended on the Emperor [5]—especially at that moment when he was negotiating a marriage with his niece, the King of Denmark's daughter, now the Dowager Duchess of Lorraine—and he could not establish open relations or intercourse with us without great prejudice to himself. A Milanese gentleman named Merveille, one of the King's equerries, was chosen for this office and was despatched with secret credentials and instructions as ambassador, also with letters of recommendation to the Duke in the matter of his own private affairs as a mask and a show. However, he was at Court so long that the Emperor began to grow suspicious; and it was this, we believe, that gave rise to the subsequent events, which were that one fine night the Duke had Merveille's head cut off on a false charge of murder, his whole trial having been hurried through in a couple of days!

[1] **Pythagoreans:** followers of a school of philosophy founded by Pythagoras in the sixth century B.C. Pythagoras, a mathematician and astronomer who traveled far in search of wisdom, believed that the purpose of earthly life is the purification of the soul.

[2] **An ancient father:** St. Augustine (?–604), founder of the Christian church in England.

[3] **King Francis the First:** King of France (1515–47).

[4] **Francesco Sforza:** Francesco II (1492–1535), the last of the dukes of Milan.

[5] **Emperor:** the Holy Roman Emperor, Charles V (1519–56). Both the King of France and the Duke of Milan were subordinate to the Emperor, as were all the other dukes and kings of western Europe.

Francesco Taverna had come with a long falsified account of the affair—for the King had addressed himself to all the princes in Christendom, as well as to the Duke, demanding satisfaction—and he was received in audience one morning. In support of his case he advanced several plausible justifications of the deed, carefully prepared for the purpose. He pleaded that his master had never taken our man for anything but a private gentleman and a subject of his own, who had come to Milan on his own business and resided there in no other character. He denied all knowledge that Merveille was a member of the King's household or was even known to the King, much less that he was his ambassador. King Francis, in his turn, pressed objections and questions upon him, attacking him from all sides and cornering him at last on the point of the execution, carried out at night and apparently in secret. To which the poor embarrassed man replied, as if to put an honest face on the matter, that out of respect for His Majesty, the Duke would have been sorry to let the execution take place in daylight. You can guess how quickly he was caught out in this clumsy self-contradiction, made in the presence of such a nose [1] as King Francis had.

Pope Julius the Second [2] having sent an ambassador to the King of England, to incite him against the French king, and having stated his case, the English king, in his reply, dwelt on the difficulties he would find in making the necessary preparations for attacking so powerful a king, and put forward certain reasons for them. The ambassador then, ill advisedly, answered that he had himself considered these difficulties, and had put them before the Pope. From this statement, so foreign to his purpose, which was to urge him to immediate war, the King of England at once inferred what he afterward found to be the case, that this ambassador was privately inclined to the French side. When he informed the Pope of this, the ambassador's property was confiscated, and he barely escaped with his life.

FOR STUDY AND DISCUSSION

1. What two kinds of falsehood does Montaigne write about? What is the difference between them?

2. The first seven paragraphs of this essay are not about liars. What are they about? Why do you think Montaigne organized the essay in this way?

3. Make a brief topic outline of paragraph 6. Then state, in a sentence, the main idea of the paragraph.

4. Is Montaigne's title "On Liars" the best title for this essay? Can you suggest a title that would be more accurate?

5. What aspects of this essay suggest that reading Montaigne is neither "frivolous" nor "unrewarding"?

USE OF ILLUSTRATION

In developing his point, Montaigne employs a valuable technique—the use of narrative illustrations. The last two paragraphs of "On Liars" contain amusing historical anecdotes related to the ideas in the first part of the essay: memory and lying. Review the essay, omitting the last two paragraphs. Do you think the essay is more or less effective without them? Why?

In your own writing, remember that a good story is often the most interesting and forceful way of supporting a point. Be certain, however, that your story is really related to your topic.

THE TOPIC SENTENCE PARAGRAPH

Montaigne makes frequent and careful use of the topic sentence. A topic sentence states the main idea or topic of a paragraph. Although it is often found at the beginning of a para-

[1] **nose:** All the portraits of Francis I agree that his nose was of unusual size.

[2] **Julius the Second:** Julius became Pope in 1503.

graph, it may also occur in the middle or at the end. See, for instance, Montaigne's paragraph beginning "Lying is indeed an accursed vice" (page 172). Note that everything in this paragraph is directly related to this concise statement.

Not all paragraphs have topic sentences that are stated directly. However, a good paragraph always has a topic. Look at some of the other paragraphs in "On Liars." What is the topic sentence for each? Are there any paragraphs in the essay that do *not* have topic sentences?

LANGUAGE AND VOCABULARY

To make the new words we come across in reading literature a meaningful part of our vocabulary, there are a few simple steps we can follow. Generally, the first step is to look up the word in a dictionary. The second step is to note carefully how the word is used in the sentence or phrase in the text. The third and most important step is to use the word in an original sentence.

Using a dictionary, find the meanings of the words italicized in the passages below. Then make sure that you understand what the words mean in the sentences of which they are a part. Finally, use these words in different sentences of your own.

"All my other *faculties* are poor and ordinary, but in this I think I am most rare and *singular* and deserve to gain name and fame thereby."

"Certainly I am *prone* enough to forgetfulness . . ."

"I might easily have let my intelligence and judgment follow *languidly* in other men's footsteps . . ."

"not seeing that the reputation and the end in view are *incompatible.*"

"The Pythagoreans regard good as certain and *finite* . . ."

FOR COMPOSITION

Write a theme on telling the truth. Select a clear main idea, and support this idea (in the manner of Montaigne) by informal, personal reference to your own beliefs.

Sir Roger and the Witches

JOSEPH ADDISON

(1672–1719)

In the eighteenth century, coffee houses, the forerunners of today's private clubs, were the gathering places of intelligent men of similar tastes and interests. Here information, opinions, and gossip were exchanged; news was spread; and the political events, the books and plays, and general business of the day were discussed.

At the turn of the century in London, many of the notable figures in the literary and political world gathered almost every day in one of the city's numerous coffee houses. Of these people, one of the most noteworthy was Joseph Addison, an Oxford graduate, classical scholar, member of Parliament, poet, dramatist, and—most important—an essayist. Addison's friend Richard Steele (1672–1729) in 1709 started a periodical of news and commentary called the *Tatler,* which appeared three times weekly and to which Addison contributed articles and essays. When in 1711 the *Tatler* was forced to discontinue, Addison and Steele together founded the *Spectator* as a daily publication. While Steele had been chiefly responsible for the *Tatler,* Addison wrote the majority of the essays for the *Spectator.*

The *Spectator* papers consisted of largely informal, conversational essays on an immense range of subjects typical of those discussed in the coffee houses. In their essays, which were usually gently satirical and often humorous, Addison and Steele wrote about literature, praised virtue, and tried to improve the manners and tastes of their readers. Some of the

most charming of the *Spectator* papers are those in which members of the fictitious Spectator Club comment upon a particular subject of interest. The essayists' own ideas are thus presented as the personal, subjective commentary of a "real" person. Their entertaining approach to their subject matter, combined with their good-natured and lively style, made these early newspapers immensely popular and influential. When we consider that English prose before Addison's time had been somewhat stiff and formal, it is easy to see why Addison enjoyed both great influence and popularity. Years later, another great English writer, Samuel Johnson, said, "Whoever wishes to attain an English style, familiar but not coarse, and elegant but not ostentatious, must give his days and nights to the volumes of Addison."

The essay which follows appeared in the *Spectator* on July 14, 1711. In it the subject of witches is discussed with Sir Roger de Coverley, the country squire who is the most prominent member of the imaginary Spectator Club and who represents the opinions and way of life of the English landed gentry.

THERE ARE some opinions in which a man should stand neuter,[1] without engaging his assent to one side or the other. Such a hovering faith as this, which refuses to settle upon any determination, is absolutely necessary in a mind that is careful to avoid errors and prepossessions. When the arguments press equally on both sides in matters that are indifferent to us, the safest method is to give up ourselves to neither.

It is with this temper of mind that I consider the subject of witchcraft. When I hear the relations that are made from all parts of the world, not only from Norway and Lapland, from the East and West Indies, but from every particular nation in Europe, I cannot forbear thinking that there is such an intercourse and commerce

[1] **neuter:** neutral.

with evil spirits as that which we express by the name of witchcraft. But when I consider that the ignorant and credulous parts of the world abound most in these relations, and that the persons among us who are supposed to engage in such an infernal commerce,[2] are people of a weak understanding and crazed imagination, and at the same time reflect upon the many impostures and delusions of this nature that have been detected in all ages, I endeavor to suspend my belief till I hear more certain accounts than any which have yet come to my knowledge. In short, when I consider the question, whether there are such persons in the world as those we call witches, my mind is divided between two opposite opinions; or rather (to speak my thoughts freely) I believe in general that there is, and has been, such a thing as witchcraft; but at the same time can give no credit to any particular instance of it.

I am engaged in this speculation, by some occurrences that I met with yesterday, which I shall give my reader an account of at large. As I was walking with my friend Sir Roger[3] by the side of one of his woods, an old woman applied herself to me for my charity. Her dress and figure put me in mind of the following description in Otway:[4]

In a close lane, as I pursued my journey,
I spied a wrinkled hag, with age grown double,
Picking dry sticks, and mumbling to herself;
Her eyes with scalding rheum were galled and red;

[2] **infernal commerce:** dealings with the devil or other evil spirits.
[3] **Sir Roger:** Sir Roger de Coverley.
[4] **Otway:** Thomas Otway (1652–1685). This passage is a description of a beggar woman in Act II of Otway's *The Orphan,* a very popular tragedy.

Cold palsy shook her head; her hands
 seemed withered,
And on her crooked shoulders had she
 wrapped
The tattered remnants of an old striped
 hanging,
Which served to keep her carcass from
 the cold;
So there was nothing of a piece about
 her:
Her lower weeds were all o'er coarsely
 patched
With different colored rags, black, red,
 white, yellow,
And seemed to speak variety of
 wretchedness.

As I was musing on this description and comparing it with the object before me, the knight told me that this very old woman had the reputation of a witch all over the country, that her lips were observed to be always in motion, and that there was not a switch [1] about her house which her neighbors did not believe had carried her several hundreds of miles. If she chanced to stumble, they always found sticks or straws that lay in the figure of a cross before her. If she made any mistake at church, and cried "Amen" in a wrong place, they never failed to conclude that she was saying her prayers backward. There was not a maid in the parish that would take a pin of her, though she should offer a bag of money with it. She goes by the name of Moll White and has made the country ring with several imaginary exploits which are palmed upon her. If the dairymaid does not make her butter to come so soon as she would have it, Moll White is at the bottom of the churn. If a horse sweats in the stable, Moll White has been upon his back. If a hare makes an unexpected

escape from the hounds, the huntsman curses Moll White. Nay (says Sir Roger), I have known the master of the pack, upon such an occasion, send one of his servants to see if Moll White had been out that morning.

This account raised my curiosity so far, that I begged my friend Sir Roger to go with me into her hovel, which stood in a solitary corner under the side of the wood. Upon our first entering, Sir Roger winked to me and pointed to something that stood behind the door, which, upon looking that way, I found to be an old broom staff. At the same time he whispered me in the ear to take notice of a tabby cat [2] that sat in the chimney corner, which, as the knight told me, lay under as bad a report as Moll White herself; for besides that Moll is said often to accompany her in the same shape, the cat is reported to have spoken twice or thrice in her life and to have played several pranks above the capacity of an ordinary cat.

I was secretly concerned to see human nature in so much wretchedness and disgrace, but at the same time could not forbear smiling to hear Sir Roger, who is a little puzzled about the old woman, advising her, as a justice of peace, to avoid all communication with the devil and never to hurt any of her neighbors' cattle. We concluded our visit with a bounty, [3] which was very acceptable.

On our return home, Sir Roger told me that old Moll had been often brought before him for making children spit pins, and giving maids the nightmare; and that the country people would be tossing her into a pond and trying experiments with her every day, if it was not for him and his chaplain.

[1] **switch:** a broom.

[2] **tabby cat:** Witches were often supposed to use cats to assist them in their "spells."

[3] **bounty:** a present of money.

I have since found, upon inquiry, that Sir Roger was several times staggered with the reports that had been brought him concerning this old woman and would frequently have bound her over to the county sessions, had not his chaplain with much ado persuaded him to the contrary.

I have been the more particular in this account, because I hear there is scarce a village in England that has not a Moll White in it. When an old woman begins to dote [1] and grow chargeable to a parish, she is generally turned into a witch and fills the whole country with extravagant fancies, imaginary distempers, and terrifying dreams. In the meantime the poor wretch that is the innocent occasion of so many evils begins to be frighted at herself, and sometimes confesses secret commerces and familiarities that her imagination forms in a delirious old age. This frequently cuts off charity from the greatest objects of compassion and inspires people with a malevolence toward those poor decrepit parts of our species, in whom human nature is defaced by infirmity and dotage.

[1] **dote:** to grow old and feebleminded.

FOR STUDY AND DISCUSSION

1. How does the essay define *witchcraft?* What is the attitude of the essayist toward the subject of witches and witchcraft? What is Sir Roger's attitude?

2. Why did the townspeople think that Moll White was a witch? What does the essay seem to be saying about the people who treat Moll White, and others like her, as they do?

3. Today it is probable that very few people sincerely believe in witches, at least not in the more "civilized" parts of the world. How can we account for the decline of interest in witchcraft since Addison's time?

4. Judging from this essay, what is your opinion of the English landed gentry of Sir Roger's time?

USE OF SPECIFIC DETAIL

Addison begins his essay with two paragraphs of "speculation"—that is, general ideas on the subject of witchcraft as he has heard about it from different parts of the world. But he does not come to a real conclusion about the topic until he comes to the story of Sir Roger and Moll White. He makes the reader *see* Moll White and *feel* for her as a specific person. How much more interesting this is than a flat statement such as: "For no good reason old women are sometimes mistaken for witches." In your own writing, remember that a specific, dramatic example will make your idea come alive. A mass of general statements is only a beginning, not a convincing argument.

LANGUAGE AND VOCABULARY

One effective and often interesting way to enlarge your working vocabulary is to learn the meaning of a word as a writer uses it and then proceed to study some of the *cognates* of the word—that is, other words formed from the same root or stem. For instance, in the first sentence of this essay Addison uses the word *neuter* as we would use *neutral*. Both words mean, literally, "not either." A much more recent word, *neutron,* looks suspiciously like both of these. What does it mean?

In the groups of words below, the italicized word is the one used by Addison. Make certain of its meaning; then use the other words in sentences which will clearly demonstrate their meanings. Whenever you are in doubt, use a dictionary.

credulous; credible
delusions; illusions, allusions
muse; amuse, bemuse
compassion; passion
malevolence; malefactor

FOR COMPOSITION

1. "There are some opinions in which a man should stand neuter [neutral] . . ." Write a short essay in which you apply this statement to a subject of your own choosing.

2. Write a brief essay in which you set forth your own beliefs about witches and witchcraft.

The Voyage

WASHINGTON IRVING
(1783–1859)

"I was always fond of visiting new scenes, and observing strange characters and manners," wrote Washington Irving at the beginning of *The Sketch Book.* "Even when a mere child I began my travels," he went on. "Books of voyages and travels became my passion, and in devouring their contents, I neglected the regular exercises of the school."

Irving did indeed travel: he spent two years in Europe, for his health, from 1804 to 1806. After the failure of an importing business which he and two of his brothers started in New York, he was back in England, where he wrote the essays and stories, such as "The Legend of Sleepy Hollow" and "Rip Van Winkle," for which he is best known. He spent several years in Spain, as writer and researcher for a series of books and as the American Minister in Madrid. It is not surprising, therefore, that the first essay in *The Sketch Book,* which follows below, is a meditation about travel.

Irving was the first American writer to establish a solid reputation in Europe. He had a deep affection for the past, a vivid imagination, and a real ability to transmit his impressions to his readers. He was "naturally a maker of legends," as one critic puts it. This ability to "spin a yarn" attracted the attention of Sir Walter Scott, the great Scottish novelist, who was so charmed with Irving's sketches that he helped to get them published in England. Irving's essays and stories have remained popular mainly because the personality of their creator can always be seen in them: the essays are familiar, personal writing

in the same way that the essays of Montaigne and Addison are familiar and personal. Irving's love of a "yarn" is evident here in his meditation about a sea voyage from New York to Liverpool.

Ships, ships, I will descrie you
 Amidst the main,
I will come and try you,
What you are protecting,
And projecting,
 What's your end and aim.
One goes abroad for merchandise and trading,
Another stays to keep his country from invading,
A third is coming home with rich and wealthy lading.
Halloo! my fancie, whither wilt thou go?
 Old Poem

To AN AMERICAN visiting Europe, the long voyage he has to make is an excellent preparative. The temporary absence of worldly scenes and employments produces a state of mind peculiarly fitted to receive new and vivid impressions. The vast space of waters that separates the hemispheres is like a blank page in existence. There is no gradual transition, by which, as in Europe, the features and population of one country blend almost imperceptibly with those of another. From the moment you lose sight of the land you have left, all is vacancy until you step on the opposite shore and are launched at once into the bustle and novelties of another world.

In traveling by land there is a continuity of scene and a connected succession of persons and incidents that carry on the story of life and lessen the effect of absence and separation. We drag, it is true, "a lengthening chain" at each remove of our pilgrimage; but the chain is unbroken: we can trace it back link by link; and we feel that the last still grapples us to home. But a wide sea voyage severs

us at once. It makes us conscious of being cast loose from the secure anchorage of settled life and sent adrift upon a doubtful world. It interposes a gulf, not merely imaginary, but real, between us and our homes—a gulf subject to tempest, and fear, and uncertainty, rendering distance palpable and return precarious.

Such, at least, was the case with myself. As I saw the last blue line of my native land fade away like a cloud in the horizon, it seemed as if I had closed one volume of the world and its concerns and had time for meditation before I opened another. That land, too, now vanishing from my view, which contained all most dear to me in life; what vicissitudes might occur in it, what changes might take place in me, before I should visit it again! Who can tell, when he sets forth to wander, whither he may be driven by the uncertain currents of existence; or when he may return; or whether it may ever be his lot to revisit the scenes of his childhood?

I said that at sea all is vacancy; I should correct the expression. To one given to daydreaming and fond of losing himself in reveries, a sea voyage is full of subjects for meditation; but then they are the wonders of the deep and of the air and rather tend to abstract the mind from worldly themes. I delighted to loll over the quarter railing, or climb to the maintop, of a calm day, and muse for hours together on the tranquil bosom of a summer's sea; to gaze upon the piles of golden clouds just peering above the horizon, fancy them some fairy realms, and people them with a creation of my own; to watch the gentle undulating billows rolling their silver volumes as if to die away on those happy shores.

There was a delicious sensation of mingled security and awe with which I looked down, from my giddy height, on the monsters of the deep at their uncouth gambols. Shoals of porpoises tumbling about the bow of the ship; the grampus [1] slowly heaving his huge form above the surface; or the ravenous shark darting, like a specter, through the blue waters. My imagination would conjure up all that I had heard or read of the watery world beneath me; of the finny herds that roam its fathomless valleys; of the shapeless monsters that lurk among the very foundations of the earth; and of those wild phantasms that swell the tales of fishermen and sailors.

Sometimes a distant sail, gliding along the edge of the ocean, would be another theme of idle speculation. How interesting this fragment of a world, hastening to rejoin the great mass of existence! What a glorious monument of human invention; which has in a manner triumphed over wind and wave; has brought the ends of the world into communion; has established an interchange of blessings, pouring into the sterile regions of the north all the luxuries of the south; has diffused the light of knowledge and the charities of cultivated life; and has thus bound together those scattered portions of the human race, between which nature seemed to have thrown an insurmountable barrier.

We one day descried some shapeless object drifting at a distance. At sea, everything that breaks the monotony of the surrounding expanse attracts attention. It proved to be the mast of a ship that must have been completely wrecked; for there were the remains of handkerchiefs, by which some of the crew had fastened themselves to this spar, to prevent their being washed off by the waves. There was no trace by which the name of the ship could be ascertained. The wreck had evidently drifted about for many months;

[1] **grampus:** a large dolphin.

clusters of shellfish had fastened about it, and long seaweeds flaunted at its sides. But where, thought I, is the crew? Their struggle has long been over, they have gone down amidst the roar of the tempest, their bones lie whitening among the caverns of the deep. Silence, oblivion, like the waves, have closed over them, and no one can tell the story of their end. What sighs have been wafted after that ship! what prayers offered up at the deserted fireside of home! How often has the wife, the mother, pored over the daily news to catch some casual intelligence of this rover of the deep! How has expectation darkened into anxiety—anxiety into dread—and dread into despair! Alas! not one memento may ever return for love to cherish. All that may ever be known is that she sailed from her port "and was never heard of more!"

The sight of this wreck, as usual, gave rise to many dismal anecdotes. This was particularly the case in the evening, when the weather, which had hitherto been fair, began to look wild and threatening and gave indications of one of those sudden storms which will sometimes break in upon the serenity of a summer voyage. As we sat round the full light of a lamp in the cabin, that made the gloom more ghastly, every one had his tale of shipwreck and disaster. I was particularly

struck with a short one related by the captain.

"As I was once sailing," said he, "in a fine stout ship across the banks of Newfoundland, one of those heavy fogs which prevail in those parts rendered it impossible for us to see far ahead even in the daytime; but at night the weather was so thick that we could not distinguish any object at twice the length of the ship. I kept lights at the masthead and a constant watch forward to look out for fishing smacks, which are accustomed to lie at anchor on the banks. The wind was blowing a smacking breeze, and we were going at a great rate through the water. Suddenly the watch gave the alarm of 'a sail ahead!'—it was scarcely uttered before we were upon her. She was a small schooner, at anchor, with her broadside toward us. The crew were all asleep and had neglected to hoist a light. We struck her just amidships. The force, the size, and weight of our vessel bore her down below the waves; we passed over her and were hurried on our course. As the crashing wreck was sinking beneath us, I had a glimpse of two or three half-naked wretches rushing from her cabin; they just started from their beds to be swallowed shrieking by the waves. I heard their drowning cry mingling with the wind. The blast that bore it to our ears swept us out

of all farther hearing. I shall never forget that cry! It was some time before we could put the ship about, she was under such headway. We returned, as nearly as we could guess, to the place where the smack had anchored. We cruised about for several hours in the dense fog. We fired signal guns and listened if we might hear the halloo of any survivors; but all was silent—we never saw or heard anything of them more.''

I confess these stories, for a time, put an end to all my fine fancies. The storm increased with the night. The sea was lashed into tremendous confusion. There was a fearful, sullen sound of rushing waves and broken surges. Deep called unto deep. At times the black volume of clouds overhead seemed rent asunder by flashes of lightning which quivered along the foaming billows and made the succeeding darkness doubly terrible. The thunders bellowed over the wild waste of waters and were echoed and prolonged by the mountain waves. As I saw the ship staggering and plunging among these roaring caverns, it seemed miraculous that she regained her balance or preserved her buoyancy. Her yards [1] would dip into the water: her bow was almost buried beneath the waves. Sometimes an impending surge appeared ready to overwhelm her, and nothing but a dexterous movement of the helm preserved her from the shock.

When I retired to my cabin, the awful scene still followed me. The whistling of the wind through the rigging sounded like funereal wailings. The creaking of the masts, the straining and groaning of bulkheads, as the ship labored in the weltering sea, were frightful. As I heard the waves rushing along the sides of the ship and roaring in my very ear, it seemed as if

Death were raging round this floating prison, seeking for his prey: the mere starting of a nail, the yawning of a seam, might give him entrance.

A fine day, however, with a tranquil sea and favoring breeze, soon put all these dismal reflections to flight. It is impossible to resist the gladdening influence of fine weather and fair wind at sea. When the ship is decked out in all her canvas, every sail swelled, and careering gaily over the curling waves, how lofty, how gallant she appears—how she seems to lord it over the deep!

I might fill a volume with the reveries of a sea voyage, for with me it is almost a continual reverie—but it is time to get to shore.

It was a fine sunny morning when the thrilling cry of "land!" was given from the masthead. None but those who have experienced it can form an idea of the delicious throng of sensations which rush into an American's bosom, when he first comes in sight of Europe. There is a volume of associations with the very name. It is the land of promise, teeming with everything of which his childhood has heard or on which his studious years have pondered.

From that time until the moment of arrival, it was all feverish excitement. The ships of war, that prowled like guardian giants along the coast; the headlands of Ireland, stretching out into the channel; the Welsh mountains, towering into the clouds: all were objects of intense interest. As we sailed up the Mersey [2] I reconnoitered the shores with a telescope. My eye dwelt with delight on neat cottages, with their trim shrubberies and green grass plots. I saw the moldering ruin of an abbey overrun with ivy and the

[1] **yards:** masts which support sails.

[2] **Mersey:** a river in northwest England, which flows into the Irish Sea; at its mouth is the port of Liverpool.

taper spire of a village church rising from the brow of a neighboring hill—all were characteristic of England.

The tide and wind were so favorable that the ship was enabled to come at once to the pier. It was thronged with people: some, idle lookers-on; others, eager expectants of friends or relatives. I could distinguish the merchant to whom the ship was consigned. I knew him by his calculating brow and restless air. His hands were thrust into his pockets; he was whistling thoughtfully and walking to and fro, a small space having been accorded him by the crowd in deference to his temporary importance. There were repeated cheerings and salutations interchanged between the shore and the ship, as friends happened to recognize each other. I particularly noticed one young woman of humble dress but interesting demeanor. She was leaning forward from among the crowd; her eye hurried over the ship as it neared the shore, to catch some wished-for countenance. She seemed disappointed and agitated; when I heard a faint voice call her name. It was from a poor sailor who had been ill all the voyage and had excited the sympathy of every one on board. When the weather was fine, his messmates had spread a mattress for him on deck in the shade; but of late his illness had so increased that he had taken to his hammock and only breathed a wish that he might see his wife before he died. He had been helped on deck as we came up the river and was now leaning against the shrouds, with a countenance so wasted, so pale, so ghastly, that it was no wonder even the eye of affection did not recognize him. But at the sound of his voice, her eye darted on his features: it read, at once, a whole volume of sorrow; she clasped her hands, uttered a faint shriek, and stood wringing them in silent agony.

All now was hurry and bustle—the meetings of acquaintances, the greeting of friends, the consultations of men of business. I alone was solitary and idle. I had no friend to meet, no cheering to receive. I stepped upon the land of my forefathers—but felt that I was a stranger in the land.

1. Does this essay have a single main idea? If so, what? Or are there several main ideas?

2. What parts of the essay are particularly personal: where does Irving most clearly talk about himself?

3. Irving calls a ship a "fragment of a world." What does he mean by this?

4. Why does the essayist use most of a long paragraph to describe a young wife waiting for her sick sailor husband? Does this episode add anything to the main idea of the essay? to the reader's understanding of Irving?

5. Why do you suppose Irving says at the end of the essay that he felt himself, after all the eager expectation of the voyage, to be a stranger in the land of his forefathers? Do you think this last paragraph upsets the unity of the essay? Why or why not?

6. For Irving, comparing travel by land and by sea meant comparing travel by stagecoach and by square-rigged ship. Are any of the things he says still valid in the age of trains, automobiles, fast ships, and jet planes?

IMAGINATIVE WRITING IN THE ESSAY

"The Voyage" is basically a very simple essay. It makes a comparison between land travel and sea travel and continues to tell about daydreaming, fish, a distant ship, a wreck, the captain's story about sinking a fishing smack, the stormy night, land sighted, and the people who meet the ship. But obviously, a routine list of this sort ignores the means by which the author holds his reader's interest. These means include the use of specific detail, of narrative anecdote, and of figurative language—all the products of the writer's vivid imagination.

Irving is not satisfied with general statements only; he supports them with specific details. For example, when he says that he looks down on the monsters of the deep, he immediately names three monsters he sees and then lets his imagination run on about those he cannot see. When a derelict ship is sighted, Irving has the captain tell the story about crashing into a fishing boat off Newfoundland, thus creating a more vivid impres-

sion of tragedy than any mere speculation about the wreck could develop.

In the essay by Joseph Addison (page 175), we have already come across an essay which makes use of narrative anecdote. Irving likewise introduces a story into his essay: the captain's story. It is probably a true story. We have no way of knowing, and it doesn't really matter, and, in any case, Irving's imagination has probably made the story better as he retells it. The important point is the contribution the anecdote makes toward lively reading.

LANGUAGE AND VOCABULARY

The *denotation* of a word is its exact, or specific, meaning; the *connotation* of a word is the meaning which the word suggests, in addition to its literal meaning. For instance, the word *rat* denotes a rodent of the genus *Rattus*. But to some people, *rat* connotes many things: any unclean, horrible animal in the barn; a person who cannot be trusted; and so on. A writer's careful control of both denotation and connotation is of great importance in all kinds of writing, but especially in description, in which the impression which the writer wishes to create must be clear.

Washington Irving was of course aware of these two aspects of word meaning. Review the fifth paragraph of "The Voyage," and be ready to explain both the denotative and the connotative meanings of the following words: *monsters, specter, fathomless, phantasms.* How is the vividness of the paragraph increased by connotation?

FOR COMPOSITION

1. To understand how figurative language helps meaning, rewrite the second paragraph of Irving's essay without changing the main idea, but using no figures of speech whatever. Compare the original and the revision. Why is Irving's a better paragraph?

2. Write a short essay about your impressions of a trip that you have taken. Do not simply recount what you did or where you went. Instead, start with a unifying main idea and support this by specific, clear illustrations of your feelings about your "voyage."

EUROPEAN PAINTING

Sixteenth-Century Painting

The early sixteenth century was a golden age for Italian art, a time when painters, sculptors, and architects created a style of exceptional power and grandeur which was soon to spread across all of Europe. This was the period known as the High Renaissance.

If any one artist could be singled out as the pioneer of this "grand style," it would have to be Leonardo da Vinci, the most versatile genius of his time. For he was not only a painter and sculptor, but also an architect, musician, engineer, and inventor. Leonardo's keen observation of nature and his prodigious artistic skills can both be seen to good advantage in the famous *Mona Lisa* (PLATE 1), a masterpiece of portraiture which astonished sixteenth-century Italy. It was an entirely new kind of portrait—not just the usual physical likeness, such as Piero della Francesca's rocklike profile of the Duke of Urbino (page 117), but also an expression of personality. The Mona Lisa looks at us with such a curious smile that we cannot help but wonder what she is thinking. Leonardo has created this mysterious effect by blurring certain details, softening parts of the mouth and eyes with hints of shadow. And he has also related the figure so intimately to the background that there is no feeling of emptiness in the composition of the picture, even in the vast open spaces of the distant mountainous landscape.

Leonardo's chief competitor in the early 1500's was a young, intense Florentine named Michelangelo Buonarroti. Like Leonardo, Michelangelo was highly skilled in a number of the arts, but he always considered himself primarily a sculptor. And it was largely for this reason that he at first refused a commission from Pope Julius II for a huge fresco that would cover the more than 10,000 square feet of ceiling in the Vatican's Sistine Chapel. But when the Pope insisted, Michelangelo resigned himself to the task. For four long years he worked flat on his back, lying on an enormous scaffold a few feet below the ceiling. Taking his theme from biblical stories, he painted over three hundred and forty human figures in many different sizes and in a great variety of poses. As you enter the chapel and look upward,

the immediate effect is overwhelming, for most of the figures seem almost bursting with energy. PLATE 2, for instance, shows the Delphic Sibyl, an ancient prophetess who lived at the sacred temple of Delphi. This massive figure (who would stand over fourteen feet tall) is shown turning suddenly, as if she had been interrupted while reading the scroll she is holding. Though her body seems solidly placed in the architectural setting, notice that the curve of her cape, her streaming hair, and the swing of her torso suggest great potential energy.

A third master of the "grand style" of the High Renaissance was the Umbrian painter Raphael, who had come to work in Florence in 1504, at the age of twenty-one. Although strongly influenced by both Leonardo and Michelangelo, Raphael soon developed a soft, graceful style of his own. Yet even his smallest paintings have a certain grandeur. A fine example is his *St. George and the Dragon,* a tiny panel less than twelve inches high (PLATE 3).

The influence of Florentine painting spread north to the island city of Venice, but painters there also had a strong native tradition, as you can see in Giorgione's *Three Philosophers* (PLATE 4). Compare the soft modeling of forms here with the hard sculptural contours in Raphael's painting. And notice that Giorgione has used his landscape background to evoke a serene, pastoral mood, which harmonizes with the quiet contemplation of the three philosophers.

The most famous of all Venetian painters was Titian, an artist of tremendous creative powers. Early in his career, Titian worked with Giorgione, but it was not until after his young friend's premature death that he developed a mature, vigorous style, more varied in its range of colors and much freer in brushwork. In his portrait, *Charles V on Horseback* (PLATE 5), Titian represented the proud emperor dressed in parade armor after a decisive victory near the North German town of Mühlberg. The landscape, however, is based on Titian's memories of the countryside near Venice, where he had spent his boyhood. The entire scene is bathed in the warm, golden light of late afternoon.

The most important developments in landscape painting, however, took place in the north of Europe, especially in the work of Pieter Bruegel, the Elder, and other Flemish painters. Bruegel was interested in the dramatic changes which take place in nature from one season to another. *Hunters in the Snow* (PLATE 6), for instance, is meant to represent January and February in a series of panels devoted to the months of the year. As in many of his other landscape pictures, Bruegel composed the main action of the composition along a diagonal leading from figures in the foreground across the valley to the mountain peaks beyond. In this vast spread of nature, the dark silhouettes of the three hunters seem almost incidental — merely three dark silhouettes, along with many others, against the snow.

186

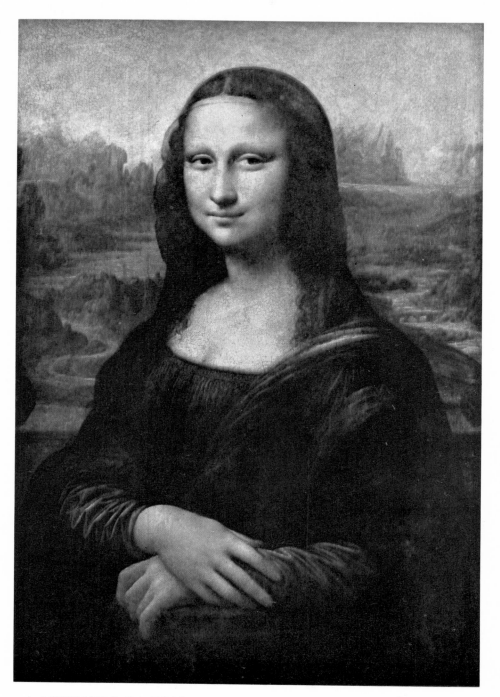

PLATE 1. LEONARDO DA VINCI (Florentine, 1452–1519): *Mona Lisa*. 1504. Oil on wood panel, 30 x 20⅝ inches. (The Louvre, Paris)

PLATE 2. MICHELANGELO (Florentine, 1475–1564): *The Delphic Sibyl*. 1509. Detail from the ceiling of the Sistine Chapel in the Vatican. Fresco. Entire ceiling is 130 feet 6 inches by 43 feet 6 inches; highest point above the floor is 59 feet. (Vatican, Rome)

PLATE 3. RAPHAEL (Umbrian, 1483–1520): *St. George and the Dragon.* 1504–1505. Oil on wood panel, $11\frac{1}{8}$ x $8\frac{3}{8}$ inches. (National Gallery of Art, Washington, D.C., Andrew Mellon Collection)

PLATE 4. GIORGIONE (Venetian, 1477/78–1510): *Three Philosophers*. 1507. Oil on canvas, $46\frac{1}{2}$ x $54\frac{7}{8}$ inches. (Kunsthistorisches Museum, Vienna)

PLATE 5. TITIAN (Venetian, 1480/90–1576): *Charles V on Horseback*. 1548. Oil on canvas, 130¾ x 109 inches. (The Prado, Madrid)

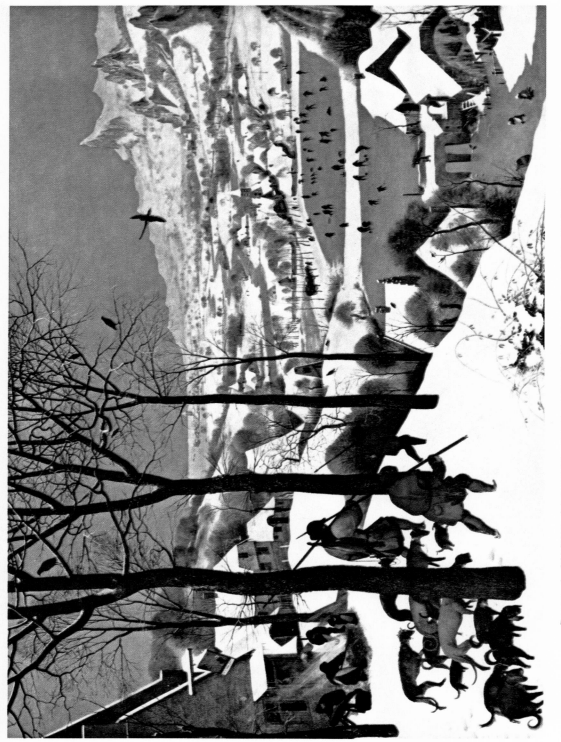

PLATE 6. PIETER BRUEGEL, THE ELDER (Flemish, about 1529–1569): *Hunters in the Snow.* 1565. Oil on wood panel, $46\frac{1}{8}$ x $63\frac{7}{8}$ inches. (Kunsthistorisches Museum, Vienna)

The Streets— Morning and Night

CHARLES DICKENS

(1812–1870)

Charles Dickens was a product of the lower middle class about which he wrote so convincingly. Because during Charles's boyhood his father was imprisoned for debt, Charles was forced to work in a factory at the age of twelve, and had therefore little schooling. A careful observer, he learned much at first-hand, however, about life in the great, teeming city of London and about the lamentable condition of the courts, prisons, hospitals, and poorhouses of his day. Hating injustice and having seen a great deal of it in his own life, Dickens later wrote about it almost every time he put pen to paper. Through books such as *Oliver Twist, Nicholas Nickleby,* and *David Copperfield,* a partly autobiographical account of the experiences of his own youth, Dickens became an effective champion of social reform.

Dickens began his first book, *Sketches by Boz,* at the age of twenty-two, while working as a newspaper reporter in London. *The Pickwick Papers,* which appeared in a monthly magazine three years later, started him on the road to fame and fortune. For the rest of his life he traveled, wrote endlessly, gave public readings of his works, appeared in theatricals, and in short, became highly successful as the most popular fiction writer of his day. Today his writings are still enjoyed by every kind of reader.

The essays which follow first appeared in *Sketches by Boz* and reveal Dickens as a wonderfully accurate observer of the world of Victorian England.

MORNING

THE APPEARANCE presented by the streets of London an hour before sunrise on a summer's morning is most striking even to the few whose unfortunate pursuits of pleasure, or scarcely less unfortunate pursuits of business, cause them to be well acquainted with the scene. There is an air of cold, solitary desolation about the noiseless streets, which we are accustomed to see thronged at other times by a busy, eager crowd, and over the quiet, closely shut buildings, which throughout the day are swarming with life and bustle, that is very impressive.

The last drunken man, who shall find his way home before sunlight, has just staggered heavily along, roaring out the burden of the drinking song of the previous night; the last houseless vagrant, whom penury and police have left in the streets, has coiled up his chilly limbs in some paved corner, to dream of food and warmth. The drunken, the dissipated, and the wretched have disappeared; the more sober and orderly part of the population have not yet awakened to the labors of the day, and the stillness of death is over the streets; its very hue seems to be imparted to them, cold and lifeless as they look in the gray, somber light of daybreak.

An occasional policeman may alone be seen at the street corners, listlessly gazing on the deserted prospect before him; and now and then a rakish-looking cat runs stealthily across the road and descends his own area with as much caution and slyness—bounding first on the water butt, then on the dust hole, and then alighting on the flagstones—as if he were conscious that his character depended on his gallantry of the preceding night escaping public observation. A partially opened bedroom window here and there bespeaks the heat of the weather and the

uneasy slumbers of its occupant; and the dim scanty flicker of the rushlight,[1] through the window blind, denotes the chamber of watching or sickness. With these few exceptions, the streets present no signs of life, nor the houses of habitation.

An hour wears away; the spires of the churches and roofs of the principal buildings are faintly tinged with the light of the rising sun; and the streets, by almost imperceptible degrees, begin to resume their bustle and animation. Market carts roll slowly along: the sleepy wagoner impatiently urging on his tired horses or vainly endeavoring to awaken the boy, who luxuriously stretched on the top of the fruit baskets, forgets, in happy oblivion, his long-cherished curiosity to behold the wonders of London.

Rough, sleepy-looking animals of strange appearance, something between ostlers[2] and hackney coachmen, begin to take down the shutters of early public houses; and little deal tables,[3] with the ordinary preparations for a street breakfast, make their appearance at the customary stations. Numbers of men and women (principally the latter), carrying upon their heads heavy baskets of fruit, toil down the park side of Piccadilly, on their way to Covent Garden, and, following each other in rapid succession, form a long straggling line from thence to the turn of the road at Knightsbridge.[4]

Here and there, a bricklayer's laborer, with the day's dinner tied up in a handkerchief, walks briskly to his work, and occasionally a little knot of three or four schoolboys on a stolen bathing expedition rattle merrily over the pavement, their boisterous mirth contrasting forcibly with the demeanor of the little sweep,[5] who, having knocked and rung till his arm aches, and being interdicted by a merciful legislature from endangering his lungs by calling out, sits patiently down on the doorstep until the housemaid may happen to awake.

Covent Garden market and the avenues leading to it are thronged with carts of all sorts, sizes, and descriptions, from the heavy lumbering wagon, with its four stout horses, to the jingling costermonger's[6] cart, with its consumptive donkey. The pavement is already strewed with decayed cabbage leaves, broken hay bands, and all the indescribable litter of a vegetable market; men are shouting, carts backing, horses neighing, boys fighting, basketwomen talking, piemen expatiating on the excellence of their pastry, and donkeys braying. These and a hundred other sounds form a compound discordant enough to a Londoner's ears and remarkably disagreeable to those of country gentlemen who are sleeping at the Hummums[7] for the first time.

Another hour passes away, and the day begins in good earnest. The servant of all work, who, under the plea of sleeping very soundly, has utterly disregarded "Missis's" ringing for half an hour previously, is warned by Master (whom Missis has sent up in his drapery to the landing place for that purpose), that it's half-past six, whereupon she awakes all of a sudden, with well-feigned astonishment, and goes downstairs very sulkily, wishing, while she strikes a light, that the principle of spontaneous combustion would extend itself to coals and kitchen range. When the fire is lighted, she opens

[1] **rushlight:** a candle made by dipping a rush, or heavy grass, in tallow.

[2] **ostlers:** stablemen or grooms.

[3] **deal tables:** tables made from plain pine boards.

[4] **Piccadilly ... Covent Garden ... Knightsbridge:** sections of London.

[5] **sweep:** a chimney sweep.

[6] **costermonger's:** A costermonger is a seller, or peddler, of vegetables and fruit.

[7] **Hummums:** a Turkish bath at Covent Garden.

A morning market scene typical of nineteenth-century London.

the street door to take in the milk, when, by the most singular coincidence in the world, she discovers that the servant next door has just taken in her milk too and that Mr. Todd's young man over the way is, by an equally extraordinary chance, taking down his master's shutters. The inevitable consequence is that she just steps, milk jug in hand, as far as next door, just to say "good morning" to Betsy Clark and that Mr. Todd's young man just steps over the way to say "good morning" to both of 'em; and as the aforesaid Mr. Todd's young man is almost as good-looking and fascinating as the baker himself, the conversation quickly becomes very interesting, and probably would become more so if Betsy Clark's Missis, who always will be a-followin' her about, didn't give an angry tap at her bedroom window, on which Mr. Todd's young man tries to whistle coolly as he goes back to his shop much faster than he came from it; and the two girls run back to their respective places and shut their street doors with surprising softness, each of them poking their heads out of the front parlor window a minute afterward, however, ostensibly with the view of looking at the mail which just then passes by, but really for the purpose of catching another glimpse of Mr. Todd's young man, who being fond of mails, but more of females, takes a short look at the mails and a long look at the girls, much to the satisfaction of all parties concerned.

The mail [1] itself goes on to the coach office in due course, and the passengers who are going out by the early coach stare with astonishment at the passengers who are coming in by the early coach, who look blue and dismal and are evidently under the influence of that odd feeling produced by traveling, which makes the events of yesterday morning seem as if they had happened at least six months ago and induces people to wonder with considerable gravity whether the friends and relations they took leave of a fortnight before have altered much since they left them. The coach office is all alive, and the coaches which are just going out are surrounded by the usual crowd of nondescripts, who seem to consider, Heaven knows why, that it is quite impossible any man can mount a coach without requiring at least sixpennyworth of oranges, a penknife, a pocketbook, a last year's annual, a pencil case, a piece of sponge, and a small series of caricatures.

[1] **mail:** the mail coach.

Half an hour more, and the sun darts his bright rays cheerfully down the still half-empty streets and shines with sufficient force to rouse the dismal laziness of the apprentice, who pauses every other minute from his task of sweeping out the shop and watering the pavement in front of it to tell another apprentice similarly employed how hot it will be today, or to stand with his right hand shading his eyes, and his left resting on the broom, gazing at the "Wonder," or the "Tally-ho," or the "Nimrod," or some other fast coach, till it is out of sight, when he reenters the shop, envying the passengers on the outside of the fast coach and thinking of the old red brick house "down in the country," where he went to school: the miseries of the milk and water and thick bread and scrapings fading into nothing before the pleasant recollection of the green field the boys used to play in, and the green pond he was caned for presuming to fall into, and other schoolboy associations.

Cabs, with trunks and bandboxes between the drivers' legs and outside the apron, rattle briskly up and down the streets on their way to the coach offices or steam-packet wharfs; and the cab drivers and hackney coachmen who are on the stand polish up the ornamental part of their dingy vehicles—the former wondering how people can prefer "them wild beast cariwans of homnibuses to a riglar cab with a fast trotter,"[1] and the latter admiring how people can trust their necks into one of "them crazy cabs, when they can have a 'spectable 'ackney cotche with a pair of 'orses as von't run away with no vun"; a consolation unquestionably founded on fact, seeing that a hackney-coach horse never was known to run at all, "except" as the smart cabman in front of the rank observes, "except one, and *he* run back'ards."

The shops are now completely opened, and apprentices and shopmen are busily engaged in cleaning and decking the windows for the day. The bakers' shops in town are filled with servants and children waiting for the drawing of the first batch of rolls—an operation which was performed a full hour ago in the suburbs, for the early clerk population of Somers and Camden towns, Islington, and Pentonville,[2] are fast pouring into the city or directing their steps towards Chancery-lane[3] and the Inns of Court.[4] Middle-aged men, whose salaries have by no means increased in the same proportion as their families, plod steadily along, apparently with no object in view but the counting house; knowing by sight almost everybody they meet or overtake, for they have seen them every morning (Sundays excepted) during the last twenty years, but speaking to no one. If they do happen to overtake a personal acquaintance, they just exchange a hurried salutation and keep walking on either by his side, or in front of him, as his rate of walking may chance to be. As to stopping to shake hands or to take the friend's arm, they seem to think that as it is not included in their salary, they have no right to do it. Small office lads in large hats, who are made men before they are boys, hurry along in pairs with their first coat carefully brushed and the white trousers of last Sunday plentifully besmeared with dust and ink. It evidently requires a considerable mental struggle to avoid investing part of the day's dinner money in the purchase of the stale

[1] To understand the meaning of these and the following phrases in Cockney dialect, read them aloud.

[2] **Somers . . . Pentonville:** suburbs of London.

[3] **Chancery-lane:** site of the London courts of law.

[4] **Inns of Court:** residences for law students in London.

tarts so temptingly exposed in dusty tins at the pastry cooks' doors; but a consciousness of their own importance and the receipt of seven shillings a week, with the prospect of an early rise to eight, comes to their aid, and they accordingly put their hats a little more on one side and look under the bonnets of all the milliners' and staymakers' apprentices they meet—poor girls!—the hardest worked, the worst paid, and too often, the worst used class of the community.

Eleven o'clock, and a new set of people fill the streets. The goods in the shop windows are invitingly arranged; the shipmen in their white neckerchiefs and spruce coats look as if they couldn't clean a window if their lives depended on it; the carts have disappeared from Covent Garden; the wagoners have returned, and the costermongers repaired to their ordinary "beats" in the suburbs; clerks are at their offices, and gigs, cabs, omnibuses, and saddle horses are conveying their masters to the same destination. The streets are thronged with a vast concourse of people, gay and shabby, rich and poor, idle and industrious; and we come to the heat, bustle, and activity of noon.

NIGHT

But the streets of London, to be beheld in the very height of their glory, should be seen on a dark, dull, murky winter's night, when there is just enough damp gently stealing down to make the pavement greasy, without cleansing it of any of its impurities; and when the heavy lazy mist, which hangs over every object, makes the gas lamps look brighter and the brilliantly lighted shops more splendid, from the contrast they present to the darkness around. All the people who are at home on such a night as this seem disposed to make themselves as snug and

comfortable as possible; and the passengers in the streets have excellent reason to envy the fortunate individuals who are seated by their own firesides.

In the larger and better kind of streets, dining parlor curtains are closely drawn, kitchen fires blaze brightly up, and savory steams of hot dinners salute the nostrils of the hungry wayfarer, as he plods wearily by the area railings. In the suburbs the muffin boy rings his way down the little street, much more slowly than he is wont to do; for Mrs. Macklin, of No. 4, has no sooner opened her little street door and screamed out "Muffins!" with all her might, than Mrs. Walker, at No. 5, puts her head out of the parlor-window and screams "Muffins!" too; and Mrs. Walker has scarcely got the words out of her lips, than Mrs. Peplow, over the way, lets loose Master Peplow, who darts down the street, with a velocity which nothing but buttered muffins in perspective could possibly inspire, and drags the boy back by main force, whereupon Mrs. Macklin and Mrs. Walker, just to save the boy trouble and to say a few neighborly words to Mrs. Peplow at the same time, run over the way and buy their muffins at Mrs. Peplow's door, when it appears from the voluntary statement of Mrs. Walker that her "kittle 's jist a-biling, and the cups and sarsers ready laid," and that, as it was such a wretched night out o' doors, she'd made up her mind to have a nice hot comfortable cup o' tea—a determination at which, by the most singular coincidence, the other two ladies had simultaneously arrived.

After a little conversation about the wretchedness of the weather and the merits of tea, with a digression relative to the viciousness of boys as a rule and the amiability of Master Peplow as an exception, Mrs. Walker sees her husband coming down the street; and as he must

want his tea, poor man, after his dirty walk from the Docks, she instantly runs across, muffins in hand, and Mrs. Macklin does the same, and after a few words to Mrs. Walker, they all pop into their little houses and slam their little street doors, which are not opened again for the remainder of the evening, except to the nine o'clock "beer," [1] who comes round with a lantern in front of his tray and says as he lends Mrs. Walker "Yesterday's 'Tiser [2]" that he's blessed if he can hardly hold the pot, much less feel the paper, for it's one of the bitterest nights he ever felt, 'cept the night when the man was frozen to death in the Brick-field.

After a little prophetic conversation with the policeman at the street corner, touching a probable change in the weather and the setting in of a hard frost, the nine o'clock beer returns to his master's house and employs himself for the remainder of the evening in assiduously stirring the taproom fire and deferentially taking part in the conversation of the worthies assembled round it.

The streets in the vicinity of the Marshgate and Victoria Theatre present an appearance of dirt and discomfort on such a night, which the groups who lounge about them in no degree tend to diminish. Even the little block-tin temple [3] sacred to baked potatoes, surmounted by a splendid design in variegated lamps, looks less gay than usual; and as to the kidney-pie stand, its glory has quite departed. The candle in the transparent lamp, manufactured of oil paper, embellished with "characters," has been blown out fifty times, so the kidney-pie merchant, tired with running backward and forward to the next wine vaults, to get a light, has given up the idea of illumination in despair, and the only signs of his "whereabout" are the bright sparks, of which a long irregular train is whirled down the street every time he opens his portable oven to hand a hot kidney pie to a customer.

Flat fish, oyster, and fruit venders linger hopelessly in the kennel, in vain endeavoring to attract customers; and the ragged boys who usually disport themselves about the streets stand crouched in little knots in some projecting doorway, or under the canvas blind of the cheesemonger's, where great flaring gaslights, unshaded by any glass, display huge piles of bright red and pale yellow cheeses, mingled with little fivepenny dabs of dingy bacon, various tubs of weekly Dorset,[4] and cloudy rolls of "best fresh."

Here they amuse themselves with theatrical converse, arising out of their last half-price visit to the Victoria gallery, admire the terrific combat, which is nightly encored, and expatiate on the inimitable manner in which Bill Thompson [5] can "come the double monkey" or go through the mysterious involutions of the sailor's hornpipe.

It is nearly eleven o'clock, and the cold thin rain, which has been drizzling so long, is beginning to pour down in good earnest; the baked-potato man has departed—the kidney-pie man has just walked away with his warehouse on his arm—the cheesemonger has drawn in his blind, and the boys have dispersed. The constant clicking of pattens [6] on the slippy and uneven pavement, and the rustling of umbrellas, as the wind blows against the shop windows, bear testimony to the inclemency of the night; and the policeman, with his oilskin cape but-

[1] **"beer":** a boy who delivers beer from a nearby tavern.

[2] **'Tiser:** *(Advertiser),* a newspaper.

[3] **block-tin temple:** a street stand made of tin.

[4] **Dorset:** a kind of cheese.

[5] **Bill Thompson:** a music-hall actor.

[6] **pattens:** thick-soled shoes.

toned closely round him, seems, as he holds his hat on his head and turns round to avoid the gust of wind and rain which drives against him at the street corner, to be very far from congratulating himself on the prospect before him.

The little chandler's [1] shop with the cracked bell behind the door, whose melancholy tinkling has been regulated by the demand for quarterns of sugar and half-ounces of coffee, is shutting up. The crowds, which have been passing to and fro during the whole day, are rapidly dwindling away; and the noise of shouting and quarreling, which issues from the public houses,[2] is almost the only sound that breaks the melancholy stillness of the night.

There was another, but it has ceased. That wretched woman with the infant in her arms, round whose meager form the remnant of her own scanty shawl is carefully wrapped, has been attempting to sing some popular ballad, in the hope of wringing a few pence from the compassionate passerby. A brutal laugh at her weak voice is all she has gained. The tears fall thick and fast down her own pale face; the child is cold and hungry, and its low half-stifled wailing adds to the misery of its wretched mother, as she moans aloud and sinks despairingly down on a cold damp doorstep.

Singing! How few of those who pass such a miserable creature as this, think of the anguish of heart, the sinking of soul and spirit, which the very effort of singing produces. Bitter mockery! Disease, neglect, and starvation, faintly articulating the words of the joyous ditty that has enlivened your hours of feasting and merriment, God knows how often! It is no subject of jeering. The weak tremulous voice tells a fearful tale of want and famishing; and the feeble singer of this roaring song may turn away, only to die of cold and hunger.

One o'clock! Parties returning from the different theaters foot it through the muddy streets; cabs, hackney coaches, carriages, and theater omnibuses roll swiftly by; watermen [3] with dim dirty lanterns in their hands and large brass plates upon their breasts, who have been shouting and rushing about for the last two hours, retire to their watering houses to solace themselves with the creature comforts of pipes and purl; [4] the half-price pit [5] and box frequenters of the theaters throng to the different houses of refreshment; and chops, kidneys, rabbits, oysters, stout, cigars, and "goes" [6] innumerable are served up amidst a noise and confusion of smoking, running, knife clattering, and waiter chattering, perfectly indescribable.

The more musical portion of the playgoing community betake themselves to some harmonic meeting. As a matter of curiosity let us follow them thither for a few moments.

In a lofty room of spacious dimensions are seated some eighty or a hundred guests, knocking little pewter measures on the tables and hammering away, with the handles of their knives, as if they were so many trunkmakers. They are applauding a glee,[7] which has just been executed by the three "professional gentlemen" at the top of the center table, one of whom is in the chair—the little pompous man with the bald head just emerging from the collar of his green coat. The others are seated on either side of him—the stout man with the

[1] **chandler's:** A chandler is a shopkeeper. Originally, a seller of candles.

[2] **public houses:** taverns.

[3] **watermen:** laborers who supply water for horses.

[4] **purl:** a beverage.

[5] **pit:** in an English theater, the "orchestra" floor, where seats are cheaper than in the boxes.

[6] **"goes":** rounds of drinks.

[7] **glee:** a song, in which different parts are sung by different voices.

small voice and the thin-faced dark man in black. The little man in the chair is a most amusing personage—*such* condescending grandeur, and *such* a voice!

"Bass!" as the young gentleman near us with the blue stock forcibly remarks to his companion, "bass! I b'lieve you; he can go down lower than any man: so low sometimes that you can't hear him." And so he does. To hear him growling away, gradually lower and lower down, till he can't get back again, is the most delightful thing in the world, and it is quite impossible to witness unmoved the impressive solemnity with which he pours forth his soul in "My 'art's in the 'ighlands" or "The brave old Hoak." The stout man is also addicted to sentimentality, and warbles "Fly, fly from the world, my Bessy with me" or some such song, with ladylike sweetness and in the most seductive tones imaginable.

"Pray give your orders, gen'l'm'n— pray give your orders"—says the pale-faced man with the red head; and demands for pints of stout and cigars of peculiar mildness are vociferously made from all parts of the room. The "professional gentlemen" are in the very height of their glory and bestow condescending nods or even a word or two of recognition on the better-known frequenters of the room, in the most bland and patronising manner possible.

That little round-faced man, with the small brown surtout,[1] white stockings and shoes, is in the comic line; the mixed air of self-denial and mental consciousness of his own powers, with which he acknowledges the call of the chair, is particularly gratifying. "Gen'l'men," says the little pompous man, accompanying the word with a knock of the president's hammer on the table—"Gen'l'men, allow me to

[1] **surtout:** overcoat.

claim your attention—our friend, Mr. Smuggins will oblige."—"Bravo!" shout the company; and Smuggins, after a considerable quantity of coughing by way of symphony, and a most facetious sniff or two, which afford general delight, sings a comic song, with a fal-de-ral—tol-de-rol chorus at the end of every verse, much longer than the verse itself. It is received with unbounded applause, and after some aspiring genius has volunteered a recitation and failed dismally therein, the little pompous man gives another knock and says, "Gen'l'men, we will attempt a glee, if you please." This announcement calls forth tumultuous applause, and the more energetic spirits express the unqualified approbation it affords them, by knocking one or two stout glasses off their legs—a humorous device, but one which frequently occasions some slight altercation when the form of paying the damage is proposed to be gone through by the waiter.

Scenes like these are continued until three or four o'clock in the morning; and even when they close, fresh ones open to the inquisitive novice. But as a description of all of them, however slight, would require a volume, the contents of which, however instructive, would be by no means pleasing, we make our bow and drop the curtain.

FOR STUDY AND DISCUSSION

1. What is the point of view in these essays? Is the essayist merely standing apart as an observer? Is he in any way involved in the scenes he describes? Explain.

2. *Caricature* is a very broad, exaggerated, usually humorous type of drawing. How does Dickens make use of caricature in writing these essays?

3. One of the most important aspects of good descriptive writing is the author's use of sensory details: details which appeal to the

senses of sound, smell, taste, touch, sight, and even motion. Find and discuss examples of details in these two essays which appeal to each of these senses.

4. Reflecting his own unhappy childhood in London in much of what he wrote, Dickens became an acute critic of the evils in English society. List a number of the episodes in these essays in which he is writing social criticism or in which he indicates his sympathy for the unfortunate.

5. What similarities to Dickens's London would you expect to find if you were to watch a big city today as it awakes, goes about its business, and turns to its evening activities? What differences would you expect to find?

CHRONOLOGICAL ORDER

After deciding on his topic, the essayist must next determine how to arrange his facts, ideas, and observations. The purpose of arrangement is to present his ideas to the reader with clarity. If a hundred different impressions are thrown down without any order, the reader will be lost. One good way to arrange details is according to the *time sequence* in which they happened: that is, in chronological order. The essays by Addison (page 175) and Irving (page 179) are largely arranged chronologically.

In this pair of essays by Dickens, we have a brilliant example of chronological order. Each of the essays is packed with literally hundreds of sights, sounds, and stories. To give shape to these impressions, Dickens arranged them according to the time at which they occurred. Notice that "Morning" begins "an hour before sunrise" and ends as "we come to the heat, bustle, and activity of noon." The essay on "Night" begins in the early evening and continues chronologically until the small hours of the morning.

Dickens's writing is so smooth that you may not have been aware of the passage of time as you read these essays, even as you are hardly aware of the movement of the sun or moon across the sky. Look again at the two essays and trace the stages of morning and night as Dickens presents them. Make a brief outline of each essay to show the time structure. Note that Dickens's use of chronological order is flexible and not too mechanical.

LANGUAGE AND VOCABULARY

At a number of points in these two essays, Dickens is writing *satire:* he is poking fun at or, more often, showing his scorn for some of the people and things he is describing. One device used in satire is a kind of vocabulary which is generally called "loaded." "Loaded" words show quite clearly the prejudiced viewpoint of the writer, and they are often used in political speeches, propaganda, and other kinds of writing in which the writer wants to make his point forcefully.

Below are a number of phrases from the Dickens's essays. Study them carefully. What is the exact meaning behind these phrases? How do the words express the writer's attitude toward his subject?

"whom penury and police have left in the streets . . ." (Page 193.)

"An occasional policeman . . . listlessly gazing . . ." (Page 193.)

"the little sweep . . . being interdicted by a merciful legislature from endangering his lungs . . ." (Page 194.)

"The little man in the chair is a most amusing personage—*such* condescending grandeur, and *such* a voice!" (Page 200.)

In all of these groups of words, Dickens makes a judgment about what he is describing. As an exercise in the use of language, try rewriting one or more of these phrases without making any judgment. That is, describe objectively. Be neutral. For example: "An occasional policeman . . . quietly gazing . . ."

FOR COMPOSITION

1. Dickens obviously not only looked at the London streets; he *saw* them. Using clear, simple English, write a brief, vivid description of something you have seen, something which made a strong impression on you.

2. Organizing your essay chronologically, write an orderly description based on careful observation. One good topic would be "Our School During the First Hour of the Day."

Julius Caesar

E. M. FORSTER

(1879–)

Edward Morgan Forster has devoted himself to writing for most of his life. He has produced essays, reviews, lectures, and broadcasts, mostly about literature. Also, although not a prolific novelist, he is the author of some of the best English novels of the early twentieth century, notably *Howard's End* and *A Passage to India*. His experience in 1921 as secretary to an Indian maharaja went into the making of the latter, which is considered his masterpiece. With the success of *A Passage to India* in 1924, Forster abruptly stopped writing novels.

Most of Forster's later writing has been essays, reviews, and articles. "Julius Caesar" is from an essay collection titled *Two Cheers for Democracy*, published in 1951. His essays are usually short and written with great economy: every word counts. The organization is clear and the style is easy and graceful. There is humor and restraint in the writing. An experienced literary critic such as Forster could have written an objective scholarly analysis of *Julius Caesar*. Instead, he has written a quiet little essay, which begins with a subjective, personal experience and says much about Shakespeare's play.

WHILE I WAS considering what to say about *Julius Caesar,* I happened to go to a school entertainment. It was a large primary school, and the boys mostly came from working class homes; little boys—the eldest couldn't have been fourteen. They acted some scenes out of this very play. They did not act them well—how should they? They had not had the time to rehearse, they forgot their words and said them too fast, also there was not the money to buy properties with: the Roman Senators wore towels and curtains and anything they could scrounge and a solitary garland of green cardboard was handed from Caesar to Brutus and from Brutus to Antony as the occasion required. The audience was more interested in identifying their offspring than in following the plot. Remarks could be heard such as, "There he is, that one's Tom," and there were squeals from babies who were lifted up in their mothers' arms to see better, and seemed critical of what they saw. I was critical myself—yet I had an odd feeling of pleasure and of awe, and certain words of Cassius after the murder came into my mind.

> How many ages hence
> Shall this our lofty scene be acted o'er
> In states unborn and accents yet unknown!

If Shakespeare had been present with us in that school, he might not have been flattered but he would not have been surprised, for what he expected to occur has occurred: the play lives.

> O Julius Caesar! thou art mighty yet!
> Thy spirit walks abroad.

It was walking with us as well as circumstances permitted: it was part of the civilization of England and of all who read English.

The general immortality of Shakespeare is too vast a subject. Let us keep to this particular play. Why has it caught on? It is about some old Romans who murdered one of their number and were finally defeated by his friends. The inci-

dent was chronicled by a Greek historian, Plutarch,[1] and Shakespeare read a translation of it and turned out a play somewhere about 1600. It seems to have been a success from the first. And we today, though we may not rank it with the Great Four— *Hamlet, Othello, Lear, Macbeth*—always hail it as a typical example of his genius, and are excited when the curtain rises.

It is exciting—that is one reason for its popularity. Although it is not carefully constructed like a Greek play or a classical French play, although it is not as cunning in its advance as *Othello* or *Macbeth,* yet it does succeed in startling us and holding us. It effects this by three well-timed explosions. The first of these explosions is of course the murder itself. The preparation for this is masterly—the growth of the conspiracy, omens, storms, apparitions, Portia's forebodings, Calpurnia's dream, the tempting of Caesar to the Senate House, the failure of Artemidorus to save him, the luring away of Antony: and then the deed. And the murder is followed by a second explosion: Antony's funeral speech. The excitement is revived and increased instead of dropping. After that indeed there is a lull and a failure to interest, until we come to the plains of Philippi and the third explosion: the quarrel in the tent between Brutus and Cassius. This is so unexpected, so natural psychologically and so touching that it produces a tremendous effect, and after it, his nerves all exhausted, Brutus beholds Caesar's ghost. I do not mean that these three explosions, these three famous scenes, are the only reason for the play's popularity. But they do provide the excitement, and if a drama does not excite the ordinary man it may satisfy its contemporaries, but it has no chance of being

acted "in states unborn and accents yet unknown."

The second reason for popularity is the character drawing, and particularly the character of Brutus. Before I come to it, I am going to risk a generalization about Shakespeare. He was an Elizabethan dramatist, and I do not think the Elizabethans were conscientious over their characters; they would often alter them in the middle in order to get on with the play. Beaumont and Fletcher [2] contain glaring examples of this. Good men become bad and then good again: traitors turn into heroes and vice versa without any internal justification. And Shakespeare sometimes does it too. There is an example—not a glaring one—in this play, in the character of Casca. Casca first appears as extremely polite and indeed servile to Caesar. "Peace ho! Caesar speaks," he cries. Then he shows himself to Brutus and Cassius as a sour blunt contradictious fellow, who snaps them up when they speak and is grumpy when they invite him to supper. You may say this is subtlety on Shakespeare's part, and that he is indicating that Casca is a dark horse. I don't think so. I don't think Shakespeare was bothering about Casca—he is merely concerned to make the action interesting and he alters the character at need. Later on, during the thunderstorm, Casca becomes different again; he walks about with a drawn sword, is deeply moved by the apparitions, and utters exalted poetry. At the murder scene he wounds Caesar in the neck, and then we hear of him no more. His usefulness is over. Contrast Shakespeare here with a modern writer, like Tolstoy.[3] Tolstoy is conscientious over his characters, he has a personal

[1] **Plutarch:** See Plutarch's "The Life of Caesar," page 231.

[2] **Beaumont and Fletcher:** Francis Beaumont (1584–1616) and John Fletcher (1579–1625) collaborated as dramatists.

[3] **Tolstoy:** Leo Tolstoy (1828–1910), Russian novelist, dramatist, and social theorist.

responsibility to each of them, he has a vital conception of them, and though they are full of contradictions, those contradictions are true to life. Contrast Casca with Dolohov[1] in *War and Peace*. Shakespeare often doesn't mind about his people. And when I am reading him, one of my difficulties is to detect when he does mind and when he doesn't. This may be heresy on my part, but it seems to me that a great deal of Shakespearean criticism is invalid because it assumes that his characters are real people, and are never put in just to make the play go. The play's the thing, I suggest.

It is delightful when the characters are real, when Shakespeare does bother about them. Brutus is real, so is Cassius, so is Antony, so perhaps is Caesar himself. Brutus is an intellectual who can do things, who is not (like Hamlet) hampered by doubts. He can do things—but he always does them wrong: his advice is invariably fatal, from the moment of the murder down to the battle of Philippi. He cannot realize that men seek their own interests, for he has never sought his own, he has lived nobly among noble thoughts, wedded to a noble wife. He is kind to his servant. Everything he does is touched with fineness. Yet Brutus is not frigid. He just avoids being a prig. We are able to take him to our hearts. And with him is associated the worldly but far from contemptible Cassius. Those two speak the same language though they sometimes use different words. And against them is opposed Mark Antony—brilliant, sensuous, devoted to Caesar, but heartless otherwise, and treacherous. These three support the play. The character of Caesar is—difficult: Shakespeare does not present him sympathetically. He makes a few fine remarks like

It seems to me most strange that men should fear;
Seeing that death, a necessary end,
Will come when it will come.

But goes on to talk bombast and to assert that he and Danger

. . . are two lions littered in one day,
And I the elder and more terrible.

Do you detect a contemporary voice here? I do. It is Mussolini's.[2] His infirmities are insisted on: his epilepsy, his deafness. He is pompous, conceited, showing off, dictatorial. Indeed, some modern producers have stressed this and have presented *Julius Caesar* as a study in fascism. But when Caesar is dead, his spirit is mighty, and haunts Brutus and wins. I don't know what to make of this. If Shakespeare were a modern writer I should be more clear about his conception. I should be certain that he has planned Caesar to be little in life and great in death. But, being an Elizabethan, is it possible that he may be altering Caesar as he alters Casca, for the sake of the play?

Excitement—and enough real people. Here are two of the reasons why *Julius Caesar* lives, and why, after more than three hundred years, it is acted by primary school boys. At the end of the performance to which I have referred, after Brutus, aged twelve, had suicided himself and fallen with rather a thump, another of the children came forward, in his little brown suit, to speak the epilogue. The epilogue was not by Shakespeare. It ran as follows:

I come to say our play is done
We hope you have enjoyed the fun.

[1] **Dolohov:** a treacherous and cruel army officer in Tolstoy's novel *War and Peace*.

[2] **Mussolini's:** Benito Mussolini (1883–1945) was dictator of Italy and leader of the country's nationalistic, anti-democratic Fascist party.

The child then retired. He had spoken briefly but justly. Shakespeare is fun. There are murders and ghosts, jealousy, remorse, despair, there is *Othello,* there is *Lear,* there is even *Timon of Athens* [1] —but—how shall I put it? Shakespeare never grumbles. He denounces life but he never complains of it; he presents even its tragedies for our comprehension and enjoyment.

[1] *Othello . . . Lear . . . Timon of Athens:* other plays by Shakespeare.

FOR STUDY AND DISCUSSION

1. Would you say that the spirit of Shakespeare might have been pleased or displeased by the performance of *Julius Caesar* which Forster describes? Explain your answer.

2. Why do you suppose Forster devotes a long paragraph to the character of Casca? Is there any clear relationship between this paragraph and the one which follows? If so, what is it?

3. What does the reference to Mussolini contribute to the reader's understanding of the essay?

4. What is the main idea behind this essay? Is there more than one main idea? Is the subject of the essay *Julius Caesar,* or is it something larger than Shakespeare's play? Explain.

ORGANIZATION OF THE ESSAY

The essay "Julius Caesar" is organized into six paragraphs, four of them rather long. Forster's plan of organization is worth studying for a moment. The first paragraph, or introduction, sets the tone of the essay and tells the reader that the topic is, in general, the fact that *Julius Caesar* has become "part of the civilization . . . of all who read English." In the second paragraph Forster simply asks a question: Why has this play been a success? And then, in the last four paragraphs, Forster answers the question.

In your study of the paragraph you have probably learned that the "topic sentence" states the main idea of the paragraph, and that

it often, but not always, comes at the beginning of the paragraph. And you know that the topic of the paragraph can be developed by the use of illustrations, facts, or reasons. What is more, many good paragraphs end with a "clincher" sentence which summarizes the ideas presented.

Review carefully the third paragraph of this essay. Note that the first sentence states the topic at once. Then follow, in order, three illustrations from the play which Forster uses to prove his point. The paragraph's concluding statement is a summary. But Forster does something more. Before his last sentence he indicates that he may go on to another reason why the play is popular. And this he does in the fourth paragraph.

The last paragraph of the essay also deserves rereading. What is its topic? Is the topic stated at the beginning of the paragraph? If not, where is it?

Notice how Forster gives the entire essay greater unity by mentioning again in the last paragraph the incident with which he began— the children's performance of *Julius Caesar.*

LANGUAGE AND VOCABULARY

The origin of a word, its *etymology,* can be very interesting. Look up in your dictionary the following words from Forster's essay. Write down the word and its origin or original meaning, together with the language from which it originally came. Then discuss the appropriateness of the meaning of the word as we now use it.

lure	bombast	pompous
dark horse	heresy	fascism

Make these words your own, if they are not already, by using them in meaningful sentences which have nothing to do with *Julius Caesar.*

FOR COMPOSITION

No two critics see a great play like *Julius Caesar* in exactly the same light. If you have read the play, write a brief essay on some point of interpretation, either major or minor, where you disagree with E. M. Forster.

The Crack of Doom

E. B. WHITE

(1899–)

Even as a college student, E. (Elwyn) B.
(Brooks) White was known as a writer of
grace and style. This reputation has increased
steadily, and today White ranks as one of our
best-known and most-admired essayists.

After working as a newspaperman in Seattle
and Alaska and in an advertising job in New
York City, White became part-time editor of
The New Yorker Magazine in 1926. Soon he
began to write "Talk of the Town," the brief
essays which many readers have considered
the best feature of the magazine.

Although White's writing has been predomi-
nately humorous, he often treats highly serious
topics. In his preface to *The Wild Flag,* a col-
lection of his *New Yorker* editorials published
at the close of the Second World War, he
writes: "Lately the most conspicuous activity
of nations has been the blowing of each other
up . . . (But) two things in the human scene
give encouragement to anyone who takes to
brooding on these matters . . . A big city is a
noisy proof of man's ability to live at peace
with strangers . . . The other encouraging
thing is that war is becoming increasingly un-
popular with warriors."

The short editorial which follows appeared
in *The New Yorker* of November 17, 1945.
Here White looks at both the discouraging
and the encouraging faces of the world which
H. G. Wells said was at the end of its tether.

THE WORLD, says Wells,[1] is at the end
of its tether. "The end of everything we
call life is close at hand," he writes in his
last literary statement, distributed by In-
ternational News Service. We note, how-
ever, that Mr. Wells went to the trouble
of taking out a world copyright on his
world's end article. A prophet who was
firmly convinced that the jig was up
wouldn't feel any need of protecting his
rights. We charge Mr. Wells with trying
to play doom both ways.

Wells has been a good prophet, as
prophets go, and his crystal gazing is not
to be sniffed at. And even lesser prophets,
these days, can feel the "frightful queer-
ness" that he says has come into life. At
the risk, however, of seeming to suggest
the continuance of life on earth, we must
admit that we found the Wells article un-
convincing in places. It is not clear yet,
at any rate, whether the world is at the
end of its tether or whether Wells is
merely at the end of his. His description
is not so much of the end of life in the
world as of the end of his ability to figure
life out. The two are not necessarily
identical.

Wells is seventy-nine, and it is possible,
of course, that he confuses his own ter-
minal sensations with universal twilight,
and that his doom is merely a case of
mistaken identity. Most writers find the
world and themselves practically inter-
changeable, and in a sense the world dies
every time a writer dies, because, if he is
any good, he has been wet nurse to hu-
manity during his entire existence and has
held earth close around him, like the little
obstetrical toad that goes about with a
cluster of eggs attached to his legs. We

[1] **Wells:** H. G. Wells (1866–1946) was a widely
read author of short stories and novels, particularly
in the field of science fiction. *The War of the Worlds*
is one of his best-known books.

hope Mr. Wells is wrong for once and that man is not the suicide he looks at the moment. Man is unpredictable, despite Mr. Wells's good record. On Monday man may be hysterical with doom, and on Tuesday you will find him opening the Doomsday Bar & Grill and settling down for another thousand years of terrifying queerness.

FOR STUDY AND DISCUSSION

1. Why, in 1945, should H. G. Wells have said what he did about the world? Why does White believe "that man is not the suicide he looks at the moment"?

2. Why do you suppose White changes Wells's "frightful queerness" to "terrifying queerness?"

3. Referring both to White's choice of words and to his ideas, cite examples of a light, familiar touch in this essay.

4. Using your own words, state the main point of the essay in one sentence.

THE EDITORIAL "WE"

The editorial writer usually calls himself "we." Who is this "we"? the writer himself? his fellow editors? the publisher? In some periodicals, such as *The New Yorker,* the editorial can be quite personal. In others, it is quite impersonal. E. B. White himself talks about this matter as follows: "An editorial writer refers to himself as 'we,' but is never sure who the other half of 'we' is. I have yet to encounter the other half of 'we,' but expect to nail him in an alley some day and beat his brains out, to see what sort of stuffing is behind such omniscience."

CONCISENESS

Because of space limitations, editorials are usually short. They compress a good deal of opinion, even on a matter of major importance, into perhaps two or three hundred words. "The Crack of Doom" is a short essay about a big idea. The question of whether the world is "at the end of its tether" could be the subject

of several volumes of formal writing. But White says a great deal about the subject in fewer than 350 words. The point is that he implies more than he says. Note, for instance, his statement that Mr. Wells took the trouble to copyright his article about the world's being at the end of its tether. What does this tell the reader about Wells? about White's opinion of Wells? about White's opinion of the state of the world?

In your own writing, never attempt to fill up space with repetition and verbiage. Give only the details you need to make your point, and stop when your point is made. Brevity is more than the soul of wit: it is the basis of all good prose style.

LANGUAGE AND VOCABULARY

Part of the magic of language is that words do not always mean what they literally say. One nonliteral use of language is called *metaphor,* in which one thing is compared to another by speaking as if it were the other thing: for example, "He is a bull in a china shop," or "He is a bear for punishment." E. B. White's short editorial contains a number of these metaphorical, nonliteral expressions:

"The world . . . is at the end of its tether."

"the jig was up . . ."

"trying to play doom both ways."

"the world dies every time a writer dies . . ."

"a writer . . . has held earth close around him . . ."

What is the literal meaning of these groups of words? What is their meaning in the editorial?

Write five sentences, each containing a metaphor.

FOR COMPOSITION

1. Without sacrificing any of his main ideas, rewrite E. B. White's editorial in about 150 words.

2. In a short essay on some controversial topic, attempt to resolve a contradiction between two different points of view. Be sure to take a stand on one point of view, so that the reader will not be confused.

The Rio Grande

PAUL HORGAN

(1903-)

Paul Horgan is a man of two worlds—upper New York State and the Southwest—and his writing reflects both of these worlds. His first published novel deals with his years in Rochester, New York, where he studied as a young man. His best-known work, however, is *Great River: The Rio Grande,* which won the Pulitzer prize for history in 1954. Most of his recent writing is set in the Southwest.

When *Great River* appeared, the critics were almost unanimous in their praise. "All of the peoples, as well as their country and their river, are re-created with poetry and integrity," said one reviewer. "There is a great deal to be explained, yet the explanations do not lag. Always the story moves," wrote another. The point, of course, is that Horgan's writing about the Rio Grande is very intimate writing, a labor of love on which he spent thirteen years. He obviously knows the river and its towns and people from careful direct observation. Thus he can be objective and accurate, while at the same time being poetic about the small details which a less interested researcher might well miss. The present essay appeared in *The New York Times* a year after *Great River* was published.

IT IS BORN of winter, this river, in the longest season of cold in the United States. The source mountains in the Colo-

"The Rio Grande" by Paul Horgan, from *The New York Times Book Review,* May 15, 1955. © 1955 by The New York Times Company. Reprinted by permission.

rado Rockies are hard and wild. The air is thin and at such altitude subject to swift, crystalline changes of condition which may bring blue darkness in midday and yield snow during nine months of the year.

Past monstrous peaks of ragged lifeless rock, clouds tear and roll from wall to wall up in the sky. Wind cries there much of the time, and when the atmosphere is overcharged with electricity, the cut and flare of lightning, the trundle and bounce of thunder after its valley-sharpened crash seem to require new senses, capacities, to be wholly heard.

The river's course—here as in its whole career—widens and narrows by turns. Where it is narrow, the slopes are dark, the stream is shadowed all day but for a little while at noon, when straight fingers of sunlight reach down through the forest. The stream is clear and icy, going rapidly over polished brown speckled stones. They remind us of something. At a glance the diamond water going over its stony bed makes the image of the fish it carries —the same speckled colors, the same watery flicker, the same half-lights of reflection and golden flecks. In and out of leaf shadow, protected by the dazzle of moving water, the trout in plain sight is safe because he and his river are so close in likeness.

The Rio Grande towns [1] in Colorado— Del Norte, Monte Vista, Alamosa—are pleasant young communities whose life in each place parallels the railroad tracks for a mile or two. About twenty miles southeast of Alamosa the first sign of Spanish adobe culture appears in a little

[1] **towns:** The names of the Rio Grande towns, Spanish in origin, have appropriate meanings: **Del Norte:** of the north; **Monte Vista:** mountain view; **Alamosa:** the poplars; **Taos:** Indian name of a Southwest tribe; **El Paso:** the ford; **Presidio:** garrison, fortress, or prison; **Española:** Spanish; **Algodones:** cotton; **Albuquerque:** the Portuguese explorer Alfonso de Albuquerque; **Belen:** Bethlehem; **Mesilla:** small mesa or plateau.

The pueblo of Taos, New Mexico, as it appears today.

village—Los Sauces, with houses built of earth, under grand cottonwoods, on a gentle slope above the river, encircled by fine hills. This scene made of slow water, bounteous tree, earthen brick, and irrigated field is like a symbolic image of much that is to follow as the river goes south. It is the kind of cell of family, primal want, and basic sustenance made visible from which, downriver, grew clusters of kinsmen, and then of neighbors, and then of material defendants, and then of parishioners, and then of descendants, in turn, until a village became a town which became a city, all originally and even now dependent upon the Rio Grande for life.

Over the three communities of Taos— the pueblo, the middle commercial town, and the old Ranchos [1]—there is a piercing sweet illimitable clarity of light and sky. Sounds carry, meadow larks, mocking birds, blackbirds have returned. Over the long plain breathes the wind, sharply sweet and already warmed, disturbing nothing but the senses. Space is so great, vision is so plain, air is so clear that human activities can be seen from afar. Small figures like humanity in Brueghel [2] go about their tasks. Earthen buildings go up. Carts travel. Winter rubble is cleared off the fields and out of the *acequias*.[3] Furrows are seeded. Out in the sagebrush of Taos plain, where the old road winds toward the canyon, tiny newborn lambs take fright and scamper before the gusty sand devils whipped up by the darting wind. Flocks move more slowly than cloud shadows. Shepherds sit on a modern culvert [4] and watch what the road brings. The valor and pity of men and women in their renewed use of a corner of the earth is as much a part of spring as everything else.

Above Albuquerque begins the lyric grace of the river in its richest passage of the pastoral life. Where life is fed by water, the landscape here recalls the opulence and grandeur and occasional

[1] **pueblo . . . Ranchos:** The pueblo, or group of original buildings, is the old center of the town; the ranchos are the country houses and farms surrounding Taos.

[2] **Brueghel:** Pieter Brueghel, a Flemish painter (1520–1569), or one of his two sons, also painters.
[3] *acequias* (Spanish): irrigation canals.
[4] **culvert:** a covered channel for water, usually under a road.

vistas of order in the image of classical country painted by Nicolas Poussin,[1] who left so many celebrations of grove and meadow, shady leaf and column of light, reflecting stream and stepped mountain and composed bodies. There is more than a reminder here, there is a real likeness. It is a likeness of grace and plenty in the midst of dramatic nature; nourishment in the desert; bounty summoned by the most ancient of agricultural rites out of the most inscrutable of antiquities; cool for the heated, slaking for the parched, food for the hungry, rest for the weary, ease for the eye blinded in the unimpeded sun.

Up to now, going south, when you looked across the river, you knew exactly how things were on the other side—just more United States of America. But at El Paso, with the new concept of a boundary between nations, things are no longer the same on the opposite bank. It is another country, with another people, and with other ways. Many manners and customs have remained common to both sides of the Rio Grande since the time a little over a century ago when the river was not a frontier—when in fact both its banks and all its courses were Spanish or Mexican. But in the United States, subject to a more powerful energy in a more technical society, such survivals remain as exotic, quaint, or commercially glamorous; while in Mexico the same expressions are sincere and not self-conscious. From El Paso southeastward, every United States town has its Mexican counterpart across the river. Commerce, appetite, and corruption draw them together. Language, national boundary, and law keep them apart. The river is hardly an obstacle anywhere, for it can be waded for most of the year, whatever else its common uses may be.

[1] **Nicolas Poussin:** a French landscape painter (1594–1665).

Seventy miles below El Paso, mountains reach in on both sides of the Rio Grande and present to it another of its many obstacles; but the stream bed passes between them and continues upon its depleted way. The river is dying. The desert finally seems ready to triumph over it and drink out of sight the last crawling trickles of the flow that was born in the Colorado Rockies.

And so it would, but relief and replenishment are on their way from another mountain system lying deep in Mexico, where the Rio Conchos with its major tributary, the Rio San Pedro, courses northeastward to join the Rio Grande at an altitude of 2,400 feet a few miles above the old Texas town of Presidio. With it comes new power for the river, to create dramatic, and even melodramatic, phases of its career, in the accomplishment of water over rock, as demonstrated by the vast implausibilities of the earth features of the Big Bend.

At Presidio the replenished river fashions another of those green and easy valleys which, as at Alamosa, Española, Algodones, Albuquerque, Belen, and Mesilla, lie on ancient fertile flats of old river bottoms between gravel terraces and outlying mountains. After the bare and voracious desert in which it nearly died, the river brings again willows and cottonwoods, lilac mountains and attendant clouds, blue sky and emerald green fields and pink sand, with a sweetness in the air made from all these together.

Summer is a long season here, after the harsh, bitter wind storms of spring, with their abrasive white dust that flies out of rocky arroyos[2] to the north, casting a steel-blue obscurity across the sun.

[2] **arroyos:** deep, usually dry, gullies which have been created by running water; a term commonly used in the Southwestern United States.

Previously the river has always been accompanied by mountains, near or far; but they lay generally parallel to its course. Now in the Big Bend the river encounters mountains in a new and extraordinary way; for they lie, chain after chain of them, directly across its way as though to impede and divert it and deny it passage to the sea. But the pull of the sea is stronger than rock, and the river was here before the mountains, and as they rose, in slowness beyond time, it cut its way against and through them.

Born in mountains, and cradled by them, and then opposed by them, the Rio Grande has always been within sight of them. But below the Big Bend they start to fall away. If you can say so, now as the river goes southeastward, mountains are getting lost, like beads of a string which has broken so the ones at the end rest separate without apparent connection with each other until finally there are no more.

Autumn is the seasonal analogy of age; and now in autumn, and here approaching the sea, the river shows its age most plainly. In its last phase with less than two feet a mile to drop, it flows slowly, making bend after bend of wide loops. Built by the drag of silt the river banks rise above the surrounding country. Everywhere are signs of former river beds which finally became too shallow and too elevated to retain the river in storm time. The river broke over, making new courses. The older ones grew grass and softened their contours. Everywhere is the green growth of semitropical climate.

The citrus, palm, garden aspect of the lower valley land begins to merge east of Brownsville into white sand and salt grass, through which the Rio Grande twists from side to side, mild and nearly exhausted. Dunes accompany it and mi-

River and cliffs in Big Bend National Park.

grate with the wind. Sometimes hurricanes formed in the West Indies slash inland over the delta. But it is too late for weather to create much downstream change in the Rio Grande in its last wandering miles.

There is evidence of marsh life. The river banks in places are hardly an inch or two above the flow. Water fowl attend— cranes, herons, geese, ducks, curlews, plover, sandpipers. The light of the sky continuously fades and brightens according to sea clouds that hardly form but hang low and filmy, as white as the wilderness of sand on which they make glistening shadows. Salt marshes and lagoons rest like misted mirrors among the low hollows bounded by dunes. The wasted flood plain is running out with the continent.

Isolated, depleted, heavy with suspended soil, the river widens gradually to a thousand feet and leaves the dunes between low shelves of sandy beach littered with driftwood that is polished to silver by wind and sun, or blackened by saturation. Through a waste of sand, misty air and silence, in the presence of no human concern, having come more than eighteen hundred miles from mountains nearly three miles high, the Rio Grande at last enters the Gulf of Mexico and the sea.

1. For what purpose do you think the author introduces the seasons of the year—winter, spring, summer, autumn—in this particular order?

2. Notice the use of the word *you* in the opening sentence of the paragraph beginning "Up to now . . ." This is the first use of *you* in the essay. What effect does Horgan achieve by using this word? Whom exactly does *you* include?

3. Cite examples of the writer's particularly keen observation. What effect does the author achieve through his fine use of detail?

ORGANIZING BY LOCATION

In studying Dickens (page 193), you saw how an essay can be organized according to a careful time sequence. Here, in Paul Horgan's essay, you have the opportunity to study an equally careful structure based on space, or location. Although Horgan also uses time, the passage of the seasons from winter to autumn, this is secondary to his use of space, or place.

Consulting an atlas as you read this essay will show you at once that the writer does not confuse his readers by following the river downstream for a while and then back upstream. The movement is orderly, from the source of the Rio Grande at the Divide to its mouth at the Gulf of Mexico. But Horgan does more than simply put things into geographical order. As in the Dickens essays, he uses many devices which help the reader follow the structure of the essay. Some of these are connectives: "Up to now, going south . . ." "But at El Paso . . ." "From El Paso southeastward . . ." "Seventy miles below El Paso . . ." Throughout the essay, phrases like these tell the reader where he is.

Horgan's essay has the characteristics of the informative magazine article: the description is orderly and objective. But the reader will surely see at once that there is a great deal of feeling added to the geographical description of this river, as is shown in striking figures of speech (for example, "straight fingers of sunlight reach down") and particularly appropriate adjectives ("*lyric* grace of the river,"

"*voracious* desert"). All of these things—the tight organization according to space, the careful attention to coherence, and the vividness of the description—give this essay a much more "personal" or "familiar" style than it might have had in the hands of a less imaginative and skillful writer.

LANGUAGE AND VOCABULARY

A student of English, who has been taught for a number of years that adjectives are words which describe and that many adverbs are derived from adjectives, is often tempted to overload his own descriptions with adjectives and adverbs. But the experienced writer, however much he may use adjectives and adverbs, knows that nouns, verbs, and "verbals," such as participles and gerunds, are likely to be the most telling words in description.

Note, for instance, the second paragraph of Paul Horgan's essay, and study the effectiveness of the italicized words:

"Past monstrous peaks of ragged lifeless rock, clouds *tear* and *roll* from wall to wall up in the sky. Wind *cries* there much of the time, and when the atmosphere is overcharged with electricity, the *cut* and *flare* of lightning, the *trundle* and *bounce* of thunder after its *valley-sharpened crash* seem to require new senses, capacities, to be wholly heard."

As an exercise in language, rewrite this passage, using as many adjectives and adverbs as you need to say the same thing Horgan says, and then compare the effectiveness of the two versions. You might begin something like this: "Past monstrous peaks of ragged lifeless rock, clouds fly very rapidly and go back and forth from wall to wall . . ."

Investigate the effective use of nouns and verbs in other passages of the Horgan essay.

FOR COMPOSITION

Write a descriptive essay about a stream, a road, or some other visible thing with which you are quite familiar. Plan your essay on an orderly, carefully worked out series of place characteristics.

My War with the Ospreys

JOHN STEINBECK
(1902–1968)

John Steinbeck is known by most readers as a deeply serious writer with a realistic view of life. During his boyhood in California and his wanderings as a young man, Steinbeck was deeply impressed by the poverty and futility that darkens many people's lives. In novels such as *The Pearl* and *The Grapes of Wrath,* he gave powerful expression to his outrage at the cruel treatment men receive from other men. Like all of us, though, Steinbeck has another side. Even in *The Grapes of Wrath,* intermixed with the tragic story of migrant farmers and their hopeless struggle, there are scenes of humor. A reading of other stories and novels by Steinbeck, such as *Tortilla Flat* and *Cannery Row,* reveals a sense of humor that is even more pronounced.

"My War with the Ospreys" is another evidence of Steinbeck's humor. Like nearly all his writing, it is based on fact, but again and again he turns aside from his story for a comment or reflection that is far from solemn. As the calm and determined narrator tries to match wits with a pair of birds and lays increasingly elaborate plots against them, his story fills with humor. In this unusual essay, a famous yet thoroughly modest writer takes direct aim at human foolishness in the person of the rarest of all targets—himself.

My war with the ospreys, like most wars, was largely accidental and had a tendency to spread in unforeseen directions. It is not over yet. The coming of winter caused an uneasy truce. I had to go into New York while the ospreys migrated to wherever they go in the winter. Spring may open new hostilities, although I can find it in my heart to wish for peace and even friendship. I hope the ospreys, wherever they may be, will read this.

I shall go back to the beginning and set down my side of the affair, trying to be as fair as I possibly can, placing truth above either propaganda or self-justification. I am confident that until near the end of the association, my motives were kind to the point of being sloppy.

Two years and a half ago I bought a little place near Sag Harbor, which is quite near to the tip of Long Island.[1] The outer end of Long Island is like the open jaws of an alligator and, deep in the mouth, about where the soft palate would be, is Sag Harbor, a wonderful village inhabited by people who have been here for a long time. It is a fishing town, a local town which has resisted the inroads of tourists by building no motor courts and putting up no hotels.

Sag Harbor was once one of the two great whaling ports of the world and was, according to local accounts, not at all second to Nantucket Island.[2] At that time no fewer than one hundred and fifty whaling bottoms roved the great seas and brought back their riches in oil. Sag Harbor and Nantucket lighted the lamps of the world until kerosene was developed and the whaling industry languished.

[1] **Long Island:** a 120-mile-long island in southeast New York State.

[2] **Nantucket Island:** a small island in the Atlantic Ocean, twenty miles off the southeast coast of Massachusetts.

With the wealth brought back by the whalers, beautiful houses were built in the village during the early 1800's, houses of neo-Greek architecture with fluted columns, Greek key decorations, with fanlights [1] and Adam [2] doors and mantels. Some of these magnificent old houses have widow's walks, those high balconies on which the women kept watch for the return of their men from their year-long voyages. Some of these old houses are being rediscovered and restored. Many of the streets of Sag Harbor are named after old whaling men. My own place is near Jesse Halsey Lane and he is still locally known as Old Cap'n Jesse. I have a picture of his rough and whiskered face.

The place I bought is not one of the great old houses but a beautiful little point of land on the inland waters, a place called Bluff Point, with its own little bay— incidentally a bay which is considered hurricane-proof. Ordinarily only two boats are moored there, mine and one other, but during hurricane warnings as many as thirty craft come in for anchorage until the all clear is broadcast.

My point, just under two acres, is shaded by great oak trees of four varieties, and there are many bushes and pines to edge it on the water side. I myself have planted a thousand Japanese black pines, furnished by the State of New York to edge my point, to hold the soil with their roots and eventually to curve beautifully inward, urged by the wind which blows every day of the year—sometimes a zephyr and sometimes a fierce and strident gale.

Greensward [3] grows on my place. On the highest point I have a small, snug cottage and in front of it a pier going out to nine feet at low water so that a fairly large boat can dock. My own boat, the *Lillymaid,* with Astolat as her port of registry, is named for my wife. She, the boat, is a utility craft twenty feet long, a clinker-built [4] Jersey sea skiff. Her eight-foot beam makes her highly dependable and seaworthy. Many of these specifications could also describe my wife. She is not clinker-built, however. The *Lillymaid* has a Navy top to put up when the weather gets too rough and she has a hundred-horsepower engine so we can run for it if a storm approaches. She is a lovely, efficient, and seaworthy craft and all we need for the fishing and coastal exploring which is our pleasure.

Our house, while very small, is double-walled and winterized so that we can drive out during cold weather when the not-so-quiet desperation of New York gets us down.

My young sons, ten and twelve, but eight and ten when the osprey war began, adore the place and spend most of their summers here, exploring about in their skiffs or quarreling happily on the pier or on the lawn under the oak trees. My wife, who I believe was realistically skeptical when I bought the place, has become its stanchest defender.

Our association with the village people of Sag Harbor is, I think, pleasant to all of us. I come originally from a small town on the West Coast, a fishing town where my people have lived for a long time. And I find that what applies in my home country is equally acceptable in Sag Harbor. If you pay your bills, trade locally as much as possible, mind your own business, and are reasonably pleasant, pretty soon they forget that you are an outlander. I feel

[1] **fanlights:** semicircular windows with radiating sash bars, like the ribs of a fan, placed over a door or window.

[2] **Adam:** Robert and James Adam were eighteenth-century furniture makers who introduced the classic style into England.

[3] **greensward:** (grēn'swôrd'): turf green with grass.

[4] **clinker-built:** having the external planks of a ship so that one edge of each overlaps the edge of the plank next to it, like clapboards on a house.

that I belong in Sag Harbor and I truly believe that the people of the village have accepted us as citizens. I do not sense the resentment from them which is reserved for tourists and summer people.

But I must get back to the ospreys, because with them I have not only failed to make friends but have, on the contrary, been insulted, have thrown down the gauntlet,[1] and had it accepted.

On the West Coast, in California's Monterey County where I was born, I learned from childhood the grasses and flowers, the insects and the fishes, the animals from gopher and ground squirrel to bobcat and coyote, deer and mountain lion, and of course the birds, the common ones at least. These are things a child absorbs as he is growing up.

When I first came to Long Island I knew none of these things. Trees, grasses, animals, and birds were all strange to me; they had to be learned. And sometimes the natives could not help me much because they knew the things so well and deeply that they could not bring them to the surface.

Thus with books and by asking questions I have begun to learn the names of trees and bushes, of berries and flowers. With a telescope, a birthday present from my wife, I have watched muskrats and a pair of otters swimming in our bay. I have tried to identify the migrating ducks and geese when they sit down in our bay to rest from their journey.

The mallards mate and nest in the reeds along our waterline and bring their ducklings for the bread we throw to them from the pier. I have watched my boys sitting quietly on the lawn with the wild ducks crawling over their legs to get pieces of doughnut from their fingers.

The baby rabbits skitter through my

vegetable garden and, since I like the rabbits better than my scrawny vegetables, I permit them not only to live but to pursue happiness on my land.

Our house has a glassed-in sun porch and outside its windows I have built a feeding station for birds. Sitting inside, I do my best to identify the different visitors with the help of an Audubon[2] and I have not always, I confess, been successful. There is one common blackish bird which looks to be of the grackle persuasion but his bill is the wrong color and I don't know what he is.

In the upper branches of a half-dead oak tree on the very tip of our point, there was, when I took possession, a tattered lump of trash which looked like an unmade bed in a motor court. In my first early spring a native named Ray Bassenden, our contractor and builder, told me, "That's an osprey's nest. They come back every year. I remember that nest since I was a little boy."

"They build a messy nest," I said.

"Messy, yes," he said professionally, "but I doubt if I could design something the winds wouldn't blow out. It isn't pretty but it's darned good architecture from a staying point of view."

Toward the end of May, to my delight, the ospreys came back from wherever

[1] **thrown down the gauntlet:** given a challenge, as to a duel.

[2] **Audubon:** a bird guide based on the books by John James Audubon (1785–1851), the first great American ornithologist.

they had been, and from the beginning they fascinated me. They are about the best fishermen in the world and I am about the worst. I watched them by the hour. They would coast along hanging on the breeze perhaps fifty feet above the water, then suddenly their wings raised like the fins of a bomb and they arrowed down and nearly always came up with a fish. Then they would turn the fish in their talons so that its head was into the wind and fly to some high dead branch to eat their catch. I became a habitual osprey watcher.

In time, two of my ospreys were nudged by love and began to install new equipment in the great nest on my point. They brought unusual material—pieces of wood, rake handles, strips of cloth, reeds, swatches of seaweed. One of them, so help me, brought a piece of two-by-four pine three feet long to put into the structure. They weren't very careful builders. The ground under the tree was strewn with the excess stuff that fell out.

I mounted my telescope permanently on the sun porch and even trimmed some branches from intervening trees, and from then on, those love-driven ospreys didn't have a moment of privacy.

Then June came and school was out and my boys trooped happily out to Sag Harbor. I warned them not to go too near the point for fear of offending the nest builders, and they promised they would not.

And then one morning the ospreys were gone and the nest abandoned. When it became apparent that they weren't coming back I walked out to the point and saw, sticking halfway out of the nest, the shaft and feathers of an arrow.

Now Catbird, my youngest son, is the archer of the family. I ran him down and gave him whatfor in spite of his plaintive protests that he had not shot at the nest.

For a week I waited for the birds to come back, but they did not. They were across the bay. I could see them through the telescope building an uneasy nest on top of a transformer on a telephone pole where they were definitely not wanted.

I got a ladder and climbed up to the nest on our point and when I came down I apologized to Catbird for my unjust suspicions. For in the nest I had found not only the arrow, but my bamboo garden rake, three T shirts belonging to my boys and a Plaza Hotel bath towel. Apparently nothing was too unusual for the ospreys to steal for their nest building. But our birds were definitely gone and showed no intention of returning. I went back to my Audubon and it told me the following:

"Osprey (fish hawk) *Pandion haliaëtus*, length 23 inches, wingspread about $6\frac{1}{2}$ feet, weight $3\frac{1}{2}$ pounds.

"Identification—in flight the wings appear long and the outer half has a characteristic backward sweep.

"Habits—(age 21 years) Provided they are not molested, ospreys will nest wherever there is a reasonably extensive body of clear water and some sort of elevated nest sites exist. The birds have little fear of man and are excellent watchdogs, cheeping loudly at intruders and driving off crows and other birds of prey. For this reason platforms on tall poles are often erected to encourage them to nest about homes and farmyards. Their food consists entirely of fish. These they spot from heights of thirty to one hundred feet, then, after hovering for a moment, they half close their wings and plunge into the water. The fish is seized in their talons, the toes of which are used in pairs, two to a side. This and the rough surface of the foot gives them a firm grip on the most slippery prey. After a catch, they rise quickly . . . and arrange the fish head first."

There followed a list of the kinds of fish they eat and their range and habits. Those were our boys, all right.

I must admit I had been pleased and a little proud to have my own osprey nest, apart from being able to watch them fish. I had planned to observe the nestlings when they arrived. The empty nest on the point was a matter of sorrow and perplexity to me. The summer was a little darkened by the empty nest, and later the winter winds ripped at its half-completed messiness.

It was in February of 1956 that the answer came to me. If people put up platforms on poles, why could I not build a nest so attractive as to be irresistible to any passing osprey with procreation on his mind? Why could I not win back my own birds from the uncomfortable nest which the power company had meanwhile torn off the transformer? I had been to Denmark and had seen what the country people there did for storks. And the storks loved them for it and had their young on the roof tops and year by year brought luck to their benefactors.

In the late winter I went to work. Climbing the oak tree on the point, I cleaned away the old debris of the nest. Then I mounted and firmly wired in place horizontally a large wagon wheel. I cut dry pampas grass stalks and bound them in long faggots. Then with the freezing blasts of winter tearing at my clothes, I reascended the tree and wove the reeds into the spokes of the wheel until I had a nest which, if I had any oviparous [1] impulses, I should have found irresistible.

My wife, dressed in warm clothing, stood dutifully on the ground under the trees and hooked bundles of reeds on the line I threw down to her. She has a highly developed satiric sense which on other occasions I have found charming. She shouted up against the howling wind: "If anybody sees you, a middle-aged man, up a tree in midwinter, building a nest, I will have trouble explaining it to a sanity commission."

Misplaced humor can, under some circumstances, almost amount to bad taste. Silently and doggedly I completed what I believe was the handsomest nest in the Western Hemisphere. Then I went back to my sun porch to await eventualities.

I did have some difficulty explaining the project to my boys. To my oldest son Thom's question, "Why do you build nests for birds?" I could only jocularly reply, "Well, I can build a better nest than they can, but I can't lay eggs, so you see we have to get together."

The winter was long and cold and there was hardly any spring at all. Summer came without warning about June first. I

[1] **oviparous** (ō·vip′ər·əs): egg-laying.

had trouble with the novel I was writing since I had to rush constantly to the telescope to see whether the ospreys, my prospective tenants, had returned.

Then school was out and my boys moved to Sag Harbor and I put them on watch.

One morning Catbird charged into my study, which is a corner of the garage.

"Ospreys!" he shouted. "Come running —ospreys!"

"Sh!" I shouted back. "Keep your voice down. You'll disturb them."

I rushed for my telescope, bowling Catbird over in my rush and tripping over Thom's feet.

There were the ospreys all right. But they weren't settling into my beautiful nest. They were dismantling it, tearing it to pieces, lifting out the carefully bound reed pads and carrying them across the bay and propping them clumsily on top of the same transformer.

Of course my feelings were hurt. Why should I deny it? And on top of all my work. But on the heels of injury came anger. Those lousy, slipshod, larcenous birds, those ingrates, those—those ospreys. My eyes strayed to the shotgun that hangs over my fireplace, but before I could reach for it a Machiavellian [1] thought came to me.

I wanted to hurt the ospreys, yes. I wanted revenge on them, but with number four shot? No. I ached to hurt them as they had hurt me—in their feelings, psychologically.

I am an adept at psychological warfare; I know well how to sink the knife into sensibilities. I was coldly quiet, even deadly in my approach and manner, so that my boys walked about under a cloud and Thom asked, "What's the matter,

[1] **Machiavellian:** cunning or crafty, after Niccolo Machi␣␣lli (1469–1527), whose book *The Prince* described a number of unscrupulous ways for a ruler to stay in power.

Father, did you lose some money playing poker?"

"You stay out of the garage," I said quietly.

I had made my plan. I declared the garage off limits to everyone. My novel came to a dead stop. Daily I worked in the garage using pieces of chicken wire and a great deal of plaster of Paris.

Then I paid a call on my neighbor, Jack Ramsey, a very good painter, and asked him to come to my work shop and to bring his palette and brushes. At the end of two days we emerged with our product—a lifesize perfect replica of a nesting whooping crane. It is my belief that there are only thirty-seven of these rare and wonderful birds in the world. Well, this was the thirty-eighth.

Chuckling evilly I hoisted the plaster bird up in the tree and wired her firmly in the nest where her blinding white body, black tail, and brilliant red mask stood out magnificently against the sky. I had even made her bill a little overlarge to take care of foreshortening.

Finally I went back to the sun porch and turned my telescope on the ospreys who pretended to go about their nest building on the transformer as though nothing had happened. But I knew what must be going on over there, although they kept up their façade [2] of listlessness, and I must say they were building an even messier nest than usual.

Mrs. Osprey was saying, "Lord almighty, George! Look who has moved into the apartment *you* didn't want. Why did I listen to you?"

To which he was replying, "*I* didn't want—what do you mean *I* didn't want? It was you who said the neighborhood wasn't good enough. Don't you put words in my mouth, Mildred."

"Everybody knows you have no taste

[2] **façade:** front, or appearance.

or background," she was replying. "Your Uncle Harry built his nest over a slaughterhouse."

And I laughed to myself. These are the wounds that never heal. This is psychological warfare as it should be fought.

Two days later, Thom came running into my study in the garage.

"The nest," he cried. "Look at the nest."

I bolted for the door. The ospreys in jealous rage were dive-bombing my whooping crane, but all they could accomplish was the breaking of their talons on the hard surface of the plaster. Finally they gave up and flew away, followed by my shouts of derision.

I did hear my oldest boy say to his brother, "Father has been working too hard. He has gone nuts."

Catbird replied, "His id [1] has been ruptured. Sometimes one broods too much on a subject and throws the whole psychic [2] pattern into an uproar."

That isn't quite where it rests.

It is true that the ospreys have not attacked any more, but we have had other visitors, human visitors.

One morning I looked out the window to see a rather stout lady in khaki trousers and a turtle-neck sweater creeping across my lawn on her hands and knees. Field glasses dangled from her neck and she held a camera in front of her. When I went out to question her, she angrily waved me away.

"Go back," she whispered hoarsely. "Do you want her to fly away?"

"But you don't understand—" I began.

"*Will* you keep your voice down," she said hoarsely. "Do you know what that is? The club will never believe me. If I

don't get a picture of her I'll kill you."

Yes, we have had bird watchers—lots of them. You see, our whooping crane can be sighted from a long way off. After a time they discovered the nature of the thing, but they would not listen to my explanation of the ruse. In fact, they became angry; not at the ospreys, where the blame rests—but at me.

As I write, it is autumn and from the coldness and the growing winds, an early winter and a cold one is indicated. I have taken my whooping crane down and restored the nest to its old beauty. When the spring comes again—we shall see what we shall see. No one can say that I am unforgiving. The nest is ready and waiting. Let us see whether the ospreys are big enough to let bygones be bygones.

My wife says that if she has to go through another year like this she will—no, I won't tell you what she says. Sometimes her sense of humor seems a little strained.

[1] **id:** a term used by psychologists to describe the unconscious part of the human make-up, that which acts independently from reason and is fulfilled by instinctive needs.

[2] **psychic:** mental.

1. By what means is the author's personality revealed directly? How is it revealed indirectly? What do you learn about the author from his comments about nature—the water, trees, birds, and animals that surround him?

2. What does the use of dialogue contribute to this essay? Why do you think an imaginary dialogue between two ospreys is included?

3. Does the essay have a main theme, either serious or not? If so, how might this main idea be stated?

4. If "My War with the Ospreys" were a short story rather than an essay, what details would the author probably omit? What details might he introduce? Do you think the short story would probably be longer or shorter than the essay?

TONE

When we speak out loud, vocal inflection has a great deal to do with what we mean. For instance, if one answers the question "Did you have a good time?" by saying "I had a great time," the answer may indicate anything from extreme pleasure to absolute boredom, depending upon the tone of voice.

In literature, *tone* can be defined as the writer's attitude, how he feels about his subject and his audience. Even though he is writing, not speaking, he uses a certain tone of voice. In written English, tone is not always easy to determine. For one thing, the way an author feels about his subject may be indicated by only a single word or phrase. The reader must read carefully. For another thing, the tone within a story or essay may shift from serious to humorous, from pleasant to unpleasant, from passionate concern to scientific detachment. This business of tone has a great deal to do with the real meaning of a piece of writing.

What about "My War with the Ospreys"? The reader may think that the use of the word *war* at the very beginning promises a serious discussion. But the first paragraph ends with "I hope the ospreys, wherever they may be, will read this." What attitude does this sentence show?

What effect do these passages have on the tone of the essay?

"two of my ospreys were nudged by love . . ."

"Why do you build nests for birds?"

"I ached to hurt them as they had hurt me —in their feelings, psychologically."

"Let us see whether the ospreys are big enough to let bygones be bygones."

The first section of Steinbeck's essay is calm, orderly, matter-of-fact. He is preparing the ground for his story. Then the tone shifts to one of excited interest in the ospreys. Next, anger and frustration: "Those lousy, slipshod, larcenous birds, those ingrates . . ." At the end the tone is calm again, but in a different way: "When the spring comes again—we shall see what we shall see."

Steinbeck's skill allows him to use his style as a mirror for his changing emotions. In your own writing, be sure that your reader can recognize your tone of voice as you intend it. Written English and spoken English are closely related, but not the same. When you speak you can change pitch, pause, or change from loud to soft. A good writer knows how to put his tone of voice down on paper.

LANGUAGE AND VOCABULARY

Look up the origins of the following words used in the first part of Steinbeck's essay. What is added to the reader's understanding of them when he knows their derivation?

osprey	strident
propaganda	zephyr

FOR COMPOSITION

1. Though you may not have had a battle with a pair of ospreys, you may have had a revealing experience with some other species of wild life—another kind of bird, a dog, a cat, a raccoon, a snake, a white rat. Write a theme in which you describe your experience with the animal and reveal your feelings about that experience.

2. As an exercise in imaginative writing, write a dialogue between two animals who have known you and who are commenting on your character or behavior.

Description

In writing a description, a writer tries to build up, with specific details, an overall impression. In reading a description, you should always try to understand the main *impression* of each paragraph. Sometimes a writer will state directly the impression he wishes to convey, but more often it will simply be suggested or implied. In a good description, every detail reinforces the writer's main impression. In the following paragraph, what impression does Charles Dickens give you of the London streets?

It is nearly eleven o'clock, and the cold thin rain, which has been drizzling so long, is beginning to pour down in good earnest; the baked-potato man has departed—the kidney-pie man has just walked away with his warehouse on his arm—the cheesemonger has drawn in his blind, and the boys have dispersed. The constant clicking of pattens on the slippy and uneven pavement, and the rustling of umbrellas, as the wind blows against the shop windows, bear testimony to the inclemency of the night; and the policeman, with his oil-skin cape buttoned closely round him, seems, as he holds his hat on his head and turns round to avoid the gust of wind and rain which drives against him at the street corner, to be very far from congratulating himself on the prospect before him. (page 198–99)

1. What kind of night is Dickens describing in this paragraph? Which details most strongly give you this impression?

2. Where does the author use a bit of narration in his description? Where does he *explain* (as in exposition) the nature of the night and the attitude of the policeman?

3. The positions of greatest emphasis in a paragraph are the beginning and the end. How does Dickens use position to emphasize the most important details in this description?

In writing a description, a writer tries to *emphasize* details that will most strongly suggest his main impression. He may emphasize a detail by placing it at the beginning or end of a paragraph, or by treating it at greater length. Which details are emphasized in this paragraph from Washington Irving's "The Voyage"?

I confess these stories, for a time, put an end to all my fine fancies. The storm increased with the night. The sea was lashed into tremendous confusion. There was a fearful, sullen sound of rushing waves and broken surges. Deep called unto deep. At times the black volume of clouds overhead seemed rent asunder by flashes of lightning which quivered along the foaming billows and made the succeeding darkness doubly terrible. The thunders bellowed over the wild waste of waters and were echoed and prolonged by the mountain waves. As I saw the ship staggering and plunging among these roaring caverns, it seemed miraculous that she regained her balance or preserved her buoyancy. Her yards would dip into the water: her bow was almost buried beneath the waves. Sometimes an impending surge appeared ready to overwhelm her, and nothing but a dexterous movement of the helm preserved her from the shock. (page 182)

1. What details are emphasized at the beginning of the paragraph? at the end?

2. Which details are emphasized by being described at greater length?

PRACTICING YOUR READING

Find four other paragraphs of description in the essays you have read. After studying these paragraphs, answer for each paragraph the two questions directly above.

READING FOR A MAIN IMPRESSION

In reading description, you should always try to gain an overall impression. Be aware of the details emphasized by the author. Open your senses to pictures and impressions and try to sense the writer's attitude and mood.

After reading each of the following paragraphs, write down answers to these questions: What is the main impression of the paragraph? Which details most strongly suggest this main impression?

Covent Garden market and the avenues leading to it are thronged with carts of all sorts, sizes, and descriptions, from the heavy lumbering wagon, with its four stout horses, to the jingling costermonger's cart, with its consumptive donkey. The pavement is already strewed with decayed cabbage leaves, broken hay bands, and all the indescribable litter of a vegetable market: men are shouting, carts backing, horses neighing, boys fighting, basket-women talking, piemen expatiating on the excellence of their pastry, and donkeys braying. These and a hundred other sounds form a compound discordant enough to a Londoner's ears and remarkably disagreeable to those of country gentlemen who are sleeping at the Hummums for the first time. ("The Streets—Morning and Night," page 194)

We one day descried some shapeless object drifting at a distance. At sea, everything that breaks the monotony of the surrounding expanse attracts attention. It proved to be the mast of a ship that must have been completely wrecked; for there were the remains of handkerchiefs, by which some of the crew had fastened themselves to this spar, to prevent their being washed off by the waves. There was no trace by which the name of the ship could be ascertained. The wreck had evidently drifted about for many months; clusters of shellfish had fastened about it, and long seaweeds flaunted at its sides. But where, thought I, is the crew? Their struggle has long been over, they have gone down amidst the roar of the tempest, their bones lie whitening among the caverns of the deep. Silence, oblivion, like the waves, have closed over them, and no one can tell the story of their end. ("The Voyage," pages 180–81)

The river's course—here as in its whole career—widens and narrows by turns. Where it is narrow, the slopes are dark, the stream is shadowed all day but for a little while at noon, when straight fingers of sunlight reach down through the forest. The stream is clear and icy, going rapidly over polished brown speckled stones. They remind us of something. At a glance the diamond water going over its stony bed makes the image of the fish it carries—the same speckled colors, the same watery flicker, the same half-lights of reflection and golden flecks. In and out of leaf shadow, protected by the dazzle of moving water, the trout in plain sight is safe because he and his river are so close in likeness. ("The Rio Grande," page 208)

WRITING TO CONVEY A MAIN IMPRESSION

In writing a description, try to choose and emphasize your details so as to give an overall impression. Think of yourself as an architect, building an impression word by word, each detail enlarging and fulfilling your design.

1. Describe a place or scene that you remember as giving you an overall impression.
2. Describe some person whose face or manner has left you with a definite impression.

ART AND LITERATURE

Sculpture, painting, and all kinds of art, of course, are directly concerned with visual impressions. Look again at the paintings on pages 187–92. Which of them gives you the strongest, most definite impression? Write a description of this painting, emphasizing those visual details that are emphasized in the painting.

BIOGRAPHY

"SOME ARE BORN great, some achieve greatness, and some have greatness thrust upon them," says a character in one of Shakespeare's comedies. In the following pages you will read about the lives of four great men. Two were writers, one was a statesman, and one was a philosopher. The philosopher was also a great teacher who was put to death by politicians. The statesman was a general and a great writer as well. Both of the writers were also famous as performers who recited their works to audiences throughout the English-speaking world. One of the writers had been a river-boat pilot.

Biography is an attempt to capture in print the greatness, complications, and fascination of a human life. Through biography we can look into the lives of all sorts of people, in all ages—men and women who, in one way or another, changed the world in which they lived. Through biography you can witness the murder of Caesar, overhear the conversation of Socrates, share a small-town boy's excitement as he leaves home for life on the Mississippi. Even in short selections you will learn much about how others have thought and felt about themselves and the world of which they were a part.

Some biographies are mainly dates, facts, and documents. Others give the reader an impression of a living man. Some are long, such as Carl Sandburg's many-volumed life of Lincoln; others are short sketches of only a few pages. The selections that follow show some of the variety of writing that comes under the heading of biography. Some of the selections are autobiography. One selection is a newspaper interview. Another is a speech at a courtroom trial. In the case of Mark Twain and Socrates, you will read different accounts of these men as they were seen from different points of view.

As you read these biographies, try to decide what made these men famous. Were they born great? Did they achieve greatness? Or was their greatness thrust upon them? Look, too, at the devices the writers have used in order to "capture" their subjects. How do they use dialogue, specific details, anecdotes? What is the purpose behind each biography? In any case, whatever the devices used by each writer to portray his subject, you will find that the lives of real people are often more interesting than fiction.

A Child's Christmas in Wales

DYLAN THOMAS

Dylan Thomas was born in 1914 in Swansea, a seaport town in southern Wales. Here he spent a happy childhood, and here, at the local grammar school, he received all his formal education. Upon leaving school, he worked for a while as a newspaper reporter, but soon turned to writing poetry full time. The brilliance of Thomas's poetry, which is full of vigor and unusual imagery, was recognized with the publication of his first book, which appeared when he was only twenty. His prose, however, was not widely read until after his death in New York at the age of thirty-nine. By this time Thomas, whose reputation had grown enormously through his poetry readings for both British and American audiences, had become a celebrated figure whom many considered one of the greatest poets of his age.

For the background of both his poetry and his prose Thomas drew heavily on his childhood years. A case in point is "A Child's Christmas in Wales," which quickly reveals Thomas's poetic gift and bears out the comment of the modern American poet Conrad Aiken, who referred to Thomas as "a born language-lover and language-juggler" with "a genuine and outrageous gift of gab." This autobiographical sketch, fantastic and realistic at the same time, is full of the joy of living.

ONE CHRISTMAS was so much like another, in those years around the sea-town corner now and out of all sound except the distant speaking of the voices I sometimes hear a moment before sleep, that I can never remember whether it snowed for six days and six nights when I was twelve or whether it snowed for twelve days and twelve nights when I was six. All the Christmases roll down toward the two-tongued sea, like a cold and headlong moon bundling down the sky that was our street; and they stop at the rim of the ice-edged, fish-freezing waves, and I plunge my hands in the snow and bring out whatever I can find. In goes my hand into that wool-white bell-tongued ball of holidays resting at the rim of the carol-singing sea, and out come Mrs. Prothero and the firemen.

It was on the afternoon of the day of Christmas Eve, and I was in Mrs. Prothero's garden, waiting for cats, with her son Jim. It was snowing. It was always snowing at Christmas. December, in my memory, is white as Lapland, though there were no reindeer. But there were cats. Patient, cold, and callous, our hands wrapped in socks, we waited to snowball the cats. Sleek and long as jaguars and horrible-whiskered, spitting and snarling, they would slink and sidle over the white back-garden walls, and the lynx-eyed hunters, Jim and I, fur-capped and moccasined trappers from Hudson Bay, off Mumbles Road, would hurl our deadly snowballs at the green of their eyes. The wise cats never appeared. We were so still, Eskimo-footed arctic marksmen in the muffling silence of the eternal snows—eternal, ever since Wednesday—that we never heard Mrs. Prothero's first cry from her igloo at the bottom of the garden. Or, if we heard it at all, it was, to us, like the far-off challenge of our enemy and prey,

Winter scene south of Swansea, Wales, where Thomas was born.

the neighbor's polar cat. But soon the voice grew louder.

"Fire!" cried Mrs. Prothero, and she beat the dinner gong.

And we ran down the garden, with the snowballs in our arms, toward the house; and smoke, indeed, was pouring out of the dining room, and the gong was bombilating,[1] and Mrs. Prothero was announcing ruin like a town crier in Pompeii.[2] This was better than all the cats in Wales standing on the wall in a row. We bounded into the house, laden with snowballs, and stopped at the open door of the smoke-filled room. Something was burning all right; perhaps it was Mr. Prothero, who always slept there after midday dinner with a newspaper over his face. But he was standing in the middle of the room, saying, "A fine Christmas!" and smacking at the smoke with a slipper.

"Call the fire brigade," cried Mrs. Prothero as she beat the gong.

[1] **bombilating:** This word means *buzzing* or *humming;* but Thomas evidently is talking about something much louder, like clanging.

[2] **Pompeii** (pom·pā'): an ancient Italian city south of Naples which was buried by an eruption of Mount Vesuvius in A.D. 79.

"They won't be there," said Mr. Prothero, "it's Christmas."

There was no fire to be seen, only clouds of smoke and Mr. Prothero standing in the middle of them, waving his slipper as though he were conducting.

"Do something," he said.

And we threw all our snowballs into the smoke—I think we missed Mr. Prothero—and ran out of the house to the telephone box.

"Let's call the police as well," Jim said.

"And the ambulance."

"And Ernie Jenkins, he likes fires."

But we only called the fire brigade, and soon the fire engine came and three tall men in helmets brought a hose into the house and Mr. Prothero got out just in time before they turned it on. Nobody could have had a noisier Christmas Eve. And when the firemen turned off the hose and were standing in the wet, smoky room, Jim's aunt, Miss Prothero, came downstairs and peered in at them. Jim and I waited, very quietly, to hear what she would say to them. She said the right thing, always. She looked at the three tall firemen in their shining helmets, standing among the smoke and cinders and dis-

solving snowballs, and she said: "Would you like anything to read?"

Years and years and years ago, when I was a boy, when there were wolves in Wales, and birds the color of red-flannel petticoats whisked past the harp-shaped hills, when we sang and wallowed all night and day in caves that smelt like Sunday afternoons in damp front farmhouse parlors, and we chased, with the jawbones of deacons, the English and the bears, before the motor car, before the wheel, before the duchess-faced horse, when we rode the daft and happy hills bareback, it snowed and it snowed. But here a small boy says: "It snowed last year, too. I made a snowman and my brother knocked it down and I knocked my brother down and then we had tea."

"But that was not the same snow," I say. "Our snow was not only shaken from whitewash buckets down the sky, it came shawling out of the ground and swam and drifted out of the arms and hands and bodies of the trees; snow grew overnight on the roofs of the houses like a pure and grandfather moss, minutely white-ivied the walls and settled on the postman, opening the gate, like a dumb, numb thunderstorm of white, torn Christmas cards."

"Were there postmen then, too?"

"With sprinkling eyes and wind-cherried noses, on spread, frozen feet they crunched up to the doors and mittened on them manfully. But all that the children could hear was a ringing of bells."

"You mean that the postman went rat-a-tat-tat and the doors rang?"

"I mean that the bells that the children could hear were inside them."

"I only hear thunder sometimes, never bells."

"There were church bells, too."

"Inside them?"

"No, no, no, in the bat-black, snow-white belfries, tugged by bishops and storks. And they rang their tidings over the bandaged town, over the frozen foam of the powder and ice-cream hills, over the crackling sea. It seemed that all the churches boomed for joy under my window; and the weathercocks crew for Christmas, on our fence."

"Get back to the postmen."

"They were just ordinary postmen, fond of walking and dogs and Christmas and the snow. They knocked on the doors with blue knuckles. . . ."

A postman of Swansea, Wales.

"Ours has got a black knocker. . . ."

"And then they stood on the white Welcome mat in the little, drifted porches and huffed and puffed, making ghosts with their breath, and jogged from foot to foot like small boys wanting to go out."

"And then the Presents?"

"And then the Presents, after the Christmas box. And the cold postman, with a rose on his button-nose, tingled down the tea-tray-slithered run of the chilly glinting hill. He went in his ice-bound boots like a man on fishmonger's slabs. He wagged his bag like a frozen camel's hump, dizzily turned the corner on one foot, and was gone."

"Get back to the Presents."

"There were the Useful Presents: engulfing mufflers of the old coach days, and mittens made for giant sloths; zebra scarfs of a substance like silky gum that could be tug-o'-warred down to the galoshes; blinding tam-o'-shanters like patchwork tea cozies [1] and bunny-suited busbies [2] and balaclavas [3] for victims of head-shrinking tribes; from aunts who always wore wool next to the skin there were mustached and rasping vests that made you wonder why the aunts had any skin left at all; and once I had a little crocheted nose bag from an aunt now, alas, no longer whinnying with us. And pictureless books in which small boys, though warned with quotations not to, *would* skate on Farmer Giles's pond and did and drowned; and books that told me everything about the wasp, except why."

"Go on to the Useless Presents."

"Bags of moist and many-colored jelly babies and a folded flag and a false nose and a tram conductor's cap and a machine that punched tickets and rang a bell; never a catapult; once, by mistake that no one could explain, a little hatchet; and a celluloid duck that made, when you pressed it, a most unducklike sound, a mewing moo that an ambitious cat might make who wished to be a cow; and a painting book in which I could make the grass, the trees, the sea and the animals any color I pleased, and still the dazzling sky-blue sheep are grazing in the red field under the rainbow-billed and pea-green birds. Hard-boileds, toffee, fudge and all-sorts, crunches, cracknels, humbugs, glaciers, marzipan, and butterwelsh [4] for the Welsh. And troops of bright tin soldiers who, if they could not fight, could always run. And Snakes-and-Families and Happy Ladders. And Easy Hobbi-Games for Little Engineers, complete with instructions. Oh, easy for Leonardo! [5] And a whistle to make the dogs bark to wake up the old man next door to make him beat on the wall with his stick to shake our picture off the wall. And a packet of cigarettes: you put one in your mouth and you stood at the corner of the street and you waited for hours, in vain, for an old lady to scold you for smoking a cigarette, and then with a smirk you ate it. And then it was breakfast under the balloons."

"Were there Uncles, like in our house?"

"There are always Uncles at Christmas. The same Uncles. And on Christmas mornings, with dog-disturbing whistle and sugar fags, [6] I would scour the swatched town for the news of the little world, and find always a dead bird by the white Post Office or by the deserted swings; perhaps a robin, all but one of his fires out. Men and women wading or scooping back from chapel, with taproom noses and wind-bussed cheeks, all albinos, huddled their stiff black jarring feathers against the irreligious snow. Mistletoe hung from the gas brackets in all the front parlors; there was sherry and walnuts and bottled beer and crackers by the dessertspoons; and cats in their furabouts watched the fires; and the high-heaped fire spat, all ready for the chestnuts and the mulling pokers. Some few large men sat in the front parlors, without their collars, Uncles almost certainly, trying their new cigars, holding them out judiciously at arms' length, returning them to their mouths, coughing, then hold-

[1] **tea cozies:** padded covers used to keep teapots hot.

[2] **busbies:** tall fur hats.

[3] **balaclavas:** knitted caps which cover the head and most of the face.

[4] **Hard-boileds . . . butterwelsh:** various kinds of candy.

[5] **Leonardo:** Leonardo da Vinci, the famous fifteenth-century Italian painter, architect, and sculptor, who was also an engineer.

[6] **sugar fags:** candy in the shape of cigarettes.

ing them out again as though waiting for the explosion; and some few small aunts, not wanted in the kitchen, nor anywhere else for that matter, sat on the very edges of their chairs, poised and brittle, afraid to break, like faded cups and saucers."

Not many those mornings trod the piling streets: an old man always, fawn-bowlered, yellow-gloved and, at this time of year, with spats of snow, would take his constitutional to the white bowling green and back, as he would take it wet or fire on Christmas Day or Doomsday; sometimes two hale young men, with big pipes blazing, no overcoats and wind-blown scarfs, would trudge, unspeaking, down to the forlorn sea, to work up an appetite, to blow away the fumes, who knows, to walk into the waves until nothing of them was left but the two curling smoke clouds of their inextinguishable briars. Then I would be slapdashing home, the gravy smell of the dinners of others, the bird smell, the brandy, the pudding and mince, coiling up to my nostrils, when out of a snow-clogged side lane would come a boy the spit of myself, with a pink-tipped cigarette and the violet past of a black eye, cocky as a bullfinch, leering all to himself. I hated him on sight and sound, and would be about to put my dog whistle to my lips and blow him off the face of Christmas when suddenly he, with a violet wink, put *his* whistle to *his* lips and blew so stridently, so high, so exquisitely loud, that gobbling faces, their cheeks bulged with goose, would press against their tinseled windows, the whole length of the white echoing street. For dinner we had turkey and blazing pudding, and after dinner the Uncles sat in front of the fire, loosened all buttons, put their large moist hands over their watch chains, groaned a little, and slept. Mothers, aunts, and sisters scuttled to and fro, bearing tureens. Auntie Bessie, who had already

been frightened, twice, by a clock-work mouse, whimpered at the sideboard and had some elderberry wine. The dog was sick. Auntie Dosie had to have three aspirins, but Auntie Hannah, who liked port, stood in the middle of the snowbound back yard, singing like a big-bosomed thrush. I would blow up balloons to see how big they would blow up to; and, when they burst, which they all did, the Uncles jumped and rumbled. In the rich and heavy afternoon, the Uncles breathing like dolphins and the snow descending, I would sit among festoons and Chinese lanterns and nibble dates and try to make a model man-o'-war, following the Instructions for Little Engineers, and produce what might be mistaken for a sea-going tramcar. Or I would go out, my bright new boots squeaking, into the white world, on to the seaward hill, to call on Jim and Dan and Jack and to pad through the still streets, leaving huge deep footprints on the hidden pavements.

"I bet people will think there's been hippos."

"What would you do if you saw a hippo coming down our street?"

"I'd go like this, bang! I'd throw him over the railings and roll him down the hill and then I'd tickle him under the ear and he'd wag his tail."

"What would you do if you saw *two* hippos?"

Iron-flanked and bellowing he-hippos clanked and battered through the scudding snow toward us as we passed Mr. Daniel's house.

"Let's post Mr. Daniel a snowball through his letter box."

"Let's write things in the snow."

"Let's write, 'Mr. Daniel looks like a spaniel' all over his lawn."

Or we walked on the white shore. "Can the fishes see it's snowing?"

The silent one-clouded heavens drifted

on to the sea. Now we were snow-blind travelers lost on the north hills, and vast dewlapped dogs, with flasks round their necks, ambled and shambled up to us, baying "Excelsior." We returned home through the poor streets where only a few children fumbled with bare red fingers in the wheel-rutted snow and cat-called after us, their voices fading away, as we trudged uphill, into the cries of the dock birds and the hooting of ships out in the whirling bay. And then, at tea the recovered Uncles would be jolly; and the ice cake loomed in the center of the table like a marble grave. Auntie Hannah laced her tea with rum, because it was only once a year.

Bring out the tall tales now that we told by the fire as the gaslight bubbled like a diver. Ghosts whooed like owls in the long nights when I dared not look over my shoulder; animals lurked in the cubby-hole under the stairs where the gas meter ticked. And I remember that we went singing carols once, when there wasn't the shaving of a moon to light the flying streets. At the end of a long road was a drive that led to a large house, and we stumbled up the darkness of the drive that night, each one of us afraid, each one holding a stone in his hand in case, and all of us too brave to say a word. The wind through the trees made noises as of old and unpleasant and maybe webfooted men wheezing in caves. We reached the black bulk of the house.

"What shall we give them? Hark the Herald?"

"No," Jack said, "Good King Wences-las. I'll count three."

One, two, three, and we began to sing, our voices high and seemingly distant in the snow-felted darkness round the house that was occupied by nobody we knew. We stood close together, near the dark door.

"Good King Wenceslas looked out
On the Feast of Stephen . . ."

And then a small, dry voice, like the voice of someone who has not spoken for a long time, joined our singing: a small, dry, eggshell voice from the other side of the door: a small dry voice through the keyhole. And when we stopped running we were outside *our* house; the front room was lovely; balloons floated under the hot-water-bottle-gulping gas; everything was good again and shone over the town.

"Perhaps it was a ghost," Jim said.

"Perhaps it was trolls," Dan said, who was always reading.

"Let's go in and see if there's any jelly left," Jack said. And we did that.

Always on Christmas night there was music. An uncle played the fiddle, a cousin sang "Cherry Ripe," and another uncle sang "Drake's Drum." It was very warm in the little house. Auntie Hannah, who had got on to the parsnip wine, sang a song about Bleeding Hearts and Death, and then another in which she said her heart was like a Bird's Nest; and then everybody laughed again; and then I went to bed. Looking through my bedroom window, out into the moonlight and the unending smoke-colored snow, I could see the lights in the windows of all the other houses on our hill and hear the music rising from them up the long, steadily falling night. I turned the gas down, I got into bed. I said some words to the close and holy darkness, and then I slept.

FOR STUDY AND DISCUSSION

1. What impression do you get of this child's Christmas? Is it happy? confused? excited? or all of these and more? Explain your answer with references to the text.

2. Thomas changes his point of view throughout this piece of writing: the first para-

graph is largely the words of an adult remembering; in the second paragraph the writer is back in his childhood, remembering as a child remembers. Find additional examples in this selection of both of these points of view.

3. Cite from this selection what seem to you to be especially vivid examples of childlike exaggeration.

4. One way in which Thomas creates vivid impressions is through his unusual use of words. For instance, note this passage at the end of the first paragraph: "In goes my hand into that *wool-white bell-tongued ball of holidays* resting at the rim of the *carol-singing sea . . .*" Find and explain other examples of Thomas's "language juggling."

5. A number of the incidents in this selection are comic. For instance: "Something was burning all right; perhaps it was Mr. Prothero . . ." Find other examples of humor, and explain what makes them funny.

AUTOBIOGRAPHY

Autobiography, like the essay, is a personal art. There are as many ways to tell the story of one's own life as there are tellers. In one autobiography the reader may find an objective day-by-day or week-by-week account of what the writer did: what his schooling was like, what jobs he held, what honors he earned, what he thought about the world around him. Dylan Thomas's "A Child's Christmas in Wales" is something else altogether. Here Thomas piles up details to create a descriptive impression of what a moment in his childhood was like. He does not try to be strictly accurate. And he looks at the child with a child's imagination, which exaggerates or makes a fantasy of such episodes as snowballing cats, calling the fire brigade, describing the presents, and talking about all the aunts and uncles. What emerges is, in a sense, a "tall tale": these things probably did not happen all at once. Thomas draws together incidents from many Christmases to give the impression of one gigantic holiday spread across his childhood. But the impression rings true, and this is what matters. How would this autobiography have been different if Thomas had confined himself only to "the facts"? Look back at two or three incidents in "A Child's Christmas in Wales" and make a list of the actual facts. What details and exaggerations has Thomas added in his account?

LANGUAGE AND VOCABULARY

One of the many ways in which Dylan Thomas introduces vivid description into his writing is through the use of compound (hyphenated) adjectives, which he makes up in order to avoid using a larger number of words to say the same thing. For instance, "fish-freezing waves," in the first paragraph, creates in a very short space as clear a feeling as could ever be produced by something like "waves so cold that they would freeze even the fish."

Below are some more of these descriptive compound words. Study them in the context of the sentences in which they appear and then describe clearly exactly what picture you think Thomas intends the reader to get from them.

"horrible-whiskered . . ." (Page 224.)
"wind-cherried . . ." (Page 226.)
"bat-black . . ." (Page 226.)
"rainbow-billed . . ." (Page 227.)
"dog-disturbing . . ." (Page 227.)
"wind-bussed . . ." (Page 227.)
"iron-flanked . . ." (Page 228.)
"one-clouded . . ." (Page 228.)
"wheel-rutted . . ." (Page 229.)

In order to give a clear visual or sound impression without using a large number of words, try making up a few such compounds of your own. You should of course note that, in the hands of an inexperienced writer, careless use, or overuse, of such made-up combinations may turn into "fancy" writing, which should be avoided.

FOR COMPOSITION

Think back to a time when you were perhaps seven or eight years old, and try to recall an incident that made a strong impression on you. Write about this incident as a fragment of your autobiography, making sure to indicate to the reader how you felt about the incident at that time. Re-create the experience through a child's eyes.

The Life of Caesar

PLUTARCH

Plutarch was the first modern biographer and the greatest biographer of the ancient world. Born around A.D. 46, about ninety years after the death of Julius Caesar, he spent most of his life in central Greece, although unlike most men of his day, he had opportunities to travel widely. He studied in Athens and traveled not only elsewhere within his own country but abroad to Egypt and to Italy.

In his own day Plutarch was known as a philosopher, by which was meant that he was a knowledgeable lecturer in many fields, including physics, natural science, rhetoric, literature, philosophy, and ethics. He also wrote voluminously and turned out many treatises on these and other subjects.

But it is as a historian and a biographer that we remember Plutarch today. In the writing of history, Plutarch's main interest was the characters of famous men and how these men shaped history. He was particularly interested in the story of the collapse of the Roman Republic, between about 100 and 30 B.C. Plutarch probably gained his knowledge of Latin and of Roman history from his years in Rome, where he lectured on philosophy. After much reading and research, he wrote biographies of ten important Romans who lived during the decline of Rome. Among them are Pompey, Caesar, Cicero, Brutus, and Antony, all of whom figure, in one way or another, in Shakespeare's play *Julius Caesar*. (Shakespeare read Plutarch in the translation by Sir Thomas North, published in England in 1579.)

From "The Life of Caesar" from *Plutarch's Lives*, translated by Rex Warner. Reprinted by permission of David Higham Associates, Ltd.

The selection which follows is a modern translation of the last part of Plutarch's *Life of Caesar*.

Julius Caesar (102?–44 B.C.) was born to a noble Roman family. His career in politics and military life started when he was about twenty years old, and it is at this point that Plutarch's *Life of Caesar* begins.

Caesar's career was full of dramatic events: wars throughout the Mediterranean world, intrigue and undercover politics at home, civil war, dictatorship, government reforms. The last five years of Caesar's life were a particularly complex period in Roman history. In 49 B.C., after years of fighting the Gallic Wars, Caesar's rivalry with Pompey, his son-in-law and principal opponent in the government, flared into civil war. Caesar, who was in the north of Italy, crossed the Rubicon, attacked the forces of Pompey, and defeated them. Pompey fled to Egypt, and Caesar was elected consul, or ruling magistrate of the republic. After defeating other opposing elements in the civil war, Caesar was elected dictator for ten years. He then sailed to Spain, defeated the sons of Pompey, and returned to Rome in triumph. The reaction of the people of Rome to Caesar's triumph is described at the beginning of this selection from Plutarch, as it is at the beginning of Shakespeare's play.

WHAT MADE CAESAR most openly and mortally hated was his passion to be made King. It was this which made the common people hate him for the first time, and it served as a most useful pretext for those others who had long hated him but had up to now disguised their feelings. Yet those who were trying to get this honor conferred on Caesar actually spread the story among the people that it was foretold in the Sibylline books [1] that

[1] **Sibylline books:** nine prophetic books, supposedly revealing the destiny of Rome. According to legend, they dated from the sixth century B.C.

Parthia could only be conquered by the Romans if the Roman army was led by a king; and as Caesar was coming down from Alba to Rome, they ventured to salute him as "King," which caused a disturbance among the people. Caesar, upset by this himself, said that his name was not King but Caesar. These words were received in total silence, and he went on his way looking far from pleased. Then there was an occasion when a number of extravagant honors had been voted for him in the senate, and Caesar happened to be sitting above the rostra. Here he was approached by the consuls and the praetors [1] with the whole senate following behind; but instead of rising to receive them, he behaved to them as though they were merely private individuals and, after receiving their message, told them that his honors ought to be cut down rather than increased. This conduct of his offended not only the senate but the people as well, who felt that his treatment of the senators was an insult to the whole state. There was a general air of the deepest dejection, and everyone who was in a position to do so went away at once. Caesar himself realized what he had done and immediately turned to go home. He drew back his toga and, uncovering his throat, cried out in a loud voice to his friends that he was ready to receive the blow from anyone who liked to give it to him. Later, however, he excused his behavior on account of his illness, saying that those who suffer from it are apt to lose control of their senses if they address a large crowd while standing; in these circumstances they are very subject to fits of giddiness and may fall into convulsions and insensibility. This excuse, however, was not true. Caesar himself was perfectly willing to rise to

receive the senate; but, so they say, one of his friends, or rather his flatterers, Cornelius Balbus, restrained him from doing so. "Remember," he said, "that you are Caesar. You are their superior and ought to let them treat you as such."

Another thing which caused offense was his insulting treatment of the tribunes. The feast of the Lupercalia [2] was being celebrated. Caesar, sitting on a golden throne above the rostra and wearing a triumphal robe, was watching this ceremony; and Antony, who was consul at the time, was one of those taking part in the sacred running. When he came running into the forum, the crowd made way for him. He was carrying a diadem [3] with a wreath of laurel tied round it, and he held this out to Caesar. His action was followed by some applause, but it was not much and it was not spontaneous. But when Caesar pushed the diadem away from him, there was a general shout of applause. Antony then offered him the diadem for the second time, and again only a few applauded, though, when Caesar again rejected it, there was applause from everyone. Caesar, finding that the experiment had proved a failure, rose from his seat and ordered the wreath to be carried to the Capitol. It was then discovered that his statues had been decorated with royal diadems, and two of the tribunes, Flavius and Marullus, went round the statues and tore down the decorations. They then found out who had been the first to salute Caesar as King, and led them off to prison. The people followed the tribunes and were loud in their applause, calling them Brutuses—because it was Brutus who first put an end to the line of Kings in Rome and gave to

[1] **praetors** (prē'tərz): A praetor was a magistrate with judicial duties, ranking just below consul.

[2] **Lupercalia:** a Roman religious festival held on February 15, during which priests, magistrates, and young noblemen raced through the streets of Rome.
[3] **diadem:** a crown.

the senate and the people the power that had previously been in the hands of one man. This made Caesar angry. He deprived Marullus and Flavius of their tribuneship and in speaking against them he insulted the people at the same time.

It was in these circumstances that people began to turn their thoughts toward Marcus Brutus. He was thought to be, on his father's side, a descendant of the Brutus who had abolished the monarchy; on his mother's side he came from another famous family, the Servilii; and he was a son-in-law and a nephew of Cato.[1] But his own zeal for destroying the new monarchy was blunted by the honors and favors which he had received from Caesar. It was not only that at Pharsalus[2] after Pompey's flight his own life had been spared and the lives of many of his friends at his request; he was also a person in whom Caesar had particular trust. He had been given the most important of the praetorships for this very year and was to be consul three years later. For this post he had been preferred to Cassius, who had been the rival candidate. Caesar, indeed, is said to have admitted that Cassius had the better claims of the two for the office. "But," he added, "I cannot pass over Brutus." And once, when the conspiracy was already formed and some people were actually accusing Brutus to Caesar of being involved in it, Caesar laid his hand on his body and said to the accusers: "Brutus will wait for this skin of mine"— implying that Brutus certainly had the qualities which would entitle him to power, but that he would not, for the sake of power, behave basely and ungratefully.

However, those who were eager for the

change and who looked to Brutus as the only, or at least the most likely, man to bring it about, used, without venturing to approach him personally, to come by night and leave papers all over the platform and the chair where he sat to do his work as praetor. Most of the messages were of this kind: "You are asleep, Brutus" or "You are no real Brutus." And when Cassius observed that they were having at least something of an effect on Brutus's personal pride, he redoubled his own efforts to incite him further. Cassius, as I have mentioned in my *Life of Brutus*, had reasons of his own for hating Caesar; moreover, Caesar was suspicious of him, and once said to his friends: "What do you think Cassius is aiming at? Personally I am not too fond of him; he is much too pale." And on another occasion it is said that, when Antony and Dolabella were accused to him of plotting a revolution, Caesar said: "I'm not much afraid of these fat, long-haired people. It's the other type I'm more frightened of, the pale thin ones" —by which he meant Brutus and Cassius.

Fate however, seems to be not so much unexpected as unavoidable. Certainly, before this event, they say that strange signs were shown and strange apparitions were seen. As for the lights in the sky, the crashing sounds heard in all sorts of directions by night, the solitary specimens of birds coming down into the forum, all these, perhaps, are scarcely worth mentioning in connection with so great an event as this. But the philosopher Strabo says that a great crowd of men all on fire were seen making a charge; also that from the hand of a soldier's slave a great flame sprang out so that the hand seemed to the spectators to be burning away; but when the flame died out, the man was uninjured. He also says that when Caesar himself was making a sacrifice, the heart of the animal being sacri-

[1] **Cato:** Marcus Porcus Cato (95–46 B.C.), famous for his courage and honor. He supported Pompey against Caesar and committed suicide when Pompey was defeated.
[2] **Pharsalus:** a city in Greece, near which Caesar defeated Pompey in 48 B.C.

ficed was missing—a very bad omen indeed, since in the ordinary course of nature no animal can exist without a heart. There is plenty of authority too for the following story: a soothsayer[1] warned Caesar to be on his guard against a great danger on the day of the month of March which the Romans call the Ides; and when this day had come, Caesar, on his way to the senate house, met the soothsayer and greeted him jestingly with the words: "Well, the Ides of March have come," to which the soothsayer replied in a soft voice: "Yes, but they have not yet gone." And on the previous day Marcus Lepidus was entertaining Caesar at supper and Caesar, according to his usual practice, happened to be signing letters as he reclined at table. Meanwhile the conversation turned to the question of what sort of death was the best, and, before anyone else could express a view on the subject, Caesar cried out: "The kind that comes unexpectedly." After this, when he was sleeping as usual by the side of his wife, all the doors and windows of the bedroom flew open at once; Caesar, startled by the noise and by the light of the moon shining down on him, noticed that Calpurnia was fast asleep, but she was saying something in her sleep which he could not make out and was groaning in an inarticulate way. In fact she was dreaming at that time that she was holding his murdered body in her arms and was weeping over it. Though some say that it was a different dream which she had. They say that she dreamed that she saw the gable ornament[2] of the house torn down and for this reason fancied that she was weeping and lamenting. In any case, when it was day, she im-

plored Caesar, if it was possible, not to go out and begged him to postpone the meeting of the senate; or if, she said, he had no confidence in her dreams, then he ought to inquire about the future by sacrifices and other methods of divination.[3] Caesar himself, it seems, was affected and by no means easy in his mind; for he had never before noticed any womanish superstition in Calpurnia and now he could see that she was in very great distress. And when the prophets, after making many sacrifices, told him that the omens were unfavorable, he decided to send for Antony and to dismiss the senate.

At this point Decimus Brutus, surnamed Albinus, intervened. Caesar had such confidence in him that he had made him the second heir in his will, yet he was in the conspiracy with the other Brutus and Cassius. Now, fearing that if Caesar escaped this day the whole plot would come to light, he spoke derisively of the prophets and told Caesar that he ought not to give the senate such a good opportunity for thinking that they were being treated discourteously; they had met, he said, on Caesar's instructions, and they were ready to vote unanimously that Caesar should be declared King of all the provinces outside Italy with the right of wearing a diadem in any other place except Italy, whether on sea or land; but if, when they were already in session, someone were to come and tell them that they must go away for the time being and come back again when Calpurnia had better dreams, it would be easy to imagine what Caesar's enemies would have to say themselves and what sort of a reception they would give to Caesar's friends when they tried to prove that Caesar was not a slave master or a tyrant. If, however, he had really made up his mind to treat this day as in-

[1] **soothsayer:** literally, truth-sayer: one who claims to be able to foretell events.

[2] **gable ornament;** This ornament was put up by decree of the senate as a mark of honor and distinction.

[3] **divination:** the act of foretelling the future.

Julius Caesar

since he had some very important information to give him.

Then there was Artemidorus, a Cnidian by birth, and a teacher of Greek philosophy who, for that reason, had become acquainted with Brutus and his friends. He had thus acquired a very full knowledge of the conspiracy and he came to Caesar with a small document in which he had written down the information which he intended to reveal to him. But when he saw that Caesar took each document that was given to him and then handed it to one of his attendants, he came close up to him and said: "Read this one, Caesar, and read it quickly and by yourself. I assure you that it is important and that it concerns you personally." Caesar then took the document and was several times on the point of reading it, but was prevented from doing so by the numbers of people who came to speak to him. It was the only document which he did keep with him and he was still holding it in his hand when he went on into the senate.

It may be said that all these things could have happened as it were by chance. But the place where the senate was meeting that day and which was to be the scene of the final struggle and of the assassination made it perfectly clear that some heavenly power was at work, guiding the action and directing that it should take place just here. For here stood a statue of Pompey, and the building had been erected and dedicated by Pompey as one of the extra amenities attached to his theater. Indeed it is said that, just before the attack was made on him, Caesar turned his eyes toward the statue of Pompey and silently prayed for its good will. This was in spite of the fact that Caesar was a follower of the doctrines of Epicurus;[1] yet the mo-

auspicious, then, Decimus Brutus said, it would be better for him to go himself to the senate, speak personally to the senators, and adjourn the meeting.

While he was speaking, Brutus took Caesar by the hand and began to lead him toward the door. And before he had gone far from the door a slave belonging to someone else tried to approach him, but being unable to get near him because of the crowds who pressed round him, forced his way into the house and put himself into the hands of Calpurnia, asking her to keep him safe until Caesar came back,

[1] **Epicurus:** A Greek philosopher who taught that happiness is achieved through the pursuit of honor, prudence, and inner peace of mind.

ment of crisis, so it would seem, and the very imminence of the dreadful deed made him forget his former rationalistic views and filled him with an emotion that was intuitive or divinely inspired.

Now Antony, who was a true friend of Caesar's and also a strong man physically, was detained outside the senate house by Brutus Albinus, who deliberately engaged him in a long conversation. Caesar himself went in and the senate rose in his honor. Some of Brutus's party took their places behind his chair and others went to meet him as though they wished to support the petition being made by Tillius Cimber on behalf of his brother who was in exile. So, all joining in with him in his entreaties, they accompanied Caesar to his chair. Caesar took his seat and continued to reject their request; as they pressed him more and more urgently, he began to grow angry with them. Tillius then took hold of his toga with both hands and pulled it down from his neck. This was the signal for the attack. The first blow was struck by Casca, who wounded Caesar in the neck with his dagger. The wound was not mortal and not even a deep one, coming as it did from a man who was no doubt much disturbed in mind at the beginning of such a daring venture. Caesar, therefore, was able to turn round and grasp the knife and hold on to it. At almost the same moment the striker of the blow and he who was struck cried out together—Caesar, in Latin, "Casca, you villain, what are you doing?" while Casca called to his brother in Greek: "Help, brother."

So it began, and those who were not in the conspiracy were so horror-struck and amazed at what was being done that they were afraid to run away and afraid to come to Caesar's help; they were too afraid even to utter a word. But those who had come prepared for the murder all bared their daggers and hemmed Caesar in on every side. Whichever way he turned he met the blows of daggers and saw the cold steel aimed at his face and at his eyes. So he was driven this way and that, and like a wild beast in the toils,[1] had to suffer from the hands of each one of them; for it had been agreed that they must all take part in this sacrifice and all flesh themselves with his blood. Because of this compact Brutus also gave him one wound in the groin. Some say that Caesar fought back against all the rest, darting this way and that to avoid the blows and crying out for help, but when he saw that Brutus had drawn his dagger, he covered his head with his toga and sank down to the ground. Either by chance or because he was pushed there by his murderers, he fell down against the pedestal on which the statue of Pompey stood, and the pedestal was drenched with his blood, so that one might have thought that Pompey himself was presiding over this act of vengeance against his enemy, who lay there at his feet struggling convulsively under so many wounds.[2]

So Caesar was done to death and, when it was over, Brutus stepped forward with the intention of making a speech to explain what had been done. The senators, however, would not wait to hear him. They rushed out through the doors of the building and fled to their homes, thus producing a state of confusion, terror, and bewilderment, amongst the people. Some bolted their doors; others left their counters and shops and could be observed either running to see the place where Caesar had been killed or, once they had seen it, running back again. Antony and

[1] **in the toils:** at bay, in a net or trap.
[2] Caesar is said to have received twenty-three wounds, and many of his assailants were wounded by each other as they tried to plant that many blows in one body.

Lepidus, who were Caesar's chief friends, stole away and hid in houses belonging to other people. Brutus and his party, on the other hand, just as they were, still hot and eager from the murder, marched all together in one body from the senate house to the Capitol, holding up their naked daggers in front of them and, far from giving the impression that they wanted to escape, looking glad and confident. They called out to the people that liberty had been restored, and they invited the more distinguished persons whom they met to join in with them. Some of these did join in the procession and go up with them to the Capitol, pretending that they had taken part in the deed and thus claiming their share in the glory of it. Among these were Caius Octavius and Lentulus Spinther who suffered later for their imposture. They were put to death by Antony and young Caesar, and did not even have the satisfaction of enjoying the fame which caused their death, since no one believed that they had taken part in the action. Even those who inflicted the death penalty on them were punishing them not for what they did but for what they would have liked to have done.

Next day Brutus and his party came down from the Capitol and Brutus made a speech. The people listened to what he said without expressing either pleasure or resentment at what had been done. Their complete silence indicated that they both pitied Caesar and respected Brutus. The senate passed a decree of amnesty [1] and tried to reconcile all parties. It was voted that Caesar should be worshiped as a god and that there should be no alteration made, however small, in any of the measures passed by him while he was in power. On the other hand, provinces and appropriate honors were given to Brutus

[1] **amnesty:** general pardon.

and his friends. Everyone thought, therefore, that things were not only settled but settled in the best possible way.

But when Caesar's will was opened and it was discovered that he had left a considerable legacy to each Roman citizen, and when the people saw his body, all disfigured with its wounds, being carried through the forum, they broke through all bounds of discipline and order. They made a great pile of benches, railings, and tables from the forum and, placing the body upon this, burned it there. Then, carrying blazing brands, they ran to set fire to the houses of the murderers, while others went up and down through the city trying to find the men themselves to tear them to pieces. They, however, were well barricaded and not one of them came in the way of the mob. But there was a man called Cinna, one of Caesar's friends, who, they say, happened to have had a strange dream during the previous night. He dreamed that Caesar invited him to supper and he declined the invitation; Caesar then led him along by the hand, though he did not want to go and was pulling in the opposite direction. Now when Cinna heard that they were burning Caesar's body in the forum he got up and went there out of respect for his memory, though he felt a certain amount of misgiving as a result of his dream and was also suffering from a fever. One of the crowd who saw him there asked who he was and, when he had learned the name, told it to another. So the name was passed on and it was quickly accepted by everyone that here was one of the men who had murdered Caesar; since among the conspirators there was in fact a man with this same name of Cinna. The crowd, thinking that this was he, rushed on him and tore him limb from limb on the spot. It was this more than anything else which frightened Brutus and Cassius, and within

a few days they withdrew from the city. What they did and what happened to them before they died has been related in my *Life of Brutus*.

Caesar was fifty-six years old when he died.[1] He had survived Pompey by not much more than four years. As for the supreme power which he had pursued during the whole course of his life throughout such dangers and which at last and with such difficulty he had achieved, the only fruit he reaped from it was an empty name and a glory which made him envied by his fellow citizens. But that great divine power or genius, which had watched over him and helped him in his life, even after his death remained active as an avenger of his murder, pursuing and tracking down the murderers over every land and sea until not one of them was left and visiting with retribution all, without exception, who were in any way concerned either with the death itself or with the planning of it.

So far as human coincidences are concerned, the most remarkable was that which concerned Cassius. After his defeat at Philippi he killed himself with the very same dagger which he had used against Caesar. And of supernatural events there was, first, the great comet, which shone very brightly for seven nights after Caesar's murder and then disappeared; and also the dimming of the sun. For the whole of that year the sun's orb rose dull and pale; the heat which came down from it was feeble and ineffective, so that the atmosphere, with insufficient warmth to penetrate it, lay dark and heavy on the earth and fruits and vegetables never properly ripened, withering away and falling off before they were mature

because of the coldness of the air.

But, more than anything else, the phantom which appeared to Brutus made it clear that the murder of Caesar was not pleasing to the gods. The story is as follows: Brutus was about to take his army across from Abydos[2] to the mainland on the other side of the straits, and one night was lying down, as usual, in his tent, not asleep, but thinking about the future. He fancied that he heard a noise at the entrance to the tent and, looking toward the light of the lamp which was almost out, he saw a terrible figure, like a man, though unnaturally large and with a very severe expression. He was frightened at first, but, finding that this apparition just stood silently by his bed without doing or saying anything, he said: "Who are you? Then the phantom replied: "Brutus, I am your evil genius. You shall see me at Philippi." On this occasion Brutus answered courageously: "Then I shall see you," and the supernatural visitor at once went away. Time passed and he drew up his army against Antony and Caesar[3] near Philippi. In the first battle he conquered the enemy divisions that were opposed to him, and, after routing them, broke through and sacked Caesar's camp. But in the night before the second battle the same phantom visited him again. It spoke no word, but Brutus realized that his fate was upon him and exposed himself to every danger in the battle. He did not die, however, in the fighting. It was after his troops had been routed that he retired to a steep rocky place, put his naked sword to his breast and with the help of a friend, so they say, who assisted him in driving the blow home, killed himself.

[1] According to Plutarch, Caesar was born in 100 B.C., but modern scholars believe that he was actually born in 102 B.C. Thus he was 58, not 56, when he died.

[2] **Abydos:** an ancient town on the Dardanelles, in Asia Minor.

[3] **Caesar:** Octavius Caesar (63 B.C.–A.D. 14), the nephew of Julius Caesar, who, in 27 B.C., under the title of Augustus Caesar, became the first Roman emperor.

FOR STUDY AND DISCUSSION

1. What do you learn about the character of Caesar from this selection?

2. In a number of instances, Plutarch puts words in the mouths of Caesar, Brutus, Casca, or someone else. What effect does this have on the dramatic situation he is describing?

3. After completing the story of Caesar's life with an account of his murder, why do you suppose Plutarch went on to tell about the fate of Cassius and Brutus?

4. In addition to recounting the life of Caesar, does Plutarch give his readers a clear impression of the characters of any other people? Why is this so?

5. Do you think any parts of Plutarch's story of Caesar might be questioned by a modern historian as not representing strict historical fact? Explain.

BIOGRAPHY AS HISTORY

History is made up of many things, and its story can be told in terms of economic forces, the development of law, discoveries and inventions, art and culture, wars and revolutions, and much else. Plutarch, however, saw history in terms of the lives of famous men. He was interested in the relation between history and human character. Whether individual men and women shape events or whether the force of events shapes their lives is always a fascinating question. Would our lives today be more or less the same if there had been no Caesar, no Columbus, no Jefferson, no Churchill?

Plutarch wrote more than forty *Lives* of famous Greeks and Romans, usually pairing a Greek and a Roman in order to show similarities and differences between them. He did not write complete biographies in the modern sense. Rather, he omitted large parts of a man's life in order to concentrate on the events that seemed to him most important. For example, he tells us practically nothing about Caesar's youth and never discusses Caesar as a writer. Yet Plutarch's *Lives* are biography. He himself insisted on this: "My design is not to write histories, but lives. A man's most glorious exploits do not always tell us most about his vices and virtues. Sometimes a smaller matter, an expression or a jest, informs us better of their characters and inclinations than the most famous sieges, the greatest armaments, or the bloodiest battles whatsoever."

LANGUAGE AND VOCABULARY

Studying the language of a translation, particularly one from Greek, is quite different from studying ways in which an English or American writer uses his own language. For one thing, no translation can ever be exactly the same as the original.

In the exercise that follows, you will not be asked to look at the original words of Plutarch. Instead, you will find printed below two English translations of the same Greek phrase, the first from the seventeenth-century translation of John Dryden and the second from the twentieth-century translation you have just read. Study these paired phrases and decide which appeals to you most. Does the wording of the recent translation tell you anything about the way people write today, as compared with how they wrote over two hundred years ago? Be sure to check the context in which these words occur.

"most specious pretense" / "most useful pretext" (Page 231.)

"procure him that title" / "get this honor conferred on [him]" (Page 231.)

"commonality" / "people" (Page 232.)

"gave a fresh occasion of resentment" / "Another thing which caused offense" (Page 232.)

"met his death"/"killed himself" (Page 238.)

FOR COMPOSITION

1. "It's the *who* that matters, not the *what*." Write a theme on this topic, illustrating from your reading or your own experience Plutarch's idea that it is the man and not his exploits that count.

2. Do some research on a famous historical character. Then write a brief biography in the form of an encyclopedia entry. Be sure to give the meaning of your subject's life and work as well as the bare facts regarding the chief events of his life.

I. MARK TWAIN

Mark Twain—or, to call him by the name his parents gave him—Samuel Langhorne Clemens, is perhaps America's most widely read author. Born in 1835 in a small Missouri town, he grew up in Hannibal, Missouri, on the Mississippi River. The river dominated the lives of the people who lived along its banks, and Twain was no exception. He lived on the Mississippi as a boy, worked on it as a young man, and wrote about it for many years thereafter. He took his pen name, Mark Twain, from the cry of the leadsman who sat at the front of the boat and measured the depth of the river waters. "By the mark, twain," indicated a depth of two fathoms, a depth which made a river pilot feel comfortable, Clemens once said, which is why he chose Mark Twain for his pen name.

In addition to working as a Mississippi River pilot, Twain was at various times of his life a printer, a mining prospector, a newspaper writer and correspondent, a lecturer and world traveler—all this in addition to being a writer of stories and books which earned him worldwide fame.

Twain first received popular recognition as a writer with the publication in 1869 of *Innocents Abroad,* a humorous travelogue based on his experiences during a trip to Europe, Egypt, and the Near East. After his return to America, Twain lived for a while in Buffalo, New York, then in Hartford, Connecticut. As the years passed, he turned out classics such as *Roughing It, The Adventures of Tom Sawyer, The Adventures of Huckleberry Finn,* and *Life on the Mississippi.* These books reflect many aspects of American life and are distinctly American in style. Twain's *Autobiography* was written late in life and was published in 1924, fourteen years after his death.

The selections which follow present a threefold portrait of Mark Twain. First, "Early Days," from the *Autobiography,* tells about his boyhood in Missouri. The selection from *Life on the Mississippi* recalls Twain's beginnings as a river pilot. Finally, "An Interview with Mark Twain" by Rudyard Kipling shows Twain as a world-famous writer—visiting with a young Englishman who also later became world-famous.

Mark Twain

Early Days

In this selection, from Mark Twain's *Auto-biography*, a seventy-year-old man with a clear memory recalls scenes from his boyhood. "I can see the farm yet," he wrote, "with perfect clearness. I can see all its belongings, all its details . . ."

I WAS BORN the 30th of November, 1835, in the almost invisible village of Florida, Monroe County, Missouri. My parents removed to Missouri in the early thirties; I do not remember just when, for I was not born then and cared nothing for such things. It was a long journey in those days and must have been a rough and tiresome one. The village contained a hundred people and I increased the population by one percent. It is more than many of the best men in history could have done for a town. It may not be modest to me to refer to this but it is true. There is no record of a person doing as much—not even Shakespeare. But I did it for Florida and it shows that I could have done it for any place—even London, I suppose.

Recently someone in Missouri has sent me a picture of the house I was born in. Heretofore I have always stated that it was a palace, but I shall be more guarded now.

The village had two streets, each a couple of hundred yards long; the rest of the avenues mere lanes, with rail fences and cornfields on either side. Both the streets and the lanes were paved with the same material—tough black mud in wet times, deep dust in dry.

Most of the houses were of logs—all of them, indeed, except three or four; these latter were frame ones. There were none of brick and none of stone. There was a log church, with a puncheon floor and slab benches. A puncheon floor is made of logs whose upper surfaces have been chipped flat with the adz.[1] The cracks between the logs were not filled; there was no carpet; consequently, if you dropped anything smaller than a peach it was likely to go through. The church was perched upon short sections of logs, which elevated it two or three feet from the ground. Hogs slept under there, and whenever the dogs got after them during services the minister had to wait till the disturbance was over. In winter there was always a refreshing breeze up through the puncheon floor; in summer there were fleas enough for all.

A slab bench is made of the outside cut of a saw log, with the bark side down; it is supported on four sticks driven into auger holes at the ends; it has no back and no cushions. The church was twi-lighted with yellow tallow candles in tin sconces hung against the walls. Week-days, the church was a schoolhouse.

There were two stores in the village. My uncle, John A. Quarles, was propri-etor of one of them. It was a very small establishment, with a few rolls of "bit" calicoes on half a dozen shelves; a few barrels of salt mackerel, coffee, and New Orleans sugar behind the counter; stacks of brooms, shovels, axes, hoes, rakes, and such things here and there; a lot of cheap hats, bonnets, and tinware strung on strings and suspended from the walls; and at the other end of the room was an-other counter with bags of shot on it, a

[1] **adz** (adz): a cutting tool with an arched blade.

From *The Autobiography of Mark Twain*, pp. 1–11, edited by Charles Neider, copyright © 1959 by The Mark Twain Company. Reprinted by permission of Harper & Row, Publishers.

cheese or two, and a keg of powder; in front of it a row of nail kegs and a few pigs of lead, and behind it a barrel or two of New Orleans molasses and native corn whisky on tap. If a boy bought five or ten cents' worth of anything, he was entitled to half a handful of sugar from the barrel; if a woman bought a few yards of calico, she was entitled to a spool of thread in addition to the usual gratis [1] "trimmin's"; if a man bought a trifle, he was at liberty to draw and swallow as big a drink of whisky as he wanted.

Everything was cheap: apples, peaches, sweet potatoes, Irish potatoes, and corn, ten cents a bushel; chickens, ten cents apiece; butter, six cents a pound; eggs, three cents a dozen; coffee and sugar, five cents a pound. I do not know how prices are out there in interior Missouri now, but I know what they are here in Hartford, Connecticut. To wit: apples, three dollars a bushel; peaches, five dollars; Irish potatoes (choice Bermudas), five dollars; chickens, a dollar to a dollar and a half apiece, according to weight; butter, forty-five to sixty cents a pound; eggs, fifty to sixty cents a dozen; coffee, forty-five cents a pound.

My uncle, John A. Quarles, was also a farmer, and his place was in the country four miles from Florida. He had eight children and was also fortunate in other ways, particularly in his character. I have not come across a better man than he was. I was his guest for two or three months every year, from the fourth year after we removed to Hannibal [2] till I was eleven or twelve years old. I have never consciously used him or his wife in a book, but his farm has come very handy to me in literature once or twice. In *Huck Finn* and in *Tom Sawyer, Detective* I moved it down

to Arkansas. It was all of six hundred miles, but it was no trouble; it was not a very large farm—five hundred acres, perhaps—but I could have done it if it had been twice as large. And as for the morality of it, I cared nothing for that; I would move a state if the exigencies of literature required it.

It was a heavenly place for a boy, that farm of my uncle John's. The house was a double log one, with a spacious floor (roofed in) connecting it with the kitchen. In the summer the table was set in the middle of that shady and breezy floor, and the sumptuous meals—well, it makes me cry to think of them. Fried chicken, roast pig; wild and tame turkeys, ducks and geese; venison just killed; squirrels, rabbits, pheasants, partridges, prairie chickens; biscuits, hot batter cakes, hot buckwheat cakes, hot "wheat bread," hot rolls, hot corn pone; fresh corn boiled on the ear, succotash, butter beans, string beans, tomatoes, peas, Irish potatoes, sweet potatoes; buttermilk, sweet milk, "clabber," [3] watermelons, muskmelons, cantaloupes—all fresh from the garden; apple pie, peach pie, pumpkin pie, apple dumplings, peach cobbler—I can't remember the rest. The way that the things were cooked was perhaps the main splendor—particularly a certain few of the dishes. For instance, the corn bread, the hot biscuits and wheat bread, and the fried chicken. These things have never been properly cooked in the North—in fact, no one there is able to learn the art, so far as my experience goes. The North thinks it knows how to make corn bread, but this is gross superstition. Perhaps no bread in the world is quite so good as Southern corn bread, and perhaps no bread in the world is quite so bad as the Northern imitation of it. The North sel-

[1] **gratis:** free of charge.

[2] **Hannibal:** When Mark Twain was three years old, the family moved to this small Missouri town.

[3] **clabber:** curdled milk.

dom tries to fry chicken, and this is well; the art cannot be learned north of the line of Mason and Dixon, nor anywhere in Europe. This is not hearsay; it is experience that is speaking. In Europe it is imagined that the custom of serving various kinds of bread blazing hot is "American," but that is too broad a spread; it is custom in the South but is much less than that in the North. In the North and in Europe hot bread is considered unhealthy. This is probably another fussy superstition, like the European superstition that ice water is unhealthy. Europe does not need ice water and does not drink it; and yet, notwithstanding this, its word for it is better than ours, because it describes it, whereas ours doesn't. Europe calls it "iced" water. Our word describes water made from melted ice—a drink which has a characterless taste and which we have but little acquaintance with.

The farmhouse stood in the middle of a very large yard and the yard was fenced on three sides with rails and on the rear side with high palings;[1] against these stood the smokehouse; beyond the palings was the orchard; beyond the orchard were the tobacco fields. The front yard was entered over a stile made of sawed-off logs of graduated heights; I do not remember any gate. In a corner of the front yard were a dozen lofty hickory trees and a dozen black walnuts, and in the nutting season riches were to be gathered there.

Down a piece, abreast the house, stood a little log cabin against the rail fence; and there the woody hill fell sharply away, past the barns, the corncrib, the stables and the tobacco-curing house, to a limpid brook which sang along over its gravelly bed and curved and frisked in and out and here and there and yonder in the deep shade of overhanging foliage and vines—

a divine place for wading, and it had swimming pools, too, which were forbidden to us and therefore much frequented by us.

I can see the farm yet, with perfect clearness. I can see all its belongings, all its details; the family room of the house, with a "trundle" bed [2] in one corner and a spinning wheel in another—a wheel whose rising and falling wail, heard from a distance, was the mournfulest of all sounds to me and made me homesick and low spirited and filled my atmosphere with the wandering spirits of the dead; the vast fireplace, piled high on winter nights with flaming hickory logs from whose ends a sugary sap bubbled out but did not go to waste, for we scraped it off and ate it; the lazy cat spread out on the rough hearthstones; the drowsy dogs braced against

the jambs and blinking; my aunt in one chimney corner, knitting; my uncle in the other, smoking his corncob pipe; the slick and carpetless oak floor faintly mirroring the dancing flame tongues and freckled with black indentations where fire coals had popped out and died a leisurely death; half a dozen children romping in the background twilight; "split"-bottomed chairs here and there, some with rockers; a cradle—out of service but waiting with confidence; in the early cold mornings a snuggle of children in shirts and chemises,

[1] **palings:** pickets, as in a picket fence.

[2] **trundle bed:** a low bed on rollers that can be pushed under another bed.

occupying the hearthstone and procrastinating — they could not bear to leave the comfortable place and go out on the windswept floor space between the house and kitchen where the general tin basin stood, and wash.

Along outside of the front fence ran the country road, dusty in the summertime and a good place for snakes—they liked to lie in it and sun themselves; when they were rattlesnakes or puff adders, we killed them; when they were black snakes or racers or belonged to the fabled "hoop" breed, we fled without shame; when they were "house snakes" or "garters," we carried them home and put them in Aunt Patsy's work basket for a surprise;[1] for she was prejudiced against snakes, and always when she took the basket in her lap and they began to climb out of it, it disordered her mind. She never could seem to get used to them; her opportunities went for nothing. And she was always cold toward bats, too, and could not bear them; and yet I think a bat is as friendly a bird as there is. My mother was Aunt Patsy's sister and had the same wild superstitions. A bat is beautifully soft and silky; I do not know any creature that is pleasanter to touch or is more grateful for caressings, if offered in the right spirit. I know all about these coleoptera[2] because our great cave, three miles below Hannibal, was multitudinously stocked with them and often I brought them home to amuse my mother with. It was easy to manage if it was a school day because then I had ostensibly been to school and hadn't any bats. She was not a suspicious person but full of trust and confidence; and when I said, "There's something in my coat pocket for you," she would put her hand in. But she always took it out again, herself; I didn't have to tell her. It was remarkable the way she couldn't learn to like private bats. The more experience she had, the more she could not change her views.

I think she was never in the cave in her life; but everybody else went there. Many excursion parties came from considerable distances up and down the river to visit the cave. It was miles in extent and was a tangled wilderness of narrow and lofty clefts[3] and passages. It was an easy place to get lost in; anybody could do it— including the bats. I got lost myself, along with a lady, and our last candle burned down to almost nothing before we glimpsed the search party's lights winding about in the distance.

"Injun Joe," the half-breed, got lost in there once and would have starved to death if the bats had run short. But there was no chance of that; there were myriads of them. He told me all his story. In the book called *Tom Sawyer* I starved him entirely to death in the cave but that was in the interest of art; it never happened. "General" Gaines, who was our first town drunkard before Jimmy Finn got the place, was lost in there for the space of a week and finally pushed his handkerchief out of a hole in a hilltop near Saverton, several miles down the river from the cave's mouth, and somebody saw it and dug him out. There is nothing the matter with his statistics except the handkerchief. I knew him for years, and he hadn't any. But it could have been his nose. That would attract attention.

Beyond the road where the snakes sunned themselves was a dense young thicket and through it a dim-lighted path led a quarter of a mile; then out of the

[1] **a surprise:** If you have read *The Adventures of Tom Sawyer,* you may be able to recall an incident or two that had their origin in such "surprises."

[2] **coleoptera:** Mark Twain is probably pretending to confuse *chiroptera,* the scientific name for bats, with *coleoptera,* an order of insects.

[3] **clefts** (klefts): cracks or openings.

dimness one emerged abruptly upon a level great prairie which was covered with wild strawberry plants, vividly starred with prairie pinks and walled in on all sides by forests. The strawberries were fragrant and fine, and in the season we were generally there in the crisp freshness of the early morning, while the dew beads still sparkled upon the grass and the woods were ringing with the first songs of the birds.

Down the forest slopes to the left were the swings. They were made of bark stripped from hickory saplings. When they became dry they were dangerous. They usually broke when a child was forty feet in the air, and this was why so many bones had to be mended every year. I had no ill luck myself but none of my cousins escaped. There were eight of them and at one time and another they broke fourteen arms among them. But it cost next to nothing, for the doctor worked by the year—twenty-five dollars for the whole family. I remember two of the Florida doctors, Chowning and Meredith. They not only tended an entire family for twenty-five dollars a year but furnished the medicines themselves. Good measure, too. Castor oil was the principal beverage. The dose was half a dipperful, with half a dipperful of New Orleans molasses added to help it down and make it taste good, which it never did. The next standby was calomel; the next rhubarb; and the next jalap.[1] Then they bled the patient and put mustard plasters on him. It was a dreadful system, and yet the death rate was not heavy. The calomel was nearly sure to salivate[2] the patient and cost him some of his teeth. There were no dentists. When teeth became touched with decay or were

otherwise ailing, the doctor knew of but one thing to do—he fetched his tongs and dragged them out. If the jaw remained, it was not his fault.

Doctor Meredith removed to Hannibal by and by and was our family physician there and saved my life several times. Still, he was a good man and meant well. Let it go.

I was always told that I was a sickly and precarious and tiresome and uncertain child and lived mainly on allopathic medicines[3] during the first seven years of my life. I asked my mother about this, in her old age—she was in her eighty-eighth year—and said:

"I suppose that during all that time you were uneasy about me?"

"Yes, the whole time."

"Afraid I wouldn't live?"

After a reflective pause—ostensibly to think out the facts—"No—afraid you would."

It sounds like plagiarism,[4] but it probably wasn't.

[3] **allopathic** (al′ə·path′ik) **medicines:** remedies that counteract symptoms rather than cure the disease itself.

[4] **plagiarism** (plā′jə·riz′əm): stealing someone else's idea or writing and passing it off as one's own.

[1] **jalap** (jal′əp): a drug prepared from the root of a Mexican plant.

[2] **salivate** (sal′ə·vāt): to produce an abnormal flow of saliva.

FOR STUDY AND DISCUSSION

1. Mark Twain often says things which, on first reading, seem simply funny, but which, on second thought, make a serious point. Find and explain one or more of these comments.

2. From this selection, do you learn more about Sam Clemens the boy, or Mark Twain the man? Give reasons for your answer.

3. Characteristic of Mark Twain's style is his use of digression. He begins "Early Days" by describing his childhood home and, before long, turns aside from his main topic to discuss, among other things, cooking in the North. Make an outline of this selection, noting Twain's development of his main topic and his various digressions from it. How does

Twain's rambling style affect the tone of his autobiography? Do you think it heightens or detracts from the effectiveness of his writing?

UNDERSTATEMENT

Understatement, the opposite of exaggeration, is a literary device in which the writer deliberately says less than he wishes to suggest. For instance, Twain notes that his aunt was "cold toward bats," when in all probability she was scared to death of them. Find other examples of understatement in this selection. What effect does the use of understatement produce?

LANGUAGE AND VOCABULARY

In a comic essay about the writings of James Fenimore Cooper, Mark Twain made up a list of rules governing literary art. One of these is this: "The author shall use the right word, not its second cousin." Twain himself, of course, almost invariably used "the right word."

To see how right his words are, study, in context, the following excerpts from "Early Days."

"in summer there were fleas enough for all." (Page 241.)

"his farm has come very handy to me . . ." (Page 242.)

"it makes me cry . . ." (Page 242.)

"this is gross superstition." (Page 242.)

"she always took it out again, herself . . ." (Page 244.)

"If the jaw remained, it was not his fault." (Page 245.)

Which is the key word—the one "right" word—in each of these statements? Write other versions of these sentences in which the meaning is the same but the words are different. What happens to the statement if any other word is substituted?

FOR COMPOSITION

Write a fragment of your own autobiography. Select a short incident or situation which you remember clearly and write about it in the first person. Use enough descriptive detail to convince your reader that what you are writing is true.

FROM *Life on the Mississippi*

The following selection from *Life on the Mississippi* is made up of three chapters which appeared originally in the *Atlantic Monthly* in 1875, when Twain was forty years old. Here, as in his *Autobiography,* Twain writes with wry humor about his youth, a part of his life that he remembered with great affection. Here too he devotes a good deal of space to descriptions of the life he saw going on around him. He writes of his early ambitions and tells about the places and people he knew. He also has a great deal to say about himself as a boy. As you read this selection, note Twain's skillful use of small details: his description of the first boy who "went away" and became the object of every other boy's jealousy, his description of the cursing of the mate on the Ohio River steamer and of Mr. Bisby's quizzing of the cub pilot. It is quite evident where the author of *Tom Sawyer* and *Huckleberry Finn* found his material: in his own colorful life.

THE BOYS' AMBITION

WHEN I WAS a boy, there was but one permanent ambition among my comrades in our village [1] on the west bank of the Mississippi River. That was, to be a steamboatman. We had transient ambitions of other sorts, but they were only transient. When a circus came and went, it left us all burning to become clowns; the first minstrel show that came to our section left us all suffering to try that kind

[1] **our village:** Hannibal, Missouri.

From *Life on the Mississippi,* Chapters 4–6, by Mark Twain. Reprinted by permission of Harper & Row, Publishers.

of life; now and then we had a hope that if we lived and were good, God would permit us to be pirates. These ambitions faded out, each in its turn; but the ambition to be a steamboatman always remained.

Once a day a cheap, gaudy packet [1] arrived upward from St. Louis, and another downward from Keokuk. Before these events, the day was glorious with expectancy; after them, the day was a dead and empty thing. Not only the boys, but the whole village, felt this. After all these years I can picture that old time to myself now, just as it was then: the white town drowsing in the sunshine of a summer's morning; the streets empty, or pretty nearly so; one or two clerks sitting in front of the Water Street stores, with their splint-bottomed chairs tilted back against the wall, chins on breasts, hats slouched over their faces, asleep—with shingle shavings enough around to show what broke them down; a sow and a litter of pigs loafing along the sidewalk, doing a good business in watermelon rinds and seeds; two or three lonely little freight piles scattered about the "levee"; a pile of "skids" [2] on the slope of the stone-paved wharf, and the fragrant town drunkard asleep in the shadow of them; two or three wood flats at the head of the wharf, but nobody to listen to the peaceful lapping of the wavelets against them; the great Mississippi, the majestic, the magnificent Mississippi, rolling its mile-wide tide along, shining in the sun; the dense forest away on the other side; the "point" above the town, and the "point" below, bounding the river glimpse and turning it into a sort of sea, and withal a very still and brilliant and lonely one. Presently a film of dark smoke appears above one of those remote "points"; instantly a drayman, famous for his quick eye and prodigious voice, lifts up the cry, "S-t-e-a-m-boat a-comin'!" and the scene changes! The town drunkard stirs, the clerks wake up, a furious clatter of drays [3] follows, every house and store pours out a human contribution, and all in a twinkling the dead town is alive and moving. Drays, carts, men, boys, all go hurrying from many quarters to a common center, the wharf. Assembled there, the people fasten their eyes upon the coming boat as upon a wonder they are seeing for the first time. And the boat *is* rather a handsome sight, too. She is long and sharp and trim and pretty; she has two tall, fancy-topped chimneys, with a gilded device of some kind swung between them; a fanciful pilothouse, all glass and "gingerbread," perched on top of the "texas" deck [4] behind them; the paddle boxes are gorgeous with a picture or with gilded rays above the boat's name; the boiler deck, the hurricane deck, [5] and the texas deck are fenced and ornamented with clean white railings; there is a flag gallantly flying from the jackstaff; the furnace doors are open and the fires glaring bravely; the upper decks are black with passengers; the captain stands by the big bell, calm, imposing, the envy of all; great volumes of the blackest smoke are rolling and tumbling out of the chimneys—a husbanded [6] grandeur created with a bit of pitch pine just before arriving at a town; the crew are grouped on the forecastle; the broad stage is run far out over the port bow, and an envied deck hand stands picturesquely on the end of it with a coil of rope in his hand;

[1] **packet:** a steamer carrying mail, passengers, and freight.
[2] **skids:** planks used as a ramp for loading cargo on a steamer.

[3] **drays:** A dray is a heavy cart.
[4] **"texas" deck:** the top deck, for the pilothouse and the officers.
[5] **hurricane deck:** the passenger deck.
[6] **husbanded:** wisely used.

the pent steam is screaming through the gauge cocks; the captain lifts his hand, a bell rings, the wheels stop; then they turn back, churning the water to foam, and the steamer is at rest. Then such a scramble as there is to get aboard, and to get ashore, and to take in freight and to discharge freight, all at one and the same time; and such a yelling and cursing as the mates facilitate it all with! Ten minutes later the steamer is underway again, with no flag on the jackstaff and no black smoke issuing from the chimneys. After ten more minutes the town is dead again, and the town drunkard asleep by the skids once more.

My father was a justice of the peace, and I supposed he possessed the power of life and death over all men and could hang anybody that offended him. This was distinction enough for me as a general thing; but the desire to be a steamboatman kept intruding, nevertheless. I first wanted to be a cabin boy, so that I could come out with a white apron on and shake a tablecloth over the side, where all my old comrades could see me; later I thought I would rather be the deck hand who stood on the end of the stage plank with the coil of rope in his hand, because he was particularly conspicuous. But these were only daydreams—they were too heavenly to be contemplated as real possibilities. By and by one of our boys went away. He was not heard of for a long time. At last he turned up as apprentice engineer or "striker" on a steamboat. This thing shook the bottom out of all my Sunday-school teachings. That boy had been notoriously worldly, and I just the reverse; yet he was exalted to this eminence, and I left in obscurity and misery. There was nothing generous about this fellow in his greatness. He would always manage to have a rusty bolt to scrub while his boat tarried at our town, and he would sit on

the inside guard and scrub it, where we could all see him and envy him and loathe him. And whenever his boat was laid up, he would come home and swell around the town in his blackest and greasiest clothes, so that nobody could help remembering that he was a steamboatman; and he used all sorts of steamboat technicalities in his talk, as if he were so used to them that he forgot common people could not understand them. He would speak of the "labboard"[1] side of a horse in an easy, natural way that would make one wish he was dead. And he was always talking about "St. Looy" like an old citizen;[2] he would refer casually to occasions when he "was coming down Fourth Street," or when he was "passing by the Planter's House," or when there was a fire and he took a turn on the brakes of "the old Big Missouri"; and then he would go on and lie about how many towns the size of ours were burned down there that day. Two or three of the boys had long been persons of consideration among us because they had been to St. Louis once and had a vague general knowledge of its wonders, but the day of their glory was over now. They lapsed into a humble silence and learned to disappear when the ruthless "cub" engineer approached. This fellow had money, too, and hair oil. Also an ignorant silver watch and a showy brass watch chain. He wore a leather belt and used no suspenders. If ever a youth was cordially admired and hated by his comrades, this one was. No girl could withstand his charms. He "cut out" every boy in the village. When his boat blew up at last, it diffused a tranquil contentment among us such as we had not known for months. But when he came home the next week, alive,

[1] **labboard:** for larboard, or portside; that is, the left side.
[2] The citizens of St. Louis today say "St. Louis" (\overline{loo}′is), never "St. Looy" (\overline{loo}′ē).

renowned, and appeared in church all battered up and bandaged, a shining hero, stared at and wondered over by everybody, it seemed to us that the partiality of Providence for an undeserving reptile had reached a point where it was open to criticism.

This creature's career could produce but one result, and it speedily followed. Boy after boy managed to get on the river. The minister's son became an engineer. The doctor's and the postmaster's sons became "mud clerks"; the wholesale liquor dealer's son became a barkeeper on a boat; four sons of the chief merchant, and two sons of the county judge, became pilots. Pilot was the grandest position of all. The pilot, even in those days of trivial wages, had a princely salary—from a hundred and fifty to two hundred and fifty dollars a month, and no board to pay. Two months of his wages would pay a preacher's salary for a year. Now some of us were left disconsolate. We could not get on the river—at least our parents would not let us.

So by and by I ran away. I said I never would come home again till I was a pilot and could come in glory. But somehow I could not manage it. I went meekly aboard a few of the boats that lay packed together like sardines at the long St. Louis wharf and very humbly inquired for the pilots, but got only a cold shoulder and short words from mates and clerks. I had to make the best of this sort of treatment for the time being, but I had comforting daydreams of the future when I should be a great and honored pilot, with plenty of money, and could kill some of these mates and clerks and pay for them.

I WANT TO BE A CUB PILOT

Months afterward the hope within me struggled to a reluctant death, and I found myself without an ambition. But I was ashamed to go home. I was in Cincinnati, and I set to work to map out a new career. I had been reading about the recent exploration of the River Amazon by an expedition sent out by our government. It was said that the expedition, owing to difficulties, had not thoroughly explored a part of the country lying about the headwaters, some four thousand miles from the mouth of the river. It was only about fifteen hundred miles from Cincinnati to New Orleans, where I could doubtless get a ship. I had thirty dollars left; I would go and complete the exploration of the Amazon. This was all the thought I gave to the subject. I never was great in matters of detail. I packed my valise and took passage on an ancient tub called the *Paul Jones,* for New Orleans. For the sum of sixteen dollars I had the scarred and tarnished splendors of "her" main saloon principally to myself, for she was not a creature to attract the eye of wiser travelers.

When we presently got underway and went poking down the broad Ohio, I became a new being, and the subject of my own admiration. I was a traveler! A word never had tasted so good in my mouth be-

fore. I had an exultant sense of being bound for mysterious lands and distant climes which I never have felt in so uplifting a degree since. I was in such a glorified condition that all ignoble feelings departed out of me, and I was able to look down and pity the untraveled with a compassion that had hardly a trace of contempt in it. Still, when we stopped at villages and woodyards, I could not help lolling carelessly upon the railings of the boiler deck to enjoy the envy of the country boys on the bank. If they did not seem to discover me, I presently sneezed to attract their attention or moved to a position where they could not help seeing me. And as soon as I knew they saw me, I gaped and stretched and gave other signs of being mightily bored with traveling.

I kept my hat off all the time and stayed where the wind and the sun could strike me, because I wanted to get the bronzed and weatherbeaten look of an old traveler. Before the second day was half gone, I experienced a joy which filled me with the purest gratitude, for I saw that the skin had begun to blister and peel off my face and neck. I wished that the boys and girls at home could see me now.

We reached Louisville in time—at least the neighborhood of it. We stuck hard and fast on the rocks in the middle of the river and lay there four days. I was now beginning to feel a strong sense of being a part of the boat's family, a sort of infant son to the captain and younger brother to the officers. There is no estimating the pride I took in this grandeur, or the affection that began to swell and grow in me for those people. I could not know how the lordly steamboatman scorns that sort of presumption in a mere landsman. I particularly longed to acquire the least trifle of notice from the big stormy mate, and I was on the alert for an opportunity to do him a service to that

end. It came at last. The riotous powwow of setting a spar [1] was going on down on the forecastle, and I went down there and stood around in the way—or mostly skipping out of it—till the mate suddenly roared a general order for somebody to bring him a capstan bar. [2] I sprang to his side and said: "Tell me where it is—I'll fetch it!"

If a ragpicker had offered to do a diplomatic service for the Emperor of Russia, the monarch could not have been more astounded than the mate was. He even stopped swearing. He stood and stared down at me. It took him ten seconds to scrape his disjointed remains together again. Then he said impressively: "Well, if this don't beat all!" and turned to his work with the air of a man who had been confronted with a problem too abstruse for solution.

I crept away and courted solitude for the rest of the day. I did not go to dinner; I stayed away from supper until everybody else had finished. I did not feel so much like a member of the boat's family now as before. However, my spirits returned, in installments, as we pursued our way down the river. I was sorry I hated the mate so, because it was not in (young) human nature not to admire him. He was huge and muscular, his face was bearded and whiskered all over; he had a red woman and a blue woman tattooed on his right arm—one on each side of a blue anchor with a red rope to it; and in the matter of profanity he was sublime. When he was getting out cargo at a landing, I was always where I could see and hear. He felt all the majesty of his great position and made the world feel it, too. When he gave even the simplest order, he dis-

[1] **setting a spar:** placing a heavy, round timber, like a mast, which formed part of a derrick or crane.
[2] **capstan bar:** a lever for turning a winch or tightening a cable.

charged it like a blast of lightning and sent a long, reverberating peal of profanity thundering after it. I could not help contrasting the way in which the average landsman would give an order with the mate's way of doing it. If the landsman should wish the gangplank moved a foot farther forward, he would probably say: "James, or William, one of you push that plank forward, please"; but put the mate in his place, and he would roar out: "Here, now, start that gangplank for'ard! Lively, now! *What*'re you about! Snatch it! *Snatch* it! There! There! Aft again! Aft again! Don't you hear me? Dash it to dash! Are you going to *sleep* over it! *'Vast* heaving. 'Vast heaving, I tell you! Going to heave it clear astern? Where're you going with that barrel! *For-ard* with it 'fore I make you swallow it, you dash-dash-dash-*dashed* split between a tired mud turtle and a crippled hearse horse!"

I wished I could talk like that.

When the soreness of my adventure with the mate had somewhat worn off, I began timidly to make up to the humblest official connected with the boat—the night watchman. He snubbed my advances at first, but I presently ventured to offer him a new chalk pipe, and that softened him. So he allowed me to sit with him by the big bell on the hurricane deck, and in time he melted into conversation. He could not well have helped it, I hung with such homage on his words and so plainly showed that I felt honored by his notice. He told me the names of dim capes and shadowy islands as we glided by them in the solemnity of the night, under the winking stars, and by and by got to talking about himself. He seemed oversentimental for a man whose salary was six dollars a week—or rather he might have seemed so to an older person than I. But I drank in his words hungrily and with a faith that might have moved mountains if it

had been applied judiciously. What was it to me that he was soiled and seedy and fragrant with gin? What was it to me that his grammar was bad, his construction worse, and his profanity so void of art that it was an element of weakness rather than strength in his conversation? He was a wronged man, a man who had seen trouble, and that was enough for me. As he mellowed into his plaintive history his tears dripped upon the lantern in his lap, and I cried, too, from sympathy. He said he was the son of an English nobleman—either an earl or an alderman, he could not remember which, but believed was both; his father, the nobleman, loved him, but his mother hated him from the cradle; and so while he was still a little boy he was sent to "one of them old, ancient colleges"—he couldn't remember which; and by and by his father died and his mother seized the property and "shook" him, as he phrased it. After his mother shook him, members of the nobility with whom he was acquainted used their influence to get him the position of "lob-lolly-boy in a ship"; and from that point my watchman threw off all trammels of date and locality and branched out into a narrative that bristled all along with incredible adventures; a narrative that was so reeking with bloodshed and so crammed with hairbreadth escapes and the most engaging and unconscious personal villainies, that I sat speechless, enjoying, shuddering, wondering, worshiping.

It was a sore blight to find out afterward that he was a low, vulgar, ignorant, sentimental, half-witted humbug, an untraveled native of the wilds of Illinois, who had absorbed wildcat literature and appropriated its marvels, until in time he had woven odds and ends of the mess into this yarn, and then gone on telling it to fledglings like me, until he had come to believe it himself.

A CUB PILOT'S EXPERIENCE

What with lying on the rocks four days at Louisville and some other delays, the poor old *Paul Jones* fooled away about two weeks in making the voyage from Cincinnati to New Orleans. This gave me a chance to get acquainted with one of the pilots, and he taught me how to steer the boat, and thus made the fascination of river life more potent than ever for me.

It also gave me a chance to get acquainted with a youth who had taken deck passage—more's the pity, for he easily borrowed six dollars of me on a promise to return to the boat and pay it back to me the day after we should arrive. But he probably died or forgot, for he never came. It was doubtless the former, since he had said his parents were wealthy, and he only traveled deck passage [1] because it was cooler.

I soon discovered two things. One was that a vessel would not be likely to sail for the mouth of the Amazon under ten or twelve years; and the other was that the nine or ten dollars still left in my pocket would not suffice for so imposing an exploration as I had planned, even if I could afford to wait for a ship. Therefore it followed that I must contrive a new career. The *Paul Jones* was now bound for St. Louis. I planned a siege against my pilot, and at the end of three hard days he surrendered. He agreed to teach me the Mississippi River from New Orleans to St. Louis for five hundred dollars, payable out of the first wages I should receive after graduating. I entered upon the small enterprise of "learning" twelve or thirteen hundred miles of the great Mississippi River with the easy confidence of my time of life. If I had really known what I was about to require of my faculties, I should

not have had the courage to begin. I supposed that all a pilot had to do was to keep his boat in the river, and I did not consider that that could be much of a trick, since it was so wide.

The boat backed out from New Orleans at four in the afternoon, and it was "our watch" until eight. Mr. Bixby, my chief, "straightened her up," plowed her along past the sterns of the other boats that lay at the levee,[2] and then said, "Here, take her; shave those steamships as close as you'd peel an apple." I took the wheel, and my heartbeat fluttered up into the hundreds; for it seemed to me that we were about to scrape the side of every ship in the line, we were so close. I held my breath and began to claw the boat away from the danger; and I had my own opinion of the pilot who had known no better than to get us into such peril, but I was too wise to express it. In half a minute I had a wide margin of safety intervening between the *Paul Jones* and the ships; and within ten seconds more I was set aside in disgrace, and Mr. Bixby was going into danger again and flaying me alive with abuse of my cowardice. I was stung, but I was obliged to admire the easy confidence with which my chief loafed from side to side of his wheel, and trimmed the ships so closely that disaster seemed ceaselessly imminent. When he had cooled a little he told me that the easy water was close ashore and the current outside, and therefore we must hug the bank, upstream, to get the benefit of the former, and stay well out, downstream, to take advantage of the latter. In my own mind I resolved to be a downstream pilot and leave the upstreaming to people dead to prudence.

Now and then Mr. Bixby called my attention to certain things. Said he, "This is Six-Mile Point." I assented. It was pleas-

[1] **deck passage:** steerage passage, the cheapest way to travel.

[2] **levee:** a landing place or pier.

ant enough information, but I could not see the bearing of it. I was not conscious that it was a matter of any interest to me. Another time he said, "This is Nine-Mile Point." Later he said, "This is Twelve-Mile Point." They were all about level with the water's edge; they all looked about alike to me; they were monotonously unpicturesque. I hoped Mr. Bixby would change the subject. But no; he would crowd up around a point, hugging the shore with affection, and then say: "The slack water ends here, abreast this bunch of China trees; now we cross over." So he crossed over. He gave me the wheel once or twice, but I had no luck. I either came near chipping off the edge of a sugar plantation, or I yawed [1] too far from shore, and so dropped back into disgrace again and got abused.

The watch was ended at last, and we took supper and went to bed. At midnight the glare of a lantern shone in my eyes, and the night watchman said:

"Come! Turn out!"

And then he left. I could not understand this extraordinary procedure; so I presently gave up trying to and dozed off to sleep. Pretty soon the watchman was back again, and this time he was gruff. I was annoyed. I said:

"What do you want to come bothering around here in the middle of the night for? Now as like as not I'll not get to sleep again tonight."

The watchman said:

"Well, if this an't good, I'm blest."

The "off watch" was just turning in, and I heard some brutal laughter from them and such remarks as "Hello, watchman! An't the new cub turned out yet? He's delicate, likely. Give him some sugar in a rag and send for the chambermaid to sing rock-a-bye-baby to him."

[1] **yawed:** steered out of the proper course.

About this time Mr. Bixby appeared on the scene. Something like a minute later I was climbing the pilothouse steps with some of my clothes on and the rest in my arms. Mr. Bixby was close behind, commenting. Here was something fresh—this thing of getting up in the middle of the night to go to work. It was a detail in piloting that had never occurred to me at all. I knew that boats ran all night, but somehow I had never happened to reflect that somebody had to get up out of a warm bed to run them. I began to fear that piloting was not quite so romantic as I had imagined it was; there was something very real and worklike about this new phase of it.

It was a rather dingy night, although a fair number of stars were out. The big mate was at the wheel, and he had the old tub pointed at a star and was holding her straight up the middle of the river. The shores on either hand were not much more than half a mile apart, but they seemed wonderfully far away and ever so vague and indistinct. The mate said:

"We've got to land at Jones's plantation, sir."

The vengeful spirit in me exulted. I said to myself, I wish you joy of your job,

Mr. Bixby; you'll have a good time finding Mr. Jones's plantation such a night as this; and I hope you never *will* find it as long as you live.

Mr. Bixby said to the mate:

"Upper end of the plantation, or the lower?"

"Upper."

"I can't do it. The stumps there are out of water at this stage. It's no great distance to the lower, and you'll have to get along with that."

"All right, sir. If Jones don't like it he'll have to lump it, I reckon."

And then the mate left. My exultation began to cool and my wonder to come up. Here was a man who not only proposed to find this plantation on such a night, but to find either end of it you preferred. I dreadfully wanted to ask a question, but I was carrying about as many short answers as my cargo room would admit of, so I held my peace. All I desired to ask Mr. Bixby was the simple question whether he was ass enough to really imagine he was going to find that plantation on a night when all plantations were exactly alike and all the same color. But I held in. I used to have fine inspirations of prudence in those days.

Mr. Bixby made for the shore and soon was scraping it, just the same as if it had been daylight. And not only that, but singing, "Father in heaven, the day is declining," etc. It seemed to me that I had put my life in the keeping of a peculiarly reckless outcast. Presently he turned on me and said:

"What's the name of the first point above New Orleans?"

I was gratified to be able to answer promptly, and I did. I said I didn't know.

"Don't *know?*"

This manner jolted me. I was down at the foot again, in a moment. But I had to say just what I had said before.

"Well, you're a smart one," said Mr. Bixby. "What's the name of the *next* point?"

Once more I didn't know.

"Well, this beats anything. Tell me the name of *any* point or place I told you."

I studied a while and decided that I couldn't.

"Look here! What do you start out from, above Twelve-Mile Point, to cross over?"

"I—I—don't know."

"You—you—don't know?" mimicking my drawling manner of speech. What *do* you know?"

"I—I—nothing, for certain."

"By the great Caesar's ghost, I believe you! You're the stupidest dunderhead I ever saw or ever heard of, so help me Moses! The idea of *you* being a pilot— *you!* Why, you don't know enough to pilot a cow down a lane."

Oh, but his wrath was up! He was a nervous man, and he shuffled from one side of his wheel to the other as if the floor was hot. He would boil a while to himself and then overflow and scald me again.

"Look here! What do you suppose I told you the names of those points for?"

I tremblingly considered a moment, and then the devil of temptation provoked me to say:

"Well—to—to—be entertaining, I thought."

This was a red rag to the bull. He raged and stormed so (he was crossing the river at the time) that I judge it made him blind, because he ran over the steering oar of a trading scow. Of course the traders sent up a volley of red-hot profanity. Never was a man so grateful as Mr. Bixby was: because he was brim full, and here were subjects who would *talk back.* He threw open a window, thrust his head out, and such an eruption followed as I never had heard before. The fainter and farther away

the scowmen's curses drifted, the higher Mr. Bixby lifted his voice and the weightier his adjectives grew. When he closed the window he was empty. You could have drawn a seine [1] through his system and not caught curses enough to disturb your mother with. Presently he said to me in the gentlest way:

"My boy, you must get a little memorandum book, and every time I tell you a thing, put it down right away. There's only one way to be a pilot, and that is to get this entire river by heart. You have to know it just like A B C."

That was a dismal revelation to me; for my memory was never loaded with anything but blank cartridges. However, I did not feel discouraged long. I judged that it was best to make some allowances, for doubtless Mr. Bixby was "stretching." Presently he pulled a rope and struck a few strokes on the big bell. The stars were all gone now, and the night was as black as ink. I could hear the wheels churn along the bank, but I was not entirely certain that I could see the shore. The voice of the invisible watchman called up from the hurricane deck:

"What's this, sir?"

"Jones's plantation."

I said to myself, I wish I might venture to offer a small bet that it isn't. But I did not chirp. I only waited to see. Mr. Bixby handled the engine bells, and in due time the boat's nose came to the land, a torch glowed from the forecastle, a man skipped ashore, and the next moment we were standing up the river again, all serene. I reflected deeply a while, and then said— but not aloud—"Well, the finding of that plantation was the luckiest accident that ever happened; but it couldn't happen again in a hundred years." And I fully believed it *was* an accident, too.

[1] **seine** (sān): a large fishnet.

By the time we had gone seven or eight hundred miles up the river, I had learned to be a tolerable plucky upstream steersman, in daylight, and before we reached St. Louis I had made a trifle of progress in night work, but only a trifle. I had a notebook that fairly bristled with the names of towns, "points," bars, islands, bends, reaches, etc.; but the information was to be found only in the notebook—none of it was in my head. It made my heart ache to think I had only got half of the river set down; for as our watch was four hours off and four hours on, day and night, there was a long four-hour gap in my book for every time I had slept since the voyage began.

My chief was presently hired to go on a big New Orleans boat, and I packed my satchel and went with him. She was a grand affair. When I stood in her pilothouse I was so far above the water that I seemed perched on a mountain; and her decks stretched so far away, fore and aft, below me, that I wondered how I could ever have considered the little *Paul Jones* a large craft. There were other differences, too. The *Paul Jones's* pilothouse was a cheap, dingy, battered rattletrap, cramped for room: but here was a sumptuous glass temple; room enough to have a dance in; showy red and gold window curtains; an imposing sofa; leather cushions and a back to the high bench where visiting pilots sit, to spin yarns and "look at the river"; bright, fanciful cuspidors instead of a broad wooden box filled with sawdust; nice new oilcloth on the floor; a hospitable big stove for winter; a wheel as high as my head, costly with inlaid work; a wire tiller rope; bright brass knobs for the bells; and a tidy, white-aproned, black "texas tender," to bring up tarts and ices and coffee during midwatch, day and night. Now this was "something like"; and so I began to take heart once more to

believe that piloting was a romantic sort of occupation after all. The moment we were underway I began to prowl about the great steamer and fill myself with joy. She was as clean and as dainty as a drawing room; when I looked down her long, gilded saloon, it was like gazing through a splendid tunnel; she had an oil picture, by some gifted sign painter, on every stateroom door; she glittered with no end of prism-fringed chandeliers; the clerk's office was elegant, the bar was marvelous, and the barkeeper had been barbered and upholstered at incredible cost. The boiler deck (i.e., the second story of the boat, so to speak) was as spacious as a church, it seemed to me; so with the forecastle; and there was no pitiful handful of deck hands, firemen, and roustabouts [1] down there, but a whole battalion of men. The fires were fiercely glaring from a long row of furnaces, and over them were eight huge boilers! This was unutterable pomp. The mighty engines—but enough of this. I had never felt so fine before. And when I found that the regiment of natty servants respectfully "sir'd" me, my satisfaction was complete.

[1] **roustabouts:** deckhands, laborers.

FOR STUDY AND DISCUSSION

1. Considering where they lived, is it surprising that the ambition of Mark Twain and his friends to be steamboatmen was permanent rather than transient? Explain.

2. What was Twain's attitude toward his chief, Mr. Bixby? What kind of man was he? What besides piloting did Twain learn from him?

3. In this selection, as in his *Autobiography,* Mark Twain often makes use of understatement, usually for comic effect. He also uses exaggeration, the opposite of understatement, to achieve comic effect. Cite several examples of both of these devices from this selection.

4. Most biographies and autobiographies which describe the early life of a person discuss the ways in which the subject grows up: the ways in which he becomes mature as he grows older. In these chapters from *Life on the Mississippi,* how does Twain seem to mature? In what ways is he still immature? Refer to specific incidents to illustrate this point.

5. One critic has said that the protagonist—that is, the leading character—in *Life on the Mississippi* is the river itself. Judging from these three chapters, in what sense is this true? In what sense is Twain the protagonist?

LANGUAGE AND VOCABULARY

Tone, the writer's attitude toward his subject, is a very subtle business. One clue to the tone of a piece of writing is the kind of language its author uses. For instance, judging from the following statements from *Life on the Mississippi,* what is the attitude of the writer toward his subject? How do the italicized words, in particular, contribute to this attitude?

"This fellow had money, too, and *hair oil.*" (Page 248.)

"A word never had *tasted* so good in my mouth before." (Page 249.)

"He was a *wronged* man, a man who had seen trouble, and that was enough for me." (Page 251.)

"I took the wheel, and my heartbeat *fluttered* up into the hundreds . . ." (Page 252.)

As an exercise in tone, write a few sentences in which a single, carefully chosen word reveals the way you feel about something. Here is an obvious example: "That was the best meal I ever choked down." Try to make your own sentences more subtle.

FOR COMPOSITION

The second paragraph of "The Boys' Ambition" is an excellent one-paragraph description of the effect on a sleepy river town of the arrival of a steamboat. Study the organization and descriptive details used by Twain in this paragraph, and write a paragraph of your own describing, perhaps, the sudden arrival of a fire engine in your neighborhood, or a celebrity at your school, or any similar incident, imaginary or real.

Seventeenth-Century Painting

Once in a while you will hear about an artist who was recognized as a master during his own lifetime but who was then almost forgotten soon after his death. A good example is the painter Domenicos Theotocopoulos, known because of his Greek ancestry as El Greco. After pursuing his early career in Italy, El Greco settled in the Spanish city of Toledo, where he prospered for the rest of his life. But after his death history forgot El Greco for nearly three hundred years, until he was rediscovered by artists and critics of the twentieth century.

The power of El Greco's intensely emotional style can be felt most strongly in his later canvases, such as the famous *View of Toledo* (PLATE 1), which he painted in 1610, only a few years before his death. Notice in this strange landscape how the eerie, silvery buildings take on a ghostlike stillness next to the explosive light of the sky and the writhing forms of the countryside below.

Curiously enough, another important artist of about this same time was scorned even by many of his own contemporaries. This artist was Caravaggio, a self-taught painter who had come to Rome around 1590 from a small town in Lombardy. Caravaggio's critics complained that he treated exalted religious subjects in a low, vulgar style, because he included in his paintings the faces and figures of common people from the streets. By using stark contrasts of light and shadow, Caravaggio managed to conjure up unforgettable scenes of dramatic realism. Look, for example, at his striking figure of David, who is shown as he holds out toward us the gruesome head of Goliath (PLATE 2).

Caravaggio was one of the founders of a complex seventeenth-century style known as the Baroque. It is not an easy style to define because it has many different aspects. We can see another kind of Baroque art in PLATE 3, *Tiger Hunt*, painted by one of Caravaggio's younger Flemish contemporaries, Peter Paul Rubens. The whole composition seems to explode with energy. Unlike Caravaggio's starkly lit scenes with motionless figures, this picture is an intricate pattern of whirling action, of violently twisting

257

shapes accented by vivid colors. Yet in spite of their differences in style, both Rubens and Caravaggio produced dynamic, theatrical spectacles which are characteristic of the Baroque.

Meanwhile, still another kind of art was developing in nearby Holland. The most popular paintings there were simple portraits and scenes of everyday life. Among the finest of these were the charming figure studies of Frans Hals, such as *A Boy with a Lute* (PLATE 4). This lively painting gives the spontaneous impression of a snapshot, since the figure seems to be caught in action rather than carefully posed. Though Hals planned his composition carefully, he has created the unlabored feeling of a quick sketch. For he did the actual painting rapidly, with short flat strokes of color, using a technique that was to become widely adopted by painters of the nineteenth century.

The most famous of all Dutch painters, however, was Rembrandt van Rijn, a generation younger than Hals. No other painter in history has ever been able to communicate profound human emotions in such an intimate way. Rembrandt's picture, *Aristotle Contemplating the Bust of Homer* (PLATE 5), for example, draws us deeply into a mood of silent meditation. There are no abrupt contrasts here, but rather a gentle modulation of brown and yellow tones which suggest so many different intensities of light that the figure of Aristotle seems to emerge gradually from the background, yet at the same time remaining part of the shadows around it. Everything builds up to the expression of the eyes, the source of this picture's unusually compelling mood. The commission for this painting was given to Rembrandt in 1653 by an Italian nobleman. Ten years later, Rembrandt painted two more canvases for the same nobleman: one, a picture of the blind Homer dictating to his pupils; the other, an imaginary portrait of Alexander the Great, who in his youth had been a pupil of the great philosopher Aristotle.

Still another important Dutch painter was Jan Vermeer of Delft. Most of his paintings, though, are rather small, showing none of the drama we find in Caravaggio and Rubens, or even in Hals and Rembrandt. *Young Woman with a Water Jug* (PLATE 6), for instance, is simply a picture of a room: a sort of still-life painting in which the human figure appears as motionless as the table and the objects upon it. What does seem to move, however, is the light. Entering from the windows at the left, it spreads softly across the back wall, gradually deepening in tone and changing in color. Vermeer has so skillfully arranged the figure and objects in this small room that we have no sense whatsoever of crowding. Our eye is led from one object to another—perhaps quickly at first, but then slowly and deliberately. Even the empty spaces between forms seem to have been harmoniously "composed."

PLATE 1. EL GRECO (Spanish, 1541–1614): *View of Toledo*. About 1610. Oil on canvas, 47¾ x 42¾ inches. (The Metropolitan Museum of Art, New York, Bequest of Mrs. H. O. Havemeyer, 1929, The H. O. Havemeyer Collection)

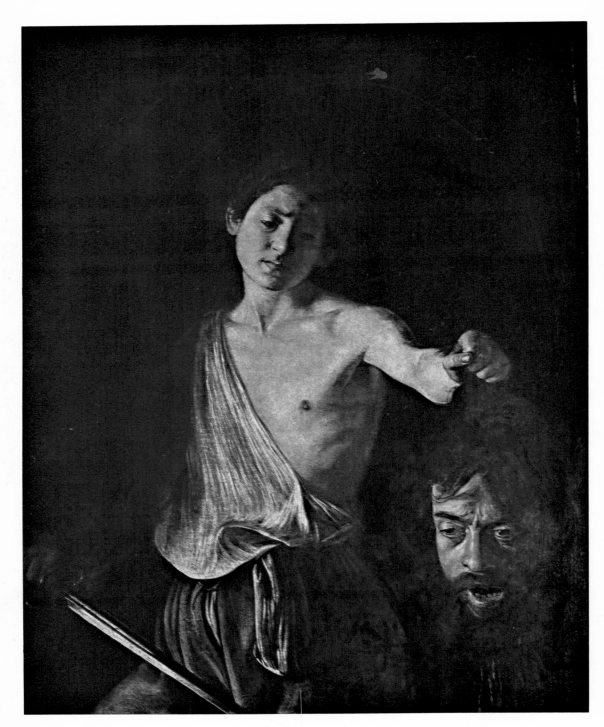

PLATE 2. CARAVAGGIO (Italian, 1573–1610): *David Holding the Head of Goliath*. 1605. Oil on canvas, 49¼ x 39¾ inches. (Villa Borghese, Rome)

PLATE 3. PETER PAUL RUBENS (Flemish, 1577–1640): *Tiger Hunt*. Oil on wood panel, 38 x 48¾ inches. (Wadsworth Atheneum, Hartford, Connecticut)

PLATE 4. FRANS HALS (Dutch, 1580/81–1666): *A Boy with a Lute*. Oil on canvas, $28\frac{3}{8}$ x $23\frac{1}{4}$ inches. (The Metropolitan Museum of Art, New York, Bequest of Benjamin Altman, 1913)

PLATE 5. REMBRANDT VAN RIJN (Dutch, 1606–1669): *Aristotle Contemplating the Bust of Homer.* 1653. Oil on canvas, $56\frac{1}{2}$ x $53\frac{3}{4}$ inches. (The Metropolitan Museum of Art, New York, Purchase, Friends of the Museum, 1961)

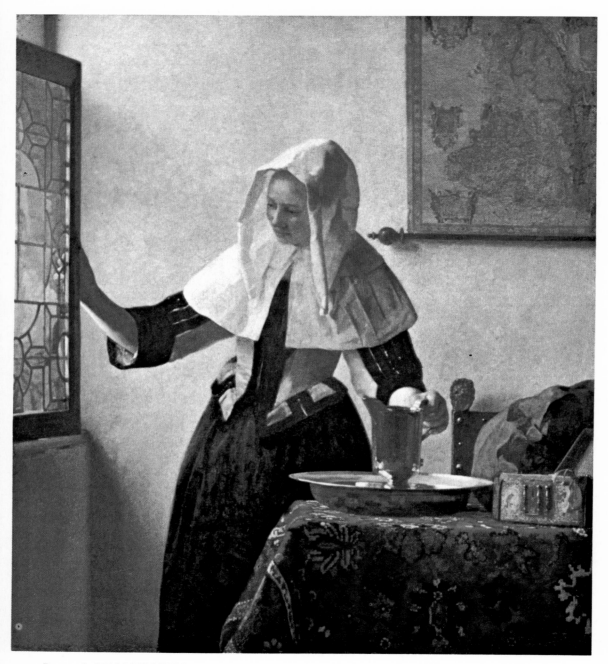

PLATE 6. JAN VERMEER (Dutch, 1632–1675): *Young Woman with a Water Jug*. Oil on canvas, 18 x 16 inches. (The Metropolitan Museum of Art, New York, Gift of Henry G. Marquand, 1889)

An Interview with Mark Twain

RUDYARD KIPLING

A young Englishman born in India, Rudyard Kipling, when he was less than twenty-five years old, left India in search of a European publisher for his stories and poems. Kipling, who later became one of England's most famous literary figures, was then still unknown as a writer, though he had already published *Departmental Ditties,* a small book of light verse, and *Plain Tales from the Hills,* a collection of stories. Stopping in New York on his way to London, Kipling was given the assignment of interviewing Mark Twain for a local newspaper. So he traveled to Elmira, New York, in search of the great man.

More than thirty years had passed since Twain had left the river he loved. In the intervening years he had become a writer and lecturer famous throughout the world. Here, then, is another portrait of Mark Twain, this time as he was seen by a young man who was just starting his literary career. This account of Kipling's visit appeared in the New York *Herald* on August 17, 1890.

I HAVE SEEN Mark Twain this golden morning, have shaken his hand, and smoked a cigar—no, two cigars—with him, and talked with him for more than two hours! Understand clearly that I do not despise you; indeed, I don't. I am only very sorry for you all. To soothe your envy and to prove that I still regard you as my equals, I will tell you all about it.

They said in Buffalo that he was in Hartford, Connecticut; and again they said perchance he is gone upon a journey to Portland, Maine; and a big, fat drummer vowed that he knew the great man intimately and that Mark was spending the summer in Europe—which information so upset me that I embarked upon the wrong train, and was incontinently [1] turned out by the conductor three quarters of a mile from the station, amid the wilderness of railway tracks. Have you ever, encumbered with greatcoat and valise, tried to dodge diversely minded locomotives when the sun was shining in your eyes? But I forgot that you have not seen Mark Twain, you people of no account!

Saved from the jaws of the cowcatcher,[2] I wandered devious, a stranger met.

"Elmira is the place. Elmira in the state of New York—this state, not two hundred miles away"; and he added, perfectly unnecessarily, "Slide, Kelly, slide."

I slid on the West Shore line, I slid till midnight, and they dumped me down at the door of a frowzy hotel in Elmira. Yes, they knew all about "that man Clemens," but reckoned he was not in town; had gone East somewhere. I had better possess my soul in patience till the morrow, and then dig up the "man Clemens's" brother-in-law, who was interested in coal.

The idea of chasing half a dozen relatives in addition to Mark Twain up and down a city of thirty thousand inhabitants kept me awake. Morning revealed Elmira, whose streets were desolated by railway tracks, and whose suburbs were given up to the manufacture of door sashes and window frames. It was surrounded by pleasant, fat little hills, trimmed with timber and topped with cul-

[1] **incontinently:** unrestrainedly.
[2] **cowcatcher:** a strong, metal frame placed on the front of a locomotive to throw obstructions off the tracks.

tivation. The Chemung River flowed generally up and down the town and had just finished flooding a few of the main streets.

The hotel man and the telephone man assured me that the much-desired brother-in-law was out of town, and no one seemed to know where "the man Clemens" abode. Later on I discovered that he had not summered in that place for more than nineteen seasons and so was comparatively a new arrival.

A friendly policeman volunteered the news that he had seen Twain or someone very like him driving a buggy on the previous day. This gave me a delightful sense of nearness to the great author. Fancy living in a town where you could see the author of *Tom Sawyer,* or "some one very like him," jolting over the pavements in a buggy!

"He lives out yonder at East Hill," said the policeman; "three miles from here."

Then the chase began—in a hired hack, up an awful hill, where sunflowers blossomed by the roadside, and crops waved, and *Harper's* Magazine cows stood in eligible and commanding attitudes knee-deep in clover, all ready to be transferred to photogravure. The great man must have been persecuted by outsiders aforetime and fled up the hill for refuge.

Presently the driver stopped at a miserable, little, white wood shanty, and demanded "Mister Clemens."

"I know he's a big bug and all that," he explained, "but you can never tell what sort of notions those sort of men take it into their heads to live in, anyways."

There rose up a young lady who was sketching thistle tops and goldenrod, amid a plentiful supply of both, and set the pilgrimage on the right path.

"It's a pretty Gothic house on the left-hand side a little way farther on."

"Gothic, heck," said the driver. "Very few of the city hacks take this drive, specially if they know they are coming out here," and he glared at me savagely.

It was a very pretty house, anything but Gothic, clothed with ivy, standing in a very big compound, and fronted by a veranda full of all sorts of chairs and hammocks for lying in all sorts of positions. The roof of the veranda was a trellis-work of creepers, and the sun peeped through and moved on the shining boards below.

Decidedly this remote place was an ideal one for working in, if a man could work among these soft airs and the murmur of the long-eared crops just across the stone wall.

Appeared suddenly a lady used to dealing with rampageous outsiders. "Mr. Clemens has just walked downtown. He is at his brother-in-law's house."

Then he was within shouting distance, after all, and the chase had not been in vain. With speed I fled, and the driver, skidding the wheel and swearing audibly, arrived at the bottom of that hill without accidents. It was in the pause that followed between ringing the brother-in-law's bell and getting an answer that it occurred to me for the first time Mark Twain might possibly have other engagements than the entertainment of escaped lunatics from India, be they ever so full of admiration. And in another man's house—anyhow, what had I come to do or say? Suppose the drawing room should be full of people, a levee of crowned heads; suppose a baby were sick anywhere, how was I to explain I only wanted to shake hands with him?

Then things happened somewhat in this order. A big, darkened drawing room; a huge chair; a man with eyes, a mane of grizzled hair, a brown moustache covering a mouth as delicate as a woman's, a

strong, square hand shaking mine, and the slowest, calmest, levelest voice in all the world saying:

"Well, you think you owe me something, and you've come to tell me so. That's what I call squaring a debt handsomely."

"Piff!" from a cob pipe (I always said that a Missouri meerschaum [1] was the best smoking in the world), and, behold! Mark Twain had curled himself up in the big armchair, and I was smoking reverently, as befits one in the presence of his superior.

The thing that struck me first was that he was an elderly man. Yet, after a minute's thought, I perceived that it was otherwise, and in five minutes, the eyes looking at me, I saw that the gray hair was an accident of the most trivial kind. He was quite young. I was shaking his hand. I was smoking his cigar, and I was hearing him talk—this man I had learned to love and admire fourteen thousand miles away.

Reading his books, I had striven to get an idea of his personality, and all my preconceived notions were wrong and beneath the reality. Blessed is the man who finds no disillusion when he is brought face to face with a revered writer. That was a moment to be remembered; the land of a twelve-pound salmon was nothing to it. I had hooked Mark Twain, and he was treating me as though, under certain circumstances, I might be an equal.

[1] **Missouri meerschaum** (mir′shəm): a corncob pipe.

Growing bold and feeling that I had a few hundred thousand folk at my back, I demanded whether Tom Sawyer married Judge Thatcher's daughter and whether we were ever going to hear of Tom Sawyer as a man.

"I haven't decided," quoth Mark Twain, getting up, filling his pipe, and walking up and down the room in his slippers. "I have a notion of writing the sequel to *Tom Sawyer* in two ways. In one I would make him rise to great honor and go to Congress, and in the other I should hang him. Then the friends and enemies of the book could take their choice."

Here I lost my reverence completely, and protested against any theory of the sort, because, to me at least, Tom Sawyer was real.

"Oh, he is real," said Mark Twain. "He's all the boys that I have known or recollect; but that would be a good way of ending the book"; then, turning around, "because, when you come to think of it, neither religion, training, nor education avails anything against the force of circumstances that drive a man. Suppose we took the next four and twenty years of Tom Sawyer's life, and gave a little joggle to the circumstances that controlled him. He would logically and according to the joggle turn out a rip or an angel."

"Do you believe that, then?"

"I think so. Isn't it what you call kismet?" [2]

"Yes; but don't give him two joggles and show the result, because he isn't your property any more. He belongs to us."

Thereat he laughed—a large, wholesome laugh—and this began a dissertation on the rights of a man to do what he liked with his own creations, which being

[2] **kismet** (kiz′met): destiny or fate, a term that is Turkish in origin but that Twain may be associating with Kipling's India.

a matter of purely professional interest, I will mercifully omit.

Returning to the big chair, he, speaking of truth and the like in literature, said that an autobiography was the one work in which a man, against his own will and in spite of his utmost striving to the contrary, revealed himself in his true light to the world.

"A good deal of your *Life on the Mississippi* is autobiographical, isn't it?" I asked.

"As near as it can be—when a man is writing to a book and about himself. But in genuine autobiography, I believe it is impossible for a man to tell the truth about himself or to avoid impressing the reader with the truth about himself.

"I made an experiment once. I got a friend of mine—a man painfully given to speak the truth on all occasions—a man who wouldn't dream of telling a lie—and I made him write his autobiography for his own amusement and mine. He did it. The manuscript would have made an octavo volume [1] but—good, honest man that he was—in every single detail of his life that I knew about he turned out, on paper, a formidable liar. He could not help himself.

"It is not in human nature to write the truth about itself. Nonetheless, the reader gets a general impression from an autobiography whether the man is a fraud or a good man. The reader can't give his reasons any more than a man can explain why a woman struck him as being lovely when he doesn't remember her hair, eyes, teeth, or figure. And the impression that the reader gets is a correct one."

"Do you ever intend writing an autobiography?"

[1] **octavo** (ok·tā′vō) **volume:** technically, a book of sheets with each one folded into eight leaves. Twain suggests that what his friend had to say would have made a complete book.

"If I do, it will be as other men have done—with the most earnest desire to make myself out to be the better man in every little business that has been to my discredit; and I shall fail, like the others, to make the readers believe anything except the truth."

Here he told me a little—such things as a man may tell a stranger—of his early life and upbringing and in what manner he had been influenced for good by the example of his parents. He spoke always through his eyes, a light under the heavy eyebrows; anon crossing the room with a step as light as a girl's, to show me some book or other; then resuming his walk up and down the room, puffing at the cob pipe. I would have given much for nerve enough to demand the gift of that pipe—value, five cents when new. I understood why certain savage tribes ardently desired the liver of brave men slain in combat. That pipe would have given me, perhaps, a hint of his keen insight into the souls of men. But he never laid it aside within stealing reach of my arms.

He recurled himself into the chair and talked of other things.

"I spend nine months of the year at Hartford. I have long ago satisfied myself that there is no hope of doing much work during those nine months. People come in and call. They call at all hours, about everything in the world. One day I thought I would keep a list of interruptions. It began this way:

"A man came and would see no one but Mr. Clemens. He was an agent for photogravure reproductions of salon pictures. I very seldom use salon pictures in my books.

"After that man, another man, who refused to see anyone but Mr. Clemens, came to make me write to Washington about something. I saw him. I saw a third man, then a fourth. By this time it was

noon. I had grown tired of keeping the list. I wished to rest.

"But the fifth man was the only one of the crowd with a card of his own. He sent up his card. 'Ben Koontz, Hannibal, Missouri.' I was raised in Hannibal. Ben was an old schoolmate of mine. Consequently I threw the house wide open and rushed with both hands out at a big, fat heavy man, who was not the Ben I had ever known nor anything like him.

"'But is it you, Ben?' I said. 'You've altered in the last thousand years.'

"The fat man said: 'Well, I'm not Koontz exactly, but I met him down in Missouri, and he told me to be sure and call on you, and he gave me his card, and'—here he acted the little scene for my benefit—'if you can wait a minute till I can get out the circulars—I'm not Koontz exactly, but I'm traveling with the fullest line of rods you ever saw.'"

"And what happened?" I asked breathlessly.

"I shut the door. He was not Ben Koontz—exactly—not my old schoolfellow, but I had shaken him by both hands in love, and . . . I had been bearded by a lightning-rod man in my own house.

"As I was saying, I do very little work in Hartford. I come here for three months every year, and I work four or five hours a day in a study down the garden of that little house on the hill. Of course, I do not object to two or three interruptions. When a man is in the full swing of his work, these little things do not affect him. Eight or ten or twenty interruptions retard composition."

I was burning to ask him all manner of impertinent questions, as to which of his works he himself preferred, and so forth; but, standing in awe of his eyes, I dared not. He spoke on, and I listened, groveling.

It was a question of mental equipment that was on the carpet, and I am still wondering whether he meant what he said.

"Personally I never care for fiction or storybooks. What I like to read about are facts and statistics of any kind. If they are only facts about the raising of radishes, they interest me. Just now, for instance, before you came in"—he pointed to an encyclopedia on the shelves—"I was reading an article about 'Mathematics.' Perfectly pure mathematics.

"My own knowledge of mathematics stops at 'twelve times twelve,' but I enjoyed that article immensely. I didn't understand a word of it; but facts, or what a man believes to be facts, are always delightful. That mathematical fellow believed in his facts. So do I. Get your facts first, and"—the voice dies away to an almost inaudible drone—"then you can distort 'em as much as you please."

Bearing this precious advice in my bosom, I left, the great man assuring me with gentle kindness that I had not interrupted him in the least. Once outside the door, I yearned to go back and ask some questions—it was easy enough to think of them now—but his time was his own, though his books belonged to me.

I should have ample time to look back to that meeting across the graves of the days. But it was sad to think of the things he had not spoken about.

FOR STUDY AND DISCUSSION

1. Review the portion of the interview which precedes Kipling's first sight of Twain. What does it tell about Kipling? What does it imply about Mark Twain as the world had come to see him?

2. Does Kipling's interview support your opinion of Mark Twain as we saw him in the two autobiographical selections? In what new light is Twain revealed?

3. In speaking of people who write autobiographies (as he himself was later to do),

Twain commented to Kipling, "I believe it is impossible for a man to tell the truth about himself or to avoid impressing the reader with the truth about himself." There is an obvious contradiction in this statement. In the two autobiographical selections preceding this statement, what are some instances to which Twain's statement might apply?

4. In your opinion, did Kipling do a good or a poor job as an interviewer? Defend your opinion with specific examples from the interview. What other questions would you have asked Mark Twain?

THE INTERVIEW AS A BASIS FOR BIOGRAPHY

When James Boswell was preparing his biography of the great English writer Samuel Johnson, he followed the great man around day after day and made careful notes on everything Johnson said. The result, which comprises three large volumes, is an amazingly detailed study of the man.

Most biographers and historians cannot live with their subjects for weeks or months at a time. This is no longer necessary, however. During the last hundred years, the rapidly increasing speed of communication and the many improvements in recording techniques (the tape recorder, for instance) have made it possible for us to become acquainted with people, so to speak, without following them around as Boswell did. The Oral History Research Office at Columbia University in New York, for instance, contains about a quarter million pages of historical material based upon interviews or spoken recollections covering events in the history of the last hundred years. More and more the interview, or recorded conversation, has become extremely important as source material for the writing of both biography and history.

You can make use of the interview technique in the writing of papers for social studies, English, science, or any other subject. What are the characteristics of a useful interview? It must be carefully planned in advance; the conversation must be carefully directed by the interviewer; and it must be accurately reported. You may be able to try out the useful-ness of the interview in your own community, recording the ideas of someone less famous, perhaps, than Mark Twain, but nevertheless of someone important to a project that either you or your community is undertaking or planning to undertake.

LANGUAGE AND VOCABULARY

Review the dictionary definitions of *denotation* and *connotation*. What are the denotations of the italicized words in the following phrases from Kipling's report of his interview with Mark Twain? What are the connotations of the same italicized words? Why do you think Kipling uses these words as he does? Which of the words tell you the most about Kipling's state of mind at the time of the interview?

"this *golden* morning . . ." (Page 265.)

"*diversely minded* locomotives . . ." (Page 265.)

"people of *no account!*" (Page 265.)

"*jaws* of the cowcatcher . . ." (Page 265.)

"*dumped* me down . . ." (Page 265.)

"pleasant, *fat* little hills . . ." (Page 265.)

"used to dealing with *rampageous* outsiders." (Page 266.)

"I was smoking *reverently* . . ." (Page 267.)

"He spoke always *through his eyes . . .*" (Page 268.)

Your study of language and vocabulary has also included a consideration of metaphor. Which of the words italicized above have connotations because they are also metaphors? To answer this question you will have to work out carefully the implied comparison in, for example, the word *golden*.

This should show you that many of the most important aspects of language—denotation, connotation, metaphor, tone, and so forth—are closely related.

FOR COMPOSITION

Write an imaginary interview with a well-known person. First look up the facts about his life. Then make a rough list of the questions you would ask the person. Finally, write the questions and the person's imagined answers.

II. SOCRATES

The great Athenian philosopher Socrates, who was born in about 470 B.C., was put to death seventy years later for "corruption of the young" and "neglect of the gods." A wise man who preached moderation, self-control, and the habit of independent thinking, Socrates dedicated his life to a search for knowledge. He was also a devoted patriot. The combination of these two qualities led to his death. He insisted on speaking out against what he considered wrong; and, although he had an opportunity both to withdraw into exile before his trial and to escape during his imprisonment, his sense of civic duty prevented him from doing either. He treated with contempt the accusations made against him, but nevertheless freely accepted the court's death penalty on the ground that it was enacted by a legitimate court and therefore must be obeyed.

Of all the men represented in this unit on biography, Socrates is the only one whose fame does not rest, at least in part, on his writings. Socrates was a philosopher and a teacher who wrote nothing. What we know of his character and his teachings is derived chiefly from the writings of Plato and of Xenophon, another of his pupils. Both men were about forty years younger than Socrates and therefore knew him for little more than the last decade of his life. Yet, through their carefully recorded accounts of their master's conversation—particularly through Plato's *Dialogues*—we have an excellent record of his character and teachings.

In the following pages we have three glimpses of Socrates from the pens of two men separated in time by more than 2,400 years: Hermann Hagedorn, a contemporary American biographer, and Plato, Socrates' famous pupil and a philosopher in his own right. First we have a description of the accusation and trial of Socrates by Mr. Hagedorn. In the following selection Plato recounts the *Apology* of Socrates. Finally, in *Phaedo,* Plato relates the story of Socrates' last hours.

Socrates—a copy of a fourth-century statue.

Socrates—His Life

HERMANN HAGEDORN

In this selection the present tense is used to tell about events which took place in the fourth century B.C. With a direct and simple prose style, the author makes Socrates come alive for twentieth-century readers.

IF YOUR Greek toga had a buttonhole, Socrates' thumb would be through it, holding you pinned in your place while the goggle-eyed and delightful old gentleman asked you exactly how clever you think you are and what in the world, in the first place, makes you think you are clever anyway.

He is the first and greatest of all buttonholers. It makes no difference where you are or how busy you are. If Socrates fixes his eyes on you, he will come lumbering across the athletic field or the marketplace, and, smiling most courteously, he will engage you in conversation. Socrates is a glutton for conversation. Money means nothing to him. Fame, power, influence mean nothing. He never knows exactly where the next meal is coming from; but he must have conversation.

It is not that he wishes to hear himself talk; but he does want to hear what you have to say. He does not seek gossip, tips on the races or the discus throwers, or stories of the dancing girls, or wails on the political situation and the state of the war between Athens and Sparta.[1] But he loves talk of fundamental things, of justice and virtue and wisdom and love and death and immortality. He can talk on these matters as no one else in his city—and it is a city of great talkers—and he can make you talk as you have never talked before.

Who is he, this man Socrates? What is his profession, his job? He is the son of a stonemason. For a while he was a stonemason himself. Yes, and he has been a soldier, not from choice, but because Athens needed all her able-bodied men in her wars with Sparta, the physical examination taking no account of height, or of eyes somewhat off center. At thirty-seven he is at the siege of Potidaea,[2] at great risk saving the life of a brilliant young fellow townsman, Alcibiades,[3] who proves, in the end, not to have been worth saving. At forty-five he is in the disastrous defeat at Delium, carrying Xenophon,[4] a young friend of his, who is to make his mark as a historian, off to safety on his broad shoulders. "He stalked along like a pelican," Alcibiades subsequently reports, "glaring around with his projecting crab's eyes, so that none of the enemy dared molest him."

But soldiering is the least important activity of this extraordinary person's life. It is as a conversationalist that Athens knows him—as the man who asks questions. If you enjoy conversation and

[1] **Athens and Sparta:** two rival city-states of ancient Greece.

[2] **Potidaea** (pot'i·di'a): The revolt of this city from the Athenian League was the immediate cause of a war between Athens and Sparta.

[3] **Alcibiades** (al'sə·bī'ə·dēz): a disciple of Socrates and for many years his devoted friend. Political ambition proved his ruination and he became a traitor to Athens.

[4] **Xenophon** (zen'ə·fən): another disciple of Socrates. His fame as a historian is based largely on his account of the *March of the Ten Thousand*—an expedition of conquest in which he took part as general.

can answer Socrates' questions with intelligence, you love him and gratefully accept his invitations to walk under the olive trees with him or to spend the night with a few other sympathetic souls, talking about courage or happiness or the ideal republic. But if you don't enjoy high talk, if you think yourself wise and are really dull and Socrates shows you up by a keen question or two, you hate him and talk of him as a public nuisance and go around growling that if the government had any sand in its gizzard it would shut him up.

He is a queer customer, unquestionably. But he has a wise mind, a humble spirit, and a voice within him which he calls his daemon,[1] which lays a check on him, he says, when he is tempted to do wrong or stupid things. His clothes are always shabby. He goes about with bare feet. How he lives no one knows. The truth is that he has a small income, much too small to keep a family on in any style which Athens would approve. But he refuses to increase it, preferring to adjust his needs to his income rather than his income to his supposed needs. His wife, a sharp-tongued lady named Xantippe,[2] rails at him as an irresponsible loafer and gadabout. At home there are arguments in which, it is rumored, all of the questioning and most of the talking is for once done by the other party.

But Socrates is not a philosopher for nothing. When a friend asks him how he happened to marry Xantippe, of all women, he replies, "Those who want to learn to ride well choose restive horses, because, if they can handle these, they can manage any others. I want to learn to associate with all mankind, and I chose Xantippe, knowing that if I could bear

her society, I should be able to get along with anyone!" Perhaps he is joking; but it would not be safe to be too sure.

He is not what would be called an established citizen, with a pleasant house to live in and taxes to growl about. He is something rarer, an institution. Everybody knows him. He has nothing to do all day except to ask questions and to talk, and as he does these things invariably in public places, he is as familiar a figure as the town constable. Even the comic writers poke fun at him in their plays. His questions always have point; that is one reason why people find them disturbing.

The oracle at Delphi, consulted by all the Greeks, has told Socrates that he is "the wisest of men." Socrates laughs at the idea. He isn't wise, he knows he isn't; that is all, in fact, that he does know. There are countless men wiser than himself, he is certain, in Athens alone. He sets about to prove it, and that is how the questioning begins. He goes to a statesman with a great reputation and asks for light on the nature of wisdom or happiness, and is most astonished to find that the statesman is as much in the dark as he is, though he thinks that he really knows.

"Well," says Socrates to himself, "I am wiser than this fellow anyway. He thinks that he knows, when he doesn't, and at least I know that I don't know."

Thereupon he calls on a great soldier, a great artist, a great philosopher. In every case his experience is the same. They all think they are wise, but when he pins them down, they do not really know anything at all, not even that they are ignorant. Men of vision, whom he thus questions, gratefully accept the light he throws into their darkness. But the men who are vain and self-important are indignant.

Young men crowd about him, however,

[1] **daemon** (dē′mən): guardian spirit.
[2] **Xantippe** (zan·tip′ē).

A restoration of the marketplace of Athens as it appeared in Socrates' day.

fascinated and thrilled. It is a period of change in Athens. Thinking people find it difficult to believe in the old gods as their fathers did. When they look coolly at the stories of Jupiter and his adventures, of Venus and Juno, of Mars and Mercury and the rest, the gods look rather shabby, a little too human in their frailties to be regarded as divine.

The young men are asking, "What is this earth made of; how did it come to be? What are we human beings here for? How can we be happy? What happens when we die?" The old myths give no answers that satisfy these eager questioners.

Socrates says to them, "Do not bother your heads overmuch with problems regarding creation or the substance of things. Here you are, a man, living for awhile in the world with other men. What you must do is to think how you can live and help others to live most nobly and wisely."

They listen, and come day after day to hear his keen questioning and to answer as intelligently as they can. Those are congenial gatherings, for Socrates loves these young men as much as they love him.

"Some men," he has a way of saying,

"have a fancy for a fine horse, or a dog, or a bird. What I fancy, and take delight in, is friends of a superior kind. If I know anything, I teach it to them. In common with them I turn over and explore the treasures of the wise men of old which have been left written in books. If we find anything good, we pick it out, and we think it a great gain if we can be beneficial to one another."

Majestic themes are discussed at those gatherings—fundamental questions of right and wrong, of the meaning of justice, the meaning of love. Questions of government are threshed through. Socrates is outspoken and spares no one. The government of Athens, splendid under the great Pericles,[1] has come to troublous times now that the leader is dead. There are wars without and revolutions within; and now the mob rules, and now a small group of powerful and wealthy citizens. The mob and the oligarchy,[2] as this small group is called, are equally unjust and despotic,[3] and in his quiet way Socrates strikes at them both.

[1] **Pericles** (per'ə·klēz): the Greek statesman under whom Athens rose to its greatest height in the fifth century B.C.
[2] **oligarchy** (ol'ə·gär'kē): a small group that rules the government.
[3] **despotic** (di·spot'ik): tyrannical.

When the Thirty Tyrants,[1] who are now ruling, send for Socrates in anger and forbid him to "discourse with the young," he merely asks them most humbly what they mean by "discourse," and whom exactly would they call "the young"? Can't he even ask directions or buy meat of anyone, say, under thirty? The Tyrants rage and threaten him with death. But Socrates pays no attention whatsoever to their orders, teaching as before.

But the old philosopher does not love a stupid mob any more than a stupid committee of tyrants. He says that democracy, if it is stupid and unjust, is as evil as stupid and cruel tyranny. Forms are comparatively unimportant; the essential thing is that government, whatever form it takes, shall be enlightened and just. It is a dangerous doctrine to preach, for it sets the stupid on both sides against him. When the Thirty Tyrants are overthrown and the popular party comes into control, Socrates is a marked man.

Slowly the feeling against him in Athens takes definite form. The men he has shown up to themselves with his straightforward questions, the ruling classes he has made fun of, the blundering mob he has refused to praise and to bow down to, begin to ask themselves why they have borne with this gadfly[2] so long. He is teaching the young men of the city that in government, majorities are not enough. You must have intelligence also. Dangerous doctrine! He is corrupting the youth!

Socrates smiles and goes quietly on, not teaching any philosophy of his own so much as stimulating his pupils to think out

an intelligent way of living for themselves. And then one day, a notice is posted in Athens:

Meletus,[3] son of Meletus, accuses Socrates, son of Sophroniscus,[4] as is underwritten. Socrates is guilty of crime—first, for neglecting the gods whom the city acknowledges, and setting forth other strange gods; next, for corrupting the youth. Penalty— death.

Meletus is a poet (or thinks he is), but there are other accusers, notably a democratic politician named Anytus[5] whose son Socrates has persuaded to give up his father's leather trade and devote himself to learning. Anytus feels strongly that to persuade any young man to give up the leather business for the shadowy rewards of scholarship is clear corruption.

Socrates seems to be the only individual in Athens who is not disturbed by the approaching trial. He does not even make any preparations for his speech of defense. All his life has been a preparation for it, he says, having been spent in learning what was right and trying to do it.

The trial is held before a jury of five hundred fifty-seven[6] citizens of Athens. Eloquently, Socrates speaks in his own behalf. He states his case as only he can state it, but his speech is not really a defense, but a lecture. If the jurymen are expecting him to back down in any respect, or to plead for his life, they are doomed to disappointment. On the contrary, he will not accept acquittal if it means that he shall stop his teaching. When he was a soldier and his commander placed him in a post of danger, there he was bound in honor to stay. It is the same now.

[1] **Thirty Tyrants:** a committee of aristocrats who governed Athens at the close of the war with Sparta. After a reign of terror, they were overthrown and a democratic government was resumed.

[2] **gadfly:** an irritating, bothersome fly that bites cattle and horses. Socrates believed that a teacher should be a gadfly to the state, criticizing it to bring about reforms.

[3] **Meletus** (mi·lē′tus).

[4] **Sophroniscus** (sō·frə·nis′kus).

[5] **Anytus** (ā·ni′tus).

[6] Some authorities say five hundred one.

"Strange indeed would be my conduct, men of Athens," he insists, "if, now when God orders me, as I believe, to fulfill the philosopher's mission of searching into myself and other men, I were to desert my post through fear of death, or any other fear. Men of Athens, I honor and love you; but I shall obey God rather than you, and while I have life and strength, I shall never cease from the practice and teaching of philosophy."

The court declares him guilty, but only by a majority of five or six. According to ancient custom, he is asked what punishment he would regard as just. Fearlessly he replies that if it is required of him to say how the public in justice ought to treat him, he can only say that he should be recognized as a public benefactor and given a pension for life; but, as an alternative, he proposes a small fine. The court regards his proposal as an insult, and he is condemned to death.

He takes the sentence with perfect calmness. Instead of pleading for mercy or sympathy, in fact, he turns about and encourages the court, as though he suspected that their consciences were pricking them for condemning him, and felt sorry for them.

"O Judges, be of good cheer about death," he says, "and know of a certainty that no evil can happen to a good man, either in life or after. I am not angry with my accusers, or with you, my condemners. The hour of departure is at hand, and we go our ways, I to die, and you to live. Which is better, God alone knows."

For a month he is in prison, with fetters on his ankles, surrounded by his friends; talking, questioning as always; refusing to escape, regretting nothing, fearing nothing. Then, one evening as the sun is setting, the young men gather around him for the last time.

One of them, Apollodorus,[1] is loud in his lamentations. "I grieve most for this, Socrates," he cries, "that I see you about to die undeservedly."

But the old gentleman's sense of humor is as active as ever. With a smile he strokes his pupil's hair. "My dearest Apollodorus," he says, "would you rather see me die deservedly?"

The last scene has all the sad beauty of autumn, or dying day. Minute by minute the shadows deepen. Xantippe, Socrates' wife, is there, wailing. For all that she abused her philosopher these many years, she loves him, and he has to send her away at last because he will have no lamentations when the end comes.

The jailer, in tears, brings him the hemlock, the poison which he is to drink. Holding the cup to his lips, he drains it and begins to walk about as the jailer has told him to do. His friends try hard to keep back the tears, but when young Apollodorus gives a sudden exclamation of grief, they lose their grip of themselves for a moment.

Socrates alone remains calm. "What is this strange outcry?" he says. "I sent away the women mainly in order that they might not offend in this way, for I have heard that a man should die in peace. Be quiet then, and have patience."

The poison is working. He can no longer walk; he lies down. They all know the end is near. But once more he uncovers his face, remembering a debt he owes to the temple of the god of medicine. "Crito,"[2] he says, turning to one of the young men, "I owe a cock to Aesculapius.[3] Will you remember to pay the debt?"

[1] **Apollodorus** (ä·pəl´ō·dōr´us).

[2] **Crito** (krī´tō).

[3] **Aesculapius** (es´kyōō·lā´pi·us): the Greek god of medicine.

"The debt shall be paid," Crito answers in low tones. "Is there anything else?"

There is nothing else, no word more. And his friends have, to comfort them, only the words which he spoke in answer to their question what they should do with his body: "You may do with it what you like, provided you do not imagine it to be me."

No, that quiet shape is not Socrates. He is elsewhere, questioning the eternities. And still he halts men in the churches and schools and marketplaces and on the buzzing highways of the world, asking them what they mean by the words they fling about so lightly; and what do they know—and are they really as wise as they imagine?

Magnificent old questioner that he was! Wisest and noblest of all the Greeks!

FOR STUDY AND DISCUSSION

1. According to Hagedorn's sketch, what sort of man was Socrates? What were his chief characteristics? What qualities of his character distinguished him as a remarkable human being?

2. What does the life of Socrates indicate about the problems of nonconformity—of acting in a manner calculated to show indifference to or contempt for accepted conventions?

3. In the next to last paragraph, what does Hagedorn mean when he says that Socrates "still halts men . . ."?

4. What does Hagedorn accomplish by his use of colloquial English ("He is a queer customer") and by his use of the present tense? Keep in mind that he is trying in a very short space to tell the life of a famous man.

5. Literally, the word *philosopher* means "lover of wisdom." Just what is a philosopher? Do you know of one or more present-day philosophers? Was Socrates more than a philosopher?

The Apology of Socrates

PLATO

We remember Plato not only as a student and devoted friend of Socrates, but as the Greek philosopher who, in about 387 B.C., founded in Athens the famous Academy, the school of philosophy where he taught for many years and where Aristotle, another great Greek philosopher, was among his students.

The *Apology* is Plato's account of the speech made by Socrates at his trial. The sequence of events at the trial was as follows. After the accusers stated their charges against Socrates and Socrates replied to them, the large jury decided by majority vote that Socrates was guilty. Since the law of Athens provided no ruling as to what the penalty should be, Socrates' accuser, Meletus, therefore proposed a penalty—death. The defendant proposed another—a small fine. The jury then voted, and the verdict was death, whereupon Socrates made his final statement.

Of the two parts of the speech that follow below, the first contains Socrates' comments upon the jury's verdict that he is guilty and Meletus' proposal of the death sentence. The second, made after the jury decides for the death penalty, is Socrates' eloquent final statement to the court.

THERE ARE a great many reasons, gentlemen, why I am not distressed by this result—I mean your condemnation of

From "The Apology of Socrates" by Plato from *The Last Days of Socrates,* translated by Hugh Tredennick. Reprinted by permission of Penguin Books Ltd.

me—but the chief reason is that the result was not unexpected. What does surprise me is the number of votes cast on the two sides. I should never have believed that it would be such a close thing; but now it seems that if a mere thirty votes had gone the other way, I should have been acquitted. Even as it is, I feel that so far as Meletus' part is concerned I have been acquitted; and not only that, but anyone can see that if Anytus and Lycon had not come forward to accuse me, Meletus would actually have forfeited his thousand drachmas for not having obtained one fifth of the votes.

However, we must face the fact that he demands the death penalty. Very good. What alternative penalty shall I propose to you, gentlemen? Obviously it must be adequate. Well, what penalty do I deserve to pay or suffer, in view of what I have done?

I have never lived an ordinary quiet life. I did not care for the things that most people care about: making money, having a comfortable home, high military or civil rank, and all the other activities—political appointments, secret societies, party organizations—which go on in our city; I thought that I was really too strict in my principles to survive if I went in for this sort of thing. So instead of taking a course which would have done no good either to you or to me, I set myself to do you individually in private what I hold to be the greatest possible service: I tried to persuade each one of you not to think more of practical advantages than of his mental and moral well-being, or in general [not] to think more of advantage than of well-being in the case of the state or of anything else. What do I deserve for behaving in this way? Some reward, gentlemen, if I am bound to suggest what I really deserve; and what is more, a reward which would be appropriate for myself. Well,

what is appropriate for a poor man who is a public benefactor and who requires leisure for giving you moral encouragement? Nothing could be more appropriate for such a person than free maintenance at the State's expense. He deserves it much more than any victor in the races at Olympia, whether he wins with a single horse or a pair or a team of four. These people give you the semblance of success, but I give you the reality; they do not need maintenance, but I do. So if I am to suggest an appropriate penalty which is strictly in accordance with justice, I suggest free maintenance by the State.

Perhaps when I say this, I may give you the impression, as I did in my remarks about exciting sympathy and making passionate appeals, that I am showing a deliberate perversity. That is not so, gentlemen; the real position is this. I am convinced that I never wrong anyone intentionally, but I cannot convince you of this, because we have had so little time for discussion. If it was your practice, as it is with other nations, to give not one day but several to the hearing of capital trials, I believe that you might have been convinced; but under present conditions it is not easy to dispose of grave allegations in a short space of time. So being convinced that I do no wrong to anybody, I can hardly be expected to wrong myself by asserting that I deserve something bad or by proposing a corresponding penalty. Why should I? For fear of suffering this penalty proposed by Meletus, when, as I said, I do not know whether it is a good thing or a bad? Do you expect me to choose something which I know very well is bad by making my counterproposal? Imprisonment? Why should I spend my days in prison, in subjection to the periodically appointed officers of the law? A fine, with imprisonment until it is paid? In my case the effect would be just the same, be-

cause I have no money to pay a fine. Or shall I suggest banishment? You would very likely accept the suggestion.

I should have to be desperately in love with life to do that, gentlemen. I am not so blind that I cannot see that you, my fellow citizens, have come to the end of your patience with my discussions and conversations; you have found them too irksome and irritating, and now you are trying to get rid of them. Will any other people find them easy to put up with? That is most unlikely, gentlemen. A fine life I should have if I left this country at my age and spent the rest of my days trying one city after another and being turned out every time! I know very well that wherever I go the young people will listen to my conversation just as they do here; and if I try to keep them off, they will make their elders drive me out, while if I do not, the fathers and other relatives will drive me out of their own accord for the sake of the young.

Perhaps someone may say, "But surely, Socrates, after you have left us you can spend the rest of your life in quietly minding your own business." This is the hardest thing of all to make some of you understand. If I say that this would be disobedience to God, and that is why I cannot "mind my own business," you will not believe that I am serious. If on the other hand I tell you that to let no day pass without discussing goodness and all the other subjects about which you hear me talking and examining both myself and others is really the very best thing that a man can do, and that life without this sort of examination is not worth living, you will be even less inclined to believe me. Nevertheless that is how it is, gentlemen, as I maintain; though it is not easy to convince you of it. Besides, I am not accustomed to think of myself as deserving punishment. If I had money, I would

have suggested a fine that I could afford, because that would not have done me any harm. As it is, I cannot, because I have none; unless of course you like to fix the penalty at what I could pay. I suppose I could probably afford one mina.[1] I suggest a fine of that amount.

One moment, gentlemen. Plato here, and Crito and Critobulus and Apollodorus, want me to propose three thousand drachmas on their security. Very well, I agree to this sum, and you can rely upon these gentlemen for its payment.

[*The jury decides for the death penalty.*]

Well, gentlemen, for the sake of a very small gain in time you are going to earn the reputation—and the blame from those who wish to disparage our city—of having put Socrates to death, "that wise man"—because they will say I am wise even if I am not, these people who want to find fault with you. If you had waited just a little while, you would have had your way in the course of nature. You can see that I am well on in life and near to death. I am saying this not to all of you but to those who voted for my execution,[2] and I have something else to say to them as well.

No doubt you think, gentlemen, that I have been condemned for lack of the arguments which I could have used if I had thought it right to leave nothing unsaid or undone to secure my acquittal. But that is very far from the truth. It is not a lack of arguments that has caused my condemnation, but a lack of effrontery and impudence, and the fact that I have refused to address you in the way which would give you most pleasure. You would have liked to hear me weep and wail,

[1] **one mina:** an amount which, even though small, would have been about a fifth of Socrates' wealth.

[2] The vote was about 360 for death, 140 for the fine.

doing and saying all sorts of things which I regard as unworthy of myself, but which you are used to hearing from other people. But I did not think then that I ought to stoop to servility because I was in danger, and I do not regret now the way in which I pleaded my case; I would much rather die as the result of this defense than live as the result of the other sort. In a court of law, just as in warfare, neither I nor any other ought to use his wits to escape death by any means. In battle it is often obvious that you could escape being killed by giving up your arms and throwing yourself upon the mercy of your pursuers; and in every kind of danger there are plenty of devices for avoiding death if you are unscrupulous enough to stick at nothing. But I suggest, gentlemen, that the difficulty is not so much to escape death; the real difficulty is to escape from doing wrong, which is far more fleet of foot. In this present instance I, the slow old man, have been overtaken by the slower of the two, but my accusers, who are clever and quick, have been overtaken by the faster: by iniquity. When I leave this court I shall go away condemned by you to death, but they will go away convicted by Truth herself of depravity and wickedness. And they accept their sentence even as I accept mine. No doubt it was bound to be so, and I think that the result is fair enough.

Having said so much, I feel moved to prophesy to you who have given your vote against me; for I am now at that point where the gift of prophecy comes most readily to men: at the point of death. I tell you, my executioners, that as soon as I am dead, vengeance shall fall upon you with a punishment far more painful than your killing of me. You have brought about my death in the belief that through it you will be delivered from submitting your conduct to criticism; but I say that the result will be just the opposite. You will have more critics, whom up till now I have restrained without your knowing it; and being younger, they will be harsher to you and will cause you more annoyance. If you expect to stop denunciation of your wrong way of life by putting people to death, there is something amiss with your reasoning. This way of escape is neither possible nor creditable; the best and easiest way is not to stop the mouths of

Socrates before his judges—based on eighteenth-century sculpture by Canova.

others, but to make yourselves as good men as you can. This is my last message to you who voted for my condemnation.

As for you who voted for my acquittal, I should very much like to say a few words to reconcile you to the result, while the officials are busy and I am not yet on my way to the place where I must die. I ask you, gentlemen, to spare me these few moments; there is no reason why we should not exchange fancies while the law permits. I look upon you as my friends, and I want you to understand the right way of regarding my present position.

Gentlemen of the jury—for *you* deserve to be so called—I have had a remarkable experience. In the past the prophetic voice to which I have become accustomed has always been my constant companion, opposing me even in quiet trivial things if I was going to take the wrong course. Now something has happened to me, as you can see, which might be thought and is commonly considered to be a supreme calamity; yet neither when I left home this morning, nor when I was taking my place here in the court, nor at any point in any part of my speech did the divine sign oppose me. In other discussions it has often checked me in the middle of a sentence; but this time it has never opposed me in any part of this business in anything that I have said or done. What do I suppose to be the explanation? I will tell you. I suspect that this thing that has happened to me is a blessing, and we are quite mistaken in supposing death to be an evil. I have good grounds for thinking this, because my accustomed sign could not have failed to oppose me if what I was doing had not been sure to bring some good result.

We should reflect that there is much reason to hope for a good result on other grounds as well. Death is one of two things. Either it is annihilation, and the dead have no consciousness of anything; or, as we are told, it is really a change: a migration of the soul from this place to another. Now if there is no consciousness but only a dreamless sleep, death must be a marvelous gain. I suppose that if anyone were told to pick out the night on which he slept so soundly as not even to dream, and then to compare it with all the other nights and days of his life, and then were told to say, after due consideration, how many better and happier days and nights than this he had spent in the course of his life—well, I think that the Great King [1] himself, to say nothing of any private person, would find these days and nights easy to count in comparison with the rest. If death is like this, then, I call it gain; because the whole of time, if you look at it in this way, can be regarded as no more than one single night. If on the other hand death is a removal from here to some other place, and if what we are told is true, that all the dead are there, what greater blessing could there be than this, gentlemen? If on arrival in the other world, beyond the reach of our so-called justice, one will find there the true judges who are said to preside in those courts, Minos and Rhadamanthys and Aeacus [2] and Triptolemus [3] and all those other half-divinities who were upright in their earthly life, would that be an unrewarding journey? Put it in this way: how much would one of you give to meet Orpheus [4] and Musaeus,[5] Hesiod [6] and Homer? I am willing to die ten times over if this account is

[1] **Great King:** the King of Persia.

[2] **Minos . . . Aeacus** (ē′ə·kus): sons of Zeus, judges in the underworld.

[3] **Triptolemus:** a founder of agriculture and priest of Demeter.

[4] **Orpheus:** son of one of the muses and a great singer and poet.

[5] **Musaeus:** a legendary early Greek poet and musician.

[6] **Hesiod:** a Greek poet, ranked second only to Homer.

true. It would be a specially interesting experience for me to join them there, to meet Palamedes and Ajax [1] the son of Telamon and any other heroes of the old days who met their death through an unfair trial, and to compare my fortunes with theirs—it would be rather amusing, I think; and above all I should like to spend my time there, as here, in examining and searching people's minds, to find out who is really wise among them, and who only thinks that he is. What would one not give, gentlemen, to be able to question the leader [2] of that great host against Troy, or Odysseus [3] or Sisyphus,[4] or the thousands of other men and women whom one could mention, to talk and mix and argue with whom would be unimaginable happiness? At any rate I presume that they do not put one to death there for such conduct; because apart from the other happiness in which their world surpasses ours, they are now immortal for the rest of time, if what we are told is true.

You too, gentlemen of the jury, must look forward to death with confidence and fix your minds on this one belief, which is certain: that nothing can harm a good man either in life or after death, and his fortunes are not a matter of indifference to the gods. This present experience of mine has not come about mechanically; I am quite clear that the time had come when it was better for me to die and be released from my distractions. That is why my sign never turned me back. For my own part I

bear no grudge at all against those who condemned me and accused me, although it was not with this kind intention that they did so, but because they thought that they were hurting me; and that is culpable of them. However, I ask them to grant me one favor. When my sons grow up, gentlemen, if you think that they are putting money or anything else before goodness, take your revenge by plaguing them as I plagued you; and if they fancy themselves for no reason, you must scold them just as I scolded you, for neglecting the important things and thinking that they are good for something when they are good for nothing. If you do this, I shall have had justice at your hands, both I myself and my children.

Now it is time that we were going, I to die and you to live; but which of us has the happier prospect is unknown to anyone but God.

[1] **Palamedes and Ajax:** Greek heroes in the Trojan War.

[2] **leader:** Agamemnon, leader of the Greek forces in the Trojan War.

[3] **Odysseus:** Greek hero of the Trojan War, who, after the fall of Troy, wandered for ten years before reaching home.

[4] **Sisyphus:** legendary king of Corinth, who, for his misdeeds, was condemned eternally to roll a heavy stone up a hill. As soon as the stone reached the top, it rolled down again.

FOR STUDY AND DISCUSSION

1. The word *apology* today usually refers to a statement expressing regret; in Greek the word means *defense*. Does Socrates indicate any regret in his *Apology?* Explain your answer. How much defense and what defense does he present?

2. After reading these speeches, what do you think of the men who accused Socrates? Do you think they were justified in doing so? Explain.

3. What was Socrates' last message to those who voted for his condemnation? Do you agree or disagree with his reasoning? Why or why not?

4. What are some of the reasons, according to Socrates, for not fearing death?

5. At the end of the selection, what is the point in Socrates' reference to his sons and their future?

6. What do these two speeches reveal about Socrates that you did not learn from Hagedorn's account of his life?

The Death of Socrates

PLATO

Plato was not present at the death of Socrates, but he heard the story directly from those who witnessed the scene. Writing about it afterward in *Phaedo,* he recounted the story in the form of a dialogue between Phaedo, who was there, and Echecrates, who was not. The moving account of the quiet way in which the great man prepared for death is the very last part of Phaedo's narrative. It reveals, as do the speeches in the *Apology,* a great deal about the man whom Hermann Hagedorn calls "wisest and noblest of all the Greeks."

SOCRATES SAID, "It is about time that I took my bath. I prefer to have a bath before drinking the poison rather than give the women the trouble of washing me when I am dead."

When he had finished speaking, Crito said, "Very well, Socrates. But have you no directions for the others or myself about your children or anything else? What can we do to please you best?"

"Nothing new, Crito," said Socrates; "just what I am always telling you. If you look after yourselves, whatever you do will please me and mine and you too, even if you don't agree with me now. On the other hand, if you neglect yourselves and fail to follow the line of life as I have laid it down both now and in the past, however

From "Phaedo" by Plato from *The Last Days of Socrates,* translated by Hugh Tredennick. Reprinted by permission of Penguin Books Ltd.

fervently you agree with me now, it will do no good at all."

"We shall try our best to do as you say," said Crito. "But how shall we bury you?"

"Any way you like," replied Socrates, "that is, if you can catch me and I don't slip through your fingers." He laughed gently as he spoke, and turning to us went on: "I can't persuade Crito that I am this Socrates here who is talking to you now and marshaling all the arguments; he thinks that I am the one whom he will see presently lying dead; and he asks how he is to bury me! As for my long and elaborate explanation that when I have drunk the poison I shall remain with you no longer, but depart to a state of heavenly happiness, this attempt to console both you and myself seems to be wasted on him. You must give an assurance to Crito for me—the opposite of the one which he gave to the court which tried me. He undertook that I should stay; but you must assure him that when I am dead I shall not stay, but depart and be gone. That will help Crito to bear it more easily and keep him from being distressed on my account when he sees my body being burned or buried, as if something dreadful were happening to me; or from saying at the funeral that it is Socrates whom he is laying out or carrying to the grave or burying. Believe me, my dear friend Crito: misstatements are not merely jarring in their immediate context; they also have a bad effect upon the soul. No, you must keep up your spirits and say that it is only my body that you are burying; and you can bury it as you please, in whatever way you think is most proper."

With these words he got up and went into another room to bathe; and Crito went after him, but told us to wait. So we waited, discussing and reviewing what had been said or else dwelling upon the great-

ness of the calamity which had befallen us; for we felt just as though we were losing a father and should be orphans for the rest of our lives. Meanwhile, when Socrates had taken his bath, his children were brought to see him—he had two little sons and one big boy—and the women of his household—you know—arrived. He talked to them in Crito's presence and gave them directions about carrying out his wishes; then he told the women and children to go away and came back himself to join us.

It was now nearly sunset, because he had spent a long time inside. He came and sat down, fresh from the bath; and he had only been talking for a few minutes when the prison officer came in and walked up to him. "Socrates," he said, "at any rate I shall not have to find fault with you, as I do with others, for getting angry with me and cursing when I tell them to drink the poison—carrying out Government orders. I have come to know during this time that you are the noblest and the gentlest and the bravest of all the men that have ever come here, and now especially I am sure that you are not angry with me, but with them; because you know who are responsible. So now—you know what I have come to say—good-by, and try to bear what must be as easily as you can." As he spoke he burst into tears, and turning round, went away.

Socrates looked up at him and said, "Good-by to you, too; we will do as you say." Then addressing us, he went on, "What a charming person! All the time I have been here he has visited me and sometimes had discussions with me and shown me the greatest kindness; and how generous of him now to shed tears for me at parting! But come, Crito, let us do as he says. Someone had better bring in the poison, if it is ready prepared; if not, tell the man to prepare it."

"But surely, Socrates," said Crito, "the sun is still upon the mountains; it has not gone down yet. Besides, I know that in other cases people have dinner and enjoy their wine, and sometimes the company of those whom they love, long after they receive the warning; and only drink the poison quite late at night. No need to hurry; there is still plenty of time."

"It is natural that these people whom you speak of should act in that way, Crito," said Socrates, "because they think that they gain by it. And it is also natural that I should not; because I believe that I should gain nothing by drinking the poison a little later—I should only make myself ridiculous in my own eyes if I clung to life and hugged it when it has no more to offer. Come, do as I say and don't make difficulties."

At this Crito made a sign to his servant, who was standing nearby. The servant went out and after spending a considerable time, returned with the man who was to administer the poison; he was carrying it ready prepared in a cup. When Socrates saw him he said, "Well, my good fellow, you understand these things; what ought I to do?"

"Just drink it," he said, "and then walk about until you feel a weight in your legs, and then lie down. Then it will act of its own accord."

As he spoke, he handed the cup to Socrates, who received it quite cheerfully, Echecrates, without a tremor, without any change of color or expression, and said, looking up under his brows with his usual steady gaze, "What do you say about pouring a libation [1] from this drink? Is it permitted, or not?"

"We only prepare what we regard as the normal dose, Socrates," he replied.

"I see," said Socrates. "But I sup-

[1] **libation** (lī·bā′shən): liquid ceremoniously poured out in honor of a deity.

"The Death of Socrates," by the French painter Jacques Louis David (1748–1825).

pose I am allowed, or rather bound, to pray the gods that my removal from this world to the other may be prosperous. This is my prayer, then; and I hope that it may be granted." With these words, quite calmly and with no sign of distaste, he drained the cup in one breath.

Up till this time most of us had been fairly successful in keeping back our tears; but when we saw that he was drinking, that he had actually drunk it, we could do so no longer; in spite of myself the tears came pouring out so that I covered my face and wept brokenheartedly—not for him, but for my own calamity in losing such a friend. Crito had given up even before me and had gone out when he could not restrain his tears. But Apollodorus, who had never stopped crying even before, now broke out into such a storm of passionate weeping that he made everyone in the room break down, except Socrates himself, who said:

"Really, my friends, what a way to behave! Why, that was my main reason for sending away the women, to prevent this sort of disturbance; because I am told that one should make one's end in a tranquil frame of mind. Calm yourselves and try to be brave."

This made us feel ashamed, and we controlled our tears. Socrates walked about, and presently, saying that his legs were heavy, lay down on his back—that was what the man recommended. The man (he was the same one who had administered the poison) kept his hand upon Socrates and after a little while examined his feet and legs; then pinched his foot hard and asked if he felt it. Socrates said no. Then he did the same to his legs; and moving gradually upward in this way, let us see that he was getting cold and numb. Presently he felt him again and said that when it reached the heart, Socrates would be gone.

The coldness was spreading about as far as his waist when Socrates uncovered his face—for he had covered it up—and said (they were his last words): "Crito, we ought to offer a cock to Asclepius.[1] See to it, and don't forget."

"No, it shall be done," said Crito. "Are you sure that there is nothing else?"

Socrates made no reply to this question, but after a little while he stirred; and when the man uncovered him, his eyes were fixed. When Crito saw this, he closed the mouth and eyes.

Such, Echecrates, was the end of our comrade, who was, we may fairly say, of all those whom we knew in our time, the bravest and also the wisest and most upright man.

[1] **a cock to Asclepius:** Asclepius (or Aesculapius) was the god of medicine. The sacrifice was made to the god by sick persons, either in the hope of waking up cured or in thanks for having been cured. In any event, Socrates here perhaps makes an almost humorous remark about the fact that his death is the cure for his life.

FOR STUDY AND DISCUSSION

1. What does this account of the last hour of Socrates' life add to your understanding of his character? of his relationship with other people? of his understanding of life and death?

2. How does Plato use contrast between Socrates and the other persons in the scene to develop Socrates' character?

3. Two or three passages in this selection indicate that Socrates had a keen sense of humor. Locate these passages and explain the humor.

4. Which of the three selections about Socrates do you think tells most about Socrates' character? Why?

THE SOCRATIC METHOD

Socrates liked to claim that he was wiser than other men only because he was aware of how little he knew. Others thought they knew more than they did. Pretending ignorance, Socrates would ask a series of questions. Sometimes these questions showed that an op-

ponent's opinions were really foolish. But Socrates' questioning, called the "Socratic" method, was mostly a way of teaching. Rather than simply tell his students what was true, Socrates liked to have his students work out problems for themselves, with direction from him. Thus, much of his teaching took the form of a dialogue between two or more people. Here is a sample from *Phaedo*. Socrates speaks first:

"Tell me, what must be present in a body to make it alive?"

"Soul."

"Is this always so?"

"Of course."

"So whenever soul takes possession of a body, it always brings life with it?"

"Yes, it does."

"Is there an opposite to life, or not?"

"Yes, there is."

"What?"

"Death."

"Does it follow, then, from our earlier agreement, that soul will never admit the opposite of that which accompanies it?"

"Most definitely," said Cebes.

"Well, now, what name did we apply just now to that which does not admit the form of even?"

"Uneven."

"And what do we call that which does not admit justice or culture?"

"Uncultured; and the other unjust."

"Very good. And what do we call that which does not admit death?"

"Immortal."

"And soul does not admit death?"

"No."

"So soul is immortal."

"Yes, it is immortal."

"Well," said Socrates, "can we say that that has been proved? What do you think?"

"Most completely, Socrates."

FOR COMPOSITION

After a careful reading of the three selections about Socrates, write a short essay about the man you believe Socrates to have been. Illustrate as necessary from one or more of the selections.

Exposition .

Exposition is the setting forth of ideas in writing. Exposition explains, instructs, or gives information, as the following paragraph from Hermann Hagedorn's "Socrates—His Life".

He is the first and greatest of all button-holers. It makes no difference where you are or how busy you are. If Socrates fixes his eyes on you, he will come lumbering across the athletic field or the marketplace, and, smiling most courteously, he will engage you in conversation. Socrates is a glutton for conversation. Money means nothing to him. Fame, power, influence mean nothing. He never knows exactly where the next meal is coming from; but he must have conversation. (page 272)

1. What is the main idea of this paragraph? What facts does the author give to support his main assertion?
2. How does the author emphasize his main idea?

A writer's aim in exposition is to communicate ideas and information, but he may use description or narration to develop his ideas and make his arguments clearer and more interesting. How does Plutarch develop his idea in the following paragraph from his "Life of Caesar"?

Another thing which caused offense was his insulting treatment of the tribunes. The feast of the Lupercalia was being celebrated. Caesar, sitting on a golden throne above the rostra and wearing a triumphal robe, was watching this ceremony; and Antony, who was consul at the time, was one of those taking part in the sacred running. When he came running into the forum, the crowd made way for him. He was carrying a diadem with a wreath of laurel tied round it, and he held this out to Caesar. His action was followed by some applause, but it was not much and it was not spontaneous. But when Caesar pushed the diadem away from him, there was a general shout of applause. Antony then offered him the diadem for the second time, and again only a few applauded, though, when Caesar again rejected it, there was applause from everyone. Caesar, finding that the experiment had proved a failure, rose from his seat and ordered the wreath to be carried to the Capitol. It was then discovered that his statues had been decorated with royal diadems, and two of the tribunes, Flavius and Marullus, went round the statues and tore down the decorations. They then found out who had been the first to salute Caesar as King, and led them off to prison. The people followed the tribunes and were loud in their applause, calling them Brutuses—because it was Brutus who first put an end to the line of Kings in Rome and gave to the senate and the people the power that had previously been in the hands of one man. This made Caesar angry. He deprived Marullus and Flavius of their tribuneship and in speaking against them he insulted the people at the same time. (pages 232–33)

1. What is the main idea of this paragraph? How has the writer used narration as an aid to exposition?
2. The author states his main idea at the beginning of the paragraph. Where does he reemphasize it at the end?

PRACTICING YOUR READING

Find four other paragraphs of exposition in the biographies that you have read. State the main idea of each and indicate how the author has supported and emphasized his main idea.

ATTITUDE AND TONE

A writer usually tries to suggest his attitude toward his subject by his use of tone. As a reader, you should be ready to infer a writer's attitude from his shadings of tone. The words a writer chooses, his sentence length and rhythm, all are clues to tone. Reread the following paragraphs, then answer these questions for each: What is the paragraph's main idea? What is the author's attitude? What clues to his attitude are revealed by his tone?

When I was a boy, there was but one permanent ambition among my comrades in our village on the west bank of the Mississippi River. That was, to be a steamboatman. We had transient ambitions of other sorts, but they were only transient. When a circus came and went, it left us all burning to become clowns; the first minstrel show that came to our section left us all suffering to try that kind of life; now and then we had a hope that if we lived and were good, God would permit us to be pirates. These ambitions faded out, each in its turn; but the ambition to be a steamboatman always remained. (FROM *Life on the Mississippi,* pages 246–47)

"But that was not the same snow," I say. "Our snow was not only shaken from whitewash buckets down the sky, it came shawling out of the ground and swam and drifted out of the arms and hands and bodies of the trees; snow grew overnight on the roofs of the houses like a pure and grandfather moss, minutely white-ivied the walls and settled on the postman, opening the gate, like a dumb, numb thunderstorm of white, torn Christmas cards." ("A Child's Christmas in Wales," page 226)

"Personally I never care for fiction or storybooks. What I like to read about are facts and statistics of any kind. If they are only facts about the raising of radishes, they interest me. Just now, for instance, before you came in"—he pointed to an encyclopedia on the shelves—"I was reading an article about 'Mathematics.' Perfectly pure mathematics.

"My own knowledge of mathematics stops at 'twelve times twelve,' but I enjoyed that article immensely. I didn't understand a word of it; but facts, or what a man believes to be facts, are always delightful. That mathematical fellow believed in his facts. So do I. Get your facts first, and"—the voice dies away to an almost inaudible drone—"then you can distort 'em as much as you please." ("An Interview with Mark Twain," page 269)

YOUR OWN TONE IN WRITING

A common weakness of many writers is that they are not careful enough in their choice of words and construction of their sentences to communicate their attitude through their tone. As a result, their ideas may not be expressed as clearly as possible. In writing the following exercises, pay close attention to your tone. Do the words and phrases express your attitude accurately? If not, revise your writing to convey your attitude as exactly as possible.

1. Write a paragraph or two about your childhood ambitions: what they were, how and when they changed, and why. Try to make clear by your tone your present attitude toward these ambitions.

2. Why is something popular? Because it satisfies a need? Because it is exciting? Express your attitude toward popularity in a short essay, using specific examples, such as popular sports or singing groups.

ART AND LITERATURE

Look again at the paintings on pages 259–64. In which are the colors brightest? In which are they dark or dull? What feeling do you get, just from the colors the artist has used, of his attitude or mood? Choose one of these paintings, and write a short essay on how the artist has used color to communicate mood.

POETRY

I N JOHN STEINBECK's story "The Leader of the People" (page 42), Grandfather says, in a moment of discouragement, "I tell those old stories, but they're not what I want to tell. I only know how I want people to feel when I tell them."

Grandfather's frustration is one that most of us have felt. Our own experience is so vivid to us, but how can we tell others about it? It's easy enough to communicate the *facts;* "I've fallen in love with Lucy Smith." But how do we communicate the *feelings?* How do we tell people *what it is like?* We can't even begin to without speaking poetically: "I feel as if I'm floating on a little pink cloud." But the words are trite from being used too often and fall short of what we want to tell. Like Grandfather, most of us have to give up the attempt as a bad job.

John Steinbeck, however, succeeds where Grandfather fails. For most readers, Steinbeck does an excellent job of making us feel how Jody felt, how Grandfather felt, how both of them felt when Carl Tiflin took the wind out of their sails, and how Jody felt an unselfish compassion for Grandfather that was something new in his experience. Jack Finney, likewise, in "Contents of the Dead Man's Pockets" (page 3) does an excellent job of communicating to us what it was like for Tom Benecke out on an eleventh-story ledge. He doesn't simply tell us, "Tom Benecke got caught on an eleventh-story ledge and was very frightened." Rather he entices us out on the ledge with Tom, puts us bodily (or rather imaginatively) into Tom's shoes, and makes us share Tom's experience.

Literature might be defined as language chosen and organized in order to communicate feelings rather than facts, to tell us what it is like, to allow us to share experience. How does it do this? Mainly by using a number of language resources not used by the writer writing merely to communicate facts. Consider the difference between a factual inning-by-inning summary of a baseball game and an account of it written by a good sportswriter. (The sportswriter is something of a poet: he wants not only to give us the facts of the game, but to make us feel as we would if we were watching it.) The

factual summary might run: "Johnson singled to left. Calvetti doubled to right, scoring Johnson." But the sportswriter writes: "Johnson smoked a grass cutter between short and third. Calvetti, after taking two strikes, drove a screaming double off the right field wall. Johnson took off like a frightened rabbit at the crack of the bat, rounded third with a full head of steam, and slid home in a cloud of dust." The sportswriter's account differs from the factual summary in a number of ways. First, it appeals to our senses, allowing us to *hear* "the crack of the bat" and *see* "a cloud of dust." Second, it uses figurative language: "smoked," "grass cutter," "screaming double," "like a frightened rabbit," "with a full head of steam." Third, its sentences are more rhythmical than those of the summary. Finally, the sportswriter's story is probably organized differently from the summary. Instead of beginning with the first inning and going straight to the end, it might begin with the high point in the seventh inning, tell of a further threat in the eighth, and only then go back to the early innings. Though it would give a fuller account of the most exciting innings, it might leave out others entirely. Like a sports story, literature achieves much of its communication through its structure and organization.

Poetry is like all other literature, only more so. Actually, there is no essential difference between poetry and any good, vivid writing. Steinbeck's account of Jody's life on the ranch and Finney's account of Tom Benecke's experience on the ledge, in a large sense, might be spoken of as poetry. Poetry, like all imaginative writing, is language put together to tell us *what it is like;* it is language that enables us to share experience. Of course, we usually use the term *poetry* to describe a piece of writing that is printed a certain way on the page—in lines of unequal length with consequently varying margins. But this is an unreliable definition. Language printed this way on the page may be less *poetical*—less expressive of feeling—than a good short story; it may indeed be such lifeless writing that it is not poetry at all. We cannot identify poetry, therefore, by the way it is printed on the page. Whether the lines are of equal or unequal length, whether the margins are straight or irregular—these considerations finally matter very little. Perhaps it is best for us to think of poetry simply as the most *concentrated* form of literature, as the purest attempt to communicate vivid experience, to give us the quality of experience, to express the "feel" of things. In order to do this, poetry uses more of the special resources of language than do other kinds of writing. (It is printed as it is because of its greater use of rhythm.) Poetry is not different from other imaginative literature; it is just more highly charged, more concentrated.

John Masefield's "Sea Fever," a poem about the powerful attractions of a life at sea for one who has once lived it, will serve as an example to show how the poet organizes language and uses all its resources in order to communicate the "feel" of things.

Sea Fever

I must go down to the seas again, to the lonely sea and the sky,
And all I ask is a tall ship and a star to steer her by,
And the wheel's kick and the wind's song and the white sail's shaking,
And a gray mist on the sea's face and a gray dawn breaking.

I must go down to the seas again, for the call of the running tide 5
Is a wild call and a clear call that may not be denied;
And all I ask is a windy day with the white clouds flying,
And the flung spray and the blown spume, and the sea gulls crying.

I must go down to the seas again to the vagrant gypsy life,
To the gull's way and the whale's way where the wind's like a whetted
 knife; 10
And all I ask is a merry yarn from a laughing fellow-rover,
And quiet sleep and a sweet dream when the long trick's° over.

If we reduce "Sea Fever" to factual language, what the poem says is this:
"A man who has been a sailor and known the sea feels forever afterward a
desire to return to the life of ships and sailing." This is the theme of the
poem: the main idea that the poem communicates to the mind. But Mase-
field wanted not only to communicate to our minds but also to our senses,
our imaginations, and our emotions, so that we too could, at least in imagina-
tion, feel and "taste" and know this desire. How does he do it?

First, of course, instead of talking abstractly about "A man who has been
a sailor," he dramatizes the experience by putting the poem into the mouth
of a specific sailor. Not "A man who," but "I" must go down to the seas
again. The "I" draws our attention as "A man who" never could.

Second, instead of talking abstractly about "the life of ships and sailing,"
he uses concrete images that appeal to our senses with sights and sounds and
physical sensations. We *see* the tall ship, the white sail, the gray mist, the
white clouds, the flung spray, and the blown spume; we see gulls, whales,
and the North Star. We *hear* the wind and the shaking of the sail, the crying
of sea gulls and the laughter of a fellow sailor. We *feel* the wheel kicking in
our hands, the spray flung in our faces, and the sharp wind "like a whetted
knife."

Third, Masefield chooses words for their power of suggestion. Words like
spume and *vagrant,* though not everyday words, seem the best words he
could have used. How much more effective *lonely* is than *uninhabited;* how
much more suggestive *gypsy* is than *tramp;* how much more of the long

12. **trick's:** A trick is a sailor's spell or turn of duty.

hours at sea and sailors' tales is called to mind by a *yarn* than by *story* or *account!* Do you know what *whetted* means? It means "sharpened"; *whetting* is what you do to a knife. Some of you may have gotten it mixed up with "wetted." If you did, little matter. In this poem, the wind is also "wetted," or mixed with spray, and part of the superiority of *whetted* to *sharpened* is that it suggests both ideas at once.

Fourth, the poem uses figurative language. The sound of the wind is a "song"; the appeal of the "running tide" is a "call"; the sailor's life is a "gypsy life"; the sea is "the gull's way and the whale's way"; the wind is like a knife. None of these expressions are exact and factual; they bypass logic and appeal directly to the imagination.

Did you notice the symbols in the last line? The "long trick" and the "quiet sleep" and the "sweet dream" all have ordinary, literal meanings; but, coming at the end of this poem about a way of life, these phrases take on symbolical significance. The "long trick" becomes life, the "quiet sleep" death, and the "sweet dream" whatever kind of consciousness may follow death. Through symbolism, the poem takes on a wider meaning.

Fifth, Masefield has chosen his words for their sound as well as their meaning. Notice how in the first line the *n* sounds in *down* and *again* and *lonely* repeat each other; how in the second line the words *star* and *steer* differ only in their vowel sound; how in the third line *wheel* and *wind* and *white* all begin with a *w*, and the *k* in *shaking* echoes the *k*'s in *kick;* how in the fourth line the words *gray, face, gray,* and *breaking* all have the same long *a* sound. Whether or not you consciously noticed these similar sounds as you read the poem, they contributed to the richness of Masefield's description and helped to give you the "feel" of his experience. Certainly you noticed the rhyme sounds at the ends of the lines—*sky, by, shaking, breaking*. These end rhymes and other similarities of sound continue throughout the poem.

Sixth, you could hardly help noticing the rhythmical quality of the language. The whole poem has a lilt and a kick to it like the roll and toss of waves at sea. This rhythm is built on a patterned base called *meter*—a regularized rhythm that allows for variation but controls the variation within the limits of the pattern.

Finally, the poem has a visual pattern: it is divided into three groups of four lines each. These line groups, or stanzas, not only give the poem an outer, visual pattern, but emphasize an inner patterning of thought. Masefield has underlined this pattern in the poem by repeating certain phrases as refrains. Each stanza begins with the words "I must go down to the seas again" and later continues "And all I ask . . ." These repetitions, besides adding to the design of the poem, underline the urgency of the sea's "wild call" that may not be denied. The repeated phrases echo in our ears as the sea's call echoes in the speaker's heart.

Poetry, we have said, is like other literature, but more highly charged. Most of the resources used by Masefield in this poem are used also, to some degree, by writers of short stories, novels, and plays. They too choose their words for maximum suggestiveness; they too use images and figures of speech; they too are conscious of rhythm and the sounds of words. Actually, the only resources of poetry not used by other writers are rhyme, meter, and stanza. Because of this, we may be tempted to think of poetry as something written in rhyme, meter, and stanzas. If we do, we make a bad mistake. The poem below has neither rhyme, meter, nor stanza, yet it is still a poem. Poetry is not created by the use of any one language resource. It simply makes richer use of all language resources.

Four Preludes on Playthings of the Wind

CARL SANDBURG

1

The woman named Tomorrow
sits with a hairpin in her teeth
and takes her time
and does her hair the way she wants it
and fastens at last the last braid and coil 5
and puts the hairpin where it belongs
and turns and drawls: "Well, what of it?
My grandmother, Yesterday, is gone.
What of it? Let the dead be dead."

2

The doors were cedar 10
and the panels strips of gold
and the girls were golden girls
and the panels read and the girls chanted:
 We are the greatest city,
 the greatest nation: 15
 nothing like us ever was.

The doors are twisted on broken hinges.
Sheets of rain swish through on the wind
 where the golden girls ran and the panels read:
 We are the greatest city,
 the greatest nation, 20
 nothing like us ever was.

It has happened before.
Strong men put up a city and got a
 nation together, 25
And paid singers to sing and women
 to warble: We are the greatest city,
 the greatest nation,
 nothing like us ever was.

And while the singers sang 30
and the strong men listened
and paid the singers well,
and felt good about it all,
 there were rats and lizards who listened
 . . . and the only listeners left now 35
 . . . are . . . the rats . . . and the lizards.

And there are black crows
crying, "Caw, caw,"
bringing mud and sticks
building a nest 40
 over the words carved
 on the doors where the panels were cedar
 and the strips on the panels were gold
 and the golden girls came singing:
 We are the greatest city, 45
 the greatest nation:
 nothing like us ever was.

The only singers now are crows crying, "Caw, caw,"
And the sheets of rain whine in the wind and doorways.
And the only listeners now are . . . the rats . . . and the lizards. 50

The feet of the rats
scribble on the doorsills;
the hieroglyphs° of the rat footprints
chatter the pedigrees of the rats
and the babble of the blood 55
and gabble of the breed
of the grandfathers and the great-grandfathers
of the rats.

53. **hieroglyphs** (hī′ər·ə-glifs′): characters in ancient picture writing; used in a general sense
to mean any sign or symbol.

And the wind shifts
and the dust on a doorsill shifts 60
and even the writing of the rat footprints
tells us nothing, nothing at all
about the greatest city, the greatest nation
where the strong men listened
and the women warbled: Nothing like us ever was. 65

This poem is written in *free verse,* a form of poetry writing that is non-metrical—"free" of the restrictions of regular meter. Is it nevertheless rhythmical? Imagine the lines of the poem written continuously like prose. What difference would this make in the way you would read the poem?

A *prelude* is a short musical composition played before an opera, a play, ceremony, or other event. Sandburg's title therefore indicates that these four pieces are like music and that they precede something. What do they precede? Are sections 2, 3, and 4 about the past? the future? or both? Do you interpret this poem as prophecy, warning, or historical record?

The Kinds of Poetry

Have you ever tried to classify pebbles you collected on a beach? You can do it by size—small, medium, and large; or by color—black, gray, blue, brown, white. But there are always some that won't fit into any classification: they are medium-large, or a shade halfway between black and gray, or brown with a streak of white.

Poems are the same way. Most of them don't fall into neat classifications: there are always some that fit into more than one category, or some that don't quite fit into any. Nevertheless, it is often helpful to be able to talk about *kinds* of poetry, even if the classifications don't always fit exactly. Classifications, even imperfect ones, give us handles we can use to pick up poems, ways by which we can approach them, and rough means of grouping them and making comparisons.

The commonest way of classifying poems is into three broad divisions: narrative, lyric, and dramatic. *Narrative* poetry tells a story. *Lyric* poetry expresses the poet's personal thoughts and feelings. *Dramatic* poetry presents one or more characters speaking, usually to other characters. We must always remember, though, that these classifications are rough and overlapping. There are dramatic narratives, dramatic lyrics, and lyric narratives, and there are other poems that won't fit into any of these categories without a liberal stretching of definitions.

NARRATIVE POETRY

A narrative poem tells a story. Early storytellers, who entertained the people in a time when hardly anyone could read or write, found that regular meter and rhyme helped them not only to remember the story but also to hold everyone's attention with a vigorous and rhythmical account. Recitations often accompanied by chords struck on a small harp or other stringed instrument took the place held by books, radio, and television in our time and were a principal form of entertainment.

One kind of narrative poetry is the *epic*—a long poem celebrating the deeds of a national hero. Most epics are lofty poems, concerned almost entirely with kings and princes and told in language that is stately and dignified. The most famous epics are the *Iliad* and *Odyssey* by the Greek poet Homer, the *Aeneid* by the Roman poet Virgil, and the *Divine Comedy* by the Italian poet Dante. The greatest epic in English is *Paradise Lost* by John Milton. Some epics are by unknown, or anonymous, poets, such as *Beowulf* by an Old English poet, *The Cid* by a Spanish poet, and *The Song of Roland* by a French poet. Epics are too long for a complete example to be included in this book; however, Sir Thomas Malory's *Morte d'Arthur,* which in some ways might be described as a prose epic, and Tennyson's *Idylls of the King,* which is often referred to as an epic, are represented on pages 537 and 540.

Another kind of narrative poem is the *ballad*—a relatively short poem originally meant for singing. The oldest ballads, known as folk or popular ballads, arose among the folk, or common people, and were passed on by word of mouth for generations. Not until centuries later were these folk ballads written down. Over the years, from being recited so often, they gradually were changed from their original form, just as coins are worn smooth by being passed from hand to hand. Many of them exist today in several different versions.

Many ballads have repeated lines or phrases called *refrains*. Originally, when ballads were sung, the ballad singer probably sang the verses and his audience joined in on the refrains. Because they were meant for singing, ballads are written in stanzas, often of four lines. Most ballads are tragic in mood and are concerned largely with physical courage, love, treachery, and the supernatural.

Literary ballads, unlike folk ballads, are composed by a known author and immediately written down. Though not always meant for singing, they preserve a stanzaic form. Literary ballads are sometimes written in imitation of folk ballads, but in general they tend to be more elaborate than folk ballads both in language and in form.

Johnny Armstrong

ANONYMOUS

This ballad, like many of our best-known folk ballads, comes from the Border country, the region along the boundary between Scotland and England. It is based on an actual incident that occurred in about 1530. The Armstrongs were a powerful clan in the fifteenth and sixteenth centuries. Though Scottish in origin, they made armed raids on both sides of the border and thus aroused the anger of the Scottish king.

There dwelt a man in fair Westmorland,
 Johnny Armstrong men did him call,
He had neither lands nor rents coming in,
 Yet he kept eight score men in his hall.

He had horse and harness for them all, 5
 Goodly steeds were all milk-white;
O the golden bands about their necks,
 And their weapons, they were all alike.

News then was brought unto the king
 That there was such a one as he, 10
That lived like a bold outlaw,
 And robbed all the north country.

The king he wrote out a letter then,
 A letter which was large and long;
He signed it with his own hand, 15
 And he promised to do him no wrong.

When this letter came Johnny unto,
 His heart it was as blithe as birds on the tree.
"Never was I sent for before any king,
 My father, my grandfather, nor none but me. 20

"And if we go the king before,
 I would we went most orderly;
Every man of you shall have his scarlet cloak,
 Laced with silver laces three.

"Every one of you shall have his velvet coat, 25
 Laced with silver lace so white;
O the golden bands about your necks,
 Black hats, white feathers, all alike."

By the morrow morning at ten of the clock,
 Toward Edinborough° gone was he, 30
And with him all his eight score men;
 Good Lord, it was a goodly sight for to see!

When Johnny came before the king,
 He fell down on his knee,
"O pardon, my sovereign liege," he said, 35
 "O pardon my eight score men and me!"

"Thou shalt have no pardon, thou traitor strong,
 For thy eight score men nor thee;
For tomorrow morning by ten of the clock,
 Both thou and them shall hang on the gallows tree." 40

But Johnny looked over his left shoulder,
 Good Lord, what a grievous look looked he!
Saying, "Asking grace of a graceless face—
 Why there is none for you nor me."

But Johnny had a bright sword by his side, 45
 And it was made of the metal so free,°
That had not the king stepped his foot aside,
 He had smitten his head from his fair body.

Saying, "Fight on, my merry men all,
 And see that none of you be ta'en; 50
For rather than men shall say we were hanged,
 Let them report how we were slain."

Then, God wot,° fair Edinborough rose,
 And so beset poor Johnny round,
That fourscore and ten of Johnny's best men 55
 Lay gasping all upon the ground.

Then like a mad man Johnny laid about,
 And like a mad man then fought he,
Until a false Scot came Johnny behind,
 And run him through the fair body. 60

Saying, "Fight on, my merry men all,
 And see that none of you be ta'en;
For I will stand by and bleed but awhile,
 And then I will come and fight again."

30. **Edinborough:** the capital of Scotland. 46. **metal . . . free:** such noble metal. 53. **wot:** knows.

News then was brought to young Johnny Armstrong, 65
 As he stood by his nurse's knee,
Who vowed if e'er he lived for to be a man,
 On the treacherous Scots revenged he'd be.

Old Christmas

ROY HELTON

This modern ballad is based on an old folk legend of the hill people in Kentucky.
Old Christmas is January 5, the date on which Christmas was celebrated until
about 1750. In some places in the Southern mountains, people still celebrate on
January 5 rather than December 25. Many superstitions are connected with Christ-
mas, such as the old belief that barnyard animals kneel in prayer at midnight on
Christmas Eve, that elderbushes bloom in honor of the Christ Child, and that, until
dawn on Christmas morning, ghosts are free to walk.

"Where you coming from, Lomey° Carter,
 So airly over the snow?
And what's them pretties you got in your hand,
 And where you aiming to go?

"Step in, honey! Old Christmas morning 5
 I ain't got nothing much;
Maybe a bite of sweetness and corn bread,
 A little ham meat and such.

"But come in, honey! Sally Anne Barton's
 Hungering after your face. 10
Wait till I light my candle up:
 Set down! There's your old place.

"Now where you been so airly this morning?"
 "Graveyard, Sally Anne.
Up by the trace° in the salt-lick meadows 15
 Where Taulbe kilt my man."

"Taulbe ain't to home this morning. . . .
 I can't scratch up a light:
Dampness gets on the heads of the matches;
 But I'll blow up the embers bright." 20

1. **Lomey:** a girl's name. 15. **trace:** path.

"Needn't trouble. I won't be stopping:
 Going a long ways still."
"You didn't see nothing, Lomey Carter,
 Up on the graveyard hill?"

"What should I see there, Sally Anne Barton?" 25
 "Well, sperits do walk last night."
"There were an elderbush a-blooming
 While the moon still give some light."

"Yes, elderbushes, they bloom, Old Christmas,
 And critters kneel down in their straw. 30
Anything else up in the graveyard?"

 "One thing more I saw:
I saw my man with his head all bleeding
 Where Taulbe's shot went through."

"What did he say?" 35
 "He stooped and kissed me."
 "What did he say to you?"

"Said, Lord Jesus forguv your Taulbe;
 But he told me another word;
He said it soft when he stooped and kissed me. 40
 That were the last I heard."

"Taulbe ain't to home this morning."

 "I know that, Sally Anne,
For I kilt him coming down through the meadow
 Where Taulbe kilt my man. 45

"I met him upon the meadow trace
 When the moon were fainting fast,
And I had my dead man's rifle gun
 And kilt him as he come past."

"But I heard two shots." 50
 "'Twas his was second:
 He shot me 'fore he died:
You'll find us at daybreak, Sally Anne Barton:
 I'm laying there dead at his side."

La Belle Dame sans Merci

JOHN KEATS

This poem uses a favorite subject of medieval poetry and romance—the supernatural lover. The French title, *"La Belle Dame sans Merci,"* means "the beautiful woman without mercy."

"O what can ail thee, knight-at-arms,
 Alone and palely loitering?
The sedge° has withered from the lake,
 And no birds sing.

"O what can ail thee, knight-at-arms! 5
 So haggard and so woebegone?
The squirrel's granary is full,
 And the harvest's done.

"I see a lily on thy brow
 With anguish moist and fever-dew, 10
And on thy cheeks a fading rose
 Fast withereth, too."

"I met a lady in the meads,
 Full beautiful—a faery's child;
Her hair was long, her foot was light, 15
 And her eyes were wild.

"I made a garland for her head,
 And bracelets, too, and fragrant zone;°
She looked at me as she did love,
 And made sweet moan. 20

"I set her on my pacing steed
 And nothing else saw all day long
For sidelong would she bend, and sing
 A faery's song.

"She found me roots of relish sweet, 25
 And honey wild and manna-dew,
And sure in language strange she said,
 'I love thee true.'

"She took me to her elfin grot,°
 And there she wept and sighed full sore;
And there I shut her wild, wild eyes 31
 With kisses four.

"And there she lullèd me asleep,
 And there I dreamed—Ah! woe betide!
The latest dream I ever dreamed 35
 On the cold hill's side.

"I saw pale kings and princes, too,
 Pale warriors, death-pale were they all;
They cried—'La belle dame sans merci
 Hath thee in thrall!'° 40

"I saw their starved lips in the gloam°
 With horrid warning gapèd wide,
And I awoke and found me here
 On the cold hill's side.

"And this is why I sojourn here, 45
 Alone and palely loitering,
Though the sedge is withered from the
 lake,
 And no birds sing."

3. **sedge** (sej): a coarse, grasslike plant. 18. **zone:** a belt or band.

29. **grot** (grot): a small cave. 40. **thrall** (thrôl): bondage, slavery. 41. **gloam** (glōm): twilight.

The Creation

JAMES WELDON JOHNSON

And God stepped out on space,
And he looked around and said:
I'm lonely—
I'll make me a world.

And far as the eye of God could see 5
Darkness covered everything,
Blacker than a hundred midnights
Down in a cypress swamp.

Then God smiled,
And the light broke, 10
And the darkness rolled up on one side,
And the light stood shining on the other,
And God said: That's good!

Then God reached out and took the light in his hands,
And God rolled the light around in his hands 15
Until he made the sun;
And he set that sun a-blazing in the heavens.
And the light that was left from making the sun
God gathered it up in a shining ball
And flung it against the darkness, 20
Spangling the night with the moon and stars.

Then down between the darkness and the light
He hurled the world;
And God said: That's good!

Then God himself stepped down— 25
And the sun was on his right hand,
And the moon was on his left;
The stars were clustered about his head,

And the earth was under his feet.
And God walked, and where he trod 30
His footsteps hollowed the valleys out
And bulged the mountains up.

Then he stopped and looked and saw
That the earth was hot and barren.
So God stepped over to the edge of the world 35
And he spat out the seven seas—
He batted his eyes, and the lightnings flashed—
He clapped his hands, and the thunders rolled—
And the waters above the earth came down,
The cooling waters came down. 40

Then the green grass sprouted,
And the little red flowers blossomed,
The pine tree pointed his finger to the sky,
And the oak spread out his arms,
The lakes cuddled down in the hollows of the ground, 45
And the rivers ran down to the sea;
And God smiled again,
And the rainbow appeared,
And curled itself around his shoulder.

Then God raised his arm and he waved his hand 50
Over the sea and over the land,
And he said: Bring forth! Bring forth!
And quicker than God could drop his hand,
Fishes and fowls
And beasts and birds 55
Swam the rivers and the seas,
Roamed the forests and the woods,
And split the air with their wings.
And God said: That's good!

Then God walked around, 60
And God looked around
On all that he had made.

He looked at his sun,
And he looked at his moon,
And he looked at his little stars; 65
He looked on his world
With all its living things,
And God said: I'm lonely still.

Then God sat down—
On the side of a hill where he could think; 70
By a deep, wide river he sat down;
With his head in his hands,
God thought and thought,
Till he thought: I'll make me a man!

Up from the bed of the river 75
God scooped the clay;
And by the bank of the river
He kneeled him down;
And there the great God Almighty
Who lit the sun and fixed it in the sky, 80
Who flung the stars to the most far corner of the night,
Who rounded the earth in the middle of his hand;
This Great God,
Like a mammy bending over her baby,
Kneeled down in the dust 85
Toiling over a lump of clay
Till he shaped it in his own image;

Then into it he blew the breath of life,
And man became a living soul.
Amen. Amen. 90

General William Booth Enters into Heaven

(To be sung to the tune of "The Blood of the Lamb"
with indicated instrument)

VACHEL LINDSAY

William Booth (1829–1912), a one-time Methodist preacher, devoted a large part of his life to evangelistic work among the poor of London. In 1878 he founded the Salvation Army to wage war on social evils and bring souls to salvation. Members of the Salvation Army, dressed in military uniforms, attract people to their meetings by playing stirring music and singing hymns on street corners. One of the Army's favorite hymns has the refrain "Are you washed in the blood of the Lamb?"

I

(Bass drum beaten loudly.)
Booth led boldly with his big bass drum—
(Are you washed in the blood of the Lamb?)
The Saints smiled gravely and they said: "He's come."
(Are you washed in the blood of the Lamb?)
Walking lepers° followed, rank on rank, 5
Lurching bravos from the ditches dank,
Drabs from the alleyways and drug fiends pale—
Minds still passion-ridden, soul-powers frail:—
Vermin-eaten saints with moldy breath,
Unwashed legions with the ways of Death— 10
(Are you washed in the blood of the Lamb?)

(Banjos.)
Every slum had sent its half-a-score
The round world over. (Booth had groaned for more.)
Every banner that the wide world flies
Bloomed with glory and transcendent dyes. 15
Big-voiced lasses made their banjos bang;
Tranced, fanatical they shrieked and sang:—
"Are you washed in the blood of the Lamb?"
Hallelujah! It was queer to see
Bull-necked convicts with that land make free. 20
Loons with trumpets blowed a blare, blare, blare
On, on upward thro' the golden air!
(Are you washed in the blood of the Lamb?)

5. **lepers:** those afflicted with leprosy, a contagious disease that causes painful sores. All of Booth's followers—"bravos," "drabs," and "loons"—are like lepers in that they are outcasts from society and avoided by everyone.

(Bass drum slower and softer.)
Booth died blind and still by faith he trod,
Eyes still dazzled by the ways of God. 25
Booth led boldly, and he looked the chief,
Eagle countenance in sharp relief,
Beard a-flying, air of high command
Unabated in that holy land.

(Sweet flute music.)
Jesus came from out the court-house door, 30
Stretched his hands above the passing poor.
Booth saw not, but led his queer ones there
Round and round the mighty court-house square.
Then, in an instant all that blear review
Marched on spotless, clad in raiment new. 35
The lame were straightened, withered limbs uncurled
And blind eyes opened on a new, sweet world.

(Bass drum louder.)
Drabs and vixens in a flash made whole!
Gone was the weasel-head, the snout, the jowl!
Sages and sibyls° now, and athletes clean, 40
Rulers of empires, and of forests green!

(Grand chorus of all instruments. Tambourines to the foreground.)
The hosts were sandaled, and their wings were fire!
(Are you washed in the blood of the Lamb?)
But their noise played havoc with the angel-choir.
(Are you washed in the blood of the Lamb?) 45
Oh, shout Salvation! It was good to see
Kings and Princes by the Lamb set free.
The banjos rattled and the tambourines
Jing-jing-jingled in the hands of Queens.

(Reverently sung, no instruments)
And when Booth halted by the curb for prayer 50
He saw his Master thro' the flag-filled air.
Christ came gently with a robe and crown
For Booth the soldier, while the throng knelt down.
He saw King Jesus. They were face to face,
And he knelt a-weeping in that holy place. 55
(Are you washed in the blood of the Lamb?)

40. **sibyls** (sib′əlz): prophets.

JOHNNY ARMSTRONG

1. Like most folk ballads, "Johnny Armstrong" is dramatic as well as narrative and contains a good deal of dialogue. How many characters speak during the course of the poem?

2. Why do you think Johnny was so willing to go before the king? What kind of person does he show himself to be? Do you admire him as a person? Why or why not?

3. Folk ballads often make abrupt narrative transitions, such as that between the last two stanzas of this poem. What missing action must we fill in here?

4. What does the last stanza add to the story? How does it deepen the tragic effect of the poem?

5. Do the poet's sympathies lie mainly with the king or with Johnny Armstrong? What in the poem makes you think so?

OLD CHRISTMAS

1. Summarize the plot of this story. How many of the characters are alive?

2. Why do you think Sally Anne is so sweet to Lomey at the beginning of the poem? Why is she so insistent in her questioning? What is ironic about the "pretties" that Lomey has in her hand? What does Lomey know that Sally Anne does not?

3. Lomey says, "I won't be stopping: / Going a long ways still." What symbolic meaning do these lines have in light of the ending of the poem?

4. What do you suppose Lomey's man told her when he stooped and kissed her? What makes you think so?

5. The story is told entirely through the dialogue of the two women. Might this poem be classified with equal appropriateness as dramatic poetry?

LA BELLE DAME SANS MERCI

1. What details in the poem suggest that the lady is supernatural? What kind of spirit do you think she is?

2. "The sedge has withered from the lake." A fading rose "fast withereth" on the knight's cheek. What do these details suggest about the knight's condition? Are the lily and the rose in stanza 3 real or figurative? How does the season of the year reinforce the mood and meaning of the poem?

3. Notice how the words *pale* and *palely* are emphasized in the poem. Who are the "death-pale" kings, princes, and warriors who appear in the knight's dream? What has happened to the knight? Why does he "sojourn" there, "palely loitering"? Is he under a spell? *Was* he under a spell? Why is he, like the other men of arms, so pale?

4. Is this poem pure fantasy, or does it suggest moods and feelings in ordinary life?

5. Like "Old Christmas," this literary ballad is told entirely through the dialogue of two speakers. There is also some similarity of subjects: both poems involve love, the supernatural, and kisses exchanged between a mortal and a spirit. Which of the two do you think is more dramatic? more haunting? why?

THE CREATION

1. Unlike a ballad, this poem has no regular meter, rhyme, or stanza. What other poem that you have read so far is it like in this respect? What is this kind of nonmetrical verse called?

2. Though not a ballad, this poem tells a story. The story itself is relatively simple, having only one character and no conflict. What are the main sources of the poem's appeal?

3. The story this poem tells is a creation myth—a story that attempts to explain the creation of things. The original Hebrew account of the creation is given in Genesis 1:2–7 and 9:8–17. This poem is a modern version of that account as it might be presented in a sermon by an old-time preacher. Compare the two versions. How do they differ?

4. What in the poem reminds you of a sermon?

5. This poem makes great use of visual imagery—of pictures presented to the eyes of the imagination. How clearly can you see each of God's actions? What picture do you see when God makes the sun? when God makes the moon and stars?

6. The early parts of the poem emphasize the power and the glory of God. What does

the last part emphasize? What characteristics of God are stressed in the last four verse paragraphs? How does this picture of God prepare us for his making man "in his own image"?

7. If you were going to read this poem aloud, what tone would you use? The closer your tone comes to the poet's attitude, the more fully you have understood his poem. Which of the following qualities do you think are part of the poet's attitude toward the events he describes in "The Creation": wonder, bitterness, reverence, contempt, amusement, awe, praise, jealousy, thankfulness?

GENERAL WILLIAM BOOTH

1. What kind of persons has Booth brought with him to heaven? What happens to them there? Why is it appropriate that it is Jesus who brings about this miracle?

2. How does Lindsay picture heaven? Do you think this is the kind of picture that the followers of William Booth would be likely to have of heaven? Why or why not?

3. This poem might be described as a spirited account of a Salvation Army parade on the streets of heaven or as a piece for jazz band, something like Sandburg's "Four Preludes" (page 293). We have classified it as narrative because it tells of an incident. Do you think some other classification, such as lyric or dramatic (see pages 309 and 317), might do as well? Why or why not?

4. The poem is intended to be accompanied by various musical instruments, and the poet has tried to suggest the sounds of these instruments in the words he has chosen. Notice, for instance, the boom of the drum in the hard *b*'s and *d*'s of the first line. What other sounds contribute to this bass-drum effect? In which lines of the second verse–paragraph is there a "twang" of banjos? How does Lindsay suggest the sound of trumpets? of tambourines? How does the flute section differ rhythmically from the drum section? What line does Lindsay use as a refrain? Why are rhyme and refrain especially appropriate for this poem?

5. What is Lindsay's attitude toward General William Booth? In what tone would you read this poem?

ABOUT THE POETS

Roy Helton (1886–), a native of Washington, D.C. and resident of Pennsylvania, learned the primitive origins of folk poetry by spending long periods in the mountains of South Carolina and Kentucky. He has earned his living as a radio commentator and free-lance writer and served in various capacities as a Pennsylvania state official.

John Keats (1795–1821) was born in London, the son of a livery stable manager. After his early schooling, he was apprenticed to a surgeon. Literature won him away from a medical career, however, and in some six years of serious writing, before his death from tuberculosis at the age of twenty-six, he wrote poems which have established him as among the greatest poets of the language. His best-known poems, besides "La Belle Dame Sans Merci," are "On First Looking into Chapman's Homer," "The Eve of St. Agnes," "Ode to a Nightingale," "Ode on Melancholy," and "Ode on a Grecian Urn."

James Weldon Johnson (1871–1938), American poet and essayist, received his B.A. and M.A. degrees from Atlanta University and studied for three years at Columbia University. During the course of an exceedingly versatile career he was a high school principal, the first Negro attorney admitted to the Florida bar since the War Between the States, a successful songwriter and opera librettist, a United States consul in Venezuela and Nicaragua, secretary of the N.A.A.C.P., and a professor of literature. His best-known book is his fictional *Autobiography of an Ex-Colored Man.*

Vachel Lindsay (1879–1931) was born in Springfield, Illinois, a city he always revered because of its associations with Lincoln. First an art student and later a poet, he illustrated some of his own books with his delicate, unique drawings. During his late twenties and early thirties, he made several vagabond walking tours through the country, reciting his poems in return for food and lodging. Later he toured the country, giving public recitations, in which he chanted his poems in his rich baritone voice. His most famous poem is "The Congo."

LYRIC POETRY

In a lyric poem the poet expresses his personal thoughts and feelings. This does not mean, of course, that lyrical poems should be read as bits of auto-biography like entries in a diary. A poet, even when he is being most personal, writes more as a representative man than as Henry A. or Arthur B. He is creating a work of art, to be read by many readers, and he feels free to change facts and circumstances for the sake of artistic truth. If he writes about something that happened on Wednesday, it may be more meaningful if he writes of it as happening on Sunday. If he is inspired to write a love poem to a girl named Mabelle Ellen Pflugmann, the intensity of his feeling may be better conveyed if he changes her name to Evelyn Hope or Annabel Lee. Also, of course, a poet is quite capable of imagining emotions that he has never directly felt at all. Just as Jack Finney in "Contents of the Dead Man's Pockets" (page 3) vividly conveys the sensations of a man trapped on an eleventh-story ledge, though he himself probably was never caught in that predicament, and just as Shakespeare in *Macbeth* vividly expresses the emotions of a murderer, although Shakespeare never murdered a man, so a lyric poet may write of feelings and emotions he has partly felt and partly guessed at or imagined. The line between lyric and dramatic poetry is very thin, and it is perhaps best to think of every poem as a fiction and of its speaker as simply a man or a woman rather than as the poet.

Originally, a lyric poem was a song accompanied by a small harp, or *lyre*. Even today, the purest lyric poems are brief and songlike and express a single thought or feeling. Since many poems are classified as lyric, however, simply because they are not either dramatic or narrative, many poems that we call lyrics have little resemblance to songs. Thus some lyric poems are more lyrical—more songlike—than others. There are many kinds and forms of lyric poem. Some of these have names; others do not and can be classified only as lyric poems. Among the best-known kinds which have names are the song (including the lullaby), the sonnet, the ode, and the elegy. All of these are illustrated in the poems that follow, as are also the haiku (a Japanese form) and the epigram, which isn't very songlike but is included in lyric poetry because it is neither narrative nor dramatic and because it expresses a thought or feeling. Some of these kinds are characterized by their special poetic form, others by a special kind of subject matter.

In some ways lyric poetry is the purest kind of poetry. A narrative poem tells a story which can be translated into prose and still retain some interest. A dramatic poem enacts a situation or a conflict which might also be cast into prose and perhaps performed as a play. A lyric poem depends for its impact, however, almost entirely on the quality of its language and the perfection of its form. To attempt to translate it into prose is to shear off its wings and to reduce it to a dead thing rather than let it sing and soar.

Sweet and Low

ALFRED, LORD TENNYSON

Sweet and low, sweet and low,
　Wind of the western sea,
Low, low, breathe and blow,
　Wind of the western sea!
　Over the rolling waters go,　　　　　　　5
　Come from the dying moon, and blow,
　Blow him again to me;
While my little one, while my pretty one sleeps.

Sleep and rest, sleep and rest,
　Father will come to thee soon;　　　　　　10
Rest, rest, on mother's breast,
　Father will come to thee soon;
　Father will come to his babe in the nest,
　Silver sails all out of the west
　Under the silver moon;　　　　　　　　15
Sleep, my little one, sleep, my pretty one, sleep.

Blow, Blow, Thou Winter Wind

WILLIAM SHAKESPEARE

Blow, blow, thou winter wind,
Thou art not so unkind
　As man's ingratitude;
Thy tooth is not so keen,
Because thou art not seen,　　　　　　　　5
　Although thy breath be rude.
Heigh-ho! sing, heigh-ho! unto the green holly:
Most friendship is feigning, most loving mere folly.
　Then heigh-ho! the holly!
　This life is most jolly.　　　　　　　　10

Freeze, freeze, thou bitter sky,
That dost not bite so nigh °
　As benefits forgot:
Though thou the waters warp,

12. **nigh:** near.

Thy sting is not so sharp
 As friend remembered not.
Heigh-ho! sing, heigh-ho! unto the green holly:
Most friendship is feigning, most loving mere folly.
 Then heigh-ho! the holly!
 This life is most jolly. 20

The Lake Isle of Innisfree

WILLIAM BUTLER YEATS

Innisfree is an island in Lough (Lake) Gill in western Ireland, where William But-
ler Yeats spent many childhood summers. The inspiration for this poem came to him
on the crowded streets of London.

I will arise and go now, and go to Innisfree,
And a small cabin build there, of clay and wattles made:
Nine bean rows will I have there, a hive for the honeybee,
And live alone in the bee-loud glade.

And I shall have some peace there, for peace comes dropping slow, 5
Dropping from the veils of the morning to where the cricket sings;
There midnight's all a glimmer, and noon a purple glow,
And evening full of the linnet's ° wings.

I will arise and go now, for always night and day
I hear lake water lapping with low sounds by the shore; 10
While I stand on the roadway, or on the pavements gray,
I hear it in the deep heart's core.

 8. **linnet's:** A linnet is a songbird.

"The Lake Isle of Innisfree" from *Collected Poems* by W. B. Yeats, copyright 1906 by The Macmillan
Company; renewed 1934 by William Butler Yeats. Reprinted by permission of the publishers, M. B.
Yeats, Miss Anne Yeats and the Macmillan Co. of London & Basingstoke.

When in Disgrace with Fortune and Men's Eyes

WILLIAM SHAKESPEARE

When in disgrace with fortune and men's eyes
I all alone beweep my outcast state,
And trouble deaf heaven with my bootless° cries,
And look upon myself, and curse my fate,
Wishing me like to one more rich in hope, 5
Featured like him, like him with friends possessed,
Desiring this man's art, and that man's scope,°
With what I most enjoy contented least;
Yet in these thoughts myself almost despising,
Haply° I think on thee—and then my state, 10
Like to the lark at break of day arising
From sullen earth, sings hymns at heaven's gate;
 For thy sweet love remembered such wealth brings
 That then I scorn to change my state with kings.

3. **bootless:** futile, useless. 7. **scope:** range of mind; wisdom. 10. **haply:** by chance.

Ode

The Dying Christian to his Soul

ALEXANDER POPE

I

Vital spark of heavenly flame!
Quit, oh quit this mortal frame:
 Trembling, hoping, lingering, flying,
 Oh the pain, the bliss of dying!
Cease, fond° Nature, cease thy strife, 5
And let me languish into life.

II

Hark! they whisper; Angels say,
Sister Spirit, come away.

5. **fond:** foolish.

What is this absorbs me quite?
 Steals my senses, shuts my sight, 10
Drowns my spirits, draws my breath?
Tell me, my Soul, can this be Death?

III

The world recedes; it disappears!
Heav'n opens on my eyes! my ears
 With sounds seraphic° ring: 15
Lend, lend your wings! I mount! I fly!
O Grave! where is thy Victory?
 O Death! where is thy Sting?

15. **seraphic:** angelic.

Elegy

ROBERT BRIDGES

An *elegy* is a poem of mourning or lamentation for the dead. Usually it expresses sorrow over the death of someone the poet admired or loved; sometimes it simply mourns the passing of all life and beauty.

> The wood is bare: a river mist is steeping
> The trees that winter's chill of life bereaves:
> Only their stiffened boughs break silence, weeping
> Over their fallen leaves;

> That lie upon the dank earth brown and rotten, 5
> Miry and matted in the soaking wet:
> Forgotten with the spring, that is forgotten
> By them that can forget.

> Yet it was here we walked when ferns were springing,
> And through the mossy bank shot bud and blade:— 10
> Here found in summer, when the birds were singing,
> A green and pleasant shade.

> 'Twas here we loved in sunnier days and greener:
> And now, in this disconsolate decay,
> I come to see her where I most have seen her, 15
> And touch the happier day.

> For on this path, at every turn and corner,
> The fancy of her figure on me falls:
> Yet walks she with the slow step of a mourner,
> Nor hears my voice that calls. 20

> So through my heart there winds a track of feeling,
> A path of memory, that is all her own:
> Whereto her phantom beauty ever stealing
> Haunts the sad spot alone.

> About her steps the trunks are bare, the branches 25
> Drip heavy tears upon her downcast head;
> And bleed from unseen wounds that no sun stanches,
> For the year's sun is dead.

> And dead leaves wrap the fruits that summer planted:
> And birds that love the South have taken wing. 30
> The wanderer, loitering o'er the scene enchanted,
> Weeps, and despairs of spring.

Six Haiku

Translated by Harold G. Henderson

Haiku (hǐ′kōō) are very brief Japanese lyric poems. Like sonnets, they have a rigid form. A haiku consists of three lines, the first having five syllables, the second having seven, and the third, five. It is impossible to properly translate haiku while preserving this syllable count. The translator of the following haiku has attempted to preserve the sense of formal structure by making the first and third lines rhyme. The essence of the art of haiku is to communicate a mood, a thought, or an emotion with the greatest possible impact within the limits of the form. Because haiku are so short, the haiku-maker relies on subtle but rich suggestion through image, symbol, and allusion. In a haiku, every word counts.

1

A fluttering swarm
 of cherry petals;—and there comes
 pursuing them, the storm!
 Sadaiye (thirteenth century)

2

The grove in spring:
 even the birds that prey on birds
 are slumbering.
 Rankō (eighteenth century)

3

Banked fires; night grows late—
 then comes a sound of rapping
 at the gate.
 Kyoroku (seventeenth century)

4

The piercing chill I feel:
 my dead wife's comb, in our bedroom,
 under my heel . . .
 Buson (eighteenth century)

5

A snake! Though it passes,
 eyes that had glared at me
 stay in the grasses.
 Kyoshi (nineteenth century)

6

Night, and the moon!
 My neighbor, playing on his flute—
 out of tune!
 Kōyō (nineteenth century)

FOR STUDY AND DISCUSSION

SWEET AND LOW
BLOW, BLOW, THOU WINTER WIND

1. These two poems, which were written to be sung as songs, are a good illustration of the perils of definition and classification. Both are unquestionably lyrics, yet Tennyson's is a lullaby sung by a mother to her baby, and Shakespeare's is the bitter lament of an exiled lord. Of course Tennyson was never a mother, and Shakespeare was never an exiled lord. Thus both poems are *dramatic* lyrics, expressing imagined rather than purely personal emotions. How do the thoughts expressed in each song reflect the situation of its singer?

2. Tennyson's poem is a prayer as well as a lullaby. The lullaby is meant to put the baby to sleep. What is the prayer for? Why are the two connected in the singer's mind?

3. What, would you guess, is the occupation of the baby's father? What evidence is there of this in the poem?

4. The speaker in Tennyson's poem asks the wind to blow gently; the speaker in Shakespeare's seems to ask it to blow sharply. Is this what he means? What does he mean? What do the winter wind and bitter sky stand for in the poem? Which disturbs the speaker more—these qualities in nature or what they remind him of in man?

5. In "Blow, Blow, Thou Winter Wind," how do the last four lines of each stanza compare in tone with the first six? In what tone of voice would you read these lines?

THE LAKE ISLE OF INNISFREE

1. This lyric expresses a personal emotion. Is it a purely private emotion, or one that many people have probably felt at one time or another? Have you ever felt such an emotion? When?

2. Why does the poet wish for a small cabin of clay and wattles rather than for a roomier house of brick or stone? What kind of life does he wish for? What in his present surroundings do you think makes him wish for this?

3. Why do you think the poet specifies *nine* bean rows? Considering that the lyric poet feels free to sacrifice factual truth to artistic truth, do you think Yeats chose the number nine for agricultural or poetic reasons?

4. This is one of the most popular poems of the last hundred years. What are the main sources of its poetic appeal? Which lines contain striking images or metaphors? How is a mood created with sound and rhythm?

WHEN IN DISGRACE

1. Into how many parts does the rhyme scheme divide this poem? How do the poet's thoughts correspond to this division? What idea is expressed in each group of lines?

2. Two of the lines of this poem end with an approximate rather than a perfect rhyme (for instance, *north* and *worth* is an approximate rhyme, whereas *north* and *forth* is a perfect rhyme). Which two? Is this a flaw in the poem, do you think, or is an off-rhyme a better echo of the meaning in the lines?

3. The lark and the nightingale are probably the two favorite birds of English poets. Look up the lark (skylark) in a bird book or encyclopedia and find out what habits it is known for. What is remarkable about its song? What does the lark suggest or symbolize as Shakespeare has used it in this poem?

THE SONNET

A *sonnet* is a lyric poem with a prescribed form. It has fourteen lines, and the lines are always iambic pentameter (that is, they consist normally of ten syllables with every second syllable accented).

There are two traditional rhyme schemes for a sonnet—the English (or Shakespearean) and the Italian. "When In Disgrace with Fortune and Men's Eyes" is an English sonnet, and so has three *quatrains* (stanzas of four lines) followed by a *couplet* (two consecutive lines that rhyme). We indicate rhyme schemes in poetry by assigning a letter of the alphabet to each rhyme sound. Thus the rhyme scheme of the first quatrain is *abab;* of the second, *cdcd.* What is the rhyme scheme of the whole poem?

FOR STUDY AND DISCUSSION

ODE: THE DYING CHRISTIAN TO HIS SOUL

1. An *ode* is an exalted lyric poem, aiming at loftier thought, more dignified expression, and a more intricate formal structure than most lyrics. Another characteristic of odes is that they are often addressed to someone or something. Who is the speaker in this ode? To whom or what is he speaking?

2. What thought is expressed in the first stanza? Why does the speaker wish the "vital spark of heavenly flame" to leave his "mortal frame"? What pain is involved in dying? what bliss? What is Nature striving against? What "life" does the speaker expect to "languish into"?

3. What happens to the speaker in the second stanza? in the third? How are his expectations fulfilled?

4. Like many odes, this poem is divided into numbered stanzas. How do these breaks between stanzas aid in reading the poem?

ELEGY

1. In this elegy the poet never speaks directly of his own sorrow. He doesn't say, "My heart is filled with pain," or "My eyes are full of tears." How does he suggest his grief?

2. What images in the first two stanzas make clear the poet's state of mind? What is implied by line 8?

3. Who is the "figure" in stanzas 5, 6, and 7? Why does this place recall it to the poet's mind? Why does it walk with "the slow step of a mourner"? How has the poet's memory "enchanted" the scene?

4. What are the "tears" in stanza 7? What "wounds" do trees have in the fall? What symbolical use of nature and the seasons is made throughout the poem?

SIX HAIKU

1. A *haiku* is intended to suggest a single mood, thought, or feeling. What mood, thought, or feeling is suggested by each of these haiku? Which did you think humorous? Which did you find most moving? Why?

2. In the fifth haiku, do the snake's eyes actually stay in the grasses? What does the poet mean? Is this an example of metaphor? Why or why not?

3. In how many of these haiku do specific objects suggest a wider, symbolic meaning? What is symbolized by each?

FOR COMPOSITION

Try your hand at writing a haiku. Recall a particular mood, thought, or feeling, and express it in a haiku of three lines. Try to use simple images that suggest a wider meaning.

ABOUT THE POETS

Alfred, Lord Tennyson (1809–1892) was England's chief poetic spokesman during the age of Queen Victoria. Brought up in Lincolnshire, the son of a clergyman, he attended Cambridge University and devoted his life to poetry. His most ambitious works were *In Memoriam* and *Idylls of the King,* but he is also known for numerous short lyrics. He was Poet Laureate of England for over forty years.

William Shakespeare (1564–1616), after a grammar school education and an early marriage, went from the market town of Stratford-on-Avon to London to become an actor and perhaps the world's greatest playwright-poet. He is known for his narrative poems, such as *Venus and Adonis;* his powerful sonnets; his comedies, such as *The Taming of the Shrew, Twelfth Night,* and *As You Like It;* his history plays, such as *Henry IV, Henry V,* and *Richard II;* and his tragedies, especially *Romeo and Juliet, Macbeth, Hamlet, Othello, King Lear,* and *Julius Caesar* (see page 386). After a highly successful career in London, he retired to Stratford and in his last years lived the life of a country gentleman.

William Butler Yeats (1865–1939) was almost single-handedly responsible for the revival of Irish literature around the turn of the century. Born in Ireland, the son of a well-known painter, he divided his life between western Ireland, Dublin, and London. As poet, as playwright, and as editor, he gained new respect for Celtic tradition and native Irish literature. Widely regarded as the greatest poet in English of the twentieth century, Yeats was awarded the Nobel prize for literature in 1923.

Alexander Pope (1688–1744) was born in London, the son of a well-to-do linen draper. A precocious lad, he early established himself as the leading poet of his time and the center of a brilliant literary group that included Jonathan Swift and John Gay. A satirist and moralist, he is remembered for *The Rape of the Lock, An Essay on Man, An Epistle to Dr. Arbuthnot,* and *The Dunciad.* Because of his gift for epigram, he is probably, after Shakespeare, the most quoted poet in the English language.

Robert Bridges (1844–1930) was born on an island in Kent, England, and was educated at Eton and Oxford. An athlete and musician, he studied medicine and served on the staffs of various London hospitals until, in 1882, he was able to retire and devote himself to poetry. In 1913 he was made Poet Laureate. One of his most important services to poetry was rescuing from obscurity the poems of his friend Gerard Manley Hopkins (see page 326), whose example has done much to introduce freer rhythms into modern poetry.

DRAMATIC POETRY

A dramatic poem presents one or more characters speaking, usually to each other, but sometimes to themselves or directly to the reader. The main characteristic of a dramatic poem is that the speaker is not the poet. Usually a dramatic poem has many of the characteristics of a play: a definite setting, a dramatic situation, emotional conflict, vigorous speech, and natural language rhythms. Just as some lyric poems are more lyrical than others, so some dramatic poems are more dramatic, or dramalike, than others. The purest example of dramatic poetry is a verse play, such as the plays of Shakespeare. Some critics, making a fine distinction, call verse plays poetic drama rather than dramatic poetry. In any case, the more dramatic a poem becomes, the more it reminds us of a play.

The dramatic monologue is a special form of dramatic poem. In a dramatic monologue one character speaks to another or other characters, whose replies are not given in the poem. The occasion is always a crucial moment in the speaker's life, and what he says on this occasion reveals his character and much of his past history. Reading a dramatic monologue is like listening to one end of a telephone conversation: from what is said at your end you must imagine what is said at the other.

The most famous dramatic monologue in English is "My Last Duchess," by Robert Browning. "The Laboratory," also by Browning, is another excellent example of this intensely dramatic kind of poem.

The Laboratory

Ancien Régime

ROBERT BROWNING

The phrase *Ancien Régime* ("The Old Order" in French) places this poem in France during the century or so before the French Revolution, when aristocrats involved in the whirl of court life had very little on their minds besides dancing, gossip, rivalries, and intrigue.

> Now that I, tying thy glass mask° tightly,
> May gaze through these faint smokes curling whitely,
> As thou pliest thy trade in this devil's smithy—
> Which is the poison to poison her, prithee?°

1. **glass mask:** a face mask worn for protection against poisonous fumes. 4. **prithee:** I pray thee.

He is with her; and they know that I know 5
Where they are, what they do. They believe my tears flow
While they laugh, laugh at me, at me fled to the drear
Empty church, to pray God in, for them!—I am here.

Grind away, moisten, and mash up thy paste,
Pound at thy powder—I am not in haste! 10
Better sit thus, and observe thy strange things,
Than go where men wait me and dance at the King's.

That in the mortar°—you call it a gum?
Ah, the brave tree whence such gold oozings come!
And yonder soft phial,° the exquisite blue, 15
Sure to taste sweetly—is that poison too?

Had I but all of them, thee and thy treasures,
What a wild crowd of invisible pleasures!
To carry pure death in an earring, a casket,
A signet, a fan mount, a filigree basket! 20

Soon, at the King's, a mere lozenge° to give,
And Pauline should have just thirty minutes to live!
But to light a pastille,° and Elise, with her head,
And her breast, and her arms, and her hands, should drop dead!

Quick—is it finished? The color's too grim! 25
Why not soft like the phial's, enticing and dim?
Let it brighten her drink, let her turn it and stir,
And try it and taste, ere she fix and prefer!

What, a drop? She's not little, no minion like me!
That's why she ensnared him; this never will free 30
The soul from those masculine eyes—say, "no!"
To that pulse's magnificent come and go.

For only last night, as they whispered, I brought
My own eyes to bear on her so, that I thought
Could I keep them one-half-minute fixed, she would fall, 35
Shriveled; she fell not; yet this does it all!

Not that I bid you spare her the pain!
Let death be felt and the proof remain;
Brand, burn up, bite into its grace—
He is sure to remember her dying face! 40

13. **mortar** (môr′tər): a very hard bowl in which softer substances are ground or pounded
to a powder. 15. **phial** (fi′əl): a small glass bottle. 21. **lozenge** (loz′inj): a cough drop or
piece of candy. 23. **pastille**: a small candle used to perfume a room.

Is it done? Take my mask off! Nay, be not morose;
It kills her, and this prevents seeing it close:
The delicate droplet, my whole fortune's fee—
If it hurts her, beside, can it ever hurt me?

Now, take all my jewels, gorge gold to your fill, 45
You may kiss me, old man, on my mouth if you will!
But brush this dust off me, lest horror it brings
Ere I know it—next moment I dance at the King's!

Lord Randal

ANONYMOUS

"O where hae ye been, Lord Randal, my son?
O where hae ye been, my handsome young man?"
"I hae been to the wild wood; mother, make my bed soon,
For I'm weary wi' hunting, and fain wald° lie down."

"Where gat ye your dinner, Lord Randal, my son? 5
Where gat ye your dinner, my handsome young man?"
"I dined wi' my true love; mother, make my bed soon,
For I'm weary wi' hunting, and fain wald lie down."

"What gat ye to your dinner, Lord Randal, my son?
What gat ye to your dinner, my handsome young man?" 10
"I gat eels boiled in broo;° mother, make my bed soon,
For I'm weary wi' hunting, and fain wald lie down."

"What became of your bloodhounds, Lord Randal, my son?
What became of your bloodhounds, my handsome young man?"
"O they swelled and they died; mother, make my bed soon, 15
For I'm weary wi' hunting, and fain wald lie down."

"O I fear ye are poisoned, Lord Randal, my son!
O I fear ye are poisoned, my handsome young man!"
"O yes! I am poisoned; mother, make my bed soon,
For I'm sick at the heart, and I fain wald lie down." 20

4. **fain wald:** would like to. 11. **broo:** broth, soup.

Danny Deever

RUDYARD KIPLING

The scene of this poem is a British army post in India at about the turn of the century. The Color Sergeant is the flag bearer of a troop. Files-on-Parade is a soldier with special duties on occasions when troops are assembled in formation.

"What are the bugles blowin' for?" said Files-on-Parade.
"To turn you out, to turn you out," the Color Sergeant said.
"What makes you look so white, so white?" said Files-on-Parade.
"I'm dreadin' what I've got to watch," the Color Sergeant said.
 For they're hangin' Danny Deever, you can 'ear the dead march play, 5
 The regiment's in 'ollow square—they're hangin' him today;
 They've taken of his buttons off an' cut his stripes away,
 An' they're hangin' Danny Deever in the mornin'.

"What makes the rear rank breathe so 'ard?" said Files-on-Parade.
"It's bitter cold, it's bitter cold," the Color Sergeant said. 10
"What makes that front-rank man fall down?" says Files-on-Parade.
"A touch o' sun, a touch o' sun," the Color Sergeant said,
 They are hangin' Danny Deever, they are marchin' of 'im round,
 They 'ave 'alted Danny Deever by 'is coffin on the ground;
 An' 'e'll swing in 'arf a minute for a sneakin', shootin' hound— 15
 O they're hangin' Danny Deever in the mornin'!

"'Is cot was right-'and cot to mine," said Files-on-Parade.
" 'E's sleepin' out an' far tonight," the Color Sergeant said.
"I've drunk 'is beer a score o' times," said Files-on-Parade.
"E's drinkin' bitter beer alone," the Color Sergeant said. 20
 They are hangin' Danny Deever, you must mark 'im to 'is place,
 For 'e shot a comrade sleepin'—you must look 'im in the face;
 Nine 'undred of 'is county an' the regiment's disgrace,
 While they're hangin' Danny Deever in the mornin'.

"What's that so black agin the sun?" said Files-on-Parade. 25
"It's Danny fightin' 'ard for life," the Color Sergeant said.
"What's that that whimpers over'ead?" said Files-on-Parade.
"It's Danny's soul that's passin' now," the Color Sergeant said.
 For they're done with Danny Deever, you can 'ear the quickstep play,
 The regiment's in column, an' they're marchin' us away; 30
 Ho! the young recruits are shakin', an' they'll want their beer today,
 After hangin' Danny Deever in the mornin'.

Bredon Hill

A. E. HOUSMAN

In summertime on Bredon
 The bells they sound so clear;
Round both the shires they ring them
 In steeples far and near,
 A happy noise to hear. 5

Here of a Sunday morning
 My love and I would lie,
And see the colored counties,
 And hear the larks so high
 About us in the sky. 10

The bells would ring to call her
 In valleys miles away:
"Come all to church, good people;
 Good people, come and pray."
 But here my love would stay. 15

And I would turn and answer
 Among the springing thyme,°
"Oh, peal upon our wedding,
 And we will hear the chime,
 And come to church in time." 20

But when the snows at Christmas
 On Bredon top were strown,
My love rose up so early
 And stole out unbeknown
 And went to church alone. 25

They tolled the one bell only,
 Groom there was none to see,
The mourners followed after,
 And so to church went she,
 And would not wait for me. 30

The bells they sound on Bredon,
 And still the steeples hum.
"Come all to church, good people,"—
 Oh, noisy bells, be dumb;
 I hear you, I will come. 35

Fear

HART CRANE

The host, he says that all is well
And the firewood glow is bright;
The food has a warm and tempting smell—
But on the window licks the night.

Pile on the logs. . . . Give me your hands, 5
Friends! No—it is not fright. . . .
But hold me . . . somewhere I heard demands. . . .
And on the window licks the night.

FOR STUDY AND DISCUSSION

THE LABORATORY

1. Who is the speaker in this dramatic monologue? Where is she? To whom is she speaking? What does she plan to do?

2. Who are the "he" and the "her" mentioned in stanza 2? Why does the speaker think they are laughing at her?

3. What does the speaker's intended victim look like? How is she unlike the speaker? Which lines tell you so?

4. What kind of person is the speaker? What passions are driving her? What do we learn about her from her reference to the church (lines 7–8)? from her remark that she is "not in haste" (line 10)? from what she dreams of doing (lines 19–24)? from her impatience (line 25)? from her self-consciousness about her size (line 29)? from the effect she wishes the poison to have on her victim (lines 37–40)? from the way she pays for the poison (lines 45–46)?

5. Notice the ironic contrast between the apothecary's shop with its fuming poisons and the King's palace, where exquisitely dressed and jeweled courtiers dance, flirt, and make elegant conversation. Does this contrast symbolically mirror a similar contrast between the inner passions and outer refinement of the speaker? Explain. How does the speaker appear to others? In what sense is she actually in hell?

LORD RANDAL

1. What is the dramatic situation in this poem?

2. Like "Johnny Armstrong" (page 297), this poem is a folk ballad and might have been classified as narrative poetry. What about the way it is told, however, makes it more dramatic—more dramalike—than "Johnny Armstrong"? Where does the poet begin, at the beginning or the climax of his tale? What does he gain by this? What does he lose?

3. If you were staging this little drama, how would you set the scene?

4. Like "The Laboratory," this is a story of poisoning. What are the main differences between the two poems? Which arouses deeper feelings? Why?

5. This ballad uses a common ballad device known as *incremental repetition*. Each stanza repeats most of the phrases of the preceding one but adds a few new details (*increments*) to advance the story. What are the advantages of this device for the singer? What are the advantages for the audience? What change in the pattern in the last stanza adds impact to the climax of the poem?

DANNY DEEVER

1. Of the Color Sergeant and Files-on-Parade, which is an old-timer in the army? Why has the regiment been called out?

2. What sort of person was Danny Deever? How do the speakers feel toward him? Is the poem primarily about Danny Deever or about the effect of his hanging on the rest of the regiment? Do his comrades regard him as a hardened criminal or as someone like themselves? What in the poem makes you think so?

3. How do you explain the apparent change in weather between lines 10 and 12? Why do you think the Color Sergeant answers as he does?

4. This modern ballad draws many of its techniques from the old folk ballads. What similarities of narrative and dramatic method do you find between "Danny Deever" and "Lord Randal"?

BREDON HILL

1. Why is it fitting that the first four stanzas of the poem are set in summer and the last three in winter? What is suggested or symbolized by this change in season? At exactly what time of year does the speaker's sweetheart die? How is this ironical?

2. For what purpose do the bells summon the people to church? For what purpose does the speaker promise he and his love will come? She actually does go—for yet another reason. What occasion does the speaker have in mind when, at the end of the poem, he once more promises to come?

3. In what tone of voice should the last two lines be spoken? Why?

4. This poem might have been classified as narrative, lyric, or dramatic. It tells a story; it is lyrical in structure and mood; and the speaker is not the poet. How is this poem less of a dramatic poem than "The Laboratory," "Lord Randal," and "Danny Deever"?

FEAR

1. This poem could be classified as a lyric and perhaps would be by most readers. Yet in it a character speaks to other persons. What else is dramatic about this poem?

2. How do you feel when you read "on the window licks the night"? How and why is this different from "night is falling" or "it is growing dark outside"?

3. Do the warm, well-lighted, well-provisioned room and the night outside suggest any symbolic meanings?

ABOUT THE POETS

Robert Browning (1812–1889) is the most outstanding writer of dramatic poems in English literature. He is particularly famous for his dramatic monologues, a form which he brought to a peak of development and for which he achieved special recognition. Browning's interest in history, music, art, and poetry is reflected in his writing. The story of his elopement with Elizabeth Barrett, at the time a much better-known poet than himself, is a famous one.

Rudyard Kipling (1865–1936) grew up in India and England, and knew at first-hand the attitudes and feelings of British soldiers stationed in the colonies. For more on his life and writings, see page 67.

Though he was born and grew up, not in Shropshire, but in the neighboring county of Worcestershire, **A. E. Housman** (1859–1936) gained fame as the author of *A Shropshire Lad,* his first book of poems. Educated at Oxford University, he worked for ten years after graduation as a clerk in the London Patent Office, then became a Professor of Latin, first in London and later at Cambridge. Housman was a severe critic of his own work, destroyed what did not meet his own high standards, and left behind him a small body of poems of unquestionable excellence.

Hart Crane (1899–1932) grew up in Ohio and is best known for a long poem about America, *The Bridge*. The child of well-to-do divorced parents, Crane had many difficulties in his personal life. He worked as an advertising copywriter, a laborer, and a clerk in his father's candy factory before going to New York to spend ten furious years working on his long epic poem. Finally, worn down by work and the feeling that his best years were behind him, he threw himself off a ship that was bringing him back to New York from Mexico.

THE LANGUAGE OF POETRY

In the nineteenth century, which often took itself too seriously, poets and critics were fond of defining poetry in terms such as "Lofty thoughts expressed in noble language" or "Beauty dressed out in melodious words." From the poems you have read so far, you know better. There is nothing lofty about the thoughts of the scheming woman in "The Laboratory" (page 317), and her emotions are no more lovely than those of the cruel and narrow-minded peasants in Maupassant's "The Piece of Yarn" (page 150). We do not expect short stories, plays, and novels to be concerned only with the lofty, the noble, and the beautiful, so why should we expect this of poetry? The subject matter of poetry, like that of all literature, is life.

If we do not limit the subject matter of poetry to the lofty and the beautiful, neither need we put any limitations on its language. Is there anything noble, or even melodious, about the language in "Old Christmas" (page 299)?

> "Step in, honey! Old Christmas morning
> I ain't got nothing much."

Your English teacher will tell you, forcefully too, that there "ain't nothing noble" about "ain't got nothing much"!

What kind of language, then, is used in poetry? What kind of words does the poet seek? The answer is simple. A poet seeks, not the most beautiful words, but the most *meaningful*—those that are most expressive, most suggestive, and fullest of life and meaning. Thus the language of poetry is almost unlimited. The most meaningful word in one context may be a lofty one; in another it may be a very common one. In "Old Christmas" the words "I ain't got nothing much" are much more expressive of character and situation than "I don't have anything much" or "I have nothing much."

The language of poetry is potentially unlimited, but there are fashions in poetic language, just as there are fashions in clothes. For centuries most readers could recognize "poetry" by its use of words like *thee* and *thou, dost* and *didst, e'en* and *o'er,* and *midst* and *'tis.* These, of course, are usually the least important words in a poem, but for a modern reader they may seem stilted and artificial. There is no reason, though, to be put off by words such as these. *Thee* and *thou, dost* and *didst* are the formal language of a more formal age, dignified by use in the King James Bible. For poets and readers of an earlier time, words like these gave a dignity to writing that could not be given by other, more ordinary terms. When we read poems of a former age today, we should respect this dignity, even though we may find such terms ridiculous in a modern poem. We do not think less of George Washington and Thomas Jefferson because they wore powdered wigs, although we would laugh at a modern man who wore one.

E'en, o'er, 'midst, and *'tis* belong to a different category. They were valued, not for their dignity, but for their usefulness in meeting the requirements of strictly regular rhythm. They belong to an age when most poetry was written in more rigid meters than is customary today. We can accept these words in the poetry of an era when women wore whalebone and stays, though in modern poetry, which permits more flexible rhythms, they would seem like museum relics. We can also be tolerant toward the inversions, or departures from normal word order, so often found in older poetry. These too were sacrifices to the strict laws of meter. Today a good poet departs from normal word order only to gain an emphasis or meaning otherwise unobtainable.

Poetry might be defined as language that "says more and talks less" than ordinary language. For poetry employs language in its most compressed, most *concentrated* form. A good poet chooses words that are rich in meaning and avoids those that are not. He does this in several ways. First, he sometimes uses words that have more than one dictionary meaning or *denotation,* as in the following two-line poem by an unknown poet:

Epitaph

This famous painter met his death
Because he could not draw his breath.

Second, the poet enriches his language by choosing words for what they suggest as well as for what they mean; that is, he uses words that are richly *connotative*—words that stir our minds with associated ideas or feelings. In the phrase "the vagrant gypsy life" from Masefield's "Sea Fever" (page 291), the word *gypsy* is richly connotative because it not only means—or *denotes*—"wandering" but also calls to mind—or *connotes*—all the color and romance and glamour associated with those picturesque people, the gypsies. In Roy Helton's "Old Christmas," the words "ain't got nothing much" are more suggestive and meaningful than "don't have anything much" because they tell us much about the speaker's social class and education. Third, the poet is impatient of words which do not carry a full freight of image or emotion. Words like *the, a, and, but, which, in,* etc., are necessary to establish logical connections, but they have little emotional and imaginative value, and the poet sometimes omits them. Finally, the poet occasionally chooses words whose sound is expressive of meaning. In "Four Preludes on Playthings of the Wind" (page 293), Carl Sandburg uses the words *chatter, babble,* and *gabble* because they sound like what they mean.

Sensitivity to words and shades of meaning is the first quality required of a good poet. It is also the first quality required of a good reader, especially a reader of poetry.

Fear No More

WILLIAM SHAKESPEARE

This poem, from the play *Cymbeline,* is
spoken by two countrymen over the appar-
ently dead body of a young stranger whom
they believe to be of noble birth but cast out by
treachery from his rightful place.

Fear no more the heat o' the sun,
 Nor the furious winter's rages;
Thou thy worldly task hast done,
 Home art gone, and ta'en thy wages.
Golden lads and girls all must, 5
As chimney sweepers, come to dust.

Fear no more the frown o' the great;
 Thou art past the tyrant's stroke;
Care no more to clothe and eat;
 To thee the reed is as the oak. 10
The scepter, learning, physic,° must
All follow this, and come to dust.

Fear no more the lightning flash,
 Nor the all-dreaded thunderstone;°
Fear not slander, censure rash; 15
 Thou hast finished joy and moan.
All lovers young, all lovers must
Consign to thee,° and come to dust.

11. **physic:** the art of healing. 14. **thunderstone:**
thunderbolt. 18. **consign to thee:** yield to your con-
dition.

Spring and Fall:
To a Young Child

GERARD MANLEY HOPKINS

Margaret, are you grieving
Over Goldengrove unleaving?
Leaves, like the things of man, yo
With your fresh thoughts care fo
 you?
Ah! as the heart grows older 5
It will come to such sights colder
By and by, nor spare a sigh
Though worlds of wanwood leafmeal lie;
And yet you will weep and know why.
Now no matter, child, the name: 10
Sorrow's springs are the same.
Nor° mouth had, no nor mind, expressed
What heart heard of, ghost° guessed:
It is the blight man was born for,
It is Margaret you mourn for. 15

12. **nor:** neither. 13. **ghost:** spirit.

The Jabberwock
as drawn
by John Tenniel.

Jabberwocky

LEWIS CARROLL

'Twas brillig, and the slithy toves
 Did gyre and gimble in the wabe:
All mimsy were the borogoves,
 And the mome raths outgrabe.

"Beware the Jabberwock, my son! 5
 The jaws that bite, the claws that catch!
Beware the Jubjub bird, and shun
 The frumious Bandersnatch!"

He took his vorpal sword in hand;
 Long time the manxome foe he sought—
So rested he by the Tumtum tree, 11
 And stood awhile in thought.

And, as in uffish thought he stood,
 The Jabberwock, with eyes of flame,
Came whiffling through the tulgey wood,
 And burbled as it came! 16

One, two! One, two! And through and
 through
 The vorpal blade went snicker-snack!
He left it dead, and with its head
 He went galumphing back. 20

"And hast thou slain the Jabberwock?
 Come to my arms, my beamish boy!
O frabjous day! Callooh, Callay!"
 He chortled in his joy.

'Twas brillig, and the slithy toves 25
 Did gyre and gimble in the wabe:
All mimsy were the borogoves,
 And the mome raths outgrabe.

in Just-

E. E. CUMMINGS

in Just-
spring when the world is mud-
luscious the little
lame balloonman

whistles far and wee 5

and eddieandbill come
running from marbles and
piracies and it's
spring

when the world is puddle-wonderful 10

the queer
old balloonman whistles
far and wee
and bettyandisbel come dancing

from hop-scotch and jump-rope and 15

it's
spring
and
 the

 goat-footed 20

balloonMan whistles
far
and
wee

EUROPEAN PAINTING

Seventeenth- and Eighteenth-Century Painting

In 1656, just three years after Rembrandt had painted *Aristotle Contemplating the Bust of Homer* (page 263), a Sevillian artist named Diego Velásquez produced in his studio at the Royal Court in Madrid one of the most remarkable paintings in the history of art: *The Maids of Honor* (PLATE 1). A huge canvas over ten feet high, it contains eleven portraits of persons attached to the Spanish Court. Two of these portraits are the faces of King Philip IV and Queen Mariana, reflected in a mirror on the back wall. Velásquez has even included his own likeness. He has shown himself at work on another large canvas at the left, presumably painting a portrait. But a portrait of whom—the King and Queen, or Princess Margarita attended by her maids of honor? This is a curious, beguiling picture. Notice how Velásquez has arranged the figures: instead of lining them up in rows, as was the custom in most family portraits, he has treated each figure individually, so that we feel any one of them could move about freely in this large room. We feel this because of the masterful way Velásquez has made use of the dimly lit empty space in the upper half of the composition. Without it the figures below would appear crowded; they would lose something of their royal dignity. You can see this for yourself by covering the upper part of the picture with your hand.

Velásquez's lighting in *The Maids of Honor* is quite different from the theatrical illumination Caravaggio had used half a century earlier in his *David Holding the Head of Goliath* (page 260). Velásquez softened the forms of his figures with the gentle tones we find in everyday indoor lighting. His approach is similar to Vermeer's (page 264), but his brushwork is much freer, as you can see by looking closely at the wispy blond hair of the little princess in the center.

The seventeenth century was an important period for French painting as well. Since by this time France had become Europe's most prosperous new monarchy, many of her artists could depend for employment upon

commissions sponsored by the state. Louis XIV had even established a Royal Academy of Fine Arts, the largest formal art school in the Western world. But curiously enough, the two greatest French painters of this period, Nicolas Poussin and Claude Lorrain, lived most of their lives in Rome, where they could study the Italian masters and the arts of classical antiquity. The painting in PLATE 2 shows Claude's vision of a great seaport, a harbor scene which combines ships and buildings from different periods of history. Notice how Claude has given depth to this scene by leading our eye out along the coastline into the rays of the sun. Yet, at the same time, the sun seems to come toward us, filling the entire harbor with the haze of late afternoon.

We find less emphasis on such atmospheric effects in Poussin's *Rebecca and Eliezer at the Well* (PLATE 3), a scene taken from the Old Testament (Genesis 24). Here, the main action moves across, rather than into, the picture. It seems measured and rhythmical—like a stately dance or procession—slowly weaving in and out, up and down, guided by the poses and gestures of the figures. But notice how Poussin has sparked the picture with clanging reds, blues, and yellows, providing a sort of "counterpoint" to the rather ponderous setting.

Around the beginning of the eighteenth century a new kind of art and decoration became fashionable throughout Europe, particularly among the French aristocracy. It was a delicate, playful style known as the Rococo. A good example of this style is Antoine Watteau's small picture of Mezzetin, a popular character of Italian repertory theater (PLATE 4). Watteau has created here a scene which appears to be from real life, yet also from the world of the theater. His light, graceful brushstrokes have harmonized every detail in the picture with the tender mood of Mezzetin's wistful love song.

Most leading French painters of the generation after Watteau worked within the accepted style of the Rococo. Jean-Baptiste Siméon Chardin, however, was a notable exception, for he painted still lifes and simple domestic scenes in a quiet, down-to-earth manner. In some ways he was more like the Dutch masters of the previous century than his own contemporaries in France. PLATE 5, *The Kitchen Maid,* shows Chardin's unique ability to make simple everyday objects appear to be more interesting in a picture than if we had actually seen the very same objects in real life.

One of the most gifted Italian Rococo painters of the eighteenth century was Francesco Guardi, best known for his picturesque views of cities. *View on the Cannaregio, Venice* (PLATE 6) shows how effectively Guardi was able to capture in paint the subtle shimmerings of light and color along the wide canals of this island seaport.

PLATE 1. DIEGO VELÁSQUEZ (Spanish, 1599–1660): *The Maids of Honor*. 1656. Oil on canvas, 10 feet 5 inches by 9 feet. (The Prado, Madrid)

PLATE 2. CLAUDE LORRAIN (French, 1600–1682): *A Seaport at Sunset*. 1639. Oil on canvas. $40\frac{1}{2}$ x $53\frac{1}{2}$ inches. (The Louvre, Paris)

PLATE 3. NICOLAS POUSSIN (French. 1594–1665): *Rebecca and Eliezer at the Well.* 1648. Oil on canvas, 46⅜ x 77½ inches. (The Louvre, Paris)

333

PLATE 4. ANTOINE WATTEAU (French, 1684–1721): *Mezzetin*. Oil on canvas, 21¾ x 17 inches. (The Metropolitan Museum of Art, New York, Munsey Fund, 1934)

PLATE 5. JEAN–BAPTISTE SIMEON CHARDIN (French, 1699–1779): *The Kitchen Maid.*
About 1738. Oil on canvas, $18\frac{1}{8}$ x $14\frac{3}{4}$ inches. (National Gallery of Art, Washington, D.C.,
Samuel H. Kress Collection)

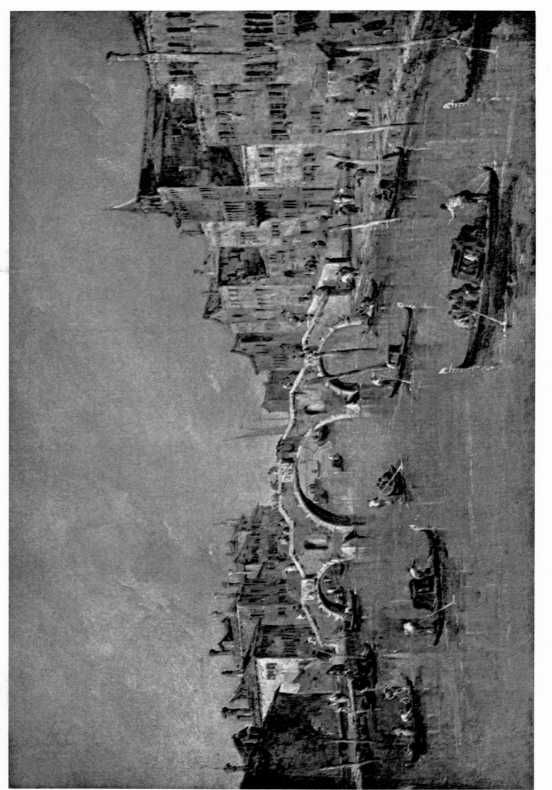

PLATE 6. FRANCESCO GUARDI (Venetian, 1712–1793): *View on the Cannaregio, Venice.* About 1770. Oil on canvas, $18\frac{3}{4}$ x $29\frac{1}{4}$ inches. (National Gallery of Art, Washington, D.C., Samuel H. Kress Collection)

The Purist

OGDEN NASH

I give you now Professor Twist,
A conscientious scientist.
Trustees exclaimed, "He never bungles!"
And sent him off to distant jungles.
Camped on a tropic riverside, 5
One day he missed his loving bride.
She had, the guide informed him later,
Been eaten by an alligator.
Professor Twist could not but smile.
"You mean," he said, "a crocodile." 10

FOR STUDY AND DISCUSSION

FEAR NO MORE

1. How do the speakers attempt to console the dead lad for his death? What theme is expressed in the first four lines of each stanza? in the last two?

2. What are the connotations or associations of *Home* in line 4? What impression do they give of the place where the speakers think of the young stranger as going?

3. How do the connotations of the word *lads* in line 5 differ from those of *juveniles, adolescents,* or *teen-agers?* Why is *lads* a better word in this poem?

4. What does the word *golden* suggest about the "lads and girls" referred to in line 5? How are they the symbolic opposite of "chimney sweepers"? Would *golden* have the same connotations if it were used in the phrase *golden calf?* How do you think words get their connotations?

5. A *pun* is the use of a word or phrase with two very different meanings. What pun does Shakespeare use in the first stanza of this poem? Which of its meanings carries over into the rest of the poem?

SPRING AND FALL: TO A YOUNG CHILD

1. A young child, Margaret, is weeping over the falling leaves. Why does the poet not think she will weep for the same reason when

she grows older? What *will* she weep over when she grows older?

2. When the poet says that Margaret will know what she is weeping for when she gets older, he implies that she does not know now, at least not consciously. What two ways of knowing sorrow are suggested in lines 11–13? What do the last two lines of the poem suggest about the sorrow for which Margaret is grieving?

3. All poets are creative in their use of language: they use old words in new ways, or invent new words by combining old ones. In this poem, Hopkins, an especially inventive poet, creates four new words. *Unleaving* (line 2) means shedding its leaves; *leafmeal* (line 8) refers to leaves ground or pulverized into small fragments like grain (meal). What do *Goldengrove* and *wanwood* suggest to you?

4. What are "sorrow's springs"? What two meanings of *spring* might fit this poem? Which meaning best fits Margaret's tears? Which is suggested in the title of the poem? How are both kinds of *spring* a beginning or source of something?

5. *Fall,* the season of the year, gets its name from the fall of leaves ("*Goldengrove* unleaving"). Both these meanings of *fall* are suggested in the poem. *Fall,* however, has still another meaning in Christian theology. Where is this meaning hinted at in the poem? How does the Biblical idea of the fall of man enrich the meaning of the poem?

JABBERWOCKY

1. In the first chapter of *Through the Looking Glass,* Alice reads this poem in a book in the Looking-Glass House. "It seems very pretty," she says when she has finished, "but it's rather hard to understand! Somehow it seems to fill my head with ideas—only I don't exactly know what they are!" Although it is a nonsense poem, "Jabberwocky" does fill one's head with ideas—partly because many of its words are ordinary English words, partly because the sentences have logical grammatical structure, and partly because all the nonsense words can be identified as to part of speech, and because many of the non-

sense words suggest meanings by their sound or their similarity to other words. Make a list of the nonsense words in the poem. What part of speech is each?

2. What, do you think, is a Jabberwock? Describe it. What about the word gives you this impression? What is the primary meaning of the title? What else does the title suggest to you?

3. What ideas are suggested to you by each of the following words: *slithy, gyre, gimble, mimsy* (stanza 1)? *vorpal* (stanza 3)? *uffish, whiffling, tulgey, burbled* (stanza 4)? *galumphing* (stanza 5)? *beamish, frabjous, Callooh, Callay* (stanza 6)?

4. In an edition of *Through the Looking Glass* illustrated by Sir John Tenniel, you will find in the first chapter Tenniel's conception of the Jabberwock, the tulgey wood, and the hero of the poem. In Chapter 6, you will find Humpty Dumpty's explanation of some of the words in the poem. For instance, *slithy,* he says, "means 'lithe and slimy.' . . . You see it's like a portmanteau—there are two meanings packed up into one word." (A portmanteau is a large suitcase.) Why could it be said of many words in good poetry that they are "like a portmanteau"?

5. Of what kind of poetry discussed in this book is "Jabberwocky" a modern example? What characteristics of this kind of poem can you find here?

IN JUST-

1. E. E. Cummings, like Gerard Manley Hopkins, handles words creatively. Why are the two compounds *mud-luscious* and *puddle-wonderful* so effective? What is *Just-spring?*

2. What is the effect of Cummings' running together of the words *eddieandbill* and *bettyandisbel?*

3. Why is *wee* more meaningful in this poem than *small* or *little?* (Give two or three reasons.)

4. What does the word *goat-footed* suggest about the balloonMan? Besides whatever is suggested by your idea of goats, the phrase has a further meaning. It is an allusion—an indirect reference—to the god Pan, who, in

Greek mythology, is pictured as having goat's ears, horns, legs, and feet. Pan was the god of woods and fields, flocks and shepherds and later became identified with all of nature. He loved music and dancing, and was supposed to have invented the syrinx or Pan-pipes. How does this allusion add to the scope and meaning of the poem?

THE PURIST

1. This poem belongs to a category of writing known as *light verse*. Light verse, as its name suggests, is light, not serious; it attempts to be amusing or entertaining rather than moving or profound. Verse can have all degrees of lightness or seriousness, of course, and the deepest light verse is not much different from the lightest serious poetry. This example belongs near the lighter end of the scale. What do the opening words "I give you" tell us about the occasion for this poem?

2. The point of the poem is made through dramatic irony. Why does Professor Twist smile? What do his words tell us about him? Why doesn't an overly conscientious scientist make a good human being?

3. Both the scientist and the poet are precise in their choice of words, but precise in different ways. What is the guiding principle of Professor Twist in choosing between *alligator* and *crocodile*? A poet describing this incident might have rejected both words and used instead *beast* or *monster*. In what ways would scientifically less precise words be poetically more precise? If the poet did decide to use either *alligator* or *crocodile,* on what basis would he choose between them?

ABOUT THE POETS

Gerard Manley Hopkins (1844–1889) was talented in music and painting as well as in poetry. A deeply religious youth, Hopkins was converted from the Church of England to Roman Catholicism while a student at Oxford. He began training as a Jesuit a year later and served the last fifteen years of his life as a priest in England and Ireland. His poetry, unpublished until almost thirty years after his death, is notable not only for its beauty but for its deep influence on the work of twentieth-century poets.

Lewis Carroll (1832–1898), whose real name was Charles Lutwidge Dodgson, was a brilliant mathematician, a professor of mathematics at Oxford University, and a writer of many mathematical treatises. As a mathematician, he became deeply interested in patterns of logic and meaning. He is most famous today however, as the author of those two delightful books, *Alice's Adventures in Wonderland* and *Through the Looking Glass.*

E. E. Cummings (1894–1962), the son of a Unitarian minister and Harvard professor, was born in Cambridge, Massachusetts, and educated at Harvard University. During World War I he went to France as an ambulance driver, where, suspected of being a German agent, he was imprisoned for several months in a French concentration camp, an experience he described in *The Enormous Room.* A painter as well as a poet, he lived the latter part of his life in New York's Greenwich Village and had several exhibitions of his paintings. As a poet, Cummings is famous for his radical experiments with punctuation, word layout, and sentence structure.

Ogden Nash (1902–1971) was born in Rye, New York, and attended Harvard University for one year. After early jobs in advertising and publishing, he made a reputation as a writer of light verse and gradually established himself as America's foremost humorous poet. In addition, he collaborated with S. J. Perelman on the libretto of the musical comedy *One Touch of Venus.*

FIGURATIVE LANGUAGE

It is a paradox that the best way of saying something is often to say something else. A paradox is an apparently self-contradictory statement that nevertheless states a truth. As such, it is one form of figurative language. Figurative language is language that says one thing and means something else. It is the opposite of literal language—language that means exactly and only what it says. The explanation of the paradox in the first sentence above is that the best way of stating factual information to the mind is not the best way of suggesting the quality of experience to the feelings and imagination.

The language of the imagination, and therefore of literature, is characteristically figurative. The wisest men and the greatest teachers have found that when they wanted to communicate the "feel" of things, to stir the emotions of their readers or listeners, they had to use figurative language. Jesus, for instance, spoke in parables and paradoxes. The core of his teaching is stated in a paradox: "For whosoever will save his life shall lose it, and whosoever will lose his life for my sake shall find it." When he wished to define the word *neighbor*, instead of giving an exact definition he instead told a story— the parable of the Good Samaritan.

Not all literature is figurative. "Johnny Armstrong" and "Lord Randal" (pages 297 and 319) tell their stories without using a single figure. Most poems, however, rely heavily on figurative language. Sometimes a whole poem will take its force from a single figure of speech. Consider, for instance, the following poem, translated from a Japanese poet, Lady Ise, of about A.D. 1000.

> The rains of spring
> Which hang to the branches
> Of the green willow,
> Look like pearls upon a string.

The simile of the final line focuses the poem visually, emotionally, and imaginatively. Visually, we see that the raindrops hanging from the slender branches look like a string of beads. Imaginatively, we are pleased by the leap of mind which notes this likeness. But, most important, our emotional response to the poem is controlled by the comparison. Rain can affect our moods in various ways. When Robert Bridges, in "Elegy" (page 313), com-

"The Rains of Spring" by Lady Ise from *Little Pictures of Japan,* arranged by Olive Beaupré Miller. Reprinted by permission of The Book House for Children.

pares raindrops dripping from the branches to tears, his metaphor reinforces the sadness of his subject. Here the effect is opposite. The comparison to pearls endows the raindrops with beauty. This ties in with the connotations of *spring* and *green* to give us a joyful sense of young nature dressed up in her beads. The whole meaning and force of the poem result from an effective figure of speech.

All degrees of emphasis are possible in figurative language. A metaphor, symbol, or personification may be lightly suggested or it may be insisted upon. In "Four Preludes on Playthings of the Wind" (page 293), Carl Sandburg describes the "woman named Tomorrow" as putting hairpins in her hair, thus making us visualize a real woman, with real hair and hands. In "The Ship That Found Herself" (page 55), however, though Kipling presents the parts of the ship as having human speech and feelings, he never asks us to imagine them in human form. In a phrase such as "the dying moon," from Tennyson's "Sweet and Low" (page 310), there is only a hint of personification.

In the pages that follow, we shall examine the use that a number of poets make of figurative language.

Roadways

JOHN MASEFIELD

One road leads to London,
 One road runs to Wales,
My road leads me seawards
 To the white dipping sails.

One road leads to the river, 5
 As it goes singing slow;
My road leads to shipping,
 Where the bronzed sailors go.

Leads me, lures me, calls me
 To salt green tossing sea; 10
A road without earth's road dust
 Is the right road for me.

A wet road heaving, shining,
 And wild with seagulls' cries,
A mad salt sea wind blowing 15
 The salt spray in my eyes.

My road calls me, lures me
 West, east, south, and north;
Most roads lead men homewards,
 My road leads me forth 20

To add more miles to the tally
 Of gray miles left behind,
In quest of that one beauty
 God put me here to find.

A Scholar Looks at an Oak

MELVIN TOLSON

Storms slug its head,
Its shoulders sag,
Its beard is shorn
Upon the crag.

In dawns and dusks 5
Its spine alone
Keeps it erect
Like Doric° stone.

A squash grows up
At a summer's stroke; 10
An age wears out
To make an oak.

8. **Doric:** one of the orders of ancient Greek architecture.

O, My Luve's like a Red, Red Rose

ROBERT BURNS

O, my luve's like a red, red rose,
 That's newly sprung in June;
O, my luve's like the melodie
 That's sweetly played in tune.

As fair art thou, my bonnie lass, 5
 So deep in luve am I;
And I will luve thee still, my dear,
 Till a' the seas gang dry.

Till a' the seas gang dry, my dear,
 And the rocks melt wi' the sun: 10
And I will luve thee still, my dear,
 While the sands o' life shall run.

And fare thee well, my only luve!
 And fare thee well a while!
And I will come again, my luve, 15
 Though it were ten thousand mile.

The Long Hill

SARA TEASDALE

I must have passed the crest a while ago
 And now I am going down—
Strange to have crossed the crest and not to know,
 But the brambles were always catching the hem of my gown.

All the morning I thought how proud I should be 5
 To stand there straight as a queen,
Wrapped in the wind and the sun with the world under me—
 But the air was dull, there was little I could have seen.

It was nearly level along the beaten track
 And the brambles caught in my gown—
But it's no use now to think of turning back, 10
 The rest of the way will be only going down.

The Tuft of Flowers

ROBERT FROST

I went to turn the grass once after one
Who mowed it in the dew before the sun.

The dew was gone that made his blade so keen
Before I came to view the leveled scene.

I looked for him behind an isle of trees; 5
I listened for his whetstone ° on the breeze.

But he had gone his way, the grass all mown,
And I must be, as he had been—alone,

"As all must be," I said within my heart,
"Whether they work together or apart." 10

But as I said it, swift there passed me by
On noiseless wing a bewildered butterfly,

Seeking with memories grown dim o'er night
Some resting flower of yesterday's delight.

And once I marked his flight go round and round, 15
As where some flower lay withering on the ground.

And then he flew as far as eye could see,
And then on tremulous wing came back to me.

I thought of questions that have no reply,
And would have turned to toss the grass to dry; 20

6. **whetstone** (hwet′stōn′): an abrasive stone for sharpening knives or other edged tools.

But he turned first, and led my eye to look
At a tall tuft of flowers beside a brook,

A leaping tongue of bloom the scythe had spared
Beside a reedy brook the scythe had bared.

The mower in the dew had loved them thus, 25
Leaving them to flourish, not for us,

Nor yet to draw one thought of ours to him,
But from sheer morning gladness at the brim.

The butterfly and I had lit upon,
Nevertheless, a message from the dawn, 30

That made me hear the wakening birds around,
And hear his long scythe whispering to the ground,

And feel a spirit kindred to my own;
So that henceforth I worked no more alone;

But glad with him, I worked as with his aid, 35
And weary, sought at noon with him the shade;

And dreaming, as it were, held brotherly speech
With one whose thought I had not hoped to reach.

"Men work together," I told him from the heart,
"Whether they work together or apart." 40

On Hygiene

HILAIRE BELLOC

Of old when folk lay sick and sorely tried . .
The doctors gave them physic,° and they died.
But here's a happier age: for now we know
Both how to make men sick and keep them so.

2. **physic:** medicine.

"On Hygiene" from *The Verse of Hilaire Belloc*. Reprinted by permission of A. D. Peters & Co.

The Glories of
Our Blood and State

JAMES SHIRLEY

In James Shirley's play *The Contention of Ajax and Ulysses for the Armor of Achilles,* this lyric is spoken by the priest and seer Calchas before an assemblage of Greek kings and princes at the funeral of Ajax, one of the great Greek warriors.

The glories of our blood and state
 Are shadows, not substantial things;
There is no armor against fate;
 Death lays his icy hand on kings.
 Scepter and crown 5
 Must tumble down,
And in the dust be equal made
With the poor crooked scythe and spade.

Some men with swords may reap the field,
 And plant fresh laurels where they
 kill; 10
But their strong nerves at last must yield,
 They tame but one another still.
 Early or late,
 They stoop to fate,
And must give up their murmuring
 breath 15
When they, pale captives, creep to death.

The garlands wither on your brow,
 Then boast no more your mighty deeds;
Upon death's purple altar now
 See where the victor-victim bleeds. 20
 Your heads must come
 To the cold tomb;
Only the actions of the just
Smell sweet and blossom in their dust.

The Sword

WILLIAM BLAKE

The sword sung on the barren heath,
The sickle in the fruitful field:
The sword he sung a song of death,
But could not make the sickle yield.

FOR STUDY AND DISCUSSION

ROADWAYS

1. An important kind of figurative language is *metaphor,* in which one thing is spoken of as if it were something else. That is, in a metaphor an implied comparison is made between two things that are essentially different. In "Roadways," Masefield repeats the word *road* eleven times. Which of these roads are literal roads? Which are metaphorical? When he uses roads in a metaphorical sense, what is the poet really speaking of?

2. Masefield personifies—gives human characteristics to—the *road* twice in the poem. In which lines? The first time it is a literal road, but, being personified, it therefore also becomes metaphorical. The second time it is a metaphorical road, which the personification makes doubly metaphorical. What else in the poem does Masefield personify?

3. Compare the theme of this poem with that of "Sea Fever" (page 291). How are they similar? How are they different? Which poem do you think is a more effective statement of the poet's theme?

O, MY LUVE'S LIKE A RED, RED ROSE

1. A *simile,* like a metaphor, is a comparison between two essentially unlike things. In a simile the comparison is *expressed,* whereas in a metaphor it is *implied.* In a simile the comparison is expressed with some word such as *like, as, than,* or *similar to.* The first line of this

poem contains one of the most famous similes in English poetry. Try to express in literal language all the ideas it suggests. Do you think it can be done? How many words does it take even to come close? Would it make any difference to the meaning if Burns had written "O, my luve's like a *yellow* rose"? What does the second line add to the simile?

2. What does the second simile in lines 3 and 4 add to the characterization of the girl?

3. Where does the speaker exaggerate in the poem? How long does he promise to love his sweetheart? Does he mean this literally? What does he mean?

4. What is the metaphor in line 12? What is the poet comparing life to in this line?

A SCHOLAR LOOKS AT AN OAK

1. What figure of speech dominates the first six lines? Which part of the tree is suggested by *head*? by *shoulders*? by *beard*? by *spine*?

2. As you know, a *symbol* is something that stands for or symbolizes more than its literal meaning. The last stanza of this poem makes a literal (botanical) statement, and also a symbolic one. State in your own words this larger meaning. Why is the poet's statement more effective than your paraphrase?

THE LONG HILL

1. What three reasons does the speaker mention for not noticing when she crossed the crest of the hill? How did the experience of crossing the crest differ from what she imagined it would be?

2. How does the poem suggest that the hill is symbolic? Of what is it a symbol? What is symbolized by the crest? the level track? the brambles? the way down?

THE TUFT OF FLOWERS

1. Why did the early mower spare the tuft of flowers? What effect does his sparing them have on the speaker? Why does he regard the tuft of flowers as "a message"?

2. The speaker's statement to himself and the mower are *paradoxes*—that is, taken literally they seem to contradict themselves, but

taken metaphorically they express a truth. What truth is expressed in each statement? Not only does each paradox seem, on the surface, to contradict itself, but the two paradoxes contradict each other. What causes the speaker's change of heart from the one view to the other? Which statement, if either, do you think is more true? Why?

3. A *dead metaphor* is a word or phrase that began as a metaphor but which has been used so often that it has come to seem literal rather than metaphorical—for example, the *eye* of a needle, the *shoulder* of a road. The phrase "A leaping tongue of bloom" combines a dead metaphor and a live one. What kind of tongue do you think the poet has in mind?

4. The verb *had lit* in line 29 has two subjects. Does it have the same meaning with each subject? Why or why not? Would you call this a live or a dead metaphor?

5. What picture or impression do you get from each of these metaphors: "an isle of trees," "sheer morning gladness at the brim," "his long scythe whispering to the ground"? Try to express these impressions in literal language, without using metaphor. Why is it so difficult to do?

ON HYGIENE

1. The first two lines of this poem present an irony of situation. Is there, perhaps, also a touch of overstatement in them? If so, how? What is ironic about the results of the doctors' treatments?

2. What word in the last two lines means the opposite of what it seems to say? What kind of irony is this?

3. An *epigram* is a short poem or saying that sums up the writer's attitude on a particular subject. Judging from "On Hygiene," what would you say is Belloc's attitude toward "progress"?

THE GLORIES OF OUR BLOOD AND STATE

1. Express in literal language the metaphors in lines 2, 9, 10, 16, and 24.

2. Where is death personified in the poem? How is he made to seem supernatural as well as human?

3. *Metonymy* is a figure of speech in which a part of a thing, or something closely associated with it in our minds, is used to stand for or suggest the thing itself. Thus a smart child might be called a *brain*. What is suggested or represented by the following examples of metonymy: *blood, scepter, crown, scythe, spade, nerves, heads, dust?*

4. What is the paradox in the third stanza? What truth does it suggest?

5. *Garlands* (line 17) is a traditional symbol for honors and victory. Why is *garlands* a symbol only, while *laurels* (line 10), which means the same thing, is also a metaphor?

6. What is the theme of this poem? (What outlasts death? What does not?)

7. What idea in stanza 1 echoes a basic idea in Shakespeare's "Fear No More" (page 326)?

THE SWORD

1. Metonymy is also used in this poem. What does the sword stand for? What does the sickle stand for?

2. How are the sword and the sickle alike? How are they different? Expressed in literal language, what is the thought of this poem? Like "On Hygiene," "The Sword" is an epigram. What is the poet's attitude toward war?

ABOUT THE POETS

John Masefield (1878–1967), left an orphan at an early age, spent three years in the merchant marine and sailed around Cape Horn at the age of fifteen as apprentice on a sailing ship. Among his best-known books of poetry are *Salt-Water Ballads, The Everlasting Mercy, The Dauber,* and *Reynard the Fox.* He was made Poet Laureate of England in 1930.

Robert Burns (1759–1796), Scotland's peasant poet, was the eldest son of a poor farmer and spent much of his own life as a plowboy, field worker, and farmer. In the last few years of his life he was a tax and customs officer. He is best known for his songs and satires in Scottish dialect verse, many of which rank among the finest romantic poetry.

Melvin Tolson (1900–1966) was born in Missouri and spent most of his life teaching drama and literature in Texas and Oklahoma. A playwright as well as a poet, he was a member of the Bread Loaf writer's workshop in Vermont and was director of the Dust Bowl Theater in Oklahoma. Tolson also was Mayor, for four terms, of Langston, Oklahoma.

Sara Teasdale (1884–1933) was born in St. Louis and lived most of her adult life there and in New York City. Though wooed by the poet Vachel Lindsay, she married a St. Louis businessman instead. A victim of ill health, she was fond of withdrawing into her own private world. She is remembered chiefly for a few graceful, simple lyrics.

Robert Frost (1874–1963) was one of America's greatest poets of the twentieth century (see pages 375–80).

Hilaire Belloc (1870–1953), a versatile man of letters, was born in Paris to a French father and an English mother. Educated in England, he served during World War I in the French artillery, but graduated from Oxford University, and later served four years in Parliament. He was a serious historian and political writer, a charming essayist, a staunch defender of Roman Catholicism, a forceful debater, a poet, a novelist, and a writer of humorous verse for children.

William Blake (1757–1827) was a great original genius both as a poet and as an artist. Born in London, the son of a hosier, he was apprenticed to an engraver, became one of the best professional engravers in England, and illustrated many of his own books. As a poet he is best known for his *Songs of Innocence* and *Songs of Experience*. Blake's later works, full of symbols and mysticism, are prophetic books based on his own complicated and unique philosophical system.

James Shirley (1596–1666) was born in London and educated at both Oxford and Cambridge Universities. He was for a while a Church of England clergyman and a schoolmaster, but after being converted to Roman Catholicism he became a playwright. During a period of eighteen years, he wrote more than thirty plays, both comedies and tragedies. When the theaters were closed by the Puritans, he supported himself chiefly by teaching.

TONE

What does it mean when someone says "Good morning"? At first, this question may sound absurd: we all know what "Good morning" means. But think of the various ways in which this greeting can be spoken. A person may say it cheerfully or surlily, cordially or grudgingly, stiffly or warmly, courteously or contemptuously, proudly or eagerly, with stiff politeness or with boisterous good will. In short, the words "Good morning" can be uttered so as to mean almost anything from "I love you" to "I don't really care to speak to you." The tone in which words are spoken may be as important to their meaning as their dictionary definitions. In fact, it is possible to communicate rich meaning by uttering sounds (*mmm-m-m,* or *ahem*) that have no dictionary meaning at all. The tone of a remark may tell you what the speaker feels about his subject ("It's really a foul morning"), what he feels about the person he is speaking to ("I consider you beneath my notice"), or what he feels about himself ("I'm a very important person"). Tone, in literature, may be defined as the emotional meaning of a work—as the author's or speaker's attitude toward his subject, his audience, or himself. In literature, however, tone cannot be indicated by voice. It therefore must be indicated by other methods: by the words chosen, by their arrangement, by the context in which they are placed. There is a difference in tone between a character's saying "Good day," or "Good morning," or "Fine day, isn't it?" or "Isn't this a marvelous morning!" There is also a difference in his saying, "Good morning, Miss Pflugmann," or "Good morning, Mabelle," or "Good morning, darling!" In poetry, tone is determined by almost everything in the poem, including rhythm, sound, images, and figures of speech.

The following two poems will indicate briefly the importance of determining tone accurately. The first, by Hilaire Belloc, is entitled "On a Dead Hostess": "Of this bad world the loveliest and best / Has smiled and said 'Good Night,' and gone to rest." The second, by John Dryden, is "Epitaph on His Wife": "Here lies my wife: here let her lie! / Now she's at rest—and so am I." Both poems are *epitaphs,* short poems in memory of a dead person. They differ sharply, however, in tone. The tone of the first poem is tender, admiring, and affectionate: the speaker deeply regrets the loss of the dead woman. The tone of the second poem is caustic and at the same time relieved: the speaker is glad to be rid of his plaguing wife. Unless we grasp this difference, we have badly missed the poets' meaning. Recognition of tone is not always easy, but it is essential to a real understanding of any poem.

The Duck

OGDEN NASH

Behold the duck.
It does not cluck.
A cluck it lacks.
It quacks.
It is specially fond 5
Of a puddle or pond.
When it dines or sups
It bottoms ups.

Duck's Ditty

KENNETH GRAHAME

All along the backwater,
Through the rushes tall,
Ducks are a-dabbling,
Up tails all!

Ducks' tails, drakes' tails, 5
Yellow feet a-quiver,
Yellow bills all out of sight
Busy in the river!

Slushy green undergrowth
Where the roach ° swim— 10
Here we keep our larder,
Cool and full and dim.

Everyone for what he likes!
We like to be
Heads down, tails up, 15
Dabbling free!

High in the blue above
Swifts ° whirl and call—
We are down a-dabbling
Up tails all! 20

10. **roach:** silver-white fish with greenish backs. 18. **swifts:** small birds that resemble swallows.

Channel Firing

THOMAS HARDY

That night your great guns, unawares,
Shook all our coffins as we lay,
And broke the chancel window squares,
We thought it was the Judgment day°

And sat upright. While drearisome 5
Arose the howl of wakened hounds:
The mouse let fall the altar crumb,
The worms drew back into the mounds,

The glebe° cow drooled. Till God called,
 "No;
It's gunnery practice out at sea 10
Just as before you went below;
The world is as it used to be:

"All nations striving strong to make
Red war yet redder. Mad as hatters
They do no more for Christès° sake 15
Than you who are helpless in such mat-
 ters.

"That this is not the judgment hour
For some of them's a blessed thing,
For if it were they'd have to scour
Hell's floor for so much threatening. . . .

"Ha, ha. It will be warmer when 21
I blow the trumpet (if indeed
I ever do; for you are men,
And rest eternal sorely need)."

So down we lay again. "I wonder, 25
Will the world ever saner be,"
Said one, "than when He sent us under
In our indifferent century!"

And many a skeleton shook his head.
"Instead of preaching forty year," 30
My neighbor Parson Thirdly said,
"I wish I had stuck to pipes and beer."

Again the guns disturbed the hour,
Roaring their readiness to avenge,
As far inland as Stourton Tower, 35
And Camelot, and starlit Stonehenge.°

4. **Judgment day:** the day when God will judge the world, punish the wicked, and reward the good. 9. **glebe:** belonging to the parish church. 15. **Christès** (kris'tez): Christ's.

35. **Stourton Tower . . . Camelot . . . Stonehenge:** Stourton Tower, near Canterbury in southeastern England, is a memorial erected on the spot where Alfred the Great resisted Danish invaders in 879. Camelot is the legendary castle of King Arthur and the Knights of the Round Table. Stonehenge is the ruins of an ancient circle of huge stones used for religious rites by the druids, or priests, of early England.

if up's the word

E. E. CUMMINGS

if up's the word;and a world grows greener
minute by second and most by more—
if death is the loser and life is the winner
(and beggars are rich but misers are poor)
—let's touch the sky: 5
 with a to and a fro
(and a here there where)and away we go

in even the laziest creature among us
a wisdom no knowledge can kill is astir—
now dull eyes are keen and now keen eyes are keener 10
(for young is the year,for young is the year)
—let's touch the sky:
 ⁄ with a great(and a gay
and a steep)deep rush through amazing day

it's brains without hearts have set saint against sinner; 15
put gain over gladness and joy under care—
let's do as an earth which can never do wrong does
(minute by second and most by more)
—let's touch the sky:
 with a strange(and a true) 20
and a climbing fall into far near blue

if beggars are rich(and a robin will sing his
robin a song)but misers are poor—
let's love until noone could quite be(and young is
the year,dear)as living as i'm and as you're 25
—let's touch the sky:
 with a you and a me
and an every(who's any who's some)one who's we

FOUR POEMS BY MARTIAL

The Latin poet Martial, writer of epigrams and biting satire, lived in the first century A.D.

Bought Locks

The golden hair that Gulla wears
 Is hers: who would have thought it?
She swears 'tis hers, and true she swears,
 For I know where she bought it.
 Translated by Sir John Harington

Critics

The readers and the hearers like my
 books,
And yet some writers cannot them digest;
But what care I? for when I make a feast,
I would my guests should praise it, not
 the cooks.
 Translated by Sir John Harington

A Hinted Wish

You told me, Maro, whilst you live
You'd not a single penny give,
But that, whene'er you chanct to die,
You'd leave a handsome legacy:
You must be mad beyond redress, 5
If my next wish you cannot guess!
 Translated by Francis Lewis

Post-Obits* and the Poets

He unto whom thou art so partial,
Oh, reader! is the well-known Martial,
The Epigrammatist:° while living,
Give him the fame thou wouldst be
 giving;
So shall he hear, and feel, and know it— 5
 Post-obits rarely reach a poet.
 Translated by Lord Byron

* **Post-Obits:** here, things said about a person after he is dead. 3. **Epigrammatist** (ep′ə·gram′-ə·tist): a writer of epigrams.

FOR STUDY AND DISCUSSION

THE DUCK
DUCK'S DITTY

1. What is the difference in tone between these two poems? What difference is there in the attitudes of the two poets toward ducks and their lives?

2. Explain as fully as you can the elements in the two poems that contribute to their difference in tone.

CHANNEL FIRING

1. Who is speaking? Where is he? To whom is he speaking?

2. Where are the guns? What effect does their firing have on the dead? on living things? on the coffins and the church windows? What do these effects suggest about the guns?

3. What meanings of the word *indifferent* (line 28) do you think the poet had in mind? What does this word suggest about our century? Why do the skeletons shake their heads?

Why does Parson Thirdly decide he might as well have "stuck to pipes and beer"?

4. In lines 25–26 one of the dead says, "I wonder, will the world ever saner be." From the tone of the poem, what do you think Hardy's answer would be? What seems to be Hardy's attitude toward mankind and human life?

5. The tone shifts in the last stanza of this poem. What are the connotations, or associations, of "Stourton Tower," "Camelot" and "starlit Stonehenge"? How do these associations emphasize the theme that Hardy is expressing in this poem?

6. Would you classify this poem as lyric or dramatic? Why?

7. How does Hardy's treatment of coffins, graves, worms, and skeletons differ in tone from that of an Edgar Allan Poe story or a book of horror tales? How does Hardy's treatment of God differ in tone from that of the Bible, a church hymn, or a poem by a deeply religious man such as the seventeenth-century English poet John Milton?

IF UP'S THE WORD

1. What season of the year does the poet celebrate in this poem? Which lines and images most vividly suggest his feelings?

2. What are the paradoxes in line 4 and 9? In each one, what does Cummings mean? What, to him, is wealth? What is wisdom? What creates conflict, pain, and care in the world? What can kill, and what gives life?

3. What kind of movement or journey is suggested in the last two lines of each stanza? What is the truth behind the paradoxes in line 21?

4. Is there an element of nonsense in the last line of the poem? What does the line mean? How does its nonsense fit in with the theme of the poem? (Do you think Cummings sees any connection between nonsense and wisdom?)

5. What is the tone of this poem? How does its tone differ from that of "Channel Firing"? How does the rhythm of each poem contribute to its tone?

FOUR POEMS BY MARTIAL

1. What are the two senses of "is hers" in "Bought Locks"? What is Martial's attitude toward Gulla? What is the tone of this poem?

2. What is the speaker's "hinted wish"? Does Maro deserve what he gets from the speaker? Do you think he will take the hint? Why or why not?

3. What is the metaphor in lines 3–4 of "Critics"? Express this idea in literal language. Which is more convincing? Why?

4. How does the theme of "Post-Obits and the Poet" compare with that of "A Hinted Wish"? What idea do the two have in common?

5. How is the tone of these poems different from those by Hardy and Cummings? What is Martial's attitude toward vanity and stinginess? Is he bitter, or amused?

ABOUT THE POETS

Kenneth Grahame (1859–1932) spent most of his adult life as an official in the Bank of England. He also wrote, however, his most famous book being the children's classic *The Wind in the Willows*. An outdoors man, Grahame was said to know the name of every horse, cow, and pig in his neighborhood.

Thomas Hardy (1840–1928) is famous for both his poetry and his novels, such as *The Return of the Native, Tess of the D'Urbervilles, Jude the Obscure, Under the Greenwood Tree,* and *The Mayor of Casterbridge.* The son of a stonemason, Hardy was born in Dorsetshire, in the "Wessex" region of England that he wrote about in his novels and poems. He spent seventeen years of his early life in architecture, first as a student and then as a practicing architect. When he found he could make a living at writing, however, he abandoned architecture and pursued the career that made him one of the great figures of English literature.

Martial (about A.D. 40–102) was born in Spain, but went to Rome in his twenties, where he quickly became known in literary circles and to the Roman emperor. He is famous as a satirist and writer of epigrams.

Five Poets

The first step in learning to like poetry is learning to read and understand a variety of poems. The second step is gaining familiarity with several outstanding poets.

Every great poet, once he has outgrown the stage of imitating others, acquires his own voice, his own manner, his own style. His uniqueness expresses itself in various ways—sometimes in his choice of verse forms, sometimes in his selection of vocabulary, sometimes in distinctive verse rhythms, sometimes in a fondness for particular images, particular figures of speech, or certain poetic devices—such as alliteration or approximate rhyme. As a result of these various choices, his poetry is stamped with his own personality, and is as distinctive as a face.

Also, like other men, the great poet has personal ideas and interests, a fondness for certain subjects, a characteristic outlook on life. These ideas and interests—broader than those of most men; deeper, too; but always his own—manifest themselves in what he writes about and in the philosophy underlying his poems or directly expressed in them. In short, his poetry has a distinctive content as well as a distinctive style. It is unique and individual, unmistakably his own.

One of the great joys of living is getting to know the personality, character, thoughts, and feelings of a few close friends. One of the great joys of reading is gaining an equally intimate knowledge of the mind, heart, and manner of particular writers. When we know a person well, we recognize his voice over the telephone without his having to identify himself. Likewise, when we know a poet well, we recognize his voice in a poem without hesitation. Of two lines in one of Wordsworth's poems, his friend Coleridge wrote: "Had I met these lines running wild in the deserts of Arabia, I should have instantly screamed out 'Wordsworth!' " To know a poet this well is to reap rewards comparable to those of friendship.

As a step in this direction, here are four poems each by five nineteenth- and twentieth-century poets—English and American.

WILLIAM WORDSWORTH

(1770–1850)

William Wordsworth was the leader of the Romantic Movement in English poetry, a movement that rebelled against the dry logic and reason of the preceding period and exalted, instead, imagination, intuition, and feeling. In addition, the Romantic poets favored democracy rather than aristocracy, valued individualism and liberty over social authority, and believed nature to be the source of truth and beauty. Their preference for the natural beauty of the country over the city as background and subject matter is one of the chief characteristics of their poetry.

Wordsworth is the supreme nature poet of English poetry. He found in nature not only beauty but strength and wisdom which nourished and sustained him and fed his imagination. Through communion with nature, much more than through scientific investigation or the study of books, Wordsworth found an avenue to the deepest truths. Nature, for Wordsworth, was divine; in it he sensed a divine "presence," a "motion and a spirit" that "rolls through all things." Nature, he believed, refined and educated those who lived close to her and sought to learn her secrets. In one of his poems he wrote:

> One impulse from a vernal wood
> May teach you more of man,
> Of moral evil and of good
> Than all the sages can.

Wordsworth's idea of poetry is set forth in his preface to the second edition of his first collection of poems, the *Lyrical Ballads,* published in 1800. In it, he tells us that his object has been "to choose incidents and situations from common life, and to relate or describe them . . . in a selection of language really used by men, and, at the same time, to throw over them a certain coloring of imagination, whereby ordinary things should be presented to the mind in an unusual aspect." In other words, he rejected the idea of language that is "poetic" and of subject matter that is exalted or high-flown.

In his choice of subject matter—"incidents and situations from common life"—we see Wordsworth's leanings toward democracy. He felt that in "humble and rustic life" the basic passions of mankind were freer to mature uncomplicated by the rules and customs of society. He felt that they could be seen more clearly in a simple setting, "incorporated with the beautiful and permanent forms of nature."

His emphasis on the "language really used by men" signals Wordsworth's rebellion against "poetic diction"—the artificial and inflated phraseology of late-eighteenth-century poets who felt that common words were undignified and that poetry had to be distinguished from prose by a superior elegance. On the contrary, Wordsworth argued, "the language of a large portion of every good poem, even of the most elevated character, must necessarily, except with reference to the meter, in no respect differ from that of good prose," and that, in fact, "there neither is, nor can be, any *essential* difference between the language of prose and metrical composition." Simple words, he said, could be used in poetry to convey the profoundest emotion and the deepest truth.

Finally, in his intention to give his poems "a certain coloring of imagination," Wordsworth suggests his deep belief in the power and importance of imagination, which he considered the highest and most trustworthy of all human faculties.

Wordsworth was born and grew up in the Lake District of northern England, a country of waters, woods, hills, and valleys that deeply affected his life and poetry. After attending Cambridge University, he took a trip to France in 1792, during the French Revolution. This experience confirmed his belief in the common man.

The publication of *Lyrical Ballads* (1798) by Wordsworth and Samuel Taylor Coleridge is generally taken as the beginning of the Romantic period in English literature. Both these poets wrote their finest poetry just before and after the turn of the century. After 1808 the quality of Wordsworth's work declined. In 1843 he was appointed Poet Laureate, an honor which he held until his death.

There Was a Boy

There was a boy; ye knew him well, ye cliffs
And islands of Winander! many a time,
At evening, when the earliest stars began
To move along the edges of the hills,
Rising or setting, would he stand alone, 5
Beneath the trees, or by the glimmering lake;
And there, with fingers interwoven, both hands
Pressed closely palm to palm and to his mouth
Uplifted, he, as through an instrument,
Blew mimic hootings to the silent owls, 10
That they might answer him. And they would shout
Across the watery vale, and shout again,
Responsive to his call, with quivering peals,
And long halloos, and screams, and echoes loud
Redoubled and redoubled; concourse wild 15
Of jocund din! And, when there came a pause
Of silence such as baffled his best skill:
Then, sometimes, in that silence, while he hung
Listening, a gentle shock of mild surprise
Has carried far into his heart the voice 20
Of mountain torrents; or the visible scene
Would enter unawares into his mind
With all its solemn imagery, its rocks,
Its woods, and that uncertain heaven received
Into the bosom of the steady lake. 25
 This boy was taken from his mates, and died
In childhood, ere he was full twelve years old.
Preeminent in beauty is the vale
Where he was born and bred: the churchyard hangs
Upon a slope above the village school; 30
And, through that churchyard when my way has led
On summer evenings, I believe, that there
A long half-hour together I have stood
Mute—looking at the grave in which he lies!

Lucy Gray

Or, Solitude

Oft I had heard of Lucy Gray:
And, when I crossed the wild,
I chanced to see at break of day
The solitary child.

No mate, no comrade Lucy knew; 5
She dwelt on a wide moor,
—The sweetest thing that ever grew
Beside a human door!

You yet may spy the fawn at play,
The hare upon the green; 10
But the sweet face of Lucy Gray
Will never more be seen.

"Tonight will be a stormy night—
You to the town must go;
And take a lantern, Child, to light 15
Your mother through the snow."

"That, Father! will I gladly do:
'Tis scarcely afternoon—
The minster clock has just struck two,
And yonder is the moon!" 20

At this the Father raised his hook,
And snapped a fagot band;
He plied his work; and Lucy took
The lantern in her hand.

Not blither is the mountain roe: °— 25
With many a wanton stroke
Her feet disperse the powdery snow,
That rises up like smoke.

The storm came on before its time:
She wandered up and down; 30
And many a hill did Lucy climb:
But never reached the town.

The wretched parents all that night
Went shouting far and wide;
But there was neither sound nor sight 35
To serve them for a guide.

At daybreak on a hill they stood
That overlooked the moor;
And thence they saw the bridge of wood,
A furlong ° from their door. 40

They wept—and, turning homeward, cried,
"In heaven we all shall meet";
When in the snow the mother spied
The print of Lucy's feet.

Then downward from the steep hill's edge
They tracked the footmarks small; 46
And through the broken hawthorn hedge,
And by the long stone wall;

And then an open field they crossed:
The marks were still the same; 50
They tracked them on, nor ever lost;
And to the bridge they came.

They followed from the snowy bank
Those footmarks, one by one,
Into the middle of the plank; 55
And further there were none!

—Yet some maintain that to this day
She is a living child;
That you may see sweet Lucy Gray
Upon the lonesome wild. 60

O'er rough and smooth she trips along,
And never looks behind;
And sings a solitary song
That whistles in the wind.

25. **roe:** deer.

40. **furlong:** an eighth of a mile.

The Solitary Reaper

Behold her, single in the field,
Yon solitary Highland° lass!
Reaping and singing by herself;
Stop here, or gently pass!
Alone she cuts and binds the grain, 5
And sings a melancholy strain;
O listen! for the vale profound
Is overflowing with the sound.

No nightingale did ever chaunt
More welcome notes to weary bands 10
Of travelers in some shady haunt
Among Arabian sands.
A voice so thrilling ne'er was heard
In springtime from the cuckoo-bird,
Breaking the silence of the seas 15
Among the farthest Hebrides.°

Will no one tell me what she sings?—
Perhaps the plaintive numbers° flow
For old, unhappy, far-off things,
And battles long ago. 20
Or is it some more humble lay,°
Familiar matter of today?
Some natural sorrow, loss, or pain,
That has been, and may be again?

Whate'er the theme, the maiden sang 25
As if her song could have no ending;
I saw her singing at her work,
And o'er the sickle bending—
I listened, motionless and still;
And, as I mounted up the hill, 30
The music in my heart I bore
Long after it was heard no more.

2. **Highland:** the Scottish upland. The girl is singing in the Highland language, a form of Gaelic. 16. **Hebrides:** islands off the northwest tip of Scotland. 18. **numbers:** measures. 21. **lay:** song.

I Wandered Lonely as a Cloud

I wandered lonely as a cloud
That floats on high o'er vales and hills,
When all at once I saw a crowd,
A host, of golden daffodils;
Beside the lake, beneath the trees, 5
Fluttering and dancing in the breeze.

Continuous as the stars that shine
And twinkle on the Milky Way,°
They stretched in never-ending line
Along the margin of a bay: 10
Ten thousand saw I at a glance,
Tossing their heads in sprightly dance.

The waves beside them danced; but they
Outdid the sparkling waves in glee:
A poet could not but be gay, 15
In such a jocund company:
I gazed—and gazed—but little thought
What wealth the show to me had brought:

For oft, when on my couch I lie
In vacant or in pensive mood, 20
They flash upon that inward eye
Which is the bliss of solitude;
And then my heart with pleasure fills,
And dances with the daffodils.

8. **the Milky Way:** an enormous cluster of stars stretching across the sky.

THERE WAS A BOY

1. What is Winander? What effect does it have upon the boy who goes there?

2. Demonstrate with your own hands exactly what the boy is doing in lines 7–10. Why does he do this? What answer does he get?

3. This poem describes a simple, often-repeated incident; tells us that the boy concerned in it died before he was twelve; and says in conclusion that the poet has often stood a long half-hour looking at the boy's grave. What do you think he was thinking of as he stood there? Why does Wordsworth not tell us in the poem?

4. Though originally published as a separate poem, these lines were later included by Wordsworth in a long autobiographical poem, *The Prelude,* as part of a discussion of education. What does the poem you have just read have to do with education? In which lines in particular does the boy learn? What kind of education is he getting? Do you think it is a good education or a poor one in Wordsworth's eyes?

LUCY GRAY

1. This poem is a modern ballad. What characteristics does it have of the ballad form? How does it differ from a folk ballad such as "Johnny Armstrong"?

2. Lucy Gray is associated with the fawn and the hare in stanza 3 and compared to the mountain deer in stanza 7. How do these associations affect our idea of her?

3. What kind of child is Lucy? Why is "solitude" a fitting subtitle for this poem? How, in the poem, is Lucy transformed into a "spirit" of solitude? From the tone of the poem, what seems to be Wordsworth's attitude toward Lucy? toward solitude?

4. Which lines in the poem present the most striking image? Which words in those lines make the image striking?

THE SOLITARY REAPER

1. In what ways is the Highland lass like Lucy Gray? What similarity is suggested in the title of the poem?

2. In how many ways is the girl's song like the song of birds? Why do you think Wordsworth speaks of birds in Arabia and the Hebrides rather than in Scotland or England?

3. What does the poet think the girl may be singing about? Why does her music have such a profound effect on him? Is this effect due only to the beauty of the song? What else might be responsible?

I WANDERED LONELY AS A CLOUD

1. There is a difference between being alone and being lonely. Why might a cloud seem "lonely"? At what points in the poem is the poet lonely? What mood is opposed to loneliness in the poem?

2. Judging from this poem, what value does nature have for man?

3. Like most poems, "I Wandered Lonely as a Cloud" expresses itself through figures of speech. Where in the poem does the poet use simile? personification? overstatement? metaphor? Why is personification especially important to the meaning of the poem?

THE POET IN THE POEMS

These four poems by Wordsworth are an excellent illustration of how a poet expresses his personality and concerns in his work. We benefit from reading a number of poems by a single poet because each poem we read deepens our understanding of the next and enables us to realize his meaning more fully.

All four of these poems by Wordsworth are concerned with the idea of solitude. In each, a solitary individual is pictured in close relationship with nature. What is the result of each of these experiences? Is the individual's relationship with nature harmonious or not? Is nature kind or hostile? Is the solitary individual in any of these poems ever entirely alone? What common theme concerning solitude seems to run through all these poems?

The selections from the poems of the poets that follow may not always cluster so closely around a single theme, but they will always reveal the poet's "voice"—his characteristic tone and attitude. Listen for this voice. Be alert for the links and similarities that reveal the poet in the poems.

WALT WHITMAN

(1819–1892)

Walt Whitman was the first poet to use free verse as the basic rhythm of his poems. Abandoning traditional meters, he wrote his poetry in long flowing lines, rhythmical but without a regular meter. He gave his lines form by using various kinds of parallel structure and repetition. Along with meter, Whitman abandoned rhyme and conventional figures of speech. His poetry was thus very new and original and to some readers seemed not like poetry at all. Nevertheless it gained a devoted audience and had a powerful influence on later poets.

In his poetry Whitman was the spokesman for the New World, as opposed to the Old World, for democracy as opposed to aristocracy, for the individual as opposed to conformity. He celebrated the common man—the craftsman, the tradesman, the sailor, the laborer—whom he considered as noble as kings and queens. He did not follow the usual poetic conventions because he believed that the New World needed a new kind of poetry; he identified the traditional meters, rhymes, and similes with Old World poetry.

Ultimately, for Whitman as for Wordsworth, the whole universe was divine. Every man, regardless of his social status was important because he contained within himself a bit of divinity. For the same reason, leaves of grass and even mice were miracles, being manifestations of a divine spirit that are unexplainable by reason. The title of his collected poems, *Leaves of Grass,* symbolizes Whitman's belief that every blade of grass is a miracle, an embodiment of divinity, a miniature symbol of the universe. Each of his poems seeks to express that divinity. His long poem "Song of Myself" is a hymn of praise, not to his own egoistic private self, but to that universal aspect of himself—and of every man and every living thing—which to Whitman was a symbol of divine power.

Whitman, like Wordsworth, believed that we learn basic truths through mystical insight or intuition. Reason and science give us facts, not truths; they deal with the body of the universe but cannot reach its soul.

Walt Whitman, the son of a carpenter, was born on Long Island, New

York, and lived his early life there and in New York City. Before turning poet, he was a teacher, a printer, a newspaper reporter, and editor of the Brooklyn *Eagle*. Not until he was thirty-six did he publish his first book of poems, the revolutionary *Leaves of Grass*. This book, which he considered his life's work, was revised and expanded in later editions. During the War Between the States, Whitman served as a volunteer nurse and wound-dresser with the Northern armies. Filled with pity for the wounded on both sides, he wrote the war poems published in *Drum Taps* and later added to *Leaves of Grass*. The assassination of Abraham Lincoln struck deeply at Whitman's sympathies and moved him to write "When Lilacs Last in the Dooryard Bloomed." He lived the last years of his life in Camden, New Jersey, finally recognized as an important poet.

FROM *Song of Myself*

Section 31

The most important poem in the first edition of *Leaves of Grass* was "Song of Myself." This is the thirty-first of the fifty-two sections of the poem.

I believe a leaf of grass is no less than the journeywork ° of the stars,
And the pismire ° is equally perfect, and a grain of sand, and the egg of the
 wren,
And the tree toad is a chef-d'œuvre ° for the highest,
And the running blackberry would adorn the parlors of heaven,
And the narrowest hinge in my hand puts to scorn all machinery, 5
And the cow crunching with depressed head surpasses any statue,
And a mouse is miracle enough to stagger sextillions of infidels.°

I find I incorporate gneiss,° coal, long-threaded moss, fruits, grains, esculent
 roots,
And am stuccoed with quadrupeds ° and birds all over,
And have distanced what is behind me for good reasons, 10
But call anything back again when I desire it.

In vain the speeding or shyness,
In vain the plutonic rocks ° send their old heat against my approach,
In vain the mastodon ° retreats beneath its own powdered bones,

1. **journeywork:** work of a craftsman. 2. **pismire:** ant. 3. **chef-d'œuvre** (she·dœ'vr'): masterpiece. 7. **sextillions of infidels:** hordes of unbelievers. 8. **gneiss (nīs):** coarse rocks. 9. **stuccoed with quadrupeds:** plastered with four-legged animals. 13. **plutonic rocks:** molten rock within the earth which has solidified. 14. **mastodon:** an extinct elephantlike animal.

In vain objects stand leagues off and assume manifold shapes, 15
In vain the ocean settling in hollows and the great monsters lying low,
In vain the buzzard houses herself with the sky,
In vain the snake slides through the creepers and logs,
In vain the elk takes to the inner passes of the woods,
In vain the razor-billed auk sails far north to Labrador, 20
I follow quickly, I ascend to the nest in the fissure of the cliff.

FROM *Song of Myself*

Section 48

I have said that the soul is not more than the body,
And I have said that the body is not more than the soul,
And nothing, not God, is greater to one than one's self is,
And whoever walks a furlong without sympathy walks to his own funeral
 dressed in his shroud,
And I or you pocketless of a dime may purchase the pick of the earth, 5
And to glance with an eye or show a bean in its pod confounds the learning
 of all times,
And there is no trade or employment but the young man following it may
 become a hero,
And there is no object so soft but it makes a hub for the wheeled universe,
And I say to any man or woman, Let your soul stand cool and composed
 before a million universes.

And I say to mankind, Be not curious about God, 10
For I who am curious about each am not curious about God,
(No array of terms can say how much I am at peace about God and about
 death.)

I hear and behold God in every object, yet understand God not in the least,
Nor do I understand who there can be more wonderful than myself.

Why should I wish to see God better than this day? 15
I see something of God each hour of the twenty-four, and each moment
 then,
In the faces of men and women I see God, and in my own face in the glass,
I find letters from God dropped in the street, and every one is signed by
 God's name,
And I leave them where they are, for I know that wheresoe'er I go
Others will punctually come for ever and ever. 20

I Hear America Singing

I hear America singing, the varied carols I hear,
Those of mechanics, each one singing his as it should be blithe and strong,
The carpenter singing his as he measures his plank or beam,
The mason singing his as he makes ready for work, or leaves off work,
The boatman singing what belongs to him in his boat, the deckhand singing
 on the steamboat deck, 5
The shoemaker singing as he sits on his bench, the hatter singing as he
 stands,
The woodcutter's song, the ploughboy's on his way in the morning, or at
 noon intermission or at sundown,
The delicious singing of the mother, or of the young wife at work, or of the
 girl sewing or washing,
Each singing what belongs to him or her and to none else,
The day what belongs to the day—at night the party of young fellows, ro-
 bust, friendly, 10
Singing with open mouths their strong melodious songs.

Cavalry Crossing a Ford

A line in long array where they wind betwixt green islands,
They take a serpentine course, their arms flash in the sun—hark to the mu-
 sical clank,
Behold the silvery river, in it the splashing horses loitering stop to drink,
Behold the brown-faced men, each group, each person a picture, the negli-
 gent rest on the saddles,
Some emerge on the opposite bank, others are just entering the ford—
 while, 5
Scarlet and blue and snowy white,
The guidon ° flags flutter gaily in the wind.

7. **guidon** (gī′don): a small flag or streamer.

SONG OF MYSELF—SECTION 31

1. What things does Whitman mention in the first part of each line in the first verse paragraph? What do these things have in common? How would Whitman's definition of a *masterpiece* or *miracle* differ from the ordinary definition?

2. In this poem Whitman speaks not literally, but figuratively. What does he mean in lines 8–11? In what way does a poet "incorporate" gneiss, coal, and moss? How is he "stuccoed with quadrupeds and birds all over"? In what sense has he "distanced" what is "behind" him? How can he "call anything back again"?

3. Why is nature's resistance to the poet "in vain"? How does he "follow" it? Why is it not separate from him?

4. How is each of the three verse paragraphs given formal structure? Would this poem resemble ordinary prose if its lines were printed continuously?

SONG OF MYSELF—SECTION 48

1. In this poem, another section of "Song of Myself," Whitman proclaims that every young man is a possible hero and that every object is "a hub for the wheeled universe." What does he mean? In what sense is every individual, to himself, the center of the universe, around which everything else revolves?

2. In this poem Whitman speaks rather slightingly of man's accumulated "learning of all times" (line 6), of his curiosity about God (lines 10–11), and of his attempts at intellec-

tual understanding (lines 13–14). Why? What do all of these have in common? What does Whitman consider superior to them?

3. Given Whitman's ideas of how we learn and grow, why does a man who walks through the world without sympathy walk "to his own funeral dressed in his shroud"? In what sense is such a man already dead? On the other hand, how may a man without money "purchase the pick of the earth"?

4. Why is Whitman able to see "letters from God dropped in the street"? What are these "letters"? Why does he let them lie?

I HEAR AMERICA SINGING

1. What do the various people mentioned in the poem have in common? What does the word *carols* suggest about the nature of their songs? What ideas from "Song of Myself" are suggested in this poem?

2. Each worker sings "what belongs to him or her and to none else." Does the result, in Whitman's poem, add up to noisy confusion or harmony? What does this result suggest about Whitman's opinion of democracy?

3. How has the poet created a sense of formal structure in this poem?

CAVALRY CROSSING A FORD

1. How does Whitman give a continuous flow of motion to this very brief picture? In which lines does he arrest our attention momentarily?

2. Though the scene described is military, the effect is peaceful. What sounds and images help to create a feeling of peace?

EMILY DICKINSON
(1830–1886)

The poems of Emily Dickinson are like little pellets of dry ice. Though nearly always brief, they burn. They are remarkable for their originality, their passion, their wit, and their extreme compression. Emily Dickinson's command of words and images enabled her to achieve, in a great many poems, the exact effect she wanted with precision and economy. In this respect she is the opposite of Walt Whitman, who was expansive and over-flowing rather than condensed and brief.

Emily Dickinson usually wrote in simple, traditional stanza forms, but she was revolutionary in her use of rhyme. She often departed from "per-fect" rhymes (such as *day, way)* and used "slant" or approximate rhymes (such as *day, why),* now a common device among poets. She was also often unconventional in her grammar—the result not of ignorance or carelessness, but of an extremely individual twist of mind.

A New England girl who all her life lived close to home, Emily Dickinson pictured great events such as love and death in terms of household tasks and her own daily preoccupations—kitchen, garden, village. Her experience was deep rather than broad and her observation close rather than wide-ranging. But her imagination soared far beyond the limits of her daily life, and though her outward existence was quiet, she lived an intense inner life of the mind and the emotions. Her poetry is whimsical, passionate, and penetrating—often all three at once. The principal subjects of her poems are love, nature, religion, and examination of her own inner feelings.

Emily Dickinson was born in Amherst, Massachusetts, the daughter of a lawyer who later became a United States congressman. After less than a year at the South Hadley Female Seminary, now Mount Holyoke College, she returned to Amherst and lived there the rest of her life, except for brief trips to Washington, Philadelphia, and Boston. It seems obvious from her poetry that she had, in her life, at least one great love, but she never spoke or wrote of it to anyone. Many readers of her poetry have tried to guess with

whom she fell in love and why she never married. Did her father forbid the match? Was the man already married? Was there one man or two in her emotional life? Whatever the answers to these questions, her later life was spent increasingly close to home, and in her last years she was practically a recluse, seldom venturing beyond her garden hedge. Though she wrote over 1,700 poems, on bits of wrapping paper, envelopes, and old grocery bills, not more than seven of her poems were published during her lifetime. To a friend of hers she once exclaimed, "How can you print a piece of your soul?"

She Sweeps with Many-Colored Brooms

She sweeps with many-colored brooms,
And leaves the shreds behind;
Oh, housewife in the evening west,
Come back, and dust the pond!

You dropped a purple raveling in, 5
You dropped an amber thread;
And now you've littered all the East
With duds of emerald!

And still she plies her spotted brooms,
And still the aprons fly, 10
Till brooms fade softly into stars—
And then I come away.

If You Were Coming in the Fall

If you were coming in the fall,
I'd brush the summer by
With half a smile, and half a spurn,
As housewives do a fly.

If I could see you in a year, 5
I'd wind the months in balls,
And put them each in separate drawers
For fear the numbers fuse.

If only centuries delayed,
I'd count them on my hand, 10
Subtracting till my fingers dropped
Into Van Diemen's land.°

If certain, when this life was out,
That yours and mine should be,
I'd toss it yonder like a rind, 15
And take eternity.

But now, uncertain of the length
Of this that is between,
It goads me, like the goblin bee,
That will not state its sting. 20

12. **Van Diemen's land:** old name for Tasmania.

I Years Had Been from Home

I years had been from home,
And now, before the door,
I dared not open, lest a face
I never saw before

Stare vacant into mine 5
And ask my business there.
My business—just a life I left,
Was such still dwelling there?

I fumbled at my nerve,
I scanned the windows o'er; 10
The silence like an ocean rolled,
And broke against my ear.

I laughed a wooden laugh
That I could fear a door,
Who danger and the dead had faced, 15
But never shook before.

I fitted to the latch
My hand, with trembling care,
Lest back the awful door should spring,
And leave me in the floor. 20

I moved my fingers off
As cautiously as glass,
And held my ears, and like a thief
Stole gasping from the house.

The Brain Within Its Groove

The brain within its groove
Runs evenly and true;
But let a splinter swerve,
'Twere easier for you

To put a current back 5
When floods have slit the hills,
And scooped a turnpike for themselves,
And trodden out the mills!

SHE SWEEPS WITH MANY-COLORED BROOMS

1. What scene in nature does the poet describe in this poem? What time of day is it? In which directions is she looking? What colors does she see?

2. Who is *She* in this poem? What does she sweep with her "many-colored brooms"? What are the "shreds," "ravelings," and "threads" she drops? What remains behind her in the East? in the pond?

3. What kind of metaphor is central to this poem? What do the pictures and imagery in the poem suggest about the kind of life most familiar to the poet?

IF YOU WERE COMING IN THE FALL

1. What seems to be the relationship between the *you* and the *I* of this poem?

2. The first four stanzas of the poem all begin with *If*. What idea do these stanzas have in common? How does each stanza increase in intensity? In the fifth stanza, how does the speaker change her tone?

3. What are the connotations of the word *goblin* in the last stanza? What does it suggest about the speaker's feelings? How is her uncertainty like a bee that "will not state its sting"?

4. What psychological truth is expressed in this poem? State its theme in a sentence.

5. How are the images in this poem like those in "She Sweeps with Many-Colored Brooms"?

I YEARS HAD BEEN FROM HOME

1. What is the situation in this poem? Why does the speaker tremble? What is he afraid of? Why does he finally steal away, "gasping," without opening the door? What does he preserve by leaving the door unopened? What does he possibly lose? discover?

2. What tone does the speaker use in saying "just a life I left" (line 7)? Is any word in this phrase ironic? If so, which? Why do the words *just* and *life* together give a shock of surprise?

3. Lines 11 and 12 contain a striking metaphor. What is *silence* pictured as in these two lines? Why is the word *broke* so effective here?

4. What irony of situation is brought out in stanza 4? What is the meaning of *awful* in line 19? What does "As cautiously as glass" (line 22) mean?

5. How is this poem like "If You Were Coming in the Fall" in subject matter? Are the two poems similar or opposite in theme?

THE BRAIN WITHIN ITS GROOVE

1. What is the brain pictured as in stanza 1? in stanza 2? What is the poet saying in this poem?

2. Once jarred from its normal functioning, what damage does the brain do? What symbolic meaning might be associated with *mills*? What connection can you see between "mills" and "the brain within its groove"?

3. In what way is the subject matter of this poem like that of "I Years Had Been from Home"?

EDWIN
ARLINGTON
ROBINSON
(1869–1935)

A quiet man given to brooding over the mysteries of man's nature and the meanings of life, Edwin Arlington Robinson began writing at a time when poetry had fallen into the doldrums. The popular poets were writing verse that was trivial and sentimental. Robinson yearned to return poetry to a concern with the central issues of man's life and to rescue it from the stilted, artificial language in which it was being written. In his own poetry he developed a lean, stripped style, stressing natural word order and language often close to the colloquial but capable of rising to eloquence. Like Wordsworth, he wanted to see poetry written in a language "really used by men."

Robinson is famous for his character portraits. Profoundly interested in human nature, he devoted his life to probing and laying bare the secret recesses of men's souls. He was particularly concerned with the puzzled and the frustrated—the misfits and the failures. They were more interesting, he said, than successful men. Robinson was teased by the paradoxes of apparent success and failure. He often discovered spiritual peace and happiness in men looked down on by their neighbors, and spiritual emptiness in those generally regarded as successful men. His characters are mostly New Englanders, inhabitants of his fictional Tilbury Town, so named because its inhabitants worshiped the *till,* or money box. He was not deeply interested in local color, however; his New Englanders are universal men.

Because of his preoccupation with failures and misfits and the darker half of life, Robinson has often been called a pessimist. It is true that nearly all his poetry is sad. Its bleakness, however, is relieved by his ironic wit and quiet humor. Robinson is seldom so sad that he cannot laugh. Moreover, at the bottom of his poetry is a transcendental faith much like that of Emerson and Whitman. Though Robinson was more of a realist than Whitman, he never lost faith in a transcendent reality that glowed within every man and thing. He used to declare himself an "insane optimist" because he saw so many possibilities of good in lives that seemed entirely bleak and evil.

Robinson grew up in Gardiner, Maine, the Tilbury Town of his poetry.

He attended Harvard University for two years, but had to leave school when his father died. He devoted his entire adult life to poetry, spending his winters in New York City and his summers at the MacDowell artists' colony in New Hampshire. Most of his life was lived in poverty. His room in New York supposedly contained a bed, a chair, a mirrorless bureau, a washstand, and a cracked water pitcher. Only after the publication in 1927 of *Tristram,* the third of three long poems on the legends of King Arthur, did his life become more comfortable. Like that of so many of his characters, Robinson's life could be described as one of material failure and spiritual success.

The House on the Hill

They are all gone away,
 The House is shut and still,
There is nothing more to say.

Through broken walls and gray
 The winds blow bleak and shrill: 5
They are all gone away.

Nor is there one today
 To speak them good or ill:
There is nothing more to say.

Why is it then we stray 10
 Around the sunken sill?
They are all gone away,

And our poor fancy-play
 For them is wasted skill:
There is nothing more to say. 15

There is ruin and decay
 In the House on the Hill:
They are all gone away,
There is nothing more to say.

Uncle Ananias

His words were magic and his heart was true,
 And everywhere he wandered he was blessed.
Out of all ancient men my childhood knew
 I choose him and I mark him for the best.
Of all authoritative liars, too, 5
 I crown him loveliest.

How fondly I remember the delight
 That always glorified him in the spring;
The joyous courage and the benedight °
 Profusion of his faith in everything! 10
He was a good old man, and it was right
 That he should have his fling.

9. **benedight** (archaic): blessed.

And often, underneath the apple trees,
 When we surprised him in the summertime,
With what superb magnificence and ease
 He sinned enough to make the day sublime! 15
And if he liked us there about his knees,
 Truly it was no crime.

All summer long we loved him for the same
 Perennial inspiration of his lies; 20
And when the russet wealth of autumn came,
 There flew but fairer visions to our eyes—
Multiple, tropical, winged with a feathery flame,
 Like birds of paradise.

So to the sheltered end of many a year 25
 He charmed the seasons out with pageantry
Wearing upon his forehead, with no fear,
 The laurel of approved iniquity.°
And every child who knew him, far or near,
 Did love him faithfully. 30

 28. **iniquity:** wickedness.

Aaron Stark

Withal° a meager man was Aaron Stark,
Cursed and unkempt, shrewd, shriveled, and morose.
A miser was he, with a miser's nose,
And eyes like little dollars in the dark.
His thin, pinched mouth was nothing but a mark; 5
And when he spoke there came like sullen blows
Through scattered fangs a few snarled words and close,°
As if a cur were chary° of its bark.

Glad for the murmur of his hard renown,
Year after year he shambled through the town, 10
A loveless exile moving with a staff;
And oftentimes there crept into his ears
A sound of alien pity, touched with tears—
And then (and only then) did Aaron laugh.

 1. **withal** (with·ôl′): also, in addition. 7. **close:** guarded, secretive. 8. **chary** (châr′ē):
stingy.

The Sheaves

Where long the shadows of the wind had rolled,
Green wheat was yielding to the change assigned;
And as by some vast magic undivined °
The world was turning slowly into gold.
Like nothing that was ever bought or sold 5
It waited there, the body and the mind;
And with a mighty meaning of a kind
That tells the more the more it is not told.

So in a land where all days are not fair,
Fair days went on till on another day 10
A thousand golden sheaves were lying there,
Shining and still, but not for long to stay—
As if a thousand girls with golden hair
Might rise from where they slept and go away.

3. **undivined:** unguessed, unexplained.

FOR STUDY AND DISCUSSION

THE HOUSE ON THE HILL

1. The poet capitalizes "the House on the Hill." What does this capitalization, and the house's location, suggest about the social status of its former owners?

2. What is the answer to the question in the fourth stanza? What is "our poor fancy-play"? Why is it wasted?

3. What comment does this poem make on human life?

UNCLE ANANIAS

1. The original Ananias, in the Bible, was a liar. Uncle Ananias also is a liar, who has "sinned" and who wears upon his forehead the sign of "iniquity." Yet he is remembered as "a good old man" whose "heart was true," and "everywhere he wandered he was blessed." How do you explain this paradox?

2. What is an "authoritative liar"? How do Ananias's lies "make the day sublime"? What about him makes the children love him?

3. What is symbolized by the progression of the seasons in the poem?

AARON STARK

1. How are Aaron Stark's name and appearance both symbolic of his nature? What is his predominant physical characteristic?

2. How does Aaron's way of speaking express his inner nature? Which words in lines 6–8 give a vivid impression of his speech?

3. When is Aaron glad? When does he laugh? How do the causes of his gladness and laughter differ from those of most people? What does this show about what has happened to his natural human feelings?

4. What kind of poem is this in form? How do you know?

THE SHEAVES

1. What does the metaphor in line 1 suggest about the wind? How does the green wheat "yield" to "the change assigned"? What time of year is described in the poem?

2. What is the poet's attitude toward nature and the changes of nature? Who or what has "assigned" the changes that take place? What "mighty meaning" does the poet see in things? How is the ripening wheat both "the body and the mind"?

ROBERT FROST
(1874–1963)

Robert Frost once pointed out that one half of what we are is where we live; the other half consists of how we talk. Or, as he put it, "One half of individuality is locality, and the other half [is] colloquiality," Although said with a smile, this remark underlines two characteristics of Frost's own poetry. First, it is rooted in place—in locality. Frost is a New England poet. He writes of the birch trees, the stone walls, the white churches, the deserted farms, the leaf-falls and the snowfalls of New England and of its farmers, its lonely hill wives, its wandering tramps and hired men. But Frost is much more than a regional poet. In writing about New England he writes about all mankind. His basic concerns are not local customs, but all human joys and griefs.

The "other half" of Frost's poetry, colloquiality, stems from his concern with the rhythms of everyday speech. Early in his writing career, he decided that the possibilities of musical variation of vowels and consonants were soon exhausted, and had in fact been exhausted by previous poets. What poetry needed, he believed, was an additional ingredient: the rise and fall of the speaking voice. Natural emphasis—"the sound of sense"—should work against the regular rise and fall of meter. "The possibilities of tune from the dramatic tones of meaning struck across the rigidity of a limited meter" were endless. Frost's great technical achievement as a poet was his ability to capture the intonations of the speaking voice in meter, as can be heard in these lines:

> "I sha'n't be gone long. You come too."

> "I doubt if even his mother could tell him, 'Sakes,
> It's only weather.' He'd think she didn't know!"

> "Earth's the right place for love:
> I don't know where it's likely to go better."

Though greatly interested in technique and form, Frost always regarded poetry as essentially "one more art of having something to say." A poem, he said, "begins in delight and ends in wisdom." It ends "in a clarification of life—not necessarily a great clarification, such as sects and cults are founded on, but in a momentary stay against confusion." This statement says much about Frost's view of life. He was not a system-builder, like Wordsworth and Whitman. Rather, he held a tentative, critical attitude toward basic problems. Though his thought was rooted in faith, it was a questioning faith, not bound up in a system of fixed rules. Life, he believed, "sways perilously at the confluence of opposing forces," and the ability to live it well—as to write poetry well or do anything well—lies largely in an inner balance that keeps us from being swept away. He believed in self-reliance and individualism, in man's dignity and life's worth and meaning. His attitude toward life is best summed up, perhaps, in the epitaph he proposed for himself in one of his poems: "I had a lover's quarrel with the world."

The spirit of play is prominent in Frost's poetry. The man himself had a roguish twinkle in his eye and loved banter in conversation. What he once wrote about Edwin Arlington Robinson applies equally to himself. "The style is the man. Rather say the style is the way the man takes himself; and to be at all charming or even bearable, the way is almost rigidly prescribed. If it is with outer seriousness, it must be with inner humor. If it is with outer humor, it must be with inner seriousness. Neither one alone without the other under it will do."

Though his poetry is characteristically of New England, Frost was born in California, where his father had gone to work on a newspaper. When he was eleven, however, his father died, and his mother took him back East to live with his father's family. In between a few months at Dartmouth College and two years at Harvard, he worked at various odd jobs and married the girl with whom he had been covaledictorian in high school. In 1900 he settled his family on a farm near Derry, New Hampshire, and began to farm, teach school, and write poetry. These early years were lonely, discouraging ones. During twenty years of writing, he earned only about ten dollars a year from his poems. Then in 1912 he took his family to England, where his first two books were published. When he returned to the United States three years later, he was widely known. For the rest of his life he combined writing poetry with "starting" farms and lecturing to students on philosophy and poetry.

Birches

When I see birches bend to left and right
Across the line of straighter darker trees,
I like to think some boy's been swinging them.
But swinging doesn't bend them down to stay
As ice storms do. Often you must have seen them 5
Loaded with ice a sunny winter morning
After a rain. They click upon themselves
As the breeze rises, and turn many-colored
As the stir cracks and crazes° their enamel.
Soon the sun's warmth makes them shed crystal shells 10
Shattering and avalanching on the snow crust—
Such heaps of broken glass to sweep away
You'd think the inner dome of heaven had fallen.
They are dragged to the withered bracken° by the load,
And they seem not to break; though once they are bowed 15
So low for long, they never right themselves:
You may see their trunks arching in the woods
Years afterward, trailing their leaves on the ground
Like girls on hands and knees that throw their hair
Before them over their heads to dry in the sun. 20
But I was going to say when Truth broke in
With all her matter of fact about the ice storm,
I should prefer to have some boy bend them
As he went out and in to fetch the cows—
Some boy too far from town to learn baseball, 25
Whose only play was what he found himself,
Summer or winter, and could play alone.
One by one he subdued his father's trees
By riding them down over and over again
Until he took the stiffness out of them, 30
And not one but hung limp, not one was left
For him to conquer. He learned all there was
To learn about not launching out too soon
And so not carrying the tree away
Clear to the ground. He always kept his poise 35
To the top branches, climbing carefully
With the same pains you use to fill a cup
Up to the brim, and even above the brim.
Then he flung outward, feet first, with a swish,
Kicking his way down through the air to the ground. 40
So was I once myself a swinger of birches.

9. **crazes:** cracks into networks of tiny lines. 14. **bracken:** large, coarse ferns.

And so I dream of going back to be.
It's when I'm weary of considerations,
And life is too much like a pathless wood
Where your face burns and tickles with the cobwebs 45
Broken across it, and one eye is weeping
From a twig's having lashed across it open.
I'd like to get away from earth awhile
And then come back to it and begin over.
May no fate willfully misunderstand me 50
And half grant what I wish and snatch me away
Not to return. Earth's the right place for love:
I don't know where it's likely to go better.
I'd like to go by climbing a birch tree,
And climb black branches up a snow-white trunk 55
Toward heaven, till the tree could bear no more,
But dipped its top and set me down again.
That would be good both going and coming back.
One could do worse than be a swinger of birches.

The Onset

Always the same, when on a fated night
At last the gathered snow lets down as white
As may be in dark woods, and with a song
It shall not make again all winter long
Of hissing on the yet uncovered ground, 5
I almost stumble looking up and round,
As one who overtaken by the end
Gives up his errand, and lets death descend
Upon him where he is, with nothing done
To evil, no important triumph won, 10
More than if life had never been begun.

Yet all the precedent is on my side:
I know that winter death has never tried
The earth but it has failed: the snow may heap
In long storms an undrifted four feet deep 15
As measured against maple, birch, and oak,
It cannot check the peeper's ° silver croak;
And I shall see the snow all go down hill
In water of a slender April rill °
That flashes tail through last year's withered brake ° 20
And dead weeds, like a disappearing snake.
Nothing will be left white but here a birch,
And there a clump of houses with a church.

17. **peeper's:** A peeper is a frog that makes a peeping noise. 19. **rill:** small stream.
20. **brake:** bracken, coarse ferns.

Departmental

An ant on the tablecloth
Ran into a dormant moth
Of many times his size.
He showed not the least surprise.
His business wasn't with such. 5
He gave it scarcely a touch,
And was off on his duty run.
Yet if he encountered one
Of the hive's enquiry squad
Whose work is to find out God 10
And the nature of time and space,
He would put him onto the case.
Ants are a curious race;
One crossing with hurried tread
The body of one of their dead 15
Isn't given a moment's arrest—
Seems not even impressed.
But he no doubt reports to any
With whom he crosses antennae,
And they no doubt report 20
To the higher up at court.
Then word goes forth in Formic:
"Death's come to Jerry McCormic,

Our selfless forager Jerry.
Will the special Janizary ° 25
Whose office it is to bury
The dead of the commissary
Go bring him home to his people.
Lay him in state on a sepal.
Wrap him for shroud in a petal. 30
Embalm him with ichor of nettle.
This is the word of your Queen."
And presently on the scene
Appears a solemn mortician;
And taking formal position, 35
With feelers calmly atwiddle,
Seizes the dead by the middle,
And heaving him high in air,
Carries him out of there.
No one stands round to stare. 40
It is nobody else's affair.

It couldn't be called ungentle.
But how thoroughly departmental.

25. **Janizary:** Turkish slave.

Reluctance

Out through the fields and the woods
 And over the walls I have wended;°
I have climbed the hills of view
 And looked at the world, and de-
 scended;
I have come by the highway home, 5
 And lo, it is ended.

The leaves are all dead on the ground,
 Save those that the oak is keeping
To ravel them one by one
 And let them go scraping and creeping
Out over the crusted snow, 11
 When others are sleeping.

2. **wended:** gone

And the dead leaves lie huddled and still,
 No longer blown hither and thither;
The last lone aster is gone; 15
 The flowers of the witch hazel wither;
The heart is still aching to seek,
 But the feet question "Whither?"

Ah, when to the heart of man
 Was it ever less than a treason 20
To go with the drift of things,
 To yield with a grace to reason,
And bow and accept the end
 Of a love or a season?

FOR STUDY AND DISCUSSION

BIRCHES

1. In structure this poem may be divided into three almost equal parts. Where does each part end? What does the poet say in each?
2. The poem contains several striking similes. Point out as many as you can. Which seems to you most fitting in this poem?
3. In the last part of the poem Frost imagines climbing the birches from earth to heaven. Do you think he means *earth* and *heaven* to be taken as literal or symbolical? What symbolic meanings do the words suggest? What does Frost feel is the right balance between the actual and the ideal? What does it mean to be a good "swinger of birches"?

THE ONSET

1. What two seasons are described in the poem? Which season symbolizes life? which death? What aspects of each season help to suggest these larger meanings?
2. There is a network of imagery in the poem. What image in stanza 2 reminds you of the snow's "hissing" in stanza 1? Do you associate the snow with life or death? with good or evil? How does this association reinforce the symbolism of the seasons?

3. What is "The Onset"? When it is over, what will have survived? In what ways are the two things in the last line unlike the white snow?

DEPARTMENTAL

1. What is the meaning of *dormant, arrest, commissary, sepal, ichor?* Why was *Formic* chosen as the name for the ant language?
2. What is *departmentalism?* Why is "Departmental" a good title for this poem?
3. How would you describe the tone of this poem? What is Frost's attitude toward the ants? What about them does he find most amusing? Is this poem only about ants? What human characteristics is Frost satirizing?

RELUCTANCE

1. What is it that has ended (line 6)?
2. In what condition are most of the oak leaves? What will happen to the rest? When?
3. What does the heart still ache to seek (line 17)? Why do the feet ask "Whither?" What does the ended season symbolize in the poem?
4. What does "reason" tell the poet? What opposes reason? What does this poem suggest about inner balance and the nature of man?

Reading and Writing About Poetry

Poetry is, in general, the most compressed and most imaginative kind of writing. A poet tries to suggest as much as possible in as few words as he can. To do this, he can use all the devices of language—such as repetition, rhythm, imagery, and rhyme—in an attempt to communicate his deepest feelings. Poetry can be difficult, but it can also be rewarding. You may find the following suggestions useful in getting at the meaning of a poem:

1. Read the poem several times. Read more slowly than you would read prose. Read in sentences rather than in lines. Read aloud at least one of these times.

2. Make sure you know the meaning of every word. Look up any words that are not clear from their context in the poem. Remember that most words have more than one meaning and that poets are aware of—and often make use of—the various meanings of a word.

3. If the meaning of a sentence is at first unclear, study its *syntax* (structure) and its punctuation. Look for key words and words that indicate transitions or turnings in the poet's thought. To be sure you understand the meaning, try rephrasing the sentence in your own words. (Be sure, though, that your rephrasing makes sense in the total context of the poem.)

4. Asking yourself questions such as the following is often useful in understanding the poem as a whole:

Does the poem make a general statement and then support that statement with details? Is there more than one general statement? If so, how are they related?

Who is the speaker in the poem? What does the character of the speaker have to do with the poem's meaning?

Is there repetition of words or phrases or ideas? Is there parallel structure of ideas or details? What is the effect of any comparisons or contrasts in the poem?

Is there more than one level of meaning in the poem? If so, which lines are most deeply concerned with which meaning?

You will probably find these procedures useful in reading any poem. As an example of how you might apply them, reread the following Shakespeare song (see pages 310–11), giving close attention to the meaning of each word and line:

> Blow, blow, thou winter wind,
> Thou art not so unkind
> As man's ingratitude;
> Thy tooth is not so keen,
> Because thou art not seen, 5
> Although thy breath be rude.
> Heigh-ho! sing, heigh-ho! unto the green holly:
> Most friendship is feigning, most loving mere
> folly.
> Then heigh-ho! the holly!
> This life is most jolly. 10
>
> Freeze, freeze, thou bitter sky,
> That dost not bite so nigh
> As benefits forgot:
> Though thou the waters warp,
> Thy sting is not so sharp 15
> As friend remembered not.
> Heigh-ho! sing, heigh-ho! unto the green holly:
> Most friendship is feigning, most loving mere
> folly.
> Then heigh ho! the holly!
> This life is most jolly. 20

1. Reread the poem several times, and at least one time aloud. What impression do you get of the tone of voice in which each line should be spoken?

2. What is the meaning of the word *rude* (line 6) in this poem? of *feigning* (line 8)? of *folly* (line 8)? of *nigh* (line 12)?

3. Express in your own words what the poet is saying in each sentence of this poem.

4. What general statements does the speaker make in each stanza of this poem? What do these statements have in common? What details in the poem make clearer and more vivid exactly what the speaker means?

What kind of person seems to be speaking? What is his mood? In what tone do you think he would speak this poem?

What is the effect of the parallel phrasing in the first line of each stanza? of the four lines repeated as a refrain? How do these repetitions emphasize the meaning of the poem?

On its deepest level, what is this poem about—winter wind and holly, or man's ingratitude to friends?

PARAPHRASING A POEM

Perhaps the best way to understand a difficult poem is to try rephrasing it in your own words, line by line. To do this, of course, you must read carefully, know the meaning of every word, and understand the syntax or structure of each line. When you can paraphrase what the poet is saying in each line, you are ready to probe for the meaning of his poem. Try paraphrasing these lines from Samuel Taylor Coleridge's "Kubla Khan":

In Xanadu did Kubla Khan
A stately pleasure dome decree:
Where Alph, the sacred river, ran
Through caverns measureless to man
 Down to a sunless sea. 5
So twice five miles of fertile ground
With walls and towers were girdled round:
And there were gardens bright with sinuous
 rills,
Where blossomed many an incense-bearing
 tree;
And here were forests ancient as the hills, 10
Enfolding sunny spots of greenery.
But oh! that deep romantic chasm which
 slanted
Down the green hill athwart a cedarn cover!
A savage place! as holy and enchanted
As e'er beneath a waning moon was haunted 15
By woman wailing for her demon lover!

1. Where is your paraphrase more direct and simple than the poet's lines? In these places, what is lost in paraphrasing?

2. Where were you forced to use more words than the poet to express his meaning?

3. What procedures would you use if you were going on to work out the full meaning of this poem?

WRITING ABOUT A POEM

Before you can write about a poem, you must understand it. Read the following poem by Emily Dickinson carefully, using the procedures described above. Read in sentences and be sure you know the meaning of each word. Look for clues in syntax and punctuation. When you feel you understand the poem, write an essay analyzing it, following your step-by-step examination. In your final paragraph explain, as fully as you can, what you think the poem means.

Success is counted sweetest
By those who ne'er succeed.
To comprehend a nectar
Requires sorest need.

Not one of all the purple Host 5
Who took the Flag today
Can tell the definition
So clear of Victory

As he defeated—dying—
On whose forbidden ear 10
The distant strains of triumph
Burst agonized and clear!

ART AND LITERATURE

Look closely at the paintings on pages 331–36. Which one gives you the strongest, most definite impression? What words would you use to create this same impression in a poem? Make a list of words, phrases, and specific details that you feel would best communicate the painting's atmosphere or mood, then try writing a free-verse poem that suggests in words what the painting makes you feel.

DRAMA

GOOD DRAMA requires three basic elements—a story, a performance, and an audience. In order to attract, interest, and hold an audience, a playwright must present a compelling, suspenseful *plot* or story, with a beginning, a middle, and an end. The beginning arouses curiosity; the middle involves us with the issues introduced at the beginning; and the end must resolve all these issues in a satisfactory manner.

In addition, a good play must have interesting *characters,* the people involved in the action. Characters should be sharply drawn and clearly motivated. Otherwise an actor will find it difficult to project that character across to the audience. Plot and character are telegraphed to the audience primarily by means of *dialogue*—that is, by what the characters say. Other important elements of the drama include *costume* and *make-up*. The villain in a Western movie is often immediately recognizable by his black clothes and drooping mustache. *Scenery, lighting,* and sometimes *music* are among the factors that combine to create the magical mood of good drama.

HISTORY OF THE DRAMA

The origins of drama are obscure, but one can assume that the form is as old as language itself. Drama was probably born when men first learned to narrate events in comprehensible words. The first theater was probably a Stone Age campfire; the first actor-playwright, a man retelling the story of a hunt to an audience made up of members of his tribe. All the ingredients were probably there: the suspenseful story, the conflict between man and beast, the electric hush in the audience, the climax, the applause.

Drama continued to evolve through the ages. The drama of the early Greeks began as simple religious celebrations, but by the time the Greeks had achieved their well-ordered civilization in the sixth and fifth centuries B.C., their theater had developed imposing and elaborate forms. The Greeks presented their plays in huge, open-air, semicircular amphitheaters which had magnificent acoustics. These amphitheaters were usually cut into the sides of hills and had a two-leveled stage area on which sumptuously cos-

tumed performers acted out the old Greek myths and legends. The large audience would spend all day at the theater, viewing a series of tragedies interspersed with comedies. When the center of Mediterranean civilization shifted from Greece to Rome, there was a decline in the range and scope of the drama. However, the Romans enjoyed bright, romantic comedies, copied from the Greeks.

During the Middle Ages, the drama was for a while confined to strolling minstrels and players, who sang or mimed their tales to small groups in marketplaces, fairs, or courts. Gradually, from the rich ritual of the medieval church grew a form of drama. Bible stories were acted out, first by priests before the altar, and later by actors on the steps of the cathedral. Biblical plays gave way to what were called "morality plays," in which abstract qualities such as vice, greed, or charity were personified in order to teach a specific lesson. Eventually, as Greek and Roman manuscripts began to be rediscovered, men began to copy and restage classical dramas. People found that inn-yards made convenient theaters. By the end of the sixteenth century, the religious, classical, and folk elements of the theater had combined into the luxurious tapestry of Elizabethan drama, whose chief exponent was William Shakespeare.

Since Shakespeare, drama has continued to have a varied career. As men's lives and thoughts have changed, so have the ways in which they express and experience drama. Since the seventeenth century, the English have used the stage primarily to laugh at themselves and to examine critically their own society; the Italians have used the theater to dramatize in grand opera the gorgeous melodies which they have been producing for centuries; French drama has remained for the most part cool, objective, and ironic—a theater of the mind. Toward the end of the nineteenth century, Scandinavia produced a series of angry, hardheaded attacks on society in general. In the second half of the nineteenth century, the drama discovered new ways of presenting itself. The stage became an arena for elaborate technical feats in lighting and scenic effects. Today motion pictures and television offer large and varied possibilities.

COMEDY AND TRAGEDY

Over the centuries, plays have generally clustered around two poles, *comedy* and *tragedy*. These poles were first established by the Greeks. Today there are many variations of these two modes of drama. We use the word *tragic* loosely today. We say it was a tragedy the Dodgers lost or the cake fell. The word has degenerated into meaning simply something rather sad. Not even the roots of the word help much as to meaning in terms of drama. *Tragos* in Greek means "goat," and *oide,* "song," or "goatsong." This image may call to mind a primitive play in which an actor, dressed in goatskin, sang his lines.

As Greek drama developed, the word *tragedy* came to be applied to the lofty, serious plays which depicted the fall and death of a noble character in conflict with forces beyond his control. It is easier, perhaps, to say what tragedy isn't than what it is: the death of a dog is not considered tragic because the animal is probably not responsible for what happened to it. Tragedy, then, must have something to do with thought, with decisions made by the hero. A man who makes a series of foolish decisions and gets himself into a position where he is killed doesn't seem tragic. Tragedy seems to require that the hero make legitimate, responsible choices which get him into a position from which there is no escape. Tragedy is the confrontation and clash between human intelligence and inexplicable forces with which intelligence doesn't seem to be able to cope. We admire the hero for trying; we feel that perhaps we might do the same things he does; and we weep when we see him fall. When we leave a truly tragic play, our feeling is one of profound sadness and yet exhilarating relief. The Greeks called this feeling *catharsis* and felt it was good politically, since it cleansed the people of their own native urges to defy authority as the tragic hero did.

Comedy, according to the Greeks, cleansed also, but in a different way. The Greek word *komos* suggests a festive procession, and *oide* is a song. Most likely, in ancient Greece, a song could be sung by a daring peasant who, with temporary immunity, poked fun at his ruler and let him know a few of his faults in the hope that he might correct them. It is thought that classical Greek comedy rose from these primitive beginnings in which a comic hero acted out a story which occasionally suggested how to improve social customs and procedures.

The best comedy of all ages seems to have continued in this tradition. It aims at the vices and follies of society, advocates changes, and elicits laughter at its boldness and veracity. Both tragic and comic heroes struggle against authority of some sort. In tragedy, the odds are usually unconquerable; in comedy, the opponent is the social environment which the hero tries to change. In both cases, the audience sympathizes with the hero's defiance of authority and feels cleansed by his sufferings or his antics.

Over the years, many different variations of comedy and tragedy developed. In *melodrama,* which is related to tragedy, the hero struggles against odds which are conquerable and which he conquers. Comedy becomes *farce* when it takes its eye off its social target and concentrates primarily on slapstick. Every age has tended to shape its own form of drama, reflecting its own particular problems, attitudes, and interests. The twentieth century, for example, has focused on psychological drama, and lately on the theater of the absurd, a form of drama whose exponents express man's attempts to face up to the absurdities of the world in which he lives. Yet the old Greek modes of tragedy and comedy still stand as yardsticks against which other forms can be compared, if not judged.

The Tragedy of Julius Caesar

WILLIAM SHAKESPEARE

For the past three hundred and fifty years Shakespeare has been regarded as the greatest writer in the English language. Not only did he express himself in language unsurpassed for its richness and beauty, but perhaps better than any other author before or after him, he understood the basic elements of human existence—the joys, fears, hopes, passions, and weaknesses common to all men in all ages. This quality of universality in his works has aroused deep emotional response from many different kinds of readers through the years. His genius is such that most people who read or see his plays feel that the author is addressing them personally, sharing secrets and discoveries which they considered theirs alone. So wide is his range of experience that one can find a quotation from his works to fit almost every occasion and mood. His lines are probably more widely quoted than those of any other single author in the history of literature. Moreover, Shakespeare's plays are so subtle and profound that they reveal new depths and insights with each reading. No writer in the English language is so enduring or so well worth careful study.

Shakespeare's Life

Although we know few facts of Shakespeare's life, it seems likely that a man who can touch us so deeply in so many ways must have lived fully and seen much. Certainly there was no better time or place to do this than in the growing, bustling England of the late sixteenth century. This was perhaps the most promising period of English history. Under the reign of Queen Elizabeth I the country developed into one of the great powers of the world. This was the age of growing sea power, of exploration, of continuing growth in scholarship and the arts.

In April 1564, in the early part of Queen Elizabeth's reign, William Shakespeare was born at Stratford-on-Avon, a small country town in the county of Warwickshire. William was the oldest son of John Shakespeare, one of the most prosperous men of Stratford, and Mary Arden, the daughter of a gentleman. At the age of eighteen Shakespeare married Anne Hathaway, the daughter of a nearby farmer, and within a few years their three children were born. Sometime after this,

Shakespeare left Stratford for London, and by 1592, when he was twenty-eight, was firmly established there as an actor and playwright. His plays became well known, and he suddenly became famous as a playwright. Two years later, in 1594, Shakespeare became a full sharer in the profits of the acting company known as the Chamberlain's Men. By the time he was thirty-two, he was generally considered "the most excellent" of the writers of both tragedy and comedy for the stage.

Early in 1599, the Chamberlain's Men moved into a new theater, built to their own specifications, just south of London. One of the first plays performed in this theater, the Globe, was *The Tragedy of Julius Caesar*. Within a few years followed *Hamlet, Othello, King Lear, Macbeth,* and *Antony and Cleopatra.* Many of these plays were performed at the royal court, for when Queen Elizabeth I died in 1603, Shakespeare's company received the enthusiastic patronage of her successor, King James, and known thereafter as the King's Men, the company rose to even greater prominence.

When in his early forties, Shakespeare apparently retired from the stage. He returned to his home in Stratford-on-Avon a prosperous man and one of the town's most honored citizens. It was in Stratford that he died on April 23, 1616.

Shakespeare's Theater

The Globe, the most famous of all Elizabethan playhouses, was an octagonal (eight-sided) building. It was a frame structure, standing on low brick supports, its roof thatched with straw. Inside, surrounding the unroofed yard, were three galleries, one above the other. The galleries looked down upon the stage, which jutted out into the yard, occupying about one third of its space. Behind the large, jutting stage was an upper stage, like a balcony, and below this was an inner stage, hidden by a curtain. These additional stages were used for indoor scenes, the upper stage being especially appropriate to represent the walls of a town or castle or to furnish a raised platform for speeches to a crowd.

A spectator entered the theater from the street by a door facing the stage. If he wished to stand in the yard to watch the play, he placed a penny in the money box before entering. If he wanted to sit in one of the upper galleries, he paid a second penny and reached the gallery by one of the staircases to the right or left. If he wished to watch the play from the lowest and most expensive gallery, he paid a third penny. Spectators in the yard stood and were known as the "groundlings." They were the noisiest and often the least desirable patrons.

In the lowest gallery, on each side of the stage, there were "gentlemen's rooms," reserved for the most distinguished spectators, who also had the privilege of sitting on a cushion. For a while it was fashionable for gallants to sit or sprawl on the stage itself.

Because the stage jutted out into the yard and was surrounded on three sides by spectators, and because there was no curtain to conceal or reveal the main stage and no light but daylight, contact between actors and spectators was close and intimate. Both shared in the experience of the play. Although costumes were lavish, there was little furniture or scenery and no realistic settings. Without elaborate scenery to be changed, scenes could follow each other much more quickly on the stage. In Elizabethan days all the illusion created in a modern theater by the scene painter and electrician had to be created by the actors and the dramatist. The actors were always before the audi-

ence, speaking and gesturing, creating, with the help of an attentive and imaginative audience, a world completely of their own and the playwright's making.

Elizabethan audiences liked noise. The texts of Elizabethan plays are full of directions for different kinds of trumpet calls. No king or royal person entered in state without a flourish on the trumpets. There was a whole series of battle sounds —alarums, retreats, and even real guns. "Chambers" (small cannon) were often shot off to rouse the audience into the proper mood of excitement. The sound of thunder was imitated by rolling cannon balls on boards.

The Elizabethan acting company was a "fellowship" consisting of ten to fifteen sharers, with perhaps another ten or a dozen extras, three or four boys, money gatherers, stagehands, and the like. The boys took the roles of girls or young women, for as yet there were no professional actresses on the English stage.

Plays were acted on the repertory system. A different play was presented every afternoon, and the company kept on their program a series of plays to which they were constantly adding. The average life of a play was about ten performances. Popular plays were generally acted more often, but unsuccessful plays were dropped from the repertory after one or two performances. This meant that the company was constantly rehearsing and was thus able to present a new play very quickly. There was little time for elaborate productions, but the players did have the advantage of being a team that played together every day. In a pinch, they could undoubtedly invent lines as they went along or call to mind lines quite similar to those they had forgotten. Thus an Elizabethan play was a very lively form of entertainment.

If by some miracle we could attend a holiday performance at the Globe, we would be surprised in many ways. The playhouse would strike us as small, uncomfortably crowded, and extraordinarily intimate. The stage would look large, bare, and overpowering. The performance might at first seem loud and crude, but we would soon become used to the trumpet

An interior view of the Globe Theater.

calls and the lack of scenery. The rate of speech would seem very rapid and the acting might at first appear overwhelmingly emotional, but it would also be very slick and professional. Actually the greatest contrast to our modern theater would be in the spectators, who in Shakespeare's theater responded quickly and violently to the play and the performance, unashamedly demonstrating their grief, pleasure, amusement, or dissatisfaction.

Shakespeare was lucky in his theater. He would undoubtedly have succeeded under any conditions, but as it happened, the kind of play that best suited his stage and audience made admirable use of all his remarkable talent for powerful and vivid poetry.

Julius Caesar

Except for *Romeo and Juliet,* which was written about five years earlier, *Julius Caesar* was the first of Shakespeare's great tragedies and the first to explore the ground in which his greatest genius would be revealed. In his earlier tragedies Shakespeare concentrated on the interworkings of events and outward actions. In *Julius Caesar* he became absorbed in the personal motives that move men to act as they do. Thus the play is not so much about the death of Caesar as it is about the causes and consequences of his death. Shakespeare shows us the many and varying motivations of the men who murder him. We see Caesar from the outside, as he appears to others, but we see Brutus and Cassius from within.

Shakespeare's source for the story of Julius Caesar was an Elizabethan translation of Plutarch's *Lives of the Noble Greeks and Romans.* Like Shakespeare, Plutarch was interested not only in narrating historical events, but in interpreting the characters of the heroes of his-tory. Because Shakespeare found Plutarch's approach so similar to his own, he was able to follow Plutarch's *Lives* very closely.

Shakespeare compressed Plutarch's material and changed some of the actions and time sequences to suit his dramatic purposes. The play opens on February 15, 44 B.C., with Caesar's entry into Rome. Historically this triumphal march of Caesar into Rome occurred in September 45 B.C., following his overthrow of the last forces which resisted his taking power as supreme leader of the Roman world.

Caesar was one of the greatest figures of world history. A brilliant statesman and politician, he also proved to be a superb general as commander of the Roman Army in Gaul. Caesar's victories in Gaul and his enormous personal popularity with his army alarmed the Roman Senate, which feared his growing power. The famous Roman general Pompey was ordered to prevent the return of Caesar and his victorious army to Rome. However, Caesar defeated Pompey and, after staying a while in Egypt, he returned briefly to Rome. After suppressing a revolt in Spain, he returned to Rome once more in September 45 B.C. and was made dictator for life. On February 15, 44 B.C., during the Feast of Lupercal, he was offered by his protégé, the Roman general Mark Antony, a royal crown of laurel, which he refused. One month later, on March 15, he was murdered by a group of the Senatorial party, headed by Caius Cassius and Marcus Brutus. Shakespeare moved the date of Caesar's triumphal entry into Rome up a few months to coincide with the Feast of Lupercal, at which time Caesar was also offered the royal crown. As the play opens, the celebration of this annual Roman holiday provides a colorful background for the spectacle of Caesar's march into the city.

Julius Caesar

WILLIAM SHAKESPEARE

The Characters

JULIUS CAESAR

OCTAVIUS CAESAR
MARCUS ANTONIUS } *triumvirs after the death of Julius Caesar*
M. AEMILIUS LEPIDUS

CICERO
PUBLIUS } *Senators*
POPILIUS LENA

MARCUS BRUTUS
CASSIUS
CASCA
TREBONIUS } *conspirators against Julius Caesar*
LIGARIUS
DECIUS BRUTUS
METELLUS CIMBER
CINNA

FLAVIUS *and* MARULLUS, *tribunes of the people*

ARTEMIDORUS *of Cnidos, a teacher of rhetoric*

A SOOTHSAYER
CINNA, *a poet*
ANOTHER POET

LUCILIUS
TITINIUS
MESSALA } *friends of Brutus and Cassius*
YOUNG CATO
VOLUMNIUS

VARRO
CLITUS
CLAUDIUS } *servants of Brutus*
STRATO
LUCIUS
DARDANIUS

PINDARUS, *servant of Cassius*

CALPURNIA, *wife of Caesar*
PORTIA, *wife of Brutus*

SENATORS, CITIZENS, GUARDS, ATTENDANTS, ETC.

SCENE—Rome; the neighborhood of Sardis; the neighborhood of Philippi.

ACT I

SCENE I

[*A street in Rome. It is the fifteenth of February, Lupercalia, a Roman holiday celebrated with dancing, feasting, and public games.* CAESAR *has recently returned to Rome.*

As the play opens, FLAVIUS *and* MARULLUS, *tribunes of the people, meet a group of* COMMONERS *on their way to the Forum. The tribunes are angered by the people's eagerness to celebrate* CAESAR'S *triumph.*

FLAVIUS. Hence! Home, you idle creatures, get you home.
 Is this a holiday? What! Know you not,
 Being mechanical,° you ought not walk
 Upon a laboring day without the sign
 Of your profession°? [*Stopping one.*] Speak, what trade art thou? 5
FIRST COMMONER. Why, sir, a carpenter.
MARULLUS. Where is thy leather apron and thy rule?
 What dost thou with thy best apparel on?
 [*To another.*] You, sir, what trade are you?
SECOND COMMONER. Truly, sir, in respect of a fine workman,° I am but, as you 10
 would say, a cobbler.°
MARULLUS. But what trade art thou? Answer me directly.
SECOND COMMONER. A trade, sir, that I hope I may use with a safe conscience,
 which is indeed, sir, a mender of bad soles.
MARULLUS. What trade, thou knave? Thou naughty knave, what trade? 15
SECOND COMMONER. Nay, I beseech you, sir, be not out° with me. Yet if you be
 out, sir, I can mend you.
MARULLUS. What mean'st thou by that? Mend me, thou saucy fellow!
SECOND COMMONER. Why, sir, cobble you.
FLAVIUS. Thou art a cobbler, art thou? 20
SECOND COMMONER. Truly, sir, all that I live by is with the awl. I meddle with no
 tradesman's matters, nor women's matters, but with awl. I am indeed,
 sir, a surgeon to old shoes. When they are in great danger, I re-cover them.
 As proper men as ever trod upon neat's leather° have gone upon my
 handiwork. 25
FLAVIUS. But wherefore art not in thy shop today? Why dost thou lead these
 men about the streets?
SECOND COMMONER. Truly, sir, to wear out their shoes, to get myself into more
 work. But indeed, sir, we make holiday, to see Caesar and to rejoice in
 his triumph. 30
MARULLUS. Wherefore rejoice? What conquest brings he home?
 What tributaries° follow him to Rome,
 To grace in captive bonds his chariot wheels?

3. **mechanical:** workmen. 4–5. **sign . . . profession:** tools and work clothes. 10. **in . . . workman:** as far as good work is concerned. 11. **cobbler:** a shoemaker. (Also, a bungler.) 16. **out:** out of temper, angry. 24. **neat's leather:** oxhide. 32. **tributaries:** captives, prisoners.

You blocks, you stones, you worse than senseless things!
O you hard hearts, you cruel men of Rome, 35
Knew you not Pompey? Many a time and oft
Have you climbed up to walls and battlements,
To towers and windows, yea, to chimney tops,
Your infants in your arms, and there have sat
The livelong day with patient expectation 40
To see great Pompey pass the streets of Rome.
And when you saw his chariot but appear,
Have you not made a universal shout,
That Tiber° trembled underneath her banks
To hear the replication° of your sounds 45
Made in her concave shores?
And do you now put on your best attire?
And do you now cull out° a holiday?
And do you now strew flowers in his way
That comes in triumph over Pompey's blood? 50
Be gone!
Run to your houses, fall upon your knees,
Pray to the gods to intermit° the plague
That needs must light on this ingratitude.
FLAVIUS. Go, go, good countrymen, and for this fault 55
Assemble all the poor men of your sort.
Draw them to Tiber banks and weep your tears
Into the channel till the lowest stream
Do kiss the most exalted shores of all.

 [Exeunt all the COMMONERS.]

See whether their basest metal° be not moved. 60
They vanish tongue-tied in their guiltiness.
Go you down that way toward the Capitol,
This way will I. Disrobe the images°
If you do find them decked with ceremonies.°
MARULLUS. May we do so? 65
You know it is the feast of Lupercal.
FLAVIUS. It is no matter. Let no images
Be hung with Caesar's trophies. I'll about,
And drive away the vulgar from the streets.
So do you too, where you perceive them thick. 70
These growing feathers plucked from Caesar's wing
Will make him fly an ordinary pitch,°
Who else would soar above the view of men
And keep us all in servile fearfulness.

 [Exeunt.]

44. **Tiber:** the river that runs through Rome. 45. **replication:** echo. 48. **cull out:** choose to take. 53. **intermit:** prevent. 60. **metal:** material, stuff of which they are made. 63. **Disrobe ... images:** strip the statues. 64. **ceremonies:** ornaments, decorations. 72. **pitch:** flight (of a soaring hawk). A term used in falconry.

SCENE II

[A public square near the Forum. A flourish of trumpets announces the approach of CAESAR. *A crowd of* COMMONERS *gathers quickly, among them a blind old man, a* SOOTHSAYER, *Enter* CAESAR, *his wife* CALPURNIA, PORTIA, DECIUS, CICERO, BRUTUS, CASSIUS, CASCA, *and* ANTONY, *stripped for running in the games.]*

CAESAR. Calpurnia!

CASCA.　　　　　　Peace, ho! Caesar speaks.

CAESAR.　　　　　　*[Music ceases.]* Calpurnia!

CALPURNIA. Here, my lord.

CAESAR. Stand you directly in Antonius' way
　　　When he doth run his course.° Antonius!

ANTONIUS. Caesar, my lord?　　　　　　　　　　　　　　　　5

CAESAR. Forget not, in your speed, Antonius,
　　　To touch Calpurnia, for our elders say
　　　The barren, touchèd in this holy chase,
　　　Shake off their sterile curse.°

ANTONIUS.　　　　　　　　I shall remember:
　　　When Caesar says "Do this," it is performed.　　　　10

CAESAR. Set on, and leave no ceremony out.

　　　[Flourish of trumpets. CAESAR *starts to leave.]*

SOOTHSAYER. Caesar!

CAESAR. Ha! Who calls?

CASCA. Bid every noise be still—peace yet again!

CAESAR. Who is it in the press° that calls on me?　　　　15
　　　I hear a tongue, shriller than all the music,
　　　Cry "Caesar." Speak. Caesar is turned to hear.

SOOTHSAYER. Beware the ides of March.°

CAESAR.　　　　　　　　　　　What man is that?

BRUTUS. A soothsayer bids you beware the ides of March.

CAESAR. Set him before me. Let me see his face.　　　　20

CASSIUS. Fellow, come from the throng. Look upon Caesar.

CAESAR. What say'st thou to me now? Speak once again.

SOOTHSAYER. Beware the ides of March.

CAESAR. He is a dreamer. Let us leave him—pass.

　　　[Trumpets sound. Exeunt all but BRUTUS *and* CASSIUS.]*

CASSIUS. Will you go see the order of the course?　　　　25

BRUTUS. Not I.

CASSIUS. I pray you, do.

4. **course:** race. 7–9. **Calpurnia . . . curse:** Caesar's wife has been unable to bear children. The Romans believed that women would bear children if touched by a whip of goat's hide carried by a racer during this feast in celebration of the return of spring. Caesar asks Antony to touch Calpurnia with his whip, hoping that this will enable her to give him a son. 15. **press:** crowd. 18. **ides of March:** March 15.

BRUTUS. I am not gamesome.° I do lack some part
 Of that quick spirit that is in Antony.
 Let me not hinder, Cassius, your desires. 30
 I'll leave you.
CASSIUS. Brutus, I do observe you now of late.
 I have not from your eyes that gentleness
 And show of love as I was wont to° have.
 You bear too stubborn and too strange a hand 35
 Over your friend that loves you.
BRUTUS. Cassius,
 Be not deceived. If I have veiled my look,
 I turn the trouble of my countenance
 Merely upon myself. Vexèd I am
 Of late with passions of some difference,° 40
 Conceptions only proper to myself,
 Which give some soil° perhaps to my behaviors.
 But let not therefore my good friends be grieved—
 Among which number, Cassius, be you one—
 Nor construe° any further my neglect 45
 Than that poor Brutus, with himself at war,
 Forgets the shows of love to other men.
CASSIUS. Then, Brutus, I have much mistook your passion,
 By means whereof° this breast of mine hath buried
 Thoughts of great value, worthy cogitations. 50
 Tell me, good Brutus, can you see your face?
BRUTUS. No, Cassius, for the eye sees not itself
 But by reflection, by some other things.
CASSIUS. 'Tis just.°
 And it is very much lamented, Brutus, 55
 That you have no such mirrors as will turn
 Your hidden worthiness into your eye,
 That you might see your shadow.° I have heard
 Where many of the best respect in Rome,
 Except immortal° Caesar, speaking of Brutus, 60
 And groaning underneath this age's yoke,
 Have wished that noble Brutus had his eyes.
BRUTUS. Into what dangers would you lead me, Cassius,
 That you would have me seek into myself
 For that which is not in me? 65
CASSIUS. Therefore, good Brutus, be prepared to hear.
 And since you know you cannot see yourself
 So well as by reflection, I your glass°

28. **gamesome:** fond of games. 34. **was wont to:** used to. 40. **passions . . . difference:** conflicting
feelings. 42. **soil:** blemish, stain. 45. **construe:** interpret, guess at. 49. **by means whereof:** be-
cause of which. 54. **just:** true. 58. **shadow:** reflection. 60. **immortal:** Cassius speaks sarcasti-
cally. 68. **glass:** mirror.

Will modestly discover to yourself
That of yourself which you yet know not of. 70
And be not jealous on° me, gentle Brutus.
Were I a common laugher,° or did use
To stale° with ordinary oaths my love
To every new protester;° if you know
That I do fawn on men and hug them hard, 75
And after scandal them; or if you know
That I profess° myself in banqueting
To all the rout°—then hold me dangerous.

[*Flourish of trumpets and a loud shout.*]

BRUTUS. What means this shouting? I do fear the people
 Choose Caesar for their king.
CASSIUS. Aye, do you fear it? 80
 Then must I think you would not have it so.
BRUTUS. I would not, Cassius, yet I love him well.
 But wherefore do you hold me here so long?
 What is it that you would impart to me?
 If it be aught toward the general good, 85
 Set honor in one eye and death i' the other,
 And I will look on both indifferently;
 For let the gods so speed me° as I love
 The name of honor more than I fear death.
CASSIUS. I know that virtue to be in you, Brutus, 90
 As well as I do know your outward favor.°
 Well, honor is the subject of my story.
 I cannot tell what you and other men
 Think of this life, but for my single self
 I had as lief° not be as live to be 95
 In awe of such a thing as I myself.
 I was born free as Caesar; so were you.
 We both have fed as well, and we can both
 Endure the winter's cold as well as he.
 For once, upon a raw and gusty day, 100
 The troubled Tiber chafing with her shores,
 Caesar said to me "Darest thou, Cassius, now
 Leap in with me into this angry flood
 And swim to yonder point?" Upon the word,
 Accoutered° as I was, I plungèd in 105
 And bade him follow. So indeed he did.
 The torrent roared, and we did buffet it

71. **jealous on:** suspicious of. 72. **laugher:** jester. 73. **stale:** make common. 74. **protester:** ne who makes solemn protestations. 77. **profess:** proclaim friendship. 78. **rout:** rabble, crowd. 8. **speed me:** give me good fortune. 91. **favor:** face, appearance. 95. **I . . . lief:** I would prefer. 05. **Accoutered:** dressed in armor.

With lusty sinews, throwing it aside
And stemming it with hearts of controversy.°
But ere we could arrive the point proposed, 110
Caesar cried, "Help me, Cassius, or I sink!"
I, as Aeneas° our great ancestor
Did from the flames of Troy upon his shoulder
The old Anchises bear, so from the waves of Tiber
Did I the tired Caesar—and this man 115
Is now become a god, and Cassius is
A wretched creature, and must bend his body
If Caesar carelessly but nod on him.
He had a fever when he was in Spain,
And when the fit was on him, I did mark 120
How he did shake. 'Tis true, this god did shake.
His coward lips did from their color fly,
And that same eye whose bend doth awe the world
Did lose his luster. I did hear him groan.
Aye, and that tongue of his that bade the Romans 125
Mark him and write his speeches in their books,
Alas, it cried, "Give me some drink, Titinius,"
As a sick girl. Ye gods! It doth amaze me
A man of such a feeble temper should
So get the start of° the majestic world 130
And bear the palm° alone.

[*Shout. Flourish.*]

BRUTUS. Another general shout!
I do believe that these applauses are
For some new honors that are heaped on Caesar.
CASSIUS. Why, man, he doth bestride the narrow world 135
Like a Colossus,° and we petty men
Walk under his huge legs and peep about
To find ourselves dishonorable graves.
Men at some time are masters of their fates.
The fault, dear Brutus, is not in our stars 140
But in ourselves, that we are underlings.
Brutus, and Caesar. What should be in that Caesar?
Why should that name be sounded more than yours?
Write them together, yours is as fair a name.
Sound them, it doth become the mouth as well. 145
Weigh them, it is as heavy. Conjure° with 'em,
Brutus will start a spirit as soon as Caesar.

109. **controversy:** competition, rivalry. 112. **Aeneas:** acknowledged as the founder of Rome. After escaping from burning Troy carrying his father, Anchises, on his back, he set sail for Italy. 130. **get ... of:** get a headstart on. 131. **palm:** prize of victory. 136. **Colossus:** a gigantic statue. The Colossus of Rhodes was one of the seven wonders of the ancient world. It stood astride the entrance to the harbor of Rhodes. 146. **Conjure:** call up spirits.

Now, in the names of all the gods at once,
Upon what meat doth this our Caesar feed
That he is grown so great? Age, thou art shamed! 150
Rome, thou hast lost the breed of noble bloods!
When went there by an age, since the great flood,
But it was famed with more than with one man?
When could they say till now that talked of Rome
That her wide walls encompassed but one man? 155
Now is it Rome indeed, and room enough,
When there is in it but one only man.
Oh, you and I have heard our fathers say
There was a Brutus° once that would have brooked°
The eternal Devil to keep his state in Rome 160
As easily as a king.
BRUTUS. That you do love me, I am nothing jealous.°
What you would work me to, I have some aim.°
How I have thought of this and of these times,
I shall recount hereafter; for this present, 165
I would not, so with love I might entreat you,
Be any further moved. What you have said
I will consider. What you have to say
I will with patience hear, and find a time
Both meet° to hear and answer such high things. 170
Till then, my noble friend, chew upon this:
Brutus had rather be a villager
Than to repute himself a son of Rome
Under these hard conditions as this time
Is like to lay upon us. 175
CASSIUS. I am glad that my weak words
Have struck but thus much show of fire from Brutus.

[*Voices and music are heard approaching.*]

BRUTUS. The games are done, and Caesar is returning.
CASSIUS. As they pass by, pluck Casca by the sleeve,
And he will, after his sour fashion, tell you
What hath proceeded worthy note today. 180

[*Reenter* CAESAR *and his train of followers.*]

BRUTUS. I will do so. But look you, Cassius,
The angry spot doth glow on Caesar's brow,
And all the rest look like a chidden train.°
Calpurnia's cheek is pale, and Cicero° 185

159. **a Brutus:** Lucius Junius Brutus, a famous Roman patriot, who expelled the last tyrant from the city and established the Republic of Rome. Marcus Brutus believed himself descended from Lucius Junius. **brooked:** put up with. 162. **am . . . jealous:** have no doubt. 163. **aim:** idea. 170. **meet:** fit, appropriate. 184. **a chidden train:** scolded followers. 185. **Cicero:** a Roman senator, famous for his oratory.

Looks with such ferret° and such fiery eyes
As we have seen him in the Capitol,
Being crossed in conference by some Senators.

CASSIUS. Casca will tell us what the matter is.

[CAESAR *looks at* CASSIUS *and turns to* ANTONY.]

CAESAR. Antonius! 190
ANTONIUS. Caesar?
CAESAR. Let me have men about me that are fat,
 Sleek-headed men, and such as sleep o' nights.
 Yond Cassius has a lean and hungry look.
 He thinks too much, such men are dangerous. 195
ANTONIUS. Fear him not, Caesar. He's not dangerous,
 He is a noble Roman, and well given.°
CAESAR. Would he were fatter! But I fear him not.
 Yet if my name were liable to fear,
 I do not know the man I should avoid 200
 So soon as that spare Cassius. He reads much,
 He is a great observer, and he looks
 Quite through the deeds of men. He loves no plays
 As thou dost, Antony; he hears no music.
 Seldom he smiles, and smiles in such a sort 205
 As if he mocked himself, and scorned his spirit
 That could be moved to smile at anything.
 Such men as he be never at heart's ease
 While they behold a greater than themselves,
 And therefore are they very dangerous. 210
 I rather tell thee what is to be feared
 Than what I fear, for always I am Caesar.
 Come on my right hand, for this ear is deaf,
 And tell me truly what thou think'st of him.

[*Trumpets sound. Exeunt* CAESAR *and all his train except* CASCA, *who stays behind.*]

CASCA. You pulled me by the cloak. Would you speak with me? 215
BRUTUS. Aye, Casca. Tell us what hath chanced today
 That Caesar looks so sad.
CASCA. Why, you were with him, were you not?
BRUTUS. I should not then ask Casca what had chanced.
CASCA. Why, there was a crown offered him; and being offered him, he 220
 put it by with the back of his hand, thus. And then the people fell
 a-shouting.
BRUTUS. What was the second noise for?
CASCA. Why, for that too.

186. **ferret:** a weasel-like animal with tiny red eyes. Here, sharp, nervous. 197. **well given:** even tempered.

CASSIUS. They shouted thrice. What was the last cry for? 225

CASCA. Why, for that too.

BRUTUS. Was the crown offered him thrice?

CASCA. Aye, marry,° was't, and he put it by thrice, every time gentler than other. And at every putting-by mine honest neighbors shouted.

CASSIUS. Who offered him the crown? 230

CASCA. Why, Antony.

BRUTUS. Tell us the manner of it, gentle Casca.

CASCA. I can as well be hanged as tell the manner of it. It was mere foolery—I did not mark it. I saw Mark Antony offer him a crown, yet 'twas not a crown neither, 'twas one of these coronets;° and, as I told you, he put it by 235 once. But for all that, to my thinking, he would fain° have had it. Then he offered it to him again, then he put it by again. But, to my thinking, he was very loath to lay his fingers off it. And then he offered it the third time, he put it the third time by. And still as he refused it the rabblement hooted and clapped their chopped° hands and threw up their sweaty nightcaps 240 and uttered such a deal of stinking breath because Caesar refused the crown that it had almost choked Caesar; for he swounded° and fell down at it. And for mine own part, I durst not laugh, for fear of opening my lips and receiving the bad air.

CASSIUS. But soft, I pray you. What, did Caesar swound? 245

CASCA. He fell down in the market place and foamed at mouth and was speechless.

BRUTUS. 'Tis very like—he hath the falling sickness.°

CASSIUS. No, Caesar hath it not. But you, and I,
And honest Casca, we have the falling sickness.

CASCA. I know not what you mean by that, but I am sure Caesar fell down. If 250 the tagrag people did not clap him and hiss him according as he pleased and displeased them, as they use to do the players in the theater, I am no true man.

BRUTUS. What said he when he came unto himself?

CASCA. Marry, before he fell down, when he perceived the common herd was 255 glad he refused the crown, he plucked me ope° his doublet and offered them his throat to cut. An I had been a man of any occupation,° if I would not have taken him at a word, I would I might go to Hell among the rogues. And so he fell. When he came to himself again, he said if he had done or said anything amiss, he desired Their Worships to think it was his in- 260 firmity. Three or four wenches where I stood cried, "Alas, good soul!" and forgave him with all their hearts: but there's no heed to be taken of them. If Caesar had stabbed their mothers, they would have done no less.

BRUTUS. And after that, he came, thus sad, away?

CASCA. Aye. 265

CASSIUS. Did Cicero say anything?

CASCA. Aye, he spoke Greek.

228. **marry:** indeed. 235. **coronets:** small crowns wreathed with laurel. 236. **fain:** gladly.
240. **chopped:** chapped. 242. **swounded:** swooned, fainted. 247. **falling sickness:** epilepsy. Cassius picks up the term and uses it with quite another meaning. 256. **ope:** open. A doublet is a short coat.
257. **An . . . occupation:** if I had been a craftsman who carried cutting tools.

CASSIUS. To what effect?

CASCA. Nay, an I tell you that, I'll ne'er look you i' the face again. But those that
 understood him smiled at one another and shook their heads—but for 270
 mine own part, it was Greek to me. I could tell you more news too. Marul-
 lus and Flavius, for pulling scarfs off Caesar's images, are put to silence.°
 Fare you well. There was more foolery yet, if I could remember it.

CASSIUS. Will you sup with me tonight, Casca?

CASCA. No, I am promised forth. 275

CASSUIS. Will you dine with me tomorrow?

CASCA. Aye, if I be alive, and your mind hold, and your dinner worth the eating.

CASSUIS. Good. I will expect you.

CASCA. Do so. Farewell, both.

 [Exit.]

BRUTUS. What a blunt fellow is this grown to be! 280
 He was quick mettle° when he went to school.

CASSIUS. So is he now in execution
 Of any bold or noble enterprise,
 However he puts on this tardy form.°
 This rudeness is a sauce to his good wit, 285
 Which gives men stomach to digest his words
 With better appetite.

BRUTUS. And so it is. For this time I will leave you.
 Tomorrow, if you please to speak with me,
 I will come home to you, or, if you will,
 Come home to me and I will wait for you. 290

CASSIUS. I will do so. Till then, think of the world. *[Exit* BRUTUS.]
 Well, Brutus, thou art noble. Yet I see
 Thy honorable mettle may be wrought
 From that it is disposed.° Therefore it is meet 295
 That noble minds keep ever with their likes,
 For who so firm that cannot be seduced?
 Caesar doth bear me hard,° but he loves Brutus.
 If I were Brutus now and he were Cassius,
 He should not humor° me. I will this night, 300
 In several hands,° in at his windows throw,
 As if they came from several citizens,
 Writings, all tending to the great opinion
 That Rome holds of his name, wherein obscurely
 Caesar's ambition shall be glancèd° at. 305
 And after this let Caesar seat him° sure,
 For we will shake him, or worse days endure. *[Exit.]*

(SCENE III FOLLOWS ON PAGE 409.)

272. **put to silence:** imprisoned. 281. **mettle:** temperament, nature. 284. **tardy form:** appearance
of stupidity. 294–95. **wrought . . . disposed:** changed from its natural inclinations. 298. **bear me
hard:** dislike me. 300. **humor:** influence, persuade. 301. **several hands:** several different hand-
writings. 305. **glancèd:** hinted. 306. **him:** himself.

EUROPEAN PAINTING

Nineteenth-Century Painting, I

During the second half of the eighteenth century, as France approached her great Revolution of 1789, the elegant style of Rococo art became more and more out of tune with the changing spirit of the times. Finally, in 1781, a Parisian painter named Jacques-Louis David introduced a new style which perfectly expressed the growing revolutionary spirit. It was a more sober, heroic style, derived largely from classical Greek and Roman sculpture.

One of the themes which David frequently used in his Neoclassical paintings was the theme of martyrdom. We find this theme, for example, in his masterpiece *The Death of Marat* (PLATE 1), a memorial tribute to one of the Revolution's leading political figures, who had been murdered while working at a desk placed across his tub. But instead of depicting the violence of the crime itself, David chose to show the moment just afterward. Of course a murder scene in real life would not be as neatly ordered as this one. Notice that none of the objects on top of the box alongside the tub seem to have been disturbed by the violence of the assassin's attack. The box itself remains exactly parallel to the back wall, strengthening the design and enhancing the dignity of the setting. By reducing the composition to only a few simplified forms, and by dramatizing Marat's eloquent dying gesture, David transformed the appearance of an unattractive corpse into an image of noble suffering.

David remained the virtual dictator of French taste well into the Empire under Napoleon. By the 1820's, however, a number of young Parisian painters known as the Romanticists had begun to rebel against the strict rules of the Neoclassical style. They proclaimed the right of the individual to paint in whatever manner best expressed his own emotions. Their acknowledged leader was Eugène Delacroix, represented here by *The Abduction of Rebecca* (PLATE 2), a painting based on a scene from Sir Walter Scott's novel *Ivanhoe*. Unlike the Neoclassicists, Delacroix deliberately left many details in a rough, sketchy state, to focus attention on the swooning figure of Rebecca. And to intensify the action in the foreground, he

echoed these swirling lines in the smoke which pours out from the burning castle in the distance.

Delacroix's chief rival in Paris was J. A. D. Ingres, a painter who had mastered the Neoclassical style through his early studies with David. But Ingres was much too original an artist to become enslaved by any one conventional approach. Look, for instance, at his lovely portrait of the Countess of Haussonville (PLATE 3). Every detail is clearly defined in the approved Neoclassical manner. Yet a subtle romantic feeling is evoked by the soft expression of the young Countess's eyes and by the graceful tilt of her head. The gently curving shapes which make this portrait so appealing are characteristic of Ingres' own highly personal style.

Though Paris was the art center of Europe at this time, there were also important painters in other countries. Spain, for instance, produced a genius named Francisco de Goya at practically the same time France produced David. PLATE 4 shows Goya's strangely romantic painting of a balcony scene in which two young Spanish beauties (called *majas*) are brightly illuminated, while their escorts, hovering mysteriously behind them, are caught up in the deep shadows of the background. Goya's handling of paint here is quite free and bold; he had even used a palette knife to build up thick layers of pigment in the dazzling ornaments of the women's costumes.

Édouard Manet, one of the most important French artists of the mid-nineteenth century, was fascinated with Spanish art and Spanish customs. Early in his career Manet painted his favorite Parisian model, Mlle. Victorine, as a bullfighter (PLATE 5). She is not very convincing in this role, and she seems unrelated to the background figures, which are sketched in roughly and lighted from the side instead of from the front. But notice how these contrasts call our attention to Manet's lively, "off-beat" color scheme —the unusual combination of pink, black, and light blue with the warm flesh tones of Mlle. Victorine's face and hands. Unfortunately, however, Manet's picture was indignantly rejected by the admissions jury of the Paris Salon of 1863. His painting proved to be much too daring for the conventional tastes of the members of the jury.

Manet's contemporary, Honoré Daumier, was a very different kind of artist from any we have seen so far. For though Daumier was one of the great French painters of the mid-nineteenth century, he was better known during his lifetime for his work as a political cartoonist and social satirist. Both in his cartoons and paintings, Daumier was able to create simple lines and shapes. You can see this in his picture *The Uprising* (PLATE 6). All but the most essential details have been eliminated from this dynamic composition. Yet Daumier has still managed to suggest the presence of a great number of people who are surging together in a mob behind their young leader.

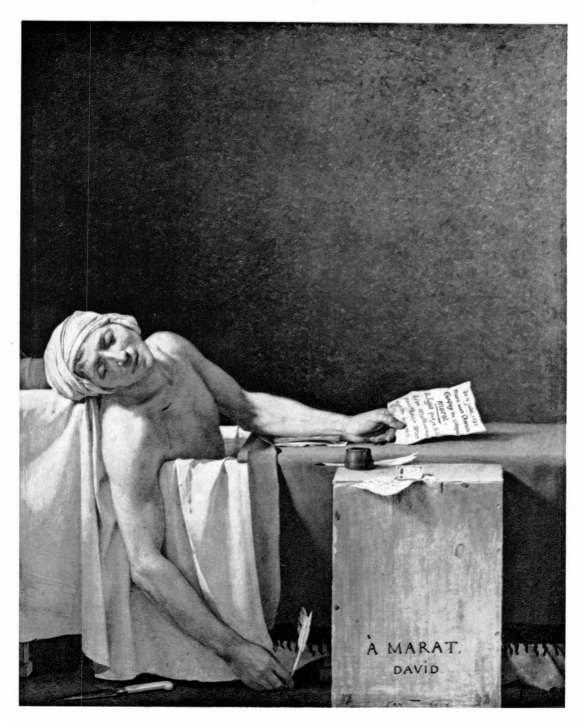

PLATE 1. JACQUES–LOUIS DAVID (French, 1748–1825): *The Death of Marat*. 1793. Oil on canvas, 65 x 50¼ inches. (Royal Museum of Fine Arts, Brussels)

PLATE 2. EUGÈNE DELACROIX (French, 1798–1863): *The Abduction of Rebecca*. 1846. Oil on canvas, 39½ x 32¼ inches. (The Metropolitan Museum of Art, New York, Wolfe Fund, 1903)

PLATE 3. JEAN AUGUSTE DOMINIQUE INGRES (French, 1780–1867): *The Countess of Haussonville*. 1845. Oil on canvas, 49¾ x 35⅜ inches. (Copyright The Frick Collection, New York)

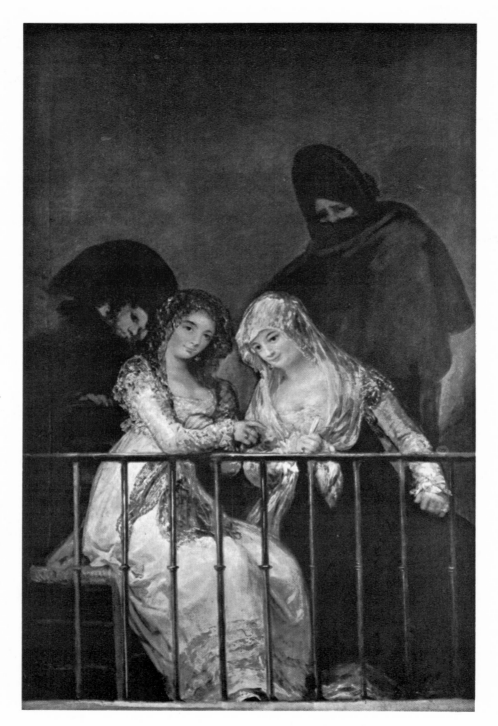

PLATE 4. FRANCISCO DE GOYA (Spanish, 1746–1828): *Majas on a Balcony*. About 1810. Oil on canvas, 76¾ x 49½ inches. (The Metropolitan Museum of Art, New York, Bequest of Mrs. H. O. Havemeyer, 1929, The H. O. Havemeyer Collection)

PLATE 5. ÉDOUARD MANET (French, 1832–1883): *Mlle, Victorine in the Costume of an Espada*. 1862. Oil on canvas, $65\frac{1}{2}$ x $50\frac{3}{4}$ inches. (The Metropolitan Museum of Art, New York, Bequest of Mrs. H. O. Havemeyer, 1929, The H. O. Havemeyer Collection)

PLATE 6. HONORÉ DAUMIER (French, 1808–1879): *The Uprising*. About 1860. Oil on canvas, $24\frac{1}{2}$ x $44\frac{1}{2}$ inches. (The Phillips Collection, Washington, D.C.)

[A street near the Capitol. Thunder and lightning. Enter, from opposite sides, CASCA, *with his sword drawn, and* CICERO. *It is the night before the ides of March.]*

CICERO. Good even, Casca. Brought you Caesar home?
 Why are you breathless? And why stare you so?

CASCA. Are not you moved, when all the sway° of earth
 Shakes like a thing unfirm? O Cicero,
 I have seen tempests when the scolding winds 5
 Have rived° the knotty oaks, and I have seen
 The ambitious ocean swell and rage and foam,
 To be exalted with° the threatening clouds.
 But never till tonight, never till now,
 Did I go through a tempest dropping fire. 10
 Either there is a civil strife in Heaven,
 Or else the world too saucy with the gods
 Incenses them to send destruction.

CICERO. Why, saw you anything more wonderful?

CASCA. A common slave—you know him well by sight— 15
 Held up his left hand, which did flame and burn
 Like twenty torches joined, and yet his hand,
 Not sensible of fire, remained unscorched.
 Besides—I ha' not since put up my sword—
 Against the Capitol I met a lion, 20
 Who glazed° upon me and went surly by
 Without annoying me. And there were drawn
 Upon a heap° a hundred ghastly women
 Transformèd with their fear, who swore they saw
 Men all in fire walk up and down the streets. 25
 And yesterday the bird of night° did sit
 Even at noonday upon the market place,
 Hooting and shrieking. When these prodigies
 Do so conjointly meet, let not men say
 "These are their reasons, they are natural." 30
 For I believe they are portentous° things
 Unto the climate° that they point upon.

CICERO. Indeed, it is a strange-disposèd time.
 But men may construe things after their fashion,
 Clean from the purpose° of the things themselves. 35
 Comes Caesar to the Capitol tomorrow?

CASCA. He doth, for he did bid Antonius
 Send word to you he would be there tomorrow.

3. **sway:** natural order. 6. **rived:** split. 8. **exalted with:** raised up to the level of. 21. **glazed:** glared. 22–23. **drawn . . . heap:** huddled together. 26. **bird of night:** screech owl. 31. **portentous:** ominous, foretelling disaster. 32. **climate:** country, place. 35. **Clean . . . purpose:** opposite to the real meaning.

CICERO. Good night then, Casca. This disturbèd sky
 Is not to walk in.
CASCA. Farewell, Cicero. 40
 [*Exit* CICERO.]

 [*Enter* CASSIUS.]

CASSIUS. Who's there?
CASCA. A Roman.
CASSIUS. Casca, by your voice.
CASCA. Your ear is good. Cassius, what night is this!
CASSIUS. A very pleasing night to honest men.
CASCA. Who ever knew the heavens menace so?
CASSIUS. Those that have known the earth so full of faults. 45
 For my part, I have walked about the streets,
 Submitting me unto the perilous night,
 And thus unbraced,° Casca, as you see,
 Have bared my bosom to the thunder stone.°
 And when the cross° blue lightning seemed to open 50
 The breast of Heaven, I did present myself
 Even in the aim and very flash of it.
CASCA. But wherefore did you so much tempt the heavens?
 It is the part of men to fear and tremble
 When the most mighty gods by tokens send 55
 Such dreadful heralds to astonish us.
CASSIUS. You are dull, Casca, and those sparks of life
 That should be in a Roman you do want,°
 Or else you use not. You look pale and gaze
 And put on fear and cast yourself in wonder, 60
 To see the strange impatience of the heavens.
 But if you would consider the true cause
 Why all these fires, why all these gliding ghosts,
 Why birds and beasts from quality and kind,°

48. **unbraced:** with clothes blowing open. 49. **thunder stone:** thunderbolt. 50. **cross:** forked.
58. **want:** lack. 64. **from . . . kind:** acting contrary to their natures.

Why old men fool and children calculate,° 65
Why all these things change from their ordinance,°
Their natures and preformèd faculties,
To monstrous quality, why, you shall find
That Heaven hath infused them with these spirits
To make them instruments of fear and warning 70
Unto some monstrous state.
Now could I, Casca, name to thee a man
Most like this dreadful night
That thunders, lightens, opens graves, and roars
As doth the lion in the Capitol— 75
A man no mightier than thyself or me
In personal action, yet prodigious grown
And fearful, as these strange eruptions are.

CASCA. 'Tis Caesar that you mean, is it not, Cassius?

CASSIUS. Let it be who it is. For Romans now 80
Have thews ° and limbs like to their ancestors.
But, woe the while!° our fathers' minds are dead,
And we are governed with our mothers' spirits,
Our yoke and sufferance show us womanish.

CASCA. Indeed they say the Senators tomorrow 85
Mean to establish Caesar as a king,
And he shall wear his crown by sea and land
In every place save here in Italy.

CASSIUS. I know where I will wear this dagger then.
Cassius from bondage will deliver Cassius. 90
Therein, ye gods, you make the weak most strong.
Therein, ye gods, you tyrants do defeat.
Nor stony tower, nor walls of beaten brass,
Nor airless dungeon, nor strong links of iron,
Can be retentive to the strength of spirit; 95
But life, being weary of these worldly bars,
Never lacks power to dismiss itself.

65. **calculate:** prophesy. 66. **ordinance:** natural order. 81. **thews:** sinews, strength. 82. **woe the while:** alas for our time.

If I know this, know all the world besides,
That part of tyranny that I do bear
I can shake off at pleasure.

[*Thunder still.*]

CASCA. So can I. 100
 So every bondman in his own hand bears
 The power to cancel his captivity.
CASSIUS. And why should Caesar be a tyrant, then?
 Poor man! I know he would not be a wolf
 But that he sees the Romans are but sheep. 105
 He were no lion were not Romans hinds.°
 Those that with haste will make a mighty fire
 Begin it with weak straws. What trash is Rome,
 What rubbish and what offal, when it serves
 For the base matter to illuminate 110
 So vile a thing as Caesar! But, O Grief,
 Where hast thou led me? I perhaps speak this
 Before a willing bondman;° then I know
 My answer must be made. But I am armed,
 And dangers are to me indifferent. 115
CASCA. You speak to Casca, and to such a man
 That is no fleering° telltale. Hold, my hand
 Be factious for redress° of all these griefs,
 And I will set this foot of mine as far
 As who goes farthest.
CASSIUS. There's a bargain made. 120
 Now know you, Casca, I have moved already
 Some certain of the noblest-minded Romans
 To undergo with me an enterprise
 Of honorable-dangerous consequence.
 And I do know, by this they stay for me 125
 In Pompey's porch;° for now, this fearful night,
 There is no stir or walking in the streets,
 And the complexion of the element
 In favor's° like the work we have in hand,
 Most bloody, fiery, and most terrible. 130

[*Enter* CINNA. *He does not see the others.*]

CASCA. Stand close° awhile, for here comes one in haste.
CASSIUS. 'Tis Cinna, I do know him by his gait—
 He is a friend. Cinna, where haste you so?
CINNA. To find out you. Who's that? Metellus Cimber?

106. **hinds:** female deer. 113. **bondman:** slave (that is, of Caesar). 117. **fleering:** sneering.
118. **factious . . . redress:** active in righting the wrongs. 126. **Pompey's porch:** the covered entrance
of the theater built by Pompey. 128–29. **element . . . favor's:** sky in appearance is. 131. **close:**
hidden.

CASSIUS. No, it is Casca, one incorporate 135
 To our attempts.° Am I not stayed for,° Cinna?
CINNA. I am glad on 't. What a fearful night is this!
 There's two or three of us have seen strange sights.
CASSIUS. Am I not stayed for? Tell me.
CINNA. Yes, you are.
 O Cassius, if you could 140
 But win the noble Brutus to our party——
CASSIUS. Be you content. Good Cinna, take this paper,
 And look you lay it in the praetor's chair,°
 Where Brutus may but find it, and throw this
 In at his window; set this up with wax 145
 Upon old Brutus'° statue. All this done,
 Repair to Pompey's porch, where you shall find us.
 Is Decius Brutus and Trebonius there?
CINNA. All but Metellus Cimber, and he's gone
 To seek you at your house. Well, I will hie,° 150
 And so bestow these papers as you bade me.
CASSIUS. That done, repair to Pompey's theater.

 [*Exit* CINNA.]

 Come, Casca, you and I will yet ere day
 See Brutus at his house. Three parts of him
 Is ours already, and the man entire 155
 Upon the next encounter yields him ours.
CASCA. Oh, he sits high in all the people's hearts,
 And that which would appear offense in us
 His countenance, like richest alchemy,°
 Will change to virtue and to worthiness. 160
CASSIUS. Him and his worth and our great need of him
 You have right well conceited.° Let us go,
 For it is after midnight, and ere day
 We will awake him and be sure of him.

 [*Exeunt.*]

 135–36. **incorporate . . . attempts:** involved in our conspiracy. 136. **stayed for:** waited for.
143. **praetor's chair:** a praetor was a high-ranking Roman official. Brutus, who was praetor at this
time, would be sure to find the paper in his chair. 146. **old Brutus':** Brutus's ancestor, Lucius Julius
Brutus. 150. **hie:** hurry. 159. **alchemy:** an ancient science that supposedly could change lesser
metals into gold. 162. **conceited:** understood.

FOR STUDY AND DISCUSSION

1. What does the opening scene show about
the affections of the mob? Are they fickle? Are
they loyal? Who was Pompey? Why do the
tribunes want to break up the people's cele-
bration of Caesar's triumphal entrance into
Rome?

2. In Scene ii, what first impression do you
get of Caesar? How does everyone act toward
him? Does he seem to take himself too seri-
ously? What do we learn about him from his
reaction to the Soothsayer?

3. What does Caesar think of Cassius?
What does Cassius think of Caesar?

4. In his scene with Cassius, Brutus's attention is divided between what Cassius is saying and what is happening in the Forum. How do offstage shouts and flourishes contribute to this scene? How do they reinforce Cassius' appeal?

5. What does Cassius do and say that makes us suspicious of his motives and his cause? Do his actions seem to support Caesar's opinion of him? In what ways is Cassius the opposite of Brutus?

6. Antony is a favorite of Caesar. What qualities does Caesar like in him? Does Antony seem sincere? Does he seem loyal to Caesar? Refer to specific lines to support your answer.

7. From Casca's description, how do you think Caesar felt when Antony offered him the crown? Why did he faint? What was the reaction of the crowd?

8. What personal defects and weaknesses of Caesar does Shakespeare emphasize in Act I? What does Cassius tell us of Caesar's frailties? What do we see? How do these defects and weaknesses affect your opinion of Caesar's fitness to rule?

9. What is the mood of Scene iii? How do stage effects throughout this scene help to create and maintain this mood? How is it intensified by the "prodigies" Casca has seen?

10. What warning does Cicero give concerning the construing or interpreting of omens? How does this warning influence our attitude toward Cassius' interpretation? From what you know about Cassius, do you think he believes his own interpretation? Why or why not?

11. In Scene iii Cassius sounds out Casca on joining the conspiracy just as in Scene ii he sounded out Brutus. In putting the question to Casca, how does Cassius appeal to his patriotism? to his courage? to his self-esteem? How is his approach to Casca different from his approach to Brutus? How is it similar?

12. At the end of Scene iii, what further arrangements does Cassius make to influence Brutus? If his cause is just, do you think he is justified in deceiving Brutus? Why or why not?

13. Why do the conspirators need Brutus in their faction? From what you know of him, do you think he will doubt that Cassius' letters genuinely represent public opinion?

ACT II

SCENE I

[*The orchard outside* BRUTUS'S *house in Rome, later the same night.* BRUTUS *enters from the orchard.*]

BRUTUS. What, Lucius, ho! [*To himself.*]
 I cannot, by the progress of the stars,
 Give guess how near to day. [*Calling.*] Lucius, I say!
 I would it were my fault to sleep so soundly.
 When, Lucius, when? Awake, I say! What, Lucius! 5

[*Enter* LUCIUS *from the house.*]

LUCIUS. Called you, my lord?
BRUTUS. Get me a taper° in my study, Lucius.
 When it is lighted, come and call me here.
LUCIUS. I will, my lord.

 [*Exit.*]

7. **taper:** candle.

[*He goes.* BRUTUS *returns to his brooding.*]

BRUTUS. It must be by his death and for my part 10
I know no personal cause to spurn at him,
But for the general.° He would be crowned.
How that might change his nature, there's the question.
It is the bright day that brings forth the adder,
And that craves wary walking. Crown him?—That— 15
And then, I grant, we put a sting in him,
That at his will he may do danger with.
The abuse of greatness is when it disjoins
Remorse from power; and to speak truth of Caesar,
I have not known when his affections swayed° 20
More than his reason. But 'tis a common proof
That lowliness is young ambition's ladder,
Whereto the climber-upward turns his face.
But when he once attains the upmost round,°
He then unto the ladder turns his back, 25
Looks in the clouds, scorning the base degrees
By which he did ascend. So Caesar may.
Then, lest he may, prevent. And since the quarrel
Will bear no color ° for the thing he is,
Fashion it thus: that what he is, augmented,° 30
Would run to these and these extremities.

12. **the general:** the general good. 20. **his affections swayed:** his personal desires ruled. 24. **round:**
rung. 29. **Will . . . color:** is unconvincing. 30. **augmented:** grown greater.

And therefore think him as a serpent's egg
Which hatched would as his kind grow mischievous,
And kill him in the shell.

[*Reenter* LUCIUS *with a letter.*]

LUCIUS. The taper burneth in your closet,° sir. 35
Searching the window for a flint,° I found
This paper thus sealed up, and I am sure
It did not lie there when I went to bed.

[*Gives him the letter.*]

BRUTUS. Get you to bed again. It is not day.
Is not tomorrow, boy, the ides of March? 40
LUCIUS. I know not, sir.
BRUTUS. Look in the calendar and bring me word.
LUCIUS. I will, sir.

[*Exit.*]

BRUTUS. The exhalations ° whizzing in the air
Give so much light that I may read by them. 45

[*Opens the letter and reads.*]

"Brutus, thou sleep'st. Awake and see thyself.
Shall Rome, etc.° Speak, strike, redress." °
"Brutus, thou sleep'st. Awake."
Such instigations have been often dropped
Where I have took them up. 50
"Shall Rome, etc." Thus must I piece it out—
Shall Rome stand under one man's awe? What, Rome?
My ancestors did from the streets of Rome
The Tarquin drive, when he was called a king.
"Speak, strike, redress." Am I entreated 55
To speak and strike? O Rome, I make thee promise,
If the redress will follow, thou receivest
Thy full petition at the hand of Brutus!

[*Reenter* LUCIUS.]

LUCIUS. Sir, March is wasted fifteen days.

[*Knocking within.*]

BRUTUS. 'Tis good. Go to the gate. Somebody knocks. 60

[*Exit* LUCIUS.]

Since Cassius first did whet me against Caesar
I have not slept.
Between the acting of a dreadful thing

35. **closet:** a small room. 36. **flint:** used to make a light. 44. **exhalations:** meteors. 47. **etc.:** The letter continues, but Shakespeare did not include it in the manuscript. **redress:** right our wrongs.

And the first motion,° all the interim is
Like a phantasma or a hideous dream. 65
The Genius ° and the mortal instruments
Are then in council, and the state of man,
Like to a little kingdom, suffers then
The nature of an insurrection.°

[*Reenter* LUCIUS.]

LUCIUS. Sir, 'tis your brother ° Cassius at the door, 70
 Who doth desire to see you.
BRUTUS. Is he alone?
LUCIUS. No, sir, there are moe ° with him.
BRUTUS. Do you know them?
LUCIUS. No, sir. Their hats are plucked about their ears,
 And half their faces buried in their cloaks,
 That by no means I may discover them 75
 By any mark of favor.°
BRUTUS. Let 'em enter.

[*Exit* LUCIUS.]

 They are the faction. O Conspiracy,
 Shamest thou to show thy dangerous brow by night,
 When evils are most free? Oh, then by day
 Where wilt thou find a cavern dark enough 80
 To mask thy monstrous visage? Seek none, Conspiracy—
 Hide it in smiles and affability.
 For if thou path, thy native semblance on,°
 Not Erebus ° itself were dim enough
 To hide thee from prevention.° 85

[*Enter the conspirators,* CASSIUS, CASCA, DECIUS, CINNA, METELLUS CIMBER,
 and TREBONIUS.]

CASSIUS. I think we are too bold upon your rest.
 Good morrow, Brutus. Do we trouble you?
BRUTUS. I have been up this hour, awake all night.
 Know I these men that come along with you?
CASSIUS. Yes, every man of them, and no man here 90
 But honors you, and every one doth wish
 You had but that opinion of yourself
 Which every noble Roman bears of you.
 This is Trebonius.
BRUTUS. He is welcome hither.
CASSIUS. This, Decius Brutus.
BRUTUS. He is welcome too. 95

64. **motion:** hint of the idea. 66. **Genius:** mind, reason. 69. **insurrection:** revolution, civil war.
70. **brother:** brother-in-law. Cassius had married Brutus's sister. 72. **moe:** more. 76. **favor:**
appearance. 83. **path . . . on:** walk openly in your usual way. 84. **Erebus:** Hell. 85. **prevention:**
detection, being seen.

CASSIUS. This, Casca, this, Cinna, and this, Metellus Cimber.
BRUTUS. They are all welcome.
　　What watchful cares do interpose themselves
　　Betwixt your eyes and night?
CASSIUS. Shall I entreat a word?　　　　　　　　　　　　　　100

　　　[*They whisper together while the others gaze up at the sky.*]

DECIUS. Here lies the east. Doth not the day break here?
CASCA. No.
CINNA. Oh, pardon, sir, it doth, and yon gray lines
　　That fret ° the clouds are messengers of day.
CASCA. You shall confess that you are both deceived.　　　　105
　　Here, as I point my sword, the sun arises,
　　Which is a great way growing on the south,
　　Weighing the youthful season of the year.
　　Some two months hence up higher toward the north
　　He first presents his fire, and the high east　　　　　　110
　　Stands as the Capitol, directly here.

　　　[BRUTUS *and* CASSIUS *rejoin the others.*]

BRUTUS. Give me your hands all over, one by one.
CASSIUS. And let us swear our resolution.
BRUTUS. No, not an oath. If not the face of men,
　　The sufferance of our souls, the time's abuse—　　　　115
　　If these be motives weak, break off betimes,°
　　And every man hence to his idle bed.
　　So let high-sighted ° tyranny range on
　　Till each man drop by lottery.° But if these,
　　As I am sure they do, bear fire enough　　　　　　　120
　　To kindle cowards and to steel with valor
　　The melting spirits of women, then, countrymen,
　　What need we any spur but our own cause
　　To prick us to redress? What other bond
　　Than secret Romans that have spoke the word,　　　　125
　　And will not palter? ° And what other oath
　　Than honesty to honesty engaged
　　That this shall be or we will fall for it?
　　Swear priests and cowards and men cautelous,°
　　Old feeble carrions ° and such suffering souls　　　　130
　　That welcome wrongs; unto bad causes swear
　　Such creatures as men doubt; but do not stain
　　The even virtue of our enterprise,
　　Nor the insuppressive mettle of our spirits,

　　104. **fret:** lace, ornament. 116. **betimes:** quickly, right now. 118. **high-sighted:** proud-eyed.
119. **lottery:** turn. 126. **palter:** play false. 129. **cautelous:** crafty, cunning. 130. **carrions:**
carcasses.

To think that or our cause or ° our performance 135
Did need an oath when every drop of blood
That every Roman bears, and nobly bears,
Is guilty of a several bastardy °
If he do break the smallest particle
Of any promise that hath passed from him. 140

CASSIUS. But what of Cicero? Shall we sound him?
 I think he will stand very strong with us.

CASCA. Let us not leave him out.

CINNA. No, by no means.

METELLUS. Oh, let us have him, for his silver hairs
 Will purchase us a good opinion, 145
 And buy men's voices to commend our deeds.
 It shall be said his judgment ruled our hands.
 Our youths and wildness shall no whit appear,
 But all be buried in his gravity.

BRUTUS. Oh, name him not. Let us not break with him, 150
 For he will never follow anything
 That other men begin.

CASSIUS. Then leave him out.

CASCA. Indeed he is not fit.

DECIUS. Shall no man else be touched but only Caesar?

CASSIUS. Decius, well urged. I think it is not meet ° 155
 Mark Antony, so well beloved of Caesar,
 Should outlive Caesar. We shall find of him
 A shrewd contriver; ° and you know his means,
 If he improve them, may well stretch so far
 As to annoy us all. Which to prevent, 160
 Let Antony and Caesar fall together.

BRUTUS. Our course will seem too bloody, Caius Cassius,
 To cut the head off and then hack the limbs,
 Like wrath in death and envy afterward.
 For Antony is but a limb of Caesar. 165
 Let us be sacrificers, but not butchers, Caius.
 We all stand up against the spirit of Caesar,
 And in the spirit of men there is no blood.
 Oh, that we then could come by Caesar's spirit,
 And not dismember Caesar! But, alas, 170
 Caesar must bleed for it! And, gentle friends,
 Let's kill him boldly, but not wrathfully.
 Let's carve him as a dish fit for the gods,
 Not hew him as a carcass fit for hounds.
 And let our hearts, as subtle masters do, 175
 Stir up their servants to an act of rage

135. **or . . . or:** either . . . or. 138. **several bastardy:** individual betrayal. 155. **meet:** fit, appropriate. 158. **contriver:** plotter.

And after seem to chide 'em. This shall make
Our purpose necessary and not envious,
Which so appearing to the common eyes,
We shall be called purgers, not murderers. 180
And for Mark Antony, think not of him,
For he can do no more than Caesar's arm
When Caesar's head is off.

CASSIUS. Yet I fear him,
For in the ingrafted love he bears to Caesar——

BRUTUS. Alas, good Cassius, do not think of him. 185
If he love Caesar, all that he can do
Is to himself, take thought and die for Caesar.
And that were much he should, for he is given
To sports, to wildness and much company.

TREBONIUS. There is no fear ° in him. Let him not die, 190
For he will live and laugh at this hereafter.

> [*Clock strikes.*]

BRUTUS. Peace! Count the clock.
CASSIUS. The clock hath stricken three.
TREBONIUS. 'Tis time to part.
CASSIUS. But it is doubtful yet
Whether Caesar will come forth today or no,
For he is superstitious grown of late, 195
Quite from the main opinion he held once
Of fantasy, of dreams and ceremonies.°
It may be these apparent prodigies,
The unaccustomed terror of this night
And the persuasion of his augurers,° 200
May hold him from the Capitol today.

DECIUS. Never fear that. If he be so resolved,
I can o'ersway him. For he loves to hear
That unicorns may be betrayed with trees
And bears with glasses, elephants with holes, 205
Lions with toils ° and men with flatterers—
But when I tell him he hates flatterers,
He says he does, being then most flattered.
Let me work,
For I can give his humor the true bent,° 210
And I will bring him to the Capitol.

CASSIUS. Nay, we will all of us be there to fetch him.
BRUTUS. By the eighth hour. Is that the uttermost? °

190. **no fear:** nothing to fear. 197. **ceremonies:** supernatural signs. 200. **augurers:** fortune-tellers. 204–06. **unicorns . . . toils:** It was believed that unicorns could be trapped by having a hunter stand in front of a tree, provoke the unicorn into charging, and then step quickly aside. Bears were supposed to be very vain and easily lured by mirrors. Elephants can still be caught in pits and lions in snares (toils). 210. **bent:** direction. 213. **uttermost:** latest.

CINNA. Be that the uttermost, and fail not then.

METELLUS. Caius Ligarius doth bear Caesar hard, 215
 Who rated ° him for speaking well of Pompey.
 I wonder none of you have thought of him.

BRUTUS. Now, good Metellus, go along by him.
 He loves me well, and I have given him reasons.
 Send him but hither and I'll fashion him. 220

CASSIUS. The morning comes upon 's. We'll leave you, Brutus.
 And friends, disperse yourselves, but all remember
 What you have said, and show yourselves true Romans.

BRUTUS. Good gentlemen, look fresh and merrily.
 Let not our looks put on our purposes, 225
 But bear it as our Roman actors do,
 With untired spirits and formal constancy.°
 And so, good morrow to you every one.

 [*Exeunt all but* BRUTUS.]

 Boy! Lucius! Fast asleep! It is no matter.
 Enjoy the honey-heavy dew of slumber. 230
 Thou hast no figures ° nor no fantasies
 Which busy care draws in the brains of men,
 Therefore thou sleep'st so sound.

 [*Enter* PORTIA, BRUTUS'S *wife.*]

PORTIA. Brutus, my lord!

BRUTUS. Portia, what mean you? Wherefore rise you now?
 It is not for your health thus to commit 235
 Your weak condition to the raw cold morning.

PORTIA. Nor for yours neither. You've ungently, Brutus,
 Stole from my bed. And yesternight at supper
 You suddenly arose and walked about,
 Musing and sighing, with your arms across. 240
 And when I asked you what the matter was,
 You stared upon me with ungentle looks.
 I urged you further, then you scratched your head,
 And too impatiently stamped with your foot.
 Yet I insisted, yet you answered not, 245
 But with an angry wafture ° of your hand
 Gave sign for me to leave you. So I did,
 Fearing to strengthen that impatience
 Which seemed too much enkindled, and withal °
 Hoping it was but an effect of humor,° 250
 Which sometime hath his hour with every man.
 It will not let you eat, nor talk, nor sleep,
 And, could it work so much upon your shape

216. **rated:** rebuked: 227. **formal constancy:** calm self-control. 231. **figures:** dreams, visions.
246. **wafture:** wave, motion. 249. **withal:** in addition. 250. **humor:** bad mood.

As it hath much prevailed on your condition,
I should not know you, Brutus. Dear my lord, 255
Make me acquainted with your cause of grief.

BRUTUS. I am not well in health, and that is all.

PORTIA. Brutus is wise, and were he not in health,
He would embrace the means to come by it.

BRUTUS. Why, so I do. Good Portia, go to bed. 260

PORTIA. Is Brutus sick, and is it physical°
To walk unbraced and suck up the humors°
Of the dank morning? What, is Brutus sick,
And will he steal out of his wholesome bed
To dare the vile contagion of the night,° 265
And tempt the rheumy and unpurgèd air
To add unto his sickness? No, my Brutus;
You have some sick offense within your mind,
Which by the right and virtue of my place
I ought to know of. And, upon my knees, 270
I charm you, by my once commended beauty,
By all your vows of love and that great vow
Which did incorporate and make us one,
That you unfold to me, yourself, your half,
Why you are heavy, and what men tonight 275
Have had resort to you; for here have been
Some six or seven who did hide their faces
Even from darkness.

BRUTUS. Kneel not, gentle Portia.

PORTIA. I should not need if you were gentle Brutus.
Within the bond of marriage, tell me, Brutus, 280
Is it excepted I should know no secrets
That appertain to you? Am I yourself°
But, as it were, in sort or limitation,
To keep with you at meals, comfort your bed,
And talk to you sometimes? Dwell I but in the suburbs 285
Of your good pleasure? If it be no more,
Portia is Brutus' harlot, not his wife.

BRUTUS. You are my true and honorable wife,
As dear to me as are the ruddy drops°
That visit my sad heart. 290

PORTIA. If this were true, then should I know this secret.
I grant I am a woman, but withal
A woman that Lord Brutus took to wife.
I grant I am a woman, but withal
A woman well reputed, Cato's daughter.° 295

261. **physical:** good for your health. 262. **humors:** mists. 265. **contagion . . . night:** It was thought that night air was unhealthy, since it was moist (rheumy) and unpurified (unpurged) by the sun. 282. **yourself:** part of you (by marriage). 289. **drops:** blood. 295. **Cato's daughter:** Cato of Utica, Portia's father, was famous for his honesty and courage.

Think you I am no stronger than my sex,
Being so fathered and so husbanded?
Tell me your counsels, I will not disclose 'em.
I have made strong proof of my constancy,
Giving myself a voluntary wound 300
Here in the thigh. Can I bear that with patience
And not my husband's secrets?

BRUTUS. O ye gods,
Render me worthy of this noble wife!

[*Knocking within.*]

Hark, hark! One knocks. Portia, go in a while,
And by and by thy bosom shall partake 305
The secrets of my heart.
All my engagements I will construe ° to thee,
All the charactery ° of my sad brows.
Leave me with haste. [*Exit* PORTIA.] Lucius, who's that knocks?

[*Reenter* LUCIUS *with* LIGARIUS.]

LUCIUS. Here is a sick man that would speak with you. 310
BRUTUS. Caius Ligarius, that Metellus spake of.
 Boy, stand aside. Caius Ligarius! How?
LIGARIUS. Vouchsafe ° good morrow from a feeble tongue.
BRUTUS. Oh, what a time have you chose out, brave Caius,
 To wear a kerchief! ° Would you were not sick! 315
LIGARIUS. I am not sick if Brutus have in hand
 Any exploit worthy the name of honor.
BRUTUS. Such an exploit have I in hand, Ligarius,
 Had you a healthful ear to hear of it.
LIGARIUS. By all the gods that Romans bow before, 320
 I here discard my sickness! Soul of Rome!
 Brave son, derived from honorable loins!
 Thou, like an exorcist,° hast conjured up
 My mortified spirit. Now bid me run,
 And I will strive with things impossible, 325
 Yea, get the better of them. What's to do?
BRUTUS. A piece of work that will make sick men whole.
LIGARIUS. But are not some whole that we must make sick?
BRUTUS. That must we also. What it is, my Caius,
 I shall unfold to thee as we are going 330
 To whom it must be done.
LIGARIUS. Set on your foot,
 And with a heart new-fired I follow you,

307. **construe:** explain. 308. **charactery:** written lines. 313. **Vouchsafe:** please accept. 315. **kerchief:** a muffler, worn by the sick. 323. **exorcist:** summoner of dead (mortified) spirits to walk again.

To do I know not what, but it sufficeth
That Brutus leads me on.
BRUTUS. Follow me, then.

 [Exeunt.]

SCENE II

[CAESAR'S *house in Rome. Early in the morning. Thunder and lightning. Enter* CAESAR *in his dressing gown.*]

CAESAR. Nor Heaven nor earth have been at peace tonight.
 Thrice hath Calpurnia in her sleep cried out,
 "Help, ho! They murder Caesar!" [*Calling.*] Who's within?

 [*Enter a* SERVANT.]

SERVANT. My lord?
CAESAR. Go bid the priests do present ° sacrifice, 5
 And bring me their opinions of success.
SERVANT. I will, my lord.

 [Exit.]

 [CALPURNIA, CAESAR'S *wife, enters, alarmed.*]

CALPURNIA. What mean you, Caesar? Think you to walk forth?
 You shall not stir out of your house today.
CAESAR. Caesar shall forth. The things that threatened me 10
 Ne'er looked but on my back. When they shall see
 The face of Caesar, they are vanishèd.
CALPURNIA. Caesar, I never stood on ceremonies,°
 Yet now they fright me. There is one within,
 Besides the things that we have heard and seen, 15
 Recounts most horrid sights seen by the watch.°
 A lioness hath whelpèd ° in the streets.
 And graves have yawned and yielded up their dead.
 Fierce fiery warriors fight upon the clouds,
 In ranks and squadrons and right form of war, 20
 Which drizzled blood upon the Capitol.
 The noise of battle hurtled in the air,
 Horses did neigh and dying men did groan,
 And ghosts did shriek and squeal about the streets.
 O Caesar! these things are beyond all use,° 25
 And I do fear them.
CAESAR. What can be avoided
 Whose end is purposed by the mighty gods?
 Yet Caesar shall go forth, for these predictions
 Are to the world in general as to Caesar.

 5. **present:** immediate. 13. **stood on ceremonies:** paid much attention to omens. 16. **the watch:** night watchmen. 17. **whelpèd:** given birth. 25. **use:** custom, usual events.

CALPURNIA. When beggars die, there are no comets seen.　　　　30
　　　The heavens themselves blaze forth the death of princes.
CAESAR. Cowards die many times before their deaths,
　　　The valiant never taste of death but once.
　　　Of all the wonders that I yet have heard,
　　　It seems to me most strange that men should fear,　　　35
　　　Seeing that death, a necessary end,
　　　Will come when it will come.

　　　　　　　　　　[*Reenter* SERVANT.]

　　　　　　　　　　　　What say the augurers?
SERVANT. They would not have you to stir forth today.
　　　Plucking the entrails of an offering forth,
　　　They could not find a heart within the beast.°　　　40
CAESAR. The gods do this in shame of cowardice.
　　　Caesar should be a beast without a heart
　　　If he should stay at home today for fear.
　　　No, Caesar shall not. Danger knows full well
　　　That Caesar is more dangerous than he,　　　45
　　　We are two lions littered in one day,
　　　And I the elder and more terrible.
　　　And Caesar shall go forth.
CALPURNIA.　　　　　　　　Alas, my lord,
　　　Your wisdom is consumed in confidence.
　　　Do not go forth today. Call it my fear　　　50
　　　That keeps you in the house, and not your own.
　　　We'll send Mark Antony to the Senate House,

　　40. **heart . . . beast:** Roman augurers predicted the future by examining the insides of animals killed for sacrifice. In this case, the lack of the heart, the most important organ, suggests that the state soon will lack its most important citizen. Caesar, however, finds another explanation.

And he shall say you are not well today.
Let me, upon my knee, prevail in this.
CAESAR. Mark Antony shall say I am not well, 55
And, for thy humor,° I will stay at home.

[*Enter* DECIUS.]

Here's Decius Brutus. He shall tell them so.
DECIUS. Caesar, all hail! Good morrow, worthy Caesar.
I come to fetch you to the Senate House.
CAESAR. And you are come in very happy time, 60
To bear my greeting to the Senators
And tell them that I will not come today.
Cannot is false, and that I dare not, falser—
I will not come today. Tell them so, Decius.
CALPURNIA. Say he is sick.
CAESAR. Shall Caesar send a lie? 65
Have I in conquest stretched mine arm so far,
To be afeared to tell graybeards the truth?
Decius, go tell them Caesar will not come.
DECIUS. Most mighty Caesar, let me know some cause,
Lest I be laughed at when I tell them so. 70
CAESAR. The cause is in my will—I will not come.
That is enough to satisfy the Senate.
But, for your private satisfaction,
Because I love you, I will let you know.
Calpurnia here, my wife, stays me at home. 75
She dreamt tonight she saw my statue,
Which like a fountain with a hundred spouts
Did run pure blood, and many lusty Romans
Came smiling and did bathe their hands in it.
And these does she apply for warnings and portents 80
And evils imminent, and on her knee
Hath begged that I will stay at home today.
DECIUS. This dream is all amiss interpreted.
It was a vision fair and fortunate.
Your statue spouting blood in many pipes, 85
In which so many smiling Romans bathed,
Signifies that from you great Rome shall suck
Reviving blood, and that great men shall press
For tinctures, stains, relics, and cognizance.°
This by Calpurnia's dream is signified. 90
CAESAR. And this way have you well expounded° it.
DECIUS. I have, when you have heard what I can say.
And know it now—the Senate have concluded

56. **humor:** whim, wish. 89. **tinctures . . . cognizance:** souvenirs of your greatness. 91. **ex-pounded:** explained.

To give this day a crown to mighty Caesar.
If you shall send them word you will not come, 95
Their minds may change. Besides, it were a mock
Apt to be rendered, for someone to say
"Break up the Senate till another time,
When Caesar's wife shall meet with better dreams,"
If Caesar hide himself, shall they not whisper 100
"Lo, Caesar is afraid"?
Pardon me, Caesar, for my dear dear love
To your proceeding bids me tell you this,
And reason to my love is liable.

CAESAR. How foolish do your fears seem now, Calpurnia! 105
 I am ashamèd I did yield to them.
 Give me my robe, for I will go.

[*Enter* PUBLIUS, BRUTUS, LIGARIUS, METELLUS, CASCA, TREBONIUS, *and* CINNA.]

 And look where Publius is come to fetch me.
PUBLIUS. Good morrow, Caesar.
CAESAR. Welcome, Publius.
 What, Brutus, are you stirred so early too? 110
 Good morrow, Casca. Caius Ligarius,
 Caesar was ne'er so much your enemy
 As that same ague° which hath made you lean.
 What is 't o'clock?
BRUTUS. Caesar, 'tis strucken eight.
CAESAR. I thank you for your pains and courtesy. 115

[*Enter* ANTONY.]

 See! Antony, that revels long o' nights,
 Is notwithstanding up. Good morrow, Antony.
ANTONY. So to most noble Caesar.
CAESAR. Bid them prepare within.
 I am to blame to be thus waited for.
 Now, Cinna, now, Metellus. What, Trebonius! 120
 I have an hour's talk in store for you.
 Remember that you call on me today.
 Be near me, that I may remember you.
TREBONIUS. Caesar, I will. [*Aside.*] And so near will I be
 That your best friends shall wish I had been further. 125
CAESAR. Good friends, go in and taste some wine with me,
 And we like friends will straightway go together.
BRUTUS. [*Aside*] That every like is not the same, O Caesar,
 The heart of Brutus yearns° to think upon!

 [*Exeunt.*]

113. **ague:** feverish sickness. 129. **yearns:** grieves.

SCENE III

[*A street near the Capitol. Enter* ARTEMIDORUS, *reading a paper.*]

ARTEMIDORUS. "Caesar, beware of Brutus; take heed of Cassius; come not near
 Casca; have an eye to Cinna; trust not Trebonius; mark well Metellus
 Cimber; Decius Brutus loves thee not; thou hast wronged Caius Ligarius.
 There is but one mind in all these men, and it is bent against Caesar. If thou
 beest not immortal, look about you. Security ° gives way to conspiracy. 5
 The mighty gods defend thee!

 "Thy lover, ARTEMIDORUS."

 Here will I stand till Caesar pass along,
 And as à suitor ° will I give him this.
 My heart laments that virtue cannot live 10
 Out of the teeth of emulation.°
 If thou read this, O Caesar, thou mayst live;
 If not, the Fates with traitors do contrive.°

 [*Exit.*]

SCENE IV

[*Another part of the same street, before the house of* BRUTUS. *Enter* PORTIA *and*
 LUCIUS.]

PORTIA. I prithee, boy, run to the Senate House.
 Stay not to answer me, but get thee gone.
 Why dost thou stay?
LUCIUS. To know my errand, madam.
PORTIA. I would have had thee there, and here again,
 Ere I can tell thee what thou shouldst do there. 5
 O Constancy, be strong upon my side!
 Set a huge mountain 'tween my heart and tongue!
 I have a man's mind, but a woman's might.
 How hard it is for women to keep counsel!
 Art thou here yet?
LUCIUS. Madam, what should I do? 10
 Run to the Capitol, and nothing else?
 And so return to you, and nothing else?
PORTIA. Yes, bring me word, boy, if thy lord look well,
 For he went sickly forth. And take good note
 What Caesar doth, what suitors press to him. 15
 Hark, boy! What noise is that?
LUCIUS. I hear none, madam.

SCENE III. 5. **Security:** overconfidence. 9. **suitor:** one who seeks a favor. 11. **emulation:** envy.
13. **contrive:** plot.

PORTIA. Prithee,° listen well.
 I heard a bustling rumor like a fray,°
 And the wind brings it from the Capitol. ·
LUCIUS. Sooth, madam, I hear nothing.

 [*Enter the* SOOTHSAYER.]

PORTIA. Come hither, fellow. 20
 Which way hast thou been?
SOOTHSAYER. At mine own house, good lady.
PORTIA. What is't o'clock?
SOOTHSAYER. About the ninth hour, lady.
PORTIA. Is Caesar yet gone to the Capitol?
SOOTHSAYER. Madam, not yet. I go to take my stand
 To see him pass on to the Capitol. 25
PORTIA. Thou hast some suit to Caesar, hast thou not?
SOOTHSAYER. That I have, lady. If it will please Caesar
 To be so good to Caesar as to hear me,
 I shall beseech him to befriend himself.
PORTIA. Why, know'st thou any harm's intended toward him? 30
SOOTHSAYER. None that I know will be, much that I fear may chance.
 Good morrow to you. Here the street is narrow,
 The throng that follows Caesar at the heels,
 Of Senators, of praetors, common suitors,

 17. **Prithee:** I pray thee. 18. **rumor . . . fray:** noise like a brawl.

Will crowd a feeble man almost to death. 35
I'll get me to a place more void,° and there
Speak to great Caesar as he comes along.

 [*Exit.*]

PORTIA. I must go in. Aye me, how weak a thing
 The heart of women is! O Brutus,
 The heavens speed thee in thine enterprise! 40
 Sure, the boy heard me. Brutus hath a suit
 That Caesar will not grant. Oh, I grow faint.
 Run, Lucius, and commend me to my lord.
 Say I am merry. Come to me again,
 And bring me word what he doth say to thee. 45

[LUCIUS *runs off toward the Capitol.* PORTIA *watches him a moment, then goes in.*]

36. **void:** empty.

FOR STUDY AND DISCUSSION

1. As Scene i begins, Brutus is walking in his orchard. What is troubling him? In his *soliloquy* (a monologue or speech given when alone), what argument does he make for killing Caesar? Is he more concerned with what Caesar is at present, or with what he might become?

2. What is Brutus's reaction to the note found in his room? Who does he think has written the note? At this point has he fully made up his mind to join the conspiracy? What makes you think so?

3. What effect does the conspirators' appearance have on Brutus? Why do you think Cassius takes him aside and whispers to him? When they return to the others, do Brutus's doubts seem to be satisfied?

4. Why does Brutus believe there is no need for the conspirators to swear an oath? What does this suggest about his character? What other decisions concerning the conspiracy does Brutus make in this scene? Are they noble and high-minded? Are they practical? Why do you think Cassius and the others let Brutus decide these important questions?

5. Why do you think Shakespeare has Portia come onstage just after Brutus's meeting with the conspirators? What kind of person is she? In what ways is she like Brutus? What does she want him to do? How do you think

she would feel about Brutus's part in the conspiracy if she knew?

6. Who is Ligarius? How does his brief scene with Brutus remind us of the respect that Brutus commands in Rome?

7. In Scene ii, why is Caesar anxious to know the results of the sacrifice? What was Calpurnia's dream? How does she interpret it? How does Decius? Which interpretation appeals most to Caesar? Why?

8. What argument finally convinces Caesar to go to the Capitol? Why does the coming of the conspirators and Antony add to his resolve to go?

9. In Scene ii, what impression do you get of Caesar? What strengths does he show? what weaknesses? Do you agree with Brutus that Caesar is dangerous as dictator of Rome?

10. How does Artemidorus plan to warn Caesar? What do you think he hopes to gain by doing this? How does Scene iii increase tension and suspense?

11. Why do you think Shakespeare turned aside from the conspirators and Caesar in Scene iv to show us Portia and Lucius? How does this scene add to our sympathy for Brutus? to our sense of Caesar's doom?

12. So far the conspiracy is going well. Do you think it will succeed? What might prevent it? If the conspirators should succeed in killing Caesar, what reaction might they expect to face in Rome?

ACT III

SCENE I

[*Rome. Before the Capitol, a great crowd. On a higher level, the Senate sits, waiting for* CAESAR *to appear. The* SOOTHSAYER *and* ARTEMIDORUS *are among the crowd.*

A flourish of trumpets. Enter CAESAR, BRUTUS, CASSIUS, CASCA, DECIUS, METEL-LUS, TREBONIUS, CINNA, ANTONY, LEPIDUS, POPILIUS, PUBLIUS, *and others.* CAESAR *stops in front of the* SOOTHSAYER *and smiles.*]

CAESAR. The ides of March are come.

SOOTHSAYER. Aye, Caesar, but not gone.

[ARTEMIDORUS *steps up to* CAESAR *with his warning.*]

ARTEMIDORUS. Hail, Caesar! Read this schedule.°

[DECIUS *steps forward quickly with another paper.*]

DECIUS. Trebonius doth desire you to o'erread,
 At your best leisure, this his humble suit. 5

ARTEMIDORUS. O Caesar, read mine first, for mine's a suit
 That touches Caesar nearer. Read it, great Caesar.

CAESAR. What touches us ourself shall be last served.

[CAESAR *pushes the paper aside and turns away.*]

ARTEMIDORUS. Delay not, Caesar. Read it instantly.

CAESAR. What, is the fellow mad?

PUBLIUS. Sirrah,° give place. 10

[PUBLIUS *and the other conspirators force* ARTEMIDORUS *away from* CAESAR.]

CASSIUS. What, urge you your petitions in the street?
 Come to the Capitol.

[CAESAR *goes up into the Senate House, the rest following.* POPILIUS *speaks to* CASSIUS *in a low voice.*]

POPILIUS. I wish your enterprise today may thrive.

CASSIUS. What enterprise, Popilius?

POPILIUS. Fare you well.

[*Advances to* CAESAR.]

BRUTUS. What said Popilius Lena? 15

CASSIUS. He wished today our enterprise might thrive.
 I fear our purpose is discovered.

BRUTUS. Look how he makes to Caesar. Mark him.

3. **schedule:** paper. 10. **Sirrah:** an insulting way of addressing an inferior.

CASSIUS. Casca,
 Be sudden, for we fear prevention.
 Brutus, what shall be done? If this be known, 20
 Cassius or Caesar never shall turn back,
 For I will slay myself.
BRUTUS. Cassius, be constant.
 Popilius Lena speaks not of our purposes,
 For look he smiles and Caesar doth not change.
CASSIUS. Trebonius knows his time, for look you, Brutus, 25
 He draws Mark Antony out of the way.

 [*Exeunt* ANTONY *and* TREBONIUS.]

DECIUS. Where is Metellus Cimber? Let him go,
 And presently prefer his suit to Caesar.
BRUTUS. He is addressed. Press near and second him.
CINNA. Casca, you are the first that rears your hand. 30

 [CAESAR *seats himself in his high Senate chair.*]

CAESAR. Are we all ready? What is now amiss
 That Caesar and his Senate must redress?
METELLUS. Most high, most mighty, and most puissant Caesar,
 Metellus Cimber throws before thy seat
 A humble heart——

 [*Kneeling.*]

CAESAR. I must prevent thee, Cimber. 35
 These couchings ° and these lowly courtesies
 Might fire the bloód of ordinary men,
 And turn preordinance and first decree °
 Into the law of children.° Be not fond,°
 To think that Caesar bears such rebel blood 40
 That will be thawed from the true quality
 With that which melteth fools—I mean sweet words,
 Low-crookèd ° curtsies, and base spaniel fawning.
 Thy brother by decree is banished.
 If thou dost bend and pray and fawn for him, 45
 I spurn thee like a cur out of my way.
 Know, Caesar doth not wrong, nor without cause
 Will he be satisfied.
METELLUS. Is there no voice more worthy than my own,
 To sound more sweetly in great Caesar's ear
 For the repealing of my banished brother? 50
BRUTUS. I kiss thy hand, but not in flattery, Caesar,
 Desiring thee that Publius Cimber may

36. **couchings:** low bowings. 38. **preordinance . . . decree:** old established laws and penalties.
39. **law of children:** that is, law or rules which change at whim. **fond:** foolish. 43. **low-crookèd:**
low-bending.

Have an immediate freedom of repeal.
CAESAR. What, Brutus!
CASSIUS. Pardon, Caesar, Caesar, pardon. 55
 As low as to thy foot doth Cassius fall,
 To beg enfranchisement° for Publius Cimber.
CAESAR. I could be well moved, if I were as you.
 If I could pray to move, prayers would move me;
 But I am constant as the Northern Star, 60
 Of whose true-fixed and resting quality
 There is no fellow in the firmament.°
 The skies are painted with unnumbered sparks,
 They are all fire, and every one doth shine,
 But there's but one in all doth hold his place. 65
 So in the world. 'Tis furnished well with men,
 And men are flesh and blood, and apprehensive;°
 Yet in the number I do know but one
 That unassailable holds on his rank,
 Unshaked of motion. And that I am he, 70
 Let me a little show it, even in this,
 That I was constant Cimber should be banished,
 And constant do remain to keep him so.
CINNA. O Caesar——
CAESAR. Hence! Wilt thou lift up Olympus?°
DECIUS. Great Caesar——
CAESAR. Doth not Brutus bootless° kneel? 75
CASCA. Speak, hands, for me!

[CASCA *first, then the other conspirators and* MARCUS BRUTUS *stab* CAESAR.]

CAESAR. *Et tu, Brute?*° Then fall, Caesar! [*Dies.*]
CINNA. Liberty! Freedom! Tyranny is dead!
 Run hence, proclaim, cry it about the streets.
CASSIUS. Some to the common pulpits, and cry out 80
 "Liberty, freedom, and enfranchisement!"
BRUTUS. People, and Senators, be not affrighted.
 Fly not, stand still. Ambition's debt is paid.
CASCA. Go to the pulpit, Brutus.
DECIUS. And Cassius too.
BRUTUS. Where's Publius?
CINNA. Here, quite confounded° with this mutiny. 85
METELLUS. Stand fast together, lest some friend of Caesar's
 Should chance——

57. **enfranchisement:** release, freedom. 62. **no . . . firmament:** no equal in the heavens. 67. **apprehensive:** capable of thought and feeling. 74. **Olympus:** a mountain in Greece, the legendary home of the gods. 75. **bootless:** uselessly, in vain. 78. *Et tu, Brute?* (broo′tā) (Latin): "And you, Brutus?" According to the historian Plutarch, these were Caesar's last words. 86. **confounded:** confused, amazed.

BRUTUS. Talk not of standing. Publius, good cheer.
 There is no harm intended to your person, 90
 Nor to no Roman else. So tell them, Publius.
CASSIUS. And leave us, Publius, lest that the people
 Rushing on us should do your age some mischief.
BRUTUS. Do so, and let no man abide° this deed
 But we the doers.

 [*Reenter* TREBONIUS.]

CASSIUS. Where is Antony? 95
TREBONIUS. Fled to his house amazed.
 Men, wives, and children stare, cry out, and run
 As it were Doomsday.
BRUTUS. Fates, we will know your pleasures.
 That we shall die, we know; 'tis but the time,
 And drawing days out, that men stand upon.° 100
CASCA. Why, he that cuts off twenty years of life
 Cuts off so many years of fearing death.
BRUTUS. Grant that, and then is death a benefit.
 So are we Caesar's friends that have abridged
 His time of fearing death. Stoop, Romans, stoop, 105
 And let us bathe our hands in Caesar's blood
 Up to the elbows, and besmear our swords.
 Then walk we forth, even to the market place,
 And waving our red weapons o'er our heads,
 Let's all cry "Peace, freedom, and liberty!" 110
CASSIUS. Stoop then, and wash. How many ages hence
 Shall this our lofty scene be acted over
 In states unborn and accents yet unknown!

 94. **abide:** pay the penalty for. 100. **stand upon:** worry about.

BRUTUS. How many times shall Caesar bleed in sport,
 That now on Pompey's basis° lies along° 115
 No worthier than the dust!
CASSIUS. So oft as that shall be,
 So often shall the knot of us be called
 The men that gave their country liberty.
DECIUS. What, shall we forth?
CASSIUS. Aye, every man away.
 Brutus shall lead, and we will grace his heels 120
 With the most boldest and best hearts of Rome.

 [*Enter a* SERVANT.]

BRUTUS. Soft! Who comes here? A friend of Antony's.
SERVANT. Thus, Brutus, did my master bid me kneel,
 Thus did Mark Antony bid me fall down,
 And, being prostrate, thus he bade me say: 125
 Brutus is noble, wise, valiant, and honest,
 Caesar was mighty, bold, royal, and loving.
 Say I love Brutus and I honor him,
 Say I feared Caesar, honored him, and loved him.
 If Brutus will vouchsafe° that Antony 130
 May safely come to him and be resolved°
 How Caesar hath deserved to lie in death,
 Mark Antony shall not love Caesar dead
 So well as Brutus living, but will follow
 The fortunes and affairs of noble Brutus 135
 Thorough the hazards of this untrod state
 With all true faith. So says my master Antony.
BRUTUS. Thy master is a wise and valiant Roman—
 I never thought him worse.
 Tell him, so please him come unto this place, 140
 He shall be satisfied and, by my honor,
 Depart untouched.
SERVANT. I'll fetch him presently.°

 [*Exit.*]

BRUTUS. I know that we shall have him well to friend.°
CASSIUS. I wish we may, but yet have I a mind
 That fears him much, and my misgiving still 145
 Falls shrewdly to the purpose.°

 [*Reenter* ANTONY.]

BRUTUS. But here comes Antony. Welcome, Mark Antony.
ANTONY. O mighty Caesar, dost thou lie so low?

 115. **Pompey's basis:** the base of Pompey's statue. **along:** stretched out. 130. **vouchsafe:** permit.
131. **resolved:** convinced. 142. **presently:** immediately. 143. **well to friend:** as a good friend.
146. **Falls . . . purpose:** doubts the wisdom of what you intend to do.

Are all thy conquests, glories, triumphs, spoils,
Shrunk to this little measure? Fare thee well. 150
I know not, gentlemen, what you intend,
Who else must be let blood, who else is rank.°
If I myself, there is no hour so fit
As Caesar's death's hour, nor no instrument
Of half that worth as those your swords, made rich 155
With the most noble blood of all this world.
I do beseech ye, if you bear me hard,
Now, whilst your purpled hands do reek and smoke,
Fulfill your pleasure. Live a thousand years,
I shall not find myself so apt to die. 160
No place will please me so, no mean° of death,
As here by Caesar, and by you cut off,
The choice and master spirits of this age.

BRUTUS. O Antony, beg not your death of us.
Though now we must appear bloody and cruel, 165
As by our hands and this our present act
You see we do. Yet see you but our hands
And this the bleeding business they have done.
Our hearts you see not. They are pitiful,
And pity to the general wrong of Rome— 170
As fire drives out fire, so pity pity—
Hath done this deed on Caesar. For your part,
To you our swords have leaden° points, Mark Antony.
Our arms in strength of malice,° and our hearts
Of brothers' temper, do receive you in 175
With all kind love, good thoughts, and reverence.

CASSIUS. Your voice shall be as strong as any man's
In the disposing of new dignities.°

BRUTUS. Only be patient till we have appeased
The multitude, beside themselves with fear, 180
And then we will deliver you the cause
Why I, that did love Caesar when I struck him,
Have thus proceeded.

ANTONY. I doubt not of your wisdom.
Let each man render me his bloody hand.
First, Marcus Brutus, will I shake with you. 185
Next, Caius Cassius, do I take your hand.
Now, Decius Brutus, yours, now yours, Metellus;
Yours, Cinna, and, my valiant Casca, yours—
Though last, not least in love, yours, good Trebonius.
Gentlemen all—alas, what shall I say? 190

152. **rank:** in need of bleeding to cure an illness. 161. **mean:** means, method. 173. **leaden:** blunt. 174. **in . . . malice:** with power to hurt you. 178. **disposing . . . dignities:** deciding who should hold high public office.

My credit° now stands on such slippery ground
That one of two bad ways you must conceit° me,
Either a coward or a flatterer.
That I did love thee, Caesar, oh, 'tis true.
If then thy spirit look upon us now, 195
Shall it not grieve thee dearer than thy death
To see thy Antony making his peace,
Shaking the bloody fingers of thy foes,
Most noble! in the presence of thy corse?°
Had I as many eyes as thou hast wounds, 200
Weeping as fast as they stream forth thy blood,
It would become me better than to close
In terms of friendship with thine enemies.
Pardon me, Julius! Here wast thou bayed,° brave hart,°
Here didst thou fall, and here thy hunters stand, 205
Signed in thy spoil° and crimsoned in thy lethe.°
O world, thou wast the forest to this hart,
And this, indeed, O world, the heart of thee.
How like a deer strucken by many princes
Dost thou here lie! 210

CASSIUS. Mark Antony——

ANTONY. Pardon me, Caius Cassius.
The enemies of Caesar shall say this;
Then, in a friend, it is cold modesty.

CASSIUS. I blame you not for praising Caesar so,
But what compact mean you to have with us? 215
Will you be pricked in number° of our friends,
Or shall we on, and not depend on you?

ANTONY. Therefore I took your hands, but was indeed
Swayed from the point by looking down on Caesar.
Friends am I with you all and love you all, 220
Upon this hope that you shall give me reasons
Why and wherein Caesar was dangerous.

BRUTUS. Or else were this a savage spectacle.
Our reasons are so full of good regard
That were you, Antony, the son of Caesar, 225
You should be satisfied.

ANTONY. That's all I seek.
And am moreover suitor that I may
Produce his body to the market place,
And in the pulpit, as becomes a friend,
Speak in the order of his funeral. 230

BRUTUS. You shall, Mark Antony.

191. **credit:** reputation. 192. **conceit:** think of. 199. **corse:** corpse. 204. **bayed:** brought to
bay, surrounded by hounds. **hart:** deer. 206. **Signed . . . spoil:** stained in your slaughter. **lethe:**
blood; death. 216. **pricked in number:** marked in the list, counted on.

CASSIUS. Brutus, a word with you.

[*Aside to* BRUTUS.] You know not what you do. Do not consent
That Antony speak in his funeral.
Know you how much the people may be moved
By that which he will utter?

BRUTUS. By your pardon, 235
I will myself into the pulpit first,
And show the reason of our Caesar's death.
What Antony shall speak, I will protest
He speaks by leave and by permission,
And that we are contented Caesar shall 240
Have all true rites and lawful ceremonies.
It shall advantage more than do us wrong.

CASSIUS. I know not what may fall. I like it not.

BRUTUS. Mark Antony, here, take you Caesar's body.
You shall not in your funeral speech blame us, 245
But speak all good you can devise of Caesar,
And say you do 't by our permission.
Else shall you not have any hand at all
About his funeral. And you shall speak
In the same pulpit whereto I am going— 250
After my speech is ended.

ANTONY. Be it so.
I do desire no more.

BRUTUS. Prepare the body then, and follow us.

[*Exeunt all but* ANTONY, *who looks down at* CAESAR'S *body.*]

ANTONY. O, pardon me, thou bleeding piece of earth,
That I am meek and gentle with these butchers! 255
Thou art the ruins of the noblest man
That ever livèd in the tide of times.
Woe to the hand that shed this costly blood!
Over thy wounds now do I prophesy,
Which like dumb mouths do ope their ruby lips 260
To beg the voice and utterance of my tongue,
A curse shall light upon the limbs of men.
Domestic fury and fierce civil strife
Shall cumber° all the parts of Italy.
Blood and destruction shall be so in use, 265
And dreadful objects so familiar,
That mothers shall but smile when they behold
Their infants quartered° with the hands of war,
All pity choked with custom of fell° deeds.
And Caesar's spirit ranging for revenge, 270

264. **cumber:** encumber, weigh down. 268. **quartered:** torn apart. 269. **fell:** cruel.

With Até° by his side come hot from Hell,
Shall in these confines with a monarch's voice
Cry "Havoc,"° and let slip the dogs of war,
That this foul deed shall smell above the earth
With carrion men, groaning for burial. 275

[*Enter a* SERVANT.]

You serve Octavius Caesar,° do you not?
SERVANT. I do, Mark Antony.
ANTONY. Caesar did write for him to come to Rome.
SERVANT. He did receive his letters, and is coming,
 And bid me say to you by word of mouth— 280
 [*Seeing the body.*] O Caesar!
ANTONY. Thy heart is big. Get thee apart and weep.
 Passion, I see, is catching, for mine eyes,
 Seeing those beads of sorrow stand in thine,
 Began to water. Is thy master coming? 285
SERVANT. He lies tonight within seven leagues of Rome.
ANTONY. Post° back with speed, and tell him what hath chanced.
 Here is a mourning Rome, a dangerous Rome,
 No Rome of safety for Octavius yet.
 Hie hence, and tell him so. Yet stay awhile. 290
 Thou shalt not back till I have borne this corse
 Into the market place. There shall I try,°
 In my oration, how the people take
 The cruel issue° of these bloody men,
 According to the which, thou shalt discourse 295
 To young Octavius of the state of things.
 Lend me your hand.

[*Exeunt with* CAESAR'S *body.*]

SCENE II

[*The Forum. Enter* BRUTUS *and* CASSIUS, *and a throng of* CITIZENS, *disturbed by the death of* CAESAR.]

CITIZENS. We will be satisfied. Let us be satisfied.
BRUTUS. Then follow me, and give me audience, friends.
 Cassius, go you into the other street,
 And part the numbers.
 Those that will hear me speak, let 'em stay here, 5
 Those that will follow Cassius, go with him,

271. **Até:** a goddess who leads men to ruin. 273. **"Havoc":** "Take no prisoners"; "Kill everyone."
276. **Octavius Caesar:** the grandson of Caesar's sister, adopted by Caesar as his official heir.
287. **Post:** ride. 292. **try:** test, find out. 294. **issue:** action, deed.

And public reasons shall be rendered
Of Caesar's death.

FIRST CITIZEN. I will hear Brutus speak.

SECOND CITIZEN. I will hear Cassius, and compare their reasons
When severally° we hear them rendered. 10

[*Exit* CASSIUS, *with some of the* CITIZENS. BRUTUS *goes into the pulpit.*]

THIRD CITIZEN. The noble Brutus is ascended. Silence!

BRUTUS. Be patient till the last.

Romans, countrymen, and lovers! Hear me for my cause, and be silent,
that you may hear. Believe me for mine honor, and have respect to mine
honor, that you may believe. Censure° me in your wisdom, and awake 15
your senses, that you may the better judge. If there be any in this assembly,
any dear friend of Caesar's, to him I say that Brutus' love to Caesar was no
less than his. If then that friend demand why Brutus rose against Caesar,
this is my answer—not that I loved Caesar less, but that I loved Rome
more. Had you rather Caesar were living, and die all slaves, than that 20
Caesar were dead, to live all freemen? As Caesar loved me, I weep for him;
as he was fortunate, I rejoice at it; as he was valiant, I honor him. But as he
was ambitious, I slew him. There is tears for his love, joy for his fortune,
honor for his valor, and death for his ambition. Who is here so base that
would be a bondman?° If any, speak, for him have I offended. Who is 25
here so rude that would not be a Roman? If any, speak, for him have I
offended. Who is here so vile that will not love his country? If any, speak,
for him have I offended. I pause for a reply.

ALL. None, Brutus, none.

BRUTUS. Then none have I offended. I have done no more to Caesar than you 30
shall do to Brutus. The question of his death is enrolled in the Capitol, his
glory not extenuated,° wherein he was worthy, nor his offenses enforced,°
for which he suffered death.

[*Enter* ANTONY *and others, with* CAESAR'S *body.*]

Here comes his body, mourned by Mark Antony, who, though he had no
hand in his death, shall receive the benefit of his dying, a place in the 35
commonwealth—as which of you shall not? With this I depart—that, as I
slew my best lover for the good of Rome, I have the same dagger for myself
when it shall please my country to need my death.

ALL. Live, Brutus! Live, live!

FIRST CITIZEN. Bring him with triumph home unto his house. 40

SECOND CITIZEN. Give him a statue with his ancestors.

THIRD CITIZEN. Let him be Caesar.

FOURTH CITIZEN. Caesar's better parts
Shall be crowned in Brutus.

FIRST CITIZEN. We'll bring him to his house with shouts and clamors.

10. **severally:** separately. 15. **Censure:** judge. 25. **bondman:** slave. 32. **extenuated:** belittled.
enforced: exaggerated.

BRUTUS. My countrymen——

SECOND CITIZEN. Peace! Silence! Brutus speaks. 45

FIRST CITIZEN. Peace, ho!

BRUTUS. Good countrymen, let me depart alone,
 And, for my sake, stay here with Antony.
 Do grace to Caesar's corpse, and grace his speech
 Tending to Caesar's glories, which Mark Antony
 By our permission is allowed to make. 50
 I do entreat you, not a man depart,
 Save I alone, till Antony have spoke.

 [*Exit.*]

FIRST CITIZEN. Stay, ho, and let us hear Mark Antony!

THIRD CITIZEN. Let him go up into the public chair. 55
 We'll hear him. Noble Antony, go up.

ANTONY. For Brutus' sake, I am beholding° to you.

 [*Goes into the pulpit.*]

FOURTH CITIZEN. What does he say of Brutus?

THIRD CITIZEN. He says, for Brutus' sake,
 He finds himself beholding to us all.

FOURTH CITIZEN. 'Twere best he speak no harm of Brutus here. 60

FIRST CITIZEN. This Caesar was a tyrant.

THIRD CITIZEN. Nay, that's certain.
 We are blest that Rome is rid of him.

SECOND CITIZEN. Peace! Let us hear what Antony can say.

57. **beholding:** indebted, grateful.

ANTONY. You gentle Romans——
ALL. Peace, ho! Let us hear him.
ANTONY. Friends, Romans, countrymen, lend me your ears. 65
 I come to bury Caesar, not to praise him.
 The evil that men do lives after them,
 The good is oft interrèd° with their bones.
 So let it be with Caesar. The noble Brutus
 Hath told you Caesar was ambitious. 70
 If it were so, it was a grievous fault.
 And grievously hath Caesar answered it.
 Here, under leave of Brutus and the rest—
 For Brutus is an honorable man,
 So are they all, all honorable men— 75
 Come I to speak in Caesar's funeral.
 He was my friend, faithful and just to me.
 But Brutus says he was ambitious,
 And Brutus is an honorable man.
 He hath brought many captives home to Rome, 80
 Whose ransoms did the general coffers° fill.
 Did this in Caesar seem ambitious?
 When that the poor have cried, Caesar hath wept—
 Ambition should be made of sterner stuff.
 Yet Brutus says he was ambitious, 85
 And Brutus is an honorable man.
 You all did see that on the Lupercal
 I thrice presented him a kingly crown,
 Which he did thrice refuse. Was this ambition?
 Yet Brutus says he was ambitious, 90
 And, sure, he is an honorable man.
 I speak not to disprove what Brutus spoke,
 But here I am to speak what I do know.
 You all did love him once, not without cause.
 What cause withholds you then to mourn for him? 95
 O judgment, thou art fled to brutish beasts,
 And men have lost their reason! Bear with me,
 My heart is in the coffin there with Caesar,
 And I must pause till it come back to me.
FIRST CITIZEN. Methinks there is much reason in his sayings. 100
SECOND CITIZEN. If thou consider rightly of the matter,
 Caesar has had great wrong.
THIRD CITIZEN. Has he, masters?
 I fear there will a worse come in his place.
FOURTH CITIZEN. Mark ye his words? He would not take the crown,
 Therefore 'tis certain he was not ambitious. 105

68. **interrèd:** buried. 81. **general coffers:** public treasury.

FIRST CITIZEN. If it be found so, some will dear abide it.°
SECOND CITIZEN. Poor soul! His eyes are red as fire with weeping.
THIRD CITIZEN. There's not a nobler man in Rome than Antony.
FOURTH CITIZEN. Now mark him, he begins again to speak.
ANTONY. But yesterday the word of Caesar might 110
 Have stood against the world. Now lies he there,
 And none so poor to do him reverence.
 O masters, if I were disposed to stir
 Your hearts and minds to mutiny and rage,
 I should do Brutus wrong and Cassius wrong, 115
 Who, you all know, are honorable men.
 I will not do them wrong; I rather choose
 To wrong the dead, to wrong myself and you,
 Than I will wrong such honorable men.
 But here's a parchment with the seal of Caesar— 120
 I found it in his closet—'tis his will.
 Let but the commons hear this testament—
 Which, pardon me, I do not mean to read—
 And they would go and kiss dead Caesar's wounds
 And dip their napkins in his sacred blood, 125
 Yea, beg a hair of him for memory,
 And, dying, mention it within their wills,
 Bequeathing it as a rich legacy
 Unto their issue.°
FOURTH CITIZEN. We'll hear the will. Read it, Mark Antony. 130
ALL. The will, the will! We will hear Caesar's will.
ANTONY. Have patience, gentle friends. I must not read it.
 It is not meet° you know how Caesar loved you.
 You are not wood, you are not stones, but men;
 And, being men, hearing the will of Caesar, 135
 It will inflame you, it will make you mad.
 'Tis good you know not that you are his heirs,
 For if you should, oh, what would come of it!
FOURTH CITIZEN. Read the will. We'll hear it, Antony.
 You shall read us the will, Caesar's will. 140
ANTONY. Will you be patient? Will you stay awhile?
 I have o'ershot myself to tell you of it.
 I fear I wrong the honorable men
 Whose daggers have stabbed Caesar. I do fear it.
FOURTH CITIZEN. They were traitors—honorable men! 145
ALL. The will! The testament!
SECOND CITIZEN. They were villains, murderers. The will! Read the will.
ANTONY. You will compel me then to read the will?
 Then make a ring about the corpse of Caesar,

106. **dear abide it:** pay for it dearly. 129. **issue:** children. 133. **meet:** fit, appropriate.

And let me show you him that made the will. 150
Shall I descend? And will you give me leave?
ALL. Come down.
SECOND CITIZEN. Descend.

[*He comes down from the pulpit.*]

THIRD CITIZEN. You shall have leave.
FOURTH CITIZEN. A ring. Stand round. 155
FIRST CITIZEN. Stand from the hearse, stand from the body.
SECOND CITIZEN. Room for Antony, most noble Antony.
ANTONY. Nay, press not so upon me. Stand far off.
ALL. Stand back. Room! Bear back.
ANTONY. If you have tears, prepare to shed them now. 160
You all do know this mantle. I remember
The first time ever Caesar put it on.
'Twas on a summer's evening, in his tent,
That day he overcame the Nervii.
Look, in this place ran Cassius' dagger through. 165
See what a rent the envious Casca made.
Through this the well-belovèd Brutus stabbed,
And as he plucked his cursèd steel away,
Mark how the blood of Caesar followed it,
As rushing out of doors, to be resolved 170
If Brutus so unkindly knocked, or no.
For Brutus, as you know, was Caesar's angel.
Judge, O you gods, how dearly Caesar loved him!
This was the most unkindest cut of all,
For when the noble Caesar saw him stab, 175
Ingratitude, more strong than traitors' arms,
Quite vanquished him. Then burst his mighty heart,
And, in his mantle muffling up his face,
Even at the base of Pompey's statue,
Which all the while ran blood, great Caesar fell. 180
Oh, what a fall was there, my countrymen!
Then I, and you, and all of us fell down,
Whilst bloody treason flourished over us.
Oh, now you weep, and I perceive you feel
The dint° of pity. These are gracious drops. 185
Kind souls, what weep you when you but behold
Our Caesar's vesture° wounded? Look you here—
Here is himself, marred, as you see, with traitors.

[*He pulls the cloak off* CAESAR'S *body*.]

FIRST CITIZEN. Oh, piteous spectacle!
SECOND CITIZEN. Oh, noble Caesar! 190

185. **dint:** blow, shock. 187. **vesture:** clothing.

THIRD CITIZEN. Oh, woeful day!

FOURTH CITIZEN. Oh, traitors, villains!

FIRST CITIZEN. Oh, most bloody sight!

SECOND CITIZEN. We will be revenged.

ALL. Revenge! About! Seek! Burn! Fire! Kill! Slay! 195
 Let not a traitor live!

ANTONY. Stay, countrymen.

FIRST CITIZEN. Peace there! Hear the noble Antony.

SECOND CITIZEN. We'll hear him, we'll follow him, we'll die with him.

ANTONY. Good friends, sweet friends, let me not stir you up 200
 To such a sudden flood of mutiny.
 They that have done this deed are honorable.
 What private griefs they have, alas, I know not,
 That made them do it. They are wise and honorable,
 And will, no doubt, with reasons answer you. 205
 I come not, friends, to steal away your hearts.
 I am no orator, as Brutus is,
 But, as you know me all, a plain blunt man
 That love my friend; and that they know full well
 That gave me public leave to speak of him. 210
 For I have neither wit, nor words, nor worth,
 Action, nor utterance, nor the power of speech,
 To stir men's blood. I only speak right on,
 I tell you that which you yourselves do know,
 Show you sweet Caesar's wounds, poor poor dumb mouths, 215
 And bid them speak for me. But were I Brutus,
 And Brutus Antony, there were an Antony
 Would ruffle up your spirits, and put a tongue
 In every wound of Caesar that should move
 The stones of Rome to rise and mutiny. 220

ALL. We'll mutiny.

FIRST CITIZEN. We'll burn the house of Brutus.

THIRD CITIZEN. Away, then! Come, seek the conspirators.

ANTONY. Yet hear me, countrymen, yet hear me speak.

ALL. Peace, ho! Hear Antony. Most noble Antony! 225

ANTONY. Why, friends, you go to do you know not what.
 Wherein hath Caesar thus deserved your loves?
 Alas, you know not. I must tell you, then—
 You have forgot the will I told you of.

ALL. Most true, the will! Let's stay and hear the will. 230

ANTONY. Here is the will, and under Caesar's seal.
 To every Roman citizen he gives,
 To every several° man, seventy-five drachmas.°

SECOND CITIZEN. Most noble Caesar! We'll revenge his death.

THIRD CITIZEN. Oh, royal Caesar! 235

 233. **several:** individual. **drachmas:** silver coins.

ANTONY. Hear me with patience.

ALL. Peace, ho!

ANTONY. Moreover, he hath left you all his walks,
His private arbors and new-planted orchards,
On this side Tiber. He hath left them you, 240
And to your heirs forever—common pleasures,
To walk abroad and recreate yourselves.
Here was a Caesar! When comes such another?

FIRST CITIZEN. Never, never. Come, away, away!
We'll burn his body in the holy place, 245
And with the brands fire the traitors' houses.
Take up the body.

SECOND CITIZEN. Go fetch fire.

THIRD CITIZEN. Pluck down benches.

FOURTH CITIZEN. Pluck down forms,° windows, anything. 250

[*Exeunt* CITIZENS *with the body.*]

ANTONY. Now let it work. Mischief, thou art afoot,
Take thou what course thou wilt.

[*Enter a* SERVANT.]

How now, fellow?

SERVANT. Sir, Octavius is already come to Rome.

ANTONY. Where is he?

SERVANT. He and Lepidus° are at Caesar's house. 255

ANTONY. And thither will I straight to visit him.
He comes upon a wish.° Fortune is merry,
And in this mood will give us anything.

SERVANT. I heard him say Brutus and Cassius
Are rid like madmen through the gates of Rome. 260

ANTONY. Belike° they had some notice of the people,
How I had moved them. Bring me to Octavius.

[*Exeunt.*]

250. **forms:** benches. 255. **Lepidus:** one of Caesar's generals and one of the three chief leaders of Caesar's party. 257. **upon a wish:** just when I wanted him. 261. **Belike:** likely, probably.

SCENE III

[*A street in Rome. Enter* CINNA *the poet.*]

CINNA. I dreamt tonight that I did feast with Caesar,
　　　And things unluckily charge my fantasy.°
　　　I have no will to wander forth of doors,
　　　Yet something leads me forth.

[*A mob of* CITIZENS, *armed with sticks, spears, and swords, enters and surrounds him.*]

FIRST CITIZEN. What is your name?　　　　　　　　　　　　　　　　5
SECOND CITIZEN. Whither are you going?
THIRD CITIZEN. Where do you dwell?
FOURTH CITIZEN. Are you a married man or a bachelor?
SECOND CITIZEN. Answer every man directly.
FIRST CITIZEN. Aye, and briefly.　　　　　　　　　　　　　　　　10
FOURTH CITIZEN. Aye, and wisely.
THIRD CITIZEN. Aye, and truly, you were best.
CINNA. What is my name? Whither am I going? Where do I dwell? Am I a married
　　　man or a bachelor? Then, to answer every man directly and briefly, wisely
　　　and truly, wisely I say I am a bachelor.　　　　　　　　　　　15
SECOND CITIZEN. That's as much as to say they are fools that marry. You'll bear
　　　me a bang° for that, I fear. Proceed, directly.
CINNA. Directly, I am going to Caesar's funeral.
FIRST CITIZEN. As a friend or an enemy?
CINNA. As a friend.　　　　　　　　　　　　　　　　　　　　20
SECOND CITIZEN. That matter is answered directly.
FOURTH CITIZEN. For your dwelling, briefly.
CINNA. Briefly, I dwell by the Capitol.

　　2. **charge my fantasy:** fill my imagination.　16–17. **bear . . . bang:** get a wallop from me.

THIRD CITIZEN. Your name, sir, truly.

CINNA. Truly, my name is Cinna. 25

FIRST CITIZEN. Tear him to pieces. He's a conspirator.

CINNA. I am Cinna the poet, I am Cinna the poet.

FOURTH CITIZEN. Tear him for his bad verses, tear him for his bad verses.

CINNA. I am not Cinna the conspirator.

FOURTH CITIZEN. It is no matter, his name's Cinna. Pluck but his name out 30
of his heart, and turn him going.

THIRD CITIZEN. Tear him, tear him! Come, brands. Ho, firebrands—to Brutus',
to Cassius'! Burn all. Some to Decius' house, and some to Casca's, some
to Ligarius'. Away, go!

[*Exeunt.*]

FOR STUDY AND DISCUSSION

1. What two threats to the conspiracy occur before Caesar takes his seat? How does Caesar's image of himself as grand and noble contribute to the failure of the warning? What do Popilius's words suggest about how some senators, at least, will react to the assassination?

2. Why do the conspirators appeal to Caesar? Does he pass their "test"? Do you think he refuses their plea out of a sense of justice or to flatter his own self-esteem? From what we have seen of him, is he as "constant" as he would like to think?

3. Why is Caesar startled to see Brutus among his murderers? How do you imagine Caesar's last words make Brutus feel?

4. What is the conspirators' first impulse after the assassination? How does Brutus argue them into a calmer mood?

5. The fact that he has been close to Caesar forces Antony to tread a tightrope in this scene. What two opposing impressions does he not want the conspirators to have of him? How does he avoid each of these extremes?

6. Antony plays a bold game in this scene. How does he impress Brutus with his frankness and sincerity? Why does Brutus so readily believe that Antony means everything he says and that he will be satisfied with reasons? Which lines might suggest, to more suspicious ears, another, ironic meaning?

7. Cassius, as usual, better understands the situation. Why do you think he avoids arguing openly with Brutus?

8. At the beginning of Scene ii, what is the mood of the crowd? Brutus appeals to their reason. Do they understand what he is saying? What is ironic about their response, "Let him be Caesar!"

9. Antony's speech is quite a different thing. What is the crowd's mood as he begins to speak? How does he use irony to arouse their feelings? How does he associate himself with Caesar in their minds?

10. *Was* Caesar ambitious? What makes you think so? In Antony's argument that he was not, what reasons does he give? How does he convince the mob?

11. Where, in a previous scene, have we seen a crowd suddenly reverse its attitude? Antony, knowing how quickly the mood of the people could change again, is not content until he has worked them up into a mad fury. How does he make dramatic use of props in building this emotion?

12. Why, given the people's mood, is it to Antony's advantage to join forces with Octavius, Caesar's heir, and Lepidus, the best known of Caesar's generals? What has happened to Brutus and Cassius by the end of this scene?

13. Why do you think Shakespeare includes the scene between the mob and Cinna the poet? What does it show us about the nature of a mob? about how fully Antony has gained the passions of the citizens of Rome?

14. Where does Shakespeare use humor in this scene? Does it increase or lessen the horror of the mob's murder of the wrong man? Explain your answer.

ACT IV

SCENE I

[A house in Rome. ANTONY, OCTAVIUS, *and* LEPIDUS, *seated at a table.]*

ANTONY. These many then shall die, their names are pricked.°
OCTAVIUS. Your brother too must die. Consent you, Lepidus?
LEPIDUS. I do consent.
OCTAVIUS. Prick him down, Antony.
LEPIDUS. Upon condition Publius shall not live,
 Who is your sister's son, Mark Antony. 5
ANTONY. He shall not live. Look, with a spot I damn him.
 But, Lepidus, go you to Caesar's house.
 Fetch the will hither, and we shall determine
 How to cut off some charge in legacies.°
LEPIDUS. What, shall I find you here? 10
OCTAVIUS. Or here or at the Capitol.

 [Exit LEPIDUS.]

ANTONY. This is a slight unmeritable man,
 Meet to be sent on errands. Is it fit,
 The threefold world divided, he should stand
 One of the three to share it?
OCTAVIUS. So you thought him, 15
 And took his voice who should be pricked to die
 In our black sentence and proscription.°
ANTONY. Octavius, I have seen more days than you.
 And though we lay these honors on this man,
 To ease ourselves of divers slanderous loads, 20
 He shall but bear them as the ass bears gold,
 To groan and sweat under the business,
 Either led or driven, as we point the way.
 And having brought our treasure where we will,
 Then take we down his load and turn him off, 25
 Like to the empty ass, to shake his ears
 And graze in commons.
OCTAVIUS. You may do your will.
 But he's a tried and valiant soldier.
ANTONY. So is my horse, Octavius, and for that
 I do appoint him store of provender.° 30
 It is a creature that I teach to fight,
 To wind,° to stop, to run directly on,
 His corporal° motion governed by my spirit.

1. **pricked:** put down on a list. 9. **cut . . . legacies:** change the will. 17. **proscription:** accusation of treason; death list. 30. **store of provender:** supply of food. 32. **wind:** turn. 33. **corporal:** bodily, physical.

And, in some taste,° is Lepidus but so.
He must be taught, and trained, and bid go forth, 35
A barren-spirited fellow, one that feeds
On abjects, orts,° and imitations,
Which, out of use and staled by other men,
Begin his fashion. Do not talk of him
But as a property.° And now, Octavius, 40
Listen great things. Brutus and Cassius
Are levying powers.° We must straight make head.°
Therefore let our alliance be combined,
Our best friends made, our means stretched,
And let us presently go sit in council 45
How covert matters may be best disclosed,
And open perils surest answered.

OCTAVIUS. Let us do so, for we are at the stake,°
And bayed about with many enemies.
And some that smile have in their hearts, I fear, 50
Millions of mischiefs.

[*Exeunt.*]

SCENE II

[*A camp near Sardis, in Greece. In front of* BRUTUS'S *tent. A sound of drums.
Enter* BRUTUS, LUCILIUS, LUCIUS, *and* SOLDIERS. TITINIUS *and* PINDARUS, *from*
CASSIUS'S *army, meet them.* BRUTUS *halts his men.*]

BRUTUS. Stand, ho!
LUCILIUS. Give the word, ho, and stand!

34. **in . . . taste:** to some extent. 37. **abjects, orts:** worthless things, scraps. 40. **property:** tool.
42. **levying powers:** gathering armies. **head:** headway; gather forces. 48. **at the stake:** like a bear
tied to a stake and "bayed about" by dogs.

BRUTUS. What now, Lucilius! Is Cassius near?

LUCILIUS. He is at hand, and Pindarus is come
To do you salutation from his master. 5

BRUTUS. He greets me well.° Your master, Pindarus,
In his own change, or by ill officers,°
Hath given me some worthy cause to wish
Things done undone. But if he be at hand,
I shall be satisfied.

PINDARUS. I do not doubt 10
But that my noble master will appear
Such as he is, full of regard and honor.

BRUTUS. He is not doubted. A word, Lucilius,
How he received you. Let me be resolved.

LUCILIUS. With courtesy and with respect enough, 15
But not with such familiar instances,°
Nor with such free and friendly conference,
As he hath used of old.

BRUTUS. Thou hast described
A hot friend cooling. Ever note, Lucilius,
When love begins to sicken and decay, 20
It useth an enforcèd ceremony.
There are no tricks in plain and simple faith.
But hollow men, like horses hot at hand,°
Make gallant show and promise of their mettle,
But when they should endure the bloody spur, 25
They fall their crests ° and like deceitful jades °
Sink in the trial. Comes his army on?

LUCILIUS. They mean this night in Sardis to be quartered.
The greater part, the horse in general,°
Are come with Cassius.

[*Low march within.*]

BRUTUS. Hark! He is arrived. 30
March gently on to meet him.

[*Enter* CASSIUS *and his army.*]

CASSIUS. Stand, ho!

BRUTUS. Stand, ho! Speak the word along.

FIRST SOLDIER. Stand!

SECOND SOLDIER. Stand! 35

THIRD SOLDIER. Stand!

CASSIUS. Most noble brother, you have done me wrong.

6. **greets ... well:** sends his greetings with a worthy man. 7. **In ... officers:** because of some change of heart in himself or because of the deeds of unworthy subordinates. 16. **familiar instances:** friendly behavior. 23. **hot at hand:** eager before the race begins. 26. **crests:** proud necks. **jades:** worn-out nags. 29. **the ... general:** all the cavalry.

BRUTUS. Judge me, you gods! Wrong I mine enemies?
 And if not so, how should I wrong a brother?
CASSIUS. Brutus, this sober form ° of yours hides wrongs, 40
 And when you do them——
BRUTUS. Cassius, be content,
 Speak your griefs softly. I do know you well.
 Before the eyes of both our armies here,
 Which should perceive nothing but love from us,
 Let us not wrangle. Bid them move away, 45
 Then in my tent, Cassius, enlarge your griefs,
 And I will give you audience.
CASSIUS. Pindarus,
 Bid our commanders lead their charges off
 A little from this ground.
BRUTUS. Lucilius, do you the like, and let no man 50
 Come to our tent till we have done our conference.
 Let Lucius and Titinius guard our door.

 [*Exeunt.*]

SCENE III

[*Inside* BRUTUS'S *tent. Enter* BRUTUS *and* CASSIUS.]

CASSIUS. That you have wronged me doth appear in this:
 You have condemned and noted ° Lucius Pella
 For taking bribes here of the Sardians,
 Wherein my letters, praying on his side,
 Because I knew the man, were slighted off. 5
BRUTUS. You wronged yourself to write in such a case.
CASSIUS. In such a time as this it is not meet
 That every nice offense should bear his comment.°
BRUTUS. Let me tell you, Cassius, you yourself
 Are much condemned to have an itching palm, 10
 To sell and mart your offices ° for gold
 To undeservers.
CASSIUS. I an itching palm!
 You know that you are Brutus that speaks this,
 Or, by the gods, this speech were else your last.
BRUTUS. The name of Cassius honors this corruption, 15
 And chastisement doth therefore hide his head.
CASSIUS. Chastisement!
BRUTUS. Remember March, the ides of March remember.
 Did not great Julius bleed for justice' sake?

SCENE II. 40. **sober form:** grave, upright appearance.
 SCENE III. 2. **noted:** publicly disgraced. 7–8. **not meet . . . comment:** not necessary for every trivial offense to be strictly punished. 11. **mart your offices:** trade your services.

What villain touched his body that did stab, 20
And not for justice? What, shall one of us,
That struck the foremost man of all this world
But for supporting robbers, shall we now
Contaminate our fingers with base bribes,
And sell the mighty space of our large honors 25
For so much trash as may be graspèd thus?
I had rather be a dog and bay the moon
Than such a Roman.

CASSIUS. Brutus, bait ° not me,
I'll not endure it. You forget yourself,
To hedge me in. I am a soldier, I, 30
Older in practice, abler than yourself
To make conditions.°

BRUTUS. Go to. You are not, Cassius.

CASSIUS. I am.

BRUTUS. I say you are not.

CASSIUS. Urge me no more, I shall forget myself. 35
Have mind upon your health, tempt me no farther.

BRUTUS. Away, slight man!

CASSIUS. Is 't possible?

BRUTUS. Hear me, for I will speak.
Must I give way and room to your rash choler? °
Shall I be frighted when a madman stares? 40

CASSIUS. O ye gods, ye gods! Must I endure all this?

BRUTUS. All this! Aye, more. Fret till your proud heart break.
Go show your slaves how choleric you are,
And make your bondmen tremble. Must I budge?
Must I observe you? Must I stand and crouch 45
Under your testy humor? ° By the gods,
You shall digest the venom of your spleen,°
Though it do split you; for, from this day forth,
I'll use you for my mirth, yea, for my laughter,
When you are waspish.

CASSIUS. Is it come to this? 50

BRUTUS. You say you are a better soldier.
Let it appear so, make your vaunting ° true
And it shall please me well. For mine own part,
I shall be glad to learn of noble men.

CASSIUS. You wrong me every way, you wrong me, Brutus. 55
I said an elder soldier, not a better.
Did I say better?

BRUTUS. If you did, I care not.

CASSIUS. When Caesar lived, he durst ° not thus have moved me.

28. **bait:** antagonize. 32. **conditions:** rules. 39. **choler:** anger. 46. **testy humor:** bad temper.
47. **spleen:** rage, temper. 52. **vaunting:** boasting. 58. **durst:** dared.

BRUTUS. Peace, peace! You durst not so have tempted him.

CASSIUS. I durst not! 60

BRUTUS. No.

CASSIUS. What, durst not tempt him!

BRUTUS. For your life you durst not.

CASSIUS. Do not presume too much upon my love.
　　　I may do that I shall be sorry for.

BRUTUS. You have done that you should be sorry for. 65
　　　There is no terror, Cassius, in your threats,
　　　For I am armed so strong in honesty
　　　That they pass by me as the idle wind
　　　Which I respect not. I did send to you
　　　For certain sums of gold, which you denied me. 70
　　　For I can raise no money by vile means—
　　　By heaven, I had rather coin my heart,
　　　And drop my blood for drachmas,° than to wring
　　　From the hard hands of peasants their vile trash
　　　By any indirection.° I did send 75
　　　To you for gold to pay my legions,
　　　Which you denied me. Was that done like Cassius?
　　　Should I have answered Caius Cassius so?
　　　When Marcus Brutus grows so covetous,
　　　To lock such rascal counters ° from his friends, 80
　　　Be ready, gods, with all your thunderbolts,
　　　Dash him to pieces!

CASSIUS. I denied you not.

BRUTUS. You did.

CASSIUS. I did not. He was but a fool
　　　That brought my answer back. Brutus hath rived ° my heart.
　　　A friend should bear his friend's infirmities. 85
　　　But Brutus makes mine greater than they are.

BRUTUS. I do not, till you practice them on me.

CASSIUS. You love me not.

BRUTUS. I do not like your faults.

CASSIUS. A friendly eye could never see such faults.

BRUTUS. A flatterer's would not, though they do appear 90
　　　As huge as high Olympus.

CASSIUS. Come, Antony, and young Octavius, come,
　　　Revenge yourselves alone on Cassius,
　　　For Cassius is aweary of the world—
　　　Hated by one he loves, braved ° by his brother, 95
　　　Checked like a bondman,° all his faults observed,
　　　Set in a notebook, learned and conned by rote,°

73. **drachmas:** coins. 75. **indirection:** underhanded means. 80. **rascal counters:** filthy coins. 84. **rived:** split. 95. **braved:** mocked. 96. **Checked . . . bondman:** chastised like a slave. 97. **conned by rote:** learned by heart.

To cast into my teeth. Oh, I could weep
My spirit from mine eyes! There is my dagger,
And here my naked breast; within, a heart 100
Dearer than Plutus'° mine, richer than gold.
If that thou be'st a Roman, take it forth,
I, that denied thee gold, will give my heart.
Strike, as thou didst at Caesar; for I know
When thou didst hate him worst, thou lovedst him better 105
Than ever thou lovedst Cassius.

BRUTUS. Sheathe your dagger.
Be angry when you will, it shall have scope; °
Do what you will, dishonor shall be humor.°
O Cassius, you are yokèd ° with a lamb
That carries anger as the flint bears fire, 110
Who, much enforcèd, shows a hasty spark
And straight is cold again.

CASSIUS. Hath Cassius lived
To be but mirth and laughter to his Brutus,
When grief and blood ill-tempered vexeth him?

BRUTUS. When I spoke that, I was ill-tempered too. 115
CASSIUS. Do you confess so much? Give me your hand.
BRUTUS. And my heart too.
CASSIUS. O Brutus!
BRUTUS. What's the matter?
CASSIUS. Have not you love enough to bear with me
When that rash humor which my mother gave me
Makes me forgetful?

BRUTUS. Yes, Cassius, and from henceforth, 120
When you are overearnest with your Brutus,
He'll think your mother chides, and leave you so.

POET. [*Within*] Let me go in to see the generals.
There is some grudge between 'em, 'tis not meet
They be alone. 125

LUCILIUS. [*Within*] You shall not come to them.
POET. [*Within*] Nothing but death shall stay me.

[*Enter* POET, *followed by* LUCILIUS, TITINIUS, *and* LUCIUS.]

CASSIUS. How now! What's the matter?
POET. For shame, you generals! What do you mean?
Love and be friends, as two such men should be, 130
For I have seen more years, I'm sure, than ye.

CASSIUS. Ha, ha! How vilely doth this cynic ° rhyme!
BRUTUS. Get you hence, sirrah. Saucy fellow, hence!
CASSIUS. Bear with him, Brutus. 'Tis his fashion.

101. **Plutus':** Plutus was the god of wealth. 107. **scope:** free range. 108. **humor:** just a mood.
109. **yokèd:** linked, harnessed. 132. **cynic:** ill-mannered fellow.

BRUTUS. I'll know his humor when he knows his time.° 135
 What should the wars do with these jigging fools?
 Companion,° hence!
CASSIUS. Away, away, be gone!

[*Exit* POET.]

BRUTUS. Lucilius and Titinius, bid the commanders
 Prepare to lodge their companies tonight.
CASSIUS. And come yourselves, and bring Messala with you 140
 Immediately to us.

[*Exeunt* LUCILIUS *and* TITINIUS.]

BRUTUS. Lucius, a bowl of wine!

[*Exit* LUCIUS.]

CASSIUS. I did not think you could have been so angry.
BRUTUS. O Cassius, I am sick of many griefs.
CASSIUS. Of your philosophy you make no use
 If you give place to accidental evils. 145
BRUTUS. No man bears sorrow better. Portia is dead.
CASSIUS. Ha! Portia!
BRUTUS. She is dead.
CASSIUS. How 'scaped I killing when I crossed you so?
 Oh, insupportable and touching loss! 150
 Upon what sickness?
BRUTUS. Impatient of my absence,
 And grief that young Octavius with Mark Antony
 Have made themselves so strong—for with her death
 That tidings came—with this she fell distract,
 And, her attendants absent, swallowed fire. 155
CASSIUS. And died so?
BRUTUS. Even so.
CASSIUS. O ye immortal gods!

[*Reenter* LUCIUS, *with wine and a taper.*]

BRUTUS. Speak no more of her. Give me a bowl of wine.
 In this I bury all unkindness, Cassius. [*Drinks.*]
CASSIUS. My heart is thirsty for that noble pledge.
 Fill, Lucius, till the wine o'erswell the cup. 160
 I cannot drink too much of Brutus' love. [*Drinks.*]
BRUTUS. Come in, Titinius!

[*Exit* LUCIUS.]

[*Reenter* TITINIUS, *with* MESSALA.]

 Welcome, good Messala.
 Now sit we close about this taper here,
 And call in question our necessities.

135. **his time:** the right time for him to speak. 137. **companion:** fellow, lout.

CASSIUS. Portia, art thou gone?

BRUTUS. No more, I pray you. 165
 Messala, I have here receivèd letters
 That young Octavius and Mark Antony
 Come down upon us with a mighty power,
 Bending their expedition toward Philippi.

MESSALA. Myself have letters of the selfsame tenor. 170

BRUTUS. With what addition?

MESSALA. That by proscription and bills of outlawry
 Octavius, Antony, and Lepidus
 Have put to death a hundred Senators.

BRUTUS. Therein our letters do not well agree. 175
 Mine speak of seventy Senators that died
 By their proscriptions, Cicero being one.

CASSIUS. Cicero one!

MESSALA. Cicero is dead,
 And by that order of proscription.
 Had you your letters from your wife, my lord? 180

BRUTUS. No, Messala.

MESSALA. Nor nothing in your letters writ of her?

BRUTUS. Nothing, Messala.

MESSALA. That, methinks, is strange.

BRUTUS. Why ask you? Hear you aught of her in yours?

MESSALA. No, my lord. 185

BRUTUS. Now, as you are a Roman, tell me true.

MESSALA. Then like a Roman bear the truth I tell—
 For certain she is dead, and by strange manner.

BRUTUS. Why, farewell, Portia. We must die, Messala.
 With meditating that she must die once 190
 I have the patience to endure it now.

MESSALA. Even so great men great losses should endure.

CASSIUS. I have as much of this in art ° as you,
 But yet my nature could not bear it so.

BRUTUS. Well, to our work alive. What do you think 195
 Of marching to Philippi presently?

CASSIUS. I do not think it good.

BRUTUS. Your reason?

CASSIUS. This it is:
 'Tis better that the enemy seek us.
 So shall he waste his means, weary his soldiers,
 Doing himself offense, whilst we lying still 200
 Are full of rest, defense, and nimbleness.

BRUTUS. Good reasons must of force give place to better.
 The people 'twixt Philippi and this ground

193. **art:** theory, philosophical belief.

Do stand in a forced affection,
For they have grudged us contribution. 205
The enemy, marching along by them,
By them shall make a fuller number up,
Come on refreshed, new-added, and encouraged.
From which advantage shall we cut him off
If at Philippi we do face him there, 210
These people at our back.
CASSIUS. Hear me, good brother——
BRUTUS. Under your pardon. You must note beside
That we have tried the utmost of our friends,
Our legions are brimful, our cause is ripe.
The enemy increaseth every day, 215
We, at the height, are ready to decline.
There is a tide in the affairs of men
Which taken at the flood leads on to fortune;
Omitted, all the voyage of their life
Is bound in shallows and in miseries. 220
On such a full sea are we now afloat,
And we must take the current when it serves,
Or lose our ventures.
CASSIUS. Then, with your will, go on.
We'll along ourselves and meet them at Philippi.
BRUTUS. The deep of night is crept upon our talk, 225
And nature must obey necessity,
Which we will niggard ° with a little rest.
There is no more to say?
CASSIUS. No more. Good night.
Early tomorrow will we rise and hence.
BRUTUS. Lucius! [*Reenter* LUCIUS.] My gown. [*Exit* LUCIUS.] Farewell, good
Messala. 230
Good night, Titinius. Noble, noble Cassius,
Good night, and good repose.
CASSIUS. O my dear brother!
This was an ill beginning of the night.
Never come such division 'tween our souls!
Let it not, Brutus.
BRUTUS. Everything is well. 235
CASSIUS. Good night, my lord.
BRUTUS. Good night, good brother.
TITINIUS. *and* MESSALA. Good night, Lord Brutus.
BRUTUS. Farewell, everyone.
 [*Exeunt all but* BRUTUS.]

227. **niggard:** satisfy reluctantly.

[Reenter LUCIUS, *with the gown.]*

Give me the gown. Where is thy instrument?

LUCIUS. Here in the tent.

BRUTUS. What, thou speak'st drowsily?

Poor knave, I blame thee not, thou art o'erwatched.° 240

Call Claudius and some other of my men.

I'll have them sleep on cushions in my tent.

LUCIUS. Varro and Claudius!

[Enter VARRO *and* CLAUDIUS.]

VARRO. Calls my lord?

BRUTUS. I pray you, sirs, lie in my tent and sleep. 245

It may be I shall raise you by and by

On business to my brother Cassius.

VARRO. So please you, we will stand and watch your pleasure.

BRUTUS. I will not have it so. Lie down, good sirs.

It may be I shall otherwise bethink me. 250

Look, Lucius, here's the book I sought for so,

I put it in the pocket of my gown.

*[*VARRO *and* CLAUDIUS *lie down.]*

LUCIUS. I was sure your lordship did not give it me.

BRUTUS. Bear with me, good boy, I am much forgetful.

Canst thou hold up thy heavy eyes awhile, 255

And touch thy instrument a strain or two?

LUCIUS. Aye, my lord, an 't please you.

BRUTUS. It does, my boy.

I trouble thee too much, but thou art willing.

LUCIUS. It is my duty, sir.

BRUTUS. I should not urge thy duty past thy might— 260

I know young bloods look for a time of rest.

LUCIUS. I have slept, my lord, already.

BRUTUS. It was well done, and thou shalt sleep again,

I will not hold thee long. If I do live,

I will be good to thee. 265

[Music, and a song. LUCIUS *falls asleep as he sings.]*

This is a sleepy tune. O murderous slumber,

Lay'st thou thy leaden mace° upon my boy,

That plays thee music? Gentle knave, good night.

I will not do thee so much wrong to wake thee.

If thou dost nod, thou break'st thy instrument, 270

I'll take it from thee, and, good boy, good night.

240. **o'erwatched:** worn out from too much watching. 267. **mace:** spiked club.

Let me see, let me see, is not the leaf turned down
Where I left reading? Here it is, I think.

[*Sits down and begins to read. Enter the* GHOST OF CAESAR.]

How ill this taper burns! Ha! Who comes here?
I think it is the weakness of mine eyes 275
That shapes this monstrous apparition.
It comes upon me. Art thou anything?
Art thou some god, some angel, or some devil,
That makest my blood cold, and my hair to stare?
Speak to me what thou art. 280
GHOST. Thy evil spirit, Brutus.
BRUTUS. Why comest thou?
GHOST. To tell thee thou shalt see me at Philippi.
BRUTUS. Well, then I shall see thee again?
GHOST. Ay, at Philippi.
BRUTUS. Why, I will see thee at Philippi then. 285

 [*Exit* GHOST.]

Now I have taken heart, thou vanishest.
Ill spirit, I would hold more talk with thee.
Boy, Lucius! Varro! Claudius! Sirs, awake!
Claudius!
LUCIUS. [*Sleepily*] The strings, my lord, are false. 290
BRUTUS. He thinks he still is at his instrument.
 Lucius, awake!
LUCIUS. My lord?
BRUTUS. Didst thou dream, Lucius, that thou so criedst out?
LUCIUS. My lord, I do not know that I did cry. 295
BRUTUS. Yes, that thou didst. Didst thou see anything?
LUCIUS. Nothing, my lord.
BRUTUS. Sleep again, Lucius. Sirrah Claudius!
 [*To* VARRO.] Fellow thou, awake!
VARRO. My lord? 300
CLAUDIUS. My lord?
BRUTUS. Why did you so cry out, sirs, in your sleep?
VARRO *and* CLAUDIUS. Did we, my lord?
BRUTUS. Aye. Saw you anything?
VARRO. No, my lord, I saw nothing.
CLAUDIUS. Nor I, my lord.
BRUTUS. Go and commend me to my brother Cassius. 305
 Bid him set on his powers betimes before,°
 And we will follow.
VARRO *and* CLAUDIUS. It shall be done, my lord.

 [*Exeunt.*]

306. **set . . . before:** lead his army on ahead of ours right away.

1. As the first scene opens, what are Antony, Octavius, and Lepidus doing? Why are they doing it? What does Antony suggest they do to lessen the payments in Caesar's will? How does this private intention compare with his public sentiment for Caesar?

2. What kind of man is Lepidus? What does Antony think of him? What does Octavius? Why does Antony feel they need to include Lepidus in their ruling group?

3. Does Octavius seem a match for Antony? How does he resist Antony's authority? What qualities of character does Octavius show in this brief scene?

4. Between the time we last saw them and their meeting in Scene ii, how have feelings changed between Brutus and Cassius? What incidents have caused these changes? Why does Cassius feel he has been wronged?

5. How does Brutus answer Cassius' charge? How are both men's arguments typical of their characters? Do you think they could ever reach real agreement on this issue?

6. During their argument, both Brutus and Cassius say many angry things. Which are true? Which are not? With whom do you sympathize most? Who, in your opinion, is most in the right?

7. What is ironic about Brutus's asking Cassius to send him money because he himself "can raise no money by vile means"? Was this a well-reasoned move? What has Brutus not considered in his reasoning?

8. How is the quarrel resolved? Who gives in? Why would you expect him to give in?

9. Brutus and Cassius are interrupted by the camp "poet," who amuses the soldiers with his rhymes. Does his rhyme give good advice? How does Cassius react to it? How does Brutus? What does each one's reaction show about his character? about his mood?

10. How has Portia died? What caused her to take her life? How do you imagine her death, and his own part in it, makes Brutus feel? Why does he hold back his feelings?

11. In Scene iii the conspirators must make one last decision. What are the choices? Does Brutus really listen to Cassius' reasons, or does it seem that he has already made up his mind? Why might Cassius, in view of what has happened, be especially reluctant to provoke a quarrel?

12. Would you guess that Brutus's decision is right or wrong? Why? Do his reasons sound persuasive? Has he proved himself a good judge of human nature?

13. How does the scene with Lucius increase our sympathy for Brutus? How does this scene help prepare us for the coming of the ghost?

14. What qualities of Brutus's character are suggested by his reaction to the ghost of Caesar? by his reading on the night before the armies march to battle?

15. As Brutus and Cassius set out for Philippi, which side do you expect to win this crucial battle? What makes you think so?

ACT V

SCENE I

[The plains of Philippi in Greece. Enter OCTAVIUS, ANTONY, *and their* ARMY.]

OCTAVIUS. Now, Antony, our hopes are answerèd.
　　You said the enemy would not come down,
　　But keep the hills and upper regions.

It proves not so, their battles° are at hand,
They mean to warn us at Philippi here, 5
Answering before we do demand of them.
ANTONY. Tut, I am in their bosoms,° and I know
Wherefore they do it. They could be content
To visit other places, and come down
With fearful bravery, thinking by this face 10
To fasten in our thoughts that they have courage.
But 'tis not so.

[*Enter a* MESSENGER.]

MESSENGER. Prepare you, generals.
The enemy comes on in gallant show.
Their bloody sign° of battle is hung out,
And something to be done immediately. 15
ANTONY. Octavius, lead your battle softly on,
Upon the left hand of the even field.
OCTAVIUS. Upon the right hand I. Keep thou the left.
ANTONY. Why do you cross me in this exigent?°
OCTAVIUS. I do not cross you, but I will do so. 20

[*March. Drum. Enter from the other side of the stage* BRUTUS, CASSIUS, *and their*
ARMY; LUCILIUS, TITINIUS, MESSALA, *and others.*]

BRUTUS. They stand, and would have parley.
CASSIUS. Stand fast, Titinius. We must out and talk.
OCTAVIUS. Mark Antony, shall we give sign of battle?
ANTONY. No, Caesar, we will answer on their charge.
Make forth, the generals would have some words. 25
OCTAVIUS. Stir not until the signal.

[BRUTUS, CASSIUS, OCTAVIUS, *and* ANTONY *meet in the center of the stage.*]

BRUTUS. Words before blows. Is it so, countrymen?
OCTAVIUS. Not that we love words better, as you do.
BRUTUS. Good words are better than bad strokes, Octavius.
ANTONY. In your bad strokes, Brutus, you give good words. 30
Witness the hole you made in Caesar's heart,
Crying "Long live! Hail, Caesar!"
CASSIUS. Antony,
The posture of your blows are yet unknown,
But for your words, they rob the Hybla° bees,
And leave them honeyless.
ANTONY. Not stingless too. 35
BRUTUS. Oh, yes, and soundless too,

 4. **battles:** armies drawn up for battle. 7. **bosoms:** inner thoughts. 14. **bloody sign:** red flag.
19. **exigent:** critical moment. 34. **Hybla:** a mountain in Sicily famous for the honey produced there.

For you have stol'n their buzzing, Antony,
And very wisely threat before you sting.
ANTONY. Villains, you did not so when your vile daggers
Hacked one another in the sides of Caesar. 40
You showed your teeth like apes, and fawned like hounds,
And bowed like bondmen, kissing Caesar's feet,
Whilst damnèd Casca, like a cur, behind
Struck Caesar on the neck. O you flatterers!
CASSIUS. Flatterers! Now, Brutus, thank yourself. 45
This tongue had not offended so today
If Cassius might have ruled.
OCTAVIUS. Come, come, the cause. If arguing make us sweat,
The proof of it will turn to redder drops.
Look, 50
I draw a sword against conspirators.
When think you that the sword goes up° again?
Never, till Caesar's three and thirty wounds
Be well avenged, or till another Caesar
Have added slaughter to the sword of traitors. 55
BRUTUS. Caesar, thou canst not die by traitors' hands,
Unless thou bring'st them with thee.
OCTAVIUS. So I hope.
I was not born to die on Brutus' sword.
BRUTUS. Oh, if thou wert the noblest of thy strain,
Young man, thou couldst not die more honorable. 60
CASSIUS. A peevish schoolboy, worthless of such honor,
Joined with a masker° and a reveler!
ANTONY. Old Cassius still!
OCTAVIUS. Come, Antony, away!
Defiance, traitors, hurl we in your teeth.
If you dare fight today, come to the field; 65
If not, when you have stomachs.°

 [*Exeunt* OCTAVIUS, ANTONY, *and their* ARMY.]
CASSIUS. Why, now, blow wind, swell billow, and swim bark!°
The storm is up, and all is on the hazard.
BRUTUS. Ho, Lucilius! Hark, a word with you.
LUCILIUS. [*Standing forth*] My lord?

 [BRUTUS *and* LUCILIUS *converse apart.*]

CASSIUS. Messala!
MESSALA. [*Standing forth*] What says my general? 70
CASSIUS. Messala,
This is my birthday, as this very day
Was Cassius born. Give me thy hand, Messala.

52. **up:** back in its scabbard. 62. **masker:** actor. 66. **stomachs:** appetites. 67. **bark:** ship.

Be thou my witness that, against my will,
As Pompey was, am I compelled to set 75
Upon one battle all our liberties.
You know that I held Epicurus° strong,
And his opinion. Now I change my mind,
And partly credit things that do presage.°
Coming from Sardis, on our former ensign° 80
Two mighty eagles fell, and there they perched,
Gorging and feeding from our soldiers' hands,
Who to Philippi here consorted° us.
This morning are they fled away and gone,
And in their steads do ravens, crows, and kites 85
Fly o'er our heads and downward look on us,
As we were sickly prey. Their shadows seem
A canopy most fatal, under which
Our army lies, ready to give up the ghost.

MESSALA. Believe not so.

CASSIUS. I but believe it partly, 90
For I am fresh of spirit and resolved
To meet all perils very constantly.

[BRUTUS *and* LUCILIUS *end their conversation.*]

BRUTUS. Even so, Lucilius.

CASSIUS. Now, most noble Brutus,
The gods today stand friendly, that we may,
Lovers in peace, lead on our days to age! 95
But since the affairs of men rest still incertain,
Let's reason with the worst that may befall.
If we do lose this battle, then is this
The very last time we shall speak together.
What are you then determinèd to do? 100

BRUTUS. Even by the rule of that philosophy
By which I did blame Cato for the death
Which he did give himself—I know not how,
But I do find it cowardly and vile,
For fear of what might fall, so to prevent 105
The time of life°—arming myself with patience
To stay° the providence of some high powers
That govern us below.

CASSIUS. Then, if we lose this battle,
You are contented to be led in triumph
Thorough the streets of Rome? 110

77. **Epicurus:** a philosopher who taught that supernatural omens were simply superstition.
79. **presage:** foretell what is to come. 80. **former ensign:** foremost battle flag. 83. **consorted:**
accompanied. 105–06. **prevent . . . life:** put off, postpone the natural end of life. 107. **stay:** await.

BRUTUS. No, Cassius, no. Think not, thou noble Roman,
 That ever Brutus will go bound to Rome.
 He bears too great a mind. But this same day
 Must end that work the ides of March begun,
 And whether we shall meet again I know not. 115
 Therefore our everlasting farewell take.
 Forever and forever, farewell, Cassius!
 If we do meet again, why, we shall smile;
 If not, why then this parting was well made.
CASSIUS. Forever and forever farewell, Brutus! 120
 If we do meet again, we'll smile indeed;
 If not, 'tis true this parting was well made.
BRUTUS. Why then, lead on. Oh, that a man might know
 The end of this day's business ere it come!
 But it sufficeth that the day will end, 125
 And then the end is known. Come, ho! Away!

 [*Exeunt.*]

SCENE II

 [*The field of battle. Alarum. Enter* BRUTUS *and* MESSALA.]

BRUTUS. Ride, ride, Messala, ride, and give these bills°
 Unto the legions on the other side.

 [*Loud alarum.*]

 Let them set on at once, for I perceive
 But cold demeanor° in Octavius' wing,
 And sudden push gives them the overthrow. 5
 Ride, ride, Messala. Let them all come down.

 [*Exeunt.*]

SCENE III

 [*Another part of the field. Alarums. Enter* CASSIUS *and* TITINIUS, *dismayed.*]

CASSIUS. Oh, look, Titinius, look, the villains fly!
 Myself have to mine own turned enemy.
 This ensign° here of mine was turning back.
 I slew the coward, and did take it from him.
TITINIUS. O Cassius, Brutus gave the word too early, 5
 Who, having some advantage on Octavius,

SCENE II. 1. **bills:** orders. 4. **cold demeanor:** lack of spirit.
SCENE III. 3. **ensign:** flag bearer.

Took it too eagerly. His soldiers fell to spoil°
Whilst we by Antony are all enclosed.

[*Enter* PINDARUS.]

PINDARUS. Fly further off, my lord, fly further off.
 Mark Antony is in your tents, my lord. 10
 Fly, therefore, noble Cassius, fly far off.
CASSIUS. This hill is far enough. Look, look, Titinius,
 Are those my tents where I perceive the fire?
TITINIUS. They are, my lord.
CASSIUS. Titinius, if thou lovest me,
 Mount thou my horse and hide thy spurs in him 15
 Till he have brought thee up to yonder troops
 And here again, that I may rest assured
 Whether yond troops are friend or enemy.
TITINIUS. I will be here again, even with a thought.

 [*Exit.*]
 20

CASSIUS. Go, Pindarus, get higher on that hill—
 My sight was ever thick.° Regard Titinius,
 And tell me what thou notest about the field.

 [PINDARUS *ascends the hill.*]

This day I breathèd first. Time is come round,
And where I did begin, there shall I end,
My life is run his compass. Sirrah, what news? 25
PINDARUS. [*Above*] O my lord!
CASSIUS. What news?
PINDARUS. [*Above*] Titinius is enclosèd round about
 With horsemen that make to him on the spur,
 Yet he spurs on. Now they are almost on him.
 Now, Titinius! Now some light.° Oh, he lights too. 30
 He's ta'en. [*Shout.*] And, hark! They shout for joy.
CASSIUS. Come down, behold no more.
 Oh, coward that I am, to live so long,
 To see my best friend ta'en before my face! 35

 [PINDARUS *descends.*]

Come hither, sirrah.
In Parthia did I take thee prisoner,
And then I swore thee, saving of thy life.
That whatsoever I did bid thee do
Thou shouldst attempt it. Come now, keep thine oath. 40
Now be a free man, and with this good sword,

7. **spoil**: looting. 21. **thick**: weak. 31. **light**: dismount.

That ran through Caesar's bowels, search this bosom.
Stand not to answer. Here, take thou the hilts,
And when my face is covered, as 'tis now,
Guide thou the sword.

[PINDARUS *stabs him.*]

 Caesar, thou art revenged, 45
Even with the sword that killed thee. [*Dies.*]
PINDARUS. So, I am free, yet would not so have been,
Durst I have done my will. O Cassius!
Far from this country Pindarus shall run,
Where never Roman shall take note of him. 50

 [*Exit.*]

[*He throws down the sword and runs.* Reenter TITINIUS *with* MESSALA.]

MESSALA. It is but change,° Titinius, for Octavius
 Is overthrown by noble Brutus' power,
 As Cassius' legions are by Antony.
TITINIUS. These tidings will well comfort Cassius.
MESSALA. Where did you leave him?
TITINIUS. All disconsolate, 55
 With Pindarus his bondman, on this hill.
MESSALA. Is not that he that lies upon the ground?
TITINIUS. He lies not like the living. Oh, my heart!
MESSALA. Is not that he?
TITINIUS. No, this was he, Messala,
 But Cassius is no more. O setting sun, 60
 As in thy red rays thou dost sink to night,
 So in his red blood Cassius' day is set,
 The sun of Rome is set! Our day is gone,
 Clouds, dews, and dangers come. Our deeds are done!
 Mistrust of my success hath done this deed. 65
MESSALA. Mistrust of good success hath done this deed.
 O hateful error, melancholy's child,
 Why dost thou show to the apt° thoughts of men
 The things that are not? O error, soon conceived,
 Thou never comest unto a happy birth, 70
 But kill'st the mother that engendered thee!
TITINIUS. What, Pindarus! Where art thou, Pindarus?
MESSALA. Seek him, Titinius, whilst I go to meet
 The noble Brutus, thrusting this report
 Into his ears. I may say "thrusting" it, 75
 For piercing steel and darts envenomèd

51. **change:** even exchange. 68. **apt:** quick, eager.

Shall be as welcome to the ears of Brutus
As tidings of this sight.
TITINIUS. Hie you, Messala,
And I will seek for Pindarus the while.

[*Exit* MESSALA. TITINIUS *looks at* CASSIUS.]

Why didst thou send me forth, brave Cassius? 80
Did I not meet thy friends? And did not they
Put on my brows this wreath of victory,
And bid me give it thee? Didst thou not hear their shouts?
Alas, thou has misconstrued° everything!
But hold thee, take this garland on thy brow. 85
Thy Brutus bid me give it thee, and I
Will do his bidding. Brutus, come apace,°
And see how I regarded Caius Cassius.
By your leave, gods, this is a Roman's part.
Come, Cassius' sword, and find Titinius' heart. 90

[*Kills himself. Alarum. Reenter* MESSALA, *with* BRUTUS, *young* CATO, *and others.*]

BRUTUS. Where, where, Messala, doth his body lie?
MESSALA. Lo, yonder, and Titinius mourning it.
BRUTUS. Titinius' face is upward.
CATO. He is slain.
BRUTUS. O Julius Caesar, thou art mighty yet!
Thy spirit walks abroad, and turns our swords 95
In our own proper entrails.

[*Low alarums.*]

CATO. Brave Titinius!
Look whether he have not crowned dead Cassius!
BRUTUS. Are yet two Romans living such as these?
The last of all the Romans, fare thee well!
It is impossible that ever Rome 100
Should breed thy fellow. Friends, I owe moe tears
To this dead man than you shall see me pay.
I shall find time, Cassius, I shall find time.
Come therefore, and to Thasos send his body.
His funerals shall not be in our camp, 105
Lest it discomfort us.° Lucilius, come,
And come, young Cato. Let us to the field.
Labeo and Flavius, set our battles on.
'Tis three o'clock, and, Romans' yet ere night
We shall try fortune in a second fight. 110

[*Exeunt.*]

84. **misconstrued:** misinterpreted, misunderstood. 87. **apace:** quickly. 106. **discomfort us:**
make us all lose heart.

SCENE IV

[*Another part of the field. Alarum. Enter, fighting,* SOLDIERS *of both armies; then* BRUTUS, *young* CATO, LUCILIUS, *and others in retreat.*]

BRUTUS. Yet, countrymen, oh, yet hold up your heads!
CATO. What fellow doth not? Who will go with me?
 I will proclaim my name about the field.
 I am the son of Marcus Cato, ho!—
 A foe to tyrants, and my country's friend. 5
 I am the son of Marcus Cato, ho!

 [*He runs off, followed by several* SOLDIERS.]

BRUTUS. And I am Brutus, Marcus Brutus, I—
 Brutus, my country's friend. Know me for Brutus!

[*He runs off in another direction, followed by all but* LUCILIUS, *who looks off in the direction taken by young* CATO. *A loud cry offstage.*]

LUCILIUS. O young and noble Cato, art thou down?
 Why, now thou diest as bravely as Titinius, 10
 And mayst be honored, being Cato's son.

 [SOLDIERS *of* ANTONY'S *army enter behind him with drawn swords.*]

FIRST SOLDIER. Yield, or thou diest.
LUCILIUS. Only I yield to die.
 [*Offering money.*] There is so much that thou wilt kill me straight.
 Kill Brutus, and be honored in his death.
FIRST SOLDIER. We must not. A noble prisoner! 15
SECOND SOLDIER. Room, ho! Tell Antony, Brutus is ta'en.
FIRST SOLDIER. I'll tell the news. Here comes the general.

 [*Enter* ANTONY.]

 Brutus is ta'en, Brutus is ta'en, my lord.
ANTONY. Where is he?
LUCILIUS. Safe, Antony, Brutus is safe enough. 20
 I dare assure thee that no enemy
 Shall ever take alive the noble Brutus.
 The gods defend him from so great a shame!
 When you do find him, or alive or dead,
 He will be found like Brutus, like himself. 25
ANTONY. This is not Brutus, friend, but, I assure you,
 A prize no less in worth. Keep this man safe,
 Give him all kindness. I had rather have
 Such men my friends than enemies. Go on,
 And see whether Brutus be alive or dead, 30
 And bring us word unto Octavius' tent
 How everything is chanced.

 [*Exeunt.*]

SCENE V

[*Another part of the field. Enter* BRUTUS, DARDANIUS, CLITUS, STRATO, *and*
VOLUMNIUS, *weary and defeated.*]

BRUTUS. Come, poor remains of friends, rest on this rock.
CLITUS. Statilius showed the torchlight, but, my lord,
 He came not back. He is or ta'en or slain.
BRUTUS. Sit thee down, Clitus. Slaying is the word,
 It is a deed in fashion. Hark thee, Clitus. [*Whispering.*] 5
CLITUS. What, I, my lord? No, not for all the world.
BRUTUS. Peace then, no words.
CLITUS. I'll rather kill myself.
BRUTUS. Hark thee, Dardanius. [*Whispering.*]
DARDANIUS. Shall I do such a deed?
CLITUS. O Dardanius!
DARDANIUS. O Clitus! 10
CLITUS. What ill request did Brutus make to thee?
DARDANIUS. To kill him, Clitus. Look, he meditates.
CLITUS. Now is that noble vessel full of grief,
 That it runs over even at his eyes.
BRUTUS. Come hither, good Volumnius, list ° a word. 15
VOLUMNIUS. What says my lord?
BRUTUS. Why, this, Volumnius.
 The ghost of Caesar hath appeared to me
 Two several ° times by night—at Sardis once,
 And this last night here in Philippi fields.
 I know my hour is come.
VOLUMNIUS. Not so, my lord. 20

 15. **list:** listen to. 18. **several:** different.

BRUTUS. Nay, I am sure it is, Volumnius.
　　Thou seest the world, Volumnius, how it goes,
　　Our enemies have beat us to the pit.

　　　　　　　　[*Low alarums.*]

　　It is more worthy to leap in ourselves
　　Than tarry till they push us. Good Volumnius,　　　　　25
　　Thou know'st that we two went to school together.
　　Even for that our love of old, I prithee
　　Hold thou my sword hilts whilst I run on it.
VOLUMNIUS. That's not an office for a friend, my lord.

　　　　　　　　[*Alarum still.*]

CLITUS. Fly, fly, my lord, there is no tarrying here.　　　30
BRUTUS. Farewell to you, and you, and you, Volumnius.
　　Strato, thou hast been all this while asleep—
　　Farewell to thee too, Strato. Countrymen,
　　My heart doth joy that yet in all my life
　　I found no man but he was true to me.　　　　　　　35
　　I shall have glory by this losing day,
　　More than Octavius and Mark Antony
　　By this vile conquest shall attain unto.
　　So, fare you well at once, for Brutus' tongue
　　Hath almost ended his life's history.　　　　　　　40
　　Night hangs upon mine eyes, my bones would rest
　　That have but labored to attain this hour.

　　　　　　[*Alarum. Cry within,* "Fly, fly, fly!"]

CLITUS. Fly, my lord, fly!
BRUTUS.　　　　　　　　Hence! I will follow.
　　　　　　　　　[*Exeunt* CLITUS, DARDANIUS, *and* VOLUMNIUS.]
　　I prithee, Strato, stay thou by thy lord.
　　Thou art a fellow of a good respect,　　　　　　　45
　　Thy life hath had some smatch° of honor in it.
　　Hold then my sword, and turn away thy face
　　While I do run upon it. Wilt thou, Strato?
STRATO. Give me your hand first. Fare you well, my lord.
BRUTUS. Farewell, good Strato. [*Runs on his sword.*] Caesar, now be still.　50
　　I killed not thee with half so good a will. [*Dies. Alarum. Retreat. Enter*
　　　　OCTAVIUS, ANTONY, MESSALA, LUCILIUS, *and the army.*]
OCTAVIUS. What man is that?
MESSALA. My master's man. Strato, where is thy master?
STRATO. Free from the bondage you are in, Messala.
　　The conquerors can but make a fire of him,　　　　55

46. **smatch:** taste.

For Brutus only overcame himself,
And no man else hath honor by his death.
LUCILIUS. So Brutus should be found. I thank thee, Brutus,
That thou hast proved Lucilius' saying true.
OCTAVIUS. All that served Brutus, I will entertain them.° 60
Fellow, wilt thou bestow thy time with me?
STRATO. Aye, if Messala will prefer° me to you.
OCTAVIUS. Do so, good Messala.
MESSALA. How died my master, Strato?
STRATO. I held the sword, and he did run on it. 65
MESSALA. Octavius, then take him to follow thee
That did the latest° service to my master.
ANTONY. This was the noblest Roman of them all.
All the conspirators, save only he,
Did that they did in envy of great Caesar. 70
He only, in a general honest thought
And common good to all, made one of them.
His life was gentle, and the elements
So mixed in him that Nature might stand up
And say to all the world, "This was a man." 75
OCTAVIUS. According to his virtue let us use him,
With all respect and rites of burial.
Within my tent his bones tonight shall lie,
Most like a soldier, ordered honorably.
So call the field to rest, and let's away, 80
To part° the glories of this happy day.

[*Exeunt.*]

60. **entertain them:** give them a place in my service. 62. **prefer:** recommend. 67. **latest:** last.
81 **part:** divide up.

FOR STUDY AND DISCUSSION

1. Why do you think Octavius refuses to advance according to Antony's plan? Why doesn't he give Antony a reason? During the parley, what kind of person does Octavius show himself to be?

2. On what question has Cassius recently changed his mind? Does this change in Cassius weaken or strengthen your expectation of who will win the battle?

3. What opinion of suicide does Brutus at first express? How does Cassius force him to face the reality of the question? How, then, does Brutus change his mind?

4. How does Scene ii affect our expectations of the battle's outcome? Where else in the play has Shakespeare used a brief scene to increase the pace of the action?

5. In the first clash between the armies, Cassius' forces find themselves confronting Antony's, and Brutus's come up against Octavius. What is the result of each of these encounters? How has Shakespeare prepared us for this outcome?

6. How does Cassius misinterpret the result of Brutus's battle? Do you think his misinterpretation is caused mostly by the misleading circumstances or by his own mood? What makes you think so?

7. Titinius is not an important character in the play. Why do you suppose Shakespeare devotes so much time to his dying? How does his eagerness to follow his master affect our opinion of Cassius?

8. What does Scene iv reveal about the progress of the battle? Why does Lucilius ask the soldiers to kill him? What orders concerning Brutus has Antony given? How does this scene resolve our doubt about whether Brutus should kill himself rather than be taken?

9. How does Shakespeare create a sense of a great battle taking place on the stage? Do the entrances and exits of the characters ever seem forced or artificial? Where does he use sound effects and offstage action as part of the action of a scene?

10. Does Brutus's friends' reaction to his request increase or lessen our respect for him? How is Brutus's way of killing himself different from Cassius'? What is the difference between their final thoughts of Caesar?

11. Has the conspiracy done Rome any good at all? What effect does their victory and Brutus's death seem to have had on Octavius and Antony? Do you think they will be better rulers than Caesar would have been?

THE PLAY AS A WHOLE

1. Would *Marcus Brutus* be a better title for this play than *Julius Caesar?* Some critics have argued that, although Caesar dies in the middle of the play, the memory of his murder and his will to rule hovers over the last half of the play and has as much effect as a living character on the play's further action and its mood. Do you agree? Make a convincing argument for or against this opinion and support it with references to the play.

2. A *tragic hero* is a leading character who is admirable, but who, because of a single fault of character, is unable successfully to oppose the overwhelming forces that bring about his destruction. Does Brutus fit these requirements? does Caesar? Who is more of a tragic hero, Brutus or Cassius? Why?

3. *Dramatic irony* is often used in tragedy, where the characters move among events and forces that they do not fully understand. A speech or action is ironic when it suggests to us, the audience, much more than is realized by the character himself. Why does a historical play such as *Julius Caesar* offer especially rich opportunities for dramatic irony? What do we know that the characters do not? Where has Shakespeare made especially powerful use of dramatic irony in this play?

4. Some critics have suggested that *Julius Caesar* tends to be misinterpreted by modern audiences because of their belief in democracy and liberty. According to these critics, Shakespeare had quite a different point of view, living as he did under a legitimate and respected ruler in a time of peace and prosperity not so long after a series of bloody civil wars. Shakespeare, say these critics, intended Brutus to be the villain of his play, not the hero, since he kills a popular ruler and disrupts law and order. Do you agree? What evidence is there in the play that Shakespeare thought of Brutus as a hero? as a villain?

5. Compare the four main characters in the play: Brutus, Cassius, Caesar, and Antony. How is each unlike the others? What traits do any two of them have in common? Which two seem most alike? Which are most nearly opposite? Which are more concerned with the public good? Which with personal advantage?

6. By the end of the play, what have the leading characters learned about themselves and others? Do any of them undergo a basic change in character? Which become more admirable during the course of the play? which less?

7. Of all the characters in the play, Brutus is the only one who consistently says what he really thinks. The play is full of grand and noble sentiments, but only Brutus suits his actions to his words. Where in the play does this lead to his misjudging others? Where does it lead to others misjudging him?

8. Is Brutus an idealist? How is this shown in his actions and motivations? What do his actions and decisions in the play show about the virtues and faults of idealism? Are there any occasions in the play where Cassius seems more likeable and human than Brutus?

9. Throughout the play Shakespeare uses supernatural omens of disaster: the Sooth-

sayer, the violent "prodigies" and storms, the animal without a heart, and the ghost of Caesar. How does each of these omens increase suspense and tension? How does Cassius react to omens at the beginning of the play? at the end? What is Brutus's reaction to predictions of disaster? What is Caesar's?

10. *Julius Caesar* is a play about politics and power. What do the play's characters, events, and outcome suggest about the kind of man that is most likely to come out on top in such a struggle? Do you think this is necessarily true? What incidents or personalities in recent world events suggest that the actual pursuit of power is, or is not, like that in the play?

11. In view of the mob's behavior, can you see why Caesar or some other powerful man might wish to rule? What do the mob's reactions in this play suggest about the qualities required of citizens if they are not to lose their freedom?

FOR COMPOSITION

1. Choose any two of the four main characters in *Julius Caesar*—Brutus, Cassius, Caesar, and Antony. Write a character sketch of each, then a final paragraph comparing the two.

2. In a short composition, analyze and compare the relationship of Brutus, Cassius, and Antony to Julius Caesar. What were their public and private feelings toward Caesar? How did each express the loyalty he owed to Caesar as the legitimate ruler of Rome?

3. Would Rome be better off under Caesar, Brutus, or Antony? Give your opinion in a short composition, supporting your argument with examples from the play of how each man behaves toward his subordinates and equals.

4. At several places in the play, especially in Act I, characters describe events that have occurred offstage. Choose one of these speeches, such as Casca's account of the crowning of Caesar or the "prodigies" he has seen, and examine the language Shakespeare uses to bring the description alive. What are some especially vivid words and images? Try to replace some of these with a word or phrase with approximately the same meaning. What

happens? Write a short report on the results of your experiment.

5. Choose one of the major scenes in the play, such as Caesar's assassination, the speeches by Brutus and Antony, or the quarrel between Brutus and Cassius, and closely examine the motives and actions behind the lines. When you have a good understanding of the scene, rewrite it as a modern playwright would, keeping Shakespeare's lines, but adding stage directions that indicate the characters' movements. Explain the motives behind the characters' lines.

6. As in all of Shakespeare's great tragedies, several ideas or themes reappear in the imagery in a kind of repeated pattern. One of these is the idea of sickness versus health; others are blood and bleeding, sleep and rest, and birth and death. Find several examples in the play of one of these uses of imagery, and suggest, in a short composition, what each contributes to the overall meaning of each passage.

7. Shakespeare followed Plutarch's "Life of Caesar" in the creation of his *Julius Caesar*. However, a comparison of the two works quickly reveals the differences between the art of the biographer and that of the dramatist. Compare, for example, Caesar's attitude toward pale, thin men in Plutarch's work ("I'm not much afraid of these fat, long-haired people. It's the other type I'm more frightened of, the pale thin ones") and his remarks on the same subject in the play where they refer directly to Cassius ("Let me have men about me that are fat . . . Yond Cassius has a lean and hungry look."). Shakespeare has transformed Caesar's words into poetry and in addition has created a brilliant thumbnail sketch of Cassius which prepares the audience for the character's subsequent behavior. Compare such parallel scenes in the "Life" and *Julius Caesar* as the warning of the soothsayer, Calpurnia's dream, the attempt of Artemidorus to warn Caesar, and the assassination scene. Select one or more examples, and in a brief composition show how Shakespeare has developed his source material to suit his dramatic purposes.

Arms and the Man

GEORGE BERNARD SHAW

The work of George Bernard Shaw (1856–1950) has earned him a place among the great dramatists of English literature. Born in Dublin, Ireland, he lived in London from early manhood and gained a reputation there as a successful critic and unsuccessful novelist before turning to playwriting at the age of thirty-five. His first popular success was *Arms and the Man,* which was soon produced in both America and Europe, and firmly established Shaw as one of the foremost dramatists and entertainers of his time. His plays not only were successful, but for the most part were acclaimed as works of remarkable distinction. They appeared in rapid succession until 1939. Some of Shaw's most famous plays are *Arms and the Man, The Devil's Disciple, Caesar and Cleopatra, Man and Superman, Major Barbara, Pygmalion,* and *Saint Joan. Pygmalion,* one of the most popular of his plays, was the basis for the musical comedy *My Fair Lady.*

Shaw's prodigious reputation, however, is due not only to his talents as a playwright. He was always concerned, both in his plays and outside of them, with hypocrisy and social injustice, and on them he brought to bear one of the great minds—and wits—of our age. An avid socialist and pacifist, he peppered his writings with condemnations of the prejudices of his day. Until his death at the age of ninety-four, he continued to be a gadfly, stinging and provoking the smugness of his generation primarily with the effective weapon of humor. Yet he was not essentially a cynic. Always in his work is the hope for a better, more just society, which he felt would someday grow out of the efforts of intelligent realists such as himself.

George Bernard Shaw

Arms and the Man

The title of this play is a quotation from the opening lines of Virgil's epic poem *The Aeneid,* which describes in lofty style and with noble sentiments its hero's struggles and the battles he fought to establish the city of Rome. During his adventures, Aeneas is detained from his goal by a romance with Dido, a Carthaginian princess, whom he ultimately rejects in favor of the grandeur that was to be Rome. Shaw's play, as its title suggests, is in many ways a burlesque of this heroic story. In *Arms and the Man,* as in *The Aeneid,* the hero is sheltered and detained by a noble lady before returning to duty, but in Shaw's play the two meet a second time. Shaw creates an amusingly complicated plot and then uses it to poke fun at love and war and romantic attitudes toward both.

The play, of course, is not only a satire on heroism and romance. It also finds time to laugh at class distinctions, at foolish customs and pretensions, and at the conventions of the drawing-room drama of the nineteenth century, with its melodramatic emphasis on overheard conversations, mistaken identities, and misplaced props. But there is a vein of seriousness underlying Shaw's wit and humor. Pompous, heroic attitudes toward war may be amusing, but war itself is a deadly serious business. Romantic postures and extravagances may be laughable, but the ending of the play seems to come out for love and marriage based on common sense and understanding.

Comedy is never simply a question of amusing remarks, exaggerated characters, and tricky situations. These ingredients are funny only when they cast a new and unexpected light on the vices and follies of the established social order. Good comedy asks society to laugh at itself.

What the audience, as members of society, takes for granted, what it considers to be its fundamental rules, are shown to be funny, foolish, or even harmful. We laugh when we see a man slip on a banana peel, but we laugh harder when he is a pompous man, whose smug, self-satisfied routine is suddenly disrupted without warning. He is revealed to be both pretentious and vulnerable.

Comedies end happily, and because they do—and we know they will—we can laugh at them all the more. If the man who slipped on the banana peel were seriously hurt, we would be less amused and more concerned. But he gets up and goes on down the street a little less pompously, just as society continues its loves and its wars on more realistic terms at the end of *Arms and the Man.*

Program for the 1926 London production.

Arms and the Man

GEORGE BERNARD SHAW

Characters

MAJOR PAUL PETKOFF
CATHERINE, *his wife*
RAINA, *his daughter*
LOUKA, *their maid*
NICOLA, *their manservant*
MAJOR SERGIUS SARANOFF
CAPTAIN BLUNTSCHLI
AN OFFICER

ACT I

Night. A lady's bedchamber in Bulgaria, in a small town near the Dragoman Pass. It is late in November in the year 1885, and through an open window with a little balcony on the left can be seen a peak of the Balkans, wonderfully white and beautiful in the starlit snow. The interior of the room is not like anything to be seen in the east of Europe. It is half-rich Bulgarian, half-cheap Viennese. The counterpane and hangings of the bed, the window curtains, the little carpet, and all the ornamental textile fabrics in the room are oriental and gorgeous: the paper on the walls is occidental and paltry. Above the head of the bed, which stands against a little wall cutting off the right-hand corner of the room diagonally, is a painted wooden shrine, blue and gold, with an ivory image of Christ, and a light hanging before it in a pierced metal ball suspended by three chains. On the left, fur-ther forward, is an ottoman. The wash-stand, against the wall on the left, consists of an enameled iron basin with a pail be-neath it in a painted metal frame, and a single towel on the rail at the side. A chair near it is Austrian bent wood, with cane seat. The dressing table, between the bed and the window, is an ordinary pine table, covered with a cloth of many colors, but with an expensive toilet mirror on it. The door is on the right; and there is a chest of drawers between the door and the bed. This chest of drawers is also covered by a variegated native cloth, and on it there is a pile of paperbacked novels, a box of chocolate creams, and a miniature easel, on which is a large photograph of an ex-tremely handsome officer, whose lofty bearing and magnetic glance can be felt even from the portrait. The room is lighted by a candle on the chest of drawers, and another on the dressing table, with a box of matches beside it.

The window is hinged doorwise and stands wide open, folding back to the left. Outside a pair of wooden shutters, open-ing outward, also stand open. On the bal-cony, a young lady, intensely conscious of the romantic beauty of the night, and of the fact that her own youth and beauty is a part of it, is on the balcony, gazing at the snowy Balkans. She is covered by a long mantle of furs, worth, on a moderate estimate, about three times the furniture of her room.

Her reverie is interrupted by her mother, CATHERINE PETKOFF, *a woman over forty, imperiously energetic, with magnificent black hair and eyes, who might be a very splendid specimen of the wife of a moun-tain farmer, but is determined to be a Viennese lady, and to that end wears a fashionable tea gown on all occasions.*

CATHERINE (*entering hastily, full of good news*). Raina—(*she pronounces it Rah-eena, with the stress on the ee*) Raina

—*(she goes to the bed, expecting to find* RAINA *there)* Why, where—*(*RAINA *looks into the room.)* Heavens! child, are you out in the night air instead of in your bed? You'll catch your death. Louka told me you were asleep.

RAINA *(coming in).* I sent her away. I wanted to be alone. The stars are so beautiful! What is the matter?

CATHERINE. Such news. There has been a battle!

RAINA *(her eyes dilating).* Ah! *(She throws the cloak on the ottoman, and comes eagerly to* CATHERINE *in her nightgown, a pretty garment, but evidently the only one she has on.)*

CATHERINE. A great battle at Slivnitza! A victory! And it was won by Sergius.

RAINA *(with a cry of delight).* Ah! *(Rapturously.)* Oh, mother! *(Then, with sudden anxiety)* Is father safe?

CATHERINE. Of course: he sent me the news. Sergius is the hero of the hour, the idol of the regiment.

RAINA. Tell me, tell me. How was it! *(Ecstatically.)* Oh, mother, mother, mother! *(*RAINA *pulls her mother down on the ottoman; and they kiss one another frantically.)*

CATHERINE *(with surging enthusiasm).* You can't guess how splendid it is. A cavalry charge—think of that! He defied our Russian commanders—acted without orders—led a charge on his own responsibility—headed it himself—was the first man to sweep through their guns. Can't you see it, Raina; our gallant splendid Bulgarians with their swords and eyes flashing, thundering down like an avalanche and scattering the wretched Servian dandies like chaff. And you—you kept Sergius waiting a year before you would be betrothed to him. Oh, if you have a drop of Bulgarian blood in your veins, you will worship him when he comes back.

RAINA. What will he care for my poor little worship after the acclamations of a whole army of heroes? But no matter: I am so happy—so proud! *(She rises and*

walks about excitedly.) It proves that all our ideas were real after all.

CATHERINE (*indignantly*). Our ideas real! What do you mean?

RAINA. Our ideas of what Sergius would do—our patriotism—our heroic ideals. Oh, what faithless little creatures girls are! I sometimes used to doubt whether they were anything but dreams. When I buckled on Sergius's sword he looked so noble: it was treason to think of disillusion or humiliation or failure. And yet—and yet—(*Quickly.*) Promise me you'll never tell him.

CATHERINE. Don't ask me for promises until I know what I am promising.

RAINA. Well, it came into my head just as he was holding me in his arms and looking into my eyes, that perhaps we only had our heroic ideas because we are so fond of reading Byron and Pushkin,[1] and because we were so delighted with the opera that season at Bucharest.[2] Real life is so seldom like that—indeed never, as far as I knew it then. (*Remorsefully.*) Only think, mother, I doubted him: I wondered whether all his heroic qualities and his soldiership might not prove mere imagination when he went into a real battle. I had an uneasy fear that he might cut a poor figure there beside all those clever Russian officers.

CATHERINE. A poor figure! Shame on you! The Servians have Austrian officers who are just as clever as our Russians; but we have beaten them in every battle for all that.

RAINA (*laughing and sitting down again*). Yes, I was only a prosaic little coward. Oh, to think that it was all true—that Sergius is just as splendid and noble as he looks—that the world is really a glorious world for women who can see its glory and men who can act its romance! What happiness! what unspeakable fulfillment! Ah! (*She throws herself on her knees beside her mother and flings her arms passionately round her. They are interrupted by the entry of* LOUKA, *a handsome, proud girl in a pretty Bulgarian peasant's dress with double apron, so defiant that her servility to* RAINA *is almost insolent. She is afraid of* CATHERINE, *but even with her goes as far as she dares. She is just now excited like the others; but she has no sympathy for* RAINA'S *raptures and looks contemptuously at the ecstasies of the two before she addresses them.*)

LOUKA. If you please, madam, all the windows are to be closed and the shutters made fast. They say there may be shooting in the streets. (RAINA *and* CATHERINE *rise together, alarmed.*) The Servians are being chased right back through the pass; and they say they may run into the town. Our cavalry will be after them; and our people will be ready for them you may be sure, now that they are running away. (*She goes out on the balcony and pulls the outside shutters to; then steps back into the room.*)

RAINA. I wish our people were not so cruel. What glory is there in killing wretched fugitives?

CATHERINE (*businesslike, her housekeeping instincts aroused*). I must see that everything is made safe downstairs.

RAINA (*to* LOUKA). Leave the shutters so that I can just close them if I hear any noise.

CATHERINE (*authoritatively, turning on her way to the door*). Oh, no, dear, you must keep them fastened. You would be sure to drop off to sleep and leave them open. Make them fast, Louka.

LOUKA. Yes, madam. (*She fastens them.*)

RAINA. Don't be anxious about me. The

[1] **Byron and Pushkin:** Romantic poets of the nineteenth century.

[2] **Bucharest** (boo′kə·rest): capital city of Rumania.

moment I hear a shot, I shall blow out the candles and roll myself up in bed with my ears well covered.

CATHERINE. Quite the wisest thing you can do, my love. Good night.

RAINA. Good night. (*They kiss one another, and* RAINA'S *emotion comes back for a moment.*) Wish me joy of the happiest night of my life—if only there are no fugitives.

CATHERINE. Go to bed, dear; and don't think of them. (*She goes out.*)

LOUKA (*secretly, to* RAINA). If you would like the shutters open, just give them a push like this. (*She pushes them: they open: she pulls them to again.*) One of them ought to be bolted at the bottom; but the bolt's gone.

RAINA (*with dignity, reproving her*). Thanks, Louka; but we must do what we are told. (LOUKA *makes a grimace.*) Good night.

LOUKA (*carelessly*). Good night. (*She goes out, swaggering.*)

[RAINA, *left alone, goes to the chest of drawers, and adores the portrait there with feelings that are beyond all expression. She does not kiss it or press it to her breast, or show it any mark of bodily affection; but she takes it in her hands and elevates it like a priestess.*]

RAINA (*looking up at the picture with worship*). Oh, I shall never be unworthy of you any more, my hero—never, never, never. (*She replaces it reverently, and selects a novel from the little pile of books. She turns over the leaves dreamily; finds her page; turns the book inside out at it; and then, with a happy sigh, gets into bed and prepares to read herself to sleep. But before abandoning herself to fiction, she raises her eyes once more, thinking of the blessed reality and murmurs*) My hero! my hero! (*A distant shot breaks the quiet of the night outside. She starts, listening;*

and two more shots, much nearer, follow, startling her so that she scrambles out of bed, and hastily blows out the candle on the chest of drawers. Then, putting her fingers in her ears, she runs to the dressing table and blows out the light there, and hurries back to bed. The room is now in darkness: nothing is visible but the glimmer of the light in the pierced ball before the image, and the starlight seen through the slits at the top of the shutters. The firing breaks out again: there is a startling fusillade [1] quite close at hand. While it is still echoing, the shutters disappear, pulled open from without, and for an instant the rectangle of snowy starlight flashes out with the figure of a man in black upon it. The shutters close immediately and the room is dark again. But the silence is now broken by the sound of panting. Then there is a scrape; and the flame of a match is seen in the middle of the room.*)

RAINA (*crouching on the bed*). Who's there? (*The match is out instantly.*) Who's there? Who is that?

A MAN'S VOICE (*in the darkness, subduedly, but threateningly*). Sh—sh! Don't call out or you'll be shot. Be good; and no harm will happen to you. (*She is heard leaving her bed, and making for the door.*) Take care, there's no use in trying to run away. Remember, if you raise your voice my pistol will go off. (*Commandingly.*) Strike a light and let me see you. Do you hear? (*Another moment of silence and darkness. Then she is heard retreating to the dressing table. She lights a candle, and the mystery is at an end. A man of about thirty-five, in a deplorable plight, bespattered with mud and blood and snow, his belt and the strap of his revolver case keeping together the torn ruins of the blue coat of a Servian artillery officer.*

[1] **fusillade:** rapid firing of shots.

As far as the candlelight and his un-washed, unkempt condition make it pos-sible to judge, he is a man of middling stature and undistinguished appearance, with strong neck and shoulders, a round-ish, obstinate-looking head covered with short crisp bronze curls, clear quick blue eyes and good brows and mouth, a hope-lessly prosaic nose like that of a strong-minded baby, trim soldierlike carriage and energetic manner, and with all his wits about him in spite of his desperate predicament—even with a sense of humor of it, without, however, the least intention of trifling with it or throwing away a chance. He reckons up what he can guess about RAINA—*her age, her social posi-tion, her character, the extent to which she is frightened—at a glance, and con-tinues, more politely but still most de-terminedly)* Excuse my disturbing you;

but you recognize my uniform—Servian. If I'm caught I shall be killed. *(Deter-minedly.)* Do you understand that?

RAINA. Yes.

MAN. Well, I don't intend to get killed if I can help it. *(Still more determinedly.)* Do you understand that? *(He locks the door with a snap.)*

RAINA *(disdainfully)*. I suppose not. *(She draws herself up superbly, and looks him straight in the face, saying with em-phasis) Some* soldiers, I know, are *afraid* of death.

MAN *(with grim goodhumor)*. All of them, dear lady, all of them, believe me. It is our duty to live as long as we can, and kill as many of the enemy as we can. Now if you raise an alarm——

RAINA *(cutting him short)*. You will shoot me. How do you know that I am afraid to die?

MAN (cunningly). Ah; but suppose I don't shoot you, what will happen then? Why, a lot of your cavalry—the greatest blackguards in your army—will burst into this pretty room of yours and slaughter me here like a pig; for I'll fight like a demon: they shan't get *me* into the street to amuse themselves with: I know what they are. Are you prepared to receive that sort of company in your present undress? (RAINA, *suddenly conscious of her nightgown, instinctively shrinks and gathers it more closely about her. He watches her, and adds, pitilessly*) It's rather scanty, eh? (*She turns to the ottoman. He raises his pistol instantly, and cries*) Stop! (*She stops.*) Where are you going?

RAINA (*with dignified patience*). Only to get my cloak.

MAN (*darting to the ottoman and snatching the cloak*). A good idea. No: I'll keep the cloak: and *you* will take care that nobody comes in and sees you without it. This is a better weapon than the pistol. (*He throws the pistol down on the ottoman.*)

RAINA (*revolted*). It is not the weapon of a gentleman!

MAN. It's good enough for a man with only you to stand between him and death. (*As they look at one another for a moment,* RAINA *hardly able to believe that even a Servian officer can be so cynically and selfishly unchivalrous, they are startled by a sharp fusillade in the street. The chill of imminent death hushes the man's voice as he adds*) Do you hear? If you are going to bring those scoundrels in on me you shall receive them as you are. (RAINA *meets his eye with unflinching scorn. Suddenly he starts, listening. There is a step outside. Someone tries the door, and then knocks hurriedly and urgently at it.* RAINA *looks at* THE MAN, *breathless. He throws up his head with the gesture of a man who sees that it is all over with him,*

and, dropping the manner which he has been assuming to intimidate her, flings the cloak to her, exclaiming, sincerely and kindly) No use: I'm done for. Quick! wrap yourself up: they're coming!

RAINA (*catching the cloak eagerly*). Oh, thank you. (*She wraps herself up with great relief. He draws his saber and turns to the door, waiting.*)

LOUKA (*outside, knocking*). My lady, my lady! Get up, quick, and open the door.

RAINA (*anxiously*). What will you do?

MAN (*grimly*). Never mind. Keep out of the way. It will not last long.

RAINA (*impulsively*). I'll help you. Hide yourself, oh, hide yourself, quick, behind the curtain. (*She seizes him by a torn strip of his sleeve, and pulls him toward the window.*)

MAN (*yielding to her*). There is just half a chance, if you keep your head. Remember: nine soldiers out of ten are born fools. (*He hides behind the curtain, looking out for a moment to say, finally*) If they find me, I promise you a fight—a devil of a fight! [*He disappears.* RAINA *takes off the cloak and throws it across the foot of the bed. Then with a sleepy, disturbed air, she opens the door.* LOUKA *enters excitedly.*]

LOUKA. A man has been seen climbing up the water pipe to your balcony—a Servian. The soliders want to search for him; and they are so wild and drunk and furious. My lady says you are to dress at once.

RAINA (*as if annoyed at being disturbed*). They shall not search here. Why have they been let in?

CATHERINE (*coming in hastily*). Raina, darling, are you safe? Have you seen anyone or heard anything?

RAINA. I heard the shooting. Surely the soldiers will not dare come in here?

CATHERINE. I have found a Russian officer, thank Heaven: he knows Sergius.

(Speaking through the door to someone outside.) Sir, will you come in now! My daughter is ready.

[*A young Russian officer, in Bulgarian uniform, enters, sword in hand.*]

THE OFFICER *(with soft, feline politeness and stiff military carriage).* Good evening, gracious lady; I am sorry to intrude, but there is a fugitive hiding on the balcony. Will you and the gracious lady your mother please to withdraw while we search?

RAINA *(petulantly).* Nonsense, sir, you can see that there is no one on the balcony. *(She throws the shutters wide open and stands with her back to the curtain where* THE MAN *is hidden, pointing to the moonlit balcony. A couple of shots are fired right under the window, and a bullet shatters the glass opposite* RAINA, *who winks and gasps, but stands her ground, while* CATHERINE *screams, and* THE OFFICER *rushes to the balcony.)*

THE OFFICER *(on the balcony, shouting savagely down to the street).* Cease firing there, you fools: do you hear? Cease firing, blast you. *(He glares down for a moment; then turns to* RAINA, *trying to resume his polite manner.)* Could anyone have got in without your knowledge? Were you asleep?

RAINA. No, I have not been to bed.

THE OFFICER *(impatiently, coming back into the room).* Your neighbors have their heads so full of runaway Servians that they see them everywhere. *(Politely.)* Gracious lady, a thousand pardons. Good night. *(Military bow, which* RAINA *returns coldly. Another to* CATHERINE, *who follows him out.* RAINA *closes the shutters. She turns and sees* LOUKA, *who has been watching the scene curiously.)*

RAINA. Don't leave my mother, Louka, while the soldiers are here. (LOUKA *glances at* RAINA, *at the ottoman, at the curtain;*

then purses her lips secretively, laughs to herself, and goes out. RAINA *follows her to the door, shuts it behind her with a slam, and locks it violently.* THE MAN *immediately steps out from behind the curtain, sheathing his saber, and dismissing the danger from his mind in a businesslike way.)*

MAN. A narrow shave; but a miss is as good as a mile. Dear young lady, your servant until death. I wish for your sake I had joined the Bulgarian army instead of the Servian. I am not a native Servian.

RAINA *(haughtily).* No, you are one of the Austrians who set the Servians on to rob us of our national liberty, and who officer their army for them. We hate them!

MAN. Austrian! not I. Don't hate me, dear young lady. I am only a Swiss, fighting merely as a professional soldier. I joined Servia because it was nearest to me. Be generous: you've beaten us hollow.

RAINA. Have I not been generous?

MAN. Noble!—heroic! But I'm not saved yet. This particular rush will soon

pass through; but the pursuit will go on all night by fits and starts. I must take my chance to get off during a quiet interval. You don't mind my waiting just a minute or two, do you?

RAINA. Oh, no: I am sorry you will have to go into danger again. (*Motioning toward ottoman.*) Won't you sit—(*She breaks off with an irrepressible cry of alarm as she catches sight of the pistol.* THE MAN, *all nerves, shies like a frightened horse.*)

MAN (*irritably*). Don't frighten me like that. What is it?

RAINA. Your pistol! It was staring that officer in the face all the time. What an escape!

MAN (*vexed at being unnecessarily terrified*). Oh, is that all?

RAINA (*staring at him rather superciliously, conceiving a poorer and poorer opinion of him, and feeling proportionately more and more at her ease with him*). I am sorry I frightened you. (*She takes up the pistol and hands it to him.*) Pray take it to protect yourself against me.

MAN (*grinning wearily at the sarcasm as he takes the pistol*). No use, dear young lady: there's nothing in it. It's not loaded. (*He makes a grimace at it, and drops it disparagingly into his revolver case.*)

RAINA. Load it by all means.

MAN. I've no ammunition. What use are cartridges in battle? I always carry chocolate instead; and I finished the last cake of that yesterday.

RAINA (*outraged in her most cherished ideals of manhood*). Chocolate! Do you stuff your pockets with *sweets*—like a schoolboy—even in the field?

MAN. Yes. Isn't it contemptible?

[RAINA *stares at him, unable to utter her feelings. Then she sails away scornfully to the chest of drawers, and returns with the box of confectionery in her hand.*]

RAINA. Allow me. I am sorry I have eaten them all except these. (*She offers him the box.*)

MAN (*ravenously*). You're an angel! (*He gobbles the comfits.*)[1] Creams! Delicious! (*He looks anxiously to see whether there are any more. There are none. He accepts the inevitable with pathetic good humor, and says, with grateful emotion*) Bless you, dear lady. You can always tell an old soldier by the inside of his holsters and cartridge boxes. The young ones carry pistols and cartridges; the old ones, grub. Thank you. (*He hands back the box. She snatches it contemptuously from him and throws it away. This impatient action is so sudden that he shies again.*) Ugh! Don't do things so suddenly, gracious lady. Don't revenge yourself because I frightened you just now.

RAINA (*superbly*). Frighten *me!* Do you know, sir, that though I am only a woman, I think I am at heart as brave as you.

MAN. I should think so. You haven't been under fire for three days as I have. I can stand two days without showing it much; but no man can stand three days: I'm as nervous as a mouse. (*He sits down on the ottoman, and takes his head in his hands.*) Would you like to see me cry?

RAINA (*quickly*). No.

MAN. If you would, all you have to do is

[1] **comfits:** sweetmeats, candy.

to scold me just as if I were a little boy and you my nurse. If I were in camp now they'd play all sorts of tricks on me.

RAINA (*a little moved*). I'm sorry. I won't scold you. (*Touched by the sympathy in her tone, he raises his head and looks gratefully at her: she immediately draws back and says stiffly*) You must excuse me: *our* soldiers are not like that. (*She moves away from the ottoman.*)

. MAN. Oh, yes, they are. There are only two sorts of soldiers: old ones and young ones. I've served fourteen years: half of your fellows never smelled powder before. Why, how is it that you've just beaten us? Sheer ignorance of the art of war, nothing else. (*Indignantly.*) I never saw anything so unprofessional.

RAINA (*ironically*). Oh, was it unprofessional to beat you?

MAN. Well, come, is it professional to throw a regiment of cavalry on a battery of machine guns, with the dead certainty that if the guns go off not a horse or man will ever get within fifty yards of the fire? I couldn't believe my eyes when I saw it.

RAINA (*eagerly turning to him, as all her enthusiasm and her dream of glory rush back on her*). Did you see the great cavalry charge? Oh, tell me about it. Describe it to me.

MAN. You never saw a cavalry charge, did you?

RAINA. How could I?

MAN. Ah, perhaps not—of course. Well, it's a funny sight. It's like slinging a handful of peas against a window pane: first one comes; then two or three close behind him; and then all the rest in a lump.

RAINA (*her eyes dilating as she raises her clasped hands ecstatically*). Yes, first One!—the bravest of the brave!

MAN (*prosaically*). Hm! you should see the poor devil pulling at his horse.

RAINA. Why should he pull at his horse?

MAN (*impatient of so stupid a question*). It's running away with him, of course: do you suppose the fellow wants to get there before the others and be killed? Then they all come. You can tell the young ones by their wildness and their slashing. The old ones come bunched up under the number-one guard: they know that they are mere projectiles, and that it's no use trying to fight. The wounds are mostly broken knees, from the horses cannoning together.

RAINA. Ugh! But I don't believe the first man is a coward. I believe he is a hero!

MAN, (*good-humoredly*). That's what you'd have said if you'd seen the first man in the charge today.

RAINA (*breathless*). Ah, I knew it! Tell me—tell me about him.

MAN. He did it like an operatic tenor—a regular handsome fellow, with flashing eyes and lovely moustache, shouting a war cry and charging like Don Quixote at the windmills.[1] We nearly burst with laughter at him; but when the sergeant ran up as white as a sheet, and told us they'd sent us the wrong cartridges, and that we couldn't fire a shot for the next ten minutes, we laughed at the other side of our mouths. I never felt so sick in my life, though I've been in one or two very tight places. And I hadn't even a revolver cartridge—nothing but chocolate. We'd no bayonets—nothing. Of course, they just cut us to bits. And there was Don Quixote flourishing like a drum major, thinking he'd done the cleverest thing ever known, whereas he ought to be court-martialed for it. Of all the fools ever let loose on a field of battle, that man must be the very maddest. He and his regiment simply committed suicide—only the pistol missed fire, that's all.

RAINA (*deeply wounded, but steadfastly

[1] **Don Quixote . . . windmills:** Don Quixote, in Cervantes' novel of the same name, does battle with a windmill, thinking it to be an enormous giant.

loyal to her ideals). Indeed! Would you know him again if you saw him?

MAN. Shall I ever forget him. *(She again goes to the chest of drawers. He watches her with a vague hope that she may have something else for him to eat. She takes the portrait from its stand and brings it to him.)*

RAINA. That is a photograph of the gentleman—the patriot and hero—to whom I am betrothed.

MAN *(looking at it).* I'm really very sorry. *(Looking at her.)* Was it fair to lead me on? *(He looks at the portrait again.)* Yes: that's him: not a doubt of it. *(He stifles a laugh.)*

RAINA *(quickly).* Why do you laugh?

MAN *(shamefacedly, but still greatly tickled).* I didn't laugh, I assure you. At least I didn't mean to. But when I think of him charging the windmills and thinking he was doing the finest thing—*(chokes with suppressed laughter).*

RAINA *(sternly).* Give me back the portrait, sir.

MAN *(with sincere remorse).* Of course. Certainly. I'm really very sorry. *(She deliberately kisses it, and looks him straight in the face, before returning to the chest of drawers to replace it. He follows her, apologizing.)* Perhaps I'm quite wrong, you know: no doubt I am. Most likely he had got wind of the cartridge business somehow and knew it was a safe job.

RAINA. That is to say, he was a pretender and a coward! You did not dare say that before.

MAN *(with a comic gesture of despair).* It's no use, dear lady: I can't make you see it from the professional point of view. *(As he turns away to get back to the ottoman, the firing begins again in the distance.)*

RAINA *(sternly, as she sees him listening to the shots).* So much the better for you.

MAN *(turning).* How?

RAINA. You are my enemy; and you are at my mercy. What would I do if I were a professional soldier?

MAN. Ah, true, dear young lady: you're always right. I know how good you have been to me: to my last hour I shall remember those three chocolate creams. It was unsoldierly; but it was angelic.

RAINA *(coldly).* Thank you. And now I will do a soldierly thing. You cannot stay here after what you have just said about my future husband; but I will go out on the balcony and see whether it is safe for you to climb down into the street. *(She turns to the window.)*

MAN *(changing countenance).* Down that waterpipe! Stop! Wait! I can't! I daren't! The very thought of it makes me giddy. I came up it fast enough with death behind me. But to face it now in cold blood!—*(He sinks on the ottoman.)* It's no use: I give up: I'm beaten. Give the alarm. *(He drops his head in his hands in the deepest dejection.)*

RAINA *(disarmed by pity).* Come, don't be disheartened. *(She stoops over him almost maternally: he shakes his head.)* Oh, you are a very poor soldier—a chocolate cream soldier. Come, cheer up: it takes less courage to climb down than to face capture—remember that.

MAN *(dreamily, lulled by her voice).* No, capture only means death; and death is sleep—oh, sleep, sleep, sleep, undisturbed sleep! Climbing down the pipe means doing something—exerting myself—thinking! Death ten times over first.

RAINA *(softly and wonderingly, catching the rhythm of his weariness).* Are you so sleepy as that?

MAN. I've not had two hours undisturbed sleep since the war began. I'm on the staff: you don't know what that means. I haven't closed my eyes for thirty-six hours.'

RAINA (*desperately*). But what am I to do with you.

MAN (*staggering up*). Of course I must do something. (*He shakes himself; pulls himself together; and speaks with rallied vigor and courage.*) You see, sleep or no sleep, hunger or no hunger, tired or not tired, you can always do a thing when you know it must be done. Well, that pipe *must* be got down—(*He hits himself on the chest, and adds*)—Do you hear that, you chocolate cream soldier? (*He turns to the window.*)

RAINA (*anxiously*). But if you fall?

MAN. I shall sleep as if the stones were a feather bed. Good-by. (*He makes boldly for the window, and his hand is on the shutter when there is a terrible burst of firing in the street beneath.*)

RAINA (*rushing to him*). Stop! (*She catches him by the shoulder, and turns him quite round.*) They'll kill you.

MAN (*coolly, but attentively*). Never mind: this sort of thing is all in my day's work. I'm bound to take my chance. (*Decisively.*) Now do what I tell you. Put out the candles, so that they shan't see the light when I open the shutters. And keep away from the window, whatever you do. If they see me, they're sure to have a shot at me.

RAINA (*clinging to him*). They're sure to see you: it's bright moonlight. I'll save you—oh, how can you be so indifferent? You want me to save you, don't you?

MAN. I really don't want to be troublesome. (*She shakes him in her impatience.*) I am not indifferent, dear young lady, I assure you. But how is it to be done?

RAINA. Come away from the window—please. (*She coaxes him back to the middle of the room. He submits humbly. She releases him, and addresses him patronizingly.*) Now listen. You must trust to our hospitality. You do not yet know in whose house you are. I am a Petkoff.

MAN. What's that?

RAINA (*rather indignantly*). I mean that I belong to the family of the Petkoffs, the richest and best known in our country.

MAN. Oh, yes, of course. I beg your pardon. The Petkoffs, to be sure. How stupid of me!

RAINA. You know you never heard of them until this minute. How can you stoop to pretend?

MAN. Forgive me: I'm too tired to think; and the change of subject was too much for me. Don't scold me.

RAINA. I forgot. It might make you cry. (*He nods, quite seriously. She pouts and then resumes her patronizing tone.*) I must tell you that my father holds the highest command of any Bulgarian in our army. He is (*proudly*) a Major.

MAN (*pretending to be deeply impressed*). A Major! Bless me! Think of that!

RAINA. You showed great ignorance in thinking that it was necessary to climb up to the balcony, because ours is the only private house that has two rows of windows. There is a flight of stairs inside to get up and down by.

MAN. Stairs! How grand! You live in great luxury indeed, dear young lady.

RAINA. Do you know what a library is?

MAN. A library? A roomful of books.

RAINA. Yes, we have one, the only one in Bulgaria.

MAN. Actually a real library! I should like to see that.

RAINA (*affectedly*). I tell you these things to show you that you are not in the house of ignorant countryfolk who would kill you the moment they saw your Servian uniform, but among civilized people. We go to Bucharest every year for the opera season; and I have spent a whole month in Vienna.

MAN. I saw that, dear young lady. I saw at once that you knew the world.

RAINA. Have you ever seen the opera of Ernani?

MAN. Is that the one with the devil in it in red velvet, and a soldier's chorus?

RAINA (contemptuously). No!

MAN (stifling a heavy sigh of weariness). Then I don't know it.

RAINA. I thought you might have remembered the great scene where Ernani, flying from his foes just as you are tonight, takes refuge in the castle of his bitterest enemy, an old Castilian noble. The noble refuses to give him up. His guest is sacred to him.

MAN (quickly waking up a little). Have your people got that notion?

RAINA (with dignity). My mother and I can understand that notion, as you call it. And if instead of threatening me with your pistol as you did, you had simply thrown yourself as a fugitive on our hospitality, you would have been as safe as in your father's house.

MAN. Quite sure?

RAINA (turning her back on him in disgust). Oh, it is useless to try and make you understand.

MAN. Don't be angry: you see how awkward it would be for me if there was any mistake. My father is a very hospitable man: he keeps six hotels; but I couldn't trust him as far as that. What about your father?

RAINA. He is away at Slivnitza fighting for his country. I answer for your safety. There is my hand in pledge of it. Will that reassure you? (She offers him her hand.)

MAN (looking dubiously at his own hand). Better not touch my hand, dear young lady. I must have a wash first.

RAINA (touched). That is very nice of you. I see that you are a gentleman.

MAN (puzzled). Eh?

RAINA. You must not think I am surprised. Bulgarians of really good standing —people in our position—wash their hands nearly every day. But I appreciate your delicacy. You may take my hand. (She offers it again.)

MAN (kissing it with his hands behind his back). Thanks, gracious young lady: I feel safe at last. And now would you mind breaking the news to your mother? I had better not stay here secretly longer than is necessary.

RAINA. If you will be so good as to keep perfectly still while I am away.

MAN. Certainly. (He sits down on the ottoman.)

[RAINA goes to the bed and wraps herself in the fur cloak. His eyes close. She goes to the door, but on turning for a last look at him, sees that he is dropping off to sleep.]

RAINA (at the door). You are not going asleep, are you? (He murmurs inarticulately: she runs to him and shakes him.) Do you hear? Wake up: you are falling asleep.

MAN. Eh? Falling aslee—? Oh, no, not the least in the world: I was only thinking. It's all right: I'm wide awake.

RAINA (severely). Will you please stand up while I am away. (He rises reluctantly.) All the time, mind.

MAN (standing unsteadily). Certainly— certainly: you may depend on me.

[RAINA looks doubtfully at him. He smiles foolishly. She goes reluctantly, turning again at the door, and almost catching him in the act of yawning. She goes out.]

MAN (drowsily). Sleep, sleep, sleep, sleep, slee—(The words trail off into a murmur. He wakes again with a shock on the point of falling.) Where am I? That's what I want to know: where am I? Must keep awake. Nothing keeps me awake except danger—remember that—(intently) danger, danger, danger, dan—Where's

danger? Must find it. *(He starts off vaguely around the room in search of it.)* What am I looking for? Sleep—danger—don't know. *(He stumbles against the bed.)* Ah, yes: now I know. All right now. I'm to go to bed, but not to sleep—be sure not to sleep—because of danger. Not to lie down, either, only sit down. *(He sits on the bed. A blissful expression comes into his face.)* Ah! *(With a happy sigh he sinks back at full length; lifts his boots into the bed with a final effort; and falls fast asleep instantly.)*

[CATHERINE *comes in, followed by* RAINA.]

RAINA *(looking at the ottoman).* He's gone! I left him here.

CATHERINE. Here! Then he must have climbed down from the——

RAINA *(seeing him).* Oh! *(She points.)*

CATHERINE *(scandalized).* Well! *(She strides to the left side of the bed,* RAINA *following and standing opposite her on the right.)* He's fast asleep. The brute!

RAINA *(anxiously).* Sh!

CATHERINE *(shaking him).* Sir! *(Shaking him again, harder.)* Sir!! *(Vehemently shaking very hard.)* Sir!!!

RAINA *(catching her arm).* Don't, mamma: the poor dear is worn out. Let him sleep.

CATHERINE *(letting him go and turning amazed to* RAINA). The poor dear! Raina!! *(She looks sternly at her daughter. The man sleeps profoundly.)*

FOR STUDY AND DISCUSSION

1. Reread the stage directions that introduce us to Raina. How does Shaw use the setting to suggest her character, even before she speaks? How does Raina act toward Sergius's portrait? What does she do just after putting it away? What connection might there be between the two?

2. In the very beginning of the play, Shaw starts to undercut the romantic expectations of his characters and his audience. How does Raina, the romantic, first hint at the foolishness of all these postures? What misgivings does she have about her heroic ideals?

3. How is Louka different from Raina? How does her behavior differ from our ordinary expectations of a servant? How does she show what she thinks of Raina?

4. After saying that she will hide under the covers the moment she hears a shot, what does Raina actually do? What makes her so brave? Why does she hide The Man?

5. Reread Shaw's description of The Man. How does his appearance fit his attitude and actions? Why is Raina so shocked by his choice of weapons?

6. What was Raina's impression of the great cavalry charge? What is The Man's description of it? Why was the charge successful? Would Sergius have any way of knowing this? How do you suppose he will think of himself when he returns?

7. According to The Man, what is the difference between an old soldier and a young one? How else are soldiers, war, and weapons made fun of in Act I?

8. What is the occupation of Raina's father? What is his rank? What does The Man's father do? How are their fathers' occupations related to their own attitudes toward life and war?

9. Shaw has a twinkle in his eye for the Petkoffs and their social and cultural pretensions. Where do his own comments suggest this attitude? What is especially amusing in Raina's description of her family's house and their social and cultural background?

10. There are a number of references in Act I to Vienna and the opera. Why does Shaw continue to remind us of these things? How are they related to Raina's romantic notions?

11. How does Shaw use props, scenery, lights, and costume in Act I to emphasize the antiromantic nature of his theme?

12. Act I contains a lot of good talk, but Shaw knows that there must be suspense as well. What is the source of most of the suspense in Act I? Throughout the act, what are we curious to know?

ACT II

The sixth of March, 1886. In the garden of MAJOR PETKOFF'S *house. It is a fine spring morning, and the garden looks fresh and pretty. Beyond the paling the tops of a couple of minarets can be seen, showing that there is a valley there, with the little town in it. A few miles further the Balkan mountains rise and shut in the view. Within the garden the side of the house is seen on the right, with a garden door reached by a little flight of steps. On the left the stable yard, with its gateway, encroaches on the garden. There are fruit bushes along the paling and house, covered with washing hung out to dry. A path runs by the house, and rises by two steps at the corner where it turns out of the sight along the front. In the middle a small table, with two bent wood chairs at it, is laid for breakfast with Turkish coffee pot, cups, rolls, etc.; but the cups have been used and the bread broken. There is a wooden garden seat against the wall on the left.*

LOUKA, *smoking a cigarette, is standing between the table and the house, turning her back with angry disdain on a manservant who is lecturing her. He is a middle-aged man of cool temperament and low but clear and keen intelligence, with the complacency of the servant who values himself on his rank in servility, and the imperturbability of the accurate calculator who has no illusions. He wears a white Bulgarian costume jacket with decorated border, sash, wide knickerbockers, and decorated gaiters. His head is shaved up to the crown, giving him a high Japanese forehead. His name is* NICOLA.

NICOLA. Be warned in time, Louka: mend your manners. I know the mistress. She is so grand that she never dreams that any servant could dare to be disrespectful to her; but if she once suspects that you are defying her, out you go.

LOUKA. I do defy her. I will defy her. What do I care for her?

NICOLA. If you quarrel with the family, I never can marry you. It's the same as if you quarreled with me!

LOUKA. You take her part against me, do you?

NICOLA (*sedately*). I shall always be dependent on the good will of the family. When I leave their service and start a shop in Sofia, their custom will be half my capital: their bad word would ruin me.

LOUKA. You have no spirit. I should like to see them dare say a word against me!

NICOLA (*pityingly*). I should have expected more sense from you, Louka. But you're young, you're young!

LOUKA. Yes; and you like me the better for it, don't you? But I know some family secrets they wouldn't care to have told, young as I am. Let them quarrel with me if they dare!

NICOLA (*with compassionate superiority*). Do you know what they would do if they heard you talk like that?

LOUKA. What could they do?

NICOLA. Discharge you for untruthfulness. Who would believe any stories you told after that? Who would give you another situation? Who in this house would dare be seen speaking to you ever again? How long would your father be left on his little farm? (*She impatiently throws away the end of her cigarette, and stamps on it.*) Child, you don't know the power such high people have over the like of you and me when we try to rise out of our poverty against them. (*He goes close to her and lowers his voice.*) Look at me, ten years in their service. Do you think I know no secrets? I know things about the mistress that she wouldn't have the

master know for a thousand levas.[1] I know things about him that she wouldn't let him hear the last of for six months if I blabbed them to her. I know things about Raina that would break off her match with Sergius if——

LOUKA (*turning on him quickly*). How do you know? I never told you!

NICOLA (*opening his eyes cunningly*). So that's your little secret, is it? I thought it might be something like that. Well, you take my advice, and be respectful; and make the mistress feel that no matter what you know or don't know, they can depend on you to hold your tongue and serve the family faithfully. That's what they like; and that's how you'll make most out of them.

LOUKA (*with searching scorn*). You have the soul of a servant, Nicola.

NICOLA (*complacently*). Yes: that's the secret of success in service.

[*A loud knocking with a whip handle on a wooden door, outside on the left, is heard.*]

¹ **levas:** The lev (plural = levas) is the gold monetary unit of Bulgaria.

MALE VOICE OUTSIDE. Hollo! Hollo there! Nicola!

LOUKA. Master! back from the war!

NICOLA (*quickly*). My word for it, Louka, the war's over. Off with you and get some fresh coffee. (*He runs out into the stable yard.*)

LOUKA (*as she puts the coffeepot and the cups upon the tray and carries it into the house*). You'll never put the soul of a servant into me.

[MAJOR PETKOFF *comes from the stable yard, followed by* NICOLA. *He is a cheerful, excitable, insignificant, un-polished man of about fifty, naturally unambitious except as to his income and his importance in local society, but just now greatly pleased with the military rank which the war has thrust on him as a man of consequence in his town. The fever of plucky patriotism which the Servian attack roused in all the Bulgarians has pulled him through the war; but he is obviously glad to be home again.*]

PETKOFF (*pointing to the table with his whip*). Breakfast out here, eh?

NICOLA. Yes, sir. The mistress and Miss Raina have just gone in.

PETKOFF *(sitting down and taking a roll)*. Go in and say I've come; and get me some fresh coffee.

NICOLA. It's coming, sir. *(He goes to the house door.* LOUKA, *with fresh coffee, a clean cup, and a brandy bottle on her tray meets him.)* Have you told the mistress?

LOUKA. Yes: she's coming.

[NICOLA *goes into the house.* LOUKA *brings the coffee to the table.*]

PETKOFF. Well, the Servians haven't run away with you, have they?

LOUKA. No, sir.

PETKOFF. That's right. Have you brought me some cognac?

LOUKA *(putting the bottle on the table)*. Here, sir.

PETKOFF. That's right. *(He pours some into his coffee.)*

[CATHERINE *who has at this early hour made only a very perfunctory toilet, and wears a Bulgarian apron over a once brilliant, but now half-worn-out red dressing gown, and a colored handkerchief tied over her thick black hair, with Turkish slippers on her bare feet, comes from the house, looking astonishingly handsome and stately under all the circumstances.* LOUKA *goes into the house.*]

CATHERINE. My dear Paul, what a surprise for us. *(She stoops over the back of his chair to kiss him.)* Have they brought you fresh coffee?

PETKOFF. Yes, Louka's been looking after me. The war's over. The treaty was signed three days ago at Bucharest; and the decree for our army to demobilize was issued yesterday.

CATHERINE *(springing erect, with flashing eyes)*. The war over! Paul: have you let the Austrians force you to make peace?

PETKOFF *(submissively)*. My dear: they didn't consult me. What could *I* do? *(She sits down and turns away from him.)* But of course we saw to it that the treaty was an honorable one. It declares peace——

CATHERINE *(outraged)*. Peace!

PETKOFF *(appeasing her)*.—but not friendly relations: remember that. They wanted to put that in; but I insisted on its being struck out. What more could I do?

CATHERINE. You could have annexed Servia and made Prince Alexander Emperor of the Balkans. That's what I would have done.

PETKOFF. I don't doubt it in the least, my dear. But I should have had to subdue the whole Austrian Empire first; and that would have kept me too long away from you. I missed you greatly.

CATHERINE *(relenting)*. Ah! *(Stretches her hand affectionately across the table to squeeze his.)*

PETKOFF. And how have you been, my dear?

CATHERINE. Oh, my usual sore throats, that's all.

PETKOFF *(with conviction)*. That comes from washing your neck every day. I've often told you so.

CATHERINE. Nonsense, Paul!

PETKOFF *(over his coffee and cigarette)*. I don't believe in going too far with these modern customs. All this washing can't be good for the health: it's not natural. There was an Englishman at Phillipopolis who used to wet himself all over with cold water every morning when he got up. Disgusting! It all comes from the English: their climate makes them so dirty that they have to be perpetually washing themselves. Look at my father: he never had a bath in his life; and he lived to be ninety-eight, the healthiest man in Bulgaria. I

don't mind a good wash once a week to keep up my position; but once a day is carrying the thing to a ridiculous extreme.

CATHERINE. You are a barbarian at heart still, Paul. I hope you behaved yourself before all those Russian officers.

PETKOFF. I did my best. I took care to let them know that we had a library.

CATHERINE. Ah; but you didn't tell them that we have an electric bell in it? I have had one put up.

PETKOFF. What's an electric bell?

CATHERINE. You touch a button; something tinkles in the kitchen; and then Nicola comes up.

PETKOFF. Why not shout for him?

CATHERINE. Civilized people never shout for their servants. I've learned that while you were away.

PETKOFF. Well, I'll tell you something I've learned, too. Civilized people don't hang out their washing to dry where visitors can see it; so you'd better have all that (*indicating the clothes on the bushes*) put somewhere else.

CATHERINE. Oh, that's absurd, Paul: I don't believe really refined people notice such things.

[*Someone is heard knocking at the stable gates.*]

PETKOFF. There's Sergius. (*Shouting.*) Hollo, Nicola!

CATHERINE. Oh, don't shout, Paul: it really isn't nice.

PETKOFF. Bosh! (*He shouts louder than before.*) Nicola!

NICOLA (*appearing at the house door*). Yes, sir.

PETKOFF. If that is Major Saranoff, bring him round this way. (*He pronounces the name with the stress on the second syllable—Sarahnoff.*)

NICOLA. Yes, sir. (*He goes into the stable yard.*)

PETKOFF. You must talk to him, my dear, until Raina takes him off our hands. He bores my life out about our not promoting him—over *my* head, mind you.

CATHERINE. He certainly ought to be promoted when he marries Raina. Besides, the country should insist on having at least one native general.

PETKOFF. Yes, so that he could throw away whole brigades instead of regiments. It's no use, my dear: he has not the slightest chance of promotion until we are quite sure that the peace will be a lasting one.

NICOLA (*at the gate, announcing*). Major Sergius Saranoff! (*He goes into the house and returns presently with a third chair, which he places at the table. He then withdraws.*)

[MAJOR SERGIUS SARANOFF, *the original of the portrait in* RAINA'S *room, is a tall, romantically handsome man, with the physical hardihood, the high spirit, and the susceptible imagination of an untamed mountaineer chieftain. But his remarkable personal distinction is of a*

characteristically civilized type. The ridges of his eyebrows, curving with a ram's horn twist round the marked projections at the outer corners, his jealously observant eye, his nose, thin, keen, and apprehensive in spite of the pugnacious high bridge and large nostril, his assertive chin, would not be out of place in a Paris salon. In short, the clever, imaginative barbarian has an acute critical faculty which has been thrown into intense activity by the arrival of Western civilization in the Balkans; and the result is precisely what the advent of nineteenth-century thought first produced in England: to wit, Byronism. By his brooding on the perpetual failure, not only of others, but of himself, to live up to his imaginative ideals, his consequent cynical scorn for humanity, the jejune[1] credulity as to the absolute validity of his ideals and the unworthiness of the world in disregarding them, his wincings and mockeries under the sting of the petty disillusions which every hour spent among men brings to his infallibly quick observation, he has acquired the half-tragic, half-ironic air, the mysterious moodiness, the suggestion of a strange and terrible history that has left him nothing but undying remorse, by which Childe Harold[2] fascinated the grandmothers of his English contemporaries. Altogether it is clear that here or nowhere is RAINA'S *ideal hero.* CATHERINE *is hardly less enthusiastic, and much less reserved in showing her enthusiasm. As he enters from the stable gate, she rises effusively to greet him.* PETKOFF *is distinctly less disposed to make a fuss about him.*]

[1] **jejune** (jə·jōōn′): here, unsophisticated, naive.
[2] **Childe Harold:** the romantic hero of a poem by Byron, whose sensitive, moody nature charmed the young women of Byron's time.

PETKOFF. Here already, Sergius. Glad to see you!

CATHERINE. My dear Sergius! (*She holds out both her hands.*)

SERGIUS (*kissing them with scrupulous gallantry*). My dear mother, if I may call you so.

PETKOFF (*drily*). Mother-in-law, Sergius; mother-in-law! Sit down, and have some coffee.

SERGIUS. Thank you, none for me. (*He gets away from the table with a certain distaste for* PETKOFF'S *enjoyment of it, and posts himself with conscious grace against the rail of the steps leading to the house.*)

CATHERINE. You look superb—splendid. The campaign has improved you. Everybody here is mad about you. We were all wild with enthusiasm about that magnificent cavalry charge.

SERGIUS (*with grave irony*). Madam: it was the cradle and the grave of my military reputation.

CATHERINE. How so?

SERGIUS. I won the battle the wrong way when our worthy Russian generals were losing it the right way. That upset their plans, and wounded their self-esteem. Two of their colonels got their regiments driven back on the correct principles of scientific warfare. Two major generals got killed strictly according to military etiquette. Those two colonels are now major generals; and I am still a simple major.

CATHERINE. You shall not remain so, Sergius. The women are on your side; and they will see that justice is done you.

SERGIUS. It is too late. I have only waited for the peace to send in my resignation.

PETKOFF (*dropping his cup in his amazement*). Your resignation!

CATHERINE. Oh, you must withdraw it!

SERGIUS (*with resolute, measured em-*

phasis, folding his arms). I never withdraw!

PETKOFF *(vexed).* Now who could have supposed you were going to do such a thing?

SERGIUS *(with fire).* Everyone that knew me. But enough of myself and my affairs. How is Raina; and where is Raina?

RAINA *(suddenly coming round the corner of the house and standing at the top of the steps in the path).* Raina is here. *(She makes a charming picture as they all turn to look at her. She wears an under-dress of pale green silk, draped with an overdress of thin ecru canvas embroidered with gold. On her head she wears a pretty Phrygian cap of gold tinsel.* SERGIUS, *with an exclamation of pleasure, goes impulsively to meet her. She stretches out her hand: he drops chivalrously on one knee and kisses it.)*

PETKOFF *(aside to* CATHERINE, *beaming with parental pride).* Pretty, isn't it? She always appears at the right moment.

CATHERINE *(impatiently).* Yes: she listens for it. It is an abominable habit.

[SERGIUS *leads* RAINA *forward with splendid gallantry, as if she were a queen. When they come to the table, she turns to him with a bend of the head; he bows; and thus they separate, he coming to his place, and she going behind her father's chair.*]

RAINA *(stooping and kissing her father).* Dear father! Welcome home!

PETKOFF *(patting her cheek).* My little pet girl. *(He kisses her; she goes to the chair left by* NICOLA *for* SERGIUS *and sits down.)*

CATHERINE. And so you're no longer a soldier, Sergius.

SERGIUS. I am no longer a soldier. Soldiering, my dear madam, is the coward's art of attacking mercilessly when you are strong, and keeping out of harm's way when you are weak. That is the whole secret of successful fighting. Get your enemy at a disadvantage; and never, on any account, fight him on equal terms. Eh, Major!

PETKOFF. They wouldn't let us make a fair stand-up fight of it. However, I suppose soldiering has to be a trade like any other trade.

SERGIUS. Precisely. But I have no ambition to succeed as a tradesman; so I have taken the advice of that bagman [1] of a captain that settled the exchange of prisoners with us at Peerot, and given it up.

PETKOFF. What, that Swiss fellow? Sergius: I've often thought of that exchange since. He overreached us about those horses.

SERGIUS. Of course he overreached us. His father was a hotel and livery stable keeper; and he owed his first step to his knowledge of horse dealing. *(With mock enthusiasm.)* Ah, he was a soldier—every inch a soldier! If only I had bought the horses for my regiment instead of foolishly leading it into danger, I should have been a field marshal now!

CATHERINE. A Swiss? What was he doing in the Servian army?

PETKOFF. A volunteer of course—keen on picking up his profession. *(Chuckling.)* We shouldn't have been able to begin fighting if these foreigners hadn't shown us how to do it: we knew nothing about it; and neither did the Servians. Egad, there'd have been no war without them.

RAINA. Are there many Swiss officers in the Servian army?

PETKOFF. No—all Austrians, just as our officers were all Russians. This was the only Swiss I came across. I'll never trust a Swiss again. He cheated us—humbugged us into giving him fifty able-

[1] **bagman:** swindler.

bodied men for two hundred confounded worn-out chargers. They weren't even eatable!

SERGIUS. We were two children in the hands of that consummate soldier, Major: simply two innocent little children.

RAINA. What was he like?

CATHERINE. Oh, Raina, what a silly question!

SERGIUS. He was like a commercial traveler[1] in uniform. Bourgeois to his boots.

PETKOFF (grinning). Sergius: tell Catherine that queer story his friend told us about him—how he escaped after Slivnitza. You remember?—about his being hid by two women.

SERGIUS (with bitter irony). Oh, yes, quite a romance. He was serving in the very battery I so unprofessionally charged. Being a thorough soldier, he ran away like the rest of them, with our cavalry at his heels. To escape their attentions, he had the good taste to take refuge in the chamber of some patriotic young Bulgarian lady. The young lady was enchanted by his persuasive commercial traveler's manners. She very modestly entertained him for an hour or so and then called in her mother lest her conduct should appear unmaidenly. The old lady was equally fascinated; and the fugitive was sent on his way in the morning, disguised in an old coat belonging to the master of the house, who was away at the war.

RAINA (rising with marked stateliness). Your life in the camp has made you coarse, Sergius. I did not think you would have repeated such a story before me. (She turns away coldly.)

CATHERINE (also rising). She is right, Sergius. If such women exist, we should be spared the knowledge of them.

PETKOFF. Pooh! nonsense! what does it matter?

SERGIUS (ashamed). No, Petkoff: I was wrong. (To RAINA, with earnest humility.) I beg your pardon. I have behaved abominably. Forgive me, Raina. (She bows reservedly.) And you, too, madam. (CATHERINE bows graciously and sits down. He proceeds solemnly, again addressing RAINA.) The glimpses I have had of the seamy side of life during the last few months have made me cynical; but I should not have brought my cynicism here—least of all into your presence, Raina. I—(Here, turning to the others, he is evidently about to begin a long speech when the MAJOR interrupts him.)

PETKOFF. Stuff and nonsense, Sergius. That's quite enough fuss about nothing: a soldier's daughter should be able to stand up without flinching to a little strong conversation. (He rises.) Come: it's time for us to get to business. We have to make up our minds how those three regiments are to get back to Phillipopolis:—there's no forage[2] for them on the Sophia route. (He goes toward the house.) Come along. (SERGIUS is about to follow him when CATHERINE rises and intervenes.)

CATHERINE. Oh, Paul, can't you spare Sergius for a few moments? Raina has hardly seen him yet. Perhaps I can help you to settle about the regiments.

SERGIUS (protesting). My dear madam, impossible: you——

CATHERINE (stopping him playfully). You stay here, my dear Sergius: there's no hurry. I have a word or two to say to Paul. (SERGIUS instantly bows and steps back.) Now, dear (taking PETKOFF's arm), come and see the electric bell.

PETKOFF. Oh, very well, very well. (They go into the house together affectionately. SERGIUS, left alone with RAINA,

[1] **commercial traveler:** traveling salesman.

[2] **forage** (fôr'ij): here, food for horses.

looks anxiously at her, fearing that she may be still offended. She smiles, and stretches out her arms to him.)

SERGIUS *(hastening to her, but refraining from touching her without express permission).* Am I forgiven?

RAINA *(placing her hands on his shoulder as she looks up at him with admiration and worship).* My hero! My king.

SERGIUS. My queen! *(He kisses her on the forehead with holy awe.)*

RAINA. How I have envied you, Sergius! You have been out in the world, on the field of battle, able to prove yourself there worthy of any woman in the world; while I have had to sit at home inactive, dreaming—useless—doing nothing that could give me the right to call myself worthy of any man.

SERGIUS. Dearest, all my deeds have been yours. You inspired me. I have gone through the war like a knight in a tournament with his lady looking on at him!

RAINA. And you have never been absent from my thoughts for a moment. *(Very solemnly.)* Sergius: I think we two have found the higher love. When I think of you, I feel that I could never do a base deed or think an ignoble thought.

SERGIUS. My lady and my saint! *(Clasping her reverently.)*

RAINA *(returning his embrace).* My lord and my g——.

SERGIUS. Sh—sh! Let *me* be the worshiper, dear. You little know how unworthy even the best man is of a girl's pure passion!

RAINA. I trust you. I love you. You will never disappoint me, Sergius. *(LOUKA is heard singing within the house. They quickly release each other.)* Hush! I can't pretend to talk indifferently before her: my heart is too full. *(LOUKA comes from the house with her tray. She goes to the table, and begins to clear it, with her back turned to them.)* I will go and get my hat; and then we can go out until lunch time. Wouldn't you like that?

SERGIUS. Be quick. If you are away five minutes, it will seem five hours. *(RAINA runs to the top of the steps and turns there to exchange a look with him and wave him a kiss with both hands. He looks after her with emotion for a moment, then turns slowly away, his face radiant with the exultation of the scene which has just passed. The movement shifts his field of vision, into the corner of which there now comes the tail of LOUKA's double apron. His eye gleams at once. He takes a stealthy look at her and begins to twirl his moustache nervously, with his left hand akimbo on his hip. Finally, striking the ground with his heels in something of a cavalry swagger, he strolls over to the left of the table, opposite her, and says)* Louka: do you know what the higher love is?

LOUKA *(astonished).* No, sir.

SERGIUS. Very fatiguing thing to keep up for any length of time, Louka. One feels the need of some relief after it.

LOUKA *(innocently).* Perhaps you would like some coffee, sir? *(She stretches her hand across the table for the coffeepot.)*

SERGIUS *(taking her hand).* Thank you, Louka.

LOUKA *(pretending to pull).* Oh, sir, you know I didn't mean that. I'm surprised at you!

SERGIUS *(coming clear of the table and drawing her with him).* I am surprised at myself, Louka. What would Sergius, the hero of Slivnitza, say if he saw me now? What would Sergius, the apostle of the higher love, say if he saw me now? What would the half-dozen Sergiuses who keep popping in and out of this handsome figure of mine say if they caught us here? *(Letting go her hand and slipping his arm dexterously round her waist.)* Do you con-

sider my figure handsome, Louka?

LOUKA. Let me·go, sir. I shall be disgraced. *(She struggles: he holds her inexorably.)* Oh, *will* you let go?

SERGIUS *(looking straight into her eyes).* No.

LOUKA. Then stand back where we can't be seen. Have you no common sense?

SERGIUS. Ah, that's reasonable. *(He takes her into the stable-yard gateway, where they are hidden from the house.)*

LOUKA *(complaining).* I may have been seen from the windows: Miss Raina is sure to be spying about after you.

SERGIUS *(stung—letting her go).* Take care, Louka. I may be worthless enough to betray the higher love; but do not you insult it.

LOUKA *(demurely).* Not for the world, sir, I'm sure. May I go on with my work please, now?

SERGIUS *(again putting his arm round her).* You are a provoking little witch, Louka. If you were in love with me, would you spy out of windows on me?

LOUKA. Well, you see, sir, since you say you are half a dozen different gentlemen all at once, I should have a great deal to look after.

SERGIUS *(charmed).* Witty as well as pretty. *(He tries to kiss her.)*

LOUKA *(avoiding him).* No, I don't want your kisses. Gentlefolk are all alike—you making love to me behind Miss Raina's back, and she doing the same behind yours.

SERGIUS *(recoiling a step).* Louka!

LOUKA. It shows how little you really care!

SERGIUS *(dropping his familiarity and speaking with freezing politeness).* If our conversation is to continue, Louka, you will please remember that a gentleman does not discuss the conduct of the lady he is engaged to with her maid.

LOUKA. It's so hard to know what a gentleman considers right. I thought from your trying to kiss me that you had given up being so particular.

SERGIUS *(turning from her and striking his forehead as he comes back into the garden from the gateway).* Devil! devil!

LOUKA. Ha! ha! I expect one of the six of you is very like me, sir, though I *am* only Miss Raina's maid. *(She goes back to her work at the table, taking no further notice of him.)*

SERGIUS *(speaking to himself).* Which of the six is the real man?—that's the question that torments me. One of them is a hero, another a buffoon, another a hum-

bug, another perhaps a bit of a black-guard. *(He pauses and looks furtively at* LOUKA, *as he adds with deep bitterness)* And one, at least, is a coward—jealous, like all cowards. *(He goes to the table.)* Louka.

LOUKA. Yes?

SERGIUS. Who is my rival?

LOUKA. You shall never get that out of me, for love or money.

SERGIUS. Why?

LOUKA. Never mind why. Besides, you would tell that I told you; and I should lose my place.

SERGIUS *(holding out his right hand in affirmation)*. No; on the honor of a—*(He checks himself, and his hand drops nerveless as he concludes, sardonically)*—of a man capable of behaving as I have been behaving for the last five minutes. Who is he?

LOUKA. I don't know. I never saw him. I only heard his voice through the door of her room.

SERGIUS. Damnation! How dare you?

LOUKA *(retreating)*. Oh, I mean no harm: you've no right to take up my words like that. The mistress knows all about it. And I tell you that if that gentleman ever comes here again, Miss Raina will marry him, whether he likes it or not. I know the difference between the sort of manner you and she put on before one another and the real manner. (SERGIUS *shivers as if she had stabbed him. Then, setting his face like iron, he strides grimly to her, and grips her above the elbows with both hands.)*

SERGIUS. Now listen you to me!

LOUKA *(mincing)*. Not so tight: you're hurting me!

SERGIUS. That doesn't matter. You have stained my honor by making me a party to your eavesdropping. And you have betrayed your mistress——

LOUKA *(writhing)*. Please——

SERGIUS. That shows that you are an abominable little clod of common clay, with the soul of a servant. *(He lets her go as if she were an unclean thing, and turns away, dusting his hands of her, to the bench by the wall, where he sits down with averted head, meditating gloomily.)*

LOUKA *(whimpering angrily with her hands up her sleeves, feeling her bruised arms)*. You know how to hurt with your tongue as well as with your hands. But I don't care, now I've found out that whatever clay I'm made of, you're made of the same. As for her, she's a liar; and her fine airs are a cheat; and I'm worth six of her. *(She shakes the pain off hardily; tosses her head; and sets to work to put the things on the tray. He looks doubtfully at her once or twice. She finishes packing the tray, and laps the cloth over the edges, so as to carry all out together. As she stoops to lift it, he rises.)*

SERGIUS. Louka! *(She stops and looks defiantly at him with the tray in her hands.)* A gentleman has no right to hurt a woman under any circumstances. *(With profound humility, uncovering his head.)* I beg your pardon.

LOUKA. That sort of apology may satisfy a lady. Of what use is it to a servant?

SERGIUS *(thus rudely crossed in his chivalry, throws it off with a bitter laugh and says slightingly)*. Oh, you wish to be paid for the hurt? *(He puts on his shako* [1] *and takes some money from his pocket.)*

LOUKA *(her eyes filling with tears in spite of herself)*. No, I want my hurt made well.

SERGIUS *(sobered by her tone)*. How?

[*She rolls up her left sleeve; clasps her arm with the thumb and fingers of her right hand; and looks down at the bruise. Then she raises her head and*

[1] **shako** (shak'ō): a high, stiff military hat with an upright plume.

looks straight at him. Finally, with a superb gesture she presents her arm to be kissed. Amazed, he looks at her; at the arm; at her again; hesitates; and then, with shuddering intensity, exclaims] Never! [*and gets away as far as possible from her.*

Her arm drops. Without a word, and with unaffected dignity, she takes her tray, and is approaching the house when RAINA *returns wearing a hat and jacket in the height of the Vienna fashion of the previous year, 1885.* LOUKA *makes way proudly for her, and then goes into the house.*]

RAINA. I'm ready! What's the matter? *(Gaily.)* Have you been flirting with Louka?

SERGIUS *(hastily)*. No, no. How can you think such a thing?

RAINA *(ashamed of herself)*. Forgive me, dear: it was only a jest. I am so happy today.

[*He goes quickly to her, and kisses her hand remorsefully.* CATHERINE *comes out and calls to them from the top of the steps.*]

CATHERINE *(coming down to them)*. I am sorry to disturb you, children; but Paul is distracted over those three regiments. He does not know how to get them to Phillipopolis; and he objects to every suggestion of mine. You must go and help him, Sergius. He is in the library.

RAINA *(disappointed)*. But we are just going out for a walk.

SERGIUS. I shall not be long. Wait for me just five minutes. *(He runs up the steps to the door.)*

RAINA *(following him to the foot of the steps and looking up at him with timid coquetry)*. I shall go round and wait in full view of the library windows. Be sure you draw father's attention to me. If you are a

moment longer than five minutes, I shall go in and fetch you, regiments or no regiments.

SERGIUS *(laughing)*. Very well. *(He goes in.* RAINA *watches him until he is out of her sight. Then, with a perceptible relaxation of manner, she begins to pace up and down about the garden in a brown study.)*

CATHERINE. Imagine their meeting that Swiss and hearing the whole story! The very first thing your father asked for was the old coat we sent him off in. A nice mess you have got us into!

RAINA *(gazing thoughtfully at the gravel as she walks)*. The little beast!

CATHERINE. Little beast! What little beast?

RAINA. To go and tell. Oh, if I had him here, I'd stuff him with chocolate creams till he couldn't ever speak again!

CATHERINE. Don't talk nonsense. Tell me the truth, Raina. How long was he in your room before you came to me?

RAINA *(whisking round and recommencing her march in the opposite direction)*. Oh, I forget.

CATHERINE. You cannot forget! Did he really climb up after the soldiers were gone, or was he there when that officer searched the room?

RAINA. No. Yes, I think he must have been there then.

CATHERINE. You *think!* Oh, Raina, Raina! Will anything ever make you straightforward? If Sergius finds out, it is all over between you.

RAINA *(with cool impertinence)*. Oh, I know Sergius is your pet. I sometimes wish you could marry him instead of me. You would just suit him. You would pet him, and spoil him, and mother him to perfection.

CATHERINE *(opening her eyes very widely indeed)*. Well, upon my word!

RAINA *(capriciously—half to herself)*.

I always feel a longing to do or say something dreadful to him—to shock his propriety—to scandalize the five senses out of him! (*To* CATHERINE *perversely.*) I don't care whether he finds out about the chocolate-cream soldier or not. I half hope he may. (*She again turns flippantly away and strolls up the path to the corner of the house.*)

CATHERINE. And what should I be able to say to your father, pray?

RAINA (*over her shoulder, from the top of the two steps*). Oh, poor father! As if *he* could help himself! (*She turns the corner and passes out of sight.*)

CATHERINE (*looking after her, her fingers itching*). Oh, if you were only ten years younger! (LOUKA *comes from the house with a salver,*[1] *which she carries hanging down by her side.*) Well?

LOUKA. There's a gentleman just called, madam—a Servian officer——

CATHERINE (*flaming*). A Servian! How dare he—(*Checking herself bitterly.*) Oh, I forgot. We are at peace now. I suppose we shall have them calling every day to pay their compliments. Well, if he is an officer why don't you tell your master? He is in the library with Major Saranoff. Why do you come to me?

LOUKA. But he asks for you, madam. And I don't think he knows who you are: he said the lady of the house. He gave me this little ticket for you. (*She takes a card out of her bosom; puts it on the salver and offers it to* CATHERINE.)

CATHERINE (*reading*). "Captain Bluntschli!" That's a German name.

LOUKA. Swiss, madam, I think.

CATHERINE (*with a bound that makes* LOUKA *jump back*). Swiss! What is he like?

LOUKA (*timidly*). He has a big carpet-bag, madam.

[1] **salver:** a tray.

CATHERINE. Oh, Heavens, he's come to return the coat! Send him away—say we're not at home—ask him to leave his address and I'll write to him—Oh, stop: that will never do. Wait! (*She throws herself into a chair to think it out.* LOUKA *waits.*) The master and Major Saranoff are busy in the library, aren't they?

LOUKA. Yes, madam.

CATHERINE (*decisively*). Bring the gentleman out here at once. (*Imperatively.*) And be very polite to him. Don't delay. Here (*impatiently snatching the salver from her*): leave that here; and go straight back to him.

LOUKA. Yes, madam. (*Going.*)

CATHERINE. Louka!

LOUKA (*stopping*). Yes, madam.

CATHERINE. Is the library door shut?

LOUKA. I think so, madam.

CATHERINE. If not, shut it as you pass through.

LOUKA. Yes, madam. (*Going.*)

CATHERINE. Stop! (LOUKA *stops.*) He will have to go out that way (*indicating the gate of the stable yard*). Tell Nicola to bring his bag here after him. Don't forget.

LOUKA (*surprised*). His bag?

CATHERINE. Yes, here, as soon as possible. (*Vehemently.*) Be quick! (LOUKA *runs into the house.* CATHERINE *snatches her apron off and throws it behind a bush. She then takes up the salver and uses it as a mirror, with the result that the handkerchief tied round her head follows the apron. A touch to her hair and a shake to her dressing gown makes her presentable.*) Oh, how—how—*how* can a man be such a fool! Such a moment to select! (LOUKA *appears at the door of the house, announcing* "Captain Bluntschli"; *and standing aside at the top of the steps to let him pass before she goes in again. He is the man of the adventure in* RAINA'S *room. He is now clean, well brushed,*

smartly uniformed, and out of trouble, but still unmistakably the same man. The moment LOUKA'S *back is turned,* CATHERINE *swoops on him with hurried, urgent, coaxing appeal.)* Captain Bluntschli, I am *very* glad to see you; but you must leave this house at once. *(He raises his eyebrows.)* My husband has just returned, with my future son-in-law; and they know nothing. If they did, the consequences would be terrible. You are a foreigner: you do not feel our national animosities as we do. We still hate the Servians: the only effect of the peace on my husband is to make him feel like a lion balked of his prey. If he discovered our secret, he would never forgive me; and my daughter's life would hardly be safe. Will you, like the chivalrous gentleman and soldier you are, leave at once before he finds you here?

BLUNTSCHLI *(disappointed, but philosophical).* At once, gracious lady. I only came to thank you and return the coat you lent me. If you will allow me to take it out of my bag and leave it with your servants as I pass out, I need detain you no further. *(He turns to go into the house.)*

CATHERINE *(catching him by the sleeve).* Oh, you must not think of going back that way. *(Coaxing him across to the stable gates.)* This is the shortest way out. Many thanks. So glad to have been of service to you. *Good-*by.

BLUNTSCHLI. But my bag?

CATHERINE. It will be sent on. You will leave me your address.

BLUNTSCHLI. True. Allow me. *(He takes out his card case, and stops to write his address, keeping* CATHERINE *in an agony of impatience. As he hands her the card,* PETKOFF, *hatless, rushes from the house in a fluster of hospitality, followed by* SERGIUS.)*

PETKOFF *(as he hurries down the steps).* My dear Captain Bluntschli——

CATHERINE. Oh Heavens! *(She sinks on the seat against the wall.)*

PETKOFF *(too preoccupied to notice her as he shakes* BLUNTSCHLI'S *hand heartily).* Those stupid people of mine thought I was out here, instead of in the—haw!—library. *(He cannot mention the library without betraying how proud he is of it.)* I saw you through the window. I was wondering why you didn't come in. Saranoff is with me: you remember him, don't you?

SERGIUS *(saluting humorously, and then offering his hand with great charm of manner).* Welcome, our friend the enemy!

PETKOFF. No longer the enemy, happily. *(Rather anxiously.)* I hope you've come as a friend, and not on business.

CATHERINE. Oh, quite as a friend, Paul. I was just asking Captain Bluntschli to stay to lunch; but he declares he must go at once.

SERGIUS *(sardonically).* Impossible, Bluntschli. We want you here badly. We have to send on three cavalry regiments to Phillipopolis; and we don't in the least know how to do it.

BLUNTSCHLI *(suddenly attentive and businesslike).* Phillipopolis! The forage is the trouble, eh?

PETKOFF *(eagerly).* Yes, that's it. *(To Sergius.)* He sees the whole thing at once.

BLUNTSCHLI. I think I can show you how to manage that.

SERGIUS. Invaluable man! Come along! *(Towering over* BLUNTSCHLI, *he puts his hand on his shoulder and takes him to the steps,* PETKOFF *following. As* BLUNTSCHLI *puts his foot on the first step,* RAINA *comes out of the house.)*

RAINA *(completely losing her presence of mind).* Oh, the chocolate-cream soldier!

[BLUNTSCHLI *stands rigid.* SERGIUS, *amazed, looks at* RAINA, *then at* PETKOFF, *who looks back at him and then at his wife.*]

CATHERINE *(with commanding presence of mind).* My dear Raina, don't you see that we have a guest here—Captain Bluntschli, one of our new Servian friends?

[RAINA *bows;* BLUNTSCHLI *bows.*]

RAINA. How silly of me! *(She comes down into the center of the group, between* BLUNTSCHLI *and* PETKOFF.*)* I made a beautiful ornament this morning for the ice pudding; and that stupid Nicola has just put down a pile of plates on it and spoiled it. *(To* BLUNTSCHLI, *winningly.)* I hope you didn't think that *you* were the chocolate-cream soldier, Captain Bluntschli.

BLUNTSCHLI *(laughing).* I assure you I did. *(Stealing a whimsical glance at her.)* Your explanation was a relief.

PETKOFF *(suspiciously, to* RAINA*).* And since when, pray, have you taken to cooking?

CATHERINE. Oh, while you were away. It is her latest fancy.

PETKOFF *(testily).* And has Nicola taken to drinking? He used to be careful enough. First he shows Captain Bluntschli out here when he knew quite well I was in the—hum!—library; and then he goes downstairs and breaks Raina's chocolate soldier. He must—*(At this moment* NICOLA *appears at the top of the steps Right, with a carpetbag. He descends; places it respectfully before* BLUNTSCHLI; *and waits for further orders. General amazement.* NICOLA, *unconscious of the effect he is producing, looks perfectly satisfied with himself. When* PETKOFF *recovers his power of speech, he breaks out at him with)* Are you mad, Nicola?

NICOLA *(taken aback).* Sir?

PETKOFF. What have you brought that for?

NICOLA. My lady's orders, sir. Louka told me that——

CATHERINE *(interrupting him).* My or-

ders! Why should I order you to bring Captain Bluntschli's luggage out here? What are you thinking of, Nicola?

NICOLA *(after a moment's bewilderment, picking up the bag as he addresses* BLUNTSCHLI *with the very perfection of servile discretion).* I beg your pardon, sir, I am sure. *(To* CATHERINE.*)* My fault, madam! I hope you'll overlook it! *(He bows, and is going to the steps with the bag, when* PETKOFF *addresses him angrily.)*

PETKOFF. You'd better go and slam that bag, too, down on Miss Raina's ice pudding! *(This is too much for* NICOLA. *The bag drops from his hands on* PETKOFF'S *corns, eliciting a roar of anguish from him.)* Begone, you butter-fingered donkey.

NICOLA *(snatching up the bag, and escaping into the house).* Yes, sir.

CATHERINE. Oh, never mind, Paul, don't be angry!

PETKOFF *(muttering).* Scoundrel. He's got out of hand while I was away. I'll

teach him. *(Recollecting his guest.)* Oh, well, never mind. Come, Bluntschli, let's have no more nonsense about you having to go away. You know very well you're not going back to Switzerland yet. Until you do go back you'll stay with us.

RAINA. Oh, do, Captain Bluntschli.

PETKOFF *(to* CATHERINE*)*. Now, Catherine, it's of you that he's afraid. Press him and he'll stay.

CATHERINE. Of course I shall be only too delighted if *(appealingly)* Captain Bluntschli really wishes to stay. He knows my wishes.

BLUNTSCHLI *(in his driest military manner)*. I am at madame's orders.

SERGIUS *(cordially)*. That settles it!

PETKOFF *(heartily)*. Of course!

RAINA. You see, you *must* stay!

BLUNTSCHLI *(smiling)*. Well, if I must, I must!

[*Gesture of despair from* CATHERINE.]

FOR STUDY AND DISCUSSION

1. How does the setting of Act II remind us of the theme of the play? What is romantic about the setting? What down-to-earth details undercut its elegance?

2. What kind of person is Major Petkoff? What does he seem to want out of life? What is the difference between his and Catherine's attitudes toward the war?

3. What attitudes and actions of Catherine and Petkoff further suggest Shaw's attitude toward Bulgarian high society? How is the social pretension of the Petkoffs more clearly revealed in this act? How are the Petkoffs' pretensions related to Raina's noble romanticism?

4. In Shaw's description of Sergius, he notes that he is a perfect example of "Byronism." Lord Byron, the famous Romantic poet, was for many years the idol of young men such as Sergius. From Shaw's description of Sergius, what Byronic qualities did these would-be heroes most wish to imitate?

5. How were Sergius and Petkoff "over-reached" in the exchange of prisoners after the war? Why hasn't Sergius been promoted? What did other officers do to gain their promotions? What other remarks and details in Act II continue Shaw's undercutting of the idea that war is a matter of heroic behavior?

6. How does Sergius act with Raina? How does he act with Louka? How does he explain his inconsistencies of character? How does he feel about "the higher love"?

7. Why do you think Louka drops hints to Sergius about Raina and another man? Where does Louka show greater common sense than Sergius in this scene?

8. At the end of Act II, all the complicated business of double standards and false heroics comes to a boil with Bluntschli's arrival. How does Bluntschli's name suggest his personality?

9. In Act II, how does Shaw show Bluntschli's professional efficiency as a soldier? What gives him stature and dignity in contrast to the blustering, posturing people around him? What other character comes closest to having this kind of dignity?

10. What kind of person does Raina show herself to be in this act? In a difficult situation, is she airily romantic or down-to-earth and practical? How does she avoid the men's discovering that she knows Bluntschli? How do you think she feels toward Bluntschli?

11. Bluntschli is absent from the stage during most of Act II. Yet he certainly is the hero of the play. How does Shaw keep us aware of him and his influence during the early and middle parts of this act?

12. Nicola, the servant who takes everyone's orders, ultimately becomes the scapegoat for the hypocrisies of the other characters. He is accused of being a liar and a blunderer by others who have lied and blundered and is showered with insults and humiliation. How does he show, in this act, that he is a born servant?

13. How does Shaw handle suspense and excitement in Act II? Which are the most exciting moments in this act? At the end of the act, what makes you want to read on?

(ACT III FOLLOWS ON PAGE 513.)

Nineteenth-Century Painting, II

Any young French painter who was eager to establish a respectable reputation in the nineteenth-century art world would have produced large monumental pictures illustrating historical events or mythological stories. He would have crammed his pictures with figures and shown off his mastery of lighting, coloring, and drawing. For this kind of display-painting was considered the highest type of art by the juries which selected pictures for the Salon exhibitions. Yet Gustave Courbet, one of the greatest French painters of the century, spent most of his career stubbornly refusing to work in this manner. He often painted simple landscapes, such as *The Forest Pool* (PLATE 1). This is no imaginary landscape, like the one we saw by Poussin (page 333). It existed in the real world much as Courbet has reproduced it here. On the other hand, this picture is no literal copy of nature. Courbet's deep and lustrous colors give this forest scene a richness far beyond what our eyes would have discovered if we had come upon it ourselves.

Certain other nineteenth-century French artists also chose to paint directly from nature. Jean-Baptiste Camille Corot, born about twenty years before Courbet, developed a rather different landscape style, which you can see in his *View Near Volterra* of 1838 (PLATE 2). Corot makes us very much aware of atmospheric effects. Instead of concentrating on the lushness of nature seen close at hand, he leads us gently back from the warmer colors of the foreground into the cool blue-gray colors of the distance.

The landscape pictures of Courbet and Corot strongly influenced a group of younger French painters who came to be known as the Impressionists. During the 1860's, these young men formed a kind of brotherhood in Paris, all agreeing that modern painting should deal exclusively with the changing aspects of everyday life. One member of this group, Claude Monet, became particularly interested in the color of shadows in foliage and in the reflections of light on water. He found that he could reproduce these effects in paint most vividly by placing small strokes of different colors side by side,

so that they would appear to blend when seen from a few feet away. A good example is his lovely view of a lake in Antibes (PLATE 3). Monet painted mainly outdoors and usually at the same hour every day, so that each time he returned to a canvas he could study his subject under similar atmospheric conditions.

Another Impressionist, Pierre Auguste Renoir, often worked alongside Monet during the late 1860's and early 1870's, painting the same quiet country scenes. But as he grew older, Renoir felt that landscape pictures could never fully express his great enjoyment of life unless they contained human figures. He turned for inspiration to places like La Moulin de la Galette (PLATE 4), a popular outdoor dance hall in Paris. This is one of the most delightful paintings in the whole history of art. The gay confusion of the crowd, the warm colors of the costumes, and the sunlight dancing over the entire scene as it filters through the trees overhead—all these effects describe a rare and beautiful moment when man and nature seem to be in perfect harmony.

It was not until the late 1880's that many art critics and collectors began to take Impressionism seriously. But by this time a number of French artists had become interested in a new kind of painting called "pointillism," developed mainly by a young Parisian named Georges Seurat. This new style refined Monet's Impressionism into an intricate system of hundreds of tiny color dots, arranged according to scientific theories of color. In *La Parade* (PLATE 5) Seurat used this method to express the strange visual effects of gaslight upon a group of musicians performing at night in an outdoor sideshow. But notice how motionless these figures appear. Rather than emphasizing gestures and movement, Seurat has frozen his figures in a flat pattern across the canvas, almost like an Egyptian wall painting. Yet the whole scene comes to life as we follow the subtle changes of the softly vibrating colors.

Edgar Degas developed a very individual kind of Impressionism. He was more interested in the gestures and attitudes of people in everyday life than in the effects of outdoor sunlight and atmosphere. In PLATE 6 we see what looks almost like a camera snapshot of a ballet rehearsal. Yet Degas never painted such a scene exactly as he saw it. First, he made quick preliminary sketches of individual figures; then later, he worked them into an organized composition. Though we seem to have just happened on this scene, each figure is carefully related to every other one. Notice, for instance, how the old woman's newspaper acts as an important "pointer," leading our eye directly back to the group of dancers at the upper left. At the same time, the angle of the old woman's slouching figure continues up into the group just behind her, tying the two halves of the design together.

PLATE 1. GUSTAVE COURBET (French, 1819–1877): *The Forest Pool*. About 1865. Oil on canvas, 61¾ x 44¾ inches. (Courtesy, Museum of Fine Arts, Boston, Gift of Mrs. Samuel Parkman Oliver)

PLATE 2. JEAN–BAPTISTE CAMILLE COROT (French, 1796–1875): *View Near Volterra*. 1838. Oil on canvas, $27\frac{1}{2}$ x $37\frac{1}{4}$ inches. (National Gallery of Art, Washington, D.C., Chester Dale Collection)

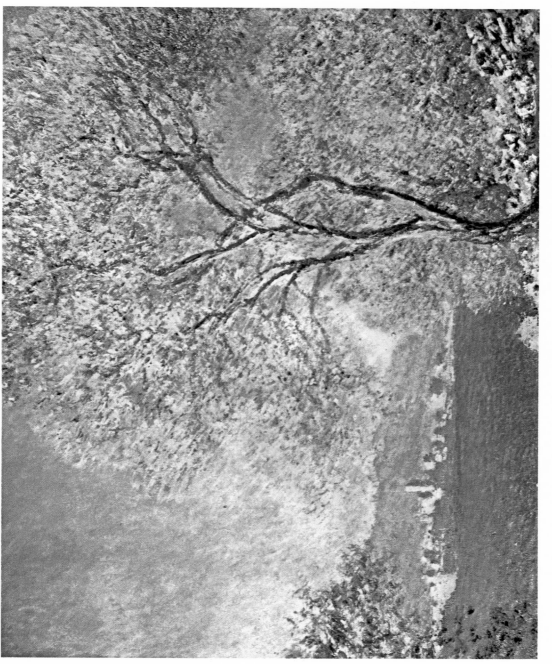

PLATE 3. CLAUDE MONET (French, 1840–1926): *Antibes*. 1888. Oil on canvas, $36\frac{1}{2}$ x $29\frac{1}{2}$ inches. (The Toledo Museum of Art, Toledo, Ohio, Gift of Edward Drummond Libbey)

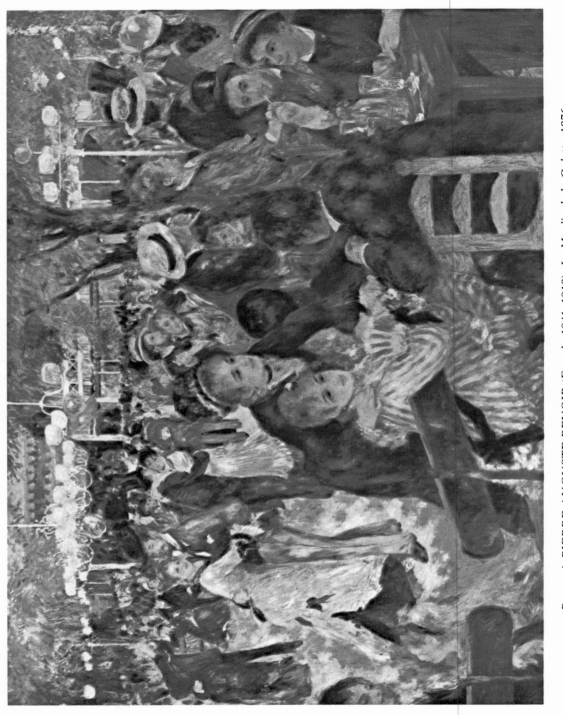

PLATE 4. PIERRE AUGUSTE RENOIR (French, 1841–1919): *Le Moulin de la Galette*. 1876. Oil on canvas, 51 9/16 x 68 7/8 inches. (The Louvre, Paris)

510

PLATE 5. GEORGES SEURAT (French, 1859–1891): *La Parade.* 1889. Oil on canvas, $39\frac{1}{2}$ x $59\frac{1}{2}$ inches. (The Metropolitan Museum of Art, New York, Bequest of Stephen C. Clark, 1960)

PLATE 6. EDGAR DEGAS (French, 1834–1917): *Ballet Class.* About 1878. Oil on canvas, 32 x 29½ inches. (Philadelphia Museum of Art, W. P. Wilstach Collection)

512

ACT III

In the library after lunch. It is not much of a library, its literary equipment consisting of a single fixed shelf stocked with old paper-covered novels, broken-backed, coffee-stained, torn and thumbed, and a couple of little hanging shelves with a few gift books on them, the rest of the wall space being occupied by trophies of war and the chase. But it is a most comfortable sitting room. A row of three large windows in the front of the house show a mountain panorama, which is just now seen in one of its softest aspects in the mellowing afternoon light. In the left-hand corner, a square earthenware stove, a perfect tower of colored pottery, rises nearly to the ceiling and guarantees plenty of warmth. The ottoman in the middle is a circular bank of decorated cushions, and the window seats are well-upholstered divans. Little Turkish tables, one of them with an elaborate hookah[1] on it, and a screen to match them, com-

plete the handsome effect of the furnishing. There is one object, however, which is hopelessly out of keeping with its surroundings. This is a small kitchen table, much the worse for wear, fitted as a writing table with an old canister full of pens, an eggcup filled with ink, and a deplorable scrap of severely used pink blotting paper.

At the side of this table, which stands on the right, BLUNTSCHLI is hard at work, with a couple of maps before him, writing orders. At the head of it sits SERGIUS, who is also supposed to be at work, but who is actually gnawing the feather of a pen and contemplating BLUNTSCHLI'S quick, sure, businesslike progress with a mixture of envious irritation at his own incapacity, and awestruck wonder at an ability which seems to him almost miraculous, though its prosaic character forbids him to esteem it. The major is comfortably established on the ottoman, with a newspaper in his hand and the tube of the hookah within his reach. CATHERINE sits at the stove, with her back to them, embroidering. RAINA, reclining on the divan under the left-hand window, is gazing in a daydream out at the Balkan landscape, with

[1] **hookah** (hōŏk′ə): an Oriental pipe with a long tube that passes through a jar of water, thus cooling the smoke.

a neglected novel in her lap.

The door is on the left. The button of the electric bell is between the door and the fireplace.

PETKOFF (*looking up from his paper to watch how they are getting on at the table*). Are you sure I can't help you in any way, Bluntschli?

BLUNTSCHLI (*without interrupting his writing or looking up*). Quite sure, thank you. Saranoff and I will manage it.

SERGIUS (*grimly*). Yes: we'll manage it. He finds out what to do; draws up the orders; and I sign 'em. Division of labor, Major. (BLUNTSCHLI *passes him a paper.*) Another one? Thank you. (*He plants the papers squarely before him; sets his chair carefully parallel to them; and signs with the air of a man resolutely performing a difficult and dangerous feat.*) This hand is more accustomed to the sword than to the pen.

PETKOFF. It's very good of you, Bluntschli, it is indeed, to let yourself be put upon in this way. Now are you *quite* sure I can do nothing?

CATHERINE (*in a low, warning tone*). You can stop interrupting, Paul.

PETKOFF (*starting and looking round at her*). Eh? Oh! Quite right, my love, quite right. (*He takes his newspaper up, but lets it drop again.*) Ah, you haven't been compaigning, Catherine: you don't know how pleasant it is for us to sit here, after a good lunch, with nothing to do but enjoy ourselves. There's only one thing I want to make me thoroughly comfortable.

CATHERINE. What is that?

PETKOFF. My old coat. I'm not at home in this one: I feel as if I were on parade.

CATHERINE. My dear Paul, how absurd you are about that old coat! It must be hanging in the blue closet where you left it.

PETKOFF. My dear Catherine, I tell you I've looked there. Am I to believe my own eyes or not? (CATHERINE *quietly rises and presses the button of the electric bell by the fireplace.*) What are you showing off that bell for? (*She looks at him majestically, and silently resumes her chair and her needlework.*) My dear: if you think the obstinacy of your sex can make a coat out of two old dressing gowns of Raina's, your waterproof, and my mackintosh, you're mistaken. That's exactly what the blue closet contains at present. (NICOLA *presents himself.*)

CATHERINE (*unmoved by* PETKOFF'S *sally*). Nicola: go to the blue closet and bring your master's old coat here—the braided one he usually wears in the house.

NICOLA. Yes, madam. (NICOLA *goes out.*)

PETKOFF. Catherine.

CATHERINE. Yes, Paul?

PETKOFF. I bet you any piece of jewelry you like to order from Sophia against a week's housekeeping money, that the coat isn't there.

CATHERINE. Done, Paul.

PETKOFF (*excited by the prospect of a gamble*). Come: here's an opportunity for some sport. Who'll bet on it? Bluntschli: I'll give you six to one.

BLUNTSCHLI (*imperturbably*). It would be robbing you, Major. Madame is sure to be right. (*Without looking up, he passes another batch of papers to* SERGIUS.)

SERGIUS (*also excited*). Bravo, Switzerland! Major: I bet my best charger against an Arab mare for Raina that Nicola finds the coat in the blue closet.

PETKOFF (*eagerly*). Your best char——

CATHERINE (*hastily interrupting him*). Don't be foolish, Paul. An Arabian mare will cost you 50,000 levas.

RAINA (*suddenly coming out of her picturesque revery*). Really, mother, if you are going to take the jewelry, I don't see why you should grudge me my Arab.

[NICOLA *comes back with the coat and brings it to* PETKOFF, *who can hardly believe his eyes.*]

CATHERINE. Where was it, Nicola?

NICOLA. Hanging in the blue closet, madam.

PETKOFF. Well, I am d——

CATHERINE (*stopping him*). Paul!

PETKOFF. I could have sworn it wasn't there. Age is beginning to tell on me. I'm getting hallucinations. (*To* NICOLA.) Here: help me to change. Excuse me, Bluntschli. (*He begins changing coats,* NICOLA *acting as valet.*) Remember: I didn't take that bet of yours, Sergius. You'd better give Raina that Arab steed yourself, since you've roused her expectations. Eh, Raina? (*He looks round at her; but she is again rapt in the landscape. With a little gush of paternal affection and pride, he points her out to them and says*) She's dreaming, as usual.

SERGIUS. Assuredly she shall not be the loser.

PETKOFF. So much the better for her. *I* shan't come off so cheap, I expect. (*The change is now complete.* NICOLA *goes out with the discarded coat.*) Ah, now I feel at home at last. (*He sits down and takes his newspaper with a grunt of relief.*)

BLUNTSCHLI (*to* SERGIUS, *handing a paper*). That's the last order.

PETKOFF (*jumping up*). What! finished?

BLUNTSCHLI. Finished.

PETKOFF (*goes beside* SERGIUS; *looks curiously over his left shoulder as he signs; and says with childlike envy*) Haven't you anything for *me* to sign?

BLUNTSCHLI. Not necessary. His signature will do.

PETKOFF. Ah, well, I think we've done a thundering good day's work. (*He goes away from the table.*) Can I do anything more?

BLUNTSCHLI. You had better both see the fellows that are to take these. (*To* SERGIUS.) Pack them off at once; and show them that I've marked on the orders the time they should hand them in by. Tell them that if they stop to drink or tell stories—if they're five minutes late, they'll have the skin taken off their backs.

SERGIUS (*rising indignantly*). I'll say so. And if one of them is man enough to spit in my face for insulting him, I'll buy his discharge and give him a pension. (*He strides out, his humanity deeply outraged.*)

BLUNTSCHLI (*confidentially*). Just see that he talks to them properly, Major, will you?

PETKOFF (*officiously*). Quite right, Bluntschli, quite right. I'll see to it. (*He goes to the door importantly, but hesitates on the threshold.*) By the by, Catherine, you may as well come, too. They'll be far more frightened of you than of me.

CATHERINE (*putting down her embroidery*). I daresay I had better. You will only splutter at them. (*She goes out,* PETKOFF *holding the door for her and following her.*)

BLUNTSCHLI. What a country! They make cannons out of cherry trees; and the officers send for their wives to keep discipline! (*He begins to fold and docket the papers.* RAINA, *who has risen from the divan, strolls down the room with her hands clasped behind her, and looks mischievously at him.*)

RAINA. You look ever so much nicer than when we last met. (*He looks up, surprised.*) What have you done to yourself?

BLUNTSCHLI. Washed; brushed; good night's sleep and breakfast. That's all.

RAINA. Did you get back safely that morning?

BLUNTSCHLI. Quite, thanks.

RAINA. Were they angry with you for running away from Sergius's charge?

BLUNTSCHLI. No, they were glad; because they'd all just run away themselves.

RAINA (*going to the table, and leaning over it toward him*). It must have made a lovely story for them—all that about me and my room.

BLUNTSCHLI. Capital story. But I only told it to one of them—a particular friend.

RAINA. On whose discretion you could absolutely rely?

BLUNTSCHLI. Absolutely.

RAINA. Hm! He told it all to my father and Sergius the day you exchanged the prisoners. (*She turns away and strolls carelessly across to the other side of the room.*)

BLUNTSCHLI(*deeply concerned and half-incredulous*). No! you don't mean that, do you?

RAINA (*turning, with sudden earnestness*). I do indeed. But they don't know that it was in this house that you hid. If Sergius knew, he would challenge you and kill you in a duel.

BLUNTSCHLI. Bless me! then don't tell him.

RAINA (*full of reproach for his levity*). Can you realize what it is to me to deceive him? I want to be quite perfect with Sergius—no meanness, no smallness, no deceit. My relation to him is the one really beautiful and noble part of my life. I hope you can understand that.

BLUNTSCHLI (*skeptically*). You mean that you wouldn't like him to find out that the story about the ice pudding was a—a—a—You know.

RAINA (*wincing*). Ah, don't talk of it in that flippant way. I lied: I know it. But I did it to save your life. He would have killed you. That was the second time I ever uttered a falsehood. (BLUNTSCHLI *rises quickly and looks doubtfully and somewhat severely at her.*) Do you remember the first time?

BLUNTSCHLI. I! No. Was I present?

RAINA. Yes; and I told the officer who was searching for you that you were not present.

BLUNTSCHLI. True. I should have remembered it.

RAINA (*greatly encouraged*). Ah, it is natural that *you* should forget it first. It cost you nothing: it cost me a lie!—a lie!! (*She sits down on the ottoman, looking straight before her with her hands clasped on her knee.* BLUNTSCHLI, *quite touched, goes to the ottoman with a particularly reassuring and considerate air, and sits down beside her.*)

BLUNTSCHLI. My dear young lady, don't let this worry you. Remember: I'm a soldier. Now what are the two things that happen to a soldier so often that he comes to think nothing of them? One is hearing people tell lies (RAINA *recoils*): the other is getting his life saved in all sorts of ways by all sorts of people.

RAINA (*rising in indignant protest*). And so he becomes a creature incapable of faith and of gratitude.

BLUNTSCHLI (*making a wry face*). Do you like gratitude? I don't. If pity is akin to love, gratitude is akin to the other thing.

RAINA. Gratitude! (*Turning on him.*) If you are incapable of gratitude you are incapable of any noble sentiment. Even animals are grateful. Oh, I see now exactly what you think of me! You were not surprised to hear me lie. To you it was something I probably did every day—every hour. That is how men think of women. (*She walks up the room melodramatically.*)

BLUNTSCHLI (*dubiously*). There's reason in everything. You said you'd told only two lies in your whole life. Dear young lady: isn't that rather a short allowance? I'm quite a straightforward man myself; but it wouldn't last me a whole morning.

RAINA (*staring haughtily at him*). Do you know, sir, that you are insulting me?

BLUNTSCHLI. I can't help it. When you get into that noble attitude and speak in that thrilling voice, I admire you; but I find it impossible to believe a single word you say.

RAINA (*superbly*). Captain Bluntschli!

BLUNTSCHLI (*unmoved*). Yes?

RAINA (*coming a little toward him, as if she could not believe her senses*). Do you mean what you said just now? Do you *know* what you said just now?

BLUNTSCHLI. I do.

RAINA (*gasping*). I! I!!! (*She points to herself incredulously, meaning "I, Raina Petkoff, tell lies!" He meets her gaze unflinchingly. She suddenly sits down beside him, and adds, with a complete change of manner from the heroic to the familiar*) How did you find me out?

BLUNTSCHLI (*promptly*). Instinct, dear young lady. Instinct, and experience of the world.

RAINA (*wonderingly*). Do you know, you are the first man I ever met who did not take me seriously?

BLUNTSCHLI. You mean, don't you, that I am the first man that has ever taken you quite seriously?

RAINA. Yes, I suppose I *do* mean that. (*Cozily, quite at her ease with him.*) How strange it is to be talked to in such a way! You know, I've always gone on like that—I mean the noble attitude and the thrilling voice. I did it when I was a tiny child to my nurse. *She* believed in it. I do it before my parents. *They* believe in it. I do it before Sergius. *He* believes in it.

BLUNTSCHLI. Yes: he's a little in that line himself, isn't he?

RAINA (*startled*). Do you think so?

BLUNTSCHLI. You know him better than I do.

RAINA. I wonder—I *wonder* is he? If I thought that—! (*Discouraged.*) Ah, well, what does it matter? I suppose, now that you've found me out, you despise me.

BLUNTSCHLI (*warmly, rising*). No, my dear young lady, no, no, no a thousand times. It's part of your youth—part of your charm. I'm like all the rest of them—the nurse—your parents—Sergius: I'm your infatuated admirer.

RAINA (*pleased*). Really?

BLUNTSCHLI (*slapping his breast smartly with his hand, German fashion*). Hand aufs Herz![1] Really and truly.

RAINA (*very happy*). But what did you think of me for giving you my portrait?

BLUNTSCHLI (*astonished*). Your portrait! You never gave me your portrait.

RAINA (*quickly*). Do you mean to say you never got it?

BLUNTSCHLI. No. (*He sits down beside her, with renewed interest, and says, with some complacency.*) When did you send it to me?

RAINA (*indignantly*). I did not send it to you. (*She turns her head away, and adds, reluctantly.*) It was in the pocket of that coat.

BLUNTSCHLI (*pursing his lips and rounding his eyes*). Oh-o-oh! I never found it. It must be there still.

RAINA (*springing up*). There still!—for my father to find the first time he puts his hand in his pocket! Oh, how could you be so stupid?

BLUNTSCHLI (*rising also*). It doesn't matter: it's only a photograph: how can he tell who it was intended for? Tell him he put it there himself.

RAINA (*impatiently*). Yes, that is so clever—*so* clever! What shall I do?

BLUNTSCHLI. Ah, I see. You wrote something on it. That was rash!

RAINA (*annoyed almost to tears*). Oh, to have done such a thing for *you*, who care no more—except to laugh at me—oh!

[1] **Hand aufs Herz** (German): Cross my heart.

Are you sure nobody has touched it?

BLUNTSCHLI. Well, I can't be quite sure. You see I couldn't carry it about with me all the time: one can't take much luggage on active service.

RAINA. What did you do with it?

BLUNTSCHLI. When I got through to Peerot I had to put it in safekeeping somehow. I thought of the railway cloak room; but that's the surest place to get looted in modern warfare. So I pawned it.

RAINA. *Pawned* it!!!

BLUNTSCHLI. I know it doesn't sound nice; but it was much the safest plan. I redeemed it the day before yesterday. Heaven only knows whether the pawnbroker cleared out the pockets or not.

RAINA (*furious—throwing the words right into his face*). You have a low, shopkeeping mind. You think of things that would never come into a gentleman's head.

BLUNTSCHLI (*phlegmatically*). That's the Swiss national character, dear lady.

RAINA. Oh, I wish I had never met you. (*She flounces away and sits at the window fuming.*)

[LOUKA *comes in with a heap of letters and telegrams on her salver, and crosses, with her bold, free gait, to the*

table. *Her left sleeve is looped up to the shoulder with a brooch, showing her naked arm, with a broad gilt bracelet covering the bruise.*]

LOUKA (*to Bluntschli*). For you. (*She empties the salver recklessly on the table.*) The messenger is waiting. (*She is determined not to be civil to a Servian, even if she must bring him his letters.*)

BLUNTSCHLI (*to Raina*). Will you excuse me: the last postal delivery that reached me was three weeks ago. These are the subsequent accumulations. Four telegrams—a week old. (*He opens one.*) Oho! Bad news!

RAINA (*rising and advancing a little remorsefully*). Bad news?

BLUNTSCHLI. My father's dead. (*He looks at the telegram with his lips pursed, musing on the unexpected change in his arrangements.*)

RAINA. Oh, how very sad!

BLUNTSCHLI. Yes: I shall have to start for home in an hour. He has left a lot of big hotels behind him to be looked after. (*Takes up a heavy letter in a long envelope.*) Here's a whacking letter from the family solicitor. (*He pulls out the enclosures and glances over them.*) Great Heavens! Seventy! Two hundred! (*In a crescendo of dismay.*) Four hundred! Four thousand!! Nine thousand six hundred!!! What on earth shall I do with them all?

RAINA (*timidly*). Nine thousand hotels?

BLUNTSCHLI. Hotels! Nonsense. If you only knew!—oh, it's too ridiculous! Excuse me: I must give my fellow orders about starting. (*He leaves the room hastily, with the documents in his hand.*)

LOUKA (*tauntingly*). He has not much heart, that Swiss, though he is so fond of the Servians. He has not a word of grief for his poor father.

RAINA (*bitterly*). Grief!—a man who has been doing nothing but killing people

for years! What does he care? What does any soldier care? (*She goes to the door, evidently restraining her tears with difficulty.*)

LOUKA. Major Saranoff has been fighting, too; and he has plenty of heart left. (RAINA, *at the door, looks haughtily at her and goes out.*) Aha! I thought you wouldn't get much feeling out of *your* soldier. (*She is following* RAINA *when* NICOLA *enters with an armful of logs for the fire.*)

NICOLA (*grinning amorously at her*). I've been trying all the afternoon to get a minute alone with you, my girl. (*His countenance changes as he notices her arm.*) Why, what fashion is that of wearing your sleeve, child?

LOUKA (*proudly*). My own fashion.

NICOLA. Indeed! If the mistress catches you, she'll talk to you. (*He throws the logs down on the ottoman, and sits comfortably beside them.*)

LOUKA. Is that any reason why *you* should take it on yourself to talk to me?

NICOLA. Come: don't be so contrary with me. I've some good news for you. (*He takes out some paper money.* LOUKA, *with an eager gleam in her eyes, comes close to look at it.*) See, a twenty-leva bill! Sergius gave me that out of pure swagger. A fool and his money are soon parted. There's ten levas more. The Swiss gave me that for backing up the mistress's and Raina's lies about him. He's no fool, he isn't. You should have heard old Catherine downstairs as polite as you please to me, telling me not to mind the Major being a little impatient; for they knew what a good servant I was—after making a fool and a liar of me before them all! The twenty will go to our savings; and you shall have the ten to spend if you'll only talk to me so as to remind me I'm a human being. I get tired of being a servant occasionally.

LOUKA (*scornfully*). Yes: sell your manhood for thirty levas, and buy me for ten! Keep your money. You were born to be a servant. I was not. When you set up your shop you will only be everybody's servant instead of somebody's servant.

NICOLA (*picking up his logs, and going to the stove*). Ah, wait till you see. We shall have our evenings to ourselves; and I shall be master in my own house, I promise you. (*He throws the logs down and kneels at the stove.*)

LOUKA. You shall never be master in mine. (*She sits down on* SERGIUS'S *chair.*)

NICOLA (*turning, still on his knees, and squatting down rather forlornly, on his calves, daunted by her implacable disdain*). You have a great ambition in you, Louka. Remember: if any luck comes to you, it was I that made a woman of you.

LOUKA. You!

NICOLA (*with dogged self-assertion*). Yes, me. Who was it made you give up wearing a couple of pounds of false black hair on your head and reddening your lips and cheeks like any other Bulgarian girl? I did. Who taught you to trim your nails, and keeps your hands clean, and be dainty about yourself, like a fine Russian lady? Me! do you hear that? me! (*She tosses her head defiantly; and he rises, ill-humoredly, adding more coolly*) I've often thought that if Raina were out of the way, and you just a little less of a fool and Sergius just a little more of one, you might come to be one of my grandest customers, instead of only being my wife and costing me money.

LOUKA. I believe you would rather be my servant than my husband. You would make more out of me. Oh, I know that soul of yours.

NICOLA (*going up close to her for greater emphasis*). Never you mind my soul; but just listen to my advice. If you want to be a lady, your present behavior to me won't do at all, unless when we're

alone. It's too sharp and impudent; and impudence is a sort of familiarity: it shows affection for me. And don't you try being high and mighty with me either. You're like all country girls: you think it's genteel to treat a servant the way I treat a stableboy. That's only your ignorance; and don't you forget it. And don't be so ready to defy everybody. Act as if you expected to have your own way, not as if you expected to be ordered about. The way to get on as a lady is the same as the way to get on as a servant: you've got to know your place; that's the secret of it. And you may depend on me to know my place if you get promoted. Think over it, my girl. I'll stand by you: one servant should always stand by another.

LOUKA (*rising impatiently*). Oh, I must behave in my own way. You take all the courage out of me with your cold-blooded wisdom. Go and put those logs on the fire: that's the sort of thing *you* understand. (*Before* NICOLA *can retort,* SERGIUS *comes in. He checks himself a moment on seeing* LOUKA; *then goes to the stove.*)

SERGIUS (*to* NICOLA). I am not in the way of your work, I hope.

NICOLA (*in a smooth, elderly manner*). Oh, no, sir, thank you kindly. I was only speaking to this foolish girl about her habit of running up here to the library whenever she gets a chance, to look at the books. That's the worst of her education. sir: it gives her habits above her station. (*To* LOUKA.) Make that table tidy, Louka, for the Major. (*He goes out sedately.*)

[LOUKA; *without looking at* SERGIUS, *begins to arrange the papers on the table. He crosses slowly to her and studies the arrangement of her sleeve reflectively.*]

SERGIUS. Let me see: is there a mark there? (*He turns up the bracelet and sees the bruise made by his grasp. She stands motionless, not looking at him: fascinated, but on her guard.*) Ffff! Does it hurt?

LOUKA. Yes.

SERGIUS. Shall I cure it?

LOUKA (*instantly withdrawing herself proudly, but still not looking at him*). No. You cannot cure it now.

SERGIUS (*masterfully*). Quite sure? (*He makes a movement as if to take her in his arms.*)

LOUKA. Don't trifle with me, please. An officer should not trifle with a servant.

SERGIUS (*touching the arm with a merciless stroke of his forefinger*). That was no trifle, Louka.

LOUKA. No. (*Looking at him for the first time.*) Are you sorry?

SERGIUS (*with measured emphasis, folding his arms*). I am *never* sorry.

LOUKA (*wistfully*). I wish I could believe a man could be so unlike a woman as that. I wonder are you really a brave man?

SERGIUS (*unaffectedly, relaxing his attitude*). Yes: I am a brave man. My heart jumped like a woman's at the first shot; but in the charge I found that I was brave. Yes: that at least is real about me.

LOUKA. Did you find in the charge that the men whose fathers are poor like mine were any less brave than the men who are rich like you?

SERGIUS (*with bitter levity*). Not a bit. They all slashed and cursed and yelled like heroes. Psha! the courage to rage and kill is cheap. I have an English bull terrier who has as much of that sort of courage as the whole Bulgarian nation and the whole Russian nation at its back. But he lets my groom thrash him, all the same. That's your soldier all over! No, Louka, your poor men can cut throats; but they are afraid of their officers; they put up with insults and blows; they stand by and see one another punished like children—aye, and help to do it when they are ordered.

And the officers!—well *(with a short, bitter laugh)* I am an officer. Oh, *(fervently)* give me the man who will defy to the death any power on earth or in heaven that sets itself up against his own will and conscience: he alone is the brave man.

LOUKA. How easy it is to talk! Men never seem to me to grow up: they all have schoolboys' ideas. You don't know what true courage is.

SERGIUS *(ironically)*. Indeed! I am willing to be instructed.

LOUKA. Look at me! how much am I allowed to have my own will? I have to get your room ready for you—to sweep and dust, to fetch and carry. How could that degrade me if it did not degrade you to have it done for you? But *(with subdued passion)* if I were Empress of Russia, above everyone in the world, then—ah, then, though according to you I could show no courage at all; you should see, you should see.

SERGIUS. What would you do, most noble Empress?

LOUKA. I would marry the man I loved, which no other queen in Europe has the courage to do. If I loved you, though you would be as far beneath me as I am beneath you, I would dare to be the equal of my inferior. Would you dare as much if you loved me? No: if you felt the beginnings of love for me you would not let it grow. You dare not: you would marry a rich man's daughter because you would be afraid of what other people would say of you.

SERGIUS *(carried away)*. You lie: it is not so, by all the stars! If I loved you, and I were the Czar himself, I would set you on the throne by my side. You know that I love another woman, a woman as high above you as heaven is above earth. And you are jealous of her.

LOUKA. I have no reason to be. She will never marry you now. The man I told

you of has come back. She will marry the Swiss.

SERGIUS *(recoiling)*. The Swiss!

LOUKA. A man worth ten of you. Then you can come to me; and I will refuse you. You are not good enough for me. *(She turns to the door.)*

SERGIUS *(springing after her and catching her fiercely in his arms)*. I will kill the Swiss; and afterward I will do as I please with you.

LOUKA *(in his arms, passive and steadfast)*. The Swiss will kill you, perhaps. He has beaten you in love. He may beat you in war.

SERGIUS *(tormentedly)*. Do you think I believe that she—*she!* whose worst thoughts are higher than your best ones, is capable of trifling with another man behind my back?

LOUKA. Do you think *she* would believe the Swiss if he told her now that I am in your arms?

SERGIUS *(releasing her in despair)*. Damnation! Oh, damnation! Mockery, mockery everywhere: everything I think is mocked by everything I do. *(He strikes himself frantically on the breast.)* Coward, liar, fool! Shall I kill myself like a man, or live and pretend to laugh at myself? *(She again turns to go.)* Louka! *(She stops near the door.)* Remember: you belong to me.

LOUKA *(quietly)*. What does that mean —an insult?

SERGIUS *(commandingly)*. It means that you love me, and that I have had you here in my arms, and will perhaps have you there again. Whether that is an insult I neither know nor care: take it as you please. But *(vehemently)* I *will* not be a coward and a trifler. If I choose to love you, I dare marry you, in spite of all Bulgaria. If these hands ever touch you again, they shall touch my affianced bride.

LOUKA. We shall see whether you dare

keep your word. But take care. I will not wait long.

SERGIUS (*again folding his arms and standing motionless in the middle of the room*). Yes, we shall see. And you shall wait my pleasure.

[BLUNTSCHLI, *much preoccupied, with his papers still in his hand, enters, leaving the door open for* LOUKA *to go out. He goes across to the table, glancing at her as he passes.* SERGIUS, *without altering his resolute attitude, watches him steadily.* LOUKA *goes out, leaving the door open.*]

BLUNTSCHLI (*absently, sitting at the table as before, and putting down his papers*). That's a remarkable-looking young woman.

SERGIUS (*gravely, without moving*). Captain Bluntschli.

BLUNTSCHLI. Eh?

SERGIUS. You have deceived me. You are my rival. I brook no rivals. At six o'clock I shall be in the drilling ground on the Klissoura road, alone, on horseback, with my saber. Do you understand?

BLUNTSCHLI (*staring, but sitting quite at his ease*). Oh, thank you: that's a cavalryman's proposal. I'm in the artillery; and I have the choice of weapons. If I go, I shall take a machine gun. And there shall be no mistake about the cartridges this time.

SERGIUS (*flushing, but with deadly coldness*). Take care, sir. It is not our custom in Bulgaria to allow invitations of that kind to be trifled with.

BLUNTSCHLI (*warmly*). Pooh! don't talk to me about Bulgaria. You don't know what fighting is. But have it your own way. Bring your saber along. I'll meet you.

SERGIUS (*fiercely delighted to find his opponent a man of spirit*). Well said, Switzer. Shall I lend you my best horse?

BLUNTSCHLI. No: blast your horse!— thank you all the same, my dear fellow. (RAINA *comes in, and hears the next sentence.*) I shall fight you on foot. Horseback's too dangerous: I don't want to kill you if I can help it.

RAINA (*hurrying forward anxiously*). I have heard what Captain Bluntschli said, Sergius. You are going to fight. Why? (SERGIUS *turns away in silence, and goes to the stove, where he stands watching her as she continues, to* BLUNTSCHLI) What about?

BLUNTSCHLI. I don't know: he hasn't told me. Better not interfere, dear young lady. No harm will be done: I've often acted as sword instructor. He won't be able to touch me; and I'll not hurt him. It will save explanations. In the morning I shall be off home; and you'll never see me or hear of me again. You and he will then make it up and live happily ever after.

RAINA (*turning away deeply hurt, almost with a sob in her voice*). I never said I wanted to see you again.

SERGIUS (*striding forward*). Ha! That is a confession.

RAINA (*haughtily*). What do you mean?

SERGIUS. You love that man!

RAINA (*scandalized*). Sergius!

SERGIUS. You allow him to make love to you behind my back, just as you accept me as your affianced husband behind his. Bluntschli: you knew our relations; and you deceived me. It is for that that I call you to account, not for having received favors that I never enjoyed.

BLUNTSCHLI (*jumping up indignantly*). Stuff! Rubbish! I have received no favors. Why, the young lady doesn't even know whether I'm married or not.

RAINA (*forgetting herself*). Oh! (*Collapsing on the ottoman.*) Are you?

SERGIUS. You see the young lady's concern, Captain Bluntschli. Denial is useless. You have enjoyed the privilege of being received in her own room, late at night——

BLUNTSCHLI (*interrupting him pepperily*). Yes; you blockhead! She received me with a pistol at her head. Your cavalry were at my heels. I'd have blown out her brains if she'd uttered a cry.

SERGIUS (*taken aback*). Bluntschli! Raina: is this true?

RAINA (*rising in wrathful majesty*). Oh, how dare you, how dare you?

BLUNTSCHLI. Apologize, man, apologize! (*He resumes his seat at the table.*)

SERGIUS (*with the old measured emphasis, folding his arms*). I *never* apologize.

RAINA (*passionately*). This is the doing of that friend of yours, Captain Bluntschli. It is he who is spreading this horrible story about me. (*She walks about excitedly.*)

BLUNTSCHLI. No: he's dead—burned alive.

RAINA (*stopping, shocked*). Burned alive!

BLUNTSCHLI. Shot in the hip in a wood yard. Couldn't drag himself out. Your fellows' shells set the timber on fire and burned him, with half a dozen other poor devils in the same predicament.

RAINA. How horrible!

SERGIUS. And how ridiculous! Oh, war! war! the dream of patriots and heroes! A fraud, Bluntschli, a hollow sham, like love.

RAINA (*outraged*). Like love! You say that before me.

BLUNTSCHLI. Come, Saranoff: that matter is explained.

SERGIUS. A hollow sham, I say. Would you have come back here if nothing had passed between you, except at the muzzle of your pistol? Raina is mistaken about our friend who was burned. He was not my informant.

RAINA. Who then? (*Suddenly guessing the truth.*) Ah, Louka! my maid, my servant! You were with her this morning all that time after—after—Oh, what sort of god is this I have been worshiping! (*He meets her gaze with sardonic enjoyment of her disenchantment. Angered all the more, she goes closer to him, and says, in a lower, intenser tone*) Do you know that I looked out of the window as I went upstairs, to have another sight of my hero; and I saw something that I did not understand then. I know now that you were making love to her.

SERGIUS (*with grim humor*). You saw that?

RAINA. Only too well. (*She turns away, and throws herself on the divan under the center window, quite overcome.*)

SERGIUS (*cynically*). Raina: our romance is shattered. Life's a farce.

BLUNTSCHLI (*to* RAINA, *good-humoredly*). You see: he's found himself out now.

SERGIUS. Bluntschli: I have allowed you

to call me a blockhead. You may now call me a coward as well. I refuse to fight you. Do you know why?

BLUNTSCHLI. No; but it doesn't matter. I didn't ask the reason when you cried on; and I don't ask the reason now that you cry off. I'm a professional soldier. I fight when I have to, and am very glad to get out of it when I haven't to. You're only an amateur: you think fighting's an amusement.

SERGIUS. You shall hear the reason all the same, my professional. The reason is that it takes two men—real men—men of heart, blood and honor—to make a genuine combat. I could no more fight with you than I could make love to an ugly woman. You've no magnetism: you're not a man, you're a machine.

BLUNTSCHLI (*apologetically*). Quite true, quite true. I always *was* that sort of chap. I'm very sorry. But now that you've found that life *isn't* a farce, but something quite sensible and serious, what further obstacle is there to your happiness?

RAINA (*rising*). You are very solicitous about my happiness and his. Do you forget his new love—Louka? It is not you that he must fight now, but his rival, Nicola.

SERGIUS. Rival!! (*Striking his forehead.*)

RAINA. Did you not know that they are engaged?

SERGIUS. Nicola! Are fresh abysses opening! Nicola!!

RAINA (*sarcastically*). A shocking sacrifice, isn't it? Such beauty, such intellect, such modesty, wasted on a middle-aged servant man! Really, Sergius, you cannot stand by and allow such a thing. It would be unworthy of your chivalry.

SERGIUS (*losing all self-control*). Viper! Viper! (*He rushes to and fro, raging.*)

BLUNTSCHLI. Look here, Saranoff; you're getting the worst of this.

RAINA (*getting angrier*). Do you realize what he has done, Captain Bluntschli? He has set this girl as a spy on us; and her reward is that he makes love to her.

SERGIUS. False! Monstrous!

RAINA. Monstrous! (*Confronting him.*) Do you deny that she told you about Captain Bluntschli being in my room?

SERGIUS. No; but——

RAINA (*interrupting*). Do you deny that you were making love to her when she told you?

SERGIUS. No; but I tell you——

RAINA (*cutting him short contemptuously*). It is unnecessary to tell us anything more. That is quite enough for us. (*She turns her back on him and sweeps majestically back to the window.*)

BLUNTSCHLI (*quietly, as* SERGIUS, *in an agony of mortification, sinks on the ottoman, clutching his averted head between his fists*). I told you you were getting the worst of it, Saranoff.

SERGIUS. Tiger cat!

RAINA (*running excitedly to* BLUNTSCHLI). You hear this man calling me names, Captain Bluntschli?

BLUNTSCHLI. What else can he do, dear lady? He must defend himself somehow. Come (*very persuasively*), don't quarrel. What good does it do? (RAINA, *with a gasp, sits down on the ottoman, and after a vain effort to look vexedly at* BLUNTSCHLI, *she falls a victim to her sense of humor, and is attacked with a disposition to laugh.*)

SERGIUS. Engaged to Nicola! (*He rises.*) Ha! ha! (*Going to the stove and standing with his back to it.*) Ah, well, Bluntschli, you are right to take this huge imposture of a world coolly.

RAINA (*to* BLUNTSCHLI *with an intuitive guess at his state of mind*). I daresay you think us a couple of grown up babies, don't you?

SERGIUS (*grinning a little*). He does,

he does. Swiss civilization nursetending Bulgarian barbarism, eh?

BLUNTSCHLI (*blushing*). Not at all, I assure you. I'm only very glad to get you two quieted. There now, let's be pleasant and talk it over in a friendly way. Where is this other young lady?

RAINA. Listening at the door, probably.

SERGIUS (*shivering as if a bullet had struck him, and speaking with quiet but deep indignation*). I will prove that that, at least, is a calumny. (*He goes with dignity to the door and opens it. A yell of fury bursts from him as he looks out. He darts into the passage, and returns dragging in* LOUKA, *whom he flings against the table, as he cries*) Judge her, Bluntschli— you, the moderate, cautious man: judge her, the eavesdropper.

[LOUKA *stands her ground, proud and silent.*]

BLUNTSCHLI (*shaking his head*). I mustn't judge her. I once listened myself outside a tent when there was a mutiny brewing. It's all a question of the degree of provocation. My life was at stake.

LOUKA. My love was at stake. (SERGIUS *flinches, ashamed of her in spite of himself.*) I am not ashamed.

RAINA (*contemptuously*). Your love! Your curiosity, you mean.

LOUKA (*facing her and retorting her contempt with interest*). My love, stronger than anything *you* can feel, even for your chocolate-cream soldier.

SERGIUS (*with quick suspicion—to* LOUKA). What does that mean?

LOUKA (*fiercely*). It means——

SERGIUS (*interrupting her slightingly*). Oh, I remember, the ice pudding. A paltry taunt, girl.

[MAJOR PETKOFF *enters, in his shirtsleeves.*]

PETKOFF. Excuse my shirtsleeves, gentlemen. Raina: somebody has been wearing that coat of mine: I'll swear it— somebody with bigger shoulders than mine. It's all burst open at the back. Your mother is mending it. I wish she'd make haste. I shall catch cold. (*He looks more attentively at them.*) Is anything the matter?

RAINA. No. (*She sits down at the stove with a tranquil air.*)

SERGIUS. Oh, no! (*He sits down at the end of the table, as at first.*)

BLUNTSCHLI (*who is already seated*). Nothing, nothing.

PETKOFF (*sitting down on the ottoman in his old place*). That's all right. (*He notices* LOUKA.) Anything the matter, Louka?

LOUKA. No, sir.

PETKOFF (*genially*). That's all right. (*He sneezes.*) Go and ask your mistress for my coat, like a good girl, will you? (*She turns to obey; but* NICOLA *enters with the coat; and she makes a pretense of having business in the room by taking the little table with the hookah away to the wall near the windows.*)

RAINA (*rising quickly, as she sees the coat on* NICOLA's *arm*). Here it is, papa. Give it to me, Nicola; and do you put some more wood on the fire. (*She takes the coat, and brings it to* THE MAJOR, *who stands up to put it on.* NICOLA *attends to the fire.*)

PETKOFF (*to* RAINA, *teasing her affectionately*). Aha! Going to be very good to poor old papa just for one day after his return from the wars, eh?

RAINA (*with solemn reproach*). Ah, how can you say that to me, father?

PETKOFF. Well, well, only a joke, little one. Come, give me a kiss. (*She kisses him.*) Now give me the coat.

RAINA. Now, I am going to put it on for you. Turn your back. (*He turns his back*

and feels behind him with his arms for the sleeves. She dexterously takes the photograph from the pocket and throws it on the table before BLUNTSCHLI, *who covers it with a sheet of paper under the very nose of* SERGIUS, *who looks on amazed, with his suspicions roused in the highest degree. She then helps* PETKOFF *on with his coat.*) There, dear! Now are you comfortable?

PETKOFF. Quite, little love. Thanks. (*He sits down; and* RAINA *returns to her seat near the stove.*) Oh, by the bye, I've found something funny. What's the meaning of this? (*He puts his hand into the picked pocket.*) Eh? Hallo! (*He tries the other pocket.*) Well, I could have sworn— (*Much puzzled, he tries the breast pocket.*) I wonder—(*Tries the original pocket.*) where can it—(*A light flashes on him; he rises, exclaiming*) Your mother's taken it.

RAINA (*very red*). Taken what?

PETKOFF. Your photograph, with the inscription: "Raina, to her Chocolate-Cream Soldier—a souvenir." Now you know there's something more in this than meets the eye; and I'm going to find it out. (*Shouting*) Nicola!

NICOLA (*dropping a log, and turning*). Sir!

PETKOFF. Did you spoil any pastry of Miss Raina's this morning?

NICOLA. You heard Miss Raina say that I did, sir.

PETKOFF. I know that, you idiot. Was it true?

NICOLA. I am sure Miss Raina is incapable of saying anything that is not true, sir.

PETKOFF. Are you? Then I'm not. (*Turning to the others.*) Come: do you think I don't see it all? (*Goes to* SERGIUS, *and slaps him on the shoulder.*) Sergius: *you're* the chocolate-cream soldier, aren't you?

SERGIUS (*starting up*). I! a chocolate-cream soldier! Certainly not.

PETKOFF. Not! (*He looks at them. They are all very serious and very conscious.*)

Do you mean to tell me that Raina sends photographic souvenirs to other men?

SERGIUS (*enigmatically.*) The world is not such an innocent place as we used to think, Petkoff.

BLUNTSCHLI (*rising*). It's all right, Major. I'm the chocolate-cream soldier. (PETKOFF *and* SERGIUS *are equally astonished.*) The gracious young lady saved my life by giving me chocolate creams when I was starving—shall I ever forget their flavor! My late friend Stolz told you the story at Peerot. I was the fugitive.

PETKOFF. You! (*He gasps.*) Sergius: do you remember how those two women went on this morning when we mentioned it? (SERGIUS *smiles cynically.* PETKOFF *confronts* RAINA *severely.*) *You're* a nice young woman, aren't you?

RAINA (*bitterly*). Major Saranoff has changed his mind. And when I wrote that on the photograph, I did not know that Captain Bluntschli was married.

BLUNTSCHLI (*much startled—protesting vehemently*). I'm *not* married.

RAINA (*with deep reproach*). You said you were.

BLUNTSCHLI. I did not. I positively did not. I never was married in my life.

PETKOFF (*exasperated*). Raina: will you kindly inform me, if I am not asking too much, which gentleman you *are* engaged to?

RAINA. To neither of them. *This* young lady (*introducing* LOUKA, *who faces them all proudly*) is the object of Major Saranoff's affections at present.

PETKOFF. Louka! Are you mad, Sergius? Why, this girl's engaged to Nicola.

NICOLA (*coming forward*). I beg your pardon, sir. There is a mistake. Louka is not engaged to me.

PETKOFF. Not engaged to you, you scoundrel! Why, you had twenty-five levas from me on the day of your be-trothal; and she had that gilt bracelet from Miss Raina.

NICOLA (*with cool unction*). We gave it out so, sir. But it was only to give Louka protection. She had a soul above her station; and I have been no more than her confidential servant. I intend, as you know, sir, to set up a shop later on in Sofia; and I look forward to her custom and recommendation should she marry into the nobility. (*He goes out with impressive discretion, leaving them all staring after him.*)

PETKOFF (*breaking the silence*). Well, I *am*—hm!

SERGIUS. This is either the finest heroism or the most crawling baseness. Which is it, Bluntschli?

BLUNTSCHLI. Never mind whether it's heroism or baseness. Nicola's the ablest man I've met in Bulgaria. I'll make him manager of a hotel if he can speak French and German.

LOUKA (*suddenly breaking out at* SERGIUS). I have been insulted by everyone here. *You* set them the example. You owe me an apology. (SERGIUS *immediately, like a repeating clock of which the spring has been touched, begins to fold his arms.*)

BLUNTSCHLI (*before he can speak*). It's no use. He never apologizes.

LOUKA. Not to you, his equal and his enemy. To me, his poor servant, he will not refuse to apologize.

SERGIUS (*approvingly*). You are right. (*He bends his knee in his grandest manner.*) Forgive me!

LOUKA. I forgive you. (*She timidly gives him her hand, which he kisses.*) That touch makes me your affianced wife.

SERGIUS (*springing up*). Ah, I forgot that!

LOUKA (*coldly*). You can withdraw if you like.

SERGIUS. Withdraw! Never! You be-

long to me! (*He puts his arm about her and draws her to him.*)

[CATHERINE *comes in and finds* LOUKA *in* SERGIUS'S *arms, and all the rest gazing at them in bewildered astonishment.*]

CATHERINE. What does this mean? (SERGIUS *releases* LOUKA.)

PETKOFF. Well, my dear, it appears that Sergius is going to marry Louka instead of Raina. (*She is about to break out indignantly at him: he stops her by exclaiming testily.*) Don't blame *me: I've* nothing to do with it. (*He retreats to the stove.*)

CATHERINE. Marry Louka! Sergius: you are bound by your word to us!

SERGIUS (*folding his arms*). Nothing binds me.

BLUNTSCHLI (*much pleased by this piece of common sense*). Saranoff: your hand. My congratulations. These heroics of yours have their practical side after all. (*To* LOUKA.) Gracious young lady: the best wishes of a good Republican![1] (*He kisses her hand, to* RAINA'S *great disgust.*)

CATHERINE (*threateningly*). Louka: you have been telling stories.

LOUKA. I have done Raina no harm.

CATHERINE (*haughtily*). Raina! (RAINA *is equally indignant at the liberty.*)

LOUKA. I have a right to call her Raina: she calls me Louka. I told Major Saranoff she would never marry him if the Swiss gentleman came back.

BLUNTSCHLI (*surprised*). Hallo!

LOUKA (*turning to* RAINA). I thought you were fonder of him than of Sergius. You know best whether I was right.

BLUNTSCHLI. What nonsense! I assure you, my dear Major, my dear Madame, the gracious young lady simply saved my life, nothing else. She never cared two

[1] **Republican:** here, one who believes in government by the people.

straws for me. Why, bless my heart and soul, look at the young lady and look at me. She, rich, young, beautiful, with her imagination full of fairy princes and noble natures and cavalry charges and goodness knows what! And I, a commonplace Swiss soldier who hardly knows what a decent life is after fifteen years of barracks and battles—a vagabond—a man who has spoiled all his chances in life through an incurably romantic disposition—a man——

SERGIUS (*starting as if a needle has pricked him and interrupting* BLUNTSCHLI *in incredulous amazement*). Excuse me, Bluntschli: *what* did you say had spoiled your chances in life?

BLUNTSCHLI (*promptly*). An incurably romantic disposition. I ran away from home twice when I was a boy. I went into the army instead of into my father's business. I climbed the balcony of this house when a man of sense would have dived into the nearest cellar. I came sneaking back here to have another look at the young lady when any other man of my age would have sent the coat back——

PETKOFF. My coat!

BLUNTSCHLI.—Yes: that's the coat I mean—would have sent it back and gone quietly home. Do you suppose I am the sort of fellow a young girl falls in love with? Why, look at our ages! I'm thirty-four: I don't suppose the young lady is much over seventeen. (*This estimate produces a marked sensation, all the rest turning and staring at one another. He proceeds innocently.*) All that adventure which was life or death to me, was only a schoolgirl's game to her—chocolate creams and hide and seek. Here's the proof! (*He takes the photograph from the table.*) Now, I ask you, would a woman who took the affair seriously have sent me this and written on it: "Raina, to her chocolate-cream soldier—a souvenir?"

(He exhibits the photograph triumphantly, as if it settled the matter beyond all possibility of refutation.)

PETKOFF. That's what I was looking for. How the deuce did it get there?

BLUNTSCHLI *(to* RAINA *complacently).* I have put everything right, I hope, gracious young lady!

RAINA *(in uncontrollable vexation).* I quite agree with your account of yourself. You are a romantic idiot. (BLUNTSCHLI *is unspeakably taken aback.)* Next time I hope you will know the difference between a schoolgirl of seventeen and a woman of twenty-three.

BLUNTSCHLI *(stupefied).* Twenty-three! *(She snaps the photograph contemptuously from his hand; tears it across; and throws the pieces at his feet.)*

SERGIUS *(with grim enjoyment of* BLUNTSCHLI'S *discomfiture).* Bluntschli: my one last belief is gone. Your sagacity is a fraud, like all the other things. You have less sense than even I have.

BLUNTSCHLI *(overwhelmed).* Twenty-three! Twenty-three!! *(He considers.)* Hm! *(Swiftly making up his mind.)* In that case, Major Petkoff, I beg to propose formally to become a suitor for your daughter's hand, in place of Major Saranoff retired.

RAINA. You dare!

BLUNTSCHLI. If you were twenty-three when you said those things to me this afternoon, I shall take them seriously.

CATHERINE *(loftily polite).* I doubt, sir, whether you quite realize either my daughter's position or that of Major Sergius Saranoff, whose place you propose to take. The Petkoffs and the Saranoffs are known as the richest and most important families in the country. Our position is almost historical: we can go back for nearly twenty years.

PETKOFF. Oh, never mind that, Catherine. *(To* BLUNTSCHLI.) We should be most happy, Bluntschli, if it were only a question of your position; but hang it, you know, Raina is accustomed to a very comfortable establishment. Sergius keeps twenty horses.

BLUNTSCHLI. But what on earth is the use of twenty horses? Why, it's a circus.

CATHERINE *(severely).* My daughter, sir, is accustomed to a first-rate stable.

RAINA. Hush, mother, you're making me ridiculous.

BLUNTSCHLI. Oh, well, if it comes to a question of an establishment, here goes! *(He goes impetuously to the table and seizes the papers in the blue envelope.)* How many horses did you say?

SERGIUS. Twenty, noble Switzer!

BLUNTSCHLI. I have two hundred horses. *(They are amazed.)* How many carriages?

SERGIUS. Three.

BLUNTSCHLI. I have seventy. Twenty-four of them will hold twelve inside, besides two on the box, without counting the driver and conductor. How many tablecloths have you?

SERGIUS. How the deuce do I know?

BLUNTSCHLI. Have you four thousand?

SERGIUS. No.

BLUNTSCHLI. I have. I have nine thousand six hundred pairs of sheets and blankets, with two thousand four hundred eiderdown quilts. I have ten thousand knives and forks and the same quantity of dessert spoons. I have six hundred servants. I have six palatial establishments, besides two livery stables, a tea garden, and a private house. I have four medals for distinguished services; I have the rank of an officer and the standing of a gentleman; and I have three native languages. Show me any man in Bulgaria that can offer as much.

PETKOFF *(with childish awe).* Are you Emperor of Switzerland?

BLUNTSCHLI. My rank is the highest

known in Switzerland: I'm a free citizen.

CATHERINE. Then Captain Bluntschli, since you are my daughter's choice, I shall not stand in the way of her happiness. (PETKOFF *is about to speak.*) That is Major Petkoff's feeling also.

PETKOFF. Oh, I shall be only too glad. Two hundred horses! Whew!

SERGIUS. What says the lady?

RAINA (*pretending to sulk*). The lady says that he can keep his tablecloths and his omnibuses. I am not here to be sold to the highest bidder.

BLUNTSCHLI. I won't take that answer. I appealed to you as a fugitive, a beggar, and a starving man. You accepted me. You gave me your hand to kiss, your bed to sleep in, and your roof to shelter me——

RAINA (*interrupting him.*) I did not give them to the Emperor of Switzerland!

BLUNTSCHLI. That's just what I say. (*He catches her hand quickly and looks her straight in the face as he adds, with confident mastery*). Now tell us who you did give them to.

RAINA (*succumbing with a shy smile*). To my chocolate-cream soldier!

BLUNTSCHLI (*with a boyish laugh of delight*). That'll do. Thank you. (*Looks at his watch and suddenly becomes business-like.*) Time's up, Major. You've managed those regiments so well that you are sure to be asked to get rid of some of the Infantry of the Teemok division. Send them home by way of Lom Palanka. Saranoff: don't get married until I come back: I shall be here punctually at five in the evening on Tuesday fortnight. Gracious ladies—good evening. (*He makes them a military bow, and goes.*)

SERGIUS. What a man! What a man!

FOR STUDY AND DISCUSSION

1. Reread Shaw's description of the assembled characters at the beginning of Act III. How does each character's position and behavior reflect his or her personality?

2. In this final act, Shaw brings all his plot strings together in a way that cuts out from under the characters all their false positions, so that each gets what he or she wants only on hard, sensible terms. What do Raina and Sergius learn about each other in this act? How do they react to this information? Do things turn out best for all concerned?

3. What has Nicola taught Louka? How does he contribute to her love affair with Sergius? Why would he rather have her marry Sergius than himself?

4. What is Louka's idea of courage? What is Sergius's? In what way are they ideally suited for each other?

5. In what way are Bluntschli and Raina alike? Do you think they will be happy together? Why?

6. Louka and Nicola contribute greatly to both the plot and theme of the play. Nicola is completely realistic and disapproves of all romantic illusions. Is this also true of Louka? Does she have good reason to be proud? What is her idea of a hero? What light does she shed on Shaw's idea of common sense and illusion?

7. Shaw uses a number of devices to keep his scenes alive in Act III—for example, the bet about the coat, the threat of a duel, and the picture in the pocket. Are these devices essential to the plot, or is Shaw simply throwing them in to add excitement? Could Act III move to its climax without these devices?

8. How does Shaw use Petkoff's coat and Raina's photograph to add to the humor in Act III? How do these props and the incidents involving them underline the conflict between the romantic and antiromantic in the play?

9. How do the following details contribute to the theme of romantic ideals and illusions: the way Sergius signs the military documents; Catherine's new electric buzzer; Louka's bracelet; Nicola's acceptance of bribes; Bluntschli's impression of Raina's age.

10. What do we learn in this act about the character of Raina? How romantic is she really? Why does she pretend she is? What is Bluntschli's answer when she tells him that he is the only man who has never taken her seriously? Do you agree with his reply?

11. Near the end of the play Bluntschli reveals that he has "an incurably romantic disposition." What does he mean? How are his "romantic" actions different from Sergius's? Would you say that Bluntschli's revelation indicates that Shaw, despite all the fun he pokes at romantic posturing, still comes out on the side of romance at the very end? Explain.

12. Why is the expression "chocolate-cream soldier" appropriate for Bluntschli? What does it suggest about him? What does it mean to Raina? Why does it make her succumb to his proposal with a shy smile?

THE PLAY AS A WHOLE

1. Is *Arms and the Man* a good title for this play? Why is the echo of *The Aeneid* (see introduction, page 476) amusing? What pun, or play on words, in the title makes it especially amusing?

2. Judging from this play, is life really ridiculous to Shaw, or do people only make it seem so by their exaggerated behavior and their role playing? What does the character of Bluntschli suggest about Shaw's attitude?

3. Do you think the attack on heroism and romanticism in this play have much meaning for a modern reader? Are we romantic or heroic today? What does this play have to say to us?

4. As you know, *dramatic irony* occurs when the audience knows more about an important fact than do the characters in a play. Where does Shaw use dramatic irony in *Arms and the Man*? Where is it especially amusing? How does Shaw's use of dramatic irony in this play compare with Shakespeare's in *Julius Caesar*?

5. Compare Shaw's attitude toward war in *Arms and the Man* with Shakespeare's in *Julius Caesar*. Compare the attitude of the two playwrights toward women, self-sacrifice, and idealism.

FOR COMPOSITION

1. Write a character sketch of Major Petkoff or Catherine. Include those details from Shaw's description that show most clearly what kind of person each one is.

2. Describe the great cavalry charge from Sergius's point of view. Use specific and exciting details to convey the thunder and confusion of the charge.

3. In Act II (page 499) Louka says to Sergius, "I know the difference between the sort of manner you and she put on before one another and the real manner." What is "the real manner"? What is "the higher love"? Answer these questions in a short essay, discussing in your final paragraph the differences between the two kinds of manners.

4. According to Nicola, having "the soul of a servant" is the secret of success as a servant. Do you agree? What exactly does he mean by this? Explain your answers in a short composition, including specific references to the relationship between Nicola and the Petkoffs in the play.

5. Many critics have objected that Shaw's characters are simply "walking ideas," not real people. Is this true of the characters in *Arms and the Man*? Write a short essay on this question, backing up your arguments with examples from the play.

Reading and Writing About Literature

Most great literary works have been the subject of considerable analysis by critics and scholars. Often, the study of literary criticism helps to further understanding of a work by providing the reader with new insights. In addition, it is interesting to a reader to compare his own ideas with those of an authority.

Literary criticism is often a highly personal form of expression. Everyone brings something of his own experience to bear upon a work which he is judging. However, personal opinion alone is not a sound basis for criticism. Sound judgments are reached only after all the evidence supporting a critical idea is carefully weighed.

Below are statements about *Julius Caesar* and *Arms and the Man* by two critics. Each critical quotation is followed by a question which you may answer in a brief essay, either attacking or defending the opinion expressed by the critic. In each case, be sure that you support your conclusions with specific references from the appropriate work.

"The mistakes of Brutus are the mistakes of a man whose nobility muffles his intelligence . . . honesty in him is humorless and edgeless; it rings a little dully in our ears, and even a little smugly . . . it is virtue . . . demonstrating itself for the benefit of others." (Mark Van Doren, quoted by Leonard F. Dean, *Julius Caesar and Modern Criticism.*)

Do you agree with this evaluation of Brutus's personality? Do you feel that his intelligence is overshadowed by his nobility? that he is humorless? smug? Explain.

Arms and the Man is rounded off not by "the disenchantment of Raina and Sergius but [by] the discovery that Bluntschli the realist is . . . an enchanted soul whom nothing will disenchant. He has destroyed their romanticism but is himself 'incurably romantic.' " [Eric Bentley, "The Making of a Dramatist (1892–1903)."]

Is Bluntschli really a romantic, or a realist—or both? Explain.

Julius Caesar and *Arms and the Man* each represent one of the modes of drama: tragedy and comedy. Below, from the introduction to this unit (pages 383–85), is a definition of tragedy.

"Tragedy . . . must have something to do with thought, with decisions made by the hero. A man who makes a series of foolish decisions and gets himself into a position where he is killed doesn't seem tragic. Tragedy seems to require that the hero make legitimate, responsible choices which get him into a position from which there is no escape."

Referring directly to the play, show how one of the chief characters in *Julius Caesar* does or does not fit this description of the tragic hero.

ART AND LITERATURE

Characterization is an important element in literature. Study the paintings on pages 403–08. In an essay, explain which paintings portray the figures most expressively. Another important element is the skill with which an artist sets or depicts a scene. In a brief composition, explain which scenes in the paintings on pages 507–12 seem to you most effectively depicted—and why.

THE KING ARTHUR LEGEND

FROM I. Sir Thomas Malory's *Morte d'Arthur*
 II. Alfred, Lord Tennyson's *Idylls of the King*
 III. T. H. White's *The Once and Future King*

> Vain was the chief's, the sage's pride!
> They had no poet and they died.
> ALEXANDER POPE

IN THESE PAGES you will read about a chief who did not die because he had many poets to tell his tale. In Greek *poet* means *maker*. The many "makers," or creators, who have helped to create the King Arthur legend include ancient historians, poets of several centuries, novelists and playwrights, and many kinds of storytellers, who sang or wrote the tale.

The King Arthur legend is the great legend of the English-speaking people. It began in England in the days before most people could read or write and before what we now call the English language existed in any form. The first "maker" of the legend was probably an old warrior telling his children or grandchildren of a great Welsh chieftain under whom he had fought. It is unlikely that Arthur was ever a real king; historians believe that he was a *dux bellorum* (a war chief) who in the year 517 led his cavalry to victory on Mount Badon, thus ending a series of twelve battles against Saxon invaders. Then the storytelling began, and during the Middle Ages the stories were copied down by scribes, often educated monks, who recorded the tales for future generations. The storytellers might have related that the Saxons later drove Arthur back into Wales and Scotland. The storytellers also might have recalled that Arthur later fell in a battle at Glastonbury in southwestern England and that he was secretly buried by his knights.

In the beginning the Arthur legend was confined mainly to the Celts and the Welsh. But the story gradually grew into legend. A witness told the story; his descendants retold it. From place to place and generation to generation, the story was carried by word of mouth and preserved in the memory. Semiprofessional storytellers—singers, bards, or minstrels, as they were called—mingled their own imaginations with their memories to make the tale satisfy the hopes and dreams of their listeners. The Celts were a defeated people. Arthur had brought them momentary glory. He was not dead, they sang. He would return someday to drive out the Saxons. Hope was fading for the Celts, however, and Arthur's tale seemed destined to die with the dreams of these hardy people.

It was one of the "makers" of the King Arthur legend who may have been responsible for bringing Arthur to the attention of the whole of England. In 817 a monk named Nennius wrote a chronicle that was a mixture of history and legend. In this account Arthur was revealed as a hero of amazing courage who had almost singlehandedly turned back the invaders. Perhaps more than any other, this account put Arthur on his way to everlasting fame and brilliance. During the next three hundred years, chiefly through the skill of the minstrels who entertained in the manor halls of the nobles, the legend began to take shape. The familiar characters appeared: Kay, Gawain, Bedivere, Gareth, Geraint, and Guinevere.

The twelfth-century writer Geoffrey of Monmouth became the first really famous maker of the Arthur legend. Geoffrey was writing a history of British kings. Geoffrey's history was actually not a history at all but an attempt to give to England, now composed of many peoples—Normans, Saxons, Angles, Celts, and others—a beginning which would link them to the ancient civilizations of classical times. In Geoffrey's chronicle, Arthur was made a descendant of Aeneas, the famous hero of the Trojan War. In this account Arthur began to lose some of the rough ways of the Celtic hero. Geoffrey wrote of him as a Norman king, modeled after Charlemagne, the great emperor of ninth-century Europe. Geoffrey was also the first to describe Arthur as a fifteen-year-old boy king and to tell about Arthur's magician-tutor, Merlin. Geoffrey, too, told of Arthur's marriage to Guinevere and of the betrayal of Arthur by the knight Modred. Wace, a Norman who wrote in French, also retold the legend of Arthur, and he based his account on Geoffrey's. Wace added the famous Round Table, "ordained by Arthur that, when his fair fellowship sat to meat, their chairs should be alike, their service equal, and none before or after his fellow."

For the next two centuries, Arthur's story changed and spread. What had been a purely British legend found its way into France, Spain, Germany, and Italy. Courtly romances and knightly adventures added a new cast of characters, among them Lancelot, Tristram, Mark, Isolde, Galahad, Percivale, and many others.

THOMAS MALORY

The King Arthur legend belonged to England, however, and in 1470 one of the most important makers of the legend, Sir Thomas Malory (?–1471), a knight himself, made it forever English. Malory, writing in English, gathered together and retold many of the French romances dealing with Arthur or the knights. He gave these stories an order, connected them all with Arthur, and unified the whole in one work which he called *Morte d'Arthur* (*The Death of Arthur*).

By Malory's time, feudalism and knighthood were dying out. People were flocking to live in the cities; gunpowder was used in warfare; a wealthy merchant class was replacing the knights and nobles as the most influential group in England; and the kings were acquiring more personal power, relying on their knights less and less for support.

Perhaps Malory was like the old warrior, trying to recapture the grandeur of the good old days. Or perhaps Malory was trying to give to the institution of knighthood an order and virtue that it had never achieved. Although the Church and the powerful kings and nobles had set down a code of conduct for knights, many knights disregarded it. Most of them were trained for little else than to fight. Unless they were kept busy, these knights could be a menace. Malory, himself, was a good example of a knight who was a law unto himself. He was sent to prison several times and the list of offenses against him was long. Perhaps, too, Malory, in his "making" of the King Arthur legend, was trying to picture the ideal knight.

In any event, it is chiefly because of Malory that today we think of a knight as one who pledged his loyalty to his lord, his service to God and man, and who always was ready to help people, especially beautiful maidens, in distress. To Malory, the knight was always striving for perfection in appearance, speech, and conduct.

ALFRED, LORD TENNYSON

Since Malory's time, scores of writers have used the Arthurian legends to please readers and to express their own views of what society should be like. The most prominent of these writers is Alfred, Lord Tennyson (1809–1892), the nineteenth-century English poet. Tennyson selected several popular Arthurian tales, changed them to suit his purpose, and retold them as poetry. He called this work the *Idylls of the King*. An idyll is characterized by its rural setting, and in Camelot, Arthur's fabled court and countryside, Tennyson found a peaceful, pastoral background against which a high-minded Arthur and the best of his knights played out a tragic story.

Tennyson, as Malory before him, was living at the end of an era. Scientific progress, particularly in the new theory of evolution, was changing man's view of life. But, for all its progress, Tennyson believed that his age

was lacking in moral stature. Thus Tennyson made his Arthur a great moral leader. Tennyson's Arthur conquers his enemies when he must, but his greatness is not in war but in moral superiority, specifically in the gathering of knights who serve him by bringing order and justice to the world.

T. H. WHITE

In our own time the English writer, T. H. White (1906–1964) has found the Arthur legend a proper setting in which to search for new hope for a world threatened by earth-wracking war. White's own "making" of the Arthur story, told in four short novels, is humorous and human. Though he shows his appreciation for the past, White's viewpoint is modern. His portrayal of Arthur as a boy shows us a boy much like every boy we know. With the help of Merlin, who introduces him to wisdom, White's Arthur grows up to be a wise, judgelike king who gropes for a solution to his world's problems. His great idea is to use the skill and valor of his knights for good—for the high ideal of a peaceful, ordered, and just world. White's four novels about King Arthur were combined in one volume with the title *The Once and Future King.*

Why have writers continued to tell the story of King Arthur? First of all, it is an exciting story. Its conflict is that age-old one of good versus evil. Its hero is a good man. He must win in his struggle against either a ravaging beast, an invader, or an idea that is evil and corrupting. He must win the struggle because good must triumph over evil. Arthur's story is never really completed: it is renewed with each age by the writers of each age, for is not the hope of mankind that good triumph over evil?

There is another reason why the legend lives. For many, Camelot is the capital of a "land of dreams." In our minds, and in the stories that are told, it shines with fairyland splendor: castles with their turrets and spires, winding streets, and lovely gardens. Who wouldn't want to live in Camelot?

We go to the story of King Arthur as we do to all great legends: not for history (it could not matter less whether Arthur ever was real), but to find what kind of dreams men dream; not, as the critic Northrup Frye has said, "to find out what a king *is,* or even what a king *could be,* but what *we would like* a king to be." The legend is, in fact, in this sense, part of our own lives.

We are told that the age of chivalry is dead. If that is so, what it has left behind is "a shining residue, like gold dust in a pan." Over the centuries readers of the Arthur legend have felt their spirits lifted in recalling that loyalty, humility, service, courage, and courtesy are still the goals of men. Mankind may never have achieved the wisp of glory that surrounds King Arthur, but its glow is unforgettable and beckoning.

I. The Storyteller:
Sir Thomas Malory

FROM *Morte d'Arthur,*
as modernized by Keith Baines

ARTHUR BECOMES KING

Uther Pendragon was King of England, but he was constantly at war with his lords. Merlin was his chief advisor and often helped Uther by predicting future events and by using his magic to control the course of battles. On one occasion Uther besieged the castle of the Duke of Cornwall at Tintagel. With Merlin's aid, Uther took the castle, slew the Duke, and soon after married the Duke's beautiful wife, Igraine. Uther was so pleased and so grateful to Merlin for his help that he promised to give him his first-born son to bring up and protect. Thus, when the child Arthur was born, he was delivered to Merlin, who took Arthur to the home of a fine old knight of the realm named Sir Ector. Here Arthur was brought up with Sir Ector's own son, Kay, and here, some years later, our story begins.

KING UTHER fell sick, and his enemies once more overran his kingdom, inflicting heavy losses on him as they advanced. Merlin prophesied that they could be checked only by the presence of the King himself on the battlefield and suggested

From Malory's *Le Morte d'Arthur,* a new rendition by Keith Baines, copyright © 1962 by Keith Baines. Reprinted by permission of The New American Library, Inc., New York.

that he should be conveyed there on a horse litter. King Uther's army met the invader on the plain at St. Albans, and the King duly appeared on the horse litter. Inspired by his presence, and by the lively leadership of Sir Brastius and Sir Jordanus, his army quickly defeated the enemy and the battle finished in a rout. The King returned to London to celebrate the victory.

But his sickness grew worse, and after he had lain speechless for three days and three nights, Merlin summoned the nobles to attend the King in his chamber on the following morning. "By the grace of God," he said, "I hope to make him speak."

In the morning, when all the nobles were assembled, Merlin addressed the King: "Sire, is it your will that Arthur shall succeed to the throne, together with all its prerogatives?"

The King stirred in his bed, and then spoke so that all could hear: "I bestow on Arthur God's blessing and my own, and Arthur shall succeed to the throne on pain of forfeiting my blessing." Then King Uther gave up the ghost. He was buried and mourned the next day, as befitted his rank, by Igraine and the nobility of Britain.

During the years that followed the death of King Uther, while Arthur was still a child, the ambitious barons fought one another for the throne, and the whole of Britain stood in jeopardy. Finally the day came when the Archbishop of Canterbury, on the advice of Merlin, summoned the nobility to London for Christmas morning. In his message the Archbishop promised that the true succession to the British throne would be miraculously revealed. Many of the nobles purified [1] themselves during their journey,

[1] **purified:** The nobles confessed their sins, attended mass, and received Communion.

in the hope that it would be to them that the succession would fall.

The Archbishop held his service in the city's greatest church (St. Paul's), and when matins [1] were done the congregation filed out to the yard. They were confronted by a marble block into which had been thrust a beautiful sword. The block was four feet square, and the sword passed through a steel anvil which had been struck in the stone and which projected a foot from it. The anvil had been inscribed with letters of gold:

WHOSO PULLETH OUTE THIS SWERD OF THIS STONE AND ANVYLD IS RIGHTWYS KYNGE BORNE OF ALL BRYTAYGNE

[1] **matins** (mat′ins): morning church service.

The congregation was awed by this miraculous sight, but the Archbishop forbade anyone to touch the sword before mass had been heard. After mass, many of the nobles tried to pull the sword out of the stone, but none was able to, so a watch of ten knights was set over the sword, and a tournament proclaimed for New Year's Day, to provide men of noble blood with the opportunity of proving their right to the succession.

Sir Ector, who had been living on an estate near London, rode to the tournament with Arthur and his own son Sir Kay, who had been recently knighted. When they arrived at the tournament, Sir Kay found to his annoyance that his sword was missing from its sheath, so he begged Arthur to ride back and fetch it from their lodging.

Arthur found the door of the lodging locked and bolted, the landlord and his wife having left for the tournament. In order not to disappoint his brother, he rode on to St. Paul's, determined to get for him the sword which was lodged in the stone. The yard was empty, the guard also having slipped off to see the tournament, so Arthur strode up to the sword, and, without troubling to read the inscription, tugged it free. He then rode straight back to Sir Kay and presented him with it.

Sir Kay recognized the sword, and taking it to Sir Ector, said, "Father, the succession falls to me, for I have here the sword that was lodged in the stone." But Sir Ector insisted that they should all ride to the churchyard, and once there bound Sir Kay by oath to tell how he had come by the sword. Sir Kay then admitted that Arthur had given it to him. Sir Ector turned to Arthur and said, "Was the sword not guarded?"

"It was not," Arthur replied.

"Would you please thrust it into the stone again?" said Sir Ector. Arthur did

so, and first Sir Ector and then Sir Kay tried to remove it, but both were unable to. Then Arthur, for the second time, pulled it out. Sir Ector and Sir Kay both knelt before him.

"Why," said Arthur, "do you both kneel before me?"

"My lord," Sir Ector replied, "there is only one man living who can draw the sword from the stone, and he is the true-born King of Britain." Sir Ector then told Arthur the story of his birth and up-bringing.

"My dear father," said Arthur, "for so I shall always think of you—if, as you say, I am to be king, please know that any request you have to make is already granted."

Sir Ector asked that Sir Kay should be made Royal Seneschal,[1] and Arthur declared that while they both lived it should be so. Then the three of them visited the Archbishop and told him what had taken place.

All those dukes and barons with ambitions to rule were present at the tournament on New Year's Day. But when all of them had failed, and Arthur alone had succeeded in drawing the sword from the stone, they protested against one so young, and of ignoble [2] blood, succeeding to the throne.

The secret of Arthur's birth was known only to a few of the nobles surviving from the days of King Uther. The Archbishop urged them to make Arthur's cause their own; but their support proved ineffective. The tournament was repeated at Candlemas and at Easter, and with the same outcome as before.

Finally at Pentecost,[3] when once more Arthur alone had been able to remove the sword, the commoners arose with a tumultuous cry and demanded that Arthur should at once be made king. The nobles, knowing in their hearts that the commoners were right, all knelt before Arthur and begged forgiveness for having delayed his succession for so long. Arthur forgave them, and then, offering his sword at the high altar, was dubbed first knight of the realm. The coronation took place a few days later, when Arthur swore to rule justly, and the nobles swore him their allegiance.

FOR STUDY AND DISCUSSION

1. What qualities of Arthur's character are revealed in this brief account? Make a list of these qualities. Do you regard all those you have listed as qualities that a king should have? Explain. What do these qualities suggest about the kind of king Arthur will be in the future?

2. Throughout the King Arthur legends, Sir Kay has a reputation for being disagreeable. How, in this selection, does he help to earn this reputation? What action does Sir Ector take? Do you think that Sir Ector acted wisely? Explain.

MIDDLE ENGLISH

Although we hardly consider Malory a modern writer, his simple and direct style places him closer to modern writers than to many writers who followed him in time. One of the important points about Malory is that he chose to write in the Midland, or Middle English, dialect. For several centuries before Malory's time, English had been a mixture of dialects. The Midland dialect was the spoken language of the people of London and its surroundings. By writing in this dialect, Malory did much to increase the chances of Middle English becoming the basis for modern English.

William Caxton, the first Englishman to use the new printing press, published an edition of Malory's *Morte d'Arthur* in 1485. Here is a

[1] **Seneschal** (sen′ə·shəl): chief administrator of the king's estate.

[2] **ignoble:** not being of noble blood.

[3] **Pentecost:** a Christian festival commemorating the coming of the Holy Spirit to the Apostles.

sample of Malory's prose as Caxton printed it. Even though the spelling is peculiar and inconsistent, and to us the use of *v* for *u* and *f* for *s* may be confusing, it is still possible for us to find in the following passage many parallels with the form of English we use today.

"It befel in the dayes of Vther Pendragon when he was kynge of all Englond/ and fo regned that there was a myzty duke of Cornewaill that helde warre ageynft hym long tyme/ And the duke was called the duke of Tyntagil/ and fo by meanes kynge Vther fend for this duk/"

FOR COMPOSITION

Retell this story of Arthur in your own words. When you have finished, compare your telling with Malory's account. For example, in writing your account, did you decide to emphasize one aspect of the story over the other? Is your account more, or less, detailed than Malory's?

ABOUT THE AUTHOR

Sir Thomas Malory (?–1471) has been the subject of considerable research. For a long time little was known about him, but modern scholars have been able to piece together a number of facts of his life. They have found, for example, that he was a knight who fought in the Hundred Years' War in France and that he was a member of the British Parliament in 1445. The great fact of Malory's life, however, was the series of disastrous civil wars fought from 1455 to 1485 between the supporters of the two great families that claimed the right to rule England: the House of Lancaster and the House of York. We call these civil wars the Wars of the Roses—the emblem of the House of Lancaster was a red rose, and that of the House of York was a white rose.

Malory's own life was caught up in this great conflict. Perhaps because he was a supporter of the party out of power, he spent many of his later years in and out of prison. It was in 1469–70, while he was in prison, and just a year before his death in 1471, that he completed his great work, the *Morte d'Arthur.*

II. The Storyteller: Alfred, Lord Tennyson

Gareth and Lynette,
FROM *Idylls of the King*

CHIVALRY AT ITS HEIGHT

When he was a boy, the nineteenth-century English poet Alfred, Lord Tennyson, read Thomas Malory's tales of Camelot. When he grew older, and in time became England's Poet Laureate, Tennyson never lost interest in the excitement, the romance, and the medieval pageantry that he found in the legend of Arthur. He himself lived at a time when people were concerned about morality, religion, and the fast-developing progress of science and industry, the evils of which many people saw as a threat to long-cherished values. These concerns were close to Tennyson, and when he wrote his twelve *Idylls of the King,* he wrote what he considered a message for his age.

To Tennyson, Arthur is a moral hero, the champion of great spiritual ideals and values, and the Round Table was society in miniature. To have leaders with high ideals and knights who would give their lives to follow those ideals—this, Tennyson felt, was the way in which a society could bring about true progress in morality.

In the *Idylls of the King,* however, Arthur fails because some men and women of his

court reject his ideals. For example, Guinevere says, "He is all fault who hath no fault." Arthur is too perfect to be human. And Tristram, second only to Lancelot, the greatest of Arthur's knights, complains, "The vow that binds too strictly, snaps itself." Finally, Lancelot himself is so weak of will that he destroys those whom he loves and with them the Round Table.

Against a backdrop of towers, which hide their spires in the clouds, and of all the color and pageantry of the tournament, Tennyson tells a human and tragic story, always conscious of its moral implications. The story is that of man from birth to death, and of the cycle in nature from the hopeful beginning of the new year to the doleful ending of the old year. Arthur is born on New Year's night, when man's hope and resolve are highest. In the springtime of his life he marries the beautiful Guinevere. Inspired by Arthur's goodness and justice and by Guinevere's beauty and grace, young and able knights flock to join Arthur's Round Table and vow to live purely, to speak truly, to right wrongs, and to follow Christ and their king. Youthful enthusiasm fills the air. The unfortunate and distressed in the kingdom ask King Arthur for boons or favors, and the knights clamor to undertake quests to assist those in need. It is a time for glorious adventure.

At this time, miles away from Camelot, a young man of noble birth, named Gareth, broods as he longs to join his brothers at the Round Table. Here, then, is the story of Gareth and Lynette, slightly abridged.

The last tall son of Lot and Bellicent,
And tallest, Gareth, in a showerful spring
Stared at the spate.° A slender-shafted pine
Lost footing, fell, and so was whirled away.
"How he went down," said Gareth, "as a false knight 5
Or evil king before my lance, if lance
Were mine to use—O senseless cataract,
Bearing all down in thy precipitancy—
And yet thou art but swollen with cold snows
And mine is living blood: thou dost His will, 10
The Maker's, and not knowest, and I that know,
Have strength and wit, in my good mother's hall
Linger with vacillating obedience,
Prisoned, and kept and coaxed and whistled to—
Since the good mother holds me still a child! 15
Good mother is bad mother unto me!
A worse were better; yet no worse would I.
Heaven yield° her for it, but in me put force
To weary her ears with one continuous prayer,
Until she let me fly discaged to sweep 20
In ever-highering eagle-circles up
To the great Sun of Glory;° and thence swoop
Down upon all things base, and dash them dead,
A knight of Arthur, working out his will,
To cleanse the world. Why, Gawain, when he came 25
With Modred hither in the summertime,

3. **spate:** a stream in flood. 18. **yield:** reward. 22. **Sun of Glory:** King Arthur.

Asked me to tilt° with him, the proven knight.
Modred for want of worthier was the judge.
Then I so shook him in the saddle, he said,
'Thou hast half prevailed against me,' said so—he— 30
Though Modred biting his thin lips was mute,
For he is always sullen—what care I?"

And Gareth went, and hovering round her chair
Asked, "Mother, though ye count me still the child,
Sweet mother, do ye love the child?" She laughed, 35
"Thou art but a wild goose to question it."
"Then, mother, an° ye love the child," he said,
"Being a goose and rather tame than wild,
Hear the child's story." "Yea, my well beloved,
An 'twere but of the goose and golden eggs." 40

And Gareth answered her with kindling eyes:
"Nay, nay, good mother, but this egg of mine
Was finer gold than any goose can lay;
For this an eagle, a royal eagle, laid
Almost beyond eye reach, on such a palm 45
As glitters gilded in thy Book of Hours.°
And there was ever haunting round the palm
A lusty youth, but poor, who often saw
The splendor sparkling from aloft, and thought,
'An I could climb and lay my hand upon it, 50
Then were I wealthier than a leash of° kings.'
But ever when he reached a hand to climb,
One that had loved him from his childhood caught
And stayed him, 'Climb not lest thou break thy neck,
I charge thee by my love,' and so the boy, 55
Sweet mother, neither clomb° nor brake his neck,
But brake his very heart in pining for it,
And passed away."

Then Bellicent bemoaned herself and said:
"Hast thou no pity upon my loneliness? 60
Lo, where thy father Lot° beside the hearth
Lies like a log, and all but smoldered out!
For ever since when traitor to the King
He fought against him in the barons' war,

27. **tilt:** fight; a mock battle on horseback. 37. **an:** if. 46. **Book of Hours:** a book containing prayers to be said at specified times during the day. 51. **a leash of:** three. 56. **clomb:** climbed. Tennyson uses archaic or obsolete words either for the effect they will have on the reader or to preserve a certain rhythm in his line of poetry. 61. **Lot:** One of the kings Arthur had defeated.

And Arthur gave him back his territory, 65
His age hath slowly dropped, and now lies there
A yet-warm corpse, and yet unburiable,
No more; nor sees, nor hears, nor speaks, nor knows.
And both thy brethren are in Arthur's hall,
Albeit° neither loved with that full love 70
I feel for thee, nor worthy such a love.
Stay therefore thou; red berries charm the bird,
And thee, mine innocent, the jousts, the wars,
Who never knewest finger ache, nor pang
Of wrenched or broken limb—an often chance 75
In those brain-stunning shocks, and tourney falls,
Frights to my heart. But stay; follow the deer
By these tall firs and our fast-falling burns;°
So make thy manhood mightier day by day.
Sweet is the chase; and I will seek thee out 80
Some comfortable bride and fair, to grace
Thy climbing life, and cherish my prone° year,
Till falling into Lot's forgetfulness
I know not thee, myself, nor anything.
Stay, my best son! ye are yet more boy than man." 85

Then Gareth: "Ye hold me yet for child.
How can ye keep me tethered to you?—Shame.
Man am I grown, a man's work must I do.
Follow the deer? follow the Christ, the King,
Live pure, speak true, right wrong, follow the King—° 90
Else, wherefore born?"

So when the Queen, who long had sought in vain
To break him from the intent to which he grew,
Found her son's will unwaveringly one,
She answered craftily: "Will ye walk through fire? 95
Who walks through fire will hardly heed the smoke.
Ay, go then, an ye must; only one proof,
Before thou ask the King to make thee knight,
Of thine obedience and thy love to me,
Thy mother, I demand."

 And Gareth cried: 100
"A hard one, or a hundred, so I go.
Nay—quick! the proof to prove me to the quick!"°

70. **Albeit:** although. 78. **burns:** brooks. 82. **prone:** declining. 90. **Live . . . King:** the oaths made by Arthur's knights. 102. **the quick:** the living. Gareth means "Try me to the utmost." Tennyson plays on words since he also used *quick* to mean *quickly*.

But slowly spake the mother looking at him:
"Prince, thou shalt go disguised to Arthur's hall,
And hire thyself to serve for meats, and drinks 105
Among the scullions° and the kitchen knaves,°
And those that hand the dish across the bar.
Nor shalt thou tell thy name to any one.
And thou shalt serve a twelvemonth and a day."

For so the Queen believed that when her son 110
Beheld his only way to glory lead
Low down thro' villain kitchen vassalage,°
Her own true Gareth was too princely proud
To pass thereby; so should he rest with her,
Closed in her castle from the sound of arms. 115

Silent awhile was Gareth, then replied:
"The thrall° in person may be free in soul,
And I shall see the jousts. Thy son am I,
And, since thou art my mother, must obey.
I therefore yield me freely to thy will; 120
For hence will I, disguised, and hire myself
To serve with scullions and with kitchen knaves;
Nor tell my name to any—no, not the King."

Gareth awhile lingered. The mother's eye
Full of the wistful fear that he would go, 125
And turning toward him wheresoe'er he turned,
Perplexed his outward purpose, till an hour
When, wakened by the wind which with full voice
Swept bellowing through the darkness on to dawn,
He rose, and out of slumber calling two 130
That still° had tended on him from his birth,
Before the wakeful mother heard him, went.

106. **scullions:** those who clean cooking utensils. **kitchen knaves:** kitchen boys. Knave originally meant boy. 112. **villain . . . vassalage:** lowborn kitchen service. 117. **thrall:** slave.
131. **still:** always.

(CONTINUED ON PAGE 553)

EUROPEAN PAINTING

The Turn of the Century

Many painters of the late nineteenth century were at one time or another fascinated with Impressionism, but very few continued to work strictly within this tradition. For example, Paul Cézanne, a regular member of the Impressionist group, suddenly left Paris in 1877 to return to his native countryside in southern France. Here, for the next eighteen years, he worked mostly by himself, attempting to make something "solid and durable" of Impressionism. He wanted to retain a feeling of light and air and at the same time give the objects he painted an appearance of weight and density. Few painters have made even mountains appear any more solid than the three seated figures in Cézanne's picture, *The Card Players* (PLATE 1). Yet his lively brushwork throughout this painting brings these sturdy, massive forms very much to life. If you look closely at the back wall, for instance, you will discover not merely a plain surface, but a gentle pattern of many lightly colored brushstrokes, which offsets the heaviness of the figures.

Another artist who became interested in Impressionism after coming to Paris was the Dutch painter Vincent van Gogh. But he too left the city to settle in the small provincial town of Arles in southern France. There he finally discovered that he was less interested in recording the shimmering effects of sunlight than in expressing the intensity of his own inner emotions. He began to thicken his outlines and to combine large areas of bright colors in highly simplified, bold patterns. A good example is his portrait of a woman of Arles, called *L'Arlésienne* (PLATE 2). Even so quiet a subject as this one seems charged with potential energy because of the way Van Gogh has painted it.

While Van Gogh was working on his portrait, *L'Arlésienne,* he had a visitor from Paris named Paul Gauguin, a former stockbroker who had given up his business connections to devote all his time to painting. Gauguin had come down to Arles to see if it really could be as charming a place for artists as Van Gogh had maintained in his letters. But Gauguin did not stay very long. What he really wanted was a tropical paradise completely

away from "overcivilized" Europe. A few years later he left France for the South Sea island of Tahiti, where, except for one short trip back home, he remained for the rest of his life. Profoundly moved by the customs and beliefs of the primitive Tahitian people, he tried to express his feelings about them through exotic combinations of colors—such as the pinks, lavenders, tans, blues, greens, and orange-reds in *La Siesta* (PLATE 3). Notice how mysteriously Gauguin seems to hide the feelings of the five women in the picture by not giving us a close look at their faces, especially of the figure in the foreground, who turns her back to us.

One of the younger painters who came to Paris in the early 1880's was a tiny dwarf of a man named Henri de Toulouse-Lautrec. This artist never considered moving to the country or to the tropics, for he became passionately interested in the night life of this gay, metropolitan city. Like Degas, Lautrec tried to capture those fleeting moments when people are so preoccupied with their own thoughts and actions that they seem quite unaware of being observed. Such a moment is revealed in *Au Moulin Rouge* (PLATE 4), his famous painting of a crowded night club. What seems to electrify this whole scene is the lurid face of the woman in the right foreground, which suddenly projects out toward us, meeting our gaze for a split second as she glances across the room.

To gain dramatic emphasis, only certain details in the last three paintings were modeled in light and shadow. Most of the shapes were painted in broad, flat colors, with thick outlines, and many of these colors were greatly intensified to produce a strong emotional impact. One of the younger artists in Paris during the late 1880's who followed this trend away from Impressionism toward a kind of emotional "expressionism" was a Norwegian painter named Edvard Munch. In *The Bridge* (PLATE 5) Munch has created a rather disturbing effect by placing the figures of four young girls in a strange and forbidding landscape. The fence and roadway seem to hurtle past them, while from along the far shore dark massive blocks of houses and trees seem to weigh down upon them oppressively. The one girl who turns in our direction has a completely blank face. In fact, the only human features in this eerie picture are those suggested by the door and windows of a house in the middle distance. Notice Munch's chilling combination of colors, especially the yellow, lavender, and green in the upper left corner.

We find a very different kind of "expressionism" in Georges Rouault's imaginary portrait, *The Old King* (PLATE 6). Here the colors are rich and warm, and the figure fills the picture space. The paint is laid on in thick slab-like strokes with a palette knife, creating an effect somewhat like that of a stained glass window in a church or of an old crusty surface deeply imbedded with jewels. Yet it is really a tragic image we see here—a lonely, troubled old monarch who pathetically clutches a tiny flower in his huge, crude hand.

PLATE 1. PAUL CEZANNE (French, 1839–1906): *The Card Players*. About 1892. Oil on canvas. 25½ x 32 inches. (The Metropolitan Museum of Art, New York, Bequest of Stephen C. Clark, 1960)

PLATE 2. VINCENT VAN GOGH (Dutch, 1853–1890): *L'Arlésienne*. 1888. Oil on canvas, 36 x 29 inches. (The Metropolitan Museum of Art, New York, Bequest of Samuel A. Lewisohn, 1951)

548

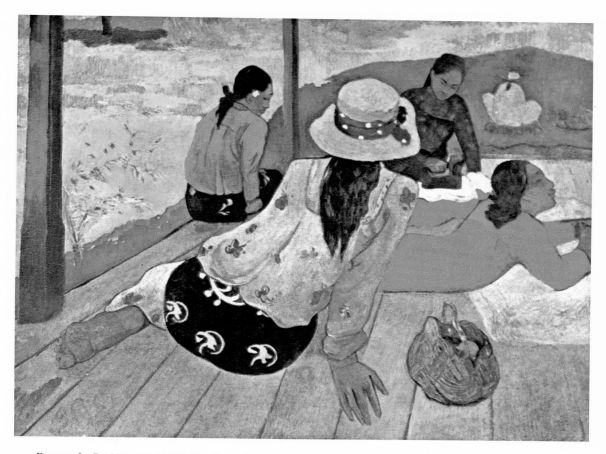

Plate 3. PAUL GAUGUIN (French, 1848–1903): *La Siesta.* 1894. Oil on canvas. 35 x 45¾ inches. (Collection of Mrs. Enid A. Haupt)

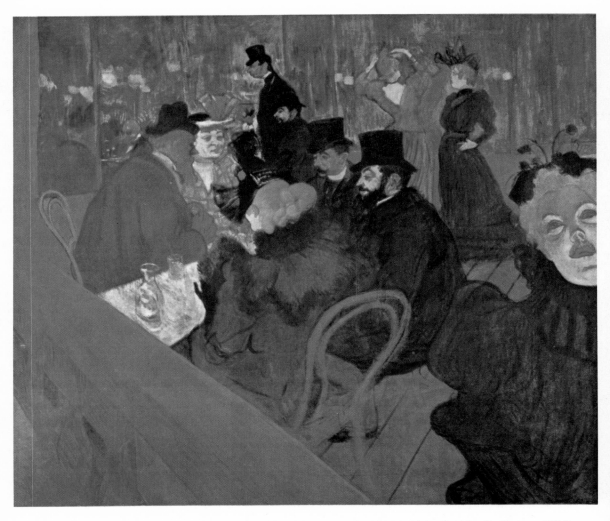

PLATE 4. HENRI DE TOULOUSE–LAUTREC (French, 1864–1901): *Au Moulin Rouge*. 1892. Oil on canvas, $48\frac{3}{8}$ x $55\frac{1}{4}$ inches. (Courtesy of The Art Institute of Chicago)

PLATE 5. EDVARD MUNCH (Norwegian, 1863–1944): *The Bridge*. 1905. Oil on canvas,
$\frac{1}{4}$ x $21\frac{1}{4}$ inches. (Wallraf-Richartz Museum, Cologne)

PLATE 6. GEORGES ROUALT (French, 1871–1958): *The Old King*. 1916, reworked 1938. Oil on canvas, $30\frac{1}{4}$ x $21\frac{1}{4}$ inches. (Collection of Museum of Art, Carnegie Institute, Pittsburgh)

The three were clad like tillers of the soil.
Southward they set their faces. The birds made
Melody on branch and melody in midair. 135
The damp hill slopes were quickened into green,
And the live green had kindled into flowers,
For it was past the time of Easter day.

So, when their feet were planted on the plain
That broadened toward the base of Camelot, 140
Far off they saw the silver-misty morn
Rolling her smoke about the royal mount,
That rose between the forest and the field.
At times the summit of the high city flashed;
At times the spires and turrets halfway down 145
Pricked through the mist; at times the great gate shone
Only, that opened on the field below;
Anon,° the whole fair city had disappeared,

Then those who went with Gareth were amazed,
One crying, "Let us go no further, lord; 150
Here is a city of enchanters, built
By fairy kings." The second echoed him,
"Lord, we have heard from our wise man at home
To northward, that this king is not the King,
But only changeling° out of Fairyland, 155
Who drave the heathen hence by sorcery
And Merlin's glamour,"° Then the first again,
"Lord, there is no such city anywhere,
But all a vision."

 Gareth answered them
With laughter, swearing he had glamour enow 160
In his own blood, his princedom, youth, and hopes,
To plunge old Merlin in the Arabian sea;°
So pushed them all unwilling toward the gate.°
He spake and laughed, then entered with his twain

148. **Anon:** at another time. 155. **changeling:** a child who is secretly exchanged for another child. In Arthur's case, fairies supposedly made the exchange. 157. **glamour:** magic. Merlin was the magician at the court. 162. **in . . . sea:** A reference perhaps to the old belief that it was possible to destroy the sorceries of a magician by plunging him into the waters of certain seas. 163. **gate:** This gate was symbolical of Arthur's ideal of Christian life. The Lady of the Lake, represented by a statue on the keystone (piece at the top center) of the arch, symbolized religion, from which poured, like drops of water, the blessings of life. The sword was a symbol of divine justice; the censer (a vessel in which incense is burned) represented worship. On her breast was a fish, the ancient symbol of Christianity (derived from the initial letters of the Greek phrase, *Jesus Christ, Son of God, Savior,* which spell the Greek word for fish). For the symbolism of the three queens, Tennyson turned to Christian sources and selected Faith, Hope, and Charity.

Camelot, a city of shadowy palaces 165
And stately, rich in emblem and the work
Of ancient kings who did their days in stone;°
Which Merlin's hand,° the Mage at Arthur's court,
Knowing all arts, had touched, and everywhere,
At Arthur's ordinance, tipped with lessening peak 170
And pinnacle, and had made it spire to heaven.
And ever and anon a knight would pass
Outward, or inward to the hall; his arms
Clashed, and the sound was good to Gareth's ear.
And out of bower and casement shyly glanced 175
Eyes of pure women, wholesome stars of love;°
And all about a healthful people stepped
As in the presence of a gracious king.

Then into hall Gareth ascending heard
A voice, the voice of Arthur, and beheld 180
Far over heads in that long-vaulted hall
The splendor of the presence of the King
Throned, and delivering doom—and looked no more—
But felt his young heart hammering in his ears,
And thought, "For this half shadow of a lie 185
The truthful King will doom me when I speak."
Yet pressing on, though all in fear to find
Sir Gawain or Sir Modred, saw nor one
Nor other, but in all the listening eyes
Of those tall knights that ranged about the throne 190
Clear honor shining like the dewy star
Of dawn, and faith in their great King, with pure
Affection, and the light of victory,
And glory gained, and evermore to gain.

Then came a widow crying to the King: 195
"A boon, Sir King! Thy father, Uther, reft
From my dead lord a field with violence;
For howsoe'er at first he proffered gold,
Yet, for the field was pleasant in our eyes,
We yielded not; and then he reft us of it. 200
Perforce and left us neither gold nor field."

167. **who . . . stone:** Kings represented in statues the events of their reigns. 168. **Which . . . hand:** The palace at Camelot supposedly was built by Merlin. 175–76. **bower . . . love:** Tennyson calls attention to the wholesome and happy life at Camelot before it was destroyed by Guinevere and Lancelot.

Said Arthur, "Whether° would ye? gold or field?"
To whom the woman weeping, "Nay, my lord,
The field was pleasant in my husband's eye."

And Arthur: "Have thy pleasant field again, 205
And thrice the gold for Uther's use thereof,
According to the years. No boon is here,
But justice, so thy say be proven true.
Accursed, who from the wrongs his father did
Would shape himself a right!" 210
And many another suppliant crying came
With noise° of ravage wrought by beast and man,
And evermore° a knight would ride away.

Last, Gareth leaning both hands heavily
Down on the shoulders of the twain, his men, 215
Approached between them toward the King, and asked,
"A boon, Sir King"—his voice was all ashamed—
"For see ye not how weak and hunger-worn
I seem—leaning on these? grant me to serve
For meat and drink among thy kitchen knaves 220
A twelvemonth and a day, nor seek my name.
Hereafter I will fight."

202. **Whether:** which. 212. **noise:** report. 213. **evermore:** each time.

ALFRED, LORD TENNYSON 555

To him the King:
"A goodly youth and worth a goodlier boon!
But so thou wilt no goodlier, then must Kay,
The master of the meats and drinks, be thine." 225

He rose and passed; then Kay, a man of mien
Wan-sallow as the plant that feels itself
Root-bitten by white lichen:

 "Lo ye now!
This fellow hath broken from some abbey where,
God wot,° he had not beef and brewis° enow, 230
However that might chance! but an he work,
Like any pigeon will I cram his crop,
And sleeker shall he shine than any hog."

Then Lancelot standing near: "Sir Seneschal,
Sleuth-hound° thou knowest, and gray, and all the hounds; 235
A horse thou knowest, a man thou dost not know.
Broad brows and fair, a fluent hair and fine,
High nose, a nostril large and fine, and hands
Large, fair, and fine!—Some young lad's mystery—
But, or° from sheepcot or king's hall, the boy 240
Is noble-natured. Treat him with all grace,
Lest he should come to shame thy judging of him."

Then Kay: "What murmurest thou of mystery?
Think ye this fellow will poison the King's dish?
Nay, for he spake too fool-like; mystery! 245
Tut, an the lad were noble, he had asked
For horse and armor; fair and fine; forsooth!
Sir Fine-face, Sir Fair-hands? but see thou to it
That thine own fineness, Lancelot, some fine day
Undo thee not—and leave my man to me." 250

So Gareth all for glory underwent
The sooty yoke of kitchen vassalage,
Ate with young lads his portion by the door,
And couched at night with grimy kitchen knaves.
And Lancelot ever spake him pleasantly, 255
But Kay the seneschal, who loved him not,
Would hustle and harry him, and labor him
Beyond his comrade of the hearth, and set
To turn the broach,° draw water, or hew wood,

230. **wot:** knows. **brewis:** broth. 235. **sleuth-hound:** bloodhound. 240. **or:** whether.
259. **broach:** spit for cooking meat over a fire.

Or grosser tasks; and Gareth bowed himself 260
With all obedience to the King, and wrought
All kind of service with a noble ease
That graced the lowliest act in doing it.

So for a month he wrought among the thralls;
But in the weeks that followed, the good Queen,° 265
Repentant of the word she made him swear,
And saddening in her childless castle, sent,
Between the increscent and decrescent moon,
Arms for her son, and loosed him from his vow.

This, Gareth hearing from a squire of Lot 270
With whom he used to play at tourney once,
When both were children, and in lonely haunts
Would scratch a ragged oval° on the sand,
And each at either dash from either end—
Shame never made girl redder than Gareth joy. 275
He laughed; he sprang. "Out of the smoke, at once
I leap from Satan's foot to Peter's knee—°
These news be mine, none other's—nay, the King's—
Descend into the city"; whereon he sought
The King alone, and found, and told him all. 280

"I have staggered thy strong Gawain in a tilt
For pastime; yea, he said it; joust can I.
Make me thy knight—in secret! let my name
Be hidden, and give me the first quest; I spring
Like flame from ashes."

265. **Queen:** Bellicent, Gareth's mother. 273. **oval:** the shape of the field where the lists
were held. 277. **Peter's knee:** a figurative expression. Gareth has gone from kitchen knave
(Hell) under Kay (Satan) to heaven's gates guarded by St. Peter (the Round Table under Ar-
thur).

Here the King's calm eye
Fell on, and checked, and made him flush, and bow
Lowly, to kiss his hand, who answered him:
"Son, the good mother let me know thee here,
And sent her wish that I would yield thee thine.
Make thee my knight? my knights are sworn to vows 290
Of utter hardihood, utter gentleness,
And, loving, utter faithfulness in love,
And uttermost obedience to the King."

Then Gareth, lightly springing from his knees:
"My King, for hardihood I can promise thee. 295
For uttermost obedience make demand
Of whom ye gave me to, the Seneschal,
No mellow master of the meats and drinks!
And as for love, God wot, I love not yet,
But love I shall, God willing."

 And the King: 300
"Make thee my knight in secret? yea, but he,
Our noblest brother, and our truest man,
And one with me in all, he needs must know."

"Let Lancelot know, my King, let Lancelot know,
Thy noblest and thy truest!"

 And the King: 305
"But wherefore would ye men should wonder at you?
Nay, rather for the sake of me, their King,
And the deed's sake my knighthood do the deed,
Than to be noised of."

 Merrily Gareth asked:
"Have I not earned my cake in baking of it? 310
Let be my name until I make my name!
My deeds will speak; it is but for a day."
So with a kindly hand on Gareth's arm
Smiled the great King, and half-unwillingly
Loving his lusty youthhood yielded to him. 315
Then, after summoning Lancelot privily:
"I have given him the first quest; he is not proven.
Look therefore, when he calls for this in hall,
Thou get to horse and follow him far away.
Cover the lions° on thy shield, and see, 320
Far as thou mayest, he be nor ta'en nor slain."

320. **lions:** Lancelot's coat of arms was azure lions crowned with gold.

Then that same day there passed into the hall
A damsel of high lineage and a brow
May-blossom, and a cheek of apple blossom,
Hawk eyes; and lightly was her slender nose 325
Tip-tilted like the petal of a flower.
She into hall passed with her page and cried:

"O King, for thou hast driven the foe without,
See to the foe within! bridge, ford, beset
By bandits, everyone that owns a tower 330
The lord for half a league.° Why sit ye there?
Rest would I not, Sir King, an I were king,
Till even the lonest hold° were all as free
From cursed bloodshed as thine altar cloth
From that best blood° it is a sin to spill." 335

"Comfort thyself," said Arthur, "I nor mine
Rest; so my knighthood keep the vows they swore,
The wastest moorland of our realm shall be
Safe, damsel, as the center of this hall.
What is thy name? thy need?"

 "My name?" she said— 340
"Lynette, my name; noble; my need, a knight
To combat for my sister, Lyonors,
A lady of high lineage, of great lands,
And comely, yea, and comelier than myself.
She lives in Castle Perilous. A river 345
Runs in three loops about her living place;
And o'er it are three passings, and three knights
Defend the passings, brethren, and a fourth,
And of that four the mightiest, holds her stayed°
In her own castle, and so besieges her 350
To break her will, and make her wed with him;
And but delays his purport° till thou send
To do the battle with him thy chief man
Sir Lancelot, whom he trusts to overthrow,
Then wed, with glory; but she will not wed 355
Save whom she loveth, or a holy life.°
Now therefore have I come for Lancelot."

331. **half a league:** Petty lords owned towers and ruled over a range of territory of about a
mile and a half. 333. **lonest hold:** loneliest stronghold or castle. 335. **best blood:** sacramental
wine. 349. **stayed:** captive. 352. **purport:** purpose. 356. **holy life:** She will become a nun
instead of marrying.

Then Arthur mindful of Sir Gareth asked:
"Damsel, ye know this Order° lives to crush
All wrongers of the realm. But say, these four, 360
Who be they? What the fashion of the men?"

"They be of foolish fashion, O Sir King,
The fashion of that old knight-errantry°
Who ride abroad, and do but what they will;
Courteous or bestial from the moment,° such 365
As have nor law nor king; and three of these
Proud in their fantasy° call themselves the Day,
Morning Star, and Noon Sun, and Evening Star,°
Being strong fools; and never a whit more wise
The fourth, who always rideth armed in black, 370
A huge man-beast of boundless savagery.
He names himself the Night and oftener Death,
And wears a helmet mounted with a skull,
And bears a skeleton figured on his arms,
To show that who may slay or scape° the three, 375
Slain by himself, shall enter endless night.
And all these four be fools, but mighty men,
And therefore am I come for Lancelot."

Hereat Sir Gareth called from where he rose,
A head with kindling eyes above the throng, 380
"A boon, Sir King—this quest!" then—for he marked
Kay near him groaning like a wounded bull—
"Yea, King, thou knowest thy kitchen knave am I,
And mighty through thy meats and drinks am I,
And I can topple over a hundred such. 385
Thy promise, King," and Arthur glancing at him,
Brought down a momentary brow.° "Rough, sudden,
And pardonable, worthy to be knight—
Go therefore," and all hearers were amazed.

But on the damsel's forehead shame, pride, wrath 390
Slew the may-white;° she lifted either arm,
"Fie on thee, King! I asked for thy chief knight,
And thou hast given me but a kitchen knave."
Then ere a man in hall could stay her, turned,

359. **Order:** the Round Table. 363. **old knight-errantry:** Before the founding of the Round Table, knights roamed the country without high purpose or the restraint of law. 365. **from the moment:** on the impulse of the moment. 367. **fantasy:** whim. 367–68. **Day ...Evening Star:** The three knights mentioned call themselves Day. 375. **scape:** elude or escape. 387. **Brought...brow:** frowned. 391. **Slew...may-white:** made her blush with anger.

Fled down the lane of access to the King, 395
Took horse, descended the slope street, and passed
The weird white gate, and paused without, beside
The field of tourney, murmuring "kitchen knave!"

Now two great entries opened from the hall,
At one end one that gave upon a range 400
Of level pavement where the King would pace
At sunrise, gazing over plain and wood;
And down from this a lordly stairway sloped
Till lost in blowing trees and tops of towers;
And out by this main doorway passed the King. 405
But one was counter° to the hearth, and rose
High that the highest-crested helm could ride
Therethrough nor graze; and by this entry fled
The damsel in her wrath, and on to this
Sir Gareth strode, and saw without the door 410
King Arthur's gift, the worth of half a town,
A war horse of the best, and near it stood
The two that out of north had followed him.
This bare a maiden shield, a casque; that held
The horse, the spear;° whereat Sir Gareth loosed 415
A cloak that dropped from collarbone to heel,
A cloth of roughest web,° and cast it down,

406. **one ... counter:** one entrance was opposite. 414–15. **This ... spear:** One servant
held a shield unmarked by a coat of arms, or other distinguishing device, and a helmet (casque).
The other servant held the horse and a spear. 417. **cloth ... web:** his knave's coat.

And from it, like a fuel-smothered fire
That looked half-dead, brake bright, and flashed as those
Dull-coated things, that making slide apart 420
Their dusk wing-cases, all beneath there burns
A jeweled harness, ere they pass and fly.
So Gareth ere he parted flashed in arms.°
Then as he donned the helm, and took the shield
And mounted horse and grasped a spear, of grain 425
Storm-strengthened on a windy site, and tipped
With trenchant steel, around him slowly pressed
The people, while from out of kitchen came
The thralls in throng, and seeing who had worked
Lustier than any, and whom they could but love, 430
Mounted in arms, threw up their caps and cried,
"God bless the King, and all his fellowship!"
And on thro' lanes of shouting Gareth rode
Down the slope street, and passed without the gate.

But by the field of tourney lingering yet 435
Muttered the damsel: "Wherefore did the King
Scorn me? for, were Sir Lancelot lacked, at least
He might have yielded to me one of those
Who tilt for lady's love and glory here,
Rather than—O sweet heaven! O fie upon him!— 440
His kitchen knave."

 To whom Sir Gareth drew—
And there were none but few goodlier than he—
Shining in arms, "Damsel, the quest is mine.
Lead, and I follow." She thereat, as one
That smells a foul-fleshed agaric in the holt,° 445
And deems it carrion° of some woodland thing,
Or shrew, or weasel, nipped her slender nose
With petulant thumb and finger, shrilling, "Hence!
Avoid,° thou smellest all of kitchen grease."
And look who comes behind"; for there was Kay. 450
"Knowest thou not me? thy master? I am Kay.
We lack thee by the hearth."

 And Gareth to him,
"Master no more! too well I know thee, ay—
The most ungentle knight in Arthur's hall."
"Have at thee then," said Kay; they shocked, and Kay 455

 423. **arms:** a full suit of glistening armor. 445. **foul-fleshed . . . holt:** a foul-smelling fungus
in the wood. 446. **carrion:** decaying flesh. 449. **Avoid:** Go away.

Fell shoulder-slipped,° and Gareth cried again,
"Lead, and I follow," and fast away she fled.

But after sod and shingle ceased to fly
Behind her, and the heart of her good horse
Was nigh to burst with violence of the beat, 460
Perforce she stayed, and overtaken spoke:

"What doest thou, scullion, in my fellowship?
Deem'st thou that I accept thee aught the more
Or love thee better, that by some device
Full cowardly, or by mere unhappiness, 465
Thou hast overthrown and slain thy master—thou!—
Dishwasher and broach-turner, loon!—to me
Thou smellest all of kitchen as before."

"Damsel," Sir Gareth answered gently, "say
Whate'er ye will, but whatsoe'er ye say, 470
I leave not till I finish this fair quest,
Or die therefore."

 "Ay, wilt thou finish it?
Sweet lord, how like a noble knight he talks
The listening rogue hath caught the manner of it.
But, knave, anon thou shalt be met with, knave, 475
And then by such a one that thou for all
The kitchen brewis that was ever supped
Shalt not once dare to look him in the face."

"I shall assay," said Gareth with a smile
That maddened her, and away she flashed again 480
Down the long avenues of a boundless wood.

456. **shoulder-slipped:** his shoulder thrown out of joint.

Then to the shore of one of those long loops
Wherethrough the serpent river coiled, they came.
Rough-thicketed were the banks and steep; the stream
Full, narrow; this a bridge of single arc 485
Took at a leap; and on the further side
Arose a silk pavilion, gay with gold
In streaks and rays, and all Lent-lily° in hue,
Save that the dome was purple, and above,
Crimson, a slender banneret fluttering. 490
And therebefore the lawless warrior paced
Unarmed, and calling, "Damsel, is this he,
The champion thou hast brought from Arthur's hall,
For whom we let thee pass?" "Nay, nay," she said,
"Sir Morning Star. The King in utter scorn 495
Of thee and thy much folly hath sent thee here
His kitchen knave; and look thou to thyself.
See that he fall not on thee suddenly,
And slay thee unarmed; he is not knight but knave."

Then at his call, "O daughters of the Dawn, 500
And servants of the Morning Star, approach,
Arm me," from out the silken curtain folds
Barefooted and bareheaded three fair girls
In gilt and rosy raiment came. Their feet
In dewy grasses glistened; and the hair 505
All over glanced with dewdrop or with gem
Like sparkles in the stone Avanturine.°
These armed him in blue arms, and gave a shield
Blue also, and thereon the morning star.
And Gareth silent gazed upon the knight, 510
Who stood a moment, ere his horse was brought,
Glorying; and in the stream beneath him shone,
Immingled with Heaven's azure waveringly,
The gay pavilion and the naked feet,
His arms, the rosy raiment, and the star. 515

Then she that watched him: "Wherefore stare ye so?
Thou shakest in thy fear. There yet is time;
Flee down the valley before he get to horse.
Who will cry shame? Thou art not knight but knave."

Said Gareth: "Damsel, whether knave or knight, 520
Far liefer had I fight a score of times

488. **Lent-lily:** the daffodil, which blooms in Lent. 507. **Avanturine** (a·ven′tyoͦor·ēn): a
kind of glass or quartz which is interspersed with scales of mica (fool's gold) or copper.

Than hear thee so missay me and revile.
Fair words were best for him who fights for thee;
But truly foul are better, for they send
That strength of anger through mine arms, I know 525
That I shall overthrow him."

 And he that bore
The star, when mounted, cried from o'er the bridge:
"A kitchen knave, and sent in scorn of me!
Such fight not I, but answer scorn with scorn.
For this were shame to do him further wrong 530
Than set him on his feet, and take his horse
And arms, and so return him to the King.
Come, therefore, leave thy lady lightly,° knave.
Avoid;° for it beseemeth not a knave
To ride with such a lady."

 "Dog, thou liest! 535
I spring from loftier lineage than thine own."
He spake; and all at fiery speed the two
Shocked on the central bridge,° and either spear
Bent but not brake, and either knight at once,
Hurled as a stone from out of a catapult 540
Beyond his horse's crupper° and the bridge,
Fell, as if dead; but quickly rose and drew,
And Gareth lashed so fiercely with his brand
He drave his enemy backward down the bridge,
The damsel crying, "Well stricken, kitchen knave!" 545
Till Gareth's shield was cloven; but one stroke
Laid him that clove it groveling on the ground.

Then cried the fallen, "Take not my life; I yield."
And Gareth, "So this damsel ask it of me
Good—I accord it easily as a grace." 550
She reddening, "Insolent scullion! I of thee?
I bound to thee for any favor asked!"
"Then shall he die." And Gareth there unlaced
His helmet as to slay him, but she shrieked,
"Be not so hardy, scullion, as to slay 555
One nobler than thyself." "Damsel, thy charge
Is an abounding pleasure to me. Knight,
Thy life is thine at her command. Arise
And quickly pass to Arthur's hall, and say

533. **lightly:** quickly. 534. **Avoid:** begone. 538. **central bridge:** the center of the bridge.
541. **crupper:** hind quarters.

His kitchen knave hath sent thee. See thou crave 560
His pardon for thy breaking of his laws.
Myself when I return will plead for thee.
Thy shield is mine°—farewell; and, damsel, thou,
Lead, and I follow."

 And fast away she fled;
Then when he came upon her, spake: "Methought, 565
Knave, when I watched thee striking on the bridge,
The savor of thy kitchen came upon me
A little faintlier; but the wind hath changed;
I scent it twentyfold." And then she sang,
"'O morning star'—not that tall felon there 570
Whom thou, by sorcery or unhappiness
Or some device, hast foully overthrown—
'O morning star that smilest in the blue,
O star, my morning dream hath proven true,
Smile sweetly, thou! my love hath smiled on me.' 575
But thou begone, take counsel, and away,
For hard by here is one that guards a ford—
The second brother in their fool's parable—°
Will pay thee all thy wages, and to boot."
So when they touched the second river loop, 580
Huge on a huge red horse, and all in mail
Burnished to blinding,° shone the Noonday Sun
Beyond a raging shallow. As if the flower°
That blows a globe of after arrowlets
Ten thousand fold had grown, flashed the fierce shield, 585
All sun; and Gareth's eyes had flying blots
Before them when he turned from watching him.
He from beyond the roaring shallow roared,
"What doest thou, brother,° in my marches° here?"
And she athwart the shallow shrilled again, 590
"Here is a kitchen knave from Arthur's hall
Hath overthrown thy brother and hath his arms."
"Ugh!" cried the Sun and, vizoring up a red
And cipher face of rounded foolishness,
Pushed horse across the foamings of the ford, 595
Whom Gareth met midstream; no room was there
For lance or tourney skill; four strokes they struck

563. **Thy . . . mine:** According to the chivalric code, the armor and horse of a defeated knight became the property of the victorious knight. 578. **fool's parable:** Lynette refers to the story of the four knights who hold her sister captive. 581–82. **mail . . . blinding:** highly polished armor. 583. **flower:** the dandelion. 589. **brother:** Gareth is mistaken for Morning Star since he carries that knight's shield. **marches:** territory.

With sword, and these were mighty; the new knight
Had fear he might be shamed; but as the Sun
Heaved up a ponderous arm to strike the fifth, 600
The hoof of his horse slipped in the stream, the stream
Descended, and the Sun was washed away.

Then Gareth laid his lance athwart the ford;
So drew him home;° but he that fought no more,
As being all bone-battered on the rock, 605
Yielded; and Gareth sent him to the King.
"Myself when I return will plead for thee."

Lead, and I follow." Quietly she led.
"Hath not the good wind, damsel, changed again?"
"Nay, not a point; nor art thou victor here. 610
There lies a ridge of slate across the ford;
His horse thereon stumbled—ay, for I saw it.

"'O sun'—not this strong fool whom thou, Sir Knave,
Hast overthrown through mere unhappiness—
'O sun, that wakenest all to bliss or pain, 615
O moon, that layest all to sleep again,
Shine sweetly; twice my love hath smiled on me.'
What knowest thou of love song or of love?
Nay, nay, God wot, so thou wert nobly born,
Thou hast a pleasant presence. Yea, perchance— 620

603–04. **lance . . . home:** Using his lance, he was able to reach solid ground.

'O dewy flowers that open to the sun,
O dewy flowers that close when day is done,
Blow sweetly; twice my love hath smiled on me.'
What knowest thou of flowers, except, belike,
To garnish meats with? hath not our good King 625
Who lent me thee, the flower of kitchendom,
A foolish love for flowers? what stick ye round
The pasty? wherewithal deck the boar's head?
Flowers? nay, the boar hath rosemaries and bay.°
'O birds that warble to the morning sky, 630
O birds that warble as the day goes by,
Sing sweetly; twice my love hath smiled on me.'
What knowest thou of birds, lark, mavis, merle,
Linnet?° what dream ye when they utter forth
May music growing with the growing light, 635
Their sweet sun worship? these be for the snare—
So runs thy fancy—these be for the spit,
Larding and basting. See thou have not now
Larded thy last, except thou turn and fly.
There stands the third fool of their allegory." 640

For there beyond a bridge of treble bow,
All in a rose-red from the west, and all
Naked it seemed, and glowing in the broad
Deep-dimpled current underneath, the knight
That named himself the Star of Evening stood. 645

And Gareth, "Wherefore waits the madman there
Naked in open dayshine?" "Nay," she cried,
"Not naked, only wrapped in hardened skins°
That fit him like his own; and so ye cleave
His armor off him, these will turn the blade." 650

Then the third brother shouted o'er the bridge,
"O brother star, why shine ye here so low?
Thy ward is higher up; but have ye slain
The damsel's champion?" and the damsel cried:

"No star of thine, but shot from Arthur's heaven 655
With all disaster unto thine and thee!
For both thy younger brethren have gone down

629. **rosemaries and bay:** herbs used to flavor meats. Lynette refers to Gareth's work in the
kitchen. 633–34. **lark . . . Linnet:** songbirds. 648. **hardened skins:** These represent evil
habits formed throughout a lifetime.

Before this youth; and so wilt thou, Sir Star,
Art thou not old?"

 "Old, damsel, old and hard,
Old, with the might and breath of twenty boys." 660
Said Gareth, "Old, and overbold in brag!
But that same strength which threw the Morning Star
Can throw the Evening."

 Then that other blew
A hard and deadly note upon the horn.
"Approach and arm me!" With slow steps from out 665
An old storm-beaten, russet, many-stained
Pavilion, forth a grizzled damsel came,
And armed him in old arms, and brought a helm
With but a drying evergreen for crest,
And gave a shield whereon the star of even 670
Half-tarnished and half-bright, his emblem, shone.
But when it glittered o'er the saddlebow,
They madly hurled together on the bridge;
And Gareth overthrew him, lighted, drew,
There met him drawn, and overthrew him again, 675
But up like fire he started; and as oft
As Gareth brought him groveling on his knees,
So many a time he vaulted up again;
Till Gareth panted hard, and his great heart,
Foredooming all his trouble was in vain, 680
Labored within him, for he seemed as one
That all in later, sadder age begins

To war against ill uses of a life,
But these from all his life arise and cry,
"Thou hast made us lords, and canst not put us down!" 685
He half despairs; so Gareth seemed to strike
Vainly, the damsel clamoring all the while,
"Well done, knave knight, well stricken, O good knight knave—
O knave, as noble as any of all the knights—
Shame me not, shame me not. I have prophesied— 690
Strike, thou art worthy of the Table Round—
His arms are old, he trusts the hardened skin—
Strike—strike—the wind will never change again."
And Gareth hearing ever stronglier smote,
And hewed great pieces of his armor off him, 695
But lashed in vain against the hardened skin,
And could not wholly bring him under, more
Than loud Southwesterns,° rolling ridge on ridge,
The buoy that rides at sea and dips and springs
Forever; till at length Sir Gareth's brand 700
Clashed his, and brake it utterly to the hilt.
"I have thee now;" but forth that other sprang,
And, all unknightlike,° writhed his wiry arms
Around him, till he felt, despite his mail,
Strangled, but straining even his uttermost 705
Cast, and so hurled him headlong o'er the bridge
Down to the river, sink or swim, and cried,
"Lead, and I follow."

 But the damsel said:
"I lead no longer; ride thou at my side;
Thou art the kingliest of all kitchen knaves. 710
'O trefoil,° sparkling on the rainy plain,
O rainbow with three colors after rain,
Shine sweetly; thrice my love hath smiled on me.'
Sir—and, good faith, I fain had added—Knight,
But that I heard thee call thyself a knave— 715
Shamed am I that I so rebuked, reviled,
Missaid thee. Noble I am; and thought the King
Scorned me and mine; and now thy pardon, friend,
For thou hast ever answered courteously,
And wholly bold thou art, and meek withal 720
As any of Arthur's best, but, being knave,
Hast mazed my wit.° I marvel what thou art."

 698. **Southwesterns:** the gales from the southwest. 703. **unknightlike:** According to the
chivalric code, as a defeated knight he should have given himself up to the victor. 711. **trefoil:**
three-leafed clover. 722. **mazed my wit:** amazed me.

"Damsel," he said, "you be not all to blame,
Saving that you mistrusted our good King
Would handle scorn, or yield you, asking, one 725
Not fit to cope your quest. You said your say;
Mine answer was my deed. Good sooth! I hold
He scarce is knight, yea but half-man, nor meet
To fight for gentle damsel, he, who lets
His heart be stirred with any foolish heat 730
At any gentle damsel's waywardness.
Shamed? care not! thy foul sayings fought for me;
And seeing now thy words are fair, methinks
There rides no knight, not Lancelot, his great self,
Hath force to quell me."

 Nigh upon that hour 735
When the lone hern° forgets his melancholy,
Lets down his other leg, and stretching dreams
Of goodly supper in the distant pool,
Then turned the noble damsel smiling at him,
And told him of a cavern hard at hand, 740
Where bread and baken meats and good red wine
Of Southland, which the Lady Lyonors
Had sent her coming champion, waited him.

Sir Lancelot, having swum the river-loops—
His blue shield lions covered—softly drew 745
Behind the twain, and when he saw the star°
Gleam, on Sir Gareth's turning to him, cried,
"Stay, felon knight, I avenge me for my friend."
And Gareth crying pricked° against the cry;
But when they closed—in a moment—at one touch 750
Of that skilled spear, the wonder of the world—
Went sliding down so easily and fell,
That when he found the grass within his hands
He laughed; the laughter jarred upon Lynette.
Harshly she asked him, "Shamed and overthrown, 755
And tumbled back into the kitchen knave,
Why laugh ye? that ye blew your boast in vain?"
"Nay, noble damsel, but that I, the son
Of old King Lot and good Queen Bellicent,
And victor of the bridges and the ford, 760
And knight of Arthur, here lie thrown by whom
I know not, all through mere unhappiness—°
Device and sorcery and unhappiness—

736. hern: heron. 746. star: Gareth was carrying the shield of Morning Star.
749. pricked: spurred on. 762. mere unhappiness: accident or mischance.

Out, sword; we are thrown!" And Lancelot answered: "Prince,
O Gareth—through the mere unhappiness 765
Of one who came to help thee, not to harm,
Lancelot, and all as glad to find thee whole
As on the day when Arthur knighted him."

Then Gareth: "Thou—Lancelot!—thine the hand
That threw me? An some chance to mar the boast° 770
Thy brethren of thee make—which could not chance—
Had sent thee down before a lesser spear,
Shamed had I been, and sad—O Lancelot—thou!"

Whereat the maiden, petulant: "Lancelot,
Why came ye not, when called? and wherefore now 775
Come ye, not called? I gloried in my knave,
Who being still rebuked would answer still
Courteous as any knight—but now, if knight,
The marvel dies, and leaves me fooled and tricked,
And only wondering wherefore played upon; 780
And doubtful whether I and mine be scorned.
Where should be truth if not in Arthur's hall,
In Arthur's presence? Knight, knave, prince, and fool,
I hate thee and forever."

 And Lancelot said:
"Blessed be thou, Sir Gareth! knight art thou 785
To the King's best wish. O damsel, be you wise,
To call him shamed who is but overthrown?
Thrown have I been, nor once, but many a time.
Well hast thou done; for all the stream is freed,
And thou hast wreaked his justice on his foes, 790
And when reviled hast answered graciously,
And makest merry when overthrown. Prince, knight,
Hail, knight and prince, and of our Table Round!"

And then when turning to Lynette he told
The tale of Gareth, petulantly she said: 795
"Ay, well—ay, well—for worse than being fooled
Of others is to fool oneself. A cave,
Sir Lancelot, is hard by, with meats and drinks
And forage for the horse, and flint for fire.
But all about it flies a honeysuckle. 800
Seek, till we find." And when they sought and found,

770. **the boast:** the boast that Lancelot has never been thrown from his horse.

Sir Gareth drank and ate, and all his life
Passed into sleep; on whom the maiden gazed:
"Sound sleep be thine! sound cause to sleep hast thou.
Wake lusty! Seem I not as tender to him 805
As any mother? Ay, but such a one
As all day long hath rated at° her child,
And vexed his day, but blesses him asleep—
Good lord, how sweetly smells the honeysuckle
In the hushed night, as if the world were one 810
Of utter peace, and love, and gentleness!
O Lancelot, Lancelot"—and she clapped her hands—
"Full merry am I to find my goodly knave
Is knight and noble. See now, sworn have I,
Else yon black felon had not let me pass, 815
To bring thee back to do the battle with him.
Thus an thou goest, he will fight thee first;
Who doubts thee victor? so will my knight knave
Miss the full flower of this accomplishment."

Said Lancelot: "Peradventure he you name 820
May know my shield. Let Gareth, an he will,
Change his for mine, and take my charger, fresh,
Not to be spurred, loving the battle as well
As he that rides him." "Lancelot-like," she said,
"Courteous in this, Lord Lancelot, as in all." 825

And Gareth, wakening, fiercely clutched the shield:
"Ramp,° ye lance-splintering lions, on whom all spears
Are rotten sticks! ye seem agape to roar!
Yea, ramp and roar at leaving of your lord!—
Care not, good beasts, so well I care for you. 830
O noble Lancelot, from my hold on these

807. **rated at:** scolded. 827. **Ramp:** The lions on Lancelot's shield were rampant—reared
on their hind legs with one foreleg raised above the other.

Streams virtue—fire—through one that will not shame
Even the shadow of Lancelot under shield.
Hence; let us go."

 Silent the silent field
They traversed. Arthur's Harp° though summer wan, 835
In countermotion to the clouds, allured
The glance of Gareth dreaming on his liege.
A star shot: "Lo," said Gareth, "the foe falls!"
An owl whooped: "Hark the victor pealing there!"
Suddenly she that rode upon his left 840
Clung to the shield that Lancelot lent him, crying:
"Yield, yield him this again; 'tis he must fight:
I curse the tongue that all through yesterday
Reviled thee, and hath wrought on Lancelot now
To lend thee horse and shield. Wonders ye have done; 845
Miracles ye cannot. Here is glory enow
In having flung the three. I see thee maimed,
Mangled; I swear thou canst not fling the fourth."

"And wherefore, damsel? tell me all ye know.
You cannot scare me; nor rough face, or voice, 850
Brute bulk of limb, or boundless savagery
Appal me from the quest."

 "Nay, prince," she cried,
"God wot, I never looked upon the face,
Seeing he never rides abroad by day;
But watched him have I like a phantom pass 855
Chilling the night; nor have I heard the voice.
Always he made his mouthpiece of a page
Who came and went, and still reported him
As closing in himself the strength of ten,
And when his anger tare him, massacring 860
Man, woman, lad, and girl—yea, the soft babe!
Some hold that he hath swallowed infant flesh,
Monster! O prince, I went for Lancelot first,
The quest is Lancelot's; give him back the shield."

Said Gareth laughing, "An he fight for this, 865
Belike he wins it as the better man;
Thus—and not else!"

835. **Arthur's Harp:** three stars—Arcturus, a star which lies near the North Star, and the North Star itself—together form a triangle which resembles a harp.

　　　　　　But Lancelot on him urged
All the devisings° of their chivalry
When one might meet a mightier than himself;
How best to manage horse, lance, sword, and shield,　　　　870
And so fill up the gap where force might fail
With skill and fineness. Instant° were his words.

Then Gareth: "Here be rules. I know but one—
To dash against mine enemy and to win.
Yet have I watched thee victor in the joust,　　　　875
And seen thy way." "Heaven help thee!" sighed Lynette.

Then for a space, and under cloud that grew
To thunder gloom palling all stars, they rode
In converse till she made her palfrey halt,
Lifted an arm, and softly whispered, "There."　　　　880
And all the three were silent seeing, pitched
Beside the Castle Perilous on flat field,
A huge pavilion like a mountain peak
Sunder the glooming crimson on the marge,
Black, with black banner, and a long black horn　　　　885
Beside it hanging; which Sir Gareth grasped,
And so, before the two could hinder him,

868. **devisings:** devices.　872. **Instant:** emphatic, urgent.

Sent all his heart and breath through all the horn.
Echoed the walls; a light twinkled; anon
Came lights and lights, and once again he blew; 890
Whereon were hollow tramplings up and down
And muffled voices heard, and shadows passed;
Till high above him, circled with her maids,
The Lady Lyonors at a window stood,
Beautiful among lights, and waving to him 895
White hands and courtesy. But when the prince
Three times had blown—after long hush—at last—
The huge pavilion slowly yielded up,
Through those black foldings, that which housed therein.
High on a night-black horse, in night-black arms, 900
With white breastbone,° and barren ribs of Death,
And crowned with fleshless laughter°—some ten steps—
In the half-light—through the dim dawn—advanced
The monster, and then paused, and spake no word.

The Lady Lyonors wrung her hands and wept, 905
As doomed to be the bride of Night and Death;
Sir Gareth's head prickled beneath his helm;
And even Sir Lancelot through his warm blood felt
Ice strike, and all that marked him were aghast.

At once Sir Lancelot's charger fiercely neighed, 910
And Death's dark war horse bounded forward with him.
Then those that did not blink° the terror saw
That Death was cast to ground, and slowly rose.
But with one stroke Sir Gareth split the skull.
Half fell to right and half to left and lay. 915

901. **With white breastbone:** with breastbone and bare ribs painted white on his armor.
902. **fleshless laughter:** a grinning skull. 912. **blink:** shrink from looking at.

Then with a stronger buffet he clove the helm
As thoroughly as the skull; and out from this
Issued the bright face of a blooming boy
Fresh as a flower newborn, and crying, "Knight,
Slay me not; my three brethren bade me do it, 920
To make a horror all about the house,
And stay the world from Lady Lyonors.
They never dreamed the passes would be passed."
Answered Sir Gareth graciously to one
Not many a moon his younger, "My fair child, 925
What madness made thee challenge the chief knight
Of Arthur's hall?" "Fair Sir, they bade me do it.
They hate the King and Lancelot, the King's friend;
They hoped to slay him somewhere on the stream;
They never dreamed the passes could be passed." 930

Then sprang the happier day from underground;°
And Lady Lyonors and her house, with dance
And revel and song, made merry over Death,
As being after all their foolish fears
And horrors only proven a blooming boy. 935
So large mirth lived, and Gareth won the quest.

And he° that told the tale in older times
Says that Sir Gareth wedded Lyonors,
But he° that told it later says Lynette.

931. **sprang . . . underground:** the sun rose. 937. **he:** Thomas Malory. 939. **he:** Tennyson.

FOR STUDY AND DISCUSSION

1. In Gareth, Tennyson has created a symbol of youth on the brink of manhood. Here is a young man who seeks to become independent and find his place in the world. Gareth's mother, Bellicent, like many parents, hates to see her son grow up and leave her. What do you think of Bellicent? Does she have selfish reasons for keeping Gareth at home? Explain. How does she try to persuade Gareth to stay with her? What are Gareth's arguments? Bellicent finally allows Gareth to go to Camelot, but what conditions does she set? Why?

2. Of all the important writers of the Arthur legend, Tennyson does most to establish an aura of mystery about Arthur. Note, for example, the quality of magic with which Tennyson surrounds Arthur's city of Camelot. How do Gareth's companions react to the city as they view it from afar? How does Gareth answer them?

3. In this poem we see Arthur as king and ruler. What boon does the widow ask of him? How does Arthur respond? Does he consider that he has granted her a favor? Explain. Judging from this episode, what is your opinion of Arthur as king and moral leader?

4. Although Gareth's life as a kitchen knave was not an easy one, he approached his tasks with as much determination as he would the tasks of a knight. What qualities of character did he display in cheerfully accepting his lowly position?

5. In the story of Gareth and Lynette, different people use different rules of judg-

ment, or criteria, to determine the worth of a person. From their actions and their words, what criteria do each of the following use to judge character?

Arthur Lancelot Sir Kay Lynette

6. In this story Gareth is more than just an individual knight following his own ideas of right and wrong. He is a representative of King Arthur's court and an example of the medieval code of chivalry in action. What incidents and actions in this selection tell you something about these aspects of chivalry:

> physical courage loyalty to a lady
> devotion to the king manners, courtesy

7. The idea of chivalry has had a considerable influence on our own society. What examples of its influence are visible in our society today? What aspects of our society today are not in the tradition of chivalry?

8. The critic Northrop Frye suggests that all heroes in literature can be divided into five general categories:

 a. those who are superior in all respects to other men and superior in all respects to their environment (called *mythic* heroes)

 b. those who are superior only in some respect or degree to other men and superior only in some respect or degree to their environment (called *romantic* heroes)

 c. those who are superior only in some respect or degree to other men but not superior to their environment (called *tragic* heroes)

 d. those who are not superior either to other men or to their environment (called *comic* or *realistic* heroes)

 e. those who are inferior to us in some respect (called *ironic* heroes)

How would you classify Gareth according to the categories suggested above? Would you say he is a mythic, romantic, tragic, comic (or realistic), or ironic hero?

FOR COMPOSITION

Rewrite the story you wrote after reading the Malory selection, this time adding some of the rich background detail that Tennyson brought to his story of Gareth and Lynette.

III. The Storyteller: T. H. White

FROM *The Once and Future King*

THE END AND THE BEGINNING

In the brief selection that follows you will see how a modern storyteller treats the legend of King Arthur. Look for changes in style and tone.

Arthur has now grown old. In his quest for justice under law, he has had to try his wife, Queen Guinevere, and sentence her to be burned at the stake for treason. Although Lancelot had exiled himself to France, he returned—just as Arthur hoped, prayed, and expected—to rescue Guinevere. During the rescue, Lancelot killed the unarmed Gareth by mistake. Because pride and loyalty demanded revenge, Arthur was forced to defend his honor. Crossing to France, Arthur and Gawain, Gareth's brother, led their forces against Lancelot. Time and time again Gawain challenged Lancelot; and time and time again he was defeated. But Lancelot always refused to kill Gawain. As the war dragged on, with neither side wanting to defeat the other, Modred, who was left to rule England in Arthur's absence, circulated the rumor of Arthur's death and declared himself King. At this point Arthur could do nothing but return to England to fight against his own nephew and his own knights.

As the following selection begins, it is winter

and the night before Arthur's last battle against Modred—the last battle for both, since both are destined to die in it. Arthur looks back on his dreams and achievements and wonders what has gone wrong.

ANOTHER WORN-OUT circle spun before him. Perhaps war was due to fear: to fear of reliability. Unless there was truth, and unless people told the truth, there was always danger in everything outside the individual. You told the truth to yourself, but you had no surety for your neighbor. This uncertainty must end by making the neighbor a menace. Such, at any rate, would have been Lancelot's explanation of the war. He had been used to say that man's most vital possession was his Word.[1] Poor Lance, he had broken his own word: all the same, there had been few men with such a good one.

Perhaps wars happened because nations had no confidence in the Word. They were frightened, and so they fought. Nations were like people—they had feelings of inferiority, or of superiority, or of revenge, or of fear. It was right to personify nations.

Suspicion and fear: possessiveness and greed: resentment for ancestral wrong: all these seemed to be a part of it. Yet they were not the solution. He could not see the real solution. He was too old and tired and miserable to think constructively. He was only a man who had meant well, who had been spurred along that course of thinking by an eccentric necromancer with a weakness for humanity. Justice had been his last attempt—to do nothing which was not just. But it had ended in failure. To do at all had proved too difficult. He was done himself.

Arthur proved that he was not quite done, by lifting his head. There was something invincible in his heart, a tincture of grandness in simplicity. He sat upright and reached for the iron bell.

"Page," he said, as the small boy trotted in, knuckling his eyes.

"My lord."

The King looked at him. Even in his own extremity he was able to notice others, especially if they were fresh or decent. When he had comforted the broken Gawaine in his tent, he had been the one who was more in need of comfort.

"My poor child," he said. "You ought to be in bed."

He observed the boy with a strained, threadbare attention. It was long since he had seen youth's innocence and certainty.

"Look," he said, "will you take this note to the bishop? Don't wake him if he is asleep."

"My lord."

"Thank you."

As the live creature went, he called it back.

"Oh, page?"

"My lord?"

"What is your name?"

"Tom, my lord," it said politely.

"Where do you live?"

"Near Warwick,[2] my lord."

"Near Warwick."

The old man seemed to be trying to imagine the place, as if it were Paradise Terrestre,[3] or a country described by Mandeville.[4]

"At a place called Newbold Revell. It is a pretty one."

"How old are you?"

"I shall be thirteen in November, my lord."

[1] **Word:** solemn promise. Note the capitalization: in one of the gospels of St. John, *Word* is used to mean Christ, or the *promise* of the Messiah fulfilled ("The *Word* was made flesh and dwelt among us.").

[2] **Warwick** (wôr′ik): Warwickshire (wôr′ik·shir), a county in central England.

[3] **Paradise Terrestre:** heaven on earth.

[4] **Mandeville** (man′də·vil): Sir John Mandeville was a fourteenth-century writer of travel books.

"And I have kept you up all night."

"No, my lord. I slept a lot on one of the saddles."

"Tom of Newbold Revell," he said with wonder. "We seem to have involved a lot of people. Tell me, Tom, what do you intend to do tomorrow?"

"I shall fight, sir. I have a good bow."

"And you will kill people with this bow?"

"Yes, my lord. A great many, I hope."

"Suppose they were to kill you?"

"Then I should be dead, my lord."

"I see."

"Shall I take the letter now?"

"No. Wait a minute. I want to talk to somebody, only my head is muddled."

"Shall I fetch a glass of wine?"

"No, Tom. Sit down and try to listen. Lift those chessmen off the stool. Can you understand things when they are said?"

"Yes, my lord. I am good at understanding."

"Could you understand if I asked you not to fight tomorrow?"

"I should want to fight," it said stoutly.

"Everybody wants to fight, Tom, but nobody knows why. Suppose I were to ask you not to fight, as a special favor to the King? Would you do that?"

"I should do what I was told."

"Listen, then. Sit for a minute and I will tell you a story. I am a very old man, Tom, and you are young. When you are old, you will be able to tell what I have told tonight, and I want you to do that. Do you understand this want?"

"Yes, sir. I think so."

"Put it like this. There was a king once, called King Arthur. That is me. When he came to the throne of England, he found that all the kings and barons were fighting against each other like madmen, and, as they could afford to fight in expensive suits of armor, there was practically noth-ing which could stop them from doing what they pleased. They did a lot of bad things, because they lived by force. Now this king had an idea, and the idea was that force ought to be used, if it were used at all, on behalf of justice, not on its own account. Follow this, young boy. He thought that if he could get his barons fighting for truth, and to help weak people, and to redress wrongs, then their fighting might not be such a bad thing as once it used to be. So he gathered together all the true and kindly people that he knew, and he dressed them in armor, and he made them knights, and taught them his idea, and set them down, at a Round Table. There were a hundred and fifty of them in the happy days, and King Arthur loved his Table with all his heart. He was prouder of it than he was of his own dear wife, and for many years his new knights went about killing ogres, and rescuing damsels and saving poor prisoners, and trying to set the world to rights. That was the King's idea."

"I think it was a good idea, my lord."

"It was, and it was not. God knows."

"What happened to the King in the end?" asked the child, when the story seemed to have dried up.

"For some reason, things went wrong. The Table split into factions, a bitter war began, and all were killed."

The boy interrupted confidently.

"No," he said, "not all. The King won. We shall win."

Arthur smiled vaguely and shook his head. He would have nothing but the truth.

"Everybody was killed," he repeated, "except a certain page. I know what I am talking about."

"My lord?"

"This page was called young Tom of Newbold Revell near Warwick, and the old King sent him off before the battle,

upon pain of dire disgrace. You see, the King wanted there to be somebody left, who would remember their famous idea. He wanted badly that Tom should go back to Newbold Revell, where he could grow into a man and live his life in Warwickshire peace—and he wanted him to tell everybody who would listen about this ancient idea, which both of them had once thought good. Do you think you could do that, Thomas, to please the King?"

The child said, with the pure eyes of absolute truth: "I would do anything for King Arthur."

"That's a brave fellow. Now listen, man. Don't get these legendary people muddled up. It is I who tell you about my idea. It is I who am going to command you to take horse to Warwickshire at once, and not to fight with your bow tomorrow at all. Do you understand all this?"

"Yes, King Arthur."

"Will you promise to be careful of yourself afterward? Will you try to remember that you are a kind of vessel to carry on the idea, when things go wrong, and that the whole hope depends on you alive?"

"I will."

"It seems selfish of me to use you for it."

"It is an honor for your poor page, good my lord."

"Thomas, my idea of those knights was a sort of candle, like these ones here. I have carried it for many years with a hand to shield it from the wind. It has flickered often. I am giving you the candle now— you won't let it out?"

"It will burn."

"Good Tom. The light bringer. How old did you say you were?"

"Nearly thirteen."

"Sixty more years then, perhaps. Half a century."

"I will give it to other people, King.

English people."

"You will say to them in Warwickshire: Eh, he wor a wonderly fine candle?"[1]

"Aye, lad, that I will."

"Then 'tis: Na, Tom, for thee must go right quickly. Thou'lt take the best son of a mare that thee kinst find, and thou wilt ride post into Warwickshire, lad, wi' nowt but the curlew?"

"I will ride post, mate, so that the candle burn."

"Good Tom, then, God bless 'ee. Doant thee ferget thick Bishop of Rochester, afore thou goest."

The little boy kneeled down to kiss his master's hand—his surcoat, with the Malory bearings, looking absurdly new.

"My lord of England," he said.

Arthur raised him gently, to kiss him on the shoulder.[2]

"Sir Thomas of Warwick," he said— and the boy was gone.

The tent was empty, tawny and magnificent. The wind wailed and the candles guttered. Waiting for the Bishop, the old, old man sat down at his reading desk. Presently his head drooped forward on the papers. The greyhound's eyes, catching the candles as she watched him, burned spectrally, two amber cups of feral[3] light. Mordred's cannonade, which he was to keep up through the darkness until the morning's battle, began to thud and bump outside. The King, drained of his last effort, gave way to sorrow. Even when his visitor's hand lifted the tent flap, the silent drops coursed down his nose and fell on the parchment with regular ticks, like an ancient clock. He turned his head aside, unwilling to be seen, unable to do better.

[1] **Eh . . . candle:** Arthur here speaks in Warwickshire dialect.

[2] **kiss . . . shoulder:** part of the ceremony of dubbing a knight.

[3] **feral** (fir′əl): wild or savage.

The flap fell, as the strange figure in cloak and hat came softly in.

"Merlyn?"

But there was nobody there: he had dreamed him in a catnap of old age.

Merlyn?

He began to think again, but now it was as clearly as it had ever been. He remembered the aged necromancer who had educated him—who had educated him with animals. There were, he remembered, something like half a million different species of animal, of which mankind was only one. Of course man was an animal —he was not a vegetable or a mineral, was he? And Merlyn had taught him about animals so that the single species might learn by looking at the problems of the thousands. He remembered the belligerent ants, who claimed their boundaries, and the pacific geese, who did not. He remembered his lesson from the badger. He remembered Lyo-lyok[1] and the island which they had seen on their migration, where all those puffins, razorbills, guillemots, and kittiwakes [2] had lived together peacefully, preserving their own kinds of civilization without war—because they claimed no boundaries. He saw the problem before him as plain as a map. The fantastic thing about war was that it was fought about nothing—literally nothing. Frontiers were imaginary lines. There was no visible line between Scotland and England, although Flodden and Bannockburn [3] had been fought about it. It was geography which was the cause—political geography. It was nothing else. Nations did not need to have the same kind of civilization, nor the same kind of leader, any more than the puffins and the guillemots did. They could keep their own civilizations, like Esquimaux [4] and Hottentots,[5]

[1] **Lyo-lyok:** the goose who guided Arthur when as a boy, in T. H. White's version of the legend, Arthur lived among geese.

[2] **puffins . . . kittiwakes:** species of seabirds.

[3] **Flodden and Bannockburn:** battles in the war between England and Scotland in the fourteenth century.

[4] **Esquimaux:** variation in spelling of *Eskimos,* though pronounced the same.

[5] **Hottentots** (hot'ən·tots): a South African people.

if they would give each other freedom of trade and free passage and access to the world. Countries would have to become counties—but counties which could keep their own culture and local laws. The imaginary lines on the earth's surface only needed to be unimagined. The airborne birds skipped them by nature. How mad the frontiers had seemed to Lyo-lyok, and would to Man if he could learn to fly.

The old King felt refreshed, clear-headed, almost ready to begin again.

There would be a day—there must be a day—when he would come back to Gramarye [1] with a new Round Table which had no corners, just as the world had none—a table without boundaries between the nations who would sit to feast there. The hope of making it would lie in culture. If people could be persuaded to read and write, not just to eat and make love, there was still a chance that they might come to reason.

But it was too late for another effort then. For that time it was his destiny to die, or, as some say, to be carried off to Avilion, [2] where he could wait for better days. For that time it was Lancelot's fate and Guenever's to take the tonsure and the veil, [3] while Mordred must be slain. The fate of this man or that man was less than a drop, although it was a sparkling one, in the great blue motion of the sunlit sea.

The cannons of his adversary were thundering in the tattered morning when the Majesty of England drew himself up to meet the future with a peaceful heart.

EXPLICIT LIBER REGIS QUONDAM REGISQUE FUTURI [4]

THE BEGINNING

FOR STUDY AND DISCUSSION

1. Compare Malory's Arthur as a young man and Tennyson's Arthur as ruler with the old Arthur of T. H. White. Are there differences in manner and in thought of these three Arthurs? If so, what are they? In what ways are these three Arthurs the same?

2. T. H. White ended his story with the words "The Beginning." What do you think he intended to suggest?

3. How does T. H. White differ from Malory and Tennyson as a storyteller? Does he write with the simplicity and directness of Malory? Does he use the rich background detail of Tennyson? How does his tone compare with that of Malory and Tennyson? Support your answers with examples from the text.

4. How does White compare with Malory and Tennyson as a "maker" of heroes? Compare the three views of Arthur as a hero. In whose account is he boldest? kindest? wisest? most human?

ABOUT THE AUTHOR

Terence Hansbury (T. H.) White (1906–1964) was born in Bombay, India. He was educated in England and published his first collection of poems when he was nineteen. He wrote several successful novels. *The Sword and the Stone,* White's novel about young Arthur, was published in 1939. His *Once and Future King* (consisting of *The Sword and the Stone* and four other novels about Arthur) took almost twenty years to prepare. This book later was used as the basis of a highly successful musical play called *Camelot,* which was first produced in 1960.

[1] **Gramarye** (gram′ər·ē): area in which Camelot was located. White names this fictional region of England with the old word for *magic.*

[2] **Avilion:** In medieval romances, this was an ocean island believed to be near an earthly paradise. Also called Avalon.

[3] **tonsure** (ton′shər) . . . **veil:** the tonsure, worn by monks, is the shaven crown of the head, indicating that Lancelot became a monk; in taking the veil Guinevere became a nun.

[4] *Explicit . . . Futuri:* Thus unfolds the book (or story) of *The Once and Future King.*

T. H. WHITE 583

Reading and Writing About Literature

The study of literary criticism often broadens a reader's understanding of a given work of literature. However, reading about literature requires careful judgment. Literary criticism can be a highly personal form of expression, but personal opinion must always be supported by convincing argument and factual evidence (see page 532).

Below are statements on the works of Malory and Tennyson by four literary critics. Each quotation is followed by a question which you may answer in a brief composition, attacking or defending the opinion expressed. Be sure to support your own conclusions with specific references from the appropriate work.

"Malory avoids realistic detail. All villages and cities are fair, all towers strong. . . . Nor are even the principal characters defined physically. We learn nothing of Arthur but that he had gray eyes." (Robert Graves, Introduction to Malory's *Morte D'Arthur.*)

Reread Malory and see if you can visualize any of the chief characters or their physical surroundings. Do you agree or disagree with Graves's view of Malory's style?

"Tennyson's picture of knighthood is distorted by his idealism. The knights, who in the days of the sixth century were often brutal, coarse, and violent, are pictured in the glamour of courtly chivalry . . . Arthur [also] is idealized . . . and knighthood is depicted as it should ideally be rather than as it was." (Hortense Levisohn, Introduction to Tennyson's *Idylls of the King.*)

"Gareth and Lynette" contains several scenes of armed conflict in which Gareth unhorses and defeats his opponents. Do he and his opponents seem to be men of flesh and blood, or do they seem to be idealized figures in an unreal world?

"In Malory . . . King Arthur's reply to Lynette, giving her a kitchen knave when she asks for Lancelot, is pleasantly irrational; but from [Tennyson's] Arthur as the perfect gentleman and ideal king we are led to expect more wisdom and less foolery. We are inclined to sympathize with Lynette, petulant though she is." (Paull F. Baum, *Tennyson Sixty Years After.*)

Defend or attack Arthur's choice of Gareth as Lynette's knight in Tennyson's poem. What agreement did Arthur and Gareth make before Gareth undertook the quest for Lynette?

In "Gareth and Lynette" "we may observe . . . the minutely accurate, carefully composed scene-painting that bears the Tennysonian hallmark . . ." (Douglas Bush in *Major British Writers.*)

What and how much background detail does Tennyson give in "Gareth and Lynette"? What visual impression do you have of the chief characters and physical surroundings in "Gareth and Lynette"? Compare Tennyson's use of background detail with Malory's.

ART AND LITERATURE

The mood or tone of a work of art or literature reflects the artist's attitude toward his material. Mood can vary according to the artist's style and his subject matter. Study the paintings on pages 547–52. Select one (or two) in which you feel that the mood of the painting best suits its subject, explaining your choice in a brief essay.

THE NOVEL

THE NOVEL is one of the most popular and familiar of all literary forms. People always enjoy a good story. They also enjoy being able to identify with the universal problems and feelings of mankind with which the novel has always concerned itself. The scope of the novel, a long story usually with many characters and more than one plot or story line, has permitted authors to present a broad picture of real life. Perhaps more than any other literary form, the novel has remained close to the changes in society, reflecting the people and customs of each of the periods through which it has passed.

The novel is a comparatively new form of writing in the English language. About three hundred years old, it came into being after a major political and social revolution that took place in England in the seventeenth century. During that revolution the English monarchy in the person of King Charles I was overthrown by the followers of Oliver Cromwell, who sought a more democratic form of government than that offered by the crown. As a result of this revolution, a new social class—the middle class of merchants, bankers, and shopkeepers—started its rise to power, firmly establishing itself by the eighteenth century. Up to this time, with the exception of a few characters in Geoffrey Chaucer's *Canterbury Tales*, the chief characters in literature were personages such as princes, dukes, and legendary heroes. The language spoken by these characters was poetic, high-sounding, and often exaggerated. Such elaborate, poetic language is known as the language of romance, and romance referred to something remote in time, place, and spirit from the experience of the ordinary man. The new middle class wanted to read about people like themselves in the everyday language with which they were familiar. They became interested in themselves as individuals and began to feel that all people, no matter how humble their position in life, had the right to be valued for their own sake.

EARLY NOVELS

One of the first authors to meet the demand for this new type of literature was Daniel Defoe. The hero of his story *Robinson Crusoe* is an ordinary trader who tells of his adventures in the everyday language of the shop, or

street, or trading ship. In this, as well as in all his other stories, Defoe concentrated on the problems and experiences of ordinary people.

Defoe's books are basically stories of adventure and travel in which the reader follows the hero or heroine from one episode to another. There is little or no *plot*, or scheme of incidents and situations which make up a story. Such rambling tales are called *picaresque* stories. (*Picaro* is the Spanish word for rogue or adventurer.) Sometimes the heroes of these stories are honest, like Robinson Crusoe. More often, though, they are crafty servants, beggars, or thieves—people who live by their wits.

Eventually, people grew tired of these rambling stories. They wanted stories from which they could learn some lesson or truth about life. They wanted the conflict between vice and virtue and between prudence and foolishness to be presented dramatically. They felt that the novel could help to reform public behavior by preaching against social ills. It was in this spirit of reform that Samuel Richardson, a printer, wrote *Pamela; or Virtue Rewarded*. In this work, a servant girl writes letters to her friends, in which she tells them how her master pursues her, how she succeeds in foiling his schemes, and how she eventually reforms and then marries him. *Pamela* is often regarded as the first English novel. It describes the problems, moral concerns, and daily lives of its characters and records what they say to each other in ordinary language. Furthermore, it has a definite shape or plot with a beginning, a middle, and an end, in which a single idea—here, the idea of virtue rewarded—is introduced, developed, and resolved.

ELEMENTS OF THE NOVEL

The novel has changed greatly since Richardson's day. His *Pamela* was written in letter form, a technique which almost nobody uses today. In addition, the novel is no longer confined only to the lives of ordinary men and women, but can be about any kind of people. However, in spite of these changes and some in language and style, the novel has retained certain fundamental elements. These include its *plot* and *subplots,* its *characters,* and its controlling idea, or *theme.* The *plot* of a novel, the pattern of events which make up the story, entangles the characters in conflict—with others, with themselves, or both. As the conflicts become more involved, the story moves toward its *climax,* or point of highest intensity. The novel ends with the author's *resolution,* or disentanglement of the conflicts.

Effective *characterization,* the creation of believable characters, is another very important element of the novel. The plot of a novel and its characters are intricately connected. In the world's great novels, the plot grows out of the development of the characters themselves. For example, the main pattern or plot of *Great Expectations* by Charles Dickens emerges from the thoughts and actions of its hero Pip, a poor boy whose head is

turned when he thinks that he is going to inherit a fortune. He sets out to make himself into a fashionable gentleman and comes to despise the poor folk who brought him up. Eventually, he achieves a balanced sense of values and finally becomes a mature, responsible adult.

Characterization can be developed to varying degrees, ranging from superficial to deep and three-dimensional in scope. In novels of action, suspense, and mystery, for example, the reader often finds engrossing, action-filled plots, but rather sketchily drawn characters. These stories, of course, do have heroes and villains, but the reader is frequently so caught up by the excitement of the story that he does not much care what the characters are like. In other types of novels, some characters, usually the principal ones, are fully realized—that is, the reader can see all around them and inside them as well. Minor characters are usually less fully developed.

One way to create a character is to describe his physical appearance and then to give him a single outstanding trait. The English novel is rich in "great characters," people who are larger than life and who portray an idea in human form. For example, in Dickens's novel *The Pickwick Papers,* Mr. Pickwick comically represents simple, innocent benevolence. Mr. Pecksniff in Dickens's *Martin Chuzzlewit* represents gross hypocrisy. Amusing situations arise when characters such as these are brought into conflict with reality. Generally, however, an author tries to create his characters by looking inside them, by examining their thoughts, feelings, and motivations. He frequently shows that people are not always what they seem: that a man who is tall and handsome and apparently courageous may in fact be a bully or a coward. The novelist portrays his characters by describing their actions, their gestures, their talk, and sometimes their physical surroundings. For example, the people in the novels of Ernest Hemingway are often characterized mainly by what they say rather than by detailed physical descriptions. When the novelist carefully plans the wording of his characters' conversation, the reader can work out a very clear picture of what the characters are really like. Taking physical surroundings as another example, the deserted stone pit near the house of George Eliot's character Silas Marner may be said to reflect the weaver's bleak life before he finds Eppie.

Another of the basic elements of the novel is its *theme.* The theme of the novel is the idea or attitude about life which the author develops throughout his work. For example, the theme of *Pamela* is that a good or virtuous person will be rewarded if he or she remains good without faltering. The theme of *Huckleberry Finn* is that of the adventurous spirit of youth, which, by breaking through the social and physical boundaries of the community, discovers new ideas and uncharted territories.

The theme of other novels is sometimes used as a protest against certain social ills. Harriet Beecher Stowe's *Uncle Tom's Cabin* was a protest against the outrage of slavery. Occasionally, as in *Uncle Tom's Cabin,*

the theme of a novel is immediately apparent to the reader. In other works, the controlling idea is introduced and developed more subtly. Sometimes the reader can get a hint of the novelist's theme from the images or symbols which the author uses. In *Huckleberry Finn,* for example, the Mississippi River—exciting, untamed, and free—is perhaps a symbol of Huck's restless desire to "light out" for new experiences and adventures.

POINT OF VIEW, STYLE, AND TONE

A novelist can approach and write his work in several ways. He selects that technique which best suits the content and nature of his work as well as his own technical skill and style. He can be an *omniscient,* or all-knowing, author, one who stands outside the story, carefully controlling his characters and determining beforehand how each one thinks, feels, and acts. Or, pretending to be a character in his own tale, he can tell his story in the first person. Or, he can tell his story through the point of view of a particular character in the novel. In this method as well as in that which uses the point of view of the first person, the actions and responses of the other characters are interpreted by the point of view of the character through whose eyes they are seen. Another possibility is the "stream of consciousness" technique, which some modern novelists use. In using this technique, the writer concentrates on the thoughts and images which flash through a person's mind as he encounters various people and situations.

An author's characteristic way of expressing himself is known as his *style*. A novelist's style is one of the major elements that distinguishes his work from that of his fellow writers. During the early years of the novel, the main styles of writing were either plain or learned. Gradually, writing styles became more flexible, and today authors express themselves in a variety of ways. Style in writing depends on the kind of vocabulary the author employs and on the kinds and lengths of sentences used, and may range from simple and direct to elaborate and involved prose, marked by difficult words and complicated grammatical constructions.

An author's style determines to a large extent his treatment of *tone,* another element of the novel. The tone of a work reflects the author's attitude both toward his readers and his subject matter. Some novelists are satirical and ridicule the follies and weaknesses of mankind in a scornful, biting manner. Comic novelists, on the other hand, tend to laugh with people rather than at them as they poke fun at society. Other variations in tone include a removed, objective attitude versus a warm, personal approach. Style and tone are closely linked. Together they make up the author's voice, his personal signature, tying his work together and making it unmistakably his own.

V. S. PRITCHETT

Silas Marner

GEORGE ELIOT

George Eliot is the penname of Mary Ann Evans. Born in 1819, Mary Ann spent the first twenty-one years of her life on a farm in Warwickshire, in central England, where her father was agent for a large estate. When Mary Ann was sixteen, her mother died, and Mary Ann became responsible for the care of the family. Despite her household duties, however, she managed to read a great deal and to study music and both classical and modern languages. She began her writing career at the age of twenty-seven by publishing anonymously a translation from German of a well-known biography of Christ. Several years later, urged by a friend to write a novel, she did just that. Her first book appeared in 1858, under the penname of George Eliot, which she adopted because women writers were still looked upon with disfavor and distrust. *Adam Bede,* her second novel and her first great success, was published the following year and won praise from several distinguished writers, among them Charles Dickens—who, by the way, guessed that "George Eliot" was a woman. In 1861 *Silas Marner* appeared. These two novels, and a number of others, were so well received that when she died in 1880, George Eliot was acclaimed one of the world's great novelists. Her earliest novels—among which *Silas Marner* is often referred to as her masterpiece—are considered George Eliot's greatest contribution not only to English literature but to English social history. In them she wrote of the people and the life of the Warwickshire countryside, which she knew so well from childhood.

The setting of *Silas Marner* is England in the early nineteenth century, near the end of the Napoleonic Wars. At this time, English society was sharply divided into two classes, with a great gap between the rich and the poor. The country squires, or landowners, lived in large manor houses and enjoyed the many pleasures afforded them by the general wartime prosperity. They not only oversaw their lands, but raised horses, hunted foxes, and gave great dinner dances on holidays. Their tenants lived in thatched-roofed cottages without such luxuries, but their life had its own rewards. In the isolated villages near the country estates lived most of the tradesmen—weavers, cobblers, blacksmiths, tavernkeepers, and others who provided goods and services. Near one of these isolated villages in central England, Raveloe, lived Silas Marner, a linen-weaver who, lacking faith in God and man, had chosen a life of solitude.

Keep this setting in mind as you begin to read the story of Silas Marner. With her portrait of the people, their customs,

their beliefs, and the details of their daily life, the author will help you visualize both time and place.

As you read, also keep in mind the other elements of fiction: plot, character, theme, irony, and symbol. Be a plot detective and watch for incidents and details that might be clues to what will happen later. George Eliot is a master of plot. In her novels every incident develops logically from what has gone before.

Listen to the many voices of the author as you read. Sometimes she speaks as though she sees and knows all. Sometimes she seems to draw you into her confidence and speak to you alone; sometimes she speaks as a lecturer. At other times she speaks indirectly through her characters. Read carefully and let your imagination take you into a world constructed by one of the most skillful of English novelists.

Silas Marner

GEORGE ELIOT

CHAPTER I

Silas Marner, Past and Present

I N THE DAYS when the spinning wheels hummed busily in the farmhouses—and even great ladies, clothed in silk and thread-lace, had their toy spinning wheels

of polished oak—there might be seen in districts far away among the lanes, or deep in the bosom of the hills, certain pallid undersized men, who, by the side of the brawny countryfolk, looked like the remnants of a disinherited race. The shepherd's dog barked fiercely when one of these alien-looking men appeared on the upland, dark against the early winter sunset—for what dog likes a figure bent under a heavy bag?—and these pale men rarely stirred abroad without that mysterious burden. The shepherd himself, though he had good reason to believe that the bag held nothing but flaxen thread, or else the long rolls of strong linen spun from that thread, was not quite sure that this trade of weaving, indispensable though it was, could be carried on entirely without the help of the Evil One. In that far-off time superstition clung easily round every person or thing that was at all unwonted,[1] or even intermittent and occasional merely, like the visits of the peddler or the knife grinder. No one knew where wandering men had their homes or their origin; and how was a man to be explained unless you at least knew somebody who knew his father and mother?

To the peasants of old times, the world outside their own direct experience was a region of vagueness and mystery: to their untraveled thought a state of wandering was a conception as dim as the winter life of the swallows that came back with the spring; and even a settler, if he came from distant parts, hardly ever ceased to be viewed with a remnant of distrust, which would have prevented any surprise if a long course of inoffensive conduct on his part had ended in the commission of a crime; especially if he had any reputation for knowledge, or showed any skill in handicraft. All cleverness, whether in the

[1] **unwonted:** unfamiliar.

rapid use of that difficult instrument the tongue, or in some other art unfamiliar to villagers, was in itself suspicious; honest folk, born and bred in a visible manner, were mostly not overwise or clever—at least, not beyond such a matter as knowing the signs of the weather; and the process by which rapidity and dexterity of any kind were acquired was so wholly hidden, that they partook of the nature of conjuring.[1] In this way it came to pass that those scattered linen-weavers—emigrants from the town into the country—were to the last regarded as aliens by their rustic neighbors, and usually contracted the eccentric habits which belong to a state of loneliness.

In the early years of this century, such a linen-weaver, named Silas Marner, worked at his vocation in a stone cottage that stood among the nutty hedgerows near the village of Raveloe, and not far from the edge of a deserted stone pit. The questionable sound of Silas's loom, so unlike the natural cheerful trotting of the winnowing machine, or the simpler rhythm of the flail,[2] had a half-fearful fascination for the Raveloe boys, who would often leave off their nutting or birds'-nesting to peep in at the window of the stone cottage, counterbalancing a certain awe at the mysterious action of the loom, by a pleasant sense of scornful superiority, drawn from the mockery of its alternating noises, along with the bent, treadmill attitude of the weaver.[3] But sometimes it happened that Marner, pausing to adjust an irregularity in his thread, became aware of the small scoundrels, and, though chary of his time, he liked their intrusion so ill that he would descend

from his loom, and, opening the door, would fix on them a gaze that was always enough to make them take to their legs in terror. For how was it possible to believe that those large brown protuberant eyes in Silas Marner's pale face really saw nothing very distinctly that was not close to them, and not rather that their dreadful stare could dart cramp, or rickets, or a wry mouth at any boy who happened to be in the rear? They had, perhaps, heard their fathers and mothers hint that Silas Marner could cure folk's rheumatism if he had a mind, and add, still more darkly, that if you could only speak the devil fair enough, he might save you the cost of the doctor. Such strange lingering echoes of the old demon worship might perhaps even now be caught by the diligent listener among the gray-haired peasantry; for the rude mind with difficulty associates the ideas of power and benignity.[4] A shadowy conception of power that by much persuasion can be induced to refrain from inflicting harm is the shape most easily taken by the sense of the Invisible in the minds of men who have always been pressed close by

[1] **conjuring:** witchcraft.
[2] **flail:** a tool used in threshing grain by hand.
[3] **bent . . . weaver:** Silas's body has become bent and misshapen from the monotonous routine of operating his loom.

[4] **benignity** (bi·nig′nə·tē): kindness, gentleness.

primitive wants and to whom a life of hard toil has never been illuminated by any enthusiastic religious faith. To them pain and mishap present a far wider range of possibilities than gladness and enjoyment; their imagination is almost barren of the images that feed desire and hope, but is all overgrown by recollections that are a·perpetual pasture to fear. "Is there anything you can fancy that you would like to eat?" I once said to an old laboring man, who was in his last illness, and who had refused all the food his wife had offered him. "No," he answered, "I've never been used to nothing but common victual, and I can't eat that." Experience had bred no fancies in him that could raise the phantasm of appetite.

And Raveloe was a village where many of the old echoes lingered, undrowned by new voices. Not that it was one of those barren parishes lying on the outskirts of civilization—inhabited by meager sheep and thinly scattered shepherds: on the contrary, it lay in the rich central plain of what we are pleased to call Merry England, and held farms which, speaking from a spiritual point of view, paid highly desirable tithes.[1] But it was nestled in a snug well-wooded hollow, quite an hour's journey on horseback from any turnpike, where it was never reached by the vibrations of the coach horn, or of public opinion. It was an important-looking village, with a fine old church and large churchyard in the heart of it, and two or three large brick-and-stone homesteads, with well-walled orchards and ornamental weather cocks standing close upon the road and lifting more imposing fronts than the rectory, which peeped from among the trees on the other side of the churchyard—a village which showed at once the summits of its social

life and told the practiced eye that there was no great park and manor house in the vicinity, but that there were several chiefs in Raveloe who could farm badly quite at their ease, drawing enough money from their bad farming, in those war-times,[2] to live in a rollicking fashion and keep a jolly Christmas, Whitsun, and Easter tide.[3]

It was fifteen years since Silas Marner had first come to Raveloe; he was then simply a pallid young man, with prominent shortsighted brown eyes, whose appearance would have had nothing strange for people of average culture and experience, but for the villagers near whom he had come to settle it had mysterious peculiarities which corresponded with the exceptional nature of his occupation and his advent from an unknown region called "North'ard." So had his way of life— he invited no comer to step across his doorsill, and he never strolled into the village to drink a pint at the Rainbow, or to gossip at the wheelwright's: he sought no man or woman, save for the purposes of his calling, or in order to supply himself with necessaries: and it was soon clear to the Raveloe lasses that he would never urge one of them to accept him against her will—quite as if he had heard them declare that they would never marry a dead man come to life again. This view of Marner's personality was not without another ground than his pale face and unexampled eyes; for Jem Rodney, the mole catcher, averred that one evening as he was returning homeward he saw Silas Marner leaning against a stile [4] with a heavy bag on his back, instead of resting the bag on the stile as a man in his senses would have done; and that, on coming up

[1] **tithes** (tīthz): taxes, amounting to one tenth of one's income, paid to the church.

[2] **war-times:** Between the years 1789 and 1815 England was at war with France.

[3] **tide:** season. Whitsuntide is the seventh week after Easter.

[4] **stile:** a set of steps leading over a wall or fence.

to him, he saw that Marner's eyes were set like a dead man's, and he spoke to him, and shook him, and his limbs were stiff, and his hands clutched the bag as if they'd been made of iron; but just as he made up his mind that the weaver was dead, he came all right again, like, as you might say, in the winking of an eye, and said "Good night," and walked off. All this Jem swore he had seen, more by token that it was the very day he had been mole catching on Squire Cass's land, down by the old saw pit. Some said Marner must have been in a "fit," a word which seemed to explain things otherwise incredible; but the argumentative Mr. Macey, clerk of the parish, shook his head, and asked if anybody was ever known to go off in a fit and not fall down. A fit was a stroke, wasn't it? and it was in the nature of a stroke to partly take away the use of a man's limbs and throw him on the parish, if he'd got no children to look to. No, no; it was no stroke that would let a man stand on his legs, like a horse between the shafts, and then walk off as soon as you can say "Gee!" But there might be such a thing as a man's soul being loose from his body, and going out and in, like a bird out of its nest and back; and that was how folks got overwise, for they went to school in this shell-less state to those who could teach them more than their neighbors could learn with their five senses and the parson. And where did Master Marner get his knowledge of herbs from—and charms too, if he liked to give them away? Jem Rodney's story was no more than what might have been expected by anybody who had seen how Marner had cured Sally Oates and made her sleep like a baby, when her heart had been beating enough to burst her body for two months and more while she had been under the doctor's care. He might cure more folks if he would; but he was worth speaking fair,[1] if it was only to keep him from doing you a mischief.

It was partly to this vague fear that Marner was indebted for protecting him from the persecution that his singularities might have drawn upon him, but still more to the fact that, the old linen-weaver in the neighboring parish of Tarley being dead, his handicraft made him a highly welcome settler to the richer housewives of the district, and even to the more provident cottagers, who had their little stock of yarn at the year's end. Their sense of his usefulness would have counteracted any repugnance or suspicion which was not confirmed by a deficiency in the quality or the tale [2] of the cloth he wove for them. And the years had rolled on without producing any change in the impressions of the neighbors concerning Marner, except the change from novelty to habit. At the end of fifteen years the Raveloe men said just the same things about Silas Marner as at the beginning: they did not say them quite so often, but they believed them much more strongly when they did say them. There was only one important addition which the years had brought: it was that Master Marner had laid by a fine sight of money somewhere, and that he could buy up "bigger men" than himself.

But while opinion concerning him had remained nearly stationary, and his daily habits had presented scarcely any visible change, Marner's inward life had been a history and a metamorphosis,[3] as that of every fervid [4] nature must be when it has fled, or been condemned to solitude. His life, before he came to Raveloe, had been filled with the movement, the mental

[1] **speaking fair:** being polite to.

[2] **tale** (archaic): amount.

[3] **metamorphosis** (met′ə·môr′fə·sis): a complete change.

[4] **fervid** (fûr′vid): intense, ardent.

activity, and the close fellowship, which, in that day as in this, marked the life of an artisan early incorporated in a narrow religious sect, where the poorest layman has the chance of distinguishing himself by gifts of speech, and has, at the very least, the weight of a silent voter in the government of his community. Marner was highly thought of in that little hidden world, known to itself as the church assembling in Lantern Yard;[1] he was believed to be a young man of exemplary life and ardent faith; and a peculiar interest had been centered in him ever since he had fallen, at a prayer meeting, into a mysterious rigidity and suspension of consciousness, which, lasting for an hour or more, had been mistaken for death. To have sought a medical explanation for this phenomenon would have been held by Silas himself, as well as by his minister and fellow members, a willful self-exclusion from the spiritual significance that might lie therein. Silas was evidently a brother selected for a peculiar discipline; and though the effort to interpret this discipline was discouraged by the absence, on his part, of any spiritual vision during his outward trance, yet it was believed by himself and others that its effect was seen in an accession of light and fervor. A less truthful man than he might have been tempted into the subsequent creation of a vision in the form of resurgent memory; a less sane man might have believed in such a creation; but Silas was both sane and honest, though, as with many honest and fervent men, culture had not defined any channels for his sense of mystery, and so it spread itself over the proper pathway of inquiry and knowledge. He had inherited from his mother some acquaintance with medicinal herbs and

their preparation—a little store of wisdom which she had imparted to him as a solemn bequest—but of late years he had had doubts about the lawfulness of applying this knowledge, believing that herbs could have no efficacy without prayer, and that prayer might suffice without herbs; so that his inherited delight to wander through the fields in search of foxglove and dandelion and coltsfoot,[2] began to wear to him the character of a temptation.

Among the members of his church there was one young man, a little older than himself, with whom he had long lived in such close friendship that it was the custom of their Lantern Yard brethren to call them David and Jonathan.[3] The real name of the friend was William Dane, and he, too, was regarded as a shining instance of youthful piety, though somewhat given to overseverity toward weaker brethren, and to be so dazzled by his own light as to hold himself wiser than his teachers. But whatever blemishes others might discern in William, to his friend's mind he was faultless; for Marner had one of those impressible self-doubting natures which, at an inexperienced age, admire imperativeness and lean on contradiction. The expression of trusting simplicity in Marner's face, heightened by that absence of special observation, that defenseless, deerlike gaze which belongs to large prominent eyes, was strongly contrasted by the self-complacent suppression of inward triumph that lurked in the narrow slanting eyes and compressed lips of William Dane. One of the most frequent topics of conversation between the two friends was assurance of salvation: Silas confessed that he could never arrive at anything higher than hope mingled with fear, and listened with longing wonder when

[1] **the church . . . Lantern Yard:** a group of religious dissenters, presumably, who had broken away from the Church of England.

[2] **foxglove . . . coltsfoot:** medicinal plants.

[3] **David and Jonathan:** in the Bible, two close friends who were always together.

William declared that he had possessed unshaken assurance ever since, in the period of his conversion, he had dreamed that he saw the words "calling and election sure"[1] standing by themselves on a white page in the open Bible. Such colloquies[2] have occupied many a pair of pale-faced weavers, whose unnurtured souls have been like young winged things, fluttering forsaken in the twilight.

It had seemed to the unsuspecting Silas that the friendship had suffered no chill even from his formation of another attachment of a closer kind. For some months he had been engaged to a young servant woman, waiting only for a little increase in their mutual savings in order to set their marriage; and it was a great delight to him that Sarah did not object to William's occasional presence in their Sunday interviews. It was at this point in their history that Silas's cataleptic[3] fit occurred during the prayer meeting; and amidst the various queries and expressions of interest addressed to him by his fellow members, William's suggestion alone jarred with the general sympathy toward a brother thus singled out for special dealings. He observed that, to him, this trance looked more like a visitation of Satan than a proof of divine favor, and exhorted his friend to see that he hid no accursed thing within his soul. Silas, feeling bound to accept rebuke and admonition as a brotherly office, felt no resentment, but only pain, at his friend's doubts concerning him; and to this was soon added some anxiety at the perception that Sarah's manner toward him began to exhibit a strange fluctuation between an effort at an increased manifestation of regard and involuntary signs of shrinking and dislike. He asked her if she wished to

[1] **calling . . . sure:** certain to be among the chosen.
[2] **colloquies:** conversations.
[3] **cataleptic:** trancelike.

break off their engagement; but she denied this: their engagement was known to the church and had been recognized in the prayer meetings; it could not be broken off without strict investigation, and Sarah could render no reason that would be sanctioned by the feeling of the community.

At this time the senior deacon was taken dangerously ill, and, being a childless widower, he was tended night and day by some of the younger brethren or sisters. Silas frequently took his turn in the night watching with William, the one relieving the other at two in the morning. The old man, contrary to expectation, seemed to be on the way to recovery, when one night Silas, sitting up by his bedside, observed that his usual audible breathing had ceased. The candle was burning low, and he had to lift it to see the patient's face distinctly. Examination convinced him that the deacon was dead—had been dead some time, for the limbs were rigid. Silas asked himself if he had been asleep, and looked at the clock: it was already four in the morning. How was it that William had not come? In much anxiety he went to seek for help, and soon there were several friends assembled in the house, the minister among them, while Silas went away to his work, wishing he could have met William to know the reason of his nonappearance. But at six o'clock, as he was thinking of going to seek his friend, William came, and with him the minister. They came to summon him to Lantern Yard, to meet the church members there; and to his inquiry concerning the cause of the summons the only reply was, "You will hear." Nothing further was said until Silas was seated in the vestry, in front of the minister, with the eyes of those who to him represented God's people fixed solemnly upon him. Then the minister, taking out a pocket

knife, showed it to Silas, and asked him if he knew where he had left that knife? Silas said, he did not know that he had left it anywhere out of his own pocket—but he was trembling at this strange interrogation. He was then exhorted not to hide his sin, but to confess and repent. The knife had been found in the bureau by the departed deacon's bedside—found in the place where the little bag of church money had lain, which the minister had seen the day before. Some hand had removed that bag; and whose hand could it be, if not that of the man to whom the knife belonged: For some time Silas was mute with astonishment: then he said: "God will clear me: I know nothing about the knife being there or the money being gone. Search me and my dwelling; you will find nothing but three pound five of my own savings, which William Dane knows I have had these six months." At this William groaned, but the minister said, "The proof is heavy against you, brother Marner. The money was taken in the night last past, and no man was with our departed brother but you, for William Dane declares to us that he was hindered by sudden sickness from going to take his place as usual, and you yourself said that he had not come; and, moreover, you neglected the dead body.

"I must have slept," said Silas. Then after a pause, he added, "Or I must have had another visitation like that which you have all seen me under, so that the thief must have come and gone while I was not in the body, but out of the body.[1] But, I say again, search me and my dwelling, for I have been nowhere else."

The search was made, and it ended—in William Dane's finding the well-known bag, empty, tucked behind the chest of drawers in Silas's chamber! On this

William exhorted his friend to confess and not to hide his sin any longer. Silas turned a look of keen reproach on him, and said, "William, for nine years that we have gone in and out together, have you ever known me tell a lie? But God will clear me."

"Brother," said William, "how do I know what you may have done in the secret chambers of your heart, to give Satan an advantage over you?"

Silas was still looking at his friend. Suddenly a deep flush came over his face, and he was about to speak impetuously, when he seemed checked again by some inward shock that sent the flush back and made him tremble. But at last he spoke feebly, looking at William.

"I remember now—the knife wasn't in my pocket."

William said, "I know nothing of what you mean." The other persons present, however, began to inquire where Silas meant to say that the knife was, but he would give no further explanation: he only said, "I am sore stricken; I can say nothing. God will clear me."

On their return to the vestry there was further deliberation. Any resort to legal measures for ascertaining the culprit was contrary to the principles of the church in Lantern Yard, according to which prosecution was forbidden to Christians, even had the case held less scandal to the community. But the members were bound to take other measures for finding out the truth, and they resolved on praying and drawing lots.[2] This resolution can be a ground of surprise only to those who are unacquainted with that obscure religious life which has gone on in the alleys of our towns. Silas knelt with his brethren, relying on his own innocence being certified

[1] **out . . . body:** in a trance.

[2] **drawing lots:** drawing pieces of paper in a lottery, one of which was marked. The person who drew the marked piece of paper was considered proven guilty.

by immediate divine interference, but feeling that there was sorrow and mourning behind for him even then—that his trust in man had been cruelly bruised. *The lots declared that Silas Marner was guilty.* He was solemnly suspended from church membership and called upon to render up the stolen money: only on confession, as the sign of repentance, could he be received once more within the folds of the church. Marner listened in silence. At last, when everyone rose to depart, he went toward William Dane and said, in a voice shaken by agitation—

"The last time I remember using my knife was when I took it out to cut a strap for you. I don't remember putting it in my pocket again. *You* stole the money, and you have woven a plot to lay the sin at my door. But you may prosper, for all that: there is no just God that governs the earth righteously, but a God of lies, that bears witness against the innocent."

There was a general shudder at this blasphemy.

William said meekly, "I leave our brethren to judge whether this is the voice of Satan or not. I can do nothing but pray for you, Silas."

Poor Marner went out with that despair in his soul—that shaken trust in God and man, which is little short of madness to a loving nature. In the bitterness of his wounded spirit, he said to himself, *"She will cast me off too."* And he reflected that, if she did not believe the testimony against him, her whole faith must be upset as his was. To people accustomed to reason about the forms in which their religious feeling has incorporated itself, it is difficult to enter into that simple, untaught state of mind in which the form and the feeling have never been severed by an act of reflection. We are apt to think it inevitable that a man in Marner's position should have begun to question

the validity of an appeal to the divine judgment by drawing lots; but to him this would have been an effort of independent thought such as he had never known; and he must have made the effort at a moment when all his energies were turned into the anguish of disappointed faith. If there is an angel who records the sorrows of men as well as their sins, he knows how many and deep are the sorrows that spring from false ideas for which no man is culpable.[1]

Marner went home, and for a whole day sat alone, stunned by despair, without any impulse to go to Sarah and attempt to win her belief in his innocence. The second day he took refuge from benumbing unbelief by getting into his loom and working away as usual; and before many hours were past, the minister and one of the deacons came to him with the message from Sarah that she held her engagement to him at an end. Silas received the message mutely and then turned away from the messengers to work at his loom again. In little more than a month from that time, Sarah was married to William Dane; and not long afterward it was known to the brethren in Lantern Yard that Silas Marner had departed from the town.

[1] **culpable:** blameable, guilty.

CHAPTER II

The Making of a Miser

EVEN PEOPLE whose lives have been made various [1] by learning sometimes find it hard to keep a fast hold on their habitual views of life, on their faith in the Invisible, nay, on the sense that their past joys and sorrows are a real experience, when they are suddenly transported to a new land, where the beings around them know nothing of their history and share none of their ideas—where their mother earth shows another lap, and human life has other forms than those on which their souls have been nourished. Minds that have been unhinged from their old faith and love have perhaps sought this Lethean influence [2] of exile, in which the past becomes dreamy because its symbols have all vanished, and the present too is dreamy because it is linked with no memories. But even *their* experience may hardly enable them thoroughly to imagine what was the effect on a simple weaver like Silas Marner, when he left his own country and people and came to settle in Raveloe. Nothing could be more unlike his native town, set within sight of the widespread hillsides, than this low, wooded region, where he felt hidden even from the heavens by the screening trees and hedgerows. There was nothing here, when he rose in the deep morning quiet and looked out on the dewy brambles and rank tufted grass, that seemed to have any relation with that life centering in Lantern Yard, which had once been to him the altar place of high dispensations. The whitewashed walls; the little pews where well-known figures entered with a subdued rustling, and where first one well-known voice and then another, pitched in a peculiar key of petition, uttered phrases at once occult and familiar, like the amulet [3] worn on the heart; the pulpit where the minister delivered unquestioned doctrine, and swayed to and fro, and handled the book in a long-accustomed manner; the very pauses between the couplets of the hymn, as it was given out, and the recurrent swell of voices in song: these things had been the channel of divine influences to Marner —they were the fostering home of his religious emotions—they were Christianity and God's kingdom upon earth. A weaver who finds hard words in his hymnbook knows nothing of abstractions; as the little child knows nothing of parental love, but only knows one face and one lap toward which it stretches its arms for refuge and nurture.

And what could be more unlike that Lantern Yard world than the world in Raveloe?—orchards looking lazy with neglected plenty; the large church in the wide churchyard, which men gazed at lounging at their own doors in service time; the purple-faced farmers jogging along the lanes or turning in at the Rainbow; homesteads, where men supped heavily and slept in the light of the evening hearth, and where women seemed to be laying up a stock of linen for the life to come. There were no lips in Raveloe from which a word could fall that would stir Silas Marner's benumbed faith to a sense of pain. In the early ages of the world, we know, it was believed that each territory was inhabited and ruled by its own divinities, so that a man could cross the bordering heights and be out of the reach of his native gods, whose presence

[1] **various:** many-sided, with broader interests.

[2] **Lethean** (lē·thē′ən) **influence:** forgetfulness. In Greek mythology, those who drank from the river Lethe became drowsy and forgot everything in their past lives.

[3] **amulet:** a charm against evil.

was confined to the streams and the groves and the hills among which he had lived from his birth. And poor Silas was vaguely conscious of something not unlike the feeling of primitive men, when they fled thus, in fear or in sullenness, from the face of an unpropitious deity.[1] It seemed to him that the Power he had vainly trusted in among the streets and at the prayer meetings, was very far away from this land in which he had taken refuge, where men lived in careless abundance, knowing and needing nothing of that trust, which, for him, had been turned to bitterness. The little light he possessed spread its beams so narrowly that frustrated belief was a curtain broad enough to create for him the blackness of night.

His first movement after the shock had been to work in his loom; and he went on with this unremittingly, never asking himself why, now he was come to Raveloe, he worked far into the night to finish the tale of Mrs. Osgood's table linen sooner than she expected—without contemplating beforehand the money she would put into his hand for the work. He seemed to weave, like the spider, from pure impulse, without reflection. Every man's work, pursued steadily, tends in this way to become an end in itself and so to bridge over the loveless chasms of his life. Silas's hand satisfied itself with throwing the shuttle, and his eye with seeing the little squares in the cloth complete themselves under his effort. Then there were the calls of hunger; and Silas, in his solitude, had to provide his own breakfast, dinner, and supper, to fetch his own water from the well, and put his own kettle on the fire; and all these immediate promptings helped, along with the weaving, to reduce his life to the unquestioning activity of a spinning insect. He hated the thought of the past; there was nothing that called out his

love and fellowship toward the strangers he had come among; and the future was all dark, for there was no Unseen Love that cared for him. Thought was arrested by utter bewilderment, now its old narrow pathway was closed, and affection seemed to have died under the bruise that had fallen on its keenest nerves.

But at last Mrs. Osgood's table linen was finished, and Silas was paid in gold. His earnings in his native town, where he worked for a wholesale dealer, had been after a lower rate; he had been paid weekly, and of his weekly earnings a large proportion had gone to objects of piety and charity.[2] Now, for the first time in his life, he had five bright guineas[3] put into his hand; no man expected a share of them, and he loved no man that he should offer him a share. But what were the guineas to him who saw no vista beyond countless days of weaving? It was needless for him to ask that, for it was pleasant to him to feel them in his palm and to look at their bright faces,

[1] **unpropitious deity** (dē'ə·tē): unkind god.

[2] **objects . . . charity:** religious contributions.
[3] **guineas** (gin'ēz): gold coins worth several dollars.

which were all his own: it was another element of life, like the weaving and the satisfaction of hunger, subsisting quite aloof from the life of belief and love from which he had been cut off. The weaver's hand had known the touch of hard-won money even before the palm had grown to its full breadth; for twenty years, mysterious money had stood to him as the symbol of earthly good and the immediate object of toil. He had seemed to love it little in the years when every penny had its purpose for him; for he loved the *purpose* then. But now, when all purpose was gone, that habit of looking toward the money and grasping it with a sense of fulfilled effort made a loam [1] that was deep enough for the seeds of desire; and as Silas walked homeward across the fields in the twilight, he drew out the money and thought it was brighter in the gathering gloom.

About this time an incident happened which seemed to open a possibility of some fellowship with his neighbors. One day, taking a pair of shoes to be mended, he saw the cobbler's wife seated by the fire, suffering from the terrible symptoms of heart disease and dropsy, [2] which he had witnessed as the precursors of his mother's death. He felt a rush of pity at the mingled sight and remembrance, and, recalling the relief his mother had found from a simple preparation of foxglove, he promised Sally Oates to bring her something that would ease her, since the doctor did her no good. In this office of charity Silas felt, for the first time since he had come to Raveloe, a sense of unity between his past and present life, which might have been the beginning of his rescue from the insectlike existence into which his nature had shrunk. But Sally

Oates's disease had raised her into a personage of much interest and importance among the neighbors, and the fact of her having found relief from drinking Silas Marner's "stuff" became a matter of general discourse. When Doctor Kimble gave physic, it was natural that it should have an effect; but when a weaver, who came from nobody knew where, worked wonders with a bottle of brown waters, the occult [3] character of the process was evident. Such a sort of thing had not been known since the Wise Woman at Tarley died; and she had charms as well as "stuff"; everybody went to her when their children had fits. Silas Marner must be a person of the same sort, for how did he know what would bring back Sally Oates's breath, if he didn't know a fine sight more than that? The Wise Woman had words that she muttered to herself, so that you couldn't hear what they were, and if she tied a bit of red thread round the child's toe the while, it would keep off the water in the head. There were women in Raveloe, at that present time, who had worn one of the Wise Woman's little bags around their necks, and, in consequence, had never had an idiot child, as Ann Coulter had. Silas Marner could very likely do as much and more; and now it was all clear how he should have come from unknown parts, and be so "comical-looking." But Sally Oates must mind and not tell the doctor, for he would be sure to set his face against Marner: he was always angry about the Wise Woman, and used to threaten those who went to her that they should have none of his help any more.

Silas now found himself and his cottage suddenly beset by mothers who wanted him to charm away the whooping cough, or bring back the milk, and by men who wanted stuff against the rheumatics or the

[1] **loam:** rich soil.
[2] **dropsy:** a swelling caused by accumulation of watery fluid.

[3] **occult:** strange, supernatural.

knots in the hands; and, to secure themselves against a refusal, the applicants brought silver in their palms. Silas might have driven a profitable trade in charms as well as in his small list of drugs; but money on this condition was no temptation to him: he had never known an impulse toward falsity, and he drove one after another away with growing irritation, for the news of him as a wise man had spread even to Tarley, and it was long before people ceased to take long walks for the sake of asking his aid. But the hope in his wisdom was at length changed into dread, for no one believed him when he said he knew no charms and could work no cures, and every man and woman who had an accident or a new attack after applying to him set the misfortune down to Master Marner's ill will and irritated glances. Thus it came to pass that his movement of pity toward Sally Oates, which had given him a transient [1] sense of brotherhood, heightened the repulsion between him and his neighbors and made his isolation more complete.

Gradually the guineas, the crowns, [2] and the half crowns grew to a heap, and Marner drew less and less for his own wants, trying to solve the problem of keeping himself strong enough to work sixteen hours a day on as small an outlay as possible. Have not men, shut up in solitary imprisonment, found an interest in marking the moments by straight strokes of a certain length on the wall, until the growth of the sum of straight strokes, arranged in triangles, has become a mastering purpose? Do we not while away moments of inanity or fatigued waiting by repeating some trivial movement or sound, until the repetition has bred a want, which is incipient [3] habit? That will help

us to understand how the love of accumulating money grows an absorbing passion in men whose imaginations, even in the very beginning of their hoard, showed them no purpose beyond it. Marner wanted the heaps of ten to grow into a square, and then into a larger square; and every added guinea, while it was itself a satisfaction, bred a new desire. In this strange world, made a hopeless riddle to him, he might, if he had had a less intense nature, have sat weaving, weaving—looking toward the end of his pattern, or toward the end of his web, till he forgot the riddle, and everything else but his immediate sensations; but the money had come to mark off his weaving into periods, and the money not only grew, but it remained with him. He began to think it was conscious of him, as his loom was, and he would on no account have exchanged those coins, which had become his familiars, for other coins with unknown faces. He handled them, he counted them, till their form and color were like the satisfaction of a thirst to him; but it was only in the night, when his work was done, that he drew them out to enjoy their companionship. He had taken up some bricks in his floor underneath his loom, and here he had made a hole in which he set the iron pot that contained his guineas and silver coins, covering the bricks with sand whenever he replaced them. Not that the idea of being robbed presented itself often or strongly to his mind: hoarding was common in country districts in those days; there were old laborers in the parish of Raveloe who were known to have their savings by them, probably inside their flock beds; [4] but their rustic neighbors, though not all of them as honest as their ancestors in the days of King Alfred, had not imaginations bold enough to lay a plan

[1] **transient:** temporary, brief.
[2] **crowns:** silver coins.
[3] **incipient:** the beginning of.

[4] **flock beds:** mattresses filled with wool.

of burglary. How could they have spent the money in their own village without betraying themselves? They would be obliged to "run away"—a course as dark and dubious as a balloon journey.

So, year after year, Silas Marner had lived in this solitude, his guineas rising in the iron pot and his life narrowing and hardening itself more and more into a mere pulsation of desire and satisfaction that had no relation to any other being. His life had reduced itself to the functions of weaving and hoarding, without any contemplation of an end toward which the functions tended. The same sort of process has perhaps been undergone by wiser men, when they have been cut off from faith and love—only, instead of a loom and a heap of guineas, they have had some erudite [1] research, some ingenious project, or some well-knit theory. Strangely Marner's face and figure shrank and bent themselves into a constant mechanical relation to the objects of his life, so that he produced the same sort of impression as a handle or a crooked tube, which has no meaning standing apart. The prominent eyes that used to look trusting and dreamy, now looked as if they had been made to see only one kind of thing that was very small, like tiny grain, for which they hunted everywhere: and he was so withered and yellow, that, though he was not yet forty, the children always called him "Old Master Marner."

Yet even in this stage of withering a little incident happened, which showed that the sap of affection was not all gone. It was one of his daily tasks to fetch his water from a well a couple of fields off, and for this purpose, ever since he came to Raveloe, he had had a brown earthenware pot, which he held as his most precious utensil among the very few conveniences

[1] **erudite:** learned.

he had granted himself. It had been his companion for twelve years, always standing on the same spot, always lending its handle to him in the early morning, so that its form had an expression for him of willing helpfulness, and the impress of its handle on his palm gave a satisfaction mingled with that of having the fresh clear water. One day as he was returning from the well, he stumbled against the step of the stile, and his brown pot, falling with force against the stones that overarched the ditch below him, was broken in three pieces. Silas picked up the pieces and carried them home with grief in his heart. The brown pot could never be of use to him any more, but he stuck the bits together and propped the ruin in its old place for a memorial.

This is the history of Silas Marner, until the fifteenth year after he came to Raveloe. The livelong day he sat in his loom, his ear filled with its monotony, his eyes bent close down on the slow growth of sameness in the brownish web, his muscles moving with such even repetition that their pause seemed almost as much a constraint as the holding of his breath. But at night came his revelry: at night he closed his shutters, and made fast his doors, and drew forth his gold. Long ago the heap of coins had become too large for

the iron pot to hold them, and he had made for them two thick leather bags, which wasted no room in their resting place, but lent themselves flexibly to every corner. How the guineas shone as they came pouring out of the dark leather mouths! The silver bore no large proportion in amount to the gold, because the long pieces of linen which formed his chief work were always partly paid for in gold, and out of the silver he supplied his own bodily wants, choosing always the shillings and sixpences to spend in this way. He loved the guineas best, but he would not change the silver—the crowns and half crowns that were his own earnings, begotten by his labor; he loved them all. He spread them out in heaps and bathed his hands in them; then he counted them and set them up in regular piles, and felt their rounded outline between his thumb and fingers, and thought fondly of the guineas that were only half-earned by the work in his loom, as if they had been unborn children—thought of the guineas that were coming slowly through the coming years, through all his life, which spread far away before him, the end quite hidden by countless days of weaving. No wonder his thoughts were still with his loom and his money when he made his journeys through the fields and the lanes to fetch and carry home his work, so that his steps never wandered to the hedge banks and the lane side in search of the once familiar herbs: these too belonged to the past, from which his life had shrunk away, like a rivulet that has sunk far down from the grassy fringe of its old breadth into a little shivering thread, that cuts a groove for itself in the barren sand.

But about the Christmas of that fifteenth year, a second great change came over Marner's life, and his history became blended in a singular manner with the life of his neighbors.

FOR STUDY AND DISCUSSION

1. What do the first few paragraphs of this novel tell about the people of Raveloe? Why do they look with suspicion upon Silas Marner?

2. How are the people of Raveloe like the people of Lantern Yard? How are they different? Why was Silas so much happier in Lantern Yard?

3. How did the people of Lantern Yard react to Silas's trance, or fit? Do you think the people of Raveloe would have had the same reaction? Why or why not?

4. Why were Silas and William Dane such good friends? What differences between them are suggested in George Eliot's description of their physical appearance?

5. Reconstruct the robbery as it occurred. What was the basic motive for the crime?

6. In what three ways did Silas lose faith as a result of the false accusation? Is Silas the type of person who would be completely disillusioned by betrayal? Why?

7. How did Silas relieve his neighbor's suffering? How did the people of Raveloe react to this action? What was ironic about the results of Silas's helpfulness?

8. How did Silas change physically as a result of his long years at the loom? How did he change spiritually? Why? What did gold and silver come to mean to him?

CHAPTER III

The Cass Brothers Quarrel

THE GREATEST MAN in Raveloe was Squire Cass, who lived in the large red house with the handsome flight of stone steps in front and the high stables behind it, nearly opposite the church. He was only one among several landed parishioners, but he alone was honored with the title of Squire; for though Mr. Osgood's family was also understood to be of time-

less origin—the Raveloe imagination having never ventured back to that fearful blank when there were no Osgoods—still, he merely owned the farm he occupied; whereas Squire Cass had a tenant or two, who complained of the game [1] to him quite as if he had been a lord.

It was still that glorious war-time which was felt to be a peculiar favor of Providence toward the landed interest,[2] and the fall of prices had not yet come to carry the race of small squires and yeomen [3] down that road to ruin for which extravagant habits and bad husbandry were plentifully anointing their wheels. I am speaking now in relation to Raveloe and the parishes that resembled it; for our old-fashioned country life had many different aspects, as all life must have when it is spread over a various surface and breathed on variously by multitudinous currents, from the winds of heaven to the thoughts of men, which are forever moving and crossing each other with incalculable results. Raveloe lay low among the bushy trees and the rutted lanes, aloof from the currents of industrial energy and Puritan earnestness: the rich ate and drank freely, accepting gout and apoplexy [4] as things that ran mysteriously in respectable families, and the poor thought that the rich were entirely in the right of it to lead a jolly life; besides, their feasting caused a multiplication of orts,[5] which were the heirlooms of the poor. Betty Jay scented the boiling of Squire Cass's hams, but her longing was arrested by the unctuous liquor in which they were boiled; and when the seasons brought round the great merrymakings, they were regarded on all

hands as a fine thing for the poor. For the Raveloe feasts were like the rounds of beef and the barrels of ale—they were on a large scale and lasted a good while, especially in the wintertime. After ladies had packed up their best gowns and topknots [6] in bandboxes, and had incurred the risk of fording streams on pillions [7] with the precious burden in rainy or snowy weather, when there was no knowing how high the water would rise, it was not to be supposed that they looked forward to a brief pleasure. On this ground it was always contrived in the dark seasons, when there was little work to be done, and the hours were long, that several neighbors should keep open house in succession. So soon as Squire Cass's standing dishes diminished in plenty and freshness, his guests had nothing to do but to walk a little higher up the village to Mr. Osgood's, at the Orchards, and they found hams and chines [8] uncut, porkpies with the scent of the fire in them, spun butter in all its freshness—everything, in fact, that appetites at leisure could desire, in perhaps greater perfection, though not in greater abundance, than at Squire Cass's.

For the Squire's wife had died long ago, and the Red House was without that presence of the wife and mother which is the fountain of wholesome love and fear in parlor and kitchen; and this helped to account not only for there being more profusion than finished excellence in the holiday provisions, but also for the frequency with which the proud Squire condescended to preside in the parlor of the Rainbow rather than under the shadow of his own dark wainscot; [9] perhaps, also, for the fact that his sons had turned out rather

[1] **game:** supply of animals for trapping, hunting, and fishing.

[2] **war-time . . . interest:** In time of war, food prices go up. Therefore, land becomes more valuable.

[3] **yeomen** (yō′mən): farmers.

[4] **gout and apoplexy:** diseases brought on by overweight and heavy eating.

[5] **orts:** scraps and leavings.

[6] **topknots:** arrangements of ribbons, flowers, and feathers for decorating the hair.

[7] **pillions:** cushions placed behind a man's saddle for a woman to ride on.

[8] **chines** (chīnz): cuts of meat including the backbone.

[9] **wainscot:** wood wall paneling.

ill. Raveloe was not a place where moral censure was severe, but it was thought a weakness in the Squire that he had kept all his sons at home in idleness; and though some license [1] was to be allowed to young men whose fathers could afford it, people shook their heads at the courses of the second son, Dunstan, commonly called Dunsey Cass, whose taste for swapping and betting might turn out to be a sowing of something worse than wild oats. To be sure, the neighbors said, it was no matter what became of Dunsey—a spiteful jeering fellow, who seemed to enjoy his drink the more when other people went dry—always provided that his doings did not bring trouble on a family like Squire Cass's, with a monument in the church, and tankards older than King George. But it would be a thousand pities if Mr. Godfrey, the eldest, a fine open-faced good-natured young man who was to come into the land some day, should take to going along the same road with his brother, as he had seemed to do of late. If he went on in that way, he would lose Miss Nancy Lammeter; for it was well known that she had looked very shyly on him ever since last Whitsuntide twelvemonth, when there was so much talk about his being away from home days and days together. There

was something wrong, more than common—that was quite clear; for Mr. Godfrey didn't look half so fresh-colored and open as he used to do. At one time everybody was saying, What a handsome couple he and Miss Nancy Lammeter would make! and if she could come to be mistress at the Red House, there would be a fine change, for the Lammeters had been brought up in that way, that they never suffered a pinch of salt to be wasted, and yet everybody in their household had of the best, according to his place. Such a daughter-in-law would be a saving to the old Squire, if she never brought a penny to her fortune; for it was to be feared that, notwithstanding his incomings, there were more holes in his pocket than the one where he put his own hand in. But if Mr. Godfrey didn't turn over a new leaf, he might say "Good-by" to Miss Nancy Lammeter.

It was the once-hopeful Godfrey who was standing, with his hands in his side pockets and his back to the fire, in the dark wainscoted parlor, one late November afternoon in that fifteenth year of Silas Marner's life at Raveloe. The fading gray light fell dimly on the walls decorated with guns, whips, and foxes' brushes,[2] on coats and hats flung on the

[1] **license:** freedom of action, special privilege.

[2] **brushes:** tails.

chairs, on tankards sending forth a scent of flat ale, and on a half-choked fire, with pipes propped up in the chimney corners: signs of a domestic life destitute of any hallowing charm, with which the look of gloomy vexation on Godfrey's blond face was in sad accordance. He seemed to be waiting and listening for someone's approach, and presently the sound of a heavy step, with an accompanying whistle, was heard across the large empty entrance hall.

The door opened, and a thickset, heavy-looking young man entered, with the flushed face and the gratuitously elated bearing which mark the first stage of intoxication. It was Dunsey, and at the sight of him Godfrey's face parted with some of its gloom to take on the more active expression of hatred. The handsome brown spaniel that lay on the hearth retreated under the chair in the chimney corner.

"Well, Master Godfrey, what do you want with me?" said Dunsey, in a mocking tone. "You're my elders and betters, you know; I was obliged to come when you sent for me."

"Why, this is what I want—and just shake yourself sober and listen, will you?" said Godfrey, savagely. He had himself been drinking more than was good for him, trying to turn his gloom into uncalculating anger. "I want to tell you, I must hand over that rent of Fowler's to the Squire, or else tell him I gave it you; for he's threatening to distrain [1] for it, and it'll all be out soon, whether I tell him or not. He said, just now, before he went out, he should send word to Cox to distrain, if Fowler didn't come and pay up his arrears this week. The Squire's short o' cash, and in no humor to stand any nonsense; and you know what he threatened, if ever he found you making away with

[1] **distrain:** seize property in payment of debt.

his money again. So, see and get the money, and pretty quickly, will you?"

"Oh!" said Dunsey, sneeringly, coming nearer to his brother and looking in his face. "Suppose, now, you get the money yourself, and save me the trouble, eh? Since you was so kind as to hand it over to me, you'll not refuse me the kindness to pay it back for me: it was your brotherly love made you do it, you know."

Godfrey bit his lip and clenched his fist. "Don't come near me with that look, else I'll knock you down."

"Oh no, you won't," said Dunsey, turning away on his heel, however. "Because I'm such a good-natured brother, you know. I might get you turned out of house and home and cut off with a shilling any day. I might tell the Squire how his handsome son was married to that nice young woman, Molly Farren, and was very unhappy because he couldn't live with his drunken wife, and I should slip into your place as comfortable as could be. But you see, I don't do it—I'm so easy and good-natured. You'll take any trouble for me. You'll get the hundred pounds for me—I know you will."

"How can I get the money?" said Godfrey, quivering. "I haven't a shilling to bless myself with. And it's a lie that you'd slip into my place: you'd get yourself turned out too, that's all. For if you begin telling tales, I'll follow. Bob's my father's favorite—you know that very well. He'd only think himself well rid of you."

"Never mind," said Dunsey, nodding his head sideways as he looked out of the window. "It 'ud be very pleasant to me to go in your company—you're such a handsome brother, and we've always been so fond of quarreling with one another, I shouldn't know what to do without you. But you'd like better for us both to stay at home together; I know you would. So you'll manage to get that little sum o'

money, and I'll bid you good-by, though I'm sorry to part."

Dunstan was moving off, but Godfrey rushed after him and seized him by the arm, saying, with an oath—

"I tell you, I have no money; I can get no money."

"Borrow of old Kimble."

"I tell you, he won't lend me any more, and I shan't ask him."

"Well, then, sell Wildfire."

"Yes, that's easy talking. I must have the money directly."

"Well, you've only got to ride him to the hunt tomorrow. There'll be Bryce and Keating there, for sure. You'll get more bids than one."

"I daresay, and get back home at eight o'clock, splashed up to the chin. I'm going to Mrs. Osgood's birthday dance."

"Oho!" said Dunsey, turning his head on one side, and trying to speak in a small mincing treble. "And there's sweet Miss Nancy coming; and we shall dance with her, and promise never to be naughty again, and be taken into favor, and——"

"Hold your tongue about Miss Nancy, you fool," said Godfrey, turning red, "else I'll throttle you."

"What for?" said Dunsey, still in an artificial tone, but taking a whip from the table and beating the butt end of it on his palm. "You've a very good chance. I'd advise you to creep up her sleeve [1] again: it 'ud be saving time if Molly should happen to take a drop too much laudanum [2] some day, and make a widower of you. Miss Nancy wouldn't mind being a second, if she didn't know it. And you've got a good-natured brother, who'll keep your secret well, because you'll be so very obliging to him."

"I'll tell you what it is," said Godfrey, quivering, and pale again, "my patience

[1] **creep . . . sleeve:** get into her good graces.
[2] **laudanum:** a drug, fatal if taken in an overdose.

is pretty near at an end. If you'd a little more sharpness in you, you might know that you may urge a man a bit too far and make one leap as easy as another. I don't know but what it is so now: I may as well tell the Squire everything myself—I should get you off my back, if I got nothing else. And, after all, he'll know sometime. She's been threatening to come herself and tell him. So, don't flatter yourself that your secrecy's worth any price you choose to ask. You drain me of money till I have got nothing to pacify *her* with, and she'll do as she threatens some.day. It's all one. I'll tell my father everything myself, and you may go to the devil."

Dunsey perceived that he had overshot his mark, and that there was a point at which even the hesitating Godfrey might be driven into decision. But he said, with an air of unconcern—

"As you please; but I'll have a draught of ale first." And ringing the bell, he threw himself across two chairs and began to rap the window seat with the handle of his whip.

Godfrey stood, still with his back to the fire, uneasily moving his fingers among the contents of his side pockets and looking at the floor. That big muscular frame of his held plenty of animal courage, but helped him to no decision when the dangers to be braved were such as could neither be knocked down nor throttled. His natural irresolution and moral cowardice were exaggerated by a position in which dreaded consequences seemed to press equally on all sides, and his irritation had no sooner provoked him to defy Dunstan and anticipate all possible betrayals, than the miseries he must bring on himself by such a step seemed more unendurable to him than the present evil. The results of confession were not contingent, they were certain; whereas betrayal was not certain. From the near

vision of that certainty he fell back on suspense and vacillation [1] with a sense of repose.

The disinherited son of a small squire, equally disinclined to dig and to beg, was almost as helpless as an uprooted tree, which, by the favor of earth and sky, has grown to a handsome bulk on the spot where it first shot upward. Perhaps it would have been possible to think of digging with some cheerfulness if Nancy Lammeter were to be won on those terms; but, since he must irrevocably lose *her* as well as the inheritance, and must break every tie but the one that degraded him and left him without motive for trying to recover his better self, he could imagine no future for himself on the other side of confession but that of "'listing for a soldier"—the most desperate step, short of suicide, in the eyes of respectable families. No! he would rather trust to casualties than to his own resolve—rather go on sitting at the feast and sipping the wine he loved, though with the sword hanging over him and terror in his heart, than rush away into the cold darkness where there was no pleasure left. The utmost concession to Dunstan about the horse began to seem easy compared with the fulfillment of his own threat. But his pride would not let him recommence the conversation otherwise than by continuing the quarrel. Dunstan was waiting for this, and took his ale in shorter draughts than usual.

"It's just like you," Godfrey burst out, in a bitter tone, "to talk about my selling Wildfire in that cool way—the last thing I've got to call my own and the best bit of horseflesh I ever had in my life. And if you'd got a spark of pride in you, you'd be ashamed to see the stables emptied and everybody sneering about it. But it's my belief you'd sell yourself, if it was only for

the pleasure of making somebody feel he'd got a bad bargain."

"Ay, ay," said Dunstan, very placably,[2] "you do me justice, I see. You know I'm a jewel for 'ticing people into bargains. For which reason I advise you to let *me* sell Wildfire. I'd ride him to the hunt tomorrow for you, with pleasure. I shouldn't look so handsome as you in the saddle, but it's the horse they'll bid for, and not the rider."

"Yes, I daresay—trust my horse to you!"

"As you please," said Dunstan, rapping the window seat again with an air of great unconcern. "It's *you* have got to pay Fowler's money; it's none of my business. You received the money from him when you went to Bramcote, and *you* told the Squire it wasn't paid. I'd nothing to do with that; you chose to be so obliging as to give it to me, that was all. If you don't want to pay the money, let it alone; it's all one to me. But I was willing to accommodate you by undertaking to sell the horse, seeing it's not convenient to you to go so far tomorrow."

Godfrey was silent for some moments. He would have liked to spring on Dunstan, wrench the whip from his hand, and flog him to within an inch of his life; and no bodily fear could have deterred him; but he was mastered by another sort of fear, which was fed by feelings stronger even than his resentment. When he spoke again it was in a half-conciliatory tone.

"Well, you mean no nonsense about the horse, eh? You'll sell him all fair and hand over the money? If you don't, you know, everything 'ull go to smash, for I've got nothing else to trust to. And you'll have less pleasure in pulling the house over my head, when your own skull's to be broken too."

[1] **vacillation:** uncertainty, wavering.

[2] **placably:** agreeably.

"Ay, ay," said Dunstan, rising; "all right. I thought you'd come round. I'm the fellow to bring old Bryce up to the scratch. I'll get you a hundred and twenty for him, if I get you a penny."

"But it'll perhaps rain cats and dogs tomorrow, as it did yesterday, and then you can't go," said Godfrey, hardly knowing whether he wished for that obstacle or not.

"Not *it*," said Dunstan. "I'm always lucky in my weather. It might rain if you wanted to go yourself. You never hold trumps,[1] you know—I always do. You've got the beauty, you see, and I've got the luck, so you must keep me by you for your crooked sixpence:[2] you'll *ne*-ver get along without me."

"Confound you, hold your tongue!" said Godfrey, impetuously. "And take care to keep sober tomorrow, else you'll get pitched on your head coming home, and Wildfire might be the worse for it."

"Make your tender heart easy," said Dunstan, opening the door. "You never knew me see double when I'd got a bargain to make; it 'ud spoil the fun. Besides, whenever I fall, I'm warranted to fall on my legs."

With that, Dunstan slammed the door behind him and left Godfrey to that bitter rumination on his personal circumstances which was now unbroken from day to day save by the excitement of sporting, drinking, card playing, or the rarer and less oblivious pleasure of seeing Miss Nancy Lammeter. The subtle and varied pains springing from the higher sensibility that accompanies higher culture, are perhaps less pitiable than that dreary absence of impersonal enjoyment and consolation which leaves ruder minds to the perpetual urgent companionship of their own griefs and discontents. The lives of those rural forefathers, whom we are apt to think very prosaic figures—men whose only work was to ride round their land, getting heavier and heavier in their saddles, and who passed the rest of their days in the half-listless gratification of senses dulled by monotony—had a certain pathos in them nevertheless. Calamities came to *them* too, and their early errors carried hard consequences: perhaps the love of some sweet maiden, the image of purity, order, and calm, had opened their eyes to the vision of a life in which the days would not seem too long, even without rioting; but the maiden was lost, and the vision passed away, and then what was left to them, especially when they had become too heavy for the hunt or for carrying a gun over the furrows, but to drink and get merry, or to drink and get angry, so that they might be independent of variety and say over again with eager emphasis the things they had said already any time that twelvemonth? Assuredly, among these flushed and dull-eyed men there were some whom—thanks to their native human kindness—even riot could never drive into brutality; men who, when their cheeks were fresh, had felt the keen point of sorrow or remorse, had been pierced by the reeds they leaned on, or had lightly put their limbs in fetters from which no struggle could loose them; and under these sad circumstances, common to us all, their thoughts could find no resting place outside the ever trodden round of their own petty history.

That, at least, was the condition of Godfrey Cass in this six-and-twentieth year of his life. A movement of compunction,[3] helped by those small indefinable influences which every personal relation exerts on a pliant nature, had urged him into a secret marriage, which was a blight on

[1] **trumps:** the winning cards.
[2] **crooked sixpence:** good-luck coin.

[3] **compunction:** a sense of guilt.

his life. It was an ugly story of low passion, delusion, and waking from delusion, which needs not to be dragged from the privacy of Godfrey's bitter memory. He had long known that the delusion was partly due to a trap laid for him by Dunstan, who saw in his brother's degrading marriage the means of gratifying at once his jealous hate and his cupidity.[1] And if Godfrey could have felt himself simply a victim, the iron bit that destiny had put into his mouth would have chafed him less intolerably. If the curses he muttered half-aloud when he was alone had had no other object than Dunstan's diabolical cunning, he might have shrunk less from the consequences of avowal.[2] But he had something else to curse—his own vicious folly, which now seemed as mad and unaccountable to him as almost all our follies and vices do when their promptings have long passed away. For four years he had thought of Nancy Lammeter and wooed her with tacit patient worship, as the woman who made him think of the future with joy: she would be his wife and would make home lovely to him, as his father's home had never been; and it would be easy, when she was always near, to shake off those foolish habits that were no pleasures, but only a feverish way of annulling vacancy. Godfrey's was an essentially domestic nature, bred up in a home where the hearth had no smiles, and where the daily habits were not chastised by the presence of household order. His easy disposition made him fall in unresistingly with the family courses, but the need of some tender permanent affection, the longing for some influence that would make the good he preferred easy to pursue, caused the neatness, purity, and liberal orderliness of the Lammeter household, sunned by the smile of Nancy, to

[1] **cupidity:** greed.
[2] **avowal:** admitting what he had done.

seem like those fresh bright hours of the morning when temptations go to sleep and leave the ear open to the voice of the good angel, inviting to industry, sobriety, and peace. And yet the hope of this paradise had not been enough to save him from a course which shut him out of it forever. Instead of keeping fast hold of the strong silken rope by which Nancy would have drawn him safe to the green banks where it was easy to step firmly, he had let himself be dragged back into mud and slime, in which it was useless to struggle. He had made ties for himself which robbed him of all wholesome motive and were a constant exasperation.

Still, there was one position worse than the present: it was the position he would be in when the ugly secret was disclosed; and the desire that continually triumphed over every other was that of warding off the evil day, when he would have to bear the consequences of his father's violent resentment for the wound inflicted on his family pride—would have, perhaps, to turn his back on that hereditary ease and dignity which, after all, was a sort of reason for living, and would carry with him the certainty that he was banished forever from the sight and esteem of Nancy Lammeter. The longer the interval, the more chance there was of deliverance from some, at least, of the hateful consequences to which he had sold himself; the more opportunities remained for him to snatch the strange gratification of seeing Nancy and gathering some faint indications of her lingering regard. Toward this gratification he was impelled, fitfully, every now and then, after having passed weeks in which he had avoided her as the far-off bright-winged prize that only made him spring forward and find his chain all the more galling. One of those fits of yearning was on him now, and it would have been strong enough to have per-

suaded him to trust Wildfire to Dunstan rather than disappoint the yearning, even if he had not had another reason for his disinclination toward the morrow's hunt. That other reason was the fact that the morning's meet was near Batherley, the market town where the unhappy woman lived, whose image became more odious to him every day; and to his thought the whole vicinage [1] was haunted by her. The yoke a man creates for himself by wrongdoing will breed hate in the kindliest nature; and the good-humored, affectionate-hearted Godfrey Cass was fast becoming a bitter man, visited by cruel wishes, that seemed to enter, and depart, and enter again, like demons who had found in him a ready-garnished home.

What was he to do this evening to pass the time? He might as well go to the Rainbow and hear the talk about the cockfighting: everybody was there, and what else was there to be done? Though, for his own part, he did not care a button for cockfighting. Snuff, the brown spaniel, who had placed herself in front of him and had been watching him for some time, now jumped up in impatience for the expected caress. But Godfrey thrust her away without looking at her and left the room, followed humbly by the unresenting Snuff—perhaps because she saw no other career open to her.

CHAPTER IV

The Theft

DUNSTAN CASS, setting off in the raw morning, at the judiciously quiet pace of a man who is obliged to ride to cover [2] on his hunter,[3] had to take his way along the lane which, at its farther extremity, passed by the piece of unenclosed ground called the stone pit, where stood the cottage, once a stonecutter's shed, now for fifteen years inhabited by Silas Marner. The spot looked very dreary at this season, with the moist trodden clay about it, and the red, muddy water high up in the deserted quarry. That was Dunstan's first thought as he approached it; the second was that the old fool of a weaver, whose loom he heard rattling already, had a great deal of money hidden somewhere. How was it that he, Dunstan Cass, who had often heard talk of Marner's miserliness, had never thought of suggesting to Godfrey that he should frighten or persuade the old fellow into lending the money on the excellent security of the young Squire's prospects? The resource occurred to him now as so easy and agreeable, especially as Marner's hoard was likely to be large enough to leave Godfrey a handsome surplus beyond his immediate needs and enable him to accommodate his faithful brother, that he had almost turned the horse's head toward home again. Godfrey would be ready enough to accept the suggestion: he would snatch eagerly at a plan that might save him from parting with Wildfire. But when Dunstan's meditation reached this point, the inclination to go on grew strong and prevailed. He didn't want to give Godfrey that pleasure: he preferred that Master Godfrey should be vexed. Moreover, Dunstan enjoyed the self-important consciousness of having a horse to sell and the opportunity of driving a bargain, swaggering, and possibly taking somebody in. He might have all the satisfaction attendant on selling his brother's horse and not the less have the further satisfaction of getting Godfrey to borrow Marner's money. So he rode on to cover.

Bryce and Keating were there, as Dunstan was quite sure they would be—he

[1] **vicinage** (vis′ə·nij): neighborhood, vicinity.
[2] **cover:** woods containing game for hunting.
[3] **hunter:** a horse ridden when hunting.

was such a lucky fellow.

"Heyday!" said Bryce, who had long had eyes on Wildfire, "you're on your brother's horse today: how's that?"

"Oh, I've swopped with him," said Dunstan, whose delight in lying, grandly independent of utility, was not to be diminished by the likelihood that his hearer would not believe him—"Wildfire's mine now."

"What! has he swopped with you for that big-boned hack of yours?" said Bryce, quite aware that he should get another lie in answer.

"Oh, there was a little account between us," said Dunsey, carelessly, "and Wildfire made it even. I accommodated him by taking the horse, though it was against my will, for I'd got an itch for a mare o' Jortin's—as rare a bit o' blood as ever you threw your leg across. But I shall keep Wildfire, now I've got him, though I'd a bid of a hundred and fifty for him the other day, from a man over at Flitton—he's buying for Lord Cromleck—a fellow with a cast in his eye and a green waistcoat. But I mean to stick to Wildfire: I shan't get a better at a fence in a hurry. The mare's got more blood, but she's a bit too weak in the hindquarters."

Bryce of course divined that Dunstan wanted to sell the horse, and Dunstan knew that he divined it (horse dealing is only one of many human transactions carried on in this ingenious manner); and they both considered that the bargain was in its first stage, when Bryce replied, ironically—

"I wonder at that now; I wonder you mean to keep him; for I never heard of a man who didn't want to sell his horse getting a bid of half as much again as the horse is worth. You'll be lucky if you get a hundred."

Keating rode up now, and the transaction became more complicated. It ended in the purchase of the horse by Bryce for a hundred and twenty, to be paid on the delivery of Wildfire, safe and sound, at the Batherley stables. It did occur to Dunsey that it might be wise for him to give up the day's hunting, proceed at once to Batherley, and, having waited for Bryce's return, hire a horse to carry him home with the money in his pocket. But the inclination for a run, encouraged by confidence in his luck, and by a draught of brandy from his pocket pistol [1] at the conclusion of the bargain, was not easy to overcome, especially with a horse under him that would take the fences to the admiration of the field. Dunstan, however, took one fence too many and got his horse pierced with a hedge stake. His own ill-favored person, which was quite unmarketable, escaped without injury; but poor Wildfire, unconscious of his price, turned on his flank and painfully panted his last. It happened that Dunstan, a short time before, having had to get down to arrange his stirrup, had muttered a good many curses at this interruption, which had thrown him in the rear of the hunt near the moment of glory, and under this exasperation had taken the fences more blindly. He would soon have been up with the hounds again, when the fatal accident happened; and hence he was between eager riders in advance, not troubling themselves about what happened behind them, and far-off stragglers who were as likely as not to pass quite aloof from the line of road in which Wildfire had fallen. Dunstan, whose nature it was to care more for immediate annoyances than for remote consequences, no sooner recovered his legs and saw that it was all over with Wildfire, than he felt a satisfaction at the absence of witnesses to a position which no swaggering could make enviable. Re-

[1] **pocket pistol:** pocket flask.

inforcing himself, after his shake, with a little brandy and much swearing, he walked as fast as he could to a coppice on his right hand, through which it occurred to him that he could make his way to Batherley without danger of encountering any member of the hunt. His first intention was to hire a horse there and ride home forthwith, for to walk many miles without a gun in his hand and along an ordinary road was as much out of the question to him as to other spirited young men of his kind. He did not much mind about taking the bad news to Godfrey, for he had to offer him at the same time the resource of Marner's money; and if Godfrey kicked, as he always did, at the notion of making a fresh debt from which he himself got the smallest share of advantage, why, he wouldn't kick long: Dunstan felt sure he could worry Godfrey into anything. The idea of Marner's money kept growing in vividness, now the want of it had become immediate; the prospect of having to make his appearance with the muddy boots of a pedestrian

at Batherley and to encounter the grinning queries of stablemen stood unpleasantly in the way of his impatience to be back at Raveloe and carry out his felicitous plan; and a casual visitation of his waistcoat pocket, as he was ruminating, awakened his memory to the fact that the two or three small coins his forefinger encountered there were of too pale a color to cover that small debt, without payment of which the stable keeper had declared he would never do any more business with Dunsey Cass. After all, according to the direction in which the run had brought him, he was not so very much farther from home than he was from Batherley; but Dunsey, not being remarkable for clearness of head, was only led to this conclusion by the gradual perception that there were other reasons for choosing the unprecedented course of walking home.

It was now nearly four o'clock, and a mist was gathering: the sooner he got into the road the better. He remembered having crossed the road and seen the finger post[1] only a little while before Wildfire broke down; so, buttoning his coat, twisting the lash of his hunting whip compactly round the handle, and rapping the tops of his boots with a self-possessed air, as if to assure himself that he was not at all taken by surprise, he set off with the sense that he was undertaking a remarkable feat of bodily exertion, which somehow and at some time he should be able to dress up and magnify to the admiration of a select circle at the Rainbow. When a young gentleman like Dunsey is reduced to so exceptional a mode of locomotion as walking, a whip in his hand is a desirable corrective to a too bewildering dreamy sense of unwontedness[2] in his position; and Dunstan, as he went along

[1] **finger post:** a guide sign shaped like a pointing finger.
[2] **unwontedness:** strangeness.

through the gathering mist, was always rapping his whip somewhere. It was Godfrey's whip, which he had chosen to take without leave because it had a gold handle; of course no one could see, when Dunstan held it, that the name *Godfrey Cass* was cut in deep letters on that gold handle—they could only see that it was a very handsome whip. Dunsey was not without fear that he might meet some acquaintance in whose eyes he would cut a pitiable figure, for mist is no screen when people get close to each other; but when he at last found himself in the well-known Raveloe lanes without having met a soul, he silently remarked that that was part of his usual good luck. But now the mist, helped by the evening darkness, was more of a screen than he desired, for it hid the ruts into which his feet were liable to slip—hid everything, so that he had to guide his steps by dragging his whip along the low bushes in advance of the hedgerow. He must soon, he thought, be getting near the opening at the stone pits: he should find it out by the break in the hedgerow. He found it out, however, by another circumstance which he had not expected —namely, by certain gleams of light, which he presently guessed to proceed from Silas Marner's cottage.

That cottage and the money hidden within it had been in his mind continually during his walk, and he had been imagining ways of cajoling and tempting the weaver to part with the immediate possession of his money for the sake of receiving interest. Dunstan felt as if there must be a little frightening added to the cajolery, for his own arithmetical convictions were not clear enough to afford him any forcible demonstration as to the advantages of interest; and as for security, he regarded it vaguely as a means of cheating a man by making him believe that he would be paid. Altogether, the operation on the

miser's mind was a task that Godfrey would be sure to hand over to his more daring and cunning brother: Dunstan had made up his mind to that; and by the time he saw the light gleaming through the chinks of Marner's shutters, the idea of a dialogue with the weaver had become so familiar to him, that it occurred to him as quite a natural thing to make the acquaintance forthwith.[1] There might be several conveniences attending this course: the weaver had possibly got a lantern, and Dunstan was tired of feeling his way. He was still nearly three quarters of a mile from home, and the lane was becoming unpleasantly slippery, for the mist was passing into rain. He turned up the bank, not without some fear lest he might miss the right way, since he was not certain whether the light were in front or on the side of the cottage. But he felt the ground before him cautiously with his whip handle, and at last arrived safely at the door. He knocked loudly, rather enjoying the idea that the old fellow would be frightened at the sudden noise. He heard no movement in reply; all was silence in the cottage. Was the weaver gone to bed, then? If so, why had he left a light? That was a strange forgetfulness in the miser. Dunstan knocked still more loudly, and, without pausing for a reply, pushed his fingers through the latch-hole, intending to shake the door and pull the latch-string up and down, not doubting that the door was fastened. But, to his surprise, at this double motion the door opened, and he found himself in front of a bright fire which lit up every corner of the cottage—the bed, the loom, the three chairs, and the table—and showed him that Marner was not there.

Nothing at that moment could be much more inviting to Dunsey than the bright

[1] **forthwith:** immediately.

fire on the brick hearth: he walked in and seated himself by it at once. There was something in front of the fire, too, that would have been inviting to a hungry man, if it had been in a different stage of cooking. It was a small bit of pork suspended from the kettle-hanger by a string passed through a large door-key, in a way known to primitive housekeepers unpossessed of jacks.[1] But the pork had been hung at the farthest extremity of the hanger, apparently to prevent the roasting from proceeding too rapidly during the owner's absence. The old staring simpleton had hot meat for his supper, then? thought Dunstan. People had always said he lived on moldy bread, on purpose to check his appetite. But where could he be at this time, and on such an evening, leaving his supper in this stage of preparation and his door unfastened? Dunstan's own recent difficulty in making his way suggested to him that the weaver had perhaps gone outside his cottage to fetch in fuel, or for some such brief purpose, and had slipped into the stone pit. That was an interesting idea to Dunstan, carrying consequences of entire novelty. If the weaver was dead, who had a right to his money? Who would know where his money was hidden? *Who would know that anybody had come to take it away?* He

went no farther into the subtleties of evidence: the pressing question, "Where *is* the money?" now took such entire possession of him as to make him quite forget that the weaver's death was not a certainty. A dull mind, once arriving at an inference that flatters a desire, is rarely able to retain the impression that the notion from which the inference started was purely problematic. And Dunstan's mind was as dull as the mind of a possible felon[2] usually is. There were only three hiding places where he had ever heard of cottagers' hoards being found: the thatch, the bed, and a hole in the floor. Marner's cottage had no thatch; and Dunstan's first act, after a train of thought made rapid by the stimulus of cupidity, was to go up to the bed; but while he did so, his eyes traveled eagerly over the floor, where the bricks, distinct in the firelight, were discernible under the sprinkling of sand. But not everywhere; for there was one spot, and one only, which was quite covered with sand, and sand showing the marks of fingers, which had apparently been careful to spread it over a given space. It was near the treddles of the loom. In an instant Dunstan darted to that spot, swept away the sand with his whip, and, inserting the thin end of the hook between the bricks, found that they were loose. In

[1] **jacks:** instruments used in roasting meat.

[2] **felon:** evildoer, criminal.

haste he lifted up two bricks and saw what he had no doubt was the object of his search; for what could there be but money in those two leathern bags? And, from their weight, they must be filled with guineas. Dunstan felt round the hole, to be certain that it held no more; then hastily replaced the bricks, and spread the sand over them. Hardly more than five minutes had passed since he entered the cottage, but it seemed to Dunstan like a long while; and though he was without any distinct recognition of the possibility that Marner might be alive and might reenter the cottage at any moment, he felt an undefinable dread laying hold on him, as he rose to his feet with the bags in his hand. He would hasten out into the darkness and then consider what he should do with the bags. He closed the door behind him immediately, that he might shut in the stream of light: a few steps would be enough to carry him beyond betrayal by the gleams from the shutter-chinks and the latch-hole. The rain and darkness had got thicker, and he was glad of it; though it was awkward

walking with both hands filled, so that it was as much as he could do to grasp his whip along with one of the bags. But when he had gone a yard or two, he might take his time. So he stepped forward into the darkness.

FOR STUDY AND DISCUSSION

1. What is the author's attitude toward the landowners of Raveloe? Why is war-time "glorious" for them?

2. How has Squire Cass raised his sons? What is Godfrey like? What is Dunsey like? What are your feelings toward each of them?

3. Why does the brown spaniel retreat under a chair when Dunsey enters the room?

4. What is Godfrey's problem? What does Dunsey tell him he can do? Would you consider this blackmail? Why or why not?

5. Why does Godfrey go along with his brother's scheme? What does he fear to lose? Why is he so afraid to stand on his own and admit what he has done?

6. How does Dunsey first come to think of Silas Marner? Why does Marner's hoard suddenly become much more important to him than it was when he first thought of it?

7. What are the causes of Dunsey's accident with Wildfire? What connection is there between the accident and Dunsey's confidence in his luck?

8. What is Dunsey's reaction to the accident? How is Dunsey's reaction indicative of his personality?

9. Why does Dunsey decide to walk home? What is the condition of the weather as he nears Raveloe? Why does he think of borrowing a lantern from Silas Marner?

10. Why is Dunsey able to find Marner's gold so easily? Why is this ironic?

11. Dunsey is always more concerned with immediate than with far-reaching consequences. What might be the consequences, for Dunsey, of taking Marner's gold? As he steps out into the night and shuts the door behind him, what do you think is in store for him?

(CHAPTER V FOLLOWS ON PAGE 625.)

EUROPEAN PAINTING

Twentieth-Century Painting, I

In the Paris Autumn Salon of 1905, several young painters exhibited a group of canvases which for sheer intensity of color and raw emotional power seemed to outdo even Van Gogh and Gauguin (pages 548 and 549). The public came to know these artists as *les fauves,* "the wild beasts," a ridiculous nickname inflicted upon them by a horrified conservative critic. This new "fauve" style was actually the result of several years' slow and deliberate experimenting by artists who had been well trained in traditional ways of painting.

One of the later masterpieces that came out of the fauve period is *The Red Studio* by Henri Matisse (PLATE 1). Almost every item of furniture in this interior has been reduced to simple outlines, directing our attention to Matisse's own brightly colored paintings and sculptures, which seem to be the only "real" objects in the room. In spite of their apparent disorder, they are carefully arranged to lead our eye in a rhythmic pattern up and down across the back walls, like the logically rising and falling notes of a melody.

As a movement, Fauvism died out in Paris about 1909. But it had an important influence in Germany right up to World War I, especially on a group of young artists in Munich who considered themselves "expressionists." One member of this group, a Russian-born painter named Wassily Kandinsky, became so fascinated with expressive qualities of line and color that he eventually stopped trying to represent nature altogether. We can sometimes make out certain resemblances to real objects, such as the cannons in his *Improvisation No. 30* (PLATE 2). But Kandinsky later pointed out that when he painted this picture, he was aware of the cannons simply as shapes to be "improvised" in an abstract composition, and not as "real" objects at all. He put together lines, shapes, and colors the way a composer of music combines different sounds that he knows will create certain emotional reactions in his audience.

Meanwhile, in Paris, another group of artists had developed a complex geometric style known as Cubism. These painters often showed the differ-

ent surfaces of an object side by side in their pictures, as if the object were seen from more than one angle at the same time. In Juan Gris' still life entitled *Breakfast* (PLATE 3), for example, each saucer and the rim of each cup are shown as perfect circles, implying that our view would have to be from directly above. Yet we can also see each cup in profile, as if it were in front of us, exactly at our eye level. Of course, in real life this would be impossible, but in Cubist paintings such visual contradictions become interesting simply as shapes and lines. Notice, however, that Gris has added a certain realistic touch to his picture by pasting actual bits of wallpaper and newspaper on the canvas, a technique known as "collage."

Around this same time, a group of artists in Milan, Italy, who called themselves "futurists" were painting images of terrific motion and energy, with which they attempted to express "the beauty of speed" in modern life. Their subjects were the roaring of motorcars, the dynamism of machines—or the motion of a cyclist, as shown in a remarkable painting by Umberto Boccioni (PLATE 4). Diagonal lines and shapes radiating from the center of the picture make it seem to explode with tremendously powerful muscular energy.

During the violent upheavals of World War I, several artists in Switzerland formed a vigorous protest movement called Dada, in which they attempted to ridicule all established institutions, including art itself. The German artist Kurt Schwitters, for example, made collages out of torn burlap, ticket stubs, and other scraps of rubbish. But unlike earlier Cubist collages, Schwitters' rubbish pictures were not meant to represent anything. *Picture with Light Center* (PLATE 5) seems to exist as a separate little world by itself, a world in which bits and pieces of discarded objects come alive together, tumbling about as if governed by certain laws of movement and balance all their own.

PLATE 6, Giorgio de Chirico's *Melancholy and Mystery of a Street* brings us back to the world of deep three-dimensional space which the Cubists had abandoned. But it is not the kind of space we can imagine entering physically. The perspective is not consistent: the converging lines of the two buildings should meet at the same vanishing point, but they do not. What Chirico has created here is a haunting *dream-image*. An almost empty square in an Italian city is menaced by a dark building and an empty wagon and by the long cast shadow of a mysterious unseen figure (perhaps a statue). A cryptic sign appears on the corner of the building at the left, adding to the mystery. In the distance a banner flutters against a clearing in the heavy green sky, suggesting an escape from this oppressive scene. Into the midst of it a little girl rushes with her hoop, but she too seems unreal. She seems like a shadow among shadows, like the one she herself casts on the pavement.

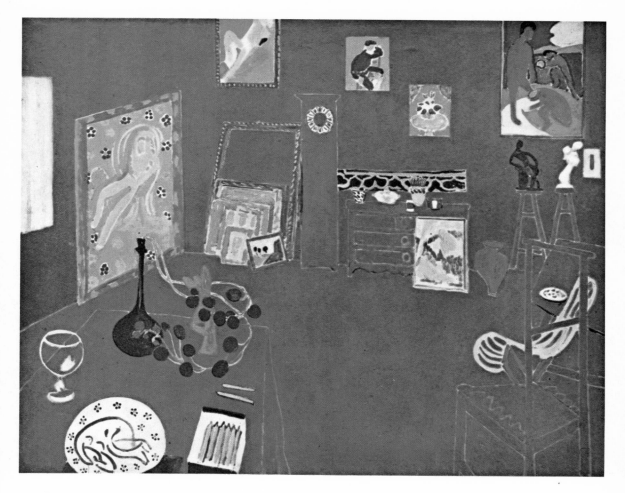

PLATE 1. HENRI MATISSE (French, 1869–1954): *The Red Studio*. 1911. Oil on canvas, $71\frac{1}{4}$ x $86\frac{1}{4}$ inches. (Collection, The Museum of Modern Art, New York, Mrs. Simon Guggenheim Fund)

PLATE 2. WASSILY KANDINSKY (Russian, 1866–1944): *Improvisation No. 30*. 1913. Oil on canvas, $43\frac{5}{8}$ x $43\frac{5}{8}$ inches. (Courtesy of The Art Institute of Chicago)

PLATE 3. JUAN GRIS (Spanish, 1887–1927): *Breakfast*. 1914. Oil on canvas with pasted paper and crayon, $31\frac{7}{8}$ x $23\frac{1}{2}$ inches. (Collection, The Museum of Modern Art, New York, acquired through Lillie Bliss Bequest)

PLATE 4. UMBERTO BOCCIONI (Italian, 1882–1916): *Dynamism of a Cyclist*. 1913. Oil on canvas, $27\frac{1}{2}$ x $37\frac{3}{8}$ inches. (Collection of Mr. G. Mattioli, Milan, Italy)

PLATE 5. KURT SCHWITTERS (German, 1887–1948): *Picture with Light Center*. 1919. Collage with oil on cardboard, $33\frac{1}{4}$ x $25\frac{7}{8}$ inches. (Collection, The Museum of Modern Art, New York)

623

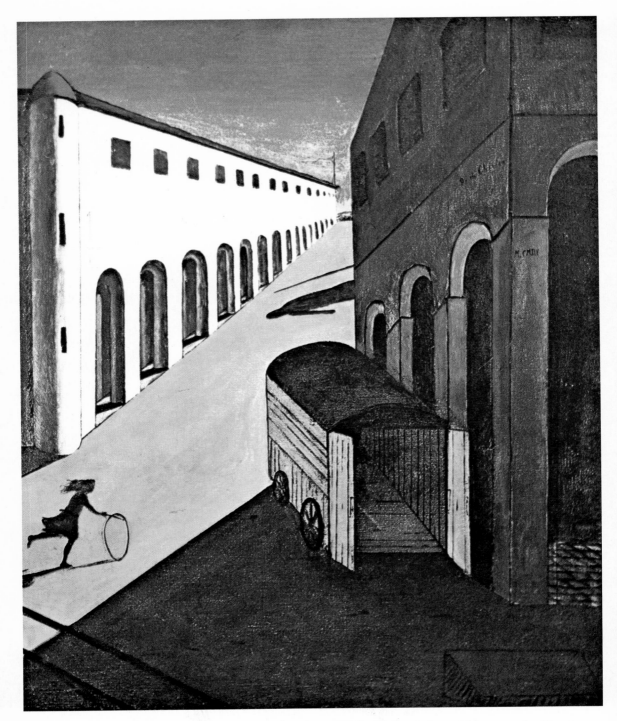

PLATE 6. GIORGIO DE CHIRICO (Italian, born 1888): *Melancholy and Mystery of a Street.*
1914. Oil on canvas, 34⅜ x 28¼ inches. (Collection of Mrs. Stanley Resor, Washington, D.C.)

CHAPTER V

The Theft Discovered

WHEN DUNSTAN CASS turned his back on the cottage, Silas Marner was not more than a hundred yards away from it, plodding along from the village with a sack thrown round his shoulders as an overcoat and with a horn lantern in his hand. His legs were weary, but his mind was at ease, free from the presentiment of change. The sense of security more frequently springs from habit than from conviction, and for this reason it often subsists after such a change in the conditions as might have been expected to suggest alarm. The lapse of time during which a given event has not happened is, in this logic of habit, constantly alleged as a reason why the event should never happen, even when the lapse of time is precisely the added condition which makes the event imminent. A man will tell you that he has worked in a mine for forty years unhurt by an accident as a reason why he should apprehend no danger, though the roof is beginning to sink; and it is often observable, that the older a man gets, the more difficult it is to him to retain a believing conception of his own death. This influence of habit was necessarily strong in a man whose life was so monotonous as Marner's—who saw no new people and heard of no new events to keep alive in him the idea of the unexpected and changeful; and it explains simply enough, why his mind could be at ease, though he had left his house and his treasure more defenseless than usual. Silas was thinking with double complacency of his supper: first, because it would be hot and savory; and secondly, because it would cost him nothing. For the little bit of pork was a present from that excellent housewife, Miss Priscilla Lammeter, to whom he had this day carried home a handsome piece of linen; and it was only on occasion of a present like this that Silas indulged himself with roast meat. Supper was his favorite meal, because it came at his time of revelry, when his heart warmed over his gold; whenever he had roast meat, he always chose to have it for supper. But this evening, he had no sooner ingeniously knotted his string fast round his bit of pork, twisted the string according to rule over his door-key, passed it through the handle, and made it fast on the hanger, than he remembered that a piece of very fine twine was indispensable to his "setting up" a new piece of work in his loom early in the morning. It had slipped his memory, because, in coming from Mr. Lammeter's he had not had to pass through the village; but to lose time by going on errands in the morning was out of the question. It was a nasty fog to turn out into, but there were things Silas loved better than his own comfort; so, drawing his pork to the extremity of the hanger, and arming himself with his lantern and his old sack, he set out on what, in ordinary weather, would have been a twenty minutes' errand. He could not have locked his door without undoing his well-knotted string and retarding his supper; it was not worth his while to make that sacrifice. What thief would find his way to the stone pits on such a night as this? and why should he come on this particular night, when he had never come through all the fifteen years before? These questions were not distinctly present in Silas's mind; they merely serve to represent the vaguely felt foundation of his freedom from anxiety.

He reached his door in much satisfaction that his errand was done: he opened it, and to his shortsighted eyes everything remained as he had left it, except that the

fire sent out a welcome increase of heat. He trod about the floor while putting by his lantern and throwing aside his hat and sack, so as to merge the marks of Dunstan's feet on the sand in the marks of his own nailed boots. Then he moved his pork nearer to the fire and sat down to the agreeable business of tending the meat and warming himself at the same time.

Anyone who had looked at him as the red light shone upon his pale face, strange straining eyes and meager form, would perhaps have understood the mixture of contemptuous pity, dread, and suspicion with which he was regarded by his neighbors in Raveloe. Yet few men could be more harmless than poor Marner. In his truthful simple soul, not even the growing greed and worship of gold could beget any vice directly injurious to others. The light of his faith quite put out and his affections made desolate, he had clung with all the force of his nature to his work and his money; and like all objects to which a man devotes himself, they had fashioned him into correspondence with themselves. His loom, as he wrought in it without ceasing, had in its turn wrought on him and confirmed more and more the monotonous craving for its monotonous response. His gold, as he hung over it and saw it grow, gathered his power of loving together into a hard isolation like its own.

As soon as he was warm he began to think it would be a long while to wait till after supper before he drew out his guineas, and it would be pleasant to see them on the table before him as he ate his unwonted feast. For joy is the best of wine, and Silas's guineas were a golden wine of that sort.

He rose and placed his candle unsuspectingly on the floor near his loom, swept away the sand without noticing any change, and removed the bricks. The sight of the empty hole made his heart leap violently, but the belief that his gold was gone could not come at once—only terror and the eager effort to put an end to the terror. He passed his trembling hand all about the hole, trying to think it possible that his eyes had deceived him; then he held the candle in the hole and examined it curiously, trembling more and more. At last he shook so violently that he let fall the candle and lifted his hands to his head, trying to steady himself, that he might think. Had he put his gold somewhere else, by a sudden resolution last night, and then forgotten it? A man falling into dark waters seeks a momentary footing even on sliding stones; and Silas, by acting as if he believed in false hopes, warded off the moment of despair. He searched in every corner, he turned his bed over, and shook it and kneaded it; he looked in his brick oven where he laid his sticks. When there was no other place to be searched, he kneeled down again and felt once more all round the hole. There was no untried refuge left for a moment's shelter from the terrible truth.

Yes, there was a sort of refuge which always comes with the prostration of thought under an overpowering passion: it was that expectation of impossibilities, that belief in contradictory images, which is still distinct from madness because it is capable of being dissipated by the external fact. Silas got up from his knees trembling and looked round at the table: didn't the gold lie there after all? The table was bare. Then he turned and looked behind him— looked all round his dwelling, seeming to strain his brown eyes after some possible appearance of the bags where he had already sought them in vain. He could see every object in his cottage—and his gold was not there.

Again he put his trembling hands to his

head and gave a wild ringing scream, the cry of desolation. For a few moments after, he stood motionless; but the cry had relieved him from the first maddening pressure of the truth. He turned, and tottered toward his loom, and got into the seat where he worked, instinctively seeking this as the strongest assurance of reality.

And now that all the false hopes had vanished, and the first shock of certainty was past, the idea of a thief began to present itself, and he entertained it eagerly, because a thief might be caught and made to restore the gold. The thought brought some new strength with it, and he started from his loom to the door. As he opened it the rain beat in upon him, for it was falling more and more heavily. There were no footsteps to be tracked on such a night—footsteps? When had the thief come? During Silas's absence in the daytime the door had been locked, and there had been no marks of any inroad on his return by daylight. And in the evening, too, he said to himself, everything was the same as when he had left it. The sand and bricks looked as if they had not been moved. *Was* it a thief who had taken the bags? or was it a cruel power that no hands could reach which had delighted in making him a second time desolate? He shrank from this vaguer dread and fixed his mind with struggling effort on the robber with hands, who could be reached by hands. His thoughts glanced at all the neighbors who had made any remarks or asked any questions which he might now regard as a ground of suspicion. There was Jem Rodney, a known poacher,[1] and otherwise disreputable: he had often met Marner in his journeys across the fields and had said something jestingly about the weaver's money; nay,

[1] **poacher:** one who steals game or fish from private lands.

he had once irritated Marner by lingering at the fire when he called to light his pipe, instead of going about his business. Jem Rodney was the man—there was ease in the thought. Jem could be found and made to restore the money: Marner did not want to punish him, but only to get back his gold which had gone from him and left his soul like a forlorn traveler on an unknown desert. The robber must be laid hold of. Marner's ideas of legal authority were confused, but he felt that he must go and proclaim his loss; and the great people in the village—the clergyman, the constable, and Squire Cass— would make Jem Rodney, or somebody else, deliver up the stolen money. He rushed out in the rain, under the stimulus of this hope, forgetting to cover his head, not caring to fasten his door; for he felt as if he had nothing left to lose. He ran swiftly, till want of breath compelled him to slacken his pace as he was entering the village at the turning close to the Rainbow.

The Rainbow, in Marner's view, was a place of luxurious resort for rich and stout husbands, whose wives had superfluous stores of linen; it was the place where he was likely to find the powers and dignities of Raveloe and where he could most speedily make his loss public. He lifted the latch and turned into the bright bar or kitchen on the right hand, where the less lofty customers of the house were in the habit of assembling, the parlor on the left being reserved for the more select society in which Squire Cass frequently enjoyed the double pleasure of convivialty and condescension. But the parlor was dark tonight, the chief personages who ornamented its circle being all at Mrs. Osgood's birthday dance, as Godfrey Cass was. And in consequence of this, the party on the high-screened seats in the kitchen was more numerous than usual; several

personages, who would otherwise have been admitted into the parlor and enlarged the opportunity of hectoring and condescension for their betters, being content this evening to vary their enjoyment by taking their spirits-and-water where they could themselves hector and condescend in company that called for beer.

CHAPTER VI

Town Talk

THE CONVERSATION, which was at a high pitch of animation when Silas approached the door of the Rainbow, had, as usual, been slow and intermittent when the company first assembled. The pipes began to be puffed in a silence which had an air of severity; the more important customers, who drank spirits and sat nearest the fire, staring at each other as if a bet were depending on the first man who winked; while the beer drinkers, chiefly men in fustian jackets and smock frocks,[1] kept their eyelids down and rubbed their hands across their mouths, as if their

draughts of beer were a funereal duty attended with embarrassing sadness. At last, Mr. Snell, the landlord, a man of a neutral disposition, accustomed to stand aloof from human differences as those of beings who were all alike in need of liquor, broke silence, by saying in a doubtful tone to his cousin the butcher—

"Some folks 'ud say that was a fine beast you druv in yesterday, Bob?"

The butcher, a jolly, smiling, red-haired man, was not disposed to answer rashly. He gave a few puffs before he spat and replied, "And they wouldn't be fur wrong, John."

After this feeble delusive thaw, the silence set in as severely as before.

"Was it a red Durham?" said the farrier,[2] taking up the thread of discourse after the lapse of a few minutes.

The farrier looked at the landlord, and the landlord looked at the butcher, as the person who must take the responsibility of answering.

"Red it was," said the butcher, in his good-humored husky treble—"and a Durham it was."

"Then you needn't tell *me* who you bought it of," said the farrier, looking round with some triumph; "I know who it is has got the red Durhams o' this countryside. And she'd a white star on her brow, I'll bet a penny?" The farrier leaned forward with his hands on his knees as he put this question, and his eyes twinkled knowingly.

"Well! yes—she might," said the butcher, slowly, considering that he was giving a decided affirmative. "I don't say contrary."

"I knew that very well," said the farrier, throwing himself backward again and speaking defiantly; "if *I* don't know Mr. Lammeter's cows, I should like to

[1] **fustian** (fus′chən) . . . **smock frocks:** jackets of heavy cotton and long, loose, shirtlike smocks.

[2] **farrier:** horseshoer and animal doctor.

know who does—that's all. And as for the cow you've bought, bargain or no bargain, I've been at the drenching [1] of her—contradick me who will."

The farrier looked fierce, and the mild butcher's conversational spirit was roused a little.

"I'm not for contradicking no man," he said; "I'm for peace and quietness. Some are for cutting long ribs—I'm for cutting 'em short myself; but *I* don't quarrel with 'em. All I say is, it's a lovely carkiss— and anybody as was reasonable, it 'ud bring tears into their eyes to look at it."

"Well, it's the cow as I drenched, whatever it is," pursued the farrier angrily; "and it was Mr. Lammeter's cow, else you told a lie when you said it was a red Durham."

"I tell no lies," said the butcher, with the same mild huskiness as before, "and I contradick none—not if a man was to swear himself black: he's no meat o' mine, nor none o' my bargains. All I say is, it's a lovely carkiss. And what I say I'll stick to; but I'll quarrel wi' no man."

"No," said the farrier, with bitter sarcasm, looking at the company generally; "and p'rhaps you aren't pigheaded; and p'rhaps you didn't say the cow was a red Durham; and p'rhaps you didn't say she'd got a star on her brow—stick to that, now you're at it."

"Come, come," said the landlord; "let the cow alone. The truth lies atween you: you're both right and both wrong, as I allays say. And as for the cow's being Mr. Lammeter's, I say nothing to that; but this I say, as the Rainbow's the Rainbow. And for the matter o' that, if the talk is to be o' the Lammeters, *you* know the most upo' that head, eh, Mr. Macey? You remember when first Mr. Lammeter's father come to these parts and took the

Warrens?"

Mr. Macey, tailor and parish clerk, the latter of which functions rheumatism had of late obliged him to share with a small-featured young man who sat opposite him, held his white head on one side and twirled his thumbs with an air of complacency, slightly seasoned with criticism. He smiled pityingly, in answer to the landlord's appeal, and said—

"Ay, ay; I know, I know; but I let other folks talk. I've laid by now, and gev up to the young uns. Ask them as have been to school at Tarley; they've learnt pernouncing; that's come up since my day."

"If you're pointing at me, Mr. Macey," said the deputy clerk, with an air of anxious propriety, "I'm nowise a man to speak out of my place. As the psalm says—

'I know what's right, nor only so,
But also practice what I know.'"

"Well, then, I wish you'd keep hold o' the tune, when it's set for you; if you're for prac*tic*ing, I wish you'd prac*tice* that," said a large jocose-looking man, an excellent wheelwright in his weekday capacity, but on Sundays leader of the choir. He winked, as he spoke, at two of the company, who were known officially as the "bassoon" and the "key bugle," in the confidence that he was expressing the sense of the musical profession in Raveloe.

Mr. Tookey, the deputy clerk, who shared the unpopularity common to deputies, turned very red, but replied, with careful moderation—"Mr. Winthrop, if you'll bring me any proof as I'm in the wrong, I'm not the man to say I won't alter. But there's people set up their own ears for a standard and expect the whole choir to follow 'em. There may be two opinions, I hope."

"Ay, ay," said Mr. Macey, who felt very well satisfied with this attack on youthful presumption; "you're right there, Tookey: there's allays two 'pinions; there's the 'pinion a man has of himsen, and there's the 'pinion other folks have on him. There'd be two 'pinions about a cracked bell, if the bell could hear itself."

"Well, Mr. Macey," said poor Tookey, serious amidst the general laughter, "I undertook to partially fill up the office of parish clerk by Mr. Crackenthorp's desire, whenever your infirmities should make you unfitting; and it's one of the rights thereof to sing in the choir—else Why have you done the same yourself?"

"Ah! but the old gentleman and you are two folks," said Ben Winthrop. "The old gentleman's got a gift. Why the Squire used to invite him to take a glass, only to hear him sing the 'Red Rovier;' didn't he, Mr. Macey? It's a nat'ral gift. There's my little lad Aaron, he's got a gift—he can sing a tune off straight, like a throstle.[1] But as for you, Master Tookey, you'd better stick to your 'Amens': your voice is well enough when you keep it up in your nose. It's your inside as isn't right made for music: it's no better nor a hollow stalk."

This kind of unflinching frankness was the most piquant form of joke to the company at the Rainbow, and Ben Winthrop's insult was felt by everybody to have capped Mr. Macey's epigram.

"I see what it is plain enough," said Mr. Tookey, unable to keep cool any longer. "There's a consperacy to turn me out o' the choir, as I shouldn't share the Christmas money—that's where it is. But I shall speak to Mr. Crackenthorp; I'll not be put upon by no man."

"Nay, nay, Tookey," said Ben Winthrop. "We'll pay you your share to keep out of it—that's what we'll do. There's things folks 'ud pay to be rid on, besides varmin."

"Come, come," said the landlord, who felt that paying people for their absence was a principle dangerous to society; "a joke's a joke. We're all good friends here, I hope. We must give and take. You're both right and you're both wrong, as I say. I agree wi' Mr. Macey here, as there's two opinions; and if mine was asked, I should say they're both right. Tookey's right and Winthrop's right, and they've only got to split the difference and make themselves even."

The farrier was puffing his pipe rather fiercely, in some contempt at this trivial discussion. He had no ear for music himself and never went to church, as being of the medical profession and likely to be in requisition for delicate cows. But the butcher, having music in his soul, had listened with a divided desire for Tookey's defeat and for the preservation of the peace.

"To be sure," he said, following up the landlord's conciliatory view, "we're fond of our old clerk; it's nat'ral, and him used to be such a singer and got a brother as is known for the first fiddler in this countryside. Eh, it's a pity but what Solomon lived in our village and could give us a tune when we liked; eh, Mr. Macey? I'd keep him in liver and lights for nothing—that I would."

"Ay, ay," said Mr. Macey, in the height of complacency; "our family's been known for musicianers as far back as anybody can tell. But them things are dying out, as I tell Solomon every time he comes round; there's no voices like what there used to be, and there's nobody remembers what we remember, if it isn't the old crows."

"Ay, you remember when first Mr. Lammeter's father come into these parts,

[1] **throstle:** thrush.

don't you, Mr. Macey?" said the landlord.

"I should think I did," said the old man, who had now gone through that complimentary process necessary to bring him up to the point of narration; "and a fine old gentleman he was—as fine and finer nor the Mr. Lammeter as now is. He came from a bit north'ard, so far as I could ever make out. But there's nobody rightly knows about those parts: only it couldn't be far north'ard, nor much different from this country, for he brought a fine breed o' sheep with him, so there must be pastures there and everything reasonable. We heared tell as he'd sold his own land to come and take the Warrens, and that seemed odd for a man as had land of his own to come and rent a farm in a strange place. But they said it was along of his wife's dying; though there's reasons in things as nobody knows on—that's pretty much what I've made out; yet some folks are so wise, they'll find you fifty reasons straight off, and all the while the real reason's winking at 'em in the corner, and they niver see't. Howsomever, it was soon seen as we'd got a new parish'ner as know'd the rights and customs o' things, and kep a good house, and was well looked on by everybody. And the young man— that's the Mr. Lammeter as now is, for he'd niver a sister—soon begun to court Miss Osgood, that's the sister o' the Mr. Osgood as now is, and a fine handsome lass she was—eh, you can't think—they pretend this young lass is like her, but that's the way wi' people as don't know what come before 'em. *I* should know, for I helped the old rector, Mr. Drumlow as was, I helped him marry 'em."

Here Mr. Macey paused; he always gave his narrative in installments, expecting to be questioned according to precedent.

"Ay, and a partic'lar thing happened, didn't it, Mr. Macey, so as you were likely to remember that marriage?" said the landlord, in a congratulatory tone.

"I should think there did—a *very* partic'lar thing," said Mr. Macey, nodding sideways. "For Mr. Drumlow—poor old gentleman, I was fond on him, though he'd got a bit confused in his head, what wi' age and wi' taking a drop o' summat warm when the service come of a cold morning. And young Mr. Lammeter he'd have no way but he must be married in Janiwary, which, to be sure, 's a unreasonable time to be married in, for it isn't like a christening or a burying, as you can't help; and so Mr. Drumlow—poor old gentleman, I was fond on him—but when he come to put the questions, he put 'em by the rule o' contrairy, like, and he says, "Wilt thou have this man to thy wedded wife?' says he, and then he says, 'Wilt thou have this woman to thy wedded husband?' says he. But the partic'larest thing of all is, as nobody took any notice on it but me, and they answered straight off 'yes,' like as if it had been me saying 'Amen' i' the right place, without listening to what went before."

"But *you* knew what was going on well enough, didn't you, Mr. Macey? You were live enough, eh?" said the butcher.

"Lor bless you!" said Mr. Macey, pausing and smiling in pity at the impotence of his hearer's imagination—"why, I was all of a tremble: it was as if I'd been a coat pulled by the two tails, like; for I couldn't stop the parson, I couldn't take upon me to do that; and yet I said to myself, I says, 'Suppose they shouldn't be fast married, 'cause the words are contrairy?' and my head went working like a mill, for I was allays uncommon for turning things over and seeing all round 'em; and I says to myself, 'Is't the meanin' or the words as makes folks fast i' wedlock?' For the parson meant right, and the bride and bride-

groom meant right. But then, when I come to think on it, meanin' goes but a little way i' most things, for you may mean to stick things together and your glue may be bad, and then where are you? And so I says to mysen, 'It isn't the meanin', it's the glue.' And I was worreted as if I'd got three bells to pull at once, when we went into the vestry, and they begun to sign their names. But where's the use o' talking?—you can't think what goes on in a 'cute [1] man's inside."

"But you held in for all that, didn't you, Mr. Macey?" said the landlord.

"Ay, I held in tight till I was by mysen wi' Mr. Drumlow, and then I out wi' everything, but respectful, as I allays did. And he made light on it, and he says, 'Pooh, pooh, Macey, make yourself easy,' he says; 'it's neither the meaning nor the words—it's the re*ges*ter does it—that's the glue.' So you see he settled it easy; for parsons and doctors know everything by heart, like, so as they aren't worreted wi' thinking what's the rights and wrongs o' things, as I'n been many and many's the time. And sure enough the wedding turned out all right, on'y poor Mrs. Lammeter— that's Miss Osgood as was—died afore the lasses was growed up; but for prosperity and everything respectable, there's no family more looked on."

Every one of Mr. Macey's audience had heard this story many times, but it was listened to as if it had been a favorite tune, and at certain points the puffing of the pipes was momentarily suspended that the listeners might give their whole minds to the expected words. But there was more to come; and Mr. Snell, the landlord, duly put the leading question.

"Why, old Mr. Lammeter had a pretty fortin' [2] didn't they say, when he come into these parts?"

"Well, yes," said Mr. Macey; "but I daresay it's as much as this Mr. Lammeter's done to keep it whole. For there was allays a talk as nobody could get rich on the Warrens: though he holds it cheap, for it's what they call Charity Land."

"Ay, and there's few folks know so well as you how it come to be Charity Land, eh, Mr. Macey?" said the butcher.

"How should they?" said the old clerk, with some contempt. "Why, my grandfather made the groom's livery for that Mr. Cliff as came and built the big stables at the Warrens. Why, they're stables four times as big as Squire Cass's, for he thought o' nothing but hosses and hunting. Cliff didn't—a Lunnon [3] tailor, some folks said, as had gone mad wi' cheating. For he couldn't ride; lor bless you! they said he'd got no more grip o' the hoss than if his legs had been cross-sticks: my grandfather heared old Squire Cass say so many and many a time. But ride he would as if Old Harry [4] had been a-driving him; and he'd a son, a lad o' sixteen; and nothing would his father have him do, but he must ride and ride—though the lad was frighted, they said. And it was a common saying as the father wanted to ride the tailor out o' the lad and make a gentleman on him—not but what I'm a tailor myself, but in respect as God made me such, I'm proud on it, for 'Macey, tailor,' 's been wrote up over our door since afore the Queen's heads went out on the shillings. But Cliff, he was ashamed o' being called a tailor, and he was sore vexed as his riding was laughed at, and nobody o' the gentlefolks hereabout could abide him. Howsomever, the poor lad got sickly and died, and the father didn't live long after him, for he got queerer nor ever, and they said he used to go out i' the dead of the night, wi' a lantern in his hand, to the

[1] **'cute:** acute, clever.
[2] **fortin':** fortune.

[3] **Lunnon:** London.
[4] **Old Harry:** the devil.

stables, and set a lot o' lights burning, for he got as he couldn't sleep; and there he'd stand, cracking his whip and looking at his hosses; and they said it was a mercy as the stables didn't get burnt down wi' the poor dumb creaturs in 'em. But at last he died raving, and they found as he'd left all his property, Warrens and all, to a Lunnon Charity, and that's how the Warrens come to be Charity Land; though, as for the stables, Mr. Lammeter never uses 'em—they're out o' all charicter—lor bless you! if you was to set the doors a-banging in 'em, it 'ud sound like thunder half o'er the parish."

"Ay, but there's more going on in the stables than what folks see by daylight, eh, Mr. Macey?" said the landlord.

"Ay, ay; go that way of a dark night, that's all," said Mr. Macey, winking mysteriously, "and then make believe, if you like, as you didn't see lights i' the stables, nor hear the stamping o' the hosses, nor the cracking o' the whips, and howling, too, if it's tow'rt daybreak. 'Cliff's Holiday' has been the name of it ever sin' I were a boy; that's to say, some said as it was the holiday Old Harry gev him from roasting, like. That's what my father told me, and he was a reasonable man, though there's folks nowadays know what happened afore they were born better nor they know their own business."

"What do you say to that, eh, Dowlas?" said the landlord, turning to the farrier, who was swelling with impatience for his cue. "There's a nut for *you* to crack."

Mr. Dowlas was the negative spirit in the company, and was proud of his position.

"Say? I say what a man *should* say as doesn't shut his eyes to look at a finger post. I say, as I'm ready to wager any man ten pound, if he'll stand out wi' me any dry night in the pasture before the Warren stables, as we shall neither see lights nor hear noises, if it isn't the blowing of our own noses. That's what I say, and I've said it many a time; but there's nobody 'ull ventur a ten-pun' note on their ghos'es [1] as they make so sure of."

"Why, Dowlas, that's easy betting, that is," said Ben Winthrop. "You might as well bet a man as he wouldn't catch the rheumatise if he stood up to's neck in the pool of a frosty night. It 'ud be fine fun for a man to win his bet as he'd catch the rheumatise. Folks as believe in Cliff's Holiday aren't a-going to ventur near it for a matter o' ten pound."

"If Master Dowlas wants to know the truth on it," said Mr. Macey, with a sarcastic smile, tapping his thumbs together, "he's no call to lay any bet—let him go and stan' by himself—there's nobody 'ull hinder him; and then he can let the parish'-ners know if they're wrong."

"Thank you! I'm obliged to you," said the farrier, with a snort of scorn. "If folks are fools, it's no business o' mine. *I* don't want to make out the truth about ghos'es: I know it a'ready. But I'm not against a bet—everything fair and open. Let any man bet me ten pound as I shall see Cliff's Holiday, and I'll go and stand by myself. I want no company. I'd as lief do it as I'd fill this pipe."

"Ah, but who's to watch you, Dowlas, and see you do it? That's no fair bet," said the butcher.

"No fair bet?" replied Mr. Dowlas, angrily. "I should like to hear any man stand up and say I want to bet unfair. Come now, Master Lundy, I should like to hear you say it."

"Very like you would," said the butcher. "But it's no business o' mine. You're none o' my bargains, and I aren't a-going to try and 'bate your price. If anybody 'll bid for you at your own vally-

[1] **ventur . . . ghos'es:** venture a ten-pound note on their ghosts.

ing, let him. I'm for peace and quietness, I am."

"Yes, that's what every yapping cur is, when you hold a stick up at him," said the farrier. "But I'm afraid o' neither man nor ghost, and I'm ready to lay a fair bet. *I aren't a turntail cur.*"

"Ay, but there's this in it, Dowlas," said the landlord, speaking in a tone of much candor and tolerance. "There's folks, i' my opinion, they can't see ghos'es, not if they stood as plain as a pikestaff before 'em. And there's reason i' that. For there's my wife, now, can't smell, not if she'd the strongest o' cheese under her nose. I never see'd a ghost myself; but then I says to myself, 'Very like I haven't got the smell for 'em.' I mean, putting a ghost for a smell, or else contrairiways. And so, I'm for holding with both sides; for, as I say, the truth lies between 'em. And if Dowlas was to go and stand and say he'd never seen a wink o' Cliff's Holiday all the night through, I'd back him; and if anybody said as Cliff's Holiday was certain sure for all that, I'd back *him* too. For the smell's what I go by."

The landlord's analogical argument [1] was not well received by the farrier—a man intensely opposed to compromise.

"Tut, tut," he said, setting down his glass with refreshed irritation; "what's the smell got to do with it? Did ever a ghost give a man a black eye? That's what I should like to know. If ghos'es want me to believe in 'em, let 'em leave off skulking i' the dark and i' lone places—let 'em come where there's company and candles."

"As if ghos'es 'ud want to be believed in by anybody so ignirant!" said Mr. Macey, in deep disgust at the farrier's crass incompetence to apprehend the conditions of ghostly phenomena.

[1] **analogical** (an′ə·loj′i·kəl) **argument:** argument by showing the likeness between two things or situations.

Excitement at the Rainbow Inn

Yет тне next moment there seemed to be some evidence that ghosts had a more condescending disposition than Mr. Macey attributed to them; for the pale thin figure of Silas Marner was suddenly seen standing in the warm light, uttering no word, but looking round at the company with his strange unearthly eyes. The long pipes gave a simultaneous movement, like the antennae of startled insects, and every man present, not excepting even the skeptical farrier, had an impression that he saw, not Silas Marner in the flesh, but an apparition; for the door by which Silas had entered was hidden by the high-screened seats, and no one had noticed his approach. Mr. Macey, sitting a long way off the ghost, might be supposed to have felt an argumentative triumph, which would tend to neutralize his share of the general alarm. Had he not always said that when Silas Marner was in that strange trance of his, his soul went loose from his body? Here was the demonstration: nevertheless, on the whole, he would have been as well contented without it. For a few moments there was a dead silence, Marner's want of breath and agitation not allowing him to speak. The landlord, under the habitual sense that he was bound to keep his house open to all company and confident in the protection of his unbroken neutrality, at last took on himself the task of adjuring [2] the ghost.

"Master Marner," he said, in a conciliatory tone, "what's lacking to you? What's your business here?"

"Robbed!" said Silas, gaspingly. "I've been robbed! I want the constable—and

[2] **adjuring:** appealing to.

the Justice—and Squire Cass—and Mr. Crackenthorp."

"Lay hold on him, Jem Rodney," said the landlord, the idea of a ghost subsiding; "he's off his head, I doubt.[1] He's wet through."

Jem Rodney was the outermost man and sat conveniently near Marner's standing place; but he declined to give his services.

"Come and lay hold on him yourself, Mr. Snell, if you've a mind," said Jem, rather sullenly. "He's been robbed, and murdered too, for what I know," he added, in a muttering tone.

"Jem Rodney!" said Silas, turning and fixing his strange eyes on the suspected man.

"Ay, Master Marner, what do ye want wi' me?" said Jem, trembling a little and seizing his drinking can as a defensive weapon.

"If it was you stole my money," said Silas, clasping his hands entreatingly and raising his voice to a cry, "give it me back—and I won't meddle with you. I won't set the constable on you. Give it me back, and I'll let you—I'll let you have a guinea."

"Me stole your money!" said Jem, angrily. "I'll pitch this can at your eye if you talk o' *my* stealing your money."

"Come, come, Master Marner," said the landlord, now rising resolutely and seizing Marner by the shoulder, "if you've got any information to lay, speak it out sensible and show as you're in your right mind, if you expect anybody to listen to you. You're as wet as a drownded rat. Sit down and dry yourself and speak straightforrard."

"Ah, to be sure, man," said the farrier, who began to feel that he had not been quite on a par with himself and the occasion. "Let's have no more staring and screaming, else we'll have you strapped for a madman. That was why I didn't speak at the first—thinks I the man's run mad."

"Ay, ay, make him sit down," said several voices at once, well pleased that the reality of ghosts remained still an open question.

The landlord forced Marner to take off his coat and then to sit down on a chair aloof from everyone else, in the center of the circle and in the direct rays of the fire. The weaver, too feeble to have any distinct purpose beyond that of getting help to recover his money, submitted unresistingly. The transient fears of the company were now forgotten in their strong curiosity, and all faces were turned toward Silas, when the landlord, having seated himself again, said—

"Now then, Master Marner, what's this you've got to say—as you've been robbed? Speak out."

"He'd better not say again as it was me robbed him," cried Jem Rodney, hastily. "What could I ha' done with his money? I could as easy steal the parson's surplice[2] and wear it."

"Hold your tongue, Jem, and let's hear what he's got to say," said the landlord. "Now then, Master Marner."

Silas now told his story, under frequent questioning as the mysterious character of the robbery became evident.

This strangely novel situation of opening his trouble to his Raveloe neighbors, of sitting in the warmth of a hearth not his own and feeling the presence of faces and voices which were his nearest promise of help, had doubtless its influence on Marner, in spite of his passionate preoccupation with his loss. Our consciousness rarely registers the beginning of a growth

[1] **I doubt:** I have no doubt.

[2] **surplice:** a loose robe worn by a priest during church services.

within us any more than without us: there have been many circulations of the sap before we detect the smallest sign of the bud.

The slight suspicion with which his hearers at first listened to him gradually melted away before the convincing simplicity of his distress: it was impossible for the neighbors to doubt that Marner was telling the truth, not because they were capable of arguing at once from the nature of his statements to the absence of any motive for making them falsely, but because, as Mr. Macey observed, "Folks as had the devil to back 'em were not likely to be so mushed" as poor Silas was. Rather, from the strange fact that the robber had left no traces and had happened to know the nick of time, utterly incalculable by mortal agents, when Silas would go away from home without locking his door, the more probable conclusion seemed to be that his disreputable intimacy in that quarter, if it ever existed, had been broken up and that, in consequence, this ill turn had been done to Marner by somebody it was quite in vain to set the constable after. Why this preternatural felon should be obliged to wait till the door was left unlocked was a question which did not present itself.

"It isn't Jem Rodney as has done this work, Master Marner," said the landlord. "You mustn't be a-casting your eye at poor Jem. There may be a bit of a reckoning against Jem for the matter of a hare or so if anybody was bound to keep their eyes staring open and niver to wink; but Jem's been a-sitting here drinking his can, like the decentest man i' the parish, since before you left your house, Master Marner, by your own account."

"Ay, ay," said Mr. Macey; "let's have no accusing o' the innicent. That isn't the law. There must be folks to swear again' a man before he can be ta'en up. Let's have

no accusing o' the innicent, Master Marner."

Memory was not so utterly torpid in Silas that it could not be wakened by these words. With a movement of compunction as new and strange to him as everything else within the last hour, he started from his chair and went close up to Jem, looking at him as if he wanted to assure himself of the expression in his face.

"I was wrong," he said—"yes, yes—I ought to have thought. There's nothing to witness against you, Jem. Only you'd been into my house oftener than anybody else, and so you came into my head. I don't accuse you—I won't accuse anybody—only," he added, lifting up his hands to his head and turning away with bewildered misery, "I try—I try to think where my guineas can be."

"Ay, ay, they're gone where it's hot enough to melt 'em, I doubt," said Mr. Macey.

"Tchuh!" said the farrier. And then he asked, with a cross-examining air, "How much money might there be in the bags, Master Marner?"

"Two hundred and seventy-two pounds, twelve and sixpence, last night when I counted it," said Silas, seating himself again, with a groan.

"Pooh! why, they'd be none so heavy to carry. Some tramp's been in, that's all; and as for the no footmarks, and the bricks and the sand being all right—why, your eyes are pretty much like a insect's, Master Marner; they're obliged to look so close, you can't see much at a time. It's my opinion as, if I'd been you or you'd been me—for it comes to the same thing—you wouldn't have thought you'd found everything as you left it. But what I vote is, as two of the sensiblest o' the company should go with you to Master Kench, the constable's—he's ill i' bed, I know that much—and get him to appoint one of us

his deppity; for that's the law, and I don't think anybody 'ull take upon him to contradick me there. It isn't much of a walk to Kench's; and then, if it's me as is deppity, I'll go back with you, Master Marner, and examine your premises; and if anybody's got any fault to find with that, I'll thank him to stand up and say it out like a man."

By this pregnant speech the farrier had reestablished his self-complacency, and waited with confidence to hear himself named as one of the superlatively sensible men.

"Let us see how the night is, though," said the landlord, who also considered himself personally concerned in this proposition. "Why, it rains heavy still," he said, returning from the door.

"Well, I'm not the man to be afraid o' the rain," said the farrier. "For it'll look bad when Justice Malam hears as respectable men like us had a information laid before 'em and took no steps."

The landlord agreed with this view, and after taking the sense of the company and duly rehearsing a small ceremony known in high ecclesiastical life as the *nolo episcopari*,[1] he consented to take on himself the chill dignity of going to Kench's. But to the farrier's strong disgust, Mr. Macey now started an objection to his proposing himself as a deputy constable; for that oracular old gentleman, claiming to know the law, stated, as a fact delivered to him by his father, that no doctor could be a constable.

"And you're a doctor, I reckon, though you're only a cow doctor, for a fly's a fly, though it may be a hoss fly," concluded Mr. Macey, wondering a little at his own "'cuteness."

[1] *nolo episcopari:* "I do not want to be a bishop," a phrase repeated by bishops when taking office in the Anglican Church. The landlord is making a pretense of taking the responsibility unwillingly, simply for the sake of doing good.

There was a hot debate upon this, the farrier being of course indisposed to renounce the quality of doctor, but contending that a doctor could be a constable if he liked—the law meant, he needn't be one if he didn't like. Mr. Macey thought this was nonsense, since the law was not likely to be fonder of doctors than of other folks. Moreover, if it was in the nature of doctors more than of other men not to like being constables, how came Mr. Dowlas to be so eager to act in that capacity?

"*I* don't want to act the constable," said the farrier, driven into a corner by this merciless reasoning; "and there's no man can say it of me, if he'd tell the truth. But if there's to be any jealousy and envying about going to Kench's in the rain, let them go as like it—you won't get me to go, I can tell you."

By the landlord's intervention, however, the dispute was accommodated.[2] Mr. Dowlas consented to go as a second person disinclined to act officially; and so poor Silas, furnished with some old coverings, turned out with his two companions into the rain again, thinking of the long night hours before him, not as those do who long to rest, but as those who expect to "watch for the morning."

[2] **accommodated:** settled.

FOR STUDY AND DISCUSSION

1. Why had Silas left home? Why had he left his door unlatched? What gave him a false sense of security? How was his sense of security like Dunsey's confidence in his luck?

2. What is Silas's reaction to the discovery that his gold is missing? Why is he so slow to realize the truth?

3. What two possible explanations does Silas see for the gold's disappearance? Why is he so eager to suspect Jem Rodney? What explanation does he most fear?

4. What is amusing about the gathering at the Rainbow? about the individual characters?

5. How does George Eliot show her sense of humor in the "argument" between the butcher and the farrier? What is the argument about? Why is it so heated? What does the argument—and its resolution—show about the character of the farrier? of the butcher? of the landlord? Why is it to the landlord's advantage, as a landlord, to smooth things over and not take sides between the two?

6. What other characters reveal their natures in this scene? What seems to be the attitude of Mr. Macey, the parish clerk, toward his deputy, Tookey? What seems to be his deputy's attitude toward him?

7. What is amusing about Mr. Macey's manner of storytelling? Where did he get his information? What question is raised by his tale of Cliff's stables? How does the landlord resolve this question?

8. What is the reaction of the villagers to Silas's announcement? How does his misfortune change their attitude toward him?

9. Why does Silas, even in this moment of great personal concern, feel moved to apologize to Jem Rodney? As Silas sits among the men at the Rainbow, what change seems to be taking place in him?

10. Why does the farrier volunteer to go with Silas? Why do the others object to this? Are they more concerned with Silas or with their own importance? What makes you think so?

CHAPTER VIII

Clues

WHEN GODFREY CASS returned from Mrs. Osgood's party at midnight, he was not much surprised to learn that Dunsey had not come home. Perhaps he had not sold Wildfire, and was waiting for another chance—perhaps, on that foggy afternoon, he had preferred housing himself at the Red Lion at Batherley for the night, if the run had kept him in that neighborhood; for

he was not likely to feel much concern about leaving his brother in suspense. Godfrey's mind was too full of Nancy Lammeter's looks and behavior, too full of the exasperation against himself and his lot, which the sight of her always produced in him, for him to give much thought to Wildfire or to the probabilities of Dunstan's conduct.

The next morning the whole village was excited by the story of the robbery, and Godfrey, like everyone else, was occupied in gathering and discussing news about it, and in visiting the stone pits. The rain had washed away all possibility of distinguishing footmarks, but a close investigation of the spot had disclosed, in the direction opposite to the village, a tinderbox,[1] with a flint and steel, half sunk in the mud. It was not Silas's tinderbox, for the only one he had ever had was still standing on his shelf; and the inference generally accepted was that the tinderbox in the ditch was somehow connected with the robbery. A small minority shook their heads and intimated their opinion that it was not a robbery to have light thrown on it by tinderboxes, that Master Marner's tale had a queer look with it, and that such things had been known as a man's doing himself a mischief and then setting the justice to look for the doer. But when questioned closely as to their grounds for this opinion, and what Master Marner had to gain by such false pretenses, they only shook their heads as before and observed that there

[1] **tinderbox:** a small box containing materials for lighting a fire.

was no knowing what some folks counted gain; moreover, that everybody had a right to their own opinions, grounds or no grounds, and that the weaver, as everybody knew, was partly crazy. Mr. Macey, though he joined in the defense of Marner against all suspicions of deceit, also poohpoohed the tinderbox; indeed, repudiated it as a rather impious suggestion, tending to imply that everything must be done by human hands and that there was no power which could make away with the guineas without moving the bricks. Nevertheless, he turned round rather sharply on Mr. Tookey, when the zealous deputy, feeling that this was a view of the case peculiarly suited to a parish clerk, carried it still further, and doubted whether it was right to inquire into a robbery at all when the circumstances were so mysterious.

"As if," concluded Mr. Tookey—"as if there was nothing but what could be made out by justices and constables."

"Now, don't you be for overshooting the mark, Tookey," said Mr. Macey, nodding his head aside, admonishingly. "That's what you're allays at; if I throw a stone and hit, you think there's summat better than hitting, and you try to throw a stone beyond. What I said was against the tinderbox; I said nothing against justices and constables, for they're o' King George's making, and it 'ud be ill becoming a man in a parish office to fly out again' King George."

While these discussions were going on amongst the group outside the Rainbow, a higher consultation was being carried on within, under the presidency of Mr. Crackenthorp, the Rector,[1] assisted by Squire Cass and other substantial parishioners. It had just occurred to Mr. Snell, the landlord—he being, as he observed, a man accustomed to put two and two together—to connect with the tinderbox, which, as deputy constable, he himself had had the honorable distinction of finding, certain recollections of a peddler who had called to drink at the house about a month before and had actually stated that he carried a tinderbox about with him to light his pipe. Here, surely, was a clue to be followed out. And as memory, when duly impregnated with ascertained facts, is sometimes surprisingly fertile, Mr. Snell gradually recovered a vivid impression of the effect produced on him by the peddler's countenance and conversation. He had a "look with his eye" which fell unpleasantly on Mr. Snell's sensitive organism. To be sure, he didn't say anything particular—no, except that about the tinderbox—but it isn't what a man says, it's the way he says it. Moreover, he had a swarthy foreignness of complexion which boded little honesty.

"Did he wear earrings?" Mr. Crackenthorp wished to know, having some acquaintance with foreign customs.

"Well—stay—let me see," said Mr. Snell, like a docile clairvoyant,[2] who would really not make a mistake if she could help it. After stretching the corners of his mouth and contracting his eyes, as if he were trying to see the earrings, he appeared to give up the effort, and said, "Well, he'd got earrings in his box to sell, so it's nat'ral to suppose he might wear 'em. But he called at every house, a'most, in the village; there's somebody else, mayhap, saw 'em in his ears, though I can't take upon me rightly to say."

Mr. Snell was correct in his surmise that somebody else would remember the peddler's earrings. For on the spread of inquiry among the villagers it was stated, with gathering emphasis that the parson had wanted to know whether the peddler

<hr>

[1] **Rector:** the minister of the parish.

[2] **docile clairvoyant:** fortuneteller who wants to say the right thing.

wore earrings in his ears, and an impression was created that a great deal depended on the eliciting of this fact. Of course, everyone who heard the question, not having any distinct image of the peddler as *without* earrings, immediately had an image of him *with* earrings, larger or smaller, as the case might be; and the image was presently taken for a vivid recollection, so that the glazier's wife, a well-intentioned woman, not given to lying, and whose house was among the cleanest in the village, was ready to declare, as sure as ever she meant to take the sacrament the very next Christmas that was ever coming, that she had seen big earrings, in the shape of the young moon, in the peddler's two ears; while Jinny Oates, the cobbler's daughter, being a more imaginative person, stated not only that she had seen them too, but that they had made her blood creep, as it did at that very moment while there she stood.

Also, by way of throwing further light on this clue of the tinderbox, a collection was made of all the articles purchased from the peddler at various houses and carried to the Rainbow to be exhibited there. In fact, there was a general feeling in the village, that for the clearing up of this robbery there must be a great deal done at the Rainbow and that no man need offer his wife an excuse for going there while it was the scene of severe public duties.

Some disappointment was felt, and perhaps a little indignation also, when it became known that Silas Marner, on being questioned by the Squire and the parson, had retained no other recollection of the peddler than that he called at his door, but had not entered his house, having turned away at once when Silas, holding the door ajar, had said that he wanted nothing. This had been Silas's testimony, though he clutched strongly at the idea of the peddler's being the culprit, if only because it gave him a definite image of a whereabout for his gold after it had been taken away from its hiding place: he could see it now in the peddler's box. But it was observed with some irritation in the village, that anybody but a "blind creatur" like Marner would have seen the man prowling about, for how came he to leave his tinderbox in the ditch close by, if he hadn't been lingering there? Doubtless, he had made his observations when he saw Marner at the door. Anybody might know—and only look at him—that the weaver was a half-crazy miser. It was a wonder the peddler hadn't murdered him; men of that sort, with rings in their ears, had been known for murderers often and often; there had been one tried at the 'sizes,[1] not so long ago but what there were people living who remembered it.

Godfrey Cass, indeed, entering the Rainbow during one of Mr. Snell's frequently repeated recitals of his testimony, had treated it lightly, stating that he himself had bought a penknife of the peddler and thought him a merry grinning fellow enough; it was all nonsense, he said, about the man's evil looks. But this was spoken of in the village as the random talk of youth, "as if it was only Mr. Snell who had seen something odd about the peddler!" On the contrary, there were at least half a dozen who were ready to go before Justice Malam and give in much more striking testimony than any the landlord could furnish. It was to be hoped Mr. Godfrey would not go to Tarley and throw cold water on what Mr. Snell said there and so prevent the justice from drawing up a warrant. He was suspected of intending this, when, after midday, he was seen setting off on horseback in the direction of Tarley.

[1] **'sizes:** assizes, court sessions.

But by this time Godfrey's interest in the robbery had faded before his growing anxiety about Dunstan and Wildfire, and he was going, not to Tarley, but to Batherley, unable to rest in uncertainty about them any longer. The possibility that Dunstan had played him the ugly trick of riding away with Wildfire, to return at the end of a month, when he had gambled away or otherwise squandered the price of the horse, was a fear that urged itself upon him more, even, than the thought of an accidental injury; and now that the dance at Mrs. Osgood's was past, he was irritated with himself that he had trusted his horse to Dunstan. Instead of trying to still his fears he encouraged them, with that superstitious impression which clings to us all, that if we expect evil very strongly it is the less likely to come; and when he heard a horse approaching at a trot and saw a hat rising above a hedge beyond an angle of the lane, he felt as if his conjuration had succeeded. But no sooner did the horse come within sight, than his heart sank again. It was not Wildfire; and in a few moments more he discerned that the rider was not Dunstan, but Bryce, who pulled up to speak, with a face that implied something disagreeable.

"Well, Mr. Godfrey, that's a lucky brother of yours, that Master Dunsey, isn't he?"

"What do you mean?" said Godfrey, hastily.

"Why, hasn't he been home yet?" said Bryce.

"Home? No. What has happened? Be quick. What has he done with my horse?"

"Ah, I thought it was yours, though he pretended you had parted with it to him."

"Has he thrown him down and broken his knees?" said Godfrey, flushed with exasperation.

"Worse than that," said Bryce. "You see, I'd made a bargain with him to buy the horse for a hundred and twenty—a swinging price,[1] but I always liked the horse. And what does he do but go and stake him—fly at a hedge with stakes in it, atop of a bank with a ditch before it. The horse had been dead a pretty good while when he was found. So he hasn't been home since, has he?"

"Home? No," said Godfrey, "and he'd better keep away. Confound me for a fool! I might have known this would be the end of it."

"Well, to tell you the truth," said Bryce, "after I'd bargained for the horse, it did come into my head that he might be riding and selling the horse without your knowledge, for I didn't believe it was his own. I knew Master Dunsey was up to his tricks sometimes. But where can he be gone? He's never been seen at Batherley. He couldn't have been hurt, for he must have walked off."

"Hurt?" said Godfrey, bitterly. "He'll never be hurt—he's made to hurt other people."

"And so you *did* give him leave to sell the horse? eh?" said Bryce.

"Yes; I wanted to part with the horse —he was always a little too hard in the mouth for me," said Godfrey; his pride making him wince under the idea that Bryce guessed the sale to be a matter of necessity. "I was going to see after him— I thought some mischief had happened. I'll go back now," he added, turning the horse's head, and wishing he could get rid of Bryce; for he felt that the long-dreaded crisis of his life was close upon him. "You're coming on to Raveloe, aren't you?"

"Well, no, not now," said Bryce. "I *was* coming round there, for I had to go to Flitton, and I thought I might as well take

[1] **a swinging price:** a good sum.

you in my way, and just let you know all I knew myself about the horse. I suppose Master Dunsey didn't like to show himself till the ill news had blown over a bit. He's perhaps gone to pay a visit at the Three Crowns, by Whitbridge—I know he's fond of the house." [1]

"Perhaps he is," said Godfrey, rather absently. Then rousing himself, he said, with an effort at carelessness, "We shall hear of him soon enough, I'll be bound."

"Well, here's my turning," said Bryce, not surprised to perceive that Godfrey was rather "down;" "so I'll bid you good-day and wish I may bring you better news another time."

Godfrey rode along slowly, representing to himself the scene of confession to his father from which he felt that there was now no longer any escape. The revelation about the money must be made the very next morning; and if he withheld the rest, Dunstan would be sure to come back shortly, and, finding that he must bear the brunt of his father's anger, would tell the whole story out of spite, even though he had nothing to gain by it. There was one step, perhaps, by which he might still win Dunstan's silence and put off the evil day: he might tell his father that he had himself spent the money paid to him by Fowler; and as he had never been guilty of such an offense before, the affair would blow over after a little storming. But Godfrey could not bend himself to this. He felt that in letting Dunstan have the money, he had already been guilty of a breach of trust hardly less culpable than that of spending the money directly for his own behoof; and yet there was a distinction between the two acts which made him feel that the one was so much more blackening than the other as to be intolerable to him.

"I don't pretend to be a good fellow," he said to himself; "but I'm not a scoundrel—at least, I'll stop short somewhere. I'll bear the consequences of what I *have* done sooner than make believe I've done what I never would have done. I'd never have spent the money for my own pleasure—I was tortured into it."

Through the remainder of this day Godfrey, with only occasional fluctuations, kept his will bent in the direction of a complete avowal to his father, and he withheld the story of Wildfire's loss till the next morning, that it might serve him as an introduction to heavier matter. The old Squire was accustomed to his son's frequent absence from home, and thought neither Dunstan's nor Wildfire's non-appearance a matter calling for remark. Godfrey said to himself again and again that if he let slip this one opportunity of confession, he might never have another; the revelation might be made even in a more odious way than by Dunstan's malignity: [2] *she* might come as she had threatened to do. And then he tried to make the scene easier to himself by rehearsal: he made up his mind how he would pass from the admission of his weakness in letting Dunstan have the money to the fact that Dunstan had a hold on him which he had been unable to shake off, and how he would work up his father to expect something very bad before he told him the fact. The old Squire was an implacable man: he made resolutions in violent anger, and he was not to be moved from them after his anger had subsided—as fiery volcanic matters cool and harden into rock. Like many violent and implacable men he allowed evils to grow under favor of his own heedlessness, till they pressed upon him with exasperating force, and then he turned round with

[1] **house:** tavern, inn.

[2] **malignity** (mə·lig′nə·tē): evil intentions.

fierce severity and became unrelentingly hard. This was his system with his tenants: he allowed them to get into arrears, neglect their fences, reduce their stock, sell their straw, and otherwise go the wrong way—and then, when he became short of money in consequence of this indulgence, he took the hardest measures and would listen to no appeal. Godfrey knew all this and felt it with the greater force because he had constantly suffered annoyance from witnessing his father's sudden fits of unrelentingness, for which his own habitual irresolution deprived him of all sympathy. (He was not critical on the faulty indulgence which preceded these fits; *that* seemed to him natural enough.) Still there was just the chance, Godfrey thought, that his father's pride might see this marriage in a light that would induce him to hush it up, rather than turn his son out and make the family the talk of the country for ten miles round.

This was the view of the case that Godfrey managed to keep before him pretty closely till midnight, and he went to sleep thinking that he had done with inward debating. But when he awoke in the still morning darkness he found it impossible to reawaken his evening thoughts; it was as if they had been tired out and were not to be roused to further work. Instead of arguments for confession, he could now feel the presence of nothing but its evil consequences: the old dread of disgrace came back—the old shrinking from the thought of raising a hopeless barrier between himself and Nancy—the old disposition to rely on chances which might be favorable to him and save him from betrayal. Why, after all, should he cut off the hope of them by his own act? He had seen the matter in a wrong light yesterday. He had been in a rage with Dunstan and had thought of nothing but a thorough breakup of their mutual understanding;

but what it would be really wisest for him to do was to try and soften his father's anger against Dunsey and keep things as nearly as possible in their old condition. If Dunsey did not come back for a few days (and Godfrey did not know but that the rascal had enough money in his pocket to enable him to keep away still longer), everything might blow over.

CHAPTER IX

The Squire Loses His Temper

GODFREY ROSE and took his own breakfast earlier than usual, but lingered in the wainscoted parlor till his younger brothers had finished their meal and gone out; awaiting his father, who always took a walk with his managing man before breakfast. Everyone breakfasted at a different hour in the Red House, and the Squire was always the latest, giving a long chance to a rather feeble morning appetite before he tried it. The table had been spread with substantial eatables nearly two hours before he presented himself—a tall, stout man of sixty, with a face in which the knit brow and rather hard glance seemed contradicted by the slack and feeble mouth. His person showed marks of habitual neglect, his dress was slovenly; and yet there was something in the presence of the old Squire distinguishable from that of the ordinary farmers in the parish, who were perhaps every whit as refined as he, but, having slouched their way through life with a consciousness of being in the vicinity of their "betters," wanted that self-possession and authoritativeness of voice and carriage which belonged to a man who thought of superiors as remote existences

with whom he had personally little more to do than with America or the stars. The Squire had been used to parish homage all his life, used to the presupposition [1] that his family, his tankards, and everything that was his, were the oldest and best; and as he never associated with any gentry higher than himself, his opinion was not disturbed by comparison.

He glanced at his son as he entered the room, and said, "What, sir! haven't *you* had your breakfast yet?" but there was no pleasant morning greeting between them: not because of any unfriendliness, but because the sweet flower of courtesy is not a growth of such homes as the Red House.

"Yes, sir," said Godfrey, "I've had my breakfast, but I was waiting to speak to you."

"Ah! well," said the Squire, throwing himself indifferently into his chair and speaking in a ponderous coughing fashion, which was felt in Raveloe to be a sort of privilege of his rank, while he cut a piece of beef and held it up before the deer-hound that had come in with him. "Ring the bell for my ale, will you? You youngsters' business is your own pleasure, mostly. There's no hurry about it for anybody but yourselves."

The Squire's life was quite as idle as his sons', but it was a fiction kept up by himself and his contemporaries in Raveloe that youth was exclusively the period of folly and that their aged wisdom was constantly in a state of endurance mitigated by sarcasm. Godfrey waited, before he spoke again, until the ale had been brought and the door closed—an interval during which Fleet, the deerhound, had consumed enough bits of beef to make a poor man's holiday dinner.

"There's been a cursed piece of ill luck

with Wildfire," he began; "happened the day before yesterday."

"What! broke his knees?" said the Squire, after taking a draught of ale. "I thought you knew how to ride better than that, sir. I never threw a horse down in my life. If I had, I might ha' whistled for another, for *my* father wasn't quite so ready to unstring [2] as some other fathers I know of. But they must turn over a new leaf—*they* must. What with mortgages and arrears, I'm as short o'. cash as a roadside pauper. And that fool Kimble says the newspaper's talking about peace. Why, the country wouldn't have a leg to stand on. Prices 'ud run down like a jack, and I should never get my arrears, not if I sold all the fellows up. And there's that Fowler, I won't put up with him any longer; I've told Winthrop to go to Cox this very day. The lying scoundrel told me he'd be sure to pay me a hundred last month. He takes advantage because he's on that outlying farm and thinks I shall forget him."

The Squire had delivered this speech in a coughing and interrupted manner, but with no pause long enough for Godfrey to make it a pretext for taking up the word again. He felt that his father meant to ward off any request for money on the ground of the misfortune with Wildfire and that the emphasis he had thus been led to lay on his shortness of cash and his arrears was likely to produce an attitude of mind the utmost unfavorable for his own disclosure. But he must go on, now he had begun.

"It's worse than breaking the horse's knees—he's been staked and killed," he said, as soon as his father was silent, and had begun to cut his meat. "But I wasn't thinking of asking you to buy me another horse; I was only thinking I'd lost the

[1] **presupposition** (prē'sup·ə·zish'ən): something assumed beforehand, or taken for granted.

[2] **unstring:** untie his purse strings.

means of paying you with the price of Wildfire, as I'd meant to do. Dunsey took him to the hunt to sell him for me the other day, and after he'd made a bargain for a hundred and twenty with Bryce, he went after the hounds, and took some fool's leap or other that did for the horse at once. If it hadn't been for that, I should have paid you a hundred pounds this morning."

The Squire had laid down his knife and fork, and was staring at his son in amazement, not being sufficiently quick of brain to form a probable guess as to what could have caused so strange an inversion of the paternal and filial relations as this proposition of his son to pay him a hundred pounds.

"The truth is,ˈsir—I'm very sorry—I was quite to blame," said Godfrey. "Fowler did pay that hundred pounds. He paid it to me, when I was over there one day last month. And Dunsey bothered me for the money, and I let him have it, because I hoped I should be able to pay it you before this."

The Squire was purple with anger before his son had done speaking, and found utterance difficult. "You let Dunsey have it, sir? And how long have you been so thick with Dunsey that you must collogue [1] with him to embezzle my money? Are you turning out a scamp? I tell you I won't have it. I'll turn the whole pack of you out of the house together, and marry again. I'd have you to remember, sir, my property's got no entail [2] on it; since my grandfather's time the Casses can do as they like with their land. Remember that, sir. Let Dunsey have the money! Why should you let Dunsey have the money? There's some lie at the bottom of it."

[1] **collogue** (kə·lōg′): plot, conspire.
[2] **entail:** a legal obligation to pass an estate on to the eldest son.

"There's no lie, sir," said Godfrey. "I wouldn't have spent the money myself, but Dunsey bothered me, and I was a fool and let him have it. But I meant to pay it, whether he did or not. That's the whole story. I never meant to embezzle money, and I'm not the man to do it. You never knew me to do a dishonest trick, sir."

"Where's Dunsey, then? What do you stand talking there for? Go and fetch Dunsey, as I tell you, and let him give account of what he wanted the money for, and what he's done with it. He shall repent. I'll turn him out. I said I would, and I'll do it. He shan't brave me. Go and fetch him!"

"Dunsey isn't come back, sir."

"What! did he break his own neck, then?" said the Squire, with some disgust at the idea that, in that case, he could not fulfill his threat.

"No, he wasn't hurt, I believe, for the horse was found dead, and Dunsey must have walked off. I daresay we shall see him again by and by. I don't know where he is."

"And what must you be letting him have my money for? Answer me that," said the Squire, attacking Godfrey again, since Dunsey was not within reach.

"Well, sir, I don't know," said Godfrey, hesitatingly. That was a feeble evasion, but Godfrey was not fond of lying, and, not being sufficiently aware that no sort of duplicity can long flourish without the help of vocal falsehoods, he was quite unprepared with invented motives.

"You don't know? I tell you what it is, sir. You've been up to some trick, and you've been bribing him not to tell," said the Squire, with a sudden acuteness which startled Godfrey, who felt his heart beat violently at the nearness of his father's guess. The sudden alarm pushed him on to take the next step—a very slight im-

pulse suffices for that on a downward road.

"Why, sir," he said, trying to speak with careless ease, "it was a little affair between me and Dunsey; it's no matter to anybody else. It's hardly worthwhile to pry into young men's fooleries: it wouldn't have made any difference to you, sir, if I'd not had the bad luck to lose Wildfire. I should have paid you the money."

"Fooleries! Pshaw! it's time you'd done with fooleries. And I'd have you know, sir, you *must* ha' done with 'em," said the Squire, frowning and casting an angry glance at his son. "Your goings on are not what I shall find money for any longer. There's my grandfather had his stables full o' horses and kept a good house, too, and in worse times, by what I can make out; and so might I, if I hadn't four good-for-nothing fellows to hang on me like horseleeches. I've been too good a father to you all—that's what it is. But I shall pull up, sir."

Godfrey was silent. He was not likely to be very penetrating in his judgments, but he had always had a sense that his father's indulgence had not been kindness, and had had a vague longing for some discipline that would have checked his own errant weakness and helped his better will. The Squire ate his bread and meat hastily, took a deep draught of ale,

then turned his chair from the table, and began to speak again.

"It'll be all the worse for you, you know—you'd need try and help me keep things together."

"Well, sir, I've often offered to take the management of things, but you know you've taken it ill always, and seemed to think I wanted to push you out of your place."

"I know nothing o' your offering or o' my taking it ill," said the Squire, whose memory consisted in certain strong impressions unmodified by detail; "but I know, one while [1] you seemed to be thinking o' marrying, and I didn't offer to put any obstacles in your way, as some fathers would. I'd as lieve you married Lammeter's daughter as anybody. I suppose, if I said you nay, you'd ha' kept on with it; but, for want o' contradiction, you've changed your mind. You're a shilly-shally fellow, you take after your poor mother. She never had a will of her own; a woman has no call for one, if she's got a proper man for her husband. But *your* wife had need have one, for you hardly know your own mind enough to make both your legs walk one way. The lass hasn't said downright she won't have you, has she?"

"No," said Godfrey, feeling very hot

[1] **one while:** at one time.

and uncomfortable; "but I don't think she will."

"Think! why haven't you the courage to ask her? Do you stick to it, you want to have *her*—that's the thing?"

"There's no other woman I want to marry," said Godfrey, evasively.

"Well, then, let me make the offer for you, that's all, if you haven't the pluck to do it yourself. Lammeter isn't likely to be loath for his daughter to marry into *my* family, I should think. And as for the pretty lass, she wouldn't have her cousin —and there's nobody else, as I see, could ha' stood in your way."

"I'd rather let it be, please sir, at present," said Godfrey in alarm. "I think she's a little offended with me just now, and I should like to speak for myself. A man must manage these things for himself."

"Well, speak, then, and manage it, and see if you can't turn over a new leaf. That's what a man must do when he thinks o' marrying."

"I don't see how I can think of it at present, sir. You wouldn't like to settle me on one of the farms, I suppose, and I don't think she'd come to live in this house with all my brothers. It's a different sort of life to what she's been used to."

"Not come to live in this house? Don't tell me. You ask her, that's all," said the Squire, with a short, scornful laugh.

"I'd rather let the thing be, at present, sir," said Godfrey. "I hope you won't try to hurry it on by saying anything."

"I shall do what I choose," said the Squire, "and I shall let you know I'm master; else you may turn out, and find an estate to drop into somewhere else. Go out and tell Winthrop not to go to Cox's, but wait for me. And tell 'em to get my horse saddled. And stop: look out and get that hack [1] o' Dunsey's sold, and hand me the money, will you? He'll keep no more hacks at my expense. And if you know where he's sneaking—I daresay you do— you may tell him to spare himself the journey o' coming back home. Let him turn ostler,[2] and keep himself. He shan't hang on me any more."

"I don't know where he is; and if I did, it isn't my place to tell him to keep away," said Godfrey, moving toward the door.

"Confound it, sir, don't stay arguing, but go and order my horse," said the Squire, taking up a pipe.

Godfrey left the room, hardly knowing whether he were more relieved by the sense that the interview was ended without having made any change in his position or more uneasy that he had entangled himself still further in prevarication and deceit. What had passed about his proposing to Nancy had raised a new alarm, lest by some afterdinner words of his father's to Mr. Lammeter he should be thrown into the embarrassment of being obliged absolutely to decline her when she seemed to be within his reach. He fled to his usual refuge, that of hoping for some unforeseen turn of fortune, some favorable chance which would save him from unpleasant consequences—perhaps even justify his insincerity by manifesting its prudence.

In this point of trusting to some throw of fortune's dice, Godfrey can hardly be called old-fashioned. Favorable Chance is the god of all men who follow their own devices instead of obeying a law they believe in. Let even a polished man of these days get into a position he is ashamed to avow, and his mind will be bent on all the possible issues that may deliver him from the calculable results of that position. Let him live outside his income, or shirk the resolute honest work that brings wages,

[1] **hack:** horse.

[2] **ostler:** stableboy, groom.

and he will presently find himself dreaming of a possible benefactor, a possible simpleton who may be cajoled into using his interest, a possible state of mind in some possible person not yet forthcoming. Let him neglect the responsibilities of his office, and he will inevitably anchor himself on the chance that the thing left undone may turn out not to be of the supposed importance. Let him betray his friend's confidence, and he will adore that same cunning complexity called Chance, which gives him the hope that his friend will never know. Let him forsake a decent craft that he may pursue the gentilities of a profession to which nature never called him, and his religion will infallibly be the worship of blessed Chance, which he will believe in as the mighty creator of success. The evil principle deprecated in that religion is the orderly sequence by which the seed brings forth a crop after its kind.

FOR STUDY AND DISCUSSION

1. The villagers seem to enjoy their roles as detectives. What clues are uncovered? What suspicions are aroused? Who finally emerges as the suspect? Why does this suspect appeal to the villagers' imagination?

2. Why doesn't anyone suspect Dunsey? What does Godfrey assume that Dunsey has done?

3. How does Godfrey find out about Wildfire? Why does he dread to tell the Squire?

4. What decision must Godfrey make? What does he decide to do? Do you think he has chosen wisely? Why does he later change his mind?

5. What kind of person is the Squire? What is his opinion of his sons?

6. What does Godfrey tell the Squire? What does he not tell him?

7. Who first mentions Nancy Lammeter? What does the Squire seem to think of her? What is Godfrey afraid that he will do? Why?

8. Do you sympathize with Godfrey in his dilemma? Why or why not? Does George Eliot? What makes you think so?

CHAPTER X

Christmas Draws Near

JUSTICE MALAM was naturally regarded in Tarley and Raveloe as a man of capacious mind, seeing that he could draw much wider conclusions without evidence than could be expected of his neighbors who were not on the Commission of the Peace. Such a man was not likely to neglect the clue of the tinderbox, and an inquiry was set on foot concerning the peddler, name unknown, with curly black hair and a foreign complexion, carrying a box of cutlery and jewelry and wearing large rings in his ears. But either because inquiry was too slowfooted to overtake him, or because the description applied to so many peddlers that inquiry did not know how to choose among them, weeks passed away, and there was no other result concerning the robbery than a gradual cessation of the excitement it had caused in Raveloe. Dunstan Cass's absence was hardly a subject of remark; he had once before had a quarrel with his father, and had gone off, nobody knew whither, to return at the end of six weeks, take up his old quarters unforbidden and swagger as usual. His own family, who equally expected this issue, with the sole difference that the Squire was determined this time to forbid him the old quarters, never mentioned his absence; and when his uncle Kimble or Mr. Osgood noticed it, the story of his having killed Wildfire and committed some offense against his father was enough to prevent surprise. To connect the fact of Dunsey's disappearance with that of the robbery occurring on the same day, lay quite away from the track of everyone's thought—even Godfrey's, who had better reason than anyone else to know what his brother was capable of.

He remembered no mention of the weaver between them since the time, twelve years ago, when it was their boyish sport to deride him; and, besides, his imagination constantly created an alibi for Dunstan: he saw him continually in some congenial haunt, to which he had walked off on leaving Wildfire—saw him sponging on chance acquaintances and meditating a return home to the old amusement of tormenting his elder brother. Even if any brain in Raveloe had put the said two facts together, I doubt whether a combination so injurious to the prescriptive respectability of a family with a mural monument and venerable tankards would not have been suppressed as of unsound tendency. But Christmas puddings, brawn,[1] and abundance of spirituous liquors, throwing the mental originality into the channel of nightmare, are great preservatives against a dangerous spontaneity of waking thought.

When the robbery was talked of at the Rainbow and elsewhere, in good company, the balance continued to waver between the rational explanation founded on the tinderbox, and the theory of an impenetrable mystery that mocked investigation. The advocates of the tinderbox-and-peddler view considered the other side a muddleheaded and credulous set, who, because they themselves were walleyed, supposed everybody else to have the same blank outlook; and the adherents of the inexplicable more than hinted that their antagonists were animals inclined to crow before they had found any corn—mere skimming dishes in point of depth—whose clearsightedness consisted in supposing there was nothing behind a barn door because they couldn't see through it; so that, though their controversy did not serve to elicit the fact concerning the robbery, it elicited some true opinions of collateral importance.

But while poor Silas's loss served thus to brush the slow current of Raveloe conversation, Silas himself was feeling the withering desolation of that bereavement about which his neighbors were arguing at their ease. To anyone who had observed him before he lost his gold, it might have seemed that so withered and shrunken a life as his could hardly be susceptible of a bruise, could hardly endure any subtraction but such as would put an end to it altogether. But in reality it had been an eager life, filled with immediate purpose which fenced him in from the wide, cheerless unknown. It had been a clinging life; and though the object round which its fibers had clung was a dead, disrupted thing, it satisfied the need for clinging. But now the fence was broken down—the support was snatched away. Marner's thoughts could no longer move in their old round, and were baffled by a blank like that which meets a plodding ant when the earth has broken away on its homeward path. The loom was there and the weaving, and the growing pattern in the cloth; but the bright treasure in the hole under his feet was gone; the prospect of handling and counting was gone: the evening had no phantasm of delight to still the poor soul's craving. The thought of the money he would get by his actual work could bring no joy, for its meager image was only a fresh reminder of his loss; and hope was too heavily crushed by the sudden blow for his imagination to dwell on the growth of a new hoard from that small beginning.

He filled up the blank with grief. As he sat weaving, he every now and then moaned low, like one in pain: it was the sign that his thoughts had come round again to the sudden chasm—to the empty evening time. And all the evening, as he

[1] **brawn:** salted boar meat.

sat in his loneliness by his dull fire, he leaned his elbows on his knees, and clasped his head with his hands, and moaned very low—not as one who seeks to be heard.

And yet he was not utterly forsaken in his trouble. The repulsion Marner had always created in his neighbors was partly dissipated [1] by the new light in which this misfortune had shown him. Instead of a man who had more cunning than honest folks could come by and, what was worse, had not the inclination to use that cunning in a neighborly way, it was now apparent that Silas had not cunning enough to keep his own. He was generally spoken of as a "poor mushed creatur"; and that avoidance of his neighbors, which had before been referred to his ill will and to a probable addiction to worse company, was now considered mere craziness.

This change to a kindlier feeling was shown in various ways. The odor of Christmas cooking being on the wind, it was the season when superfluous pork and black puddings are suggestive of charity in well-to-do families; and Silas's misfortune had brought him uppermost in the memory of housekeepers like Mrs. Osgood. Mr. Crackenthorp, too, while he admonished Silas that his money had probably been taken from him because he thought too much of it and never came to church, enforced the doctrine by a present

of pigs' pettitoes,[2] well calculated to dissipate unfounded prejudices against the clerical character. Neighbors who had nothing but verbal consolation to give showed a disposition not only to greet Silas and discuss his misfortune at some length when they encountered him in the village, but also to take the trouble of calling at his cottage and getting him to repeat all the details on the very spot; and then they would try to cheer him by saying, "Well, Master Marner, you're no worse off nor other poor folks, after all; and if you was to be crippled, the parish 'ud give you a 'lowance."

I suppose one reason why we are seldom able to comfort our neighbors with our words is that our good will gets adulterated, in spite of ourselves, before it can pass our lips. We can send black puddings and pettitoes, without giving them a flavor of our own egoism; but language is a stream that is almost sure to smack of a mingled soil. There was a fair proportion of kindness in Raveloe; but it was often of a beery and bungling sort, and took the shape least allied to the complimentary and hypocritical.

Mr. Macey, for example, coming one evening expressly to let Silas know that recent events had given him the advantage of standing more favorably in the opinion of a man whose judgment was not formed lightly, opened the conversation by saying, as soon as he had seated himself and adjusted his thumbs—

"Come, Master Marner, why, you've no call to sit amoaning. You're a deal better off to ha' lost your money, nor to ha' kep it by foul means. I used to think, when you first come into these parts, as you were no better nor you should be; you were younger a deal than what you are now; but you were allays a staring, white-

faced creatur, partly like a bald-faced calf, as I may say. But there's no knowing: it isn't every queer-looksed thing as Old Harry's had the making of—I mean, speaking o' toads and such; for they're often harmless, and useful against varmin. And it's pretty much the same wi' you, as fur as I can see. Though as to the yarbs [1] and stuff to cure the breathing, if you brought that sort o' knowledge from distant parts, you might ha' been a bit freer of it. And if the knowledge wasn't well come by, why, you might ha' made up for it by coming to church reg'lar; for as for the children as the Wise Woman charmed, I've been at the christening of 'em again and again, and they took the water just as well. And that's reasonable; for if Old Harry's a mind to do a bit o' kindness for a holiday, like, who's got anything against it? That's my thinking; and I've been clerk o' this parish forty year, and I know, when the parson and me does the cussing of a Ash Wednesday,[2] there's no cussing o' folks as have a mind to be cured without a doctor, let Kimble say what he will. And so, Master Marner, as I was saying—for there's windings i' things as they may carry you to the fur end o' the prayer book afore you get back to 'em—my advice is, as you keep up your sperrits; for as for thinking you're a deep un, and ha' got more inside you nor 'ull bear daylight, I'm not o' that opinion at all, and so I tell the neighbors. For, says I, you talk o' Master Marner making out a tale— why, it's nonsense, that is: it 'ud take a 'cute man to make a tale like that; and, says I, he looked as scared as a rabbit."

During this discursive address Silas had continued motionless in his previous attitude, leaning his elbows on his knees and pressing his hands against his head. Mr. Macey, not doubting that he had been listened to, paused, in the expectation of some appreciatory reply, but Marner remained silent. He had a sense that the old man meant to be good-natured and neighborly; but the kindness fell on him as sunshine falls on the wretched—he had no heart to taste it and felt that it was very far off him.

"Come, Master Marner, have you got nothing to say to that?" said Mr. Macey at last, with a slight accent of impatience.

"Oh," said Marner, slowly, shaking his head between his hands, "I thank you— thank you—kindly."

"Ay, ay, to be sure: I thought you would," said Mr. Macey; "and my advice is—have you got a Sunday suit?"

"No," said Marner.

"I doubted it was so," said Mr. Macey. "Now, let me advise you to get a Sunday suit: there's Tookey, he's a poor creatur, but he's got my tailoring business and some o' my money in it, and he shall make a suit at a low price, and give you trust,[3] and then you can come to church and be a bit neighborly. Why, you've never heared me say 'Amen' since you come into these parts, and I recommend you to lose no time, for it'll be poor work when Tookey has it all to himself, for I mayn't be equil to stand i' the desk at all, come another winter." Here Mr. Macey paused, perhaps expecting some sign of emotion in his hearer; but not observing any, he went on. "And as for the money for the suit o' clothes, why, you get a matter of a pound a week at your weaving, Master Marner, and you're a young man, eh, for all you look so mushed. Why, you couldn't ha' been five-and-twenty when you come into these parts, eh?"

Silas started a little at the change to a

[1] yarbs: herbs.

[2] cussing . . . Wednesday: A reference to the customary acknowledgment on Ash Wednesday of man's faults.

[3] trust: credit.

questioning tone, and answered mildly, "I don't know; I can't rightly say—it's a long while since."

After receiving such an answer as this, it is not surprising that Mr. Macey observed, later on in the evening at the Rainbow, that Marner's head was "all of a muddle," and that it was to be doubted if he ever knew when Sunday came round, which showed him a worse heathen than many a dog.

Another of Silas's comforters, besides Mr. Macey, came to him with a mind highly charged on the same topic. This was Mrs. Winthrop, the wheelwright's wife. The inhabitants of Raveloe were not severely regular in their churchgoing, and perhaps there was hardly a person in the parish who would not have held that to go to church every Sunday in the calendar would have shown a greedy desire to stand well with Heaven and get an undue advantage over their neighbors—a wish to be better than the "common run," that would have implied a reflection on those who had had godfathers and godmothers as well as themselves and had an equal right to the burying service. At the same time, it was understood to be requisite for all who were not household servants or young men to take the sacrament at one of the great festivals: Squire Cass himself took it on Christmas Day; while those who were held to be "good livers" went to church with greater, though still with moderate, frequency.

Mrs. Winthrop was one of these: she was in all respects a woman of scrupulous conscience, so eager for duties that life seemed to offer them too scantily unless she rose at half-past four, though this threw a scarcity of work over the more advanced hours of the morning, which it was a constant problem with her to remove. Yet she had not the vixenish temper which is sometimes supposed to be a necessary condition of such habits: she was a very mild, patient woman, whose nature it was to seek out all the sadder and more serious elements of life, and pasture her mind upon them. She was the person always first thought of in Raveloe when there was illness or death in the family, when leeches were to be applied,[1] or there was a sudden disappointment in a monthly nurse. She was a "comfortable woman"— good-looking, fresh-complexioned, having her lips always slightly screwed, as if she felt herself in a sickroom with a doctor or the clergyman present. But she was never whimpering; no one had seen her shed tears; she was simply grave and inclined to shake her head and sigh, almost imperceptibly, like a funereal mourner who is not a relation. It seemed surprising that Ben Winthrop, who loved his quart pot and his joke, got along so well with Dolly; but she took her husband's jokes and joviality as patiently as everything else, considering that "men *would* be so," and viewing the stronger sex in the light of animals whom it had pleased Heaven to make naturally troublesome, like bulls and turkey cocks.

This good, wholesome woman could hardly fail to have her mind drawn strongly toward Silas Marner, now that he appeared in the light of a sufferer; and one Sunday afternoon she took her little boy Aaron with her and went to call on Silas, carrying in her hand some small lard cakes, flat, pastelike articles much esteemed in Raveloe. Aaron, an apple-cheeked youngster of seven, with a clean starched frill which looked like a plate for the apples, needed all his adventurous curiosity to embolden him against the possibility that the big-eyed weaver might do him some bodily injury; and his dubi-

[1] **leeches . . . applied:** that is, when blood is drawn from a sick person—a common method of treating diseases.

ety was much increased when, on arriving at the stone pits, they heard the mysterious sound of the loom.

"Ah, it is as I thought," said Mrs. Winthrop, sadly. ·

They had to knock loudly before Silas heard them; but when he did come to the door he showed no impatience, as he would once have done, at a visit that had been unasked for and unexpected. Formerly, his heart had been as a locked casket with its treasure inside; but now the casket was empty, and the lock was broken. Left groping in darkness, with his prop utterly gone, Silas had inevitably a sense, though a dull and half-despairing one, that if any help came to him it must come from without; and there was a slight stirring of expectation at the sight of his fellowmen, a faint consciousness of dependence on their goodwill. He opened the door wide to admit Dolly, but without otherwise returning her greeting than by moving the armchair a few inches as a sign that she was to sit down in it. Dolly, as soon as she was seated, removed the white cloth that covered her lard cakes, and said in her gravest way—

"I'd a baking yisterday, Master Marner, and the lard cakes turned out better nor common, and I'd ha' asked you to accept some, if you'd thought well. I don't eat such things myself, for a bit o' bread's what I like from one year's end to the other; but men's stomichs are made so comical, they want a change—they do, I know, God help 'em."

Dolly sighed gently as she held out the cakes to Silas, who thanked her kindly and looked very close at them, absently, being accustomed to look so at everything he took into his hand—eyed all the while by the wondering bright orbs of the small Aaron, who had made an outwork of his mother's chair, and was peeping from behind it.

"There's letters pricked on 'em," said Dolly. "I can't read 'em myself, and there's nobody, not Mr. Macey himself, rightly knows what they mean; but they've a good meaning, for they're the same as is on the pulpit cloth at church. What are they, Aaron, my dear?"

Aaron retreated completely behind his outwork.

"Oh go, that's naughty," said his mother, mildly. "Well, whativer the letters are, they've a good meaning; and it's a stamp as has been in our house, Ben says, ever since he was a little un and his mother used to put it on the cakes and I've allays put it on too; for if there's any good, we've need of it i' this world."

"It's I.H.S.," [1] said Silas, at which proof of learning Aaron peeped round the chair again.

"Well, to be sure, you can read 'em off," said Dolly. "Ben's read 'em to me many and many a time, but they slip out o' my mind again; the more's the pity, for they're good letters, else they wouldn't be in the church; and so I prick 'em on all the loaves and all the cakes, though sometimes they won't hold, because o' the rising—for, as I said if there's any good to

[1] **I.H.S.:** an ancient symbol of Christianity, a Latin version of the Greek letters spelling "Jesus."

be got we've need of it i' this world—that we have; and I hope they'll bring good to you, Master Marner, for it's wi' that will I brought you the cakes; and you see the letters have held better nor common."

Silas was as unable to interpret the letters as Dolly, but there was no possibility of misunderstanding the desire to give comfort that made itself heard in her quiet tones. He said, with more feeling than before—"Thank you—thank you kindly." But he laid down the cakes and seated himself absently—drearily unconscious of any distinct benefit toward which the cakes and the letters, or even Dolly's kindness, could tend for him.

"Ah, if there's good anywhere, we've need of it," repeated Dolly, who did not lightly forsake a serviceable phrase. She looked at Silas pityingly as she went on. "But you didn't hear the church bells this morning, Master Marner? I doubt you didn't know it was Sunday. Living so lone here, you lose your count, I daresay; and then, when your loom makes a noise, you can't hear the bells, more partic'lar now the frost kills the sound."

"Yes, I did; I heard 'em," said Silas, to whom Sunday bells were a mere accident of the day and not part of its sacredness. There had been no bells in Lantern Yard.

"Dear heart!" said Dolly, pausing before she spoke again. "But what a pity it is you should work of a Sunday, and not clean yourself—if you *didn't* go to church; for if you'd a roasting bit,[1] it might be as you couldn't leave it, being a lone man. But there's the bakehus, if you could make up your mind to spend a twopence on the oven now and then—not every week, in course—I shouldn't like to do that myself —you might carry your bit o' dinner there, for it's nothing but right to have a bit o' summat hot of a Sunday, and not to make

it as you can't know your dinner from Saturday. But now, upo' Christmas Day, this blessed Christmas as is ever coming, if you was to take your dinner to the bakehus, and go to church, and see the holly and the yew, and hear the anthim, and then take the sacramen', you'd be a deal the better, and you'd know which end you stood on, and you could put your trust i' Them as knows better nor we do, seein' you'd ha' done what it lies on us all to do."

Dolly's exhortation, which was an unusually long effort of speech for her, was uttered in the soothing, persuasive tone with which she would have tried to prevail on a sick man to take his medicine, or a basin of gruel for which he had no appetite. Silas had never before been closely urged on the point of his absence from church, which had only been thought of as a part of his general queerness; and he was too direct and simple to evade Dolly's appeal.

"Nay, nay," he said, "I know nothing o' church. I've never been to church."

"No!" said Dolly, in a low tone of wonderment. Then bethinking herself of Silas's advent from an unknown country, she said, "Could it ha' been as they'd no church where you was born?"

"Oh yes," said Silas, meditatively, sitting in his usual posture of leaning on his knees, and supporting his head. "There was churches—a many—it was a big town. But I knew nothing of 'em—I went to chapel."[2]

Dolly was much puzzled at this new word, but she was rather afraid of inquiring further, lest "chapel" might mean some haunt of wickedness. After a little thought, she said—

[1] **bit:** piece of meat.

[2] **went to chapel:** Silas Marner was formerly a religious dissenter; that is, he belonged to a sect which had broken away from the Church of England. Dissenters worshiped in "chapels" rather than in "churches."

"Well, Master Marner, it's niver too late to turn over a new leaf, and if you've niver had no church, there's no telling the good it'll do you. For I feels so set up and comfortable as niver was, when I've been and heard the prayers, and the singing to the praise and glory o' God, as Mr. Macey gives out—and Mr. Crackenthorp saying good words, and more partic'lar on Sacramen' Day; and if a bit o' trouble comes, I feel as I can put up wi' it, for I've looked for help i' the right quarter, and gev myself up to Them as we must all give ourselves up to at the last; and if we'n done our part, it isn't to be believed as Them as are above us 'ull be worse nor we are and come short o' Their'n."

Poor Dolly's exposition of her simple Raveloe theology [1] fell rather unmeaningly on Silas's ears, for there was no word in it that could rouse a memory of what he had known as religion, and his comprehension was quite baffled by the plural pronoun, which was no heresy of Dolly's, but only her way of avoiding a presumptuous familiarity. He remained silent, not feeling inclined to assent to the part of Dolly's speech which he fully understood—her recommendation that he should go to church. Indeed, Silas was so unaccustomed to talk beyond the brief questions and answers necessary for the transaction of his simple business, that words did not easily come to him without the urgency of a distinct purpose.

But now, little Aaron, having become used to the weaver's awful presence, had advanced to his mother's side, and Silas, seeming to notice him for the first time, tried to return Dolly's signs of goodwill by offering the lad a bit of lard cake. Aaron shrank back a little and rubbed his head against his mother's shoulder, but still thought the piece of cake worth the risk of putting his hand out for it.

"Oh, for shame, Aaron," said his mother, taking him on her lap, however; "why, you don't want cake again yet awhile. He's wonderful hearty," she went on, with a little sigh—"that he is, God knows. He's my youngest, and we spoil him sadly, for either me or the father must allays hev him in our sight—that we must."

She stroked Aaron's brown head and thought it must do Master Marner good to see such a "pictur of a child." But Marner, on the other side of the hearth, saw the neat-featured rosy face as a mere dim round, with two dark spots in it.

"And he's got a voice like a bird—you wouldn't think," Dolly went on; "he can sing a Christmas carril as his father's taught him; and I take it for a token as he'll come to good, as he can learn the good tunes so quick. Come, Aaron, stan' up and sing the carril to Master Marner, come."

Aaron replied by rubbing his forehead against his mother's shoulder.

"Oh, that's naughty," said Dolly, gently. "Stan' up, when mother tells you, and let me hold the cake till you've done."

Aaron was not indisposed to display his talents, even to an ogre,[2] under protecting circumstances: and after a few more signs of coyness,[3] consisting chiefly in rubbing the backs of his hands over his eyes and then peeping between them at Master Marner to see if he looked anxious for the "carril," he at length allowed his head to be duly adjusted, and standing behind the table, which let him appear above it only as far as his broad frill, so that he looked like a cherubic head untroubled with a body, he began with a clear chirp and in a melody that

[1] **theology** (thē·ol'ə·jē): religious belief.

[2] **ogre** (ō'gər): in fairy tales, a giant or monster said to eat people.

[3] **coyness** (koi'nes): pretended bashfulness.

had the rhythm of an industrious hammer—

"God rest you, merry gentlemen,
Let nothing you dismay,
For Jesus Christ our Saviour
Was born on Christmas Day."

Dolly listened with a devout look, glancing at Marner in some confidence that this strain would help to allure him to church.

"That's Christmas music," she said, when Aaron had ended and had secured his piece of cake again. "There's no other music equil to the Christmas music— 'Hark the erol angils sing.' And you may judge what it is at church, Master Marner, with the bassoon and the voices, as you can't help thinking you've got to a better place a'ready—for I wouldn't speak ill o' this world, seeing as Them put us in it as knows best—but what wi' the drink, and the quarreling, and the bad illnesses, and the hard dying, as I've seen times and times, one's thankful to hear of a better. The boy sings pretty, don't he, Master Marner?"

"Yes," said Silas, absently, "very pretty."

The Christmas carol, with its hammer-like rhythm, had fallen on his ears as strange music, quite unlike a hymn, and could have none of the effect Dolly contemplated. But he wanted to show her that he was grateful, and the only mode that occurred to him was to offer Aaron a bit more cake.

"Oh no, thank you, Master Marner," said Dolly, holding down Aaron's willing hands. "We must be going home now. And so I wish you good-by, Master Marner; and if you ever feel anyways bad in your inside, as you can't fend for yourself, I'll come and clean up for you, and get you a bit o' victual, and willing. But

I beg and pray of you to leave off weaving of a Sunday, for it's bad for soul and body—and the money as comes i' that way 'ull be a bad bed to lie down on at the last, if it doesn't fly away, nobody knows where, like the white frost. And you'll excuse me being that free with you, Master Marner, for I wish you well— I do. Make your bow, Aaron."

Silas said "Good-by, and thank you kindly," as he opened the door for Dolly, but he couldn't help feeling relieved when she was gone—relieved that he might weave again and moan at his ease. Her simple view of life and its comforts, by which she had tried to cheer him, was only like a report of unknown objects, which his imagination could not fashion. The fountains of human love and of faith in a divine love had not yet been unlocked, and his soul was still the shrunken rivulet, with only this difference, that its little groove of sand was blocked up, and it wandered confusedly against dark obstruction.

And so, notwithstanding the honest persuasions of Mr. Macey and Dolly Winthrop, Silas spent his Christmas Day in loneliness, eating his meat in sadness of heart, though the meat had come to him as a neighborly present. In the morning he looked out on the black frost that seemed to press cruelly on every blade of grass, while the half-icy red pool shivered under the bitter wind; but toward evening the snow began to fall and curtained from him even that dreary outlook, shutting him close up with his narrow grief. And he sat in his robbed home through the livelong evening, not caring to close his shutters or lock his door, pressing his head between his hands and moaning, till the cold grasped him and told him that his fire was gray.

Nobody in this world but himself knew that he was the same Silas Marner who

had once loved his fellow with tender love and trusted in an unseen goodness. Even to himself that past experience had become dim.

But in Raveloe village the bells rang merrily, and the church was fuller than all through the rest of the year, with red faces among the abundant dark-green boughs—faces prepared for a longer service than usual by an odorous breakfast of toast and ale. Those green boughs, the hymn and anthem never heard but at Christmas—even the Athanasian Creed,[1] which was discriminated from the others only as being longer and of exceptional virtue, since it was only read on rare occasions—brought a vague exulting sense, for which the grown men could as little have found words as the children, that something great and mysterious had been done for them in heaven above and in earth below, which they were appropriating by their presence. And then the red faces made their way through the black biting frost to their own homes,

feeling themselves free for the rest of the day to eat, drink, and be merry, and using that Christian freedom without diffidence.

At Squire Cass's family party that day nobody mentioned Dunstan—nobody was sorry for his absence, or feared it would be too long. The doctor and his wife, uncle and aunt Kimble, were there, and the annual Christmas talk was carried through without any omissions, rising to the climax of Mr. Kimble's experience when he walked the London hospitals thirty years back, together with striking professional anecdotes then gathered. Whereupon cards followed, with aunt Kimble's annual failure to follow suit, and uncle Kimble's irascibility concerning the odd trick, which was rarely explicable to him, when it was not on his side, without a general visitation of tricks to see that they were formed on sound principles: the whole being accompanied by a strong steaming odor of spirits-and-water.

But the party on Christmas Day, being a strictly family party, was not the preeminently brilliant celebration of the

[1] **Athanasian** (ath·ə·nā′zhən) **Creed:** a Latin confession of faith.

season at the Red House. It was the great dance on New Year's Eve that made the glory of Squire Cass's hospitality, as of his forefathers', time out of mind. This was the occasion when all the society of Raveloe and Tarley, whether old acquaintances separated by long rutty distances, or cooled acquaintances separated by misunderstandings concerning runaway calves, or acquaintances founded on intermittent condescension, counted on meeting and on comporting themselves with mutual appropriateness. This was the occasion on which fair dames who came on pillions sent their bandboxes before them, supplied with more than their evening costume; for the feast was not to end with a single evening, like a paltry town entertainment, where the whole supply of eatables is put on the table at once, and bedding is scanty. The Red House was provisioned as if for a siege; and as for the spare featherbeds ready to be laid on floors, they were as plentiful as might naturally be expected in a family that had killed its own geese for many generations.

Godfrey Cass was looking forward to this New Year's Eve with a foolish reckless longing that made him half deaf to his importunate companion, Anxiety.

"Dunsey will be coming home soon: there will be a great blowup, and how will you bribe his spite to silence?" said Anxiety.

"Oh, he won't come before New Year's Eve, perhaps," said Godfrey; "and I shall sit by Nancy then, and dance with her, and get a kind look from her in spite of herself."

"But money is wanted in another quarter," said Anxiety in a louder voice, "and how will you get it without selling your mother's diamond pin? And if you don't get it . . . ?"

"Well, but something may happen to make things easier. At any rate, there's one pleasure for me close at hand: Nancy is coming."

"Yes, and suppose your father should bring matters to a pass that will oblige you to decline marrying her—and to give your reasons?"

"Hold your tongue, and don't worry me. I can see Nancy's eyes, just as they will look at me, and feel her hand in mine already."

But Anxiety went on, though in noisy Christmas company; refusing to be utterly quieted even by much drinking.

FOR STUDY AND DISCUSSION

1. What is ironic about George Eliot's description of Justice Malam? What inquiry does he "set on foot"? What opinions about the robbery are held to by the villagers? What does each group think of those holding the opposing view?

2. What is "the blank" that Silas Marner must somehow fill? How do his neighbors attempt to help him? What does the Rector, Mr. Crackenthorp, do?

3. Why does Mr. Macey visit Silas? What do his words say that he did not mean them to? What kind of irony is this? Why is it amusing?

4. How is Dolly Winthrop different from the others who have called on Silas? Why is she drawn to him? What does she urge him to do? Why does she believe it would be good for him?

5. How does Silas react to Dolly's kindness and concern? Why does he keep giving Aaron pieces of the cake she has brought him? What kind of change seems to be taking place in him?

6. Dolly's church is the Church of England, while Silas's was a small, separate sect of dissenters. What is amusing about their misunderstanding of the words *church* and *chapel?* What does this misunderstanding suggest about the dangers of distrust and ignorance?

7. Godfrey looks forward to New Year's Eve with mixed feelings. What does he long for? What does he fear?

CHAPTER XI

New Year's Eve

SOME WOMEN, I grant, would not appear to advantage seated on a pillion and attired in a drab joseph [1] and a drab beaver bonnet, with a crown resembling a small stew pan; for a garment suggesting a coachman's greatcoat, cut out under an exiguity [2] of cloth that would only allow of miniature capes, is not well adapted to conceal deficiencies of contour, nor is drab a color that will throw sallow cheeks into lively contrast. It was all the greater triumph to Miss Nancy Lammeter's beauty that she looked thoroughly bewitching in that costume, as seated on the pillion behind her tall, erect father, she held one arm around him and looked down, with open-eyed anxiety, at the treacherous snow-covered pools and puddles, which sent up formidable splashings of mud under the stamp of Dobbin's foot. A painter would, perhaps, have preferred her in those moments when she was free from self-consciousness; but certainly the bloom on her cheeks was at its highest point of contrast with the surrounding drab when she arrived at the door of the Red House and saw Mr. Godfrey Cass ready to lift her from the pillion. She wished her sister Priscilla had come up at the same time behind the servant, for then she would have contrived that Mr. Godfrey should have lifted off Priscilla first, and, in the meantime, she would have persuaded her father to go round to the horse block instead of alighting at the doorsteps. It was very painful, when you had made it quite clear to a young man that you were determined not to marry him, however much he might

[1] **joseph:** riding cloak.
[2] **exiguity** (ek'sə·gyo͞o'ə·tē): scarceness.

wish it, that he would still continue to pay you marked attentions; besides, why didn't he always show the same attentions, if he meant them sincerely, instead of being so strange as Mr. Godfrey Cass was, sometimes behaving as if he didn't want to speak to her, and taking no notice of her for weeks and weeks, and then, all on a sudden, almost making love again? Moreover, it was quite plain he had no real love for her, else he would not let people have *that* to say of him which they did say. Did he suppose that Miss Nancy Lammeter was to be won by any man, squire or no squire, who led a bad life? That was not what she had been used to see in her own father, who was the soberest and best man in that countryside, only a little hot and hasty now and then, if things were not done to the minute.

All these thoughts rushed through Miss Nancy's mind, in their habitual succession, in the moments between her first sight of Mr. Godfrey Cass standing at the door and her own arrival there. Happily, the Squire came out too and gave a loud greeting to her father, so that, somehow, under cover of this noise she seemed to

find concealment for her confusion and neglect of any suitably formal behavior, while she was being lifted from the pillion by strong arms which seemed to find her ridiculously small and light. And there was the best reason for hastening into the house at once, since the snow was beginning to fall again, threatening an unpleasant journey for such guests as were still on the road. These were a small minority: for already the afternoon was beginning to decline, and there would not be too much time for the ladies who came from a distance to attire themselves in readiness for the early tea which was to inspirit them for the dance.

There was a buzz of voices through the house, as Miss Nancy entered, mingled with the scrape of a fiddle preluding in the kitchen; but the Lammeters were guests whose arrival had evidently been thought of so much that it hád been watched for from the windows, for Mrs. Kimble, who did the honors at the Red House on these great occasions, came forward to meet Miss Nancy in the hall and conduct her upstairs. Mrs. Kimble was the Squire's sister, as well as the doctor's wife—a double dignity, with which her diameter was in direct proportion; so that, a journey upstairs being rather fatiguing to her, she did not oppose Miss Nancy's request to be allowed to find her way alone to the Blue Room, where the Miss Lammeters' bandboxes had been deposited on their arrival in the morning.

There was hardly a bedroom in the house where feminine compliments were not passing and feminine toilettes going forward, in various stages, in space made scanty by extra beds spread upon the floor; and Miss Nancy, as she entered the Blue Room, had to make her little formal curtsy to a group of six. On the one hand, there were ladies no less important than the two Miss Gunns, the wine merchant's

daughters from Lytherly, dressed in the height of fashion, with the tightest skirts and the shortest waists, and gazed at by Miss Ladbrook (of the Old Pastures) with a shyness not unsustained by inward criticism. Partly, Miss Ladbrook felt that her own skirt must be regarded as unduly lax by the Miss Gunns, and partly, that it was a pity the Miss Gunns did not show that judgment which she herself would show if she were in their place, by stopping a little on this side of the fashion. On the other hand, Mrs. Ladbrook was standing in skullcap and front, with her turban in her hand, curtsying and smiling blandly and saying, "After you, ma'am," to another lady in similar circumstances, who had politely offered the precedence at the looking glass.

But Miss Nancy had no sooner made her curtsy than an elderly lady came forward, whose full white muslin kerchief and mobcap round her curls of smooth gray hair were in daring contrast with the puffed yellow satins and topknotted caps of her neighbors. She approached Miss Nancy with much primness and said, with a slow, treble suavity—

"Niece, I hope I see you well in health." Miss Nancy kissed her aunt's cheek dutifully and answered, with the same sort of amiable primness, "Quite well, I thank you, aunt; and I hope I see you the same."

"Thank you, niece; I keep my health for the present. And how is my brother-in-law?"

These dutiful questions and answers were continued until it was ascertained in detail that the Lammeters were all as well as usual, and the Osgoods likewise, also that niece Priscilla must certainly arrive shortly, and that traveling on pillions in snowy weather was unpleasant, though a joseph was a great protection. Then Nancy was formally introduced to her aunt's visitors, the Miss Gunns, as

being the daughters of a mother known to *their* mother, though now for the first time induced to make a journey into these parts; and these ladies were so taken by surprise at finding such a lovely face and figure in an out-of-the-way country place, that they began to feel some curiosity about the dress she would put on when she took off her joseph. Miss Nancy, whose thoughts were always conducted with the propriety and moderation conspicuous in her manners, remarked to herself that the Miss Gunns were rather hard-featured than otherwise, and that such very low dresses as they wore might have been attributed to vanity if their shoulders had been pretty, but that, being as they were, it was not reasonable to suppose that they showed their necks from a love of display, but rather from some obligation not inconsistent with sense and modesty. She felt convinced, as she opened her box, that this must be her aunt Osgood's opinion, for Miss Nancy's mind resembled her aunt's to a degree that everybody said was surprising, considering the kinship was on Mr. Osgood's side; and though you might not have supposed it from the formality of their greeting, there was a devoted attachment and mutual admiration between aunt and niece. Even Miss Nancy's refusal of her cousin Gilbert Osgood (on the ground solely that he was her cousin), though it had grieved her aunt greatly, had not in the least cooled the preference which had determined her to leave Nancy several of her hereditary

ornaments,[1] let Gilbert's future wife be whom she might.

Three of the ladies quickly retired, but the Miss Gunns were quite content that Mrs. Osgood's inclination to remain with her niece gave them also a reason for staying to see the rustic beauty's toilette. And it was really a pleasure—from the first opening of the bandbox, where everything smelled of lavender and rose leaves, to the clasping of the small coral necklace that fitted closely round her little white neck. Everything belonging to Miss Nancy was of delicate purity and nattiness: not a crease was where it had no business to be, not a bit of her linen professed whiteness without fulfilling its profession; the very pins on her pincushion were stuck in after a pattern from which she was careful to allow no aberration; and as for her own person, it gave the same idea of perfect unvarying neatness as the body of a little bird. It is true that her light brown hair was cropped behind like a boy's and was dressed in front in a number of flat rings that lay quite away from her face; but there was no sort of coiffure that could make Miss Nancy's cheek and neck look otherwise than pretty; and when at last she stood complete in her silvery twilled silk, her lace tucker,[2] her coral necklace, and coral eardrops, the Miss Gunns could see nothing to criticize except her hands, which

[1] **hereditary ornaments:** family jewels, handed down from generation to generation.
[2] **tucker:** scarf.

bore the traces of butter-making, cheese-crushing, and even still coarser work. But Miss Nancy was not ashamed of that, for while she was dressing she narrated to her aunt how she and Priscilla had packed their boxes yesterday, because this morning was baking morning, and since they were leaving home, it was desirable to make a good supply of meat pies for the kitchen; and as she concluded this judicious remark, she turned to the Miss Gunns that she might not commit the rudeness of not including them in the conversation. The Miss Gunns smiled stiffly and thought what a pity it was that these rich country people, who could afford to buy such good clothes (really Miss Nancy's lace and silk were very costly), should be brought up in utter ignorance and vulgarity. She actually said "mate" for "meat," "'appen" for "perhaps," and "oss" for "horse," which to young ladies living in good Lytherly society, who habitually said 'orse, even in domestic privacy, and only said 'appen on the right occasions, was necessarily shocking. Miss Nancy, indeed, had never been to any school higher than Dame Tedman's; her acquaintance with profane literature hardly went beyond the rhymes she had worked in her large sampler [1] under the lamb and the shepherdess; and in order to balance an account, she was obliged to effect her subtraction by removing visible metallic shillings and sixpences from a visible metallic total. There is hardly a servant maid in these days who is not better informed than Miss Nancy; yet she had the essential attributes of a lady—high veracity, delicate honor in her dealings, deference to others, and refined personal habits; and lest these should not suffice to convince grammatical [2] fair ones that her feelings can at all resemble theirs,

I will add that she was slightly proud and exacting and as constant in her affection toward a baseless opinion as toward an erring lover.

The anxiety about sister Priscilla, which had grown rather active by the time the coral necklace was clasped, was happily ended by the entrance of that cheerful-looking lady herself, with a face made blowsy by cold and damp. After the first questions and greetings, she turned to Nancy and surveyed her from head to foot—then wheeled her round, to ascertain that the back view was equally faultless.

"What do you think o' *these* gowns, aunt Osgood?" said Priscilla, while Nancy helped her to unrobe.

"Very handsome indeed, niece," said Mrs. Osgood, with a slight increase of formality. She always thought niece Priscilla too rough.

"I'm obliged to have the same as Nancy, you know, for all I'm five years older, and it makes me look yellow; for she never *will* have anything without I have mine just like it, because she wants us to look like sisters. And I tell her, folks 'ull think it's my weakness makes me fancy as I shall look pretty in what she looks pretty in. For I *am* ugly—there's no denying that; I feature my father's family. But, law! I don't mind, do you?" Priscilla here turned to the Miss Gunns, rattling on in too much preoccupation with the delight of talking to notice that her candor was not appreciated. "The pretty uns do for fly catchers—they keep the men off us. I've no opinion o' the men, Miss Gunn—I don't know what *you* have. And as for fretting and stewing about what *they*'ll think of you from morning till night, and making your life uneasy about what they're doing when they're out o' your sight—as I tell Nancy, it's a folly no woman need be guilty of, if she's got a good

¹ **sampler:** an embroidered piece of needlework.
² **grammatical:** educated.

662　THE NOVEL

father and a good home; let her leave it to them as have got no fortin and can't help themselves. As I say, Mr. Have-your-own-way is the best husband and the only one I'd ever promise to obey. I know it isn't pleasant, when you've been used to living in a big way, and managing hogs-heads and all that, to go and put your nose in by somebody else's fireside, or to sit down by yourself to a scrag or a knuckle;[1] but, thank God! my father's a sober man and likely to live; and if you've got a man by the chimney corner, it doesn't matter if he's childish—the business needn't be broke up."

The delicate process of getting her narrow gown over her head without injury to her smooth curls obliged Miss Priscilla to pause in this rapid survey of life, and Mrs. Osgood seized the opportunity of rising and saying—

"Well, niece, you'll follow us. The Miss Gunns will like to go down."

"Sister," said Nancy, when they were alone, "you've offended the Miss Gunns, I'm sure."

"What have I done, child?" said Priscilla, in some alarm.

"Why, you asked them if they minded about being ugly—you're so very blunt."

"Law, did I? Well, it popped out: it's a mercy I said no more, for I'm a bad un to live with folks when they don't like the truth. But as for being ugly, look at me, child, in this silver-colored silk—I told you how it 'ud be—I look yellow as a daffodil. Anybody 'ud say you wanted to make a mawkin[2] of me."

"No, Priscy, don't say so. I begged and prayed of you not to let us have this silk if you'd like another better. I was willing to have *your* choice, you know I was," said Nancy, in anxious self-vindication.

"Nonsense, child! you know you'd set

your heart on this; and reason good, for you're the color o' cream. It 'ud be fine doings for you to dress yourself to suit *my* skin. What I find fault with is that notion o' yours as I must dress myself just like you. But you do as you like with me—you always did, from when first you begun to walk. If you wanted to go the field's length, the field's length you'd go; and there was no whipping you, for you looked as prim and innicent as a daisy all the while."

"Priscy," said Nancy, gently, as she fastened a coral necklace, exactly like her own, round Priscilla's neck, which was very far from being like her own, "I'm sure I'm willing to give way as far as is right, but who shouldn't dress alike if it isn't sisters? Would you have us go about looking as if we were no kin to one another—us that have got no mother and not another sister in the world? I'd do what was right, if I dressed in a gown dyed with cheese-coloring; and I'd rather you'd choose and let me wear what pleases you."

"There you go again! You'd come round to the same thing if one talked to you from Saturday night till Saturday morning. It'll be fine fun to see how you'll master your husband and never raise your voice above the singing o' the kettle all the while. I like to see the men mastered!"

"Don't talk *so,* Priscy," said Nancy, blushing. "You know I don't mean ever to be married."

"Oh, you never mean a fiddlestick's end!" said Priscilla, as she arranged her discarded dress and closed her bandbox. "Who shall *I* have to work for when father's gone, if you are to go and take notions in your head and be an old maid, because some folks are no better than they should be? I haven't a bit o' patience with you—sitting on an addled egg forever, as if there was never a fresh un in the world.

[1] **scrag . . . knuckle:** a bony piece of meat.
[2] **mawkin:** scarecrow.

One old maid's enough out o' two sisters; and I shall do credit to a single life, for God A'mighty meant me for it. Come, we can go down now. I'm as ready as a mawkin *can* be—there's nothing a-wanting to frighten the crows, now I've got my eardroppers in."

As the two Miss Lammeters walked into the large parlor together, anyone who did not know the character of both might certainly have supposed that the reason why the square-shouldered, clumsy, high-featured Priscilla wore a dress the facsimile of her pretty sister's was either the mistaken vanity of the one or the malicious contrivance of the other in order to set off her own rare beauty. But the good-natured self-forgetful cheeriness and common sense of Priscilla would soon have dissipated the one suspicion; and the modest calm of Nancy's speech and manners told clearly of a mind free from all disavowed devices.

Places of honor had been kept for the Miss Lammeters near the head of the principal tea table in the wainscoted parlor, now looking fresh and pleasant with handsome branches of holly, yew, and laurel from the abundant growths of the old garden; and Nancy felt an inward flutter that no firmness of purpose could prevent when she saw Mr. Godfrey Cass advancing to lead her to a seat between himself and Mr. Crackenthorp, while Priscilla was called to the opposite side between her father and the Squire. It certainly did make some difference to Nancy that the lover she had given up was the young man of quite the highest consequence in the parish—at home in a venerable and unique parlor, which was the extremity of grandeur in her experience, a parlor where *she* might one day have been mistress, with the consciousness that she was spoken of as "Madam Cass," the Squire's wife. These circumstances exalted her inward drama in her own eyes and deepened the emphasis with which she declared to herself that not the most dazzling rank should induce her to marry a man whose conduct showed him careless of his character, but that "love once, love always" was the motto of a true and pure woman, and no man should ever have any right over her which would be a call on her to destroy the dried flowers that she treasured, and always would treasure, for Godfrey Cass's sake. And Nancy was capable of keeping her word to herself under very trying conditions. Nothing but a becoming blush betrayed the moving thoughts that urged themselves upon her as she accepted the seat next to Mr. Crackenthorp; for she was so instinctively neat and adroit in all her actions, and her pretty lips met each other with such quiet firmness, that it would have been difficult for her to appear agitated.

It was not the Rector's practice to let a charming blush pass without an appropriate compliment. He was not in the least lofty or aristocratic, but simply a merry-eyed, small-featured, gray-haired man, with his chin propped by an ample many-creased white neckcloth which

seemed to predominate over every other point in his person and somehow to impress its peculiar character on his remarks; so that to have considered his amenities [1] apart from his cravat would have been a severe, and perhaps a dangerous, effort of abstraction.

"Ha, Miss Nancy," he said, turning his head within his cravat and smiling down pleasantly upon her, "when anybody pretends this has been a severe winter, I shall tell them I saw the roses blooming on New Year's Eve—eh, Godfrey, what do *you* say?"

Godfrey made no reply and avoided looking at Nancy very markedly; for though these complimentary personalities were held to be in excellent taste in old-fashioned Raveloe society, reverent love has a politeness of its own which it teaches to men otherwise of small schooling. But the Squire was rather impatient at Godfrey's showing himself a dull spark in this way. By this advanced hour of the day, the Squire was always in higher spirits than we have seen him in at the breakfast table and felt it quite pleasant to fulfill the hereditary duty of being noisily jovial and patronizing: the large silver snuffbox was in active service and was offered without fail to all neighbors from time to time, however often they might have declined the favor. At present, the Squire had only given an express welcome to the heads of families as they appeared; but always as the evening deepened, his hospitality rayed out more widely, till he had tapped the youngest guests on the back and shown a peculiar fondness for their presence, in the full belief that they must feel their lives made happy by their belonging to a parish where there was such a hearty man as Squire Cass to invite them and wish them well.

Even in this early stage of the jovial mood, it was natural that he should wish to supply his son's deficiencies by looking and speaking for him.

"Ay, ay," he began, offering his snuffbox to Mr. Lammeter, who for the second time bowed his head and waved his hand in stiff rejection of the offer, "us old fellows may wish ourselves young tonight, when we see the mistletoe bough in the White Parlor. It's true, most things are gone back'ard in these last thirty years—the country's going down since the old king [2] fell ill. But when I look at Miss Nancy here, I begin to think the lasses keep up their quality; ding me if I remember a sample to match her, not when I was a fine young fellow and thought a deal about my pigtail. No offense to you, madam," he added, bending to Mrs. Crackenthorp, who sat by him; "I didn't know *you* when you were as young as Miss Nancy here."

Mrs. Crackenthorp—a small blinking woman, who fidgeted incessantly with her lace, ribbons, and gold chain, turning her head about and making subdued noises, very much like a guinea pig that twitches its nose and soliloquizes in all company indiscriminately—now blinked and fidgeted toward the Squire, and said, "Oh no—no offense."

This emphatic compliment of the Squire's to Nancy was felt by others besides Godfrey to have a diplomatic significance; and her father gave a slight additional erectness to his back, as he looked across the table at her with complacent gravity. That grave and orderly senior was not going to bate a jot of his dignity by seeming elated at the notion of a match between his family and the Squire's: he was gratified by any honor paid to his daughter; but he must see an

[1] **amenities:** pleasant qualities.

[2] **old king:** George III, who fell ill in 1810.

alteration in several ways before his consent would be vouchsafed. His spare but healthy person and high-featured firm face, that looked as if it had never been flushed by excess, was in strong contrast, not only with the Squire's, but with the appearance of the Raveloe farmers generally—in accordance with a favorite saying of his own, that "breed was stronger than pasture."

"Miss Nancy's wonderful like what her mother was, though; isn't she, Kimble?" said the stout lady of that name, looking round for her husband.

But Doctor Kimble (country apothecaries in old days enjoyed that title without authority of diploma), being a thin and agile man, was flitting about the room with his hands in his pockets, making himself agreeable to his feminine patients, with medical impartiality, and being welcomed everywhere as a doctor by hereditary right —not one of those miserable apothecaries who canvass for practice in strange neighborhoods and spend all their income in starving their one horse, but a man of substance, able to keep an extravagant table like the best of his patients. Time out of mind the Raveloe doctor had been a Kimble; Kimble was inherently a doctor's name; and it was difficult to contemplate firmly the melancholy fact that the actual Kimble had no son, so that his practice might one day be handed over to a successor with the incongruous name of Taylor or Johnson. But in that case the wiser people in Raveloe would employ Dr. Blick of Flitton—as less unnatural. "Did you speak to me, my dear?" said the authentic doctor, coming quickly to his wife's side; but, as if foreseeing that she would be too much out of breath to repeat her remark, he went on immediately— "Ha, Miss Priscilla, the sight of you revives the taste of that superexcellent pork pie. I hope the batch isn't near an end."

"Yes, indeed, it is, doctor," said Priscilla; "but I'll answer for it the next shall be as good. My pork pies don't turn out well by chance."

"Not as your doctoring does, eh, Kimble!—because folks forget to take your physic, eh?" said the Squire, who regarded physic and doctors as many loyal churchmen regard the church and the clergy— tasting a joke against them when he was in health, but impatiently eager for their aid when anything was the matter with him. He tapped his box and looked round with a triumphant laugh.

"Ah, she has a quick wit, my friend Priscilla has," said the doctor, choosing to attribute the epigram to a lady rather than allow a brother-in-law that advantage over him. "She saves a little pepper to sprinkle over her talk—that's the reason why she never puts too much into her pies. There's my wife, now, she never has an answer at her tongue's end; but if I offend her, she's sure to scarify [1] my throat with black pepper the next day or else give me the colic [2] with watery greens. That's an awful tit-for-tat." Here the vivacious doctor made a pathetic grimace.

"Did you ever hear the like?" said Mrs. Kimble, laughing above her double chin with much good humor, aside to Mrs. Crackenthorp, who blinked and nodded, and amiably intended to smile, but the intention lost itself in small twitchings and noises.

"I suppose that's the sort of tit-for-tat adopted in your profession, Kimble, if you've a grudge against a patient," said the rector.

"Never do have a grudge against our patients," said Mr. Kimble, "except when they leave us: and then, you see, we haven't the chance of prescribing for 'em. Ha, Miss Nancy," he continued, suddenly

[1] **scarify** (skar′ə·fī): mark with scars.
[2] **colic** (kol′ik): stomach pains.

skipping to Nancy's side, "you won't forget your promise? You're to save a dance for me, you know."

"Come, come, Kimble, don't you be too for'ard," said the Squire. "Give the young uns fair play. There's my son Godfrey'll be wanting to have a round with you if you run off with Miss Nancy. He's bespoke her for the first dance, I'll be bound. Eh, sir! what do you say?" he continued, throwing himself backward, and looking at Godfrey. "Haven't you asked Miss Nancy to open the dance with you?"

Godfrey, sorely uncomfortable under this significant insistence about Nancy and afraid to think where it would end by the time his father had set his usual hospitable example of drinking before and after supper saw no course open but to turn to Nancy and say, with as little awkwardness as possible—

"No, I've not asked her yet, but I hope she'll consent—if somebody else hasn't been before me."

"No, I've not engaged myself," said Nancy, quietly, though blushingly. (If Mr. Godfrey founded any hopes on her consenting to dance with him, he would soon be undeceived; but there was no need for her to be uncivil.)

"Then I hope you've no objections to dancing with me," said Godfrey, beginning to lose the sense that there was anything uncomfortable in this arrangement.

"No, no objections," said Nancy, in a cold tone.

"Ah, well, you're a lucky fellow, Godfrey," said uncle Kimble; "but you're my godson, so I won't stand in your way. Else I'm not so very old, eh, my dear?" he went on, skipping to his wife's side again. "You wouldn't mind my having a second after you were gone—not if I cried a good deal first?"

"Come, come, take a cup o' tea and stop your tongue, do," said good-humored Mrs. Kimble, feeling some pride in a husband who must be regarded as so clever and amusing by the company generally. If he had only not been irritable at cards!

While safe, well-tested personalities were enlivening the tea in this way, the sound of the fiddle approaching within a distance at which it could be heard distinctly made the young people look at each other with sympathetic impatience for the end of the meal.

"Why, there's Solomon in the hall," said the Squire, "and playing my fav'rite tune, I believe—'The flaxen-headed ploughboy'—he's for giving us a hint as we aren't enough in a hurry to hear him play. Bob," he called out to his third long-legged son, who was at the other end of the room, "open the door, and tell Solomon to come in. He shall give us a tune here."

Bob obeyed, and Solomon walked in, fiddling as he walked, for he would on no account break off in the middle of a tune.

"Here, Solomon," said the Squire, with loud patronage. "Round here, my man. Ah, I knew it was 'The flaxen-headed ploughboy': there's no finer tune."

Solomon Macey, a small hale old man, with an abundant crop of long white hair reaching nearly to his shoulders, advanced to the indicated spot, bowing reverently while he fiddled, as much as to say that he respected the company though he respected the keynote more. As soon as he had repeated the tune and lowered his fiddle, he bowed again to the Squire and the Rector and said, "I hope I see your honor and your reverence well, and wishing you health and long life and a happy New Year. And wishing the same to you, Mr. Lammeter, sir; and to the other gentlemen, and the madams, and the young lasses."

As Solomon uttered the last words, he bowed in all directions solicitously, lest

he should be wanting in due respect. But thereupon he immediately began to prelude and fell into the tune which he knew would be taken as a special compliment by Mr. Lammeter.

"Thank ye, Solomon, thank ye," said Mr. Lammeter when the fiddle paused again. "That's 'Over the hills and far away,' that is. My father used to say to me, whenever we heard that tune, 'Ah, lad, *I* come from over the hills and far away.' There's a many tunes I don't make head or tail of; but that speaks to me like the blackbird's whistle. I suppose it's the name: there's a deal in the name of a tune."

But Solomon was already impatient to prelude again, and presently broke with much spirit into "Sir Roger de Coverley," at which there was a sound of chairs pushed back and laughing voices.

"Ay, ay, Solomon, we know what that means," said the Squire, rising. "It's time to begin the dance, eh? Lead the way, then, and we'll all follow you."

So Solomon, holding his white head on one side, and playing vigorously, marched forward at the head of the gay procession into the White Parlor, where the mistletoe bough was hung, and multitudinous tallow candles made rather a brilliant effect, gleaming from among the berried holly boughs and reflected in the old-fashioned oval mirrors fastened in the panels of the white wainscot. A quaint procession! Old Solomon, in his seedy clothes and long white locks seemed to be luring that decent company by the magic scream of his fiddle—luring discreet matrons in turban-shaped caps, nay, Mrs. Crackenthorp herself, the summit of whose perpendicular feather was on a level with the Squire's shoulder—luring fair lasses complacently conscious of very short waists and skirts blameless of front folds—luring burly fathers in large variegated waistcoats, and

ruddy sons, for the most part shy and sheepish, in short nether garments and very long coattails.

Already Mr. Macey and a few other privileged villagers, who were allowed to be spectators on these great occasions, were seated on benches placed for them near the door; and great was the admiration and satisfaction in that quarter when the couples had formed themselves for the dance, and the Squire led off with Mrs. Crackenthorp, joining hands with the Rector and Mrs. Osgood. That was as it should be—that was what everybody had been used to—and the charter of Raveloe seemed to be renewed by the ceremony. It was not thought of as an unbecoming levity for the old and middle-aged people to dance a little before sitting down to cards, but rather as part of their social duties. For what were these if not to be merry at appropriate times, interchanging visits and poultry with due frequency, paying each other old-established compliments in sound traditional phrases, passing well-tried personal jokes, urging your guests to eat and drink too much out of hospitality, and eating and drinking too much in your neighbor's house to show that you liked your cheer? And the parson naturally set an example in these social duties. For it would not have been possible for the Raveloe mind, without a peculiar revelation, to know that a clergyman should be a palefaced memento of solemnities, instead of a reasonably faulty man whose exclusive authority to read prayers and preach, to christen, marry, and bury you, necessarily coexisted with the right to sell you the ground to be buried in and to take tithe in kind; [1] on which last point, of course, there was a little grumbling, but not to the extent of irreligion—not of deeper significance than

[1] **tithe in kind:** one tenth of a person's income, in any kind of merchandise.

the grumbling at the rain, which was by no means accompanied with a spirit of impious defiance, but with a desire that the prayer for fine weather might be read forthwith.

There was no reason, then, why the Rector's dancing should not be received as part of the fitness of things quite as much as the Squire's, or why, on the other hand, Mr. Macey's official respect should restrain him from subjecting the parson's performance to that criticism with which minds of extraordinary acuteness must necessarily contemplate the doings of their fallible fellowmen.

"The Squire's pretty springe,[1] considering his weight," said Mr. Macey, "and he stamps uncommon well. But Mr. Lammeter beats 'em all for shapes: you see he holds his head like a sodger,[2] and he isn't so cushiony as most o' the oldish gentlefolks—they run fat in general; and he's got a fine leg. The parson's nimble enough, but he hasn't got much of a leg: it's a bit too thick down'ard, and his knees might be a bit nearer wi'out damage; but he might do worse, he might do worse. Though he hasn't that grand way o' waving his hand as the Squire has."

"Talk o' nimbleness, look at Mrs. Osgood," said Ben Winthrop, who was holding his son Aaron between his knees. "She trips along with her little steps, so as nobody can see how she goes—it's like as if she had little wheels to her feet. She doesn't look a day older nor last year: she's the finest made woman as is, let the next be where she will."

"I don't heed how the women are made," said Mr. Macey, with some contempt. "They wear nayther coat nor breeches; you can't make much out o' their shapes."

"Fayder," said Aaron, whose feet were

¹ **springe:** spry.
² **sodger:** soldier.

busy beating out the tune, "how does that big cock's feather stick in Mrs. Crackenthorp's yead? Is there a little hole for it, like in my shuttlecock?"

"Hush, lad, hush; that's the way the ladies dress theirselves, that is," said the father, adding, however, in an undertone to Mr. Macey, "it does make her look funny, though—partly like a short-necked bottle wi' a long quill in it. Hey, by jingo, there's the young Squire leading off now, wi' Miss Nancy for partners! There's a lass for you!—like a pink and white posy there's nobody 'ud think as anybody could be so pritty. I shouldn't wonder if she's Madam Cass some day, arter all—and nobody more rightfuller, for they'd make a fine match. You can find nothing against Master Godfrey's shapes, Macey, I'll bet a penny."

Mr. Macey screwed up his mouth, leaned his head further on one side, and twirled his thumbs with a presto movement as his eyes followed Godfrey up the dance. At last he summed up his opinion.

"Pretty well down'ard, but a bit too round i' the shoulderblades. And as for them coats as he gets from the Flitton tailor, they're a poor cut to pay double money for."

"Ah, Mr. Macey, you and me are two

folks," said Ben, slightly indignant at this carping. "When I've got a pot o' good ale, I like to swaller it, and do my inside good, i'stead o' smelling and staring at it to see if I can't find faut wi' the brewing. I should like you to pick me out a finer-limbed young fellow nor Master Godfrey—one as 'ud knock you down easier, or 's more pleasanter looksed when he's piert and merry."

"Tchuh!" said Mr. Macey, provoked to increased severity, "he isn't come to his right color yet: he's partly like a slack-baked [1] pie. And I doubt he's got a soft place in his head, else why should he be turned round the finger by that offal Dunsey as nobody's seen o' late and let him kill that fine hunting hoss as was the talk o' the country? And one while he was allays after Miss Nancy, and then it all went off again, like a smell o' hot porridge, as I may say. That wasn't my way when *I* went a-coorting."

"Ah, but mayhap Miss Nancy hung off like, and your lass didn't," said Ben.

"I should say she didn't," said Mr. Macey, significantly. "Before I said 'sniff,' I took care to know as she'd say 'snaff,' and pretty quick too. I wasn't a-going to open *my* mouth, like a dog at a fly and snap it to again, wi' nothing to swaller."

"Well, I think Miss Nancy's a-coming round again," said Ben, "for Master Godfrey doesn't look so downhearted tonight. And I see he's for taking her away to sit down, now they're at the end o' the dance: that looks like sweethearting, that does."

The reason why Godfrey and Nancy had left the dance was not so tender as Ben imagined. In the close press of couples a slight accident had happened to Nancy's dress, which, while it was short enough to show her neat ankle in front,

[1] **slack-baked:** underdone.

was long enough behind to be caught under the stately stamp of the Squire's foot, so as to rend certain stitches at the waist and cause much sisterly agitation in Priscilla's mind, as well as serious concern in Nancy's. One's thoughts may be much occupied with love struggles, but hardly so as to be insensible to a disorder in the general framework of things. Nancy had no sooner completed her duty in the figure they were dancing than she said to Godfrey, with a deep blush, that she must go and sit down till Priscilla could come to her; for the sisters had already exchanged a short whisper and an open-eyed glance full of meaning. No reason less urgent than this could have prevailed on Nancy to give Godfrey this opportunity of sitting apart with her. As for Godfrey, he was feeling so happy and oblivious under the long charm of the country dance with Nancy, that he got rather bold on the strength of her confusion and was capable of leading her straight away, without leave asked, into the adjoining small parlor, where the card tables were set.

"O no, thank you," said Nancy, coldly, as soon as she perceived where he was going, "not in there. I'll wait here till Priscilla's ready to come to me. I'm sorry to bring you out of the dance and make myself troublesome."

"Why, you'll be more comfortable here by yourself," said the artful Godfrey: "I'll leave you here till your sister can come." He spoke in an indifferent tone.

That was an agreeable proposition and just what Nancy desired; why, then, was she a little hurt that Mr. Godfrey should make it? They entered, and she seated herself on a chair against one of the card tables, as the stiffest and most unapproachable position she could choose.

"Thank you, sir," she said immediately. "I needn't give you any more trouble. I'm

sorry you've had such an unlucky partner."

"That's very ill-natured of you," said Godfrey, standing by her without any sign of intended departure, "to be sorry you've danced with me."

"Oh no, sir, I don't mean to say what's ill-natured at all," said Nancy, looking distractingly prim and pretty. "When gentlemen have so many pleasures, one dance can matter but very little."

"You know that isn't true. You know one dance with you matters more to me than all the other pleasures in the world."

It was a long, long while since Godfrey had said anything so direct as that, and Nancy was startled. But her instinctive dignity and repugnance to any show of emotion made her sit perfectly still and only throw a little more decision into her voice, as she said—

"No, indeed, Mr. Godfrey, that's not known to me, and I have very good reasons for thinking different. But if it's true, I don't wish to hear it."

"Would you never forgive me, then, Nancy—never think well of me, let what would happen—would you never think the present made amends for the past? Not if I turned a good fellow and gave up everything you didn't like?"

Godfrey was half-conscious that this sudden opportunity of speaking to Nancy alone had driven him beside himself; but blind feeling had got the mastery of his tongue. Nancy really felt much agitated by the possibility Godfrey's words suggested, but this very pressure of emotion that she was in danger of finding too strong for her roused all her power of self-command.

"I should be glad to see a good change in anybody, Mr. Godfrey," she answered, with the slightest discernible difference of tone, "but it 'ud be better if no change was wanted."

"You are very hardhearted, Nancy," said Godfrey, pettishly. "You might encourage me to be a better fellow. I'm very miserable—but you've no feeling."

"I think those have the least feeling that act wrong to begin with," said Nancy, sending out a flash in spite of herself. Godfrey was delighted with that little flash, and would have liked to go on and make her quarrel with him; Nancy was so exasperatingly quiet and firm. But she was not indifferent to him *yet*.

The entrance of Priscilla, bustling forward and saying, "Dear heart alive, child, let us look at this gown," cut off Godfrey's hopes of a quarrel.

"I suppose I must go now," he said to Priscilla.

"It's no matter to me whether you go or stay," said that frank lady, searching for something in her pocket, with a preoccupied brow.

"Do *you* want me to go?" said Godfrey, looking at Nancy, who was now standing up by Priscilla's order.

"As you like," said Nancy, trying to recover all her former coldness, and looking down carefully at the hem of her gown.

"Then I like to stay," said Godfrey, with a reckless determination to get as much of this joy as he could tonight and think nothing of the morrow.

FOR STUDY AND DISCUSSION

1. What is your first impression of Nancy Lammeter? What is her attitude toward Godfrey? Why does she blush when she sees him waiting to lift her off her horse?

2. What do the Gunn sisters think of Nancy? What do you think of them?

3. What kind of person is Priscilla? What impression does she make on the Miss Gunns? What are her views on men and marriage? Do you think she is right or wrong?

4. Why does Nancy insist that she and Priscilla dress alike? What does this show about her character?

5. Why does Nancy blush on entering the Cass's parlor? How does the Squire act toward her? how does Godfrey? Why?

6. What more do you learn about the Squire from this chapter?

7. What do the onlookers at the dance think of Godfrey and Nancy? Does Godfrey seem to be making any progress with her? Why are they so stiff and awkward with each other? Does Godfrey have a right to think of Nancy as his possible future wife?

8. Which characters and incidents in this chapter did you find most humorous? What about them was amusing?

CHAPTER XII

Gold on Silas's Hearth

W<small>HILE</small> G<small>ODFREY</small> C<small>ASS</small> was taking drafts of forgetfulness from the sweet presence of Nancy, willingly losing all sense of that hidden bond which at other moments galled and fretted him so as to mingle irritation with the very sunshine, Godfrey's wife was walking with slow uncertain steps through the snow-covered Raveloe lanes, carrying her child in her arms.

This journey on New Year's Eve was a premeditated act of vengeance which she had kept in her heart ever since Godfrey, in a fit of passion, had told her he would sooner die than acknowledge her as his wife. There would be a great party at the Red House on New Year's Eve, she knew: her husband would be smiling and smiled upon, hiding *her* existence in the darkest corner of his heart. But she would mar his pleasure: she would go in her dingy rags, with her faded face, once as handsome as the best, with her little child that had its father's hair and eyes, and disclose herself to the Squire as his eldest son's wife. It is seldom that the miserable can help regarding their misery as a wrong inflicted by those who are less miserable. Molly knew that the cause of her dingy rags was not her husband's neglect, but the demon Opium, to whom she was enslaved, body and soul, except in the lingering mother's tenderness that refused to give him her hungry child. She knew this well; and yet, in the moments of wretched unbenumbed consciousness, the sense of her want and degradation transformed itself continually into bitterness toward Godfrey. *He* was well off; and if she had her rights she would be well off too. The belief that he repented his marriage and suffered from it only aggravated her vindictiveness. Just and self-reproving thoughts do not come to us too thickly, even in the purest air and with the best lessons of heaven and earth; how should those white-winged delicate messengers make their way to Molly's poisoned chamber, inhabited by no higher memories than those of a barmaid's paradise of pink ribbons and gentlemen's jokes?

She had set out at an early hour, but had lingered on the road, inclined by her indolence to believe that if she waited under a warm shed the snow would cease to fall. She had waited longer than she knew, and now that she found herself belated in the snow-hidden ruggedness of the long lanes, even the animation of a vindictive purpose could not keep her spirit from failing. It was seven o'clock, and by this time she was not very far from Raveloe, but she was not familiar enough with those monotonous lanes to know how near she was to her journey's end. She needed comfort, and she knew but one comforter—the familiar demon in her bosom; but she hesitated a moment, after drawing out the black remnant, before she raised it to her lips. In that moment the mother's love pleaded for painful con-

sciousness rather than oblivion—pleaded to be left in aching weariness rather than to have the encircling arms benumbed so that they could not feel the dear burden. In another moment Molly had flung something away, but it was not the black remnant—it was an empty phial. And she walked on again under the breaking cloud, from which there came now and then the light of a quickly veiled star, for a freezing wind had sprung up since the snowing had ceased. But she walked always more and more drowsily and clutched more and more automatically the sleeping child at her bosom.

Slowly the demon was working his will, and cold and weariness were his helpers. Soon she felt nothing but a supreme immediate longing that curtained off all futurity—the longing to lie down and sleep. She had arrived at a spot where her footsteps were no longer checked by a hedgerow, and she had wandered vaguely, unable to distinguish any objects, notwithstanding the wide whiteness around her, and the growing starlight. She sank down against a straggling furze bush, an easy pillow enough; and the bed of snow, too, was soft. She did not feel that the bed was cold, and did not heed whether the child would wake and cry for her. But her arms had not yet relaxed their instinctive clutch; and the little one slumbered on as gently as if it had been rocked in a lace-trimmed cradle.

But the complete torpor [1] came at last: the fingers lost their tension, the arms unbent; then the little head fell away from the bosom, and the blue eyes opened wide on the cold starlight. At first there was a little peevish cry of "mammy," and an effort to regain the pillowing arm and bosom; but mammy's ear was deaf, and the pillow seemed to be slipping away

[1] **torpor:** unconsciousness, stupor.

backward. Suddenly, as the child rolled downward on its mother's knees, all wet with snow, its eyes were caught by a bright glancing light on the white ground, and, with the ready transition of infancy, it was immediately absorbed in watching the bright living thing running toward it, yet never arriving. That bright living thing must be caught; and in an instant the child had slipped on all fours and held out one little hand to catch the gleam. But the gleam would not be caught in that way, and now the head was held up to see where the cunning gleam came from. It came from a very bright place; and the little one, rising on its legs, toddled through the snow, the old grimy shawl in which it was wrapped trailing behind it, and the queer little bonnet dangling at its back—toddled on to the open door of Silas Marner's cottage and right up to the warm hearth, where there was a bright fire of logs and sticks, which had thoroughly warmed the old sack (Silas's greatcoat) spread out on the bricks to dry. The little one, accustomed to be left to itself for long hours without notice from its mother, squatted down on the sack and spread its tiny hands toward the blaze, in perfect contentment, gurgling and making many inarticulate communications to the cheerful fire, like a new-hatched gosling beginning to find itself comfortable. But presently the warmth had a lulling effect, and the little golden head sank down on the old sack, and the blue eyes were veiled by their delicate half-transparent lids.

But where was Silas Marner while this strange visitor had come to his hearth? He was in the cottage, but he did not see the child. During the last few weeks, since he had lost his money, he had contracted the habit of opening his door and looking out from time to time, as if he thought that his money might be somehow coming back to

him, or that some trace, some news of it, might be mysteriously on the road and be caught by the listening ear or the straining eye. It was chiefly at night, when he was not occupied in his loom, that he fell into this repetition of an act for which he could have assigned no definite purpose, and which can hardly be understood except by those who have undergone a bewildering separation from a supremely loved object. In the evening twilight, and later whenever the night was not dark, Silas looked out on that narrow prospect round the stone pits, listening and gazing, not with hope, but with mere yearning and unrest.

This morning he had been told by some of his neighbors that it was New Year's Eve and that he must sit up and hear the old year rung out and the new rung in, because that was good luck, and might bring his money back again. This was only a friendly Raveloe way of jesting with the half-crazy oddities of a miser, but it had perhaps helped to throw Silas into a more than usually excited state. Since the oncoming of twilight he had opened his door again and again, though only to shut it immediately at seeing all distance veiled by the falling snow. But the last time he opened it the snow had ceased, and the clouds were parting here and there. He stood and listened, and gazed for a long while—there was really something on the road coming toward him then, but he caught no sign of it; and the stillness and the wide trackless snow seemed to narrow his solitude and touched his yearning with the chill of despair. He went in again and put his right hand on the latch of the door to close it—but he did not close it: he was arrested, as he had been already since his loss, by the invisible wand of catalepsy,[1] and stood like a graven image,

[1] **catalepsy:** suddenly rigid muscles; trance.

with wide but sightless eyes, holding open his door, powerless to resist either the good or evil that might enter there.

When Marner's sensibility returned, he continued the action which had been arrested, and closed his door, unaware of the chasm in his consciousness, unaware of any intermediate change, except that the light had grown dim and that he was chilled and faint. He thought he had been too long standing at the door and looking out. Turning toward the hearth, where the two logs had fallen apart and sent forth only a red uncertain glimmer, he seated himself on his fireside chair, and was stooping to push his logs together, when, to his blurred vision, it seemed as if there were gold on the floor in front of the hearth. Gold!—his own gold—brought back to him as mysteriously as it had been taken away! He felt his heart begin to beat violently, and for a few moments he was unable to stretch out his hand and grasp the restored treasure. The heap of gold seemed to glow and get larger beneath his agitated gaze. He leaned forward at last and stretched forth his hand; but instead of the hard coin with the familiar resisting outline, his fingers encountered soft warm curls. In utter amazement, Silas fell on his knees and bent his head low to examine the marvel: it was a sleeping child—a round, fair thing, with soft yellow rings all over its head. Could this be his little sister come back to him in a dream—his little sister whom he had carried about in his arms for a year before she died, when he was a small boy without shoes or stockings? That was the first thought that darted across Silas's blank wonderment. *Was* it a dream? He rose to his feet again, pushed his logs together, and, throwing on some dried leaves and sticks, raised a flame; but the flame did not disperse the vision—it only lit up more distinctly the

little round form of the child and its shabby clothing. It was very much like his little sister. Silas sank into his chair, powerless under the double presence of an inexplicable surprise and a hurrying influx of memories. How and when had the child come in without his knowledge? He had never been beyond the door. But along with that question, and almost thrusting it away, there was a vision of the old home and the old streets leading to Lantern Yard—and within that vision another, of the thoughts which had been present with him in those far-off scenes. The thoughts were strange to him now, like old friendships impossible to revive; and yet he had a dreamy feeling that this child was somehow a message come to him from that far-off life: it stirred fibers that had never been moved in Raveloe— old quiverings of tenderness—old impressions of awe at the presentiment of some Power presiding over his life; for his imagination had not yet extricated [1] itself from the sense of mystery in the child's sudden presence and had formed no conjectures of ordinary, natural means by which the event could have been brought about.

But there was a cry on the hearth: the child had awaked, and Marner stooped to lift it on his knee. It clung round his neck and burst louder and louder into that mingling of inarticulate cries with "mammy" by which little children express the bewilderment of waking. Silas pressed it to him and almost unconsciously uttered sounds of hushing tenderness, while he bethought himself that some of his porridge, which had got cool by the dying fire, would do to feed the child with if it were only warmed up a little.

He had plenty to do through the next hour. The porridge, sweetened with some

[1] **extricated** (eks′trə·kāt′ed): freed, disentangled.

dry brown sugar from an old store which he had refrained from using for himself, stopped the cries of the little one and made her lift her blue eyes with a wide, quiet gaze at Silas, as he put the spoon into her mouth. Presently she slipped from his knee and began to toddle about, but with a pretty stagger that made Silas jump up and follow her lest she should fall against anything that would hurt her. But she only fell in a sitting posture on the ground and began to pull at her boots, looking up at him with a crying face as if the boots hurt her. He took her on his knee again, but it was some time before it occurred to Silas's dull, bachelor mind that the wet boots were the grievance, pressing on her warm ankles. He got them off with difficulty, and baby was at once happily occupied with the primary mystery of her own toes, inviting Silas, with much chuckling, to consider the mystery too. But the wet boots had at last suggested to Silas that the child had been walking on the snow, and this roused him from his entire oblivion of an ordinary means by which it could have entered or been brought into his house. Under the prompting of this new idea, and without waiting to form conjectures, he raised the child in his arms and went to the door. As soon as he had opened it, there was the cry of "mammy" again, which Silas had not heard since the child's first hungry waking. Bending forward, he could just discern the marks made by the little feet on the virgin snow, and he followed their track to the furze bushes. "Mammy!" the little one cried again and again, stretching itself forward so as almost to escape from Silas's arms, before he himself was aware that there was something more than the bush before him—that there was a human body, with the head sunk low in the furze, and half-covered with the shaken snow.

CHAPTER XIII

A Crisis

IT WAS after the early suppertime at the Red House, and the entertainment was in that stage when bashfulness itself had passed into easy jollity, when gentlemen, conscious of unusual accomplishments, could at length be prevailed on to dance a hornpipe,[1] and when the Squire preferred talking loudly, scattering snuff, and patting his visitors' backs, to sitting longer at the whist table—a choice exasperating to uncle Kimble, who, being always volatile in sober business hours, became intense and bitter over cards and brandy, shuffled before his adversary's deal with a glare of suspicion, and turned up a mean trump card with an air of inexpressible disgust, as if in a world where such things could happen one might as well enter on a course of reckless profligacy. When the evening had advanced to this pitch of freedom and enjoyment, it was usual for the servants, the heavy duties of supper being well over, to get their share of amusement by coming to look on at the dancing; so that the back regions of the house were left in solitude.

There were two doors by which the White Parlor was entered from the hall, and they were both standing open for the sake of air; but the lower one was crowded with the servants and villagers, and only the upper doorway was left free. Bob Cass was figuring in a hornpipe, and his father, very proud of this lithe son, whom he repeatedly declared to be just like himself in his young days in a tone that implied this to be the very highest stamp of juvenile merit, was the center of a group who had placed themselves opposite the performer, not far from the upper door. Godfrey was standing a little way off, not to admire his brother's dancing, but to keep sight of Nancy, who was seated in the group, near her father. He stood aloof, because he wished to avoid suggesting himself as a subject for the Squire's fatherly jokes in connection with matrimony and Miss Nancy Lammeter's beauty, which were likely to become more and more explicit. But he had the prospect of dancing with her again when the hornpipe was concluded, and in the meanwhile it was very pleasant to get long glances at her quite unobserved.

But when Godfrey was lifting his eyes from one of those long glances, they encountered an object as startling to him at that moment as if it had been an apparition from the dead. It *was* an apparition from that hidden life which lies, like a dark bystreet, behind the goodly ornamented façade that meets the sunlight and the gaze of respectable admirers. It was his own child carried in Silas Marner's arms. That was his instantaneous impression, unaccompanied by doubt, though he had not seen the child for months past; and when the hope was rising that he might possibly be mistaken, Mr. Crackenthorp and Mr. Lammeter had already advanced to Silas, in astonishment at this strange advent. Godfrey joined them immediately, unable to rest without hearing every word—trying to control himself, but conscious that if anyone noticed him, they must see that he was white-lipped and trembling.

But now all eyes at that end of the room were bent on Silas Marner; the Squire himself had risen, and asked angrily, "How's this?—what's this?—what do you do coming in here in this way?"

"I'm come for the doctor—I want the doctor," Silas had said, in the first moment, to Mr. Crackenthorp.

"Why, what's the matter, Marner?"

[1] **hornpipe:** a lively, energetic dance.

said the Rector. "The doctor's here; but say quietly what you want him for."

"It's a woman," said Silas, speaking low, and half-breathlessly, just as Godfrey came up. "She's dead, I think—dead in the snow at the stone pits—not far from my door."

Godfrey felt a great throb: there was one terror in his mind at that moment: it was, that the woman might *not* be dead. That was an evil terror—an ugly inmate to have found a nestling place in Godfrey's kindly disposition; but no disposition is a security from evil wishes to a man whose happiness hangs on duplicity.[1]

"Hush, hush!" said Mr. Crackenthorp. "Go out into the hall there. I'll fetch the doctor to you. Found a woman in the snow—and thinks she's dead," he added, speaking low, to the Squire. "Better say as little about it as possible: it will shock the ladies. Just tell them a poor woman is ill from cold and hunger. I'll go and fetch Kimble."

By this time, however, the ladies had pressed forward, curious to know what could have brought the solitary linen-weaver there under such strange circumstances, and interested in the pretty child, who, half-alarmed and half-attracted by the brightness and the numerous company, now frowned and hid her face, now lifted up her head again and looked round placably, until a touch or a coaxing word brought back the frown and made her bury her face with new determination.

"What child is it?" said several ladies at once, and, among the rest, Nancy Lammeter, addressing Godfrey.

"I don't know—some poor woman's who has been found in the snow, I believe," was the answer Godfrey wrung from himself with a terrible effort. ("After all, *am* I certain?" he hastened to add, in

[1] **duplicity:** deceit, lying.

anticipation of his own conscience.)

"Why, you'd better leave the child here, then, Master Marner," said good-natured Mrs. Kimble, hesitating, however, to take those dingy clothes into contact with her own ornamental satin bodice. "I'll tell one o' the girls to fetch it."

"No—no—I can't part with it, I can't let it go," said Silas, abruptly. "It's come to me—I've a right to keep it."

The proposition to take the child from him had come to Silas quite unexpectedly, and his speech, uttered under a strong, sudden impulse, was almost like a revelation to himself: a minute before, he had no distinct intention about the child.

"Did you ever hear the like?" said Mrs. Kimble, in mild surprise, to her neighbor.

"Now, ladies, I must trouble you to stand aside," said Mr. Kimble, coming from the card room, in some bitterness at the interruption, but drilled by the long habit of his profession into obedience to unpleasant calls, even when he was hardly sober.

"It's a nasty business turning out now, eh, Kimble?" said the Squire. "He might ha' gone for your young fellow—the 'prentice, there—what's his name?"

"Might? ay—what's the use of talking about might?" growled uncle Kimble, hastening out with Marner and followed by Mr. Crackenthorp and Godfrey. "Get me a pair of thick boots, Godfrey, will you? And stay, let somebody run to Winthrop's and fetch Dolly—she's the best woman to get. Ben was here himself before supper; is he gone?"

"Yes, sir, I met him," said Marner; "but I couldn't stop to tell him anything, only I said I was going for the doctor, and he said the doctor was at the Squire's. And I made haste and ran, and there was nobody to be seen at the back o' the house, and so I went in to where the company was."

The child, no longer distracted by the bright light and the smiling women's faces, began to cry and call for "mammy," though always clinging to Marner, who had apparently won her thorough confidence. Godfrey had come back with the boots, and felt the cry as if some fiber were drawn tight within him.

"I'll go," he said, hastily, eager for some movement; "I'll go and fetch the woman—Mrs. Winthrop."

"O, pooh—send somebody else," said uncle Kimble, hurrying away with Marner.

"You'll let me know if I can be of any use, Kimble," said Mr. Crackenthorp. But the doctor was out of hearing.

Godfrey, too, had disappeared: he was gone to snatch his hat and coat, having just reflection enough to remember that he must not look like a madman; but he rushed out of the house into the snow without heeding his thin shoes.

In a few minutes he was on his rapid way to the stone pits by the side of Dolly, who, though feeling that she was entirely in her place in encountering cold and snow on an errand of mercy, was much concerned at a young gentleman's getting his feet wet under a like impulse.

"You'd a deal better go back, sir," said Dolly, with respectful compassion. "You've no call to catch cold; and I'd ask you if you'd be so good as tell my husband to come, on your way back—he's at the Rainbow, I doubt—if you found him anyway sober enough to be o' use. Or else, there's Mrs. Snell 'ud happen send the boy up to fetch and carry, for there may be things wanted from the doctor's."

"No, I'll stay, now I'm once out—I'll stay outside here," said Godfrey, when they came opposite Marner's cottage. "You can come and tell me if I can do anything."

"Well, sir, you're very good: you've a tender heart," said Dolly, going to the door.

Godfrey was too painfully preoccupied to feel a twinge of self-reproach at this undeserved praise. He walked up and down, unconscious that he was plunging ankle deep in snow, unconscious of everything but trembling suspense about what was going on in the cottage and the effect of each alternative on his future lot. No, not quite unconscious of everything else. Deeper down, and half-smothered by passionate desire and dread, there was the sense that he ought not to be waiting on these alternatives; that he ought to accept the consequences of his deeds, own the miserable wife, and fulfill the claims of the helpless child. But he had not moral courage enough to contemplate that active renunciation of Nancy as possible for him: he had only conscience and heart enough to make him forever uneasy under the weakness that forbade the renunciation. And at this moment his mind leaped away from all restraint toward the sudden prospect of deliverance from his long bondage.

"Is she dead?" said the voice that predominated over every other within him. "If she is, I may marry Nancy; and then I shall be a good fellow in future, and have no secrets, and the child—shall be taken care of somehow." But across that vision came the other possibility—"She may live, and then it's all up with me."

Godfrey never knew how long it was before the door of the cottage opened and Mr. Kimble came out. He went forward to meet his uncle, prepared to suppress the agitation he must feel, whatever news he was to hear.

"I waited for you, as I'd come so far," he said, speaking first.

"Pooh, it was nonsense for you to come out: why didn't you send one of the men?

There's nothing to be done. She's dead—has been dead for hours, I should say."

"What sort of woman is she?" said Godfrey, feeling the blood rush to his face.

"A young woman, but emaciated, with long black hair. Some vagrant—quite in rags. She's got a wedding ring on, however. They must fetch her away to the workhouse tomorrow. Come, come along."

"I want to look at her," said Godfrey. "I think I saw such a woman yesterday. I'll overtake you in a minute or two."

Mr. Kimble went on, and Godfrey turned back to the cottage. He cast only one glance at the dead face on the pillow, which Dolly had smoothed with decent care; but he remembered that last look at his unhappy hated wife so well, that at the end of sixteen years every line in the worn face was present to him when he told the full story of this night.

He turned immediately toward the hearth, where Silas Marner sat lulling the child. She was perfectly quiet now, but not asleep—only soothed by sweet porridge and warmth into that wide-gazing calm which makes us older human beings, with our inward turmoil, feel a certain awe in the presence of a little child, such as we feel before some quiet majesty or beauty in the earth or sky—before a steady glowing planet, or a full-flowered eglantine,[1] or the bending trees over a silent pathway. The wide-open blue eyes looked up at Godfrey's without any uneasiness or sign of recognition: the child could make no visible audible claim on its father; and the father felt a strange mixture of feelings, a conflict of regret and joy that the pulse of that little heart had no response for the half-jealous yearning in his own, when the blue eyes turned away from him slowly and fixed themselves on the weaver's queer face, which was bent low down to look at them, while the small hand began to pull Marner's withered cheek with loving disfiguration.

"You'll take the child to the parish tomorrow?" asked Godfrey, speaking as indifferently as he could.

"Who says so?" said Marner, sharply. "Will they make me take her?"

"Why, you wouldn't like to keep her, should you—an old bachelor like you?"

"Till anybody shows they've a right to take her away from me," said Marner. "The mother's dead, and I reckon it's got no father: it's a lone thing—and I'm a lone thing. My money's gone, I don't know where—and this is come from I don't know where. I know nothing—I'm partly mazed."

"Poor little thing!" said Godfrey. "Let me give something toward finding it clothes."

He had put his hand in his pocket and found half a guinea, and, thrusting it into Silas's hand, he hurried out of the cottage to overtake Mr. Kimble.

"Ah, I see it's not the same woman I saw," he said, as he came up. "It's a pretty little child: the old fellow seems to want to keep it; that's strange for a miser like him. But I gave him a trifle to help him out: the parish isn't likely to quarrel with him for the right to keep the child."

"No; but I've seen the time when I might have quarreled with him for it myself. It's too late now, though. If the child ran into the fire, your aunt's too fat to overtake it: she could only sit and grunt like an alarmed sow. But what a fool you are, Godfrey, to come out in your dancing shoes and stockings in this way—and you one of the beaux of the evening and at your own house! What do you mean by such freaks, young fellow? Has Miss Nancy been cruel, and do you want to

[1] **eglantine:** honeysuckle.

spite her by spoiling your pumps?" [1]

"Oh, everything has been disagreeable tonight. I was tired to death of jigging and gallanting and that bother about the hornpipes. And I'd got to dance with the other Miss Gunn," said Godfrey, glad of the subterfuge [2] his uncle had suggested to him.

The prevarication and white lies which a mind that keeps itself ambitiously pure is as uneasy under as a great artist under the false touches that no eye detects but his own are worn as lightly as mere trimmings when once the actions have become a lie.

Godfrey reappeared in the White Parlor with dry feet, and, since the truth must be told, with a sense of relief and gladness that was too strong for painful thoughts to struggle with. For could he not venture now, whenever opportunity offered, to say the tenderest things to Nancy Lammeter —to promise her and himself that he would always be just what she would desire to see him? There was no danger that his dead wife would be recognized: those were not days of active inquiry and wide report; and as for the registry of their marriage, that was a long way off, buried in unturned pages, away from everyone's interest but his own. Dunsey might betray him if he came back; but Dunsey might be won to silence.

And when events turn out so much better for a man than he has had reason to dread, is it not a proof that his conduct has been less foolish and blameworthy than it might otherwise have appeared? When we are treated well, we naturally begin to think that we are not altogether unmeritorious, and that it is only just we should treat ourselves well, and not mar our own good fortune. Where, after all, would be the use of his confessing the past

to Nancy Lammeter, and throwing away his happiness?—nay, hers? for he felt some confidence that she loved him. As for the child, he would see that it was cared for: he would never forsake it; he would do everything but own it. Perhaps it would be just as happy in life without being owned by its father, seeing that nobody could tell how things would turn out, and that—is there any other reason wanted?—well, then, that the father would be much happier without owning the child.

FOR STUDY AND DISCUSSION

1. Why does Molly plan to go to Raveloe on the day of Squire Cass's New Year's dance? Is she right about what she thinks Godfrey will be doing? What condition is she in? In what way is she responsible for her own doom?

2. What attracts the child to Silas's cottage? Why is his door open? Why is she able to enter without his seeing her?

3. When Silas discovers the child, what is his first thought? Why is he reminded of Lantern Yard? What effect does this reminder have on him?

4. What does Silas do with some of the brown sugar he has hoarded and would not allow himself to use? What effect does the coming of the child seem to have had on him?

5. Why does Silas's appearance startle the gathering at the Red House? This is the second time Silas has interrupted an evening gathering. How is it like the first time? How is it different?

6. How does Godfrey react to Silas's breathless announcement? to the child in his arms? Why is he silent? Do you think he should be?

7. Why doesn't Mrs. Kimble or some other lady take the child out of Silas's arms? How does Silas feel about the child? Do you think she is better off with him than with someone else?

8. At the end of the episode, what position is Godfrey in? What is the only thing he has to fear? What is his final thought?

[1] **pumps:** boots.
[2] **subterfuge:** excuse, false reason.

CHAPTER XIV

Eppie

THERE WAS a pauper's burial that week in Raveloe, and up Kench Yard at Batherley it was known that the dark-haired woman with the fair child, who had lately come to lodge there, was gone away again. That was all the express note taken that Molly had disappeared from the eyes of men. But the unwept death which, to the general lot, seemed as trivial as the summer-shed leaf, was charged with the force of destiny to certain human lives that we know of, shaping their joys and sorrows even to the end.

Silas Marner's determination to keep the "tramp's child" was matter of hardly less surprise and iterated talk in the village than the robbery of his money. That softening of feeling toward him which dated from his misfortune, that merging of suspicion and dislike in a rather contemptuous pity for him as lone and crazy, was now accompanied with a more active sympathy, especially among the women. Notable mothers, who knew what it was to keep children "whole and sweet"; lazy mothers, who knew what it was to be interrupted in folding their arms and scratching their elbows by the mischievous propensities of children just firm on their legs, were equally interested in conjecturing how a lone man would manage with a two-year-old child on his hands and were equally ready with their suggestions: the notable chiefly telling him what he had better do, and the lazy ones being emphatic in telling him what he would never be able to do.

Among the notable mothers, Dolly Winthrop was the one whose neighborly offices were the most acceptable to Marner, for they were rendered without any show of bustling instruction. Silas had shown her the half guinea given to him by Godfrey and had asked her what he should do about getting some clothes for the child.

"Eh, Master Marner," said Dolly, "there's no call to buy no more nor a pair o' shoes; for I've got the little petticoats as Aaron wore five years ago, and it's ill spending the money on them baby clothes, for the child 'ull grow like grass i' May, bless it—that it will."

And the same day Dolly brought her bundle and displayed to Marner, one by one, the tiny garments in their due order of succession, most of them patched and darned, but clean and neat as fresh-sprung herbs. This was the introduction to a great ceremony with soap and water, from which baby came out in new beauty and sat on Dolly's knee, handling her toes and chuckling and patting her palms together with an air of having made several discoveries about herself, which she communicated by alternate sounds of "gug-gug-gug" and "mammy." The "mammy" was not a cry of need or uneasiness: Baby had been used to utter it without expecting either tender sound or touch to follow.

"Anybody 'ud think the angils in heaven couldn't be prettier," said Dolly, rubbing the golden curls and kissing them. "And to think of its being covered wi' them

dirty rags—and the poor mother—froze to death; but there's Them as took care of it and brought it to your door, Master Marner. The door was open, and it walked in over the snow, like as if it had been a little starved robin. Didn't you say the door was open?"

"Yes," said Silas, meditatively. "Yes—the door was open. The money's gone I don't know where, and this is come from I don't know where."

He had not mentioned to anyone his unconsciousness of the child's entrance, shrinking from questions which might lead to the fact he himself suspected—namely, that he had been in one of his trances.

"Ah," said Dolly, with soothing gravity, "it's like the night and morning, and the sleeping and the waking, and the rain and the harvest—one goes and the other comes, and we know nothing how nor where. We may strive and scrat and fend, but it's little we can do arter all—the big things come and go wi' no striving o' our'n —they do, that they do; and I think you're in the right on it to keep the little un, Master Marner, seeing as it's been sent to you, though there's folks as thinks different. You'll happen be a bit moithered [1] with it while it's so little; but I'll come, and welcome, and see to it for you; I've a bit o' time to spare most days, for when one gets up betimes [2] i' the morning, the clock seems to stan' still tow'rt ten, afore it's time to go about the victual. So, as I say, I'll come and see to the child for you, and welcome."

"Thank you . . . kindly," said Silas, hesitating a little. "I'll be glad if you'll tell me things. But," he added, uneasily, leaning forward to look at Baby with some jealousy, as she was resting her head backward against Dolly's arm and eyeing him contentedly from a distance—"But I

want to do things for it myself, else it may get fond o' somebody else, and not fond o' me. I've been used to fending for myself in the house—I can learn, I can learn."

"Eh, to be sure," said Dolly, gently. "I've seen men as are wonderful handy wi' children. The men are awk'ard and contrairy mostly, God help 'em—but when the drink's out of 'em, they aren't unsensible, though they're bad for leeching and bandaging—so fiery and unpatient. You see this goes first, next the skin," proceeded Dolly, taking up the little shirt, and putting it on.

"Yes," said Marner, docilely, bringing his eyes very close, that they might be initiated in the mysteries; whereupon Baby seized his head with both her small arms and put her lips against his face with purring noises.

"See there," said Dolly, with a woman's tender tact, "she's fondest o' you. She wants to go o' your lap, I'll be bound. Go, then: take her, Master Marner; you can put the things on, and then you can say as you've done for her from the first of her coming to you."

Marner took her on his lap, trembling with an emotion mysterious to himself, at something unknown dawning on his life. Thought and feeling were so confused within him, that if he had tried to give them utterance, he could only have said that the child was come instead of the gold—that the gold had turned into the child. He took the garments from Dolly and put them on under her teaching; interrupted, of course, by Baby's gymnastics.

"There, then! why, you take to it quite easy, Master Marner," said Dolly; "but what shall you do when you're forced to sit in your loom? For she'll get busier and mischievouser every day—she will, bless her. It's lucky as you've got that high hearth i'stead of a grate, for that keeps the fire more out of her reach: but if

[1] **moithered:** bothered, worried.
[2] **betimes:** early.

you've got anything as can be split or broke, or as is fit to cut her fingers off, she'll be at it—and it is but right you should know."

Silas meditated a little while in some perplexity. "I'll tie her to the leg o' the loom," he said at last—"tie her with a good long strip o' something."

"Well, mayhap that'll do, as it's a little gell, for they're easier persuaded to sit i' one place nor the lads. I know what the lads are; for I've had four—four I've had, God knows—and if you was to take and tie 'em up, they'd make a fighting and crying as if you was ringing the pigs.[1] But I'll bring you my little chair, and some bits o' red rag and things for her to play wi'; an' she'll sit and chatter to 'em as if they was alive. Eh, if it wasn't a sin to the lads to wish 'em made different, bless 'em, I should ha' been glad for one of 'em to be a little gell; and to think as I could ha' taught her to scour, and mend, and the knitting, and everything. But I can teach 'em this little un, Master Marner, when she gets old enough."

"But she'll be *my* little un," said Marner, rather hastily. "She'll be nobody else's."

"No, to be sure; you'll have a right to her, if you're a father to her and bring her up according. But," added Dolly, coming to a point which she had determined beforehand to touch upon, "you must bring her up like christened folks's children, and take her to church, and let her learn her catechize,[2] as my little Aaron can say off—the 'I believe,' and everything, and 'hurt nobody by word or deed'—as well as if he was the clerk. That's what you must do, Master Marner, if you'd do the right thing by the orphin child."

Marner's pale face flushed suddenly under a new anxiety. His mind was too busy trying to give some definite bearing to Dolly's words for him to think of answering her.

"And it's my belief," she went on, "as the poor little creature has never been christened, and it's nothing but right as the parson should be spoke to; and if you was noways unwilling, I'd talk to Mr. Macey about it this very day. For if the child ever went anyways wrong, and you hadn't done your part by it, Master Marner—'noculation,[3] and everything to save it from harm—it 'ud be a thorn i' your bed for ever o' this side the grave; and I can't think as it 'ud be easy lying down for anybody when they'd got to another world, if they hadn't done their part by the helpless children as come wi'out their own asking."

Dolly herself was disposed to be silent for some time now, for she had spoken from the depths of her own simple belief, and was much concerned to know whether her words would produce the desired effect on Silas. He was puzzled and anxious, for Dolly's word "christened" conveyed no distinct meaning to him. He had only heard of baptism and had only seen the baptism of grown-up men and women.

"What is it as you mean by 'christened'?" he said at last, timidly. "Won't folks be good to her without it?"

"Dear, dear! Master Marner," said Dolly, with gentle distress and compassion. "Had you never no father nor mother as taught you to say your prayers, and as there's good words and good things to keep us from harm?"

"Yes," said Silas, in a low voice; "I know a deal about that—used to, used to. But your ways are different: my country was a good way off." He paused a few moments, and then added, more decidedly,

[1] **ringing the pigs:** putting rings in pigs' noses.
[2] **catechize** (kat′ə·kīz): catechism (kat′ə·kiz′əm), a set of questions and answers used for religious instruction.

[3] **'noculation:** inoculation.

"But I want to do everything as can be done for the child. And whatever's right for it i' this country, and you think 'ull do it good, I'll act according, if you'll tell me."

"Well, then, Master Marner," said Dolly, inwardly rejoiced, "I'll ask Mr. Macey to speak to the parson about it; and you must fix on a name for it, because it must have a name giv' it when it's christened."

"My mother's name was Hephzibah," said Silas, "and my little sister was named after her."

"Eh, that's a hard name," said Dolly. "I partly think it isn't a christened name."

"It's a Bible name," said Silas, old ideas recurring.

"Then I've no call to speak again' it," said Dolly, rather startled by Silas's knowledge on this head; "but you see I'm no scholard, and I'm slow at catching the words. My husband says I'm allays like as if I was putting the haft for the handle—that's what he says—for he's very sharp, God help him. But it was awk'ard calling your little sister by such a hard name, when you'd got nothing big to say, like—wasn't it, Master Marner?"

"We called her Eppie," said Silas.

"Well, if it was noways wrong to shorten the name, it 'ud be a deal handier. And so I'll go now, Master Marner, and I'll speak about the christening afore dark, and I wish you the best o' luck, and it's my belief as it'll come to you, if you do what's right by the orphin child; and there's the 'noculation to be seen to; and as to washing its bits o' things, you need look to nobody but me, for I can do 'em wi' one hand when I've got my suds about. Eh, the blessed angil! You'll let me bring my Aaron one o' these days, and he'll show her his little cart as his father's made for him, and the black and white pup as he's got a-rearing."

Baby *was* christened, the Rector deciding that a double baptism was the lesser risk to incur; and on this occasion Silas, making himself as clean and tidy as he could, appeared for the first time within the church and shared in the observances held sacred by his neighbors. He was quite unable, by means of anything he heard or saw, to identify the Raveloe religion with his old faith; if he could at any time in his previous life have done so, it must have been by the aid of a strong feeling ready to vibrate with sympathy, rather than by a comparison of phrases and ideas: and now for long years that feeling had been dormant. He had no distinct idea about the baptism and the church-going, except that Dolly had said it was for the good of the child; and in this way, as the weeks grew to months, the child created fresh and fresh links between this life and the lives from which he had hitherto shrunk continually into narrower isolation. Unlike the gold which needed nothing, and must be worshiped in close-locked solitude—which was hidden away from the daylight, was deaf to the song of birds, and started to no human tones—Eppie was a creature of endless claims and ever-growing desires, seeking and loving sunshine, and living sounds, and living movements; making trial of everything, with trust in new joy, and stirring the human kindness in all eyes that looked on her. The gold had kept his thoughts in an ever-repeated circle, leading to nothing beyond itself; but Eppie was an object compacted of changes and hopes that forced his thoughts onward and carried them far away from their old eager pacing toward the same blank limit—carried them away to the new things that would come with the coming years, when Eppie would have learned to understand how her father Silas cared for her; and made him look for images of that time in

the ties and charities that bound together the families of his neighbors. The gold had asked that he should sit weaving longer and longer, deafened and blinded more and more to all things except the monotony of his loom and the repetition of his web; but Eppie called him away from his weaving and made him think all its pauses a holiday, reawakening his senses with her fresh life, even to the old winter flies that came crawling forth in the early spring sunshine, and warming him into joy because *she* had joy.

And when the sunshine grew strong and lasting, so that the buttercups were thick in the meadows, Silas might be seen in the sunny midday, or in the late afternoon when the shadows were lengthening under the hedgerows, strolling out with uncovered head to carry Eppie beyond the stone pits to where the flowers grew, till they reached some favorite bank where he could sit down, while Eppie toddled to pluck the flowers, and made remarks to the winged things that murmured happily above the bright petals, calling "Dad-dad's" attention continually by bringing him the flowers. Then she would turn her ear to some sudden bird note, and Silas learned to please her by making signs of hushed stillness, that they might listen for the note to come again: so that when it came, she set up her small back and

laughed with gurgling triumph. Sitting on the banks in this way, Silas began to look for the once-familiar herbs again; and as the leaves, with their unchanged outline and markings, lay on his palm, there was a sense of crowding remembrances from which he turned away timidly, taking refuge in Eppie's little world, that lay lightly on his enfeebled spirit.

As the child's mind was growing into knowledge, his mind was growing into memory: as her life unfolded, his soul, long stupefied in a cold narrow prison, was unfolding too and trembling gradually into full consciousness.

It was an influence which must gather force with every new year: the tones that stirred Silas's heart grew articulate and called for more distinct answers; shapes and sounds grew clearer for Eppie's eyes and ears, and there was more that "Dad-dad" was imperatively required to notice and account for. Also, by the time Eppie was three years old, she developed a fine capacity for mischief and for devising ingenious ways of being troublesome, which found much exercise, not only for Silas's patience, but for his watchfulness and penetration. Sorely was poor Silas puzzled on such occasions by the incompatible demands of love. Dolly Winthrop told him that punishment was good for Eppie, and that, as for rearing a child without making

it tingle a little in soft and safe places now and then, it was not to be done.

"To be sure, there's another thing you might do, Master Marner," added Dolly, meditatively: "you might shut her up once i' the coal hole. That was what I did wi' Aaron; for I was that silly wi' the youngest lad, as I could never bear to smack him. Not as I could find i' my heart to let him stay i' the coal hole more nor a minute, but it was enough to colly [1] him all over, so as he must be new washed and dressed, and it was as good as a rod to him—that was. But I put it upo' your conscience, Master Marner, as there's one of 'em you must choose—ayther smacking or the coal hole—else she'll get so masterful, there'll be no holding her."

Silas was impressed with the melancholy truth of this last remark; but his force of mind failed before the only two penal methods open to him, not only because it was painful to him to hurt Eppie, but because he trembled at a moment's contention with her, lest she should love him the less for it. Let even an affectionate Goliath get himself tied to a small tender thing, dreading to hurt it by pulling, and dreading still more to snap the cord, and which of the two, pray, will be master? It was clear that Eppie, with her short toddling steps must lead father Silas a pretty dance on any fine morning when circumstances favored mischief.

For example. He had wisely chosen a broad strip of linen as a means of fastening her to his loom when he was busy: it made a broad belt round her waist and was long enough to allow of her reaching the truckle bed [2] and sitting down on it, but not long enough for her to attempt any dangerous climbing. One bright summer's morning Silas had been more engrossed than usual in "setting up" a new piece of work, an occasion on which his scissors were in requisition. These scissors, owing to an especial warning of Dolly's, had been kept carefully out of Eppie's reach; but the click of them had had a peculiar attraction for her ear, and watching the results of that click, she had derived the philosophic lesson that the same cause would produce the same effect. Silas had seated himself in his loom, and the noise of weaving had begun; but he had left his scissors on a ledge which Eppie's arm was long enough to reach; and now, like a small mouse, watching her opportunity, she stole quietly from her corner, secured the scissors, and toddled to the bed again, setting up her back as a mode of concealing the fact. She had a distinct intention as to the use of the scissors; and having cut the linen strip in a jagged but effectual manner, in two moments she had run out at the open door where the sunshine was inviting her, while poor Silas believed her to be a better child than usual. It was not until he happened to need his scissors that the terrible fact burst upon him; Eppie had run out by herself—had perhaps fallen into the stone pit. Silas, shaken by the worst fear that could have befallen him, rushed out, calling "Eppie!" and ran eagerly about the unenclosed space, exploring the dry cavities into which she might have fallen, and then gazing with questioning dread at the smooth red surface of the water. The cold drops stood on his brow. How long had she been out? There was one hope—that she had crept through the stile and got into the fields, where he habitually took her to stroll. But the grass was high in the meadow, and there was no descrying [3] her, if she were there, except by a close search that would be a trespass on Mr. Osgood's

[1] **colly:** dirty with coal dust.
[2] **truckle bed:** a low bed that can be slid under a high one when not in use.

[3] **descrying:** seeing.

crop. Still, that misdemeanor must be committed; and poor Silas, after peering all round the hedgerows, traversed the grass, beginning with perturbed vision to see Eppie behind every group of red sorrel, and to see her moving always farther off as he approached. The meadow was searched in vain; and he got over the stile into the next field, looking with dying hope toward a small pond which was now reduced to its summer shallowness, so as to leave a wide margin of good adhesive mud. Here, however, sat Eppie, discoursing cheerfully to her own small boot, which she was using as a bucket to convey the water into a deep hoof-mark, while her little naked foot was planted comfortably on a cushion of olive-green mud. A red-headed calf was observing her with alarmed doubt through the opposite hedge.

Here was clearly a case of aberration in a christened child which demanded severe treatment; but Silas, overcome with convulsive joy at finding his treasure again, could do nothing but snatch her up and cover her with half-sobbing kisses. It was not until he had carried her home and had begun to think of the necessary washing, that he recollected the need that he should punish Eppie, and "make her remember." The idea that she might run away again and come to harm, gave him unusual resolution, and for the first time he determined to try the coal hole—a small closet near the hearth.

"Naughty, naughty Eppie," he suddenly began, holding her on his knee, and pointing to her muddy feet and clothes—"naughty to cut with the scissors and run away. Eppie must go into the coal hole for being naughty. Daddy must put her in the coal hole."

He half expected that this would be shock enough, and that Eppie would begin to cry. But instead of that, she began to shake herself on his knee, as if the proposition opened a pleasing novelty. Seeing that he must proceed to extremities, he put her into the coal hole and held the door closed, with a trembling sense that he was using a strong measure. For a moment there was silence, but then came a little cry, "Opy, opy!" and Silas let her out again, saying, "Now Eppie 'ull never be naughty again, else she must go into the coal hole—a black naughty place."

The weaving must stand still a long while this morning, for now Eppie must be washed, and have clean clothes on; but it was to be hoped that this punishment would have a lasting effect and save time in future—though, perhaps, it would have been better if Eppie had cried more.

In half an hour she was clean again, and Silas having turned his back to see what he could do with the linen band, threw it down again, with the reflection that Eppie would be good without fastening for the rest of the morning. He turned round again, and was going to place her in

her little chair near the loom, when she peeped out at him with black face and hands again, and said, "Eppie in de toal hole!"

This total failure of the coal-hole discipline shook Silas's belief in the efficacy of punishment. "She'd take it all for fun," he observed to Dolly, "if I didn't hurt her, and that I can't do, Mrs. Winthrop. If she makes me a bit o' trouble, I can bear it. And she's got no tricks but what she'll grow out of."

"Well, that's partly true, Master Marner," said Dolly, sympathetically; "and if you can't bring your mind to frighten her off touching things, you must do what you can to keep 'em out of her way. That's what I do wi' the pups as the lads are allays a-rearing. They *will* worry and gnaw—worry and gnaw they will, if it was one's Sunday cap as hung anywhere so they could drag it. They know no difference, God help 'em: it's the pushing o' the teeth as sets 'em on, that's what it is."

So Eppie was reared without punishment, the burden of her misdeeds being borne vicariously by father Silas. The stone hut was made a soft nest for her, lined with downy patience: and also in the world that lay beyond the stone hut she knew nothing of frowns and denials.

Notwithstanding the difficulty of carrying her and his yarn or linen at the same time, Silas took her with him in most of his journeys to the farmhouses, unwilling to leave her behind at Dolly Winthrop's, who was always ready to take care of her; and little curly-headed Eppie, the weaver's child, became an object of interest at several outlying homesteads, as well as in the village. Hitherto he had been treated very much as if he had been a useful gnome or brownie—a queer and unaccountable creature, who must necessarily be looked at with wondering curiosity and repulsion, and with whom one would be glad to make all greetings and bargains as brief as possible, but who must be dealt with in a propitiatory way, and occasionally have a present of pork or garden stuff to carry home with him, seeing that without him there was no getting the yarn woven. But now Silas met with open smiling faces and cheerful questioning, as a person whose satisfaction and difficulties could be understood. Everywhere he must sit a little and talk about the child, and words of interest were always ready for him: "Ah, Master Marner, you'll be lucky if she takes the measles soon and easy!"—or, "Why, there isn't many lone men 'ud ha' been wishing to take up with a little un like that: but I reckon the weaving makes you handier than men as do outdoor work— you're partly as handy as a woman, for weaving comes next to spinning." Elderly masters and mistresses, seated observantly in large kitchen armchairs, shook their heads over the difficulties attendant on rearing children, felt Eppie's round arms and legs, and pronounced them remarkably firm, and told Silas that, if she turned out well (which, however, there was no telling), it would be a fine thing for him to have a steady lass to do for him when he got helpless. Servant maidens were fond of carrying her out to look at the hens and chickens, or to see if any cherries could be shaken down in the orchard; and the small boys and girls approached her slowly, with cautious movement and steady gaze, like little dogs face to face with one of their own kind, till attraction had reached the point at which the soft lips were put out for a kiss. No child was afraid of approaching Silas when Eppie was near him: there was no repulsion around him now, either for young or old: for the little child had come to link him once more with the

whole world. There was love between him and the child that blended them into one, and there was love between the child and the world—from men and women with parental looks and tones, to the red ladybirds and the round pebbles.

Silas began now to think of Raveloe life entirely in relation to Eppie; she must have everything that was good in Raveloe; and he listened docilely, that he might come to understand better what this life was, from which, for fifteen years, he had stood aloof as from a strange thing, wherewith he could have no communion: as some man who has a precious plant to which he would give a nurturing home in a new soil thinks of the rain, and the sunshine, and all influences, in relation to his nursling, and asks industriously for all knowledge that will help him to satisfy the wants of the searching roots, or to guard leaf and bud from invading harm. The disposition to hoard had been utterly crushed at the very first by the loss of his long-stored gold: the coins he earned afterward seemed as irrelevant as stones brought to complete a house suddenly buried by an earthquake; the sense of bereavement was too heavy upon him for the old thrill of satisfaction to arise again at the touch of the newly earned coin. And now something had come to replace his hoard which gave a growing purpose to the earnings, drawing his hope and joy continually onward beyond the money.

In old days there were angels who came and took men by the hand and led them away from the city of destruction. We see no white-winged angels now. But yet men are led away from threatening destruction: a hand is put into theirs, which leads them forth gently toward a calm and bright land, so that they look no more backward; and the hand may be a little child's.

CHAPTER XV

Brighter Days

THERE WAS one person, as you will believe, who watched with keener though more hidden interest than any other the prosperous growth of Eppie under the weaver's care. He dared not do anything that would imply a stronger interest in a poor man's adopted child than could be expected from the kindliness of the young Squire, when a chance meeting suggested a little present to a simple old fellow whom others noticed with goodwill; but he told himself that the time would come when he might do something toward furthering the welfare of his daughter without incurring suspicion. Was he very uneasy in the meantime at his inability to give his daughter her birthright? I cannot say that he was. The child was being taken care of, and would very likely be happy, as people in humble stations often were—happier, perhaps, than those brought up in luxury.

That famous ring that pricked its owner when he forgot duty and followed desire— I wonder if it pricked very hard when he set out on the chase, or whether it pricked but lightly then, and only pierced to the quick when the chase had long been ended, and hope, folding her wings, looked backward and became regret?

Godfrey Cass's cheek and eye were brighter than ever now. He was so undivided in his aims, that he seemed like a man of firmness. No Dunsey had come back: people had made up their minds that he was gone for a soldier, or gone "out of the country," and no one cared to be specific in their inquiries on a subject delicate to a respectable family. Godfrey had ceased to see the shadow of Dunsey across his path; and the path now lay

straight forward to the accomplishment of his best, longest-cherished wishes. Everybody said Mr. Godfrey had taken the right turn; and it was pretty clear what would be the end of things, for there were not many days in the week that he was not seen riding to the Warrens. Godfrey himself, when he was asked jocosely if the day had been fixed, smiled with the pleasant consciousness of a lover who could say "yes," if he liked. He felt a reformed man, delivered from temptation; and the vision of his future life seemed to him as a promised land for which he had no cause to fight. He saw himself with all his happiness centered on his own hearth, while Nancy would smile on him as he played with the children.

And that other child, not on the hearth —he would not forget it; he would see that it was well provided for. That was a father's duty.

FOR STUDY AND DISCUSSION

1. How do the villagers react to Silas's decision to keep the child? How does the child bring Silas closer to the villagers?

2. How does Dolly Winthrop help Silas with the child? Why does he not want her to help him too much?

3. For whom is Eppie named? What memories in Silas does she stir? How does she make him "grow" with her?

4. How is Silas's life changed by Eppie? How does he feel when she disappears? Why is his attempted punishment of Eppie amusing?

5. What effect does Dolly Winthrop have on Silas's thinking? Do you think she helps Silas more than she helps Eppie? What do you think of her advice and her warnings? Explain.

6. Godfrey remains in the background during all the excitement about the orphan child. Does he make any effort to help? How does he feel about the way things have turned out? Why?

PART TWO

CHAPTER XVI

A Sunday Afternoon

IT WAS a bright autumn Sunday, sixteen years after Silas Marner had found his new treasure on the hearth. The bells of the old Raveloe church were ringing the cheerful peal that told that the morning service was ended; and out of the arched doorway in the tower came slowly, retarded by friendly greetings and questions, the richer parishioners who had chosen this bright Sunday morning as eligible for church-going. It was the rural fashion of that time for the more important members of the congregation to depart first, while their humbler neighbors waited and looked on, stroking their bent heads or dropping their curtsies to any large ratepayer who turned to notice them.

Foremost among these advancing groups of well-clad people, there are some whom we shall recognize, in spite of Time, who has laid his hand on them all. The tall, blond man of forty is not much changed in features from the Godfrey Cass of six-and-twenty: he is only fuller in flesh, and has only lost the indefinable look of youth—a loss which is marked even when the eye is undulled and the wrinkles are not yet come. Perhaps the pretty woman, not much younger than he, who is leaning on his arm, is more changed than her husband: the lovely bloom that used to be always on her cheek now comes but fitfully, with the fresh morning air or with some strong surprise; yet to all who love human faces best for what they tell of human experience, Nancy's beauty has a heightened interest. Often the soul is ripened into fuller goodness while age

has spread an ugly film, so that mere glances can never divine the preciousness of the fruit. But the years have not been so cruel to Nancy. The firm yet placid mouth, the clear veracious [1] glance of the brown eyes, speak now of a nature that has been tested and has kept its highest qualitites; and even the costume, with its dainty neatness and purity, has more significance now the coquetries [2] of youth can have nothing to do with it.

Mr. and Mrs. Godfrey Cass (any higher title has died away from Raveloe lips since the old Squire was gathered to his fathers and his inheritance was divided) have turned round to look for the tall aged man and the plainly dressed woman who are a little behind—Nancy having observed that they must wait for "father and Priscilla"—and now they all turn into a narrower path leading across the churchyard to a small gate opposite the Red House. We will not follow them now; for may there not be some others in this departing congregation whom we should like to see again—some of those who are not likely to be handsomely clad, and whom we may not recognize so easily as the master and mistress of the Red House?

But it is impossible to mistake Silas Marner. His large brown eyes seem to have gathered a longer vision, as is the way with eyes that have been shortsighted in early life, and they have a less vague, a more answering gaze; but in everything else one sees signs of a frame much enfeebled by the lapse of the sixteen years. The weaver's bent shoulders and white hair give him almost the look of advanced age, though he is not more than five-and-fifty; but there is the freshest blossom of youth close by his side—a blond dimpled

girl of eighteen, who has vainly tried to chastise her curly auburn hair into smoothness under her brown bonnet: the hair ripples as obstinately as a brooklet under the March breeze, and the little ringlets burst away from the restraining comb behind and show themselves below the bonnet crown. Eppie cannot help being rather vexed about her hair, for there is no other girl in Raveloe who has hair at all like it, and she thinks hair ought to be smooth. She does not like to be blameworthy even in small things: you see how neatly her prayer book is folded in her spotted handkerchief.

That good-looking young fellow, in a new fustian suit, who walks behind her, is not quite sure upon the question of hair in the abstract, when Eppie puts it to him, and thinks that perhaps straight hair is the best in general, but he doesn't want Eppie's hair to be different. She surely divines that there is someone behind her who is thinking about her very particularly and mustering courage to come to her side as soon as they are out in the lane, else why should she look rather shy, and take care not to turn away her head from her father Silas, to whom she keeps mur-

[1] **veracious:** truthful.

[2] **coquetries:** actions intended to attract attention and admiration.

muring little sentences as to who was at church, and who was not at church, and how pretty the red mountain ash is over the Rectory wall!

"I wish *we* had a little garden, father, with double daisies in it, like Mrs. Winthrop's," said Eppie, when they were out in the lane; "only they say it 'ud take a deal of digging and bringing fresh soil— and you couldn't do that, could you, father? Anyhow, I shouldn't like you to do it, for it 'ud be too hard work for you."

"Yes, I could do it, child, if you want a bit o' garden: these long evenings, I could work at taking in a little bit o' the waste, just enough for a root or two o' flowers for you; and again, i' the morning, I could have a turn wi' the spade before I sat down to the loom. Why didn't you tell me before as you wanted a bit o' garden?"

"*I* can dig it for you, Master Marner," said the young man in fustian, who was now by Eppie's side, entering into the conversation without the trouble of formalities. "It'll be play to me after I've done my day's work, or any odd bits o' time when the work's slack. And I'll bring you some soil from Mr. Cass's garden—he'll let me, and willing."

"Eh, Aaron, my lad, are you there?" said Silas; "I wasn't aware of you; for when Eppie's talking o' things, I see nothing but what she's a-saying. Well, if you could help me with the digging, we might ger her a bit o' garden all the sooner."

"Then, if you think well and good," said Aaron, "I'll come to the stone pits this afternoon, and we'll settle what land's to be taken in, and I'll get up an hour earlier i' the morning and begin on it."

"But not if you don't promise me not to work at the hard digging, father," said Eppie. "For I shouldn't ha' said anything about it," she added, half-bashfully, half-roguishly, "only Mrs. Winthrop said as Aaron 'ud be so good, and——"

"And you might ha' known it without her telling you," said Aaron. "And Master Marner knows too, I hope, as I'm able and willing to do a turn o' work for him, and he won't do me the unkindness to anyways take it out o' my hands."

"There, now, father, you won't work in it till it's all easy," said Eppie, "and you and me can mark out the beds and make holes and plant the roots. It'll be a deal livelier at the stone pits when we've got some flowers, for I always think the flowers can see us and know what we're talking about. And I'll have a bit of rosemary, and bergamot, and thyme, because they're so sweet-smelling; but there's no lavender only in the gentlefolks' gardens, I think."

"That's no reason why you shouldn't have some," said Aaron, "for I can bring you slips of anything; I'm forced to cut no end of 'em when I'm gardening, and I throw 'em away mostly. There's a big bed o' lavender at the Red House; the missus is very fond of it."

"Well," said Silas, gravely, "so as you don't make free for us, or ask for anything as is worth much at the Red House: for Mr. Cass's been so good to us, and built us up the new end o' the cottage, and given us beds and things, as I couldn't abide to be imposin' for garden stuff or anything else."

"No, no, there's no imposin'," said Aaron; "there's never a garden in all the parish but what there's endless waste in it for want o' somebody as could use everything up. It's what I think to myself sometimes, as there need nobody run short o' victuals if the land was made the most on, and there was never a morsel but what could find its way to a mouth. It sets one thinking o' that—gardening does. But I must go back now, else mother 'ull be in trouble as I aren't there."

"Bring her with you this afternoon,

Aaron," said Eppie; "I shouldn't like to fix about the garden, and her not know everything from the first—should *you*, father?"

"Ay, bring her if you can, Aaron," said Silas; "she's sure to have a word to say as'll help us to set things on their right end."

Aaron turned back up the village, while Silas and Eppie went on up the lonely sheltered lane.

"Oh daddy!" she began, when they were in privacy, clasping and squeezing Silas's arm, and skipping round to give him an energetic kiss. "My little old daddy! I'm so glad. I don't think I shall want anything else when we've got a little garden; and I knew Aaron would dig it for us," she went on with roguish triumph —"I knew that very well."

"You're a deep little puss, you are," said Silas, with the mild passive happiness of love-crowned age in his face; "but you'll make yourself fine and beholden to Aaron."

"Oh, no, I shan't," said Eppie, laughing and frisking; "he likes it."

"Come, come, let me carry your prayer book, else you'll be dropping it, jumping i' that way."

Eppie was now aware that her behavior was under observation, but it was only the observation of a friendly donkey, browsing with a log fastened to his foot—a meek donkey, not scornfully critical of human trivialities, but thankful to share in them, if possible, by getting his nose scratched; and Eppie did not fail to gratify him with her usual notice, though it was attended with the inconvenience of his following them, painfully, up to the very door of their home.

But the sound of a sharp bark inside, as Eppie put the key in the door, modified the donkey's views, and he limped away again without bidding. The sharp bark was the sign of an excited welcome that was awaiting them from a knowing brown terrier, who, after dancing at their legs in a hysterical manner, rushed with a worrying noise at a tortoise-shell kitten under the loom, and then rushed back with a sharp bark again, as much as to say, "I have done my duty by this feeble creature, you perceive"; while the lady mother of the kitten sat sunning her white bosom in the window and looked round with a sleepy air of expecting caresses, though she was not going to take any trouble for them.

The presence of this happy animal life was not the only change which had come over the interior of the stone cottage. There was no bed now in the living room, and the small space was well filled with decent furniture, all bright and clean enough to satisfy Dolly Winthrop's eye. The oaken table and three-cornered oaken chair were hardly what was likely to be seen in so poor a cottage: they had come, with the beds and other things, from the Red House; for Mr. Godfrey Cass, as everyone said in the village, did very kindly by the weaver; and it was nothing but right a man should be looked on and helped by those who could afford it, when he had brought up an orphan child, and father and mother to her—and had lost his money too, so as he had nothing but what he worked for week by week, and when the weaving was going down too— for there was less and less flax spun—and Master Marner was none so young. Nobody was jealous of the weaver, for he was regarded as an exceptional person whose claims on neighborly help were not to be matched in Raveloe. Any superstition that remained concerning him had taken an entirely new color; and Mr. Macey, now a very feeble old man of fourscore and six, never seen except in his chimney corner or sitting in the sun-

shine at his doorsill, was of opinion that
when a man had done what Silas had
done by an orphan child, it was a sign that
his money would come to light again, or
leastwise that the robber would be made
to answer for it—for, as Mr. Macey ob-
served of himself, his faculties were as
strong as ever.

Silas sat down now and watched Eppie
with a satisfied gaze as she spread the
clean cloth and set on it the potato pie,
warmed up slowly in a safe Sunday
fashion by being put into a dry pot over a
slowly dying fire as the best substitute for
an oven. For Silas would not consent to
have a grate and oven added to his con-
veniences: he loved the old brick hearth
as he had loved his brown pot—and was
it not there when he had found Eppie? The
gods of the hearth exist for us still; and
let all new faith be tolerant of that
fetishism, lest it bruise its own roots.

Silas ate his dinner more silently than
usual, soon laying down his knife and fork
and watching half-abstractedly Eppie's
play with Snap and the cat, by which her
own dining was made rather a lengthy
business. Yet it was a sight that might well
arrest wandering thoughts: Eppie, with
the rippling radiance of her hair and the
whiteness of her rounded chin and throat
set off by the dark-blue cotton gown,
laughing merrily as the kitten held on with

her four claws to one shoulder, like a de-
sign for a jug handle, while Snap on the
right hand and Puss on the other put up
their paws toward a morsel which she held
out of the reach of both—Snap occa-
sionally desisting in order to remonstrate
with the cat by a cogent worrying growl on
the greediness and futility of her conduct;
till Eppie relented, caressed them both,
and divided the morsel between them.

But at last Eppie, glancing at the clock,
checked the play and said, "Oh, daddy,
you're wanting to go into the sunshine to
smoke your pipe. But I must clear away
first, so as the house may be tidy when
godmother comes. I'll make haste—I
won't be long."

Silas had taken to smoking a pipe daily
during the last two years, having been
strongly urged to it by the sages of
Raveloe, as a practice "good for the fits";
and this advice was sanctioned by Dr.
Kimble, on the ground that it was as well
to try what could do no harm—a principle
which was made to answer for a great deal
of work in that gentleman's medical prac-
tice. Silas did not highly enjoy smoking
and often wondered how his neighbors
could be so fond of it; but a humble sort
of acquiescence in what was held to be
good, had become a strong habit of that
new self which had been developed in him
since he had found Eppie on his hearth: it

had been the only clue his bewildered mind could hold by in cherishing this young life that had been sent to him out of the darkness into which his gold had departed. By seeking what was needful for Eppie, by sharing the effect that everything produced on her, he had himself come to appropriate the forms of custom and belief which were the mold of Raveloe life; and as, with reawakening sensibilities, memory also reawakened, he had begun to ponder over the elements of his old faith and blend them with his new impressions, till he recovered a consciousness of unity between his past and present. The sense of presiding goodness and the human trust which come with all pure peace and joy had given him a dim impression that there had been some error, some mistake, which had thrown that dark shadow over the days of his best years; and as it grew more and more easy to him to open his mind to Dolly Winthrop, he gradually communicated to her all he could describe of his early life. The communication was necessarily a slow and difficult process, for Silas's meager power of explanation was not aided by any readiness of interpretation in Dolly, whose narrow outward experience gave her no key to strange customs and made every novelty a source of wonder that arrested them at every step of the narrative. It was only by fragments, and at intervals which left Dolly time to revolve what she had heard till it acquired some familiarity for her, that Silas at last arrived at the climax of the sad story —the drawing of lots, and its false testimony concerning him; and this had to be repeated in several interviews, under new questions on her part as to the nature of this plan for detecting the guilty and clearing the innocent.

"And yourn's the same Bible, you're sure o' that, Master Marner—the Bible as you brought wi' you from that country —it's the same as what they've got at church, and what Eppie's a-learning to read in?"

"Yes," said Silas, "every bit the same; and there's drawing o' lots in the Bible, mind you," he added in a lower tone.

"Oh dear, dear," said Dolly in a grieved voice, as if she were hearing an unfavorable report of a sick man's case. She was silent for some minutes; at last she said:

"There's wise folks, happen, as know how it all is; the parson knows, I'll be bound; but it takes big words to tell them things, and such as poor folks can't make much out on. I can never rightly know the meaning o' what I hear at church, only a bit here and there, but I know it's good words—I do. But what lies upo' your mind—it's this, Master Marner: as, if Them above had done the right thing by you, They'd never ha' let you be turned out for a wicked thief when you was innicent."

"Ah!" said Silas, who had now come to understand Dolly's phraseology, "that was what fell on me like as if it had been red-hot iron; because, you see, there was nobody as cared for me or clave [1] to me above nor below. And him as I'd gone out and in wi' for ten year and more, since when we was lads and went halves— mine own familiar friend in whom I trusted had lifted up his heel again' me and worked to ruin me."

"Eh, but he was a bad un—I can't think as there's another such," said Dolly. "But I'm o'ercome, Master Marner; I'm like as if I'd waked and didn't know whether it was night or morning. I feel somehow as sure as I do when I've laid something up, though I can't justly put my hand on it, as there was a rights in what happened to you, if one could but make it out; and

[1] **clave:** cleaved—held fast, was faithful.

you'd no call to lose heart as you did. But we'll talk on it again; for sometimes things come into my head when I'm leeching or poulticing,[1] or such, as I could never think on when I was sitting still."

Dolly was too useful a woman not to have many opportunities of illumination of the kind she alluded to, and she was not long before she recurred to the subject.

"Master Marner," she said one day that she came to bring home Eppie's washing, "I've been sore puzzled for a good bit wi' that trouble o' yourn and the drawing o' lots; and it got twisted back-'ards and for'ards, as I didn't know which end to lay hold on. But it come to me all clear like, that night when I was sitting up wi' poor Bessy Fawkes, as is dead and left her children behind, God help 'em—it come to me as clear as daylight; but whether I've got hold on it now, or can anyways bring it to my tongue's end, that I don't know. For I've often a deal inside me as 'll never come out; and for what you talk o' your folks in your old country niver saying prayers by heart nor saying 'em out of a book, they must be wonderful cliver; for if I didn't know 'Our Father,' and little bits o' good words as I can carry out o' church wi' me, I might down o' my knees every night, but nothing could I say."

"But you can mostly say something as I can make sense on, Mrs. Winthrop," said Silas.

"Well, then, Master Marner, it come to me summat like this: I can make nothing o' the drawing o' lots and the answer coming wrong; it 'ud mayhap take the parson to tell that, and he could only tell us i' big words. But what come to me as clear as the daylight, it was when I was troubling over poor Bessy Fawkes, and it allays

[1] **leeching or poulticing:** Formerly common household remedies, leeches were used for bloodletting and poultices (hot compresses) to relieve soreness.

comes into my head when I'm sorry for folks and feel as I can't do a power to help 'em, not if I was to get up i' the middle o' the night—it comes into my head as Them above has got a deal tenderer heart nor what I've got—for I can't be anyways better nor Them as made me; and if anything looks hard to me, it's because there's things I don't know on; and for the matter o' that, there may be plenty o' things I don't know on, for it's little as I know—that it is. And so, while I was thinking o' that, you come into my mind, Master Marner, and it all come pouring in: if *I* felt i' my inside what was the right and just thing by you, and them as prayed and drawed the lots, all but that wicked un, if *they*'d ha' done the right thing by you if they could, isn't there Them as was at the making on us, and knows better and has a better will? And that's all as ever I can be sure on, and everything else is a big puzzle to me when I think on it. For there was the fever come and took off them as were full-growed, and left the helpless children; and there's the breaking o' limbs; and them as 'ud do right and be sober have to suffer by them as are con-trairy—eh, there's trouble i' this world, and there's things as we can niver make out the rights on. And all as we've got to do is to trusten, Master Marner—to do the right thing as fur as we know, and to trusten. For if us as knows so little can see a bit o' good and rights, we may be sure as there's a good and a rights bigger nor what we can know—I feel it i' my own inside as it must be so. And if you could but ha' gone on trustening, Master Marner, you wouldn't ha' run away from your fellow creatures and been so lone."

"Ah, but that 'ud ha' been hard," said Silas, in an undertone; "it 'ud ha' been hard to trusten then."

"And so it would," said Dolly, almost with compunction; "them things are easier

said nor done; and I'm partly ashamed o' talking."

"Nay, nay," said Silas, "you're i' the right, Mrs. Winthrop—you're i' the right. There's good i' this world—I've a feeling o' that now; and it makes a man feel as there's a good more nor he can see, i' spite o' the trouble and the wickedness. That drawing o' the lots is dark; but the child was sent to me: there's dealings with us—there's dealings."

This dialogue took place in Eppie's earlier years, when Silas had to part with her for two hours every day, that she might learn to read at the dame school,[1] after he had vainly tried himself to guide her in that first step to learning. Now that she was grown up, Silas had often been led, in those moments of quiet outpouring which come to people who live together in perfect love, to talk with *her* too of the past, and how and why he had lived a lonely man until she had been sent to him. For it would have been impossible for him to hide from Eppie that she was not his own child: even if the most delicate reticence on the point could have been expected from Raveloe gossips in her presence, her own questions about her mother could not have been parried, as she grew up, without that complete shrouding of the past which would have made a painful barrier between their minds. So Eppie had long known how her mother had died on the snowy ground, and how she herself had been found on the hearth by father Silas, who had taken her golden curls for his lost guineas brought back to him. The tender and peculiar love with which Silas had reared her in almost inseparable companionship with himself, aided by the seclusion of their dwelling, had preserved her from the lowering influences of the village talk and habits, and had kept her

[1] **dame school:** a primary school taught by a neighborhood woman.

mind in that freshness which is sometimes falsely supposed to be an invariable attribute of rusticity. Perfect love has a breath of poetry which can exalt the relations of the least-instructed human beings; and this breath of poetry had surrounded Eppie from the time when she had followed the bright gleam that beckoned her to Silas's hearth; so that it is not surprising if, in other things besides her delicate prettiness, she was not quite a common village maiden, but had a touch of refinement and fervor which came from no other teaching than that of tenderly nurtured unvitiated feeling. She was too childish and simple for her imagination to rove into questions about her unknown father; for a long while it did not even occur to her that she must have had a father; and the first time that the idea of her mother having had a husband presented itself to her was when Silas showed her the wedding ring which had been taken from the wasted finger and had been carefully preserved by him in a little lacquered box shaped like a shoe. He delivered this box into Eppie's charge when she had grown up, and she often opened it to look at the ring; but still she thought hardly at all about the father of whom it was the symbol. Had she not a father very close to her, who loved her better than any real fathers in the village seemed to love their daughters? On the contrary, who her mother was, and how she came to die in that forlornness, were questions that often pressed on Eppie's mind. Her knowledge of Mrs. Winthrop, who was her nearest friend next to Silas, made her feel that a mother must be very precious; and she had again and again asked Silas to tell her how her mother looked, whom she was like, and how he had found her against the furze bush, led toward it by the little footsteps and the outstretched arms. The furze bush was

there still; and this afternoon, when Eppie came out with Silas into the sunshine, it was the first object that arrested her eyes and thoughts.

"Father," she said, in a tone of gentle gravity, which sometimes came like a sadder, slower cadence across her playfulness, "we shall take the furze bush into the garden; it'll come into the corner, and just against it I'll put snowdrops and crocuses, 'cause Aaron says they won't die out, but'll always get more and more."

"Ah, child," said Silas, always ready to talk when he had his pipe in his hand, apparently enjoying the pauses more than the puffs, "it wouldn't do to leave out the furze bush; and there's nothing prettier to my thinking, when it's yellow with flowers. But it's just come into my head what we're to do for a fence—mayhap Aaron can help us to a thought; but a fence we must have, else the donkeys and things 'ull come and trample everything down. And fencing's hard to be got at, by what I can make out."

"Oh, I'll tell you, daddy," said Eppie, clasping her hands suddenly, after a minute's thought. "There's lots o' loose stones about, some of 'em not big, and we might lay 'em atop of one another, and make a wall. You and me could carry the smallest, and Aaron 'ud carry the rest—I know he would."

"Eh, my precious un," said Silas, "there isn't enough stones to go all round; and as for you carrying, why, wi' your little arms you couldn't carry a stone no bigger than a turnip. You're dillicate made, my dear," he added, with a tender intonation—"that's what Mrs. Winthrop says."

"Oh, I'm stronger than you think, daddy," said Eppie; "and if there wasn't stones enough to go all round, why they'll go part o' the way, and then it'll be easier to get sticks and things for the rest. See here, round the big pit, what a many stones!"

She skipped forward to the pit, meaning to lift one of the stones and exhibit her strength, but she started back in surprise.

"Oh, father, just come and look here," she exclaimed—"come and see how the water's gone down since yesterday. Why, yesterday the pit was ever so full!"

"Well, to be sure," said Silas, coming to her side. "Why, that's the draining they've begun on, since harvest, i' Mr. Osgood's fields, I reckon. The foreman said to me the other day, when I passed by 'em, 'Master Marner,' he said, 'I shouldn't wonder if we lay your bit o' waste as dry as a bone.' It was Mr. Godfrey Cass, he said, had gone into the draining: he'd been taking these fields o' Mr. Osgood."

"How odd it'll seem to have the old pit dried up!" said Eppie, turning away, and stopping to lift rather a large stone. "See, daddy, I can carry this quite well," she said, going along with much energy for a few steps, but presently letting it fall.

"Ah, you're fine and strong, aren't you?" said Silas, while Eppie shook her aching arms and laughed. "Come, come, let us go and sit down on the bank against the stile there and have no more lifting. You might hurt yourself, child. You need have somebody to work for you—and my arm isn't overstrong."

Silas uttered the last sentence slowly, as if it implied more than met the ear; and

Eppie, when they sat down on the bank, nestled close to his side, and, taking hold caressingly of the arm that was not over-strong, held it on her lap, while Silas puffed again dutifully at the pipe, which occupied his other arm. An ash in the hedgerow behind made a fretted screen from the sun and threw happy playful shadows all about them.

"Father," said Eppie, very gently, after they had been sitting in silence a little while, "if I was to be married, ought I to be married with my mother's ring?"

Silas gave an almost imperceptible start, though the question fell in with the under-current of thought in his own mind, and then said, in a subdued tone, "Why, Eppie, have you been a-thinking on it?"

"Only this last week, father," said Eppie, ingenuously, "since Aaron talked to me about it."

"And what did he say?" said Silas, still in the same subdued way, as if he were anxious lest he should fall into the slight-est tone that was not for Eppie's good.

"He said he should like to be married, because he was a-going on four-and-twenty and had got a deal of gardening work, now Mr. Mott's given up; and he goes twice a week regular to Mr. Cass's, and once to Mr. Osgood's, and they're going to take him on at the Rectory."

"And who is it as he's wanting to marry?" said Silas, with rather a sad smile.

"Why, me, to be sure, daddy," said Eppie, with dimpling laughter, kissing her father's cheek; "as if he'd want to marry anybody else!"

"And you mean to have him, do you?" said Silas.

"Yes, sometime," said Eppie, "I don't know when. Everybody's married some-time, Aaron says. But I told him that wasn't true: for, I said, look at father—he's never been married."

"No, child," said Silas, "your father was a lone man till you was sent to him."

"But you'll never be lone again, father," said Eppie, tenderly. "That was what Aaron said—'I could never think o' taking you away from Master Marner, Eppie.' And I said, 'It 'ud be no use if you did, Aaron.' And he wants us all to live to-gether, so as you needn't work a bit, only what's for your own pleasure; and he'd be as good as a son to you—that was what he said."

"And should you like that, Eppie?" said Silas, looking at her.

"I shouldn't mind it, father," said Eppie, quite simply. "And I should like things to be so as you needn't work much. But if it wasn't for that, I'd sooner things didn't change. I'm very happy: I like Aaron to be fond of me and come and see us often and behave pretty to you—he always *does* behave pretty to you, doesn't he, father?"

"Yes, child, nobody could behave better," said Silas, emphatically. "He's his mother's lad."

"But I don't want any change," said Eppie. "I should like to go on a long, long while, just as we are. Only Aaron does want a change; and he made me cry a bit —only a bit—because he said I didn't care for him, for if I cared for him I should want us to be married, as he did."

"Eh, my blessed child," said Silas, laying down his pipe as if it were useless to pretend to smoke any longer, "you're o'er young to be married. We'll ask Mrs. Winthrop—we'll ask Aaron's mother what *she* thinks: if there's a right thing to do, she'll come at it. But there's this to be thought on, Eppie: things *will* change, whether we like it or no; things won't go on for a long while just as they are and no difference. I shall get older and helplesser, and be a burden on you, belike, if I don't go away from you altogether. Not as I

mean you'd think me a burden—I know you wouldn't—but it 'ud be hard upon you; and when I look for'ard to that, I like to think as you'd have somebody else besides me—somebody young and strong, as'll outlast your own life, and take care on you to the end." Silas paused and, resting his wrists on his knees, lifted his hands up and down meditatively as he looked on the ground.

"Then, would, you like me to be married, father?" said Eppie, with a little trembling in her voice.

"I'll not be the man to say no, Eppie," said Silas, emphatically; "but we'll ask your godmother. She'll wish the right thing by you and her son too."

"There they come then," said Eppie. "Let us go and meet 'em. Oh, the pipe! won't you have it lit again, father?" said Eppie, lifting that medicinal appliance from the ground.

"Nay, child," said Silas, "I've done enough for today. I think, mayhap, a little of it does me more good than so much at once."

CHAPTER XVII

The Childless Home

WHILE SILAS and Eppie were seated on the bank discoursing in the fleckered shade of the ash tree, Miss Priscilla Lammeter was resisting her sister's arguments that it would be better to take tea at the Red House and let her father have a long nap than drive home to the Warrens so soon after dinner. The family party (of four only) were seated round the table in the dark wainscoted parlor, with the Sunday dessert before them, of fresh filberts, apples, and pears, duly ornamented with

leaves by Nancy's own hand before the bells had rung for church.

A great change has come over the dark wainscoted parlor since we saw it in Godfrey's bachelor days and under the wifeless reign of the old Squire. Now all is polish, on which no yesterday's dust is ever allowed to rest, from the yard's width of oaken boards round the carpet, to the old Squire's gun and whips and walking sticks, ranged on the stag's antlers above the mantelpiece. All other signs of sporting and outdoor occupation Nancy has removed to another room; but she has brought into the Red House the habit of filial reverence, and preserves sacredly in a place of honor these relics of her husband's departed father. The tankards are on the side table still, but the bossed silver is undimmed by handling, and there are no dregs to send forth unpleasant suggestions: the only prevailing scent is of the lavender and rose leaves that fill the vases of Derbyshire spar. All is purity and order in this once dreary room, for, fifteen years ago, it was entered by a new presiding spirit.

"Now, father," said Nancy, "*is* there any call for you to go home to tea? Mayn't you just as well stay with us?—such a beautiful evening as it's likely to be."

The old gentleman had been talking with Godfrey about the increasing poor rate [1] and the ruinous times and had not heard the dialogue between his daughters.

"My dear, you must ask Priscilla," he said, in the once firm voice, now become rather broken. "She manages me and the farm too."

"And reason good as I should manage you, father," said Priscilla, "else you'd be giving yourself your death with rheumatism. And as for the farm, if anything turns out wrong, as it can't but do in these times,

[1] **poor rate:** a tax on the rich for the welfare of the poor.

there's nothing kills a man so soon as having nobody to find fault with but himself. It's a deal the best way o' being master, to let somebody else do the ordering, and keep the blaming in your own hands. It 'ud save many a man a stroke, *I* believe."

"Well, well, my dear," said her father, with a quiet laugh, "I didn't say you don't manage for everybody's good."

"Then manage so as you may stay tea, Priscilla," said Nancy, putting her hand on her sister's arm affectionately. "Come now; and we'll go round the garden while father has his nap."

"My dear child, he'll have a beautiful nap in the gig,[1] for I shall drive. And as for staying tea, I can't hear of it; for there's this dairymaid, now she knows she's to be married turned Michaelmas,[2] she'd as lief pour the new milk into the pig trough as into the pans. That's the way with 'em all: it's as if they thought the world 'ud be new made because they're to be married. So come and let me put my bonnet on, and there'll be time for us to walk round the garden while the horse is being put in."

When the sisters were treading the neatly swept garden walks, between the bright turf that contrasted pleasantly with the dark cones and arches and wall-like hedges of yew, Priscilla said—

[1] **gig:** a light, two-wheeled carriage.
[2] **Michaelmas:** September 29, the feast of Michael the Archangel.

"I'm as glad as anything at your husband's making that exchange o' land with cousin Osgood and beginning the dairying. It's a thousand pities you didn't do it before; for it'll give you something to fill your mind. There's nothing like a dairy if folks want a bit of worrit[3] to make the days pass. For as for rubbing furniture, when you can once see your face in a table there's nothing else to look for; but there's always something fresh with the dairy; for even in the depths o' winter there's some pleasure in conquering the butter and making it come whether or no. My dear," added Priscilla, pressing her sister's hand affectionately as they walked side by side, "you'll never be low when you've got a dairy."

"Ah, Priscilla," said Nancy, returning the pressure with a grateful glance of her clear eyes, "but it won't make up to Godfrey: a dairy's not so much to a man. And it's only what he cares for that ever makes me low. I'm contented with the blessings we have, if he could be contented."

"It drives me past patience," said Priscilla, impetuously, "that way o' the men—always wanting and wanting and never easy with what they've got: they can't sit comfortable in their chairs when they've neither ache nor pain, but either they must stick a pipe in their mouths, to make 'em better than well, or else they must be

[3] **worrit:** worry or trouble.

swallowing something strong, though they're forced to make haste before the next meal comes in. But joyful be it spoken, our father was never that sort o' man. And if it had pleased God to make you ugly, like me, so as the men wouldn't ha' run after you, we might have kept to our own family and had nothing to do with folks as have got uneasy blood in their veins."

"Oh don't say so, Priscilla," said Nancy, repenting that she had called forth this outburst; "nobody has any occasion to find fault with Godfrey. It's natural he should be disappointed at not having any children: every man likes to have somebody to work for and lay by for, and he always counted so on making a fuss with 'em when they were little. There's many another man 'ud hanker more than he does. He's the best of husbands."

"Oh, I know," said Priscilla, smiling sarcastically, "I know the way o' wives; they set one to abuse their husbands, and then they turn round on one and praise 'em as if they wanted to sell 'em. But father'll be waiting for me; we must turn now."

The large gig with the steady old gray was at the front door, and Mr. Lammeter was already on the stone steps, passing the time in recalling to Godfrey what very fine points Speckle had when his master used to ride him.

"I always *would* have a good horse, you know," said the old gentleman, not liking that spirited time to be quite effaced from the memory of his juniors.

"Mind you bring Nancy to the Warrens before the week's out, Mr. Cass," was Priscilla's parting injunction, as she took the reins and shook them gently, by way of friendly incitement to Speckle.

"I shall just take a turn to the fields against the stone pits, Nancy, and look at the draining," said Godfrey.

"You'll be in again by tea time, dear?"

"Oh, yes, I shall be back in an hour."

It was Godfrey's custom on a Sunday afternoon to do a little contemplative farming in a leisurely walk. Nancy seldom accompanied him; for the women of her generation—unless, like Priscilla, they took to outdoor management—were not given to much walking beyond their own house and garden, finding sufficient exercise in domestic duties. So, when Priscilla was not with her, she usually sat with Mant's Bible [1] before her, and after following the text with her eyes for a little while, she would gradually permit them to wander as her thoughts had already insisted on wandering.

But Nancy's Sunday thoughts were rarely quite out of keeping with the devout and reverential intention implied by the book spread open before her. She was not theologically instructed enough to discern very clearly the relation between the sacred documents of the past which she opened without method, and her own obscure, simple life; but the spirit of rectitude and the sense of responsibility for the effect of her conduct on others, which were strong elements in Nancy's character, had made it a habit with her to scrutinize her past feelings and actions with self-questioning solicitude. Her mind not being courted by a great variety of subjects, she filled the vacant moments by living inwardly, again and again, through all her remembered experience, especially through the fifteen years of her married time, in which her life and its significance had been doubled. She recalled the small details, the words, tones, and looks, in the critical scenes which had opened a new epoch for her by giving her a deeper insight into the relations and trials of life, or which had called on her for some little

[1] **Mant's Bible:** a Bible published by Richard Mant.

effort of forbearance, or of painful adherence to an imagined or real duty—asking herself continually whether she had been in any respect blamable. This excessive rumination and self-questioning is perhaps a morbid habit inevitable to a mind of much moral sensibility when shut out from its due share of outward activity and of practical claims on its affections—inevitable to a noble-hearted, childless woman, when her lot is narrow. "I can do so little—have I done it all well?" is the perpetually recurring thought; and there are no voices calling her away from that soliloquy, no peremptory demands to divert energy from vain regret or superfluous scruple.

There was one main thread of painful experience in Nancy's married life, and on it hung certain deeply felt scenes, which were the oftenest revived in retrospect. The short dialogue with Priscilla in the garden had determined the current of retrospect in that frequent direction this particular Sunday afternoon. The first wandering of her thought from the text, which she still attempted dutifully to follow with her eyes and silent lips, was into an imaginary enlargement of the defense she had set up for her husband against Priscilla's implied blame. The vindication of the loved object is the best balm affection can find for its wounds: "A man must have so much on his mind" is the belief by which a wife often supports a cheerful face under rough answers and unfeeling words. And Nancy's deepest wounds had all come from the perception that the absence of children from their hearth was dwelt on in her husband's mind as a privation to which he could not reconcile himself.

Yet sweet Nancy might have been expected to feel still more keenly the denial of a blessing to which she had looked forward with all the varied expectations and preparations, solemn and prettily trivial, which fill the mind of a loving woman when she expects to become a mother. Was there not a drawer filled with the neat work of her hands, all unworn and untouched, just as she had arranged it there fourteen years ago—just, but for one little dress, which had been made the burial dress? But under this immediate personal trial Nancy was so firmly unmurmuring that years ago she had suddenly renounced the habit of visiting this drawer, lest she should in this way be cherishing a longing for what was not given.

Perhaps it was this very severity toward any indulgence of what she held to be sinful regret in herself that made her shrink from applying her own standard to her husband. "It is very different—it is much worse for a man to be disappointed in that way: a woman can always be satisfied with devoting herself to her husband, but a man wants something that will make him look forward more—and sitting by the fire is so much duller to him than to a woman." And always, when Nancy reached this point in her meditations—trying, with predetermined sympathy, to see everything as Godfrey saw it—there came a renewal of self-questioning. *Had* she done everything in her power to lighten Godfrey's privation? Had she really been right in the resistance which had cost her so much pain six years ago, and again four years ago— the resistance to her husband's wish that they should adopt a child? Adoption was more remote from the ideas and habits of that time than of our own; still Nancy had her opinion on it. It was as necessary to her mind to have an opinion on all topics, not exclusively masculine, that had come under her notice as for her to have a precisely marked place for every article of her personal property: and her opinions were always principles to be unwaveringly

acted on. They were firm, not because of their basis, but because she held them with a tenacity inseparable from her mental action. On all the duties and proprieties of life, from filial behavior to the arrangements of the evening toilet, pretty Nancy Lammeter, by the time she was three-and-twenty, had her unalterable little code and had formed every one of her habits in strict accordance with that code. She carried these decided judgments within her in the most unobtrusive way: they rooted themselves in her mind and grew there as quietly as grass. Years ago, we know, she insisted on dressing like Priscilla, because "it was right for sisters to dress alike," and because "she would do what was right if she wore a gown dyed with cheese-coloring."

That was a trivial but typical instance of the mode in which Nancy's life was regulated.

It was one of those rigid principles, and no petty egoistic feeling, which had been the ground of Nancy's difficult resistance to her husband's wish. To adopt a child, because children of your own had been denied you, was to try and choose your lot in spite of Providence: the adopted child, she was convinced, would never turn out well and would be a curse to those who had willfully and rebelliously sought what it was clear that, for some high reason, they were better without. When you saw a thing was not meant to be, said Nancy, it was a bounden duty to leave off so much as wishing for it. And so far, perhaps, the wisest of men could scarcely make more than a verbal improvement in her principle. But the conditions under which she held it apparent that a thing was not meant to be depended on a more peculiar mode of thinking. She would have given up making a purchase at a particular place if, on three successive times, rain, or some other cause of

Heaven's sending, had formed an obstacle; and she would have anticipated a broken limb or other heavy misfortune to anyone who persisted in spite of such indications.

"But why should you think the child would turn out ill?" said Godfrey, in his remonstrances. "She has thriven as well as child can do with the weaver; and *he* adopted her. There isn't such a pretty little girl anywhere else in the parish, or one fitter for the station we could give her. Where can be the likelihood of her being a curse to anybody?"

"Yes, my dear Godfrey," said Nancy, who was sitting with her hands tightly clasped together, and with yearning, regretful affection in her eyes. "The child may not turn out ill with the weaver. But, then, he didn't go to seek her, as we should be doing. It will be wrong: I feel sure it will. Don't you remember what that lady we met at the Royston Baths told us about the child her sister adopted? That was the only adopting I ever heard of: and the child was transported [1] when it was twenty-three. Dear Godfrey, don't ask me to do what I know is wrong: I should never be happy again. I know it's very hard for *you*—it's easier for me—but it's the will of Providence."

It might seem singular that Nancy—with her religious theory pieced together out of narrow social traditions, fragments of church doctrine imperfectly understood, and girlish reasonings on her small experience—should have arrived by herself at a way of thinking so nearly akin to that of many devout people whose beliefs are held in the shape of a system quite remote from her knowledge: singular, if we did not know that human beliefs, like all other natural growths, elude the barriers of system.

[1] **transported:** as used here, sent to a penal colony in Australia after conviction as a criminal.

Godfrey had from the first specified Eppie, then about twelve years old, as a child suitable for them to adopt. It had never occurred to him that Silas would rather part with his life than with Eppie. Surely the weaver would wish the best to the child he had taken so much trouble with and would be glad that such good fortune should happen to her: she would always be very grateful to him, and he would be well provided for to the end of his life—provided for as the excellent part he had done by the child deserved. Was it not an appropriate thing for people in a higher station to take a charge off the hands of a man in a lower? It seemed an eminently appropriate thing to Godfrey, for reasons that were known only to himself; and by a common fallacy, he imagined the measure would be easy because he had private motives for desiring it. This was rather a coarse mode of estimating Silas's relation to Eppie; but we must remember that many of the impressions which Godfrey was likely to gather concerning the laboring people around him would favor the idea that deep affections can hardly go along with callous palms and scant means; and he had not had the opportunity, even if he had had the power, of entering intimately into all that was exceptional in the weaver's experience. It was only the want of adequate knowledge that could have made it possible for Godfrey deliberately to entertain an unfeeling project: his natural kindness had outlived that blighting time of cruel wishes, and Nancy's praise of him as a husband was not founded entirely on a willful illusion.

"I was right," she said to herself, when she had recalled all their scenes of discussion—"I feel I was right to say him nay, though it hurt me more than anything; but how good Godfrey has been about it! Many men would have been very angry with me for standing out against their wishes; and they might have thrown out that they'd had ill luck in marrying me; but Godfrey has never been the man to say me an unkind word. It's only what he can't hide; everything seems so blank to him, I know; and the land—what a difference it 'ud make to him, when he goes to see after things, if he'd children growing up that he was doing it all for! But I won't murmur; and perhaps if he'd married a woman who'd have had children, she'd have vexed him in other ways."

This possibility was Nancy's chief comfort; and to give it greater strength, she labored to make it impossible that any other wife should have had more perfect tenderness. She had been *forced* to vex him by that one denial. Godfrey was not insensible to her loving effort and did Nancy no injustice as to the motives of her obstinacy. It was impossible to have lived with her fifteen years and not be aware that an unselfish clinging to the right and a sincerity clear as the flower-born dew were her main characteristics; indeed, Godfrey felt this so strongly that his own more wavering nature, too averse to facing difficulty to be unvaryingly simple and truthful, was kept in a certain awe of this gentle wife who watched his looks with a yearning to obey them. It seemed to him impossible that he should ever confess to her the truth about Eppie: she would never recover from the repulsion the story of his earlier marriage would create, told to her now, after that long concealment. And the child, too, he thought, must become an object of repulsion: the very sight of her would be painful. The shock to Nancy's mingled pride and ignorance of the world's evil might even be too much for her delicate frame. Since he had married her with that secret on his heart, he must keep it there to the last. Whatever else he did, he could not make

an irreparable breach between himself and this long-loved wife.

Meanwhile, why could he not make up his mind to the absence of children from a hearth brightened by such a wife? Why did his mind fly uneasily to that void, as if it were the sole reason why life was not thoroughly joyous to him? I suppose it is the way with all men and women who reach middle age without the clear perception that life never *can* be thoroughly joyous: under the vague dullness of the gray hours, dissatisfaction seeks a definite object and finds it in the privation of an untried good. Dissatisfaction seated musingly on a childless hearth thinks with envy of the father whose return is greeted by young voices—seated at the meal where the little heads rise one above another like nursery plants, it sees a black care hovering behind every one of them and thinks the impulses by which men abandon freedom and seek for ties are surely nothing but a brief madness. In Godfrey's case there were further reasons why this thought would be continually solicited by this one point in his lot: his conscience, never thoroughly easy about Eppie, now gave his childless home the aspect of a retribution; and as the time passed on, under Nancy's refusal to adopt her, any retrieval of his error became more and more difficult.

On this Sunday afternoon it was already four years since there had been any allusion to the subject between them, and Nancy supposed that it was forever buried.

"I wonder if he'll mind it less or more as he gets older," she thought; "I'm afraid more. Aged people feel the miss of children; what would father do without Priscilla? And if I die, Godfrey will be very lonely—not holding together with his brothers much. But I won't be over-anxious and trying to make things out

beforehand: I must do my best for the present."

With that last thought Nancy roused herself from her reverie and turned her eyes again toward the forsaken page. It had been forsaken longer than she imagined, for she was presently surprised by the appearance of the servant with the tea things. It was, in fact, a little before the usual time for tea; but Jane had her reasons.

"Is your master come into the yard, Jane?"

"No'm, he isn't," said Jane, with a slight emphasis, of which, however, her mistress took no notice.

"I don't know whether you've seen 'em, 'm," continued Jane, after a pause, "but there's folks making haste all one way, afore the front window. I doubt something's happened. There's niver a man to be seen i' the yard, else I'd send and see. I've been up into the top attic, but there's no seeing anything for trees. I hope nobody's hurt, that's all."

"Oh, no, I daresay there's nothing much the matter," said Nancy. "It's perhaps Mr. Snell's bull got out again, as he did before."

"I wish he mayn't gore anybody then, that's all," said Jane, not altogether despising a hypothesis which covered a few imaginary calamities.

"That girl is always terrifying me," thought Nancy; "I wish Godfrey would come in."

She went to the front window and looked as far as she could see along the road, with an uneasiness which she felt to be childish, for there were now no such signs of excitement as Jane had spoken of, and Godfrey would not be likely to return by the village road, but by the fields. She continued to stand, however, looking at the placid churchyard with the long shadows of the gravestones across the

bright green hillocks and at the glowing autumn colors of the Rectory trees beyond. Before such calm external beauty the presence of a vague fear is more distinctly felt—like a raven flapping its slow wing across the sunny air. Nancy wished more and more that Godfrey would come in.

CHAPTER XVIII

Revelations

SOMEONE OPENED the door at the other end of the room, and Nancy felt that it was her husband. She turned from the window with gladness in her eyes, for the wife's chief dread was stilled.

"Dear, I'm so thankful you're come," she said, going toward him. "I began to get . . ."

She paused abruptly, for Godfrey was laying down his hat with trembling hands, and turned toward her with a pale face and a strange unanswering glance, as if he saw her indeed, but saw her as part of a scene invisible to herself. She laid her hand on his arm, not daring to speak again; but he left the touch unnoticed and threw himself into his chair.

Jane was already at the door with the hissing urn. "Tell her to keep away, will you?" said Godfrey; and when the door was closed again he exerted himself to speak more distinctly.

"Sit down, Nancy—there," he said, pointing to a chair opposite him. "I came back as soon as I could, to hinder anybody's telling you but me. I've had a great shock—but I care most about the shock it'll be to you."

"It isn't father and Priscilla?" said Nancy, with quivering lips, clasping her hands together tightly on her lap.

"No, it's nobody living," said Godfrey, unequal to the considerate skill with which he would have wished to make his revelation. "It's Dunstan—my brother Dunstan, that we lost sight of sixteen years ago. We've found him—found his body—his skeleton."

The deep dread Godfrey's look had created in Nancy made her feel these words a relief. She sat in comparative calmness to hear what else he had to tell. He went on:

"The stone pit has gone dry suddenly—from the draining, I suppose; and there he lies—has lain for sixteen years, wedged between two great stones. There's his watch and seals, and there's my gold-handled hunting whip, with my name on: he took it away, without my knowing, the day he went hunting on Wildfire, the last time he was seen."

Godfrey paused: it was not so easy to say what came next. "Do you think he drowned himself?" said Nancy almost wondering that her husband should be so deeply shaken by what had happened all those years ago to an unloved brother, of whom worse things had been augured.

"No, he fell in," said Godfrey, in a low but distinct voice, as if he felt some deep meaning in the fact. Presently he added: "Dunstan was the man that robbed Silas Marner."

The blood rushed to Nancy's face and neck at this surprise and shame, for she had been bred up to regard even a distant kinship with crime as a dishonor.

"Oh Godfrey!" she said, with compassion in her tone, for she had immediately reflected that the dishonor must be felt still more keenly by her husband.

"There was the money in the pit," he continued—"all the weaver's money. Everything's been gathered up, and they're taking the skeleton to the Rain-

bow. But I came back to tell you: there was no hindering it; you must know."

He was silent, looking on the ground for two long minutes. Nancy would have said some words of comfort under this disgrace, but she refrained, from an instinctive sense that there was something behind—that Godfrey had something else to tell her. Presently he lifted his eyes to her face and kept them fixed on her as he said:

"Everything comes to light, Nancy, sooner or later. When God Almighty wills it, our secrets are found out. I've lived with a secret on my mind, but I'll keep it from you no longer. I wouldn't have you know it by somebody else, and not by me—I wouldn't have you find it out after I'm dead. I'll tell you now. It's been 'I will' and 'I won't' with me all my life—I'll make sure of myself now."

Nancy's utmost dread had returned. The eyes of the husband and wife met with awe in them, as at a crisis which suspended affection.

"Nancy," said Godfrey, slowly, "when I married you, I hid something from you—something I ought to have told you. That woman Marner found dead in the snow—Eppie's mother—that wretched woman—was my wife: Eppie is my child."

He paused, dreading the effect of his confession. But Nancy sat quite still, only that her eyes dropped and ceased to meet his. She was pale and quiet as a meditative statue, clasping her hands on her lap.

"You'll never think the same of me again," said Godfrey, after a little while, with some tremor in his voice.

She was silent.

"I oughtn't to have left the child unowned: I oughtn't to have kept it from you. But I couldn't bear to give you up, Nancy. I was led away into marrying her—I suffered for it."

Still Nancy was silent, looking down; and he almost expected that she would presently get up and say she would go to her father's. How could she have any mercy for faults that must seem so black to her, with her simple severe notions?

But at last she lifted up her eyes to his again and spoke. There was no indignation in her voice—only deep regret.

"Godfrey, if you had but told me this six years ago, we could have done some of our duty by the child. Do you think I'd have refused to take her in, if I'd known she was yours?"

At that moment Godfrey felt all the bitterness of an error that was not simply futile, but had defeated its own end. He had not measured this wife with whom he had lived so long. But she spoke again, with more agitation.

"And—Oh, Godfrey—if we'd had her from the first, if you'd taken to her as you ought, she'd have loved me for her mother—and you'd have been happier with me: I could better have bore my little baby dying, and our life might have been more like what we used to think it 'ud be."

The tears fell, and Nancy ceased to speak.

"But you wouldn't have married me then, Nancy, if I'd told you," said Godfrey, urged, in the bitterness of his self-reproach, to prove to himself that his conduct had not been utter folly. "You may think you would now, but you wouldn't then. With your pride and your father's, you'd have hated having anything to do with me after the talk there'd have been."

"I can't say what I should have done about that, Godfrey. I should never have married anybody else. But I wasn't worth doing wrong for—nothing is in this world. Nothing is so good as it seems beforehand—not even our marrying wasn't, you see." There was a faint sad smile on Nancy's face as she said the last words.

"I'm a worse man than you thought I was, Nancy," said Godfrey, rather tremulously. "Can you forgive me ever?"

"The wrong to me is but little, Godfrey: you've made it up to me—you've been good to me for fifteen years. It's another you did the wrong to; and I doubt it can never be all made up for."

"But we can take Eppie now," said Godfrey. "I won't mind the world knowing at last. I'll be plain and open for the rest o' my life."

"It'll be different coming to us, now she's grown up," said Nancy, shaking her head sadly. "But it's your duty to acknowledge her and provide for her; and I'll do my part by her and pray to God Almighty to make her love me."

"Then we'll go together to Silas Marner's this very night, as soon as everything's quiet at the stone pits."

FOR STUDY AND DISCUSSION

1. How many years have passed between Part I and Part II? What changes have taken place in Silas? in Godfrey? in Nancy?

2. What is Eppie like as a young woman? What does she reveal about herself in what she says? in what she does? How has her life with Silas made her different from the village girls?

3. Where have we seen Aaron before in the novel? Why is he a good choice for Eppie? How does he feel about her? How does she feel about him? What kind of life do you foresee for them?

4. When Dolly Winthrop heard the story of Silas's past, what was her reaction to the lottery? to William Dane? What did she feel Silas should have done?

5. By suddenly shifting scenes, George Eliot points up the contrast between life at Silas's cottage and life at the Red House. What is the most striking difference? What does Godfrey desperately want? How has he been disappointed? Why can Nancy bear the disappointment so much more calmly?

6. Why had Nancy opposed adopting a child? Do you think her reasons were good? Why does she now regret her firmness? Is she more sorry for her own sake or for Godfrey's?

7. How is Dunsey's body discovered? How did he die? Why is this discovery such a shock to Godfrey?

8. Why does Godfrey finally reveal his secret to Nancy? Did she react as he expected? Why?

9. What does Godfrey want to do for Eppie? Why does Nancy agree that this is the right thing to do?

10. What do you think will happen when Godfrey and Nancy claim Eppie from Silas Marner?

CHAPTER XIX

Eppie Makes Her Choice

BETWEEN EIGHT and nine o'clock that evening, Eppie and Silas were seated alone in the cottage. After the great excitement the weaver had undergone from the events of the afternoon, he had felt a longing for this quietude and had even begged Mrs. Winthrop and Aaron, who had naturally lingered behind everyone else, to leave him alone with his child. The excitement had not passed away: it had only reached that stage when the keenness of the susceptibility makes external stimulus intolerable—when there is no sense of weariness, but rather an intensity of inward life, under which sleep is an impossibility. Anyone who has watched such moments in other men remembers the brightness of the eyes and the strange definiteness that comes over coarse features from that transient influence. It is as if a new fineness of ear for all spiritual voices had sent wonder-working vibrations through the heavy mortal frame—as if "beauty born of murmuring sound" had passed into the face of the listener.

Silas's face showed that sort of trans-figuration, as he sat in his armchair and looked at Eppie. She had drawn her own chair toward his knees and leaned forward, holding both his hands, while she looked up at him. On the table near them, lit by a candle, lay the recovered gold—the old long-loved gold, ranged in orderly heaps, as Silas used to range it in the days when it was his only joy. He had been telling her how he used to count it every night, and how his soul was utterly desolate till she was sent to him.

"At first, I'd a sort o' feeling come across me now and then," he was saying in a subdued tone, "as if you might be changed into the gold again; for sometimes, turn my head which way I would, I seemed to see the gold; and I thought I should be glad if I could feel it and find it was come back. But that didn't last long. After a bit, I should have thought it was a curse come again, if it had drove you from me, for I'd got to feel the need o' your looks and your voice and the touch o' your little fingers. You didn't know then, Eppie, when you were such a little un—you didn't know what your old father Silas felt for you."

"But I know now, father," said Eppie. "If it hadn't been for you, they'd have taken me to the workhouse, and there'd have been nobody to love me."

"Eh, my precious child, the blessing was mine. If you hadn't been sent to save me, I should ha' gone to the grave in my misery. The money was taken away from me in time; and you see it's been kept—kept till it was wanted for you. It's wonderful—our life is wonderful."

Silas sat in silence a few minutes, looking at the money. "It takes no hold of me now," he said, ponderingly—"the money doesn't. I wonder if it ever could again—I doubt it might, if I lost you, Eppie. I might come to think I was forsaken again and lose the feeling that God was good to me."

At that moment there was a knocking at the door; and Eppie was obliged to rise without answering Silas. Beautiful she looked, with the tenderness of gathering tears in her eyes and a slight flush on her cheeks, as she stepped to open the door. The flush deepened when she saw Mr. and Mrs. Godfrey Cass. She made her little rustic curtsy and held the door wide for them to enter.

"We're disturbing you very late, my dear," said Mrs. Cass, taking Eppie's hand, and looking in her face with an expression of anxious interest and admiration. Nancy herself was pale and tremulous.

Eppie, after placing chairs for Mr. and Mrs. Cass, went to stand against Silas, opposite to them.

"Well, Marner," said Godfrey, trying to speak with perfect firmness, "it's a great comfort to me to see you with your money again, that you've been deprived of so many years. It was one of my family did you the wrong—the more grief to me—and I feel bound to make up to you for it in every way. Whatever I can do for you will be nothing but paying a debt, even if I looked no further than the robbery. But there are other things I'm beholden—shall be beholden to you for, Marner."

Godfrey checked himself. It had been agreed between him and his wife that the subject of his fatherhood should be approached very carefully, and that, if possible, the disclosure should be reserved for the future, so that it might be made to Eppie gradually. Nancy had urged this, because she felt strongly the painful light in which Eppie must inevitably see the relation between her father and mother.

Silas, always ill at ease when he was being spoken to by "betters," such as Mr. Cass—tall, powerful, florid men, seen chiefly on horseback—answered with some constraint—

"Sir, I've a deal to thank you for a'ready. As for the robbery, I count it no loss to me. And if I did, you couldn't help it: you aren't answerable for it."

"You may look at it in that way, Marner, but I never can; and I hope you'll let me act according to my own feeling of what's just. I know you're easily contented: you've been a hard-working man all your life."

"Yes, sir, yes," said Marner, meditatively. "I should ha' been bad off without my work: it was what I held by when everything else was gone from me."

"Ah," said Godfrey, applying Marner's words simply to his bodily wants, "it was a good trade for you in this country, because there's been a great deal of linen-weaving to be done. But you're getting rather past such close work, Marner: it's time you laid by and had some rest. You look a good deal pulled down, though you're not an old man, *are* you?"

"Fifty-five, as near as I can say, sir," said Silas.

"Oh, why, you may live thirty years longer—look at old Macey! And that money on the table, after all, is but little. It won't go far either way—whether it's put out to interest, or you were to live on it as long as it would last: it wouldn't go far if you'd nobody to keep but yourself, and you've had two to keep for a good many years now."

"Eh, sir," said Silas, unaffected by anything Godfrey was saying, "I'm in no fear o' want. We shall do very well—Eppie and me 'ull do well enough. There's few working folks have got so much laid by as that. I don't know what it is to gentlefolks, but I look upon it as a deal—almost too much. And as for us, it's little we want."

"Only the garden, father," said Eppie, blushing up to the ears the moment after.

"You love a garden, do you, my dear?" said Nancy, thinking that this turn in the point of view might help her husband. "We should agree in that: I give a deal of time to the garden."

"Ah, there's plenty of gardening at the Red House," said Godfrey, surprised at the difficulty he found in approaching a proposition which had seemed so easy to him in the distance. "You've done a good part by Eppie, Marner, for sixteen years. It 'ud be a great comfort to you to see her well provided for, wouldn't it? She looks blooming and healthy, but not fit for any hardships: she doesn't look like a strapping girl come of working parents. You'd like to see her taken care of by those who can leave her well off and make a lady of her; she's more fit for it than for a rough life, such as she might come to have in a few years' time."

A slight flush came over Marner's face and disappeared, like a passing gleam. Eppie was simply wondering Mr. Cass should talk so about things that seemed to have nothing to do with reality, but Silas was hurt and uneasy.

"I don't take your meaning, sir," he answered, not having words at command to express the mingled feelings with which he had heard Mr. Cass's words.

"Well, my meaning is this, Marner," said Godfrey, determined to come to the

point. "Mrs. Cass and I, you know, have no children—nobody to be the better for our good home and everything else we have—more than enough for ourselves. And we should like to have somebody in the place of a daughter to us—we should like to have Eppie and treat her in every way as our own child. It 'ud be a great comfort to you in your old age, I hope, to see her fortune made in that way, after you've been at the trouble of bringing her up so well. And it's right you should have every reward for that. And Eppie, I'm sure, will always love you and be grateful to you: she'd come and see you very often, and we should all be on the lookout to do everything we could toward making you comfortable."

A plain man like Godfrey Cass, speaking under some embarrassment, necessarily blunders on words that are coarser than his intentions and that are likely to fall gratingly on susceptible feelings. While he had been speaking, Eppie had quietly passed her arm behind Silas's head, and let her hand rest against it caressingly: she felt him trembling violently. He was silent for some moments when Mr. Cass had ended—powerless under the conflict of emotions, all alike painful. Eppie's heart was swelling at the sense that her father was in distress; and she was just going to lean down and speak to him, when one struggling dread at last gained the mastery over every other in Silas, and he said, faintly:

"Eppie, my child, speak. I won't stand in your way. Thank Mr. and Mrs. Cass."

Eppie took her hand from her father's head and came forward a step. Her cheeks were flushed, but not with shyness this time: the sense that her father was in doubt and suffering banished that sort of self-consciousness. She dropped a low curtsy, first to Mrs. Cass and then to Mr. Cass, and said:

"Thank you, ma'am—thank you, sir. But I can't leave my father nor own anybody nearer than him. And I don't want to be a lady—thank you all the same" (here Eppie dropped another curtsy). "I couldn't give up the folks I've been used to."

Eppie's lip began to tremble a little at the last words. She retreated to her father's chair again and held him round the neck: while Silas, with a subdued sob, put up his hand to grasp hers.

The tears were in Nancy's eyes, but her sympathy with Eppie was, naturally, divided with distress on her husband's account. She dared not speak, wondering what was going on in her husband's mind.

Godfrey felt an irritation inevitable to almost all of us when we encounter an unexpected obstacle. He had been full of his own penitence and resolution to retrieve his error as far as the time was left to him; he was possessed with all-important feelings that were to lead to a predetermined course of action which he had fixed on as the right, and he was not prepared to enter with lively appreciation into other people's feelings counteracting his virtuous resolves. The agitation with which he spoke again was not quite unmixed with anger.

"But I've a claim on you, Eppie—the strongest of all claims. It's my duty, Marner, to own Eppie as my child and provide for her. She's my own child: her mother was my wife. I've a natural claim on her that must stand before every other."

Eppie had given a violent start and turned quite pale. Silas, on the contrary, who had been relieved, by Eppie's answer, from the dread lest his mind should be in opposition to hers, felt the spirit of resistance in him set free, not without a touch of parental fierceness. "Then, sir," he answered, with an accent of bitterness

that had been silent in him since the memorable day when his youthful hope had perished—"then, sir, why didn't you say so sixteen year ago, and claim her before I'd come to love her, i'stead o' coming to take her from me now, when you might as well take the heart out o' my body? God gave her to me because you turned your back upon her, and He looks upon her as mine: you've no right to her! When a man turns a blessing from his door, it falls to them as take it in."

"I know that, Marner. I was wrong. I've repented of my conduct in that matter," said Godfrey, who could not help feeling the edge of Silas's words.

"I'm glad to hear it, sir," said Marner, with gathering excitement; "but repentance doesn't alter what's been going on for sixteen year. Your coming now and saying 'I'm her father' doesn't alter the feelings inside us. It's me she's been calling her father ever since she could say the word."

"But I think you might look at the thing more reasonably, Marner," said Godfrey, unexpectedly awed by the weaver's direct truth-speaking. "It isn't as if she was to be taken quite away from you so that you'd never see her again. She'll be very near you and come to see you very often. She'll feel just the same toward you."

"Just the same?" said Marner, more bitterly than ever. "How'll she feel just the same for me as she does now, when we eat o' the same bit, and drink o' the same cup, and think o' the same things from one day's end to another? Just the same? that's idle talk. You'd cut us i' two."

Godfrey, unqualified by experience to discern the pregnancy of Marner's simple words, felt rather angry again. It seemed to him that the weaver was very selfish (a judgment readily passed by those who have never tested their own power of sacrifice) to oppose what was undoubtedly for Eppie's welfare; and he felt himself called upon, for her sake, to assert his authority.

"I should have thought, Marner," he said, severely—"I should have thought your affection for Eppie would make you rejoice in what was for her good, even if it did call upon you to give up something. You ought to remember your own life's uncertain, and she's at an age now when her lot may soon be fixed in a way very different from what it would be in her father's home: she may marry some low workingman, and then, whatever I might do for her, I couldn't make her well off. You're putting yourself in the way of her welfare; and though I'm sorry to hurt you after what you've done and what I've left undone, I feel now it's my duty to insist on taking care of my own daughter. I want to do my duty."

It would be difficult to say whether it were Silas or Eppie that was more deeply stirred by this last speech of Godfrey's. Thought had been very busy in Eppie as she listened to the contest between her old, long-loved father and this new, unfamiliar father who had suddenly come to fill the place of that black, featureless shadow which had held the ring and placed it on her mother's finger. Her imagination had darted backward in conjectures, and forward in previsions, of what this revealed fatherhood implied; and there were words in Godfrey's last speech which helped to make the previsions especially definite. Not that these thoughts, either of past or future, determined her resolution —*that* was determined by the feelings which vibrated to every word Silas had uttered; but they raised, even apart from these feelings, a repulsion toward the offered lot and the newly revealed father.

Silas, on the other hand, was again stricken in conscience and alarmed lest

Godfrey's accusation should be true—lest he should be raising his own will as an obstacle to Eppie's good. For many moments he was mute, struggling for the self-conquest necessary to the uttering of the difficult words. They came out tremulously.

"I'll say no more. Let it be as you will. Speak to the child. I'll hinder nothing."

Even Nancy, with all the acute sensibility of her own affections, shared her husband's view that Marner was not justifiable in his wish to retain Eppie after her real father had avowed himself. She felt that it was a very hard trial for the poor weaver, but her code allowed no question that a father by blood must have a claim above that of any foster father. Besides, Nancy, used all her life to plenteous circumstances and the privileges of "respectability," could not enter into the pleasures which early nurture and habit connect with all the little aims and efforts of the poor who are born poor: to her mind, Eppie, in being restored to her birthright, was entering on a too long withheld but unquestionable good. Hence she heard Silas's last words with relief, and thought, as Godfrey did, that their wish was achieved.

"Eppie, my dear," said Godfrey, looking at his daughter, not without some embarrassment, under the sense that she was old enough to judge him, "it'll always be our wish that you should show your love and gratitude to one who's been a father to you so many years, and we shall want to help you to make him comfortable in every way. But we hope you'll come to love us as well; and though I haven't been what a father should ha' been to you all these years, I wish to do the utmost in my power for you for the rest of my life and provide for you as my only child. And you'll have the best of mothers in my wife—that'll be a blessing you haven't known since you were old enough to know it."

"My dear, you'll be a treasure to me," said Nancy, in her gentle voice. "We shall want for nothing when we have our daughter."

Eppie did not come forward and curtsy, as she had done before. She held Silas's hand in hers and grasped it firmly—it was a weaver's hand, with a palm and finger tips that were sensitive to such pressure—while she spoke with colder decision than before.

"Thank you, ma'am—thank you, sir, for your offers—they're very great and far above my wish. For I should have no delight i' life any more if I was forced to go away from my father and knew he was sitting at home, a'thinking of me and feeling lone. We've been used to be happy together every day, and I can't think o' no happiness without him. And he says he'd nobody i' the world till I was sent to him, and he'd have nothing when I was gone. And he's took care of me and loved me from the first, and I'll cleave to him as long as he lives, and nobody shall ever come between him and me."

"But you must make sure, Eppie," said Silas, in a low voice—"you must make sure as you won't ever be sorry because you've made your choice to stay among poor folks, and with poor clothes and things, when you might ha' had everything o' the best."

His sensitiveness on this point had increased as he listened to Eppie's words of faithful affection.

"I can never be sorry, father," said Eppie. "I shouldn't know what to think on or to wish for with fine things about me as I haven't been used to. And it 'ud be poor work for me to put on things, and ride in a gig, and sit in a place at church, as 'ud make them as I'm fond of think me unfitting company for 'em. What could I care for then?"

Nancy looked at Godfrey with a pained, questioning glance. But his eyes were fixed on the floor, where he was moving the end of his stick, as if he were pondering on something absently. She thought there was a word which might perhaps come better from her lips than from his.

"What you say is natural, my dear child —it's natural you should cling to those who've brought you up," she said, mildly; "but there's a duty you owe to your lawful father. There's perhaps something to be given up on more sides than one. When your father opens his home to you, I think it's right you shouldn't turn your back on it."

"I can't feel as I've got any father but one," said Eppie, impetuously, while the tears gathered. "I've always thought of a little home where he'd sit i' the corner, and I should fend and do everything for him: I can't think o' no other home. I wasn't brought up to be a lady, and I can't turn my mind to it. I like the working folks, and their victuals, and their ways. And," she ended passionately, while the tears fell, "I'm promised to marry a working man as 'll live with father and help me to take care of him."

Godfrey looked up at Nancy with a flushed face and smarting, dilated eyes. This frustration of a purpose toward which he had set out under the exalted consciousness that he was about to compensate in some degree for the greatest demerit of his life made him feel the air of the room stifling.

"Let us go," he said, in an undertone.

"We won't talk of this any longer now," said Nancy, rising. "We're your well-wishers, my dear—and yours too, Marner. We shall come and see you again. It's getting late now."

In this way she covered her husband's abrupt departure, for Godfrey had gone straight to the door, unable to say more.

CHAPTER XX

The Dead Past

Nancy and Godfrey walked home under the starlight in silence. When they entered the oaken parlor, Godfrey threw himself into his chair, while Nancy laid down her bonnet and shawl and stood on the hearth near her husband, unwilling to leave him even for a few minutes and yet fearing to utter any word lest it might jar on his feelings. At last Godfrey turned his head toward her, and their eyes met, dwelling in that meeting without any movement on either side. That quiet mutual gaze of a trusting husband and wife is like the first moment of rest or refuge from a great weariness or a great danger—not to be interfered with by speech or action which would distract the sensations from the fresh enjoyment of repose.

But presently he put out his hand, and as Nancy placed hers within it, he drew her toward him, and said—"that's ended!"

She bent to kiss him and then said, as she stood by his side, "Yes, I'm afraid we must give up the hope of having her for a daughter. It wouldn't be right to want to force her to come to us against her will. We can't alter her bringing up and what's come of it."

"No," said Godfrey, with a keen decisiveness of tone, in contrast with his usually careless and unemphatic speech— "there's debts we can't pay like money debts, by paying extra for the years that have slipped by. While I've been putting off and putting off, the trees have been growing—it's too late now. Marner was in the right in what he said about a man's turning away a blessing from his door; it falls to somebody else. I wanted to pass

for childless once, Nancy—I shall pass for childless now against my wish."

Nancy did not speak immediately, but after a little while she asked—"You won't make it known, then, about Eppie's being your daughter?"

"No: where would be the good to anybody?—only harm. I must do what I can for her in the state of life she chooses. I must see who it is she's thinking of marrying."

"If it won't do any good to make the thing known," said Nancy, who thought she might now allow herself the relief of entertaining a feeling which she had tried to silence before, "I should be very thankful for father and Priscilla never to be troubled with knowing what was done in the past, more than about Dunsey: it can't be helped, their knowing that."

"I shall put it in my will—I think I shall put it in my will. I shouldn't like to leave anything to be found out, like this about Dunsey," said Godfrey meditatively. "But I can't see anything but difficulties that 'ud come from telling it now. I must do what I can to make her happy in her own way. I've a notion," he added, after a moment's pause, "it's Aaron Winthrop she meant she was engaged to. I remember seeing him with her and Marner going away from church."

"Well, he's very sober and industrious," said Nancy, trying to view the matter as cheerfully as possible.

Godfrey fell into thoughtfulness again. Presently he looked up at Nancy sorrowfully and said—

"She's a very pretty, nice girl, isn't she, Nancy?"

"Yes, dear; and with just your hair and eyes: I wondered it had never struck me before."

"I think she took a dislike to me at the thought of my being her father: I could see a change in her manner after that."

"She couldn't bear to think of not looking on Marner as her father," said Nancy, not wishing to confirm her husband's painful impression.

"She thinks I did wrong by her mother as well as by her. She thinks me worse than I am. But she *must* think it: she can never know all. It's part of my punishment, Nancy, for my daughter to dislike me. I should never have got into that trouble if I'd been true to you—if I hadn't been a fool. I'd no right to expect anything but evil could come of that marriage—and when I shirked doing a father's part too."

Nancy was silent: her spirit of rectitude [1] would not let her try to soften the edge of what she felt to be a just compunction. He spoke again after a little while, but the tone was rather changed: there was tenderness mingled with the previous self-reproach.

"And I got *you,* Nancy, in spite of all; and yet I've been grumbling and uneasy because I hadn't something else—as if I deserved it."

"You've never been wanting to me, Godfrey," said Nancy, with quiet sincerity. "My only trouble would be gone if you resigned yourself to the lot that's been given us."

"Well, perhaps it isn't too late to mend a bit there. Though it *is* too late to mend some things, say what they will."

CHAPTER XXI

Return to Lantern Yard

THE NEXT MORNING, when Silas and Eppie were seated at their breakfast, he said to her—

[1] **rectitude:** strict observance of standards of integrity and honesty.

"Eppie, there's a thing I've had on my mind to do this two year, and now the money's been brought back to us, we can do it. I've been turning it over and over in the night, and I think we'll set out tomorrow, while the fine days last. We'll leave the house and everything for your godmother to take care on, and we'll make a little bundle o' things and set out."

"Where to go, daddy?" said Eppie, in much surprise.

"To my old country—to the town where I was born—up Lantern Yard. I want to see Mr. Paston, the minister: something may ha' come out to make 'em know I was innicent o' the robbery. And Mr. Paston was a man with a deal o' light—I want to speak to him about the drawing o' the lots. And I should like to talk to him about the religion o' this countryside, for I partly think he doesn't know on it."

Eppie was very joyful, for there was the prospect not only of wonder and delight at seeing a strange country, but also of coming back to tell Aaron all about it. Aaron was so much wiser than she was about most things—it would be rather pleasant to have this little advantage over him. Mrs. Winthrop, though possessed with a dim fear of dangers attendant on so long a journey, and requiring many assurances that it would not take them out of the region of carriers' carts and slow wagons, was nevertheless well pleased that Silas should revisit his own country and find out if he had been cleared from that false accusation.

"You'd be easier in your mind for the rest o' your life, Master Marner," said Dolly—"that you would. And if there's any light to be got up the Yard as you talk on, we've need of it i' this world, and I'd be glad on it myself, if you could bring it back."

So on the fourth day from that time, Silas and Eppie, in their Sunday clothes, with a small bundle tied in a blue linen handkerchief, were making their way through the streets of a great manufacturing town. Silas, bewildered by the changes thirty years had brought over his native place, had stopped several persons in succession to ask them the name of this town, that he might be sure he was not under a mistake about it.

"Ask for Lantern Yard, father—ask this gentleman with the tassels on his shoulders a-standing at the shop door; he isn't in a hurry like the rest," said Eppie, in some distress at her father's bewilderment and ill at ease, besides, amidst the noise, the movement, and the multitude of strange, indifferent faces.

"Eh, my child, he won't know anything about it," said Silas; "gentlefolks didn't ever go up the Yard. But happen somebody can tell me which is the way to Prison Street, where the jail is. I know the way out o' that as if I'd seen it yesterday."

With some difficulty, after many turnings and new inquiries, they reached Prison Street; and the grim walls of the jail, the first object that answered to any image in Silas's memory, cheered him with the certitude which no assurance of the town's name had hitherto given him, that he was in his native place.

"Ah," he said, drawing a long breath, "there's the jail, Eppie; that's just the same: I aren't afraid now. It's the third turning on the left hand from the jail doors—that's the way we must go."

"Oh, what a dark, ugly place!" said Eppie. "How it hides the sky! It's worse than the workhouse. I'm glad you don't live in this town now, father. Is Lantern Yard like this street?"

"My precious child," said Silas, smiling, "it isn't a big street like this. I never was easy i' this street myself, but I was fond o' Lantern Yard. The shops here are all altered, I think—I can't make 'em out;

but I shall know the turning, because it's the third."

"Here it is," he said, in a tone of satisfaction, as they came to a narrow alley. "And then we must go to the left again, and then straight for'ard for a bit, up Shoe Lane: and then we shall be at the entry next to the o'erhanging window, where there's the nick in the road for the water to run. Eh, I can see it all."

"O father, I'm like as if I was stifled," said Eppie. "I couldn't ha' thought as any folks lived i' this way, so close together. How pretty the stone pits 'ull look when we get back!"

"It looks comical to *me,* child, now—and smells bad. I can't think as it usened to smell so."

Here and there a sallow, begrimed face looked out from a gloomy doorway at the strangers and increased Eppie's uneasiness, so that it was a longed-for relief when they issued from the alleys into Shoe Lane, where there was a broader strip of sky.

"Dear heart!" said Silas, "why, there's people coming out o' the Yard as if they'd been to chapel at this time o' day—a weekday noon!"

Suddenly he started and stood still, with a look of distressed amazement that alarmed Eppie. They were before an opening in front of a large factory, from which men and women were streaming for their midday meal.

"Father," said Eppie, clasping his arm, "what's the matter?"

But she had to speak again and again before Silas could answer her.

"It's gone, child," he said, at last, in strong agitation—"Lantern Yard's gone. It must ha' been here, because here's the house with the o'erhanging window—I know that—it's just the same; but they've made this new opening; and see that big factory! It's all gone—chapel and all."

"Come into that little brush shop and sit down, father—they'll let you sit down," said Eppie, always on the watch lest one of her father's strange attacks should come on. "Perhaps the people can tell you all about it."

But neither from the brushmaker, who had come to Shoe Lane only ten years ago, when the factory was already built, nor from any other source within his reach, could Silas learn anything of the old Lantern Yard friends, or of Mr. Paston, the minister.

"The old place is all swep' away," Silas said to Dolly Winthrop on the night of his return—"the little graveyard and everything. The old home's gone; I've no home but this now. I shall never know whether they got at the truth o' the robbery, nor whether Mr. Paston could ha' given me any light about the drawing o' the lots. It's dark to me, Mrs. Winthrop, that is; I doubt it'll be dark to the last."

"Well, yes, Master Marner," said Dolly, who sat with a placid, listening face, now bordered by gray hairs; "I doubt it may. It's the will o' Them above as a many

things should be dark to us; but there's some things as I've never felt i' the dark about, and they're mostly what comes i' the day's work. You were hard done by that once, Master Marner, and it seems as you'll never know the rights of it; but that doesn't hinder there *being* a rights, Master Marner, for all it's dark to you and me."

"No," said Silas, "no; that doesn't hinder. Since the time the child was sent to me and I've come to love her as myself, I've had light enough to trusten by; and now she says she'll never leave me, I think I shall trusten till I die."

CONCLUSION

The Wedding

THERE WAS one time of the year which was held in Raveloe to be especially suitable for a wedding. It was when the great lilacs and laburnums [1] in the old-fashioned gardens showed their golden and purple wealth above the lichen-tinted walls, and when there were calves still young enough to want bucketfuls of fragrant milk. People were not so busy then as they must become when the full cheese-making and the mowing had set in; and besides, it was a time when a light bridal dress could be worn with comfort and seen to advantage.

Happily the sunshine fell more warmly than usual on the lilac tufts the morning that Eppie was married, for her dress was a very light one. She had often thought, though with a feeling of renunciation, that the perfection of a wedding dress would be a white cotton, with the tiniest pink

[1] **laburnums** (lə·bûr′nəmz): The laburnum is a small, poisonous shrub or tree with flowers of a bright yellow color.

sprig at wide intervals; so that when Mrs. Godfrey Cass begged to provide one and asked Eppie to choose what it should be, previous meditation had enabled her to give a decided answer at once.

Seen at a little distance as she walked across the churchyard and down the village, she seemed to be attired in pure white, and her hair looked like the dash of gold on a lily. One hand was on her husband's arm, and with the other she clasped the hand of her father, Silas.

"You won't be giving me away, father," she had said before they went to church; "you'll only be taking Aaron to be a son to you."

Dolly Winthrop walked behind with her husband; and there ended the little bridal procession.

There were many eyes to look at it, and Miss Priscilla Lammeter was glad that she and her father had happened to drive up to the door of the Red House just in time to see this pretty sight. They had come to keep Nancy company today, because Mr. Cass had had to go away to Lytherley, for special reasons. That seemed to be a pity, for otherwise he might have gone, as Mr. Crackenthorp and Mr. Osgood certainly would, to look on at the wedding feast which he had ordered at the Rainbow, naturally feeling a great interest in the weaver who had been wronged by one of his own family.

"I could ha' wished Nancy had had the luck to find a child like that and bring her up," said Priscilla to her father, as they sat in the gig; "I should ha' had something young to think of then, besides the lambs and the calves."

"Yes, my dear, yes," said Mr. Lammeter; "one feels that as one gets older. Things look dim to old folks; they'd need have some young eyes about 'em, to let 'em know the world's the same as it used to be."

Nancy came out now to welcome her father and sister; and the wedding group had passed on beyond the Red House to the humbler part of the village.

Dolly Winthrop was the first to divine that old Mr. Macey, who had been set in his armchair outside his own door, would expect some special notice as they passed, since he was too old to be at the wedding feast.

"Mr. Macey's looking for a word from us," said Dolly; "he'll be hurt if we pass him and say nothing—and him so racked with rheumatiz."

So they turned aside to shake hands with the old man. He had looked forward to the occasion and had his premeditated speech.

"Well, Master Marner," he said, in a voice that quavered a good deal, "I've lived to see my words come true. I was the first to say there was no harm in you, though your looks might be again' you; and I was the first to say you'd get your money back. And it's nothing but rightful as you should. And I'd ha' said the 'Amens,' and willing, at the holy matrimony; but Tookey's done it a good while

now, and I hope you'll have none the worse luck."

In the open yard before the Rainbow the party of guests were already assembled, though it was still nearly an hour before the appointed feast time. But by this means they could not only enjoy the slow advent of their pleasure; they had also ample leisure to talk of Silas Marner's strange history and arrive by due degrees at the conclusion that he had brought a blessing on himself by acting like a father to a lone motherless child. Even the farrier did not negative this sentiment: on the contrary, he took it up as peculiarly his own and invited any hardy person present to contradict him. But he met with no contradiction; and all differences among the company were merged in a general agreement with Mr. Snell's sentiment that when a man had deserved his good luck, it was the part of his neighbors to wish him joy.

As the bridal group approached, a hearty cheer was raised in the Rainbow yard; and Ben Winthrop, whose jokes had retained their acceptable flavor, found it agreeable to turn in there and receive congratulations; not requiring the proposed

interval of quiet at the stone pits before joining the company.

Eppie had a larger garden than she had ever expected there now; and in other ways there had been alterations at the expense of Mr. Cass, the landlord, to suit Silas's larger family. For he and Eppie had declared that they would rather stay at the stone pits than go to any new home. The garden was fenced with stones on two sides, but in front there was an open fence, through which the flowers shone with answering gladness, as the four united people came within sight of them.

"Oh father," said Eppie, "what a pretty home ours is! I think nobody could be happier than we are."

FOR STUDY AND DISCUSSION

1. How does Silas feel about his money? What does he tell Eppie about how his feelings toward the money have changed?

2. What does Silas say just before Godfrey and Nancy arrive? What effect do his words have on Eppie?

3. Why does Godfrey state his proposal so awkwardly? What is Eppie's reaction? What does it provoke Godfrey to reveal?

4. How does Silas answer Godfrey? Do you think his answer is a statement of George Eliot's own view? Who do you think has the right to Eppie? Why?

5. Do you think Eppie makes the right decision? What effect does it have on everyone?

6. Why was Godfrey going to make public that Eppie was his child? Why does he change his mind? What has he learned from the incident?

7. Why does Silas return to Lantern Yard? What change does he find there? What does this change suggest has happened?

8. How do Godfrey and Nancy contribute to Eppie's wedding? Why does Godfrey go away at the time of the wedding?

9. Many critics consider Eppie's closing words too sentimental. Do you agree? Why or why not?

THE NOVEL AS A WHOLE

1. There are two plots in this novel. Which characters are involved in each? Cite examples to show how the actions of a character in one group affect the destiny of those in the other.

2. In many ways Godfrey Cass is the opposite of Silas Marner. Silas is falsely and publicly accused; Godfrey, in spite of his guilt, continues in public esteem. Silas is betrayed by his best friend; Godfrey betrays himself. How do the two differ in their attitude toward Eppie? in their tolerance of evil? How do the actions of each bring about his own reward or punishment?

3. In this novel, which characters bring about their own destruction? How do other characters earn happiness? In reading the novel, did you feel that the author pulled strings to guarantee a certain outcome, or did the characters' actions seem natural and real to you? Support your opinion with specific illustrations from the text.

4. What is the great difference in outlook between Dolly Winthrop and William Dane? between Dolly and Molly Farren? between Dolly and Squire Cass? What is Dolly's philosophy of life? How does it differ from the attitude of Dunsey? of Godfrey? of a modern scientist?

5. What are the causes of Silas Marner's spiritual regeneration? What part in this awakening is played by Eppie? by Dolly Winthrop? by the people of Raveloe? How does Silas's concern for Eppie open his eyes to what is good around him? Try to sum up in a sentence or two what brought about Silas's new sense of happiness and peace.

6. George Eliot did not supply chapter titles for this novel. Do you agree with the titles supplied in this text? Why or why not? Make up titles of your own, and then compare them with those of your classmates.

THE CRAFT OF THE NOVELIST

1. The *theme,* or central idea, of a story expresses a general outlook on life. What, would you say, is the theme of *Silas Marner?*

2. As you know, *plot* is the sequence of

incidents or actions which make up a story. Before the plot begins to unfold, however, first of all, in the very beginning of the novel, the background or *exposition* introduces us to the setting of the story and to the characters. How is this done in *Silas Marner?*

3. As one event leads to another, the plot progresses step by step to the *climax,* or point of highest interest, which is usually the turning point in the fortune of the major character. What event in Silas's life signals the climax in this novel?

4. An important skill of the novelist is *foreshadowing*—that is, preparing us for what will happen later in the novel. A careful writer weaves into his story hints that suggest or foretell future actions. George Eliot foreshadows the finding of Dunsey by reminding us throughout the novel of the stone pit next to Silas's cottage. How often is the pit mentioned in the chapter leading up to Dunsey's theft? What incident later in the novel forcefully reminds us of the danger of the stone pit?

5. In a good novel, plot and *characterization* are closely connected, and characters usually change during the course of the novel. Review how the major events in *Silas Marner* cause a change of outlook, habit, or feeling in Silas, in Godfrey, in Nancy.

6. George Eliot has established the character of Silas as a miser who is jealously protective of his hoard of gold. When Dunsey finds Marner's door unlatched, the author must explain this fact and make it seem believable. What is George Eliot's explanation? Is it convincing?

7. At the Rainbow and at the New Year's dance, George Eliot uses minor characters to comment on the major ones. What do minor characters add to your impression of Godfrey, Nancy, the Casses, and the Lammeters? At the dance, what do the minor characters contribute to the scene? Which character's remarks are most amusing?

8. *Atmosphere* and *mood* play a large part in any novel. In *Silas Marner* there are scenes of gaiety and scenes of danger and foreboding. On two important occasions, the weather influences the course of the plot and at the same time contributes to the mood or atmosphere of the scene. For example, what is the weather when Dunsey comes to Marner's door? What part does the weather play in Dunsey's doom? Where else in the novel does the weather decisively affect the action? How does the atmosphere conveyed by the author contribute to each of these scenes?

9. George Eliot uses several *points of view* in this novel. For the most part, she tells her tale as an *omniscient,* or all-knowing observer. At times, however, she seems to speak through one of her characters. Find two or three places where this happens in *Silas Marner.* Where is the story told through Silas's mind? through Godfrey's mind? In these places, how does the author ease us into direct contact with the character's thoughts and feelings?

10. Between Parts I and II of the novel, sixteen years have elapsed. Why are the events of these sixteen years unnecessary to the story? What does the author gain by omitting them?

FOR COMPOSITION

1. What kind of a father is the Squire? What effect has his character had on his sons? How might he have acted differently? Write a short essay on how—and why—the Squire failed his sons.

2. George Eliot believed that people are what they are largely because of the conditions under which they live. Consider the circumstances that have shaped the character of Godfrey Cass, of Dunsey, or of Nancy Lammeter, and write a short essay on one of these, explaining what influences have made that person what he is.

3. What do you learn from *Silas Marner* about life in nineteenth-century England? How does the life of a landowner differ from that of one of the villagers of Raveloe? Discuss these questions in a short composition, using examples from the novel.

4. What do you think became of William Dane after his betrayal of Silas? What happens to other characters of his kind in the novel? Tell the story of Dane's later life as you think it might have happened. Write as if you were someone who knew Dane well and as if you were telling your story to Silas Marner.

The Bridge
of San Luis Rey

THORNTON WILDER

Novels bear the stamp of their creators. In contrast to the rather isolated life of George Eliot, Thornton Wilder was a world traveler before he reached the age of ten. Born in Madison, Wisconsin, in 1897, he attended a German-speaking school in Hong Kong, where his father served as United States Consul General. Later, he attended a missionary school in Shanghai. Ever since those early days, Wilder has successfully combined travel, study, writing, and teaching.

Contrary to George Eliot, who drew the subject matter for her novels mainly from her own experiences, Wilder draws his mainly from research and study, chiefly from history and literature. He is especially fond of presenting the past from the viewpoint of the present. Although his best plays are about typical modern men, they too reveal his sense of history: how the past affects the present, how small incidents in life may turn out to have the most profound significance. Wilder's two best plays are *Our Town*—a Pulitzer prize winner—and *The Skin of Our Teeth. The Matchmaker,* perhaps his funniest play, was revived as a successful musical play, *Hello Dolly.*

The Bridge of San Luis Rey is set in Lima, Peru, at the beginning of the eighteenth century. By 1714, when the story begins, Spain had established a powerful system of control over her colonies in the New World, with viceroys or royal governors as the direct link to the king. The viceroy of Peru was the most influential and powerful Spanish official overseas, holding court in Lima much as the king did in Spain. He surrounded himself with a small native-born Spanish aristocracy, and, to keep from becoming bored in his exile, imported the finest Spanish art, literature, and theater for his court. The Church, with the archbishop in Lima as its head, was another powerful force in the colonies. Thousands of missionaries had come to the New World, and, shocked by the rawness of life in the colonies, many of them came to feel the need for new affirmations of their faith.

Out of this background step the characters of Wilder's novel: the humble Brother Juniper; the Marquesa and her daughter, Doña Clara; Don Andrés, the viceroy; the Perichole, the actress, and her manager, Uncle Pio; the Abbess and the orphans—Pepita, Esteban, and Manuel.

The Bridge of San Luis Rey

THORNTON WILDER

PART ONE

Perhaps an Accident

ON FRIDAY NOON, July the twentieth,
1714, the finest bridge in all Peru broke
and precipitated five travelers into the
gulf below. This bridge was on the high-
road between Lima [1] and Cuzco [2] and
hundreds of persons passed over it every
day. It had been woven of osier [3] by the
Incas more than a century before and
visitors to the city were always led out to
see it. It was a mere ladder of thin slats
swung out over the gorge, with handrails
of dried vine. Horses and coaches and
chairs had to go down hundreds of feet
below and pass over the narrow torrent
on rafts, but no one, not even the Viceroy,
not even the Archbishop of Lima, had
descended with the baggage rather than
cross by the famous bridge of San Luis
Rey. [4] St. Louis of France himself pro-
tected it, by his name and by the little
mud church on the further side. The
bridge seemed to be among the things that
last forever; it was unthinkable that it
should break. The moment a Peruvian
heard of the accident, he signed [5] himself
and made a mental calculation as to how
recently he had crossed by it and how
soon he had intended crossing it again.
People wandered about in a trancelike
state, muttering; they had the hallucina-
tion of seeing themselves falling into a
gulf.

There was a great service in the Ca-
thedral. The bodies of the victims were
approximately collected and approxi-
mately separated from one another, and
there was great searching of hearts in
the beautiful city of Lima. Servant girls
returned bracelets which they had stolen
from their mistresses, and usurers ha-
rangued their wives angrily, in defense of
usury. [6] Yet it was rather strange that this
event should have so impressed the Li-
means, [7] for in that country those catas-
trophes which lawyers shockingly call the
"acts of God" were more than usually
frequent. Tidal waves were continually
washing away cities; earthquakes arrived
every week and towers fell upon good
men and women all the time. Diseases
were forever flitting in and out of the prov-
inces and old age carried away some of
the most admirable citizens. That is why
it was so surprising that the Peruvians
should have been especially touched by
the rent in the bridge of San Luis Rey.

Everyone was very deeply impressed,
but only one person did anything about it,
and that was Brother Juniper. By a series
of coincidences so extraordinary that one
almost suspects the presence of some In-

[1] **Lima** (lē′mə): capital of Peru.
[2] **Cuzco** (kōōs′kō): once the capital of the Incan
empire, now a city in Peru.
[3] **osier** (ō′zhər): willow twigs woven together as
in a basket.
[4] **San Luis Rey** (sän lōō′ē rā).

The Bridge of San Luis Rey by Thornton Wilder, copyright 1927 by
Albert & Charles Boni, Inc.; copyright renewed 1955 by Thornton
Wilder. Reprinted by permission of Brandt & Brandt.

[5] **signed:** crossed.
[6] **usury** (yōō′zhər·ē): the lending of money at large
rates of interest.
[7] **Limeans** (lē·mā′ənz): people of Lima.

tention, this little red-haired Franciscan from northern Italy happened to be in Peru converting the Indians and happened to witness the accident.

It was a very hot noon, that fatal noon, and coming around the shoulder of a hill, Brother Juniper stopped to wipe his forehead and to gaze upon the screen of snowy peaks in the distance, then into the gorge below him filled with the dark plumage of green trees and green birds and traversed by its ladder of osier. Joy was in him; things were not going badly. He had opened several little abandoned churches and the Indians were crawling in to early Mass and groaning at the moment of miracle as though their hearts would break. Perhaps it was the pure air from the snows before him; perhaps it was the memory that brushed him for a moment of the poem that bade him raise his eyes to the helpful hills.[1] At all events he felt at peace. Then his glance fell upon the bridge, and at that moment a twanging noise filled the air, as when the string of some musical instrument snaps in a disused room, and he saw the bridge divide

[1] **the poem . . . hills:** Psalm 121, which begins, "I will lift up my eyes unto the hills, from whence cometh my help."

and fling five gesticulating ants into the valley below.

Anyone else would have said to himself with secret joy, "Within ten minutes myself . . . !" But it was another thought that visited Brother Juniper: "Why did this happen to *those* five?" If there were any plan in the universe at all, if there were any pattern in a human life, surely it could be discovered mysteriously latent in those lives so suddenly cut off. Either we live by accident and die by accident, or we live by plan and die by plan. And on that instant Brother Juniper made the resolve to inquire into the secret lives of those five persons, that moment falling through the air, and to surprise the reason of their taking off.

It seemed to Brother Juniper that it was high time for theology to take its place among the exact sciences and he had long intended putting it there. What he had lacked hitherto was a laboratory. Oh, there had never been any lack of specimens; any number of his charges had met calamity: spiders had stung them; their lungs had been touched; their houses had burned down; and things had happened to their children from which one averts

the mind. But these occasions of human woe had never been quite fit for scientific examination. They had lacked what our good savants[1] were later to call *proper control*. The accident had been dependent upon human error, for example, or had contained elements of probability. But this collapse of the bridge of San Luis Rey was a sheer Act of God. It afforded a perfect laboratory. Here at last one could surprise His intentions in a pure state.

You and I can see that coming from anyone but Brother Juniper this plan would be the flower of a perfect skepticism. It resembled the effort of those presumptuous souls who wanted to walk on the pavements of Heaven and built the Tower of Babel[2] to get there. But to our Franciscan there was no element of doubt in the experiment. He knew the answer. He merely wanted to prove it, historically, mathematically, to his converts—poor obstinate converts, so slow to believe that their pains were inserted into their lives for their own good. People were always asking for good sound proofs; doubt springs eternal in the human breast, even in countries where the Inquisition[3] can read your very thoughts in your eyes.

This was not the first time that Brother Juniper had tried to resort to such methods. Often on the long trips he had to make (scurrying from parish to parish, his robe tucked up about his knees, for haste) he would fall to dreaming of experiments that justify the ways of God to man. For instance, a complete record of the Prayers for Rain and their results.

Often he had stood on the steps of one of his little churches, his flock kneeling before him on the baked street. Often he had stretched his arms to the sky and declaimed the splendid ritual. Not often, but several times, he had felt the virtue enter him and seen the little cloud forming on the horizon. But there were many times when weeks went by . . . but why think of them? It was not himself he was trying to convince that rain and drought were wisely apportioned.

Thus it was that the determination rose within him at the moment of the accident. It prompted him to busy himself for six years, knocking at all the doors in Lima, asking thousands of questions, filling scores of notebooks, in his effort at establishing the fact that each of the five lost lives was a perfect whole. Everyone knew that he was working on some sort of memorial of the accident and everyone was very helpful and misleading. A few even knew the principal aim of his activity and there were patrons in high places.

The result of all this diligence was an enormous book, which, as we shall see later, was publicly burned on a beautiful spring morning in the great square. But there was a secret copy and after a great many years and without much notice it found its way to the library of the University of San Marco.[4] There it lies between two great wooden covers collecting dust in a cupboard. It deals with one after another of the victims of the accident, cataloging thousands of little facts and anecdotes and testimonies, and concluding with a dignified passage describing why God had settled upon that person and upon that day for His demonstration of wisdom. Yet for all his diligence Brother Juniper never knew the central passion of

[1] **savants** (sə·vänts'): men of learning.

[2] **Tower of Babel** (bā'bəl): a Biblical reference (Genesis 11:4) to a tower which was intended to reach to heaven; any structure impossibly high.

[3] **Inquisition:** a tribunal established to stamp out heresy and punish those who questioned the teachings of the Church. The Spanish Inquisition, put under state control in 1480, conducted its proceedings with extreme severity.

[4] **University of San Marco:** a university in Lima.

Doña María's life, nor of Uncle Pío's, not even of Esteban's. And I, who claim to know so much more, isn't it possible that even I have missed the very spring within the spring?

Some say that we shall never know and that to the gods we are like the flies that the boys kill on a summer day, and some say, on the contrary, that the very sparrows do not lose a feather that has not been brushed away by the finger of God.

FOR STUDY AND DISCUSSION

1. What effect did the accident have on the people of Lima? Would you call their reactions selfish or unselfish? Why?

2. What did Brother Juniper set out to prove? Why was this accident such a good "laboratory" for scientific investigation? Why did he fail to find a convincing answer to his question?

3. Why does the narrator think he might succeed where Brother Juniper failed? What is he aware of that Brother Juniper was not? Why, as he admits, is it possible that he might fail too?

PART TWO

The Marquesa de Montemayor

ANY SPANISH schoolboy is required to know today more about Doña María, Marquesa de Montemayor,[1] than Brother Juniper was to discover in years of research. Within a century of her death her letters had become one of the monuments of Spanish literature and her life and times have ever since been the object of long studies. But her biographers have erred in one direction as greatly as the Franciscan did in another; they have tried to

[1] **Doña María, Marquesa de Montemayor** (dō'nyä mä·rē'ä mär·kä'sä dā mōn·tā·mī·yôr').

invest her with a host of graces, to read back into her life and person some of the beauties that abound in her letters, whereas all real knowledge of this wonderful woman must proceed from the act of humiliating her and of divesting her of all beauties save one.

She was the daughter of a cloth merchant who had acquired the money and the hatred of the Limeans within a stone's throw of the Plaza. Her childhood was unhappy: she was ugly; she stuttered; her mother persecuted her with sarcasms in an effort to arouse some social charms and forced her to go about the town in a veritable harness of jewels. She lived alone and she thought alone. Many suitors presented themselves, but as long as she could she fought against the convention of her time and was determined to remain single. There were hysterical scenes with her mother, recriminations, screams, and slamming of doors. At last at twenty-six she found herself penned into marriage with a supercilious and ruined nobleman, and the Cathedral of Lima fairly buzzed with the sneers of her guests. Still she lived alone and thought alone, and when an exquisite daughter was born to her she fastened upon her an idolatrous love. But little Clara took after her father; she was cold and intellectual. At the age of eight she was calmly correcting her mother's speech and presently regarding her with astonishment and repulsion. The frightened mother became meek and obsequious, but she could not prevent herself from persecuting Doña Clara with nervous attention and a fatiguing love. Again there were hysterical recriminations, screams, and slamming of doors. From the offers of marriage that fell to her, Doña Clara deliberately chose the one that required her removal to Spain. So to Spain she went, to that land from which it takes six months to receive an answer

to one's letter. The leavetaking before so long a voyage became in Peru one of the formal services of the Church. The ship was blessed and as the space widened between the vessel and the beach, both companies knelt and sang a hymn that never failed to sound weak and timid in all that open air. Doña Clara sailed with most admirable composure, leaving her mother to gaze after the bright ship, her hand pressing now her heart and now her mouth. Blurred and streaked became her view of the serene Pacific and the enormous clouds of pearl that hang forever motionless above it.

Left alone in Lima, the Marquesa's life grew more and more inward. She became increasingly negligent in her dress and like all lonely people she talked to herself audibly. All her existence lay in the burning center of her mind. On that stage were performed endless dialogues with her daughter, impossible reconciliations, scenes eternally recommenced of remorse and forgiveness. On the street you beheld an old woman, her red wig fallen a little over one ear, her left cheek angry with a leprous affection, her right with a complementary adjustment of rouge. Her chin was never dry; her lips were never still. Lima was a city of eccentrics, but even there she became its jest as she drove through the streets or shuffled up the steps of its churches. She was thought to be continuously drunk. Worse things were said of her and petitions were afloat that she be locked up. She had been denounced three times before the Inquisition. It is not impossible that she might have been burned had her son-in-law been less influential in Spain and had she not somehow collected a few friends about the viceregal court who suffered her for her oddity and her wide reading.

The distressing character of the relations between mother and daughter was further embittered by misunderstandings over money. The Condesa [1] received a handsome allowance from her mother and frequent gifts. Doña Clara soon became the outstanding woman of intelligence at the Spanish court. All the wealth of Peru would have been insufficient to maintain her in the grandiose style she fancied for herself. Strangely enough, her extravagance proceeded from one of the best traits in her nature: she regarded her friends, her servants, and all the interesting people in the capital, as her children. In fact there seemed only one person in the world toward whom she did not expend herself in kind offices. Among her protégés [2] was the cartographer De Blasiis (whose *Maps of the New World* was dedicated to the Marquesa de Montemayor amid the roars of the courtiers at Lima who read that she was the *"admiration of her city and a rising sun in the West")*; another was the scientist Azuarius, whose treatise on the laws of hydraulics was suppressed by the Inquisition as being too exciting. For a decade the Condesa literally sustained all the arts and sciences of Spain; it was not her fault that nothing memorable was produced in that time.

About four years after Doña Clara's departure, Doña María received her permission to visit Europe. On both sides the visit was anticipated with resolutions well nourished on self-reproach: the one to be patient, the other to be undemonstrative. Both failed. Each tortured the other and was on the point of losing her mind under the alternations of self-rebuke and the outbursts of passion. At length one day Doña María rose before dawn, daring no more than to kiss the door behind which her daughter was sleeping, took ship and

[1] **Condesa** (kōn·dä′sä): countess.
[2] **protégés** (prō′tə·zhāz): A protégé is one who is under the care or protection of another.

returned to America. Henceforth letter writing had to take the place of all the affection that could not be lived.

Hers were the letters that in an astonishing world have become the textbook of schoolboys and the anthill of the grammarians.[1] Doña María would have invented her genius had she not been born with it; so necessary was it to her love that she attract the attention, perhaps the admiration, of her distant child. She forced herself to go out into society in order to cull its ridicules; she taught her eye to observe; she read the masterpieces of her language to discover its effects; she insinuated herself into the company of those who were celebrated for their conversation. Night after night in her baroque [2] palace she wrote and rewrote the incredible pages, forcing from her despairing mind those miracles of wit and grace, those distilled chronicles of the viceregal court. We know now that her daughter barely glanced at the letters and that it is to the son-in-law that we owe their preservation.

The Marquesa would have been astonished to learn that her letters were immortal. Yet many critics have accused her of keeping one eye on posterity and point to a number of letters that have all the air of being bravura pieces.[3] To them it seems impossible that Doña María should have put herself to the same pains to dazzle her daughter that most artists expend on dazzling the public. Like her son-in-law they misunderstood her: the Conde [4] delighted in her letters, but he thought that when he had enjoyed the style, he had ex-

tracted all their richness and intention, missing (as most readers do) the whole purport of literature, which is the notation of the heart. Style is but the faintly contemptible vessel in which the bitter liquid is recommended to the world. The Marquesa would even have been astonished to learn that her letters were very good, for such authors live always in the noble weather of their own minds and those productions which seem remarkable to us are little better than a day's routine to them.

This was the old woman who hour by hour would sit upon her balcony, her odd straw hat casting a purple shadow across her lined and yellow face. How often as she turned her pages with her gemmed hands, she would ask herself, almost with amusement, whether the constant pain at her heart had an organic seat. She won-

[1] **grammarians:** specialists in grammar who are greatly concerned that rules be strictly followed.

[2] **baroque** (bə·rōk′): the style of art and architecture prevailing from the mid-sixteenth to the late eighteenth century and characterized by the use of curved and contorted forms.

[3] **bravura pieces:** dazzling displays of style.

[4] **Conde** (kōn′dä).

dered whether a subtle doctor cutting through to that battered throne could at last discover a sign and lifting his face to the amphitheater cry out to his students, "This woman has suffered, and her suffering has left its mark upon the structure of her heart." This idea had so often visited her that one day she wrote it into a letter and her daughter scolded her for an introspective and for making a cult of sorrow.

The knowledge that she would never be loved in return acted upon her ideas as a tide acts upon cliffs. Her religious beliefs went first, for all she could ask of a god, or of immortality, was the gift of a place where daughters love their mothers; the other attributes of Heaven you could have for a song. Next she lost her belief in the sincerity of those about her. She secretly refused to believe that anyone (herself excepted) loved anyone. All families lived in a wasteful atmosphere of custom and kissed one another with secret indifference. She saw that the people of this world moved about in an armor of egotism, drunk with self-gazing, athirst for compliments, hearing little of what was said to them, unmoved by the accidents that befell their closest friends, in dread of all appeals that might interrupt their long communion with their own desires. These were the sons and daughters of Adam from Cathay [1] to Peru. And when on the balcony her thoughts reached this turn, her mouth would contract with shame for she knew that she too sinned and that though her love for her daughter was vast enough to include all the colors of love, it was not without a shade of tyranny: she loved her daughter not for her daughter's sake, but for her own. She longed to free herself from this ignoble bond, but the passion was too fierce to

[1] **Cathay:** ancient name for China.

cope with. And then on that green balcony a strange warfare would shake the hideous old lady, a singularly futile struggle against a temptation to which she would never have the opportunity of succumbing. How could she rule her daughter when her daughter saw to it that four thousand miles lay between them? Nevertheless Doña María wrestled with the ghost of her temptation and was worsted on every occasion. She wanted her daughter for herself; she wanted to hear her say, "You are the best of all possible mothers"; she longed to hear her whisper, "Forgive me."

About two years after her return from Spain there took place a series of inconspicuous events that had a great deal to tell about the inner life of the Marquesa. Only the faintest allusion to them occurs in the Correspondence, but as that is found in Letter XXII which contains other signs, I shall do my best to give a translation and commentary of the first part of the letter:

"Are there no doctors in Spain? Where are those good men from Flanders that used to help you so? Oh, my treasure, how can we punish you enough for letting your cold endure so many weeks? Don Vicente, I implore you to make my child see reason. Angels of Heaven, I implore you to make my child see reason. Now that you are better, I beg of you, resolve that when the first warning of a cold comes you will steam yourself well and go to bed. Here in Peru I am helpless; I can do nothing. Do not be self-willed, my beloved. God bless you. I am enclosing in today's packet the gum of some tree which the sisters of San Tomás peddle from door to door. Whether it be of much use I know not. It can do no harm. I am told that in the convent the silly sisters inhale it so diligently that one cannot smell the incense at Mass. Whether it be worth anything I know not; try it.

"*Rest easy, my love, I am sending His Most Catholic Majesty the perfect gold chain.*" (Her daughter had written her: "*The chain arrived in good condition and I wore it at the christening of the Infante.[1] His Most Catholic Majesty was gracious enough to admire it and when I told Him that you had given it me He sent you His compliments upon your taste. Do not fail to send Him one as like it as possible; send it at once, by way of the Chamberlain.*") "*He need never know that in order to obtain it I had to walk into a picture. Do you remember that in the sacristy of San Martín there is a portrait by Velásquez[2] of the Viceroy who founded the monastery and of his wife and brat? and that his wife is wearing a gold chain? I resolved that only that chain would do. So one midnight I slipped into the sacristy, climbed upon the robing table like a girl of twelve, and walked in. The canvas resisted for a moment, but the painter himself came forward to lift me through the pigment. I told him that the most beautiful girl in Spain wished to present the finest gold chain that could be found to the most gracious king in the world. It was as simple as that, and there we stood talking, we four, in the gray and silvery air that makes a Velásquez. Now I keep thinking about a more golden light; I keep looking at the Palace: I must pass the evening in a Titian.[3] Would the Viceroy let me?*

"*But His Excellency has the gout[4] again. I say 'again' because the flattery of the court insists that there are times when he is free of it. This being Saint Mark's day, His Excellency started out* to visit the University where twenty-two new doctors were being brought into the world. He had hardly been carried from his divan to his coach when he screamed and refused to go any farther. He was carried back to his bed where he broke a most delicious cigar and sent for the Perichole.[5] And while we listened to long doctrinal addresses, more or less in Latin, he heard all about us, more or less in Spanish, from the reddest and cruelest lips in town.*" (Doña María permitted herself this passage, although she had just read in her daughter's last letter: "*How many times must I tell you to be more cautious in the things you say in your letters? They often show signs of having been opened on the journey. Nothing could be more ill-judged than your remarks on the you-know-what-I-mean at Cuzco. Such remarks are not funny, even though Vicente did compliment you upon them in his postscript, and they might get us into a great deal of trouble with Certain Persons here in Spain. I continue to be astonished that your indiscretions have not long since led to your being ordered to retire to your farm.*")

"*There was a great press at the Exercises and two women fell from the balcony, but God in His goodness saw that they fell on Doña Merced. All three are badly hurt, but will be thinking of other things within a year. The President was speaking at the moment of the accident and being shortsighted could not imagine what the disturbance of cries and talk and falling bodies could be about. It was very pleasant to see him bowing, under the impression that he was being applauded.*

"*Speaking of the Perichole, and of applause, you should know that Pepita and I decided to go to the Comedia this evening. The public still idolizes its Peri-*

[1] **Infante** (in·fan′tā): any son of a king of Spain or Portugal except the eldest.
[2] **Velásquez** (və·las′kwiz): Spanish painter (1599–1660).
[3] **Titian** (tish′ən): Italian painter (1477–1576).
[4] **gout:** a disease marked by painful swellings of the joints.

[5] **Perichole** (per·i·kōl′).

chole; it even forgives her her years. We are told that she saves what she can, every morning, by passing alternate pencils of ice and fire across her cheeks." (Translation falls especially short of this conceit [1] which carries the whole flamboyance [2] of the Spanish language. It was intended as an obsequious flattery of the Condesa, and was untrue. The great actress was twenty-eight at this time; her cheeks had the smoothness and polish of dark yellow marble and would certainly have retained that quality for many years. Apart from the cosmetics required by her performances, the only treatment Camila Perichole afforded her face was to throw cold water at it twice a day, like a peasant woman at a horse trough.) *"That curious man they call Uncle Pio is by her all the time. Don Rubío says that he cannot make out whether Uncle Pio is her father, her lover, or her son. The Perichole gave a wonderful performance. Scold me all you like for a provincial ninny, you have no such actresses in Spain."* And so on.

It is on this visit to the theater that further matter hangs. She decided to go to the Comedia where the Perichole was playing Doña Leonor in Moreto's *Trampa Adelante;* [3] perhaps some material could be derived from the visit for her daughter's next letter. She took with her Pepita, a little girl about whom later we shall learn much. Doña María had borrowed her from the orphanage connected with the Convent of Santa María Rosa de las Rosas to be her companion. The Marquesa sat in her box gazing with flagging attention at the brilliant stage. Between the acts it was the Perichole's custom to lay aside the courtly role and appear

[1] **conceit:** idea, conception.
[2] **flamboyance:** ornateness.
[3] **Moreto's Trampa Adelante:** *Deceitful Procrastination* by Moreto, Spanish dramatist (1618?–1669).

before the curtain to sing a few topical songs. The malicious actress had seen the Marquesa arrive and presently began improvising couplets alluding to her appearance, her avarice, her drunkenness, and even to her daughter's flight from her. The attention of the house was subtly directed to the old woman and a rising murmur of contempt accompanied the laughter of the audience. But the Marquesa, deeply moved by the first two acts of the comedy, scarcely saw the singer and sat staring before her, thinking about Spain. Camila Perichole became bolder and the air was electric with the hatred and glee of the crowd. At last Pepita plucked the Marquesa's sleeve and whispered to her that they should go. As they left the box the house arose and burst into a roar of triumph; the Perichole flung herself into a frenzied dance, for she saw the manager at the back of the hall and knew that her salary had been increased. But the Marquesa remained unaware of what had taken place; in fact she was quite pleased, for during the visit she had contrived a few felicitous phrases, phrases (who knows) that might bring a smile to her daughter's face and might make her murmur, "Really, my mother is charming."

In due time the report reached the Viceroy's ears that one of his aristocrats had been openly baited in the theater. He summoned the Perichole to the Palace and ordered her to call upon the Marquesa and to apologize. The trip was to be made barefoot and in a black dress. Camila argued and fought, but all she gained was a pair of shoes.

The Viceroy had three reasons for insisting. In the first place the singer had taken liberties with his court. Don Andrés had contrived to make exile endurable by building up a ceremonial so complicated that it could be remembered only by a society that had nothing else to think

about. He nursed his little aristocracy and its minute distinctions and any insult paid to a Marquesa was an insult to His Person. In the second place, Doña María's son-in-law was an increasingly important personage in Spain, laden with possibilities of injury to the Viceroy, nay with the possibility of supplanting him. The Conde Vicente d'Abuirre [1] must not be vexed, even through his half-wit mother-in-law. Finally, the Viceroy was delighted to humble the actress. He suspected that she was deceiving him with a matador,[2] perhaps with an actor—between the flattery of the court and the inertia of gout he could not quite make out who it was; at all events, it was clear that the singer was beginning to forget that he was one of the first men in the world.

The Marquesa, beside not having heard the scurrilous songs, was in other ways unprepared for the actress's visit. You should know that after the departure of her daughter, Doña María had lighted upon a certain consolation: she had taken to drinking. Everyone drank *chicha* [3] in Peru and there was no particular disgrace in being found unconscious on a feast day. Doña María had begun to discover that her feverish monologues had a way of keeping her awake all night. Once she took a delicate fluted glassful of *chicha* on retiring. Oblivion was so sweet that presently she stole larger amounts and tried dissimulating their effects from Pepita; she hinted that she was not well, and represented herself as going into a decline. At last she resigned all pretense. The boats that carried her letter to Spain did not leave oftener than once a month. During the week that preceded the making

of the packet she observed a strict regimen and cultivated the city assiduously for material. At last on the eve of the post she wrote the letter, making up the bundle toward dawn and leaving it for Pepita to deliver to the agent. Then as the sun rose she would shut herself up in her room with some flagons and drift through the next few weeks without the burden of consciousness. Finally she would emerge from her happiness and prepare to go into a state of "training" in preparation for the writing of another letter.

Thus on the night following the scandal in the theater, she wrote Letter XXII and retired to bed with a carafe. All next day Pepita moved about the room, glancing anxiously at the figure on the bed. The next afternoon Pepita brought her needlework into the room. The Marquesa lay staring at the ceiling with wide-open eyes, talking to herself. Toward dusk Pepita was called to the door and informed that the Perichole had come to see the mistress. Pepita remembered the theater very well and sent back word angrily that the mistress refused to see her. The man carried the message to the street door, but returned awe-struck with the news that the Señora Perichole was armed with a letter from the Viceroy presenting her to the lady. Pepita tiptoed to the bed-and started talking to the Marquesa. The glazed eyes moved to the girl's face. Pepita shook her

gently. With great effort Doña María tried to fix her mind on what was being said to her. Twice she lay back, refusing to seize the meaning, but at last, like a general calling together in a rain and by night the dispersed division of his army, she assembled memory and attention and a few other faculties and painfully pressing her hand to her forehead, she asked for a bowl of snow. When it was brought her, she long and drowsily pressed handfuls of it against her temples and cheeks; then rising, she stood for a long time leaning against the bed and looking at her shoes. At last she raised her head with decision, she called for her fur-trimmed cloak and a veil. She put them on and tottered into her handsomest reception room where the actress stood waiting for her.

Camila had intended to be perfunctory and if possible impudent, but now she was struck for the first time with the dignity of the old woman. The mercer's daughter could carry herself at times with all the distinction of the Montemayors and when she was drunk she wore the grandeur of Hecuba.[1] For Camila the half-closed eyes had the air of weary authority and she began almost timidly:

"I come, señora, to make sure that you could not have misunderstood anything I said on the evening that Your Grace did me the honor to visit my theater."

"Misunderstood? Misunderstood?" said the Marquesa.

"Your Grace might have misunderstood and thought that my words were intended to be disrespectful to Your Grace."

"To me?"

"Your Grace is not offended at her humble servant? Your Grace is aware that a poor actress in my position may be carried beyond her intentions . . . that it is very difficult . . . that everything. . . ."

"How can I be offended, señora? All that I can remember is that you gave a beautiful performance. You are a great artist. You should be happy, happy. My handkerchief, Pepita. . . ."

The Marquesa brought out these words very rapidly and vaguely, but the Perichole was confounded. A piercing sense of shame filled her. She turned crimson. At last she was able to murmur:

"It was in the songs between the acts of the comedy. I was afraid Your Grace. . . ."

"Yes, yes. I remember now. I left early. Pepita, we left early, did we not? But, señora, you are good enough to forgive my leaving early, yes, even in the middle of your admirable performance. I forget why we left. Pepita . . . oh, some indisposition. . . ."

It was impossible that anyone in the theater could have missed the intention of the songs. Camila could only assume that the Marquesa, out of a sort of fantastic magnanimity, was playing the farce of not having noticed it. She was almost in tears: "But you are so good to overlook my childishness, señora—I mean Your Grace. I did not know. I did not know your goodness. Señora, permit me to kiss your hand."

Doña María held out her hand, astonished. She had not for a long time been addressed with such consideration. Her neighbors, her tradespeople, her servants —for even Pepita lived in awe of her—her very daughter had never approached her thus. It induced a new mood in her, one that must very likely be called maudlin.[2] She became loquacious:

"Offended, offended at you, my beautiful . . . my gifted child? Who am I, a . . . an unwise and unloved old woman, to be offended at you? I felt, my daughter, as

[1] **Hecuba** (hek′yo͞o·bə): in Greek mythology, the wife of Priam, last king of Troy.

[2] **maudlin** (môd′lin): overly sentimental.

though I were—what says the poet?—*surprising through a cloud the conversation of the angels.* Your voice kept finding new wonders in our Moreto. When you said:

'*Don Juan, si mi amor estimas,*
Y la fe segura es necia,
Enojarte mis temores
Es no quererme discreta.
¿Tan seguros . . . ?' [1]

and so on—that was true! And what a gesture you made at the close of the First Day. There, with your hand *so*. Such a gesture as the Virgin made, saying to Gabriel, *How is it possible that I shall have a child?* No, no, you will begin to have resentment at me, for I am going to tell you about a gesture that you may remember to use someday. Yes, it would fit well into that scene where you forgive your Don Juan de Lara. Perhaps I should tell you that I saw it made one day by my daughter. My daughter is a very beautiful woman . . . everyone thinks. Did . . . did you know my Doña Clara, señora?"

"Her Grace often did me the honor of visiting my theater. I knew the Condesa well by sight."

"Do not remain so, on one knee, my child.—Pepita, tell Jenarito to bring this lady some sweet cakes at once. Think, one day we fell out, I forget over what. Oh, there is nothing strange in that; all we mothers from time to time. . . . Look, can you come a little closer? You must not believe the town that says she was unkind to me. You are a great woman with a beautiful nature and you can see further than the crowd sees in these matters.—It is a pleasure to talk to you. What beautiful hair you have! What beautiful hair!—She had not a warm impulsive nature, I know that. But, oh, my child, she has such a store of intelligence and graciousness. Any misunderstandings between us are so plainly my fault; is it not wonderful that she is so quick to forgive me? This day there fell one of those little moments. We both said hasty things and went off to our rooms. Then each turned back to be forgiven. Finally only a door separated us and there we were pulling it in contrary ways. But at last she . . . took my . . . face . . . thus, in her two white hands. So! Look!"

The Marquesa almost fell out of her chair as she leaned forward, her face streaming with happy tears, and made the beatific gesture. I should say the mythical gesture, for the incident was but a recurring dream.

"I am glad you are here," she continued, "for now you have heard from my own lips that she is not unkind to me, as some people say. Listen, señora, the fault was mine. Look at me. Look at me. There was some mistake that made me the mother of so beautiful a girl. I am difficult. I am trying. You and she are great women. No, do not stop me: you are rare women, and I am only a nervous . . . a foolish . . . a stupid woman. Let me kiss your feet. I am impossible. I am impossible. I am impossible."

Here indeed the old woman did fall out of her chair and was gathered up by Pepita and led back to her bed. The Perichole walked home in consternation and sat for a long time gazing into her eyes in the mirror, her palms pressed against her cheeks.

But the person who saw most of the difficult hours of the Marquesa was her little companion, Pepita. Pepita was an orphan and had been brought up by that strange genius of Lima, the Abbess Madre

[1] 'Don Juan, if you value my love,
And if blind faith is foolish,
The fact that my fears annoy you,
Means that you wish me less than wise.
So certain . . . ?'

María del Pilar. The only occasion upon which the two great women of Peru (as the perspective of history was to reveal them) met face to face was on the day when Doña María called upon the directress of the Convent of Santa María Rosa de las Rosas and asked if she might borrow some bright girl from the orphanage to be her companion. The Abbess gazed hard at the grotesque old woman. Even the wisest people in the world are not perfectly wise and Madre María del Pilar, who was able to divine the poor human heart behind all the masks of folly and defiance, had always refused to concede one to the Marquesa de Montemayor. She asked her a great many questions and then paused to think. She wanted to give Pepita the worldly experience of living in the palace. She also wanted to bend the old woman to her own interests. And she was filled with a somber indignation, for she knew she was gazing at one of the richest women in Peru, and the blindest.

She was one of those persons who have allowed their lives to be gnawed away because they have fallen in love with an idea several centuries before its appointed appearance in the history of civilization. She hurled herself against the obstinacy of her time in her desire to attach a little dignity to women. At midnight when she had finished adding up the accounts of the House, she would fall into insane vision of an age when women could be organized to protect women, women traveling, women as servants, women when they are old or ill, the women she had discovered in the mines of Potosí, or in the workrooms of the cloth merchants, the girls she had collected out of doorways on rainy nights. But always the next morning she had to face the fact that the women in Peru, even her nuns, went through life with two notions: one, that all the misfortunes that might befall them were merely due to the fact that they were not sufficiently attractive to bind some man to their maintenance, and two, that all the misery in the world was worth his caress. She had never known any country but the environs of Lima and she assumed that all its corruption was the normal state of mankind. Looking back from our century, we can see the whole folly of her hope. Twenty such women would have failed to make any impression on that age. Yet she continued diligently in her task. She resembled the swallow in the fable who once every thousand years transferred a grain of wheat, in the hope of rearing a mountain to reach the moon. Such persons are raised up in every age; they obstinately insist on transporting their grains of wheat and they derive a certain exhilaration from the sneers of the bystanders. "How queerly they dress!" we cry. "How queerly they dress!"

Her plain red face had great kindliness, and more idealism than kindliness, and more generalship than idealism. All her work, her hospitals, her orphanage, her convent, her sudden journeys of rescue, depended upon money. No one harbored a fairer admiration for mere goodness, but she had been obliged to watch herself sacrificing her kindliness, almost her idealism, to generalship, so dreadful were the struggles to obtain her subsidies from her superiors in the church. The Archbishop of Lima, whom we shall know later in a more graceful connection, hated her with what he called a Vatinian hate [1] and counted the cessation of her visits among the compensations for dying.

Lately she had felt not only the breath of old age against her cheek, but a graver warning. A chill of terror went through her, not for herself, but for her work. Who

[1] **Vatinian hate:** dislike like that of Vatinius, an unpopular Roman who hated people for no particular reason.

was there in Peru to value the things she had valued? And rising one day at dawn, she had made a rapid journey through her hospital and convent and orphanage, looking for a soul she might train to be her successor. She hurried from empty face to empty face, occasionally pausing more from hope than conviction. In the courtyard she came upon a company of girls at work over the linen and her eyes fell at once upon a girl of twelve who was directing the others at the trough and at the same time recounting to them with great dramatic fire the less probable miracles in the life of Saint Rose of Lima. So it was that the search ended with Pepita. The education for greatness is difficult enough at any time, but amid the sensibilities and jealousies of a convent it must be conducted with fantastic indirection. Pepita was assigned to the most disliked tasks in the House, but she came to understand all the aspects of its administration. She accompanied the Abbess on her journeys, even though it was in the capacity of custodian of the eggs and vegetables. And everywhere, by surprise, hours would open up in which the directress suddenly appeared and talked to her at great length, not only on religious experience, but on how to manage women and how to plan contagious wards and how to beg for money. It was a step in this education for greatness that led to Pepita's arriving one day and entering upon the crazy duties of being Doña María's companion. For the first two years she merely came for occasional afternoons, but finally she came to the palace to live. She never had been taught to expect happiness, and the inconveniences, not to say terrors, of her new position did not seem to her excessive for a girl of fourteen. She did not suspect that the Abbess, even there, was hovering above the house, herself estimating the stresses and watching for the

moment when a burden harms and not strengthens.

A few of Pepita's trials were physical: for example, the servants in the house took advantage of Doña María's indisposition; they opened up the bedrooms of the palace to their relatives; they stole freely. Alone Pepita stood out against them and suffered a persecution of small discomforts and practical jokes. Her mind, similarly, had its distresses: when she accompanied Doña María on her errands in the city, the older woman would be seized with the desire to dash into a church, for what she had lost of religion as faith she had replaced with religion as magic. "Stay here in the sunlight, my dear child; I shall not be long," she would say. Doña María would then forget herself in a reverie before the altar and leave the church by another door. Pepita had been brought up by Madre María del Pilar to an almost morbid obedience and when after many hours she ventured into the church and made sure that her mistress was no longer there, still she returned to the street corner and waited while the shadows fell gradually across the square. Thus waiting in public, she suffered all the torture of a little girl's self-consciousness. She still wore the uniform of the orphanage (which a minute's thoughtfulness on the part of Doña María could have altered) and she suffered hallucinations wherein men seemed to be staring at her and whispering—nor were these always hallucinations. No less her heart suffered, for on some days Doña María would suddenly become aware of her and would talk to her cordially and humorously, would let appear for a few hours all the exquisite sensibility of the Letters; then, on the morrow she would withdraw into herself again and, while never harsh, would become impersonal and unseeing. The beginnings of hope and affection that Pepita

had such need to expend would be wounded. She tiptoed about the palace, silent, bewildered, clinging only to her sense of duty and her loyalty to her "mother in the Lord," Madre María del Pilar, who had sent her there.

Finally a new fact appeared that was to have considerable effect on the lives of both the Marquesa and her companion: *"My dear mother,"* wrote the Condesa, *"the weather has been most exhausting and the fact that the orchards and gardens are in bloom only makes it the more trying. I could endure flowers if only they had no perfume. I shall therefore ask your permission to write you at less length than usual. If Vicente returns before the post leaves he will be delighted to finish out the leaf and supply you with those tiresome details about myself which you seem to enjoy so. I shall not go to Grignan in Provence [1] as I expected this Fall, as my child will be born in early October."*

What child? The Marquesa leaned against the wall. Doña Clara had foreseen the exhausting importunities [2] that this news would waken in her mother and had sought to mitigate them by the casualness of her announcement. The ruse did not succeed. The famous Letter XLII was the answer.

Now at length the Marquesa had something to be anxious about: her daughter was to become a mother. This event, which merely bored Doña Clara, discovered a whole new scale of emotions in the Marquesa. She became a mine of medical knowledge and suggestion. She combed the city for wise old women and poured into her letters the whole folk wisdom of the New World. She fell into

the most abominable superstition. She practiced a degrading system of taboos for her child's protection. She refused to allow a knot in the house. The maids were forbidden to tie up their hair and she concealed upon her person ridiculous symbols of a happy delivery. On the stairs the even steps were marked with red chalk and a maid who accidentally stepped upon an even step was driven from the house with tears and screams. Doña Clara was in the hands of malignant Nature who reserves the right to inflict upon her children the most terrifying jests. There was an etiquette of propitiation [3] which generations of peasant women had found comforting. So vast an army of witnesses surely implied that there was some truth in it. At least it could do no harm, and perhaps it did good. But the Marquesa did not only satisfy the rites of paganism; she studied the prescriptions of Christianity as well. She arose in the dark and stumbled through the streets to the earliest Masses. She hysterically hugged the altar rails, trying to rend from the gaudy statuettes a sign, only a sign, the ghost of a smile, the furtive nod of a waxen head. Would all be well? Sweet, sweet Mother, would all be well?

At times, after a day's frantic resort to such invocations, a revulsion would sweep over her. Nature is deaf. God is indifferent. Nothing in man's power can alter the course of law. Then on some street corner she would stop, dizzy with despair, and leaning against a wall, would long to be taken from a world that had no plan in it. But soon a belief in the great Perhaps would surge up from the depths of her nature and she would fairly run home to renew the candles above her daughter's bed.

At last the time came to satisfy the su-

[1] **Provence** (prô·väṅs'): region bordering on the Mediterranean in southeastern France.

[2] **importunities** (im'pôr·tōō'nə·tēz): continuous requests or demands.

[3] **propitiation:** appeasement, attempting to win the favor of the gods.

preme rite of Peruvian households look-
ing forward to this event: she made the
pilgrimage to the shrine of Santa María de
Cluxambuqua.[1] If there resided any effi-
cacy in devotion at all, surely it lay in a
visit to this great shrine. The ground had
been holy through three religions; even
before the Incan civilization, distraught
human beings had hugged the rocks and
lashed themselves with whips to wring
their will from the skies. Thither the
Marquesa was carried in her chair, cross-
ing the bridge of San Luis Rey and as-
cending up into the hills toward that city
of large-girdled women; a tranquil town,
slow-moving and slow-smiling; a city of
crystal air, cold as the springs that fed its
many fountains; a city of bells, soft and
musical, and tuned to carry on with one
another the happiest quarrels. If anything
turned out for disappointment in the town
of Cluxambuqua, the grief was somehow
assimilated by the overwhelming imma-
nence of the Andes and by the weather of
quiet joy that flowed in and about the side
streets. No sooner did the Marquesa see
from a distance the white walls of this
town perched on the knees of the highest
peaks than her fingers ceased turning the
beads and the busy prayers of her fright
were cut short on her lips.

She did not even alight at the inn, but
leaving Pepita to arrange for their stay,
she went on to the church and knelt for a
long time patting her hands softly together.
She was listening to the new tide of resig-
nation that was rising within her. Perhaps
she would learn in time to permit both her
daughter and her gods to govern their own
affairs. She was not annoyed by the
whispering of the old women in padded
garments who sold candles and medals
and talked about money from dawn to
dark. She was not even distracted by an

officious sacristan who tried to collect a
fee for something or other and who, from
spite, made her change her place under the
pretext of repairing a tile on the floor.
Presently she went out into the sunshine
and sat on the steps of the fountain. She
watched the little processions of invalids
slowly revolving about the gardens. She
watched three hawks plunging about the
sky. The children who had been playing
by the fountain stared at her for a moment
and went away alarmed, but a llama [2] (a
lady with a long neck and sweet shallow
eyes, burdened down by a fur cape too
heavy for her and picking her way deli-
cately down an interminable staircase)
came over and offered her a velvet cleft
nose to stroke. The llama is deeply in-
terested in the men about her, is even fond
of pretending that she too is one of them
and of inserting her head into their con-
versations as though in a moment she
would lift her voice and contribute a wan
and helpful comment. Soon Doña María

[1] **de Cluxambuqua** (dā clōōk·säm·bōō′kwä).

[2] **llama** (lä′mə): a camel-like, humpless animal
sometimes used as a beast of burden in the Andes.

was surrounded by a number of these sisters who seemed on the point of asking her why she clapped her hands so and how much her veiling cost a yard.

Doña María had arranged that any letters arriving from Spain should be brought to her at once by a special messenger. She had traveled slowly from Lima and even now as she sat in the square, a boy from her farm ran up and put into her hand a large packet wrapped in parchment and dangling some nuggets of sealing wax. Slowly she undid the wrappings. With measured stoic gestures she read first an affectionate and jocose note from her son-in-law; then her daughter's letter. It was full of wounding remarks rather brilliantly said, perhaps said for the sheer virtuosity [1] of giving pain neatly. Each of its phrases found its way through the eyes of the Marquesa, then, carefully wrapped in understanding and forgiveness, it sank into her heart. At last she arose, gently dispersed the sympathetic llamas, and with a grave face returned to the shrine.

While Doña María was passing the late afternoon in the church and in the square, Pepita was left to prepare their lodging. She showed the porters where to lay down the great wicker hampers and set about unpacking the altar, the brazier, [2] the tapestries, and the portraits of Doña Clara. She descended into the kitchen and gave the cook exact instructions as to the preparations of a certain porridge upon which the Marquesa principally subsisted. Then she returned to the rooms and waited. She resolved to write a letter to the Abbess. She hung for a long time over the quill, staring into the distance with trembling lip. She saw the face of Madre María del Pilar, so red and scrubbed, and the

wonderful black eyes. She heard her voice as at the close of supper (the orphans sitting with lowered eyes and folded hands) she commented on the events of the day or as, by candlelight, she stood among the beds of the hospital and announced the theme for meditation during the night. But most clearly of all Pepita remembered the sudden interviews when the Abbess (not daring to wait until the girl was older) had discussed with her the duties of her office. She had talked to Pepita as to an equal. Such speech is troubling and wonderful to an intelligent child and Madre María del Pilar had abused it. She had expanded Pepita's vision of how she should feel and act beyond the measure of her years. And she had unthinkingly turned upon Pepita the full blaze of her personality, as Jupiter had turned his upon Semele. [3] Pepita was frightened by her sense of insufficiency; she hid it and wept. And then the Abbess had cast the child into the discipline of this long solitude, where Pepita struggled, refusing to let herself believe that she had been abandoned. And now from this strange inn in these strange mountains, where the altitude was making her lightheaded, Pepita longed for the dear presence, the only real thing in her life.

She wrote a letter, all ink stains and incoherence. Then she went downstairs to see about fresh charcoal and to taste the porridge.

The Marquesa came in and sat down at the table. "I can do no more. What will be, will be," she whispered. She unbound from her neck the amulets of her superstition and dropped them into the glowing brazier. She had a strange sense of having antagonized God by too much prayer and so addressed Him now obliquely. "After

[1] **virtuosity:** great technical skill.
[2] **brazier** (brā′zhər): a pan for holding burning coals.

[3] **Semele** (sĕm′ə·lē): a Theban princess, who, according to legend, met her death when she looked upon Jupiter in his full glory as King of the Gods.

all it is in the hands of another. I no longer claim the least influence. What will be, will be." She sat for a long time, her palms against her cheeks, making a blank of her mind. Her eyes fell on Pepita's letter. She opened it mechanically and started to read. She had read a full half of it before her attention was aware of the meaning of the words: "... *but all this is nothing if you like me and wish me to stay with her. I oughtn't to tell you but every now and then the bad chambermaids lock me up in rooms and steal things and perhaps My Lady will think that I steal them. I hope not. I hope you are well and not having any trouble in the hospital or anywhere. Though I never see you I think of you all the time and I remember what you told me, my dear mother in God. I want to do only what you want, but if you could let me come back for a few days to the convent, but not if you do not wish it. But I am so much alone and not talking to anyone, and everything. Sometimes I do not know whether you have forgotten me and if you could find a minute to write me a little letter or something, I could keep it, but I know how busy you are. . . ."*

Doña María read no further. She folded the letter and put it aside. For a moment she was filled with envy: she longed to command another's soul as completely as this nun was able to do. Most of all she longed to be back in this simplicity of love, to throw off the burden of pride and vanity that hers had always carried. To quiet the tumult in her mind she picked up a book of devotion and tried to fix her attention upon the words. But after a moment she suddenly felt the need to reread the whole letter, to surprise, if possible, the secret of so much felicity.

Pepita returned bringing the supper in her hands, followed by a maid. Doña María watched her over the top of her book as she would have watched a visitor

from Heaven. Pepita tiptoed about the room, laying the table and whispering directions to her assistant.

"Your supper is ready, My Lady," she said at last.

"But, my child, you are going to eat with me?" In Lima, Pepita generally sat down at the table with her mistress.

"I thought you would be tired, My Lady. I had my supper downstairs."

"She does not wish to eat with me," thought the Marquesa. "She knows me and has rejected me."

"Would you like me to read aloud to you while you are eating, My Lady?" asked Pepita, who felt that she had made a mistake.

"No. You may go to bed, if you choose."

"Thank you, My Lady."

Doña María had risen and approached the table. With one hand on the back of the chair she said haltingly, "My dear child, I am sending off a letter to Lima in the morning. If you have one you can enclose it with mine."

"No, I have none," said Pepita. She added hastily, "I must go downstairs and get you the new charcoal."

"But, my dear, you have one for . . . Madre María del Pilar. Wouldn't you . . . ?"

Pepita pretended to be busy over the brazier. "No, I'm not going to send it," she said. She was aware during the long pause that followed that the Marquesa was staring at her in stupefaction. "I've changed my mind."

"I know she would like a letter from you, Pepita. It would make her very happy. I know."

Pepita was reddening. She said loudly, "The innkeeper said that there would be some new charcoal ready for you at dark. I'll tell them to bring it up now." She glanced hastily at the old woman and saw that she had not ceased from staring at

her with great, sad, inquiring eyes. Pepita felt that these were not things one talked about, but the strange woman seemed to be feeling the matter so strongly that Pepita was willing to concede one more answer: "No, it was a bad letter. It wasn't a good letter."

Doña María fairly gasped. "Why, my dear Pepita, I think it was very beautiful. Believe me, I know. No, no; what could have made it a bad letter?"

Pepita frowned, hunting for a word that would close the matter.

"It wasn't . . . it wasn't . . . brave," she said. And then she would say no more. She carried the letter off into her own room and could be heard tearing it up. Then she got into bed and lay staring into the darkness, still uncomfortable at having talked in such a fashion. And Doña María sat down to her dish amazed.

She had never brought courage to either life or love. Her eyes ransacked her heart. She thought of the amulets and of her beads, her drunkenness . . . she thought of her daughter. She remembered the long relationship, crowded with the wreckage of exhumed conversations, of fancied slights, of inopportune confidences, of charges of neglect and exclusion (but she must have been mad that day; she remembered beating upon the table). "But it's not my fault," she cried. "It's not my fault that I was so. It was circumstance. It was the way I was brought up. Tomorrow I begin a new life. Wait and see, oh my child." At last she cleared away the table and sitting down, wrote what she called her first letter, her first stumbling misspelled letter in courage. She remembered with shame that in the previous one she had piteously asked her daughter how much she loved her and had greedily quoted the few and hesitant endearments that Doña Clara had lately ventured to her. Doña María could not recall those

pages, but she could write some new ones, free and generous. No one else has regarded them as stumbling. It is the famous letter LVI, known to the Encyclopedists as her First Corinthians [1] because of its immortal paragraph about love: "Of the thousands of persons we meet in a lifetime, my child . . ." and so on. It was almost dawn when she finished the letter. She opened the door upon her balcony and looked at the great tiers of stars that glittered above the Andes. Throughout the hours of the night, though there had been few to hear it, the whole sky had been loud with the singing of these constellations. Then she took a candle into the next room and looked at Pepita as she slept, and pushed back the damp hair from the girl's face. "Let me live now," she whispered. "Let me begin again."

Two days later they started back to Lima, and while crossing the bridge of San Luis Rey the accident which we know befell them.

[1] **First Corinthians:** in the Bible, the first epistle of Paul the apostle to the people of Corinth, a letter famous for its teachings on love and charity.

FOR STUDY AND DISCUSSION

1. How was the Marquesa treated as a child? What effect did this have on her later life? on the life of her child?

2. What happened to the Marquesa when Doña Clara went to Spain? How did she change? What was her attitude toward her own suffering? toward the sincerity and suffering of others?

3. When did the Marquesa begin her letter writing? Why were her letters so remarkable? What did her son-in-law appreciate about them? What about them does the author appreciate? Why is Doña Clara's barely glancing at the letters ironic, in view of her generosity at court? Why was she blind to the merits of her mother's letters?

4. Why did the Perichole make fun of the Marquesa in the theater? Why did the audi-

ence laugh so gleefully? Why was the Marquesa unaware of the insults? Why was she pleased as she left the theater?

5. Why did the Viceroy force the Perichole to apologize to the Marquesa? When she does apologize, what misunderstanding broke down the barriers between them? What effect did this have on the Marquesa? What effect did it have on the Perichole?

6. What kind of person is the Abbess? In what ways is she the opposite of the Marquesa? Why does she send Pepita to live with the Marquesa?

7. Do you think Pepita would have been a good successor to the Abbess? Why or why not? What trials did she undergo? What did the Abbess give her? What did she not give her?

8. Why did the Marquesa cross the bridge to the shrine? Why did Pepita's letter stir her so deeply? What lesson about love did she learn from Pepita?

PART THREE

Esteban

ONE MORNING twin boys were discovered in the foundlings' basket before the door of the Convent of Santa María Rosa del las Rosas. Names were found for them almost before the arrival of the wet nurse, but the names were not as useful to them as our names are to most of us, for no one ever succeeded in telling the boys apart. There was no way of knowing who their parents were, but Limean gossips, noticing as the boys grew older how straight they held themselves and how silent and somber they were, declared them to be Castilian and laid them in turn at all sorts of crested doorways.[1] The person in the

world who came nearest to being their guardian was the Abbess of the Convent. Madre María del Pilar had come to hate all men, but she grew fond of Manuel and Esteban. In the late afternoon she would call them into her office, send for some cakes from the kitchen, and tell them stories about the Cid [2] and Judas Maccabeus [3] and the thirty-six misfortunes of Harlequin.[4] She grew to love them so that she would catch herself gazing deep into their black and frowning eyes, looking for those traits that would appear when they grew to be men, all that ugliness, all that soullessness that made hideous the world she worked in. They grew up about the convent until they were a little past the age when their presence began to be a slight distraction to the dedicated sisters. From thence they became vaguely attached to all the sacristies in town: they trimmed all the cloister hedges; they polished every possible crucifix; they passed a damp cloth once a year over most of the ecclesiastical ceilings. All Lima knew them well. When the priest rushed through

[1] **crested doorways:** doorways of the nobility, which bore the crests or emblems of Castilian aristocracy.

[2] **Cid** (sid): a title of Rodrigo Díaz de Bivar, an eleventh-century champion of Christianity.

[3] **Judas Maccabeus:** a Jewish patriot.

[4] **Harlequin:** a character in comedy and pantomime.

the streets carrying his precious burden into a sickroom, either Esteban or Manuel was to be seen striding behind him, swinging a censer.[1] As they grew older, however, they showed no desire for the clerical life. They gradually assumed the profession of the scribe. There were few printing presses in the New World and the boys soon made a fair living transcribing comedies for the theater, ballads for the crowds, and advertisements for the merchants. Above all they were the copyists of the choirmasters and made endless parts of the motets[2] of Morales and Vittoria.

Because they had no family, because they were twins, and because they were brought up by women, they were silent. There was in them a curious shame in regard to their resemblance. They had to live in a world where it was the subject of continual comment and joking. It was never funny to them and they suffered the eternal pleasantries with stolid patience. From the years when they first learned to speak they invented a secret language for themselves, one that was scarcely dependent on the Spanish for its vocabulary, or even for its syntax. They resorted to it only when they were alone or at great intervals in moments of stress whispered it in the presence of others. The Archbishop of Lima was something of a philologist;[3] he dabbled in dialects; he had even evolved quite a brilliant table for the vowel and consonant changes from Latin into Spanish and from Spanish into Indian-Spanish. He was storing up notebooks of quaint lore against an amusing old age he planned to offer himself back on his estates outside Segovia.[4] So when

he heard one day about the secret language of the twin brothers, he trimmed some quills and sent for them. The boys stood humiliated upon the rich carpets of his study while he tried to extract from them their *bread* and *tree* and their *I see* and *I saw*. They did not know why the experience was so horrible to them. They bled. Long, shocked silences followed each of the Archbishop's questions, until finally one or the other mumbled an answer. The priest thought for a while that they were merely in awe before his rank and before the luxury of his apartment, but at last, much perplexed, he divined the presence of some deeper reluctance and sadly let them go.

This language was the symbol of their profound identity with one another, for just as resignation was a word insufficient to describe the spiritual change that came over the Marquesa de Montemayor on that night in the inn at Cluxambuqua, so *love* is inadequate to describe the tacit almost ashamed oneness of these brothers. What relationship is it in which few words are exchanged, and those only about the details of food, clothing, and occupation; in which the two persons have a curious reluctance even to glance at one another; and in which there is a tacit arrangement not to appear together in the city, and to go on the same errand by different streets? And yet side by side with this there existed a need of one another so terrible that it produced miracles as naturally as the charged air of a sultry day produces lightning. The brothers were scarcely aware of it themselves, but telepathy was a common occurrence in their lives, and when one returned home the other was always aware of it when his brother was still several streets away.

Suddenly they discovered that they were tired of writing. They went down to the sea and found an occupation in loading

[1] **censer:** a vessel for burning incense.
[2] **motets** (mō·tets'): choral compositions on a sacred text.
[3] **philologist:** a student of languages.
[4] **Segovia:** a city in Spain.

and unloading vessels, not ashamed of working side by side with Indians. They drove teams across the provinces. They picked fruit. They were ferrymen. And always they were silent. Their somber faces took on from these labors a male and gypsy cast. Their hair was seldom cut and under the dark mat their eyes looked up suddenly surprised and a little sullen. All the world was remote and strange and hostile except one's brother.

But at last the first shadow fell across this unity and the shadow was cast by the love of women. They had returned to the city and resumed the copying of parts for the theater. One night the manager, foreseeing a thinning house, gave them a free admission. The boys did not like what they found there. Even speech was for them a debased form of silence; how much more futile is poetry which is a debased form of speech. All those allusions to honor, reputation, and the flame of love, all the metaphors about birds, Achilles, and the jewels of Ceylon were fatiguing. In the presence of literature they had the same darkling intelligence that stirs for a time behind the eyes of a dog, but they sat on patiently, gazing at the bright candles and the rich clothes. Between the acts of the comedy the Perichole stepped out of her role, put on twelve petticoats, and danced before the curtain. Esteban had some copying still to do, or pretended so, and went home early; but Manuel stayed on. The red stockings and shoes of the Perichole had made their impression.

Both brothers had fetched and carried their manuscripts up and down the dusty stairs behind the stage. There they had seen an irritable girl in a soiled bodice mending her stockings before a mirror while her stage director read aloud her lines for memorization. She had let fall upon the boys for a moment the detonation of her amazing eyes, immediately dissipated in her amused recognition that they were twins. Forthwith she had dragged them into the room and placed them side by side. Carefully, amusedly, and remorselessly she had peered into every square inch of their faces, until finally, laying one hand on Esteban's shoulder, she had cried out, "This one is the younger!" That had been several years before and neither brother had thought of the episode again.

Henceforth all Manuel's errands seemed to lead him past the theater. Late at night he would drift about among the trees beneath her dressing room window. It was not the first time that Manuel had been fascinated by a woman, but it was the first time that his will and imagination had been thus overwhelmed. He had lost that privilege of simple nature, the dissociation of love and pleasure. Pleasure was no longer as simple as eating; it was being complicated by love. Now was beginning that crazy loss of one's self, that neglect of everything but one's dramatic thoughts about the beloved, that feverish inner life all turning upon the Perichole and which would so have astonished and disgusted her had she been permitted to divine it. This Manuel had not fallen in love through any imitation of literature. It was not of him, at all events, that the bitterest tongue in France [1] had remarked only fifty years before: that many people would never have fallen in love if they had not heard about it. Manuel read little; he had only been once to the theater (where above all there reigns the legend that love is a devotion), and the Peruvian tavern songs that he might have heard, unlike those of Spain, reflected very little of the romantic cult of an idealized woman. When he said over to himself that she was

[1] **the bitterest . . . France:** a reference to La Rochefoucauld (la rôsh·foo·kō′) (1613–1680), a satirical French writer.

beautiful and rich and fatiguingly witty and the Viceroy's mistress, none of these attributes that made her less obtainable had the power to quench his curious and tender excitement. So he leaned against the trees in the dark, his knuckles between his teeth, and listened to his loud heart-beats.

But the life that Esteban was leading had been full enough for him. There was no room in his imagination for a new loyalty, not because his heart was less large than Manuel's, but because it was of a simpler texture. Now he discovered that secret from which one never quite recovers, that even in the most perfect love one person loves less profoundly than the other. There may be two equally good, equally gifted, equally beautiful, but there may never be two that love one another equally well. So Esteban sat up in their room by a guttering candle, his knuckles between his teeth, and wondered why Manuel was so changed and why the whole meaning had gone out of their life.

One evening Manuel was stopped on the street by a small boy who announced to him that the Perichole wished him to call upon her at once. Manuel turned in his path and went to the theater. Straight, somber, and impersonal, he entered the actress's room and stood waiting. Camila had a service to ask of Manuel, and she thought a few preliminary blandishments were necessary, but she scarcely paused in combing a blond wig that was dressed upon the table before her.

"You write letters for people, don't you? I want you to write a letter for me, please. Please come in."

He came forward two steps.

"You never pay me the least visit either of you. That's not Spanish of you" (meaning "courteous"). "Which are you, Manuel or Esteban?"

"Manuel."

"It doesn't matter. You are both unfriendly. Neither of you ever comes to see me. Here I sit learning stupid lines all day and no one ever comes to see me but a lot of peddlers. It is because I am an actress, no?"

This was not very artful, but for Manuel it was unspeakably complicated. He merely stared at her from the shadows of his long hair and left her to improvise.

"I am going to engage you to write a letter for me, a very secret letter. But now I can see that you don't like me and that to ask you to write a letter would be as good as reading it aloud in all the wineshops. What does that look mean, Manuel? Are you my friend?"

"Yes, señora."

"Go away. Send me Esteban. You do not even say *Yes, señora* as a friend would say it."

Long pause. Presently she raised her head: "Are you still there, Unfriendly?"

"Yes, señora . . . you can trust me to do anything for you . . . you can trust . . ."

"If I ask you to write one letter for me, or two letters, you promise never to mention to a human being what is in them, or even that you wrote them?"

"Yes, señora."

"What do you promise by?—by the Virgin Mary?"

"Yes, señora."

"And by the heart of Saint Rose of Lima?"

"Yes, señora."

"Name of the Name, Manuel, anyone would think you were stupid as an ox. Manuel, I am very angry with you. You are not stupid. You don't look stupid. Please don't say just *Yes, señora* again. Don't be stupid or I'll send for Esteban. Is anything the matter with you?"

Here Manuel cast himself upon the Spanish language and exclaimed with unnecessary vigor, "I swear by the Virgin

Mary and the heart of Saint Rose of Lima that all that has to do with the letter will be secret."

"Even from Esteban," prompted the Perichole.

"Even from Esteban."

"Well, that's better." She motioned him to sit down at a table where writing materials were already laid out. As she dictated, she strode about the room, frowning, swinging her hips. With her arms akimbo, she hugged her shawl about her shoulders defiantly.

"*Camila Perichole kisses the hands of Your Excellency and says*—No, take another piece of paper and begin again. *The señora Micaela Villegas,*[1] *artist, kisses the hands of Your Excellency and says that, being the victim of the envious and lying friends that Y.E.'s goodness permits about him, she can no longer endure Y.E.'s suspicions and jealousy. Y.E.'s servant has always valued Y.E.'s friendship and has never committed, nor even thought, an offense against it, but she can no longer fight against the calumnies*[2] *that Y.E. believes so readily. Señora Villegas, artist, called the Perichole, therefore returns herewith such of Y.E.'s gifts as have not been placed beyond recall, since without Y.E.'s confidence, Y.E.'s servant can take no pleasure in them.*"

[1] **Micaela Villegas** (mē·kä·ä′lə vēl·yä′gäs).
[2] **calumnies** (kal′əm·nēz): slanders.

Camila continued walking about the room for several minutes, consumed by her thoughts. Presently, without so much as glancing at her secretary, she commanded, "Take another leaf. *Have you gone mad? Do not ever think of dedicating another bull to me again. It has caused a frightful war. Heaven protect you, my colt. Friday night, the same place, the same time. I may be a little late, for the fox is wide-awake.* That will be all."

Manuel rose.

"You swear that you have made no errors?"

"Yes, I swear."

"There is your money."

Manuel took the money.

"I shall want you to write me more letters from time to time. My uncle Pio generally writes my letters; these I do not wish him to know about. Good night. Go with God."

"Go with God."

Manuel descended the stairs and stood for a long time among the trees, not thinking, not moving.

Esteban knew that his brother was continually brooding over the Perichole, but he never suspected that he saw her. From time to time during the next two months, a small boy would approach him in great haste and ask whether he were Manuel or Esteban, and being informed that he was only Esteban, the boy would add that

Manuel was wanted at the theater. Esteban assumed that the call was for copyist's work and was therefore utterly unprepared for a visit that they received one night in their room.

It was almost midnight. Esteban had gone to bed and lay gazing out from under the blanket at the candle beside which his brother was working. There was a light tap at the door and Manuel opened to admit a lady heavily veiled, out of breath, and nervous. She threw back the scarf from her face and said hurriedly:

"Quick, ink and paper. You are Manuel, yes? You must do a letter for me at once."

For a moment her glance fell on the two bright eyes that glared at her from the edge of the cot. She murmured, "Eu . . . you must excuse me. I know it is late. It was necessary . . . I must come." Then turning to Manuel, she whispered into his ear: "Write this, *I, the Perichole, am not accustomed to wait at a rendezvous.* Have you finished that? *You are only a cholo,*[1] *and there are better matadors than you, even in Lima. I am half Castilian and there are no better actresses in the world. You shall not have the opportunity*—Have you got that?—*to keep me waiting again, cholo, and I shall laugh the last, for even an actress does not grow old as fast as a bullfighter.*"

To Esteban in the shadows the picture of Camila leaning over his brother's hand and whispering into his ear was complete evidence that a new congeniality had formed such as he would never know. He seemed to shrink away into space, infinitely tiny, infinitely unwanted. He took one more glance at the tableau of love, all the paradise from which he was shut out, and turned his face to the wall.

Camila seized the note the moment it

[1] **cholo** (chō′lō): half-breed.

was done, pushed a coin along the table, and in a last flurry of black lace, scarlet beads, and excited whispers left the room. Manuel turned from the door with his candle. He sat down, put his hands over his ears, his elbows on his knees. He worshiped her. He murmured to himself over and over again that he worshiped her, making of the sound a sort of incantation and an obstacle to thought.

He emptied his mind of everything but a singsong, and it was this vacancy that permitted him to become aware of Esteban's mood. He seemed to hear a voice that proceeded from the shadows saying, "Go and follow her, Manuel. Don't stay here. You'll be happy. There's room for us all in the world." Then the realization became even more intense and he received a mental image of Esteban going a long way off and saying good-by many times as he went. He was filled with terror; by the light of it he saw that all the other attachments in the world were shadows, or the illusions of fever, even Madre María del Pilar, even the Perichole. He could not understand why Esteban's misery should present itself as demanding a choice between him and the Perichole, but he could understand Esteban's misery as misery. And at once he sacrificed everything to it, if it can be said we ever sacrifice anything save what we know we can never attain, or what some secret wisdom tells us it would be uncomfortable or saddening to possess. To be sure, there was nothing on which Esteban could base a complaint. It was not jealousy, for in their earlier affairs it had never occurred to either of them that their loyalty to one another had been diminished. It was merely that in the heart of one of them there was left room for an elaborate imaginative attachment and in the heart of the other there was not. Manuel could not quite understand this and, as we shall see, he nourished a dim

sense of being accused unjustly. But he did understand that Esteban was suffering. In his excitement he groped for a means of holding this brother who seemed to be receding into the distance. And at once, in one unhesitating stroke of the will, he removed the Perichole from his heart.

He blew out the candle and lay down on his bed. He was trembling. He said aloud, with exaggerated casualness, "Well, that's the last letter I write for that woman. She can go and find a pander [1] somewhere else. If ever she calls here or sends for me when I'm out, tell her so. Make it plain. That's the last I have to do with her," and with that he began reciting his evening psalm aloud. But he had hardly reached *A sagitta volante in die* [2] when he became aware that Esteban had risen and was lighting the candle.

"What's the matter?" he asked.

"I'm going out for a walk," replied Esteban somberly, fastening his belt. After a moment, he broke out with an assumption of anger, "You don't have to say . . . what you just said, for me. I don't care whether you write her letters or not. You don't have to change for me. I haven't anything to do with that."

"Go to bed, you fool. God, you're a fool, Esteban. What made you think I said that for you? Don't you believe I mean it when I say I'm through with her? Do you think I want to write any more of her dirty letters and get paid for them like that?"

"It's all right. You love her. You don't have to change because of me."

"'*Love* her?' *Love* her? You're crazy, Esteban. How could I love her? What

chance would there be for me? Do you suppose she'd give me those letters to write if there were any chance? Do you suppose she'd push a piece of money across the table every time. . . . You're crazy, Esteban, that's all."

There was a long pause. Esteban would not go to bed. He sat by the candle in the middle of the room, tapping with his hand on the edge of the table.

"Go to bed, you fool," shouted Manuel, rising on one elbow under the blanket. He was talking in their secret language and the new pain at his heart gave a greater ring of reality to his assumption of rage. "I'm all right."

"I won't. I'm going out for a walk," replied Esteban, picking up his coat.

"You can't go out for a walk. It's two o'clock. It's raining. You can't go and walk about for hours like that. Look, Esteban, I swear to you there's nothing left to all that. I don't love her. I only did for a time."

By now Esteban stood in the dark of the open door. In the unnatural voice with which we make the greatest declarations of our lives, he muttered: "I'm in your way," and turned to go.

Manuel leaped out of his bed. His head seemed to be full of a great din, a voice crying out that Esteban was going away forever. "In the name of God, in the name of God, Esteban, come back here."

Esteban came back and went to bed and the matter was not mentioned again for many weeks. The very next evening Manuel had an opportunity of declaring his position. A messenger arrived from the Perichole and was told harshly to inform the actress that Manuel would write no more letters for her.

One evening Manuel tore open the flesh on his knee against a piece of metal. Neither brother had ever been ill for as

[1] **pander:** a go-between in love intrigues.

[2] *A sagitta . . . die:* "for the arrow that flieth by day," a phrase from Psalm 91. The whole verse reads, "Thou shalt not be afraid for the terror by night; nor for the arrow that flieth by day."

much as a day in his life, and now Manuel, utterly bewildered, watched his leg swell and felt the waves of pain rise and fall in his body. Esteban sat by and stared at his face trying to imagine what great pain was. At last one midnight Manuel remembered that the signboard of a certain hairdresser in the city described the proprietor as an experienced barber and surgeon. Esteban ran through the streets to fetch him. He pounded on the door. Presently a woman leaned out of a window and announced that her husband would be back in the morning. During the fearful hours that followed they told one another that when the doctor had seen the leg all would be well. He would do something about it, and Manuel would be out around the town in a day or two, even in a day perhaps, even less than a day.

The barber arrived and prescribed various drafts and ointments. Esteban was instructed to lay cold cloths on his brother's leg every hour. The barber withdrew and the brothers sat down to wait for the pain to subside. But while they continued staring into one another's face, waiting for the miracle of science, the pain grew worse. Hour after hour Esteban approached with his dripping towel and they discovered that the moment of its application was the worst of all. With all the fortitude in the world Manuel could not prevent himself from shouting and from flinging himself about upon the bed. Night came on and still Esteban stolidly waited and watched and worked. Nine, ten, eleven. Now when the time drew near to apply the cloths (the hour struck so musically from all those towers) Manuel would plead with Esteban not to do his work. He would resort to guile and declare that he scarcely felt it. But Esteban, his heart bursting with pain and his lips a line of iron, would roll back the blanket and bind the towel fiercely in its place. Manuel gradually be-

came delirious and under this application all the thoughts he did not permit himself in his right mind would burst magnified from his mouth.

Finally at two o'clock, out of his mind with rage and pain, and flinging himself half out of the bed until his head struck the floor, Manuel cried, "God condemn your soul to the hottest hell there is. A thousand devils torture you forever, Esteban. God cóndemn your soul, do you hear?" At first, the air gone out of his body, Esteban went out into the hall and leaned against the door, his mouth and eyes, wide open. Still he heard from within, "Yes, Esteban, may God damn your beastly soul forever, do you hear that? For coming between me and what was mine by right. She was mine, do you hear, and what right had you . . ." and he would go off into an elaborate description of the Perichole.

These outbursts recurred hourly. It was some time before Esteban was able to realize that his brother's mind was not then clear. After some moments of horror, in which his being a devout believer had its part, he would return to the room and go about his duties with bent head.

Toward dawn his brother became serener. (For what human ill does not dawn seem to be an alleviation?) It was in one of these intervals that Manuel said quite calmly:

"God's son! I feel better, Esteban. Those cloths must be good after all. You'll see. I'll be up and around tomorrow. You haven't slept for days. You'll see I won't cause you any more trouble, Esteban."

"It's no trouble, you fool."

"You mustn't take me seriously when I try and stop you putting on the old cloths, Esteban."

A long pause. At last Esteban brought out, barely audible:

"I think . . . Don't you think it would

be fine if I sent for the Perichole? She could just come and see you for a few minutes, I mean . . ."

"Her? You still thinking about her? I wouldn't have her here for anything. No."

But Esteban was not content yet. He dragged up a few more phrases from the very center of his being:

"Manuel, you still feel, don't you, that I came between you and the Perichole and you don't remember that I told you it was all right with me. I swear to you I'd have been glad if you'd gone away with her, or anything."

"What are you bringing that up for, Esteban? I tell you, in God's own name, I never think of that. She's nothing to me. When are you going to forget that, Esteban? I tell you I'm glad things are as they are. Look, I got to get angry when you keep going back to that."

"Manuel, I wouldn't speak of it again, only when you get angry at me about the cloths . . . you, you get angry at me about that, too. And you talk about it and you . . ."

"Look, I'm not responsible what I say. My old leg hurts then, see."

"Then you don't damn me to hell because . . . it looks like I came between you and the Perichole?"

"Damn you to . . . ? What makes you say that? You're going crazy, Esteban; you're imagining things. You haven't had any sleep, Esteban. I've been a curse to you and you're losing your health because of me. But you'll see, I won't trouble you much more. How could I damn you to hell, Esteban, when you're all I've got? Understand, see, that when the cold cloths go on, I just lose myself, see. You know. Don't think about it twice. It's time to put them on now. I won't say a word."

"No, Manuel, I'll skip this time. It won't do you any harm. I'll just skip this time."

"I've got to get well, Esteban. I've got to get up soon, you know. Put them on. But one minute—give me the crucifix. I swear by the blood and body of Christ that if I say anything against Esteban, I don't mean it and it's just the foolish words when I'm dreaming because of the pain in my leg. God make me well again soon, amen. Put it back. There. Now I'm ready."

"Look, Manuel, it won't hurt if I skip just this once, see. It'll be good for you, sure, to not get it all stirred up just this once."

"No, I've got to get well. The doctor said it had to be done. I won't say a word, Esteban."

And it would begin all over again.

During the second night a prostitute in the next room started beating on the wall, outraged at such language. A priest in the room on the other side would come out into the hall and beat on the door. The whole floor would gather before the room in exasperation. The innkeeper came up the stairs, loudly promising his guests that the brothers would be dumped into the street the very next morning. Esteban, holding his candle, would go into the hall and permit them to rage at him for as long as they pleased; but after that he took to pressing his hand firmly over his brother's mouth during the moments of greatest stress. This increased Manuel's personal rage at him and he would babble all through the night.

On the third night, Esteban sent for the priest, and amidst the enormous shadows Manuel received the sacrament and died.

Thereafter, Esteban refused to come near the building. He would start off upon long walks, but presently drifting back, would hang about, staring at passers-by, within two streets of where his brother lay. The innkeeper failing to make any impression upon him and remembering

that the boys were brought up at the Convent of Santa María Rosa de las Rosas, sent for the Abbess. Simply and soundly she directed all that was to be done. At last she went down to the street corner and spoke to Esteban. He watched her approach him, a glance mixed of longing and distrust. But when she stood near him, he turned sideways and looked away.

"I want you to help me. Won't you come in and see your brother? Won't you come in and help me?"

"No."

"You won't help me!" A long pause. Suddenly, as she stood there full of her helplessness, there flashed through her mind an incident of many years before: the twin brothers about fifteen years old were sitting at her knee and she was telling them the story of the crucifixion. Their large grave eyes were fixed upon her lips. Suddenly Manuel had cried out loudly, "If Esteban and I had been there, we would have prevented it."

"Well, then, if you won't help me, will you tell me which you are?"

"Manuel," said Esteban.

"Manuel, won't you come and sit with me up there for just a short time?"

After a long pause: "No."

"But, Manuel, dear Manuel, can't you remember as children how you did so many things for me? You were willing to go across the town on some little errand. When I was ill you made the cook let you bring me my soup?" Another woman would have said, "Do you remember how much I did for you?"

"Yes."

"I, too, Manuel, have lost. I too . . . once. We know that God has taken them into His hands. . . ." But this did not do at all. Esteban turned vaguely and walked away from her. When he had gone about twenty paces, he stopped and stared down a side street, like a dog who wants to go away but is reluctant to offend the master who calls him back.

That was all they could get out of him. When the fearful procession passed through the city, with its black hoods and masks, its candles in broad daylight, its display of heaped-up skulls, its terrifying psalms, Esteban followed it in the parallel streets, catching glimpses of it from a distance, like a savage.

(CONTINUED ON PAGE 761)

Twentieth-Century Painting, II

Among the many foreign artists living in Paris just before World War I was a young Russian named Marc Chagall. Like other young painters of that time, he quickly became interested in Cubism and adapted certain aspects of this new style to suit his own needs. For example, look at the thin geometric planes of color in his painting *I and the Village* (PLATE 1). Notice, however, that this is a world of complete fantasy, a world of images considered from childhood memories. Things appear upside down, out of proportion, and even transparent, as if they were drifting among our thoughts like the disconnected images of a dream. Do we actually see *through* the large head of a cow to find another cow in the distance, or is the cow in the foreground simply dreaming of being milked? Chagall teases the mind; but by offering a feast of rich, warm colors, he also delights the eye of the beholder.

In 1924 a number of artists signed a manifesto in Paris which proclaimed the birth of a new movement known as Surrealism. They called for the abandonment of all traditional ideas, insisting that art should deal exclusively with the irrational workings of the subconscious mind. PLATE 2, *Dog Barking at the Moon,* shows a painting by one of the original Surrealists, the Spanish artist Joan Miró. At first, this bright, colorful picture seems to be just pure fun, somewhat like an animated cartoon. But the longer we look at it, the more it takes on the uncertainties of a dream or hallucination. The little dog appears hopelessly alone out on the edge of infinite space. And why is the ladder there—and where is it leading us? After a while, these forms seem to become luminous abstract shapes, magically suspended in space.

Almost everyone has heard of the great Spanish painter Pablo Picasso. For over fifty years his genius has influenced artists all over the world. In fact, he was largely responsible for the development of Cubism, which he brought to one of its high points in two large canvases of 1921, both titled *Three Musicians*. In the version shown here, (PLATE 3), two musicians are playing instruments, while the third seems to be singing from a sheet of

music he is holding in his lap. How thin and weightless these figures appear, almost like cutouts from a magazine! When we look through the eye-slots of their masks, we see only the dark brown color of the back wall. Various parts of each figure seem to be mixed up with parts of another. For instance, the area of bright blue that defines the upper half of Pierrot's face becomes part of Harlequin, and also the space between them. Nothing seems quite real here, yet every shape fits perfectly into place, like part of an ingeniously designed jigsaw puzzle. And despite all the dark, somber browns and blacks, there are just enough areas of bright, gay colors to bring this picture very much to life. PLATE 4 shows a much smaller, quieter painting: the delightful *Fish Magic* by the Swiss artist Paul Klee. In this dream world we see various types of fish swimming among vases of flowers in a moonlit sea, past a clock in a fishnet, while a clown and a girl with two faces peer curiously out toward us from beneath. We can only guess what all this means. The clock suggests a certain moment in time, like the moment of perfect stillness before a fish darts suddenly through the water. The vases look also like hourglasses (another symbol of time), and the net holding the clock also resembles a steeple. But perhaps we should take this picture simply as Klee has titled it, as a kind of visual "magic" which turns a strange collection of objects into a colorful pattern of predominantly round and oval shapes.

Salvador Dali, the most widely known of all Surrealists, brought to modern painting the exquisite technical perfection of a great miniaturist like Jan van Eyck (page 120). Dali's little portrait of his wife Gala (PLATE 5) has the kind of sharpness of detail we sometimes experience in an unusually vivid dream. But what makes this portrait especially compelling is the way Gala is shown facing herself, without any suggestion of a mirror between the two figures. (Notice that each of the two figures is, in fact, seated on a different kind of object.) The melancholy mood of the dusky picture on the back wall is used as a foil to set off by contrast the startling clarity of the double portrait.

Probably no single artist in the twentieth century has so profoundly influenced modern design as the Dutch painter Piet Mondrian. At first a traditional landscape painter, he quickly absorbed both Fauvism and Cubism, and by 1915 had evolved a completely abstract style. The picture in PLATE 6, *Broadway Boogie-Woogie,* is a much later work in this style, painted several years after Mondrian had settled in New York City. Its grid pattern of small brightly colored rectangles evokes the excitement of a modern city—vibrating neon lights, darting traffic, blocks of skyscrapers, and the lively rhythms of jazz. Mondrian's style appears simple, but it is deceptively so. For when a picture is reduced to nothing but rectangles of pure color, the exact position, size, proportion, and color of every shape become tremendously important.

PLATE 1. MARC CHAGALL (Russian, born 1887): *I and the Village*. 1911. Oil on canvas, $75\frac{5}{8}$ x $59\frac{5}{8}$ inches. (Collection, The Museum of Modern Art, New York, Mrs. Simon Guggenheim Fund)

PLATE 2. JOAN MIRÓ (Spanish, born 1893): *Dog Barking at the Moon*. 1926. Oil on canvas, 28¾ x 36¼ inches. (Philadelphia Museum of Art, A. E. Gallatin Collection)

PLATE 3. PABLO PICASSO (Spanish, born 1881): *Three Musicians*. 1921. Oil on canvas, 79 x 87¾ inches. (Collection, The Museum of Modern Art, New York, Mrs. Simon Guggenheim Fund)

PLATE 4. PAUL KLEE (Swiss, 1879–1940): *Fish Magic*. 1925. Oil on canvas mounted on board, $30\frac{3}{8}$ x $38\frac{1}{2}$ inches. (Philadelphia Museum of Art, The Louise and Walter Arensberg Collection)

PLATE 5. SALVADOR DALI (Spanish, born 1904): *Portrait of Gala*. 1935. Oil on wood, $12\frac{3}{4}$ x $10\frac{1}{2}$ inches. (Collection, The Museum of Modern Art, New York, Gift of Abby Aldrich Rockefeller)

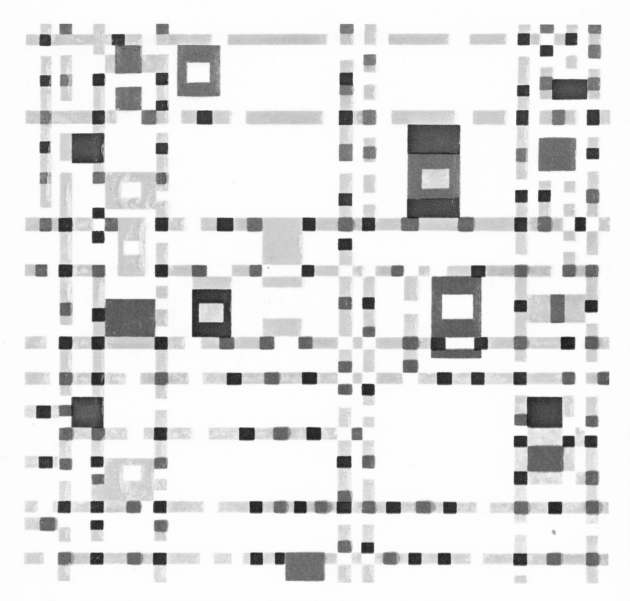

PLATE 6. PIET MONDRIAN (Dutch, 1872–1944): *Broadway Boogie-Woogie*. 1942–1943. Oil on canvas, 50 x 50 inches. (Collection, The Museum of Modern Art, New York)

All Lima was interested in this separation of the brothers. Housewives whispered together sympathetically about it as they unfurled their carpets from the balconies. The men in the wineshops, alluding to it, shook their heads and smoked in silence for a while. Travelers from the interior told of seeing Esteban as he strayed with eyes like coals along the dried-up beds of rivers or through the great ruins of the old race. A herder of llamas had come upon him standing upon a hilltop, asleep or dazed, wet with dew under the stars. Some fishermen surprised him swimming far out from shore. From time to time he would find work to do, he would become a shepherd or a carter, but after a few months he would disappear and stride from province to province. But he always returned to Lima. One day he appeared at the door of the Perichole's dressing room; he made as though to speak, gazed earnestly at her and vanished. One day a sister came running into the office of Madre María del Pilar with the news that Esteban (whom the world called Manuel) was lingering about the door of the convent. The Abbess hurried out into the street. For months she had been asking herself what strategy could reconcile this half-demented boy to living among them again. She assembled as grave and calm a manner as she was able and, appearing at the street door, murmured "My friend" and looked at him. He gazed back at her with the same glance of longing and distrust that he had shown her before, and stood trembling. Again she whispered "My friend" and moved a step forward. Suddenly Esteban turned and, breaking into a run, disappeared. Madre María del Pilar rushed, stumbling, back to her desk and fell upon her knees, exclaiming angrily, "I have prayed for wisdom and You have given me none. You have not chosen to give me the least grace.

I am a mere scrubber of floors. . . ." But during the penance she set herself for this impudence the thought came to her to send for Captain Alvarado. Three weeks later she had a ten-minute conversation with him. And the next day he started for Cuzco where, it was said, Esteban was doing some copying for the University.

There was this strange and noble figure in Peru during these years, the Captain Alvarado, the traveler. He was blackened and cured by all weathers. He stood in the square with feet apart as though they were planted on a shifting deck. His eyes were strange, unaccustomed to the shorter range, too used to seizing the appearances of a constellation between a cloud and a cloud, and the outline of a cape in rain. His reticence was sufficiently explained for most of us by his voyages, but the Marquesa de Montemayor had other light on the matter. *"Captain Alvarado is bringing you this letter in person,"* she wrote to her daughter. *"Introduce him to some of your geographers, my treasure, though it may make them a little uncomfortable, for he is the diamond of sincerity. They will never see anyone who has traveled so far. Last night he described to me some of his voyages. Imagine him pushing his prow through a sea of weeds, stirring up a cloud of fish like grasshoppers in June; or sailing between islands of ice. Oh, he has been to China and up the rivers of Africa. But he is not merely an adventurer and he seems to take no pride in discovering new places; nor is he a mere merchant. One day I asked him narrowly why he lived so, and he avoided my question. I found out from my laundress what I think is the reason of his wandering: My child, he had a child; my daughter, he had a daughter. She was just old enough to cook a holiday meal and do a little sewing for him. In those days he merely sailed between Mexico and Peru and hundreds*

*of times she waved him farewell or wel-
come. We have no way of knowing
whether she was more beautiful or intel-
ligent than the thousands of other girls
that lived about him, but she was his. I
suppose it seems ignoble to you that a
great oak of a man should go about the
world like a blind man about an empty
house merely because a chit of a girl has
been withdrawn from it. No, no, you can-
not understand this, my adored one, but
I understand and grow pale. Last night
he sat with me and talked of her. He laid
his cheek against his hand and, looking
into the fire, he said, 'It sometimes seems
to me that she is away upon a voyage and
that I shall see her again. It seems to me
that she is in England.' You will laugh at
me, but I think he goes about the hemi-
spheres to pass the time between now and
his old age."*

The brothers had always entertained a
great respect for Captain Alvarado. They
had worked for him a short time, and the
silence of the three of them had made a
little kernel of sense in a world of boast-
ing, self-excuse, and rhetoric.[1] So now
when the great traveler came into the
dark kitchen where Esteban was eating,
the boy drew his chair farther into the
shadow, but at a distance, he was glad.
The Captain gave no sign of recognizing
or even of seeing him until he had finished
his meal. Esteban had finished long before
but, not wishing to be spoken to, waited
until the Captain should have left the
cave. At last the Captain walked over to
him and said:

"You are Esteban or Manuel. You
helped me once with some unloading. I
am Captain Alvarado."

"Yes," said Esteban.

"How are you?"

Esteban muttered something.

[1] **rhetoric:** here, empty words.

"I am looking for some strong fellows
to go on my next trip with me." Pause.
"Would you like to come?" Longer pause.
"England. And Russia. . . . Hard work.
Good wages. . . . A long way from Peru—
Well?"

Apparently Esteban had not been lis-
tening. He sat with his eyes on the table.
At last the Captain raised his voice, as to
a deaf person:

"I said: Do you want to go on my next
trip with me. . . ."

"Yes, I'll go," answered Esteban sud-
denly.

"Fine. That's fine. I want your brother,
too, of course."

"No."

"What's the matter? Wouldn't he want
to come?"

Esteban mumbled something, looking
away. Then, half-rising, he said, "I got
to go now. I've got to see somebody about
something."

"Let me see your brother myself. Where
is he?"

". . .'dead," said Esteban.

"Oh, I didn't know. I didn't know. I'm
sorry."

"Yes," said Esteban. "I got to go."

"Hmm—Which are you? What's your
name?"

"Esteban."

"When did Manuel die?"

"Oh, just a . . . just a few weeks. He
hit his knee against something and . . . just
a few weeks ago."

They both kept their eyes on the floor.

"How old are you, Esteban?"

"Twenty-two."

"Well, that's settled then, you're com-
ing with me?"

"Yes."

"You may not be used to the cold."

"Yes, I'm used to it—I've got to go
now. I got to go in the city and see some-
body about something."

"Well, Esteban. Come back here for supper and we'll talk about the trip. Come back and have some wine with me, see. Will you?"

"Yes, I will."

"Go with God."

"Go with God."

They had supper together and it was arranged that they were to start for Lima the next morning. The Captain got him very drunk. At first they poured and drank in silence. Then the Captain began to talk about ships and their courses. He asked Esteban questions about tackle and about the guide stars. Then Esteban began to talk about other things, and to talk very loudly:

"On the ship you must give me something to do all the time. I'll do anything, anything. I'll climb up high and fix ropes; and I'll watch all night—because, you know, I don't sleep well anyway. And, Captain Alvarado, on the ship you must pretend that you don't know me. Pretend that you hate me the most. So that you'll always give me things to do. I can't sit still and write at a table any more—And don't tell the other men about me . . . that is, about . . ."

"I hear you went into a burning house, Esteban, and pulled someone out."

"Yes. I didn't get burned or anything. You know," cried Esteban, leaning across the table, "you're not allowed to kill yourself; you know you're not allowed. Everybody knows that. But if you jump into a burning house to save somebody, that wouldn't be killing yourself. And if you became a matador and the bull caught you, that wouldn't be killing yourself. Only you mustn't put yourself in the bull's way on purpose. Did you ever notice that animals never kill themselves, even when they're sure to lose? They never jump into a river or anything, even when they're sure to lose. Some people say that horses run into bonfires. Is that true?"

"No, I don't think that's true."

"I don't think it's true. We had a dog once. Well, I mustn't think of that—Captain Alvarado, do you know Madre María del Pilar?"

"Yes."

"I want to give her a present before I go away. Captain Alvarado, I want you to give me all my wages before I start—I won't need any money anywhere—and I want to buy her a present now. The present isn't from me only. She was . . . was . . ." Here Esteban wished to say his brother's name, but was unable to. Instead he continued in a lower voice, "She had a kind of a . . . she had a serious loss once. She said so. I don't know who it was, and I want to give her a present. Women can't bear that kind of a thing like we can."

The Captain promised him that they would choose something in the morning. Esteban talked about it at great length. At last the Captain saw him slip under the table, and himself, rising up, went out into the square before the inn. He looked at the line of the Andes and at the streams of stars crowding forever across the sky. And there was that wraith [1] hanging in midair and smiling at him, the wraith with the silvery voice that said for the thousandth time, "Don't be gone long. But I'll be a big girl when you get back." Then he went within and carried Esteban to his room and sat looking at him for a long while.

The next morning he was waiting at the bottom of the stairs when Esteban appeared:

"We're starting when you're ready," said the Captain.

The strange glitter had returned to the boy's eyes. He blurted out, "No, I'm

[1] **wraith** (rāth): a ghost or apparition.

not coming. I'm not coming after all."

"Aïe! Esteban! But you have promised me that you would come."

"It's impossible. I can't come with you," and he turned back up the stairs.

"Come here a moment, Esteban, just a moment."

"I can't come with you. I can't leave Peru."

"I want to tell you something."

Esteban came down to the foot of the stairs.

"How about that present for Madre María del Pilar?" asked the Captain in a low voice. Esteban was silent, looking over the mountains. "You aren't going to take that present away from her? It might mean a lot to her . . . you know."

"All right," murmured Esteban, as though much impressed.

"Yes. Besides, the ocean's better than Peru. You know Lima and Cuzco and the road. You have nothing more to know about them. You see it's the ocean you want. Besides, on the boat you'll have something to do every minute. I'll see to that. Go and get your things and we'll start."

Esteban was trying to make a decision. It had always been Manuel who had made the decisions, and even Manuel had never been forced to make as great a one as this. Esteban went slowly upstairs. The Captain waited for him and waited so long that presently he ventured half the way up the stairs and listened. At first there was silence; then a series of noises that his imagination was able to identify at once. Esteban had scraped away the plaster about a beam and was adjusting a rope about it. The Captain stood on the stairs trembling: "Perhaps it's best," he said to himself. "Perhaps I should leave him alone. Perhaps it's the only thing possible for him." Then, on hearing another sound, he flung himself against the door, fell into the room, and caught the boy. "Go away," cried Esteban. "Let me be. Don't come in now."

Esteban fell face downward upon the floor. "I am alone, alone, alone," he cried. The Captain stood above him, his great plain face ridged and gray with pain; it was his own old hours he was reliving. He was the awkwardest speaker in the world apart from the lore of the sea, but there are times when it requires a high courage to speak the banal.[1] He could not be sure the figure on the floor was listening, but he said, "We do what we can. We push on, Esteban, as best we can. It isn't for long, you know. Time keeps going by. You'll be surprised at the way time passes."

They started for Lima. When they reached the bridge of San Luis Rey, the Captain descended to the stream below in order to supervise the passage of some merchandise, but Esteban crossed by the bridge and fell with it.

[1] **banal** (bā′nəl): commonplace, trite.

FOR STUDY AND DISCUSSION

1. In what ways was the relationship of Manuel and Esteban like a perfect love? Why were they silent in the presence of others? Why did the Archbishop's questions embarrass them? How did their love for each other affect their freedom to go where they wanted and do what they wanted to do?

2. How was Manuel's love for the Perichole different from his love for Esteban? What, do you think, is the author's attitude toward this new love: is he shocked? condemning? regretful? amused? What makes you think so?

3. What differences in the two brothers and their love for each other are revealed by Manuel's passion for the Perichole? In what ways was Manuel "older"? Why couldn't Esteban understand how his brother felt? What false impression did he get of his brother's relationship with the Perichole?

4. What do we learn about the Perichole from the letters that Manuel writes for her? What is her attitude toward love?

5. What does the author suggest was the real reason Manuel gave up the Perichole? Did he succeed in giving her up entirely? in convincing Esteban that he had done so? What makes you think so?

6. What do you think were the causes of Manuel's death? Why did Esteban continue to apply the cold cloths when Manuel begged him not to? Why did Manuel later insist that he continue to apply them?

7. After Manuel's death, why do you think Esteban told everyone that he was Manuel? Why did he admit his true identity to the Captain? What did Esteban and the Captain have in common?

8. Why was Esteban's grief so much more unbearable than the Captain's? Do you think that, in time, Esteban would have learned to bear his grief as did the Captain? Why or why not?

PART FOUR

Uncle Pio

In one of her letters (the XXIXth) the Marquesa de Montemayor tries to describe the impression that Uncle Pio *"our aged Harlequin"* made upon her: *"I have been sitting all morning on the green balcony making you a pair of slippers, my soul,"* she tells her daughter. *"As the golden wire did not take up my whole attention, I was able to follow the activity of a coterie of ants in the wall beside me. Somewhere behind the partition they were patiently destroying my house. Every three minutes a little workman would appear between two boards and drop a grain of wood upon the floor below. Then he would wave his antennae at me and*
back busily into his mysterious corridor. In the meantime various brothers and sisters of his were trotting back and forth on a certain highway, stopping to massage one another's heads, or if the messages they bore were of first importance, refusing angrily to massage or to be massaged. And at once I thought of Uncle Pio. Why? Where else but with him had I seen that very gesture with which he arrests a passing abbé or a courtier's valet, and whispers, his lips laid against his victim's ear? And surely enough, before noon I saw him hurry by on one of those mysterious errands of his. As I am the idlest and silliest of women, I sent Pepita to get me a piece of nougat, which I placed on the ant's highway. Similarly I sent word to the Café Pizarro, asking them to send Uncle Pio to see me if he dropped in before sunset. I shall give him that old bent salad fork with the turquoise in it, and he will bring me a copy of the new ballad that everyone is singing about the d—q—a of Ol—v—s. My child, you shall have the best of everything, and you shall have it first."*

And in the next letter: *"My dear, Uncle Pio is the most delightful man in the world, your husband excepted. He is the second most delightful man in the world. His conversation is enchanting. If he weren't so disreputable, I should make him my secretary. He could write all my letters for me and generations would rise up and call me witty. Alas, however, he is so moth-eaten by disease and bad company that I shall have to leave him to his underworld. He is not only like an ant, he is like a soiled pack of cards. And I doubt whether the whole Pacific could wash him sweet and fragrant again. But what divine Spanish he speaks and what exquisite things he says in it! That's what one gets by hanging around a theater and hearing nothing but the conversation of*

Calderón.[1] *Alas, what is the matter with this world, my soul, that it should treat such a being so ill! His eyes are as sad as those of a cow that has been separated from its tenth calf."*

You should know first that this Uncle Pio was Camila Perichole's maid. He was also her singing master, her coiffeur, her masseur, her reader, her errand boy, her banker; rumor added: her father. For example, he taught her her parts. There was a whisper around town that Camila could read and write. The compliment was unfounded; Uncle Pio did her reading and writing for her. At the height of the season the company put on two or three new plays a week, and as each one contained a long and flowery part for the Perichole, the mere task of memorization was not a trifle.

Peru had passed within fifty years from a frontier state to a state in renaissance. Its interest in music and the theater was intense. Lima celebrated its feast days by hearing a Mass of Tomás Luis de Victoria in the morning and the glittering poetry of Calderón in the evening. It is true that the Limeans were given to interpolating trivial songs into the most exquisite comedies and some lachrymose[2] effects into the austerest music; but at least they never submitted to the boredom of a misplaced veneration. If they had disliked heroic comedy the Limeans would not have hesitated to remain at home; and if they had been deaf to polyphony[3] nothing would have prevented their going to an earlier service. When the Archbishop returned from a short trip to Spain, all Lima kept asking, "What has he brought?" The

news finally spread abroad that he had returned with tomes[4] of masses and motets by Palestrina, Morales, and Victoria, as well as thirty-five plays by Tirso de Molina and Ruiz de Alarçon and Moreto. There was a civic fete in his honor. The choirboys' school and the greenroom of the Comedia were swamped with the gifts of vegetables and wheat. All the world was eager to nourish the interpreters of so much beauty.

This was the theater in which Camila Perichole gradually made her reputation. So rich was the repertory and so dependable the prompter's box that few plays were given more than four times a season. The manager had the whole flowering of the seventeenth-century Spanish drama to draw upon, including many that are now lost to us. The Perichole had appeared in a hundred plays of Lope de Vega[5] alone. There were many admirable actresses in Lima during these years, but none better. The citizens were too far away from the theaters of Spain to realize that she was the best in the Spanish world. They kept sighing for a glimpse of the stars of Madrid whom they had never seen and to whom they assigned vague new excellences. Only one person knew for certain that the Perichole was a great performer and that was her tutor, Uncle Pio.

Uncle Pio came of a good Castilian house, illegitimately. At the age of ten he ran away to Madrid from his father's hacienda[6] and was pursued without diligence. He lived ever after by his wits. He possessed the six attributes of the adventurer—a memory for names and faces, with the aptitude for altering his own; the gift of tongues; inexhaustible invention; secrecy; the talent for falling into conver-

[1] **Calderón** (käl·dā·rôn′): Spanish dramatist and poet (1600–1681).

[2] **lachrymose** (lak′rə·mōs): tearful.

[3] **polyphony** (pə·lif′ə·nē): the harmonizing of melodically independent parts, or voices, in a musical composition.

[4] **tomes:** large books.

[5] **Lope de Vega** (lō′pā dā vā·gä): a well-known Spanish dramatist and poet (1562–1635).

[6] **hacienda** (hä′sē·en′də): estate.

sation with strangers; and that freedom from conscience that springs from a contempt for the dozing rich he preyed upon. From ten to fifteen he distributed handbills for merchants, held horses, and ran confidential errands. From fifteen to twenty he trained bears and snakes for traveling circuses; he cooked, and mixed punches; he hung about the entries of the more expensive taverns and whispered informations into the travelers' ears— sometimes nothing more dubious than that a certain noble house was reduced to selling its plate and could thus dispense with the commission of a silversmith. He was attached to all the theaters in town and could applaud like ten. He spread slanders at so much a slander. He sold rumors about crops and about the value of land. From twenty to thirty his services came to be recognized in very high circles —he was sent out by the government to inspirit some half-hearted rebellions in the mountains, so that the government could presently arrive and wholeheartedly crush them. His discretion was so profound that the French party used him even when they knew that the Austrian party used him also. He had long interviews with the Princesse des Ursins, but he came and went by the back stairs. During this phase he was no longer obliged to ar-

range gentlemen's pleasures, nor to plant little harvests of calumny.

He never did one thing for more than two weeks at a time even when enormous gains seemed likely to follow upon it. He could have become a circus manager, a theatrical director, a dealer in antiquities, an importer of Italian silks, a secretary in the Palace or the Cathedral, a dealer in provisions for the army, a speculator in houses and farms, a merchant in dissipations and pleasures. But there seemed to have been written into his personality, through some accident or early admiration of his childhood, a reluctance to own anything, to be tied down, to be held to a long engagement. It was this that prevented his thieving, for example. He had stolen several times, but the gains had not been sufficient to offset his dread of being locked up; he had sufficient ingenuity to escape on the field itself all the police in the world, but nothing could protect him against the talebearing of his enemies. Similarly he had been reduced for a time to making investigations for the Inquisition, but when he had seen several of his victims led off in hoods, he felt that he might be involving himself in an institution whose movements were not evenly predictable.

As he approached twenty, Uncle Pio

came to see quite clearly that his life had three aims. There was first this need of independence, cast into a curious pattern, namely: the desire to be varied, secret, and omniscient.[1] He was willing to renounce the dignities of public life, if in secret he might feel that he looked down upon men from a great distance, knowing more about them than they knew themselves; and with a knowledge which occasionally passed into action and rendered him an agent in the affairs of states and persons. In the second place he wanted to be always near beautiful women, of whom he was always in the best and worst sense the worshiper. To be near them was as necessary to him as breathing. His reverence for beauty and charm was there for anyone to see and to laugh at, and the ladies of the theater and the court and the houses of pleasure loved his connoisseurship. They tormented him and insulted him and asked his advice and were singularly comforted by his absurd devotion. He suffered greatly their rages and their meannesses and their confiding tears; all he asked was to be accepted casually, to be trusted, to be allowed like a friendly and slightly foolish dog to come and go in their rooms and to write their letters for them. He was insatiably curious about their minds and their hearts. He never expected to be loved by them; for that, he carried his money to the obscurer parts of the city; he was always desperately unprepossessing, with his wisp of a mustache and his wisp of a beard and his big ridiculous sad eyes. They constituted his parish; it was from them that he acquired the name of Uncle Pio, and it was when they were in trouble that he most revealed himself; when they fell from favor he lent them money, when they were ill he outlasted the flagging devotion of their lovers

and the exasperation of their maids; when time or disease robbed them of their beauty, he served them still for their beauty's memory; and when they died his was the honest grief that saw them as far as possible on their journey.

In the third place he wanted to be near those that loved Spanish literature and its masterpieces, especially in the theater. He had discovered all that treasure for himself, borrowing or stealing from the libraries of his patrons, feeding himself upon it in secrecy—behind the scenes, as it were, of his mad life. He was contemptuous of the great persons who, for all their education and usage, exhibited no care or astonishment before the miracles of word order in Calderón and Cervantes.[2] He longed himself to make verses. He never realized that many of the satirical songs he had written for the vaudevilles passed into folk music and have been borne everywhere along the highroads.

As the result of one of those quarrels that arise so naturally in brothels, his life became too complicated and he removed to Peru. Uncle Pio in Peru was even more versatile than Uncle Pio in Europe. Here too he touched upon real estate, circuses, pleasures, insurrections, and antiques. A Chinese junk had been blown from Canton to America; he dragged up the beach

the bales of deep-red porcelain and sold the bowls to the collectors of virtu.[3] He

[1] **omniscient** (om·nish′ənt): all-knowing, infinitely wise.

[2] **Cervantes** (sər·van′tēz): Spanish novelist (1547–1616), author of *Don Quixote*.
[3] **virtu** (vər·tōo′): curios or antiques.

traced down the sovereign remedies of the Incas and started a smart trade in pills. Within four months he knew practically everyone in Lima. He presently added to this acquaintance the inhabitants of scores of seacoast towns, mining camps, and settlements in the interior. His pretensions to omniscience became more and more plausible. The Viceroy discovered Uncle Pio and all this richness of reference; he engaged his services in many affairs. In the decay of his judgment Don Andrés had retained one talent: he was a master of the technique of handling confidential servants. He treated Uncle Pio with great tact and some deference; he understood which errands the other should not be asked to undertake and he understood his need for variety and intermission. Uncle Pio in turn was perpetually astonished that a prince should make so little use of his position, for power, or for fantasy, or for sheer delight in the manipulation of other men's destinies; but the servant loved the master because he could quote from any of Cervantes' prefaces and because his tongue had a little Castilian salt about it still. Many a morning Uncle Pio entered the Palace through corridors where there was no one to cross but a confessor or a confidential bully and sat with the Viceroy over his morning chocolate.

But for all his activity nothing made Uncle Pio rich. One would have said that he abandoned a venture when it threatened to prosper. Although no one knew it, he owned a house. It was full of dogs that could add and multiply, and the top floor was reserved for birds. But even in this kingdom he was lonely, and proud in his loneliness, as though there resided a certain superiority in such a solitude. Finally he stumbled upon an adventure that came like some strange gift from the skies and that combined the three great aims of his life: his passion for overseeing the lives of others, his worship of beautiful women, and his admiration for the treasures of Spanish literature. He discovered Camila Perichole. Her real name was Micaela Villegas. She was singing in cafés at the age of twelve and Uncle Pio had always been the very soul of cafés. Now as he sat among the guitarists and watched this awkward girl singing ballads, imitating every inflection of the more experienced singers who had preceded her, the determination entered his mind to play Pygmalion.[1] He bought her. Instead of sleeping locked up in the wine bin, she inherited a cot in his house. He wrote songs for her, he taught her how to listen to the quality of her tone, and bought her a new dress. At first all she noticed was that it was wonderful not to be whipped, to be offered hot soups, and to be taught something. But it was Uncle Pio who was really dazzled. His rash experiment flourished beyond all prophecy. The little twelve-year-old, silent and always a little sullen, devoured work. He set her endless exercises in acting and mimicry; he set her problems in conveying the atmosphere of a song; he took her to the theaters and made her notice all the details of a performance. But it was from Camila as a woman that he was to receive his greatest shock. The long arms and legs were finally harmonized into a body of perfect grace. The almost grotesque and hungry face became beautiful. Her whole nature became gentle and mysterious and oddly wise; and it all turned to him. She could find no fault in him and she was sturdily loyal. They loved one another deeply but without passion. He respected the slight nervous shadow that crossed her face

[1] **Pygmalion:** in Greek mythology, a king of Cyprus who fell in love with a statue of a beautiful young girl that he had made. Pitying his hopeless love, the gods brought the statue to life.

when he came too near her. But there arose out of this denial itself the perfume of a tenderness, that ghost of passion which, in the most unexpected relationship, can make even a whole lifetime devoted to irksome duty pass like a gracious dream.

They traveled a great deal, seeking new taverns, for the highest attribute of a café singer will always be her novelty. They went to Mexico, their odd clothes wrapped up in the selfsame shawl. They slept on beaches, they were whipped at Panama and shipwrecked on some tiny Pacific islands plastered with the droppings of birds. They tramped through jungles, delicately picking their way among snakes and beetles. They sold themselves out as harvesters in a hard season. Nothing in the world was very surprising to them.

Then began an even harder course of training for the girl, a regimen that resembled more the preparation for an acrobat. The instruction was a little complicated by the fact that her rise to favor was very rapid; and there was some danger that the applause she received would make her content with her work too soon.

Uncle Pio never exactly beat her, but he resorted to a sarcasm that had terrors of its own.

At the close of a performance Camila would return to her dressing room to find Uncle Pio whistling nonchalantly in one corner. She would divine his attitude at once and cry angrily:

"Now what is it? Mother of God, Mother of God, what is it now?"

"Nothing, little pearl. My little Camila of Camilas, nothing."

"There was something you didn't like. Ugly faultfinding thing that you are. Come on now, what was it? Look, I'm ready."

"No, little fish. Adorable morning star, I suppose you did as well as you could."

The suggestion that she was a limited artist and that certain felicities would be forever closed to her never failed to make Camila frantic. She would burst into tears: "I wish I had never known you. You poison my whole life. You just think I did badly. It pleases you to pretend that I was bad. All right then, be quiet."

Uncle Pio went on whistling.

"The fact is I know I was weak tonight, and don't need you to tell me so. So there. Now go away. I don't want to see you around. It's hard enough to play that part without coming back and finding you this way."

Suddenly Uncle Pio would lean forward and ask with angry intensity, "Why did you take that speech to the prisoner so fast?"

More tears from the Perichole: "Oh, God, let me die in peace! One day you tell me to go faster and another to go slower. Anyway, I shall be crazy in a year or two and then it won't matter."

More whistling.

"Besides, the audience applauded as never before. Do you hear me? *As never before*. There! Too fast or too slow is nothing to them. They wept. I was divine.

That's all I care for. Now be silent. Be silent."

He was absolutely silent.

"You may comb my hair, but if you say another word I shall never play again. You can find some other girl, that's all."

Thereupon he would comb her hair soothingly for ten minutes, pretending not to notice the sobs that were shaking her exhausted body. At last she would turn quickly and, catching one of his hands, would kiss it frantically: "Uncle Pio, was I so bad? Was I a disgrace to you? Was it so awful *that you left the theater?*"

After a long pause Uncle Pio would admit judiciously, "You were good in the scene on the ship."

"But I've been better, Uncle Pio. You remember the night you came back from Cuzco—?"

"You were pretty good at the close."

"Was I?"

"But, my flower, my pearl, *what was the matter in the speech to the prisoner?*"

Here the Perichole would fling her face and arms upon the table amid the pomades,[1] caught up into a tremendous fit of weeping. Only perfection would do, only perfection. And that had never come.

Then beginning in a low voice Uncle Pio would talk for an hour, analyzing the play, entering into a world of finesse in matters of voice and gesture and tempo, and often until dawn they would remain there declaiming to one another the lordly conversation of Calderón.

Whom were these two seeking to please? Not the audiences of Lima. They had long since been satisfied. We come from a world where we have known incredible standards of excellence, and we dimly remember beauties which we have not seized again; and we go back to that world. Uncle Pio and Camila Perichole

were tormenting themselves in an effort to establish in Peru the standards of the theaters in some heaven whither Calderón had preceded them. The public for which masterpieces are intended is not on this earth.

With the passing of time Camila lost some of this absorption in her art. A certain intermittent contempt for acting made her negligent. It was due to the poverty of interest in women's roles throughout Spanish classical drama. At a time when the playwrights grouped about the courts of England and France (a little later, of Venice) were enriching the parts of women with studies in wit, charm, passion, and hysteria, the dramatists of Spain kept their eyes on their heroes, on gentlemen torn between the conflicting claims of honor, or, as sinners, returning at the last moment to the cross. For a number of years Uncle Pio spent himself in discovering ways to interest the Perichole in the roles that fell to her. Upon one occasion he was able to announce to Camila that a granddaughter of Vico de Barrera had arrived in Peru. Uncle Pio had long since communicated to Camila his veneration for great poets, and Camila never questioned the view that they were a little above the kings and not below the saints. So it was in great excitement that the two of them chose one of the master's plays to perform before his granddaughter. They rehearsed the poem a hundred times, now in the great joy of invention, now in dejection. On the night of the performance Camila, peering out between the folds of the curtain, had Uncle Pio point out to her the little middle-aged woman worn with the cares of penury and a large family; but it seemed to Camila that she was looking at all the beauty and dignity in the world. As she waited for the lines that preceded her entrance, she clung to Uncle Pio in reverent silence, her heart

[1] **pomades:** perfumed ointments.

beating loudly. Between the acts she retired to the dusty corner of the warehouse where no one would find her and sat staring into the corners. At the close of the performance Uncle Pio brought the granddaughter of Vico de Barrera into Camila's room. Camila stood among the clothes that hung upon the wall, weeping with happiness and shame. Finally she flung herself on her knees and kissed the older woman's hands, and the older woman kissed hers, and while the audience went home and went to bed, the visitor remained, telling Camila the little stories that had remained in the family of Vico's work and of his habits.

Uncle Pio was at his happiest when a new actress entered the company, for the discovery of a new talent at her side never failed to bestir the Perichole. To Uncle Pio (standing at the back of the auditorium, bent double with joy and malice) it seemed that the body of the Perichole had become an alabaster lamp in which a strong light had been placed. Without any resort to tricks or to false emphasis, she set herself to efface the newcomer. If the play were a comedy, she became the very abstraction of wit, and (as was more likely) if it was a drama of wronged ladies and implacable hates, the stage fairly smoldered with her emotion. Her personality became so electric that if she so much as laid her hand upon that of a fellow actor a sympathetic shudder ran through the audience. But such occasions of excellence became less and less frequent. As her technique became sounder, Camila's sincerity became less necessary. Even when she was absent-minded the audience did not notice the difference and only Uncle Pio grieved.

Camila had a very beautiful face, or rather a face beautiful save in repose. In repose one was startled to discover that the nose was long and thin, the mouth tired and a little childish, the eyes unsatisfied—a rather pinched peasant girl, dragged from the cafés chantants [1] and quite incapable of establishing any harmony between the claims of her art, of her appetites, of her dreams, and of her crowded daily routine. Each of these was a world in itself, and the warfare between them would soon have reduced to idiocy (or triviality) a less tenacious physique. We have seen that in spite of her discontent with her parts, the Perichole knew very well the joy that might reside in acting and warmed herself from time to time at that flame. But that of love attracted her more often, though with no greater assurance of happiness, until Jupiter himself sent her some pearls.

Don Andrés de Ribera, the Viceroy of Peru, was the remnant of a delightful man, broken by the table, the alcove, a grandeeship, and ten years of exile. As a youth he had accompanied embassies to Versailles and Rome; he had fought in the wars in Austria; he had been in Jerusalem. He was a widower, and childless, of an enormous and wealthy woman; he had collected coins a little, wines, actresses, orders, and maps. From the table he had

received the gout; from the alcove a tendency to convulsions; from the grandeeship a pride so vast and puerile [2] that he seldom heard anything that was said to

[1] **cafés chantants** (ka·fā′ shän′tän′): concert halls or gardens where refreshments are served.
[2] **puerile** (pyŏo′ər·il): childish.

him and talked to the ceiling in a perpetual monologue; from the exile, oceans of boredom, a boredom so persuasive that it was like pain—he woke up with it and spent the day with it, and it sat by his bed all night watching his sleep. Camila was passing the years in the hardworking routine of the theater, savored by a few untidy love affairs, when this Olympian personage (for he had a face and port [1] fit to play gods and heroes on the scene) suddenly transported her to the most delicious midnight suppers at the Palace. Contrary to all the traditions of the stage and state, she adored her elderly admirer; she thought she was going to be happy forever. Don Andrés taught the Perichole a great many things and to her bright eager mind that was one of the sweetest ingredients of love. He taught her a little French; to be neat and clean; the modes of address. Uncle Pio had taught her how great ladies carry themselves on great occasions; he taught her how they relax. Uncle Pio and Calderón had trained her in beautiful Spanish; Don Andrés furnished her with the smart slang of *El Buen Retiro*.[2]

Uncle Pio was made anxious by Camila's invitation from the Palace. He would have much preferred that she continue with her little vulgarian love affairs in the theatrical warehouse. But when he saw that her art was gaining a new finish, he was well content. He would sit in the back of the theater, rolling about in his seat for sheer joy and amusement, watching the Perichole intimate to the audience that she frequented the great world about whom the dramatists wrote. She had a new way of fingering a wineglass, of exchanging an adieu, a new way of entering a door that told everything. To Uncle

Pio nothing else mattered. What was there in the world more lovely than a beautiful woman doing justice to a Spanish masterpiece—a performance (he asks you), packed with observation, in which the very spacing of the words revealed a comment on life and on the text—delivered by a beautiful voice—illustrated by a faultless carriage, considerable personal beauty, and irresistible charm? "We are almost ready to take this marvel to Spain," he would murmur to himself. After the performance he would go around to her dressing room and say "Very good!" But before taking his leave he would manage to ask her where, in the name of the eleven thousand virgins of Cologne,[3] she had acquired that affected way of saying *Excelencia*.

After a time the Viceroy asked the Perichole whether it would amuse her to invite a few discreet guests to their midnight suppers, and he asked her whether she would like to meet the Archbishop. Camila was delighted. The Archbishop was delighted. On the eve of their first meeting he sent the actress an emerald pendant as big as a playing card.

There was something in Lima that was wrapped up in yards of violet satin from which protruded a great dropsical [4] head and two fat pearly hands; and that was its archbishop. Between the rolls of flesh that surrounded them looked out two black eyes speaking discomfort, kindliness, and wit. A curious and eager soul was imprisoned in all this lard, but by dint of never refusing himself a pheasant or a goose or his daily procession of Roman wines, he was his own bitter jailer. He loved his cathedral; he loved his duties;

[1] **port:** carriage or bearing.
[2] *El Buen Retiro:* a park in Madrid, a fashionable gathering place.

[3] **eleven . . . Cologne:** the reference is to the legend of St. Ursula, who, accompanied by 11,000 virgins, was massacred in Cologne by the Huns.
[4] **dropsical:** swollen with dropsy, an excess of bodily fluids.

he was very devout. Some days he regarded his bulk ruefully; but the distress of remorse was less poignant than the distress of fasting, and he was presently found deliberating over the secret messages that a certain roast sends to the certain salad that will follow it. And to punish himself he led an exemplary life in every other respect.

He had read all the literature of antiquity and forgotten all about it except a general aroma of charm and disillusion. He had been learned in the Fathers and the Councils and forgotten all about them save a floating impression of dissensions that had no application to Peru. He had read all the libertine masterpieces of Italy and France and reread them annually; even in the torments of the stone (happily dissolved by drinking the water from the springs of Santa María de Cluxambuqua), he could find nothing more nourishing than the anecdotes of Brantôme [1] and the divine Aretino. [2]

The Archbishop knew that most of the priests of Peru were scoundrels. It required all his delicate Epicurean [3] education to prevent his doing something about it; he had to repeat over to himself his favorite notions: that the injustice and unhappiness in the world is a constant; that the theory of progress is a delusion; that the poor, never having known happiness, are insensible to misfortune. Like all the rich, he could not bring himself to believe that the poor (look at their houses, look at their clothes) could really suffer. Like all the cultivated, he believed that only the widely read could be said to *know*

that they were unhappy. On one occasion, the iniquities in his see [4] having been called to his notice, he almost did something about it. He had just heard that it was becoming a rule in Peru for priests to exact two measures of meal for a fairly good absolution and five measures for a really effective one. He trembled with indignation; he roared to his secretary and, bidding him bring up his writing materials, announced that he was going to dictate an overwhelming message to his shepherds. But there was no ink left in the inkwell; there was no ink left in the next room; there was no ink to be found in the whole palace. This state of things in his household so upset the good man that he fell ill of the combined rages and learned to guard himself against indignations.

The addition of the Archbishop to the suppers was so successful that Don Andrés began to think of new names. He had grown increasingly dependent upon Uncle Pio, but waited until Camila should propose his inclusion of her own accord. And in due time Uncle Pio brought with him that courser of the seas, the Captain Alvarado. Generally, the reunion had been several hours underway before Camila was able to join them after her performance at the theater. She would arrive toward one o'clock, radiant and bejeweled and very tired. The four men received her as they would a great queen. For an hour or so she would carry the conversation, but gradually reclining more and more against Don Andrés' shoulder she would follow the talk as it flitted from one humorous lined face to the other. All night they talked, secretly comforting their hearts that longed always for Spain and telling themselves that such a symposium was after the manner of the high Spanish soul. They talked about ghosts and second

[1] **Brantôme** (brän·tōm'): French soldier and historian (1540–1614).

[2] **Aretino** (ä·rä·tē'nō): an Italian satirist of the sixteenth century.

[3] **Epicurean** (ep'ə·kyo͞o·rē'ən): pertaining to the philosophy of Epicurus, a Greek who taught that pleasure is the goal of life and that genuine pleasure is derived from a life of prudence, honor, and justice.

[4] **see:** area over which a bishop or archbishop exercises authority.

sight, and about the earth before man appeared upon it, and about the possibility of the planets striking against one another; about whether the soul can be seen, like a dove, fluttering away at the moment of death; they wondered whether at the second coming of Christ to Jerusalem, Peru would be long in receiving the news. They talked until the sun rose, about wars and kings, about poets and scholars, and about strange countries. Each one poured into the conversation his store of wise, sad anecdotes and his dry regret about the race of men. The flood of golden light struck across the Andes and, entering the great window, fell upon the piles of fruit, the stained brocade upon the table, and the sweet thoughtful forehead of the Perichole as she lay sleeping against the sleeve of her protector. There would ensue a long pause, no one wishing to make the first move to go, and the glances of them all would rest upon this strange beautiful bird who lived among them. But Uncle Pio's glance had been upon her all night, a quick glance from his black eyes, full of tenderness and anxiety, resting on the great secret and reason of his life.

But Uncle Pio never ceased watching Camila. He divided the inhabitants of this world into two groups: into those who had loved and those who had not. It was a horrible aristocracy, apparently, for those who had no capacity for love (or rather for suffering in love) could not be said to be alive and certainly would not live again after their death. They were a kind of straw population, filling the world with their meaningless laughter and tears and chatter and disappearing, still lovable and vain, into thin air. For this distinction he cultivated his own definition of love that was like no other and that had gathered all its bitterness and pride from his odd life. He regarded love as a sort of cruel malady through which the elect are required to pass in their late youth and from which they emerge, pale and wrung, but ready for the business of living. There was (he believed) a great repertory of errors mercifully impossible to human beings who had recovered from this illness. Unfortunately there remained to them a host of failings, but at least (from among many illustrations) they never mistook a protracted amiability for the whole conduct of life, they never again regarded any human being, from a prince to a servant, as a mechanical object. Uncle Pio never ceased watching Camila because it seemed to him that she had never undergone this initiation. In the months that followed her introduction to the Viceroy, he held his breath and waited. He held his breath for years. Camila bore the Viceroy three children, yet remained the same. He knew that the first sign of her entrance into the true possession of the world would be the mastery of certain effects in her acting. There were certain passages in the plays that she would compass someday, simply, easily, and with secret joy, because they alluded to the new rich wisdom of her heart; but her treatment of such passages became more and more cursory, not to say embarrassed. He presently saw that she had tired of Don Andrés and had returned to a series of furtive love affairs with the actors and matadors and merchants of the town.

She became more and more impatient of acting and another parasite found its way into her mind. She wanted to be a lady. She slowly contracted a greed for respectability and began to refer to her acting as a pastime. She acquired a duenna [1] and some footmen and went to church at the fashionable hours. She attended the prize days at the University and appeared among the donors of the

[1] **duenna:** an older woman who serves as companion and chaperone to a young lady.

great charities. She even learned to read and write a little. Any faint discrimination against her as a Bohemian [1] she challenged with fury. She led the Viceroy a horrible life with her passion for concessions and her gradual usurpation of privileges. The new vice displaced the old and she became noisily virtuous. She invented some parents and produced some cousins. She obtained an undocumented legitimatization of her children. In society she cultivated a delicate and languid magdalenism,[2] as a great lady might, and she carried a candle in the penitential parades, side by side with ladies who had nothing to regret but an outburst of temper and a furtive glance into Descartes.[3] Her sin had been acting and everyone knows that there were even saints who had been actors—there was Saint Gelasius and Saint Genesius and Saint Margaret of Antioch and Saint Pelagia.

There was a fashionable watering place in the hills not far from Santa María de Cluxambuqua. Don Andrés had traveled in France and had thought to build himself a little mock Vichy; [4] there was a pagoda, some drawing rooms, a theater, a little arena for bullfights, and some French gardens. Camila's health had never known a shadow, but she built herself a villa in the vicinity and sipped the hateful waters at eleven o'clock. The Marquesa de Montemayor has left a brilliant picture of this *opéra bouffe* [5] paradise with the reigning divinity parading her fierce sensitiveness along the avenues of powdered shell and receiving the homage of all those who could not afford to offend the Viceroy.

Doña María draws a portrait of this ruler, stately and weary, gambling all through the night in sums that would have raised another Escurial.[6] And beside him she sets the portrait of his son, Camila's little Don Jaime. Don Jaime, at seven years, was a rachitic [7] little body who seemed to have inherited not only his mother's forehead and eyes, but his father's liability to convulsions. He bore his pain with the silent bewilderment of an animal, and like an animal he was mortally ashamed when any evidences of it occurred in public. He was so beautiful that the more trivial forms of pity were hushed in his presence and his long thoughts about his difficulties had given his face a patient and startling dignity. His mother dressed him in garnet velvet, and when he was able he followed her about at a distance of several yards, extricating himself gravely from the ladies who tried to detain him in conversation. Camila was never cross to Don Jaime and she was never demonstrative. When the sun was shining the two could be seen walking along those artificial terraces in silence, Camila wondering when the felicity would begin that she had always associated with social position, Don Jaime rejoicing merely in the sunlight and anxiously estimating the approach of a cloud. They looked like figures that had strayed there from some remote country, or out of an old ballad, that had not yet learned the new language and had not yet found any friends.

Camila was about thirty when she left the stage, and it required five years for her to achieve her place in society. She gradually became almost stout, though her head seemed to grow more beautiful every

[1] **Bohemian:** someone who lives in an unconventional manner.

[2] **magdalenism:** here, sudden virtue and reform.

[3] **Descartes** (dā·kärt′): seventeenth-century French mathematician and philosopher.

[4] **Vichy:** a French resort with mineral springs.

[5] **opéra bouffe** (ô·pā·rȧ bo͞of′): a farcical comic opera.

[6] **Escurial:** usually spelled Escorial, the sixteenth-century palace and mausoleum of Spanish kings, near Madrid.

[7] **rachitic** (rȧ·kit′ik): suffering from rickets, an inflammation of the spine.

year. She took to overdressing, and the floors of the drawing rooms reflected a veritable tower of jewels and scarves and plumes. Her face and hands were covered with a bluish powder against which she drew an irritable mouth in scarlet and orange. The almost distraught fury of her temper was varied by the unnatural sweetness of her address in the company of the dowagers. In the earliest stages of her progress upward she had intimated to Uncle Pio that he was not to be seen with her in public, but finally she became impatient even of his discreeter visits. She conducted the interviews with formality and evasion. Her eyes never crossed his and she angled for pretexts to quarrel with him. Still he ventured out once a month to try her patience and when the call had become impossible he would climb the stairs and finish the hour among her children.

One day he arrived at her villa in the hills and, through her maid, begged for an opportunity to talk with her. He was told that she would see him in the French gardens a little before sunset. He had come up from Lima on a strange sentimental impulse. Like all solitary persons, he had invested friendship with a divine glamour: he imagined that the people he passed on the street, laughing together and embracing when they parted, the people who dined together with so many smiles—you will scarcely believe me, but he imagined that they were extracting from all that congeniality great store of satisfaction. So that suddenly he was filled with the excitement of seeing her again, of being called "Uncle Pio," and of reviving for a moment the trust and humor of their long vagabondage.

The French gardens were at the southern end of the town. Behind them rose the higher Andes and before them there was a parapet overlooking a deep valley and overlooking wave after wave of hills that stretched toward the Pacific. It was the hour when bats fly low and the smaller animals play recklessly underfoot. A few solitaries lingered about the gardens, gazing dreamily into the sky that was being gradually emptied of its color, or leaned upon the balustrade and looked down into the valley, noting in which village a dog was barking. It was the hour when the father returns home from the fields and plays for a moment in the yard with the dog that jumps upon him, holding his muzzle closed or throwing him upon his back. The young girls look about for the first star to fix a wish upon it, and the boys

grow restless for supper. Even the busiest mother stands for a moment idle-handed, smiling at her dear and exasperating family.

Uncle Pio stood against one of the chipped marble benches and watched Camila coming toward him:

"I am late," she said. "I am sorry. What is it you wish to say to me?"

"Camila—" he began.

"My name is Doña Micaela."

"I do not wish to offend you, Doña Micaela, but when you let me call you Camila for twenty years, I should think——"

"Oh, do as you like. Do as you like."

"Camila, promise me that you will listen to me. Promise me that you will not run away at my first sentence."

At once she burst out with unexpected passion, "Uncle Pio, listen to me. You are mad if you think you can make me return to the theater. I look back at the theater with horror. Understand that. The theater! The theater, indeed! The daily payment of insults in that filthy place. Understand that you are wasting your time."

He answered gently, "I would not have you come back if you are happy with these new friends."

"You don't like my new friends, then?" she answered quickly. "Whom do you offer me in their stead?"

"Camila, I only remember . . ."

"I will not be criticized. I don't want any advice. It will be cold in a moment. I must go back to my house. Just give me up, that's all. Just put me out of your mind."

"Dear Camila, don't be angry. Let me talk to you. Just suffer me for ten minutes."

He did not understand why she was weeping. He did not know what to say. He talked at random. "You never even come to see the theater, and they all notice it.

The audiences are falling away now, too. They only put on the Old Comedy twice a week; all the other nights there are these new farces in prose. All is dull and childish and indecent. No one can speak Spanish any more. No one can even walk correctly any more. On Corpus Christi Day they gave *Belshazzar's Feast* where you were so wonderful. Now it was shameful."

There was a pause. A beautiful procession of clouds, like a flock of sheep, was straying up from the sea, slipping up the valleys between the hills. Camila suddenly touched his knee, and her face was like her face twenty years before: "Forgive me, Uncle Pio, for being so bad. Jaime was ill this afternoon. There's nothing one can do. He lies there, so white and . . . so surprised. One must just think of other things. Uncle Pio, it would be no good if I went back to the theater. The audiences come for the prose farces. We were foolish to try and keep alive the Old Comedy. Let people read the old plays in books if they choose to. It is not worthwhile fighting with the crowd."

"Wonderful Camila, I was not just to you when you were on the stage. It was some foolish pride in me. I grudged you the praise that you deserved. Forgive me. You have always been a very great artist. If you come to see that you are not happy among these people you might think about going to Madrid. You would have a great triumph there. You are still young and beautiful. There will be time later to be called Doña Micaela. We shall be old soon. We shall be dead soon."

"No, I shall never see Spain. All the world is alike, Madrid or Lima."

"Oh, if we could go away to some island where the people would know you for yourself. And love you."

"You are fifty years old and you are still dreaming of such islands, Uncle Pio."

He bent his head and mumbled, "Of

course I love you, Camila, as I always must and more than I can say. To have known you is enough for my whole life. You are a great lady now. And you are rich. There is no longer any way that I can help you. But I am always ready."

"How absurd you are," she said, smiling. "You said that as boys say it. You don't seem to learn as you grow older, Uncle Pio. There is no such thing as that kind of love and that kind of island. It's in the theater you find such things."

He looked shamefaced, but unconvinced.

At last she rose and said sadly, "What are we talking about! It is growing cold. I must be going in. You must be resigned. I have no heart for the theater." There was a pause. "And for the rest? . . . Oh, I do not understand. It is just circumstance. I must be what I must. Do not try to understand either. Don't think about me, Uncle Pio. Just forgive, that's all. Just try to forgive."

She stood still a moment, searching for something deeply felt to say to him. The first cloud reached the terrace; it was dark; the last stragglers were leaving the gardens. She was thinking of Don Jaime, and of Don Andrés, and of himself. She could not find the words. Suddenly she went down and kissed his fingers and went quickly away. But he sat for a long time in the gathering clouds trembling with happiness and trying to penetrate into the meaning of these things.

Suddenly the news was all over Lima. Doña Micaela Villegas, the lady that used to be Camila the Perichole, had the smallpox. Several hundred other persons had the smallpox also, but popular interest and malignity were concentrated upon the actress. A wild hope ran about the town that the beauty would be impaired that had enabled her to despise the class from which she sprang. The news escaped from the sickroom that Camila had become ludicrous in homeliness and the cup of the envious overflowed. As soon as she was able, she had herself carried from the city to her villa in the hills; she ordered the sale of her elegant little palace. She returned her jewels to their givers and she sold her fine clothes. The Viceroy, the Archbishop, and the few men at court who had been her sincerest admirers besieged her door still with messages and gifts; the messages were ignored and the gifts were returned without comment. No one but her nurse and maids had been permitted to see her since the commencement of her illness. As an answer to his repeated attempts, Don Andrés received a large sum of money from her with a letter compounded of all that is possible in bitterness and pride.

Like all beautiful women who have been brought up amid continual tributes to her beauty, she assumed without cynicism that it must necessarily be the basis of anyone's attachment to herself; henceforth any attention paid to her must spring from a pity full of condescension and faintly perfumed with satisfaction at so complete a reversal. This assumption that she need look for no more devotion now that her beauty had passed proceeded

from the fact that she had never realized any love save love as passion. Such love, though it expends itself in generosity and thoughtfulness, though it give birth to visions and to great poetry, remains among the sharpest expressions of self-interest. Not until it has passed through a long servitude, through its own self-hatred, through mockery, through great doubts, can it take its place among the loyalties. Many who have spent a lifetime in it can tell us less of love than the child that lost a dog yesterday. As her friends continued in their efforts to draw her again into society, she grew more and more angry and dispatched insulting messages to the city. It was said for a time that she was retiring into religion. But new rumors that all was fury and despair on the little farm contradicted the old. For those near to her the despair was fearful to behold. She was convinced that her life was over, her life and her children's. In her hysterical pride she had given back more than she owed and the approach of poverty was added to the loneliness and the gloom of her future. There was nothing left for her to do but to draw out her days in jealous solitude in the center of the little farm that was falling into decay. She brooded for hours upon the joy of her enemies and could be heard striding about her room with strange cries.

Uncle Pio did not allow himself to be discouraged. By dint of making himself useful to the children, by taking a hand in the management of the farm, and by discreetly lending her some money, he obtained his entrance into the house and even into the presence of its veiled mistress. But even then Camila, convinced in her pride that he *pitied* her, lashed him with the blade of her tongue and derived some strange comfort from heaping him with sneers. He loved her the more, understanding better than she did herself all the stages in the convalescence of her humiliated spirit. But one day an accident befell that lost him his share in her progress. He pushed open a door.

She thought she had locked it. For just one hour a foolish secret hope had come to her; she wondered whether she could make a paste of chalk and cream to spread upon her face. She who had sneered so often at the befloured grandmothers of the court wondered for a few moments whether she had learned anything on the stage that would aid her now. She thought she had locked the door and with hurried hands and beating heart she laid on the coat, the grotesque pallor, and as she gazed into the mirror and recognized the futility of her attempt she caught the image of Uncle Pio standing in the door amazed. She rose from the chair with a

cry and covered her face with her hands.

"Go away. Go away out of my house forever," she screamed. "I never want to see you again." In her shame she drove him out with blasphemy and hatred, she pursued him down the corridor and hurled objects down the stairs. She gave her farmer orders that Uncle Pio was forbidden to come into the grounds. But he continued for a week trying to see her again. At last he went back to Lima; he filled in the time as best he could, but he longed to be by her as a boy of eighteen would long. At last he devised a stratagem and returned up into the hills to put it into effect.

One morning before dawn he arose and lay on the ground below her window. He imitated in the darkness the sound of weeping, and, as nearly as he could, of a young girl's weeping. He continued in this for the whole quarter of an hour. He did not let his voice rise above that degree of loudness which Italian musicians would represent by the direction *piano*,[1] but he frequently intermitted the sound, trusting that if she were asleep it would insinuate itself into her mind as well by duration as by degree. The air was cool and agreeable. The first faint streak of sapphire was appearing behind the peaks and in the east the star of morning was pulsating every moment with a more tender intention. A profound silence wrapped all the farm buildings, only an occasional breeze set all the grasses sighing. Suddenly a lamp was lighted in her room and a moment later the shutter was thrown back and a head wrapped in veils leaned far out.

"Who is there?" asked the beautiful voice.

Uncle Pio remained silent.

Camila said again in a tone edged with impatience:

"Who is there? Who is there weeping?"

"Doña Micaela, my lady, I beg of you to come here to me."

"Who are you and what do you want?"

"I am a poor girl. I am Estrella. I beg of you to come and help me. Do not call your maid. I pray you, Doña Micaela, to come yourself."

Camila was silent a moment, then said abruptly, "Very well," and closed the shutter. Presently she appeared around the corner of the house. She wore a thick cloak that dragged in the dew. She stood at a distance and said, "Come over here to where I am standing—Who are you?"

Uncle Pio rose up. "Camila, it is I— Uncle Pio. Forgive me, but I must speak to you."

"Mother of God, when shall I be free of this dreadful person! Understand: I want to see no one. I don't want to speak to a soul. My life is over. That is all."

"Camila, by our long life together, I beg of you to grant me one thing. I shall go away and never trouble you again."

"I grant you nothing, nothing. Stay away from me."

"I promise you I shall never trouble you again if you listen to me this once." She was hurrying around to the door on the other side of the house and Uncle Pio was obliged to run beside her to make sure that she heard what he was saying. She stopped:

"What is it then? Hurry. It is cold. I am not well. I must go back to my room."

"Camila, let me take Don Jaime for a year to live with me in Lima. Let me be his teacher. Let me teach him the Castilian. Here he is left among the servants. He is learning nothing."

"No."

"Camila, what will become of him? He has a good mind and he wants to learn."

"He is sick. He is delicate. Your house is a sty. Only the country is good for him."

[1] **piano:** soft, softly.

"But he has been much better these last few months. I promise you I shall clean out my house. I shall apply to Madre María del Pilar for a housekeeper. Here he is in your stables all day. I shall teach him all that a gentleman should know—fencing and Latin and music. We shall read all . . ."

"A mother cannot be separated from her child like that. It is impossible. You are crazy to have thought of it. Give up thinking of me and of everything about me. I no longer exist. I and my children will get on as best we can. Do not try to disturb me again. I do not want to see any human being."

Now it was that Uncle Pio felt obliged to use a hard measure. "Then pay me the money that you owe me," he said.

Camila stood still, confounded. To herself she said, "Life is too fearful to bear. When may I die?" After a moment she answered him, in a hoarse voice, "I have very little money. I will pay you what I can. I will pay you now. I have a few jewels here. Then we need never see one another again." She was ashamed of her poverty. She took a few steps, then turned and said, "Now I see that you are a very hard man. But it is right that I pay you what I owe you."

"No, Camila, I only said that to enforce my request. I shall take no money from you. But lend me Don Jaime for one year. I shall love him and take every care of him. Did I harm you? Was I a bad teacher to you in those other years?"

"It is cruel of you to keep urging gratitude, gratitude, gratitude. I was grateful—good, good! But now that I am no longer the same woman there remains nothing to be grateful for." There was a silence. Her eyes were resting on the star that seemed to be leading forth the whole sky in its wonder. A great pain lay at her heart, the pain of a world that was meaningless.

Then she said, "If Jaime wishes to go with you, very well. I shall talk to him in the morning. If he wishes to go with you, you will find him at the Inn about noon. Good night. Go with God."

"Go with God."

She returned to the house. The next day the grave little boy appeared at the Inn. His fine clothes were torn and stained now and he carried a small bundle for change. His mother had given him a gold piece for spending money and a little stone that shone in the dark to look at in his sleepless nights. They set off together in a cart, but soon Uncle Pio became

aware that the jolting was not good for the boy. He carried him on his shoulder. As they drew near to the bridge of San Luis Rey, Jaime tried to conceal his shame, for he knew that one of those moments was coming that separated him from other people. He was especially ashamed because Uncle Pio had just overtaken a friend of his, a sea captain. And just as they got to the bridge he spoke to an old

lady who was traveling with a little girl. Uncle Pio said that when they had crossed the bridge they would sit down and rest, but it turned out not to be necessary.

FOR STUDY AND DISCUSSION

1. What picture do you get of Uncle Pio from the Marquesa's letter? Why does she compare him to an ant? Which qualities in him does she admire? Which does she dislike?

2. What were Uncle Pio's three great aims in life? How did he satisfy them by becoming the tutor of Camila Perichole? What qualities made her a great actress? Why was tutoring her so painful? What is the answer to the question, "Whom were these two seeking to please?"

3. Uncle Pio is one of the few characters Wilder describes physically. What are his outstanding features? What facts in his past explain the sadness in his eyes?

4. What kind of person was the Viceroy? What kind of love did Camila feel for him? How was she changed as a result of their association? What attitude toward life did she hear expressed at their midnight suppers?

5. Into what two kinds of people did Uncle Pio divide everyone? Why did he feel that Camila had never really loved? What change in her did he expect to see had she truly loved?

6. As Camila became more and more "respectable," how did her attitude toward Uncle Pio change? Why did he continue to see her? What would he have liked her to do?

7. What was Camila's idea of love? What was Uncle Pio's? Do you agree that "there is no such thing as that kind of love and that kind of island"? Do you think the author does? Why or why not?

8. After having had smallpox, what did Camila's behavior show about her pride? Why was she so furious at Uncle Pio? Do you think his offer to teach Don Jaime was due to his desire for "overseeing the lives of others" or that it was an act of love?

9. What decision did Jaime make on the morning of his death? Do you think it was the right one? As he approached the bridge with Uncle Pio, why was he suddenly ashamed?

Perhaps an Intention

A NEW BRIDGE of stone has been built in the place of the old, but the event has not been forgotten. It has passed into proverbial expressions. "I may see you Tuesday," says a Limean, "unless the bridge falls." "My cousin lives by the bridge of San Luis Rey," says another, and a smile goes around the company, for that also means: under the sword of Damocles.[1] There are some poems about the accident, classics to be found in every Peruvian anthology, but the real literary monument is Brother Juniper's book.

There are a hundred ways of wondering at circumstances. Brother Juniper would never have arrived at his method had it not been for his friendship with a certain master in the University of San Martín. This student's wife had stolen away one morning on a boat for Spain, following a soldier, and had left him the care of two daughters in their cradle. He was possessed of all the bitterness that Brother Juniper lacked and derived a sort of joy from the conviction that all was wrong in the world. He whispered into the Franciscan's ear such thoughts and anecdotes as belied the notion of a guided world. For a moment a look of distress, almost of defeat, would come into the Brother's eyes; then he would begin patiently explaining why such stories held no difficulty for a believer. "There was a queen of Naples and Sicily," the student would say,

[1] **sword of Damocles:** Damocles was a courtier who attempted to flatter King Dionysius of Syracuse by repeatedly praising the happiness of kings. Dionysius, in answer, invited Damocles to a royal banquet and seated him directly under a sword suspended by a single hair.

"who discovered that she was carrying an angry tumor in her side. In great dismay she commanded her subjects to fall to their prayers and ordered that all the garments in Sicily and Naples be sewn with votive crosses. She was well loved by her people and all their prayers and embroideries were sincere, but ineffectual. Now she lies in the splendor of Monreale, and a few inches above her heart may be read the words: *I shall fear no evil.*"

It was by dint of hearing a great many such sneers at faith that Brother Juniper became convinced that the world's time had come for proof, tabulated proof, of the conviction that was so bright and exciting within him. When the pestilence visited his dear village of Puerto and carried off a large number of peasants, he secretly drew up a diagram of the characteristics of fifteen victims and fifteen survivors, the statistics of their value *sub specie aeternitatis*.[1] Each soul was rated upon a basis of ten as regards its goodness, its diligence in religious observance, and its importance to its family group.

[1] ***sub specie aeternitatis*** (sub spē·shi i·tûr·ni-tā′tis): in the eyes of eternity.

Here is a fragment of this ambitious chart:

	Goodness	Piety	Usefulness
Alfonso G.	4	4	10
Nina	2	5	10
Manuel B.	10	10	0
Alfonso V.	−8	−10	10
Vera N.	0	10	10

The thing was more difficult than he had foreseen. Almost every soul in a difficult frontier community turned out to be indispensable economically, and the third column was all but useless. The examiner was driven to the use of minus terms when he confronted the personal character of Alfonso V., who was not, like Vera N., merely bad: he was a propagandist for badness and not merely avoided church but led others to avoid it. Vera N. was indeed bad, but she was a model worshiper and the mainstay of a full hut. From all this saddening data Brother Juniper contrived an index for each peasant. He added up the total for victims and compared it with the total for survivors, to discover that the dead were five times more worth saving. It almost looked as though the pestilence had been directed

against the really valuable people in the village of Puerto. And on that afternoon Brother Juniper took a walk along the edge of the Pacific. He tore up his findings and cast them into the waves; he gazed for an hour upon the great clouds of pearl that hang forever upon the horizon of that sea, and extracted from their beauty a resignation that he did not permit his reason to examine. The discrepancy between faith and the facts is greater than is generally assumed.

But there was another story of the master of San Martín (not so subversive, this one) that probably gave to Brother Juniper the hint for his procedure after the fall of the bridge of San Luis Rey.

This master was one day walking through the Cathedral of Lima and stopped to read the epitaph of a lady. He read with an increasingly prominent lower lip that she had been for twenty years the center and joy of her home, that she had been the delight of her friends, that all who met her went away in astonishment at her goodness and beauty, and that there she lay awaiting the return of her Lord. Now on the day that he read these words, the master of San Martín had had much to fret him, and raising his eyes from the tablet he spoke aloud in his rage. "The shame of it, the persecution of it! Everyone knows that in the world we do nothing but feed our wills. Why perpetuate this legend of self-lessness? Why keep this thing alive, this rumor of disinterestedness?"

And so saying, he resolved to expose this conspiracy of the stonecutters. The lady had been dead only twelve years. He sought out her servants, her children, and her friends. And everywhere he went, like a perfume, her dear traits had survived her and wherever she was mentioned there arose a suffering smile and the protest that words could not describe the gracious ways of her. Even the eager youth of her grandchildren, who had never seen her, was made more difficult by the news that it was possible to be as good as that. And the man stood amazed; only at last he muttered, "Nevertheless, what I said was true. This woman was an exception, perhaps an exception."

In compiling his book about these people Brother Juniper seemed to be pursued by the fear that in omitting the slightest detail he might lose some guiding hint. The longer he worked, the more he felt that he was stumbling about among great dim imitations. He was forever being cheated by details that looked as though they were significant if only he could find their setting. So he put everything down on the notion perhaps that if he (or a keener head) reread the book twenty times, the countless facts would suddenly start to move, to assemble, and to betray their secret. The Marquesa de Monte-mayor's cook told him that she lived almost entirely on rice, fish, and a little fruit, and Brother Juniper put it down on the chance that it would someday reveal a spiritual trait. Don Rubío said of her that she used to appear at his receptions without invitation in order to steal the spoons. A midwife on the edge of the town declared that Doña María called upon her with morbid questions until she had been obliged to order her away from the door like a beggar. The bookseller of the town reported that she was one of the three most cultivated persons in Lima. Her farmer's wife declared that she was absent-minded, but compact of goodness. The art of biography is more difficult than is generally supposed.

Brother Juniper found that there was least to be learned from those who had been most closely associated with the subjects of his inquiry. Madre María del Pilar talked to him at length about Pepita,

but she did not tell him of her own ambitions for her. The Perichole was at first difficult óf approach, but presently even liked the Franciscan. Her characterization of Uncle Pio flatly contradicted the stores of unsavory testimonies that he had acquired elsewhere. Her allusions to her son were few and conceded with pain. They closed the interview abruptly. The Captain Alvarado told what he could of Esteban and of Uncle Pio. Those who know most in this realm, venture least.

I shall spare you Brother Juniper's generalizations. They are always with us. He thought he saw in the same accident the wicked visited by destruction and the good called early to Heaven. He thought he saw pride and wealth confounded as an object lesson to the world, and he thought he saw humility crowned and rewarded for the edification of the city. But Brother Juniper was not satisfied with his reasons. It was just possible that the Marquesa de Montemayor was not a monster of avarice and Uncle Pio of self-indulgence.

The book being done fell under the eyes of some judges and was suddenly pronounced heretical. It was ordered to be burned in the Square with its author. Brother Juniper submitted to the decision that the devil had made use of him to effect a brilliant campaign in Peru. He sat in his cell that last night trying to seek in his own life the pattern that had escaped him in five others. He was not rebellious. He was willing to lay down his life for the purity of the church, but he longed for one voice somewhere to testify for him that his intention, at least, had been for faith; he thought there was no one in the world who believed him. But the next morning in all that crowd and sunlight there were many who believed, for he was much loved.

There was a little delegation from the village of Puerto, and Nina (Goodness 2, Piety 5, Usefulness 10) and others stood with drawn, puzzled faces while their little friar was given to the congenial flames. Even then, even then, there remained in his heart an obstinate nerve insisting that at least St. Francis would not utterly have condemned him, and (not daring to call upon a greater name, since he seemed so open to error in these matters) he called twice upon St. Francis and, leaning upon a flame, he smiled and died.

The day of the service was clear and warm. The Limeans, their black eyes wide with awe, poured through the streets into their Cathedral and stood gazing at the mound of black velvet and silver. The

Archbishop, enclosed in his wonderful and almost wooden vestments, perspired upon his throne, lending from time to time a connoisseur's ear to the felicities of Victoria's counterpoint. The choir had restudied the pages that, as his farewell to music, Tomás Luis [1] had composed for his friend and patron, the Empress of Austria, and all that grief and sweetness, all that Spanish realism filtering through an Italian mode, rose and fell above the sea of man-

[1] **Tomás Luis:** the composer Tomás Luis Victoria.

tillas. Don Andrés, under the colors and feathered hangings of his office, knelt, ill and troubled. He knew that the crowd was furtively glancing at him, expecting him to play the father who has lost his only son. He wondered whether the Perichole was present. He had never been obliged to go so long without smoking. The Captain Alvarado pushed in from the sunny square for a moment. He looked across the fields of black hair and lace at the trooping of the candles and the ropes of incense. "How false, how unreal," he said, and pushed his way out. He descended to the sea and sat on the edge of his boat, gazing down into the clear water. "Happy are the drowned, Esteban," he said.

Behind the screen the Abbess sat among her girls. The night before she had torn an idol from her heart and the experience had left her pale but firm. She had accepted the fact that it was of no importance whether her work went on or not; it was enough to work. She was the nurse who tends the sick who never recover; she was the priest who perpetually renews the office [1] before an altar to which no worshipers come. There would be no Pepita to enlarge her work; it would relapse into the indolence and the indifference of her colleagues. It seemed to be sufficient for Heaven that for a while in Peru a disinterested love had flowered and faded. She leaned her forehead upon her hand, following the long tender curve that the soprano lifts in the Kyrie. [2] "My affection should have had more of that color, Pepita. My whole life should have had more of that quality. I have been too busy," she added ruefully, and her mind drifted into prayer.

Camila had started from the farm to attend the service. Her heart was filled with consternation and amazement. Here was another comment from the skies; that was the third time she had been spoken to. Her smallpox, Jaime's illness, and now the fall of the bridge—oh, these were not accidents. She was as ashamed as though letters had appeared on her forehead. An order from the Palace announced that the Viceroy was sending her two daughters to a convent school in Spain. That was right. She was alone. She gathered a few things together mechanically and started to the city for the service. But she fell to thinking of the crowds gaping over her Uncle Pio and over her son; she thought of the vast ritual of the church, like a chasm into which the beloved falls, and of the storm of the *dies irae,* [3] where the individual is lost among the millions of the dead, features grow dim, and traits fade. At a little more than half the journey, at the mud church of San Luis Rey, she slipped in and knelt against a pillar to rest. She wandered through her memory, searching for the faces of her two. She waited for some emotion to appear. "But I feel nothing," she whispered to herself. "I have no heart. I am a poor meaningless woman, that's all. I am shut out. I have no heart. Look, I won't try and think of anything; let me just rest here." And scarcely had she paused when again that terrible incommunicable pain swept through her, the pain that could not speak once to Uncle Pio and tell him of her love and just once offer her courage to Jaime in his sufferings. She started up wildly: "I fail everybody," she cried. "They love me and I fail them." She returned to the farm and carried for a year the mood of her self-despair. One day she heard by accident that the wonderful Abbess had lost two persons whom she loved

[1] **renews the office:** performs the service.
[2] **the Kyrie:** the musical setting of the Latin mass *Kyrie eleison* (kir′i·ē i·lā′i·sən)—"Lord, have mercy on us."

[3] *dies irae* (dī′ēz ī′rē): literally, day of wrath, a Latin hymn sung in requiem masses.

in the same accident. Her sewing fell from her hand: then *she* would know, she would explain. "But no, what would she say to me! She would not even believe that such a person as I could love or could lose." Camila decided to go to Lima and look at the Abbess from a distance. "If her face tells me that she would not despise me, I will speak to her," she said.

Camila lurked about the convent church and fell humbly in love with the homely old face, though it frightened her a little. At last she called upon her.

"Mother," she said, "I . . . I . . ."

"Do I know you, my daughter?"

"I was the actress, I was the Perichole."

"Oh, yes. Oh, I have wished to know you for a long while, but they told me you did not wish to be seen. You too, I know, lost in the fall of the bridge of San . . ."

Camila rose and swayed. There! again that access of pain, the hands of the dead she could not reach. Her lips were white. Her head brushed the Abbess's knee. "Mother, what shall I do? I am all alone. I have nothing in the world. I love them. What shall I do?"

The Abbess looked at her closely. "My daughter, it is warm here. Let us go into the garden. You can rest there." She made a sign to a girl in the cloister to bring some water. She continued talking mechanically to Camila. "I have wished to know you for a long while, señora. Even before the accident I had wished much to know you. They told me that in the *autos sacramentales*[1] you were a very great and beautiful actress, in *Belshazzar's Feast*."

"Oh, Mother, you must not say that. I am a sinner. You must not say that."

"Here, drink this, my child. We have a beautiful garden, do you not think so? You will come and see us often and someday you will meet Sister Juana who is our

gardener-in-chief. Before she entered religion she had almost never seen a garden, for she worked in the mines high up in the mountains. Now everything grows under her hand—A year has gone by, señora, since our accident. I lost two who had been children in my orphanage, but you lost a real child of your own?"

"Yes, Mother."

"And a great friend?"

"Yes, Mother."

"Tell me. . . ."

And then the whole tide of Camila's long despair, her lonely obstinate despair since her girlhood, found its rest on that dusty friendly lap among Sister Juana's fountains and roses.

But where are sufficient books to contain the events that would not have been the same without the fall of the bridge? From such a number I choose one more.

"The Condesa d'Abuirre wishes to see you," said a lay sister at the door of the Abbess's office.

"Well," said the Abbess, laying down her pen, "who is she?"

[1] *autos sacramentales:* poems on religious subjects, presented as a play.

"She has just come from Spain. I don't know."

"Oh, it is some money, Inez, some money for my house for the blind. Quick, bid her come in."

The tall, rather languorous beauty entered the room. Doña Clara, who was generally so adequate, seemed constrained for once. "Are you busy, dear Mother, may I talk to you for a while?"

"I am quite free, my daughter. You will excuse an old woman's memory; have I known you before?"

"My mother was the Marquesa de Montemayor. . . ." Doña Clara suspected that the Abbess had not admired her mother and would not let the older woman speak until she herself had made a long passionate defense of Doña María. The languor fell away in her self-reproach. At last the Abbess told her of Pepita and Esteban, and of Camila's visit. "All, all of us have failed. One wishes to be punished. One is willing to assume all kinds of penance, but do you know, my daughter, that in love—I scarcely dare say it—but in love our very mistakes don't seem to be able to last long?"

The Condesa showed the Abbess Doña María's last letter. Madre María dared not say aloud how great her astonishment was that such words (words that since then the whole world has murmured over with joy) could spring in the heart of Pepita's mistress. "Now learn," she commanded herself, "learn at last that anywhere you may expect grace." And she was filled with happiness like a girl at this new proof that the traits she lived for were everywhere, that the world was ready. "Will you do me a kindness, my daughter? Will you let me show you my work?"

The sun had gone down, but the Abbess led the way with a lantern down corridor after corridor. Doña Clara saw the old and the young, the sick and the blind, but most of all she saw the tired, bright old woman who was leading her. The Abbess would stop in a passageway and say suddenly, "I can't help thinking that something could be done for the deaf-and-dumb. It seems to me that some patient person could . . . could study out a language for them. You know there are hundreds and hundreds in Peru. Do you remember whether anyone in Spain has found a way for them? Well, someday they will." Or a little later: "Do you know, I keep thinking that something can be done for the insane. I am old, you know, and I cannot go where these things are talked about, but I watch them sometimes and it seems to me . . . In Spain, now, they are gentle with them? It seems to me that there is a secret about it, just hidden from us, just around the corner. Someday, back in Spain, if you hear of anything that would help us, you will write me a letter . . . if you are not too busy?"

At last after Doña Clara had seen even the kitchens, the Abbess said, "Now will you excuse me, for I must go into the room of the very sick and say a few words for them to think about when they cannot sleep. I will not ask you to come with me there, for you are not accustomed to such . . . such sounds and things. And besides, I only talk to them as one talks to children." She looked up at her with her modest rueful smile. Suddenly she disappeared a moment to return with one of her helpers, one who had likewise been involved in the affair of the bridge and who had formerly been an actress. "She is leaving me," said the Abbess, "for some work across the city and when I have spoken here I must leave you both, for the flour broker will not wait for me any longer, and our argument will take a long time."

But Doña Clara stood in the door as

the Abbess talked to them, the lamp placed on the floor beside her. Madre María stood with her back against a post; the sick lay in rows gazing at the ceiling and trying to hold their breaths. She talked that night of all those out in the dark (she was thinking of Esteban alone, she was thinking of Pepita alone) who had no one to turn to, for whom the world perhaps was more than difficult, without meaning. And those who lay in their beds there felt that they were within a wall that the Abbess had built for them; within all was light and warmth, and without was the darkness they would not exchange even for a relief from pain and from dying. But even while she was talking, other thoughts were passing in the back of her mind. "Even now," she thought, "almost no one remembers Esteban and Pepita, but myself. Camila alone remembers her Uncle Pio and her son; this woman, her mother. But soon we shall die and all memory of those five will have left the earth, and we ourselves shall be loved for a while and forgotten. But the love will have been enough; all those impulses of love return to the love that made them. Even memory is not necessary for love. There is a land of the living and a land of the dead and the bridge is love, the only survival, the only meaning."

FOR STUDY AND DISCUSSION

1. Why was Brother Juniper's fellow student so bitter? What effect did his attitude have on Brother Juniper? What was the ultimate result of Brother Juniper's dedicated quest for proof?

2. What were the results of Brother Juniper's experiment in the village of Puerto? In what ways is his chart amusing? Why did he destroy his findings?

3. How did Brother Juniper's efforts illustrate the truth of Wilder's statement that "The art of biography is more difficult than is generally supposed"? At the end of his investigation, what were Brother Juniper's generalizations? What does the author think of them?

4. The accident brings together at the end of the novel three women who never would have met otherwise. What new realization has each of them come to since the accident?

5. What is the Abbess's conclusion about death and love? Do you agree? does the author? What in the novel makes you think so?

THE NOVEL AS A WHOLE

1. How does the novel answer Brother Juniper's question: Do we live by chance or by divine plan? Where in the novel would you say chance affects the characters' lives and actions? In what events and outcomes can you see some sort of pattern? Is the evidence heavier on the side of chance or of pattern? How do you think the author would answer Brother Juniper's question?

2. What appears to be Wilder's attitude toward science and the scientific method? Why did Brother Juniper fail in his attempt to prove scientifically that the accident was an act of God? Should he have known better? Why? What do the following quotes suggest about the author's attitude:

"The discrepancy between faith and the facts is greater than is generally assumed."

"And I, who claim to know so much more, isn't it possible that even I have missed the very spring within the spring?"

3. Throughout the novel Wilder contrasts the *external* (the physical, which can be sensed or seen) with the *internal* (the intuitive, which can be guessed but not explained). Which characters' outward appearance is farthest from their inner nature? Which characters most drastically misjudge each others' real nature? Do you think it is possible to truly know another person?

4. What does the Marquesa learn about pride? about love? about loyalty? What does Esteban learn? What does Camila Perichole learn? What, in this novel, seems to be the relationship between suffering and love? How does it compare with the relationship between suffering and love in *Silas Marner*?

5. What decision does each of the victims of the accident make shortly before crossing the bridge of San Luis Rey? What commitment is made by each of them? What crisis does each overcome? What connection do you see between these personal decisions and the Abbess's final benediction, "There is a land of the living and a land of the dead and the bridge is love, the only survival, the only meaning"?

THE CRAFT OF THE NOVELIST

1. The fall of the bridge is the major element of unity in Wilder's plot. How does he use the relationship of the characters to each other to further unify the plot?

2. How does Wilder tell his story so as to make his characters believable and real? Are most of the characters introduced directly, or are they seen first through the eyes of others? How are the Marquesa's letters used throughout the novel?

3. An author must make believable any change of heart in his characters. Do you think Wilder succeeded or failed in the case of the Marquesa? of Doña Clara? of the Perichole? Why?

4. Camila Perichole changes before our very eyes. What picture do we get of her through the eyes of the Marquesa? of Manuel? of Esteban? of Uncle Pio? What was your first opinion of her? What is your final opinion?

5. How does the way Wilder tells his story compare with the way George Eliot tells her story in *Silas Marner?* Which novel is more strictly chronological? Would you say that the method used by Wilder in *The Bridge of San Luis Rey* is more effective than a more traditional one would have been for this particular story? Explain.

FOR COMPOSITION

1. Which character in *The Bridge of San Luis Rey* did you like best or consider most admirable? Why? Write a short essay, stating your choice and explaining your reasons.

2. The Archbishop and the Abbess held somewhat similar positions. Were they alike as persons in any way? How did they differ in their attitude toward right and wrong? Compare the two in a short composition, discussing fully the character of each.

3. In speaking of Doña Clara, the Marquesa said to the Perichole: "Any misunderstandings between us are so plainly my fault . . ." Do you agree? Discuss the relationship between the Marquesa and Doña Clara in a short composition, arguing for or against this view.

4. Wilder gives only a few suggestive words of the Marquesa's immortal paragraph on love. How would you complete it? Continue from where Wilder leaves off, beginning, "Of the thousands of persons we meet in a lifetime, my child . . ."

SILAS MARNER AND *THE BRIDGE OF SAN LUIS REY*

The major theme of both *Silas Marner* and *The Bridge of San Luis Rey* is the redeeming power of love. The authors of both novels show that there are many kinds of love, from selfish possessiveness to unselfish devotion. In answering the following questions, try to come to an understanding of what these authors meant by love.

1. How is the love between Silas and Eppie like the love between Manuel and Esteban? Which of the twins—Manuel or Esteban—is more like Eppie in his love?

2. Pepita, the Abbess, Dolly Winthrop, and Nancy Lammeter are all unselfish characters. Which of them are most alike in the way they love?

3. How is Godfrey's relationship to Eppie like that of the Marquesa to Pepita? What lesson do both Godfrey and the Marquesa learn about moral courage and real love?

4. Both the Captain and Nancy, Godfrey's wife, have been deeply disillusioned. Which of them was more responsible for his (or her) own predicament? How do they differ in their attitudes toward their misfortune?

5. Eppie and Uncle Pio differ in age, sex, character, and way of life, yet they have a very similar idea of love. How is this shown in their actions toward others? in what they say to others about happiness and love?

Reading and Writing About Literature

Literary criticism helps to give a reader new insights about a work of literature. It also often stimulates a reader to form his own ideas about a given work. However, the reader should always remember to check the critic's interpretation against the facts as they are presented in the work itself (see pages 532 and 584).

Below are some statements on *Silas Marner* and *The Bridge of San Luis Rey*. Each quotation is followed by a question which you may answer in a brief essay, attacking or defending the opinion expressed. Be sure to support your own conclusions with specific references from the appropriate work.

"Within the neatly articulated simple ... plot of *Silas Marner* George Eliot creates a little world of sharply individualized characters. She presents them mainly by their own words and acts and her own commentary on their behavior is never overelaborate and never patronizing." (Joan Bennett, *George Eliot: Her Mind and Her Art.*)

Which characters in *Silas Marner* are most sharply individualized? How does Eliot reveal her attitude toward them through their words and acts, and her commentary?

"... we always see him [Silas] ... as the pathetic figure he ... is, which is how George Eliot shows him, and as the essentially alien creature, the outsider, that he is for the villagers." (Walter Allen, *The English Novel.*)

How do the men at the Rainbow Inn feel about Silas? How is he regarded by the Cass family? Dolly Winthrop? the Raveloe boys who peep in his window?

"He [Wilder] shows that those who remain alive as well as those who die on the bridge suffer through the preliminary stages of love until they reach an enlightenment that brings the full knowledge and reward of love ..." (Oscar H. Fidell, ed., *The Bridge of San Luis Rey.*)

What discovery about the nature of real love is made by those who die on the bridge? What discovery is made by those whose lives are spared? In *Silas Marner,* how has the suffering experienced by Silas prepared him to love Eppie with complete selflessness?

"... Wilder speaks out for the ... pursuit of purely human relationships. If the five characters are tragic, they are so not ... because they die, but because they have not truly lived ..." (Malcolm Goldstein, *The Art of Thornton Wilder.*)

In Wilder's opinion, what qualities would characterize someone who "truly lived"? How does Wilder's idea of what makes a meaningful life compare with Eliot's?

ART AND LITERATURE

The work of the painter, unlike that of the writer, has an immediate visual impact. Its many elements, including form and color, can all be seen at once. Study the paintings on pages 619–24, and in a brief composition explain which painting appeals to you most in terms of its overall impact—and why.

Humor and whimsy are delightful ingredients in both art and literature. Study the paintings on pages 755–60, and select the ones you find especially amusing. Explain your choices in a brief essay.

THE COMPOSITION AND LANGUAGE PROGRAM

Assignments Based on Selections

All assignments are presented in the anthology under the heading *For Composition*. Numbers in parentheses refer to the numbered items in the text under the heading *For Composition*.

Writing About Literature: Assignments in Literary Criticism

Essay interpreting one aspect of the drama *Julius Caesar* that is in conflict with one of critic E. M. Forster's views 205

Julius Caesar (For Composition)

Essay on Shakespeare's use of imagery to develop a theme 474

Julius Caesar (For Composition, number 6)

Explanation, using specific examples, of how Shakespeare developed Plutarch's work into the play *Julius Caesar* 474

Julius Caesar (For Composition, number 7)

Essay on characterization in *Arms and the Man* 531

Arms and the Man (For Composition, number 5)

Relating a definition of tragedy to the play *Julius Caesar* 532

Reading and Writing About Literature

Essay supporting or refuting a professional critic's opinion on the works of either Malory or Tennyson 584

Reading and Writing About Literature

Comparison of similar themes in two novels 791

Silas Marner and The Bridge of San Luis Rey (For Composition, number 5)

Essay supporting or refuting a professional critic's views on *Silas Marner* or *The Bridge of San Luis Rey* 792

Reading and Writing About Literature

Practice in Reading and Writing

A list of the sections in the anthology which provide model paragraphs and writing exercises based on models of description, narration, and exposition, and on literary criticism.

Narration 167–68

Writing Dialogue 168

Description 221–22

Writing to Convey a Main Impression 222

Exposition 287–88

Your Own Tone in Writing 288

Reading and Writing About Poetry 381–82

Writing About a Poem 382

Reading and Writing About Literature 532, 584, 792

Assignments relating statements by professional critics to specific literary works

Study of Expository Skills

Use of narrative illustrations 174, 184

"On Liars" 174

"The Voyage" 184

Topic sentences 174

"On Liars"

Arrangement of details in chronological order 201

"The Streets—Morning and Night"

Organization and unity 205

"Julius Caesar"

Conciseness 207

"The Crack of Doom"

Organization, coherence, and clarity 212

"The Rio Grande"

796

Literary Terms and Techniques

Glossary of Literary Terms

Numbers after entries are page references indicating location of principal discussions of literary terms.

ALLEGORY A tale in verse or prose in which the characters represent abstract ideas or moral qualities.

ALLITERATION The repetition of initial consonant sounds of words as in "*w*ild and *w*oolly" or "*th*ick and *th*in."

ALLUSION A reference to something in history, mythology, literature, etc., which the author expects the reader to recognize.

ANALOGY A comparison between two objects to show the similarities between them. Analogies are often used for illustration (to explain something unfamiliar by comparing it to something familiar) or for argument (to persuade that what holds true for one thing should hold true for the thing to which it is compared).

ANAPEST A poetic foot consisting of two unstressed syllables followed by a stressed syllable.

ANTAGONIST A person opposing the protagonist (see page 800) in a dramatic or narrative work.

APPROXIMATE RHYME Rhyme in which only the final consonant sounds of the words are identical (as opposed to *exact rhyme*). *Cook-look* is an exact rhyme; *cook-lack* is an approximate rhyme.

ASSONANCE The repetition of vowel sounds, especially in poetry, as in t*ea* l*ea*f.

ATMOSPHERE The prevailing mood of a literary work. 722

AUTOBIOGRAPHY An author's account of his own life. 230

BALLAD A story told in verse. *Folk ballads,* by unknown authors, have come down from the Middle Ages or the early modern period. The *literary ballad* is the work of an author who is imitating folk ballads. Almost all ballads use the BALLAD STANZA. 296

BALLAD STANZA A stanza of four lines. The first and third lines have four stresses, or beats. The second and fourth lines each have three stresses. Lines two and four rhyme.

BIOGRAPHY The detailed story of a person's life. 223

BLANK VERSE A line of poetry that usually contains ten syllables in which every other syllable, beginning with the second, is stressed. Blank verse is often used in verse plays and in narrative poems.

CAESURA A break or pause in a line of poetry.

CHARACTER A person in a story, novel, play, or narrative poem. 28, 586–87, 722

CHARACTERIZATION The sort of personality a character displays; also the means by which the author reveals those characteristics. 28, 586–87, 722

CLIMAX The crisis or turning point in a play or story; the point of greatest intensity or interest. 586, 722

COMEDY In general, a literary work or situation which is amusing rather than weighty or painful. 384–85

CONFLICT A clash of purposes or viewpoints in a story, a novel, and especially in a play. Usually the whole action of a play is built up from a basic conflict. 2

CONNOTATION All emotions and associations that a word may arouse. Connotation is usually opposed to *denotation,* the literal meaning of a word. 184

CONNOTE To suggest or imply a meaning.

CONSONANCE The repetition of consonant sounds, especially in poetry, as in "wo*rl*d of me*rr*iment."

CONTEXT The situation in which a word occurs: that is, the words surrounding it and the general meaning of the passage. Context clarifies and deepens the meaning of a word or a passage.

COUPLET Two consecutive lines of poetry that rhyme. 315

DACTYL A poetic foot consisting of a stressed syllable followed by two unstressed syllables.

DEAD METAPHOR A metaphor which has become so commonplace that it seems literal rather than metaphorical (e.g., the *foot* of a hill). 347

DENOTATION See CONNOTATION.

DIALOGUE The speech exchanged between characters in a literary work. 383

DICTION An author's choice of words, particularly for clearness, effectiveness, and correctness.

DRAMATIC MONOLOGUE A form of dramatic poem in which one character speaks either to himself or to another character. The occasion is usually a crucial and self-revealing moment in the speaker's life. 317

DRAMATIC POETRY Poetry which presents one or more characters speaking, usually to other characters. 295, 317

ELEGY A poem mourning the death of an individual. See, for example, "Elegy" by Robert Bridges (page 313).

END RHYME Rhyme that occurs at the ends of lines of poetry.

EPIC A long narrative poem that relates the deeds of a hero. 296

EPIGRAM A short, often witty, poem or saying that sums up a writer's attitude on a particular subject. 347

EPITAPH A short poem in memory of some one who has died. 349

ESSAY A piece of prose, usually short, that expresses a personal point of view. 169

EXAGGERATION Overstatement or overemphasis; hyperbole. The opposite of understatement. 246

EXPOSITION The kind of writing that seeks primarily to present information. Also the part of a story, novel, and especially a play that helps the reader to understand the situation. 722

FARCE A humorous play with highly improbable characters and situations. 385

FIGURATIVE LANGUAGE Language that departs from the strictly literal to achieve special effects. Such language makes use of devices called figures of speech (see FIGURE OF SPEECH). 340

FIGURE OF SPEECH A device that permits an author to say one thing and mean another. The two most common kinds of figures of speech—SIMILE (see page 801) and METAPHOR (see page 800)—depend on a comparison of different things. 346

FLASHBACK A scene in a story or novel that goes back to an event in the past.

FORESHADOW To suggest what will come later in a story, novel, or play by means of hints or by showing events of a similar nature. 722

FORM The arrangement of all aspects of a work of art to make a unified whole. The form of a work is frequently opposed to its *content*. In such a case, content refers to what the work is about, while *form* refers to the way the work is organized and designed.

FORMAL ESSAY An essay that is carefully organized, methodical, and serious in manner.

FORMS OF DISCOURSE A way of classifying writing under four types: *exposition, description, persuasion,* and *narration*. This approach to writing seeks to determine the special skills and procedures necessary for each kind of writing.

FREE VERSE Poetry that does not have a fixed rhythmical pattern, rhyme scheme, or length of line.

HAIKU Japanese lyric poems consisting of three lines, the first line having five syllables, the second, seven syllables, and the third, five. 314, 316

IAMB A poetic foot consisting of an unstressed syllable followed by a stressed syllable.

IMAGE A picture aroused in the mind; words that summon up the picture or that appeal to any of the senses.

IMAGERY The words and phrases that summon up the picture in the mind.

IMPRESSIONISM The rendering of events or details as they immediately appear to the senses.

INCREMENTAL REPETITION A device commonly used in ballads in which each stanza repeats most of the phrases of the previous stanza but adds a few new details (*increments*) to advance the story. 322

INFORMAL ESSAY An essay written in a highly personal way. The author may allow himself to ramble and to express amusing, startling, or absurd opinions.

IN MEDIAS RES A Latin phrase meaning "in the middle of things." The phrase refers to the practice of some writers of plunging into the middle of a story and only later telling what has happened previously.

INTERNAL RHYME Rhyme that occurs within a single line of poetry, as in the following line by Tennyson: "the splendor *falls* on castle *walls*."

IRONY An attitude or a way of writing that depends on a difference between what is real and what only seems to be real. 85, 102 Irony which depends on words is called *verbal irony;* the author may say one thing and mean another. 85 Another kind of irony is *dramatic irony.* 85, 473, 531 Here the reader of a story or audience of a play may perceive a special meaning in a character's words which the character himself does not perceive.

LIGHT VERSE Verse which intends to be humorous or entertaining rather than serious or profound. 339

LITERARY ALLUSION A reference to some feature of a literary work that the author expects the reader to recognize.

LOCAL COLOR In fiction, the use of details associated with a particular region or section of the country.

LYRIC A short poem in which the expression of personal emotion is more important than any idea or information that is conveyed. Originally, *lyric* referred to any short poem meant to be set to music. Many lyrics do have musical qualities.

LYRIC POETRY Poetry which expresses the poet's personal thoughts and feeling. 295, 309

MELODRAMA A dramatic form related to tragedy in which the hero struggles and overcomes conquerable odds. 385

METAPHOR A figure of speech that suggests a resemblance between two different things without using any word of comparison (such as *like* or *as*). Two examples are "laughing daffodils" and "the ship plowed through the waves." 346

METER A regular pattern of rhythm in poetry.

METONYMY A figure of speech in which a part of a thing is used to stand for or suggest the thing itself (e.g., three *sails* came into the harbor). 348

MORAL The ethical or practical lesson that may be learned from a literary work. This lesson may be stated or implied.

MOTIF A recurring feature (for example, a phrase or a symbol) in a work of art.

MOTIVE The reasons, either revealed or hidden, for a character acting as he does.

MYTH A traditional story, connected with religious beliefs or practices, which attempts to explain or justify them. Also, any story that is felt to have a deep, general significance.

NARRATIVE POETRY Poetry which tells a story. 295, 296

NATURALISM An extreme form of realism. Naturalist writers begin with a view of man's place in the universe and seek to show how man is affected by his heredity and environment.

NOVEL A fictional prose narrative of considerable length. 585–88

ODE A serious, dignified lyric poem, often addressed to someone or something. 315

ONOMATOPOEIA The use of a word, especially in poetry, whose sound imitates or suggests its meaning, such as "clang."

PARABLE A short tale that illustrates a moral or religious principle.

PARADOX A statement that is true in fact although it seems to contradict itself, such as "a fortunate accident." 347

PARALLELISM The repetition of phrases that are similar in structure or meaning.

PATHOS A feeling of sympathetic pity; also the qualities in a literary work that arouse such a feeling.

PENTAMETER A poetic line consisting of five verse feet.

PERSONIFICATION A figure of speech in which an animal, object, or idea is treated as if it had human characteristics. 346

PLOT Everything that happens in a story, novel, or play. Plots may be simple or complicated, loosely constructed or close-knit. But to satisfy us, every plot must appear to be made of incidents that are related to each other. 2, 586, 721

POETIC INVERSION Words arranged in an unusual or confusing order in a poetic line, usually to force the line into a particular metrical pattern or to have the line end with a particular word for the sake of rhyme. Modern poets generally try to avoid such inversions.

POINT OF VIEW The vantage point from which a story or novel is told. A work of fiction may use a *first-person* point of view, in which the story is told by one of the characters ("I locked the door and went up the stairs.") or it may be told from a *third-person* point of view ("He locked the door and went up the stairs."). 588, 722

PROTAGONIST The main character or hero of a dramatic or narrative work.

PUN A word or phrase which suggests two or more meanings simultaneously. 337

QUATRAIN A stanza of four lines. 315

REALISM The attempt to represent life as it really is, without sentimentalizing or idealizing it. This had led, sometimes, to a preoccupation with petty or sordid details.

REFRAIN A line or two that are repeated at regular intervals in a poem, especially at the end of each stanza. 296

RHYME The repetition of sounds at the ends of words, as in *coat* and *boat* or *river* and *shiver*.

RHYTHM The sequence of strong and weak syllables in speech and writing; the pattern made by this sequence.

ROMANCE A tale, written in medieval times, dealing with the loves and adventures of kings and heroes and with unlikely or supernatural happenings.

SATIRE A piece of writing, usually dealing with current affairs, that holds up to ridicule or contempt the weakness and wrong doing of individuals, groups, or humanity in general.

SETTING The place and time of a story, poem, novel, or play.

SIMILE A comparison between two things in which a word of comparison (such as *like* or *as*) is used. 346

SOLILOQUY A speech, usually in a drama, in which a character speaks his thoughts aloud while alone. 430

SONNET A fourteen-line lyric poem with a rhyme scheme that may follow one of several patterns. 315

STYLE The manner of writing rather than the content (*how* rather than *what* is said); an author's characteristic way of writing, which is determined by his choice of words, his arrangement of words in sentences, and the relationship of the sentences to each other. 588

SYMBOL Something specific that is used to stand for an idea. A literary symbol, for example, may be a thing (an old tower) or an action (climbing stairs), and is so used that it becomes highly suggestive. (Climbing stairs, for example, may symbolize the struggle to gain wisdom.) 103, 126, 347

TETRAMETER A poetic line consisting of four verse feet.

THEME The underlying idea or ideas of a literary work. 54, 84, 586–87, 721

TONE The attitude of the author as this attitude is revealed through his written words. 220, 256, 349, 588

TOTAL EFFECT The final, overall impression that a story, novel, poem, or play leaves on the reader or spectator.

TRAGEDY In general, a literary work or situation which ends with the fall or death of a hero in conflict with forces beyond his control. 384–85

TRAGIC HERO A leading character who, because of a flaw in his character, is destroyed by overwhelming forces which he cannot overcome. 473

TROCHEE A poetic foot consisting of a stressed syllable followed by an unstressed syllable.

UNDERSTATEMENT A restrained statement whose mildness serves to contrast with, and thus emphasize, what is really meant. 246

VERSE PLAY A drama written in verse form, such as the plays of Shakespeare. 317

Exercises in the Text

The page numbers cited in this index indicate the location of the major exercises on the topics listed below.

Index of Fine Art

Glossary

Listed below are words from selections in this book that you will find useful to add to your vocabulary. Proper names and words that are specialized, archaic, or not generally useful are not included in this glossary but have been footnoted, as appropriate, in the text. The pronunciation key is that of the Funk and Wagnalls *Standard College Dictionary* and the definitions are based on those given in the *Standard College Dictionary*.

A

abbey (ab'ē) *n.* A monastery or convent.

aberration (ab'ə·rā'shən) *n.* Deviation from a right, customary, prescribed, or natural course or condition.

abominable (ə·bom'in·ə·bəl) *adj.* Very hateful.

abound (ə·bound') *v.* To be plentiful.

abrasive (ə·brā'siv, -ziv) *adj.* Tending to rub or wear off by friction.

absolution (ab'sə·lōo'shən) *n.* A remission of sin and its penalties pronounced by a priest.

abstainer (ab·stā'nər) *n.* One who abstains, particularly one who keeps himself back from using alcoholic beverages.

abstruse (ab·strōōs') *adj.* Hard to understand.

abyss (ə·bis') *n.* Chasm.

accelerate (ak·sel'ə·rāt) *v.* To increase the speed of.

access (ak'ses) *n.* **1.** Admittance. **2.** An outburst of passion, emotion, etc.

acclamation (ak'lə·mā'shən) *n.* A shout or other manifestation of applause, approval, or welcome.

accost (ə·kôst', ə·kost') *v.* To speak to first; greet.

accredit (ə·kred'it) *v.* To authorize.

accursed (ə·kûr'sid, ə·kûrst') *adj.* Lying under a curse; doomed.

acquiescence (ak'wē·es'əns) *n.* Quiet submission.

acquittal (ə·kwit'l) *n.* The act of declaring innocent.

adept (ə·dept', ad'ept) *n.* An expert.

adherent (ad·hir'ənt) *adj.* Clinging or sticking fast.

admonish (ad·mon'ish) *v.* To advise of a fault. **—admonition** *n.*

adornment (ə·dôrn'mənt) *n.* A decoration.

adroit (ə·droit') *adj.* Skillful.

adulterate (ə·dul'tə·rāt) *v.* To make impure or inferior by admixture of other ingredients.

advent (ad'vent) *n.* A coming or arrival, as of any important event or person.

affiance (ə·fī'əns) *v.* To promise in marriage.

agape (ə·gāp', ə·gap') *adv. & adj.* Gaping.

aghast (ə·gast', ə·gäst') *adj.* Struck dumb with horror.

akimbo (ə·kim'bō) *adv. & adj.* With hands on hips and elbows outward.

alabaster (al'ə·bas'tər, -bäs'-) *n.* A white or tinted fine-grained gypsum.

alien (āl'yən, ā'lē·ən) *adj.* Strange.

allege (ə·lej') *v.* To assert to be true without proving. **—allegation** *n.*

alleviate (ə·lē'vē·āt) *v.* To make lighter or easier to bear.

allude (ə·lōōd') *v.* Make indirect or casual reference.

aloof (ə·lōōf') *adj.* Distant, especially in manner or interest.

altercation (ôl'tər·kā'shən, al'-) *n.* A heated dispute.

amass (ə·mas') *v.* To heap up.

amber (am'bər) *n.* **1.** A yellow, reddish-yellow, or brownish-yellow fossilized vegetable resin, used in jewelry. **2.** The color of amber.

amiable (ā'mē·ə·bəl) *adj.* Agreeable; friendly; pleasing in disposition.

amulet (am'yə·lit) *n.* A charm.

analogy (ə·nal'ə·jē) *n.* Agreement or resemblance in certain aspects, as form or function, between otherwise dissimilar things.

anecdote (an'ik·dōt) *n.* A brief account of some incident.

angelus (an'jə·ləs) *n.* A bell rung at morning, noon, and night as a call to prayers.

anguish (ang'gwish) *n.* Agony; torture.

animation (an'ə·mā'shən) *n.* The quality of being lively or quick.

animosity (an'ə·mos'ə·tē) *n.* Hatred.

annals (an'əlz) *n.* History or records in general.

PRONUNCIATION: add, āce, câre, pälm; end, ēven; it, īce; odd, ōpen, ôrder; tŏŏk, pōōl; up, bûrn; ə = a in *above*, e in *sicken*, i in *flexible*, o in *melon*, u in *focus*; yōō = u in *fuse*; oil; pout; check; go; ring; thin; ̱this; zh, vision.

803

annul (ə·nul′) v. To reduce to nothing; put an end to.

anoint (ə·noint′) v. To smear with oil or any soft substance.

anvil (an′vil, -vəl) n. A heavy block of iron on which metal may be worked into shape.

apathetic (ap′ə·thet′ik) adj. Indifferent; unconcerned. —**apathetically** adv.

apothecary (ə·poth′ə·ker′ē) n. A druggist.

appalling (ə·pô′ling) adj. Causing terror. —**appallingly** adv.

apparition (ap′ə·rish′ən) n. Ghost.

appease (ə·pēz′) v. To bring to peace. —**appeasingly** adv.

appendage (ə·pen′dij) n. Anything hung or attached.

appertain (ap′ər·tān′) v. Relate: with to.

apportion (ə·pôr′shən, ə·pōr′-) v. To divide and assign proportionally.

apprehend (ap′rə·hend′) v. 1. To understand. 2. To arrest.

apprehension (ap′rə·hen′shən) n. Fear concerning the future.

approbation (ap′rə·bā′shən) n. The act of approving.

arabesque (ar′ə·besk′) adj. Fanciful; ornamental.

ardent (är′dənt) adj. Passionate; zealous; intense.

arrear (ə·rir′) n. Usually pl. A part, as of a debt, overdue and unpaid.

arrogant (ar′ə·gənt) adj. Overly proud; haughty.

artful (ärt′fəl) adj. Crafty; cunning.

articulate (adj. är·tik′yə·lit, v. är·tik′yə·lāt) adj. Able to speak well. —v. To express in words.

artisan (är′tə·zən) n. A trained or skilled workman.

ascertain (as′ər·tān′) v. To learn with certainty.

ascetic (ə·set′ik) n. One who leads a very austere and self-denying life.

aspiration (as′pə·rā′shən) n. High ambition.

assail (ə·sāl′) v. To attack violently.

assay (ə·sā′) v. 1. To subject to chemical analysis. 2. To prove; test.

assent (ə·sent′) v. To express agreement.

assert (ə·sûrt′) v. 1. To state positively. 2. To maintain as a right or claim.

assessor (ə·ses′ər) n. One who determines the amount of a tax.

assiduous (ə·sij′o͞o·əs) adj. Devoted; attentive. —**assiduously** adv.

assimilate (ə·sim′ə·lāt) v. To become absorbed.

astound (ə·stound′) v. To overwhelm with wonder.

asunder (ə·sun′dər) adv. Apart.

attain (ə·tān′) v. 1. To gain. 2. To arrive at.

attribute (ə·trib′yo͞ot) v. To consider or ascribe as belonging to, resulting from, owing to, or caused by. —**attribute** (at′rə·byo͞ot) n. A quality or characteristic of a person or thing.

augur (ô′gər, -gyər) v. To be an omen of.

august (ô·gust′) adj. Majestic; imposing.

auk (ôk) n. A short-winged, web-footed diving bird of northern seas.

aureole (ôr′ē·ōl) n. Halo.

austere (ô·stir′) adj. Solemn and dignified in appearance.

authentic (ô·then′tik) adj. 1. Trustworthy. 2. Genuine.

avalanche (av′ə·lanch, -länch) n. The fall of a mass of snow or ice.

avarice (av′ə·ris) n. Greed.

avenge (ə·venj′) v. To inflict punishment, injury, or loss in return for.

averse (ə·vûrs′) adj. Opposed: with to.

avert (ə·vûrt′) v. To turn or direct away or aside.

avowal (ə·vou′əl) n. Frank admission.

awesome (ô′səm) adj. Inspiring reverential fear.

azure (azh′ər, ā′zhər) n. A clear, sky-blue color.

B

backwater (bak′wô′tər, -wot′ər) n. Water turned or held back, as by a dam, a current, etc.

bait (bāt) v. To torment.

balustrade (bal′ə·strād′, bal′ə·strād) n. A handrail.

baroque (ba·rōk′) adj. Of a style of art and architecture developed in Europe in the late sixteenth and seventeenth centuries, characterized by extravagantly contorted classical forms, dynamic curvilinear ornament, and theatrical effects.

bate (bāt) v. To lessen the force or intensity of.

beatific (bē′ə·tif′ik) adj. Imparting or expressing bliss or blessedness.

beguile (bi·gīl′) v. To charm; please. —**beguiling** adj. Charming; pleasing.

beholden (bi·hōl′dən) adj. Indebted.

belie (bi·lī′) v. To prove false.

belligerent (bə·lij′ər·ənt) adj. Warlike; inclined to fight.

benefactor (ben′ə·fak′tər, ben′ə·fak′-) n. One who gives help or confers a benefit.

benevolent (bə·nev′ə·lənt) adj. Kindly.

benign (bi·nīn′) adj. Kindly.

benumb (bi·num′) v. To make numb; deaden.

bequest (bi·kwest′) n. The act of handing down.

bereave (bi·rēv′) v. To deprive. —**bereavement** n.

besiege (bi·sēj′) v. To attack on all sides.

blackguard (blag′ərd, -ärd) n. A rogue.

PRONUNCIATION: add, āce, câre, pälm; end, ēven; it, īce; odd, ōpen, ôrder; to͝ok, po͞ol; up, bûrn; ə = a in *above*, e in *sicken*, i in *flexible*, o in *melon*, u in *focus*; yo͞o = u in *fuse*; oil; pout; check; go; ring; thin; this; zh, vision.

bland (bland) *adj.* Gentle and soothing in manner.

blandishment (blan'dish·mənt) *n.* Flattering speech or action.

blasphemous (blas'fə·məs) *adj.* Irreverent; profane. **—blasphemy** *n.*

blear (blir) *adj.* Blurred; dim.

blemish (blem'ish) *v.* To mar the perfection of.

blench (blench) *v.* To make or become pale.

blight (blīt) *n.* Anything that withers hopes, destroys prospects, or impairs growth.

blithe (blīth, blīth) *adj.* Joyous.

blunder (blun'dər) *v.* To act or move blindly, awkwardly, or stupidly.

bode (bōd) *v.* To be a foretoken of.

bohemian (bō·hē'mē·ən) *adj.* A person, usually of artistic or literary tastes, who lives in an unconventional manner.

boisterous (bois'ter·əs, -trəs) *adj.* Noisy and unrestrained.

bray (brā) *v.* To utter the loud, harsh call which donkeys make.

brazen (brā'zən) *adj.* Shameless.

brazier (brā'zhər) *n.* An open pan for holding live coals.

brigand (brig'ənd) *n.* A robber.

brimstone (brim'stōn') *n.* Sulfur.

brocade (brō·kād') *n.* A rich fabric interwoven with a raised design, as in silken or gold or silver thread.

brook brook) *v.* To put up with.

buoy (boi, boo'ē) *n.* A warning float.

buoyancy (boi'ən·sē, boo'yən·sē) *n.* The tendency or ability to keep afloat.

burnish (bûr'nish) *v.* To polish by friction.

byre (bīr) *n.* A cow stable.

C

cadence (kād'ns) *n.* Rhythmic or measured flow, as of poetry or oratory.

cajole (kə·jōl') *v.* To coax with flattery.

calcimine (kal'sə·mīn, -min) *n.* A white or tinted wash for ceilings, walls, etc.

callous (kal'əs) *adj.* Hardened in feelings.

calumny (kal'əm·nē) *n.* A false and malicious accusation or report.

cambric (kām'brik) *n.* A fine white linen.

candelabrum (kan'də·lä'brəm, -lā-) *n. pl.* **·bra** (-brə) or **·brums** A large, branched candlestick. Also **candelabra** (-brə) *pl.* **·bras.**

candor (kan'dər) *n.* Openness; frankness.

capacious (kə·pā'shəs) *adj.* Roomy.

caper (kā'pər) *n.* The flower bud of a low shrub of Mediterranean countries, pickled and used as a condiment.

capricious (kə·prish'əs) *adj.* Fickle. **—capriciously** *adv.*

capsize (kap·sīz', kap'sīz) *v.* To upset or overturn.

carafe (kə·raf', -räf') *n.* A glass water bottle; decanter.

cartography (kär·tog'rə·fē) *n.* The art of drawing or compiling maps or charts. **—cartographer** *n.*

casing (kā'sing) *n.* The framework around a window or door.

castellated (kas'tə·lā'tid) *adj.* Built like a castle.

catapult (kat'ə·pult) *n.* An ancient military engine for throwing stones, arrows, etc.

cataract (kat'ə·rakt) *n.* A flood of water.

censure (sen'shər) *n.* The expression of disapproval or blame.

centipede (sen'tə·pēd) *n.* A long, many-legged insect.

centrifugal (sen·trif'yə·gəl, -trif'ə·gəl) *adj.* Directed away from a center.

cerement (sir'mənt) *n.* A dress for the dead.

certified (sûr'tə·fīd) *adj.* Vouched for in writing.

cessation (se·sā'shən) *n.* A stop.

chafe (chāf) *v.* To scrape away by rubbing.

chaff (chaf, chäf) *n.* Straw or hay cut fine.

chancel (chan'səl, chän'-) *n.* The space near the altar of a church.

chary (châr'ē) *adj.* Cautious; careful.

chasten (chā'sən) *v.* To soften.

chastise (chas·tīz') *v.* To punish, especially by beating.

chide (chīd) *v.* Scold.

chitter (chit'ər) *v.* To twitter.

cholera (kol'ər·ə) *n.* An acute disease, usually fatal.

chortle (chôr'təl) *v.* To utter with sounds of glee.

christen (kris'ən) *v.* To give a name to in a ceremony.

chronicle (kron'i·kəl) *n.* A register of events in the order of time. **—v.** To record in, or in the manner of a chronicle.

cipher (sī'fər) *n.* **1.** The figure 0; zero. **2.** A person or thing of no value or importance.

cleave (klēv) *v.* To split or sunder.

clod (klod) *n.* A lump of earth.

cloister (klois'tər) *n.* A building devoted to religious seclusion.

cogent (kō'jənt) *adj.* Convincing.

coil (koil) *n.* A series of concentric rings or spirals.

colloquy (kol'ə·kwē) *n.* A conversation.

comely (kum'lē) *adj.* Handsome.

commend (kə·mend') *v.* To praise.

commodious (kə·mō'dē·əs) *adj.* Containing ample room.

compact (kəm·pakt') *adj.* **1.** Pressed together. **2.** Composed; made up: with *of.*

PRONUNCIATION: add, āce, câre, pälm; end, ēven; it, īce; odd, ōpen, ôrder; took, pool; up, bûrn; ə = a in *above*, e in *sicken*, i in *flexible*, o in *melon*, u in *focus*; yoo = u in *fuse*; oil; pout; check; go; ring; thin; this; zh, vision.

805

compact (kom'pakt) *n.* An agreement.

compassion (kəm·pash'ən) *n.* Pity for the suffering of others.

compensate (kom'pən·sāt) *v.* To make suitable amends to or for.

compile (kəm·pīl') *v.* To gather various materials) into a volume.

complacent (kəm·plā'sənt) *adj.* Feeling or showing satisfaction, especially self-satisfaction. —**complacency** *n.* Also **complacence.**

comport (kəm·pôrt', -pōrt') *v.* To conduct or behave (oneself).

compunction (kəm·pungk'shən) *n.* A sense of guilt or remorse.

concede (kən·sēd') *v.* To admit.

conceive (kən·sēv') *v.* To form in the mind. —**conceivable** *adj.* —**conceivably** *adv.*

conception (kən·sep'shən) *n.* A concept, idea, plan, or design.

conciliate (kən·sil'ē·āt) *v.* To win over. —**conciliatory** *adj.*

conclusive (kən·kloo'siv) *adj.* Putting an end to doubt.

concourse (kon'kôrs, -kōrs, kong'-) *n.* A coming together.

condescend (kon'di·send') *v.* To come down voluntarily to equal terms with inferiors.

condescending (kon'di·sen'ding) *adj.* Showing conscious courtesy toward inferiors.

confer (kən·fûr') *v.* To grant as a gift.

confirmation (kon'fər·mā'shən) *n.* Proof.

confiscate (kon'fis·kāt) *v.* To seize for the public use.

conflagration (kon'flə·grā'shən) *n.* A great fire.

confound (kon·found', kən-) *v.* To confuse, amaze, or bewilder.

congenial (kən·jēn'yəl) *adj.* Having similar character or tastes.

conjecture (kən·jek'chər) *v.* To guess. —*n.* A tentative judgment; a guess. —**conjectural** *adj.*

conjure (kon'jər) *v.* To accomplish or effect by or as by magic. —**conjuration** *n.*

connoisseur (kon'ə·sûr') *n.* One competent to judge critically because of thorough knowledge, especially in matters of art and taste.

consign (kən·sīn') *v.* To forward or deliver, as merchandise.

consolation (kon'sə·lā'shən) *n.* The state of being comforted.

conspicuous (kən·spik'yoo·əs) *adj.* Easy to be seen.

conspiracy (kən·spir'ə·sē) *n.* A planning of two or more persons to do an evil act. —**conspiratorial** *adj.*

consternation (kon'stər·nə'shən) *n.* Sudden, paralyzing fear or amazement.

constitute (kon'stə·toot, -tyoot) *v.* To make up; compose

constitutional (kon'stə·too'shən·əl, -tyoo'-) *n.* A walk or exercise taken for one's health.

constrained (kən·strānd') *adj.* Forced.

constraint (kən·strānt') *n.* The use of force.

construe (kən·stroo') *v.* To interpret; explain.

consummate (kən·sum'it) *adj.* Of the highest degree.

consumptive (kən·sump'tiv) *adj.* Pertaining to tuberculosis.

contemplate (kon'təm·plāt) *v.* 1. To gaze at. 2. To consider thoughtfully. —**contemplative** *adj.*

contempt (kən·tempt') *n.* Scorn. —**contemptuous** *adj.* —**contemptuously** *adv.*

contemptible (kən·temp'tə·bəl) *adj.* Despicable.

contention (kən·ten'shən) *n.* 1. Strife or argument. 2. A point asserted in an argument.

contour (kon'toor) *n.* The outline of a figure or body.

contract (kən·trakt') *v.* 1. To cause to draw together. 2. To acquire or become affected with, as a disease or habit.

contrive (kən·trīv') *v.* To plan ingeniously; devise.

convene (kən·vēn') *v.* To come together.

convent (kon'vent, -vənt) *n.* A religious community, especially of nuns.

convivial (kən·viv'ē·əl) *adj.* Fond of feasting and good fellowship. —**conviviality** (kən·viv'ē·al'ətē) *n.*

convolute (kon'və·loot) *v.* To coil up.

convulse (kən·vuls') *v.* To affect with violent movements. —**convulsive** *adj.* —**convulsion** *n.*

coordination (kō·ôr'də·nā'shən) *n.* The act of making things work in harmony.

coquetry (kō'kə·trē, kō·ket'rē) *n.* The behavior or practices of a flirtatious woman.

coquette (kō·ket') *n.* A flirt. —**coquettish** *adj.*

corollary (kôr'ə·ler'ē, kor'-) *n.* A natural result.

corruption (kə·rup'shən) *n.* Dishonesty.

countenance (koun'tə·nəns) *n.* The face.

counteract (koun'tər·akt') *v.* To act in opposition to.

course (kôrs, kōrs) *v.* To run through or over.

covert (kuv'ərt, kō'vərt) *adj.* Secret.

covetous (kuv'ə·təs) *adj.* Excessively desirious (of something).

cozen (kuz'ən) *v.* To cheat.

crass (kras) *adj.* Grossly vulgar or stupid.

cravat (krə·vat') *n.* 1. A necktie. 2. A scarf.

crave (krāv) *v.* 1. To long for; desire greatly. 2. To ask for earnestly, beg.

credentials (kri·den'shəlz) *n.* A certificate or letter giving evidence of one's authority, identity, or claim to confidence.

credulous (krej′ŏŏ·ləs) *adj.* Disposed to believe on slight evidence. —**credulity** (krə·dŏŏ′lə·tē, -dyŏŏ′-) *n.*

crucify (krŏŏ′sə·fī) *v.* To torture.

crypt (kript) *n.* A vault.

cull (kul) *v.* **1.** To pick or sort out. **2.** To gather.

culpable (kul′pə·bəl) *adj.* Deserving of blame.

cult (kult) *n.* A system of religious rites and observances.

cupidity (kyŏŏ·pid′ə·tē) *n.* Greed.

curate (kyŏŏr′it) *n.* A clergyman assisting a parish priest.

cursory (kûr′sər·ē) *adj.* Not thorough.

cuspidor (kus′pə·dôr) *n.* A spittoon.

cynicism (sin′ə·siz′əm, -i-) *n.* Contempt for or disbelief in the virtues of others.

D

dank (dangk) *adj.* Unpleasantly damp.

darkling (därk′ling) *Poetic adj.* Occurring or being in the dark; dim.

dauntless (dônt′lis) *adj.* Fearless; brave.

debase (di·bās′) *v.* To lower in character, quality, or worth.

debility (di·bil′ə·tē) *n.* Abnormal weakness; feebleness.

decanter (di·kan′tər) *n.* A bottle.

declaim (di·klām′) *v.* To speak loudly and rhetorically.

decrepit (di·krep′it) *adj.* Enfeebled or worn out by old age.

deferential (def′ə·ren′shəl) *adj.* Respectful; courteous. —**deferentially** *adv.* —**deference** *n.*

deficiency (di·fish′ən·sē) *n.* A lack.

degrade (di·grād′) *v.* To debase or lower in character, morals, etc.

deign (dān) *v.* To lower oneself.

dejection (di·jek′shən) *n.* Lowness of spirits.

delectable (di·lek′tə·bəl) *adj.* Delightful; giving pleasure.

delirious (di·lir′ē·əs) *adj.* Wildly excited.

delusion (di·lŏŏ′zhən) *n.* A false belief. —**delusive** *adj.*

demean (di·mēn′) *v.* To lower in dignity.

demented (di·men′tid) *adj.* Deprived of reason; insane.

demolish (di·mol′ish) *v.* To destroy utterly.

demure (di·myŏŏr′) *adj.* Affecting modesty; prim.

deplete (di·plēt′) *v.* To reduce or lessen.

deplorable (di·plôr′ə·bəl, -plō′rə-) *adj.* Regrettable.

depopulate (dē·pop′yə·lāt) *v.* To remove the inhabitants from.

deportment (di·pôrt′mənt, -pōrt′-) *n.* Conduct or behavior.

depravity (di·prav′ə·tē) *n.* Wickedness.

deprecate (dep′rə·kāt) *v.* To express disapproval of or regret for; plead earnestly against.

deride (di·rīd′) *v.* To ridicule. —**derisive** *adj.* —**derision** *n.*

desist (di·zist′) *v.* To cease, as from an action or proceeding.

desolation (des′ə·lā′shən) *n.* A lonely or deserted condition.

destitute (des′tə·tŏŏt, -tyŏŏt) *adj.* **1.** Entirely lacking. **2.** Extremely poor.

detonation (det′ə·nā′shən, dē′tə-) *n.* A violent and sudden explosion.

devastate (dev′ə·stāt) *v.* To lay waste.

deviation (dē′vē·ā′shən) *n.* The act of turning aside from a straight or appointed way.

devour (di·vour′) *v.* To eat up.

devout (di·vout′) *adj.* Earnestly religious.

dexterous (dek′strəs, -stər·əs) *adj.* Skillful. —**dexterity** *n.*

diabolic (dī′ə·bol′ik) *adj.* Befitting the devil; atrociously wicked or inhuman. Also **diabolical.**

diadem (dī′ə·dem) *n.* A crown.

diffident (dif′ə·dənt) *adj.* Timid. —**diffidently** *adv.* —**diffidence** *n.*

dilate (dī·lāt′, di-) *v.* To make wider or larger; cause to swell or expand.

dilatory (dil′ə·tôr′ē, -tō′rē) *adj.* Slow.

diligence (dil′ə·jəns) *n.* Persistent application to one's work or duty. —**diligent** *adj.*

diminish (di·min′ish) *v.* To make smaller or less.

dint (dint) *n.* Means; force.

dirge (dûrj) *n.* A song expressing mourning.

disapprobation (dis′ap·rə·bā′shən) *n.* Disapproval.

disarming (dis·är′ming) *adj.* Charming and attractive.

discern (di·sûrn′, di·zûrn′) *v.* To perceive, as with sight or mind; recognize; apprehend. —**discernible** *adj.*

discharge (dis·chärj′) *v.* To send forth.

disconcert (dis′kən·sûrt′) *v.* To confuse.

disconsolate (dis·kon′sə·lit) *adj.* **1.** Dejected. **2.** Saddening. —**disconsolately** *adv.*

discourse (dis·kôrs′, -kōrs′) *v.* To converse; confer.

discreet (dis·krēt′) *adj.* Careful not to say or do the wrong thing. —**discretion** *n.*

discrepancy (dis·krep′ən·sē) *n.* Lack of agreement or consistency.

discursive (dis·kûr′siv) *adj.* Wandering from the main point.

disfigure (dis·fig′yər) *v.* To mar or destroy the appearance or form of. —**disfiguration** *n.*

PRONUNCIATION: add, āce, câre, pälm; end, ēven; it, īce; odd, ōpen, ôrder; tŏŏk, pŏŏl; up, bûrn; ə = a in *above,* e in *sicken,* i in *flexible,* o in *melon,* u in *focus;* yŏŏ = u in *fuse;* oil; pout; check; go; ring; thin; this; zh, vision.

807

disheveled (di·shev′əld) *adj.* Untidy.

disincline (dis′in·klīn′) *v.* To make or be unwilling or averse.

dismantle (dis·man′təl) *v.* To take apart or strip bare.

disparage (dis·par′ij) *v.* To belittle.

dispassionate (dis·pash′ən·it) *adj.* Free from personal feelings.

dispensation (dis′pən·sā′shən) *n.* A dealing out.

disperse (dis·pûrs′) *v.* To cause to scatter.

dispirited (dis·pir′it·id) *adj.* Downhearted.

disreputable (dis·rep′yə·tə·bəl) *adj.* Not respectable.

dissension (di·sen′shən) *n.* Difference of opinion.

dissentient (di·sen′shənt) *adj.* Differing in thought.

dissertation (dis′ər·tā′shən) *n.* An extended formal treatise or discourse.

dissimulate (di·sim′yə·lāt) *v.* To conceal (intentions, feelings, etc.) by pretense.

dissipate (dis′ə·pāt) *v.* To disperse or drive away.

distemper (dis·tem′pər) *n.* Illness.

distraught (dis·trôt′) *adj.* Worried, tense, and bewildered.

divert (di·vûrt′, dī-) *v.* **1.** To turn aside. **2.** To entertain. ·

divest (di·vest′, dī-) *v.* To strip.

divine (di·vīn′) *v.* To guess by instinct.

docile (dos′əl) *adj.* Easy to manage. —**docilely** *adv.*

docket (dok′it) *v.* To put a tag or label on.

doctrine (dok′trin) *n.* Teachings, as of a religious or political group. —**doctrinal** *adj.*

dogged (dôg′id, dog′-) *adj.* Stubborn. —**doggedly** *adv.*

domicile (dom′ə·səl, -sīl) *v.* To establish in a place to live.

dormant (dôr′mənt) *adj.* Asleep or as if asleep.

dotage (dō′tij) *n.* Feebleness of mind as a result of old age.

dour (door, dour) *adj.* Ill-tempered.

dowager (dou′ə·jər) *n.* An elderly woman of dignified bearing.

dragoon (drə·goon′) *v.* To browbeat.

drake (drāk) *n.* A male duck.

draught (draft, dräft) *n.* A quantity of liquid for drinking.

drear (drir) *adj. Poetic* Dreary.

dregs (dregz) *n. pl.* A small amount left over.

drone (drōn) *v.* To speak in a dull, monotonous manner. —*n.* A low humming or buzzing sound.

dubious (doo′bē·əs, dyoo′-) *adj.* Doubtful. —**dubiously** *adv.* —**dubiety** (doo·bī′ə·tē, dy-oo) *n.*

ducal (doo′kəl, dyoo′-) *adj.* Pertaining to a duke or a duchy.

duly (doo′lē, dyoo′-) *adv.* **1.** In due or proper manner. **2.** At the proper time.

duplicity (doo·plis′ə·tē, dyoo-) *n.* Double-dealing.

E

ebb (eb) *v.* To recede, as the tide.

ecclesiastical (i·klē′zē·as′ti·kəl) *adj.* Of the church.

ecru (ek′roo, ā′kroo) *adj.* A light, yellowish brown.

ecstatic (ek·stat′ik) *adj.* In a state of rapture. —**ecstatically** *adv.*

edification (ed′ə·fə·kā′shən) *n.* Intellectual or moral enlightenment and improvement.

edifice (ed′ə·fis) *n.* A building.

efface (i·fās′) *v.* To obliterate or destroy.

efficacy (ef′ə·kə·sē) *n.* Power to produce a desired or intended result.

effrontery (i·frun′tər·ē) *n.* Shameless or insolent boldness.

effusive (i·fyoo′siv) *adj.* Gushing. —**effusively** *adv.*

egoism (ē′gō·iz′əm) *n.* The tendency to think mainly of one's own welfare; selfishness.

egress (ē′gres) *n.* A place of exit.

elicit (i·lis′it) *v.* To draw out or forth.

eloquence (el′ə·kwəns) *n.* Effective use of language.

elusive (i·loo′siv) *adj.* Tending to slip away.

emaciated (i·mā′shē·ā′tid) *adj.* Very thin; wasted away.

emanate (em′ə·nāt) *v.* To flow forth from a source.

embellishment (im·bel′ish·mənt) *n.* Decoration.

eminence (em′ə·nəns) *n.* Superiority in rank.

emissary (em′ə·ser′ē) *n.* A person sent on a mission.

emit (i·mit′) *v.* To send forth or give off (light, heat, sound, etc.).

emphatic (em·fat′ik) *adj.* Striking; decisive.

endurance (in·door′əns, -dyoor′-) *n.* The act of putting up with.

enfranchise (in·fran′chīz) *v.* **1.** To endow with a franchise, as with the right to vote. **2.** To set free, as from bondage or legal liabilities. —**enfranchisement** *n.*

engender (in·jen′dər) *v.* To cause to exist.

engross (in·grōs′) *v.* To occupy completely; absorb.

enigmatic (en′ig·mat′ik, ē′nig-) *adj.* Puzzling. —**enigmatically** *adv.*

enkindle (en·kin′dəl) *v.* To excite; stir to action.

ensue (en·soo′) *v.* Occur afterward.

entice (in·tīs′) *v.* To lead on; allure.

PRONUNCIATION: add, āce, câre, pälm; end, ēven; it, īce; odd, ōpen, ôrder; took, pool; up, bûrn; ə = a in *above*, e in *sicken*, i in *flexible*, o in *melon*, u in *focus*; yoo = u in *fuse*; oil; pout; check; go; ring; thin; this; zh, vision.

808

entreat (in·trēt′) *v.* To beg. **—entreatingly** *adv.* **—entreaty** *n.*

environs (in·vī′rəns) *n. pl.* A surrounding, outlying area, as about a city.

epilepsy (ep′ə·lep′sē) *n.* A disorder of cerebral function marked primarily by recurring attacks of unconsciousness with or without convulsions.

epoch (ep′ək) *n.* A point in time marked by the beginning of a new development or state of things: the atomic *epoch* in history. **—epochal** *adj.*

esculent (es′kyə·lənt) *adj.* Suitable for food.

excruciating (iks·krōo′shē·ā′ting) *adj.* Causing or inflicting intense pain.

exemplary (ig·zem′plər·ē) *adj.* Serving as a model or example worthy of imitation.

exert (ig·zûrt′) *v.* To put forth or put into action.

exhilaration (ig·zil′ə·rā′shən) *n.* The state of being set aglow with happiness.

exhort (ig·zôrt′) *v.* To urge by earnest appeal or argument. **—exhortation** *n.*

exhume (ig·zyōom′, iks·hyōom′) *v.* To dig up.

exigency (ek′sə·jən·sē) *n. Usually pl.* A pressing need or necessity.

expatiate (ik·spā′shē·āt) *v.* To speak at considerable length.

expend (ik·spend′) *v.* To pay out or spend.

exploit (eks′ploit, ik·sploit′) *n.* A deed or act.

exploitation (eks′ploi·tā′shən) *n.* The act of using someone or something for purely selfish ends.

exposition (eks′pə·zish′ən) *n.* A written or spoken explanation of an idea or process.

extremity (ik·strem′ə·tē) *n. pl.* **·ties 1.** The farthest point. **2.** *pl.* The hands or feet.

extricate (eks′trə·kāt) *v.* To free from entanglement.

exultant (ig·zul′tənt) *adj.* Joyful.

F

façade (fə·säd′) *n.* The front or visible part of anything; especially, a false front.

facsimile (fak·sim′ə·lē) *n.* An exact copy.

faction (fak′shən) *n.* A distinct group within a larger group, working against other parts of the main group to gain its own ends.

faculty (fak′əl·tē) *n.* One of the inherent powers or capabilities of the body or mind: the *faculty* of seeing, reasoning, speech, etc.

fallacy (fal′ə·sē) *n.* Unsoundness or incorrectness.

fallible (fal′ə·bəl) *adj.* Liable to err.

fanatical (fə·nat′i·kəl) *adj.* Unreasonably enthusiastic.

fancy (fan′sē) *n.* An extravagant, odd, or whimsical invention or image.

fang (fang) *n.* A long, pointed tooth.

farce (färs) *n.* A comedy.

fastidious (fas·tid′ē·əs, fəs-) *adj.* Overnice.

fatuous (fach′ōo·əs) *adj.* Foolish and silly

fawn (fôn) *v.* To seek favor or advantage by humbling oneself and flattering.

feign (fān) *v.* To make a false show of.

felicitous (fə·lis′ə·təs) *adj.* Particularly well chosen.

felicity (fə·lis′ə·tē) *n.* Happiness.

feline (fē′līn) *adj.* Resembling a cat.

felon (fel′ən) *n.* **1.** *Law* One who has committed a felony. **2.** *Rare* A wicked or villainous individual.

ferocity (fə·ros′ə·tē) *n.* Fierceness.

fervid (fûr′vid) *adj.* Fervent, especially to an extreme degree.

fervor (fûr′vər) *n.* Great warmth or intensity, as of emotion.

fetter (fet′ər) *n. Usually pl.* Anything checking freedom of movement or expression.

filial (fil′ē·əl, fil′yəl) *adj.* Of, pertaining to, or fitting a son or daughter.

filigree (fil′ə·grē) *n.* Delicate ornamental work formed of intertwisted gold or silver wire.

finesse (fi·nes′) *n.* Highly refined skill; subtlety of style or performance.

finite (fī′nīt) *adj.* Having bounds, ends, or limits.

fissure (fish′ər) *n.* A narrow opening.

flagging (flag′ing) *adj.* Growing weak.

flamboyant (flam·boi′ənt) *adj.* Showy. **—flamboyance** *n.*

flaunt (flônt) *v.* **1.** To make a brazen or gaudy display. **2.** To wave or flutter freely.

flaxen (flak′sən) *adj.* Having a light golden color.

fledgling (flej′ling) *n.* A beginner.

flint (flint) *n.* A very hard, dull-colored variety of quartz that produces a spark when struck with steel.

florid (flôr′id, flor′-) *adj.* Flushed with redness.

flotsam (flot′səm) *n.* Any objects floating on a body of water.

flounder (floun′dər) *v.* To move awkwardly.

fluctuation (fluk′chōo·ā′shən) *n.* Varying movement or action.

fluted (flōo′tid) *adj.* Having parallel grooves.

font (font) *n.* A receptacle for the water used in baptism.

forage (fôr′ij, for′-) *v.* To search about, especially for food. **—forager** *n.*

forbear (fôr·bâr′) *v.* To refrain or abstain from.

forfeit (fôr′fit) *v.* To bring about the loss of.

forlorn (fôr·lôrn′, fər-) *adj.* Cheerless; desolate.

formidable (fôr′mi·də·bəl) *adj.* Exciting fear or dread by reason of strength, size, etc.

founder (foun′dər) *v.* To sink after filling with water.

PRONUNCIATION: add, āce, câre, pälm; end, ēven; it, īce; odd, ōpen, ôrder; tŏŏk, pōol; up, bûrn; ə = a in *above*, e in *sicken*, i in *flexible*, o in *melon*, u in *focus*; yōo = u in *fuse*; oil; pout; check; go; ring; thin; this; zh, vision.

809

fret (fret) *v.* To vex, annoy, or trouble.

frivolous (friv'ə·ləs) *adj.* Not serious; silly.

frowzy (frou'zē) *adj.* Looking slovenly and unkempt; slatternly.

frugal (frōō'gəl) *adj.* **1.** Avoiding waste. **2.** Costing little money.

frustrate (frus'trāt) *v.* To keep, as plans or schemes, from being fulfilled.

funereal (fyōō·nir'ē·əl) *adj.* Depressingly sad or gloomy.

furlong (fûr'lông, -long) *n.* A measure of length, equal to ⅛ mile.

furtive (fûr'tiv) *adj.* Done in secret. **—furtively** *adv.*

fusillade (fyōō'zə·lād') *n.* A quickly repeated discharge of firearms.

G

gadfly (gad'flī) *n.* An irritating, bothersome individual.

gait (gāt) *n.* One's particular manner of walking.

gall (gôl) *n.* Something bitter and disagreeable. **—v.** To vex or irritate.

garnet (gär'nit) *n.* A deep red color.

garnish (gär'nish) *v.* To add something to by way of decoration.

gaunt (gônt) *adj.* Gloomy in appearance.

gentility (jen·til'ə·tē) *n.* Refinement.

genuflect (jen'yə·flekt) *v.* To bend the knee, as in worship.

glazier (glā'zhər) *n.* One who fits windows, doors, etc., with panes of glass.

glimmer (glim'ər) *v.* To shine with a faint unsteady light.

gloaming (glō'ming) *n.* Twilight.

goad (gōd) *v.* To prick or drive with or as with a pointed stick.

gradation (grā·dā'shən) *n.* A step or degree in a series or progression, as of shades of color or tones of light and shadow in art.

granary (gran'ər·ē, grā'nər-) *n.* A storehouse for threshed grain.

grandiose (gran'dē·ōs, gran'dē·ōs') *adj.* Producing an effect of grandeur.

gratify (grat'ə·fī) *v.* To give pleasure or satisfaction to. **—gratification** *n.*

gratuitous (grə·tōō'ə·təs, -tyōō'-) *adj.* **1.** Free. **2.** Uncalled-for.

grimace (gri·mās') *n.* A distorted facial expression.

grizzled (griz'əld) *adj.* Having gray or graying hair.

grotesque (grō·tesk') *adj.* Distorted, incongruous, or fantastically ugly in appearance or style. **—grotesquely** *adv.*

grovel (gruv'əl, grov'-) *v.* To abase oneself, as from fear.

grub (grub) *v.* To dig from the ground.

guile (gīl) *n.* Falseness.

guinea (gin'ē) *n.* Formerly, an English gold coin.

H

habiliment (hə·bil'ə·mənt) *n. Usually pl.* Clothing.

habituate (hə·bich'ōō·āt) *v.* To accustom to a given experience.

hacienda (hä'sē·en'də) *n.* A country house; a landed estate.

haft (haft, häft) *n.* A handle.

hale (hāl) *adj.* Having sound and vigorous health; robust.

hallow (hal'ō) *v.* To make holy.

harangue (hə·rang') *v.* To address in a lengthy, loud, and vehement manner.

hardihood (här'dē·hŏŏd) *n.* Boldness.

havoc (hav'ək) *n.* Ruin. **—to play havoc with** To ruin; destroy.

hector (hek'tər) *v.* **1.** To bully. **2.** To tease.

hereditary (hə·red'ə·ter'ē) *adj.* Derived from ancestors; inherited.

heresy (her'ə·sē) *n.* A belief or opinion contrary to the established doctrines of a church or religious system.

hew (hyōō) *v.* To cut or strike with an ax.

hideously (hid'ē·əs·lē) *adv.* Frightfully; horribly.

hoist (hoist) *v.* To raise, lift, or heave up.

homage (hom'ij, om'-) *n.* Respect or honor given or shown.

hostler (hos'lər, os'-) *n.* A stableman.

hover (huv'ər, hov'-) *v.* **1.** To linger or remain nearby. **2.** To remain in an uncertain state.

hue (hyōō) *n.* Color.

husbandry (huz'bən·drē) *n.* The occupation or business of farming.

hydraulics (hī·drô'liks) *n. pl.* The science of the laws governing the motion of water and other liquids and of their practical applications in engineering.

I

idolatrous (ī·dol'ə·trəs) *adj.* Blindly devoted.

ignoble (ig·nō'bəl) *adj.* Dishonorable in purpose or character.

ill-favored (il'fā'vərd) *adj.* Ugly.

illimitable (i·lim'it·ə·bəl) *adj.* Having no limit.

illusion (i·lōō'zhən) *n.* A false idea.

immanence (im'ə·nəns) *n.* The presence of God pervading all creation.

immerse (i·mûrs') *v.* To dip into water.

imminent (im'ə·nənt) *adj.* About to happen.

immortality (im'ôr·tal'ə·tē) *n.* Eternal life.

immune (i·myōōn') *adj.* Protected against a disease, poison, or the like.

impede (im·pēd') *v.* To put obstacles in the way of.

PRONUNCIATION: add, āce, câre, pälm; end, ēven; it, īce; odd, ōpen, ôrder; tŏŏk, pōōl; up, bûrn; ə = a in *above*, e in *sicken*, i in *flexible*, o in *melon*, u in *focus*; yōō = u in *fuse*; oil; pout; check; go; ring; thin; this; zh, vision.

imperative (im·per′ə·tiv) *adj.* Urgently and absolutely necessary; unavoidable.

imperceptible (im′pər·sep′tə·bəl) *adj.* Barely noticeable. **—imperceptibly** *adv.*

imperial (im·pir′ē·əl) *adj.* Suitable to the rank of an emperor.

imperious (im·pir′ē·əs) *adj.* Domineering. **—imperiously** *adv.*

imperturbable (im′pər·tûr′bə·bəl) *adj.* Incapable of being disturbed. **—imperturbability** *n.* **—imperturbably** *adv.*

impetuous (im·pech′ōō·əs) *adj.* Rashly hasty. **—impetuosity** *n.*

impious (im′pē·əs) *adj.* Lacking in reverence.

implacable (im·plā′kə·bəl, -plak′ə-) *adj.* That cannot be appeased or pacified.

implausible (im·plô′zə·bəl) *adj.* Lacking the appearance of truth. **—implausibility** *n.*

importunate (im·pôr′chə·nit) *adj.* Urgently stubborn or persistent in demand.

imposture (im·pos′chər) *n.* Deception by means of false pretenses.

impotence (im′pə·təns) *n.* Helplessness.

impregnate (im·preg′nāt) *v.* To fill or imbue, as with ideas, etc.

improvise (im′prə·vīz) *v.* To invent; make up.

inanimate (in·an′ə·mit) *adj.* Showing no signs of life.

inanity (in·an′ə·tē) *n.* Foolishness.

inarticulate (in′är·tik′yə·lit) *adj.* Uttered without the distinct sounds of spoken language.

inaudible (in·ô′də·bəl) *adj.* Incapable of being heard.

inauspicious (in′ô·spish′əs) *adj.* Not favorable, or unlucky.

incalculable (in·kal′kyə·lə·bəl) *adj.* Too great or numerous to be determined.

incantation (in′kan·tā′shən) *n.* The uttering or intoning of words or syllables supposed to produce magical results.

incessant (in·ses′ənt) *adj.* Never ceasing. **—incessantly** *adv.*

incite (in·sīt′) *v.* To spur to action. **—incitement** *n.*

inclement (in·klem′ənt) *adj.* Of the weather, stormy.

incoherent (in′kō·hir′ənt) *adj.* Disjointed; confused. **—incoherently** *adv.*

incompatible (in′kəm·pat′ə·bəl) *adj.* Incapable of coexisting harmoniously.

incomprehensible (in′kom·pri·hen′sə·bəl, in·kom′-) *adj.* Incapable of being understood.

incongruous (in·kong′grōō·əs) *adj.* Out of place; not suited to the circumstances.

inconsequent (in·kon′sə·kwənt) *adj.* Illogical.

incontrovertible (in′kon·trə·vûr′tə·bəl) *adj.* Undeniable.

incorporate (in·kôr′pə·rāt) *v.* To combine or merge into a whole.

incredulous (in·krej′ə·ləs) *adj.* Not willing to believe.

incur (in·kûr′) *v.* To bring (something unpleasant) on oneself.

indispensable (in′dis·pen′sə·bəl) *adj.* Essential.

indisposition (in′dis·pə·zish′ən) *n.* Slight illness.

indolence (in′də·ləns) *n.* The state of being lazy.

induce (in·dōōs′, -dyōōs′) *v.* To cause to act, speak, etc., by convincing or other influence.

indulgence (in·dul′jəns) *n.* Something granted as a favor.

ineffectual (in′i·fek′chōō·əl) *adj.* Not able to produce a proper or intended result.

inertia (in·ûr′shə) *n.* Inactivity.

inexorable (in·ek′sər·ə·bəl) *adj.* Unyielding. **—inexorably** *adv.*

inexplicable (in·eks′pli·kə·bəl, in′iks·plik′ə·bəl) *adj.* Impossible to explain.

infallible (in·fal′ə·bəl) *adj.* Exempt from fallacy or error of judgment.

infer (in·fûr′) *v.* To derive by reasoning.

infinitesimal (in′fin·ə·tes′ə·məl) *adj.* Extremely small.

infirm (in·fûrm′) *adj.* Feeble or weak.

inflict (in·flikt′) *v.* To impose (something disagreeable): to *inflict* punishment.

ingenious (in·jēn′yəs) *adj.* Having inventive ability; clever.

ingenuity (in′jə·nōō′ə·tē, -nyōō′-) *n.* Inventiveness; cleverness.

ingenuous (in·jen′yōō·əs) *adj.* **1.** straightforward. **2.** Innocent and simple.

ingraft (in·graft′, -gräft′) *v.* To engraft; to set firmly; implant.

ingrate (in′grāt) *n.* An ungrateful person.

ingress (in′gres) *n.* A place of entrance.

inherent (in·hir′ənt, -her′-) *adj.* Forming a permanent and essential element or quality of something. **—inherently** *adv.*

inimitable (in·im′ə·tə·bəl) *adj.* Defying imitation.

iniquity (in·ik′wə·tē) *n.* Wickedness.

injunction (in·jungk′shən) *n.* The act of directing or commanding (a person or group) to a course of action, conduct, etc.

innovator (in′ə·vā′tər) *n.* A person who introduces new ideas, methods, or devices.

inroad (in′rōd′) *n.* A harmful tresspass: with *on* or *upon.*

insatiable (in·sā′shə·bəl, -shē·ə·bəl) *adj.* Incapable of being sated or satisfied.

inscrutable (in·skrōō′tə·bəl) *adj.* That cannot be searched into or understood.

insensible (in·sen′sə·bəl) *adj.* Unconscious. **—insensibility** *n.*

insight (in'sīt) *n.* Perception into the inner nature or real character of a thing.

insinuate (in·sin'yōō·āt) *v.* To introduce subtly and gradually by devious means.

insolence (in'sə·ləns) *n.* Disrespectfulness. **—insolent** *adj.*

insurmountable (in'sər·moun'tə·bəl) *adj.* Incapable of being passed over.

insurrection (in'sə·rek'shən) *n.* An organized resistance to established government.

intangible (in·tan'jə·bəl) *adj.* Incapable of being perceived by touch.

intellect (in'tə·lekt) *n.* The power of the mind to grasp ideas.

interdict (in'tər·dikt') *v.* To prohibit.

interlace (in'tər·lās') *v.* To weave together.

interminable (in·tûr'mə·nə·bəl) *adj.* Seeming endless; never ending.

intermittent (in'tər·mit'ənt) *adj.* Coming at intervals.

interpolate (in·tûr'pə·lāt) *v.* To make additions, insertions, interruptions, etc., in a discourse, process, or series.

interpose (in'tər·pōz') *v.* To put between.

interrogation (in·ter'ə·gā'shən) *n.* The act of questioning.

intervene (in'tər·vēn') *v.* To be located between.

intimate (in'tə·māt) *v.* To hint.

intimidate (in·tim'ə·dāt) *v.* To scare.

intolerable (in·tol'ər·ə·bəl) *adj.* That cannot be borne or endured.

intonation (in'tō·nā'shən) *n.* Way of speaking a language or utterance.

intrigue (in·trēg', in'trēg) *n.* A plot or scheme.

intrude (in·trōōd') *v.* To thrust or force in. **—intrusive** *adj.* **intrusion** *n.*

intuitive (in·tōō'ə·tiv, -tyōō'-) *adj.* Perceived without conscious attention or reasoning.

invalid (in·val'id) *adj.* Having no force, weight or cogency.

inversion (in·vûr'zhən, -shən) *n.* The act of turning upside down.

invincible (in·vin'sə·bəl) *adj.* Not to be overcome.

invocation (in'və·kā'shən, -vō-) *n.* The act of invoking or appealing to a deity.

involuntary (in·vol'ən·ter'ē) *adj.* Done or occurring contrary to one's wish or will.

irascible (i·ras'ə·bəl, ī·ras'-) *adj.* Easily provoked to anger. **—irascibility** *n.*

irrelevant (i·rel'ə·vənt) *adj.* Having no bearing on the matter at hand. **—irrelevantly** *adv.*

irreparable (i·rep'ər·ə·bəl) *adj.* Incapable of being repaired, rectified, remedied, or made good.

irreproachable (ir'i·prō'chə·bəl) *adj.* Blameless.

irresolution (i·rez'ə·lōō'shən) *n.* Indecision.

irrevocable (i·rev'ə·kə·bəl) *adj.* Incapable of being brought back.

iterate (it'ə·rāt) *v.* To state or utter again.

J

jejune (jə·jōōn') *adj.* Naive.

jeopardy (jep'ər·dē) *n.* Danger.

jocose (jō·kōs') *adj.* Disposed to jesting or joking.

jocund (jok'ənd, jō'kənd) *adj.* Jovial.

jounce (jouns) *v.* To shake or move roughly, up and down; bounce.

joust (just, joust, jōōst) *n.* A formal combat between two mounted knights armed with lances.

jowl (joul, jōl) *n.* The fleshy part under the lower jaw, especially when fat and pendulous.

jubilant (jōō'bə·lənt) *adj.* Joyful.

judicious (jōō·dish'əs) *adj.* Having, showing, or using good judgment. **—judiciously** *adv.*

juncture (jungk'chər) *n.* A point in time.

justify (jus'tə·fī) *v.* To show to be just, right, or reasonable. **—justification** *n.*

K

keen (kēn) *adj.* Of senses or sense organs, having great acuity and sensitivity.

kindle (kin'dəl) *v.* To become bright or glowing.

kindred (kin'drid) *adj.* Having a like nature or character.

knead (nēd) *v.* To mix and work (dough, clay, etc.).

L

lachrymose (lak'rə·mōs) *adj.* Tearful.

lamentable (lam'ən·tə·bəl, lə·ment'ə-) *adj.* Bad enough or unfortunate enough to arouse pity or regret.

languid (lang'gwid) *adj.* Lacking animation; listless.

languorous (lang'gər·əs) *adj.* Listless.

larcenous (lär'sə·nəs) *adj.* Guilty of thieving or addicted to theft.

larder (lär'dər) *n.* A room or cupboard where articles of food are stored.

latent (lā'tənt) *adj.* Not visible or apparent.

lath (lath, läth) *n.* One of a number of thin strips of wood used to support plaster.

latitude (lat'ə·tōōd, -tyōōd) *n.* Freedom from narrow restrictions.

league (lēg) *n.* A measure of distance usually reckoned as approximately 3 miles.

legacy (leg'ə·sē) *n.* Anything received from or passed on by an ancestor or predecessor.

levee (lev'ē, lə·vē') *n.* A reception or formal gathering of visitors.

levity (lev'ə·tē) *n.* Frivolity.

liability (lī'ə·bil'ə·tē) *n.* The state or condition of being liable.

libertine (lib'ər·tēn) *n.* One completely lacking in moral restraint. **—adj.** Morally unrestrained.

PRONUNCIATION: add, āce, câre, pälm; end, ēven; it, īce; odd, ōpen, ôrder; tŏŏk, pōōl; up, bûrn; ə = a in *above*, e in *sicken*, i in *flexible*, o in *melon*, u in *focus*; yōō = u in *fuse*; oil; pout; check; go; ring; thin; this; zh, vision.

812

liege (lēj) *n.* A lord to whom allegiance is due.

limpid (lim′pid) *adj.* Characterized by liquid clearness.

lineage (lin′ē·ij) *n.* Those descended from the same ancestor.

linguist (ling′gwist) *n.* One who speaks several languages.

listless (list′lis) *adj.* Characterized by or exhibiting lack of energy or interest.

loftily (lôf′tə·lē) *adv.* Arrogantly; proudly.

loiter (loi′tər) *v.* To linger idly.

loll (lol) *v.* To lie in a relaxed manner.

lope (lōp) *v.* To run with a steady, swinging stride or gallop.

loquacious (lō·kwā′shəs) *adj.* Talkative.

lurid (loor′id) *adj.* Shocking; sensational; vivid.

luster (lus′tər) *n.* Brightness or brilliance of light.

M

maculate (mak′yə·lāt, -lit) *adj.* Stained.

magnanimity (mag′nə·nim′ə·tē) *n.* The quality of being generous in forgiving insults or injuries.

mail (māl) *n.* Flexible armor.

malevolent (mə·lev′ə·lənt) *adj.* Wishing evil toward others. **—malevolence** *n.*

malice (mal′is) *n.* Ill will; spite. **—malicious** *adj.*

malignant (mə·lig′nənt) *adj.* Tending to do great harm.

malignity (mə·lig′nə·tē) *n.* Intense ill will.

manifest (man′ə·fest) *v.* To show. **—manifestation** *n.*

manifold (man′ə·fōld) *adj.* Having many and varied forms.

manipulation (mə·nip′yə·lā′shən) *n.* The act of using the hands skillfully.

mantilla (man·til′ə) *n.* A light scarf often of black lace worn over the head and shoulders.

mantle (man′təl) *n.* A loose and usually sleeveless garment worn over other garments.

maritime (mar′ə·tīm) *adj.* Of or pertaining to the sea.

masque (mask, mäsk) *n.* A disguise.

masseur (ma·sûr′) *n.* A man who practices or gives massage.

material (mə·tir′ē·əl) *adj.* Concerned with things physical.

matriarch (mā′trē·ärk) *n.* The female leader of a family or tribe.

maunder (môn′dər) *v.* To talk in a wandering or incoherent manner.

maxim (mak′sim) *n.* A brief statement of a general principle, truth, or rule of conduct.

mead (mēd) *n.* A meadow.

menagerie (mə·naj′ər·ē) *n.* A collection of wild animals.

metamorphosis (met′ə·môr′fə·sis) *n.* Change from one form, shape, or substance into another by any means.

metaphysical (met′ə·fiz′i·kəl) *adj.* Beyond or above the physical or the laws of nature.

meteorology (mē′tē·ə·rol′ə·jē) *n.* The weather conditions of any particular place. **—meteorological** *adj.*

mettle (met′l) *n.* Courage.

mien (mēn) *n.* Manner.

mimic (mim′ik) *v.* To copy closely. **—adj.** Mock.

mincing (min′sing) *adj.* Affectedly precise, refined, or dainty, as in manner, gait, etc. **—mincingly** *adv.*

mingle (ming′gəl) *v.* To mix or unite together.

minion (min′yən) *n.* A servile favorite or follower.

mire (mīr) *n.* Deep mud or slush. **—miry** *adj.*

mirth (mûrth) *n.* Spirited gaiety.

mitigate (mit′ə·gāt) *v.* To make or become less severe.

mode (mōd) *n.* Manner or form.

modify (mod′ə·fī) *v.* To make somewhat different in form.

modulation (moj′oo·lā′shən) *n.* Regulation or adjustment, as in passing from one musical key to another, or in the management of tones of color in art.

molder (mōl′dər) *v.* To decay gradually.

monosyllable (mon′ə·sil′ə·bəl) *n.* A word of one syllable.

morbid (môr′bid) *adj.* **1.** Grisly; gruesome. **2.** Pertaining to, arising from, or affected by disease.

mordant (mor′dənt) *adj.* Biting; cutting.

morose (mə·rōs′) *adj.* Gloomy.

mortician (môr·tish′ən) *n.* Undertaker.

mortify (môr′tə·fī) *v.* To affect with shame.

multitudinous (mul′tə·too′də·nəs, -tyoo′) *adj.* Existing in great numbers.

mummer (mum′ər) *n.* One who wears a mask or disguise.

musing (myoo′zing) *adj.* Thoughtful. **—musingly** *adv.*

mute (myoot) *adj.* Silent.

N

natty (nat′ē) *adj.* Neat and smart, as in dress or appearance. **—nattiness** *n.*

necromancy (nek′rə·man′sē) *n.* Black magic. **—necromancer** *n.*

negligent (neg′lə·jənt) *adj.* **1.** Neglectful. **2.** Nonchalant.

notorious (nō·tôr′ē·əs, -tō′rē-) *adj.* Widely known and generally disapproved. **—notoriously** *adv.*

PRONUNCIATION: add, āce, câre, pälm; end, ēven; it, īce; odd, ōpen, ôrder; took, pool; up, bûrn; ə = a in *above*, e in *sicken*, i in *flexible*, o in *melon*, u in *focus*; yoo = u in *fuse*; oil; pout; check; go; ring; thin; this; zh, vision.

nucleus (nōō'klē-əs, nyōō'-) *n.* Core.

nurture (nûr'chər) *v.* To feed or support.

O

oblique (ə-blēk') *adj.* Not direct or straightforward.

oblivious (ə-bliv'ē-əs) *adj.* Not conscious or aware.

obscene (əb-sēn', ob-) *adj.* Indecent. —**obscenity** *n.*

obscure (əb-skyōōr') *adj.* 1. Not clear or plain to the mind. 2. Hidden.

obsequious (əb-sē'kwē-əs) *adj.* Excessively obedient; fawning.

obstinate (ob'stə-nit) *adj.* Stubborn. —**obstinacy** *n.*

occidental (ok'sə-den'təl) *adj.* Of or belonging to the western hemisphere.

odious (ō'dē-əs) *adj.* Exciting hate, repugnance, or disgust.

office (ô'fis, of'is) *n.* A service; a favor.

officious (ə-fish'əs, ō-) *adj.* Unduly forward in offering one's services or advice. —**officiously** *adv.*

ominous (om'ə-nəs) *adj.* Threatening. —**ominously** *adv.*

omniscience (om-nish'əns) *n.* Infinite knowledge.

oppressive (ə-pres'iv) *adj.* Producing a state of mental depression.

opulence (op'yə-ləns) *n.* Luxuriance.

ornithology (ôr'nə-thol'ə-jē) *n.* The branch of zoology that treats of birds. —**ornithologist** *n.*

ostensible (os-ten'sə-bəl) *adj.* Offered as real or genuine. —**ostensibly** *adv.*

ottoman (ot'ə-mən) *n.* A cushioned footrest.

overbearing (ō'vər-bâr'ing) *adj.* Dictatorial.

own (ōn) *v.* To admit.

P

pacify (pas'ə-fī) *v.* To allay the anger or agitation of.

pagoda (pə-gō'də) *n.* In the Far East, a sacred tower or temple.

painstaking (pānz'tā'king, pān'stā'-) *adj.* Careful.

paling (pā'ling) *n.* A fence.

pall (pôl) *n.* Something that covers, especially something that is dark or gloomy.

pallid (pal'id) *adj.* Of a pale or wan appearance.

pallor (pal'ər) *n.* Paleness.

palpable (pal'pə-bəl) *adj.* Readily perceived; obvious.

paltry (pôl'trē) *adj.* Having little or no worth or value.

parapet (par'ə-pit, -pet) *n.* A low wall about the edge of a roof, terrace, bridge, etc.

parley (pär'lē) *n.* A conference.

parry (par'ē) *v.* To avoid or evade.

partiality (pär'shē-al'ə-tē) *n.* A particular fondness.

passive (pas'iv) *adj.* Not acting, working, or operating.

pastoral (pas'tər-əl, päs'-) *adj.* 1. Pertaining to rural life. 2. Pertaining to a clergyman.

patent (pāt'nt) *adj.* Apparent to everybody.

pathos (pā'thos) *n.* The quality that arouses feelings of pity, sorrow, compassion, etc.

patrimony (pat'rə-mō'nē) *n.* Anything inherited.

patronize (pā'trən-īz, pat'rən-) *v.* To treat in a consciously courteous manner. —**patronizingly** *adv.*

paucity (pô'sə-tē) *n.* Smallness of number or quantity.

peal (pēl) *n.* A loud, full, echoing sound, as of a bell or of thunder.

peat (pēt) *n.* A block of moss pressed and dried for fuel.

pedigree (ped'ə-grē) *n.* 1. A line of ancestors. 2. A list or table of descent and relationship.

peeress (pir'is) *n.* A woman who holds a title of nobility.

penal (pē'nəl) *adj.* Of or pertaining to punishment.

penance (pen'əns) *n.* Any penalty, mortification, or act of piety, imposed or voluntarily undertaken as an atonement.

penitence (pen'ə-təns) *n.* The state of being affected by a sense of one's own guilt, and resolved on amendment. —**penitential** *adj.*

pensioner (pen'shən-ər) *n.* One who receives a pension.

pensive (pen'siv) *adj.* Engaged in serious, quiet thought.

penury (pen'yə-rē) *n.* Extreme poverty.

perceive (pər-sēv') *v.* To come to understand. —**perception** *n.*

peremptory (pə-remp'tər-ē, per'əmp-tôr'ē, -tō'rē) *adj.* Positive and assured in manner. —**peremptorily** *adv.*

perennial (pə-ren'ē-əl) *adj.* Everlasting.

perforce (pər-fôrs', -fōrs') *adv.* Of necessity.

perfunctory (pər-fungk'tər-ē) *adj.* Done merely for the sake of getting through.

perpetuate (pər-pech'ōō-āt) *v.* To cause to remain known.

perplexed (pər-plekst') *adj.* Confused; puzzled; bewildered.

persecution (pûr'sə-kyōō'shən) *n.* The act or process of harassing with cruel or oppressive treatment.

perturb (pər-tûrb') *v.* To disturb.

pervade (pər-vād') *v.* To spread through every part of.

perversity (pər·vûr′sə·tē) *n.* The state of being waywardly or unreasonably nonconforming.

pestilence (pes′tə·ləns) *n.* Any widespread, often fatal, infectious or contagious disease.

petrify (pet′rə·fī) *v.* To convert (organic material) into a substance of stony character.

pettish (pet′ish) *adj.* Ill-tempered. **—pettishly** *adv.*

petulant (pech′ōō·lənt) *adj.* Peevish.

phantasm (fan′taz·əm) *n.* A mental image.

phenomenon (fi·nom′ə·non) *n. pl.* phenomena (-nə) Something visible or directly observable, as an appearance, action, change, etc.

philanthropy (fi·lan′thrə·pē) *n.* Love toward mankind. **—philanthropic** *adj.*

phlegmatic (fleg·mat′ik) *adj.* Sluggish. **—phlegmatically** *adv.*

physic (fiz′ik) *n.* **1.** Medicine in general. **2.** A cathartic; a purge.

piety (pī′ə·tē) *n.* Reverence toward God or the gods.

pillion (pil′yən) *n.* A pad or seat behind the saddle of a horse or motorcycle for a second rider.

pinafore (pin′ə·fôr, -fōr) *n.* A sleeveless apronlike garment.

pincers (pin′sərz) *n.* An instrument having two handles and a pair of jaws working on a pivot, used for holding objects.

pine (pīn) *v.* To have great desire or longing.

pinion (pin′yən) *n.* The wing of a bird.

piquant (pē′kant, -känt, -kwant, pē·känt′) *adj.* Lively and entertaining. **—piquancy** *n.*

pitch (pich) *n.* A thick, dark substance obtained by boiling down tar.

pitch (pich) *v.* To fall forward.

pith (pith) *n.* The soft, spongy tissue in the center of the stems of certain plants.

placable (plā′kə·bəl, plak′ə-) *adj.* Appeasable; yielding; forgiving. **—placably** *adv.*

plaintive (plān′tiv) *adj.* Mournful.

plausible (plô′zə·bəl) *adj.* Seeming to be likely or probable, but open to doubt.

pliant (plī′ənt) *adj.* Capable of being bent or twisted with ease.

poignant (poin′yənt, poi′nənt) *adj.* Painful to the feelings.

pompous (pom′pəs) *adj.* Marked by exaggerated dignity or self-importance.

ponderous (pon′dər·əs) *adj.* Having great weight.

portentous (pôr·ten′təs, pōr-) *adj.* Extraordinary.

posterity (pos·ter′ə·tē) *n.* Future generations taken collectively.

potent (pōt′nt) *adj.* Capable of influencing greatly.

precarious (pri·kâr′ē·əs) *adj.* Uncertain.

precedent (pres′ə·dənt) *n.* An act or instance capable of being used as a guide or standard in evaluating future actions.

precipitancy (pri·sip′ə·tən·sē) *n.* The quality of rushing.

preclude (pri·klōōd′) *v.* To make impossible.

precursor (pri·kûr′sər) *n.* One who or that which precedes and suggests the course of future events.

predecessor (pred′ə·ses′ər) *n.* One who goes before another in point of time.

preeminent (prē·em′ə·nənt) *adj.* Outstanding.

premonition (prē′mə·nish′ən, prem′ə-) *n.* A presentiment of the future not based on information received.

prerogative (pri·rog′ə·tiv) *n.* A hereditary or official right.

preternatural (prē′tər·nach′ər·əl) *adj.* Diverging from or exceeding the common order of nature.

pretext (prē′tekst) *n.* A fictitious reason or motive advanced to conceal a real one.

prevarication (pri·var′ə·kā′shən) *n.* A lie.

primal (prī′məl) *adj.* First; original.

privation (prī·vā′shən) *n.* The state of lacking something necessary or desirable.

privily (priv′ə·lē) *adv.* Privately.

probe (prōb) *v.* To investigate or examine thoroughly.

procrastinate (prō·kras′tə·nāt) *v.* To put off doing something until a future time.

prodigious (prə·dij′əs) *adj.* Enormous in size, quantity, or degree.

profanity (prə·fan′ə·tē) *n.* Vulgar or coarse speech or action.

proffer (prof′ər) *v.* To offer for acceptance.

profligacy (prof′lə·gə·sē) *n.* Reckless extravagance.

profound (prə·found′, prō-) *adj.* Deep.

profuse (prə·fyōōs′, prō-) *adj.* Abundant. **—profusion** *n.*

project (prə·jekt′) *v.* To cause to extend forward or out.

projectile (prə·jek′təl) *n.* A missile for discharge from a gun or cannon.

prone (prōn) *adj.* Mentally inclined.

propensity (prə·pen′sə·tē) *n.* A natural tendency.

prophetic (prə·fet′ik) *adj.* Pertaining to or involving prediction.

propitiate (prō·pish′ē·āt) *v.* To cause to be favorably disposed. **—propitiation** *n.*

propriety (prə·prī′ə·tē) *n.* The character or quality of being proper.

prosaic (prō·zā′ik) *adj.* Dull.

proscription (prō·skrip′shən) *n.* The act of prohibiting.

prostrate (pros′trāt) *adj.* Lying with the face to

PRONUNCIATION: add, āce, câre, pälm; end, ēven; it, īce; odd, ōpen, ôrder; tŏŏk, pōōl; up, bûrn; ə = a in *above*, e in *sicken*, i in *flexible*, o in *melon*, u in *focus*; yōō = u in *fuse*; oil; pout; check; go; ring; thin; this; zh, vision.

815

the ground. *v.* To make helpless.

protract (prō·trakt′) *v.* To extend in time.

protrude (prō·trōōd′) *v.* To push or thrust out.

protuberant (prō·tōō′bər·ənt, -tyoō-) *adj.* Bulging.

provident (prov′ə·dənt) *adj.* Exercising foresight.

provincial (prə·vin′shəl) *adj.* Narrow; uncultured.

provision (prə·vizh′ən) *v.* To provide with food.

provoke (prə·vōk′) *v.* To irritate.

prudence (prōōd′ns) *n.* The quality or state of being careful. **—prudent** *adj.*

puerile (pyōō′ər·il, pyōō′rəl, -rīl, pwer′əl, -īl) *adj.* Pertaining to or characteristic of childhood.

pugnacious (pug·nā′shəs) *adj.* Quarrelsome.

puissant (pyōō′ə·sənt, pyōō·is′ənt, pwis′ənt) *adj.* Powerful.

pulsation (pul′sā′shən) *n.* Throbbing.

pungent (pun′jənt) *adj.* Sharp or piercing to smell or taste.

purport (pûr′pôrt, -pōrt) *n.* That which is conveyed or suggested to the mind as the meaning or intention.

Q

quaver (kwā′vər) *v.* To tremble or shake.

R

rail (rāl) *v.* To complain in angry, bitter, or scornful words.

raiment (rā′mənt) *n.* Clothing.

rampage (ram′pāj) *n.* A dashing about with anger or violence. **—rampageous** *adj.*

rancor (rang′kər) *n.* Spitefulness.

rankle (rang′kəl) *v.* To irritate.

rationalism (rash′ən·əl·iz′əm) *n.* The formation of opinions by relying upon reason alone. **—rationalistic** *adj.*

raveling (rav′əl·ing) *n.* A thread.

rebuke (ri·byōōk′) *v.* To reprimand.

recede (ri·sēd′) *v.* To move or fade away.

recluse (ri·klōōs′, rek′lōōs) *n.* A person who lives alone, shut away from the world.

recoil (ri·koil′) *v.* To move or draw back.

recrimination (ri·krim′ə·nā′shən) *n.* An accusation made in return.

rectitude (rek′tə·tōōd, -tyōōd) *n.* Uprightness in principles and conduct.

rector (rek′tər) *n.* In the Church of England, a priest.

rectory (rek′tər·ē) *n.* The dwelling of a priest.

recurrent (ri·kûr′ənt) *adj.* Happening or appearing again or repeatedly.

redress (ri·dres′) *v.* To set right. **—***n.* Correction.

reflective (ri·flek′tiv) *adj.* Given to thought.

—reflectively *adv.*

refutation (ref′yōō·tā′shən) *n.* The act of proving to be in error.

regimen (rej′ə·mən) *n.* A systematized course of living, as to food, clothing, etc.

reiterate (rē·it′ə·rāt) *v.* To say again and again; repeat.

relent (ri·lent′) *v.* Become more gentle.

remonstrate (ri·mon′strāt) *v.* To say or plead in protest or opposition. **—remonstrance** *n.*

remorse (ri·môrs′) *n.* The keen or hopeless anguish caused by a sense of guilt.

remorseless (ri·môrs′lis) *adj.* Pitiless; cruel.

rend (rend) *v.* To tear apart.

renunciation (ri·nun′sē·ā′shən, -shē-) *n.* The act of giving up.

repertory (rep′ər·tôr′ē, -tō′rē) *n.* Repertoire; a list of songs, plays, operas, or the like, that a person or company is prepared to perform.

replenish (ri·plen′ish) *v.* To fill again.

reprove (ri′prōōv′) *v.* To express disapproval of (an act).

repudiate (ri·pyōō′dē·āt) *v.* To refuse to accept as binding or valid.

repugnance (ri·pug′nəns) *n.* The state of feeling aversion and resistance.

requisition (rek′wə·zish′ən) *n.* A formal request, summons, or demand, as by a government.

resolute (rez′ə·lōōt) *adj.* Determined.

restrain (ri·strān′) *v.* To hold back from acting. **—restraint** *n.*

resurgent (ri·sûr′jənt) *adj.* Rising again.

retentive (ri·ten′tiv) *adj.* Having the power or tendency to retain.

reticence (ret′ə·sens) *n.* The quality of being habitually silent or reserved in utterance.

retract (ri·trakt′) *v.* To take back.

retribution (ret′rə·byōō′shən) *n.* The act of repaying in kind.

retrieve (ri·trēv′) *v.* To get back. **—retrieval** *n.*

retrospect (ret′rə·spekt) *n.* A view or contemplation of something past.

revel (rev′əl) *v.* To make merry.

reverie (rev′ər·e) *n.* Abstracted dreaming. Also **revery.**

revile (ri·vīl′) *v.* To assail with abusive language.

rheum (rōōm) *n.* A thin, watery catarrhal discharge from the nose and eyes. **—rheumy** *adj.*

rheumatism (rōō′mə·tiz′əm) *n.* A painful inflammation and stiffness of the muscles, joints, etc.

rivulet (riv′yə·lit) *n.* A small stream or brook.

roister (rois′tər) *v.* To engage in merrymaking.

rollicking (rol′ik·ing) *adj.* Jovial; light-hearted.

rueful (rōō′fəl) *adj.* Sorrowful. **—ruefully** *adv.*

ruminate (rōō′mə·nāt) *v.* **1.** To chew over again. **2.** To meditate or reflect (upon). **—rumination** *n.*

PRONUNCIATION: add, āce, câre, pälm; end, ēven; it, īce; odd, ōpen, ôrder; tŏŏk, pōōl; up, bûrn; ə = a in *above*, e in *sicken*, i in *flexible*, o in *melon*, u in *focus*; yōō = u in *fuse*; oil; pout; check; go; ring; thin; ṯhis; zh, vision.

816

ruse (rōoz) *n.* A trick.

russet (rus'it) *adj.* Of a reddish or yellowish brown color.

rustic (rus'tik) *adj.* Typical of simple country life.

S

sacrament (sak'rǝ-mǝnt) *n.* A rite ordained by the church as an outward and visible sign of an inward and spiritual grace.

sacristy (sak'ris-tē) *n.* A room in a religious house for the sacred vessels and vestments.

sagacity (sǝ-gas'ǝ-tē) *n.* Shrewdness.

sage (sāj) *n.* A wise man.

sallow (sal'ō) *adj.* Of an unhealthy yellowish color.

sally (sal'ē) *n.* A bantering remark.

sanction (sangk'shǝn) *v.* To approve.

sardonic (sär-don'ik) *adj.* Scornful. **—sardonically** *adv.*

savory (sā'vǝr-ē) *adj.* Of an agreeable taste and odor.

scarify (skar'ǝ-fī) *v.* **1.** To scratch or make slight incisions in. **2.** To criticize severely; make cutting comments on.

scepter (sep'tǝr) *n.* Kingly office or power.

score (skôr, skōr) *n.* A set of twenty.

scour (skour) *v.* To clean or brighten by thorough washing and rubbing.

scourge (skûrj) *v.* To whip severely.

scrabble (skrab'ǝl) *v.* To scratch, scrape, or paw.

scribe (skrīb) *n.* One who writes or copies manuscripts.

scrupulous (skrōo'pyǝ-lǝs) *adj.* Exact; careful.

scud (skud) *v.* To move, run, or fly swiftly, especially when driven by the wind.

scurrilous (skûr'ǝ-lǝs) *adj.* Grossly and offensively abusive.

scuttle (skut'ǝl) *v.* To scurry; run quickly.

scythe (sīth, *sometimes* sī) *n.* An implement used for mowing, consisting of a long, curved blade fixed at an angle to a long bent handle.

sear (sir) *v.* To scorch.

seclusion (si-klōo'zhǝn) *n.* The act of living apart from others.

sect (sekt) *n.* The adherents collectively of a particular religious creed or confession.

sedate (si-dāt') *adj.* Unhurried; calm. **—sedately** *adv.*

sedulous (sej'ōo-lǝs) *adj.* Constant in attention.

semblance (sem'blǝns) *n.* Outward appearance.

sensation (sen-sā'shǝn) *n.* The aspect of consciousness resulting from the stimulation of any of the sense organs, as hearing, taste, touch, smell, or sight; an excited condition.

sensibility (sen'sǝ-bil'ǝ-tē) *n.* Power to perceive or feel.

sentry (sen'trē) *n.* A soldier placed on guard duty.

serenity (si-ren'ǝ-tē) *n.* Peacefulness.

serpentine (sûr'pǝn-tēn, -tīn) *adj.* Winding.

servile (sûr'vīl, -vil) *adj.* Having the spirit of a slave. **—servility** *n.*

sever (sev'ǝr) *v.* To put or keep apart; separate.

shard (shärd) *n.* A broken piece of a brittle substance.

sheaf (shēf) *n.* A bundle of stalks of cut grain.

shingle (shing'gǝl) *n.* A thin, tapering, oblong piece of wood or other material, used in courses to cover roofs.

shoal (shōl) *n.* A shallow place in any body of water.

shorn (shôrn, shōrn) Alternative past participle of SHEAR.

shrew (shrōo) *n.* Any of numerous diminutive, chiefly insectivorous mammals having a long pointed snout and soft fur.

shroud (shroud) *n.* A dress or garment for the dead. **—v.** To envelop, as with a garment.

shy (shī) *v.* To start suddenly aside, as in fear.

sickle (sik'ǝl) *n.* An implement for cutting tall grass, grains, etc.

sidle (sīd'l) *v.* To move sideways.

simultaneous (sī'mǝl-tā'nē-ǝs, sim'ǝl-) *adj.* Occurring, done, or existing at the same time.

sinewy (sin'yōo-ē) *adj.* Having sinews; firm or tough.

singe (sinj) *v.* To burn slightly; scorch.

singular (sing'gyǝ-lǝr) *adj.* Not customary or usual. **—singularity** *n.*

skeptical (skep'ti-kǝl) *adj.* Doubting.

slattern (slat'ǝrn) *adj.* Untidy; slovenly.

slaver (slav'ǝr) *v.* To dribble saliva from the mouth; drool.

slew (slōo) *v.* To move sideways.

slip (slip) *n.* A cutting from a plant for planting or grafting.

slovenly (sluv'ǝn-lē) *adj.* Untidy; careless.

sluice (slōos) *v.* To wet or drench.

smite (smīt) *v.* **1.** To strike. **2.** To cut, sever, or break by a blow.

smithy (smith'ē, smith'ē) *n.* A blacksmith's shop; a forge.

smolder (smōl'dǝr) *v.* To burn and smoke.

smug (smug) *adj.* Having a self-satisfied air.

sobriety (sō-brī'ǝ-tē) *n.* **1.** The state or quality of being sober. **2.** Seriousness.

sod (sod) *n.* A piece of grassy surface soil.

solicitous (se-lis'ǝ-tǝs) *adj.* Full of anxiety or concern. **—solicitude** *n.*

soliloquy (sǝ-lil'ǝ-kwē) *n.* A talking or discourse to oneself.

PRONUNCIATION: add, āce, câre, pälm; end, ēven; it, īce; odd, ōpen, ôrder; tŏŏk, pōōl; up, bûrn; ǝ = a in *above*, e in *sicken*, i in *flexible*, o in *melon*, u in *focus*; yōō = u in *fuse*; oil; pout; check; go; ring; thin; this; zh, vision.

sophistication (sə·fis'tə·kā'shən) *n.* Quality of being worldly-wise.

soporific (sō'pə·rif'ik, sop'ə-) *adj.* Causing sleep.

sordid (sôr'did) *adj.* Filthy; dirty. **—sordidly** *adv.*

sorely (sôr'lē, sōr'-) *adv.* Greatly.

sovereign (sov'rən, suv'-) *n.* A monarch; ruler. **—**adj.* **1.** Exercising or possessing supreme authority. **2.** Potent.

spangle (spang'gəl) *v.* To adorn with or as with small bits of sparkling metal.

spasmodic (spaz·mod'ik) *adj.* Of the nature of a sudden, temporary burst of energy or activity. **—spasmodically** *adv.*

spawn (spôn) *n.* Very small fish.

specter (spek'tər) *n.* A ghost. **—spectral** adj.

speculate (spek'yə·lāt) *v.* To guess.

speculator (spek'yə·lā'tər) *n.* One who makes an investment involving risk with hope of large profit.

spindrift (spin'drift) *n.* Blown sea spray.

spontaneous (spon·tā'nē·əs) *adj.* Done or resulting from one's own impulse, prompting, or desire. **—spontaneity** *n.*

sprightly (sprīt'lē) *adj.* Lively.

spume (spyōom) *n.* Foam.

spurn (spûrn) *v.* To reject with disdain. **—**n.* A kick.

squabble (skwob'əl) *n.* A petty quarrel.

squalor (skwol'ər) *n.* Filth and wretched poverty.

staid (stād) *adj.* Steady.

stanch (stanch, stänch) *v.* To stop or check the flow of (blood, etc.).

stanchion (stan'shən) *n.* An upright bar forming a principal support.

staunch (stônch, stänch) *adj.* Firm and dependable. **—staunchness** *n.*

steadfast (sted'fast', -fäst', -fəst) *adj.* Unchanging.

stealthy (stel'thē) *adj.* Moving or acting secretly. **stealthily** *adv.*

steep (stēp) *v.* To soak in a liquid.

sterile (ster'əl) *adj.* Barren.

stile (stīl) *n.* A step, or series of steps, on each side of a fence or wall to aid in surmounting it.

stoic (stō'ik) *adj.* Indifferent to pleasure or pain; impassive.

stolid (stol'id) *adj.* Having or showing little feeling. **—stolidly** *adv.*

strain (strān) *n.* A passage of music.

stratagem (strat'ə·jəm) *n.* A device for obtaining advantage.

stricken (strik'ən) *adj.* Strongly affected or afflicted.

strident (strīd'nt) *adv.* Shrill.

strife (strīf) *n.* Fighting.

stripping (strip'ing) *n.* A narrow piece of wood.

stupefy (stōo'pə·fī, styōo') *v.* To stun. **—stupefaction** *n.*

sty (stī) *n.* A pen for swine.

suavity (swä'və·tē, swav'ə) *n.* The state or quality of being smoothly pleasant and ingratiating in manner.

subdue (sub·dōo', -dyōo') *v.* To soften.

sublime (sə·blīm') *adj.* Grand.

subside (səb·sīd') *v.* To become less violent or agitated.

subsidy (sub'sə·dē) *n.* Financial assistance.

subsist (səb·sist') *v.* To continue to exist.

succumb (sə·kum') *v.* To give away.

sufferance (suf'ər·əns, suf'rəns) *n.* Permission given or implied by failure to prohibit.

suffice (sə·fīs') *v.* Meet the requirements or answer the purpose.

sullen (sul'ən) *adj.* Ill-humored; glum.

sultry (sul'trē) *adj.* Hot, moist, and still.

sumptuous (sump'chōo·əs) *adj.* Luxurious; magnificent.

supercilious (sōo'pər·sil'ē·əs) *adj.* Arrogant. **—superciliously** *adv.*

superficial (sōo'pər·fish'əl) *adj.* Of the surface. **—superficially** *adv.*

superfluous (sōo·pûr'flōo·əs) *adj.* Exceeding what is needed.

superlative (sə·pûr'lə·tiv, sōo-) *adj.* Elevated to the highest degree. **—superlatively** *adv.*

supplant (sə·plant', plänt') *v.* To take the place of.

suppliant (sup'lē·ənt) *n.* One who makes an earnest request.

suppress (sə·pres') *v.* To put a stop to.

surlily (sûr'lə·lē) *adv.* Rudely and crossly.

surmise (sər·mīz') *v.* To guess.

surpliced (sûr'plist) *adj.* Wearing a clergyman's robe.

susceptible (sə·sep'tə·bəl) *adj.* Capable of being influenced, acted on, or determined.

symposium (sim·pō'zē·əm) *n.* A meeting for discussion of a particular subject.

T

tableau (tab'lō, ta·blō') *n.* Any picture or picturesque representation.

tabloid (tab'loid) *adj.* Compact; condensed.

tacit (tas'it) *adj.* Existing, inferred, or implied without being directly stated.

tale (tāl) *n. Archaic* An amount.

tally (tal'ē) *n.* A reckoning; account.

tarnish (tär'nish) *v.* To dim the luster of.

taunt (tônt) *n.* A sarcastic, biting speech or remark.

tauten (tôt'n) *v.* To tighten.

PRONUNCIATION: add, āce, câre, pälm; end, ēven; it, īce; odd, ōpen, ôrder; tŏŏk, pōōl; up, bûrn; ə = a in *above*, e in *sicken*, i in *flexible*, o in *melon*, u in *focus*; yōō = u in *fuse*; oil; pout; check; go; ring; thin; this; zh, vision.

teeter (tē′tər) *v.* To rock back and forth, as if about to fall.

temperament (tem′pər·ə·mənt, -prə-) *n.* Mental makeup; disposition. —**temperamental** *adj.*

tenacious (ti·nā′shəs) *adj.* Having great cohesiveness of parts. —**tenacity** *n.*

testy (tes′tē) *adj.* Touchy. —**testily** *adv.*

tether (teth′ər) *n.* Something used to check or confine, as a rope for fastening an animal. —*v.* To fasten or confine by a tether.

theology (thē·ol′ə·jē) *n.* The study of religion, culminating in a synthesis or philosophy of religion; also a critical survey of religion.

tincture (tingk′chər) *n.* A slight additional quality.

toilette (toi·let′, *Fr.* twȧ·let′) *n.* **1.** The act or process of grooming oneself. **2.** A person's actual dress or style of dress.

token (tō′kən) *n.* A visible sign.

tome (tōm) *n.* A large book.

topical (top′i·kəl) *adj.* Pertaining to matters of present interest.

torpid (tôr′pid) *adj.* Inactive, as a hibernating animal.

tourney (tûr′nē, tōor′-) *n.* A tournament.

trammel (tram′əl) *n. Usually pl.* That which limits freedom or activity.

transcendent (tran·sen′dənt) *adj.* Of very high and remarkable degree.

transcribe (tran·skrīb′) *v.* To write over again.

transfer (trans′fər) *n.* An order transferring money or securities.

transfigure (trans·fig′yər) *v.* To change the outward form or appearance of. —**transfiguration** *n.*

transient (tran′shənt) *adj.* Passing away quickly.

traverse (trav′ərs, tra·vûrs′) *v.* **1.** To pass over, across, or through. **2.** To move back and forth over or along.

treacherous (trech′ər·əs) *adj.* Disloyal.

treadle (tred′l) *n.* A lever operated by the foot.

treadmill (tred′mil′) *n.* **1.** A mechanism rotated by the walking motion of one or more persons. **2.** Any wearisome or monotonous work.

treatise (trē′tis) *n.* A formal and systematic written account of some subject.

treble (treb′əl) *v.* To multiply by three.

tremulous (trem′yə·ləs) *adj.* **1.** Characterized or affected by trembling. **2.** Showing timidity or fear. —**tremulously** *adv.*

trenchant (tren′chənt) *adj.* Cutting.

tributary (trib′yə·ter′ē) *n.* A stream flowing into a larger stream or body of water.

tripod (trī′pod) *n.* A three-legged stand.

truculence (truk′yə·ləns) *n.* Savageness of character. —**truculent** *adj.*

tuft (tuft) *n.* A clump.

U

unabated (un′ə·bāt′id) *adj.* Not made less.

uncanny (un·kan′ē) *adj.* Weird; unnatural.

unctuous (ungk′chōo·əs) *adj.* Characterized by affected emotion. —**unction** *n.*

undefinable (un′di·fīn′ə·bəl) *adj.* Incapable of being explained or interpreted.

undemonstrative (un′di·mon′strə·tiv) *adj.* Not disposed to show the feelings.

undermine (un′dər·mīn′, un′dər·mīn) *v.* To weaken.

undulate (un′dyə·lāt, -də-) *v.* To cause to move like a wave or in waves. —**undulation** *n.*

unenterprising (un·en′tər·prī′zing) *adj.* Not energetic, bold, and full of initiative.

unexampled (un′ig·zam′pəld) *adj.* Having no precedent, analogy, or parallel example.

unimpeachable (un′im·pē′chə·bəl) *adj.* Faultless.

unimpeded (un′im·pēd′id) *adj.* Having nothing in the way of.

unkempt (un·kempt′) *adj.* Not clean or neat; untidy; rough.

unlettered (un·let′ərd) *adj.* Not educated.

unmeritorious (un·mer′ə·tôr′ē·əs, -tō′rē-) *adj.* Not deserving of reward or praise.

unmodified (un·mod′ə·fīd) *adj.* Not made different in form.

unnurtured (un·nûr′chərd) *adj.* Not fed or supported.

unprecedented (un·pres′ə·den′tid) *adj.* Unheard-of.

unprepossessing (un′prē·pə·zes′ing) *adj.* Not inspiring a favorable opinion.

unrelentingly (un′ri·len′ting·lē) *adv.* Pitilessly; with no relaxation, no diminishing.

unremitting (un′ri·mit′ing) *adj.* Not relaxing or stopping.

unscrupulous (un·skrōo′pyə·ləs) *adj.* Having no morals.

unseemly (un·sēm′lē) *adj.* Not proper.

unsolicited (un′sə·lis′it·id) *adj.* Not asked for.

unsustained (un′sə·stānd′) *adj.* Not kept up.

untenanted (un·ten′ənt·id) *adj.* Not occupied.

unutterable (un·ut′ər·ə·bəl) *adj.* That cannot be spoken.

usurpation (yōo′zər·pā′shən, -sər-) *n.* The act of seizing and holding without right or legal authority.

V

vacillating (vas′ə·lā′ting) *adj.* Wavering.

vagrant (vā′grənt) *n.* A person without a settled home.

vale (vāl) *n.* A valley: used mainly in poems.

validity (və·lid′ə·tē) *n.* Soundness, as in law or reasoning.

PRONUNCIATION: add, āce, câre, pälm; end, ēven; it, īce; odd, ōpen, ôrder; tōok, pōol; **up**, bûrn; ə = a in *above*, e in *sicken*, i in *flexible*, o in *melon*, u in *focus*; **yōo** = u in *fuse*; **oil**; **pout**; **check**; **go**; **ring**; **thin**; **this**; **zh**, vision.

variegated (vâr′ē·ə·gā′tid) *adj.* Varied in color, as with streaks or blotches.

vehement (vē′ə·mənt) *adj.* Violent. —**vehemently** *adv.*

venerable (ven′ər·ə·bəl) *adj.* Meriting or commanding respect and deference.

veneration (ven′ə·rā′shən) *n.* A feeling of profound respect and awe.

veracity (və·ras′ə·tē) *n.* Truthfulness.

verify (ver′ə·fī) *v.* To prove to be true.

veritable (ver′ə·tə·bəl) *adj.* Properly so called.

vested (ves′tid) *adj.* Established as a permanent right.

vex (veks) *v.* To provoke to anger; annoy.

vexation (vek·sā′shən) *n.* Irritation.

vibration (vī·brā′shən) *n.* The act of moving back and forth rapidly.

vicarious (vī·kâr′ē·əs, vi-) *adj.* Suffered or done in place of another. —**vicariously** *adv.*

vicinage (vis′ə·nij) *n.* Neighboring places collectively.

vicissitude (vi·sis′ə·tood, -tyood) *n. pl.* Irregular changes or variations.

victual (vit′l) *n. pl.* Food for human beings.

vindication (vin′də·kā′shən) *n.* The act of clearing of an accusation.

vindictive (vin·dik′tiv) *adj.* Spiteful.

visage (viz′ij) *n.* The face.

visitation (viz′ə·tā′shən) *n.* The act or fact of visiting.

vivacious (vi·vā′shəs, vī-) *adj.* Full of life and spirits.

vixen (vik′sən) *n.* **1.** A female fox. **2.** A turbulent, quarrelsome woman.

vocation (vō·kā′shən) *n.* A stated or regular occupation; a calling.

volatile (vol′ə·til) *adj.* Fickle; changeable.

voluptuous (və·lup′choo·əs) *adj.* Devoted to the enjoyment of pleasures or luxuries.

voracious (vô·rā′shəs, vō-, və-) *adj.* Ready to swallow up.

votive (vō′tiv) *adj.* Performed in fulfillment of a vow.

vouchsafe (vouch′sāf′) *v.* To permit. *Obs.* To assure or guarantee.

W

wan (won) *adj.* Indicating illness, unhappiness, etc.

wane (wān) *v.* Draw to an end.

wanton (won′tən) *adj.* Without moral restraints.

warrant (wôr′ənt, wor′-) *v.* **1.** To assure or guarantee. **2.** To say confidently; feel sure.

wary (wâr′ē) *adj.* Carefully watching.

whet (hwet) *v.* To sharpen.

wistful (wist′fəl) *adj.* Wishful; longing. —**wistfulness** *n.*

wither (with′ər) *v.* To droop.

wizened (wiz′ənd) *adj.* Shrunken.

worldly (wûrld′lē) *adj.* Pertaining to the world; earthly; not spiritual.

wraith (rāth) *n.* Any ghost.

writhe (rīth) *v.* **1.** To twist or contort the body. **2.** To move by such twisting and contortion.

wrought (rôt) *adj.* Worked; molded.

Z

zealous (zel′əs) *adj.* Enthusiastic.

zephyr (zef′ər) *n.* Any soft, gentle wind.

Index of Authors and Titles

Numbers in italics designate pages on which biographical data appear.

PICTURE ACKNOWLEDGMENTS

p. 116, Scala from Shostal; p. 117, Scala from Shostal; p. 118, Photo by John R. Freeman, L. H. London; p. 119, Scala from Shostal; p. 171, Culver Pictures, Inc.; p. 187, Photo from Musées Nationaux; p. 190, Photo by Meyer Erwin; p. 191, Scala from Shostal; p. 192, Photo by Meyer Erwin; p. 195, Historical Pictures Service, Chicago; p. 209, Don Knight, Alpha Photo Associates, Inc.; p. 211, United States Department of the Interior, National Park Service Photo; p. 225, Dennis Stock, Magnum; p. 226, Dennis Stock, Magnum; p. 235, Alinari, Art Reference Bureau; p. 240, The Bettmann Archive; p. 260, De Antonis, Roma; p. 271, British Museum; p. 274, Historical Pictures Service, Chicago; p. 280, Historical Pictures Service, Chicago; p. 285, The Metropolitan Museum of Art, Wolfe Fund, 1931; p. 302, The Mount Wilson and Palomar Observatories; p. 304, Ebony Magazine; p. 331, Art Reference Bureau; p. 332, Photo from Musées Nationaux; p. 333, Photo from Musées Nationaux; p. 356, The Bettmann Archive; p. 362, The Bettmann Archive; p. 367, The Bettmann Archive; p. 371, The Bettmann Archive; p. 375, Culver Pictures, Inc.; p. 408, Henry B. Beville; p. 475, Culver Pictures, Inc.; p. 476, Playbill, Inc.; p. 510, Photo from Musées Nationaux; p. 552, Photo: Elton Schnellbacher; p. 624, Harbrace Photo.

ART CREDITS

VAN BALET. 43, 47, 48, 51

HUNTLEY BROWN. 478, 481, 483, 484, 491, 493, 498, 503, 513, 518, 522, 526, 530

NAIAD EINSEL. 311, top 342, bottom 342

JOHN GRETZER. 69, 71, 73, 75, 78, 80, 82, 328

JOE GREY. 30, 33, 34, 36, 38, 725, 729, 733, 739, 743, 747, 752, 767, 768, 770, 772, 777, 779, 780, 782, 784, 786, 788

MANNY HALLER. 143, 388, 410 and 411, 415, 425, 429, 434, 441, 446, 447, 450, 470

PAT KENT. 132, 136, 138, 337

AL LEINER. 87, 91, 94, 95, 96, 97, 99, 100, 343, 344, 357, 368, 376

KEN LONGTEMPS. 122, 124, 125, 157, 158, 159, 161, 162, 163, 351, 369

JAMES AND RUTH MC CREA. 321, 326, 378, 538, 544, 555, 557, 561, 563, 567, 569, 573, 575, 576, 582

MARIE NONAST. 5, 10, 13, 591, 597, 599, 602, 605, 613, 615, 616, 628, 638, 646, 650, 653, 657, 659, 661, 664, 669, 681, 685, 687, 691, 694, 698, 701, 710, 718, 720

SHANNON STIRNWEIS. 215, 216, 219, 243, 365

EARL THOLLANDER. 105, 106, 109, 110, 147, 148

HAND ZANDER. 16, 18, 20, 21, 23, 24, 56, 65, 66, 151, 152, 154, 181, 183, 249, 253, 267